Scholars International Publishing Corp.

Mastercam® Book for Windows©

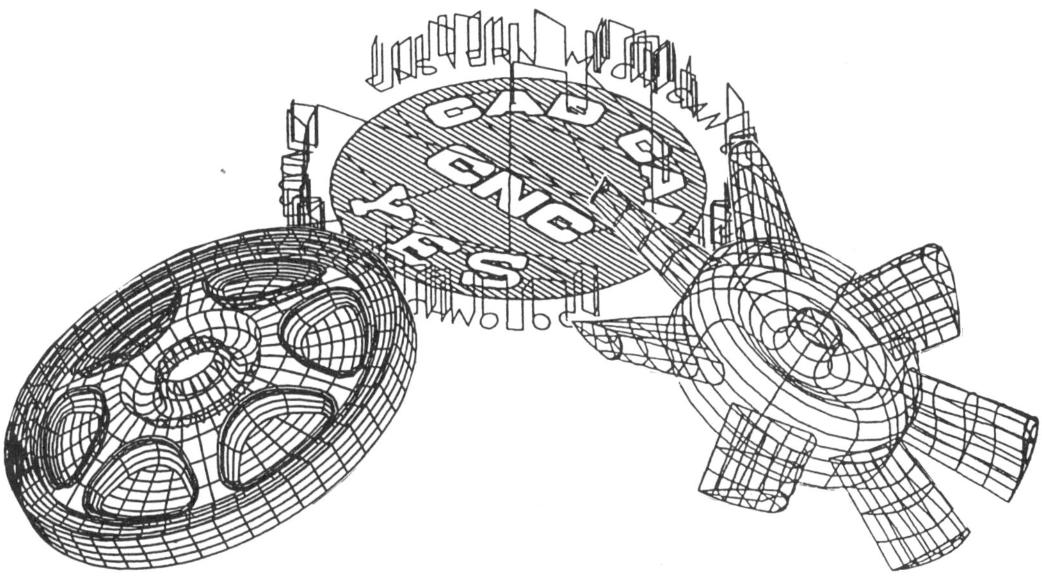

by Dr. S.C. Jonathon Lin
and Dr. F.C. Tony Shiue

Scholars International Publishing Corp.

2675 Georgetown Blvd.
Ann Arbor, MI 48105

Scholars staff:
Marketing manager: Grace Lin
Chief editor: Jonathon Lin
Project editor: Karen L. Sterzik
Illustrator: Joy Chou
Cover Designers: Karen L. Sterzik and Jonathon Lin
Printer/Binder: BookCrafters, Chelsea, MI

Printed and bound in the United States of America
95 96 97 98 99 -- 10 9 8 7 6 5 4 3 2 1

To request more information on this publication, contact:

Scholars International Publishing Corp.
2675 Georgetown Blvd.
Ann Arbor, MI 48105
Phone: (313) 930-0813 or FAX: (313) 741-1927

Lin, Su-Chen Jonathon, and Shiue, Fuh-Cwo Tony.
Mastercam Book for Windows
Includes index.
ISBN 1-886552-01-0
Library of Congress Catalog Number: 95-069374

Preface

CAD/CAM technology has emerged as one of the major driving forces in our modern manufacturing industry. Due to the increased computer power and the advancement of CAD/CAM software, manual CNC programming has been replaced by CAD/CAM programming in recent years. Mastercam CNC programming software has become the leading PC-based CAM software due to its power and ease of use.

Mastercam software is widely used in industry and in schools. It has become a leading tool for teaching CNC programming. Additionally, there is a need for a comprehensive text to teach students of all skill levels to effectively use Mastercam. This text is intended to be used to teach CNC programming with Mastercam software in schools and in industrial training classes. It is also a valuable reference for all levels of Mastercam users.

Mastercam Book for Windows is derived from its predecessor, CNC Programming Using Mastercam Version 4 and 5 which was written for the DOS version of Mastercam software. As suggested by readers, we kept the same format and style, as well as most of the contents, for this new text which is written for the Windows version. Two new chapters have been added in addition to many significant changes throughout the book to reflect the new features in Version 5. Readers should find this new text a valuable learning tool for mastering CNC programming with Mastercam Software.

This book is suitable for a two-semester course. It is appropriate for industrial technology, engineering technology, and engineering courses at many levels; universities and colleges, junior colleges, trade schools, high schools, as well as for courses offered by industry.

The following is a list of suggested topics to be covered in two semesters:

First semester:

Chapters 1 and 2 : CNC programming and machining fundamentals
Chapters 3 through 10: 2-D toolpath programming
Chapter 18: Milling tools construction and definition
Chapters 19 and 20: Lathe programming

Second semester:

Chapter 11 through 17: 3-D (surfaces) toolpath programming
Chapter 21: Post processor customization

Chapters 3, 5, 6, and 10 were written by Dr. Fuh-Cwo (Tony) Shiue.

Su-Chen Jonathon Lin

Acknowledgements

The author is indebted to many persons and organizations for their help and contributions in making this book idea into a reality. First, I wish to express my sincere appreciation to Iven May of CNC Software, Inc. He is the person who initiated the book idea and gave numerous suggestions toward making it possible. His two colleagues in the Educational Division of CNC Software, Dan Newby and Rick Meyers, also provided a lot of assistance and especially helped by reviewing the manuscript.

Special thanks are due to Jack, Brian and Mark Summers who reviewed the manuscript and helped tremendously in marketing the book to Mastercam users. Because they are so friendly and easy to work with, they made the project progress smoothly.

I also owe Paul Zwarka a thank you for reviewing the manuscript.

Thanks are also extended to Ms. Joy Chou, who prepared several hundred illustrations using AutoCAD and Mastercam. Without her great skill, care and amazing speed, the book would never have been finished.

I greatly appreciate the excellent work Ms. Karen Sterzik has contributed to this book in editing, and using PageMaker to do the page layout design. Her endeavor in many long-hour nights has made this book possible in only a few months.

I am greatly indebted to my dear wife, Grace, for her continuous support and encouragement. I am also grateful to my son, Andrew, and daughter, Carol, for their understanding when they couldn't see me very often because I was preparing the manuscript at my office.

A credit needs to be given also to Delmar Publishers, Inc. for granting me their permission to use the following seventeen figures and tables:

Figure 1.2 Direct Numerical Control
Figure 1.3 Distributive numerical control
Figure 2.6 Toolholder system for machining centers
Figure 2.11 Insert identification system
Figure 2.20 Drilling
Figure 2.21 Milling
Figure 2.22 Turning
Figure 2.9 Unit horsepower required for drilling AISI 1112 steels
Figure 2.10 Approximate conversion factor for unit horsepower required to drill other materials
Figure 2.11 Unit horsepower for milling
Figure 2.12 Unit horsepower for turning various materials
Figure 7.39 Pocket cutting direction
Figure 19.5 Cutting direction in the left-handed coordinate direction
Figure 19.6 Cutting direction in the right-handed coordinate direction
Figure 19.7 Tool nose of a turning tool
Figure 19.8 Imaginary tool nose
Figure 19.9 OFT number for tool nose direction

All the above illustrations are Reproduced by Permission.
COMPUTER NUMERICAL CONTROL: FROM PROGRAMMING TO NETWORKING
by Jonathon Lin
Delmar Publishers Inc., Albany, New York, Copyright 1994

Machine photographs are provided by the following companies:
Bridgeport Machines, Inc.
Leadwell CNC Machines Mfg. Co.
Mori Seiki Co., Ltd.
Okuma Machinery, Inc.
Peddinghaus Corporation

Table of Contents

Chapter 1

CNC Programming Fundamentals

Objectives:

1. Understand the basic concepts required in CNC programming and operation.
2. Know the career opportunities in NC related jobs.
3. Know NC programming words and commands.
4. Be familialized with CNC machines and their axes designation.
5. Know various reference zero points in CNC programming.

1.1 NC, CNC and DNC, What are they ?

Four terms are often used in describing the emerging technology dealt with in this book:

- numerical control (NC)
- computer numerical control (CNC),
- direct numerical control (DNC)
- distributive numerical control (DNC).

Numerical Control (NC)

Numerical control (NC) is a technique for controlling machine tools or processes by using coded command instructions. The NC controller interprets these instructions and then converts them into two types of control signals: **motion control signals** and **miscellaneous control signals** (Figure 1.1).

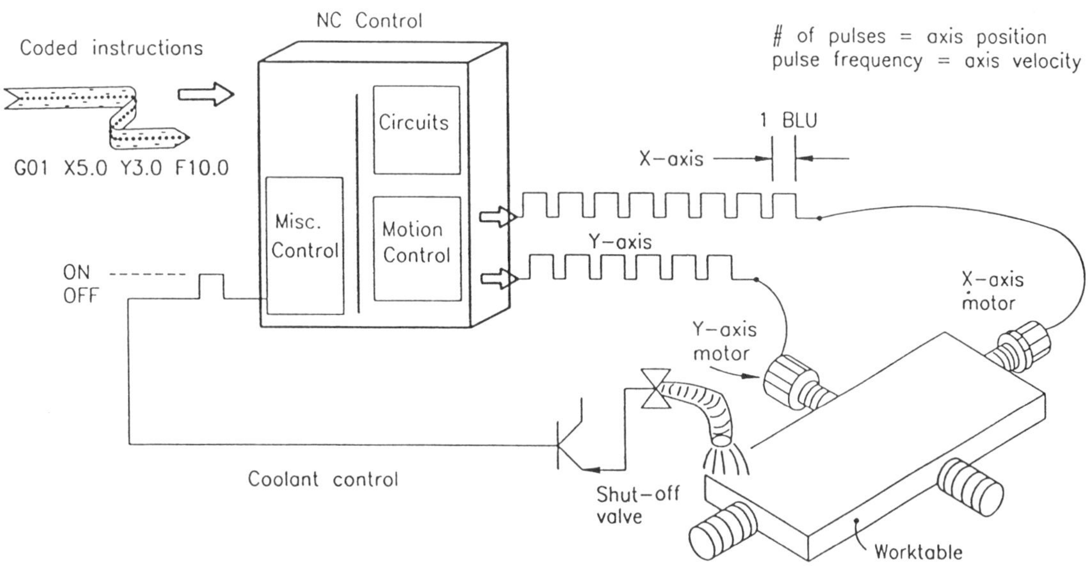

Figure 1.1 Numerical control

Motion control signals are a series of electric pulse trains that are used to control the position and the speed of the machine table and spindle. Each pulse activates a motion of one basic length-unit (BLU) which is the minimum increment size of the NC control system. The typical increment for one BLU in the old generation of NC controls is 0.001in. (or 0.01 mm), while in modern CNC controls, the increment resolution can reach 0.0001 in. (or 0.001 mm). The number of pulses transmitted to each axis determines the incremental axis position, and the frequency of these pulses regulates the axis speed.

Miscellaneous control functions are a set of on/off signals to implement the control of the speed and direction of the spindle rotation, control of coolant supply, selection of cutting tool, automatic clamping and unclamping, etc.

NC is often referred to as the older generation of numerical control technology. NC systems are hard-wired controls in which most functions are implemented by electronic hardware based upon digital circuit technology.

Computer Numerical Control (CNC)

Computer numerical control (CNC) is the numerical control system in which a dedicated, stored program computer is built into the control to perform basic and advanced NC functions. CNC controls are also referred to as soft-wired NC systems because most of their control functions are implemented by the *control software programs.* All numerical control machines manufactured since the seventies are of CNC type. The control signals in CNC systems are in the form of binary words. Each word contains a fixed number of bits, 32 bits or 64 bits are commonly used. Each bit of data produces one BLU motion in the controlled axis. Theoretically a 32-bit word could represent one of up to 2^{32} = 4,294,967,296 different axial positions. If the system resolution is, for example, BLU = 0.0001 in., this number can represent up to 429,969 in. possible motions, which is more than enough for all types of applications.

Direct Numerical Control (DNC)

Direct numerical control uses a shared computer to simultaneously control the operation of a group of NC machine tools (Figure 1.2). The main tasks performed by the computer are to program and edit part programs as well as download part programs to NC machines. The idea of direct numerical control began in the mid-1960s in Cincinnati Milacron and General Electric. In 1970 about a half-dozen vendors marketed their DNC systems.

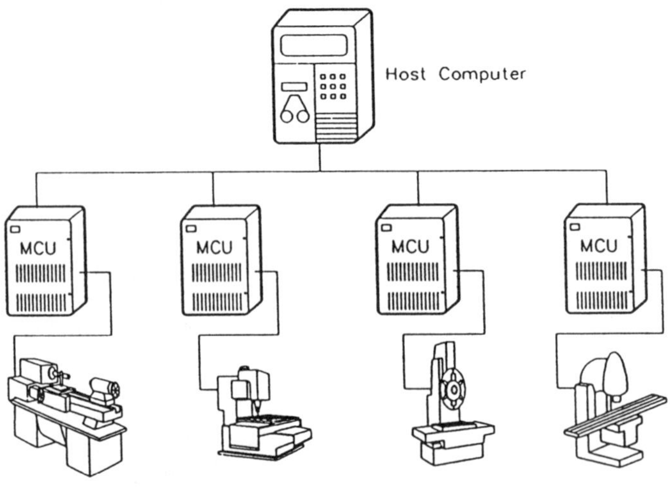

Figure 1.2 Direct numerical control (Source: S. C. Jonathon Lin, Computer Numerical Control: From Programming to Networking, 1994.Courtesy of Delmar Publishers, Inc.)

Direct numerical control was not widely used in industry mainly due to two reasons. The industry could not afford the expensive mainframe computers which could cost as much as a million dollars each. The other reason was the introduction of CNC in 1970s. The capacity of stored memory and enhanced intelligence of the built-in low cost dedicated computer replaced the desirable features of the DNC systems.

Distributive Numerical Control (DNC)

The main concept of distributive numerical control is to use a network of computers to coordinate the operation of a group of CNC machine tools (Figure 1.3). This new form of DNC systems began to evolve in the early 1980s and grew with the development of computer and communication technologies. Today many CNC machines together with robots, programmable logic controllers, and other computer-based controllers have been integrated into DNC systems to make automated manufacturing systems possible.

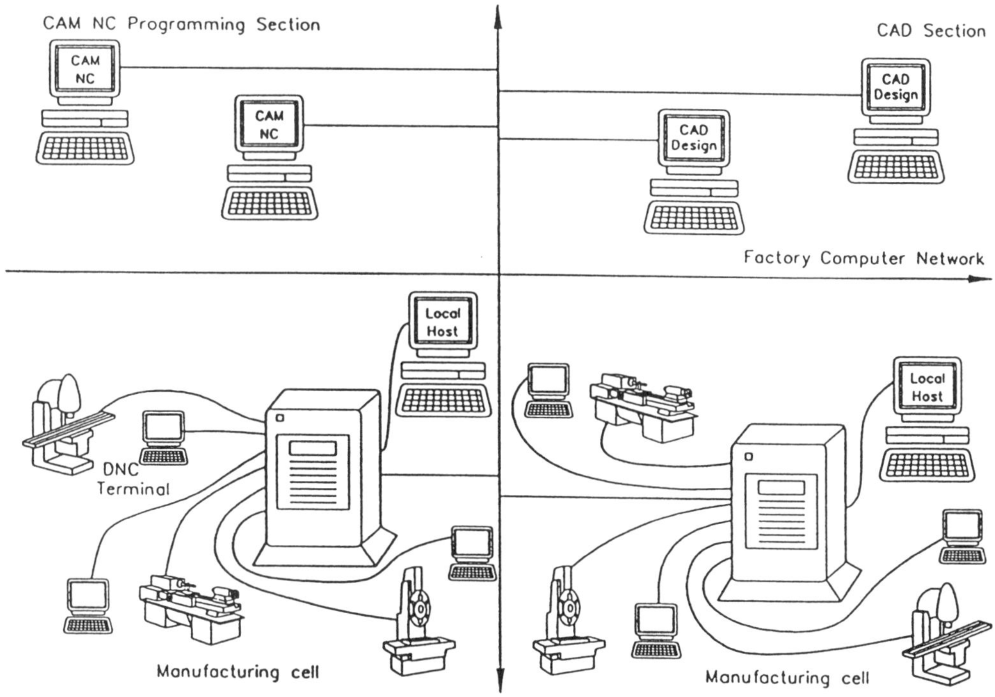

Figure 1.3 Distributive numerical control (Source: S. C. Jonathon Lin, Computer Numerical Control: From Programming to Networking, Courtesy of Delmar Publishers, Inc.)

1.2 Advantages and Limitations of CNC Technology

The main advantages of using CNC technology are to **reduce product cost, improve product quality, and facilitate production planning and control**. These benefits can be realized through these **nine** causes:

- Increased productivity
- Reduced production costs
- Facilitation of complex machining operations
- Improved production planning and control
- Facilitation of flexible automation
- High accuracy and repeatability
- Reduced indirect operating costs
- Greater flexibility
- Lower operator skill requirement

Three main drawbacks of using CNC technology include **high initial investment, high maintenance requirement, and not cost-effective for low productions runs**.

1.3 CNC Operations

The orgnizational structure for implementing computer numerical control operations varies throughout the industry. The larger the operation, the greater the need for organization. The functions found within a CNC group are the same no matter how large the group is; the only difference is how those functions are delegated. A small shop might have only one or two people performing all of the NC department functions, while a medium to large operation will divide the NC functions into groups or even assign them to departments (Figure 1.4):

- NC shop management
- NC part programming
- Tool and fixture design
- Machine maintenance
- NC machine operation

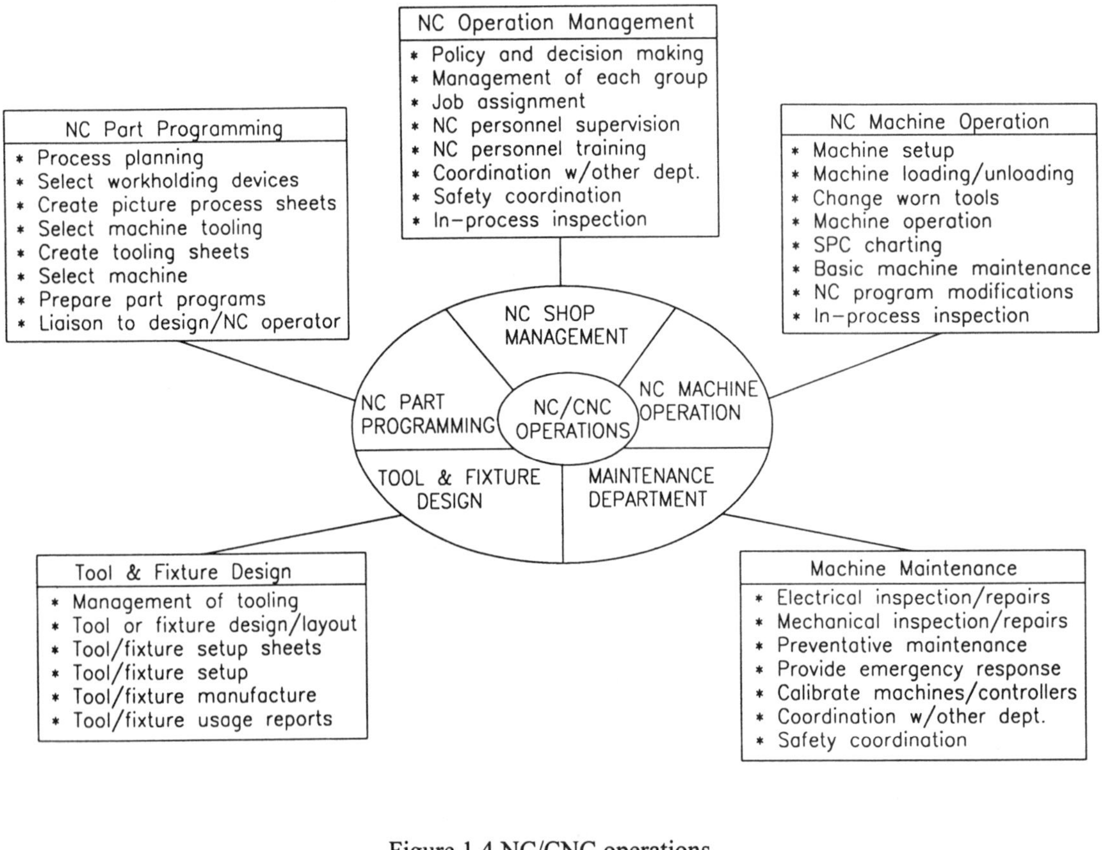

Figure 1.4 NC/CNC operations

1.4 Career Opportunities

There are about three hundred thousand NC related jobs available to service 170,000 NC/CNC machine tools in the U.S. industry today. The demand for NC related personnel has increased in a very steady pace as industry moves further into automated manufacturing. The job titles associated with NC personnel may appear as NC manager or supervisor, process planner, part programmer, tool designer, tool maker, machine setup person, machine operator, or maintenance person. The major responsibilities, required job skills, as well as education and experience of each job title are summarized in Table 1.1.

Table 1.1 CNC Career Opportunities

Job Title	Responsibility	Required Job Skills	Education/Experience
NC manager or supervisor	• Oversee NC operations • NC personnel hiring, training and job assignment • Coordination with other departments • Evaluate and acquire new CNC machine tools and CAD/CAM software	— Management skills — Machining knowledge — NC programming and operation background	4-year college degree with several years of manufacturing experience
Process planner	• Determine what machining processes to be used, with what sequence, and in what machines • Select cutting tools and workholders and fixtures • Prepare operation sheets and tooling sheets	— Overall knowledge of machining, tooling, and capability of available equipment — Good background in manufacturing and CNC	At least 2-year college degree, 4-year college degree preferred
Part programmer	• Prepare part programs • Prepare NC documents concerning setup instructions • Prepare process plan if needed	— Good command at math, geometry and trigonometry — Sound knowledge of machining — Blue-print reading — Computer skills — Use of CAD/CAM software	2-year college degree or vocational technical school
Tool designer	• Select standard tooling • Design special-purpose tooling	— Good command at locating and clamping knowledge — Knowledge of tool making — Understanding of standard tooling and fixturing	At least 2-year college degree with tool and machine experience 4-year college degree preferred
Tool maker	• Assemble and preset standard tooling • Make special-purpose tooling • Repair damaged tooling items	— Highly skilled in machining — Knowledge in CNC — Print reading and making	4-year apprenticeship program
Machine setup person	• Set up fixture and cutting tools on the machine • Coordinate the machine • Determine and enter offset and compensation values • Correct errors in tooling and program • Tryout run the program	— Good knowledge in machining and tooling — Understanding of part program and machine functions	Machinist experience with extensive CNC knowledge
Machine operator	• Load and unload workpieces • Monitor machining in progress • Finished part inspection • SPC charting • Regular check-up	— General knowledge of machining	Technical programs in vocational technical school, area occupational school, community college

1.5 CNC System Elements

A typical CNC system consists of the following **six** elements shown in Figure 1.5:

- •Part program
- •Program input device
- •Machine control unit
- •Drive system
- •Machine tool
- •Feedback system

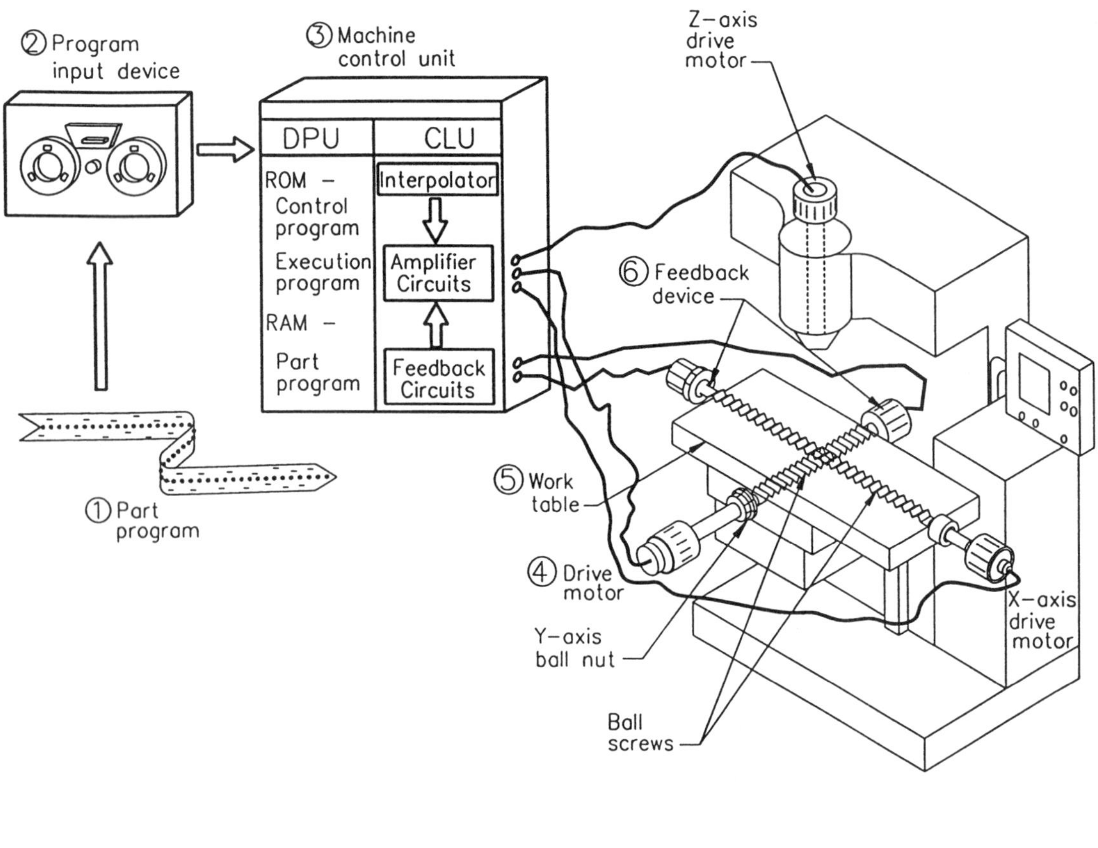

Figure 1.5 CNC system elements

Mastercam Book for Windows,
Scholar's International Publishing Corp., 1995

Part Program

A part program is a series of coded instructions required to produce a part. It controls the movement of the machine tool and the on/off control of auxiliary functions such as spindle rotation and coolant. The coded instructions are composed of letters, numbers and symbols and are arranged in a format of functional blocks as in the following example.

N10 G01 X5.0 Y2.5 F15.0

- F15.0 — Feed rate (15 in/min)
- Y2.5 — Y-coordinate (2.5")
- X5.0 — X-coordinate (5.0")
- G01 — Linear interpolation mode
- N10 — Sequence number

Program Input Device

The program input device is the mechanism for part programs to be entered into the CNC control. **Three** commonly used program input devices are **punch tape reader, magnetic tape reader, and computer via RS-232-C communication.**

Machine Control Unit

The machine control unit (MCU) is the heart of a CNC system. It is used to perform the following functions:

- Read coded instructions
- Decode coded instructions
- Implement interpolations (linear, circular, and helical) to generate axis motion commands
- Feed axis motion commands to the amplifier circuits for driving the axis mechanisms
- Receive the feedback signals of position and speed for each drive axis
- Implement auxiliary control functions such as coolant or spindle on/off, and tool change

Drive System

A drive system consists of **amplifier circuits, drive motors, and ball lead-screws**. The MCU feeds control signals (position and speed) of each axis to the amplifier circuits. The control signals are augmented to actuate drive motors which in turn rotate the ball lead-screws to position the machine table.

Machine Tool

CNC controls are used to control various types of machine tools. Regardless of which type of machine tool is controlled, it always has a **slide table and a spindle to control of position and speed.** The machine table is controlled in the X and Y axes, while the spindle runs along the Z axis.

Feedback System

The feedback system is also referred to as the *measuring system.* It uses position and speed transducers to continuously monitor the position at which the cutting tool is located at any particular time. The MCU uses the difference between reference signals and feedback signals to generate the control signals for correcting position and speed errors.

1.6 CNC Applications and Machines

CNC technology has been successfully applied to almost every aspect of the manufacturing industry. Their applications are often classified in these five categories:

- Chip removal (metal cutting)
- Grinding
- Unconventional machining
- Fabrication
- Special-purpose applications

The machines controlled by CNC can be classified into the following **eight** categories:

- CNC mills and machining centers
- CNC lathes and turning centers
- CNC EDMs
- CNC grinding machines
- CNC cutting machines (laser, plasma, electron, or flame)
- CNC fabrication machines (sheet metal punch press, bending machine, or press brake)
- CNC welding machines
- CNC coordinate measuring machines

Figures 1.6 to 1.14 show some typical CNC controlled machine tools used in industry.

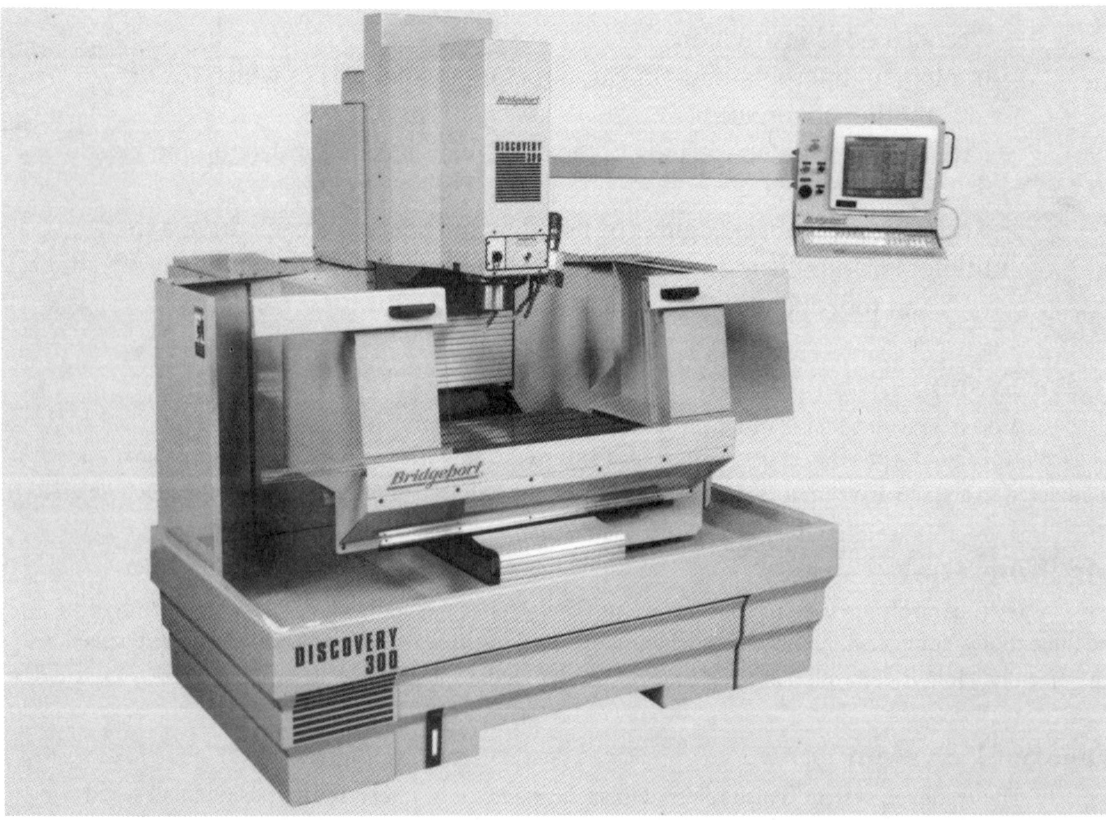

Figure 1.6 CNC milling machine (Courtesy of Bridgeport Machines, Inc.)

Figure 1.7 CNC Vertical machining center (Courtesy of Mori Seiki Co., LTD.)

Figure 1.8 CNC Horizontal machining center (Courtesy of Mori Seiki Co.,LTD.)

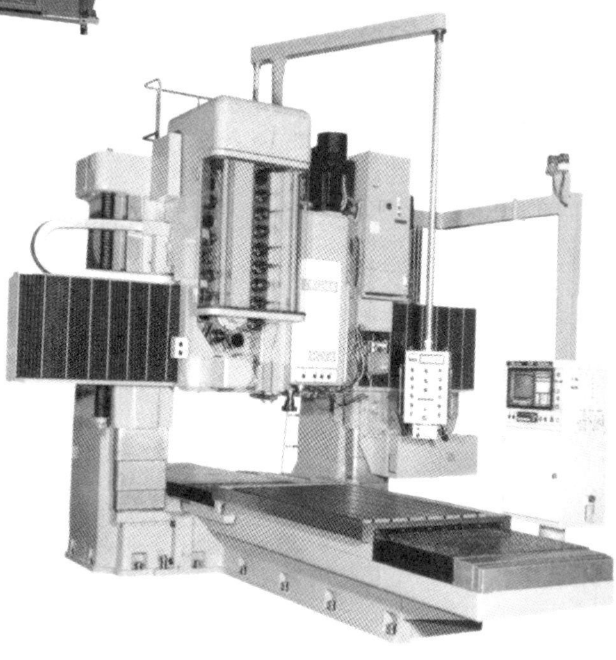

Figure 1.9 Double-column machining center (Courtesy of Okuma Machincry, Inc.)

Figure 1.10 CNC Turning center (Courtesy of Leadwell CNC Machines Mfg. Corp.)

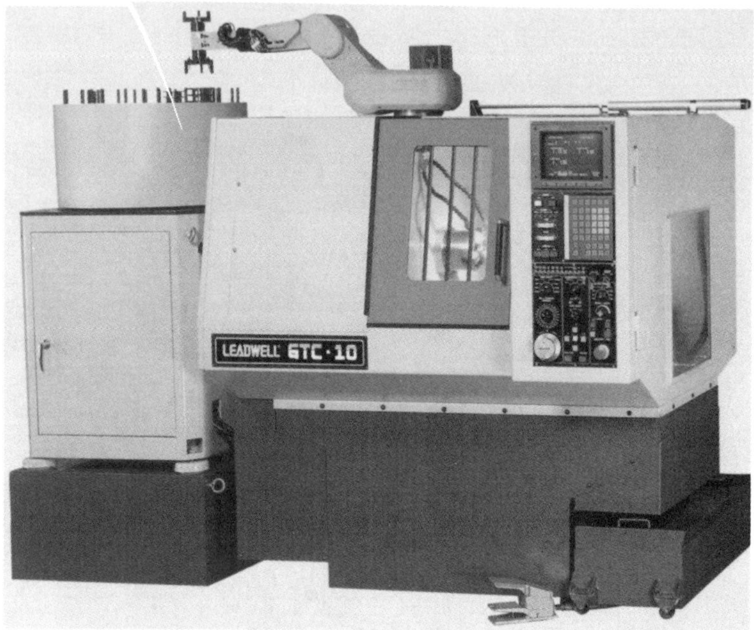

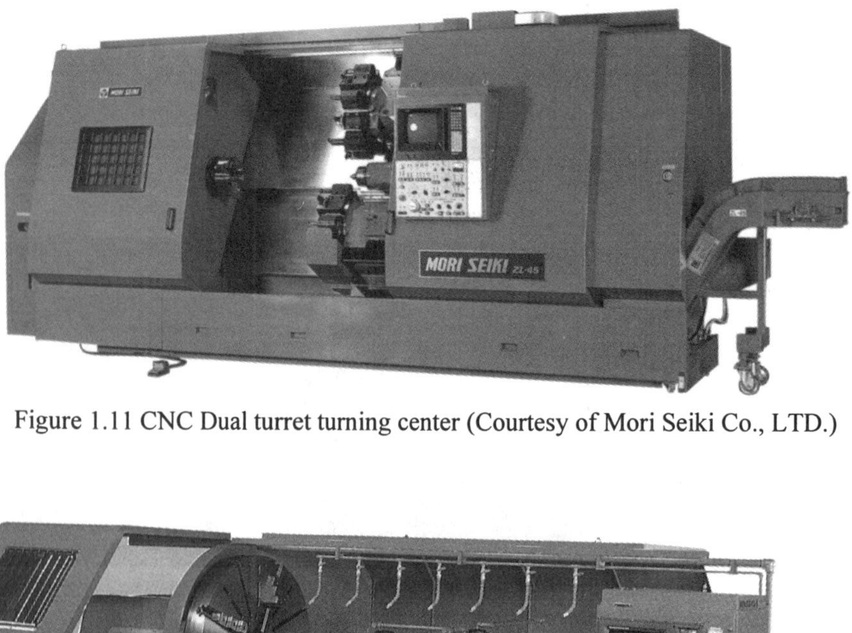

Figure 1.11 CNC Dual turret turning center (Courtesy of Mori Seiki Co., LTD.)

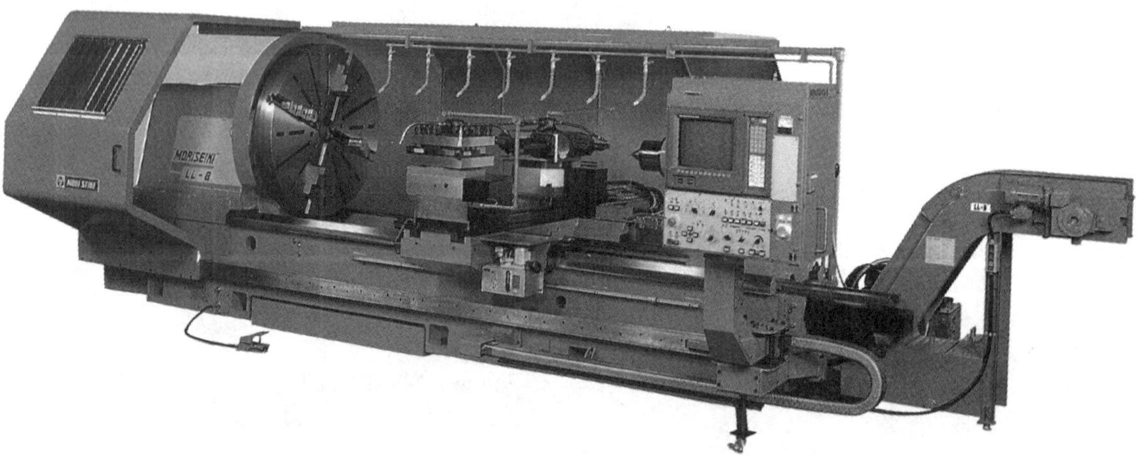

Figure 1.12 Heavy-duty CNC lathe (Courtesy of Mori Seiki Co., LTD.)

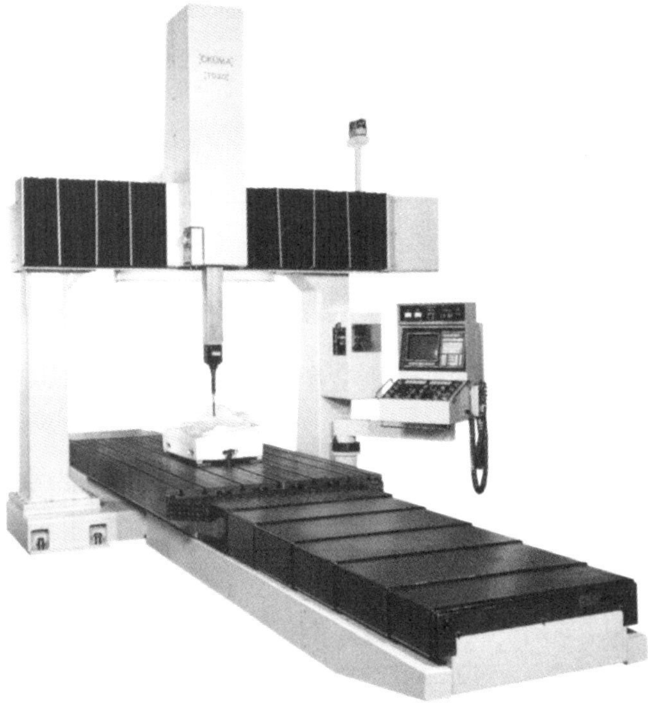

Figure 1.13 CNC Measuring machine (Courtesy of Okuma Machinery, Inc.)

Figure 1.14 CNC fabrication machine (Courtesy of Peddington Corp.)

1.7 NC Coding Systems

There are **two** coding systems used in NC/CNC controls: **EIA and ASCII standards.** The EIA coding system is established by the EIA standard 244-B. This code was widely adopted in North America before the ASCII code was established. The hole pattern assignment of EIA codes is given in the **left column** of the Figure 1.15.

ASCII is an acronym for the American Standard Code for Information Interchange. It refers to the code used to represent common keyboard characters. The ASCII NC code for punched tape was established by the RS-358-B standard. It is also referred to as the ISO code. The hole pattern of ASCII codes is given in the **right column** of Figure 1.15.

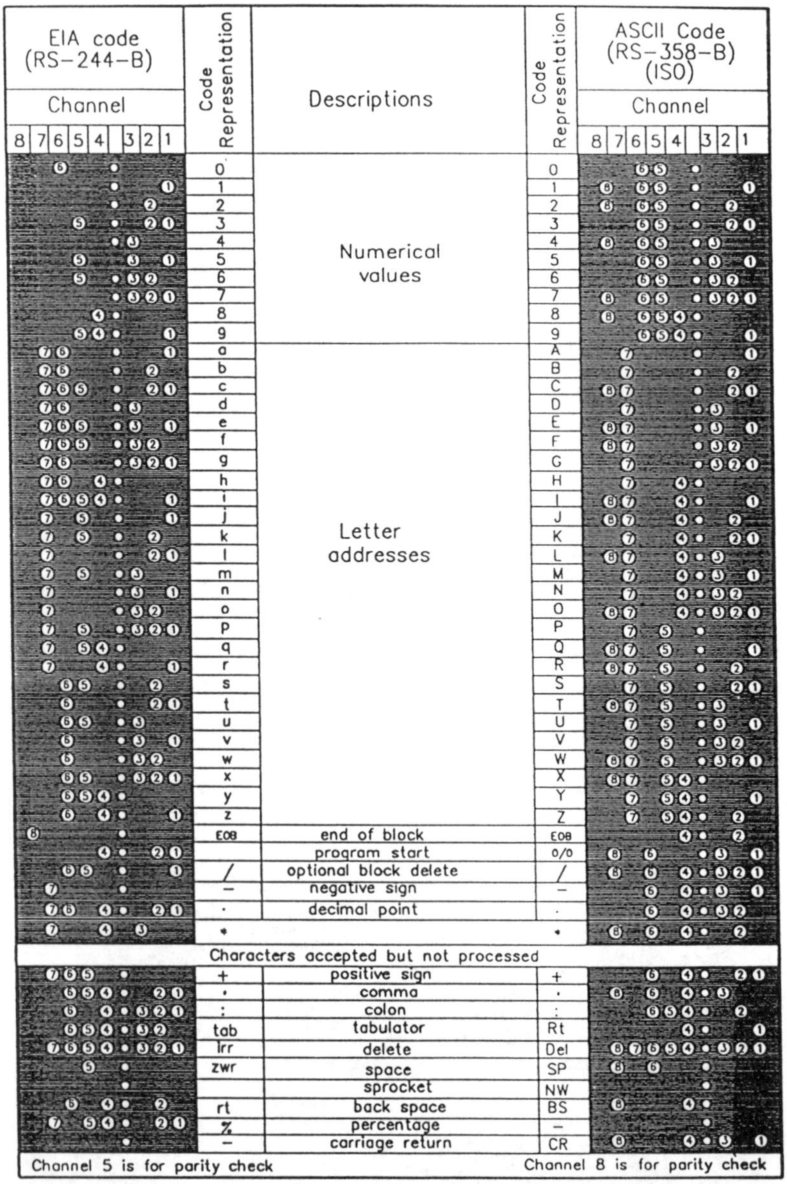

Figure 1.15 EIA and ASCII NC Coding systems

1.8 NC Addresses

An address is the letter at the beginning of each word which defines the meaning or purpose of the numerical data. The addresses used in NC programming have been specified by ANSI's EIA RS-274-B standard. Most of the letters are assigned to a unique function, but some have two functions. The NC addresses can be classified into the seven groups according to their functionality, refer to Table 1.2.

Table 1.2 NC Addresses

Address Type	Description	Illustration
1. Dimension		
a. Primary linear dimensions		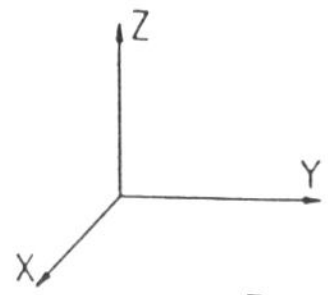
X Y Z	Primary X motion dimension Primary Y motion dimension Primary Z motion dimension	
b. Secondary linear dimensions		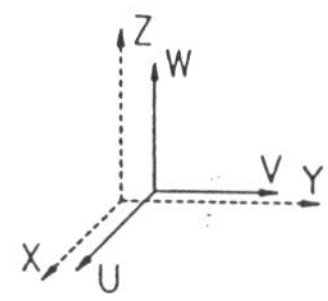
U V W	Secondary dimension parallel to X axis Secondary dimension parallel to Y axis Secondary dimension parallel to Z axis	
c. Tertiary linear dimensions		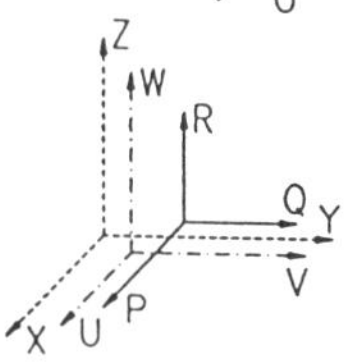
P Q R	Third dimension parallel to X axis Third dimension parallel to Y axis Third dimension parallel to Z axis	
d. Primary rotary dimensions		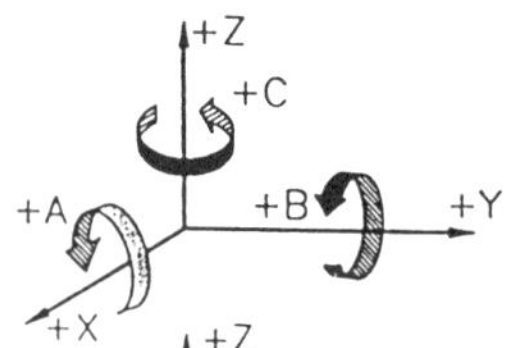
A B C	Angular dimension around X axis Angular dimension around Y axis Angular dimension around Z axis	
e. Special rotary dimensions		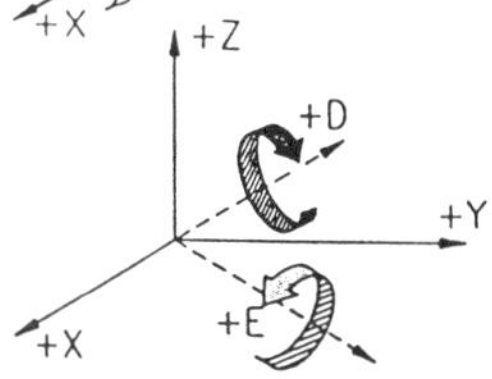
D E	Angular dimension around a special axis or line Angular dimension around a special axis or line	
2. Arc center		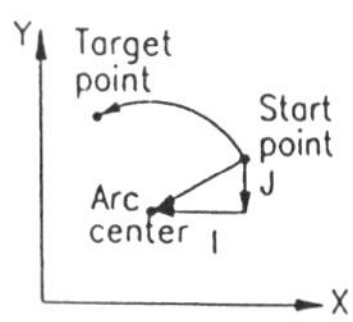
I J K	X dimension for circular arc center Y dimension for circular arc center Z dimension for circular arc center	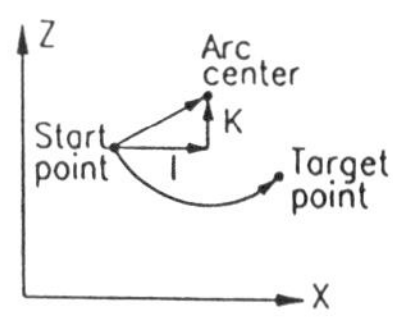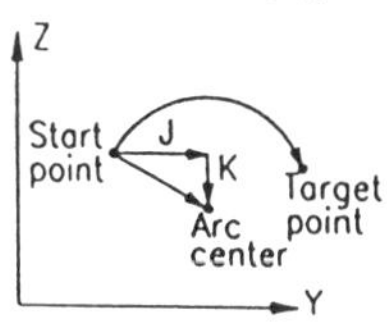

Table 1.2 (Continued)

Address Type		Description	Illustration
3. Feed			
	F	Primary feed function (applied to the main slide table)	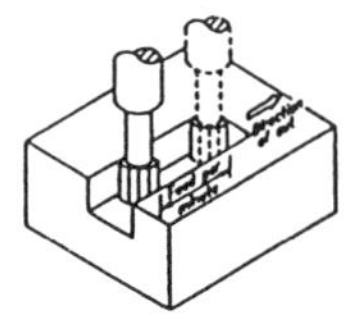
	E	Secondary feed function (applied to the second slide table)	
	D	Third feed function (applied to the third slide table)	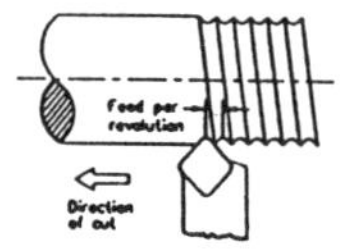
4. Thread pitches			
	I	Thread pitch in the X axis	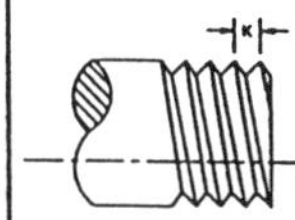 Straight thread
	J	Thread pitch in the Y axis	
	K	Thread pitch in the Z axis	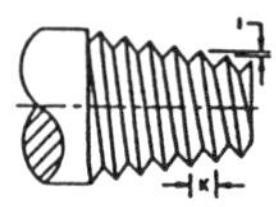 Taper thread
5. Preparatory functions	GXX		A preparatory function is defined by the address G followed by two digits to specify the control mode of the operation. (see Tables 1.4 and 1.5 for detail)
a. Motion commands		G00, G01, G02, and G03	
b. Plane selection commands		G17, G18, and G19	
c. Cutter compensation commands		G40, G41, and G42	
d. Tool length offset commands		G43–G49	
e. Fixed cycle commands		G80–G89	
f. Unit selection commands		G20 (or G70) and G21 (or G71)	
g. Positioning system commands		G90 and G91	
h. Coordinate system setting commands		G92, G54–G59	
6. Miscellaneous function	MXX		A miscellaneous function is defined by the address M followed by two digits to specify the type of machine control. (see Table 1.6 for detail)
a. Program stop		M00 and M01	
b. End of program		M02 and M30	
c. Spindle rotation		M03, M04, and M05	
d. Tool change		M06	
e. Coolant control		M07; M08, and M09	
7. Other functions			
	N	Sequence number of program block	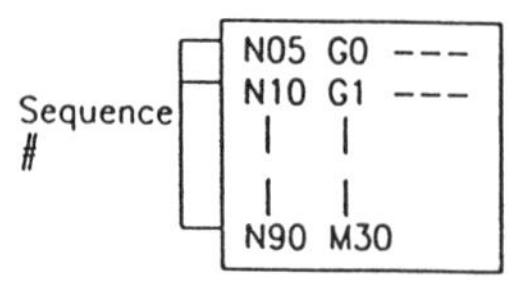
	S	Spindle speed function	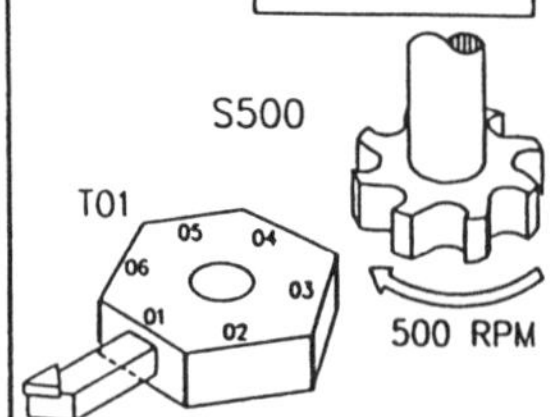
	T	Tool function	

1.9 NC Words

NC part programs are coded instructions that are organized into functional blocks. Each **block** consists of one or more NC words. An **NC word** is a collection of characters that begins with an address followed by numbers. A **character** is one byte (8 bits) of information representing a number, letter, or symbol. The sequence and arrangement of NC words in part programs must follow a certain pattern that is called the **tape format** or program format.

An NC word is the collection of characters arranged in a certain order to cause a special action by an NC machine. NC words always begin with a letter address followed by a numerical value. Table 1.3 lists seven groups of NC words.

Table 1.3 NC words

NC Words	Description	Typical Examples
1. Dimension words	Specify coordinates of a tool path.	X10.5 Y4.5 Z-1.0
2. Arc center words	Indicate coordinates of an arc center.	I3.0 J1.5 or R3.5
3. Feed words	Specify the feed rate of machining.	F15.0
4. Preparatory words	Specify command modes, the information of the block to be executed.	G90 G1 G2 G43
5. Miscellaneous words	Indicate control modes such as program stop, spindle rotation, tool change, coolant control, end of program, etc.	M0 M3 M6 M7M30
6. Spindle words	Specify spindle rotation speed in RPM	S3000
7. Tool words	Indicate the tool number to be selected	T5

Preparatory Words

The term "preparatory" in NC means that it "prepares" the control system to be ready for implementing the information that follows in the next block of instructions. A **preparatory function** is designated in a program by the word address G followed by two digits. Preparatory functions are also called **G-codes** and they specify the control mode of the operation. On the next page, Table 1.4 illustrates **eight groups** of commonly used G-codes in CNC milling machines. Following that, Table 1.5 lists the G-codes for CNC turning machines.

Table 1.4 G-Codes for Milling

Command Group	G-code	Function and Command statement	Illustration
Tool motion	G00	Rapid traverse G00 Xx Yy Zz	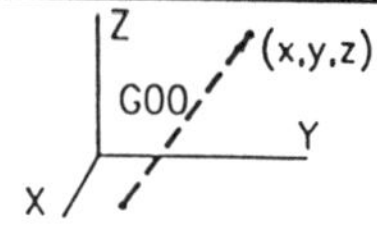
	G01	Linear interpolation G01 Xx Yy Zz Ff	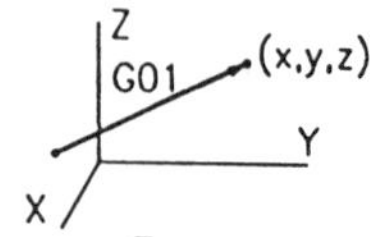
	G02	Circular interpolation in clockwise direction G02 Xx Yy Ii Jj G02 Xx Zz Ii Kk G02 Yy Zz Jj Kk	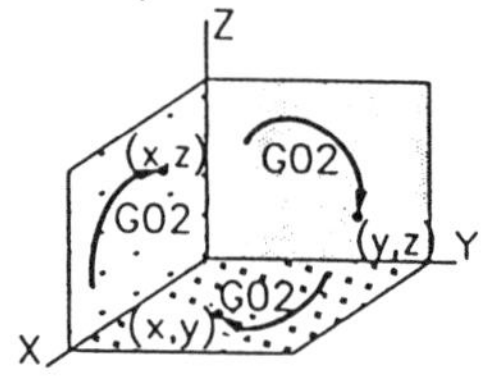
	G03	Circular interpolation in counter-clockwise direction G03 Xx Yy Ii Jj G03 Xx Zz Ii Kk G03 Yy Zz Jj Kk	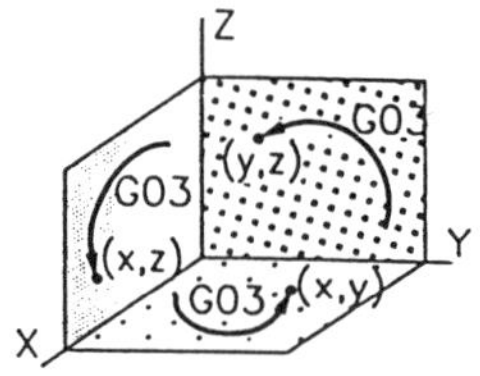
Plan selection	G17	XY-plane selection	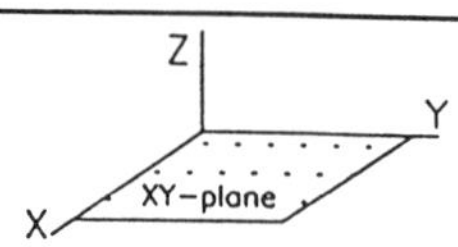
	G18	ZX-plane selection	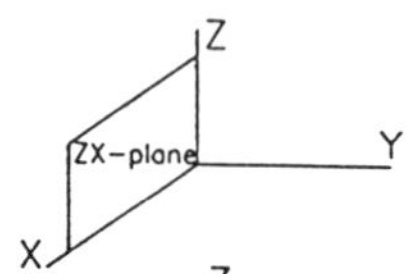
	G19	YZ-plane selection	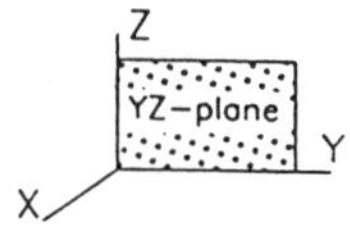
Unit selection	G20 or G70	Inch unit selection G20 or G70	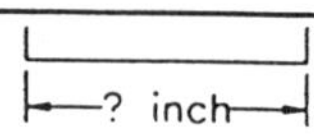
	G21 or G71	Metric unit selection G21 or G71	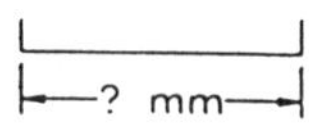
Offset and compensation	G40	Cutter diameter compensation cancel G40 G0 (or G1) Xx Yy	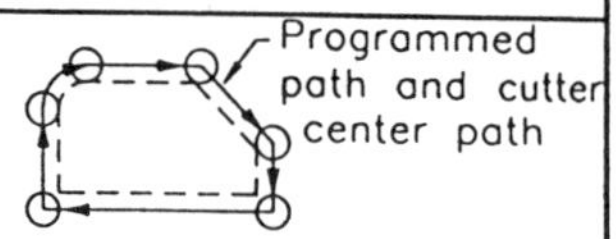
	G41	Cutter diameter compensation left G41 G0 (or G1) Xx Yy Dd	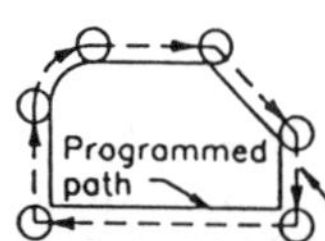
	G42	Cutter diameter compensation right G42 G0 (or G1) Xx Yy Dd	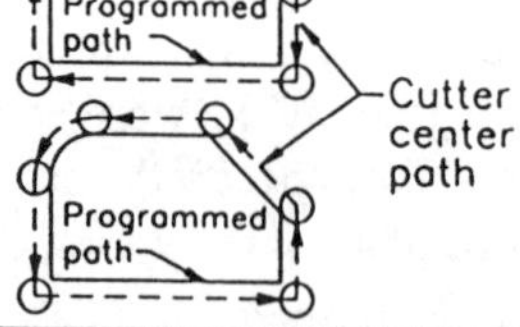

Table 1.4 (Continued)

<table>
<tr><th>Command Group</th><th>G-code</th><th>Function and Command statement</th><th>Illustration</th></tr>
<tr><td></td><td>G43</td><td>Tool length offset
G43 Hh</td><td>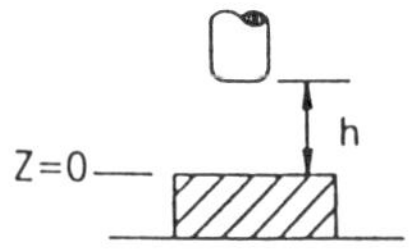
</td></tr>
<tr><td rowspan="2">Positioning system</td><td>G90</td><td>Absolute positioning system

G90 Xx Yy Zz</td><td>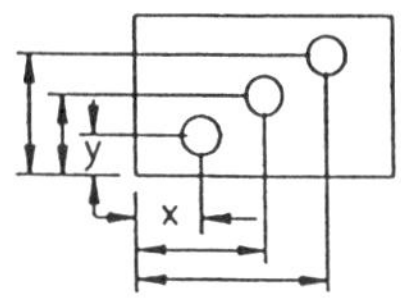
</td></tr>
<tr><td>G91</td><td>Incremental positioning system

G91 Xx Yy Zz</td><td>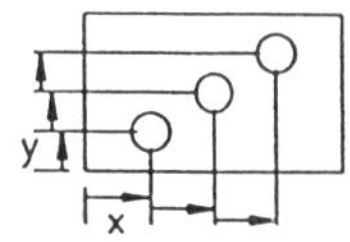
</td></tr>
<tr><td rowspan="2">Feed unit selection</td><td>G94</td><td>Feed per minute system

G94 Ff</td><td rowspan="2">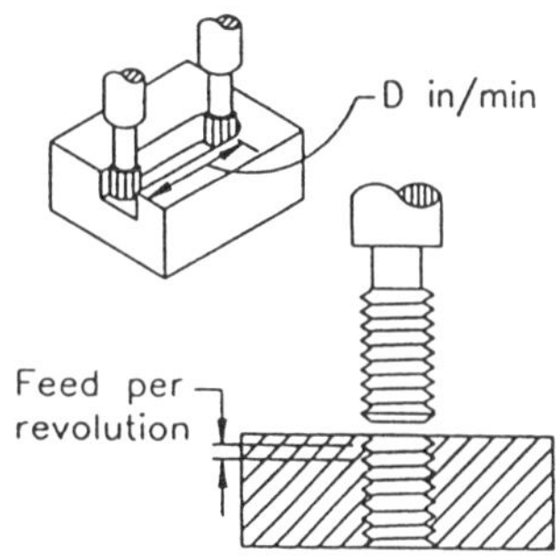
</td></tr>
<tr><td>G95</td><td>Feed per revolution system

G95 Ff</td></tr>
<tr><td rowspan="2">Work Coordinate Definition</td><td>G92</td><td>Absolute zero setting

G92 Xx Yy Zz</td><td>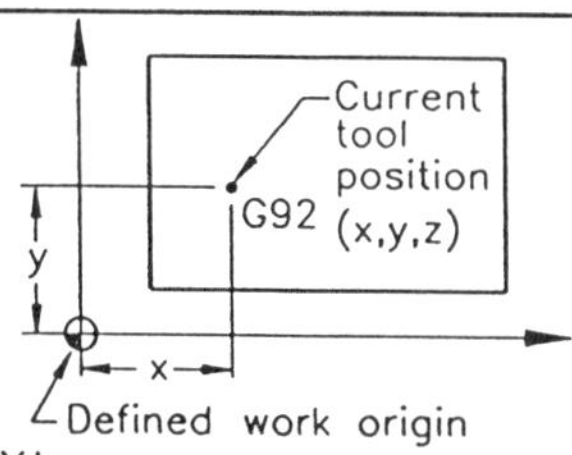
</td></tr>
<tr><td>G54 – G59</td><td>Work Coordinate setting
G54 Xx Yy Zz</td><td>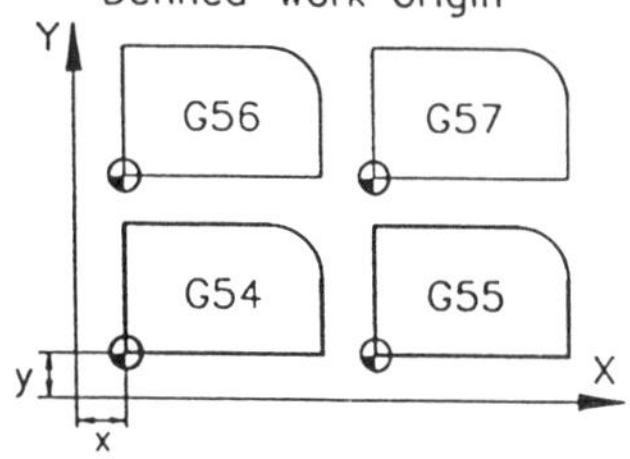
</td></tr>
<tr><td rowspan="2">Fixed cycles selection</td><td>G80 –</td><td>Fixed cycle cancel</td><td rowspan="2">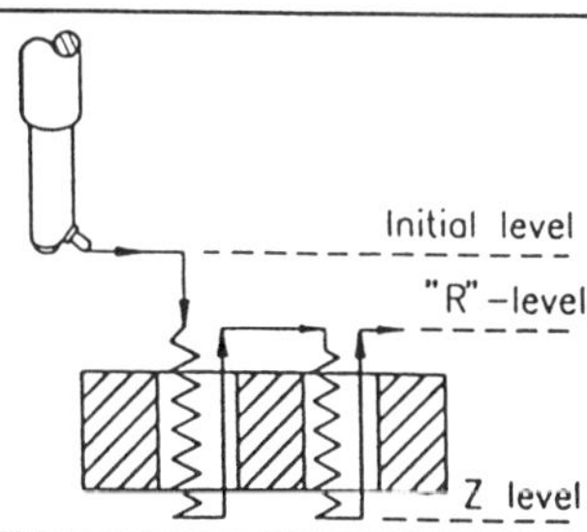
</td></tr>
<tr><td>G81 – G89</td><td>Fixed cycle

G99/G98 G8_ Xx Yy Zz Rr Ff Qq Pp</td></tr>
</table>

Table 1.5 G-Codes for Turning

Command Group	G-code	Function and Command Statement	Illustration
1. Tool motion	G00	Rapid traverse G00 Xx Zz	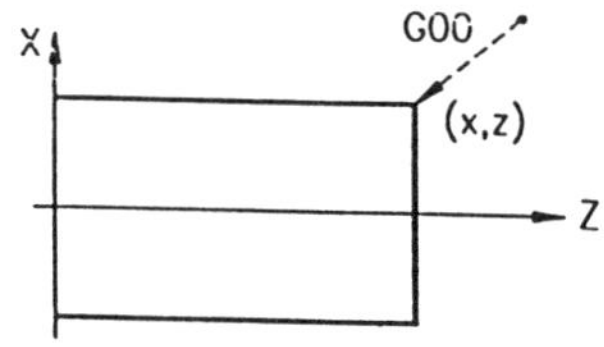
	G01	Linear interpolation G01 Xx Zz	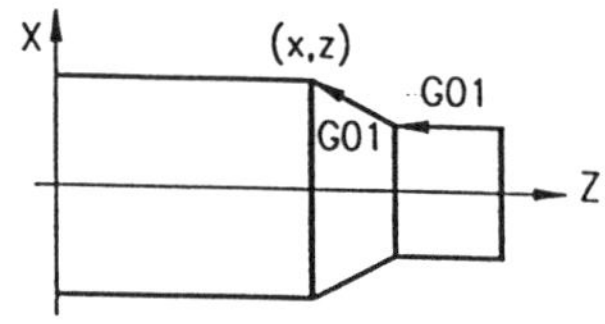
	G02	Circular interpolation in clockwise direction a. IJK method G02 Xx Zz Ii Kk b. R-method G02 Xx Zz Rr	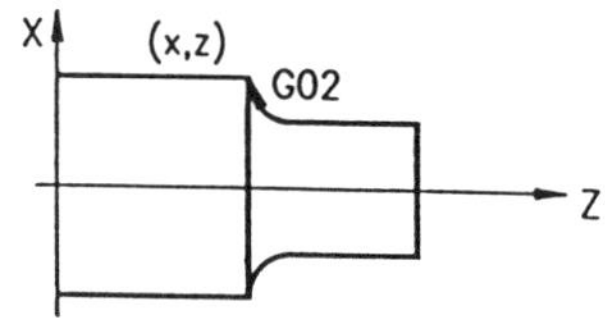
	G03	Circular interpolation in counter-clockwise direction a. IJK method G03 Xx Zz Ii Kk b. R-method G03 Xx Zz Rr	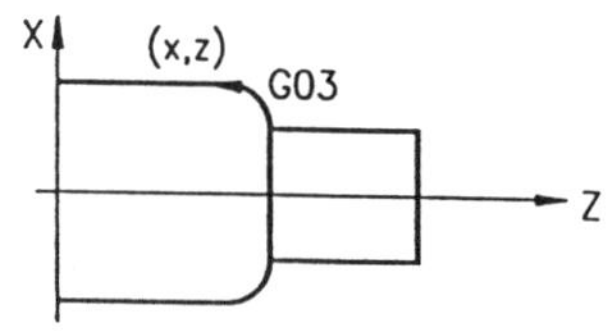
2. Work coordinate definition	G50 or G92 in some controls	(Work zero setting) G50 Xx Zz	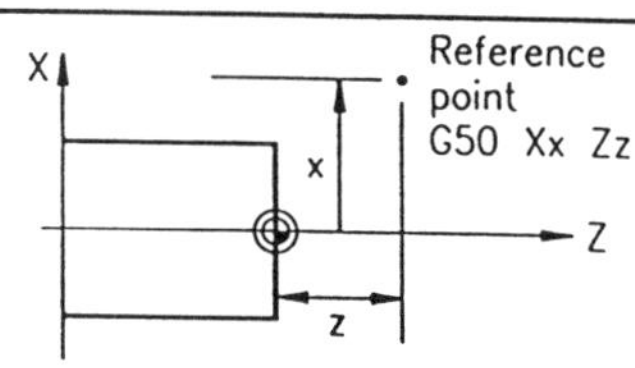
3. Spindle speed control	G50 G96 G97	Maximum spindle speed G50 Ss in RPM Constant surface speed setting G96 Ss in FPM Fixed spindle speed G97 Ss in RPM	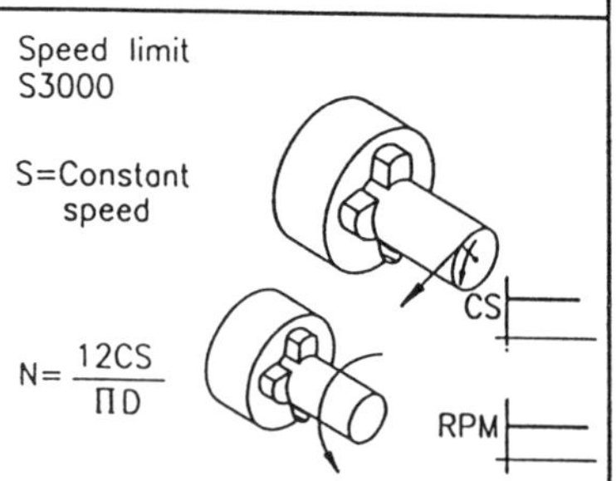
4. Unit selection	G20/G70 G21/G71	Inch unit selection Metric unit selection	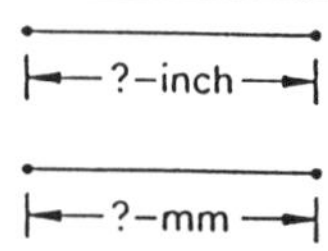

Table 1.5 (Continued)

<table>
<tr><th>Command Group</th><th>G-code</th><th>Function and Command Statement</th><th>Illustration</th></tr>
<tr><td rowspan="2">5. Feed Unit Selection</td><td>G98</td><td>Feed per minute</td><td>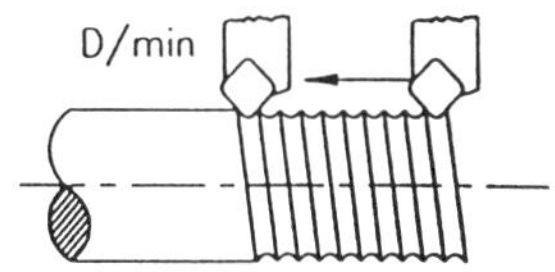
</td></tr>
<tr><td>G99</td><td>Feed per revolution</td><td>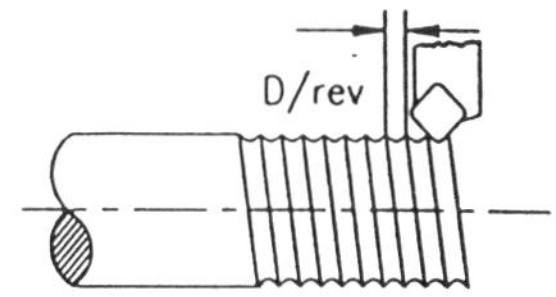
</td></tr>
<tr><td rowspan="3">6. Tool nose radius compen-sation</td><td>G40</td><td>Tool nose radius compensation cancel
G40 G0/G1 Xx Zz</td><td>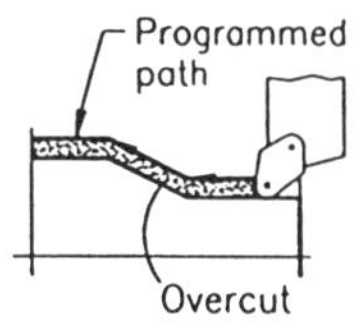
</td></tr>
<tr><td>G41</td><td>Tool nose radius compensation left
G41 G0/G1 Xx Zz Txxxx</td><td>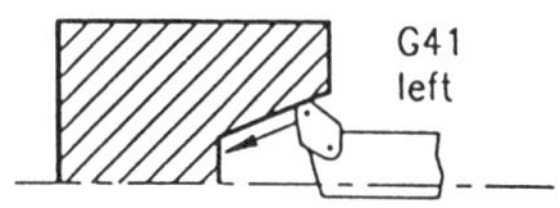
</td></tr>
<tr><td>G42</td><td>Tool nose radius compensation right
G42 G0/G1 Xx Zz Txxxx</td><td>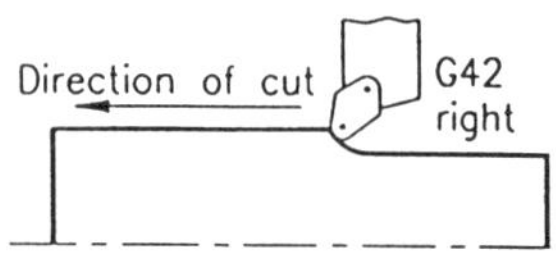
</td></tr>
<tr><td>7. Fixed cycles
A. Single cycles</td><td>G90
G94</td><td>Generate one pass of four toolpath moves</td><td>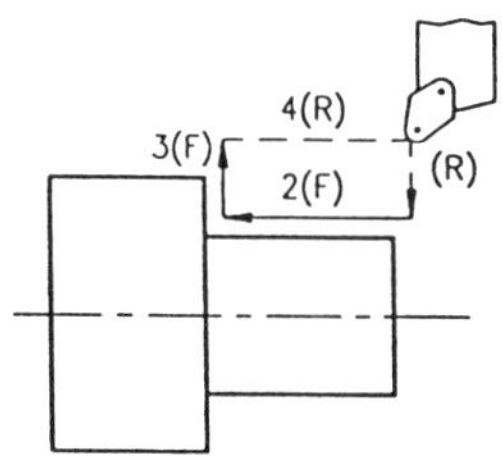
</td></tr>
<tr><td>B. Multiple-pass cycles</td><td>G71
G72</td><td>Generate multiple passes of four toolpath moves</td><td>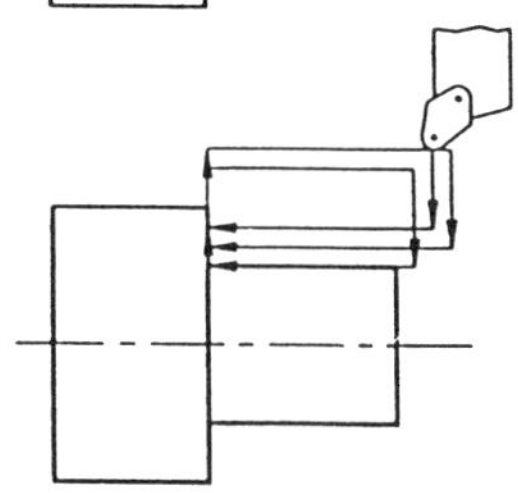</td></tr>
</table>

Miscellaneous Words

Miscellaneous functions use the address letter M followed by two digits. They perform a group of instructions such as coolant on/off, spindle on/off, tool change, program stop, or program end. They are often referred to as machine functions or **M-functions**. Table 1.6 illustrates common M-functions used in both milling and turning machines.

Table 1.6 Miscellaneous Functions

Function Group	M-function	Function and Command statement	Illustration
Program Stop	M00	Program stop	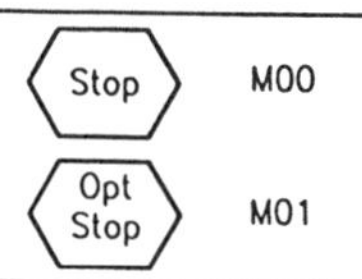
	M01	Optional stop	
Spindle Control	M03	Spindle on (rotation in clockwise direction)	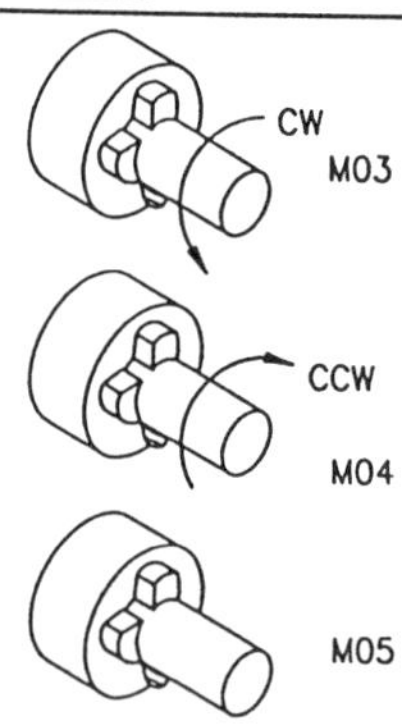
	M04	Spindle on (rotation in counter-clockwise direction)	
	M05	Spindle off	
Tool Change	M06	Too change to the specified tool number T__ M06	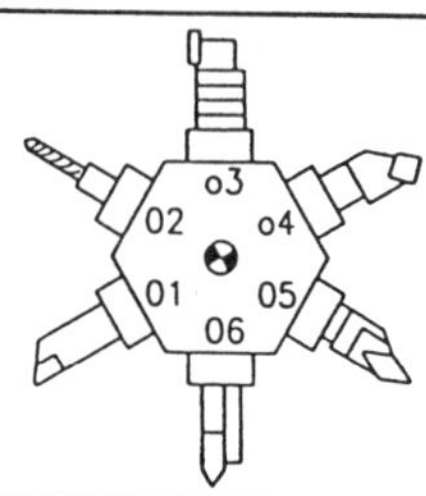
Coolant Control	M07	Coolant on (midst)	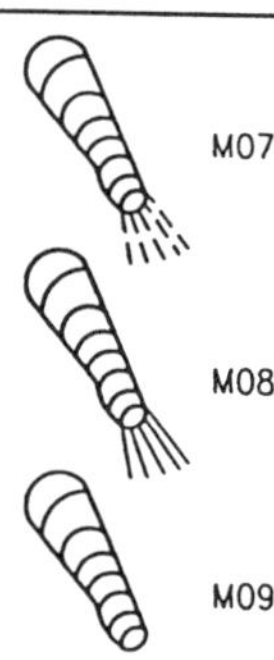
	M08	Coolant on (flood)	
	M09	Coolant off	
End of Program	M02	End of program and tape rewind	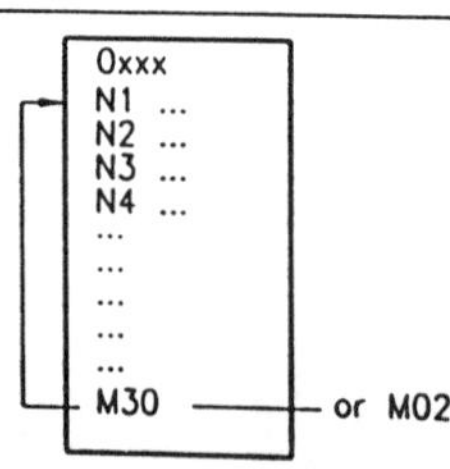
	M30	End of program and memory return	

1.10 NC Functional Blocks

NC controls simultaneously execute **all NC words contained in a block**. Therefore, NC blocks are normally organized according to their tasks. Table 1.7 gives some common functional blocks used in part programming.

Table 1.7 CNC functional blocks

Functional Block	Explanation	Typical Examples
1. Safety feature	Set the control to proper operating modes at the beginning of a part program. This block is also used after a tool change.	G90 G80 G40 G17
2. Coordinate system setting	Define the work zero point.	G92 Xx Yy Zz G54
3. Tool length offset	Offset the difference between the programmed tool length and the acutal tool length.	G43 Hh
4. Tool motion	Generate tool paths to machine the workpiece.	G0 Xx Yy Zz G1 Xx Yy Zz G2/G3 Xx Yy Zz
5. Cutter diameter compensation	Offset the cutter in a specified direction by a given amount of distance.	G41/G42 Xx Yy Hh/Dd G40 Xx Yy
6. Fixed cycle	Generate a series of tool paths to perform hole operations.	G8_ Xx Yy Zz Rr Ff
7. Tool change	Select a tool and cause a tool change.	Tt M6
8. Spindle control	Command spindle rotation speed and direction.	Ss M3/M4 M5
9. Reference point return	Return the tool to the machine home position.	G91 G28 Z0 G91 G28 X0 Y0
10. Program end	Specify the end of part program	M2 M30

1.11 NC Programming Methods

NC part programming methods can be classified into two main categories: **manual programming and computer-assisted programming**. In the manual method, a part program is prepared by manually inputting the coded instructions into the controller by either using a tape-punching unit, via manual data input (MDI) mode on the CNC unit, or using a computer with a text editor.

The computer-assisted NC programming method uses a computer to help automatically generate the tool path for producing a part. It can appear in one of the following three forms:

- NC processor languages (APT, Compact II, etc.)
- CAD/CAM NC software systems
- Conversational programming software as part of the CNC unit

Using NC processor languages to generate part programs is gradually being replaced by CAD/CAM software. More than one-third of the plants use CAD/CAM software systems to generate part programs. This approach is gaining ground and eventually will become the major method of NC programming. Conversational programming, also referred to as interactive programming, has found use in about one-fifth of plants. This type of programming software is provided by the CNC unit builder and is part of the CNC unit. This method is adequate for programming simple workpieces.

1.12 CNC Control Systems

CNC controls can be either a **point-to-point system or a continuous path system**. The point-to-point (PTP) control moves the tool to the programmed point, normally in rapid traverse, without engaging the workpiece. Once the programmed point is reached, machining is then executed in the Z axis direction.

The PTP sytem is also called the positioning system because its exact tool path normally cannot be controlled. Depending on the control type, the PTP tool path (Figure 1.16) may follow one of the following three modes:

- Axial path (Figure 1.16a)
- 45° line path (Figure 1.16b)
- Linear path (Figure 1.16c)

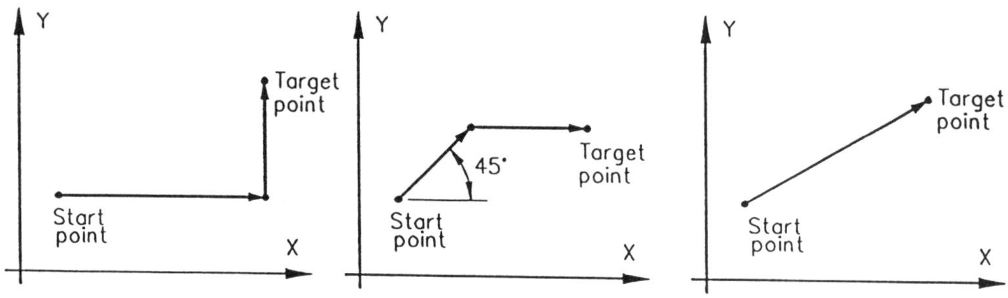

a. axial path b. 45° line path c. linear path

Figure 1.16 PTP tool path

PTP systems are typically used in drilling machines, punch presses, and spot welders which require positioning in the XY-plane in rapid traverse mode while executing machining in the Z axis (see Figure 1.17). PTP control systems are less expensive and are simple in control structure. They are also easy to maintain.

The continuous path control system is also called the contouring system. A **contouring system** is capable of synchronizing two or more axial drives to produce a prescribed path. Depending on the control type, a contouring system can be one of these four types: **2-D contouring, 2½-D contouring, 3-D contouring and 4-D contouring.**

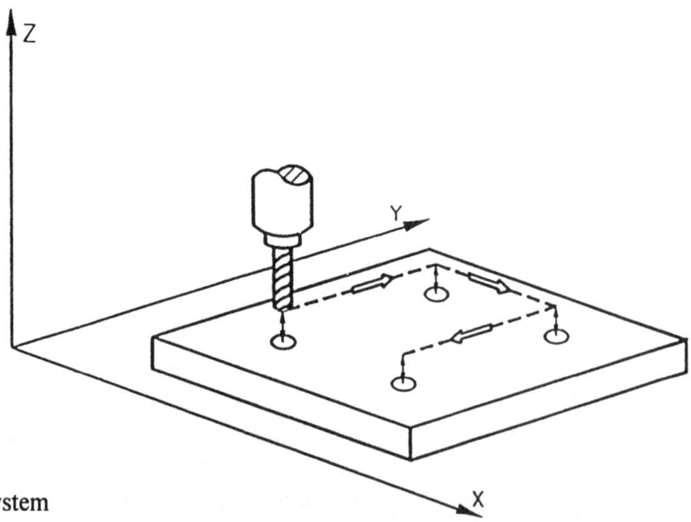

Figure 1.17 Application of a PTP system

2-D Contouring Control

A 2-D contouring system implements linear and circular tool paths in the two-axis (XY-) plane (Figure 1.18). The third (Z) axis is controlled independently of the other two axes. Contouring can be implemented in only one plane, in most cases the XY-plane (in a 2-D system). In other words, a 2-D contouring system can synchronize the feed of only two axes simultaneously. In practice, the feeding to desired depth in the Z axis should be made before contouring in the XY-plane.

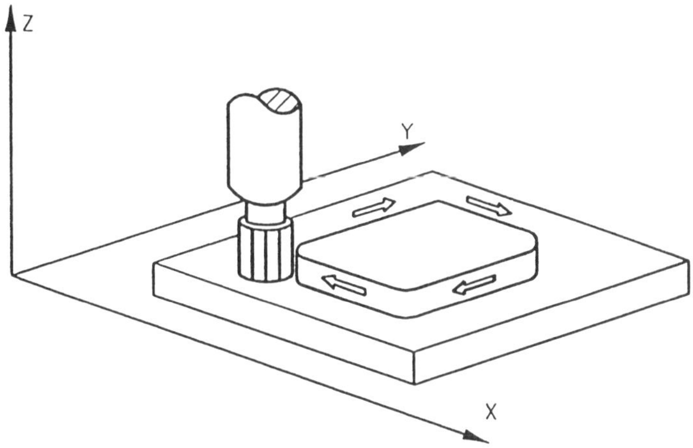

Figure 1.18 2-D contouring

2½-D Contouring Control

In a 2½-D contouring system, **any two** of three axes can be controlled simultaneously. Thus, the contouring can be implemented either in the XY-plane, ZX-plane, or YZ-plane. In practice, the feed can be executed in any one of the three axis, then followed by contouring in any two-axis plane. Figure 1.19 shows contouring in the ZX- and YZ- planes, respectively.

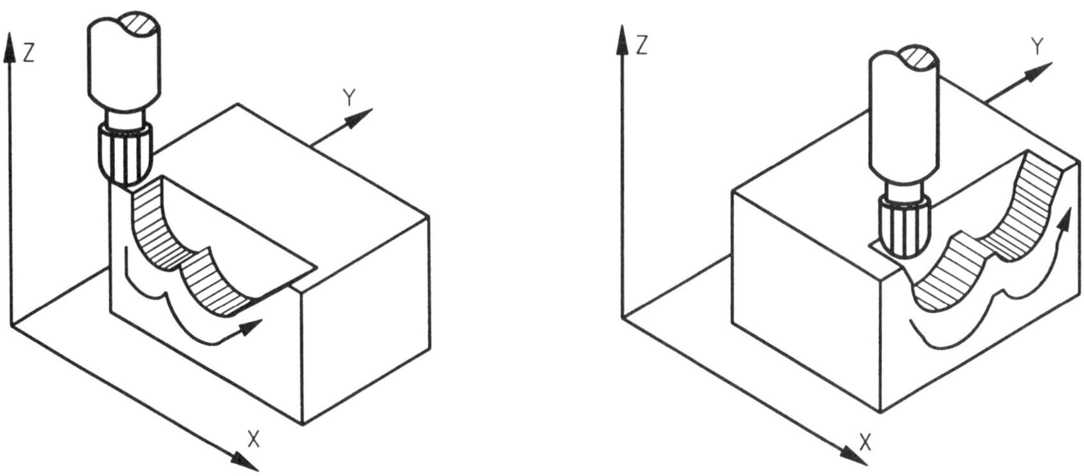

a. in the ZX- plane b. in the YZ- plane

Figure 1.19 2 ½-D Contouring

3-D Contouring Control

A 3-D contouring system is capable of synchronizing **three axes** simultaneously to produce linear and circular tool paths in 3-D space. It can be used to produce any 3-D surface as shown in Figure 1.20.

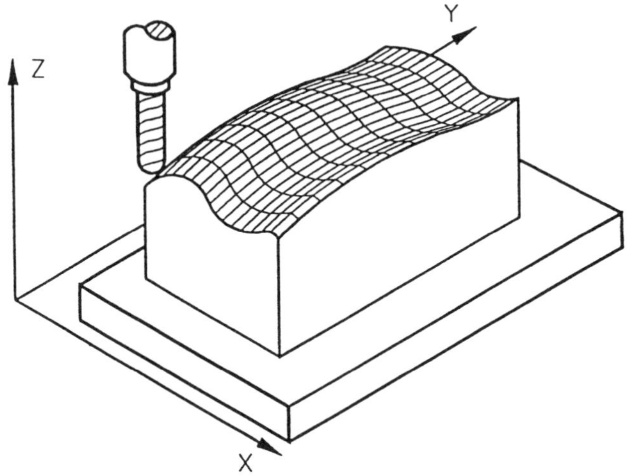

Figure 1.20 3-D contouring

4-D Contouring Control

Some controls furnish an additional axial control for the regular 3-axial control system. The fourth axial control is normally the **rotary axis** which is used for indexing the rotary table. Figure 1.21 shows a 4-D contouring example.

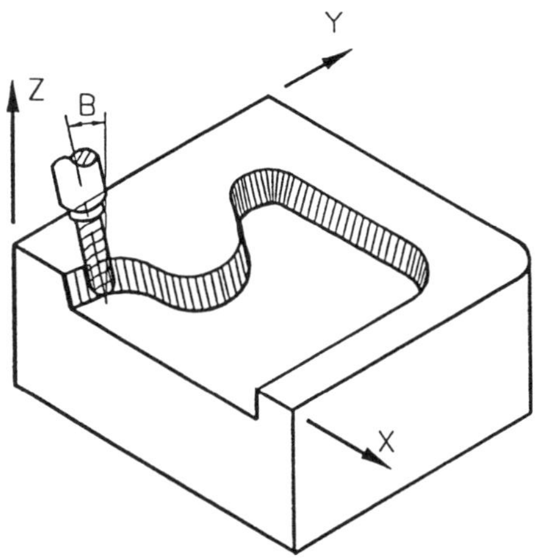

Figure 1.21 4-D contouring

1.13 CNC Drive Systems

The CNC drive systems can be either **open loop or closed loop** type. The main difference between the two systems depends on whether the system has a **feedback loop** to insure the accuracy of system performance.

Open Loop System

No feedback loop is used in open loop drive systems. The drive motor acts upon the control commands from the machine control unit (MCU). The system simply assumes the machine table will reach the target position. There is no way for the MCU to know the actual performance of the system. An open loop system is very sensitive to the load resistance. Position and velocity error may occur when a heavy cutting resistance is encountered. Figure 1.22 shows an open loop CNC drive system. Open loop drives are typically used in PTP systems in which the cutting tool does not engage with the workpiece during positioning. They can also be used in light-loaded cutting machines. Open loop systems are less expensive, but they are prone to load resistances during machining.

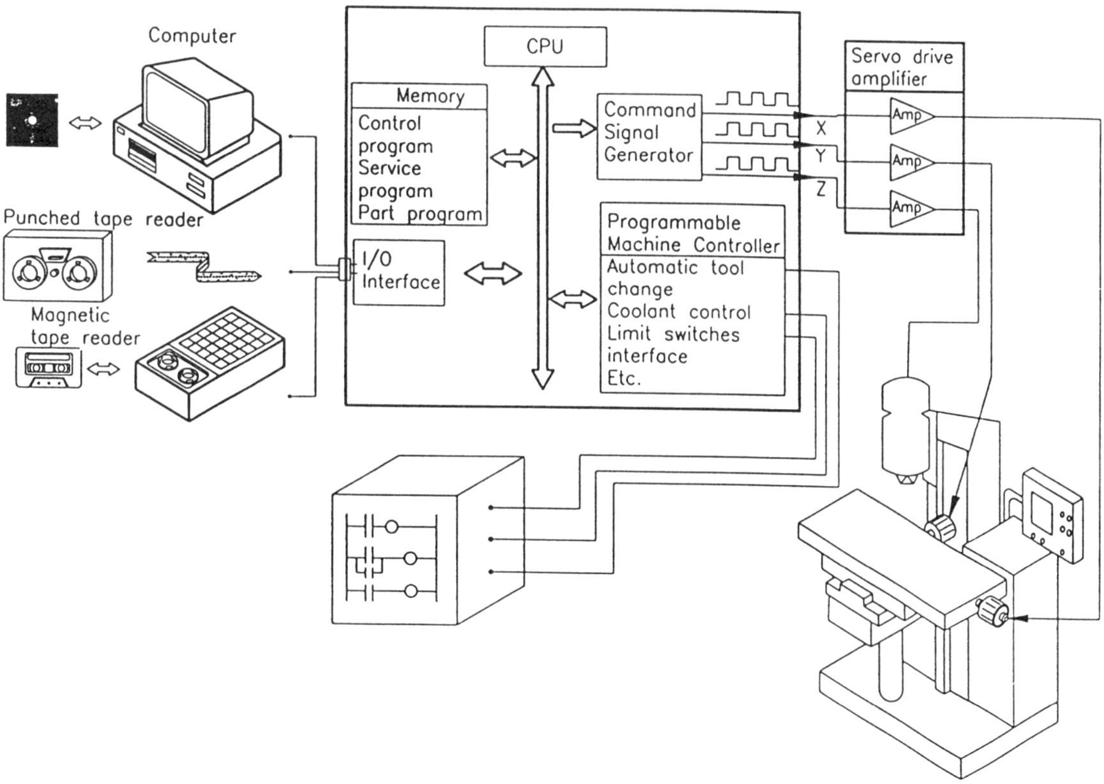

Figure 1.22 An open loop CNC drive system

Closed Loop System

With closed loop drive systems, feedback sub-systems are used to monitor the actual output and correct any discrepancy between desired and actual system performance. Feedback sub-systems may be either an analog or digital type. **Analog systems** measure the variation of physical systems such as position and velocity in voltage level. Tachometers are typically used to measure the velocity, while resolvers for position.

There are two feedback loops in CNC drive systems: **position loop and velocity loop** (Figure 1.23). The **position loop** is the outer loop that consists of a comparator, an amplifier ciurcuit, a velocity loop, a resolver, and a resolver interface. In operation, the comparator receives the reference signal from CNC control and the position feedback signal from the resolver. The difference of these two signals represents the existing positional error. The comparator produces the positional error signal and feeds this signal to the amplifier to drive the servo motor for correcting the error.

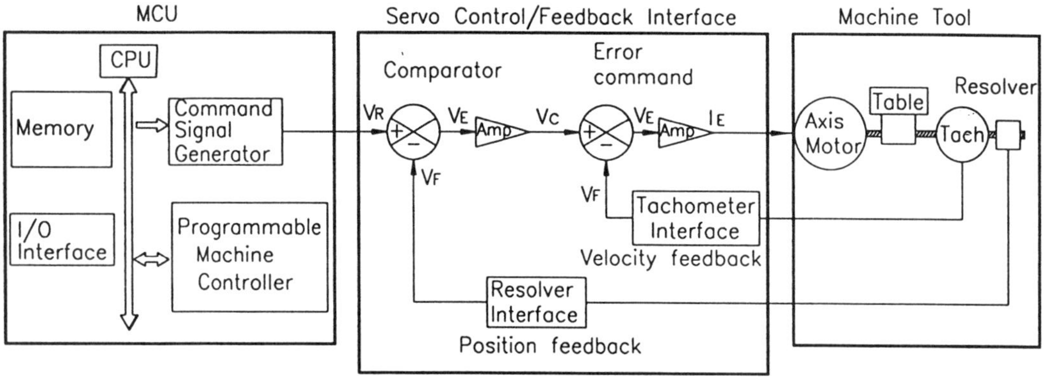

Figure 1.23 Analog type closed loop CNC drive system

The **velocity loop** is the sub-loop within the position loop. It consists of a comparator, an amplifier circuit, a tachometer attached to either the leadscrew or the servo motor, and a tachometer interface.

Digital feedback systems (Figure 1.24) use a digital position transducer to measure the position. Encoders are popular digital position transducers. An up-down counter and a digital-to-analog converter are used in place of the comparator and amplifier. The velocity loop in a digital feedback system is the same as that found in the analog feedback system.

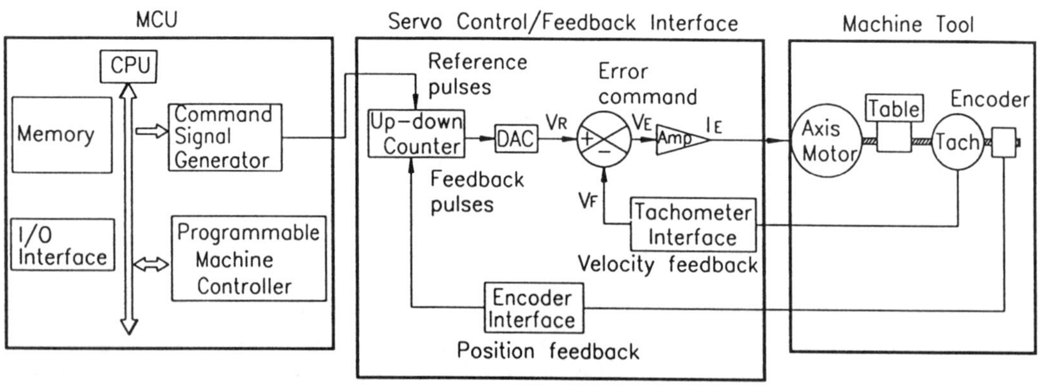

Figure 1.24 Digital type closed loop CNC drive system

1.14 CNC Interpolations

CNC controls use various forms of interpolation to execute contouring tool paths. **Interpolation** is the process of producing a series of intermediate data points between given coordinate positions. The interpolation points are implemented by various types of CNC control interpolators.
The **two** main functions provided by an interpolator are:

Compute intermediate coordinate positions along the programmed path
Compute the axial velocity of an individual axis along the contour path

CNC controls furnish the following **five** possible types of interpolations:

- Linear interpolation
- Circular interpolation
- Helical interpolation
- Parabolic interpolation
- Cubic interpolation

All modern CNC controls furnish linear, circular, and helical interpolation; very few controls support parabolic and cubic interpolations.

Linear Interpolation

Linear interpolation moves the tool from the starting point to the target point along a straight line. Linear interpolation can be implemented in a 2-D plane or 3-D space. It is used in two categories of applications: machine lines (Figure 1.25) and on the following page, approximate irregular curves (Figure 1.26) and surfaces (Figure 1.27).

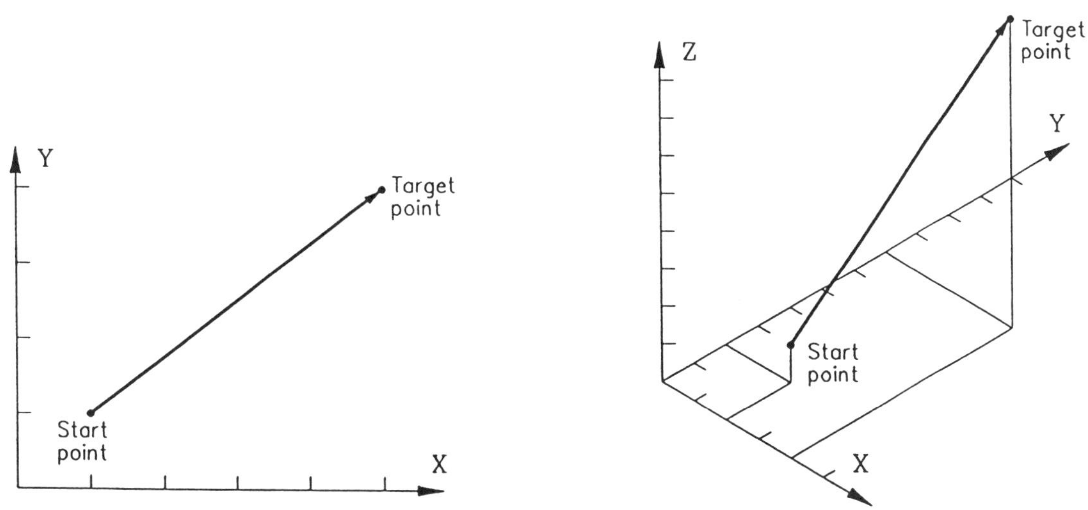

a. in 2-D b. in 3-D

Figure 1.25 Straight line cutting

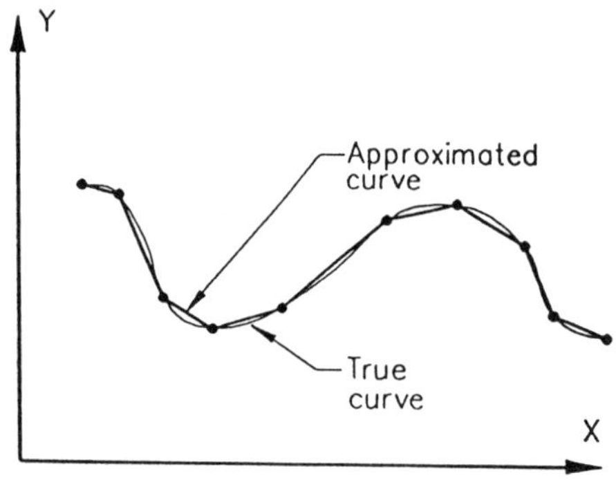

Figure 1.26 Cutting irregular curve

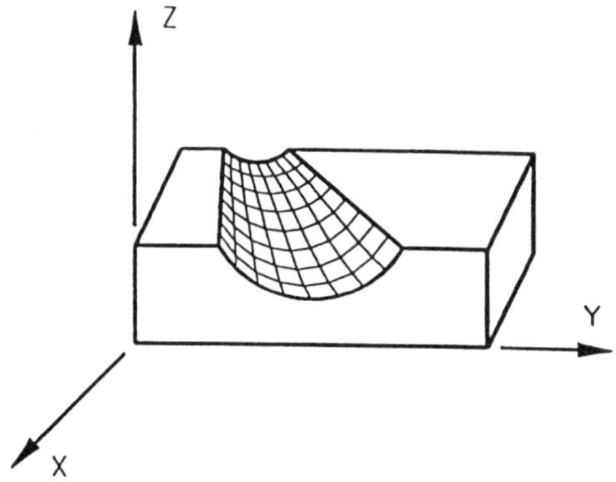

Figure 1.27 Surface cutting

Circular Interpolation

Circular interpolation is programmed to cut circular arcs in one of three principal planes (XY-plane, ZX-plane, or YZ-plane) (Figure 1.28).

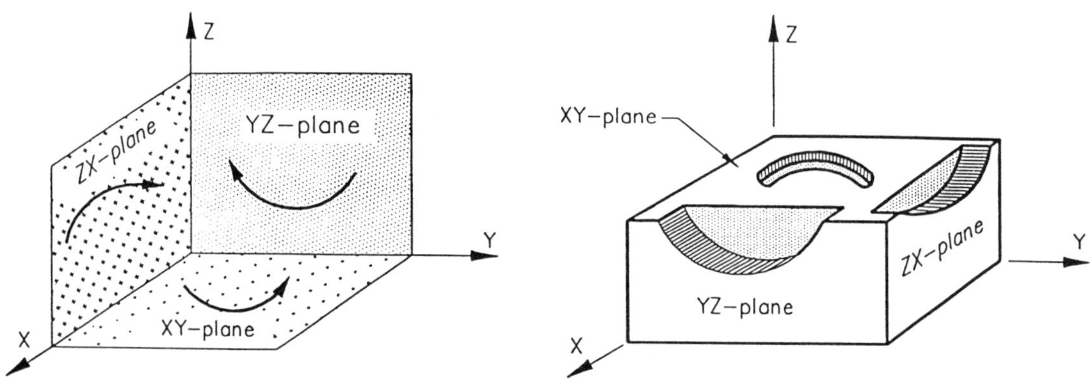

Figure 1.28 Circular interpolation

Helical Interpolation

Helical interpolation combines the two-axis circular interpolation and a linear interpolation in the third axis. It can be used in the following three configurations:

•Circular arc in XY-plane and linear interpolation in Z axis (Figure 1.29**a**)

•Circular arc in ZX-plane and linear interpolation in Y axis (Figure 1.29**b**)

•Circular arc in YZ-plane and linear interpolation in X axis (Figure 1.29**c**)

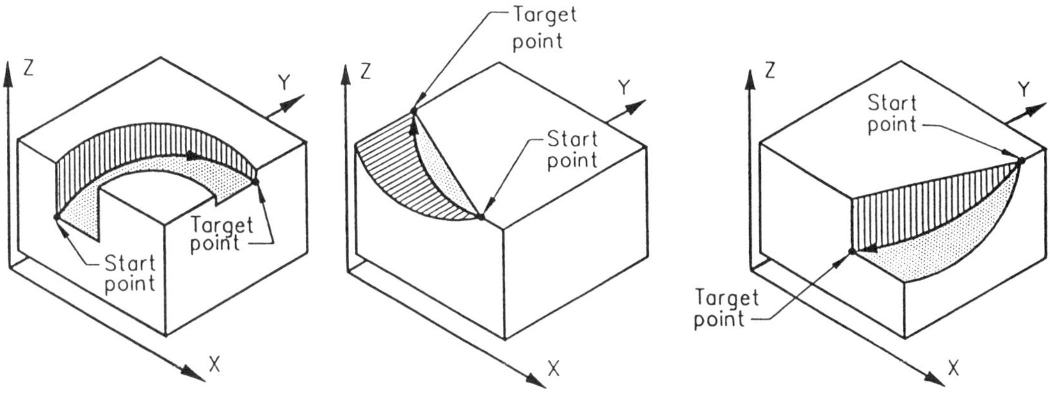

a. Arc in the XY-plane b. Arc in the ZX-plane c. Arc in the YZ-plane

Figure 1.29 Helical interpolation

Parabolic Interpolation

Parabolic interpolation uses three non-collinear points to approximate curves that are of free form (Figure 1.30). It is mainly used in mold and die making where free form designed, rather than precisely defined shapes, are preferred. The use of two or more successive parabolic interpolations can approximate higher-order curves (Figure 1.31). The advantage of using parabolic interpolation is the reduction of programmed points by as much as 50 times that required by the linear interpolation mode.

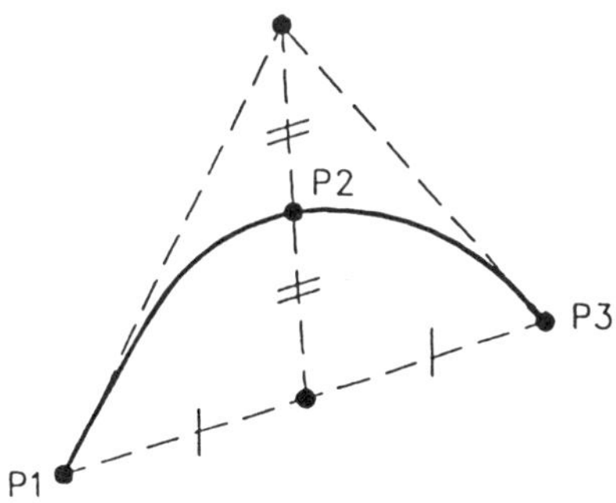

Figures 1.30 Parabolic interpolation

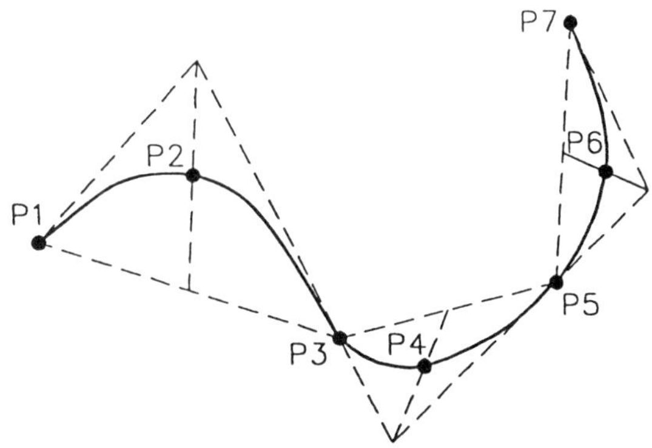

Figure1.31 Parabolic interpolation of a higher order curve

Cubic Interpolation

Cubic interpolation approximates the surfaces defined by third-order geometry. It involves the motion of three axes to machine complex shapes such as automobile sheet metal dies.

1.15 Machine Axes Designation and Direction

The EIA-267-B standard specifies fourteen axes for describing the linear and rotary motions of CNC machines. This includes nine linear axes and five rotary axes. The nine linear axes are further divided into the following three groups: (Figure 1.32)

- Primary linear axes (X,Y, and Z)
- Secondary linear axes (U, V, and W)
- Tertiary linear axes (P, Q, and R)

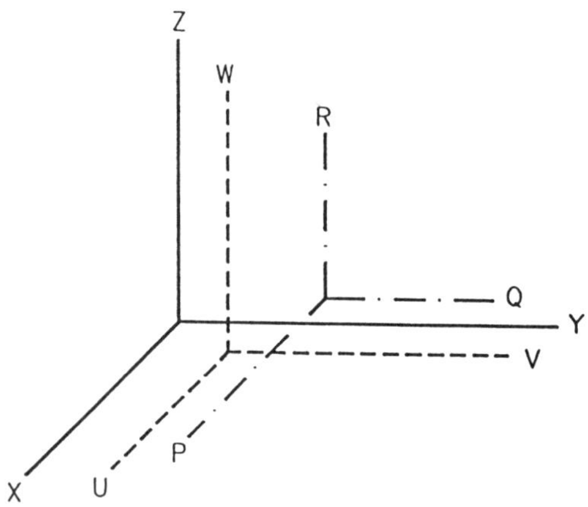

Figure 1.32 Nine linear axes

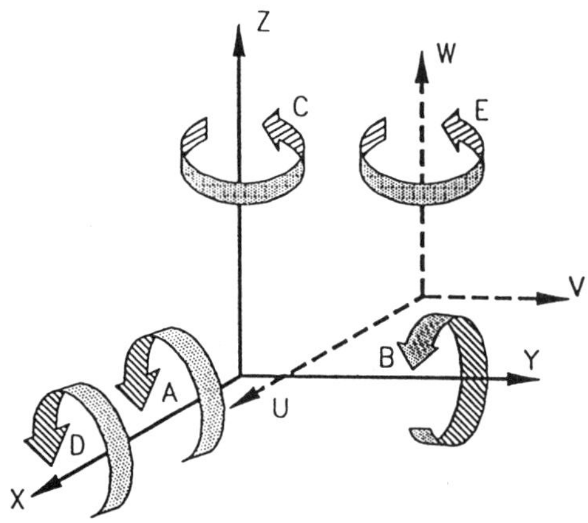

Figure 1.33 Five rotary axes

The primary axes (X, Y, and Z) are assigned to the primary slide table. The secondary linear axes (U, V, and W) are added to the primary axes for defining the movement of the second moving slide or spindle. Similarly, the tertiary linear axes (P, Q, and R) are used to represent the linear motion of the third slide or spindle.

The five rotary axes consist of three primary rotary axes (A, B, and C) and two special axes (D and E) (Figure 1.33). Their definitions are:

Axis A:	rotary motion around the primary linear axis X
Axis B:	rotary motion around the primary linear axis Y
Axis C:	rotary motion around the primary linear axis Z
Axis D:	rotary motion around any linear axis
Axis E:	rotary motion around any linear axis

Machine Axes Designation

Machine axes are designated according to the "right-hand rule". When the thumb of right hand points in the direction of the positive X axis, the index finger points toward the positive Y axis, and the middle finger toward the positive Z aixs. Figure 1.34 shows the right-hand rule applied to vertical machines, while Figure 1.35 applies to horizontal machines.

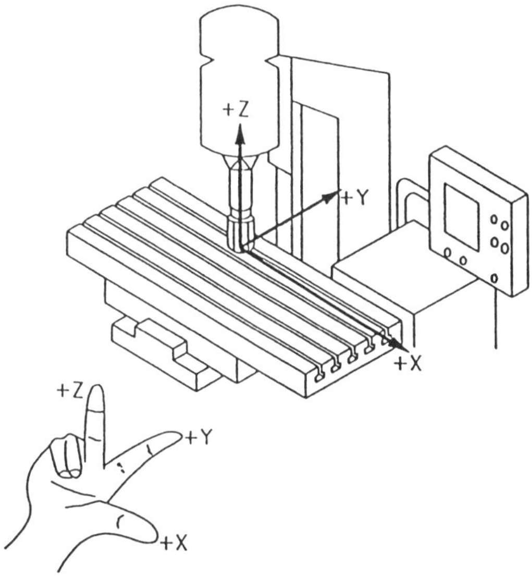

Figures 1.34 Right hand rule: vertical machine

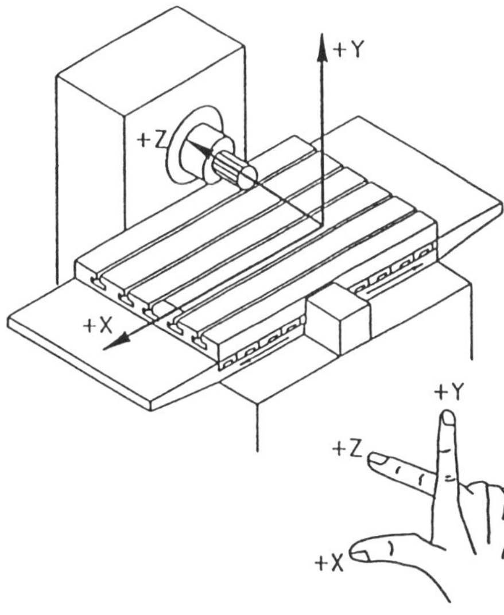

Figure 1.35 Right hand rule: horizontal machine

Direction of Machine Axes

CNC controls use the positive (+) and negative (-) sign to indicate the motion direction of the machine axes. This is how we define the directions.

+Z direction: is the direction which increases the distance between the workpiece and the cutting tool.

-Z direction: is in the opposite direction of +Z.

+X direction: (a) In vertical machines, it is the direction to the right when observed *from* the spindle *toward* its supporting column.
(b) In horizontal machines, it is pointed to the right when viewed *from* the spindle axis *toward* the workpiece.

-X direction: is in the opposite direction of +X.

+Y direction: follows the right-hand rule: when the thumb points *toward* the +X axis and the middle finger is directed *toward* the +Z axis, the index finger points in the direction of the +Y axis.

-Y direction: is in the opposite direction of +Y.

1.16 Reference Zero Points

Reference zero points are the base or starting points that are chosen as the reference for calculating the coordinates of the other points. Also, reference zero points are called the **zero points**. CNC controls use the following **four** types of reference zero points to facilitate the programming of tool paths:

- Machine zero point
- Reference return point
- Work zero point
- Program zero point

Machine Zero Point

The machine zero point is the origin of the machine coordinate system. It is set by the machine tool manufacturer and can not be changed.

The machine zero is labelled with an **M** and represented by this symbol: 

The location of the machine zero point varies from manufacturer to manufacturer. For turning machines, the machine zero is normally located at the center of the spindle end face (Figure 1.36). In milling machines, the machine zero is usually at the extreme limit of each axis travel (Figure 1.37).

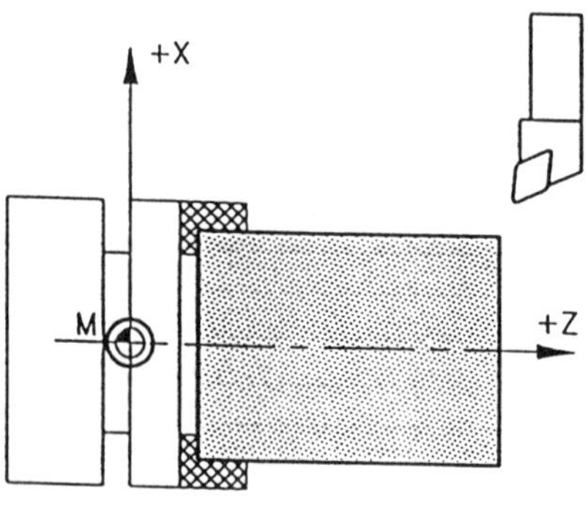

Figures 1.36 Machine zero point of a turning machine

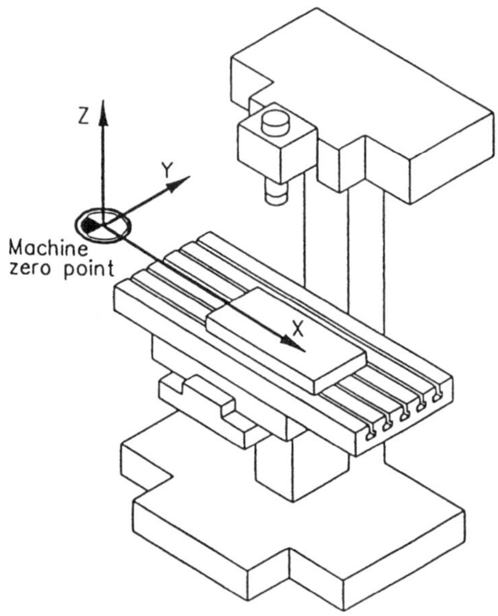

Figure 1.37 Machine zero point of a milling machine

Normally the machine zero is not directly used as the reference point for writing part programs. It may be used in one of the following **three** applications:

1. Initial setup of the machine
2. As the reference point for other reference points such as reference return points, work zeros, and program zeros
3. As the tool change position

Reference Return Point

Reference return points are the locations to which the machine table or the spindle is returned. They are identified by the letter **R** and are represented by the symbol: 

Some CNC controls allow defining up to four reference return points. Normally, the machine zero is set to be the first reference return point in milling machines (Figure 1.38). The second, third, and fourth reference return points are specified by setting their parameter values. They can be set at any convenient location within the work envelope. In turning machines, the reference return point is located in the extreme end of the work envelope (Figure 1.39)

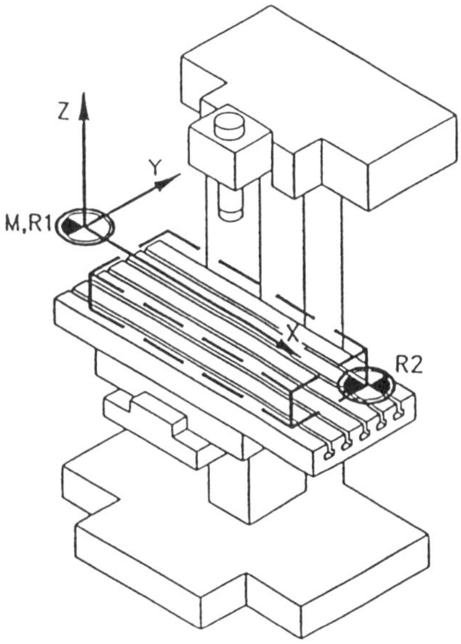

Figures 1.38 Reference return point of a milling machine

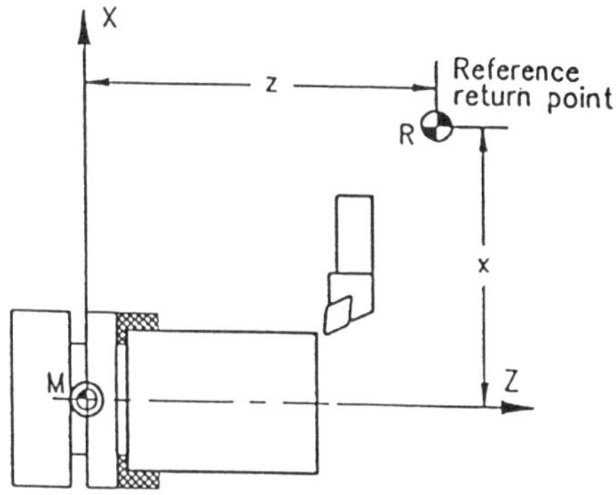

Figure 1.39 Reference return point of a turning machine

The location of the first reference return point is precisely predetermined in each moving axis in relation to the machine zero point. Because of this, it can be used for **calibrating and regulating** the measuring system of the slide table and spindle.

Specifically, the reference point is used in **four** situations:

1. When the control is powered up, all axes always must be positioned at the reference return point to calibrate the measuring system.

2. The machine must be re-positioned to the reference return point for re-establish ing the proper coordinate values in situations such as losing the current position data due to electrical failure or improper machine operation.

3. All axes must be retracted to the reference point before the tool change can take place.

4. At the end of the part program, all axes must be retracted to the reference return point to reset the control system for re-running the part program or running a new part program.

Work Zero Point

A work zero point is the origin of the workpiece's coordinate system. It is used to determine the work's coordinate system in relation to the machine zero point. The work's zero points are often referred to as setup points because they are the locations for setting up the workpiece on the machine table. Some CNC controls allow the use of multiple work zero points in one machine setup or operation. The work zero point is labelled by **W** and represented by the symbol: 

The work zero point can be chosen by the programmer at any convenient location within the working envelope of the machine. It is recommended that you place the work zero point in a way that it can be easily located and measured on the workpiece. Figure 1.40 shows two common methods of choosing the work zero point for turnings and Figure 1.41 shows milling examples.

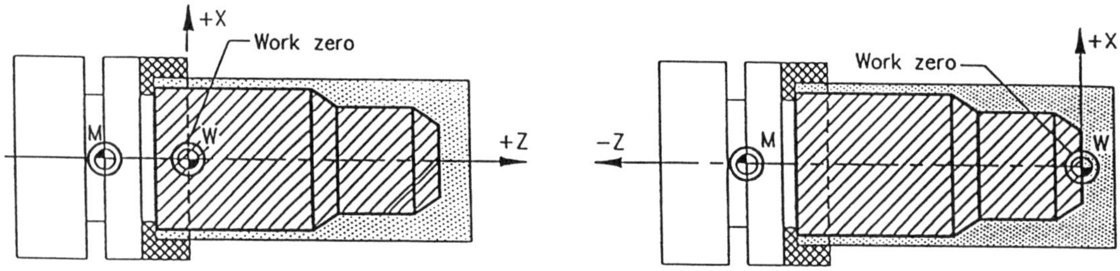

a. located at the chuck face b. located at right workpiece face

Figures 1.40 Selecting work zero for turning

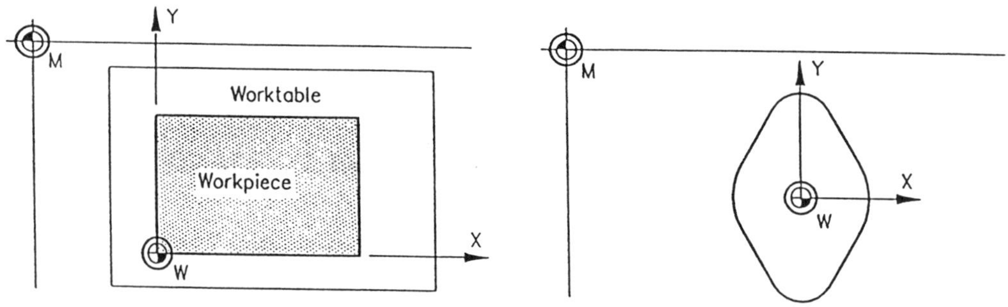

a. located at intersecting point of two datum surfaces b. located at workpiece center

Figure 1.41 Selecting work zero for milling

Program Zero Points

A program zero point is the **origin** of the part program. It is used to locate all other points in the part program. Therefore, it must be chosen before any programming can proceed. The program zero point is labelled by P and represented by the symbol: 

The program zero point normally coincides with the work zero point. However, it can be located at any convenient position. On the next page, Figure 1.42 shows the situation of the program zero point and the work zero point coinciding, while these two points are located separately in Figure 1.43.

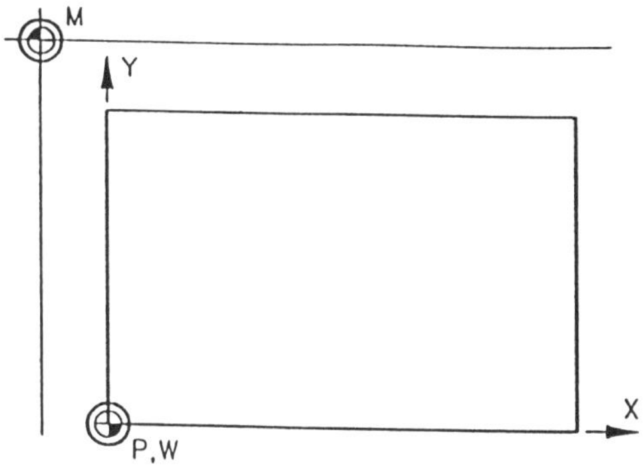

Figures 1.42 Program zero point and work zero point coincide

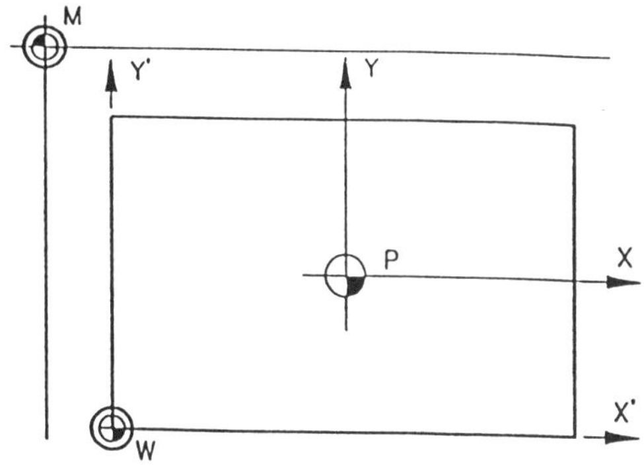

Figure 1.43 Separate program zero point and work zero point

It is possible to define multiple program zero points to facilitate the programming of workpieces with complex features. The **first** program zero point is the **program zero** and the **second** program zero point and **all succeeding points** are referred to as the **local zero point**. Figure 1.44 illustrates using two zero points to write a part program.

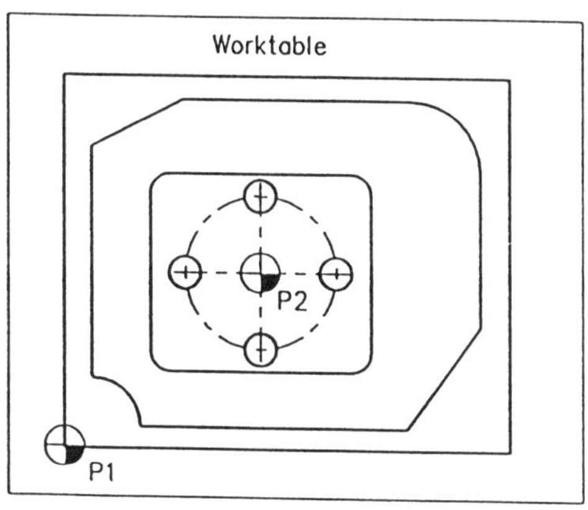

Figure 1.44 Multiple program zero points

1.17 Positioning Systems

We use a positioning system to determine the locations of the positioning points on the workpiece to which the cutting tool is moved. Two methods of positioning systems are used in NC part programming:

- absolute positioning system and
- incremental positioning system.

Absolute Positioning System

We always measure the dimension data of all positions from a **fixed reference point** in the absolute positioning system. In fact, this point is the program zero point. The absolute positioning system is sometimes referred to as the reference positioning system. Figure 1.45 shows an example using absolute positioning system.

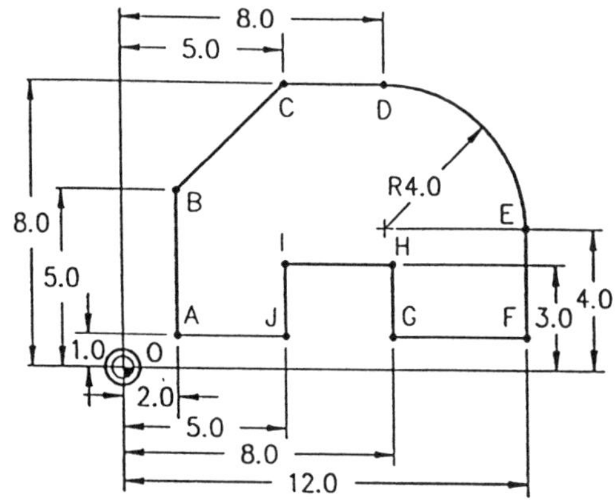

Figure 1.45 Absolute positioning system

Incremental Positioning System

When using the incremental positioning system, the dimension data of a point always refers to the immediately **preceding** point. Each position is measured in relation to the previous one and the coordinate system shifts from point to point. Some important features of the incremental positioning system are given below:

a. The program zero point is used as the reference point only for the first programmed point.
b. The plus (+) and minus (-) sign should be used to indicate the direction of tool motion even though points may be located only in the first quadrant.
c. The positioning sequence of the tool path affects the dimension data of a point. This feature is illustrated in Figure 1.46.

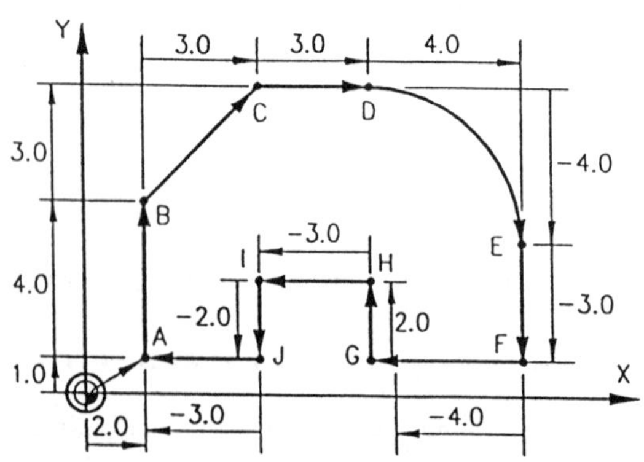

a. Clockwise sequence

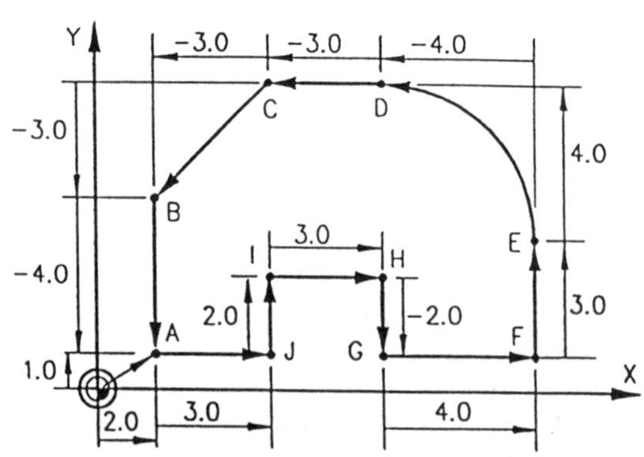

b. Counter-clockwise sequence

Figure 1.46 Incremental positioning system

Selection of the Positioning System

Using the **absolute positioning system** in part programming is recommended for the following **two** reasons:

1. The positioning error encountered with an individual point has no effect on subsequent positions.
2. The absolute system is easier to use to trace the cutter locations for check -ing errors because all dimensions are referenced to the same fixed point.

The **incremental positioning system** is preferred when common patterns (holes, pockets, or contour patterns) in a workpiece are repeated several times. **Three** main disadvantages of using the incremental positioning system are:

1. Any positioning error will be continued throughout the rest of the program. A positioning error of 1.0" in H1 as shown in Figure 1.47 below, for example, is carried to all succeeding programming positions.
2. A compound error is progressively accumulated if more than one error is encountered in a part program. Figure 1.48 below depicts this feature. A positioning error of 0.5" in H1 continues on to H2. An additional error of 1.5" is encountered in H3, the accumulated error of 2.0" then appears throughout the rest of the program.
3. It is very difficult to check for any position error, especially in large part programs.

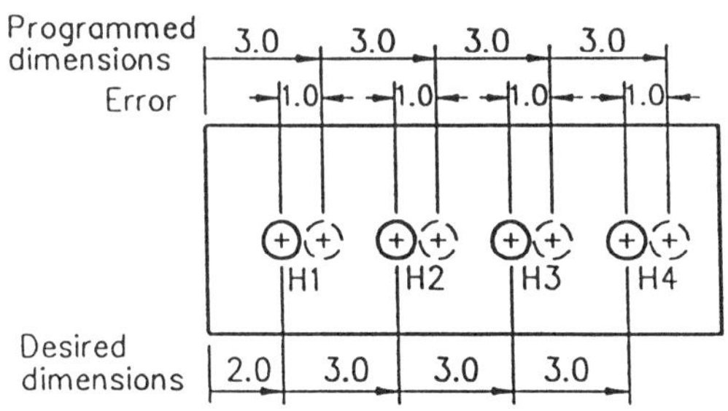

Figure 1.47 A position error is extended to all succeeding programming positions

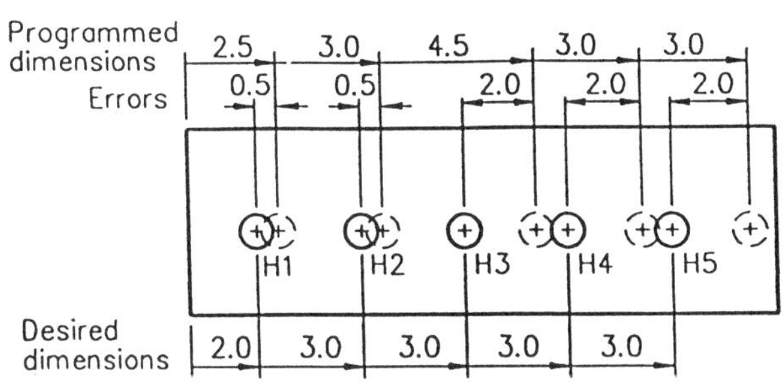

Figure 1.48 Accummulated errors

Chapter 2

Machining Fundamentals

Objectives:

1. Be familiar with the machining processes performed by CNC milling and turning machines.
2. Know cutting tools and tooling systems for CNC machines.
3. Select machining parameters for various machining processes.
4. Provide useful tips for various machining processes.

2.1 CNC Milling Processes

CNC milling machines and machining centers are used to perform **six** types of machining processes. Table 2.1 illustrates these six types of machining processes on the following two pages.

- Facing
- Profiling
- Pocketing
- Slot cutting
- Hole machining
- 3-D surface machining

2.2 CNC Turning Processes

CNC turning machines and turning centers implement the following **ten** types of machining processes:

- Facing
- Profiling
- Drilling
- Threading
- Cutting off
- Turning
- Grooving
- Boring
- Chamfering
- Milling

All ten processes are illustrated in Table 2.2 on the following pages 2-4 and 2-5.

Table 2.1 Milling Processes

Process Type	Tool	Illustration
1. Facing Producing flat surfaces	Face mill for larger surfaces End mill for small surfaces	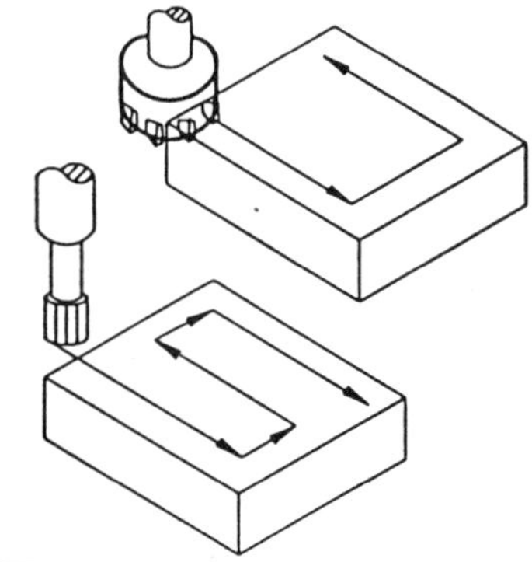
2. Profiling Producing part contours	End mill	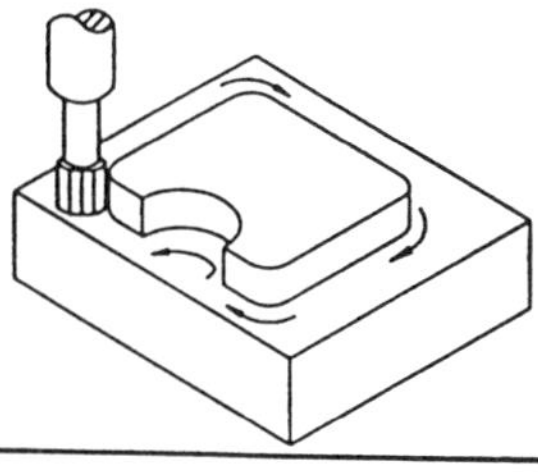
3. Pocketing Removing the material enclosed by a closed boundary	End mill	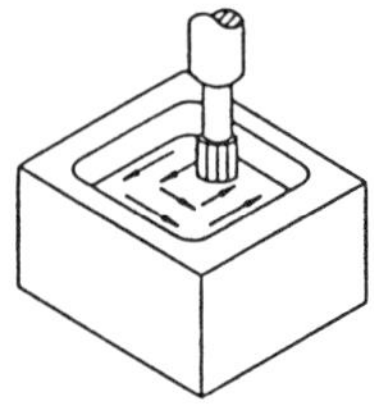
4. Slot cutting Producing various types of slots	End mill	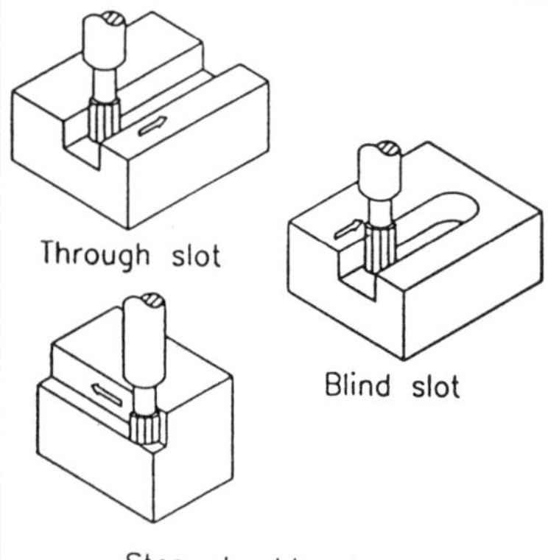
5. Hole machining a. Drilling	Drill	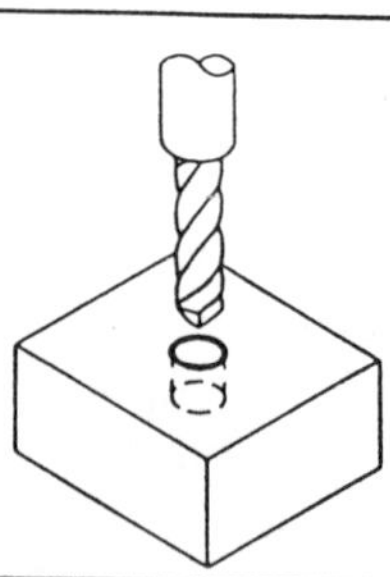

Table 2.1 (Continued)

Process Type	Tool	Illustration
b. Countersinking	Countersink tool	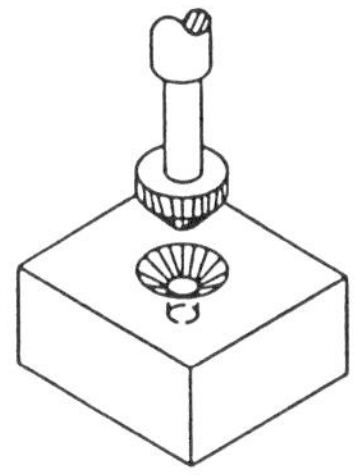
c. Counterboring	Counterbore tool	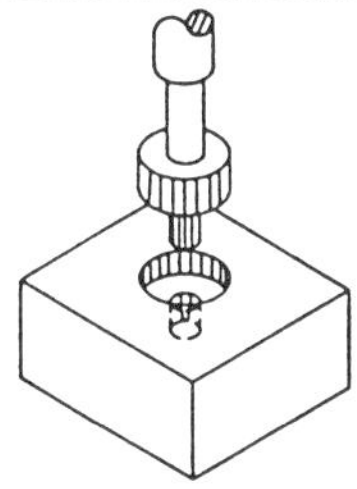
d. Boring	Boring tool	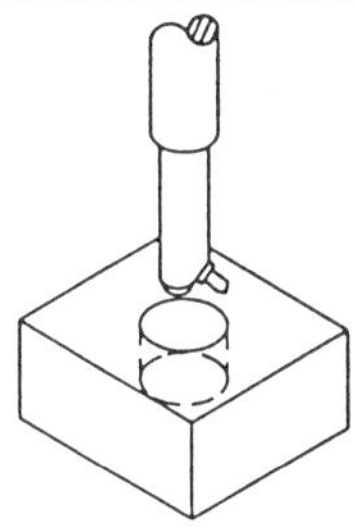
e. Tapping	Tap	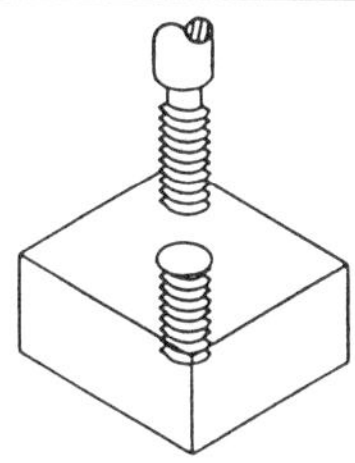
f. Reaming Producing smooth and precise holes	Reamer	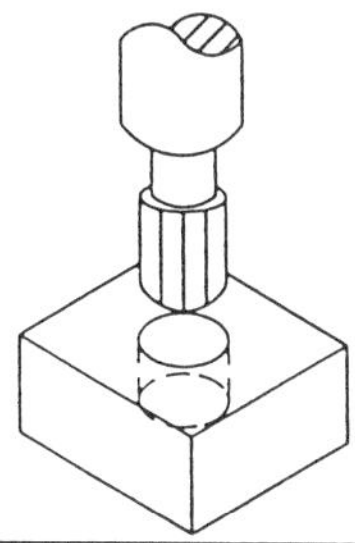
6. 3-D Surface machining Cutting various types of surfaces	Ball-end mill	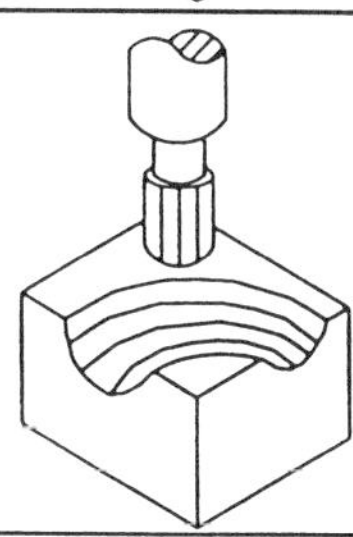

Table 2.2 Turning Machining Processes

Process Type	Tool	Illustration
1. Facing: Producing flat end face a. Facing to center b. Facing to shoulder	Facing tool	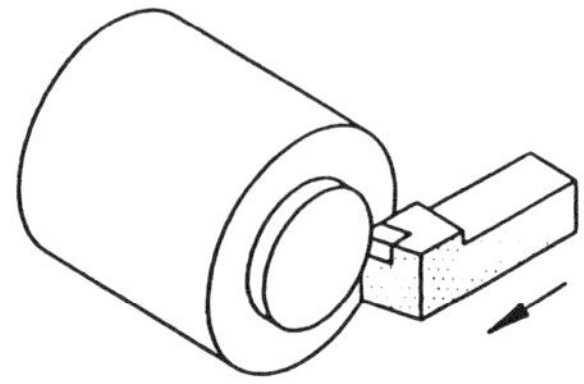
2. Turning: Producing line profiles a. Straight turning	Turning tool	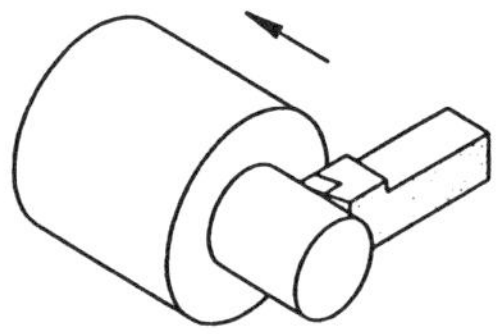
b. Taper turning		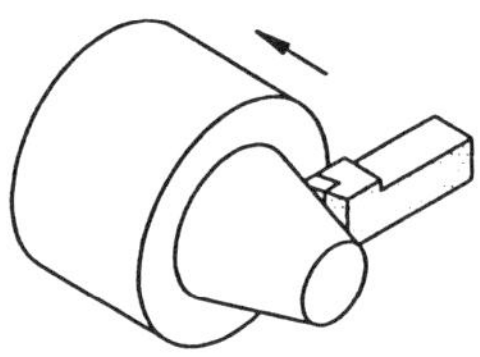
3. Profiling Producing external line and circular profiles	Profiling tool	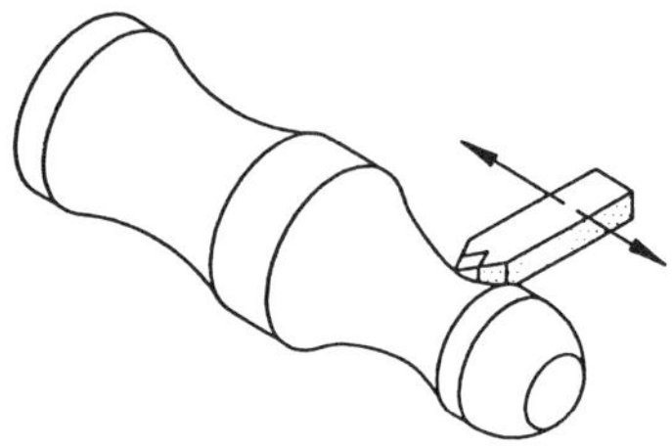
4. Grooving: Cutting various forms of grooves a. Side grooving	Grooving tool	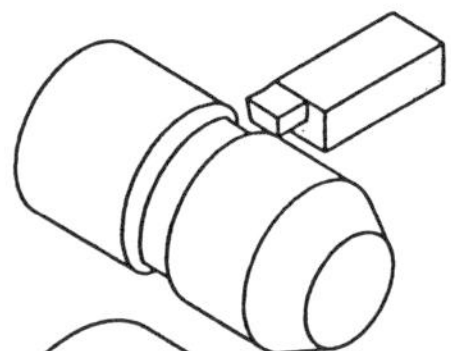 Side grooving
b. Face grooving		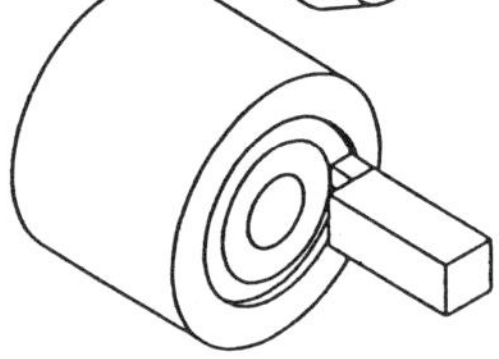 Face grooving
5. Drilling Producing holes in the spindle axis	Drill	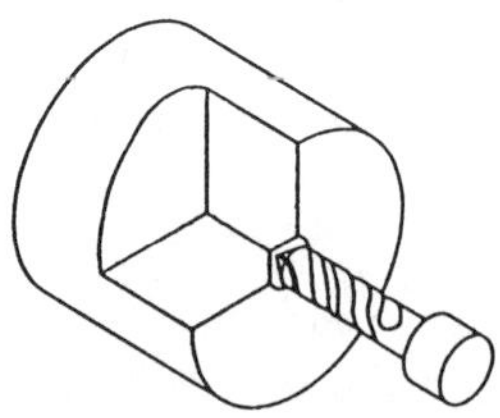

Table 2.2 (Continued)

Process Type	Tool	Illustration
6. Boring Producing internal line and circular profiles	Boring tool	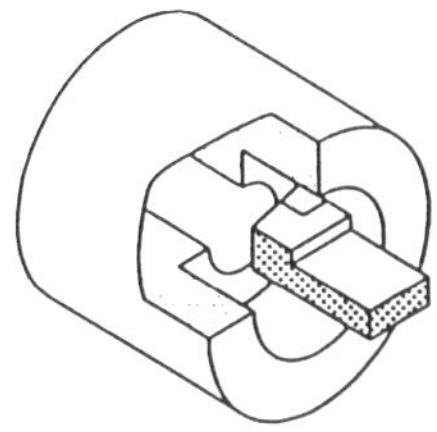
7. Threading: Cutting various thread forms a. External thread	Threading tool	External thread 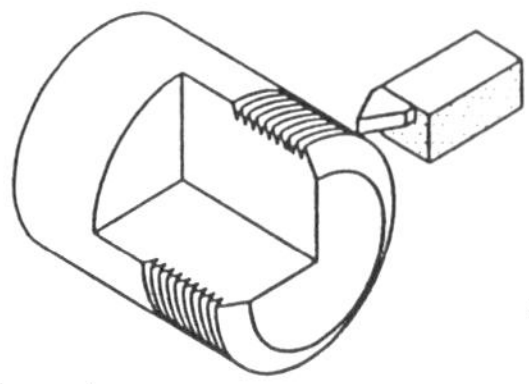
b. Internal thread		Internal thread 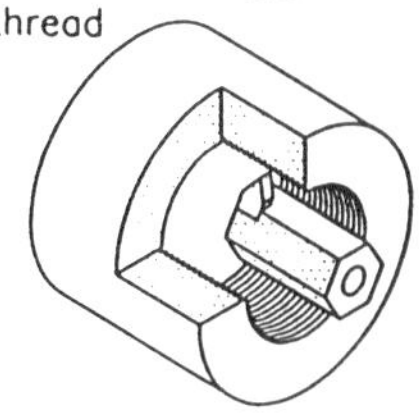
8. Chamfering Generating chamfers at sharp corners	Chamfering tool	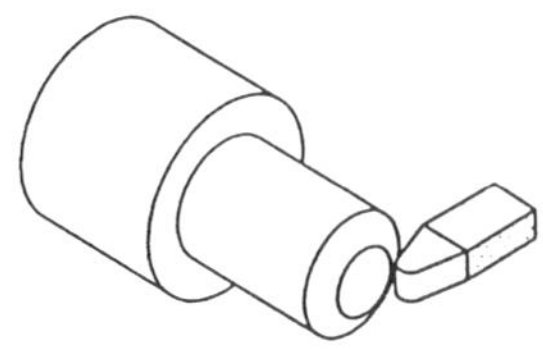
9. Cutting off Separating the workpiece from the stock	Cut-off tool	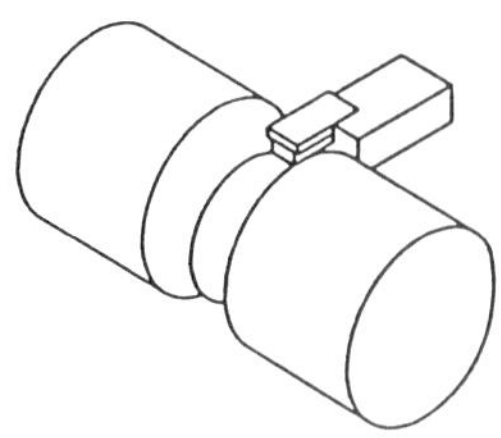
10. Milling Producing slots and surfaces	End mill	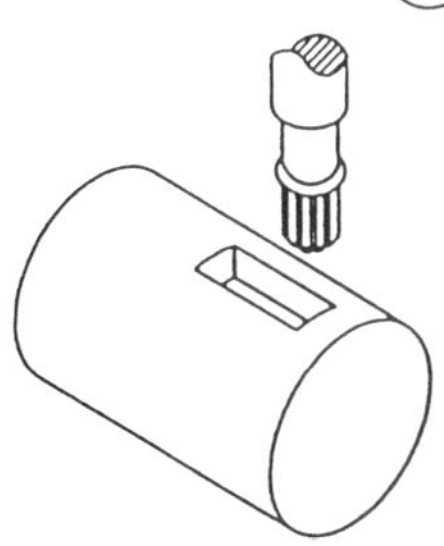

2.3 Cutting Tool Materials

Required Properties of Cutting Tool Materials

Three important properties of any cutting tool material are:

1. Wear resistance (resistance to the various wear mechanism)
2. Toughness (the ability to absorb energy and withstand plastic deformation without fracturing under compressive loading)
3. Hot hardness (the ability to resist stresses and maintain hardness and cutting efficiency at elevated temperatures)

Cutting Tool Materials

The common cutting tool materials used for CNC machining are **high speed steel (HSS), tungsten carbides, cermets, ceramics, and polycrystalline.** Table 2.3 summarizes the characteristics and applications of various cutting tool materials.

Table 2.3 Characteristics and applications of various cutting tool materials

Material	Principal Characteristics	Typical Applications	Advantages
HSS	Tougher than carbides	Low speed machining, and interrupted cuts.	Lower cost than carbide, longer tool life, better surface finish.
Uncoated carbide	Very tough, excellent edge wear resistance.	Roughing to finishing virtually any material including iron, steel, stainless steel, high temp-erature alloy, non ferrous metals and non- metallic materials.	Higher cutting speed than HSS and tougher than coated carbides.
PVD coated carbide	Very tough, good thermal shock resistance and crater resistance. High retained edge strength. Excellent resistance to buildup on the cutting edge.	Machining of steels, high temperature alloys, stainless steels, difficult to machine materials, aluminum, carbon and alloy steels.	Permit speeds to be in-creased up to 15% when compared to uncoated with no loss of tool life.
Cermet	Excellent resistance to wear, shock and heat.	Finishing operations on malle able cast irons, carbon steels, alloy steels, stainless steels, and aluminum alloys.	Up to 20 times the tool life of conventional carbide grades.
Ceramics (alumina base)	High hardness, excellent chemical wear resistance.	For high speed rouging and finishing of cast irons and steels.	Better finishes at higher machining rates.
Ceramics (silicon base)	High hardness plus high fracture toughness and thermal shock esistance.	Roughing and finishing operations on cast irons.	Machining speeds up to 5000 sfm and beyond.
Polycrystalline diamond (PCV)	Hardness of diamond plus toughness, excellent wear resistance.	Roughing to finishing operations on aluminum and other soft or abrasive non-ferrous or non-metallic materials.	Better than 30 times the tool life of carbide, even on high silicon aluminum.
Cubic born nitride (CBN)	Exceptional hardness, excellent wear resistance and mechanical shock resistance.	High speed machining on hardened ferrous materials in the 50 65 Rc (480 740 Bhn) range.	Provide many times the edge life of carbide, eliminate the need for costly alternative grinding operations.

ANSI and ISO Carbide Grade Classifications

There are two commonly used classification systems for carbide cutting tools:

ANSI system and ISO system.

ANSI System

The ANSI carbide classification system was initiated in the U.S. automotive industry and more commonly used in the United States. It is also called U.S. **C-system** because it uses the letter C with a numeric digit ranging from 1 to 8 to indicate the carbide grade (Table 2.4)

Table 2.4 ANSI Carbide Classification System

Class	Class	Material to be cut	Application	Characteristics of cutting	Characteristics of carbide
C1	Tungsten	Cast iron, nonferrous metals, and nonmetallics	Roughing cuts	Increasing cutting speed ↓ / Increasing feed rate ↑	Increasing hardness & wear resistance ↓ / Increasing strength ↑
C2	Tungsten		General-purpose		
C3	Tungsten		Finishing		
C4	Tungsten		Roughing cuts		
C5	Tungsten	Steels and steel alloys	Tungsten	Increasing cutting speed ↓ / Increasing feed rate ↑	Increasing hardness & wear resistance ↓ / Increasing strength ↑
C6	Titanium		General-purpose		
C7	Tungsten Titanium and Tantalum in varying amounts		Finishing		
C8			Fine finishing		

Carbide tools are classified into **two** major categories. One category is composed of the **straight tungsten carbides** (classes 1 to 4), which are hard and have very good wear resistance. They are best suited to machining cast iron, non-ferrous metals, and some nonmetallic materials that are abrasive. The second category (classes 5 to 8) includes the combinations of **tungsten and tantalum or titanium carbide**. These carbides are generally used for machining steels. They are resistant to cratering, which is a serious problem when tungsten carbide is used to machine steels.

ISO System

The ISO (International Organization for Standardization) system is based on the ISO Standard 513-1975(E) which is widely used in Europe. It uses **three** main categories: **P, M, and K** (Table 2.5 on the next page).

P category:	for machining	ferrous metals with long chips
M category:	for machining	(1) ferrous metals with long or short chips (2) non-ferrous metals
K category:	for machining	(1) ferrous metals with short chips (2) non-ferrous metals (3) non-metallic materials

Table 2.5 ISO Carbide Classification System

Symbol and color	Broad material categories to be cut	Class	Application	Characteristics of cutting	Characteristics of carbide
P (Blue)	Ferrous metals with long chips	P01	Finish turning and boring under vibration free operations	Increasing cutting speed (↑); Increasing feed rate (↓)	Increasing wear resistance (↑); Increasing toughness (↓)
		P10	Turning, copying, threading and milling of light roughing and finishing		
		P20	Turning, copying and milling at medium cutting speeds		
		P30	Turning and milling under heavy feeds and shocks		
		P40	Turning, planning and milling under unfavorable conditions		
		P50	Machining operations demanding very tough carbide		
M (Yellow)	Ferrous metals with long and short chips	M10	Finish turning alloy steels and cast iron	Increasing cutting speed (↑); Increasing feed rate (↓)	Increasing wear resistance (↑); Increasing toughness (↓)
		M20	General grade for machining of alloy steels and gray cast iron		
	Nonferrous metals	M30	Rough machining of tough materials		
		M40	Turning and parting off of mild steel, nonferrous metals and light alloys		
K (Red)	Ferrous metals with short chips	K01	Finish turning, boring and milling of very hard materials, abrasive plastics and ceramics		
	Nonferrous metals	K10	Turning, milling, drilling, and boring of malleable cast iron, nonferrous alloys, plastics, rubber, etc.		
	Nonmetallic materials	K20	Machining of copper, brass, and aluminum demanding tough carbide		
		K30	Rough machining of soft cast iron, low tensile steel in unfavorable conditions		
		K40	Machining of wood and nonferrous metals in unfavorable conditions		

Table 2.6 shows the relationship between ISO designation system and ANSI designation system.

Table 2.6 Relationship between ANSI and ISO Carbide Classification Systems

	Carbide grade		
ISO	P01 P05 P10 P20 P25 P30 P40 P50	M10 M20 M30 M40	K01 K05 K10 K20 K30 K40
ANSI	C8 C7 C6 C5		C4 C3 C2 C1

Increasing toughness →

← Increasing hardness

Note that both ISO and ANSI designation systems for various types and grades of cutting tool materials are not precise. They can only serve as a general guide in selecting cutting tool materials for specific applications. Cutting tool manufacturers often use their own classification systems with ANSI and ISO equivalent grades for their products.

Cutting Tool Material Selection

Selecting proper cutting tool materials for a specific machining application can provide significant advantages including **increased productivity, improved quality, and reduced costs**. The following factors should be carefully considered in selecting cutting tool materials:

1. Type of material to be machined (ferrous or non-ferrous type)

   Select grade C5 - C8 for steel materials

   Select grade C1 - C4 for cast iron, non-ferrous metals, and non-metallic materials

2. Machining types

   Roughing: C1 for non-steel materials
   C5 for steel materials

   General Purpose: C2 for non-steel materials
   C6 for steel materials

   Finishing: C3 for non-steel materials
   C7 for steel materials

   Precision boring and fine finishing: C4 for non-steel materials
   C8 for steel materials

Figure 2.1 is a comparision chart of the cutting speed range for various cutting tool materials for machining different metals.

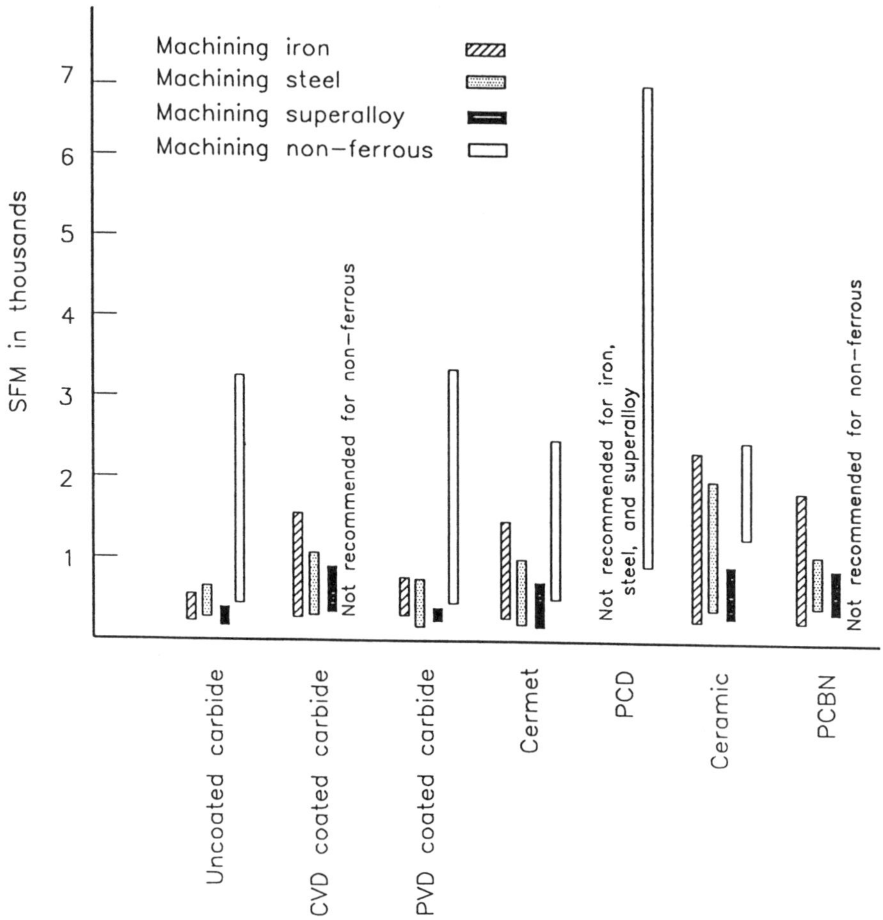

Figure 2.1

2.4 Tooling for Milling

A typical tooling system for machining centers consists of the **four** major components; **automatic tool changer, toolholders, adaptors, and cutting tools.** Any tooling system for CNC machine tools must meet the following **three** requirements:

- capable of holding multiple tools
- automatic tool change to shorten tool change time
- interchangeability

Automatic Tool Changer

An automatic tool changer (ATC) facilitates the quick change of tools in and out of the machine spindle. The tools are stored in the **automatic tool magazine** which is an indexable storage component part of the machine tool. The tools can be selected and changed under the control of the part program. Figure 2.2 on the following page shows a machining center with a chain type of ATC.

Figure 2.2 A chain type automatic tool changer

Toolholders

Toolholders are used to facilitate the switching of a broad range of cutting tools in and out of the spindle automatically. A toolholder consists of **five** basic components (Figure 2.3):

1. Tapered shank
2. Flange
3. Retention knob
4. Opposed slots
5. Adaptor

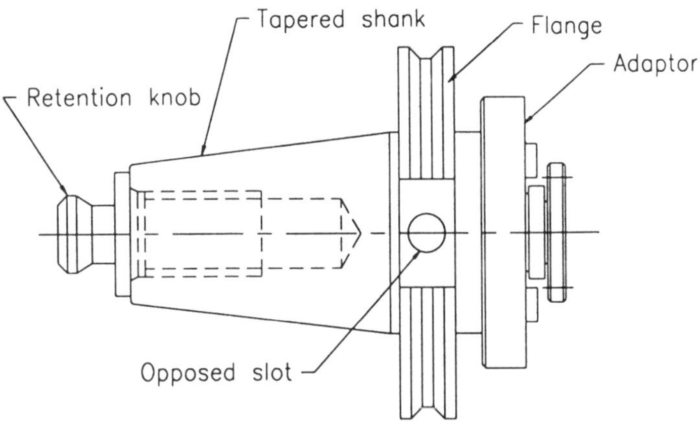

Figure 2.3

Tapered Shank

The tapered shank fits the toolholder to the spindle. The ANSI standard defines **six basic taper shank sizes** including #30, #35, #40, #45, #50, and #60. Larger machines use toolholders that have larger shank taper numbers. The taper of the shank is made to 3.5 in./ft (or a ratio of 7:24).

Taper Shank No.	Type of Machine
#60	Very large machines
#50	Medium size machines (20 to 50 HPs)
#40	Small size machines
#30	Very small machines

Flange Type

The flange allows the toolholder to be grabbed by the tool gripper or the machine spindle. There are **two** commonly used flange types: **V-flange and BT-flange** (Figure 2.4). V-falnges are often referred to as Caterpillar V-flanges. They use inch threads for the retention knob and are used to hold inch-dimensioned cutting tools. BT-flanges have metric threads for the retention knob, but their adaptors can be designed to accommodate a wide range of inch-dimensioned cutting tools. BT-flange holders are widely used in Japanese and European made machining centers.

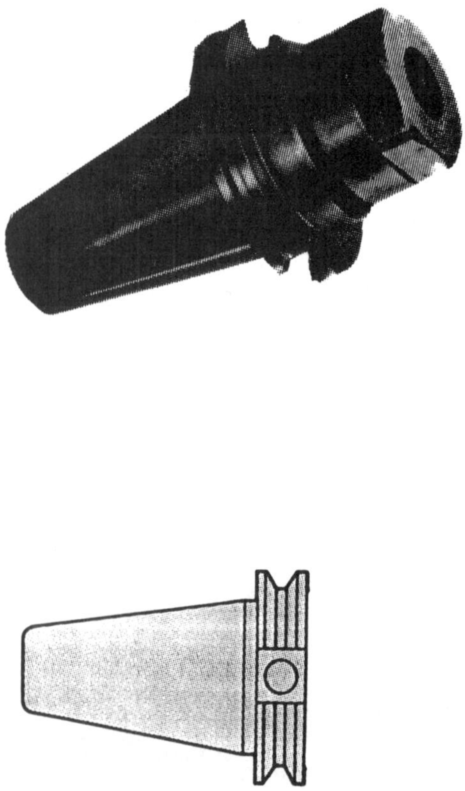

Figure 2.4a V-flange

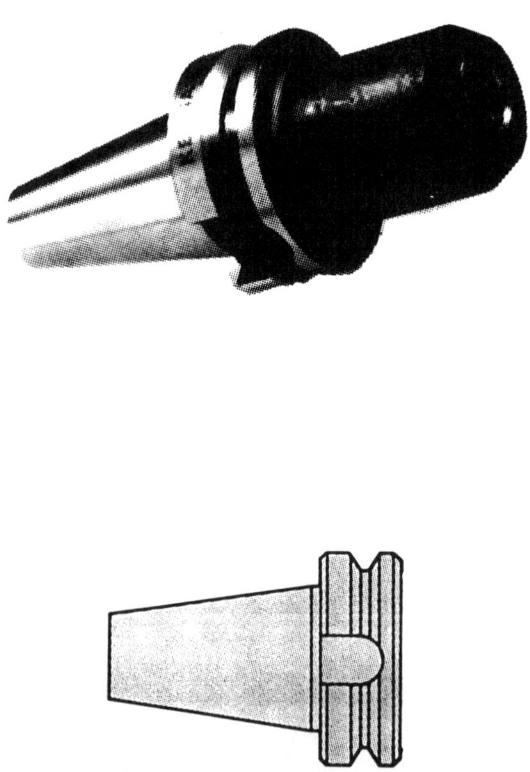

Figure 2.4b BT-flange

Retention Knob

The retention knob allows the locking drawbar of the spindle to pull the toolholder firmly into the spindle and to release the toolholder automatically (Figure 2.5). Retention knobs are made in various styles and sizes. They are not necessarily interchangeable. Only use the retention knobs that are specified by the machine tool manufacturer.

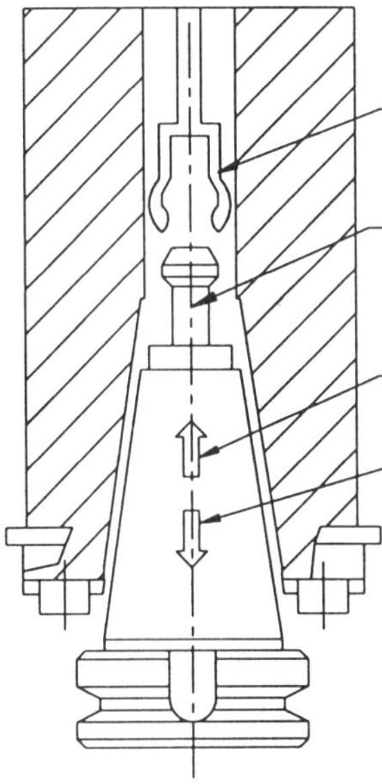

Figure 2.5

Adaptors

Adaptors are designed with various configurations to accommodate different types and sizes of cutting tools. Toolholders are often named according to their adaptor type. Commonly used adaptors include; **end mill holders, face mill holders, tap holders, collet holders, boring bar holders, Morse taper holders, Jacob taper holders, and straight shank holders.** Figure 2.6 on the next page shows a toolholder selection chart. There is no established standard for specifying the configuration and size of adaptors.

2.5 Tooling System for Turning

The tooling system for turning centers consists of **six** basic components (Figure 2.7):

1. Turret head
2. Mounting blocks
3. Mounting plates
4. Tool holders
5. Sleeves and sockets
6. Inserts or cutting tools

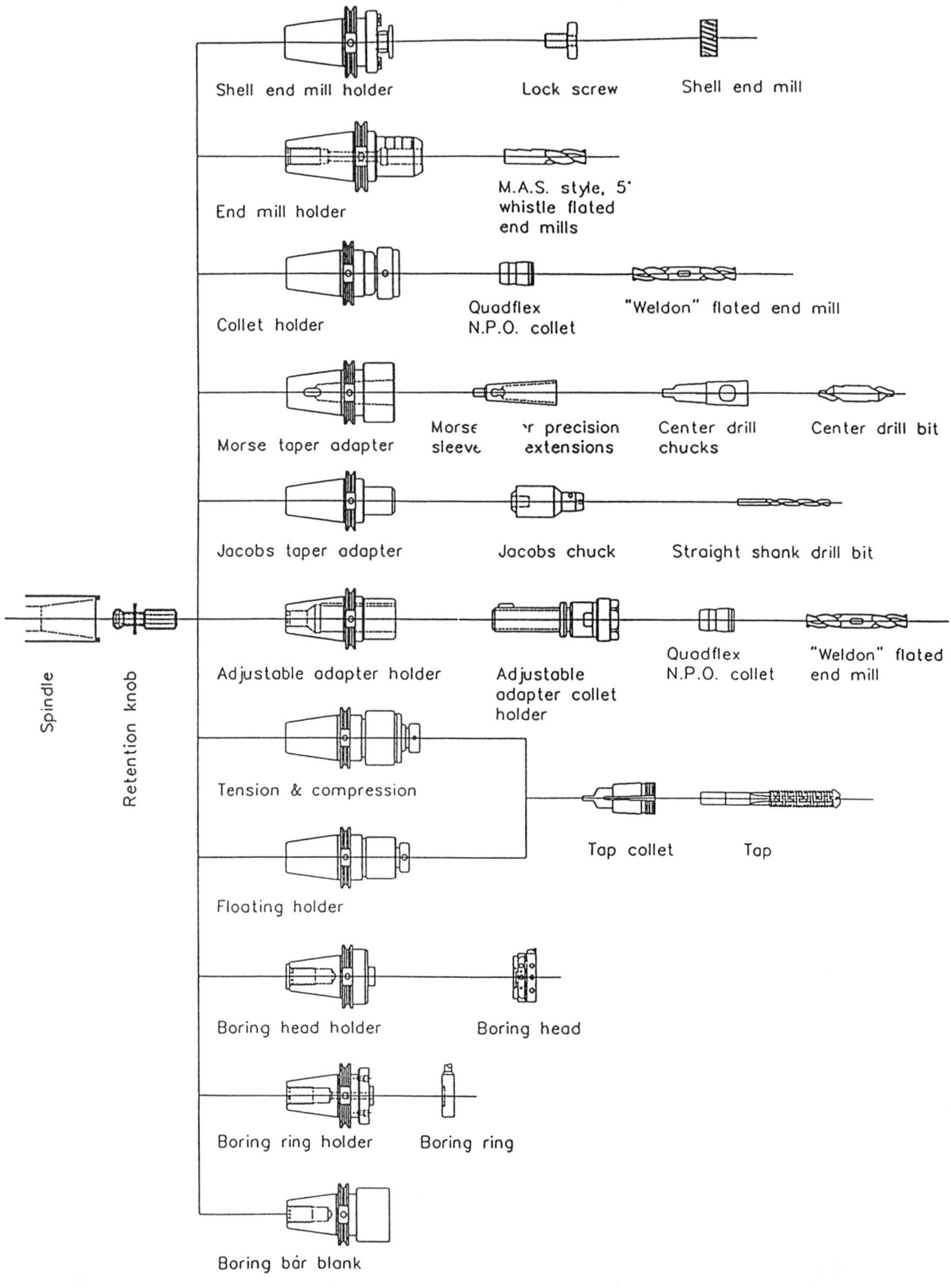

Figure 2.6 Tooling system for milling machines (Source: S.C. Jonathon Lin, Computer Numerical Control: From Programming to Networking, 1994. Courtesy of Delmar Publishers, Inc.)

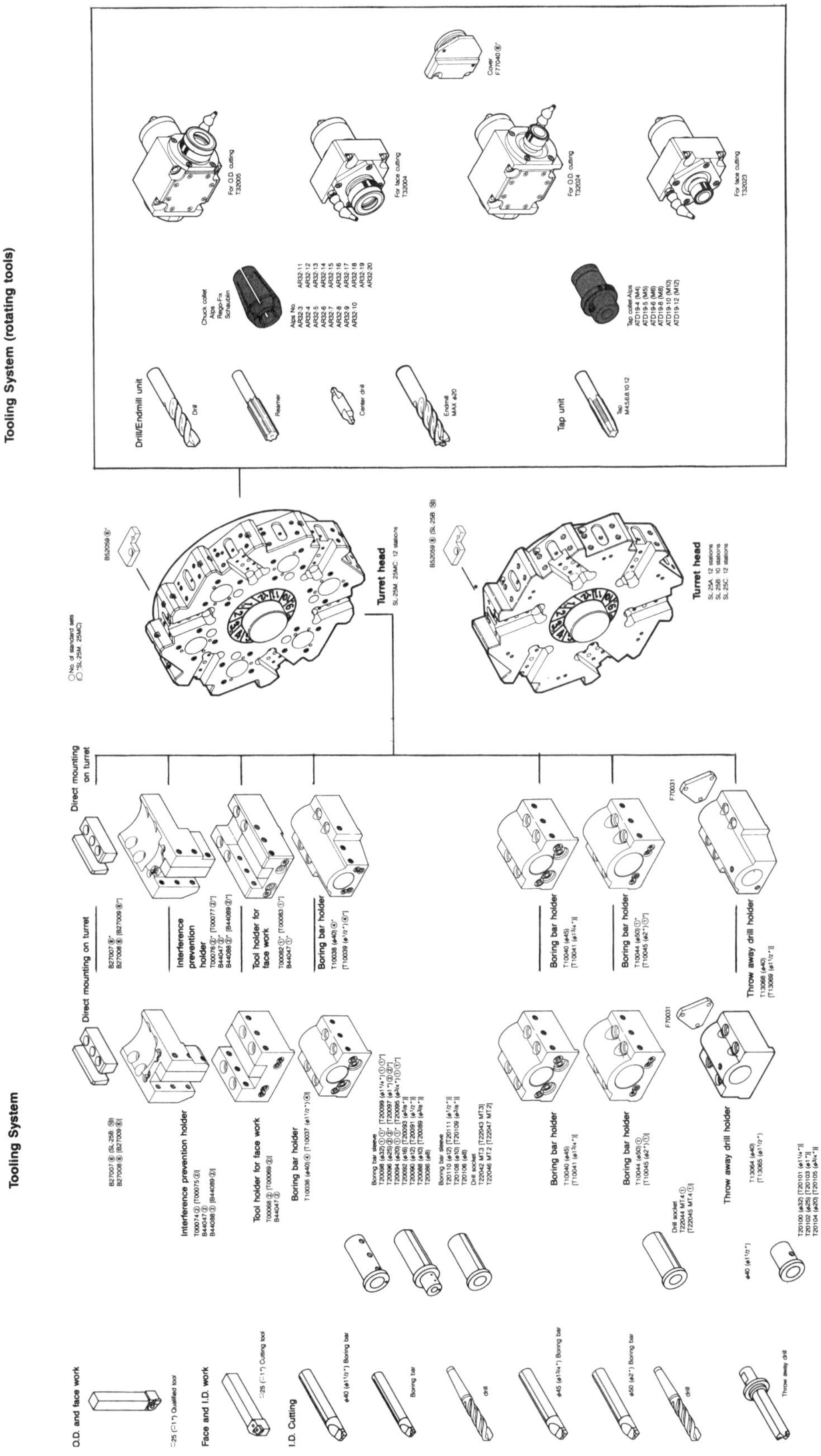

Figure 2.7 Tooling system for turning centers (Courtesy of Mori Seiki Co. Ltd.)

A turret head provides from 6 to 12 tool stations that can be automatically indexed by the control. Depending on the type of cutting tool used, mounting plates or mounting blocks are needed to attach the cutting tools to turret head. Normally, tools for OD turning and facing operations use mounting plates. Boring tools and drills use mounting blocks. Usually sleeves or sockets are needed to allow for different tool shank size. Figure 2.8 shows a 12-station turret head with a variety of cutting tools. Some turning centers provide simultaneous 3-axis control (X, Z, and spindle angular orientation). The spindle C axis can give as small as 0.001° of spindle rotation. Spindle axis control combined with rotating tools allows the machine to turn, bore, drill, mill, tap, and ream the workpiece in any direction in one machine setup. These turning centers have simultaneous 3-axis control which allows the machining of the rotating tools and they are often referred to as mill-turn. Figure 2.9 shows a turret used in a mill turn.

Figure 2.8
(Source of photograph: Mori Seiki Co. Ltd.)

Figure 2.9
(Source of photograph: Mori Seiki Co. Ltd.)

2.6 Inserts Identification and Selection

Indexable inserts are widely used in CNC machines. They are made with various shapes and sizes (Figure 2.10). The ANSI standard provides an identification system to describe the features of inserts. The identification consists of up to 10 symbol codes. Each code defines a feature of the insert (Figure 2.11). The first 7 symbols are mandatory, the following 2 symbols are optional, and the last symbol is for the manufacturer's use. The ISO standard basically follows the ANSI standard except the dimensions are specified in millimeters.

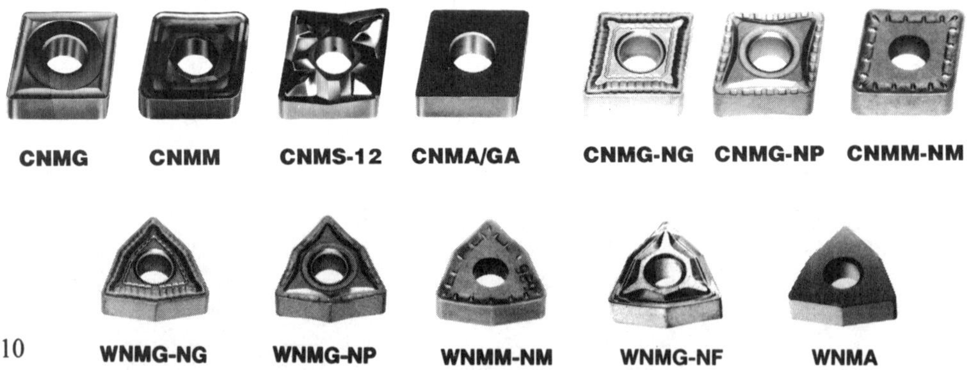

Figure 2.10

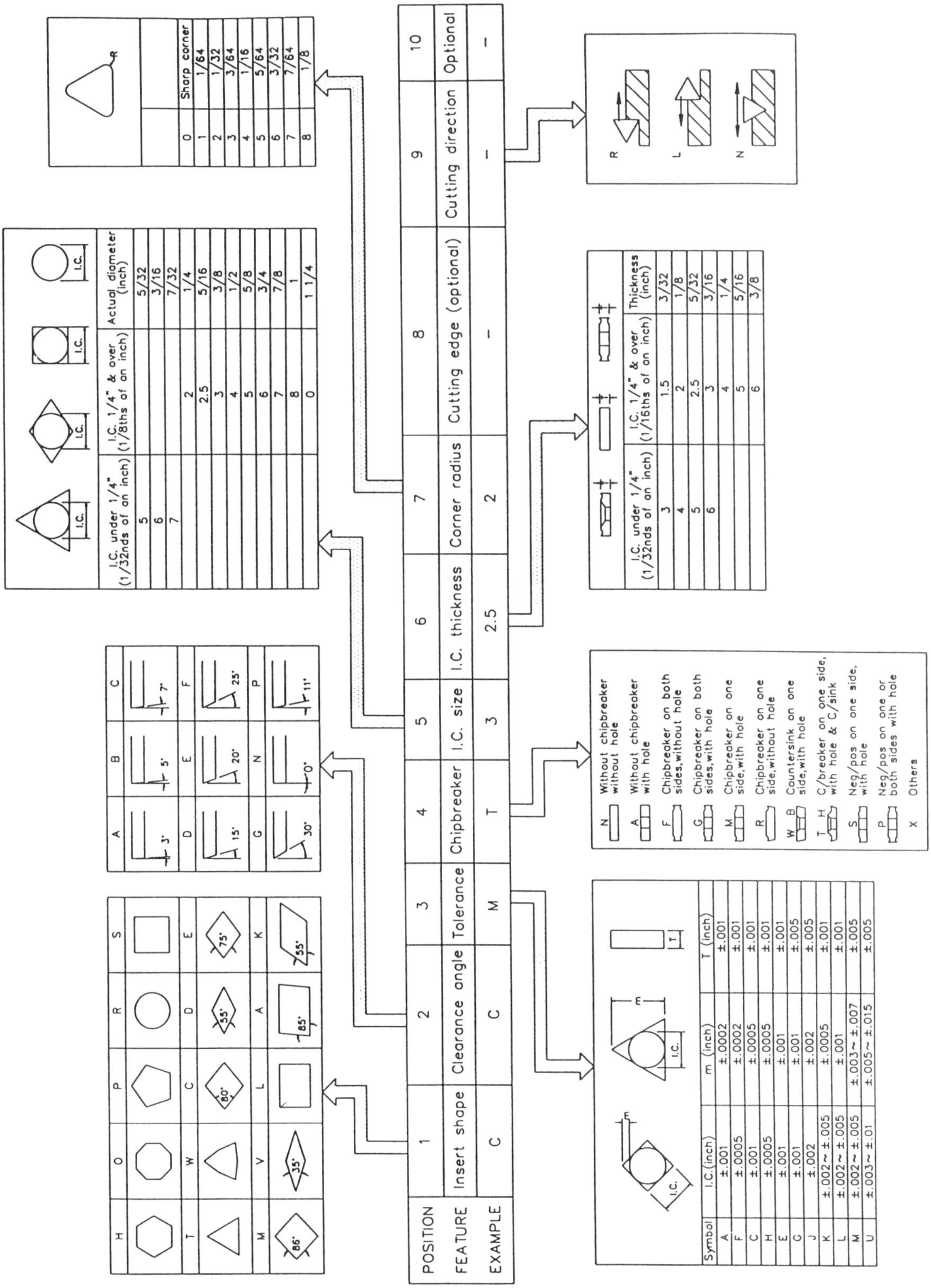

Figure 2.11 Insert identification system (Source: S.C. Jonathon Lin, <u>Computer Numerical Control: From Programming to Networking</u>, 1994. Courtesy of Delmar Publishers Inc.)

Insert Selection

Several factors must be carefully considered in selecting proper inserts for specific applications. These factors include **insert shape, insert size, and chip breaker.**

Insert Shape

Inserts are made in various shapes. The insert shape affects **insert strength, insert angle, maximum number of cutting edges available, power consumption, and versatility**. The larger the included insert angle, the stronger the insert. A round insert is the strongest, while the 35° diamond insert is the weakest type.

The inserts with more sides provide a greater number of cutting edges. A hexagonal shaped insert has six cutting edges, while a triangle shape only furnishes three edges. The cutting edges of those inserts with a zero clearance angle are twice those with a non-zero clearance angle. The zero clearance triangle inserts, for example, have 6 possible edges.

The more commonly used insert types in turning applications include:

80° diamond shape:	for OD turning, ID boring, and facing
55° diamond shape:	for OD turning, profiling, and ID boring
35° diamond shape:	for OD profiling and ID profiling
60° shape:	for OD turning, ID boring, and facing
Round shape:	for OD turning, and ID boring

Insert Size

Three dimensions used to describe the insert size are the **inscribed circle (IC), thickness (T), and nose radius (R)** (Figure 2.12).

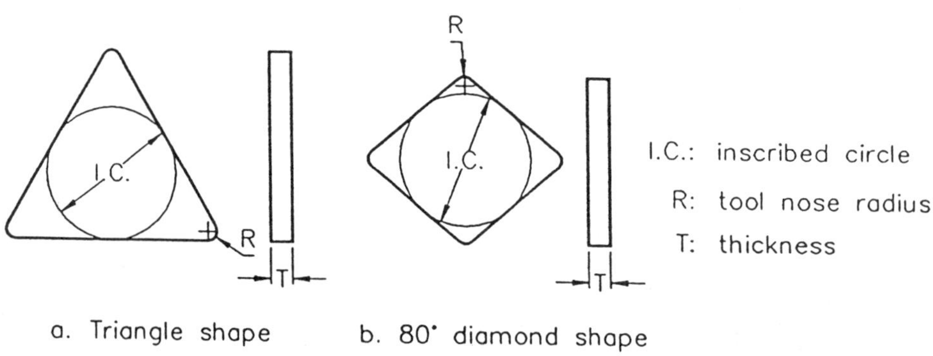

Figure 2.12

The selection of IC size depends on the maximum depth of cut to be taken. The rule of thumb is that the maximum cutting edge engagement is one-half the insert edge length. The cutting edge length is normally longer than the IC size except for square and round inserts as shown in Figure 2.13. The cutting edge length of commonly used inserts can be computed from the formulas given in Table 2.7.

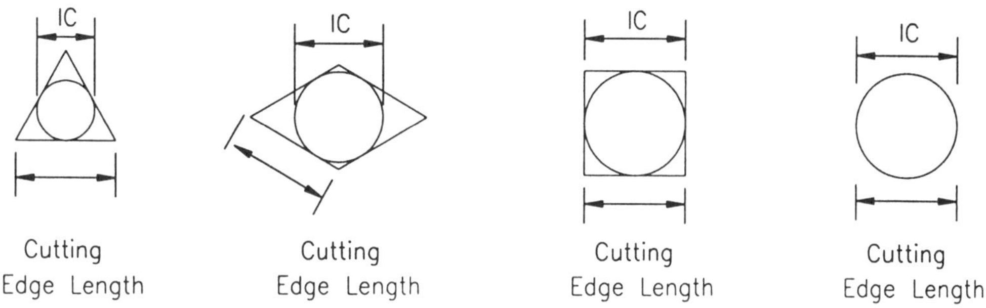

IC And Cutting Edge Length

Figure 2.13

Table 2.7 The cutting edge length of various insert shapes

Insert Shape	Cutting Edge Length (L)
Square	L = IC
Round	L = IC
Triangle	L = 1.732 IC
80° diamond	L = 1.015 IC
55° diamond	L = 1.221 IC
35° diamond	L = 1.744 IC

Insert Thickness

The factors affecting the selection of insert thickness are the **feed rate** and the **cutting edge engagement**. The nomograph shown in Figure 2.14 provides a reference guide for selecting the insert thickness to meet the strength requirement. To use this nomograph, connect a line between the selected feed rate and the actual maximum cutting edge engagement. This line intersects with the insert thickness line at one point which is the proper insert thickness. Two scales are given in the insert thickness line, one for regular cuts and thc other for interrupted cuts.

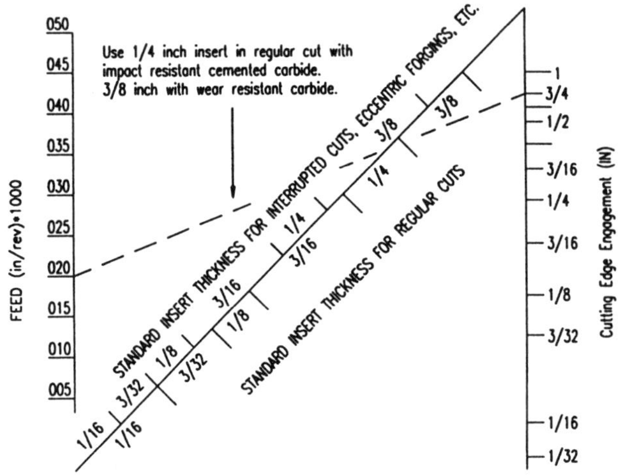

Insert Thickness Selection Chart

Figure 2.14

Insert Nose Radius

The selection of insert nose radius for an operation is mainly determined by two factors: **feed rate and required surface finish.** The surface finish (or roughness) is normally expressed by an arithmetic average (AA) value or the root mean square (RMS) value. Figure 2.15 provides a nomograph for selecting the proper insert nose radius based on the given feed rate and the required surface finish either in AA or RMS value.

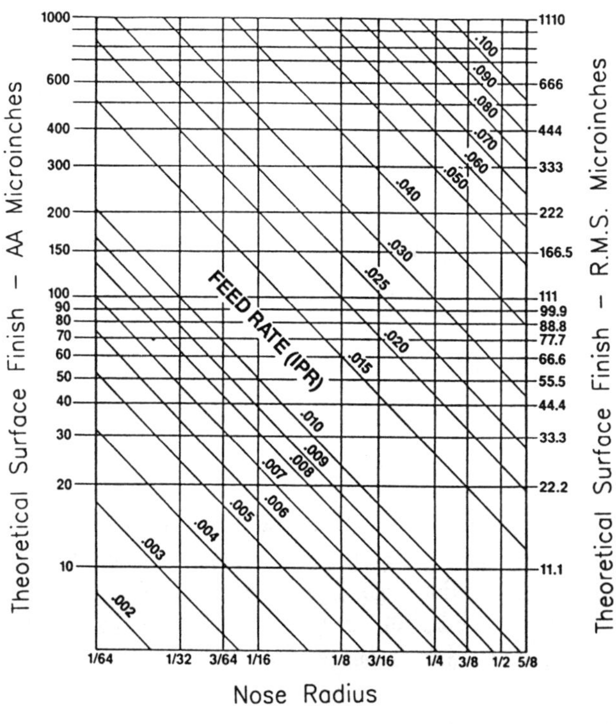

Nose Radius

Figure 2.15

Follow these steps to select the nose radius using the nomograph:

1. Locate the required surface finish (AA or RMS) on the vertical line.
2. Follow the horizontal line corresponding to the desired surface finish to the point at which the line intersects the diagonal line representing the feed rate.
3. Project a line from this point downward to the nose radius scale.
4. If this line falls between two values, select the larger value.
5. If no available nose radius generates the required finish, reduce the feed rate.

Chip Breakers

Follow these **two** guidelines when selecting the proper chip breaker:

a. No chip breaker is required for:
   - interrupted cuts
   - turning brittle materials such as cast iron

b. Chip breakers are needed for turning tough, stringy matrials such as steels, aluminum, and non-ferrous materials.

2.7 Toolholders

The ANSI standard for insert toolholder identification system is given in Figure 2.16 on the next page. The ANSI identification system describes the following features of an insert toolholder:

1. Clamping method
2. Insert shape
3. Holder style
4. Rake angle
5. Hand of tool
6. Shank size
7. Insert IC size
8. Qualified condition

An insert toolholder is specifically designed to match only one insert shape and size. Therefore, it is very important to choose the right insert toolholder for a particular job. There are **five factors** to be considered in selecting an insert toolholder. They are:

1. Holder style
2. Insert shape and size
3. Rake angle
4. Shank dimension
5. Hand type

The **lead angle** defines the style of the insert toolholder. The lead angle is also referred to as the side cutting edge angle. It is formed between the side cutting edge and one of the principal axis (Figure 2.17). **Three** types of lead angle are **negative lead angle, zero lead angle, and positive lead angle** (Figure 2.18).

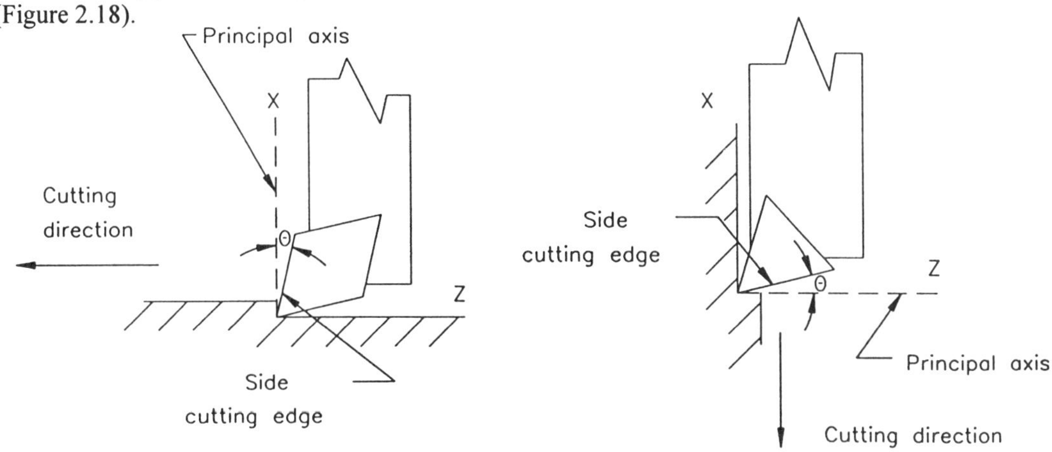

Figure 2.17 Definition of lead angles

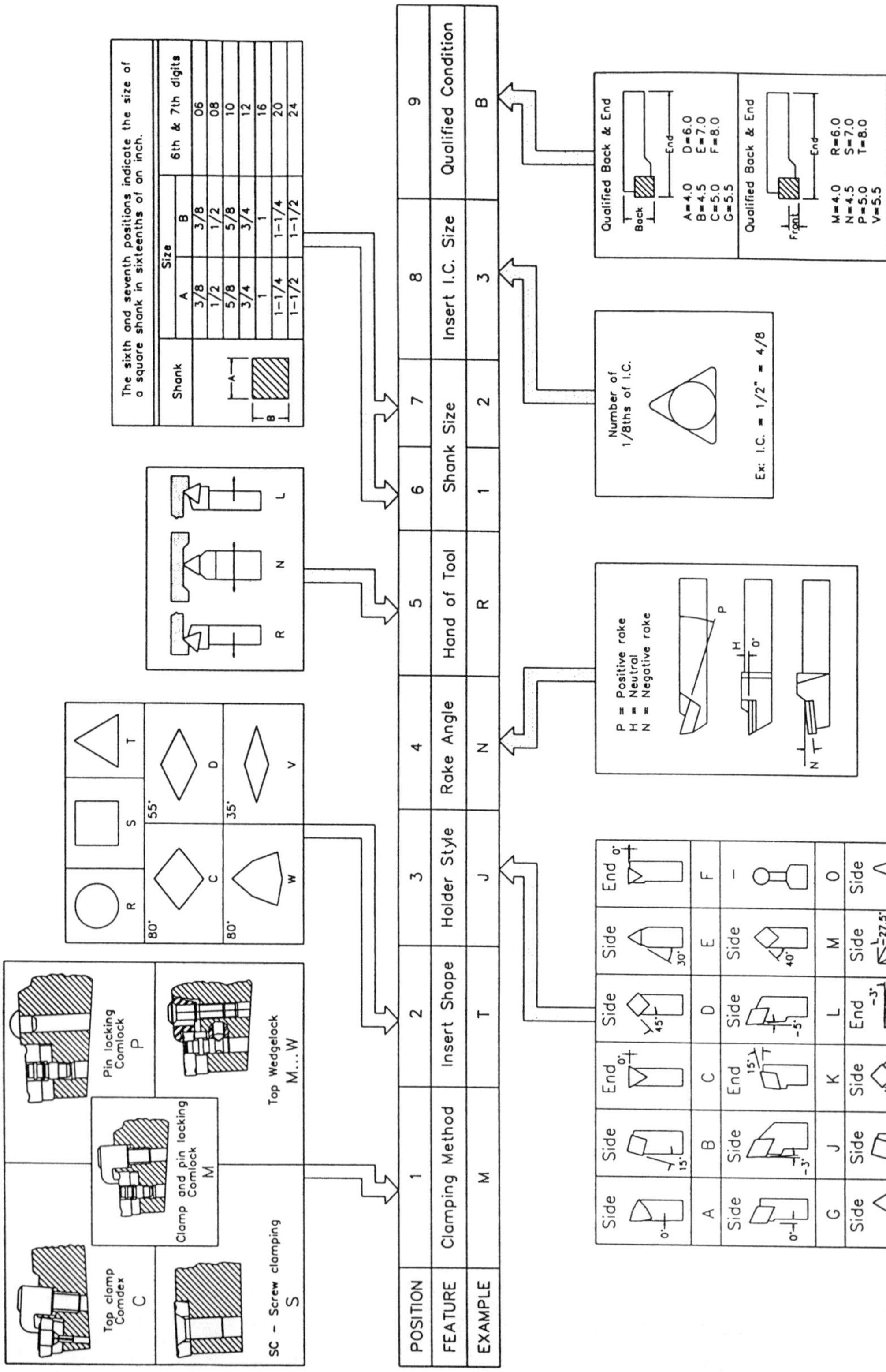

Figure 2.16 Insert toolholder identification system

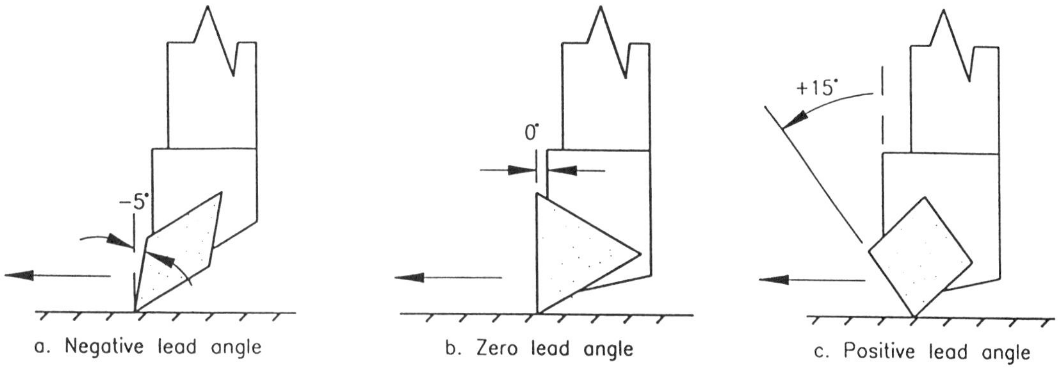

Figure 2.18 Three types of lead angles

The other important angle to be considered in selecting a toolholder type is the **profile** angle. The profile angle is the maximum slope angle that the combination of insert and toolholder can produce in profiling (Figure 2.19). A profile angle can be calculated from the following formula:

$$\text{Profile angle} = 90° + \text{lead angle} - \text{insert angle}$$

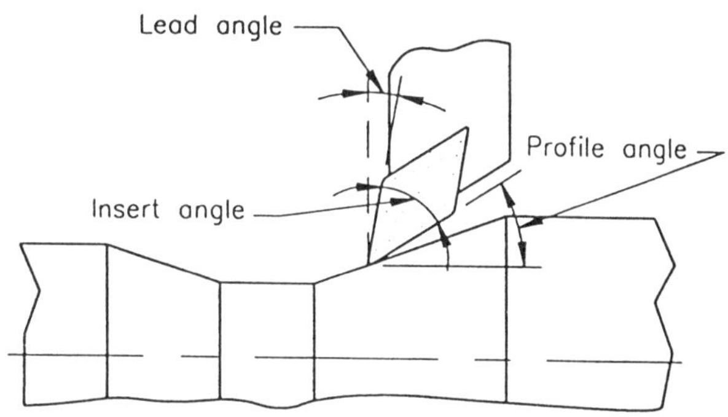

Figure 2.19

In practice, the maximum profile angle to be produced should be at least *2° smaller* than the computed profile angle.

Boring Bar Indentification System

A boring bar identification system is actually very similar to that of regular toolholders. The main difference is that a bar composition code is added to the beginning of the identification codes. The bar composition indicates what materials are in the boring bar. Two common boring bar materials are **steel (S)** and **carbide (C)**. The sixth and seventh positions specify the cross section of the shank for regular toolholders, and they are used to represent the bar diameter for boring bars.

The selection of boring bars for specific applications depends on the following seven factors:

1. Bar compositon
2. Boring bar style
3. Minimum bore diameter
4. Bar diameter
5. Insert shape and size
6. Hand type
7. Rake angle

Table 2.8 on the next two pages presents a list of combinations of toolholder styles and inserts commonly used in industry. Their typical applications are also included.

2.8 Machining Parameters

Three variables that dictate the efficiency of a machining process include **cutting speed, feed rate, and depth of cut**. These three variables are often referred to as machining parameters. The following factors should be carefully considered in selecting machining parameters:

- Operating capacity of the cutting tool
- Machine's available spindle horsepower
- Machinability of the workpiece material
- Rigidity of the part and fixture

Cutting Speed and Spindle Speed

Cutting speed, also called surface speed, refers to the speed at which the cutting edge of the tool passes over the surface of the workpiece. The cutting speed of a machining operation can be determined by the following two formulas:

$$CS = \frac{\pi \cdot D \cdot N}{12} \quad \text{(unit: FPM in inch units)}$$

$$CS = \frac{\pi \cdot D \cdot N}{1000} \quad \text{(unit: MPM in metric units)}$$

where CS = surface cutting speed, feet/minute (FPM) or meter/minute (MPM)
D = diameter of the rotating part, either the cutting tool or workpiece, in. or mm
N = RPM (rotation speed at which workpiece or cutter will turn)

In drilling (Figure 2.20) and milling (Figure 2.21), the diameter of the rotating part refers to the cutter diameter. In turning (Figure 2.22), the diameter represents the workpiece major diameter.

Table 2.8 Selection of Indexable Insert Holders

Operation Pattern	Holder Illustration	Holder Style	Insert Shape	Applications
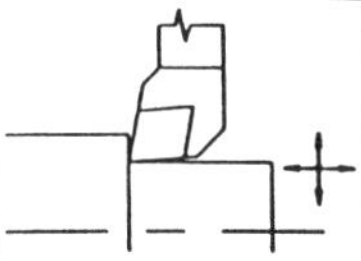	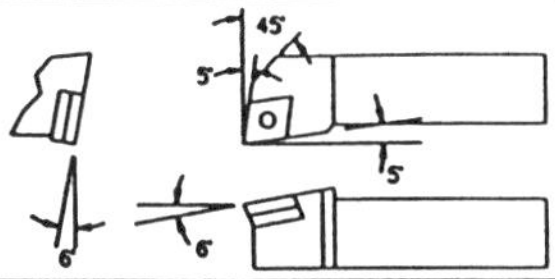	L −5°	C 80° diamond	• OD turning • Facing
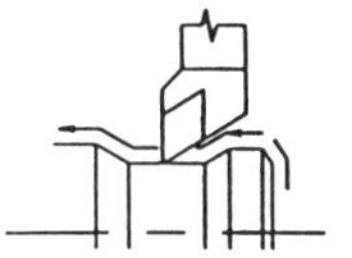	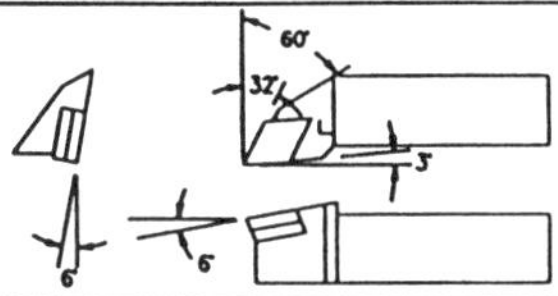	J −3°	D 55° diamond	• OD turning • Profiling with a max. of 30° profile angle
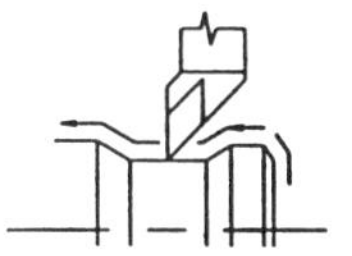	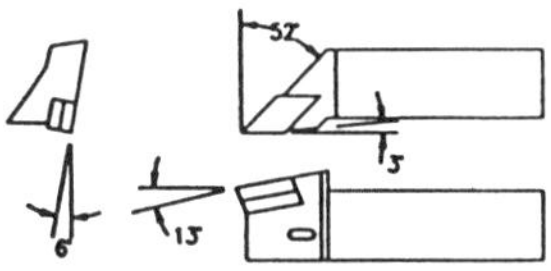	J −3°	V 35° diamond	• OD Profiling with a max. of 50° profile angle
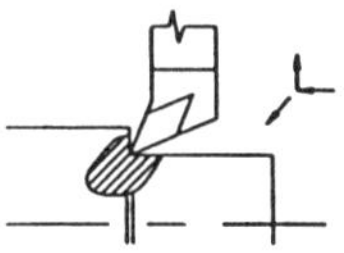	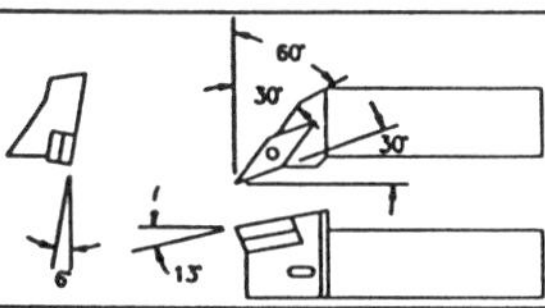	T	V 35° diamond	• Turning and undercutting
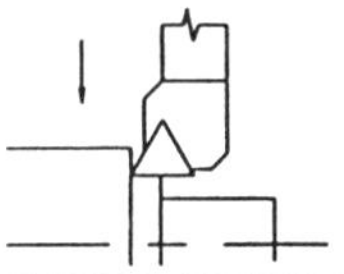	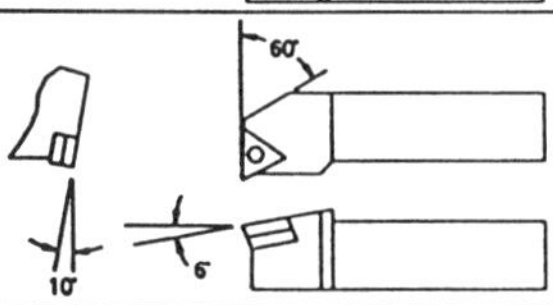	F 0°	T 60°	• Facing with square shoulder cutting
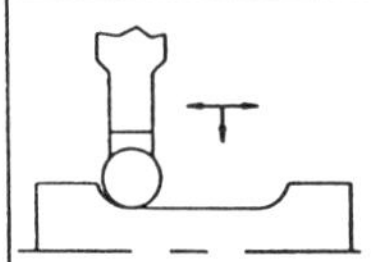	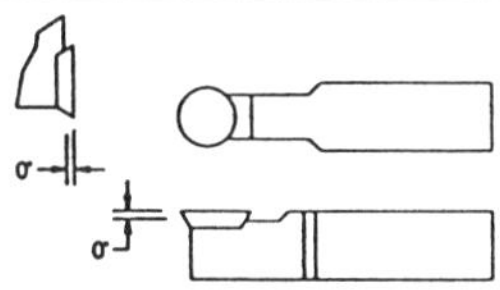	N	R round	• Profiling
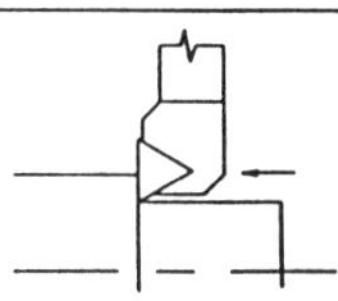	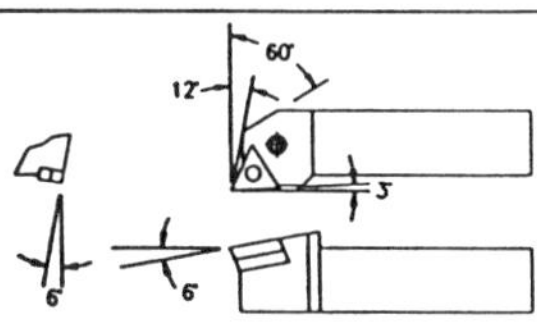	J −3°	T 60°	• OD turning with Square shoulder cutting
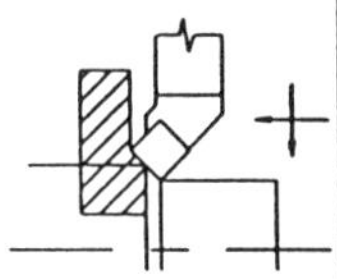	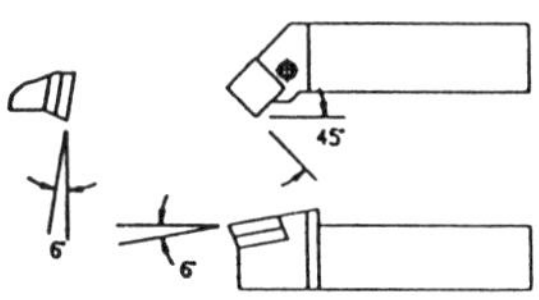	D 45°	T 90° square	• OD turning Facing
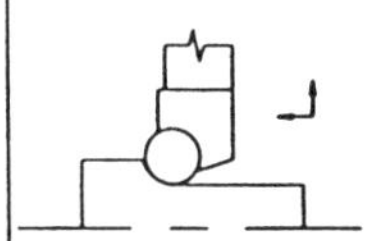	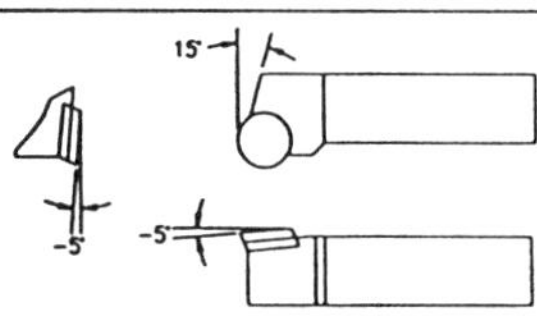	G 0°	R round	• OD turning Facing

Table 2.8 (Continued)

Operation Pattern	Holder Illustration	Holder Style	Insert Shape	Applications
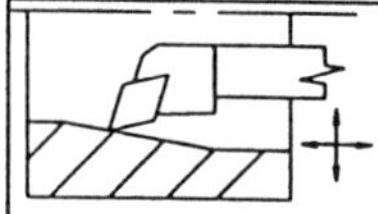	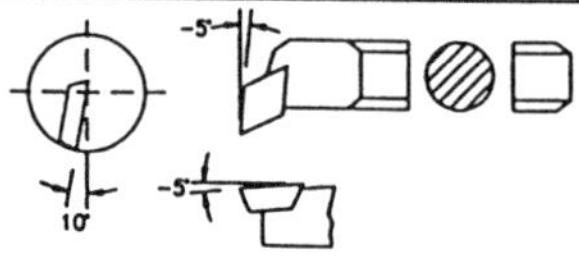	L –5°	C 80° diamond	• Straight surfaces and boring profiles positive
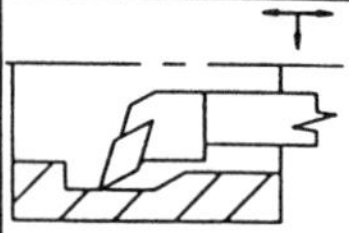	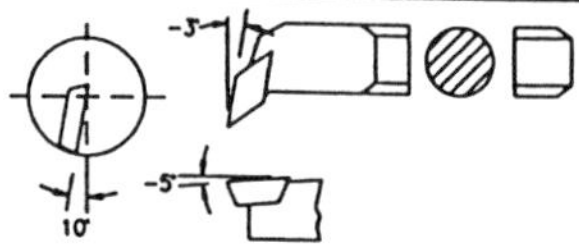	J –3°	D 55° diamond	• Boring internal profiles with the max. profile angle of 30°
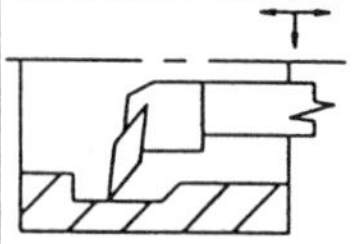	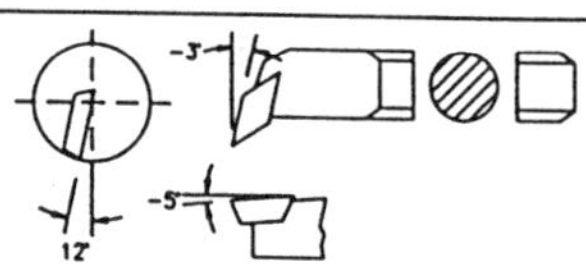	J –3°	V 35° diamond	• Boring internal profiles with the max. profile angle of 50°
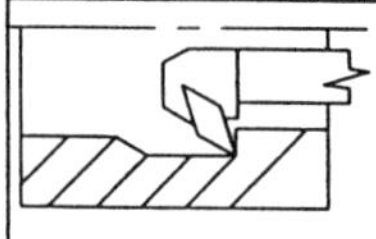	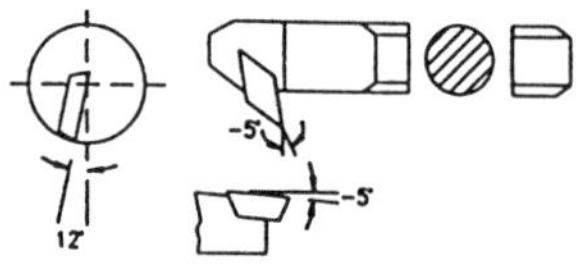	L –5°	V 35° diamond	• Back boring internal profiles
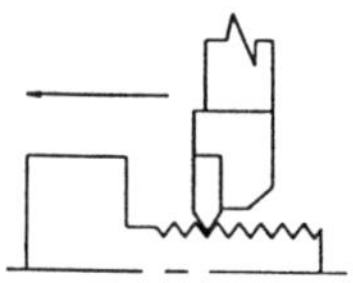	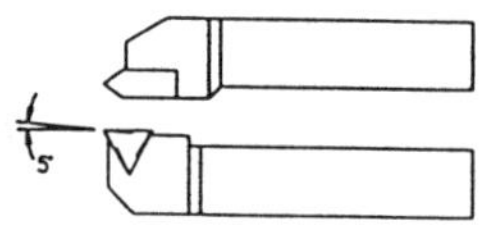	Vertical	Threading insert	• External threads cutting
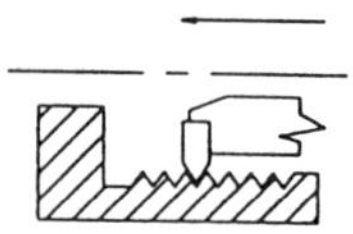	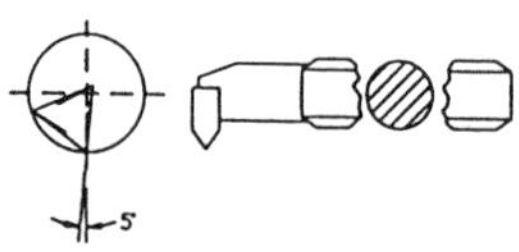	Horizontal	Threading insert	• Internal threads cutting
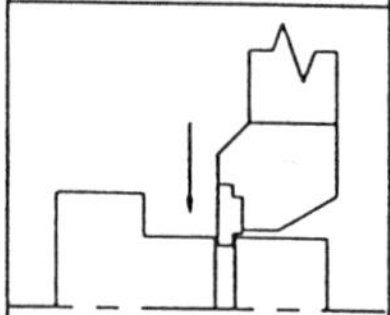	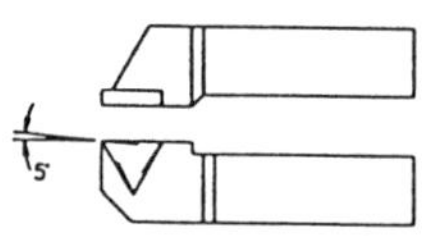	Vertical	Grooving insert	• External grooves cutting
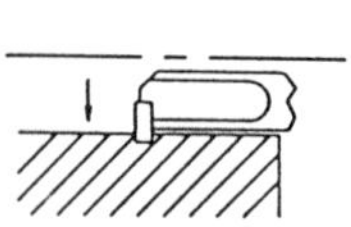	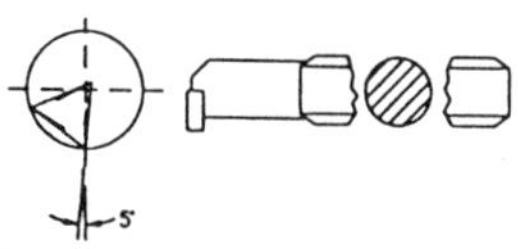	Horizontal	Grooving insert	• Internal grooves cutting

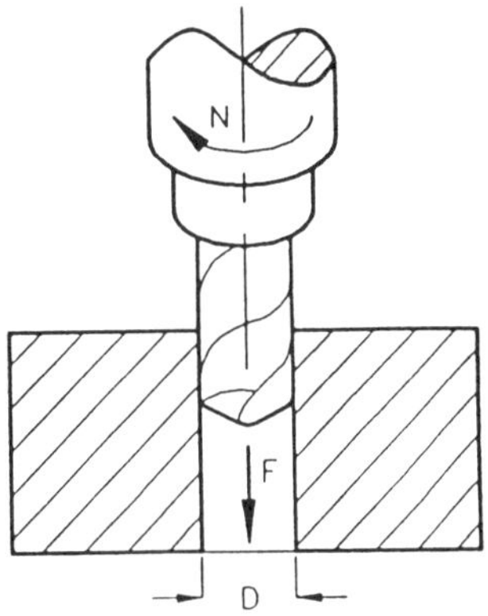

Figure 2.20 Drilling

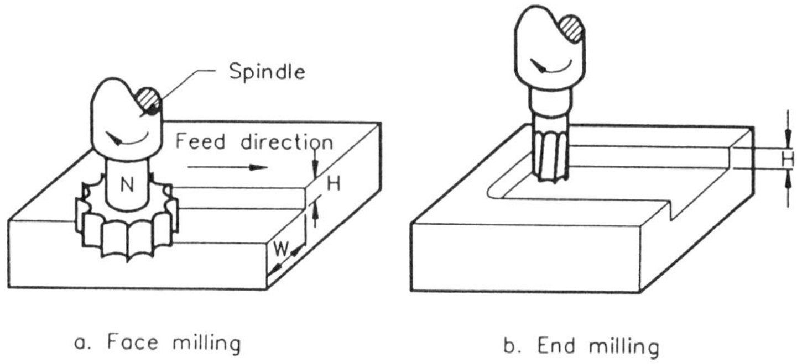

Figure 2.21 Milling

(Source: S.C. Jonathon Lin, Computer Numerical Control: From Programming to Networking, 1994. Courtesy of Delmar Publishers, Inc.)

The surface cutting speed at which a material is machined is a given quantity and is normally obtained from a machining data handbook or experience. We can use the given surface cutting speed value to find the spindle speed by re-arranged the above two formulas as follows:

$$N = \frac{12 \cdot CS}{\pi \cdot D} \quad \text{(Inch unit)}$$

$$N = \frac{1000 \cdot CS}{\pi \cdot D} \quad \text{(Metric unit)}$$

where N = rotation speed in RPM

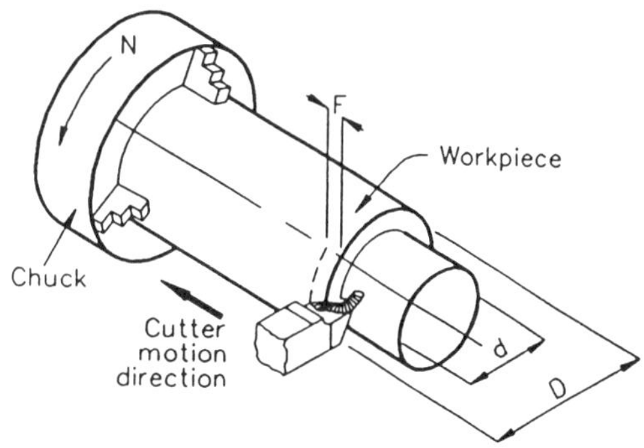

Figure 2.22 Turning (Source: S.C. Jonathon Lin, Computer Numerical Control: From Programming to Networking, 1994. Courtesy of Delmar Publishers, Inc.)

Feed Rate

The **feed** is the movement of the cutting tool in the cutting direction. The **feed rate** is the speed of feed that is normally specified by the following **three** units:

- Feed per tooth, inches per tooth (IPT) or millimeters per tooth (MMPT)
- Feed per revolution, inches per revolution (IPR) or millimeters per revolution (MMPR)
- Feed per minutc, inches per minute (IPM) or millimeters per minute (MMPM)

The feed rate *recommended* by machining handbooks or cutting tool manufacturers is normally given in feed per tooth. However, the feed is *programmed* in the units of feed per revolution or feed per minute in NC machines.

The following three formulas can be used to convert the feed rate from feed per tooth to feed per revolution or feed per minute:

$$f_r = f_t \cdot T$$

$$f_m = f_r \cdot N$$

$$f_m = f_t \cdot T \cdot N$$

where f_r = feed per revolution (unit: IPR or MMPR)
f_t = feed per tooth (or flute) (unit: IPT or MMPT)
f_m = feed per minute (unit: IPM or MMPM)
T = number of teeth (or flutes) of the cutter
N = RPM

Depth of Cut

Depth of cut is the distance the cutter penetrates into the workpiece and is measured in the direction perpendicular to the cutter motion direction. The depth of cut is mainly determined by two factors: **available spindle horsepower** and **rigidity of cutter and machine.**

Material Removal Rate

The material removal rate refers to the amount of material removed per unit time. It is normally expressed in the units of **cubic inch per minute** or **cubic meter per minute**. The formulas to compute the material removal rate for three commonly used machining processes are given below:

1. **For Drilling** (see Figure 2.20):

$$MRR = \frac{\pi \cdot D^2 \cdot f_r \cdot N}{4}$$

where MRR = material removal rate, in^3/min.
D = drill diameter, inches
f_r = feed rate, IPR
N = spindle speed, RPM

2. **For Milling** (see Figure 2.21):

$$MRR = W \cdot H \cdot f_m$$

where W = width of cut, inches
H = depth of cut, inches
f_m = feed rate, inches/minute

3. **For Turning** (see Figure 2.22):

$$MRR = \frac{\pi \cdot (D^2 - d^2) \cdot f_r \cdot N}{4}$$

where D = original (major) diameter of workpiece
d = diameter after cut
f_r = feed (IPR)
N = revolutions per minute

Horsepower Requirement

It is important to know the required power for machining a workpiece under a set of machining conditions. The required horsepower in machining can not exceed the machine spindle power rating. The unit horsepower concept is widely used to calculate the required power for machining a workpiece. The amount of power needed to remove 1 cubic inch per minute of a certain material is called the **unit horsepower** (UHP). It is determined experimentally and is provided in tables for practical use.

The required horsepower can be obtained from the following formula:

$$HP_c = UHP \cdot MRR \cdot C$$

where HP_c = required horsepower at cutter
UHP = unit horsepower
MRR = material removal rate
C = feed correction factor

Tables 2.9 and 2.10 give the unit horsepower for drilling various materials. Tables 2.11 and 2.12 on the next page provide unit horsepower for milling, and turning operations, respectively.

Drill Size, in.	Feed, ipr										
	0.001	0.002	0.004	0.006	0.008	0.010	0.013	0.016	0.020	0.025	0.030
1/8	1.63	1.63	1.22	1.22							
1/4	1.43	1.32	1.17	1.02	0.94	0.86					
3/8	1.40	1.22	1.09	1.02	0.91	0.85					
1/2	1.38	1.07	1.03	0.98	0.86	0.83	0.78	0.75	0.71		
3/4	1.36	1.13	1.02	0.94	0.90	0.86	0.78	0.74	0.70		
1	1.27	1.08	0.99	0.89	0.83	0.82	0.74	0.72	0.70	0.66	
1 1/4	1.22	1.06	0.92	0.87	0.80	0.77	0.72	0.69	0.65	0.62	
1 1/2	1.24	1.02	0.88	0.83	0.78	0.74	0.70	0.67	0.62	0.59	
1 3/4	1.25	1.04	0.85	0.83	0.78	0.71	0.70	0.65	0.62	0.58	
2	1.18	0.99	0.88	0.80	0.76	0.70	0.66	0.64	0.61	0.57	0.55
2 1/2	—	—	—	—	0.71	0.67	0.63	0.61	0.54	0.56	0.53
3	—	—	—	—	—	—	—	0.61	0.57	0.52	0.52

Table 2.9 Unit horsepower required for drilling AISI 1112 steels (Source: S.C. Jonathon Lin, Computer Numerical Control: From Programming to Networking, 1994. Courtesy of Delmar Publishers, Inc.)

Material	Factor
AISI 1020	1.6
AISI 1035	1.3
1.99% C Tool Steel	1.7
AISI 3150	1.6
Gray Cast Iron	0.5
Malleable Iron	0.6
Stainless Steel	
AISI 416 free-machining martensitic	1.2
AISI 303 free-machining austenitic	1.6
AISI 304 austenitic	1.8
17-7 Plt precipitation-hardened austenitic	2.0
4340 Steel heat-treated to 240,000-260,000 psi	2.3

Table 2.10 Approximate conversion factor for unit horsepower required to drill other materials (Source: S.C. Jonathon Lin, Computer Numerical Control: From Programming to Networking, 1994. Courtesy of Delmar Publishers,Inc.)

Material	UHP	Material	UHP
Magnesium	0.25	Stainless	
Aluminum	0.25	Free machining	1.0
Copper	0.5	Other	1.7
Brass	0.4	Titanium	
Bronze	0.5	Under 100,000 psi	1.3
Malleable iron	1.0	100,000–135,000 psi	1.7
Cast iron		135,000 and over	2.5
Ferrite	0.7	High–tensile alloys	
Pearlitic	1.0	180,000–220,000 psi	2.0
Chilled	0.7	220,000–260,000 psi	2.5
Steel		260,000–300,000 psi	3.3
Up to 150 BHN	1.4	High–temperature alloys	
300 BHN	1.7	Ferritic low alloys	1.7
400 BHN	2.0	Austenitic alloys	2.0
500 BHN	2.5	Nickel–based alloys	2.5
		Cobalt–based alloys	2.5

Table 2.11 Unit horsepower for milling (Source: S.C. Jonathon Lin, Computer Numerical Control: From Programming to Networking, 1994. Courtesy of Delmar Publishers, Inc.)

(a) Ferrous Metals and Alloys

Materials	BHN 150–175	176–200	201–250	251–300	301–350	351–400
	Unit Horsepower (UHP)					
AISI						
1010–1025	0.58	0.67				
1030–1055	0.58	0.67	0.80	0.96		
1060–1095			0.75	0.88	1.00	
1112–1120	0.50					
1314–1340	0.42	0.46	0.50			
1330–1350		0.67	0.75	0.92	1.10	
2015–2115	0.67					
2315–2335	0.54	0.58	0.62	0.75	0.92	
2340–2350		0.50	0.58	0.70	0.83	1.00
2512–2515	0.50	0.58	0.67	0.80	0.92	
3115–3130	0.50	0.58	0.70	0.83	1.00	
3160–3450		0.50	0.62	0.75	0.87	1.00
4130–4345		0.46	0.58	0.70	0.83	1.00
4615–4820	0.46	0.50	0.58	0.70	0.83	0.87
5120–5150	0.46	0.50	0.62	0.75	0.87	1.00
52100		0.58	0.67	0.83	1.00	
6115–6140	0.46	0.54	0.67	0.83	1.00	
6145–6195		0.70	0.83	1.00	1.20	1.30
Plain cast iron	0.30	0.33	0.42	0.50		
Alloy cast iron	0.30	0.42	0.52			
Malleable cast iron	0.42					
Cast steel	0.62	0.67	0.80			

(b) High–Temperature Alloys

Material	BHN	UHP	Material	BHN	UHP	Material	BHN	UHP
A286	165	0.82	Hastelloy B	230	1.10	Ti–150A	340	0.65
A286	285	0.93	Inco 700	300	1.12	U–500	375	1.10
Chromoloy	200	0.78	Inco 702	230	1.10	4340	200	0.78
Chromoloy	310	1.18	M–252	230	1.10	4340	340	0.93
			M–252	310	1.20			

(c) Nonferrous Metals and Alloys

Material	UHP	Material	UHP	Material	UHP
Brass		Bronze		Aluminum	
Hard	0.83	Hard	0.83	Cast	0.25
Medium	0.50	Med.	0.50	Hard	0.33
Soft	0.33	Soft	0.33	Monel	1.00
Free–machining	0.25	Copper	0.90	Zinc(die cast)	0.25

Table 2.12 Unit horsepower for turning various materials (Source: S.C. Jonathon Lin, Computer Numerical Control: From Programming to Networking, 1994. Courtesy of Delmar Publishers, Inc.)

The feed correction factor C is used to compensate for the effect of feed on horsepower because **high** feed rates require **less** unit horsepower. Figure 2.23 shows the feed correction factors.

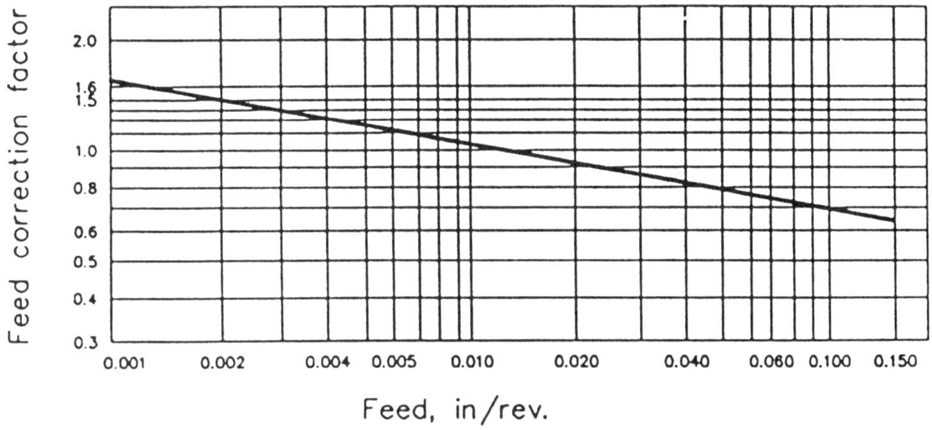

Adjustment for lead angle as follows:

If tool cuts with a lead angle of	Reduce the actual feed by this amount and use the feed correction factor for the finer feed
30°	10%
45°	30%
60°	50%
If the depth of cut is less than the nose radius	30%

Figure 2.23 Feed conversion facator
(Source: Application Data Manual, Courtesy of Carboloy Inc., a Seco Tools Company)

The efficiency of the machine must be considered when calculating the required horsepower because power is needed to overcome friction in the machine. The formula for calculating the required horsepower at the spindle motor is:

$$HP_m = \frac{HP_c}{E}$$

where HP_m = required horsepower at the spindle motor
E = machine efficiency

2.9 Face Milling

Face milling is normally used in two situations:

1. where a large amount of material must be removed in a short period of time
2. a good surface finishing is required.

Cutter Size

When possible, use a larger effective diameter to shorten the machining time. The larger the flat surface to be machined, the larger the effective diameter should be used.

The cutter height determines the allowable maximum depth of cut. The depth of cut should be smaller than the cutter height.

Cutting Width Selection

The selection of cutting width is dictated by two considerations, **tool life and machining efficiency**. The *larger* the cutting width, the *shorter* the tool life and the *better* the machining efficiency. Cutting width must be chosen in such a way that it produces efficient machining, yet tool life is not significantly sacrificed. The engage angle, the angle between the initial contact point and the exit point (Figure 2.24), is often used to relate the cutting width to tool life.

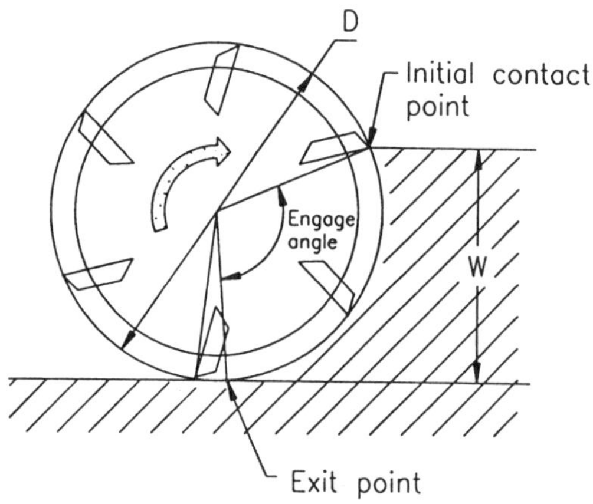

Figure 2.24 Engage angle

Figure 2.25 shows the relationship between the **ratio of W/D to the engage angle.** The engage angle ranges from 0 to 180° depending on the amount of cutting width. The engage angle is 180° for W/D = 1, and 90° for W/D = 0.5.

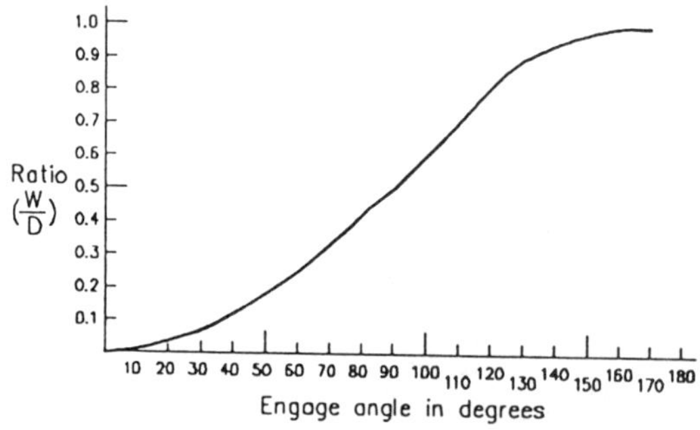

Figure 2.25

Figure 2.26 shows how the engage angle affects the tool life. Tool life decreases drastically after the engage angle exceeding 105°. Also, note that the relationship between the tool life and the engage angle varies from one material to another.

Figure 2.26 ☞

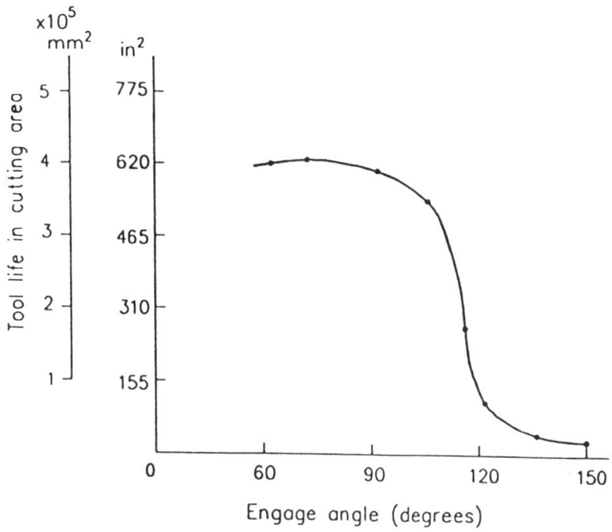

The following two rules are used to determine the maximum cutting width in face milling:

$$W = (.6)\,D \quad \text{(for face milling steels)}$$

$$W = (.75)\,D \quad \text{(for face milling cast irons)}$$

where W = cutting width
D = diameter of face mill

The maximum depth of cut for most face milling operations is **0.1 in.** and the feed rate is approximately **0.001 - 0.01 in./revolution.**

2.10 End Milling

End mills can be used to perform five types of operations: plunge milling, peripheral shoulder milling, slot milling, pocket milling, and profile milling (Table 2.13) on the next page.

Table 2.13 End Milling Operations

Operation Type	Features	Application	Illustration
1. Plunge milling	Repeatly plunges to a predetermined depth retracts, then advances and plunges again. The maximum cutting force acts in the axial (Z) direction where the machine is strongest.	Rapidly remove large quantity of material.	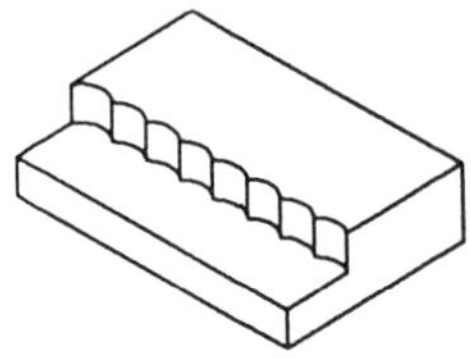
2. Peripheral shoulder milling	Uses end mill's to produce side edges shoulders or steps.	The maximum width of cutter engagement is 3D/4 where D is the cutter diameter.	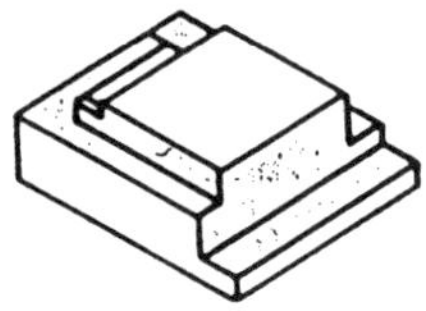
3. slot milling	Uses cutter's side edges to produce blind slot and through slot.	To cut various forms of slots.	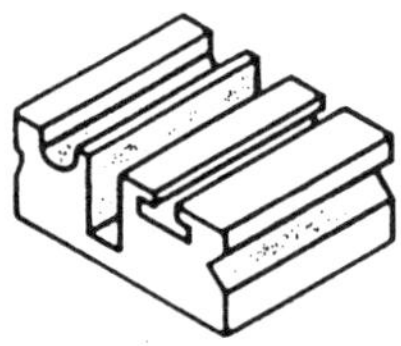
4. Pocket milling	Takes a zig zag or spiral out pattern of cuts in sequence.	To produce a deep cavity.	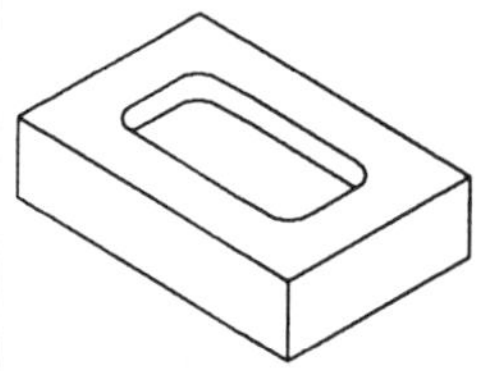
5. Profile milling	Takes the cutter along a predetermined contour.	To machine part profiles that consist of a series of lines and arcs.	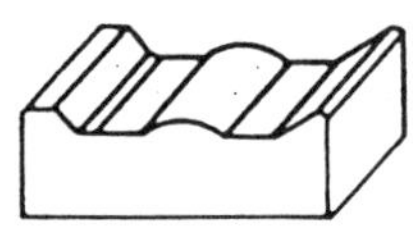

End Mills Selection

End mills are made in various forms, configurations, number of flutes, and end face center types. End mills are availbale in three forms: **solid end mills, carbide-tipped end mills and indexable inserts.** Solid end mills are made from high speed steel or sintered cabide. They are double or single ended. Carbide-tipped end mills have carbide inserts brazed on the tool body to form the cutting edges. In CNC applications, the end mills with indexable inserts are the most widely used.

End mills are made in a variety of configurations including straight end mills for general purpose applications, waved-formed end mills for roughing operation, ball end mills for machining dies, molds, and surfaces, and shell end mills for producing deep slots, shoulders, or profiles (Figure 2.27 on the next page)

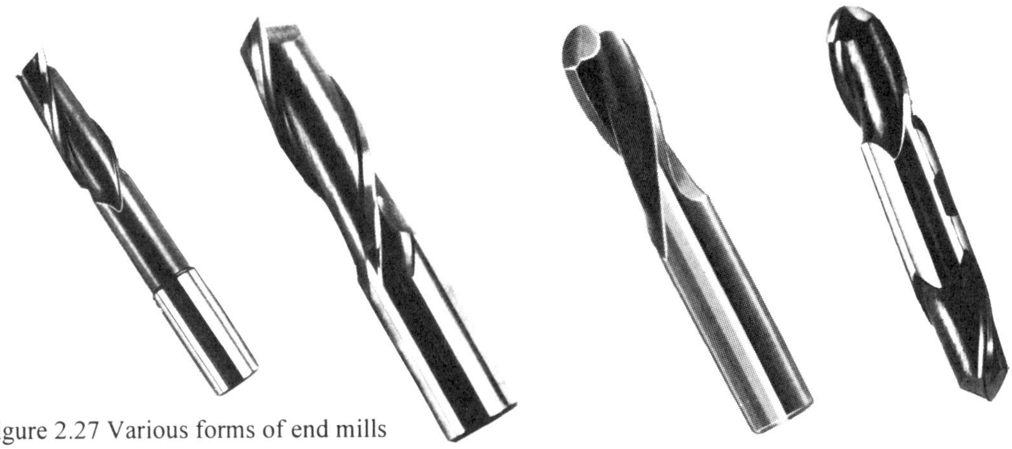

Figure 2.27 Various forms of end mills

End mills have two, three, four, or more flutes to allow for the removal of chips. The fewer the number of flutes means the bigger the cutting pocket.

The end face center of an end mill can be made as either a cutting type or hole type. End mills with a **center cutting** type, have one or two end-cutting edges extending past the center of the cutter (Figure 2.28) so that they can be used for plunging purposes. With the **center hole** type (Figure 2.29), no end-cutting edge is extended to the center of the cutter, therefore, they can not be used to perform plunging operations.

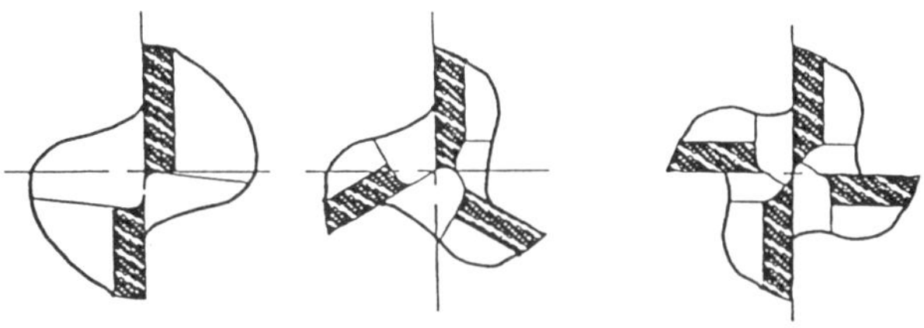

Figure 2.28 Center cutting type

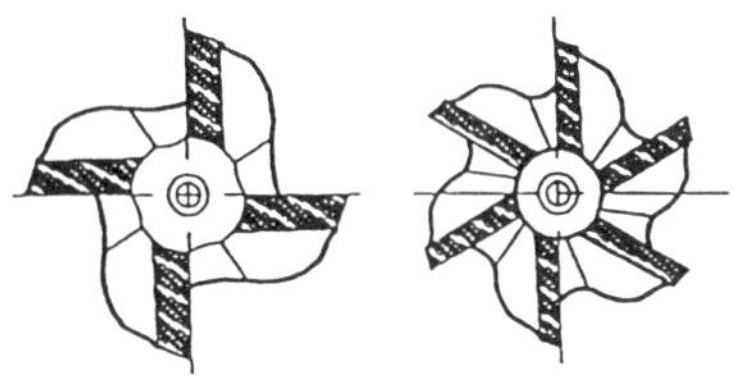

Figure 2.29 Center hole type

The following criteria are used to select end mills for a particular application:

1. Use end mills with 30° helical angle for general applications. Use 40°-45° helical angle and 15° of axial helical angle at the end face to perform heavy cuttings.

2. Use end mills with waved-shaped cutting edges for roughing cuts to obtain rapid metal removal.

3. Select end mills with a smaller number of flutes for roughing cuts because they provide larger cutting pockets. Tools with a larger number of flutes are used for finishing cuts.

4. Choose tools with the end face of center cutting type for cutting involving plunging. Tools with the end face of center hole type can perform only side cutting.

The **width of cut** for end milling operations affects the tool life. The maximum width of cut is 75 percent of the cutter diameter (or 3D/4).

2.11 Milling with Ball End Mills

A ball end mill, also known as spherical end mill or ball nose end mill, has a semi-sphere at the tool end. Ball end mills are used extensively in the machining of dies, molds, and workpieces with complex surfaces in the automotive, aerospace, and defense industries.

Effective diameter is the main factor used in the calculation of the required spindle speed. Effective diameter is defined as the **actual diameter of the cutter at the axial depth-of-cut line** (Figure 2.30). The effective diameter is affected by two parameters: **tool radius and axial depth of cut**.

The effective diameter can be calculated from:

$$D_E = 2[R^2-(R-H)^2]^{1/2}$$

where D_E = effective diameter
R = tool radius
H = axial depth of cut

The **effective** radius replaces the cutter radius when calculating the cutting speed for ball end milling. The formula becomes:

$$CS = \frac{\pi \cdot D_E \cdot N}{12}$$

where D_E = effective diameter (in.)
CS = cutting speed (feet/minute)
N = rotation speed (revolution/minute)

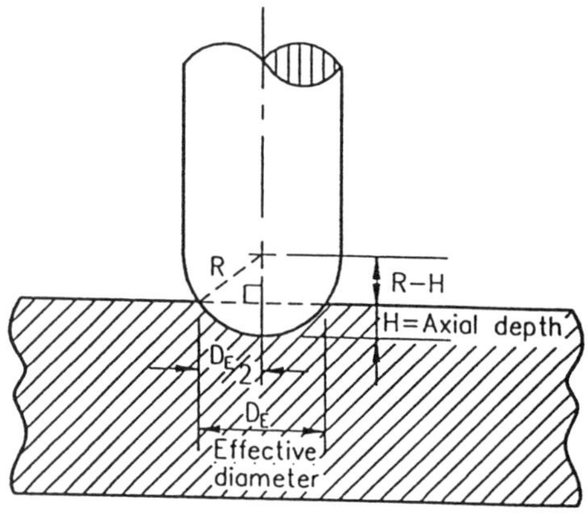

Figure 2.30

When a cutter with a non-flat end, such as a ball end mill, is used to cut a surface in a zigzag pattern, an uncut strip is created between the two cutting passes (Figure 2.31). The height of these undesirable strips is called cusp height.

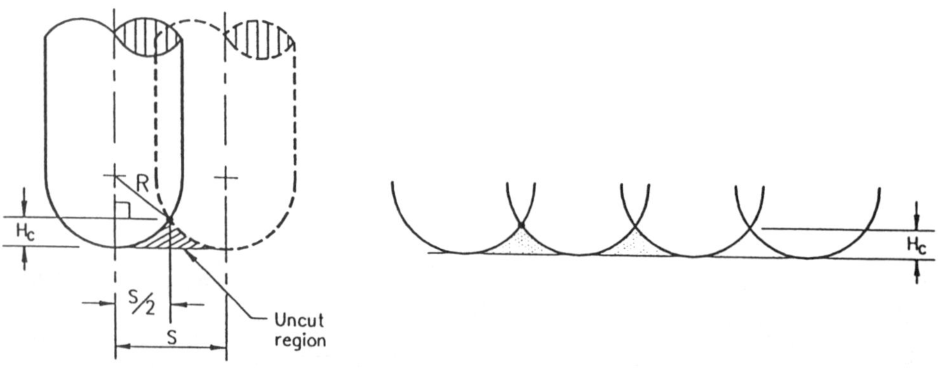

Figure 2.31

The cusp height can be calculated from

$$H_C = R - [R^2 - (S/2)^2]^{1/2}$$

or

$$S = 2[R^2 - (R - H_C)^2]^{1/2}$$

where H_c = cusp height (in.)
R = tool nose radius (in.)
S = stepover value between two cutting passes (in.)

2.12 Drilling Operations

Drilling is the process to produce holes or enlarge existing holes. Commonly used drilling operations include drilling, center drilling, countersinking, and counterboring.

Factors to Be Considered in Drilling

1. **Initial condition of holes**: The initial state of holes may have one of three forms:
   - Casted holes or forged holes in which rough hole dimension has been formed. These holes can be produced by using a correct-size drill or a two-flute end mill.
   - Pre-drilled holes in which holes, normally of large diameter, have been drilled by a small drill. The final drilling is done by using a correct size of drill.
   - Blank stock. Drilling holes on blank stock may require using more than one drill depending on the size, accuracy, and surface roughness of the holes.

2. **Required accuracy of holes**

   Drilling tends to produce oversized holes with a dislocation of hole centers. Hole oversize and runout are two parameters in measuring the hole accuracy. When the required accuracy of hole, with respect to diameter and runout, is within ±0.005 in., a center drilling is required to locate the hole center.

3. **Hole size**

   The hole **diameter** decides the number of drillings required to produce the hole. Generally speaking, a 1 in. diameter is used as the critical dimension. Only one drilling is required for any hole size that is smaller than **1 in.** of diameter. To drill a 1¼ in. hole, for example, requires two drillings, first drilling with a 3/8 in. drill and then a final drilling with 1¼ in. drill to produce the finished size.

4. **Hole depth**

   Only one drilling pass is required to drill shallow holes. As the depth of hole **increases**, peck drilling is used to clear chips and avoid packing. Peck drilling is recommended when the depth of hole is greater than three to four times the diameter of drills. The distance (depth) of each peck ranges from ½ to 1½ times the drill diameter,depending upon the chip formation and rate of drill breakage encountered.

Note: that the cutting speed and feed rate for drilling deep holes should be reduced according to the ratio of hole depth to drill diameter.

Safety, drill lip, and penetration distance

In drilling with NC machines, the tool moves rapidly to the reference level (**R**) and then feeds into the workpiece until it reaches the hole bottom. **Three** distances should be carefully determined to optimize NC use: **safety, drill lip, and penetration distance** (Figure 2.32).

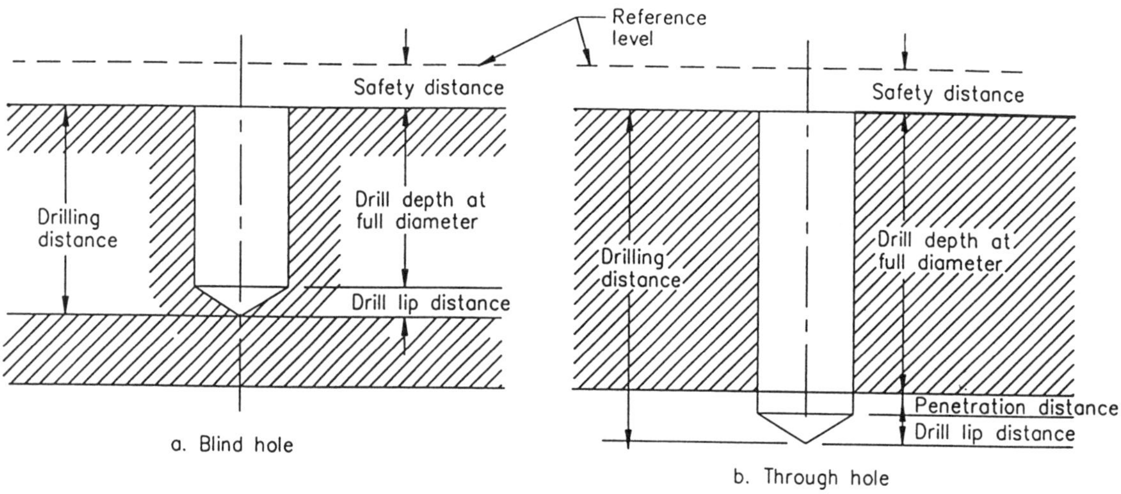

Figure 2.32 Drilling distances

Safety distance

The safety distance is measured from the reference (R) level to the work surface and should be as short as possible to increase NC efficiency. The safety distance is determined by the surface condition of the workpiece and is calculated as follows:

$L_S = 0.15$ in. (or 4 mm) for flat casted, and machined surfaces

$L_S = 0.2$ in. (or 5 mm) for rough surfaces

Drill lip distance

The drill point angle is generally ground to 118° or 59° on each side of the centerline. The drill lip distance can be calculated from:

$$L_L = \frac{D}{2(\tan 59°)}$$

or $$L_L = 0.3\ D$$

where D = drill diameter (in. or mm)

L_L = drill lip distance (in. or mm)

Penetration distance

Penetration distance is the allowance that permits the drill to move to extra depth to remove the burs produced during the time when the drill penetrated through the hole. Generally speaking, the penetration distance is equal to the safety distance that is:

L_P = 0.15 in. (or 4 mm) for flat casted, and machined surfaces
L_P = 0.2 in. (or 5 mm) for rough surfaces

The drilling distance of a blind hole consists of **three** components: **safety distance, depth at full diameter, and depth of drill lip** (Figure 2.32a).

$$L = L_S + L_D + L_L$$

where L = drilling distance
L_S = safety distance
L_D = drill depth at full diameter
L_L = depth of drill lip

The drilling distance for a through hole is the sum of **four** components (Figure 2.32b) and can be found from:

$$L = L_S + L_D + L_P + L_L$$

where L_D = depth of hole
L_P = penetration distance

2.13 Boring Operations

Boring is a precision machining process for producing internal holes by removing metal with single-point tools or tools with multiple cutting edges. Common applications for boring include the enlarging or finishing of existing holes that were drilled, pierced, casted, or forged. Boring operations can be of **two** categories; **single-stage** (Figure 2.33) **and multiple-stage** (Figure 2.34).

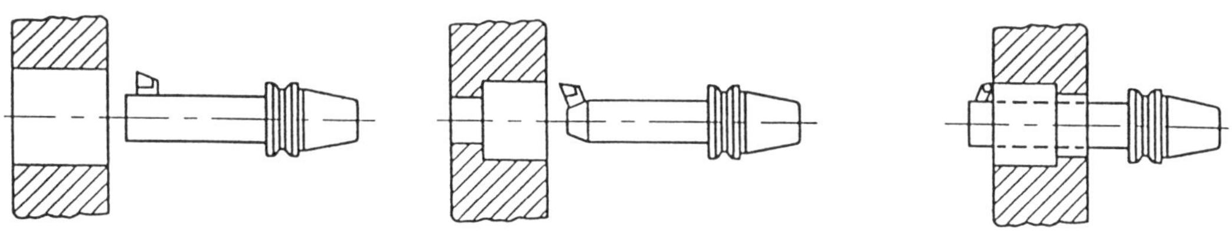

a. through hole b. Blind hole c Back hole

Figures 2.33Single stage boring operations

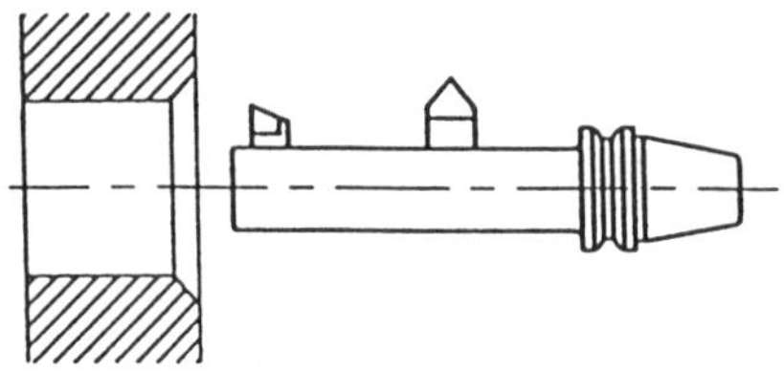

a. Boring and chamfering

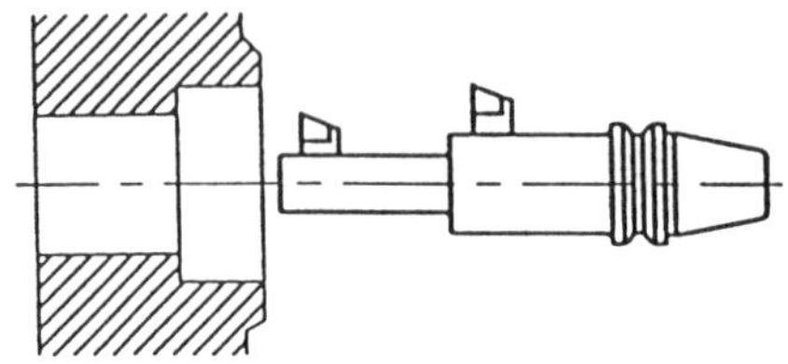

b. Boring two-step hole

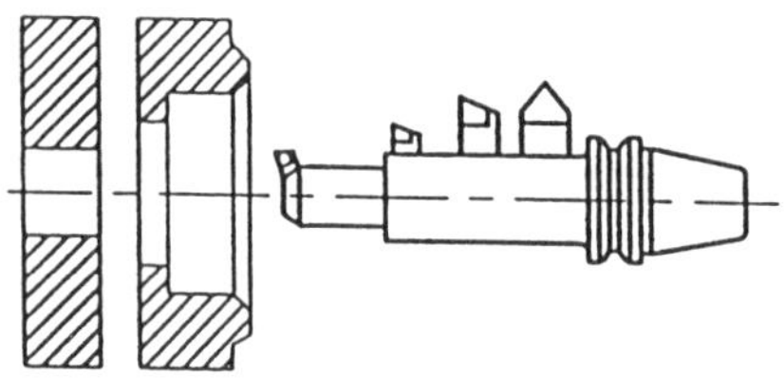

c. Boring three-step hole and chamfering

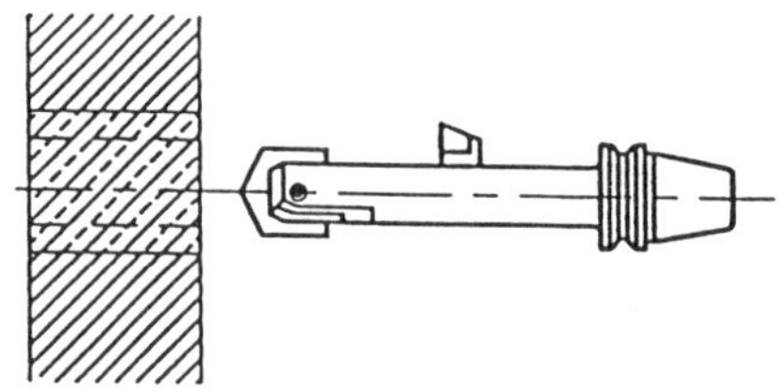

d. Spade drilling and boring

Figure 2.34 Multiple stage boring operaitons

Boring bars are made of various sizes and types. The most common type is the single-stage boring bar that is a round boring bar with one cutting edge mounted at the end of the bar to perform a single-diameter boring operation. The ratio of length to diameter of the shank (L/D) is the main measure of the boring capability for a boring bar. As a general rule, a L/D ratio of 4 - 5 would provide a stable machining under normal boring conditions. Chatter may occur when this ratio is larger than 5. Actually, chatter results from the deflection of the boring bar that is subjected to the cutting resistant force. The larger the cutting resistant force, the larger the deflection results. In some critical applications, this deflection must be kept within an allowable limit.

Selection of Feed and Depth of Cut

The selection of feed and depth of cut depends on the following factors:

1. Deflection should not exceed 0.001 in. (or 0.02 mm).

2. Use the formula, $F = (8HR)^{1/2}$
   to determine the feed for the required surface roughness,
   where H = surface roughness (in.),
   R = tool nose radius (in.)
   F = feed (in./rev).

3. Depth of cut for rough borings ranges from 0.04 - 0.24 in. (1 - 6 mm).
   Use 0.02 - 0.04 in. (0.5 - 1 mm) for finish borings.

2.14 Tapping Operations

Tapping is a process of using a tap to produce internal threads in existing holes by a combination of axial and rotary motions. CNC milling machines use hand taps, spiral-pointed taps, spiral-fluted taps, and metric taps for cutting straight threads.

Tap selection

Several types of taps are used in CNC machines to produce internal threads. Table 2.14 on the next page summarizes various tap types and their applications.

Tap drill selection

A tap drill is used to produce the minor diameter of the internal threads. The percentage of thread engagement, or thread height, is an important factor in determining the tap drill size. Figure 2.35 illustrates the definition of thread height percentage. Table 2.15 gives a range of thread height percentage for general applications of classes 1B and 2B.

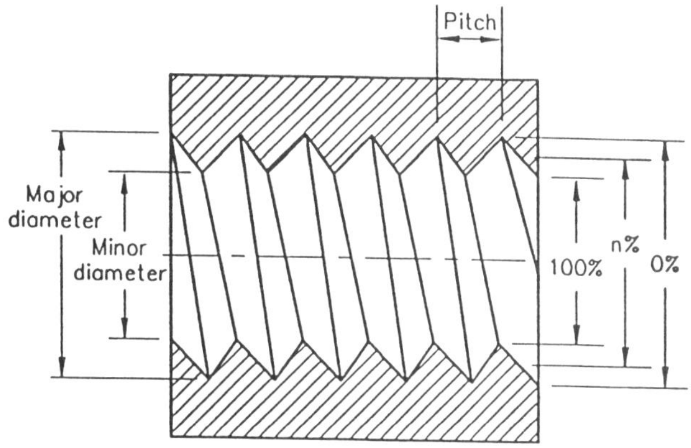

Figure 2.35

Table 2.15 Thread height percentages for various thread sizes

Thread Size	Thread Height, %
#0 to #12	53 to 65
1/4 to 1/2"	64 to 66.5
1/2 to 1"	64 to 67
1 to 2"	66 to 71

Note that the **tougher** the material, the less percentage of thread should be produced. The **closer** the tolerance, the greater percentage of thread is required.

The tap hole diameter can be roughly calculated by the formula:

$$D = D_M - P$$

where D = tap hole diameter
D_M = tap major diameter
P = thread pitch

Table 2.14 Tap Types and Their Applications

Tap Type	Feature	Application	Illustration
A. Hand Tap			
1. Taper Tap	Having first 8 to 10 threads chamfered.	For starting the threads in a deep hole or for tapping through holes.	
2. Plug Tap	Having a 3 to 5 thread chamfer length.	Tapping through holes, general tapping application.	
3. Bottoming Tap	Having only 1 thread chamfer length.	Tapping blind holes where limited lengths of imperfect threads are allowed. They should be used only a taper or plug tap has been used to thread a blind hole as far as possible.	
B. Spiral-pointed tap	Having a left-hand spiral flute at the point to force the chips ahead of the tap. More rigid than conventional taps. Low cutting resistance.	Tapping short through holes in mild steel and stainless steel where chips do not easily break. Produce high precision threads.	
C. Spiral-fluted taps			
1. Spiral-flute taps	Having right hand helical flutes with a helix angle ranging from 25° to 35° to increase lifting action in ejecting chips backward.	Tapping blind holes where chips have to be ejected backward through the open end of the hole.	
2. Fast spiral-flute taps	45°-60° helix angle to increase lifting action in ejecting chips backward.	Tapping deep blind holes in materials that produce long curling chips.	

The following formulas are used to calculate the tap drill size when the thread height percentage is considered:

Unified Threads:

$$D = D_M - \frac{2 \cdot H \cdot Q}{100}$$

$$H = 0.6495\ P$$

$$P = 1/N$$

or

$$D = D_M - 0.01299 \times (Q/N)$$

where D = tap drill size (diameter)
D_M = major diameter of tap (threads)
H = thread height
P = thread pitch
Q = thread height percentage
N = number of threads per in.

Metric threads:

$$D = D_M - \frac{2 \cdot H \cdot Q}{100}$$

$$H = 0.6403\ P$$

or

$$D = D_M - 0.01281\ P \cdot Q$$

Depth of tap holes

The depth of tap holes must be deep enough to allow the tap to produce threads to the desired depth. In tapping blind holes, the depth of holes is the sum of the **four** distances: **thread length, deceleration length, clearance length, and drill tip length** (Figure 2.36).

$$L = L_l + L_d + L_c + L_t$$

$$L_t = 0.3\ D$$

where L = depth of tap hole
L_l = thread length
L_d = deceleration length (1 -2 thread pitch)
L_c = clearance length (0.5 thread pitch)
L_t = drill tip length
D = tap drill diameter

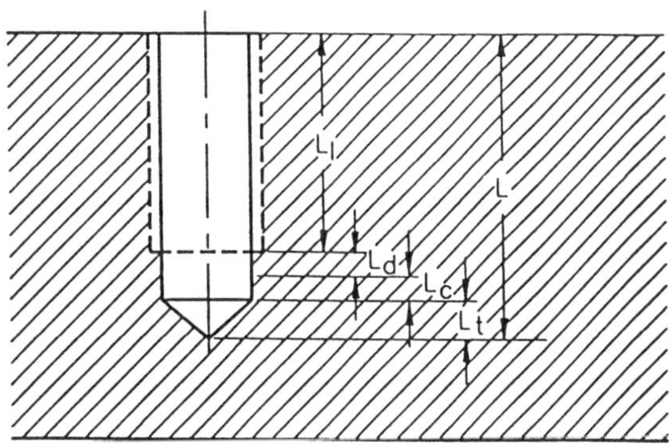

Figure 2.36

2.15 Turning Operation

Turning is an improtant machining process for producing external and internal profiles and surfaces on a turning machine. Several important factors should be considered in turning operation are presented in this section. They include **feed selection, depth of cut, error resulting from off center of the cutter, and chip breaker.**

Feed selection and surface roughness

Feed is one of important factors in determining the machining efficiency. The selection of feed for turning is mainly governed by the required surface roughness. The theoretical formula for calculating the roughness is: (Figure 2.37):

$$H = R - (R^2 - (F/2)^2)^{1/2}$$

where H = surface roughness (in. or mm)
R = tool nose radius (in. or mm)
F = feed (in./rev or mm/rev)

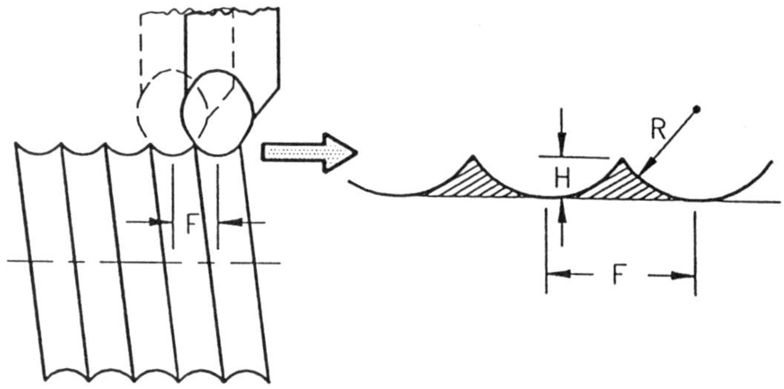

Figure 2.37

This equation can be expanded as:

$$H^2 - 2RH = -F^2/4$$

Since the value of H is very small, the term H^2 can be overlooked and the equation becomes:

$$H = \frac{F^2}{8R}$$

or $$F = (8RH)^{1/2}$$

The surface roughness can be improved either by **reducing** the feed rate or by **increasing** the tool nose radius. It is preferred to use a larger tool nose radius to obtain better roughness than to reduce the feed rate because chips may congest on the insert tip and cause damage to the surface when too small a feed is used.

Depth of cut and deflection

Generally speaking, the depth of cut for roughing all materials, excluding stainless steels, is about 0.15 in. (4 mm). Roughing stainless steels uses 0.1 in. depth of cut.

The deeper cut requires a larger cutting force. The cutting resistant force causes the workpiece to be deflected. This deflection produces chatter when the workpiece rotates at a relatively high speed. When this deflection is greater than 0.001 in. (or 0.02mm), chatter may be severe enough to make the surface finish requirements impossible to obtain.

Error resulted from off center of the cutter

In most cases, we like to have the cutter tip located at the center in turning operations. The turned diameter is slightly larger than the programmed dimension when the tip of the cutter is off center by a distance (Figure 2.38 on the next page).

The resultant diameter error can be calculated from:

$$\Delta X = (X^2 + Y^2)^{1/2} - X$$

where ΔX = error amount
X = X-coordinate of the programmed point
Y = amount of center offset

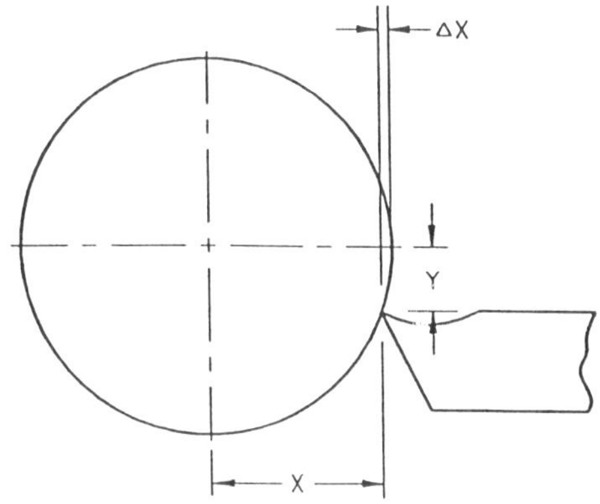

Figure 2.38

Chip breaker

Chips should be broken into pieces or curled into small coils to facilitate the removal from the workpiece and the cutter. When turning brittle materials such as cast iron and intermittent cuttings, the chips are automatically broken, so no chip breaker is required. A chip breaker must be given to the cutter which is used to turn the stingy, tough materials such as steels, aluminum, and so on. Chip breakers can appear in various forms. Figure 2.39 illustrates the basic principle of a chip breaker.

The theoretical radius of curled chips can be determined by two variables: **width of the chip breaker (W) and depth of the chip breaker (H)**, and can be calculated by using the relationship of two similar triangles ABD and ACB.

$$\frac{AC}{AB} = \frac{AB}{AD}$$

Since $AC = 2R$, $AD = H$, and $AB = (H^2 + W^2)^{1/2}$

Therefore, $2RH = H^2 + W^2$

or
$$R = \frac{W^2}{2H} + \frac{H}{2}$$

where W = width of the chip breaker
H = depth of the chip breaker
R = radius of curled chips

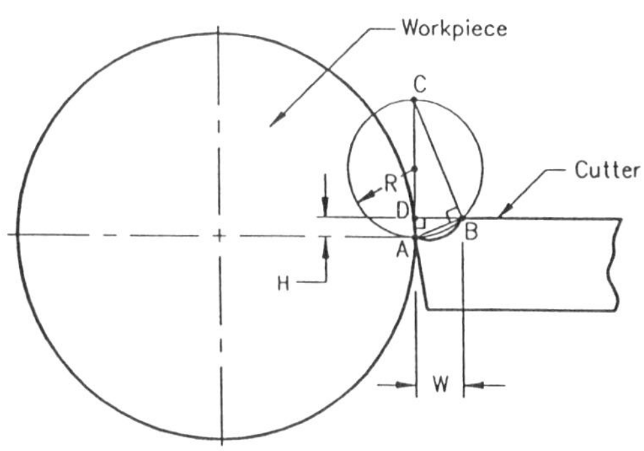

Figure 2.39

The actual chip size is also affected by the feed used in cutting. Larger feed causes chips to be broken easily, whereas smaller feed reduces the effect of chip breaking.

Chapter 3

Mastercam Environments

Objectives:

1. Start the Mastercam program.
2. Understand screen menus and how to move from one to another.
3. Know the function of the SAVE, FILE and EXIT commands.

3.1 Working with Windows

Entering Windows Applications

At the DOS prompt, type **WIN** to enter Windows applications. When working with Windows applications (Figure 3.1), you might have several different applications and icons on your screen. This section briefly describes some fundamentals for the application of Mastercam. Refer to the "Basic Skills" chapter of the Microsoft Windows User's Guide for further information on Windows.

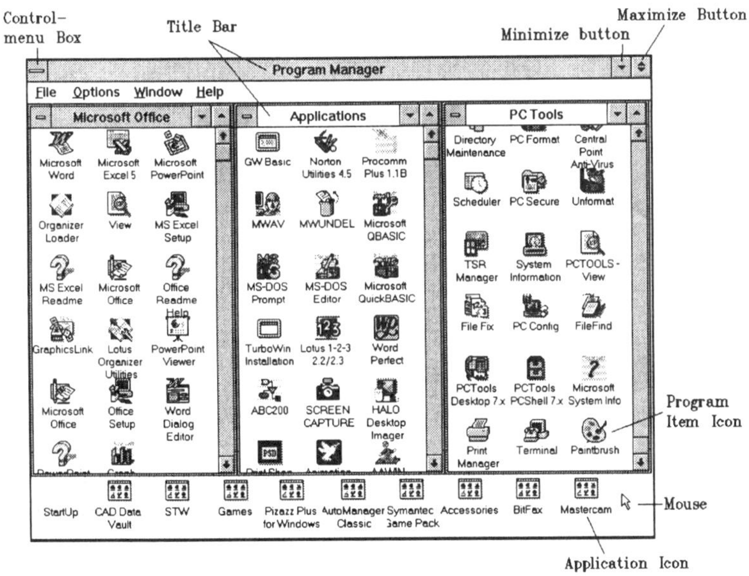

Figure 3.1

Activating a Windows Application

1. Double-click the Mastercam Icon in the Program Manager Group Window and you will see the enlarged application window shown in Figure 3.2 on the next page.

Tip: Double-clicking is performed by quickly pressing and releasing the left mouse button twice. Double-clicking is frequently used as a shortcut for other actions, such as starting an application from an icon.

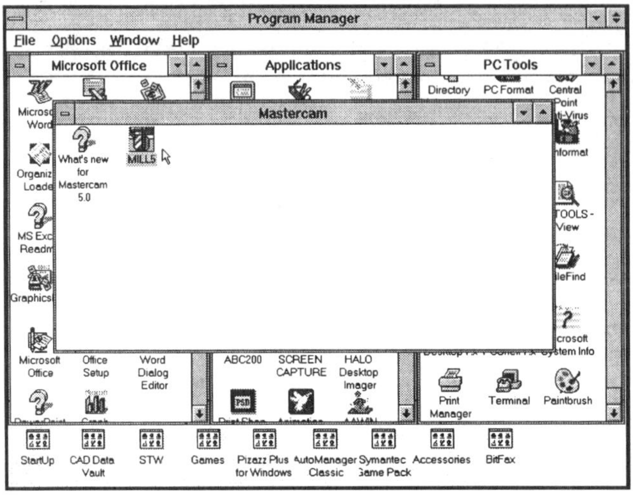

Figure 3.2

2. Double-click the MILL5 icon in Figure 3.2 to start Mastercam.

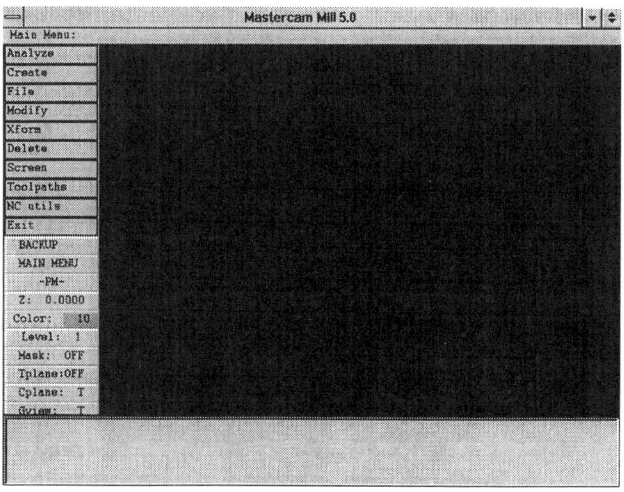

Figure 3.3

Changing the Size of the Window

To maximize the Mastercam window to the full screen, click the maximize button on the title bar as shown in Figure 3.4.

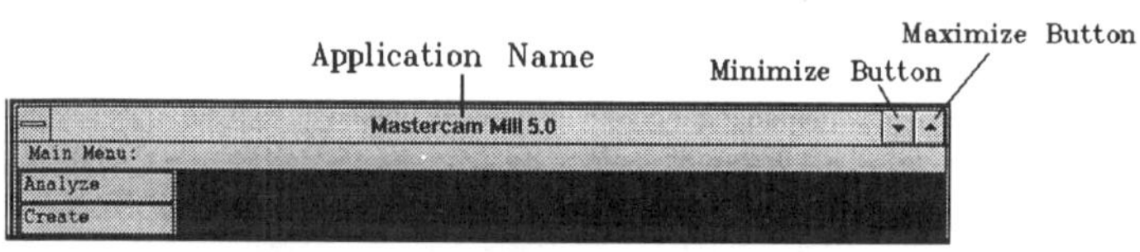

Figure 3.4: The Title Bar of Mastercam

To minimize the Mastercam window to an icon, click the minimize button on the title bar shown in Figure 3.4 above.

To change the size of the window, follow this procedure:

1. Point to the Mastercam border, or corner, and the pointer will change to a two headed arrow.

2. Press and hold the pick (left) mouse button while dragging the corner or border of the Mastercam screen.

3. Release the pick button when you have the desired window size.

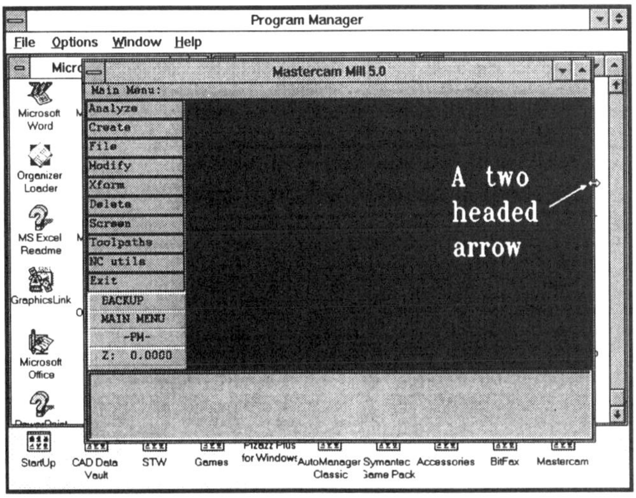

Figure 3.5

Moving a Window

To move a window, position your mouse pointer in the bar at the top of your window that contains the application name (or the title bar), press the pick button, and keep the button down. Drag the window to its new position, and release the pick button.

Exiting Windows Applications

To exit Windows and return to DOS, you can choose one of the following three methods.

1. In Program Manager, select File → Exit Windows... → OK

- or -

2. In Program Manager, double-click the Control-menu Box (see Figure 3.1), and select OK

- or -

3. Press Alt-F4, and select OK.

3.2 Entering Mastercam (WINDOWS version)

In the WINDOWs version, the way to enter Mastercam has only two steps:

Step 1. Enter the WINDOWS environment

Type WIN at the DOS prompt.

Step 2. Enter the Mastercam mill application

Use the mouse to pick the MILL5 icon (or the Mastercam Mill icon) under the Mastercam application.

3.3 Mastercam Screen

After you enter Mastercam, the system will display the Mastercam screen which is divided into **three sections**: a graphics display, a screen menu and a system response area.

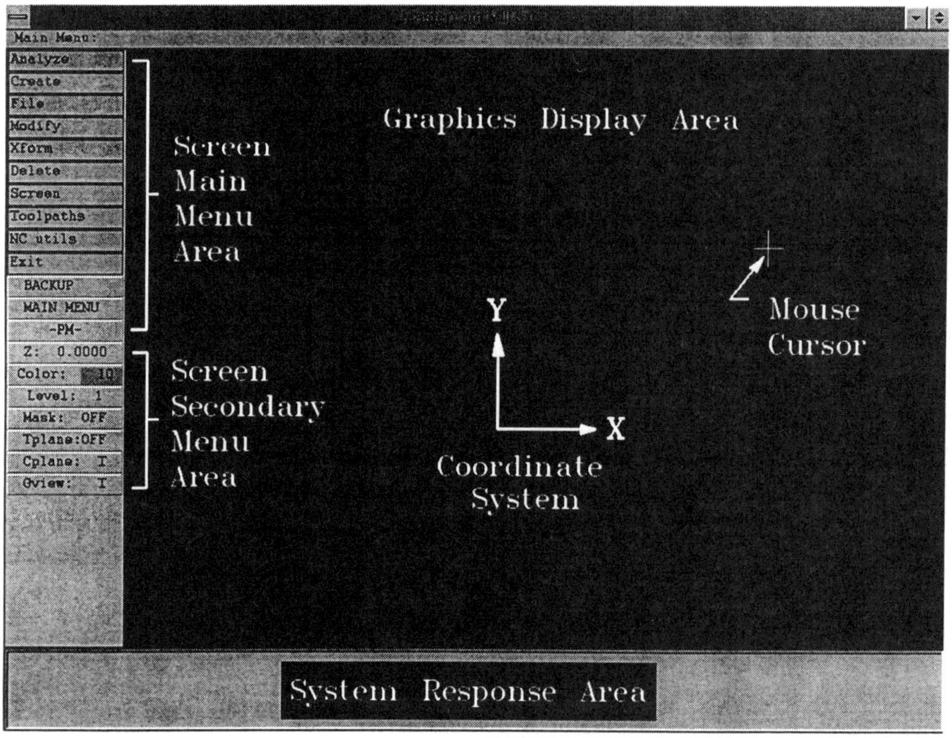

Figure 3.6 Mastercam Screen Display

Graphics Display Area

This is the working area where your drawing geometry can be created, retrieved or modified.

Screen Menu Area

This area is located at the left of the screen and consists of a main menu and a secondary menu. The **main menu** is used to select the system's main functions such as create, modify, or toolpaths. The **secondary menu** is used to change the system's parameters such as the Z depth or color which is frequently revised by the user. All the commands used in Mastercam can be selected from this area.

Selecting a Menu Option

In Mastercam, there are two ways to select a menu option:

1. Moving the mouse or pointing devices into the menu area. After the desired menu box is highlighted, press any mouse button to activate the command.

2. Pressing the first capital letter of the command.

The first menu to appear on the Mastercam main menu screen is the Mastercam **Root Menu**. It is shown in Figure 3.6. Some of these menu items have a more detailed submenu from which an item must be selected. A brief description of the commands available from the main menu and secondary menu is listed below.

Table 3.1 The Main Menu

Main Item	Description
Analyze	Displays coordinate and database information for selected object such as point,line, arc, spline, surface or dimension on the screen. It is helpful to identify objects that had already been created. For example, it can be used to determine the angle of an existing line or the radius of a specified circle.
Create	Creates geometry to the drawing database and draws it on the Graphics Display Area. These geometries include line, arc, circle, rectangle, etc.
File	Manipulates disk **files** such as SAVE, GET, CONVERT, TRANSMIT, or RECEIVE.
Modify	Modifies screen geometry with the fillet, trim, break and join commands.
Xform	Transforms already created geometry with the mirror, rotate, scale, and offset commands.
Delete	Deletes an entity or group of entities from the screen and the system's database.
Screen	Plots or views the drawing geometry, shows the number of drawing entities, zooms in and out, changes the viewport number and configuration.
Toolpaths	Creates NC toolpaths using drill, contour, pocket, etc.
NC utils	Manipulates and processes NC toolpaths.
Exit	Exits Mastercam.
BACKUP*	Brings the main menu item to its upper level.
MAIN MENU	Brings the main menu item to its root page.

* Refer to section 3.5.2 for short-cut keys.

Table 3.2 The Secondary Menu

Main	Item	Description
Z:	0.0000	Displays and changes the current working depth.
Color	10	Sets the current system default color.
Level	1	Sets the current system active level.
Mask:	OFF	Sets the system masking level.
Tplane:	OFF	Sets a tool plane.
Cplane:	T	Sets a construction plane.
Gview:	T	Changes the graphic view. Note that the graphic view can be independent of construction plane.

The menu, command, and option structure of Mastercam is a *tree* (or *hierarchy*) arrangement. For example, the actual tree arrangement to Create a Rectangle using the 2 points option is shown in Figure 3.7.

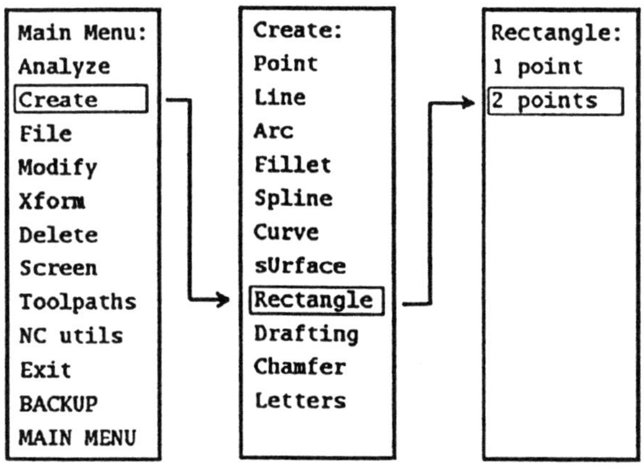

Figure 3.7 The tree arrangement of the CREATE menu

Select the **Create** menu with your mouse pointer. The menu changes and now consists of the submenu of **Create**. Select **Rectangle** and the menu changes to the submenu of **Rectangle**. Select **2 points** to activate the option. Notice the prompts in the system response area. It provides important information for you to follow through.

To conserve space and still allow you to access the commands properly, the convention used in this book for the command selections shown in Figure 3.7 will be indicated as,

Create → Rectangle → 2 points

The entire Mastercam command hierarchy is organized systematically. Take your time to review it. You will have more opportunity to learn and practice some of the screen commands in the upcoming chapters.

System Response Area

One or two text lines at the bottom of the screen indicate the status of the commands. This is where you will receive messages from Mastercam. Watch this area carefully; it might require some input from the keyboard.

3.4 Exiting Mastercam

To exit Mastercam, follow the steps shown here. The same steps also apply to the DOS version.

Step 1. Go to the root page of the main menu.
Select MAIN MENU

Step 2. Select the Exit option.
Select Exit

Step 3. Confirm to exit Mastercam.
Select Yes

3.5 Using Mastercam Navigation Commands

Understanding Mastercam navigation commands is essential to operating the system effectively. In section 3.3, we explained how to select a menu option from the Screen Menu Area. To speed up the drawing construction, other commands such as accepting the default value and short-cut keys are described as follows:

3.5.1 In Mastercam, the **default value** set up by the system (or from previous user input) is indicated in a dialog box in the system response area, e.g.,

Enter the radius

0.5

If you decide to use this default value, you don't have to re-type it and the value can be accepted in two ways:

(a) press the (Enter) key, or
(b) press any mouse button.

If you want to change the default value at any time, you don't have to erase the old value, just type the new value in its place.

3.5.2 BACKUP and MAIN MENU

BACKUP backs up one menu level at a time and **MAIN MENU** jumps back to main menu options are used constantly and are available from every menu option. You can use mouse to select the option or use the following **short-cut keys.**

Menu option	Key(s)
BACKUP	Esc
MAIN MENU	Press Esc key continuously

3.5.3 Mastercam short-cut keys

Ten short-cut keys have special uses in Mastercam.

Alt-C	Run C-Hook application program[*1]
Alt-D	Access drafting parameters
Alt-F	Set menu fonts
Alt-H	Display on-line help
Alt-L	Set current line style
Alt-S	Display surface
Alt-T	Toggle NC toolpath display (CAM system only)
Alt-U	Undo
Alt-V	Display Mastercam version and serial numbers
Alt-W	Set viewport windows

[*1]: C-Hook programs are a customized application program written by CNC Software Inc. or other professionals using Watcom C/C++32 and the Mastercam C-Hooks library.

3.5.4 Mastercam function keys

Nineteen function keys have special uses in Mastercam. Using Mastercam's short-cut commands and function keys is a fast way to step into an operation and can reduce your drawing time remarkably.

	Function Key	Alt + Function key
F1	Zoom	Fit to extents of the screen
F2	Zoom Previous or Scale by 0.5	Scale by 0.8
F3	Repaint	Analyze at Cursor Position
F4	Analyze	Exit Mastercam
F5	Delete	Delete Window
F6	File	Edit
F7	Modify	(Blank)
F8	Create	Configuration
F9	Display System Information	Draw Axes
F10	Help Screen	Help Screen

3.6 Getting Help

If you need help for a Mastercam function key, use the **F10** function key. A limited help screen is displayed. See Figure 3.8.

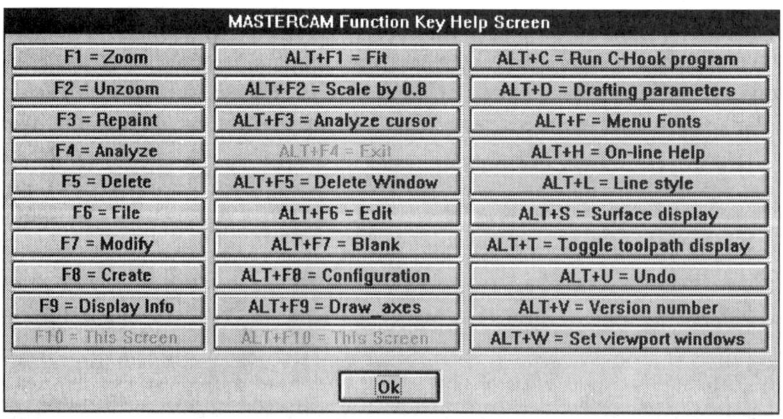

Figure 3.8 Mastercam Function Key Help Screen

As of Mastercam Version 5.0, you will notice that the on-line help screen can be accessed by pressing Alt-H. This on-line help, shown in Figure 3.9, provides you with information in great detail. Therefore, it is highly recommended to step into this new utility. You can select a topic with the mouse or press ESC to exit the help. An example showing help on Xform → Translate is shown in figure 3.10.

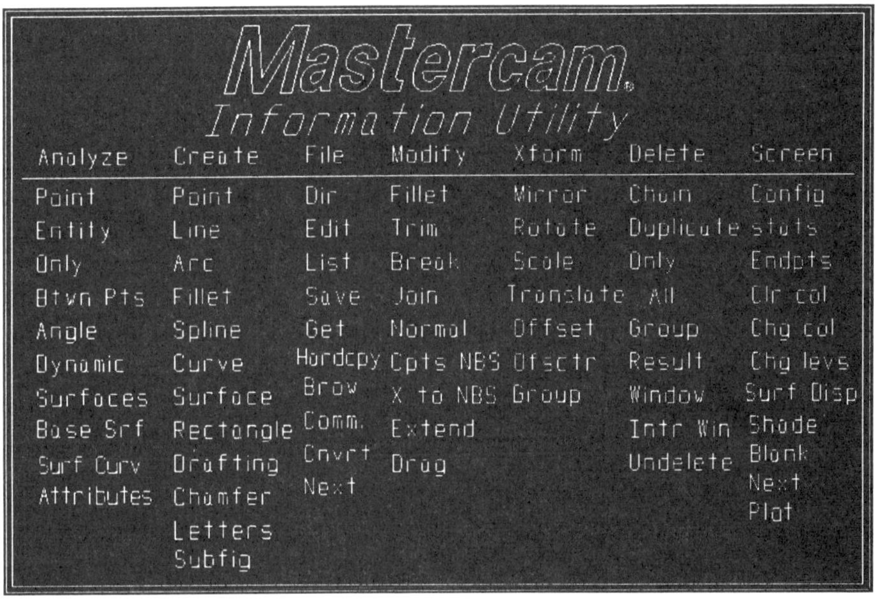

Figure 3.9

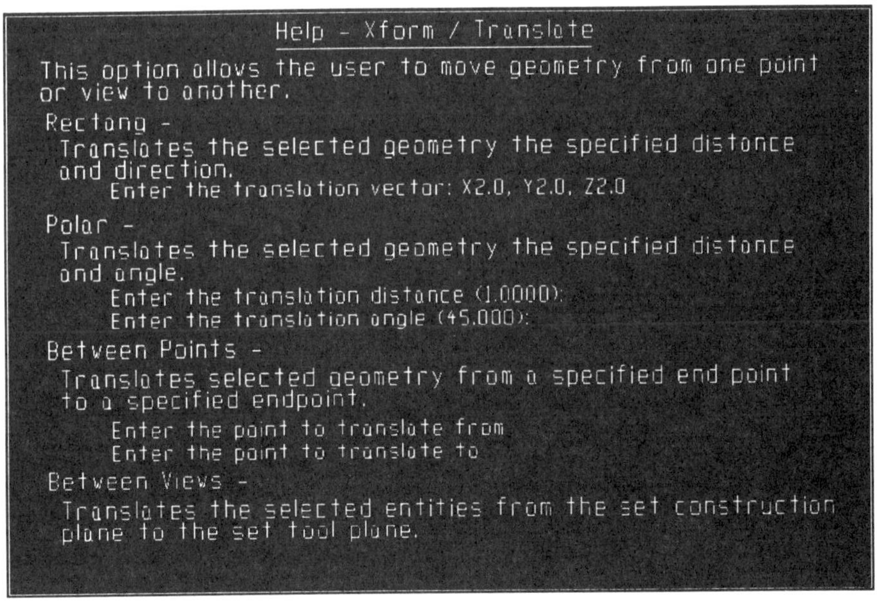

Figure 3.10

Example

In the following example, you will practice the essential commands introduced in this chapter to work with Mastercam. You will enter the Mastercam environment, complete a simple drawing as shown in Figure 3.11, save the drawing and retrieve it. Don't worry about exact sizes or dimensions, but do try to make them look as much like the drawing as possible.

Figure 3.11 Example drawing: Mastercam to go

In the process of creating this drawing, you will learn to use the mouse, select the screen menu commands and enter other input from the keyboard. This hands-on experience is important for you to be familiar with Mastercam and its applications. The learning objectives can be itemized as:

- Entering Mastercam
- Analyzing the drawing entities
- Creating a simple geometry
- Saving to a file
- Exiting Mastercam
- Restarting Mastercam
- Retrieving previous file

Step 1. Entering Mastercam

Follow the procedures shown in Section 3.2.

Step 2. Analyzing the drawing entities

In order to construct the drawing, the first procedure is to identify the drawing entities as shown in Figure 3.12, and the construction sequences. Although this chapter does not cover this procedure, it is important to include it in your practice before you start constructing your drawing.

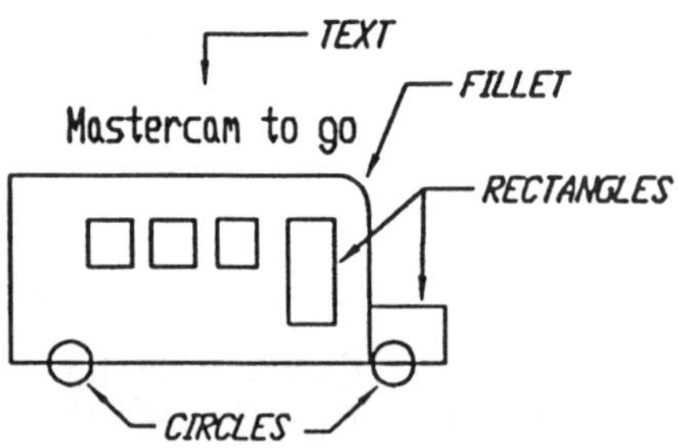

Figure 3.12

Step 3. Creating a simple geometry

For steps 3.1 - 3.6, you should refer to the pick points shown in Figure 3.13.

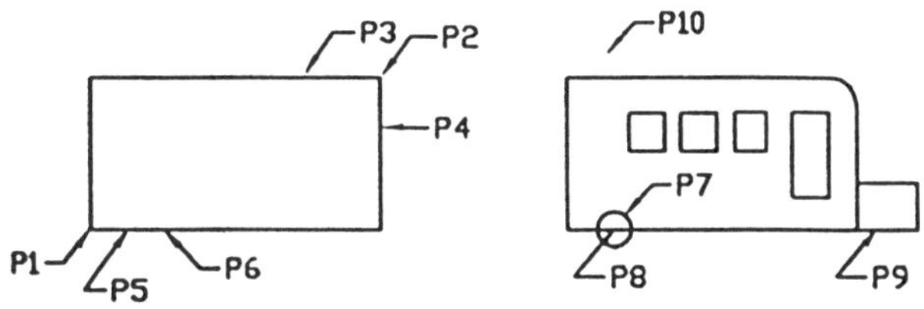

Figure 3.13 Pick points for the example drawing

Step 3.1 Create a rectangle

Select the menu items:

Main Menu → Create → Rectangle → 2 points

(Notice and switch to the prompt in the System Response Area)

Enter the lower left corner: Pick at P1

Enter the upper right corner: Pick at P2

Step 3.2 Create a fillet

Select the menu items:

Main Menu → Create → Fillet

(Notice the default values in the System Response Area)

Select an entity: Pick at P3

Select another entity: Pick at P4

Step 3.3 Create a circle

Select the menu items:

Main Menu → Create → Arc → 2 pt cir

(Notice the prompt in the System Response Area)

Enter the first point: Pick at P5

Enter the second point: Pick at P6

Step 3.4 Create rectangles

Follow Step 3.1 and create the rest of the five rectangles using rectangle commands.

Step 3.5 Copy a circle

Select the menu items:

Main Menu → Xform → Translate → Entity

Select an entity: Pick at P7

Select the menu items:

Backup → Done → Between pts

(Notice the pop-up dialog box on screen)

Enter the points to translate from: Pick at P8

Enter the points to translate to: Pick at P9

Set the Translate menu as shown:☞

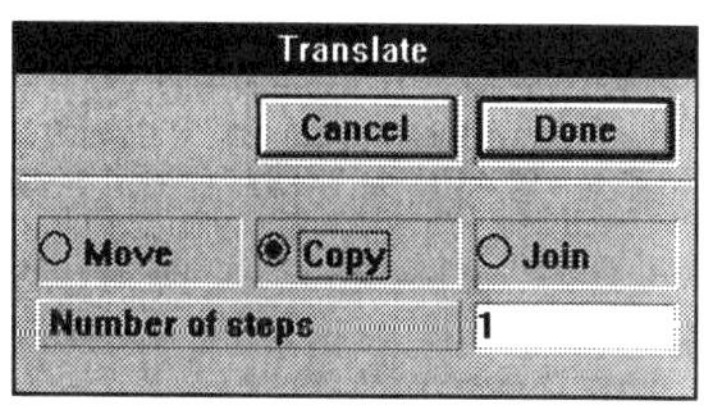

Select **Done** to return from the Translate menu.

Step 3.6 Create a text note

Select the menu items:

Main Menu → Create → Drafting → Note → Keyin

(Notice the prompt in the System Response Area)

Text: Enter **Mastercam to go**

Enter line 2 (press Enter when done): press Enter

Create note: Indicate text position: Pick at P10

Step 4. Saving to a file

Main Menu → File → Save

Enter file name (Drive:\NC\GE3\T.GE3): Enter **BUS**

Step 5. Exiting Mastercam

Main Menu → Exit → Yes

Step 6. Restarting Mastercam

Follow the procedures outlined in Section 3.2.

Step 7. Retrieving previous file

Main Menu → File → Get

Enter file name (Drive:\NC\GE3\T.GE3): Enter **BUS**

Note: The drawing you just created in this example should appear much like Figure 3.11 at the top of page 3-10.

3.7 Exercises

In the following steps, you are to review and practice the essential commands presented in the previous example.

1. Turn on your computer and load Mastercam to access the drawing editor.

2. Begin a new drawing using your own variables.
   Draw six connected lines. (Hint: Create → Line → Multi → sKetch)
   Draw two rectangle boxes.
   Draw four circles.
   Draw two text notes.
   Delete a line, a rectangle box, a circle, and a text note.

3. Save the drawing as **EX** and exit Mastercam.

4. Enter Mastercam and load **EX**.

3.7.1 Short Answer

1. Explain the overall purpose of the Graphics Display Area, System Response Area and Screen Menu Area in Mastercam.

2. Briefly describe the ways to select a menu option.

3. What is the short-cut function key for DELETE?

4. Briefly explain the purpose of the following commands: Create, Modify, Xform

Chapter 4

Mastercam Process Overview

Objectives:

1. Provide an overview of CAD/CAM NC programming.
2. Use a simple example to step through the main tasks of CAD/CAM NC programming.
3. Be familiarized with the process of CAD/CAM NC programming.

4.1 CAD/CAM NC Programming Process

The intent of this chapter is to provide an overview of the processing steps required to generate NC codes in a CAD/CAM system. CAD/CAM NC programming involves **three** major components: **CAD, CAM, and a postprocessor**. Figure 4.1 illustrates the CAD/CAM NC programming steps. Each step indicates the input data and output data. Studying the part drawing is the first step of the process. We need to identify what part features need to be produced and determine the size of the raw material. From these, we should be able to determine how much material needs to be removed. The next step is to create a CAD drawing. The main task of the CAD program is to create the part geometry of the final finished part and its raw material shape if necessary.

The CAM program requires **two** types of input data, **part geometry and machining data**, to generate the tool path to machine the part. The output of the CAM program is a generic file called a cutter location data file (NCI) which contains the coordinate values of a series of cutter paths, machining information such as feed rate, spindle speed, coolant control command, etc. The postprocessor converts the NCI file into NC codes readable to CNC controllers. Since CNC controllers vary from vendor to vendor, this requires us to create a dedicated postprocessor for a particular CNC controller/machine combination. We need to know which CNC machine will be used for machining the part in order to select the appropriate postprocessor.

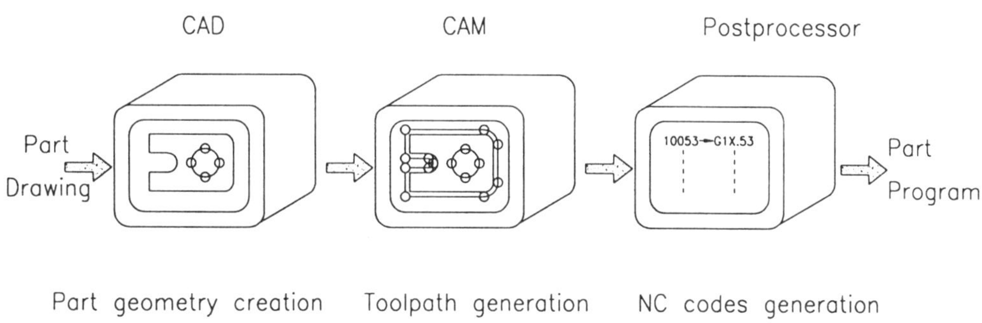

Figure 4.1

4.2 Mastercam Process Overview

This section presents the step-by-step procedure that generates the toolpath to machine a simple part shown in Figure 4.2. This exercise will help you to understand the overall process of CAD/CAM NC programming.

The project involves creating a 6" x 4" rectangle, a blind slot, and four holes. The contour module is used to generate the toolpaths for the outer profile, and the drill module is used for generating the toolpaths for drilling four holes.

Note: If the working envelope of your machine is smaller than 6" x 4", scale all the dimensions by one-half.

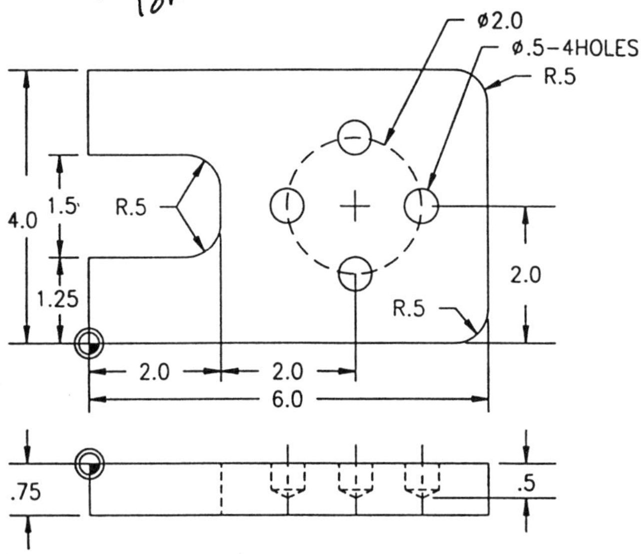

Figure 4.2

Tips: **Creating part geometry:**

1. Create a rectangle with 6" x 4" dimensions.

2. Create two horizontal lines and one vertical line.

3. Break the left vertical line of the rectangle into two pieces. This allows the line to be trimmed.
4. Add four fillets.

5. Trim the left vertical line of the rectangle and two horizontal lines.

6. Create four circles.

⌛**Tips: Generating toolpaths:**

1. Use the contour module to generate the toolpaths for the outer profile with a 1" end mill.

2. Use the drill module to generate the toolpaths for drilling four holes with a 0.5" drill.

3. Set the NC parameters according to the following tooling and machining specifications:

Tool No.	Tool Dia.	Feedrate	Plunge Rate	Spindle Speed
1	1.0"	15.0 ipm	10.0 ipm	3000 rpm
2	0.5"	15.0 ipm	-	1500 rpm

Step 1. Enter Mastercam Mill. Following the procedure given in Chapter 3.

Step 2. Create a rectangle. The rectangle should appear as Figure 4.3.

Select **MAIN MENU →Create → Rectangle → 1 point**
Enter the lower left corner: **0,0** ←
Enter the width: **6** ←
Enter the height: **4** ←
Press **ALT + F1** simultaneously then press **F2** to fit the drawing to the screen.

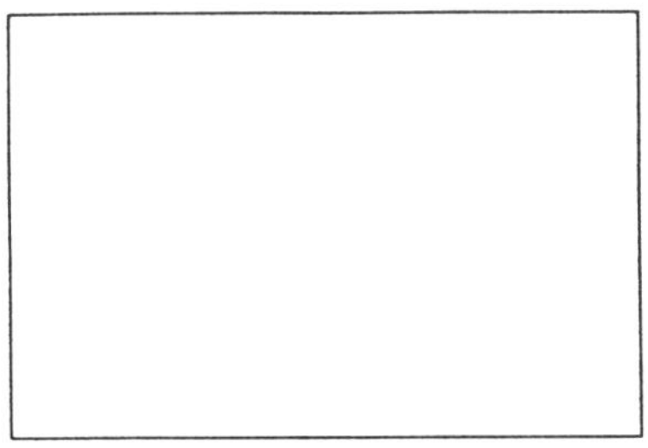

Figure 4.3

Step 3. Create two horizontal lines and one vertical line. The three lines should add to the drawing as shown in Figure 4.4.

Select **MAIN MENU → Create → Line → Endpoints**
Specify the first endpoint: **-0.5, 2.75** ←
Specify the second endpoint: **2.5, 2.75** ← to complete the first line
Specify the first endpoint: **-0.5, 1.25** ←
Specify the second endpoint: **2.5,1.25** ← to complete the second line
Specify the first endpoint: **2.0, 3.0** ←
Specify the second endpoint: **2.0, 1** ← to complete the third line

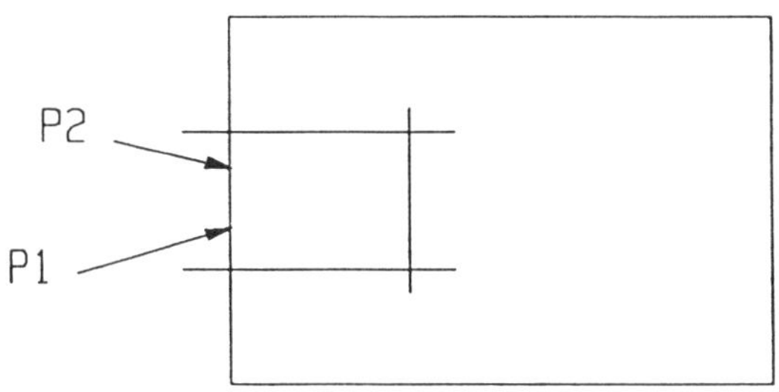

Figure 4.4

Step 4. Break the left vertical line of the rectangle into two pieces. Use the pick points in Figure 4.4 on the previous page.

Select **MAIN MENU → Modify → Break → 2 pieces**
Select an entity: pick at **P1** ←
Enter the breakpoint: pick at **P2** ←

The left vertical line is broken into two pieces, but you may not see this on the screen. The new drawing should look identical to Figure 4.4 which is redrawn in Figure 4.5.

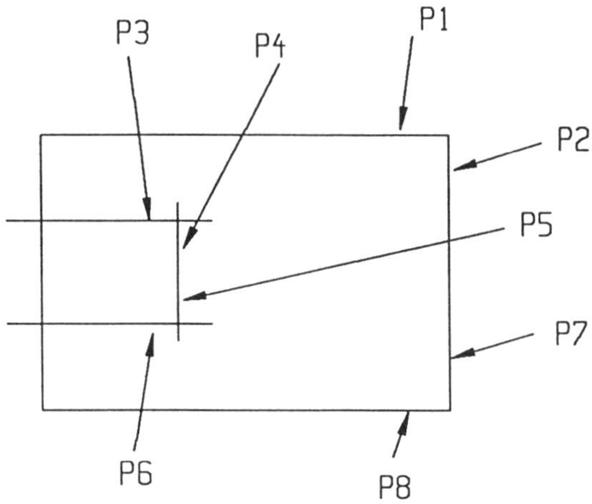

Figure 4.5

Step 5. Add four fillets using the pick points in Figure 4.5. The four fillets should appear as in Figure 4.6.

Select **BACKUP → BACKUP → Fillet → Radius**
Enter the fillet radius: **0.5** ←
Pick points at **P1** and **P2** to complete the first fillet
Sequentially pick points at **P3 - P8** to complete the three remaining fillets

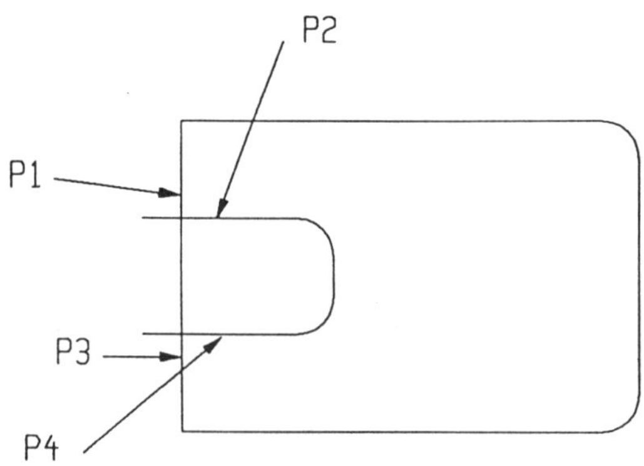

Figure 4.6

Step 6. Trim the left vertical line of the rectangle and two horizontal lines using the pick points in Figure 4.6. The trimmed drawing should look like Figure 4.7 on the next page.

Select **BACKUP → Trim → 2 entities**
Select the entity to trim: pick at **P1**
Select the entity to trim to: pick at **P2** to trim the upper half of the vertical line
Select the entity to trim: pick at **P3**
Select the entity to trim to: pick at **P4** to complete the trimming

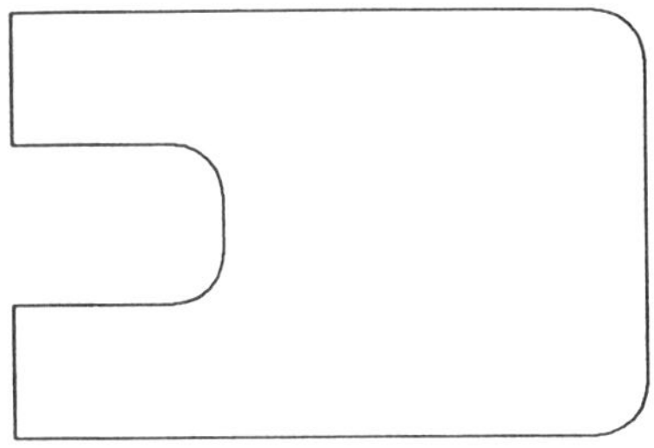

Figure 4.7

Step 7. Create four circles. The four circles are added to the drawing as shown in Figure 4.8.

Select **MAIN MENU → Create → Arc → pt Dia cir**
Enter the center point: **5,2** ←
Enter the diameter: **.5** ←
Enter the center point: **4,3** ←
Enter the diameter (0.5): press ← to accept the default value
Enter the center point: **3,2** ←
Enter the diameter (0.5): press ←
Enter the center point: **4,1** ←
Enter the diameter (0.5); press ←

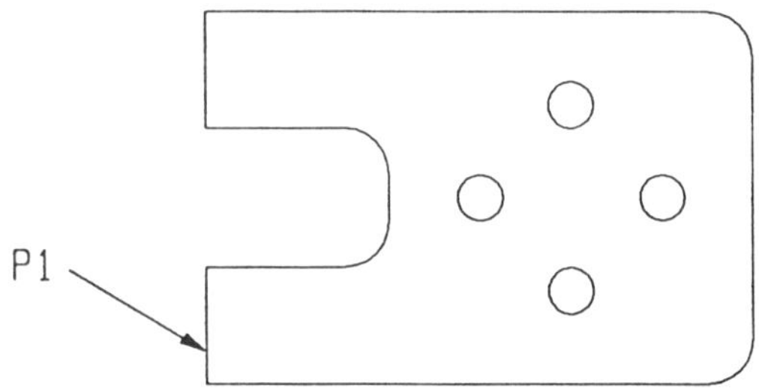

Figure 4.8

Step 8. Initiate the Contour module to generate the toolpath for the outer profile. Use the pick points in Figure 4.8.

Select **MAIN MENU → Toolpaths → Contour**
Enter file name (C:\NC\NCI\T.NCI): **overview** ←
Define contour 1: select **Chain** from the chaining method menu
Select the first entity in the contour: pick at **P1**
Note: The chaining diamond will go in the clockwise direction
Select **Close → End here → Done** to complete the contour chaining

Step 9. Set the contour parameters.

Select **Params** from the menu.Set the parameters to the following settings:

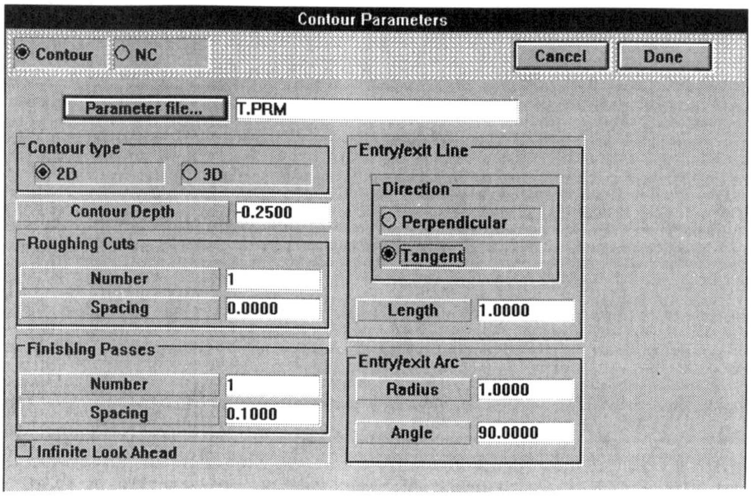

Select the **NC Button** to advance to the next parameter page.

Step 10. Set the NC common parameters. Set parameters to the following settings:

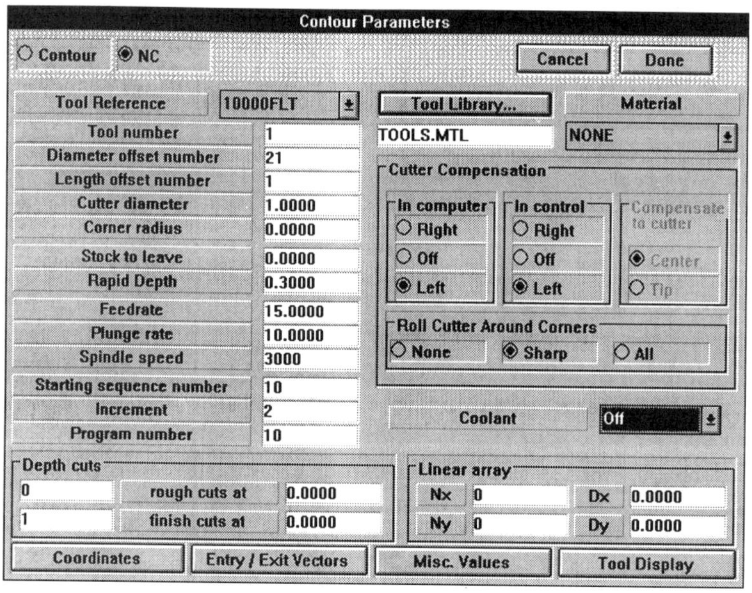

Select the **Done Button** to complete the parameter settings.
The toolpath should appear as Figure 4.9 on the next page.

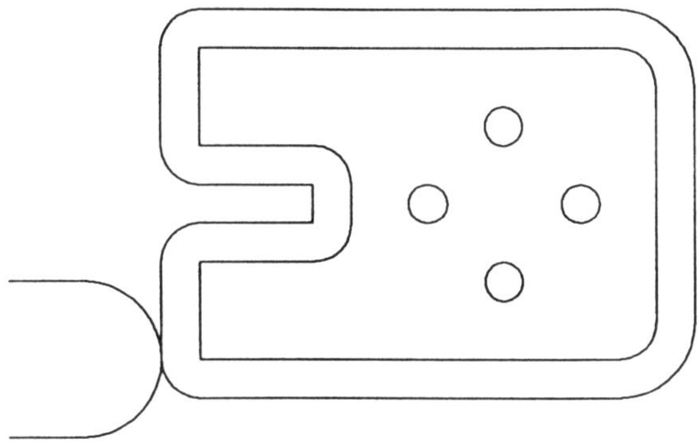

Figure 4.9

Step 11. Write the toolpath.

Select **Write** from the Change menu
Select **Yes** to accept the tool paths

The tool paths for cutting the outer profile are shown in Figure 4.10.

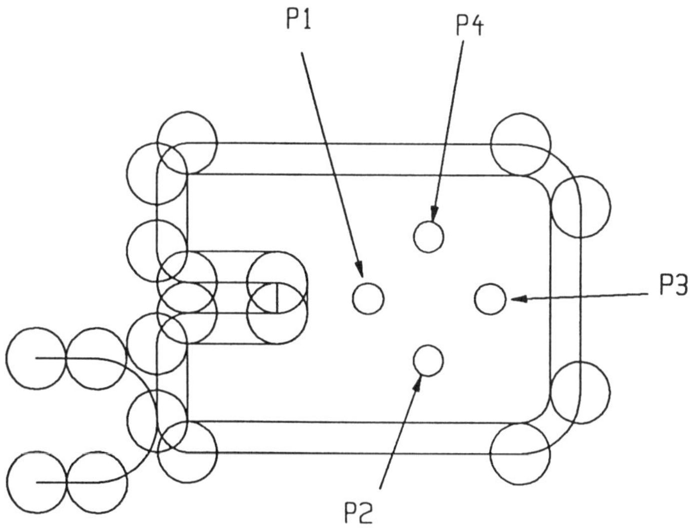

Figure 4.10

Step 12. Initiate the Drill module and select four locations for drilling using the pick points in Figure 4.10.

Select **Drill**
Select **Manual** from the Select points menu
Select **Center** from the point menu
Sequentially pick at **P1, P2, P3,** and **P4,**
then press **Esc** to complete the points selection
Select **Yes** for Draw the path between points?
Select **Yes** for Is the path OK?

Step 13. Set the Drill parameters.

Define the Drill parameters to the following settings:

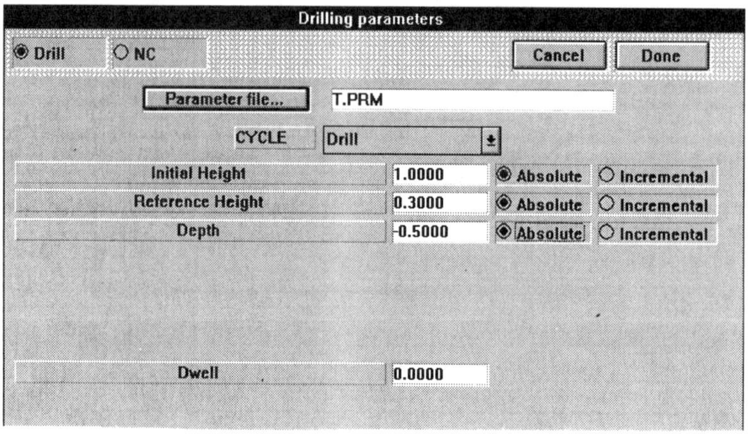

Select the **NC Button** to advance to the NC parameters menu.

Step 14. Set the NC parameters.

Set the NC parameters to the following settings:

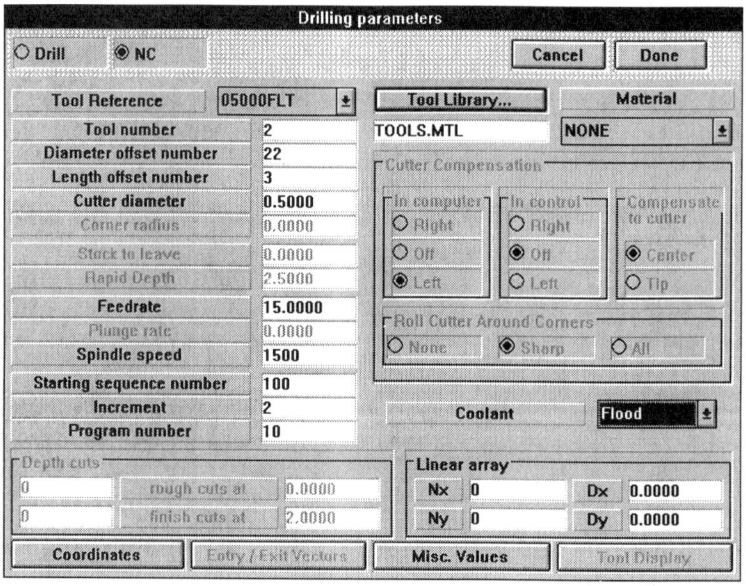

Select the **Done Button** to complete the parameter settings.

Step 15. Write the drilling toolpaths.

Select **Write** from the Change menu
Select **Yes** for Accept this toolpath segment?
Select **No** for Repeat with same points?

The drilling toolpaths are added to the drawing as shown in Figure 4.11.

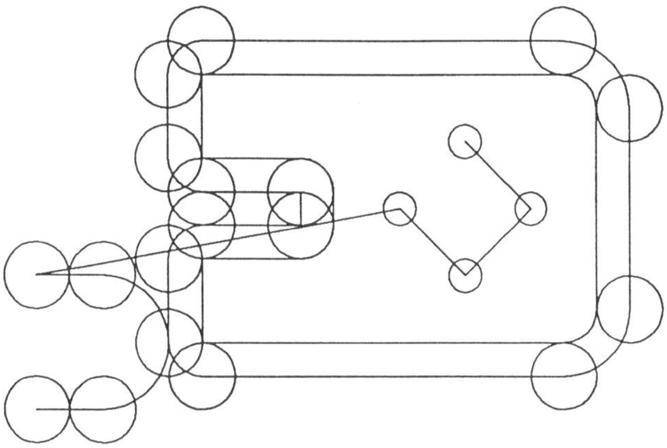

Figure 4.11

Step 16. Change to isometric view.

Select **Gview** from the Secondary menu
Select **Isometric** from the Gview menu
Press **Alt** + **F1** simultaneously
then press **F2** to fit the drawing on the screen if necessary.

The drawing should look like Figure 4.12.

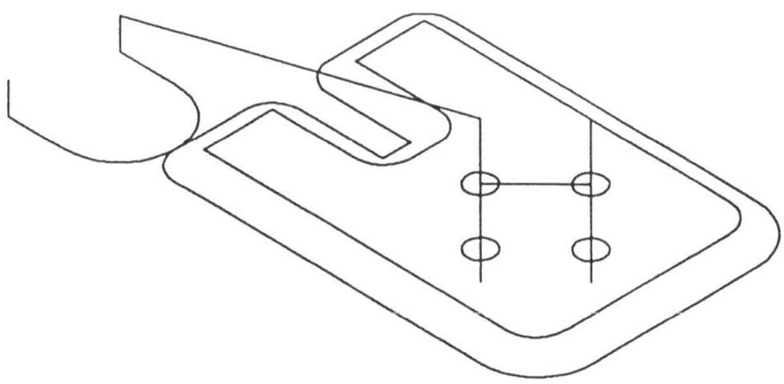

Figure 4.12

Step 17. Close the toolpath file.

Select **End program** to close the toolpath file (.NCI)
Select **No** for "Run the post processor?"

Step 18. Select the Post Processor.

Select **MAIN MENU →NC utils → Post Proc →Change**
Enter file pattern (c:\NC*.pst): **mpfan** (or the post processor name you select)

Step 19. Run the post processor to convert the toolpath file (.NCI) into the NC Codes (.NC).

Select **Run**

Enter file pattern (C:\NC\NCI*.NCI): Overview ←

Enter file name (c:\NC\overview.NC): ← to accept the default name

The part program should appear on the screen. Double-click the window button to return back to graphic mode.

Step 20. List the NC codes.

Select **MAIN MENU → File → Edit → NC**

Enter file name (C:\NC\T.NC): **overview**

The part program generated from this process is listed below:

```
%
O10
N1 G90 G80 G40 G0
N2 T1 M6
N3 G54 G0 X-2.5 Y-1.
N4 S3000 M3
N5 G43 H1 Z.3
N6 G1 Z-.25 F10.0
N7 X-1.5 F15.0
N8 G3 X-.5 Y0. R1.
N9 G1 Y1.25
N10 G2 X0. Y1.75 R.5
N11 G1 X1.5
N12 Y2.25
N13 X0.
N14 G2 X-.5 Y2.75 R.5
N15 G1 Y4.
N16 G2 X0. Y4.5 R.5
N17 G1 X5.5
N18 G2 X6.5 Y3.5 R1.
N19 G1 Y.5
N20 G2 X5.5 Y-.5 R1.
N21 G1 X0.
N22 G2 X-.5 Y0. R.5
N23 G3 X-1.5 Y1. R1.
N24 G1 X-2.5
N25 G0 Z.3
N26 G28 Z.3
N27 T2 M6
```

Part program continued:

```
N28 M1
N29 G54 G0 X3. Y2.
N30 S1500 M3 T1
N31 G43 H2 Z1.
N32 G0 X3. Y2.
N33 G98 G81 X3. Y2. Z-.5 R.3 F15.0
N34 X4. Y1.
N35 X5. Y2.
N36 X4. Y3.
N37 G80
N38 G28 Z1.
N39 G28 X0. Z0.
N40 M30
```

Press **F10 Twice** to return to graphic mode.

4.3 Exercises

1. What are the three major components involved in CAD/CAM NC programming?

2. What should be included in generating CAD drawing?

3. What are the two types of data that should be entered into any CAM program to generate NC toolpath?

4. Describe the output of the CAM program.

5. Explain the main task performed in a postprocessor.

6. Explain why a dedicated postprocessor is needed for a unique combination of CNC controller/machine.

Chapter 5

Basic (2-D) Geometry Construction

Objectives:

1. Understand the function of POINT, LINE, ARC, CIRCLES, RECTANGLE, CHAMFER, SPLINE, ELLIPSE and LETTERS commands.
2. Practice using Mastercam **CREATE** commands to construct entities on screen.
3. Construct part geometries using basic create commands.

Overview

The part geometry of the final finished part and its raw material shape should be defined in the CAD program. This geometric file is then used in the CAM program to generate the toolpaths for producing the part. An accurate and complete CAD geometry model is very essential in implementing any CAD/CAM software for producing a part program. The focus of this chapter is to show how to use Mastercam's CAD functions to create basic 2-D part geometries. The commands presented in this chapter include Point, Line, Arc, Circles, Rectangle, Chamfer, Spline, Ellipse, and Letters. Advanced geometry modification functions are presented in chapter 6. Three-D wireframe geometric model construction is covered in chapter 11.

5.1 Create Menu

Mastercam groups geometry entity construction functions under the Create menu. To create a geometric entity, we have to follow a proper cascaded menu sequence which starts at the MAIN MENU, followed by the Create menu and necessary sub-menus. Figure 5.1 shows a cascaded sequence for the Create function.

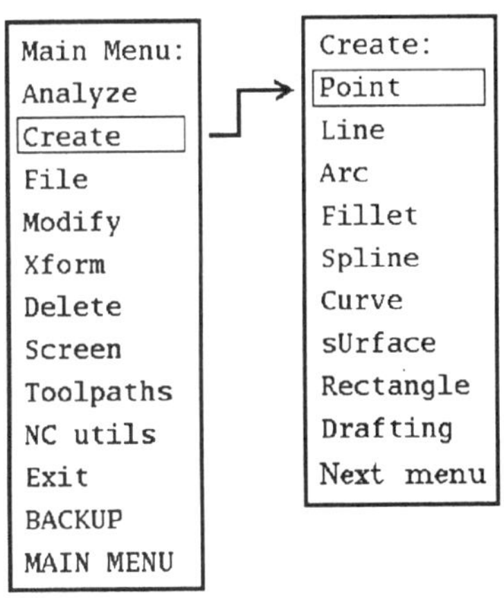

Figure 5.1: Menu for Create

5.2 Point and The Point Submenu

The **Point** command marks points on the drawing with a plus (+) mark. These points can be used as reference points for other geometric constructions when needed.

Select **Create → Point** from the main menu and you will see the following options (Figure 5.2).

```
Create:            Point:
[Point]  ───────>  Position
Line               Along ent
Arc                Node pts
Fillet             Cpts NBS
Spline             Dynamic
Curve              Length
sUrface            Boltcir*
Rectangle          cSinkpt*
Drafting           dRillpt*
Next menu          proJpt*
```

Figure 5.2: Menu for Point

A brief description for the POINT options follows:

Point Option	Description	
Position:	Create a point by selecting from the following submenu	
	Value:	<Refer to the next table for detailed descriptions of these options.>
	Center:	
	Endpoint:	
	Intersec:	
	Midpoint:	
	Point:	
	Last:	
	Relative:	
	sKetch:	
Along ent:	Create a series of points along an entity with equal distance	
Node pts:	Recall the node points used to create a parametric spline curve	
Cpts pts:	Recall the control points of NURBS curve or 3-D surface	
Dynamic:	Create points along an existing entity using the pointing device	
Length:	Create a point on an entity by a given distance from the end point.	
Boltcir*:	Create points in a bolt circle	
cSinkpt*:	Create countersink point	
dRillpts*:	Place points at the center of all circles	

Note: * indicates this topic will not be discussed in this chapter.

5.2.1 Create → Point → Position

Use the Position command to create points on the screen. As shown in Figure 5.3, there are **nine** options available and they will be referred as the **<using position menu>** in the future.

Position:	
Value:	Enter coordinates.
Center:	Select an entity which has a geometric center, e.g., arc, circle.
Endpoint:	Select an entity which has end points, e.g., line, arc, spline, etc. Pick a location closest to the end point you intend to select.
Intersec:	Select two entities which have an intersection point, e.g., line-line, line-arc, etc.
Midpoint:	Select an entity which has a midpoint.
Point:	Select an existing point.
Last:	Select the last point created.
Relative:	Create a point by giving a relative distance to an existing point. Input the distance as either Rectangular or Polar coordinates.
sKetch:	Use the mouse to pick the point to be created.

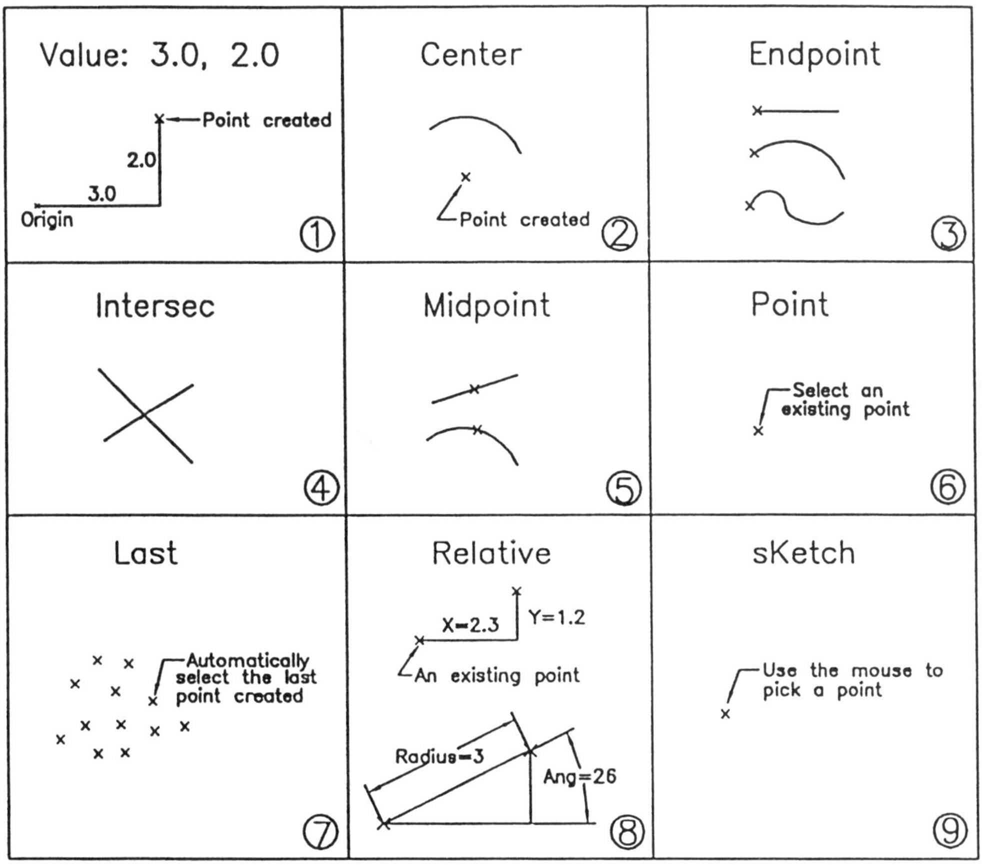

Figure 5.3 Mastercam position menu

5.2.2 Create → Point → Along ent

Create a series of points along an entity with equal distance between the points.

Procedure:

Create an entity such as line, arc, circle, fillet or spline.

Select an entity

Use the mouse to select an entity including line, arc, circle, fillet or spline.

Enter the number of points to create (def val): **6** ←

Note: **def val** stands for default value from the system, see section **3.5.1** for more detailed information. The points created are spaced at an equal distance along the entity selected as shown in Figure 5.4.

Tip If you want to break an entity into 3 equal sections, this is the command you can use. The number of points to create should be set to 4.

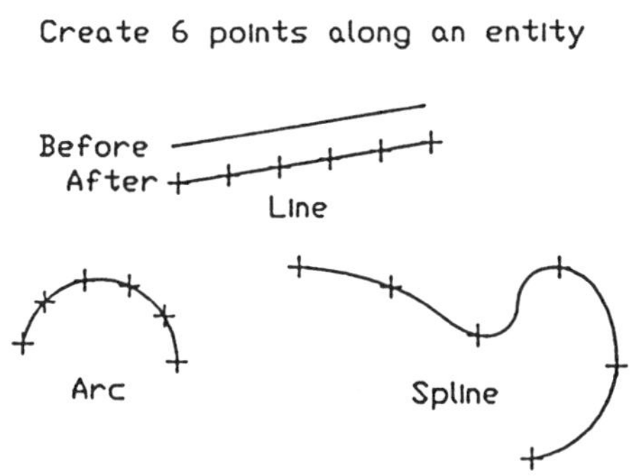

Figure 5.4

5.2.3 Create → Point → Node pts

Recall the node points used to create a parametric spline curve (Figure 5.5).

Procedure:

Create a spline curve. Refer to Section 5.6 for the steps in the construction of a spline curve.

Select a parametric spline.

Tips 1. These points are the node points used to define the spline.

2. If a wrong entity is selected, (other than spline), the system will respond "try again". Use the **Esc** key to quit the selection.

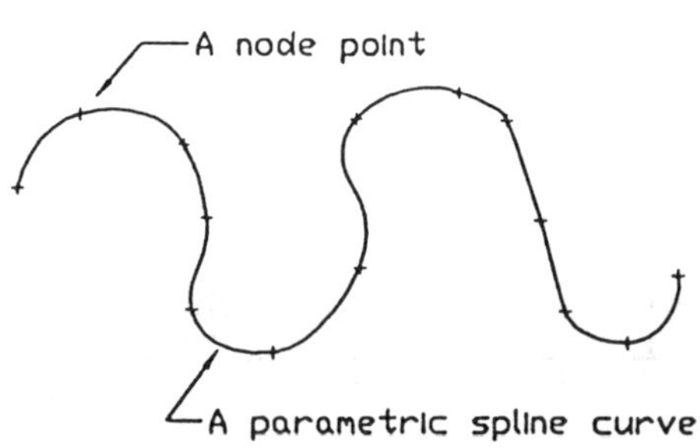

Figure 5.5

5.2.4 Create → Point → Cpts pts

Recall the control points of NURBS curve or 3-D surface.

Procedure:

Create a NURBS curve.

Refer to Section 5.6 for the construction of a NURBS curve.

Select a NURBS curve (or a 3-D surface).

Tips 1. These points are the control points used to define the curve or surface (Figure 5.6).

2. If you select a wrong entity (other than NURBS curve or surface), the system will response "try again". Use Esc key to quit the selection.

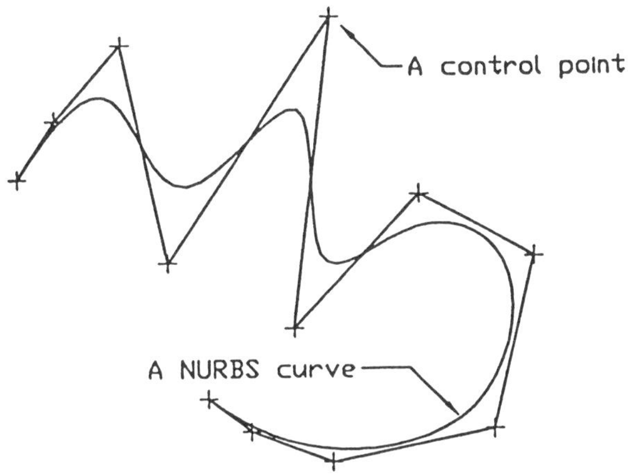

Figure 5.6

5.2.5 Create → Point → Dynamic

Create points along an existing entity with the mouse or pointing device (Figure 5.7).

Procedure:

Select an entity such as line, circle or spline.

Move the mouse around the entity and then press <Enter> to create a point (click any mouse button or press Esc when done).

Note: You can use this function to create as many points as you want in any position along the entity selected.

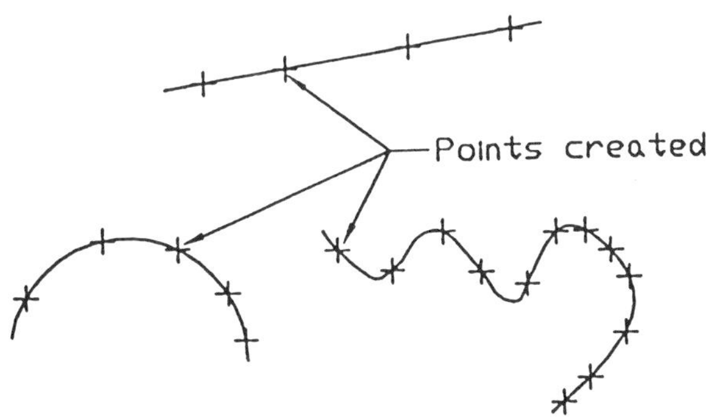

Figure 5.7

5.2.6 Create → Point → Length

Create a point on an entity at given distance from the end point. (Figure 5.8).

Procedure:

Create an entity such as a line, arc, etc.

Select an entity: Pick at **P1**

Length = **1.5←**

Press **ESC** to quit

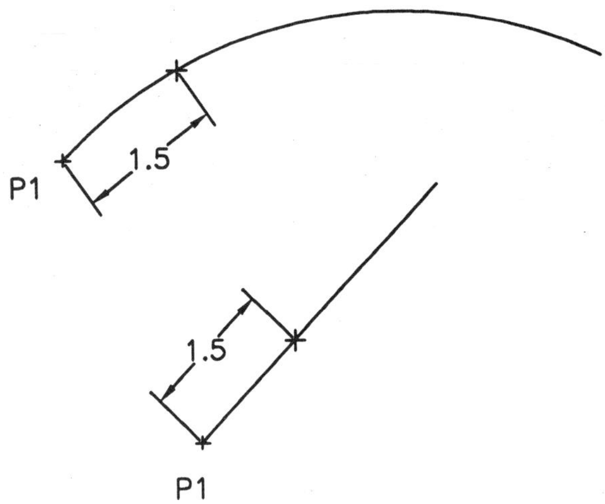

Figure 5.8

5.3 Line and Its Submenu

The **Line** command draws lines on the screen. These lines can be horizontal, vertical, or with any other orientation. It can be used to construct geometries such as those shown in Figure 5.9.

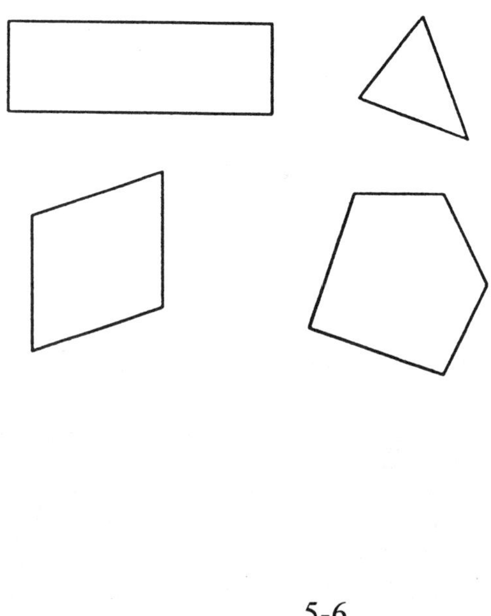

Figure 5.9

Select **Create → Line** from the main menu and you will see the following submenu options.

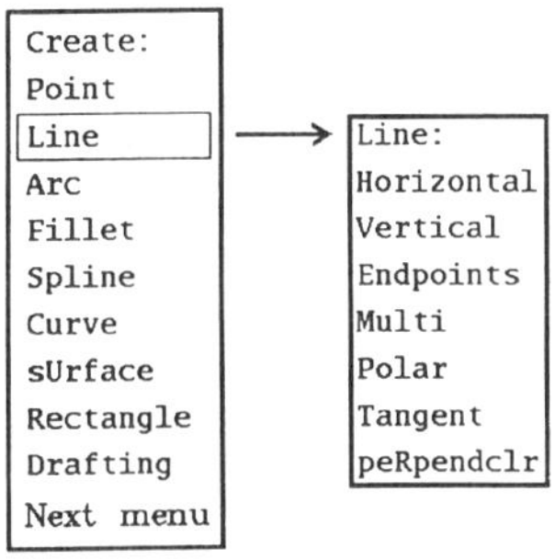

Figure 5.10: Submenu options for Line

In the LINE submenu, there are **seven** options. A brief description of each option is given below and its examples are provided in Figure 5.11.

Line Option	Description
Horizontal:	Create a horizontal line.
Vertical:	Create a vertical line.
Endpoints:	Create a line by specifying its two endpoints.
Multi:	Construct multi-line segments by specifying segment endpoints.
Polar:	Create a line using polar coordinate.
Tangent:	Create a line which is tangent to an arc or arcs.
peRpendclr:	Create a line which is perpendicular to a line or an arc.

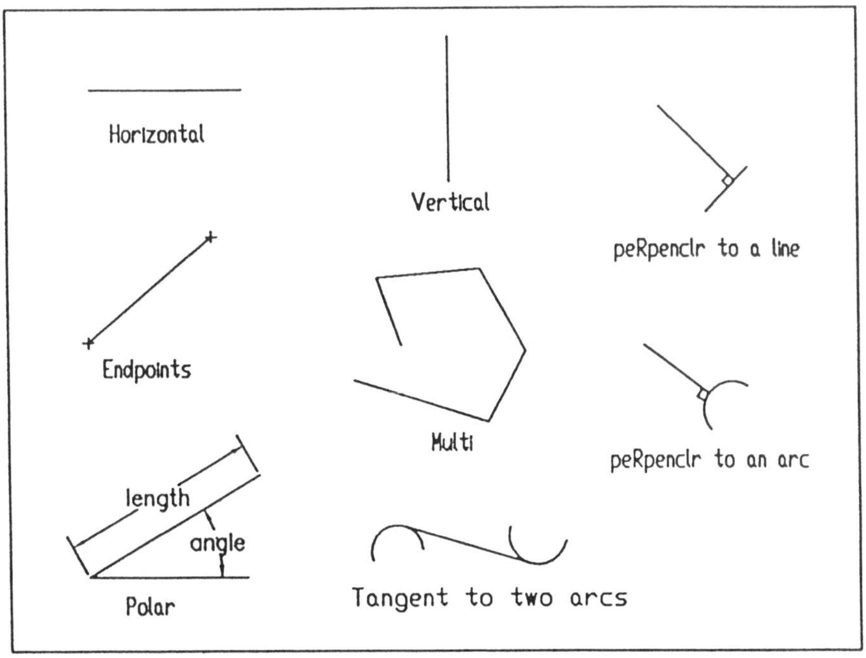

Figure 5.11

Note: The default line style can be changed by pressing Alt-D or picking **-PM-** (Drafting Parameters) from the Menu Area (See Figure 3.3). The available line styles are solid, hidden, center, phantom and Zbreak.

5.3.1 Create → Line → Horizontal

Create a horizontal line (Figure 5.12).

Procedure:

Specify the first endpoint <using position menu>: Pick at **P1**
Specify the second endpoint <using position menu>: Pick at **P2**
Enter the y coordinate (def val): **3.0** ←
(Press Esc to quit this procedure.)

Note: The default value inside the dialog box is the Y coordinate of the first selected endpoint.

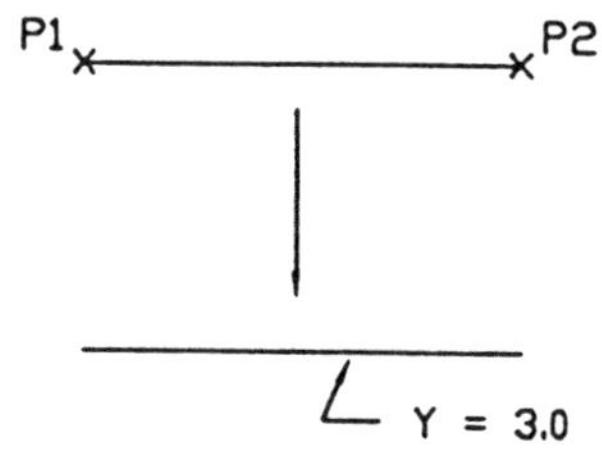

Figure 5.12

5.3.2 Create → Line → Vertical

Create a vertical line (Figure 5.13).

Procedure:

Specify the first endpoint <using position menu>: Pick at **P1**
Specify the second endpoint <using position menu>: Pick at **P2**
Enter the x coordinate (def val): **3.0** ←
(Press Esc to quit this procedure.)

Note: The default value inside the dialog box is the X coordinate of the first selected endpoint.

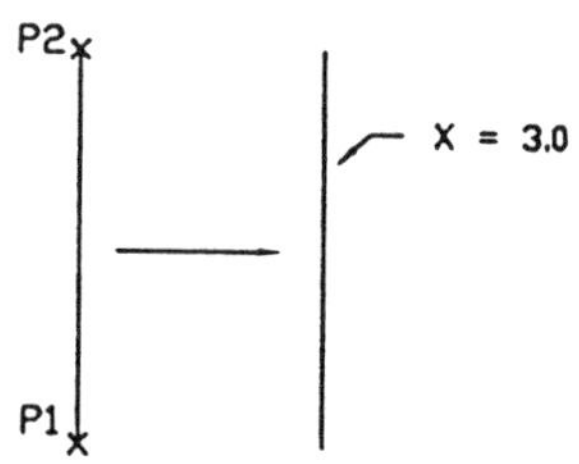

Figure 5.13

5.3.3 Create → Line → Endpoints

Create a line by specifying its two endpoints (Figure 5.14).

Procedure:

Specify the first endpoint <using position menu>: Pick at **P1**
Specify the second endpoint <using position menu>: Pick at **P2**

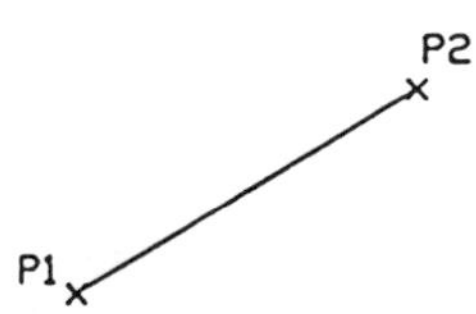

Figure 5.14

5.3.4 Create → Line → Multi

Construct multi-line segments by specifying their segment endpoints (Figure 5.15).

Procedure:

Select endpoint 1 <using position menu>: Pick at **P1**
Select endpoint 2 <using position menu>: Pick at **P2**
Select endpoint 3 <using position menu>: Pick at **P3**
Continue with endpoint selection(s): Pick at **P4**, **P5** and **P6**
Select **BACKUP** or press **Esc** key to exit the selection.

Note: As of Mastercam V5.0, the **UNDO** key will undo only the last line segment created.

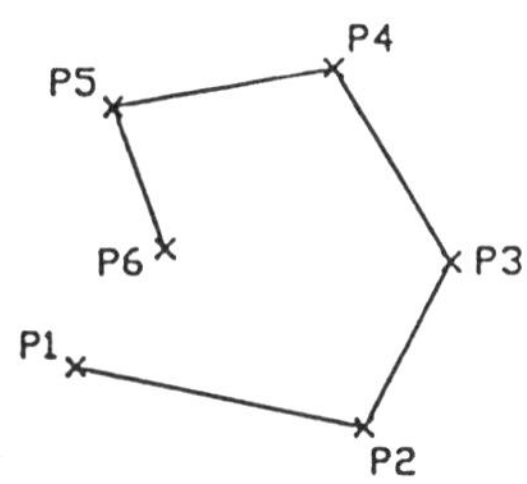

Figure 5.15

5.3.5 Create → Line → Polar

Create a line using polar coordinate (Figure 5.16).

Procedure:

Specify an endpoint <using position menu>: Pick at **P1**
Enter the angle in degrees (def val): **30**←
Enter the line length (def val): **2.5** ←

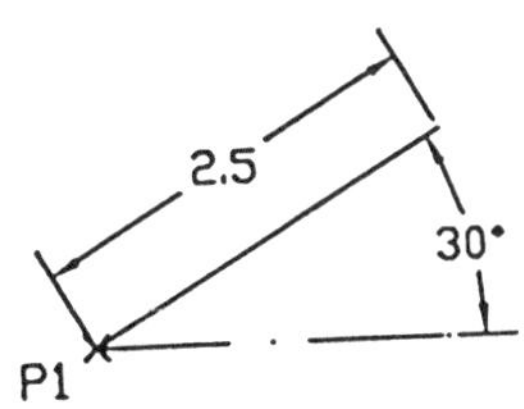

Figure 5.16

5.3.6 Create → Line → Tangent

Create a line which is tangent to an arc or arcs. It has **three** options:

Angle:	Create a line with a specified angle and length and tangent to a arc.
2 arcs:	Create a line tangent to two arcs.
Point:	Create a line tangent to an arc through a specified point.

Create → Line → Tangent → Angle

Create a line with a specified angle and length tangent to an arc.
Procedure:
Create an arc or a circle similar to the one shown in Figure 5.17.
(Refer to section 5.4 for the construction of arcs.)
Select an arc: Pick at **P1**
Enter the angle in degrees (def val): **30←**
Enter the line length (def val): **2.0** ←
Select line to keep: **Pick** the correct line segment.

Note: There are two line segments created in this procedure. Choose the one you want to keep.

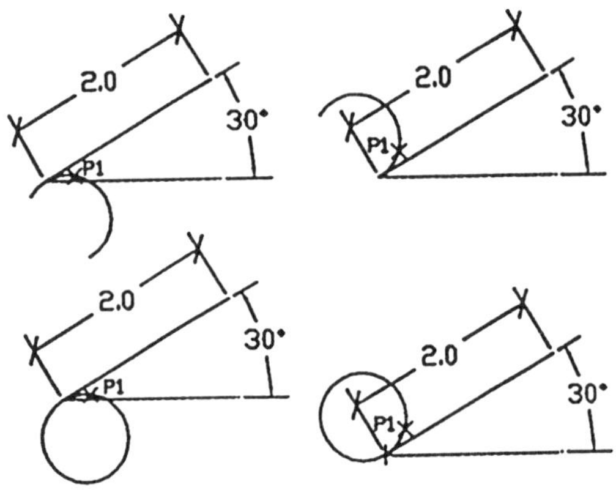

Figure 5.17

Create → Line → Tangent → 2 arcs

Create a line tangent to two arcs (Figure 5.18).
Procedure:
Create two arcs.
Select an arc: Pick at **P1**
Select another arc: Pick at **P2**

Tip There are several possibilities when a line is tangent to two arcs. In procedure 1 and 2, choose the points close to the arcs where you want the line to be created.

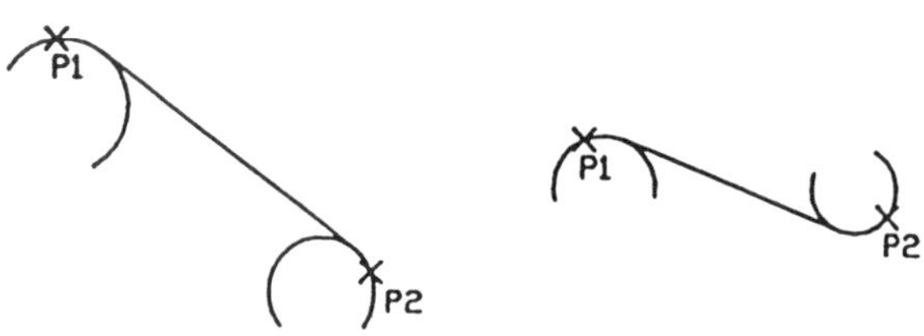

Figure 5.18

Create → Line → Tangent → Point

Create a line tangent to an arc through a specified point (Figure 5.19).

Procedure:

Create an arc.

Select an arc: Pick at **P1**

Specify an endpoint <using position option>: Pick at **P2**

Enter the line lenght (def val): ←

Note: The default value is calculated automatically from the tangent point to P2.

Tip Generally speaking, there are two possibilities in this case. In procedure 1, choose the points close to the arcs where you want the line to be tangent to.

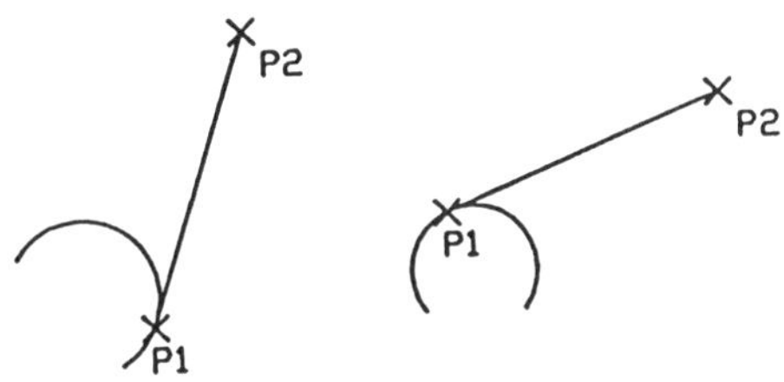

Figure 5.19

5.3.7 Create → Line → peRpendclr

Create a line which is perpendicular to a line or an arc.

Procedure:

Create a line or an arc.

Select a line or an arc: Pick at **P1**

Specify an endpoint <using position menu>: Pick at **P2**

Enter the line length (def val): ←

Note: As shown in Figure 5.20, in some cases the line created does not have an explicit intersection with the line or the arc selected. Mastercam will automatically extend the line or the arc to calculate intersected point.

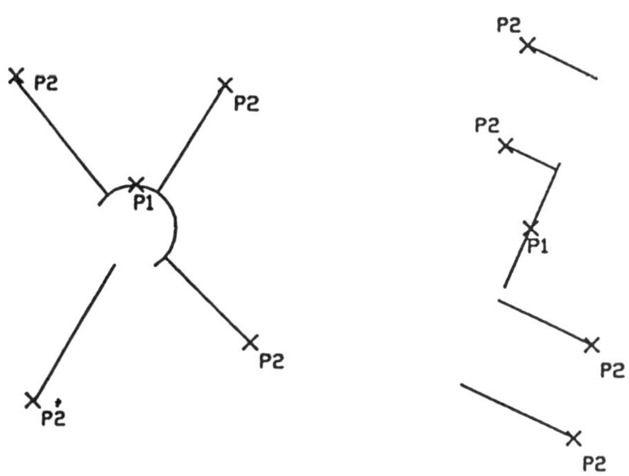

Figure 5.20

Line Exercise

Using the LINE Command and your mouse, draw each of the following objects as shown in Figure 5.21. Don't worry about exact sizes, but do try to make them look like these drawings as much as possible. Practice the various options covered in this section.

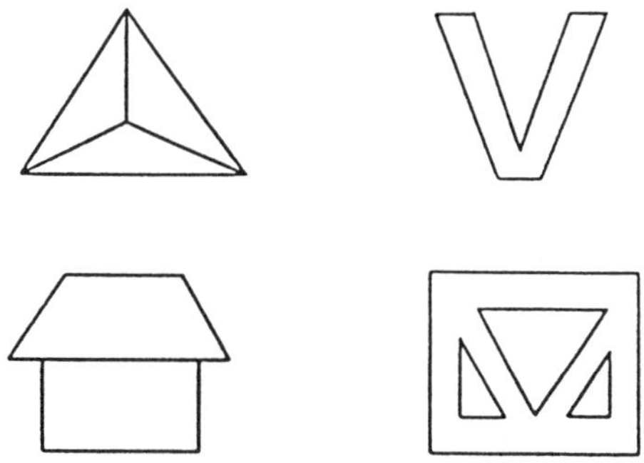

Figure 5.21

Practice LINE commands to draw the the objects shown in Figure 5.22.

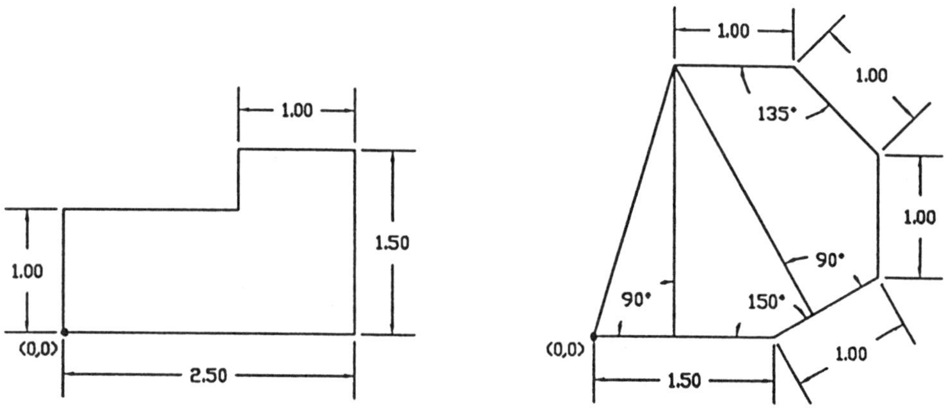

Use Polar coordinates if needed.

Figure 5.22

5.4 Arc and the Arc Submenu

The Arc command is used to create arcs and circles. Figure 5.23 shows some of the arcs and circles that will be created in this section. Mastercam provides **four** methods to create arcs and **five** methods for drawing circles.

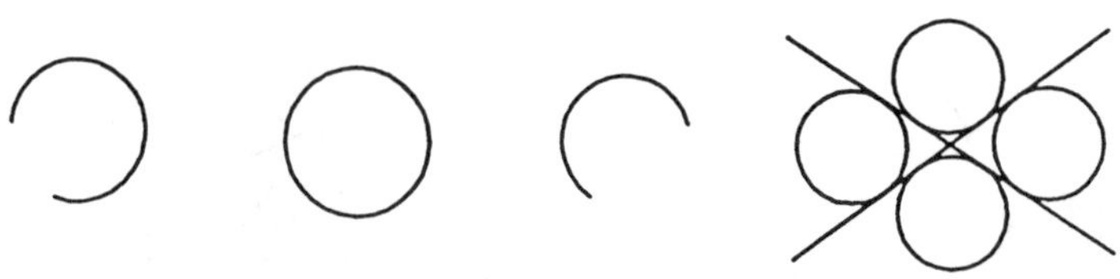

Figure 5.23

In Mastercam, these arcs and circles can be created using several options. Select **Create → Arc** from the main menu and you will see the following **Arc submenu**. A short description of each menu item follows.

```
Create:              Arc:
Point                Polar
Line                 Endpoints
Arc  ──────────→     3 points
Fillet               Tangent
Spline               2 pt cir
Curve                3 pt cIr
sUrface              pt Rad cir
Rectangle            pt Dia cir
Drafting             pt edG cir
Next menu
```

Figure 5.24: Submenu for arc

Arc option	Description
Polar:	Create an arc using polar coordinates
Endpoint:	Create an arc with known two endpoints and its radius.
3 points:	Create an arc with known 3 points
Tangent:	Create an arc that passes through tangent points of select entities
2 pt cir:	Create a circle by giving two diameter points
3 pt cIr	Create a circle that passes through 3 known points
pt Rad cir:	Create a circle with a given center point and a radius
pt Dia cir:	Create a circle with a given center point and a diameter
pt edG cir:	Create a circle with a given center point and a point on the circumference

5.4.1 Create → Arc → Polar

Create an arc using polar coordinates. In Mastercam, there are **four** options under polar. They are:

Ctr point:
sKetch:
Strt point:
End point:

These options are explained in the following procedures:

Create → Arc → Polar → **Ctr point**

Create an arc with a given center point, radius, initial and final angles. The angles are entered from the keyboard.

Procedure:

Enter the center point <using position menu>: **0,0** ←
Enter the radius (def val): **1.5** ←
Enter the initial angle (def val): **30** ←
Enter the final angle (def val): **280** ←

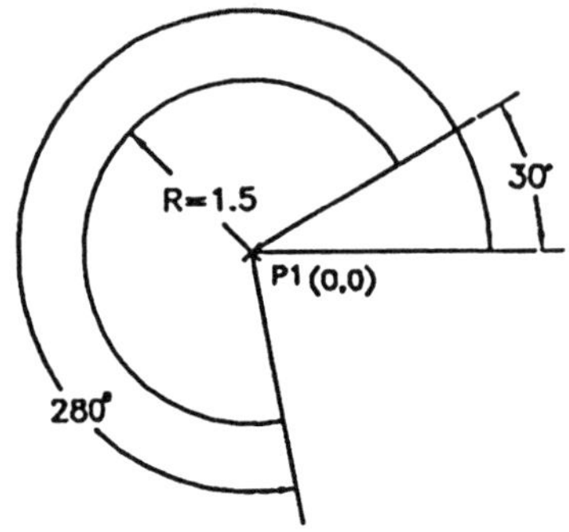

Figure 5.25

Create → Arc → Polar → **sKetch**

Create an arc with a given center point, radius, initial and final angles. The angles are selected by the mouse.

Procedure:

Enter the center point <using position menu>: Pick at **P1**
Enter the radius (def val): **1.5** ←
Sketch the initial angle: Pick at **P2**
Sketch the final angle: Pick at **P3**

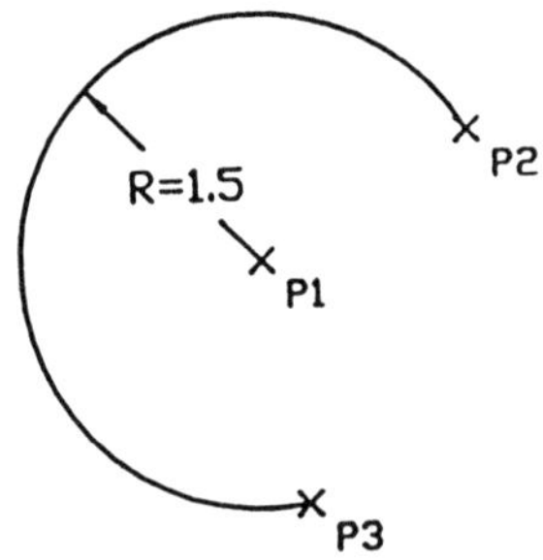

Figure 5.26

Create → Arc → Polar → **Strt point**

Create an arc with given starting point, radius, initial and final angles. The angles are entered from the keyboard.

Procedure:

Enter the start point <using position menu>: Pick at **P1**
Enter the radius (def val): **1.0** ←
Enter the initial angle (def val): **30** ←
Enter the final angle (def val): **280** ←

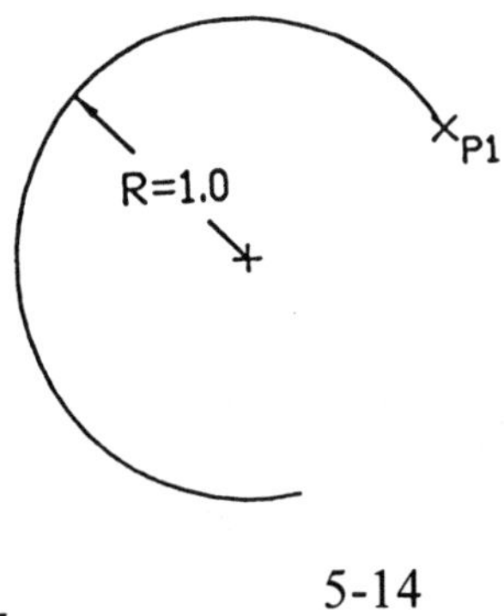

Figure 5.27

Create → Arc → Polar → **End point**

Create an arc with a given end point, radius, initial and final angles. The angles are entered from the keyboard.

Procedure:

Enter the end point <using position menu>: Pick at **P1**
Enter the radius (def val): **1.0** ←
Enter the initial angle (def val): **30** ←
Enter the final angle (def val): **280** ←

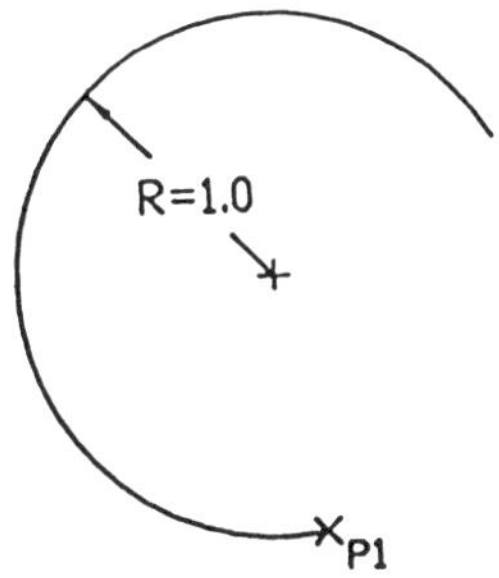

Figure 5.28

5.4.2 Create → Arc → Endpoints

Create an arc with two given endpoints and a radius. In general, there is more than one possible choice for the arc. You will have chance to pick the desired one.

Procedure:

Enter the first point <using position menu>: Pick at **P1**
Enter the second point <using position menu>: Pick at **P2**
Enter the radius (def val): **1.0** ←
Select an arc: Pick at **P3** <pick the desired arc>

Tip In this example, there are four possible arcs to be selected. To pick the desired arc, you need to use the mouse to select a point closest to the arc.

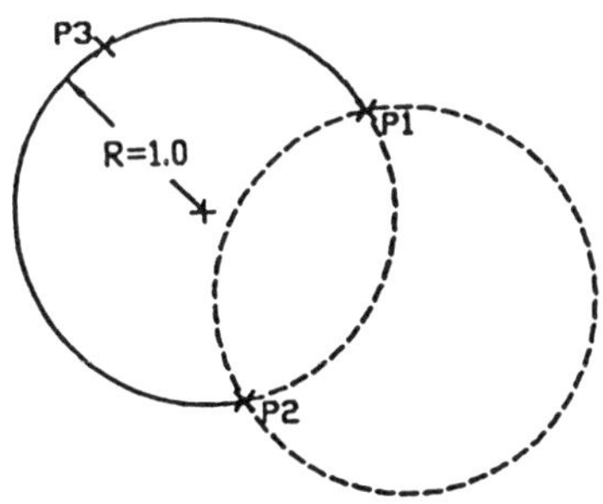

Figure 5.29

5.4.3 Create → Arc → 3 points

Create an arc that passes through three points selected. The first and third points become the endpoints of the arc.

Procedure:

Enter the first point <using position menu>: Pick at **P1**
Enter the second point <using position menu>: Pick at **P2**
Enter the third point <using position menu>: Pick at **P3**

Note: These three points should not be on the same line.

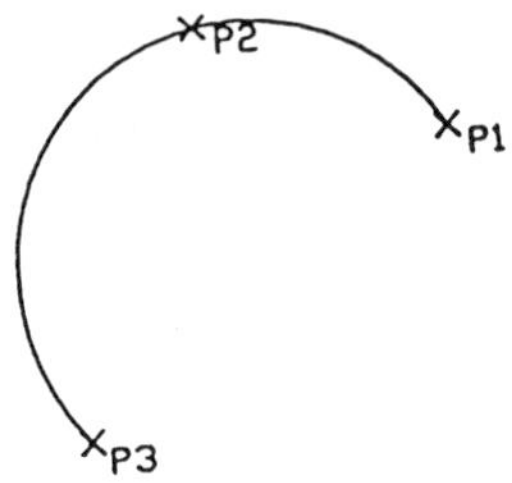

Figure 5.30

5.4.4 Create → Arc → Tangent

Create an arc tangent to one or three entities. There are **three** options under tangent:

1 entity:	Create a 180-degree arc which is tangent to a selected entity.
3 entities:	Create an arc that passes through three tangent points of three selected entities.
Point:	Create an arc that is tangent to an entity through another entity.

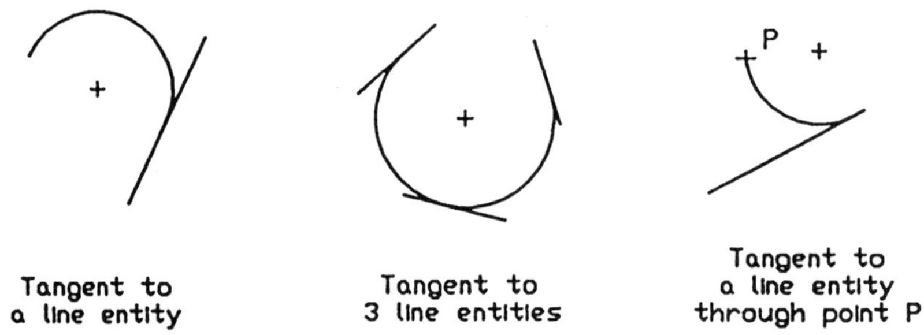

Figure 5.31

Create → Arc → Tangent → **1 entity**

Create a 180-degree arc which is tangent to a selected entity.

Procedure:

Create a line entity.

Select the entity that the arc is to be tangent to: Pick at **P1**

Specify the tangent point: Pick at **P2**

Enter the radius (def val): **1.0** ←

Select an arc: Pick at **P3**

Tip In this example, there are four possible choices. To pick the desired arc, you need to use the mouse and pick on the desired arc.

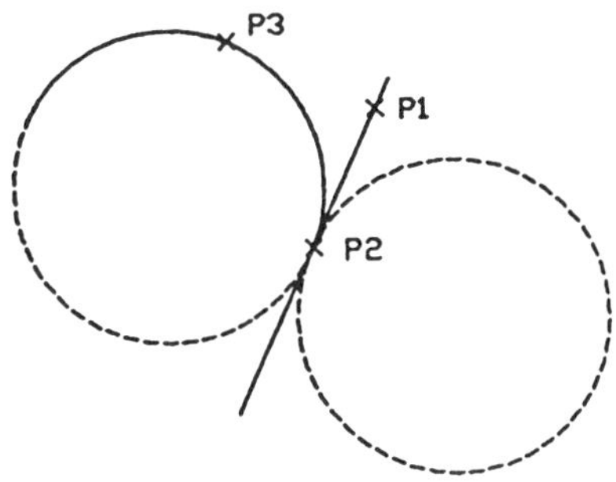

Figure 5.32

Create → Arc → Tangent → **3 entities**

Create an arc that passes through three tangent points of three selected entities. The arc will start at the first entity and end at the third entity.

Procedure:

Create 3 lines and/or three arcs.
Select the first entity: Pick at **P1**
Select the second entity: Pick at **P2**
Select the third entity: Pick at **P3**

Tips 1. Select each entity near its tangent point.

2. The order of the selection will determine the arc.

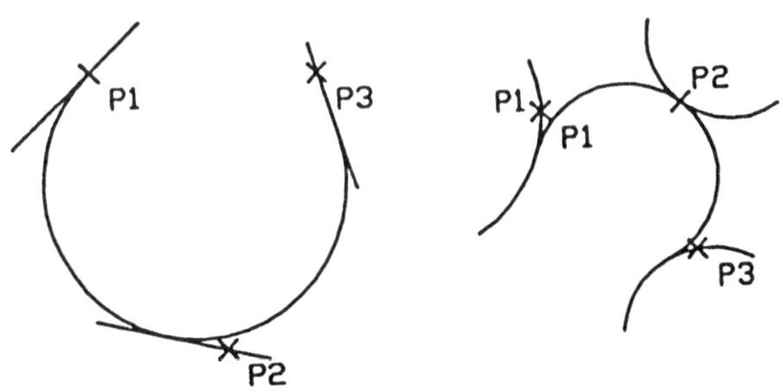

Figure 5.33

Create → Arc → Tangent → **Point**

Create an arc that is tangent to an entity and passes through a point.

Procedure:

Create a line and/or an arc.
Select the entity that the arc is to be tangent to: Pick at **P1**
Enter the thru point: Pick at **P2**
Enter the radius (def val): **1.0** ←
Select an arc: Pick at **P3**

Tips 1. Select each entity near its tangent point.

2. If there is more than one possible choice, use the mouse to select a point on the closest arc.

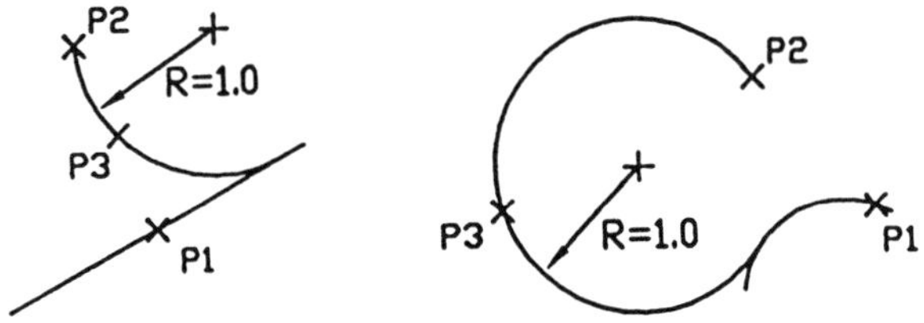

Figure 5.34

5.4.5 Create → Arc → 2 pt cir

Create a circle by giving two points which lie 180-degree apart on its circumference; or in other words, pick the endpoints of the circle's diameter.

Procedure:

Enter the first point <using position menu>: Pick at **P1**

Enter the second point <using position menu>: Pick at **P2**

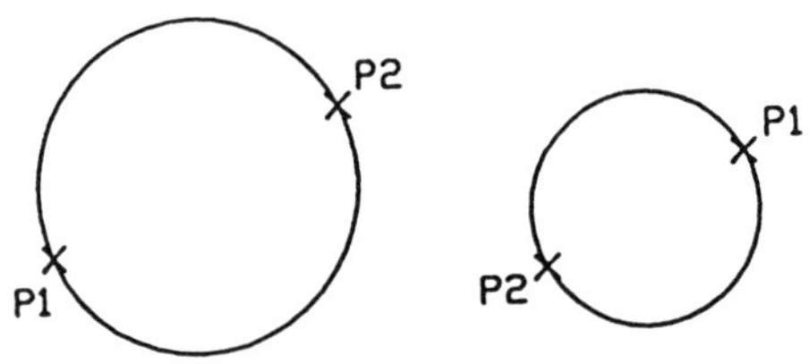

Figure 5.35

5.4.6 Create → Arc → 3 pt cir

Create a circle by specifying three points on its circumference. These three points should **not** be in a straight line. The selection order is not important.

Procedure:

Enter the first point <using position menu>: Pick at **P1**

Enter the second point <using position menu>: Pick at **P2**

Enter the third point <using position menu>: Pick at **P3**

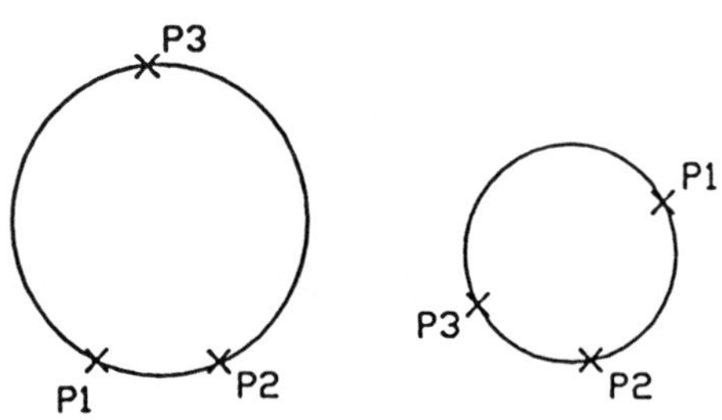

Figure 5.36

5.4.7 Create → Arc → pt Rad cir

Create a circle with a given center point and a radius.

Procedure:

Enter the center point <using position menu>: Pick at **P1**

Enter the radius (def val): **1.0** ←

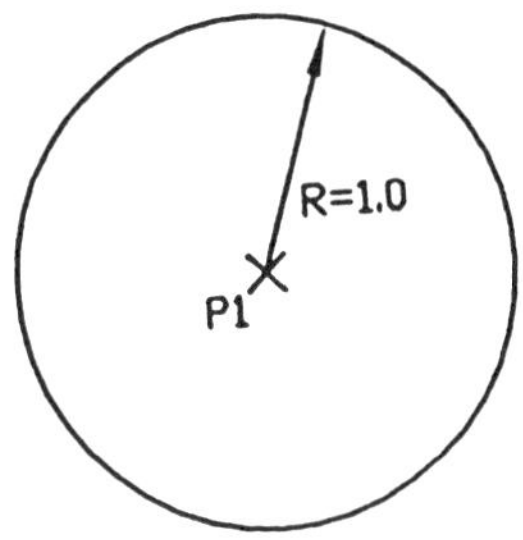

Figure 5.37

5.4.8 Create → Arc → pt Dia cir

Create a circle with a given center point and a diameter.

Procedure:

Enter the center point <using position menu>: Pick at **P1**

Enter the diameter (def val): **2.0** ←

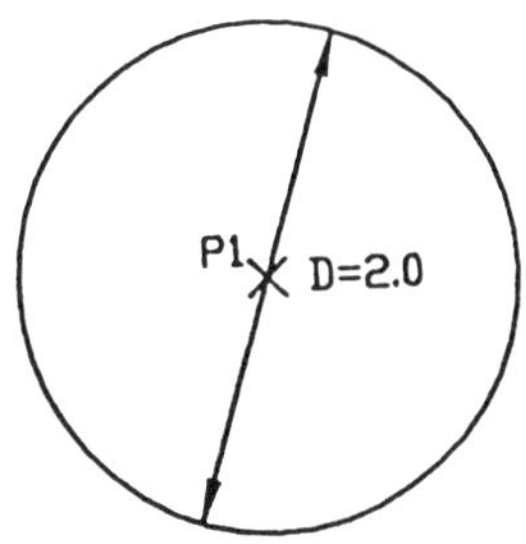

Figure 5.38

5.4.9 Create → Arc → pt edG cir

Create a circle with a given center point and a point on the circumference.

Procedure:

Enter the center point <using position menu>: Pick at **P1**

Enter the edge point <using position menu>: Pick at **P2**

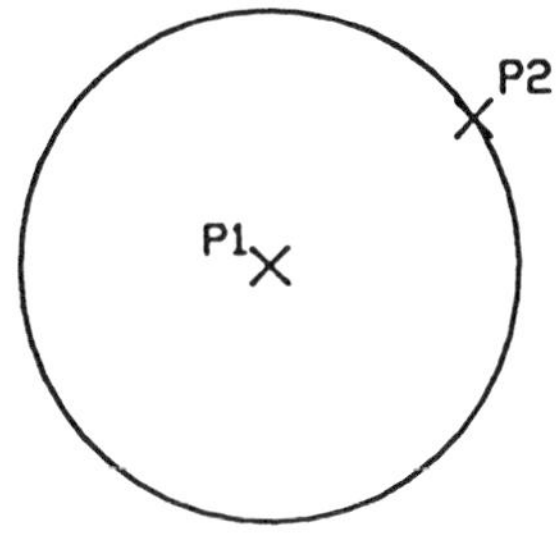

Figure 5.39

Arc and Circle Exercise

Using the ARC Command and your mouse, draw each of the following objects. Don't worry about exact sizes, but do try to make them look as much as these drawings as possible. Practice the various options covered in this section.

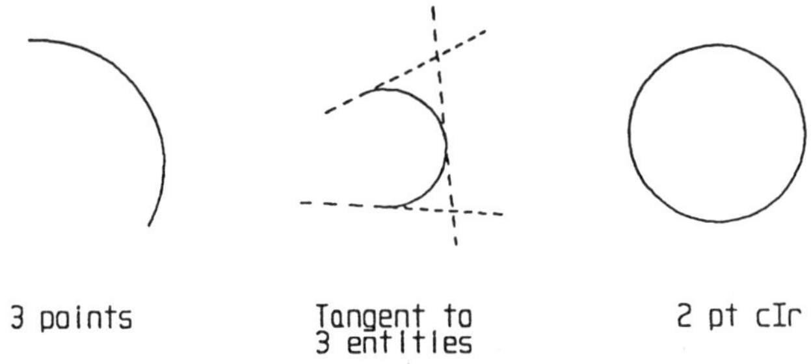

Figure 5.40

Practice using ARC command to draw the following objects.

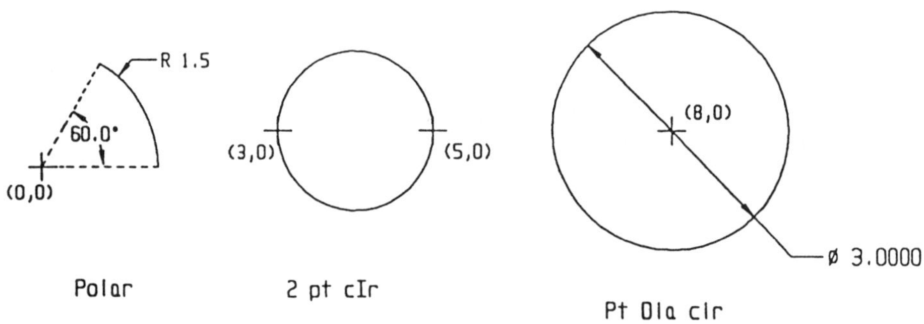

Figure 5.41

5.5 Fillet and the Fillet Submenu

The menu sequence for Fillet command is **Create → Fillet**.

Create one or more fillets for two or more entities by specifying the following **four** fillet parameters:

Radius: Change to a new radius.
Angle: Toggle the angle option. The angle options can be either greater than 180-degrees or less than 180-degrees.
Trim: Toggle the trim option to either keep or delete the trimmed line after filleting.
Chain: Create one or more fillets by chaining several entities at once.

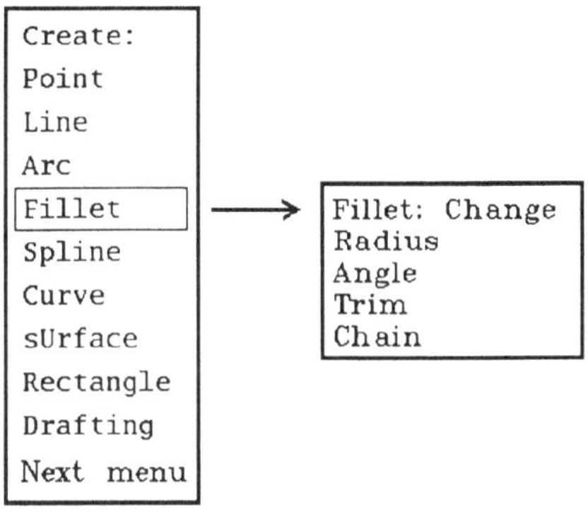

Figure 5.42: Submenu for Fillet

Create a fillet between two lines.
Procedure:
Create two lines.
Choose and change fillet parameters (radius, angle and trim options) if needed.
Select the first entity: Pick at **P1**
Select the second entity: Pick at **P2**

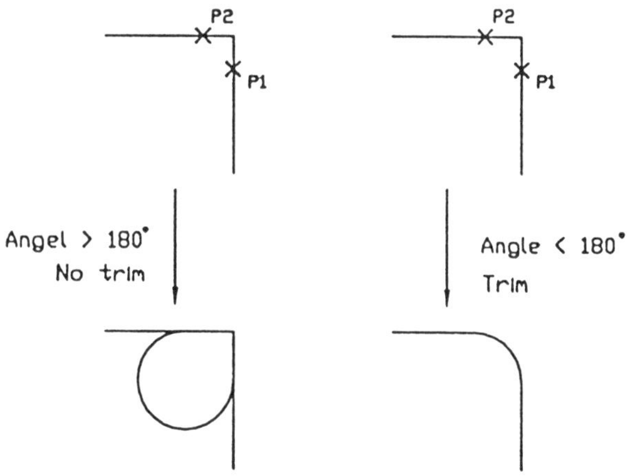

Figure 5.43

Create several fillets by chaining several entities at once.
Procedure:
Create several lines using **Create→ Line→ Multi.**
Choose and change fillet parameters (radius, angle and trim options) if needed.
Select **Chain**
Select the first entity in the chain: Pick at **P1**
Select **Close →** **End here.**

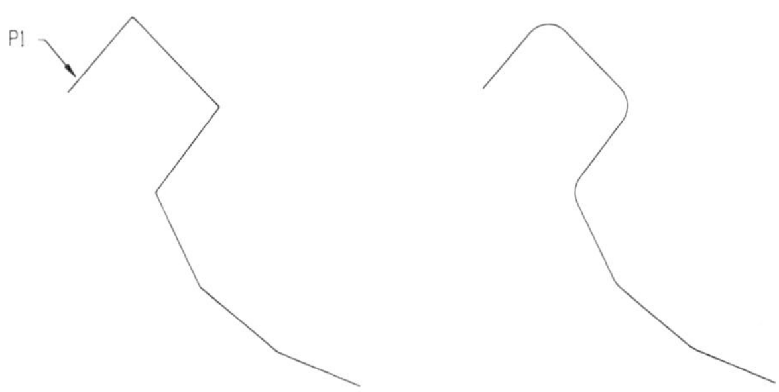

Figure 5.44 Original entities After Create, Fillet and Chain

5.6 Spline and the Spline Submenu

In Mastercam, the Spline command creates a smooth spline curve that passes through all the node points selected, and there are **two** spline curve options: **Parametric spline** (Type P) and **NURBS spline** (Type N). The user is able to toggle this option by selecting the first option (Type) in the menu (Figure 5.45).

A parametric spline curve is a flexible strip which can be held by weights so that it passes through each of the given points. Corresponding to a draftman's spline, the present mathematical procedure requires that both the slope and the curvature be the same on both sides of the node points.

NURBS is abbreviated from Non-Uniform Rational B-Spline curve or surface. In general, NURBS is smoother than the regular spline curve and may be edited more easily by pulling its control points (see section 6.2.6 and Figure 6.14). It is a useful tool to general curves and surfaces for the automotive industry.

There are three ways to generate a spline curve:

Manual:	Manually select all the points for the spline curve.
Automatic:	Automatically select the points for the spline curve.
Curves:	Create a spline by chaining existing geometry.

The menu sequence for spline is **Create → Spline**.

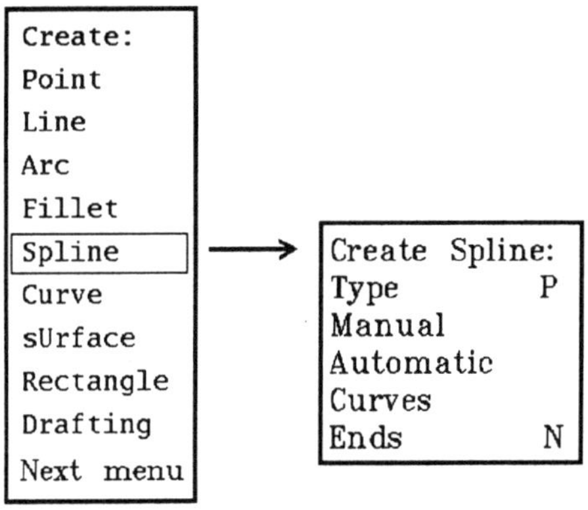

Figure 5.45: Submenu for Spline

The last option in the menu is the **Ends** option. This is a toggle option which allows you to modify the slope of the spline at the start and end points. The default value is **N.**

Tips 1. Default maximum value of 250 node points can be changed in the MILL5.CFG file.

2. To generate a closed spline curve, pick the same point for the first and last node points for the curve. This node point should be an existing point which was created by the **Create → Point** command.

5.6.1 Create → Spline → Manual

Manually select all the points for the spline curve. The user needs to select all the points in a proper order.

Procedure:

Select all the node points <using position menu>: Pick at **P1**, **P2**, **P3**, etc.
Select BACKUP to finish selection and create the spline.

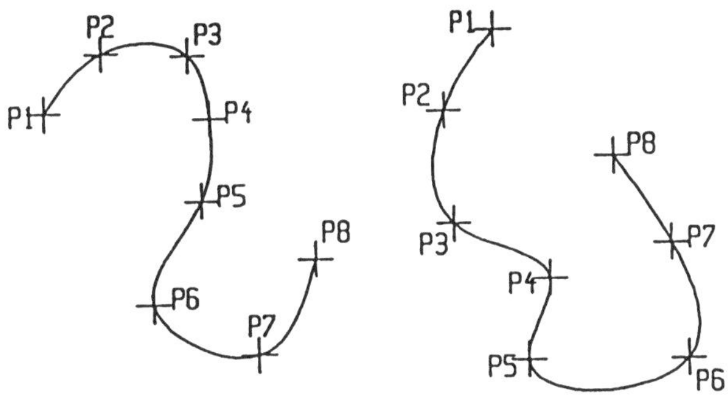

Figure 5.46

5.6.2 Create → Spline → Automatic

Automatically select the points for the spline curve. The user needs to select the first, second, and last point on the curve. The system will automatically select other points which stay within the system's curve tolerance.

Tips 1. The first, second and last point should be existing points created by the Create → Point command.
2. Use Create → Spline → Manual option if it doesn't work as you desired.

Procedure:

Create several points as shown in Figure 5.47.
Select the first point: Pick at **P1**
Select the second point: Pick at **P2**
Select the last point: Pick at **P3**

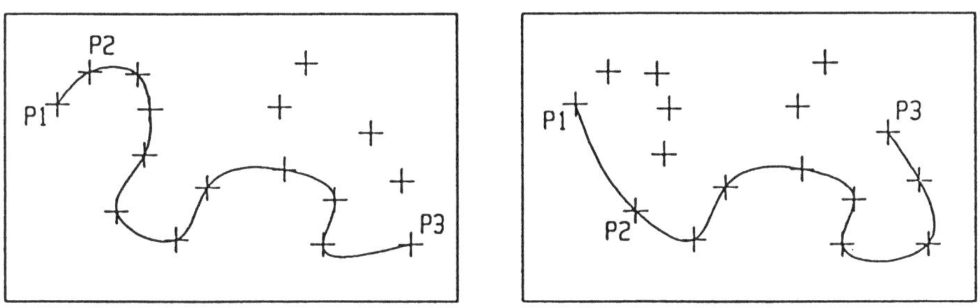

Figure 5.47

When a curve's geometry changes dramatically, create more points around that area to better control the direction of the spline. This is shown in Figure 5.48 on the next page.

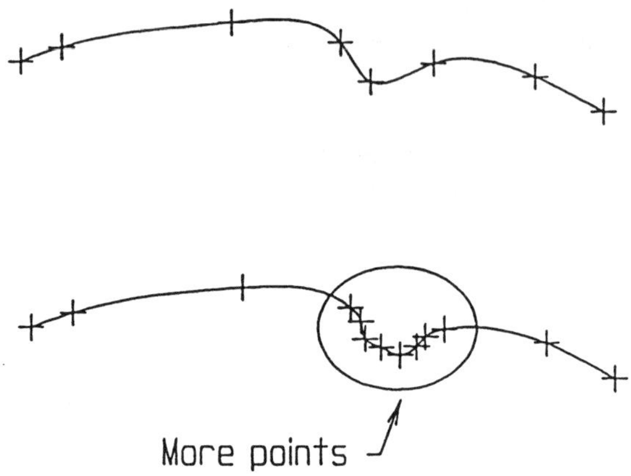

Figure 5.48

A comparison of a NURBS and a parametric spline curve created by the same points are shown in Figure 5.49. Notice the difference at the beginning and ending point.

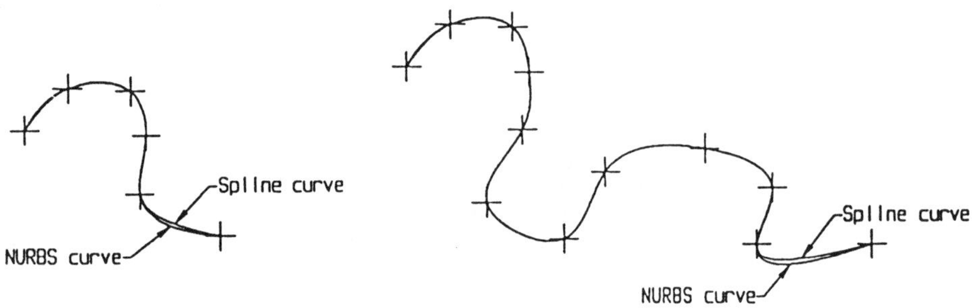

Figure 5.49

5.7 Curve and the Curve Submenu

In Mastercam, the only type of curve for 2-D applications is the ellipse. The curve menu sequence is **Create → Curve**. There is only one submenu item under Create → Curve:

Ellipse: Create an ellipse or an elliptical arc.

```
Create:            Curve:
Point              Ellipse
Line
Arc
Fillet             ON SURFACE
Spline             Intersect
Curve      ──→     pAtch bnd
sUrface            Flowline
Rectangle          Project
Drafting           Dynamic
Next menu          paRt line
```

Figure 5.50: Submenu for Curve

5.7.1 Create → Curve → Ellipse

Create an ellipse or an elliptical arc. Here are two examples:

Procedure:	Example 1	Example 2
Enter a (x axis radius) (def val):	**3.0**	**3.0**
Enter b (y axis radius) (def val):	**1.5**	**1.5**
Enter the starting angle (def val):	**30**	**0**
Enter the final angle (def val):	**300**	**360**
Enter the rotational angle (ccw) in degrees (def val):	**0**	**15**

Note: CCW stands for counterclockwise direction.

Enter the center <using position menu>:	Pick at **P1**	Pick at **P1**

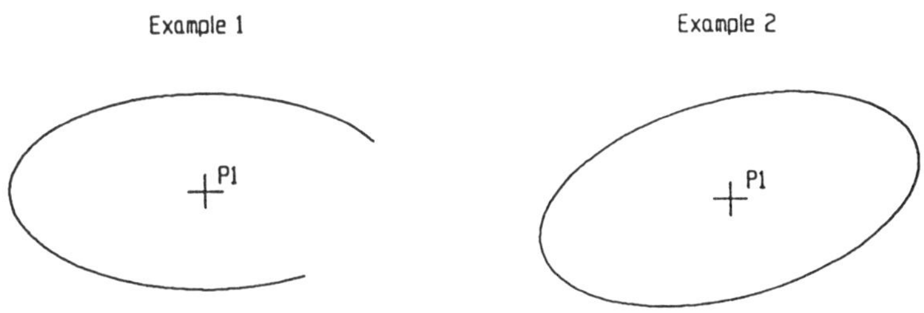

Figure 5.51

5.8 Rectangle and the Rectangle Submenu

The rectangle menu sequence is **Create → Rectangle**.
In Mastercam, there are **two** options to generate a rectangle:

1 point: Create a rectangle by giving corner point, the width and the height.
2 points: Create a rectangle by giving its two corner points.

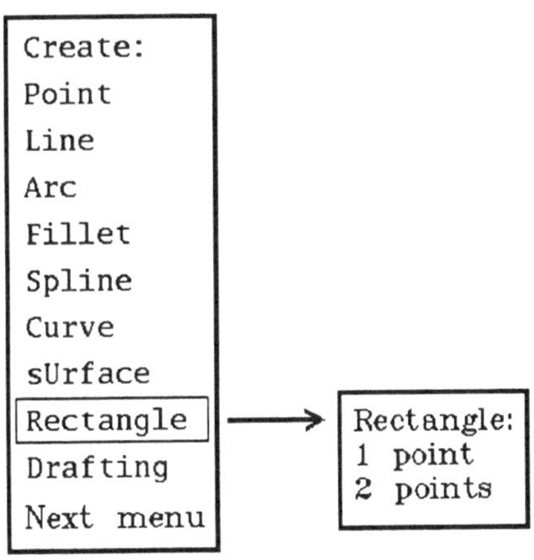

Figure 5.52: Submenu for Rectangle

5.8.1 Create → Rectangle → 1 point

Create a rectangle by giving corner point, the width and the height.

Procedure:

Enter the lower left corner <using position menu>: Pick at **P1**

Enter the width <def val>: **3.0** ←

Enter the height <def val>: **2.0** ←

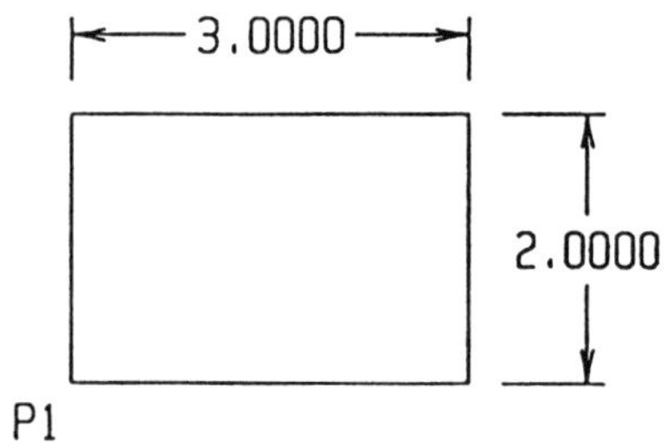

Figure 5.53

Tip The width and the height can be negative values. If both of them are negative, the point selected in Procedure 1 becomes the upper right corner.

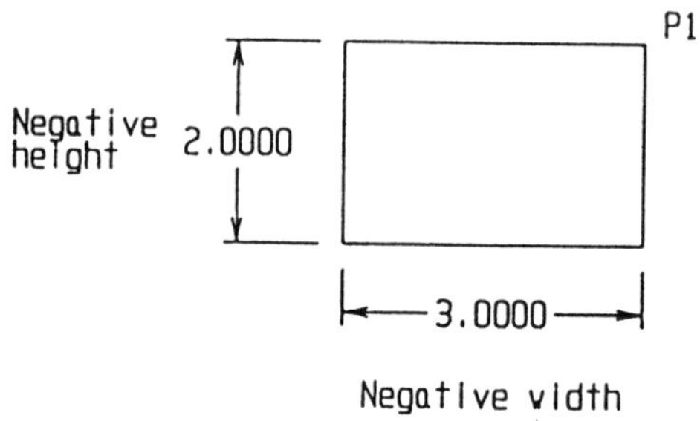

Figure 5.54

5.8.2 Create → Rectangle → 2 points

Create a rectangle by giving its two corner points.

Procedure:

Enter the lower left corner <using position menu>: Pick at **P1**

Enter the upper right corner <using position menu>: Pick at **P2**

Tip The selection sequence is not that important. For example, you can select the upper right corner first, then, the lower left corner.

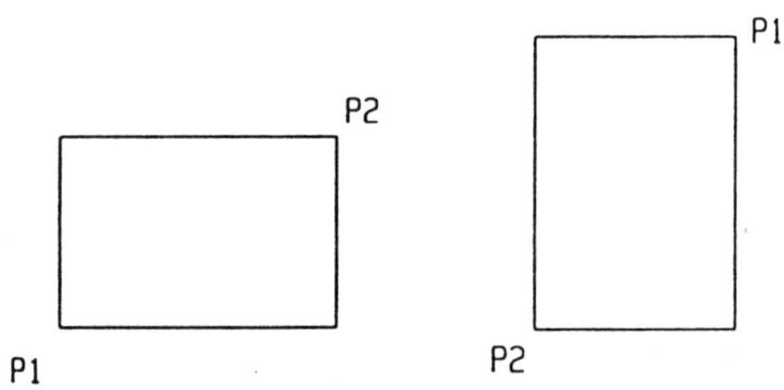

Figure 5.55

5.9 Chamfer and the Chamfer Submenu

The chamfer menu sequence is **Create → Next menu → Chamfer**. This command is used to create a chamfer between two non-parallel lines with two given distances. There is an option under the Chamfer command to change the chamfer distance:

Distances:	To change the default chamfer distance(s) of the chamfer. In general, there are two distances can be changed. The first distance related to the first picked point (**P1**), and the second distance related to the second picked point (**P2**).

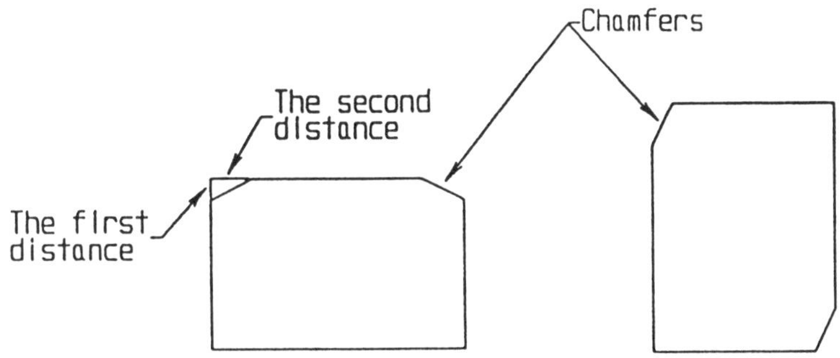

Figure 5.56

Tips 1. The chamfer command operates very similar to the Fillet command.

2. To change the distances, select Distances or enter D at the keyboard, and specify the first and second chamfer distance.

Procedure:

Note: The system prompts the following message for default values in the System Response Area:

first distance = (def value)
second distance = (def val)

(Make sure the first distance = 0.25 and the second distance = 0.50)

Create a rectangle.
Select the first line: Pick at **P1**
Select the second line: Pick at **P2**

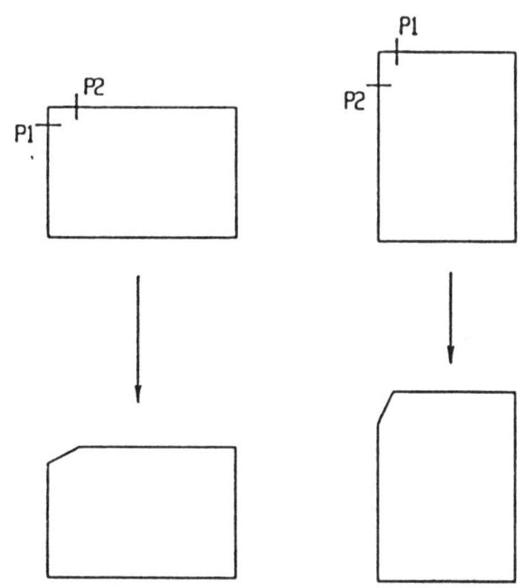

Figure 5.57

5.10. Letters and the Letter Submenu

Letter geometries can be useful for cutting letters on plaques. In Mastercam, there are two methods to create these letter geometries. The first method is to create the geometry using Mastercam's system fonts. Note that this method creates only upper case letter geometries. The second method is much more flexible and works on both upper- and lower-case letters. The user first creates "Note" in Drafting, and then changes its attributes and repositions it. The details of these two methods are described in this section.

Method 1: Using the Letters Command

The letters command sequence is **Create → Next menu → Letters**.

The submenu for Letters includes the choice of system fonts. As shown in Figure 5.58 on the next page, there are four font styles available in Mastercam V5.0. In addition, the user can provide other customized fonts by selecting the **Other** option in the same menu.

Box:	Box font
bLock:	Block font
Roman:	Roman font
Slant:	Slant font
Other:	User customized font. A file name should be provided.

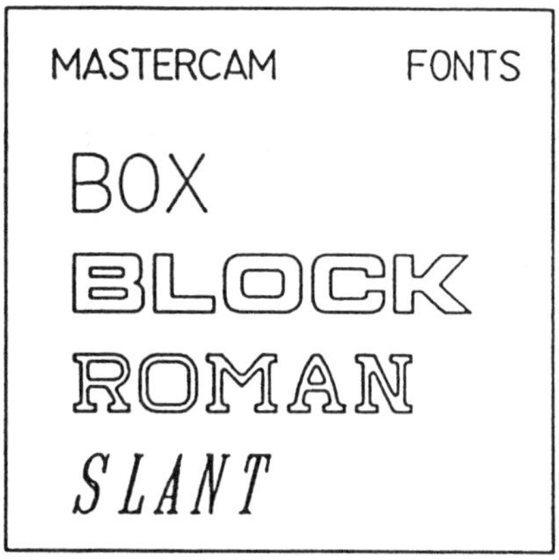

Figure 5.58

Procedure:
Select the font style.
Enter letter height (def val): **1.0** ←
Enter letter spacing (def val): **0.2** ←
Write letters on an arc (Y/N)?
  Select **Yes** to accept an arc letter.
  Select **No** to accept a line letter.

Note: The system will have different prompts after this step. There are **four** more steps for arc letters and **two** more steps for line letters.

<u>For arc letters</u>
Enter coordinates of arc center. Pick at **P1**
Enter arc radius (def val): **5.0** ←
Enter type of arc (Top=0, Bottom=1) (def val): **0** or **1** ←

Note: Refer to Figure 5.59 on the next page for the type of arc.
Enter letters: **ARC LETTERS** ←

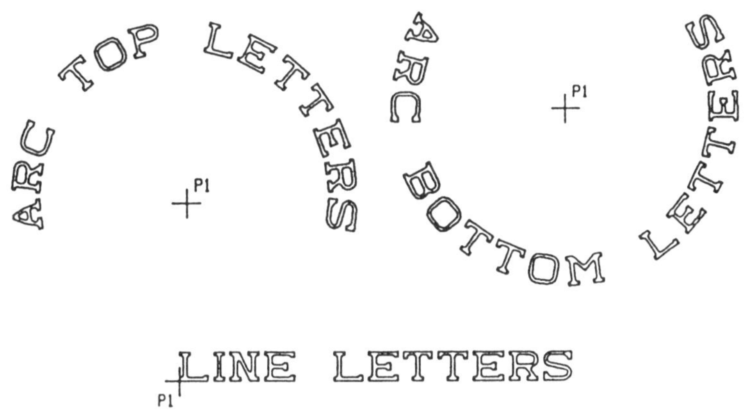

Figure 5.59: Arc and line letters

<u>**For line letters**</u>
Enter starting location of letters: Pick at **P1**
Enter letters: **LINE LETTERS** ←

Method 2: Using Note and Modify Commands

In this method, you will create a string of letters using the "Note" command in Drafting. Follow this procedure to create letters:

1. Create a string of letters using the "Note" command in the drafting section.
2. Change the attributes including the height, aspect ratio, font type and spacing.
3. Convert the Note into chains of geometry entities by using
   Modify → Break → Note/Let → Geometry → Entity commands.
4. Reposition the letters string to a new position, if necessary.

In the following example, we are creating a letter geometry (Mastercam) using a European font with height = 0.5, aspect = 0.6 and spacing = 0.25.

The sequence is **Create → Drafting → Note → Keyin**
Text: **Mastercam** ←
Enter line 2 (press Enter when done): ←
Create note: Indicate text position: Pick at **P1**

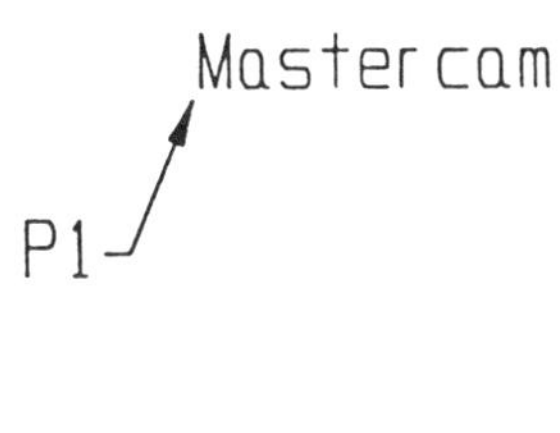

Figure 5.60

Select **BACKUP → Edit → Note**
Select note to edit: Pick at **the note**
Select **Attribs**
Select **Height**
Character height: **0.5 ←**
Select **Aspect**
Character aspect ratio: **0.6 ←**
Select **Font → Next → Next**.
(Notice the changes in System Response Area: Attribute style: **European**)
Select **BACKUP → Spacing → Character**
Enter character spacing factor: **0.25 ←**

Figure 5.61

Select **MAIN MENU → Modify → Break → Note/Lel → Geometry → Entity**
Select note: Pick at **the note** (After this step the note is turned into geometry. You can select **MAIN MENU** to exit the sequence.)
Note: Use the **Analyze** (F4) key to see if the original note has changed to geometries.

5.11 2-D Geometry Construction Project

In the following five projects, you will practice a combination of commands introduced in this chapter. A step by step procedure is provided. Save each project under the file name specified. You will retrieve these files to generate the toolpaths for producing the part in chapters 7 and 8.

Project 1.

1

We are here

Part Geometry Creation

(Contour1)

Go to

Toolpath Generation

Project 1 of Chapter 7

(Contour1)

Create a part geometry as shown in Figure 5.62. Save the file as **contour1.** This file will be used in project 1 of chapter 7.

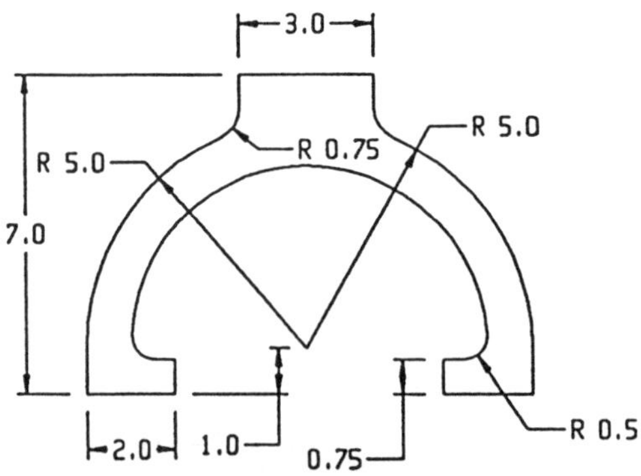

Figure 5.62

⌛**Tips** 1. The geometry is symmetrical about the Y-axis. Create one-half of the geometry and then use the Mirror command (see section 6.3.1) to create the other half.
2. The basic geometry consists of two rectangles, two arcs and two fillets.

Step 1. Create two rectangles.

Select **MAIN MENU → Create → Rectangle → 2 points**
Enter the lower left corner: **3,-1** ←
Enter the upper right corner: **5,-.25** ← for the first rectangle
Enter the lower left corner: **0,6** ←
Enter the upper right corner: **1.5,5** ← for the second rectangle

Press Alt and F1 simultaneously, then F2 to fit the geometry on the screen

The two rectangles should appear as Figure 5.63.

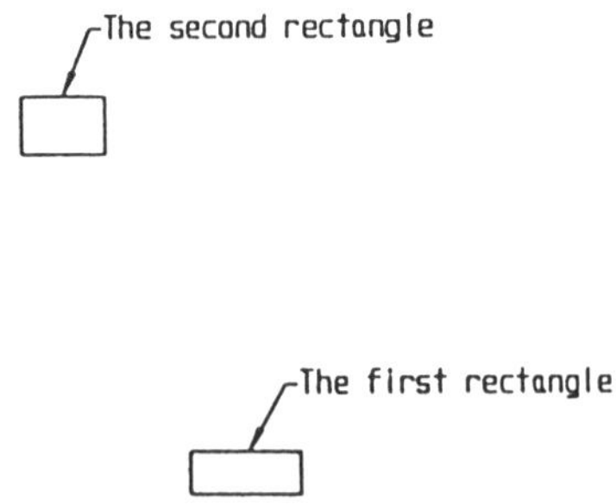

Figure 5.63

Step 2. Create two arcs.

Select **MAIN MENU → Create → Arc → Polar → Ctr point**
Enter the center point: **0,0** ←
Enter the radius: **5** ←
Enter the initial angle: **0** ←
Enter the final angle: **90** ← for the first arc
Enter the center point: **0,0** ←
Enter the radius: **4** ←
Enter the initial angle: **0** ←
Enter the final angle: **90** ← for the second arc

The new drawing becomes Figure 5.64

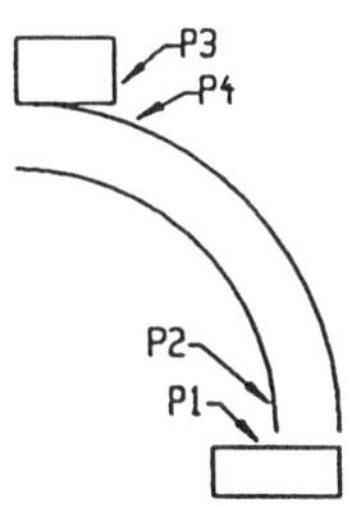

Figure 5.64

Step 3. Create two fillets using the pick points in Figure 5.64.

Select **MAIN MENU → Create → Fillet → Radius**
Enter the fillet radius: **0.5**

Note: Make certain the other two options are correct. If the fillet angle is less than 180; trim to fillet.

Select an entity: Pick at **P1**
Select another entity: Pick at **P2**
Select **Radius**
Enter the radius: **0.75 ←**
Select an entity: Pick at **P3**
Select another entity: Pick at **P4**

The two fillets are added as shown in Figure 5.65.

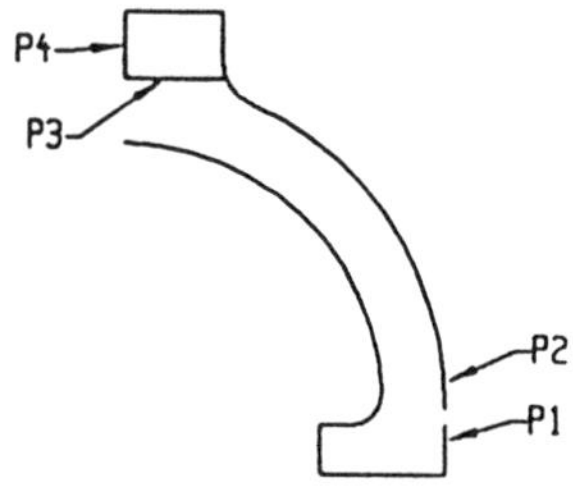

Figure 5.65

Step 4. Trim and delete the unnecessary lines using the pick points in Figure 5.65.

Select **MAIN MENU → Modify → Trim → 1 entity**
Select the entity to trim: Pick at **P1**
Select the entity to trim to: Pick at **P2**
Select **MAIN MENU → Delete**
Select an entity or: Pick at **P3**
Select an entity or: Pick at **P4**
The half geometry should look like Figure 5.66.

Figure 5.66

Step 5. Mirror about the Y axis.

Select **MAIN MENU→Xform→ Mirror→ All→Entities→Done→Y axis→Copy →Done**
The complete geometry appears as Figure 5.67.

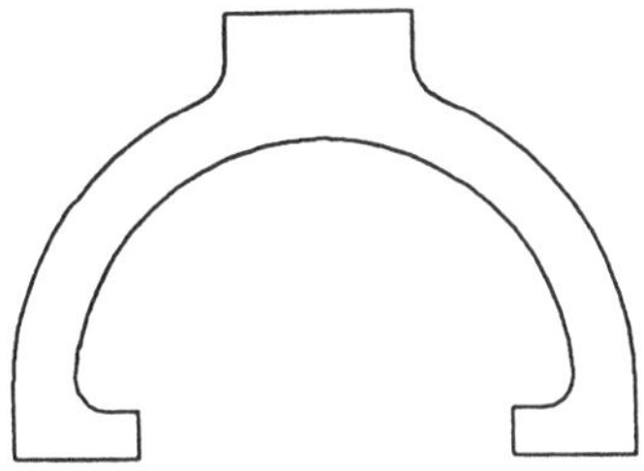

Figure 5.67

Step 6. Save to a file.

Select **MAIN MENU → File → Save**
Enter file name: **contour1**

Project 2.

2

We are here

Part Geometry Creation

(Contour3)

Go to

Toolpath Generation

Project 3 of Chapter 7

(Contour3)

Create a part geometry as shown in Figure 5.68. Save the file as **contour3**. This file will be used to generate the toolpaths for contouring in project 3 of chapter 7.

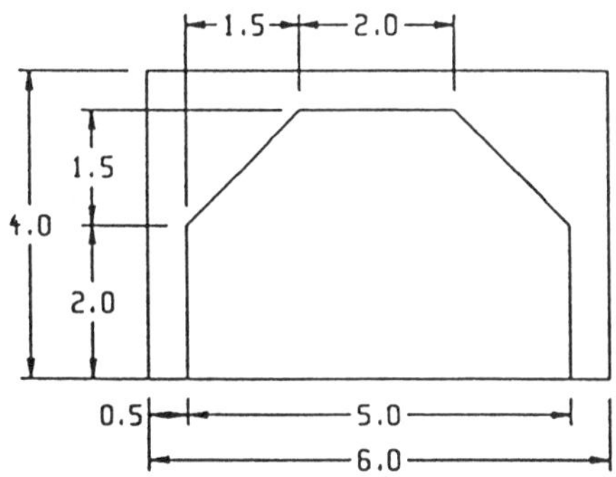

Figure 5.68

Tips 1. This geometry can be created using a rectangle and several lines.

2. The coordinates of keypoints are shown in Figure 5.69.

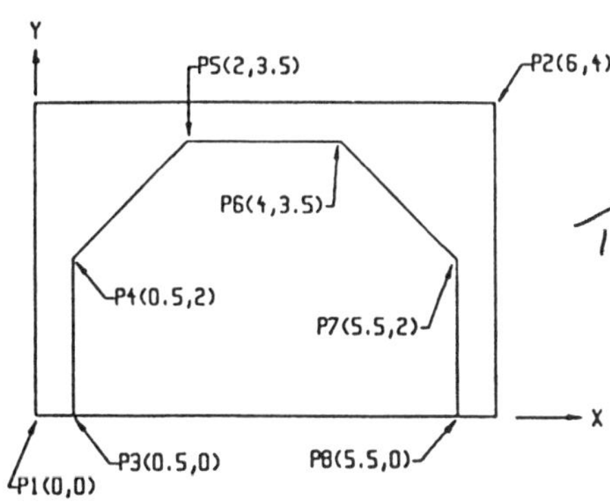

Figure 5.69

Step 1. Create a rectangle.

Select **MAIN MENU →Create → Rectangle → 2 points**
Enter the lower left corner: **0,0** ←
Enter the upper right corner: **6,4** ←

Step 2. Create five lines.

Select **MAIN MENU → Create → Line → Multi**
Specify endpoint 1: Enter **0.5,0** ←
Specify endpoint 2: Enter **0.5,2** ←
Specify endpoint 3: Enter **2,3.5** ←
Specify endpoint 4: Enter **4,3.5** ←
Specify endpoint 5: Enter **5.5,2** ←
Specify endpoint 6: Enter **5.5,0** ←

Step 3. Save to a file.

Select **MAIN MENU → File → Save**
Enter file name: **contour3**

Project 3.

Construct a geometry as shown in Figure 5.70. Save the file as **pocket1**. This file will be used to generate the toolpaths for pocketing in project 5 of chapter 7.

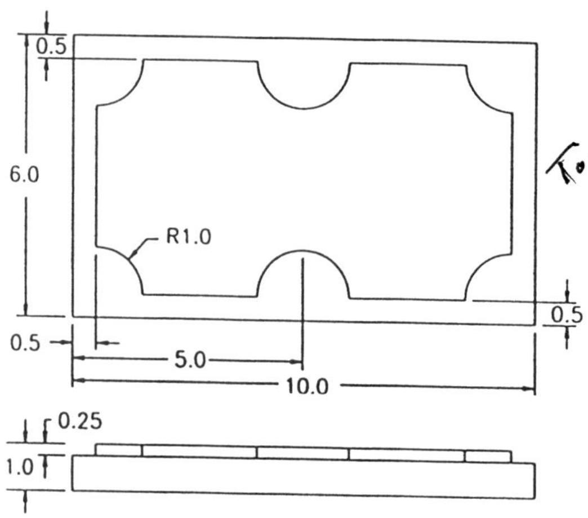

Figure 5.70

Tips 1. Create two rectangles and six circles.

2. Break the two horizontal lines of the inside rectangle into two pieces to allow for the trimming of the two circles in the middle.
3. Trim the six circles and four lines using 3 entities command.

3

We are here

Part Geometry Creation

(Pocket1) (Drill2)

Go to

Toolpath Generation

Project 5 of Chapter 7 (Pocket1)

- or Go to

Toolpath Generation

Project 8 of Chapter 7 (Drill2)

Step 1. Create two rectangles.

Select **MAIN MENU → Create → Rectangle → 2 points**
Enter the lower left corner: **0,0** ←
Enter the upper right corner: **10,6** ← for the first rectangle
Enter the lower left corner: **0.5,0.5** ←
Enter the upper right corner: **9.5,5.5** ← for the second rectangle
Press **Alt + F1** simultaneously and then **F2** to fit the drawing in the screen

The two rectangles should look like Figure 5.71.

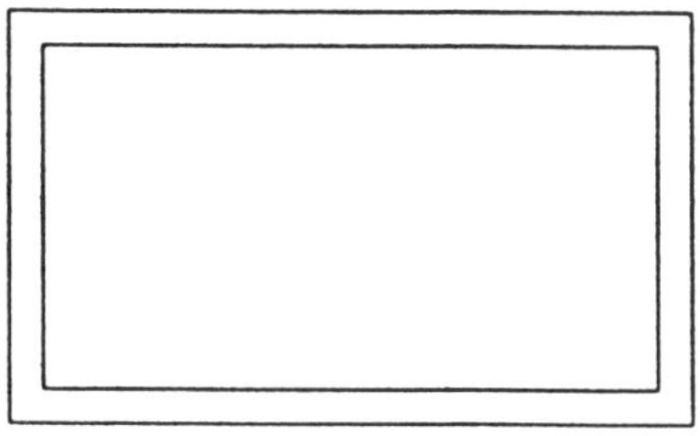

Figure 5.71

Step 2. Create six circles.

Select **MAIN MENU → Create → Arc → pt Rad cir**
Enter the center point: **0.5,0.5** ←
Enter the radius: **1** ←
Enter the center point: **5,0.5** ←
Enter the radius: **1** ←
Enter the center point: **9.5,0.5** ←
Enter the radius: **1** ←
Enter the center point: **0.5,5.5** ←
Enter the radius: **1** ←
Enter the center point: **5,5.5** ←
Enter the radius: **1** ←
Enter the center point: **9.5,5.5** ←
Enter the radius: **1** ←

The six circles are added as shown in Figure 5.72.

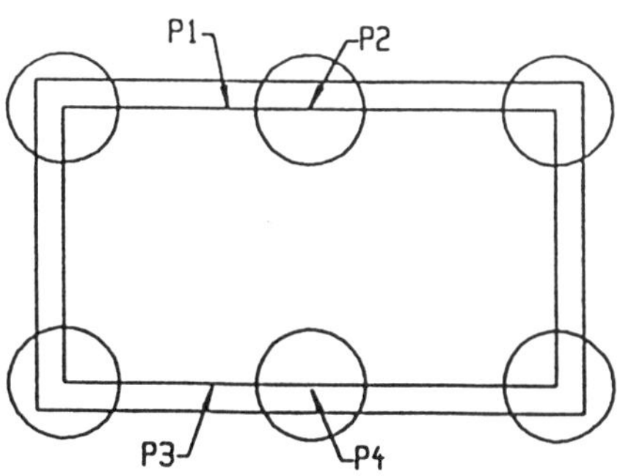

Figure 5.72

Step 3. Break two horizontal lines of the inside rectangle into two pieces.

Use the pick points in Figure 5.72.
Select **MAIN MENU → Modify → Break → 2 pieces**
Select an entity: pick at **P1**
Enter the break point: pick at **P2** to break the first line
Select an entity: pick at **P3**
Enter the break point: pick at **P4** to break the second line

After breaking two lines the drawing still looks the same as before breaking. This drawing is redrawn in Figure 5.73.

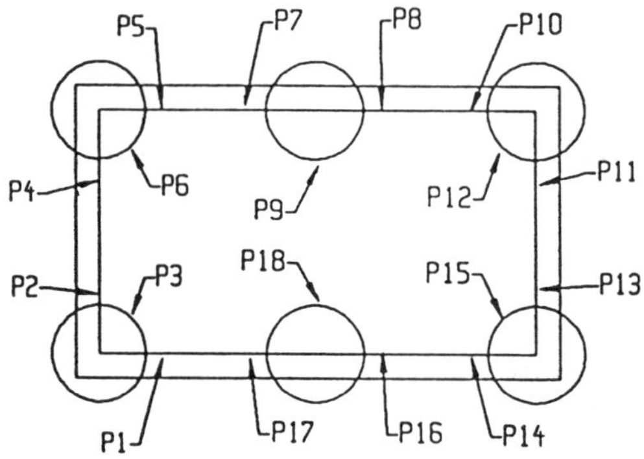

Figure 5.73

Step 4. Trim the six circles using the pick points in Figure 5.73.

Select **MAIN MENU → Modify → Trim → 3 entities**
Select the first entity to trim: pick at **P1**
Select the second entity to trim: pick at **P2**
Select the entity to trim to: pick at **P3** to complete the trimming of first circle

Sequentially pick at **P4 - P18** to complete the trimming of the remaining five circles

The final geometry should look like Figure 5.74.

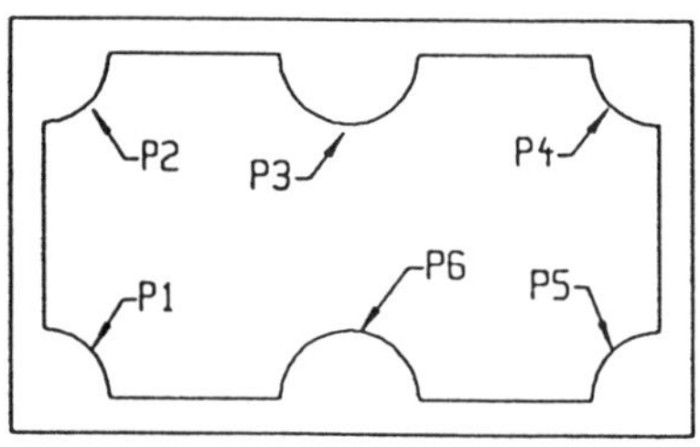

Figure 5.74

Step 5. Save the file (pocket1).

Select **MAIN MENU → File → Save**
Enter file name: **pocket1**

Note: Continue steps 6 and 7 to add six points for another project.

Step 6. Create six points at the center of each arc. Use the pick points labeled in Figure 5.74 above.

Select **MAIN MENU → Create → Point → Position → Center**
Specify a point: pick at **P1** to create the first point

Step 6, continued.

Sequentially pick at **P2 - P6** to create the remaining five points
The six points are added as shown in Figure 5.75.

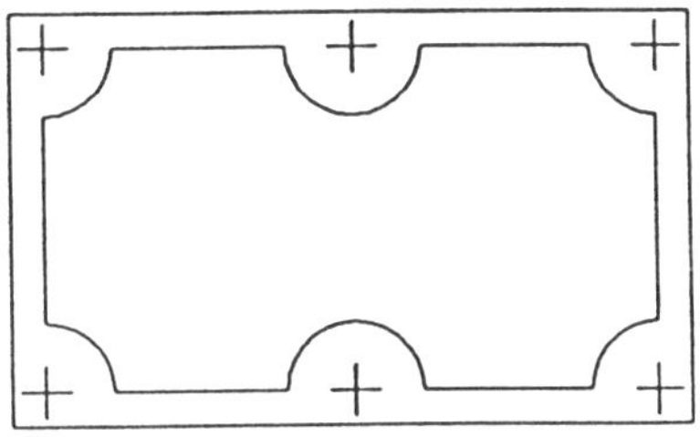

Figure 5.75

Step 7. Save to another file (drill2).

Select **MAIN MENU → File → Save**
Enter file name: **drill2**

Note: The geometry file **drill2** is used to drilling and tapping six holes in project 8 of chapter 7.

Project 4.

We are here

Part Geometry Creation
(Drill3)

Go to

Toolpath Generation
Project 9 of Chapter 7 **(Drill3)**

Create a rectangle and four points as shown in Figure 5.76. Save this file as **drill3**. This file will be used in project 9 of chapter 7.

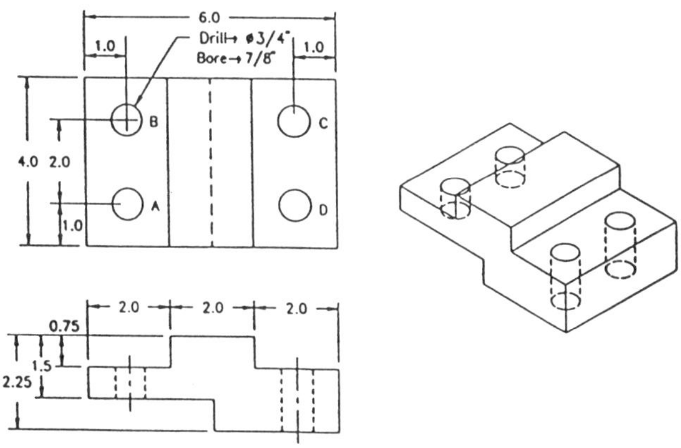

Figure 5.76

This geometry consists of a rectangle and four points. The coordinates of keypoints are shown in Figure 5.77.

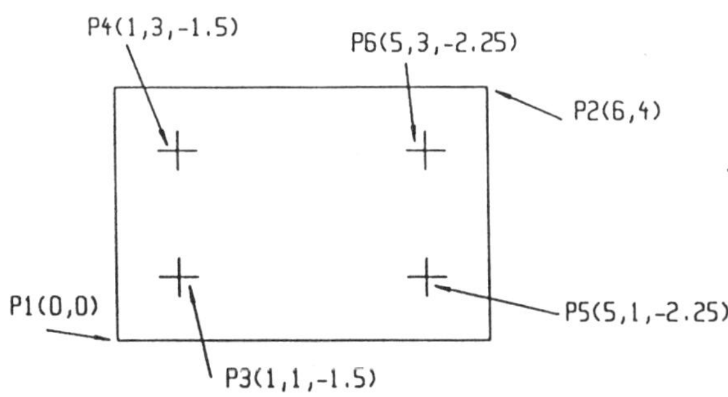

Figure 5.77

Step 1. Create a rectangle.

Select **MAIN MENU → Create → Rectangle → 2 points**
Enter the lower left corner: **0,0** ←
Enter the upper right corner: **6,4** ←

Step 2. Create four points.

Select **MAIN MENU → Create → Point → Position → Value**
Enter coordinates: **1,1, -1.5** ←
Enter coordinates: **1,3, -1.5** ←
Enter coordinates: **5,1, -2.25** ←
Enter coordinates: **5,3, -2.25** ←

Step 3. Save to a file.

Select **MAIN MENU → File → Save**
Enter file name: **drill3**

Project 5.

Use the Letters command to create a geometry as shown in Figure 5.78. This geometry consists of two circles and five strings of letters in **three** font types; box, block and roman. These three fonts are used to create letters as follows:

We are here

Part Geometry Creation
(Letter3)

Go to

Toolpath Generation
Project 12 of Chapter 7 **(Letter3)**

1. EASTERN MICHIGAN UNIVERSITY and INDUSTRIAL TECHNOLOGY
   Font = Box
   Height = 0.3
   Spacing = 0.1
   Arc Radius=2.5
2. CADCAM
   Font=Block
   Height=0.4
   Spacing=0.1
   Arc Radius=1.5
3. CNC
   Font=Block
   Height=0.5
   Spacing=0.15
   Starting point= (-1.125,-.4)
4. YES
   Font=Roman
   Height=0.6
   Spacing=0.2
   Arc Radius=1.35

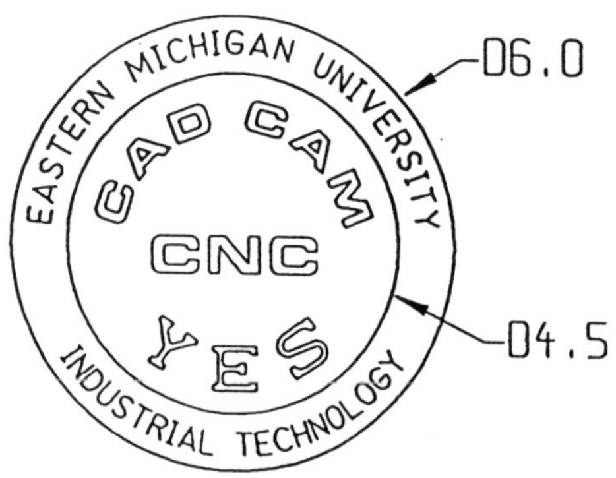

Figure 5.78

⌛**Tips** 1. Use different levels and colors for different groups of geometry and letters.

2. The letter strings EASTERN MICHIGAN UNIVERSITY and INDUSTRIAL TECHNOLOGY can be changed to your school name and department name.

Step 1. Create two circles

Select **MAIN MENU → Create → Arc → pt Dia cir**
Enter the center point: **0,0** ←
Enter the diameter: **6**←
Enter the center point: **0,0** ←
Enter the diameter: **4.5** ←

The two circles appear as Figure 5.79.

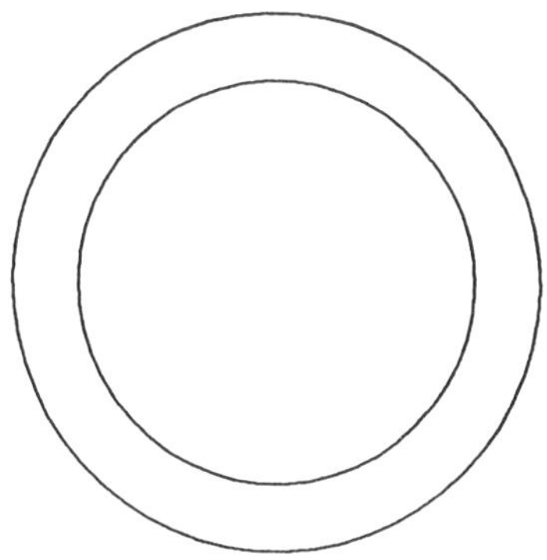

Figure 5.79

Step 2. Create a string of box letters using level 2 and color 12.

Select **Level** then enter **2** ←
Select **Color** then enter **12** ←
Select **MAIN MENU → Create → Next menu → Letters → Box**
Enter letter height: **0.3** ←
Enter letter spacing: **0.1** ←
Select **Yes** to write letters on an arc
Enter coordinates of arc center: **0,0**←
Enter arc radius: **2.5** ←
Enter type of arc: **0** ← to select the top arc
Enter letters: **EASTERN MICHIGAN UNIVERSITY** (or your school name)

Step 3. Create a string of box letters in the bottom arc.

Select **Letters → Box**
Enter letter height: **0.3** ←
Enter letter spacing: **0.1** ←
Select **Yes** to write letters on an arc
Enter coordinates of arc center: **0,0** ←
Enter arc radius: **2.5**←
Enter type of arc: **1** ← to select the bottom arc
Enter letters: **INDUSTRIAL TECHNOLOGY** (or your department name)

Two strings of box letters should look like Figure 5.80 on the next page.

Figure 5.80

Step 4. Change level to 3 and color to 13.

Select **Level** then enter **3** ←
Select **Color** then enter **13** ←

Step 5. Create a string of block letters on an arc.

Select **Letters** → **bLock**
Enter letter height: **0.4** ←
Enter letter spacing: **0.1** ←
Select **Yes** to write letters on an arc
Enter coordinates of arc center: **0,0** ←
Enter arc radius: **1.5** ←
Enter type of arc: **0** ← to select the top arc
Enter letters: **CAD CAM** ←

The letter string of block font appears as Figure 5.81.

Figure 5.81

Step 6. Create the letters string CNC along a line.

Select **Letters** → **bLock**
Enter letter height: **0.5** ←
Enter letter spacing: **0.15** ←
Select **No** to "Write letters on an arc (Y/N)?"
Enter starting location of letters: **-1.125,-.4** ←
Enter letters: **CNC** ←

The CNC letters are added as in Figure 5.82.

Figure 5.82

Step 7. Create the letters string YES along a bottom arc.

Select **Letters → Roman**
Enter letter height: **0.6** ←
Enter letter spacing: **0.2** ←
Select **Yes** to write letters on an arc
Enter coordinates of arc center: **0,0** ←
Enter arc radius: **1.35** ←
Enter type of arc: **1** ← to select the bottom arc
Enter letters: **YES** ←

The final drawing should look like Figure 5.83.

Figure 5.83

Step 8. Save to a file.

Select **MAIN MENU → File → Save**
Enter file name: **letter2**

5.12 Exercises

5.12.1 Short Answer

1. Use a drawing to show how Mastercam uses cascaded menus for creating geometry entities.
2. A point can be defined in Mastercam with how many options ?
3. How many options can be used to create a line in Mastercam?
4. Describe how the feature of the Multi command creates lines.
5. Describe the difference between arcs and circles.
6. How many options can define an arc in Mastercam?
7. How many options can define a circle in Mastercam?
8. What are the three fillet parameters? Describe, with drawings, how these three parameters change the fillets.
9. What is a spline?
10. What is the minimum number of points required to define a spline?
11. What are two common types of curves for 2-D geometry in Mastercam?
12. What is the full name of NURBS?
13. Describe the major difference between splines and NURBS curves.
14. Use a drawing to show how Mastercam creates a rectangle with (a)one point and (b)two points options.
15. List the four standard fonts used in Mastercam for creating letter geometry.

5.12.2 Problems

16. Create the geometry shown in Figure 5.84. Save the file as **contour8.** This file is used in problem 66 of chapter 7.

Tom '18

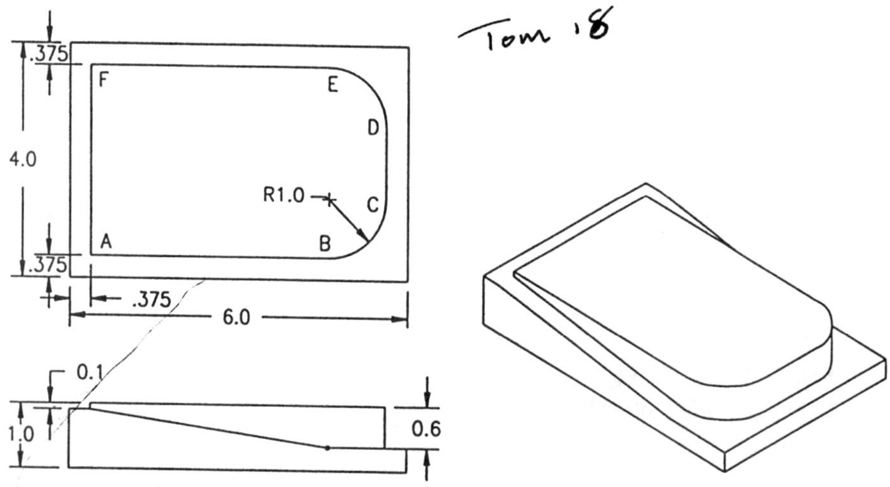

Figure 5.84

17. Create the geometry shown in Figure 5.85. Save the file as contour9. This file is used in problem 67 of chapter 7.

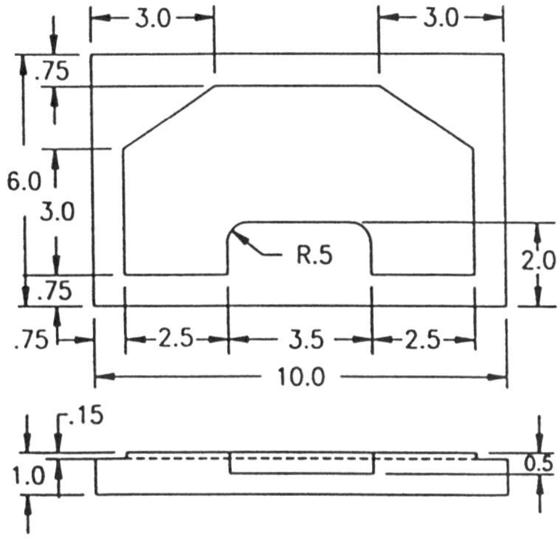

Figure 5.85

18. Create the geometry shown in Figure 5.86. Save the file as **drill4.** This file is used in problem 71 of chapter 7.

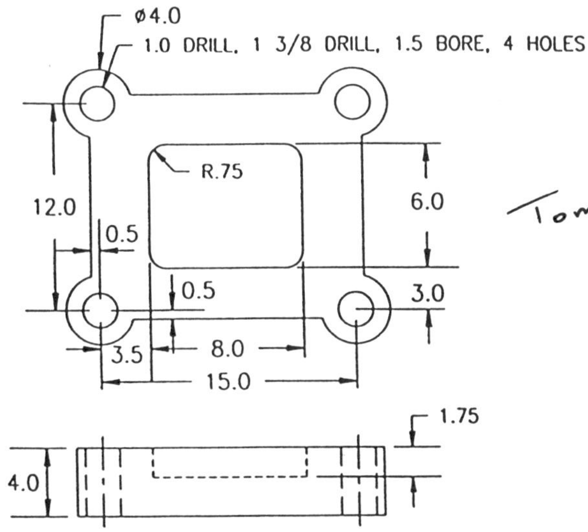

Figure 5.86

19. Create the geometry shown in Figure 5.87. Save the file as **comb2**. This file is used in problem 73 of chapter 7.

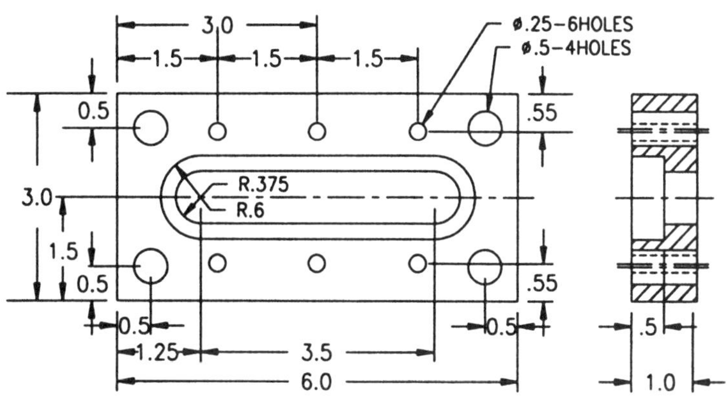

Figure 5.87

20. Create the part geometry shown in Figure 5.88. and save the files as **trans2.** This file is used later in problem 19 of chapter 8.

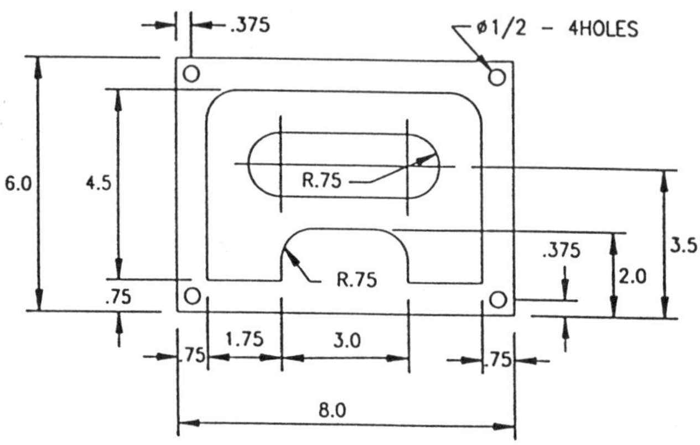

Figure 5.88

21. Create the geometry and letter strings as shown in Figure 5.89. Save the file as letters4 which will be used in problem 77 in chapter 7. Replace the string EMU IT with your school name and department name. Some helpful tips are listed.

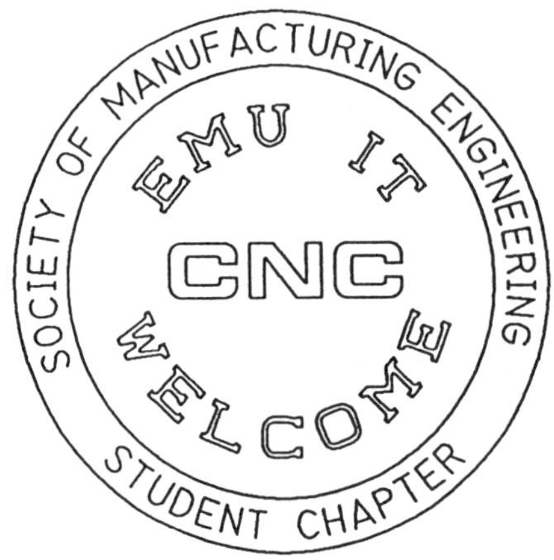

Figure 5.89

1. The geometry file is organized by level and color as below:

Two circles:	level 1 and color 10
Box font:	level 2 and color 12
Roman font:	level 3 and color 13
Block font:	level 4 and color 14

2. Box font: SOCIETY OF MANUFACTURING ENGINEERING and STUDENT CHAPTER

Roman font:	EMU IT and WELCOME
Block font:	CNC

3. Height,spacing, radius, and starting point:

Box font:	height = 0.5"	Spacing = 0.15"	Radius = 4.25"
Roman font:	height = 0.75"	Spacing = 0.2"	Radius = 2.5"
Block font:	height = 1.0"	Spacing = 0.25"	Starting point is (-2.1,-0.3)

Chapter 6

Modification of Existing Geometry

Objectives:

1. Understand the features of geometry modification functions and know when to apply them.
2. Apply geometry modification functions, Delete, Modify, and Xform, to simplify the geometric creation process.

Overview

The geometry creation functions presented in chapter 5 are used to produce simple part geometries. It would be very time consuming, if not impossible, to use those basic functions to create complex part geometries. Like most CAD software, Mastercam provides a variety of functions to modify existing geometric entities. All of these modifying functions make geometric construction easier and faster. Three groups of modifying functions are covered in this chapter including delete, modify, and Xform.

6.1 Delete Function

The delete function is used for removing a single entity or a group of entities from the screen and the system's database. Select **Delete** from the main menu (or press **F5** on the keyboard), and you will be given an option to select an entity or use its submenu options shown in Figure 6.1.

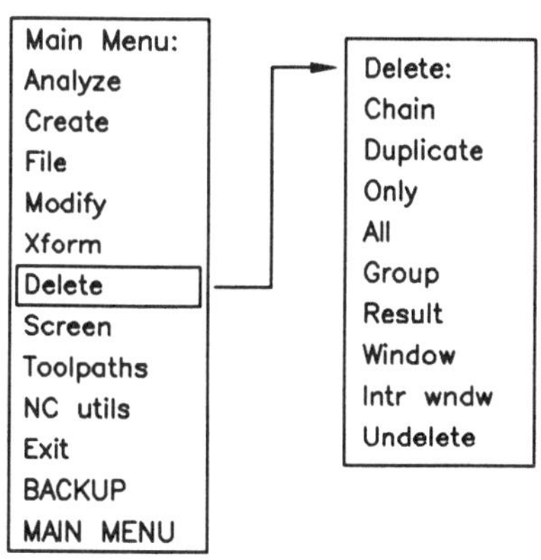

Figure 6.1: Submenu for Delete

The submenu options for Delete can be described as follows:

Chain -	deletes a chain of connected entities.
Duplicate -	deletes duplicate entities occupying the same space.
Only -	deletes only a certain type of entities such as points, lines, splines, etc. User selection is required.
All -	deletes all entities of a certain type. User selection is not required.
Group -	deletes the current group defined by the Xform→ Group function.
Result -	deletes the result of the transformed entities.
Window -	deletes all the entities fully included in the Window. **Alt-F5** is a short-cut key for this operation.
Intr wndw -	deletes all the entities inside or intersected with a rectangular window defined by the mouse.
Undelete -	undeletes previously deleted entities.

Undelete

Undelete recreates the deleted entities in the order they were deleted. This function is under the submenu of Delete.

6.2 Modify Functions

A group of modifying functions are grouped under the **Modify** menu. They are used to change existing entities. Select Modify from the main menu and you will have the submenu options shown in Figure 6.2.

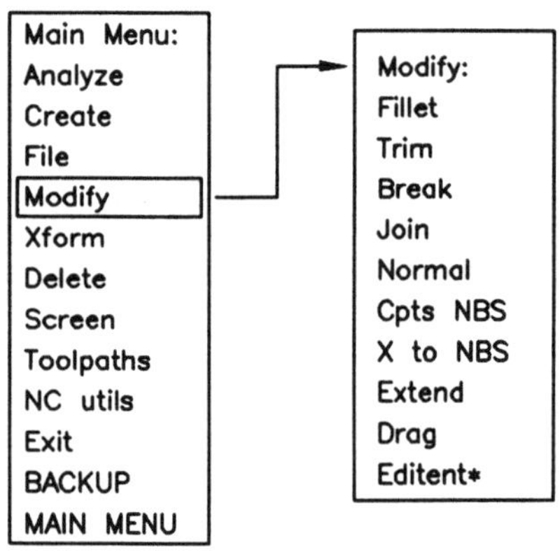

Figure 6.2: Submenu for Modify

The submenu options for **Modify** can be described as follows:

Fillet -	creates a fillet between two intersected entities.
Trim -	trims up to three entities to specified boundaries.
Break -	divides entities (lines, arcs, or splines) into two or more segments.
Join -	joins two segments into one entity. It undos what Break does.
Normal -	modifies the normal directions of a 3-D surface.
Cpts NBS -	modifies the control points of a NURBS curve.
X to NBS	transforms arcs or lines into NURBS format.
Extend -	extend a line or arc by a desired length
Drag -	dynamically drags (moves or copies) entities on screen.
Editent* -	edits attributes such endpoint, color and level for an entity.

6.2.1 Fillet Function

This function is used to create a fillet between two entities. The procedures for filleting are the same as shown in section 5.5. Figure 6.3 shows two filleting examples.

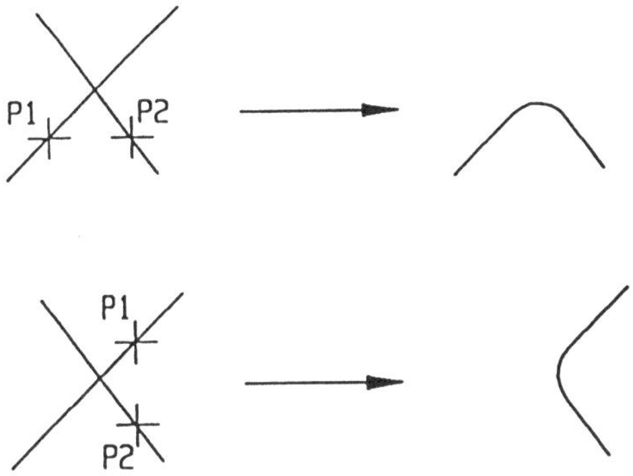

Figure 6.3

6.2.2 Trim Function

The Trim function is used to trim up to three entities to a specified boundaries. The trimming can trim or extend entities to their intersection points. **Seven** options are available:

1 entity-	trims an entity by selecting the entity and an entity to trim to.
2 entities-	trims two entities at the same time at their intersection point.
3 entities-	trims three entities in the same time at their intersection point(s).
To point-	trims or extends the selected entity to a point selected.
Many -	trims several entities at once.
Close arc -	converts any arc to a full circle.
Divide -	trims a line or curve between two other lines or curves.

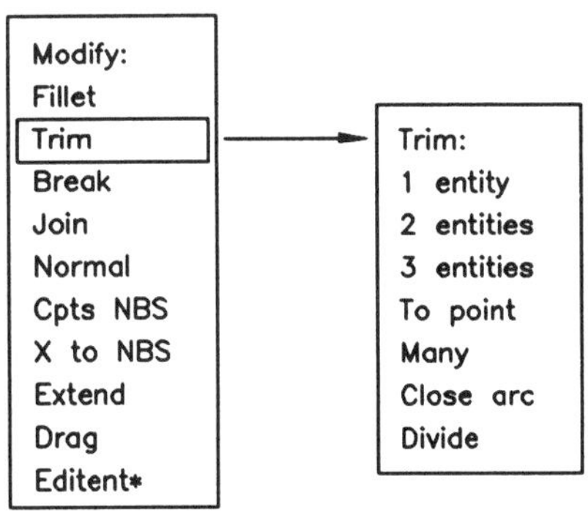

Figure 6.4

1 Entity Trimming

Menu selection sequence is **Modify → Trim → 1 entity**.

This function trims an entity by selecting the segment of the object you wish to retain first, then pick the entity you wish to trim to.

Procedure: (Figure 6.5)

1. Select the entity to trim: Pick at **P1**
2. Select the entity to trim to: Pick at **P2**

Tip On step 1, pick the segment of the entity you wish to retain first.

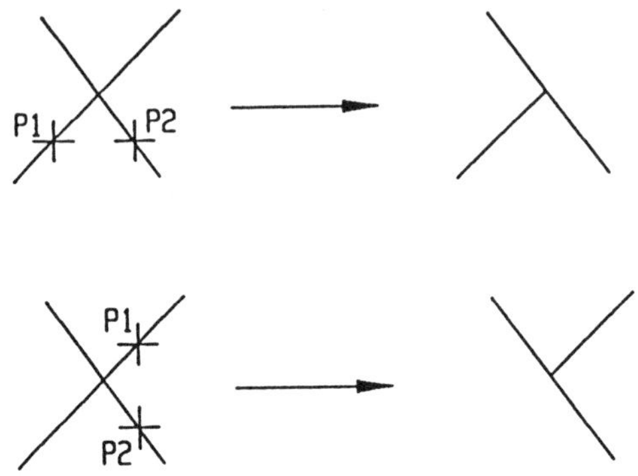

Figure 6.5

2 Entities Trimming

Menu selection sequence is **Modify → Trim → 2 entities.**

This function trims two entities simultaneously to their intersection point.
Procedure: (Figure 6.6)
1. Select the entity to trim: Pick at **P1**
2. Select the entity to trim to: Pick at **P2**

Tips 1. These two entities need to have an intersection point.

2. Pick the segments to be kept on both entities.

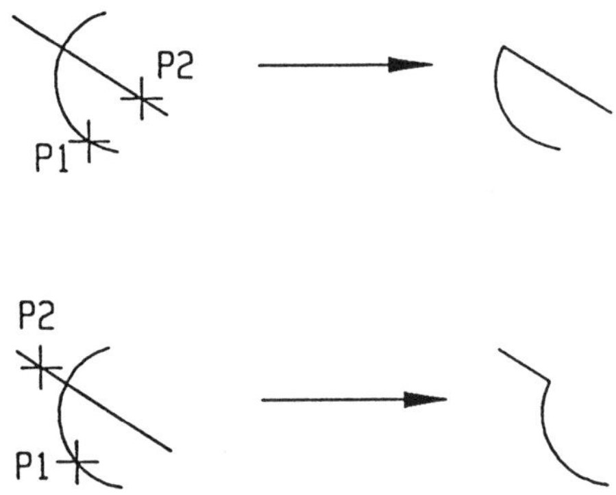

Figure 6.6

3 Entities Trimming

Menu selection sequence is **Modify → Trim → 3 entities.**

This function trims three entities simultaneously to their intersection points.
Procedure: (Figure 6.7 on next page)
1.Select the first entity to trim: Pick at **P1**
2.Select the second entity to trim: Pick at **P2**
3.Select the third entity to trim: Pick at **P3**

Tips 1. These three entities need to intersect with one another at three different points.

2. The first two entities will become the boundaries of the third entity.

3. Pick the segments to be kept on these three entities.

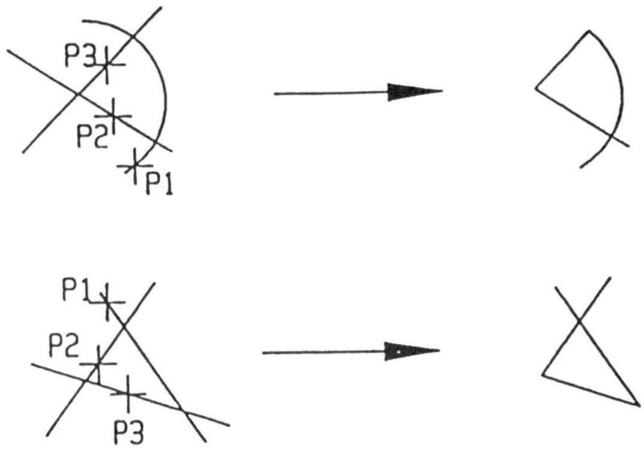

Figure 6.7

Trimming An Entity To a Point

Menu selection is **Modify → Trim → To point.**

This command trims or extends the selected line or arc entity to a point selected. The selected entity will be trimmed at or extended to the point where the perpendicular relationship occurs.

Procedure: (Figure 6.8)

1. Select entity to TRIM/EXTEND: Pick at **P1**
2. Indicate TRIM/EXTEND location <position option>: Pick at **P2**

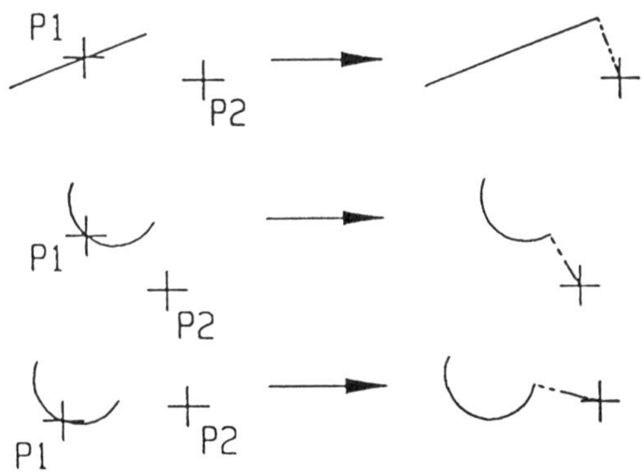

Figure 6.8

Trimming Many Entities at a time

Menu select is **Modify → Trim → Many**

This command trims several entities at once.

Procedure: (Figure 6.9)

1. Select Curves to trim <entity selection options>: Sequentially pick at **P1 - P6.**
2. Select **Done**
3. Select Trimming Curve: Pick at **P7**
4. Indicate Side of Trimming Curve: Pick at **P8**

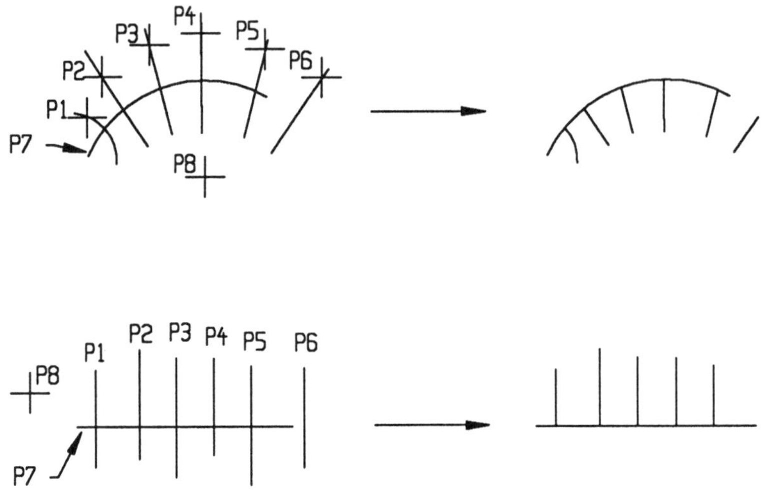

Figure 6.9

Convert an Arc to a Full Circle

Menu select is **Modify → Trim → Close arc**

This command converts an arc to a full circle.

Procedure: (Figure 6.10)

1. Select an Arc to convert to a full circle: Pick at **P1**

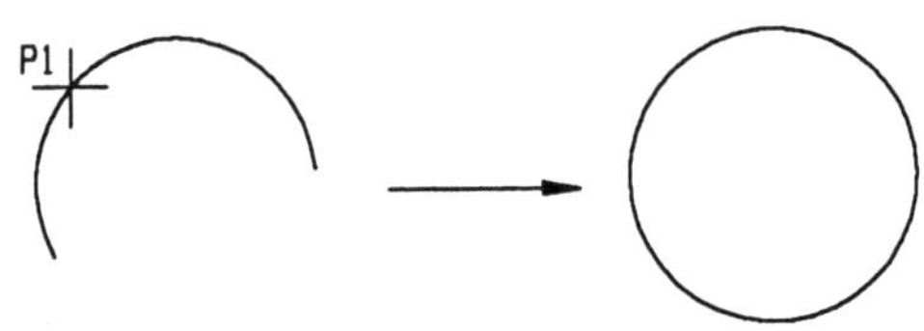

Figure 6.10

Trimming a Curve Between Two Other Curves

Menu select is **Modify → Trim → Divide**

This command trims a line or curve between two other lines or curves.

Procedure: (Figure 6.11)

1. Select curve to divide: Pick at **P1**
2. Select first dividing curve: Pick at **P2**
3. Select second dividing curve: Pick at **P3**

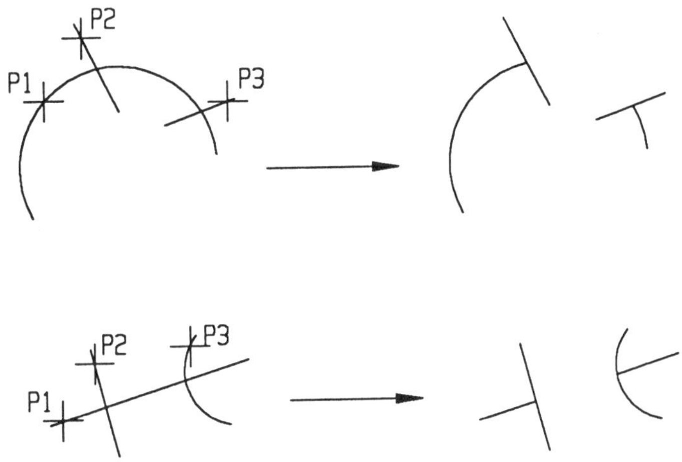

Figure 6.11

Project 1. 1

Filleting and Trimming

Create the geometry shown in Figure 6.12a. Save the file as **array1**. This file is used in project 6 of chapter 8 to generate a set of toolpaths to produce three pockets as shown in Figure 6.12b.

We are here

Part Geometry Creation

(Array 1)

Go to

Toolpath Generation

Project 6 of Chapter 8 (Array 1)

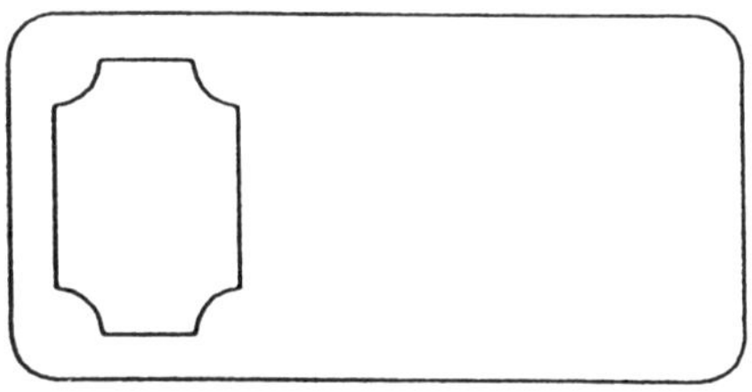

Figure 6.12a

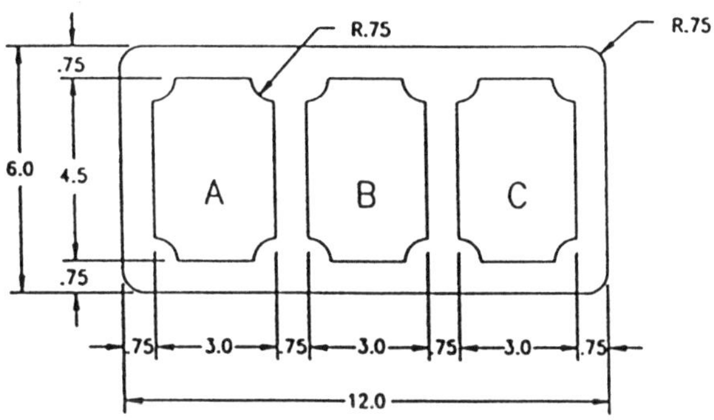

Figure 6.12.b

Tips 1. Create two rectangles.

2. Add four fillets at the corners of the outer rectangle.

3. Create four circles at the corners of the inside rectangle.

4. Use Trim → 3 entities commands to trim the four circles to their desired arcs.

Step 1. Create two rectangles.

Select **MAIN MENU → Create → Rectangle → 2 points**
Enter the lower left corner: **0,0** ←
Enter the upper right corner: **12,6** ← for the outer rectangle
Enter the lower left corner: **0.75,0.75** ←
Enter the upper right corner: **3.75,5.25** ← for the inside rectangle

Press **Alt** and **F1** simultaneously to fit the drawing.

The two rectangles appear as Figure 6.13.

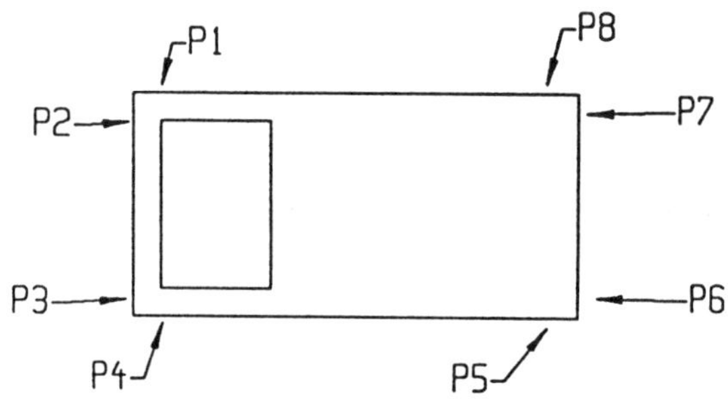

Figure 6.13

Step 2. Create four fillets at corners of outer rectangle. Use the pick points in Figure 6.13.

Select **MAIN MENU → Create → Fillet → Radius**
Enter the first radius: **0.75** ←
*Note:*Make sure the other two parameters' settings are correct. The fillet angle is less than 180; trim to fillet.

Select an entity: pick at **P1**
Select another entity: pick at **P2** to complete the first fillet
Sequentially pick at **P3 - P8** to complete the remaining three fillets

The four fillets are added as in Figure 6.14.

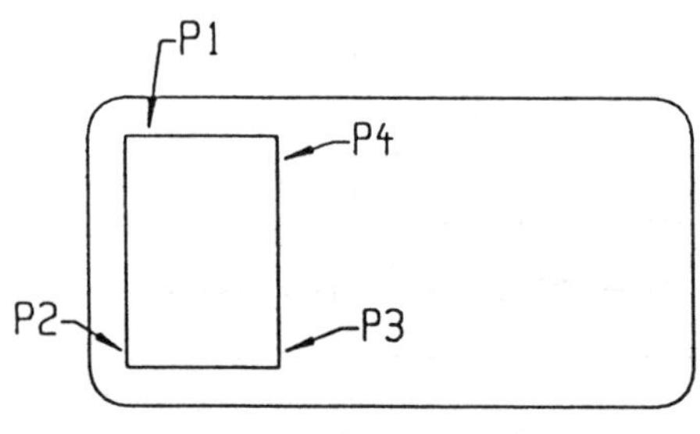

Figure 6.14

Step 3. Create four circles at corners of the inner rectangle. Use the pick points from the Figure 6.14 on the previous page.

Select **MAIN MENU → Create → Arc → pt Rad cir → Endpoint**
Enter the center point: Pick at **P1**
Enter the radius: **0.75** ← to complete the first circle
Enter the center point: Pick at **P2**
Enter the radius: **0.75** ← for the second circle
Enter the center point: Pick at **P3**
Enter the radius: **0.75** ← for the third circle
Enter the center point: Pick at **P4**
Enter the radius: **0.75** ← for the fourth circle

Four circles are added as in Figure 6.15.

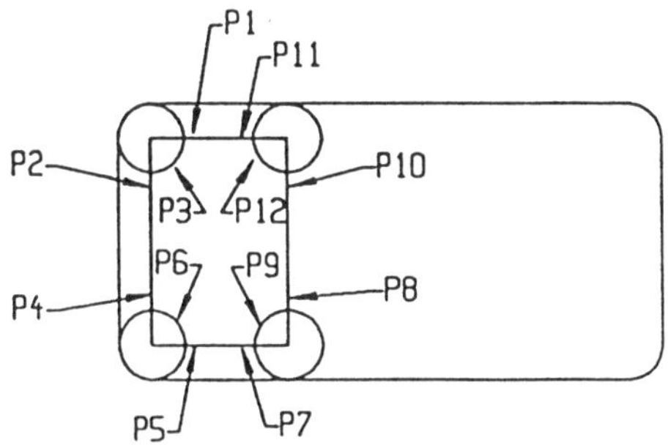

Figure 6.15

Step 4. Trim four circles to become arcs. Use the pick points in Figure 6.15.

Select **MAIN MENU → Modify → Trim → 3 entities**
Select the first entity to trim: pick at **P1**
Select the second entity to trim: pick at **P2**
Select the entity to trim to: pick at **P3** to complete the trimming of the first corner
Sequentially pick at **P4 - P12** to trim the remaining three corners

The final drawing should look like Figure 6.16.

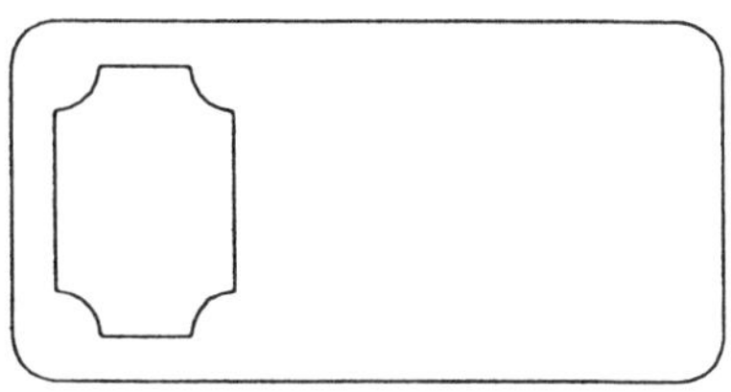

Figure 6.16

Step 5. Save to a file (array1).

Select **MAIN MENU → File → Save**
Enter file name: **array1**

6.2.3 Break Function

This function separates an entity into two or more entities. The new entities can be different from the original entity type. The options under Break are:

Arcs-	breaks a 2-D spline or 2-D NURBS curve into lines and arcs.
Mny pieces-	breaks lines, arcs, splines and NURBS curve into more than two line segments.
2 pieces-	breaks lines, arcs, splines and NURBS curve into two pieces.
at Length -	breaks a line, arc or spline at a distance along the entity.
Note/let -	breaks a note into geometry.
Hatch/line-	breaks a cross-hatch entity into line segments.
Cdata/line-	breaks a copious data entity into points or line segments.
Breakcir*-	not available.

⌛**Tip** These new line and arc segments are difficult to distinguish on screen. Use **Analyze** (F4) command to examine these segments.

6.2.4 Join Function

Join combines two separated entities together to become a new entity.

⌛**Tips** 1. NURBS curves can not be joined.

2. Note that these two entities have to be compatible. The system checks the database for each entity and tries to join them together. An error message displays if the two entities selected are not compatible. For example:
   "Cannot join the lines - they are not collinear."
   "Cannot join the arcs - they do not have the same center and radius."

6.2.5 Normal Function

This function is used to change the normal direction of surfaces.

6.2.6 Cpts NBS Function

This function modifies the control points of NURBS curves and surfaces, and creates a new NURBS curve and surface.

Procedure: (Figure 6.17 on the next page)

1. Select a NURBS curve or surface: Pick at **P1**
   The control points and control lines will be highlighted on the screen.
2. Select a control point: Pick at **P2**
3. Modify NURBS: Select **Dynamic**

Dynamic	- dynamically drag the control point and see the new curve in blue.
XYZ	- input a new XYZ coordinates for the control points.
Weight	- not available for NURBS yet.

4. Enter the starting point: Pick at **P2** again.
5. Drag to **P3**

⌛**Tip** **F3** key repaints the drawing.

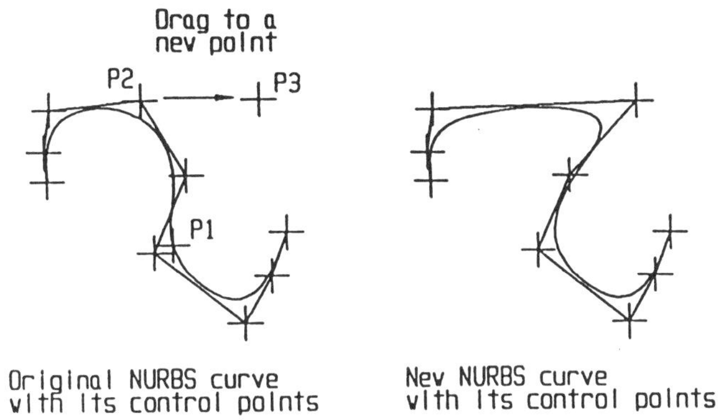

Figure 6.17.

6.2.7 X to NBS Function

This function converts lines, arcs, splines and surfaces to the NURBS format. The new entities are saved to the drawing database as NURBS curves.

Procedure:

1. Select line, spline, surface or arc to convert to NURBS.
2. Select **Done**

Tip Use **Analyze F4** to confirm the changes.

6.2.8 Extend Function

This function allows the user to extend a line or arc by a desired length. The user types in the desired length and selects a line or arc near the endpoint to direct the extension.

6.2.9 Drag Function

This function dynamically moves or copies drawing entities when given the new location. Drag helps you see the results of the command before it is finished.

6.2.10 Editent* Function

This function edits attributes such as an endpoint, color and level for an entity. After the modification, MasterCAM will update the geometry automatically.

6.3 Xform Functions

Mastercam provides eight very useful editing functions to change the position, orientation, and size of exiting geometries. These **eight** functions are mirror, rotate, scale, scalexyz, translate, offset, ofs ctour and group. They are grouped under the Xform command. The submenu of Xform is shown in Figure 6.18 on the next page.

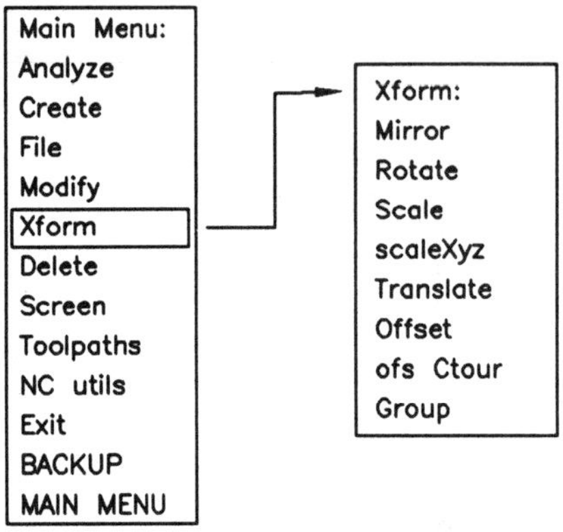

Figure 6.18

The eight editing functions are described below:

Mirror -	produces a mirror image of a drawing, detail, or part.
Rotate-	rotates the selected entities about any point.
Scale -	scales the selected entities to increase or decrease their sizes.
scale Xyz -	scales the selected entities by the given x, y and z values.
ofs Ctour -	offsets several connected lines or arcs by chaining their entities.
Translate -	moves or copies objects to new location(s).
Offset -	moves or copies a line or arc away from itself in a perpendicular direction with an offset distance to the line or arc.
Group -	selects and defines a group of entities to be transformed. The selected entities will be highlighted in red.

Entity Selection Option and Its Procedures

When Mirror, Rotate, Scale, scaleXyz, Translate or Offset is selected, the following **entity selection option** will appear on the Main Menu Area. You can select an entity one after another, use chain, window, or combine different options in the menu. The selected entity will be highlighted in yellow. You can select **Done** to finish the selection process and proceed to the next step, or select **Backup** to abort the selected entities.

Entity -	selects entity one after another. These entities are added into the selection database. Select Backup/Done to finish the selection.
Chain -	selects a group of entities that are chained together.
Only -	selects a group of entities with a specific entity type, i.e., lines,arcs, etc. Select the specific kind of entity one after another to add into the database.
All -	selects a group of entities of a specific entity type, i.e., lines,arcs, splines, etc. The options automatically selects all the entities in that particular entity type.
Group -	retrieves and selects the previous group from the database.
Results -	shows the current selected group in Magenta.
Window -	selects all the entities that are inside the window.
Intr wndw -	selects all the entities that are either inside or intersect with the window.
Done -	closes the selection process.

Transformation Parameters

Mastercam uses different dialog boxes with different parameters to to perform a transformation. An example for rotate is shown in the following figure.

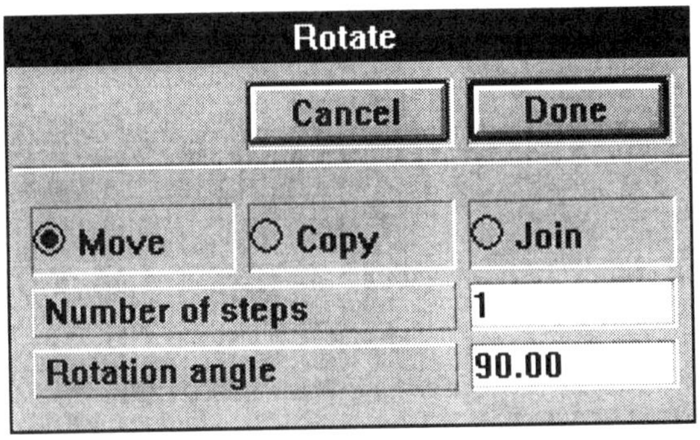

Firgure 6.19

Move - moves the original entities.
Copy - copies the original entities.
Join - joins the new transformed entities to original entities at their end points.
Number of Steps - specifies the number of steps to be performed by the transformation function.
Rotation Angle - specifies the angle of rotation.

6.3.1 Mirror Function

This function produces a **mirror** image of selected entities about the X axis, Y axis or an existing line. It is best suited for those parts that have identical features being symmetrical about an axis or a line.

Procedure: (Figure 6.20)

1. Entity selection option: Pick at **P1**
2. Entity selection option: Select **Done**
3. Mirror about: Select **Line**

X axis - mirrors with respect to X axis.
Y axis - mirrors with respect to Y axis.
Line - mirrors with respect to an existing line. The system will prompt after this selection.

4. Select line to mirror across: Pick at **P2**
5. Select **Copy** → **Done** from the pop-up dialog box.

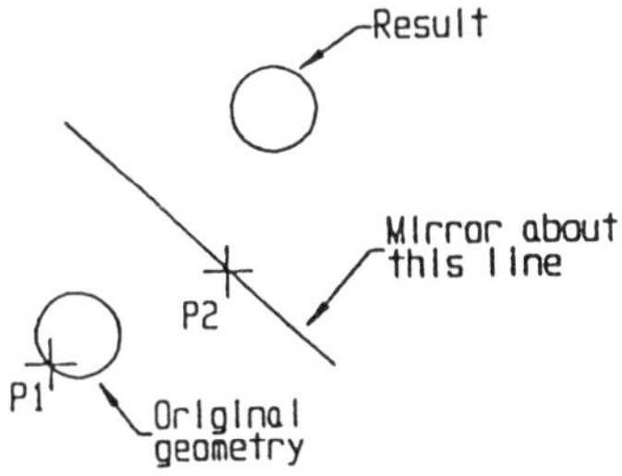

Figure 6.20: Mirroring an entity about an existing line

Tips 1. Select **Move → Done** or **Copy → Done** in step 5 to delete or retain the original entities.
2. Use the **Repaint** (F3) command to see the complete drawing after modification.

Project 2.

2

Mirroring

We are here

Part Geometry Creation
(Scale 1)

Go to

Toolpath Generation
Project 4 of Chapter 8 (Scale 1)

Create a hexagon and a rectangle as shown in Figure 6.21. Save the file as **scale1**. This file is used in project 4 of chapter 8 to generate a set of toolpaths for pocketing three hexagons at different depths.

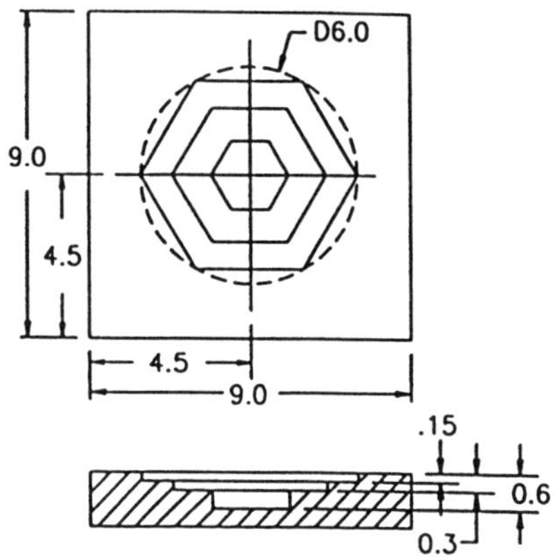

Figure 6.21

Tips 1. Create three sides of upper half of hexagon.

2. Mirror the three sides of hexagon about the X-axis to form the hexagon.

Step 1. Create two lines.

Select **MAIN MENU → Create → Line → Polar**
Specify an endpoint: **3,0** ←
Enter the angle in degree: **120** ←
Enter the length: **3** ←
Specify an endpoint: **-3,0** ←
Enter the angle in degree: **60** ←
Enter the length: **3** ←

The drawing appears as Figure 6.22.

Figure 6.22

Step 2. Create another line using the pick points in Figure 6.22 on page 6-14.

Select **BACKUP → Endpoints → Endpoint**
Specify the first endpoint: Pick at **P1**
Specify the second endpoint: Pick at **P2**

The new drawing becomes Figure 6.23.

Figure 6.23

Step 3. Mirror about X axis.

Select **MAIN MENU → Xform → Mirror → All → Entities → Done → X axis → Copy →Done**

The hexagon appears as in Figure 6.24.

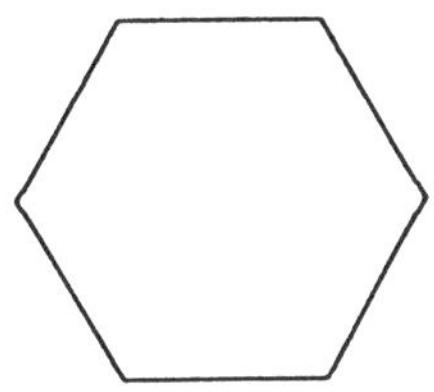

Figure 6.24

Step 4. Create a rectangle.

Select **MAIN MENU → Create → Rectangle → 2 points**
Enter the lower left corner: **-4.5,-4.5** ←
Enter the upper right corner: **4.5,4.5** ←

The final drawing shall look like Figure 6.25.

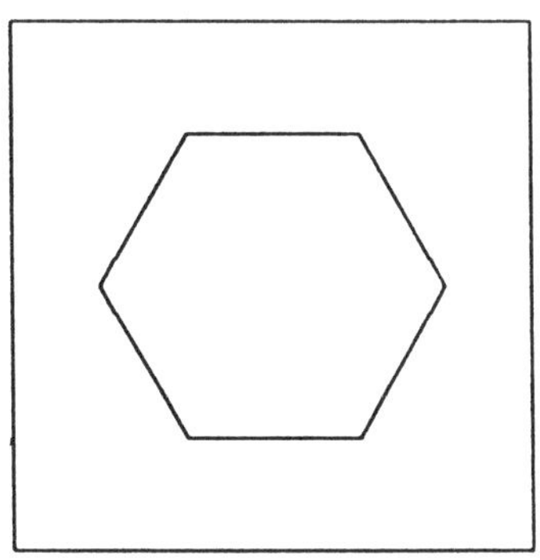

Figure 6.25

Step 5. Save to a file (scale1).

Select **MAIN MENU → File → Save**
Enter file name: **Scale1**

Project 3.

Mirroring

Create a geometry as shown in Figure 6.26. Save the file as **contour2.** This file is used in project 2 of chapter 7 to generate the toolpaths to cut the internal profile.

3

We are here

Part Geometry Creation

(Contour2)

Go to

Toolpath Generation

Project 2 of Chapter 7

(Contour2)

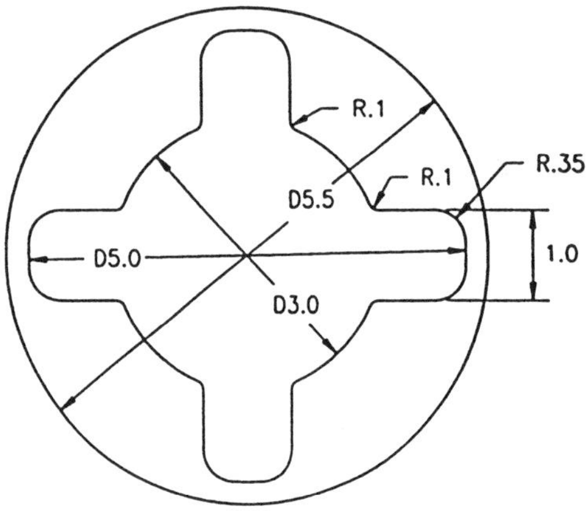

Figure 6.26

Tips 1. Create three 45° construction arcs and one construction line at 45° with the X axis.

2. Add two fillets to form the basic profile.

3. Mirror the basic profile about the 45° line to form a quarter of the part profile.

4. The quarter profile is then mirrored twice to complete the final part profile. The first time mirror about the Y axis. The second time mirror about the X axis.

Step 1. Create three 45° arcs.

Select **MAIN MENU → Create → Arc → Polar → Ctr point**
Enter the center point: **0,0** ←
Enter the radius: **2.75** ←
Enter the initial angle: **0** ←
Enter the final angle: **45** ←
Enter the center point: **0,0** ←
Enter the radius: **2.5** ←
Enter the initial angle: **0** ←
Enter the final angle: **45** ←
Enter the center point: **0,0** ←
Enter the radius: **1.5** ←
Enter the initial angle: **0** ←
Enter the final angle: **45** ←

The three 45° arcs are shown in Figure 6.27.

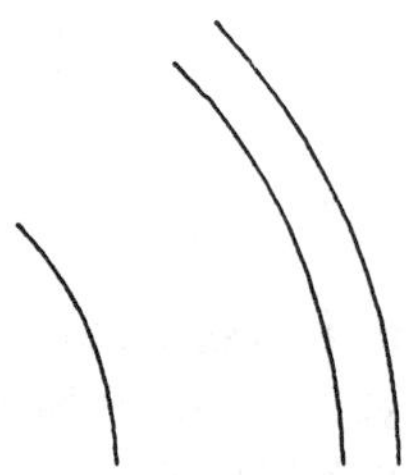

Figure 6.27

Step 2. Create a horizontal line at y = 0.5 and a 45° line.

Select **MAIN MENU → Create → Line → Endpoints**
Specify the first endpoint: Enter **0,0.5** ←
Specify the second endpoint: Enter **2.5,0.5** ←
Specify the first endpoint: Enter **0,0** ←
Specify the second endpoint: Enter **3,3** ←

Two lines are added as in Figure 6.28.

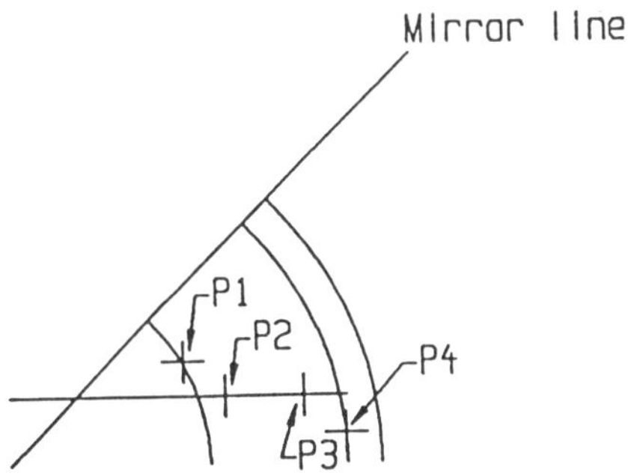

Figure 6.28

Step 3. Create two fillets using the pick points in Figure 6.28.

Select **MAIN MENU → Create → Fillet → Radius**
Enter the fillet radius: **0.1** ←

Note: Be sure the other two options are correct. The fillet angle is less than 180; trim to the fillet.

Select an entity: pick at **P1**
Select another entity: pick at **P2**
Select **Radius**
Enter the radius: **0.35** ←
Select an entity: pick at **P3**
Select another entity: pick at **P4**

Two fillets are added as in Figure 6.29.

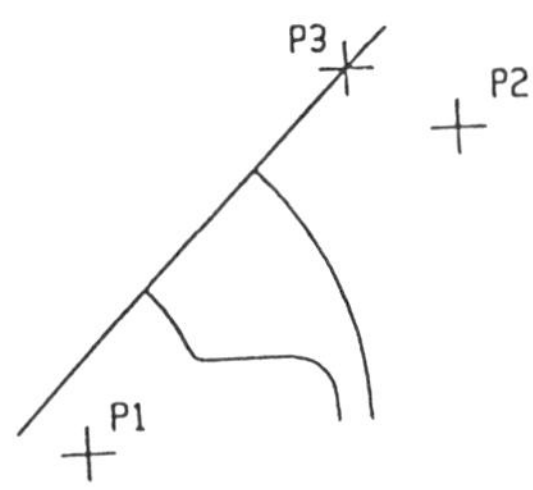

Figure 6.29

Step 4. Mirror the basic profile about the 45° line using the pick points in Figure 6.29.

Select **MAIN MENU → Xform → Mirror → Window**
Select the first corner: pick at **P1**
Select the second corner: pick at **P2**
Select **Done → Line**
Select line about which to mirror: pick at **P3**
Select **Copy→ Done**

The mirrored profile should look like Figure 6.30.

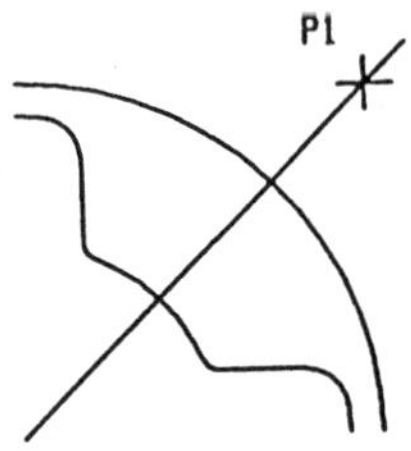

Figure 6.30

Step 5. Delete the mirror line using the pick point in Figure 6.30.

Select **MAIN MENU → Delete**
Select an entity or: pick at **P1**

The new drawing appears as Figure 6.31.

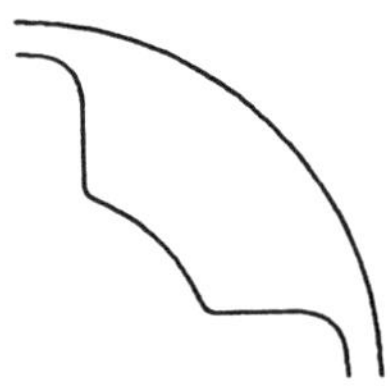

Figure 6.31

Step 6. Complete the geometry by using the Mirror command twice.

Select **MAIN MENU → Xform → Mirror → All → Entities → Done → Y axis → Copy → Done→ All → Entities → Done → X axis→Copy → Done**

The final drawing should resemble Figure 6.32.

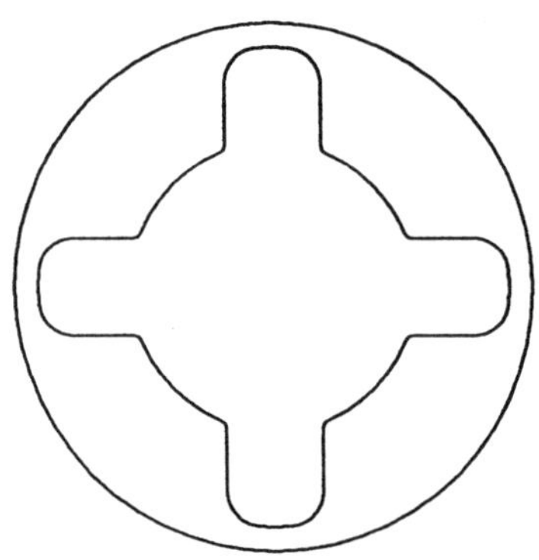

Figure 6.32

Step 7. Save to a file.

Select **MAIN MENU → File → Save**
Enter file name: **contour2**

Project 4.

4

Mirroring

We are here

Part Geometry Creation

(Rotate1)

Go to

Toolpath Generation

Project 3 of Chapter 8

(Rotate1)

Create a geometry as shown in Figure 6.33. Save the file as **rotate1.** This file is used in project 3 of chapter 8 to generate toolpaths.

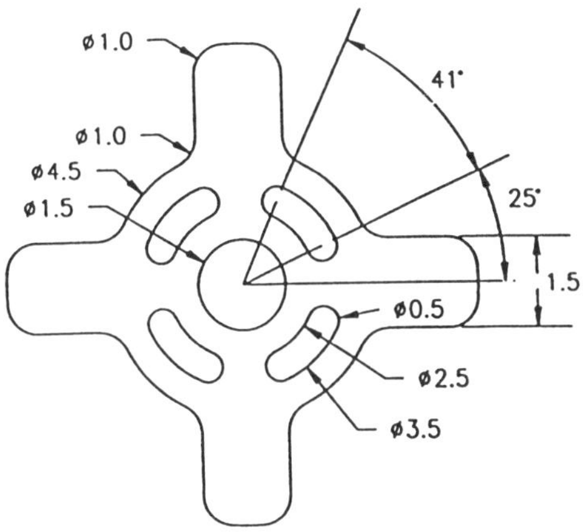

Figure 6.33

Tips 1. Create a basic profile that encompasses 45° of the profile.

2. Mirror the basic profile about the 45° line to complete a profile of 90°.

3. Mirror the profile of 90° about the Y axis to generate another profile of 180°.

4. Mirror the 180° profile about the X axis to complete the geometry.

Step 1. Create five circles.

Select **MAIN MENU** → **Create** → **Arc** → **pt Rad cir**
Enter the center point: **0,0** ←
Enter the radius: **4.0** ←
Enter the center point: **0,0** ←
Enter the radius: **2.25** ←
Enter the center point: **0,0** ←
Enter the radius: **1.75** ←
Enter the center point: **0,0** ←
Enter the radius: **1.25** ←
Enter the center point: **0,0** ←
Enter the radius: **0.75** ←

Step 2. Create a 45° line.

Select **MAIN MENU** → **Create** → **Line** → **Polar**
Specify an endpoint: Enter **0,0** ←
Enter angle in degrees: **45** ←
Enter the line length: **4.5** ←

The drawing should look like Figure 6.34.

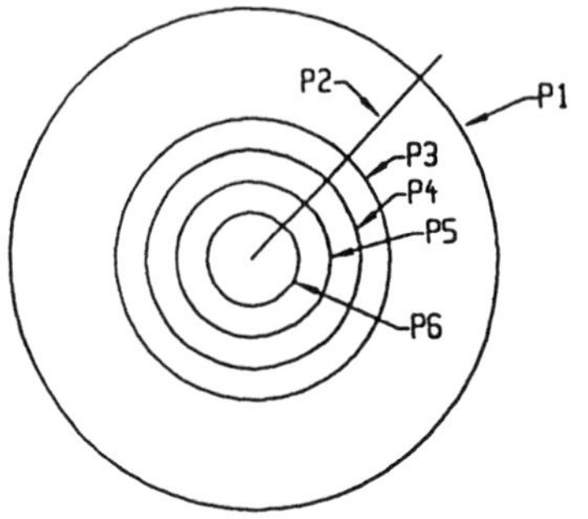

Figure 6.34

Step 3. Trim the circles to the line. Use pick points in Figure 6.34.

Select **MAIN MENU → Modify → Trim → 1 entity**
Select the entity to trim: pick at **P1**
Select the entity to trim to: pick at **P2**
Select the entity to trim: pick at **P3**
Select the entity to trim to: pick at **P2**
Select the entity to trim: pick at **P4**
Select the entity to trim to: pick at **P2**
Select the entity to trim: pick at **P5**
Select the entity to trim to: pick at **P2**
Select the entity to trim: pick at **P6**
Select the entity to trim to: pick at **P2**

These trimmed arcs should appear as Figure 6.35.

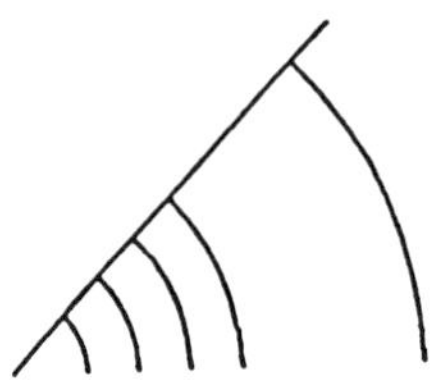

Figure 6.35

Tip Step 3 can be done by the following procedures: (use the pick points in 6.34 above)

Select **MAIN MENU → Modify → Trim → Many→ All →Arcs →Done**
Select trimming curve: pick at **P2**
Indicate side of the trimming curve: pick at **P1**

Step 4. Create two lines for fillets.

Select **MAIN MENU → Create → Line → Polar**
Specify an endpoint: Enter **0,0** ←
Enter angle in degrees: **25.0** ←
Enter the line length: **2.5** ←
Select **BACKUP → Endpoints**
Specify the first endpoint: Enter **2.25,.75** ←
Specify the second endpoint: Enter **4,.75** ←

The two lines are added as in Figure 6.36.

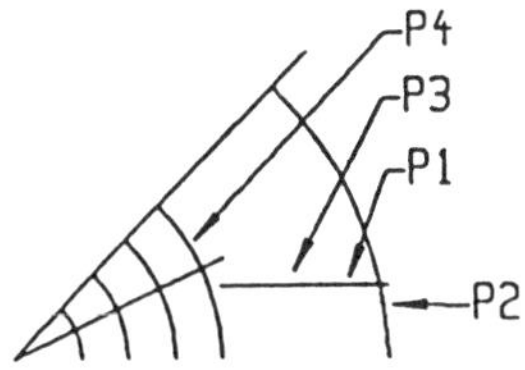

Figure 6.36

Step 5. Create two fillets using the pick points in Figure 6.36.

Select **MAIN MENU → Create → Fillet → Radius**
Enter the fillet radius: **0.5 ←**

Note: Make sure the other two options are correct. The fillet angle is less than 180;trim to fillet.
Select an entity: pick at **P1**
Select another entity: pick at **P2**
Select an entity: pick at **P3**
Select another entity: pick at **P4**

The new drawing becomes Figure 6.37.

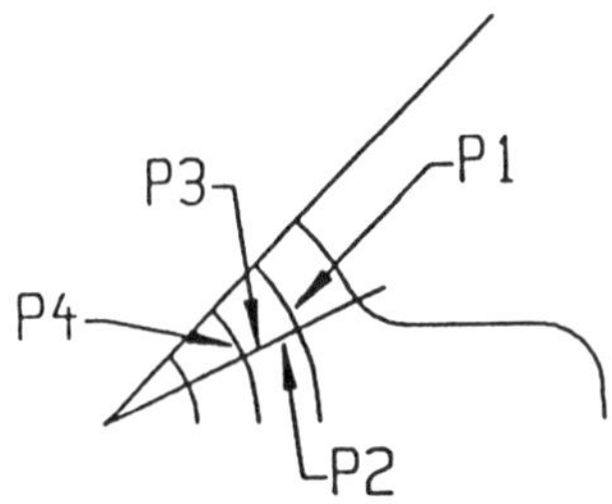

Figure 6.37

Step 6. Trim entities using the pick points in Figure 6.37.

Select **MAIN MENU → Modify → Trim → 2 entities**
Select the entity to trim: pick at **P1**
Select the entity to trim to: pick at **P2**
Select the entity to trim: pick at **P3**
Select the entity to trim to: pick at **P4**

The drawing should look like Figure 6.38.

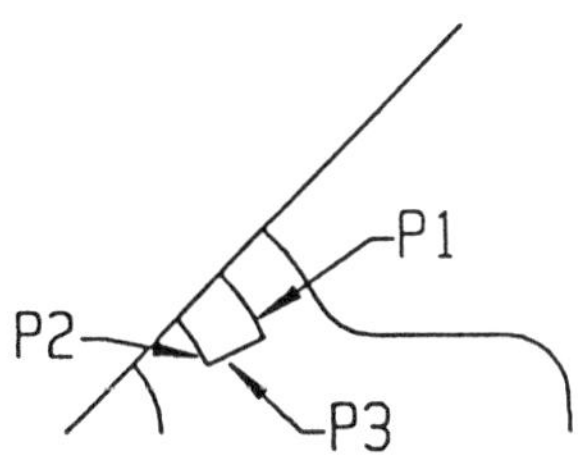

Figure 6.38

Step 7. Create an arc and delete a line using the pick points in Figure 6.38.

Select **MAIN MENU → Create → Arc → Endpoints → Endpoint**
Enter the first point: pick at **P1**
Enter the second point: pick at **P2**
Enter the radius: **0.25** ←
Select an arc: pick at the bottom arc
Select **MAIN MENU → Delete**
Select an entity or: pick at **P3**

The arc should appear in Figure 6.39.

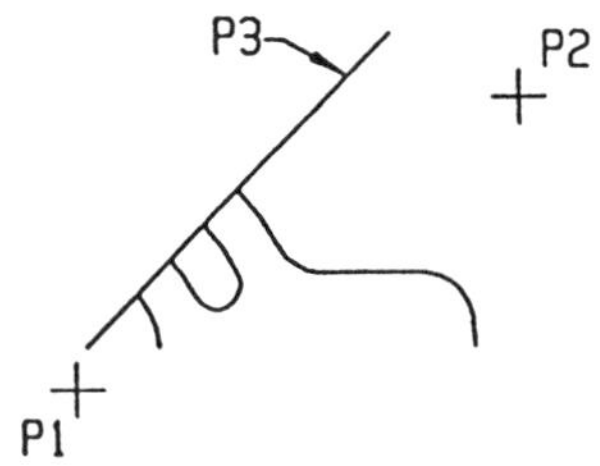

Figure 6.39

Step 8. Mirror about the 45° line. Use the pick points in Figure 6.39.

Select **MAIN MENU → Xform → Leave → Mirror → Window**
Select the first corner: pick at **P1**
Select the second corner: pick at **P2**
Select **Done → Line**
Select line about which to mirror: pick at **P3**
Select **Copy → Done**

The mirrored drawing should look like Figure 6.40.

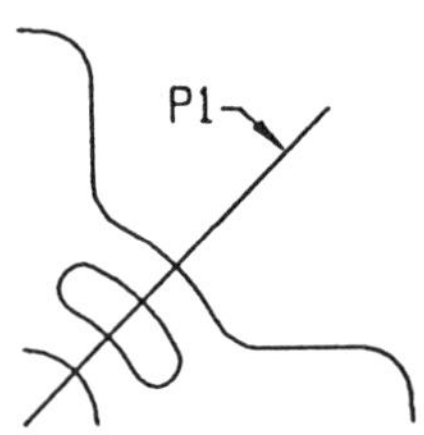

Figure 6.40

Step 9. Delete the 45° line using the pick point in Figure 6.40.

Select **MAIN MENU → Delete**
Select an entity or: pick at **P1**

The new drawing becomes Figure 6.41.

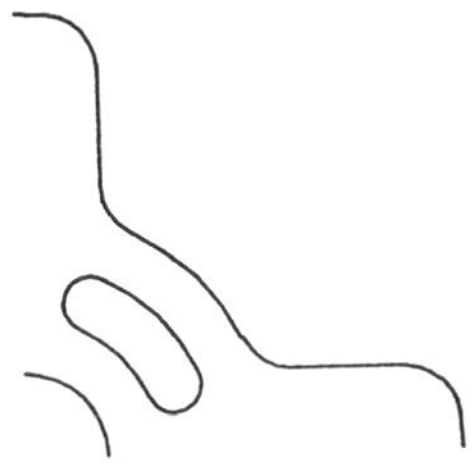

Figure 6.41

Step 10. Mirror all entities twice. The first time about the Y axis and second time about the X axis.
Select **MAIN MENU → Xform → Mirror → All → Entities →Done → Y axis → Copy → Done → All → Entities → Done → X axis → Copy → Done**

The final drawing should resemble Figure 6.42.

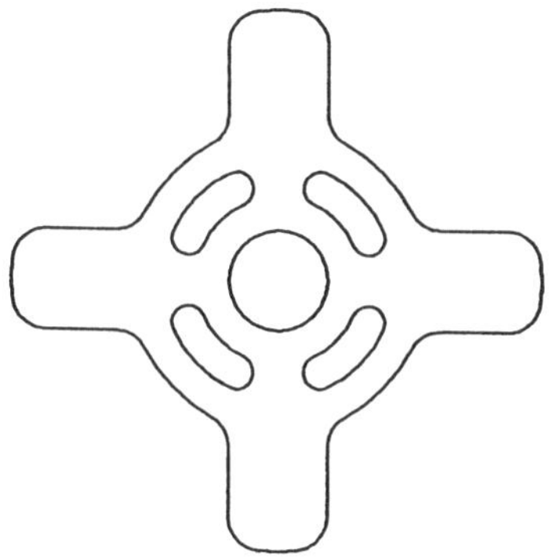

Figure 6.42

Step 11. Save to a file.
Select **MAIN MENU → File → Save**
Enter file name: **rotate1**

Project 5.

Mirroring

Create a part geometry as shown in Figure 6.43. Save the file as **pocket2**. This file is used in project 6 of chapter 7 to generate a set of toolpaths for pocketing the internal profile with an island.

5

We are here

Part Geometry Creation

(Pocket2)

Go to

Toolpath Generation

Project 6 of Chapter 7

(Pocket2)

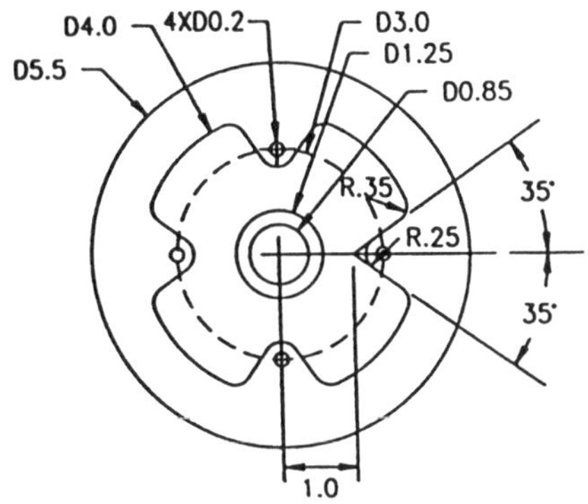

Figure 6.43

⌛**Tips** 1. Create a basic (partial) profile. This basic profile is then mirrored about a 45° line from the +X axis to form a quarter profile.
2. Mirror the quarter profile twice, first with the Y axis and then with the X axis.

3. Create the remaining seven circles.

Step 1. Create a circle.

Select **MAIN MENU → Create → Arc → pt Dia cir**
Enter the center point: **0,0 ←**
Enter the diameter: **4 ←**

Step 2. Create two lines for fillets and another two lines for trimming and mirroring.

Select **MAIN MENU → Create → Line → Polar**
Specify an endpoint: **1.0,0 ←**
Enter angle in degrees: **35 ←**
Enter the line length: **1.5 ←**
Specify an endpoint: **1.0,0 ←**
Enter angle in degrees: **-35 ←**
Enter the line length: **1.5 ←**
Specify an endpoint: **0,0 ←**
Enter angle in degrees: **45 ←**
Enter the line length: **3 ←**
Specify an endpoint: **0,0 ←**
Enter angle in degrees: **0 ←**
Enter the line length: **3 ←**

The drawing should look like Figure 6.44.

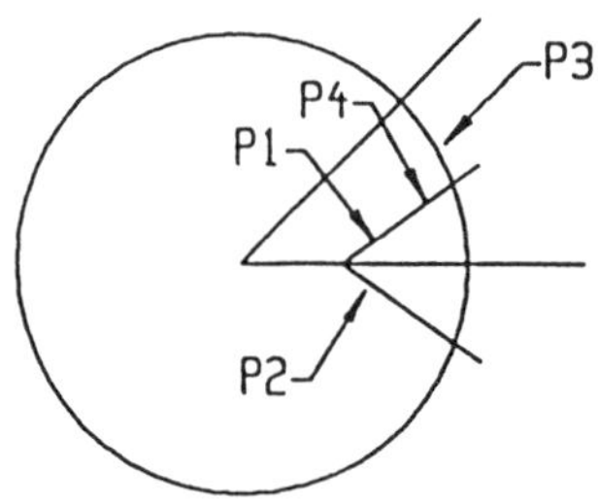

Figure 6.44

Step 3. Create two fillets. Use the pick points in Figure 6.44.

Select **MAIN MENU → Create → Fillet → Radius**
Enter the fillet radius: **0.25 ←**
Select an entity: pick at **P1**
Select another entity: pick at **P2**
Select **Radius**
Enter the fillet radius: **0.35 ←**
Select an entity: pick at **P3**
Select another entity: pick at **P4**

The new drawing appears as Figure 6.45.

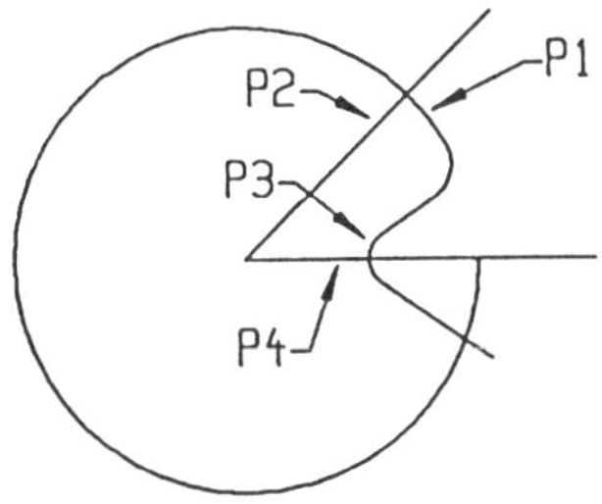

Figure 6.45

Step 4. Trim entities using the pick points in Figure 6.45 above.

Select **MAIN MENU → Modify → Trim → 1 entity**
Select the entity to trim: pick at **P1**
Select the entity to trim to: pick at **P2**
Select the entity to trim: pick at **P3**
Select the entity to trim to: pick at **P4**

The trimmed geometry appears as Figure 6.46.

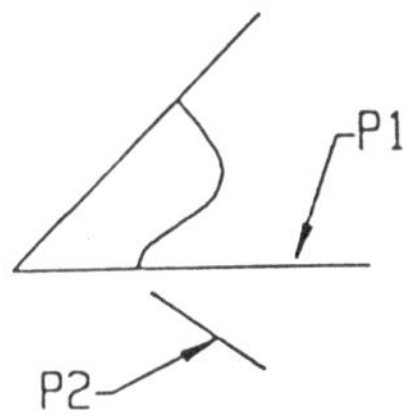

Figure 6.46

Step 5. Delete two construction entities using the pick points in Figure 6.46.

Select **MAIN MENU → Delete**
Select an entity: pick at **P1**
Select an entity: pick at **P2**

New drawing with the basic profile should resemble Figure 6.47.

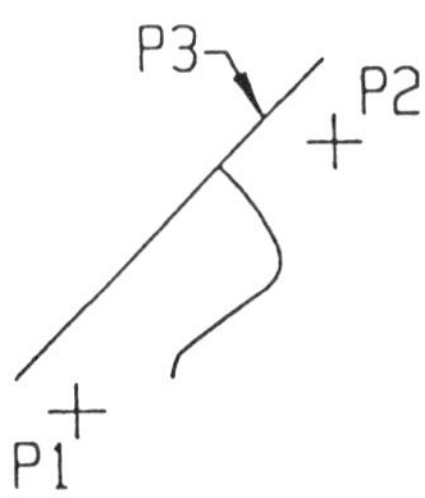

Figure 6.47

Step 6. Mirror the basic profile about the 45° line. Use the pick points marked in Figure 6.47 on the previous page.

Select **MAIN MENU → Xform → Mirror → Window**
Select the first corner: pick at **P1**
Select the second corner: pick at **P2**
Select **Done → Line**
Select line about which to mirror: pick at **P3**
Select Copy → Done

The new profile becomes as shown in Figure 6.48.

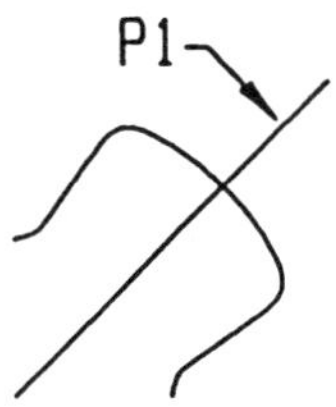

Figure 6.48

Step 7. Delete the 45° construction line using the pick point in Figure 6.48.

Select **MAIN MENU → Delete**
Select an entity or: pick at **P1**

The profile should resemble Figure 6.49.

Figure 6.49

Step 8. Mirror the profile twice.

Select **MAIN MENU → Xform → Mirror → All → Entities → Done → Y axis → Copy → Done →All → Entities → Done → X axis→Copy → Done**

The complete profile should look like Figure 6.50.

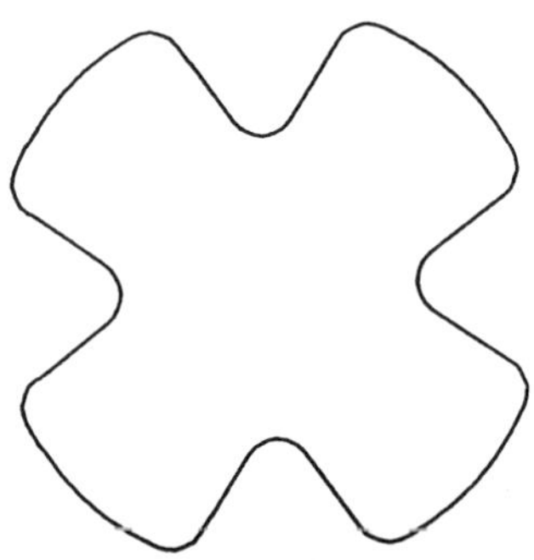

Figure 6.50

Step 9. Create the remaining seven circles.

Select **MAIN MENU → Create → Arc → pt Dia cir**
Enter the center point: **0,0** ←
Enter the diameter: **5.5** ←
Enter the center point: **0,0** ←
Enter the diameter: **1.25** ←
Enter the center point: **0,0** ←
Enter the diameter: **0.85** ←
Enter the center point: **1.5,0** ←
Enter the diameter: **0.2** ←
Enter the center point: **0,1.5** ←
Enter the diameter: **0.2** ←
Enter the center point: **-1.5,0** ←
Enter the diameter: **0.2** ←
Enter the center point: **0,-1.5** ←
Enter the diameter: **0.2** ←

The seven circles are added as in Figure 6.51.

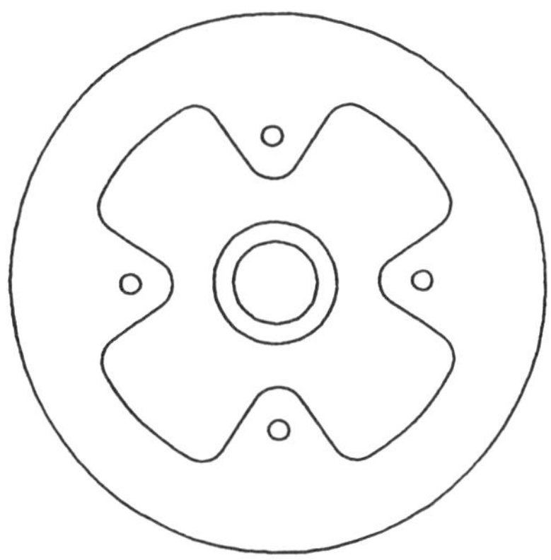

Figure 6.51

Step 10. Save to a file.

Select **MAIN MENU → File → Save**
Enter file name: **pocket2**

6.3.2 Rotate Function

The rotate function moves or copies existing entities by rotating about the origin or any given point. It is best suited to generating geometries for identical patterns or features that are symmetrical about a point.

Procedure: (Figure 6.52)

1. Entity selection option: pick at **P1**
2. Entity selection option: select **Done**
3. Rotate about: select **Point**

Origin - system origin or Construction origin. Point - for a specific point with a <position options>.

4. Enter the point to rotate about: Pick at **P2**
5. Select **Rotation angle** option in the dialogue box = **90** ←
   (Make sure the Number of steps =1.)
6. Select **Copy** → **Done**

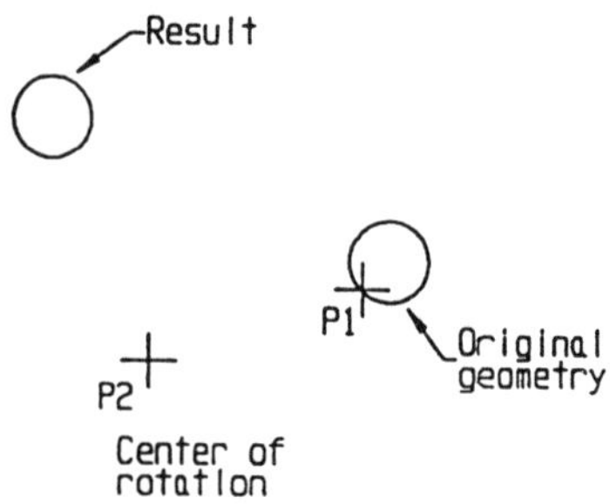

Figure 6.52: Rotating an entity about an existing point for 90-degree

Project 6.

Rotating

Create the geometry as shown in Figure 6.53a. Save the file as **mirror1**. This geometry file is used in project 2 of chapter 8 to generate the toolpaths to cut the four pockets shown in Figure 6.53b.

We are here

Part Geometry Creation

(Mirror1)

Go to

Toolpath Generation

Project 2 of Chapter 8

(Mirror1)

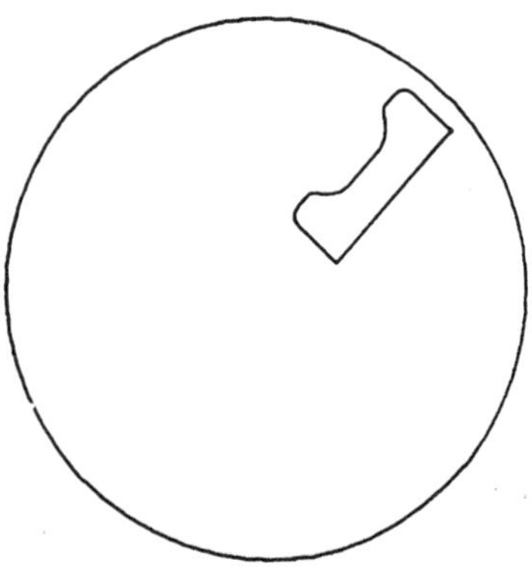

Figure 6.53a

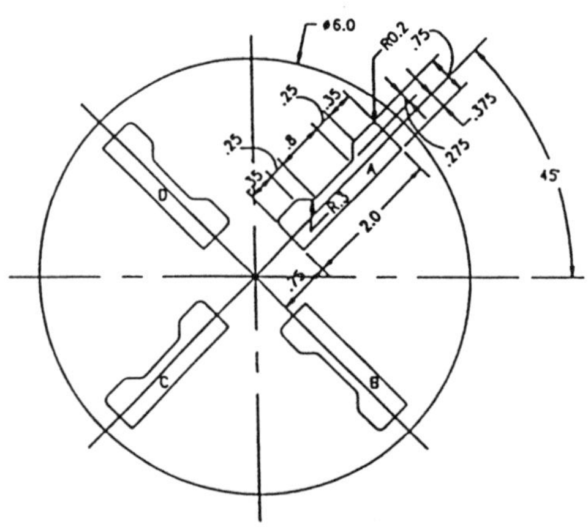

Figure 6.53b

Tips 1. Create the entities of the pocket profile in the +X direction. Then rotate them 45° in the counterclockwise direction.

2. Use the Multi line command to create the basic pocket profile consisting of eight lines. Their end coordinates are illustrated in Figure 6.54 .

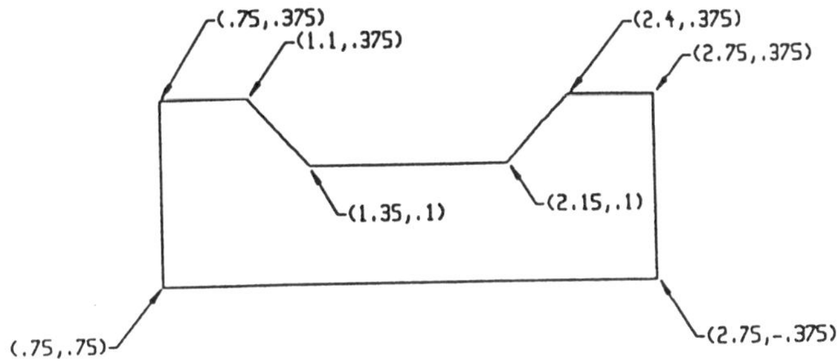

Figure 6.54

Step 1. Create eight lines

Select **MAIN MENU → Create → Line → Multi**
Specify endpoint 1: Enter **.75,-.375** ←
Specify endpoint 2: Enter **2.75,-.375** ←
Specify endpoint 3: Enter **2.75,.375** ←
Specify endpoint 4: Enter **2.4,.375** ←
Specify endpoint 5: Enter **2.15,.1** ←
Specify endpoint 6: Enter **1.35,.1** ←
Specify endpoint 7: Enter **1.1,.375** ←
Specify endpoint 8: Enter **.75,.375** ←
Specify endpoint 9: Enter **.75,-.375** ←

The basic pocket profile appears as Figure 6.55.

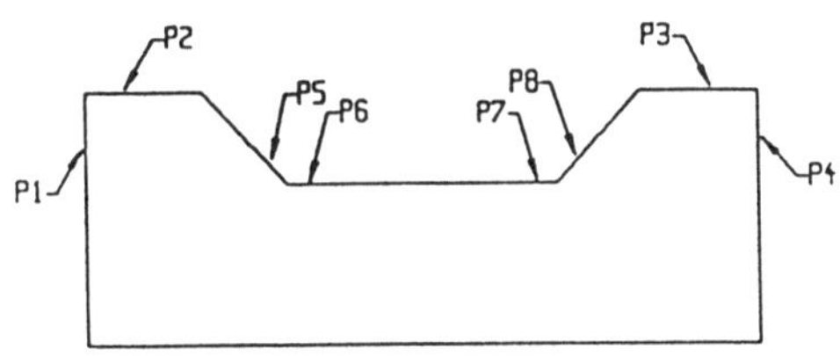

Figure 6.55

Step 2. Create four fillets using the pick points in Figure 6.55.

Select **MAIN MENU → Create → Fillet → Radius**
Enter the fillet radius: **0.15** ←

Note: Make sure the other two options are correct. The fillet angle is less than 180; trim to fillet.
Select an entity: Pick at **P1**
Select another entity: Pick at **P2**
Select an entity: Pick at **P3**
Select another entity: Pick at **P4**
Select **Radius**
Enter the fillet radius: **0.3** ←
Select an entity: Pick at **P5**
Select another entity: Pick at **P6**
Select an entity: Pick at **P7**
Select another entity: Pick at **P8**

The four fillets are added to the drawing as shown in Figure 6.56 below.

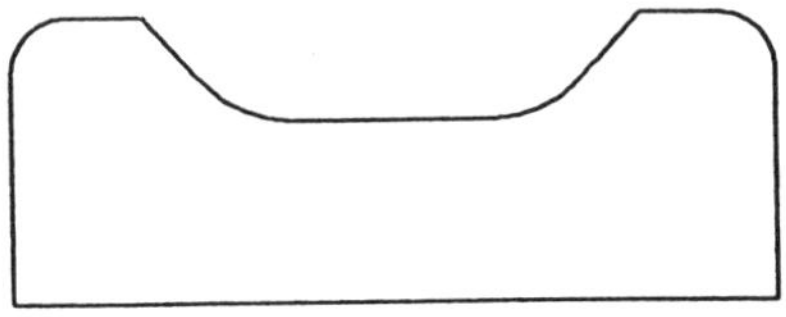

Figure 6.56

Step 3. Rotate the geometry for 45° in counterclockwise direction about the origin.

Select **MAIN MENU → Xform → Rotate → All → Entities → Done → Origin**
Select Rotation angle option in the dialog box: **45 ←**
(Make sure the Number of steps = 1)
Select **Move →Done**

The rotated geometry entities are shown in Figure 6.57.

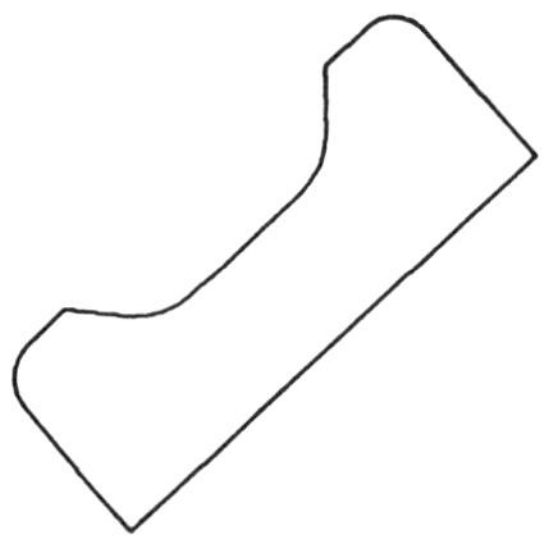

Figure 6.57

Step 4. Create an outside circle.

Select **MAIN MENU → Create → Arc → pt Dia cir**
Enter the center point: **0,0** ←
Enter the diameter: **6** ←

The complete drawing should resemble Figure 6.58.

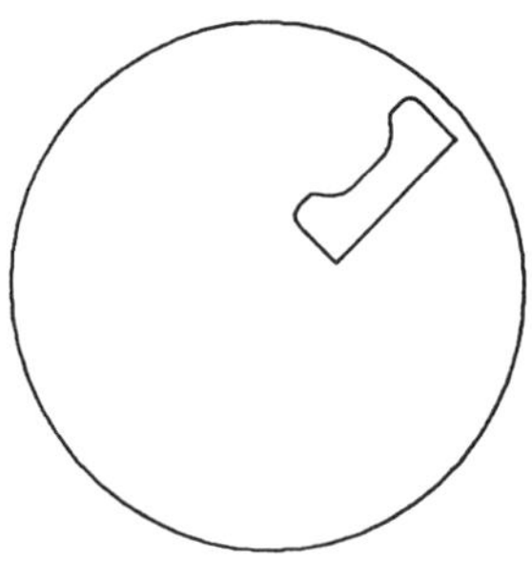

Figure 6.58

Step 5. Save to a file.

Select **MAIN MENU → File → Save**
Enter file name: **mirror1**

Project 7.

We are here

Part Geometry Creation
(Trans1)

Go to

Toolpath Generation
Project 5 of Chapter 8 (Trans1)

Rotating

Use the basic create commands and the rotate function to create a geometry as shown in Figure 6.59a. The file is saved as **trans1**. This file is used in project 5 of chapter 8 to generate a set of toolpaths for producing three pockets as shown in figure 6.59b.

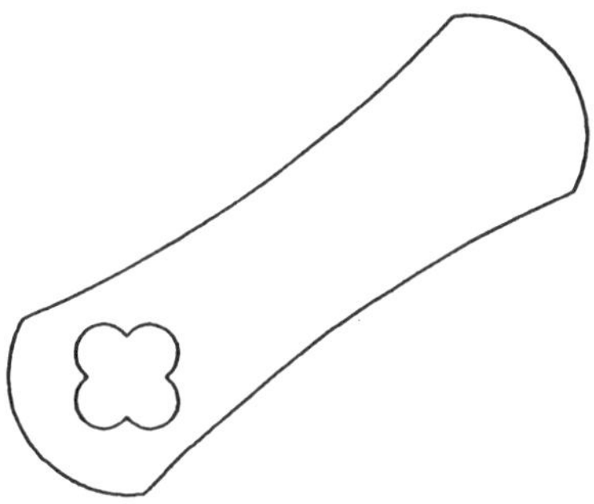

Figure 6.59a

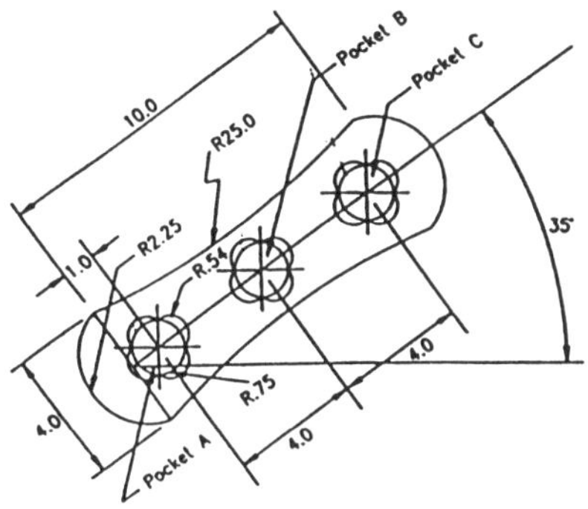

Figure 6.59b

Tips

1. Create the outer curved profile in the X direction. This profile is then rotated 35° in the counterclockwise direction to its desired location.
2. Create a consturction circle and two construction lines to create an arc. This arc is then rotated by 90° to three other locations.

Step 1. Create a construction rectangle.

Select **MAIN MENU → Create → Rectangle → 2 points**
Enter the lower left corner: **0,-2** ←
Enter the upper right corner: **10,2** ←

Note: Press Alt-F1 (Fit) to see the whole geometry

The rectangle should appear as Figure 6.60.

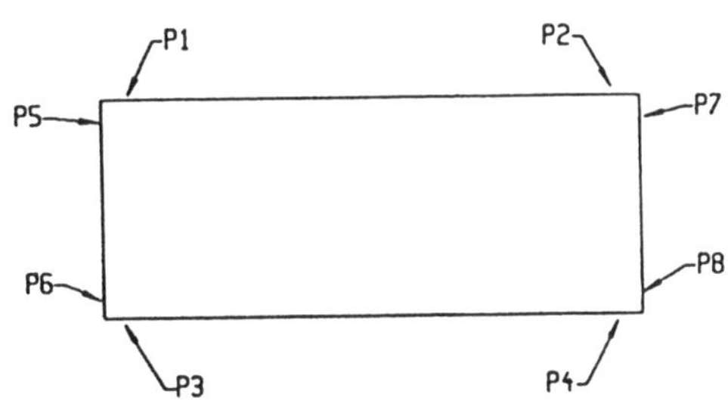

Figure 6.60

Step 2. Create four arcs using the pick points in Figure 6.60.

Select **MAIN MENU → Create → Arc → Endpoints → Endpoint**
Enter the first point: Pick at **P1**
Enter the second point: Pick at **P2**
Enter the radius: **25** ←
Select an arc: Pick at the correct arc *Note:* there are four choices

Step 2, continued.

Enter the first point: Pick at **P3**
Enter the second point: Pick at **P4**
Enter the radius: **25** ←
Select an arc: Pick at the correct arc
Enter the first point: Pick at **P5**
Enter the second point: Pick at **P6**
Enter the radius: **2.25** ←
Select an arc: Pick at the correct arc
Enter the first point: Pick at **P7**
Enter the second point: Pick at **P8**
Enter the radius: **2.25** ←
Select an arc: Pick at the correct arc

The four arcs are added as in Figure 6.61.

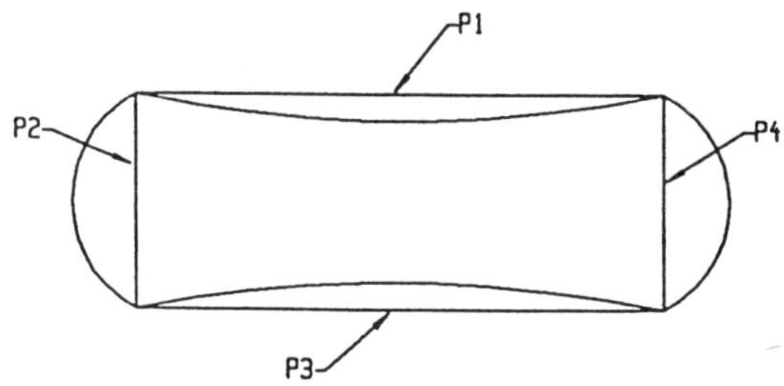

Figure 6.61

Step 3. Delete the rectangle using the pick points in Figure 6.61.

Select **MAIN MENU** → **Delete**
Select an entity or: pick at **P1**
Select an entity or: pick at **P2**
Select an entity or: pick at **P3**
Select an entity or: pick at **P4**

The outer profile should look like Figure 6.62.

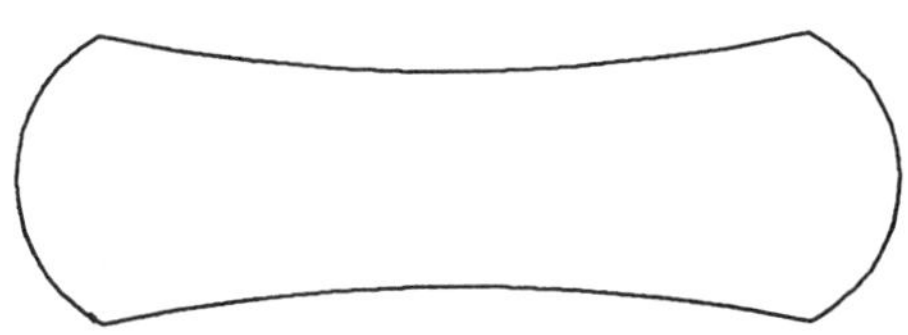

Figure 6.62

Step 4. Create a construction circle.

Select **MAIN MENU** → **Create** → **Arc** → **pt Rad cir**
Enter the center point: **1,0** ←
Enter the radius: **.75** ←

The circle is added as in Figure 6.63.

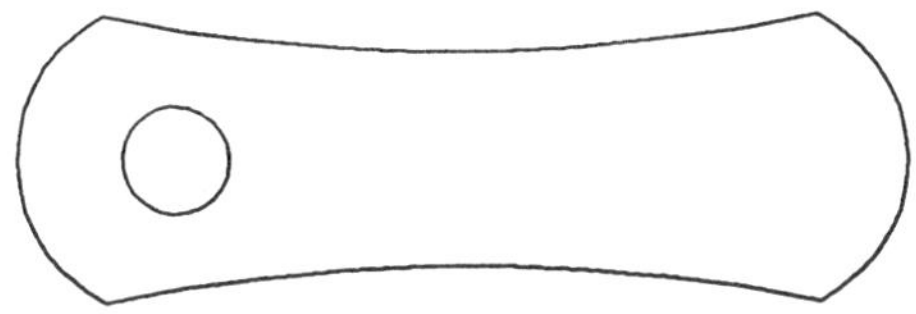

Figure 6.63

Step 5. Rotate all entities for 35° in the counterclockwise direction.

Select **MAIN MENU → Xform → Rotate → All → Entities → Done → Point**
Enter the point to rotate about: **1,0** ←
Select the Rotation angle option in the dialog box= **35** ←
(Make sure the Number of steps = 1)
Select **Move →Done**

The rotated geometry becomes Figure 6.64.

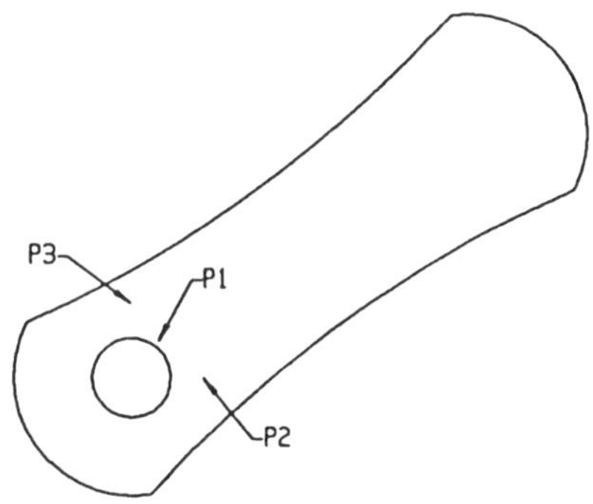

Figure 6.64

Step 6. Create two construction lines. Use the pick points in Figure 6.64.

Select **MAIN MENU → Create → Line → Horizontal → Center**
Specify the first endpoint: pick at **P1**
Select **sKetch**
Specify the second endpoint: pick at **P2**
Enter the Y coordinate: 0 ←
Select **BACKUP → Vertical → Center**
Specify the first endpoint: Pick at **P1**
Select **sKetch**
Specify the second endpoint: Pick at **P3**
Enter the X coordinate: 1 ←

The two lines are added as in Figure 6.65.

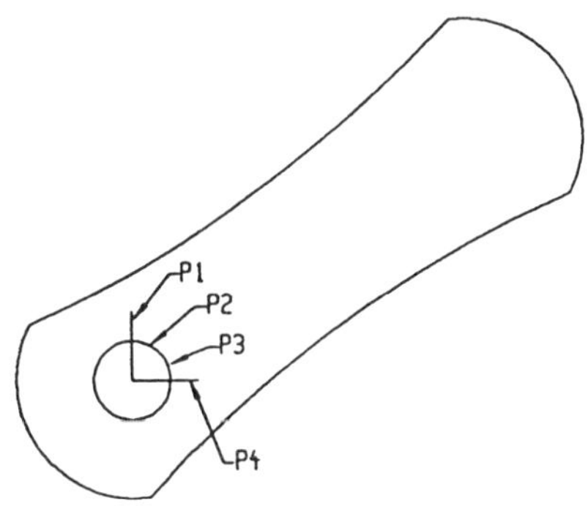

Figure 6.65

Step 7. Create an arc using the pick points in Figure 6.65 on the previous page.

Select **MAIN MENU → Create → Arc → Endpoints → Intersec**
Enter the first point: pick at **P1**
Enter the first point: pick at **P2**
Enter the second point: pick at **P3**
Enter the second point: pick at **P4**
Enter the radius: **.54** ←
Select an arc: Pick at the outside one on the upper-right corner
Note: there are four choices

The arc is added as in Figure 6.66.

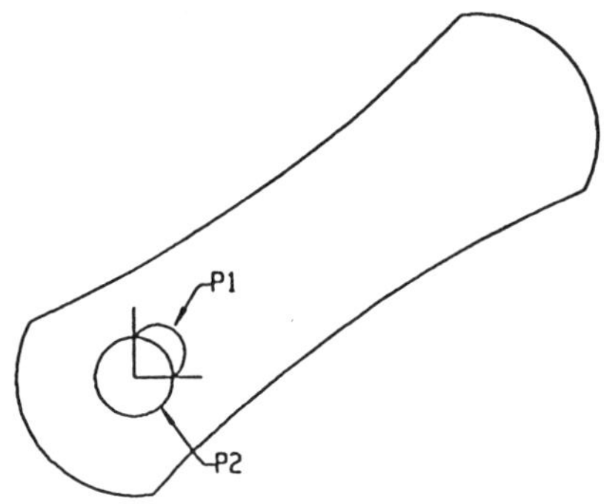

Figure 6.66

Step 8. Rotate the arc by 90° to other three locations. Use the pick points in Figure 6.66.

Select **MAIN MENU → Xform → Rotate → Entity**
Pick at **P1** to select the arc to be rotated
Select **BACKUP → Done → Point → Center**
Pick at **P2**
Select Rotation angle option in the dialog box = **90** ←
Select the Number of steps option in the dialog box = **3** ←
Select **Copy → Done**

Three arcs are added as shown in Figure 6.67.

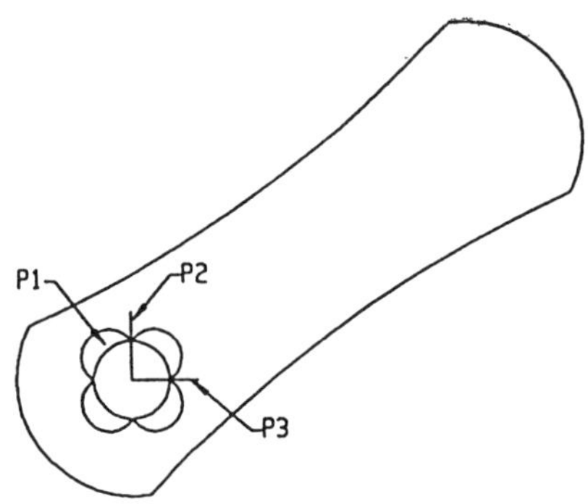

Figure 6.67

Step 9. Delete a construction circle and two construction lines. Use the pick points in Figure 6.67.

Select **MAIN MENU → Delete**
Select an entity or: pick at **P1**
Select an entity or: pick at **P2**
Select an entity or: pick at **P3**

The final drawing should look like Figure 6.68.

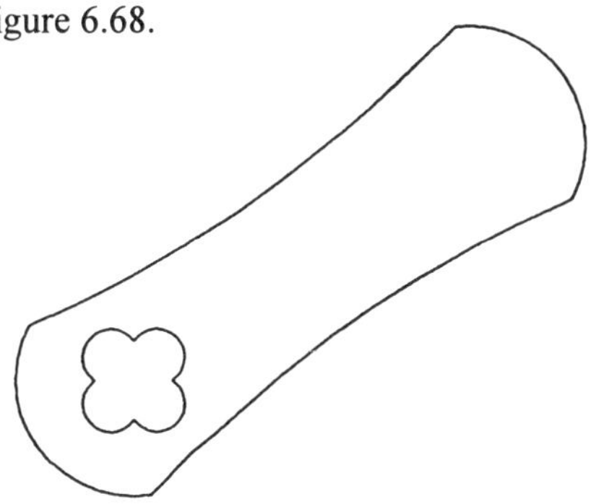

Figure 6.68

Step 10. Save to a file.

Select **MAIN MENU → File → Save**
Enter file name: **trans1**

Project 8.

Rotating

Create 24 circles and 24 points at their centers (Figure 6.69). Three construction circles are added to show their positions. Save the file as **drill1**. This file will be used to generate the drilling toolpaths in project 7 of chapter 7.

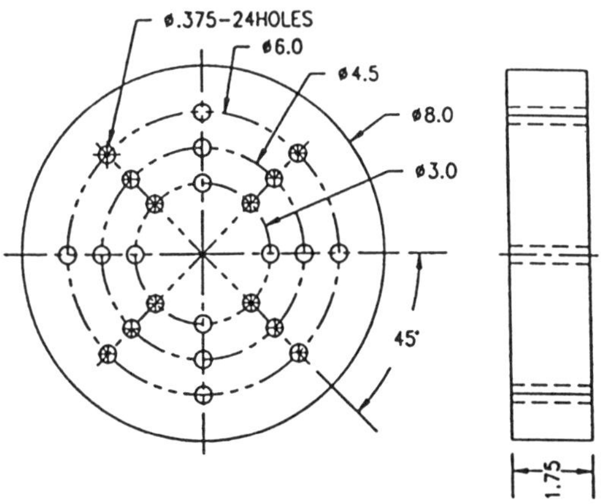

Figure 6.69

Tips 1. Create 3 circles and three points at their centers in the X axis.

2. Rotate these 3 circles and 3 points by 45° to the other 7 locations.

3. Construct three construction circles. Set the line type to hidden.

Step 1. Create three circles.

Select **MAIN MENU → Create → Arc → pt Dia cir**
Enter the center point: **1.5,0** ←
Enter the diameter: **0.375** ←
Enter the center point: **2.25,0** ←
Enter the diameter: **0.375** ←
Enter the center point: **3,0** ←
Enter the diameter: **0.375** ←

8

We are here

Part Geometry Creation

(Drill 1)

Go to

Toolpath Generation

Project 7 of Chapter 7

(Drill 1)

Three arcs appear as in figure 6.70.

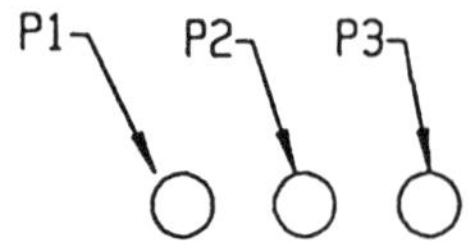

Figure 6.70

Step 2. Create points at the center of the circles using the pick points in Figure 6.70.

Select **MAIN MENU → Create → Point → Position → Center**
Pick at **P1, P2,** and **P3** to define three points

Three points are added as in Figure 6.71.

Figure 6.71

Step 3. Rotate these six entities 45° about the origin, seven times.

Select **MAIN MENU → Xform → Rotate → All → Entities → Done → Origin**
Enter the rotation angle in degrees: **45** ←
In the pop-up dialog box:

Number of steps: **7**
Rotation angle: **45**

Select **Copy → Done**

Twenty-four circles are created as shown in Figure 6.72.

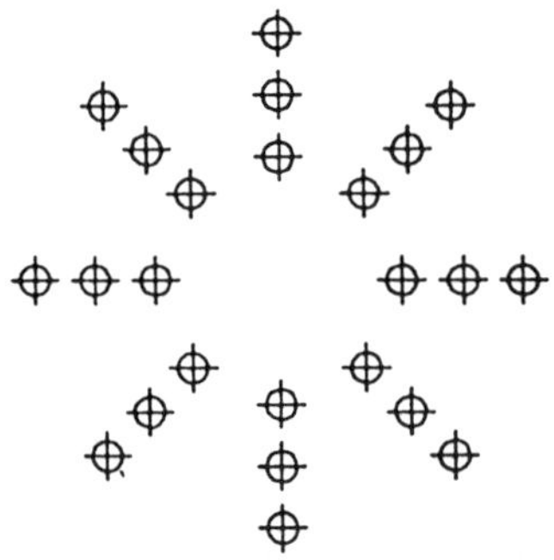

Figure 6.72

Step 4. Create three construction circles.

Select **PM** from the left Menu
Select the line style parameter to **hidden**
Select **Done** to complete the setting
Select **MAIN MENU →Create → Arc → pt Dia cir**
Enter the center point: **0,0** ←
Enter the diameter: **3** ←
Enter the center point: **0,0** ←
Enter the diameter: **4.5** ←
Enter the center point: **0,0** ←
Enter the diameter: **6.0** ←

The final drawing should resemble Figure 6.73.

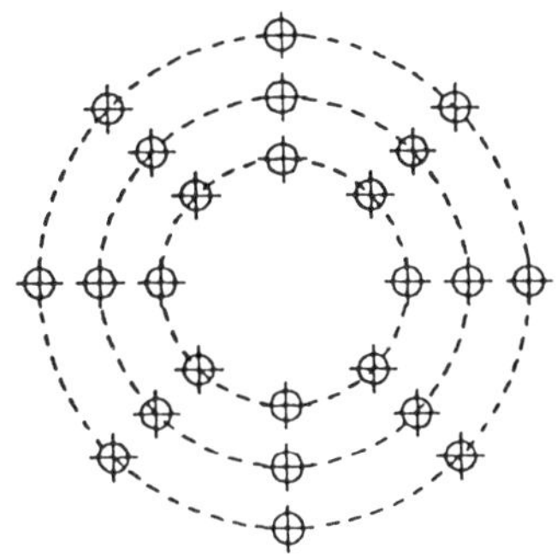

Figure 6.73

Step 5. Save to a file.

Select **MAIN MENU → File → Save**
Enter file name: **drill1**

6.3.3 Scale Function

The scale function increases or decreases the sizes of geometry entities by a specified scale factor. Two important factors to be determined in scaling are the scaling center and the scaling factor. The scaling center is the point from which the scaling of the geometric entity starts. The scaling factor determines the size.

Scaling factor > 1	enlarges the entity size
Scaling factor = 1	sizes do not change
Scaling factor < 1	reduces the entity size

Procedure: (Figure 6.74)

1. Entity selection option (see section 6.3): Pick at **P1**
2. Entity selection option: Select **Done**
3. Scale about: Select **Point**

Origin - system origin or Construction origin. Point - for a specific point with a <position options>.

4. Enter the point for scaling: Pick at **P2**
5. Adjust the parameters in the pop-up dialog box:

Number of steps = 1 Scale factor = 2.0

6. Select **Copy → Done**

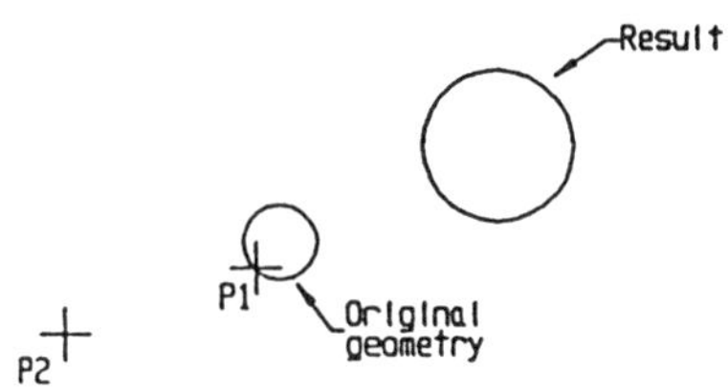

Figure 6.74: Scaling an entity about an existing point for a factor of 2

6.3.4 ScaleXyz Function

The scaleXyz is the other scale function and is similar to the Scale discussed in section 6.3.3. It gives the user an opportunity to specify the x, y and z scale factors individually. By adjusting the scale factors properly, it is possible to transform a circle into an ellipse.

Procedure: (Figure 6.75)
1. Select entities to scale <entity selection options>: Pick at **P1**
2. Select **Done → Point → Center**
3. Enter the point to scale about: Pick at **P1**
4. In the dialog box:

X scale factor: **0.5**
Y scale factor: **2.0**
Z scale factor: **1.0**

5. Select **Move → Done**
6. Press <Enter> to continue: ←

Note: The original circle was converted to a NURBS curve.

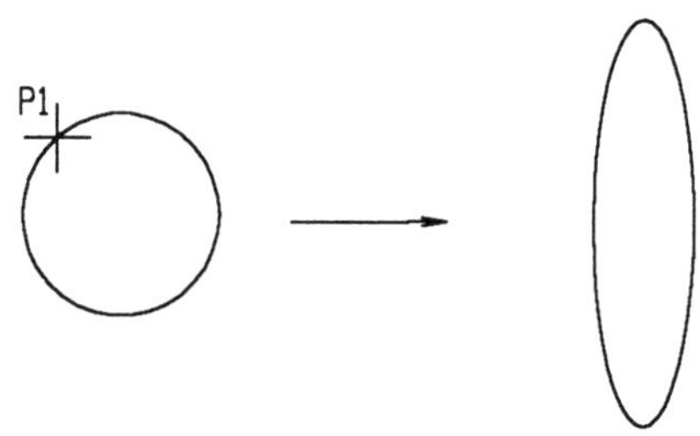

Figure 6.75

6.3.5 Translate Function

The translate function moves or copies the selected geometric entities to new locations. You might need to adjust **Delete** or **Leave** option in the Xform menu.

Procedure: (Figure 6.76 on the next page)
1. Entity selection option (see section 6.3): Pick at **P1**
2. Entity selection option: Select **Done**
3. Translate: Refer to Figure 6.71 to select **an appropriate method**

Rectang -	enters a rectangular (Cartesian) coordinate vector for the X and Y translation.
Polar -	enters a polar coordinate vector for the translation.
Btween pts -	selects the beginning and ending points for the translation.
btween Vws -	translates the entities between viewport.

For Rectang
4. Enter the translation vector: **1,0.5** ←

For Polar
4. Enter the translation distance: **1.5** ←
5. Enter the translation angle: **30** ←

For Btween pts
4. Enter the point to translate from <position option>: Pick at **P2**
5. Enter the point to translate to <position option>: Pick at **P3**
6. In the pop-up dialog box:

Number of steps = **1** Select **Copy →Done**

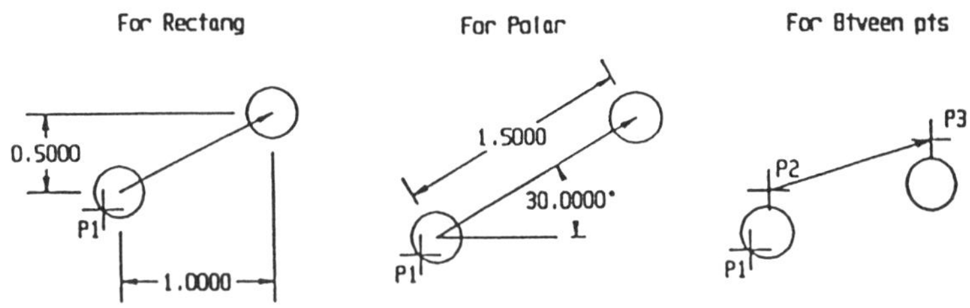

Figure 6.76: Translating using different methods

Project 9.

Translating

Copy the inside pocket contour of the drawing shown in Figure 6.77a to two locations by using the **Translate → Rectang** commands. The file for Figure 6.77a is **array1** which is created in project 1 of this chapter. The complete part geometry is shown in Figure 6.77b.

9

Part Geometry Creation
(Array 1)

We are here

Geometry Translation

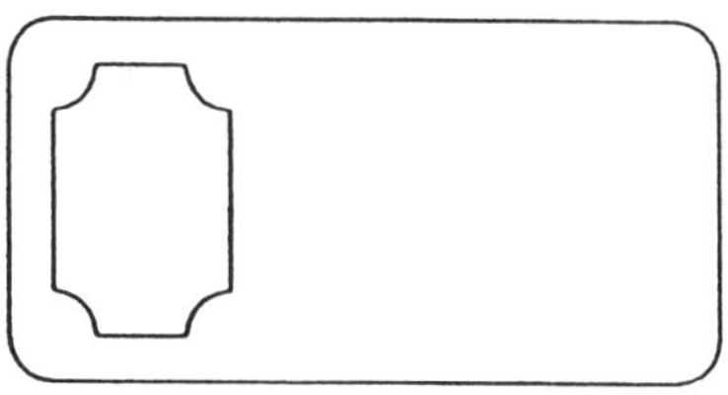

Figure 6.77a

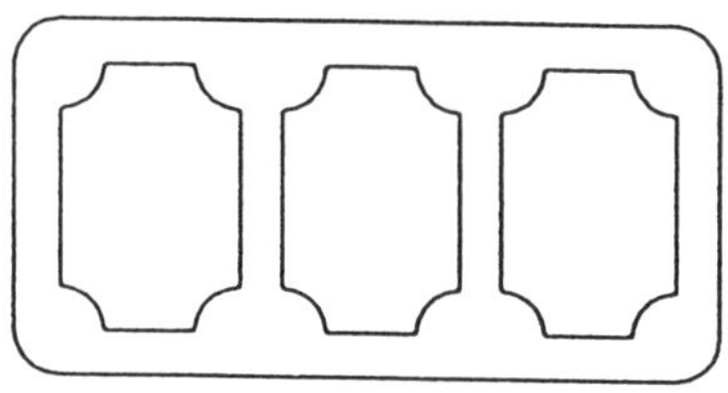

Figure 6.77b

Tips 1. Use the file array1 which is created in project 1 of this chapter.

2. Use Xform → Translate → Rectang commands to copy the pocket profile.

3. Set the number of steps to 2.

Step 1. Load the geometry file array1.

Select **MAIN MENU → File → Get**
Enter file name: **array1**
Select **Yes** to delete the current part
The part geometry should appear as Figure 6.78 on the next page.

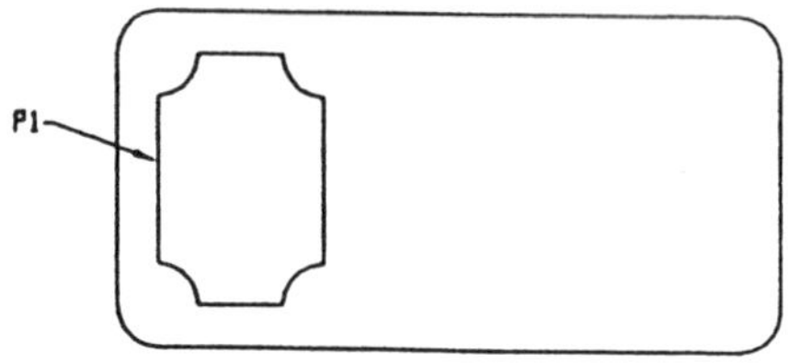

Figure 6.78

Step 2. Initiate the Translate command.

Select **MAIN MENU → Xform →Translate → Chain**

Step 3. Define the contour using the pick point in Figure 6.78.

Pick at **P1**
Select **Close → End here → Done**

Step 4. Define Translate parameters.

Select **Rectang**
Enter the translation vector: **X3.75** ←
In the pop-up dialog box:

> Set the Number of steps = **2**
> Select **Copy →Done**

The two translated profiles are shown in Figure 6.79.

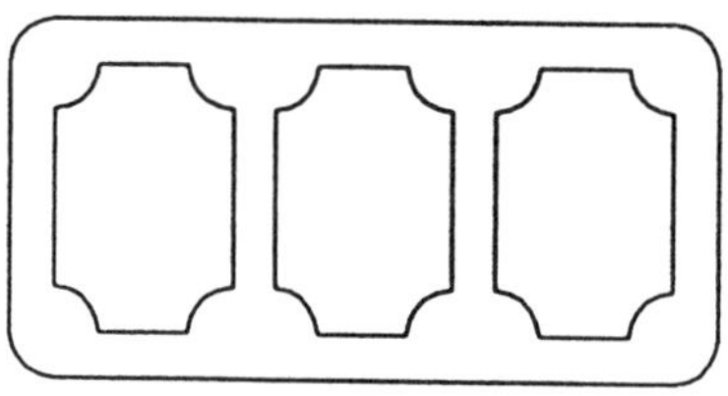

Figure 6.79

6.3.6 Offset Function

The offset function moves or copies a line or arc away from itself in a perpendicular direction with an offset distance to the line or arc. *Note:* this function only works for line or arc entities.

Procedure: (Figure 6.80)

1. In the pop-up dialog box:

> Number of steps = **1**
> Offset distance (def val): **0.5** ←
> Select **Copy → Done**

2. Select the line or arc to offset: Pick at **P1**
3. Indicate the offset direction: Pick at **P2**

Note: In general, there are two perpendicular directions. Indicate the appropriate direction using the mouse.

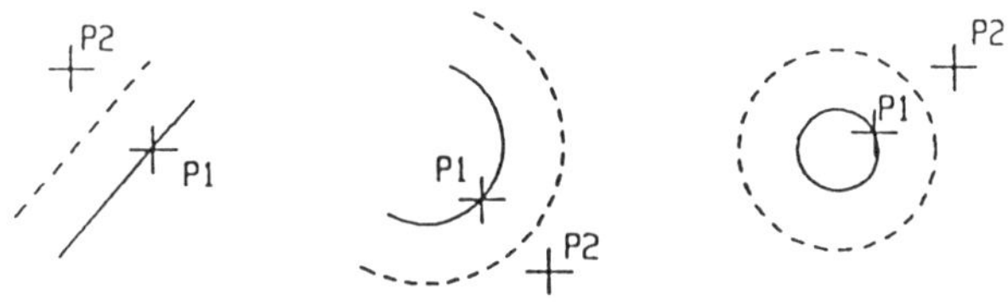

Figure 6.80

6.3.7 ofs Ctour Function

This option allows the user to offset several connected lines or arcs by chaining the entities. The process is similar to the toolpath contour function. This function will offset only lines and arcs.

Procedure: (Figure 6.81)

1. Chaining method: Select **Chain**
2. Select the first entity in the contour: Pick at **P1**
3. Select **Close → End here → Done**
4. In the dialog box:

Offset distance: **0.5**
Corners: **None**
Side: **Right**
Select **Done**

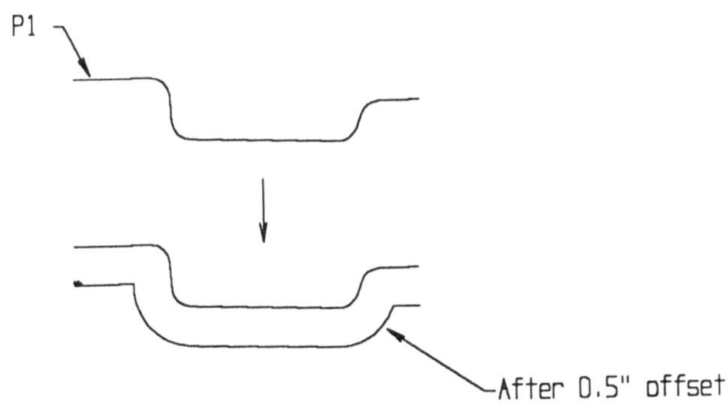

Figure 6.81

Group Parameter

Group selects and defines a collection of entities to be used in Xform. The last Group is saved in the database and can be used in other Xform functions such as Mirror, Rotate, Scale, scaleXyz and Translate. Note that Offset can not take advantage of Group since it only works with line or arc.

When **Group** is selected, these Group Entity Selection Options appear on the Main Menu Area:

New -	clears the existing groups.
Entities -	adds or deletes a single entity to or from the database.
Chain -	adds or deletes a group of entities to or from the database.
Only -	adds or deletes a specific type of entities to or from the database.
All -	adds or deletes all entities of a specific type to or from the database.
Results -	shows the current selected group in Magenta.
Window -	selects all the entities that are inside the window to or from the database.
Intr wndw -	selects all the entities that are either inside or intersect with the window to or from the database.
UnGroup (Y/N) -	toggles the system to group (add) or ungroup (delete) the selected entities for previous operations.

You can combine different methods to select the entities for the group, then select **Backup** to exit and save the database.

6.4 Exercises

1. What does the delete function do?
2. What does the undelete function do?
3. What does the trim function do?
4. Describe the difference between the following three trim commands:
   1 entity
   2 entities
   3 entities
5. Describe what the break function does?
6. Describe what the join function does?
7. List the five editing functions under the Xform command.
8. List the five transformation parameters and describe what they are.
9. When should you use the mirror function?
10. When should you use rotate function?

11. Explain how to use the scale function to increase or decrease the size of geometry entities.

12. When should you use the translate function.

13. When should you use the offset function.

14. Create the geometry shown in Figure 6.82. Save the file as **contour5**. This file is used in problem 63 of chapter 7.

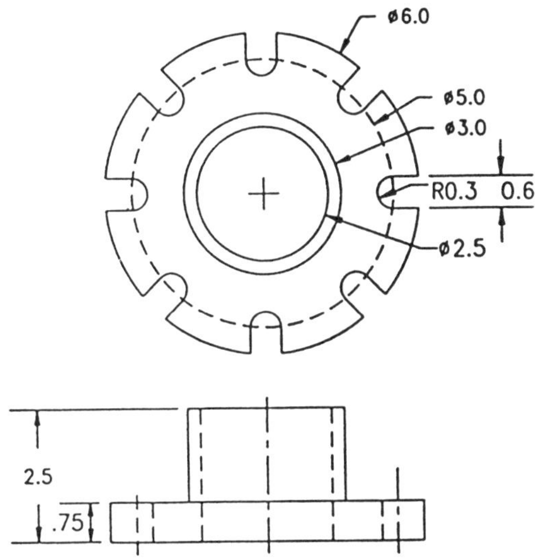

Figure 6.82

15. Create the geometry shown in Figure 6.83 and save the file as **contour6**. This file is used to generate the toolpath in problem 64 of chapter 7.

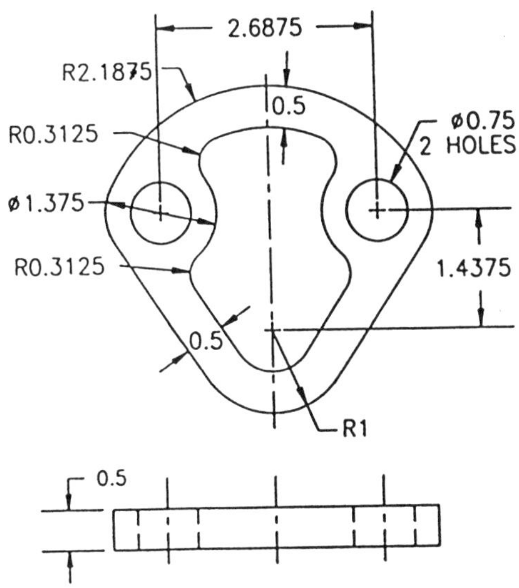

Figure 6.83

16. Create the part geometry as shown in Figure 6.84. Save the file as **contour7**. This part geometry is used to generate the toolpath for problem 65 in chapter 7.

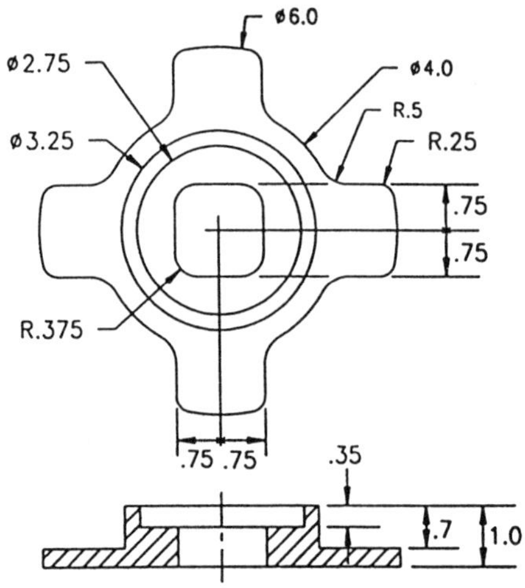

Figure 6.84

17. Create the part geometry for Figure 6.85. Save the geometry file as **pocket3**. This geometry file is used to generate the pocketing toolpath for problem 68 in chapter 7.

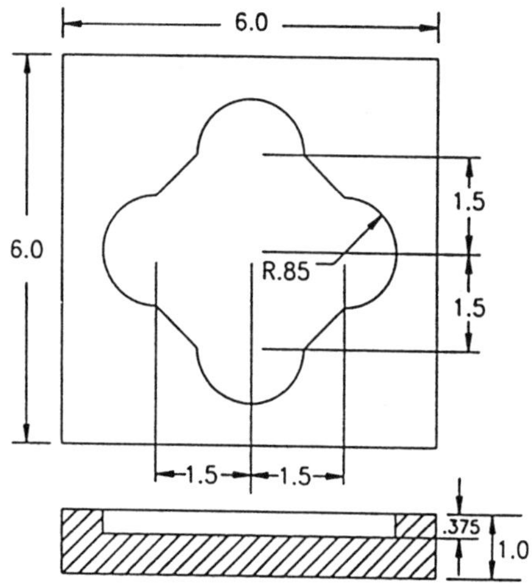

Figure 6.85

18. Create the geometry shown in Figure 6.86. Save the geometry as **pocket4**. This file is used to generate the pocketing toolpaths in problem 69 of chapter 7.

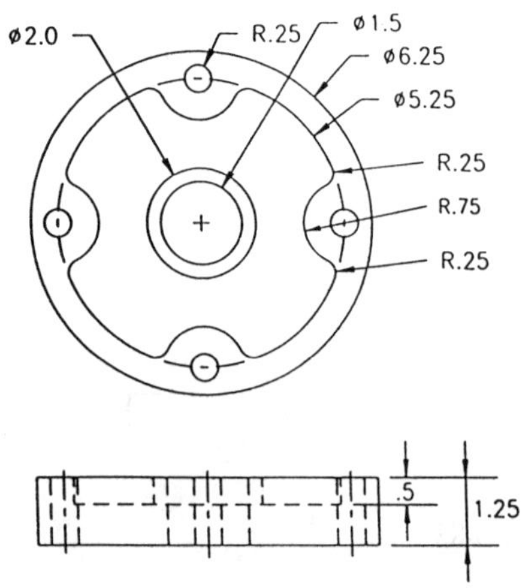

Figure 6.86

19. Create the part geometry as shown in Figure 6.87 and save the file as **pocket5**. This geometry will be used to generate the toolpath for pocketing with an island in problem 70 of chapter 7.

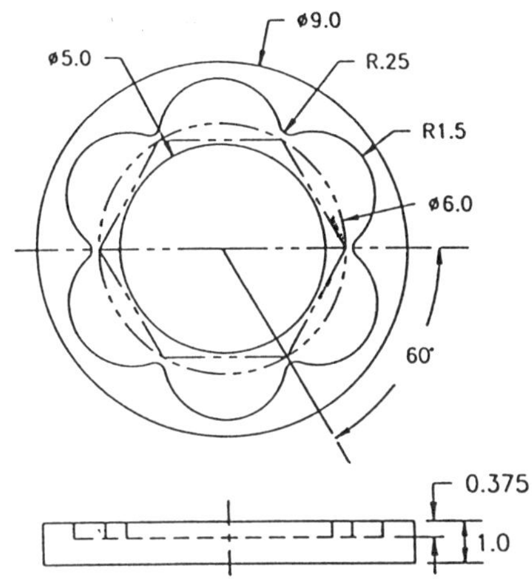

Figure 6.87

20. Create the part geometry shown in Figure 6.88. Save the file as **comb1**. This geometry will be used to generate the toolpaths for contouring, pocketing, and drilling in problem 72 of chapter 7.

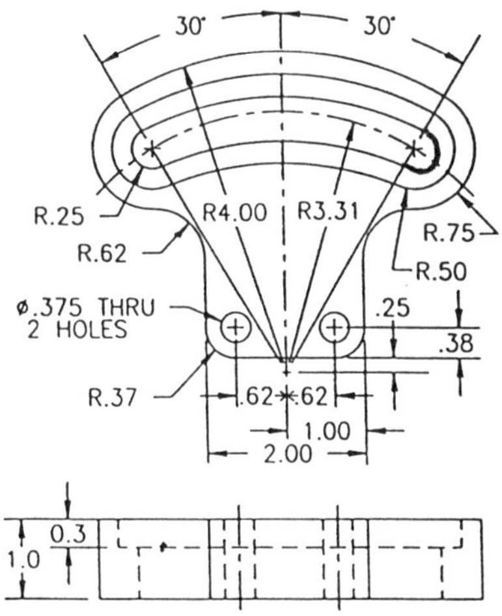

Figure 6.88

21. Create the part geometry shown in Figure 6.89 and save the file as **comb3**. The file is used to generate the toolpaths in problem 74 of chapter 7.

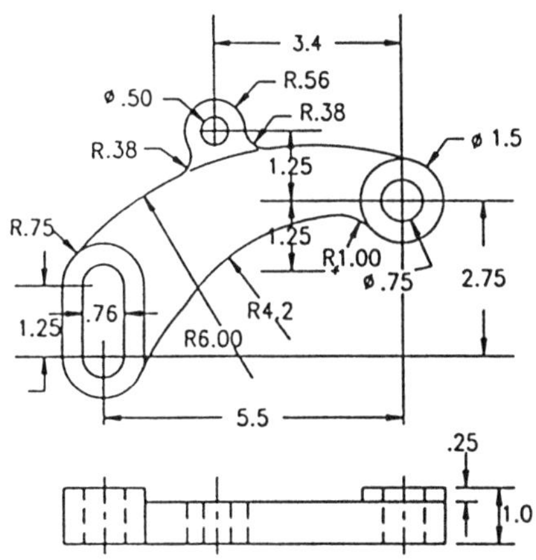

Figure 6.89

22. Create the geometry as shown in Figure 6.90 and save this file as **comb4**. This geometry is used to generate the toolpaths in problem 75 of chapter 7.

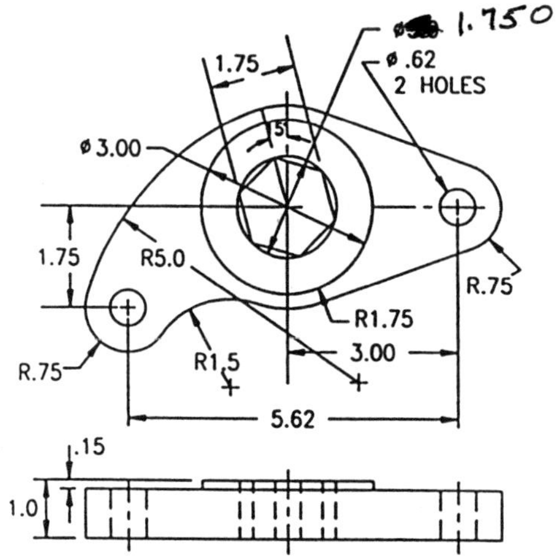

Figure 6.90

Tom #1

23. Create the part geometry shown in Figure 6.91 and save the file as **rotate2**. This geometry is used to generate the toolpaths in problem 16 of chapter 8.

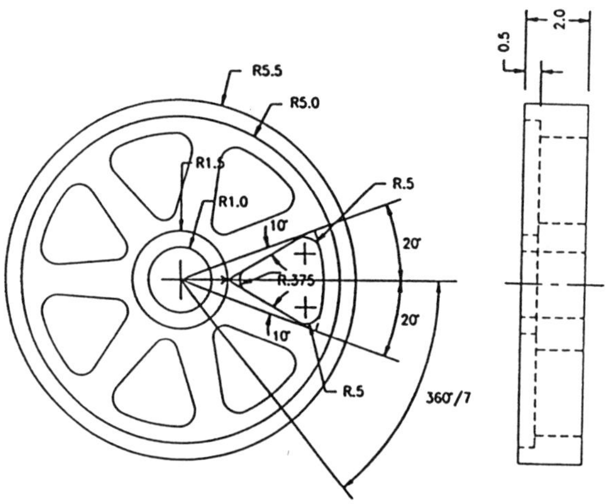

Figure 6.91

Tom #2

24. Create the part geometry shown in Figure 6.92 and save the file as **mirror2**. The file is used to generate a set of toolpaths to machine one part and then copy to machine another part by using the mirror function in problem 17 of chapter 8.

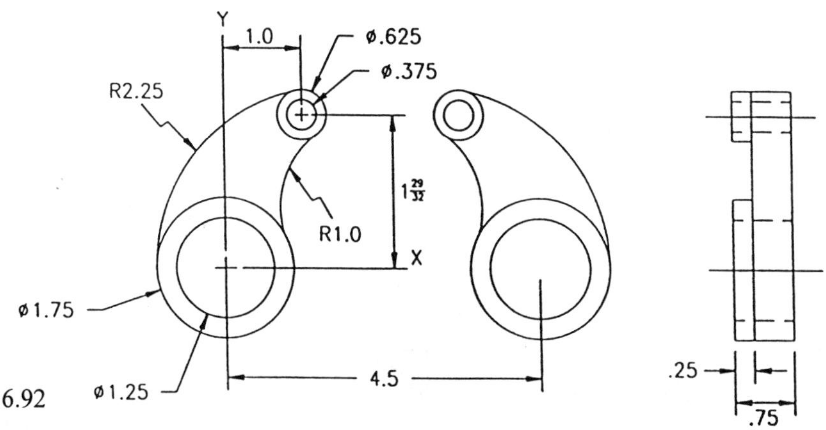

Figure 6.92

Tom #3

Chapter 7

2-D Toolpaths Generation From Print to Part

Objectives:

1. Identify four types of 2-D toolpath modules and know when to use them.
2. Define common parameters used in 2-D toolpath modules.
3. Apply four 2-D toolpath modules to generate NC programs for producing parts.

7.1 2-D Toolpath Modules

Mastercam provides **two groups** of toolpath modules for generating toolpaths: 2-D toolpath modules and 3-D toolpath modules. Use 2-D toolpath modules to generate toolpaths for machining workpieces in a 2-D plane, and 3-D toolpath modules for machining various forms of 3-D surfaces. This chapter presents 2-D toolpath modules. Mastercam has **four 2-D toolpath modules**: contour, pocket, drill, and letters. Table 7.1 summaries the features and applications of these.

Table 7.1 2-D Toolpath Modules

Module	Description	Application	Illustration
Contour	Generate the toolpaths along a series of geometric entities chained as a contour. Required geometry: lines and arcs	· Cutting external and internal part profiles	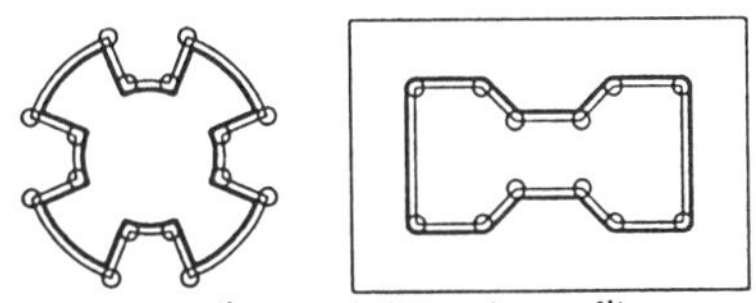 External profile; Internal profile
Pocket	Generate the toolpaths to remove the material enclosed by a closed contour. Required geometry: Closed boundary	· Cutting pockets · Facing large flat surfaces	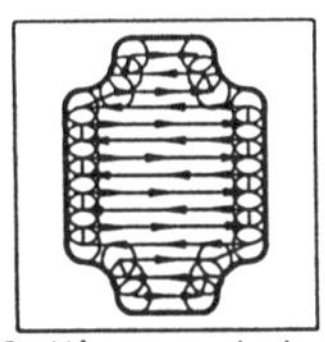 Cutting pockets; 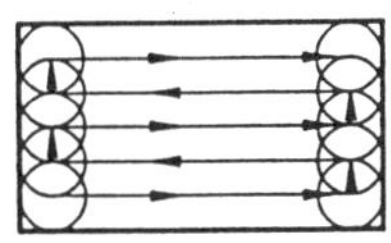 Facing
Drill	Generate the toolpaths to perform drilling, boring, or tapping holes. Required geometry: points	· Drilling · Boring · Tapping	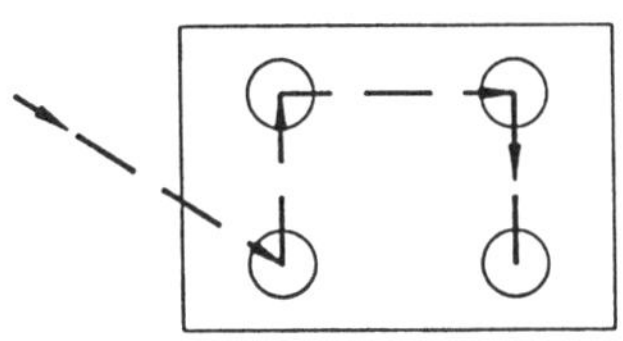
Letters	Generate the toolpaths to engrave a string of letters. Required geometry: letters, lines and arcs	· Engraving letters	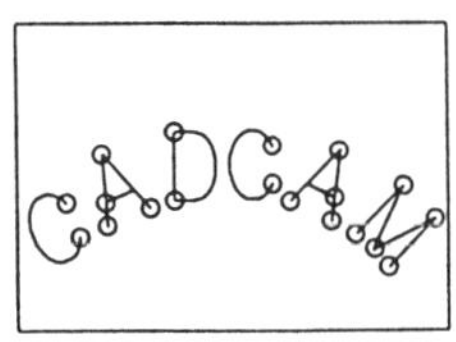

7.2 Common Parameters

Mastercam uses various types of parameters to define the information required to generate toolpaths. These parameters can be classified into **two groups**: common parameters and module specific parameters. As their names imply, common parameters are commonly used in all toolpath modules, while module specific parameters are unique to the particular module and are not applicable to any other modules. Common parameters referred to as NC parameters in Mastercam, can be classified into **six groups**:

- Cutter compensation
- Tooling information
- Machining parameters
- Coordinate settings
- Tool and toolpath display
- Others

Common parameters are listed below:

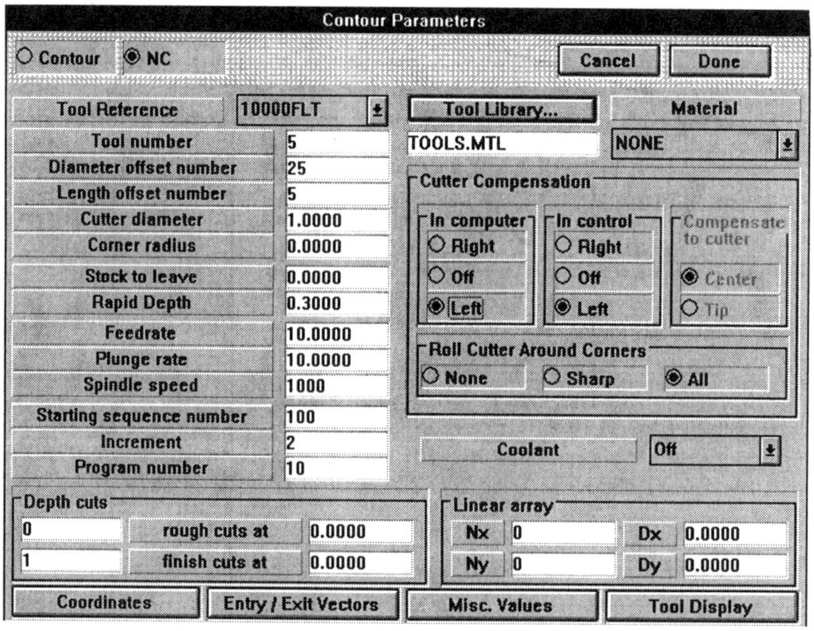

Cutter Compensation

Cutter compensation displaces the cutter center by a distance from the specified side of the programmed path. It is often referred to as cutter diameter compensation (CDC) or cutter radius compensation. It can be used in the following applications:

1. Allow the programmer to prepare the required tool path with reference to part coordinates directly.
2. Allow to use a cutter whose diameter differs from that specified by the part programmer without rewritting the program.
3. Compensate the variation in tool size due to wear, regrinding, or refurnishment.
4. Allow roughing and finishing cuts to be done with the same part program. Clearance or stock for the finishing cuts has to be set aside during the roughing cuts.

Cutter compensation parameters in Mastercam can be toggled to one of **three options**: tool left (CDC left), tool right (CDC right), and tool on (CDC off).

Tool left:	The cutting edge of the tool is offset to the left of the programmed path
Tool right:	The cutting edge of the tool is offset to the right of the programmed path
Tool on:	The cutter center is on the programmed path

Figure 7.1 shows the effect of these three commands on the tool paths. To determine the cutter compensation option, look in the chaining direction. Use **tool left** if the cutter is offset to the left of the contour. Use **tool right** when the cutter is displaced to the right of the contour path. Use **tool on** when the cutter coincides with the contour.

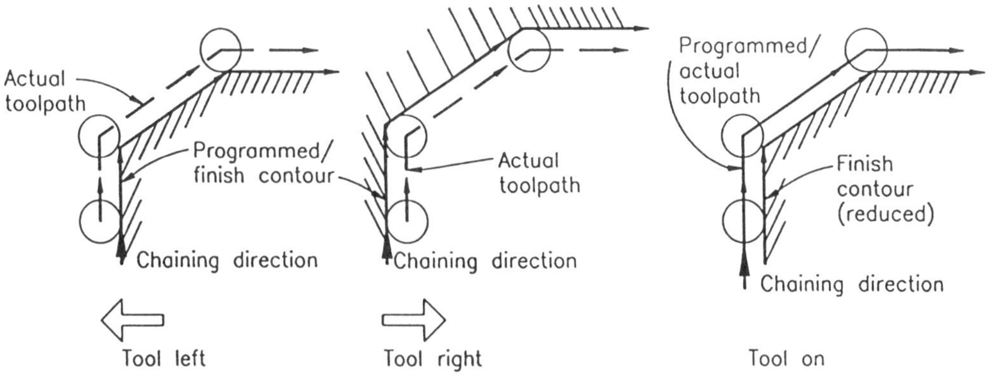

Figure 7.1

These three cutter compensation commands are converted into the following three G-codes during post processing stage:

CDC left:	G41
CDC right:	G42
CDC off:	G40

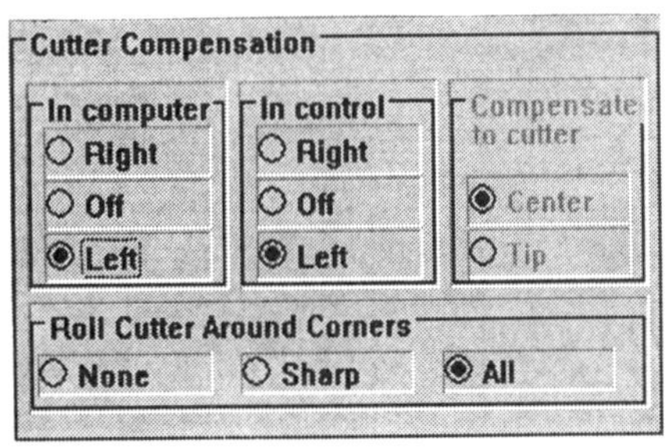

Mastercam uses **three cutter compensation parameters** to specify cutter compensation: cutter compensation in control,cutter compensation in computer and compensate to cutter.

Cutter Compensation in Control

This parameter generates a cutter compensation command (G40, G41, or G42) for the part program according to the selection. You can set this parameter to "**off**", "**left**", or "**right**". A compensation register number (Dia. ofst. n.) is assigned to the compensation in control. The compensation value is stored in the specified register. The compensation value can be (1) the **actual tool diameter**, or (2) the **variation value** between the designated tool diameter and the actual tool diameter.

Cutter compensation in control	**Commands in part program**
Left	G41 Dd
Right	G42 Dd
Off	G40

where d is the diameter offset number (Dia. ofst. n.).
The offset value is stored in this register in the CNC control

Figure 7.2 shows the effect of an offset value on the programmed tool paths.

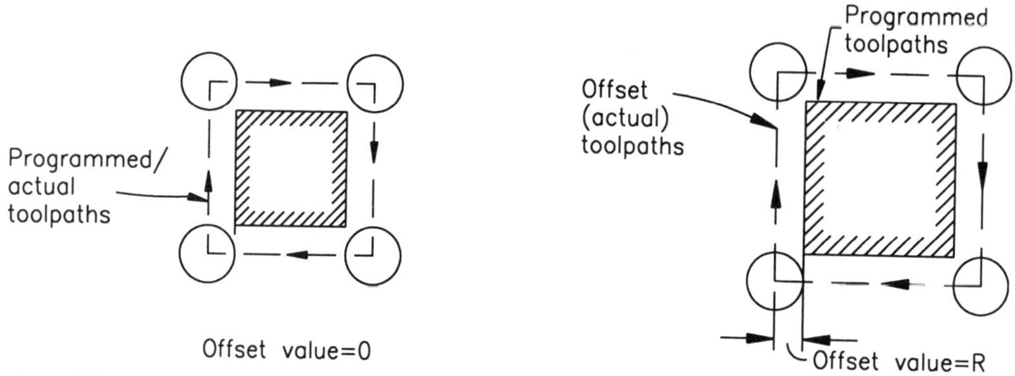

Figure 7.2

Note: On the computer screen, the cutter center does not offset even though the cutter compensation in the control parameter is set to the right or left.

Cutter Compensation in Computer

This parameter causes the cutter center to be displaced in the specified direction by the designated cutter radius distance. This parameter can be selected to **left**, **right**, or **off**. No cutter diameter compensation code will be inserted into the part program even though the compensation in the system parameter is toggled to the left or right. Note that this parameter changes the coordinate values of the cutter center paths. Figure 7.3 shows the effect of cutter compensation in computer on the tool path.

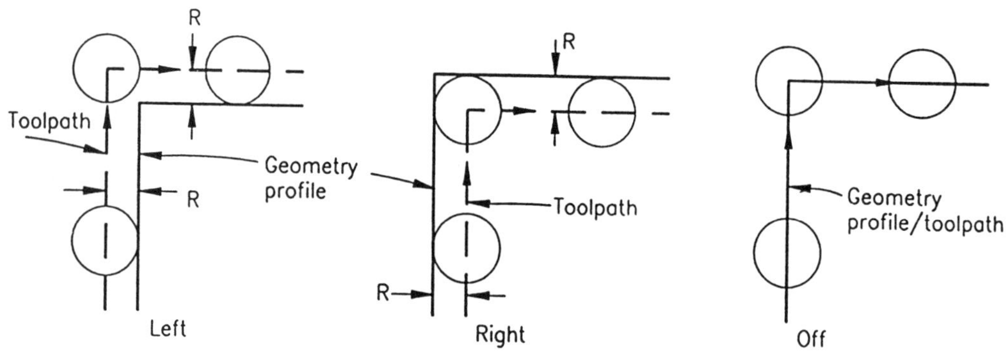

Figure 7.3

Note: Selecting the proper setting of cutter compensation parameters for a particular application is often very confusing.

Two factors to be considered in selecting cutter compensation are:

1. Is the actual cutter diameter identical to the programmed diameter ?
2. Is tool wear present ?

Table 7.2 shows combinations in which two cutter compensation parameters can be applied.

Table 7.2 The use of cutter compensation in control and in system

<table>
<tr><th colspan="2">Compensation in</th><th rowspan="2">CDC command</th><th rowspan="2">Remark</th><th rowspan="2">Illustration</th></tr>
<tr><th>control</th><th>system</th></tr>
<tr><td>Off</td><td>Off</td><td>None</td><td>Produces an inaccurate part profile. The dimensional error in all sides is equal to the value of the tool radius.</td><td>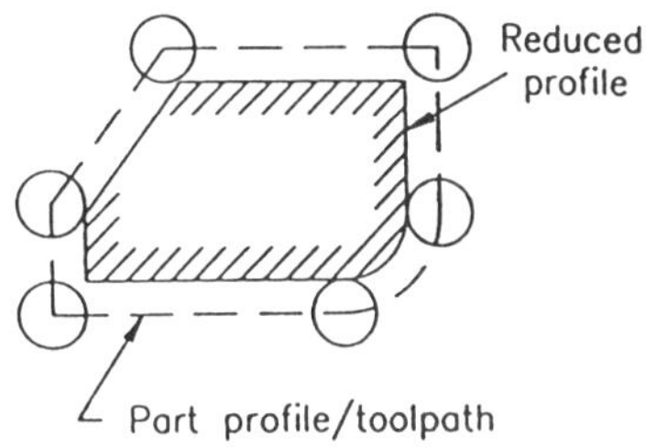
</td></tr>
<tr><td>Off</td><td>On (Right or Left)</td><td>None</td><td>Actual tool diameter must be the same as designated diameter, otherwise a positional error will be encountered. The positional error is equal to one-half of the difference between the designated diameter and actual diameter.</td><td>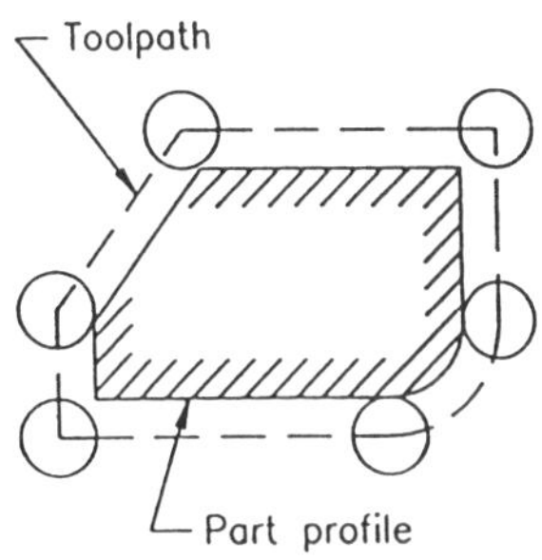
</td></tr>
<tr><td>On (Right or Left)</td><td>Off</td><td>G41 Dxx or G42 Dxx</td><td>The actual cutter diameter must be input to the specified register (Dxx) to produce an accurate part profile.</td><td>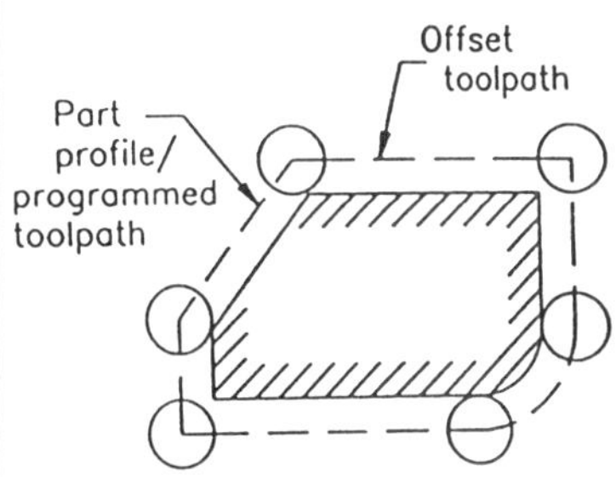
</td></tr>
<tr><td>On (Right or Left)</td><td>On (Right or Left)</td><td>G41 Dxx or G42 Dxx</td><td>The difference between the actual and designated tool diameter should be input to the selected register.</td><td>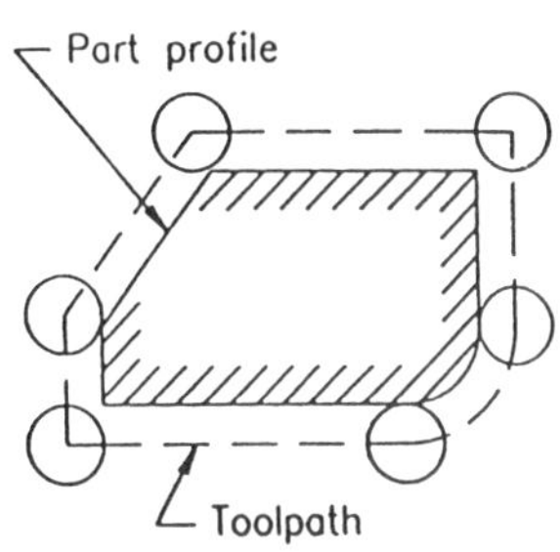
</td></tr>
</table>

⌛**Tip:** Set **both** compensation in system and compensation in control to **On** (Right or Left). This allows the tool to be offset to the proper locations by the compensation in system, and also permits the variation between the actual and designated cutter diameter to be compensated by using the compensation in control. The compensation value given in the register should be zero when no diameter variation exists, otherwise, the compensation value is the difference between the two diameters.

It should be noted that some toolpath modules do not have all three cutter compensation parameters. The availability of cutter compensation parameters for various toolpath modules is summarized in Table 7.3.

Table 7.3 Cutter Compensation for various toolpath modules

Toolpath Modules	Cutter compensation		
	In Computer	In Control	Compensation to center
Contour 2D	Yes	Yes	No
3D	No	No	No
Pocket	No	No	No
Drill	No	No	No
Letters 2D	Yes	Yes	No
3D	No	No	No
Coons	Yes	No	Yes
Loft	Yes	No	Yes
Ruled	Yes	No	Yes
Swept 2D	Yes	No	Yes
3D	Yes	No	Yes
Revolution	Yes	No	Yes
Flowline	No	No	Yes
Multisurf	No	No	Yes

Compensate to Cutter Parameter

This parameter allows you to select cutter compensation to the cutter's center or tip. To make a selection, click on "Center" or "Tip" from the Compensate to Cutter area in the NC Window.

Figure 7.4 shows the definition of cutter center and tip for three common cutter types: flat end, ball end (spherical) and bull nose.

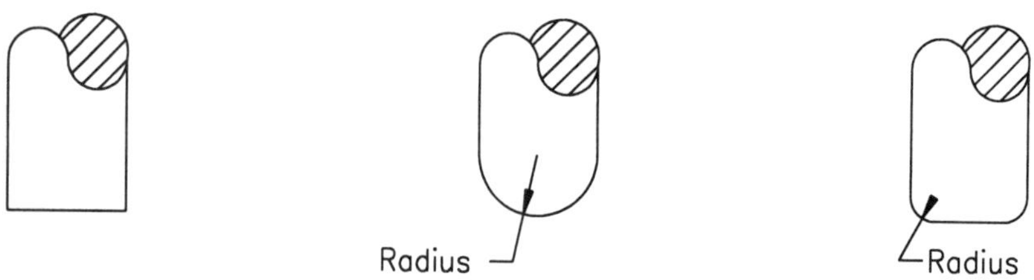

a. Flat end b.Ball end c. Bull nose

Figure 7.4 Definition of cutter center and tip

Figure 7.5 illustrates the effect of selection of cutter center and tip on 3D toolpaths.

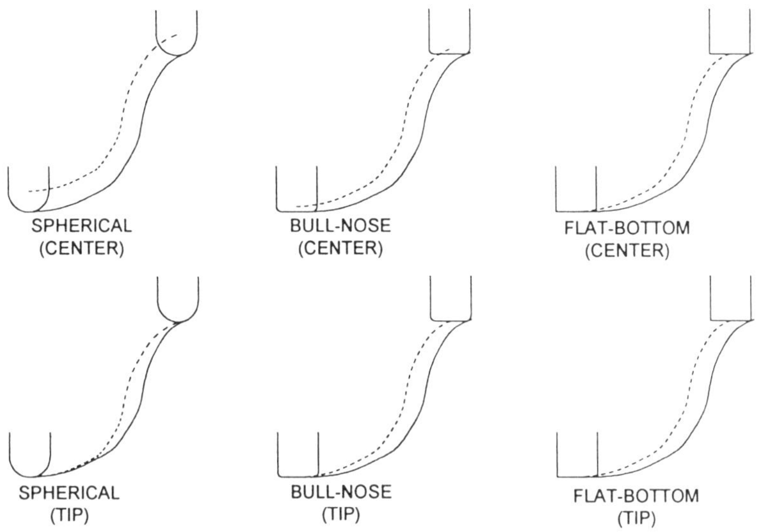

Figure 7.5

Tooling Information

Tooling information is defined by a group of parameters for specifying tool reference, tool number, diameter offset number, length, offset number, tool library and material.

Tool reference: recalls the tool information stored in the current tool library under the specified reference. The information includes tool number, diameter offset number, length offset number, cutter diameter and corner radius.
It is recommended that a tool reference consist of a combination of a number and a legend to describe the cutter size; and type, respectively. Use the input format of 44 without a decimal point to specify the diameter of the cutter. For example, 5000 is equivalent to 0.5 and 12500 is equivalent to 1.25.

Use the following legends to indicate the cutter type or shape:

FLT:	flat end (bottom) cutter
SPH:	spherical (ball end) cutter
DRL:	drill
TAP:	tap
FAC:	face mill
BOR:	boring tool

Examples:

1250 FLT:	1/8" flat end mill
10000FLT:	1" flat end mill
5000 SPH:	1/2" ball end mill
7500 DRL:	3/4" drill

Tool number: indicates the selected tool number in the tool magazine or tool turret. The number given to this parameter causes the system to insert tool change commands into the part program. For example, a value of 2 will cause the command T2 M6 in the part program.

Diameter offset number (Dia. ofst. n.) specifies the register number in which the cutter compensation value is stored. The register number is in the form of Dxx. A value of 25 given to this parameter, for example, will cause the register number to become D25. This parameter is used only when "Cutter compensation in control" is set to either left or right. The table shown below illustrates the effect on commands given to the part program by a combination of cutter compensation in control and diameter offset number.

Length offset number (Len. ofst. n.) This parameter specifies the register number in which the cutter length offset value is stored. The register number has the form Hxx. A value of 5 given to this parameter, for example, will cause the register number to become H5. The cutter length offset value is the distance measured from the tip of the tool held at machine zero to the reference zero plane as shown in Figure 7.6.

Cutter diameter: specifies the designated diameter of the cutter to be used.

Corner radius: specifies the corner radius of the cutter to be used.

Cutter Compensation in control	Diameter offset number	Commands to be issued to part program
Off	21	None
Left	21	G41 D21
Right	25	G42 D25

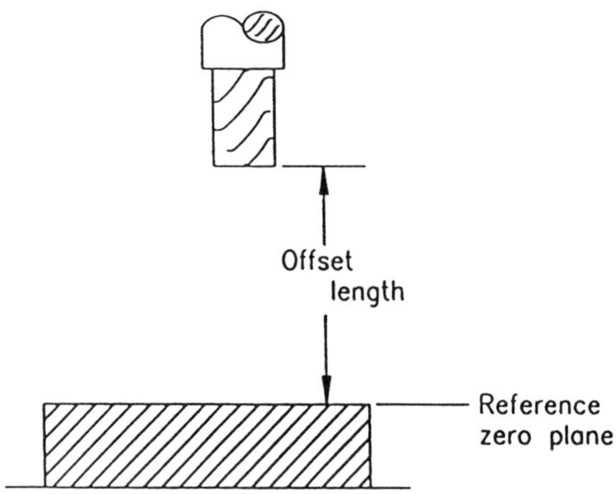

Figure 7.6

Machining Parameters

The machining parameters used in Mastercam include:

- Stock allowance (Stock to Leave)
- Feed (feedrate and plunge rate)
- Spindle speed
- Rapid depth
- Depth cuts
- Linear array

Stock allowance

This parameter specifies a certain thickness of material to be left on the workpiece for further machining. Figure 7.7 illustrates the effect of the stock on the tool path. In Mastercam, the direction of stock allowance is determined by setting compensation in the computer parameter. The stock is left on the **left** side when the compensation in computer is set to left, likewise, when it is set to **right** the compensation is on the right. If the compensation in computer is set to **off**, the stock direction is then decided by the parameter of compensation in control. If **both** compensation in computer and compensation in control are set to off, the stock allowance is ignored.

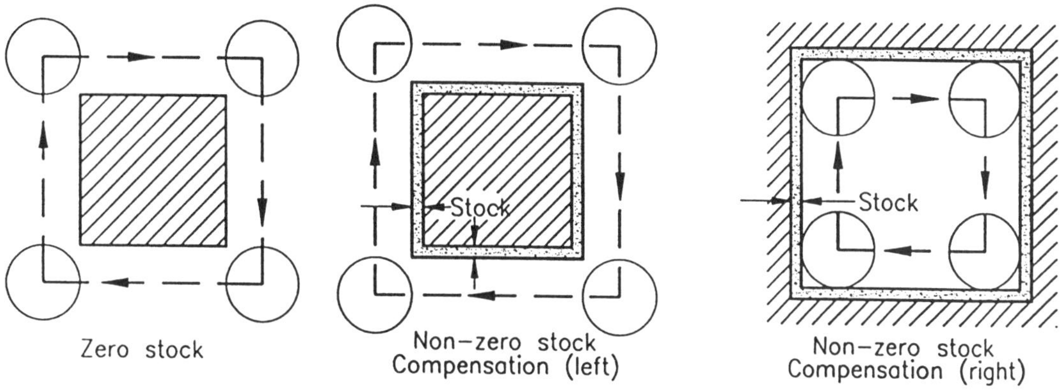

Figure 7.7

Feed

Mastercam uses two types of feed to control the machining speed: feedrate and plunge rate. The plunge rate applies to motions in Z direction only; feed rate applies to all other motions. The unit is normally in IPM (inches per minute).

Spindle Speed

This parameter specifies the desired speed in revolutions per minute (RPM). An S-code with the given RPM will be inserted into the part program to control the spindle speed of the machine.

Rapid Depth

Rapid depth is also referred to as the clearance plane, plunge reference plane, or initial level. It specifies a **Z coordinate** for (1) the cutter to **rapid down to** before starting cutting, (2) the cutter to **rapidly retract to** at the end of the machining motion, and (3) the cutter to **move to** this rapid depth between separate machining contours. Figure 7.8 illustrates the use of rapid depth in machining.

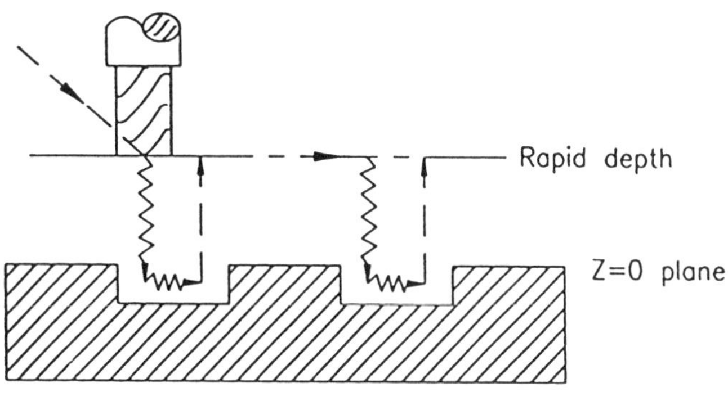

Figure 7.8

Depth Cuts

This parameter specifies the number of roughing and finish cuts to be taken in the Z direction. It allows us to set the number of roughing cuts with the specified depth of each roughing cut and the number of finish cuts with the specified depth of each finish cut. The total number of cutting passes is the **sum** of the roughing cuts and finish cuts. The four parameters defined at this step are shown below:

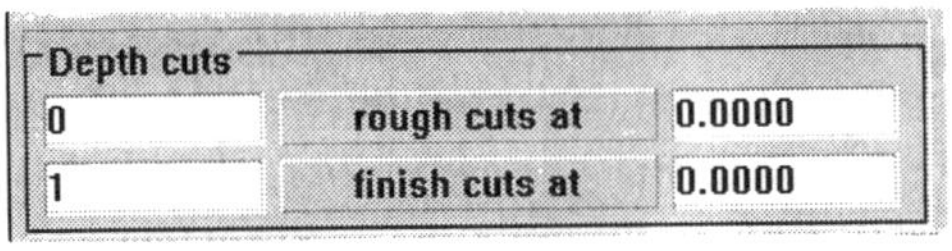

The cutting sequence is determined from the bottom up as defined below (Figure 7.9):

Last finish cut - cut at final depth
Second to last finish cut - cut at depth that is a finish cut spacing above final depth
Subsequent finish cut - cut at depth that is a finish cut spacing above previous finish cut
Last roughing cut - cut at depth that is a roughing cut spacing above first finish cut
Next to last roughing cut - cut at depth that is a roughing cut spacing above last roughing cut
Subsequent roughing cuts - cut at depth that is a roughing cut spacing above previous roughing cut

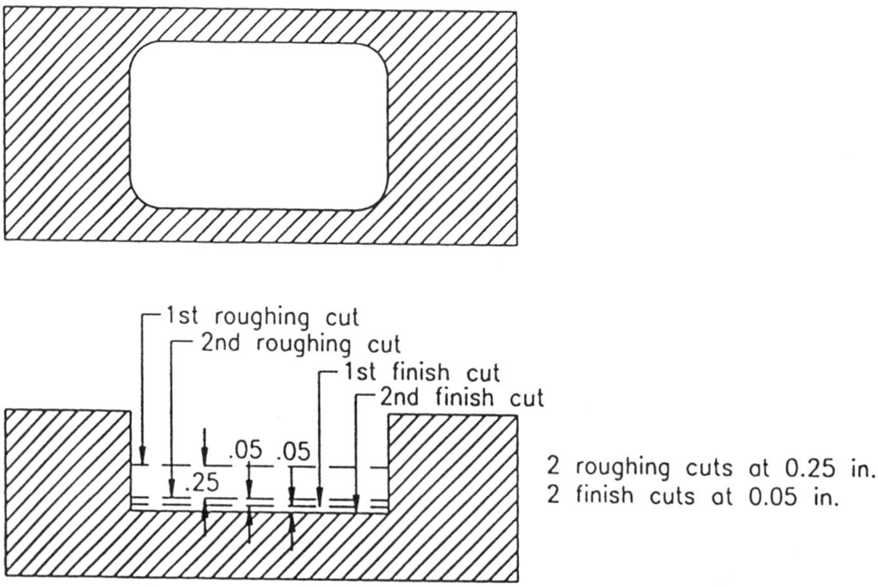

Figure 7.9

Linear array

This array is used to generate a set of repeated machining toolpaths along the X or Y axis of the current construction plane with a given spacing. It uses the following parameters:

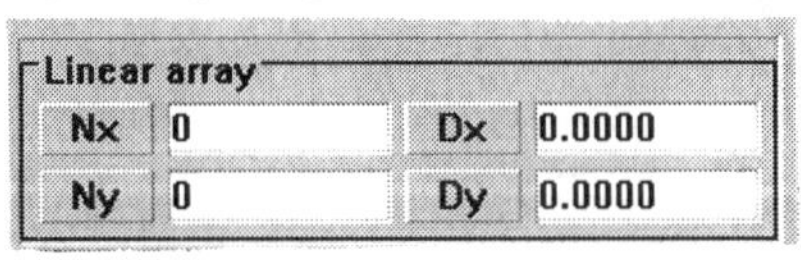

Nx - specifies the number of times to step and repeat the toolpath along the X axis
Ny - specifies the number of times to step and repeat the toolpath along the Y axis
Dx - specifies the distance to step the toolpath along the X axis
Dy - specifies the distance to step the toolpath along the Y axis

Figure 7.10 shows the toolpaths repeated to the other five locations using the linear array parameter.

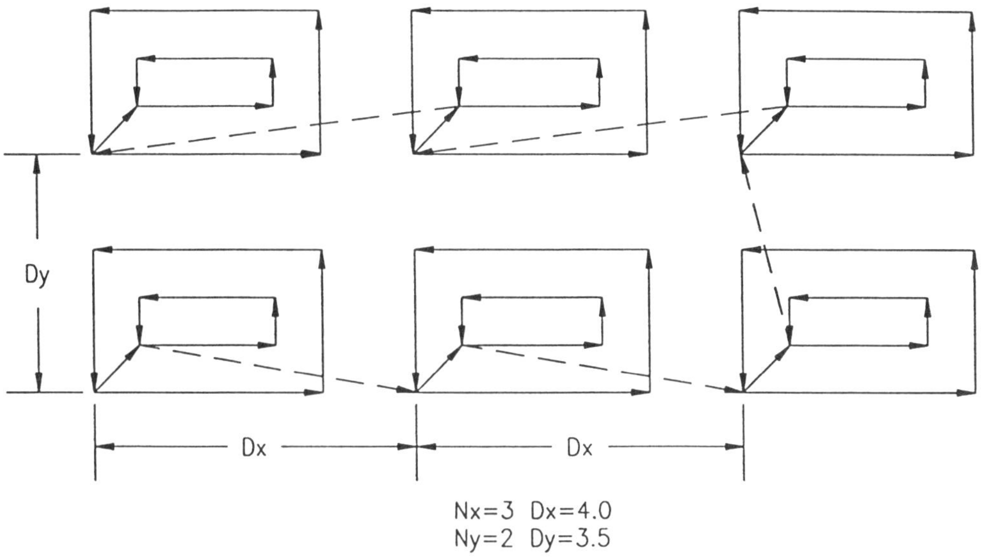

Figure 7.10

Coordinate Setting

Mastercam uses **three** parameters to define the work coordinates of the part program. They are home position, tool origin, and tool plane.

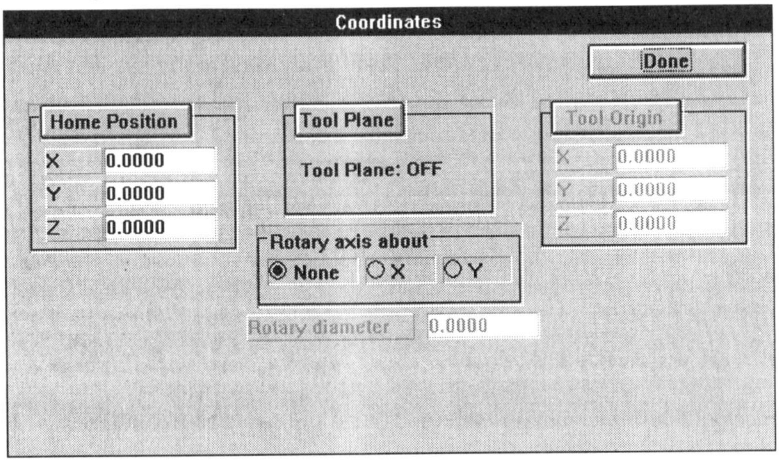

Home Position

This parameter specifies the intermediate position for reference point return. Most CNC controls use reference return commands to generate paths for the spindle and worktable to return to machine origin. Reference point return commands have the following formats:

G90 G28 Xx Yy Zz (absolute positioning mode)

or G91 G28 Xx Yy Zz (incremental positioning mode)

where G90: absolute positioning mode

G91: incremental positioning mode

G28: reference point return command

x, y, and z are the coordinate values of the intermediate point

The toolpath pattern of the reference point return G28 is shown in figure 7.11. In fact, we arrange the reference return point command into two block statements as below:

G91 G28 Zz
G91 G28 Xx Yy

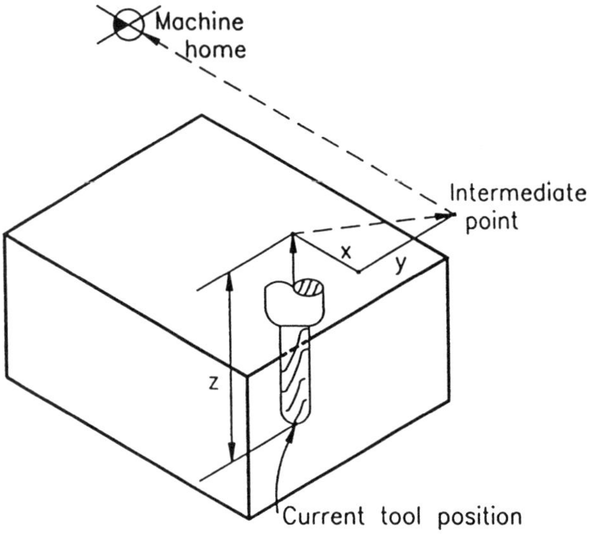

Figure 7.11

This arrangement allows the cutter to be retracted in the Z direction before the worktable moves in the X and Y plane, and avoids interference.

In Mastercam the coordinate values of Home Position are used as the x, y and z values of the reference return point. With the default value (X0 Y0 Z0) of Home Position, the reference return point commands become:

G91 G28 Z0
G91 G28 X0 Y0

With the coordinate value of (X1.0 Y1.0 Z2.0), the reference return point commands become:

G91 G28 Z2.0
G91 G28 X1.0 Y1.0

The reference point return commands are used in the following two conditions:

1. Execution of tool change. Tool change has to be implemented at the machine origin in most CNC machines.

2. At the end of the part program. The spindle and worktable should be moved to machine origin to (1) make the control ready for the next operation and
(2) load and unload the workpieces.

Tip Always use (X0 Y0 Z0) for Home Position and set the positioning system command to incremental mode in the postprocessor. This setting can be used in any workpiece machining. Care must be exercised when other coordinate values are given to this parameter, otherwise an undesirable toolpath may result.

Tool Origin

Mastercam allows to define **three possible origins**: system origin, construction origin, and tool origin. The system origin is the fixed coordinate system automatically setup by the system. The construction origin is used to redefine the origin for geometry construction. The tool origin is to redefine the tool path origin. All three origins locate at the system origin unless they are redefined.

The principle of redefining tool origin is the same as programming the work coordinate setting command G92. The coordinate values given in this parameter indicate the coordinate values of the system origin in the tool coordinate system. Figure 7.12 shows three cases of tool origin setup.

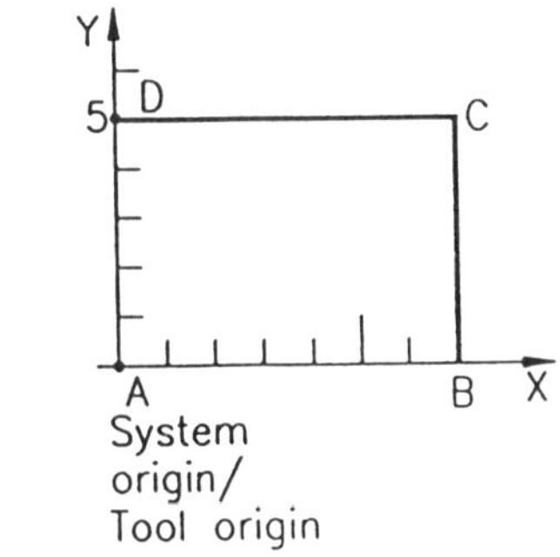

	Toolpath Coord.	
	X–Coord.	Y–Coord.
A	0	0
B	7.0	0.0
C	7.0	5.0
D	0	5.0

a. Tool origin: X0 Y0

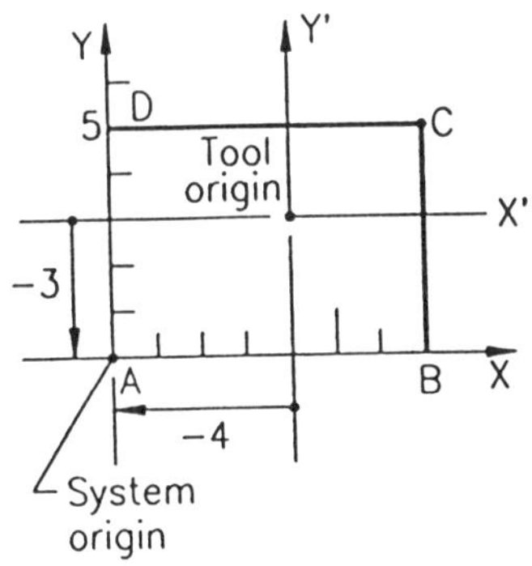

	Toolpath Coord.	
	X–Coord.	Y–Coord.
A	–4.0	–3.0
B	3.0	–3.0
C	3.0	2.0
D	–4.0	2.0

b. Tool origin: X–4.0 Y–3.0

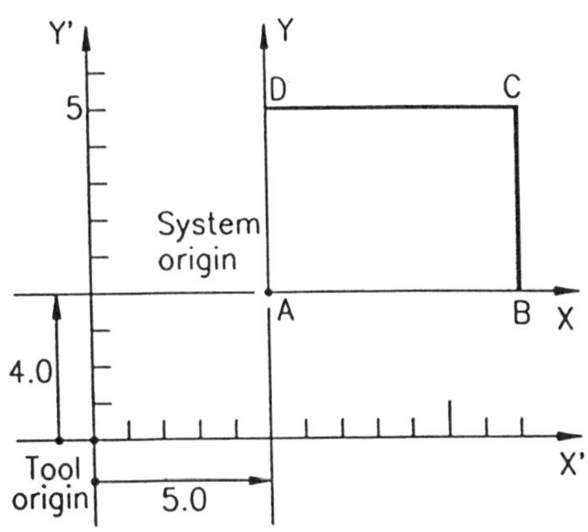

	Toolpath Coord.	
	X–Coord.	Y–Coord.
A	5.0	4.0
B	12.0	4.0
C	12.0	9.0
D	5.0	9.0

c. Tool origin: X5.0 Y4.0

Figure 7.12

Tool Plane

This parameter is used to select the tool plane for the current operation. There are three principal tool planes: XY-plane, ZX-plane, and YZ-plane. The system will issue a plane selection command code to the part program as below:

Plane selection	Command code
XY-plane	G17
ZX-plane	G18
YZ-plane	G19

Tool plane (Tplane) parameters can be toggled to these options:

Off	Tool plane defaulted to Top view
Top	Top view
Front	Front view
Side	Side view
Number	View identified by its number
2 Lines	View defined by two mutually perpendicular lines
Arc	View contained an arc
Rotate	View defined by rotating a construction plane about an axis
Normal	View which is perpendicular to a normal vector

Figure 7.13 shows a number of examples of selecting proper tool plane.

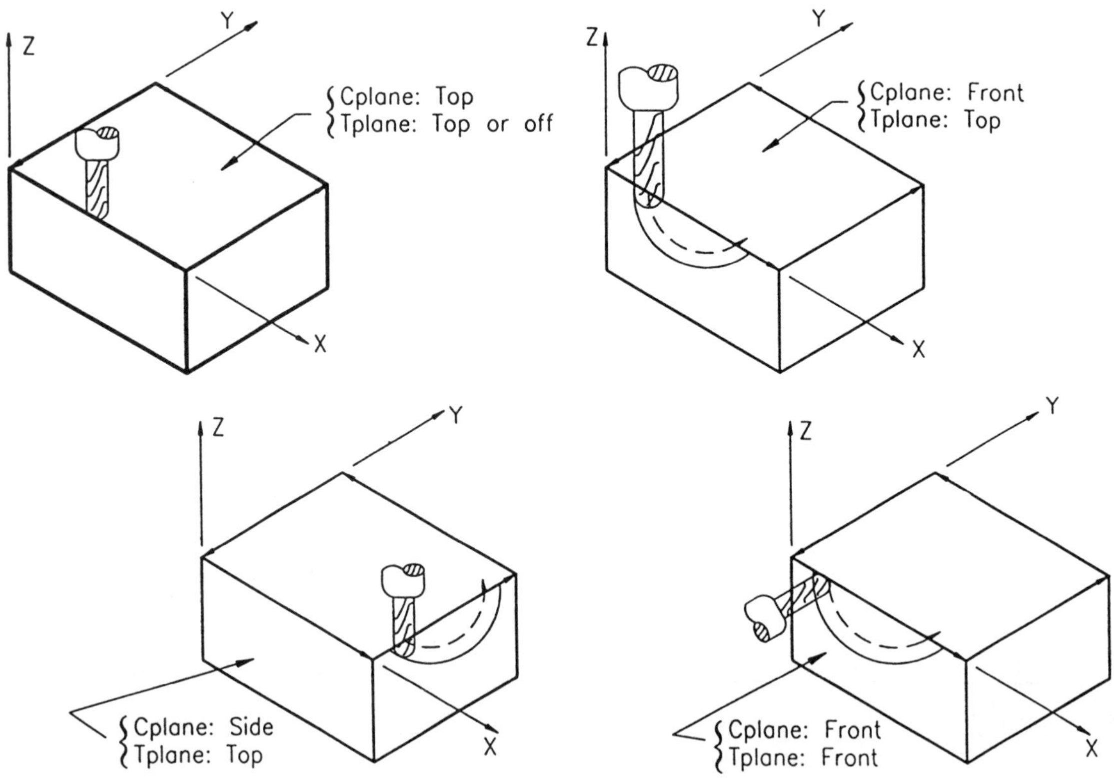

Figure 7.13

Display

The display parameter allows us to select the display mode for tool and toolpath. The tool motion can be shown in **animated mode** or **static mode**. In animated mode, the tool will appear and disappear at each point along the toolpath and as if it were moving. In static mode, the tool will appear at every point along the toolpath and will not be erased.

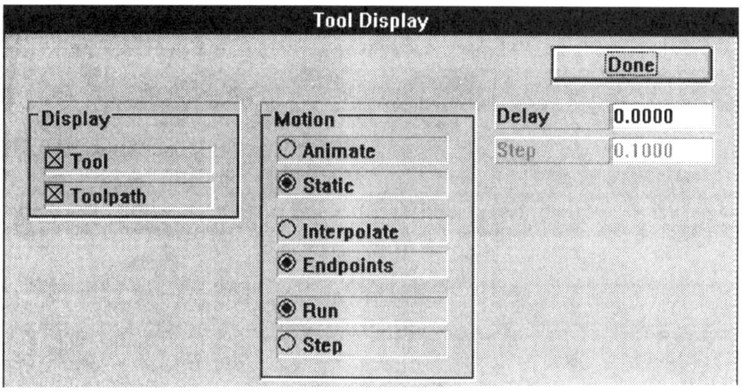

The tool display can be set one of the following two modes (Figure 7.14):

•Interpolate: tool is shown at increments of specified step size
•Endpoints: tool is shown at each endpoint of the toolpath

The system uses the Delay function to allow for specifying how long the tool will be displayed each time it appears on the screen. Use delay of 0.0 for large files. The Step option allows you to specify the step distance for the tool display.

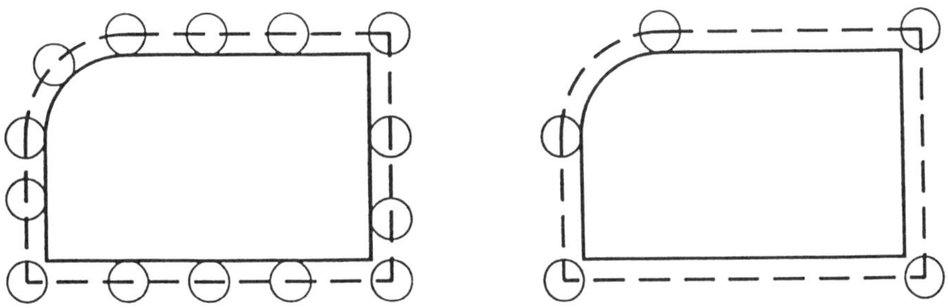

Figure 7.14

Entry/Exit Vectors

Mastercam version 5 provides a new feature called Entry/Exit Vectors (Table 7.4). It allows you to add an incremental line to the beginning (entry) and/or end (exit) of the toolpath (Figure 12.15). Its main purpose is to prevent gouging and burrs.

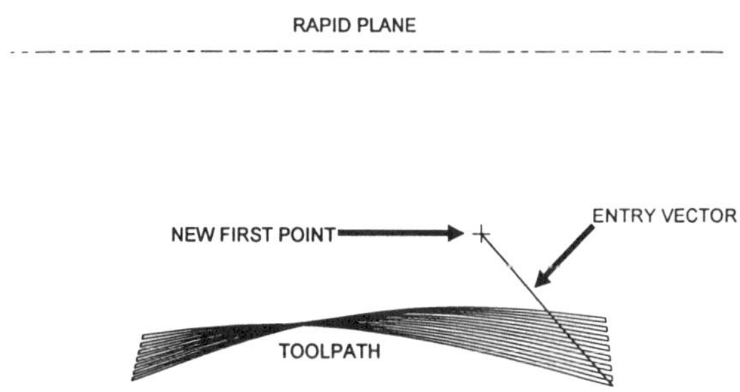

Figure 7.15 ☞
(Courtesy of CNC Software, Inc.)

Table 7.4 Format of Entry/Exit Vectors

<table>
<tr><th>Format</th><th>Description</th><th>Illustration</th></tr>
<tr><td>XYZ</td><td>The added line-segment vector is defined by incremental x,y and z values.
ex. X1.0 Y0 Z-0.5</td><td>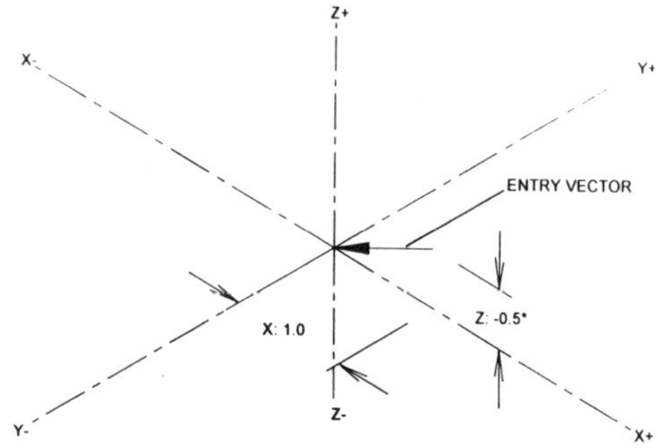
</td></tr>
<tr><td>Polar</td><td>The added line segment vector is defined in the polar coordinate system by specifying the angle and length.
ex. Angle = 25
Length = 2</td><td>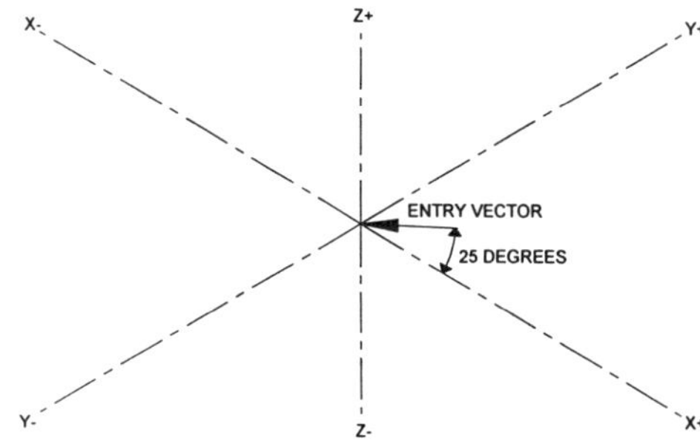
</td></tr>
<tr><td>Single</td><td>The added line-segment vector is determined by selecting a line. The system will automatically determine the start or end point of the toolpath.</td><td>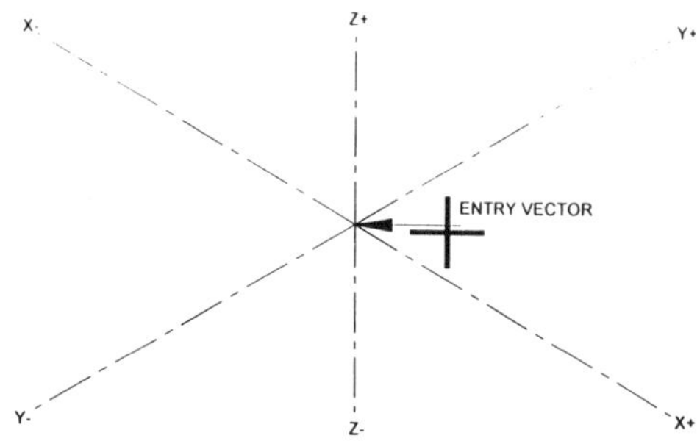
</td></tr>
<tr><td>Chain</td><td>The chain option allows you to define up to 10 line segments from which the start or end point of the toolpath is determined.</td><td>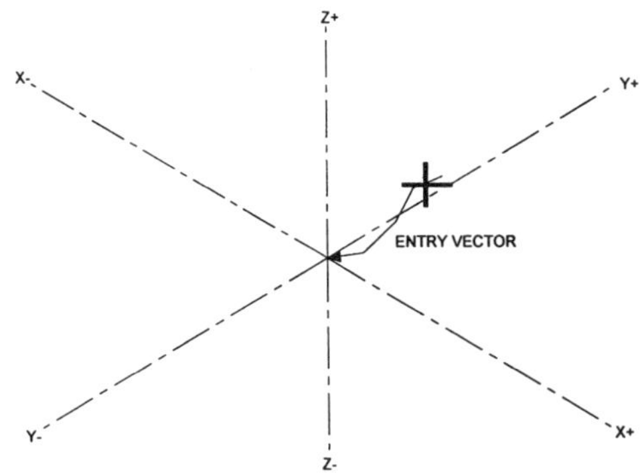
</td></tr>
</table>

(Courtesy of CNC Software, Inc.)

7.3 Contour Definition

A contour consists of a number of connected geometric entities to form a part profile for machining. The benefit of defining a contour is to allow multiple entities of a part shape to be formed as a single entity. This facilitates profile or pocket cutting in one tool motion command.

Chaining direction

The pick point of the first entity of the contour determines the starting position of the contour and the chaining direction of the contour. The chaining direction is also the contour direction. The chaining direction starts at one entity end point, traps the end point that is closer to the picked position, and points to the other end point (Figure 7.16).

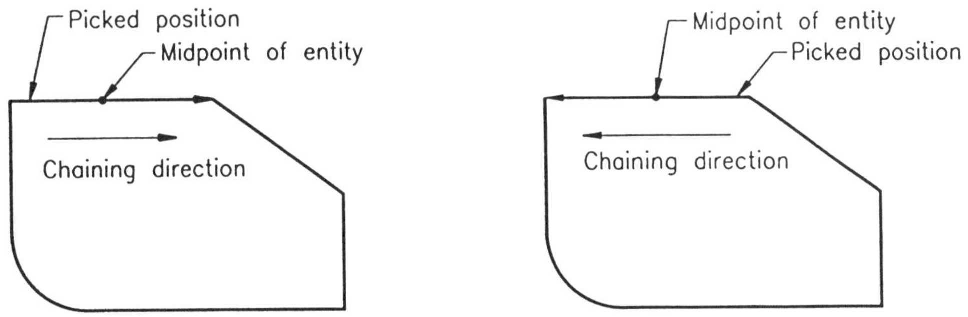

Figure 7.16

There are **two** types of contours: closed and open. In a closed contour, the first and last entities are connected (Figure 7.17a). In an open contour, the first and last entities are not connected (Figure 7.17b). The contours used in pocketing must be the closed type.

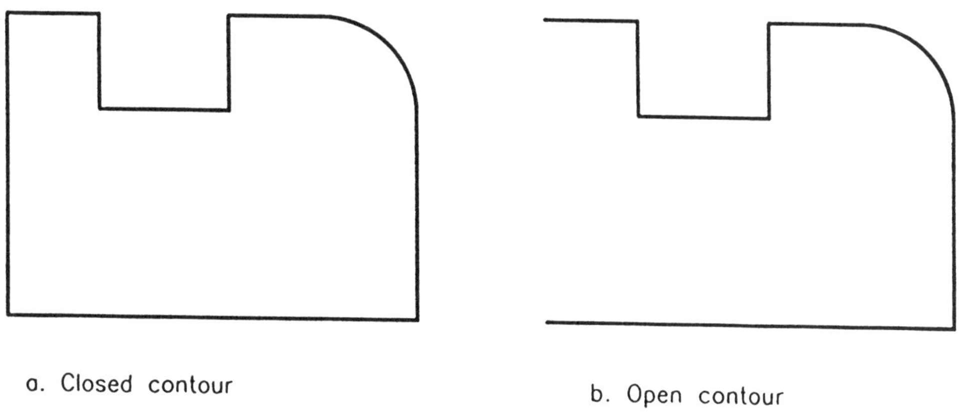

Figure 7.17

Chaining methods

Mastercam provides various methods for defining contours. Table 7.4 describes these chaining methods.

Table 7.4 Contour Chaining Methods

Chaining method	Description	Illustration
Chain	Defining a contour consisting of one or more entities	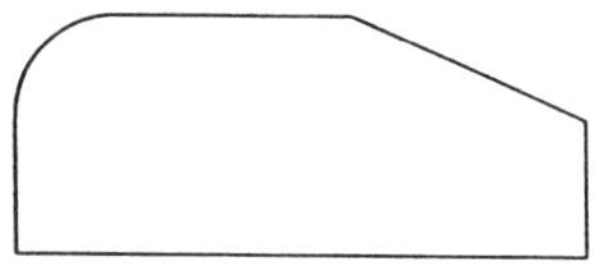
Single	Defining a contour consisting of only one entity	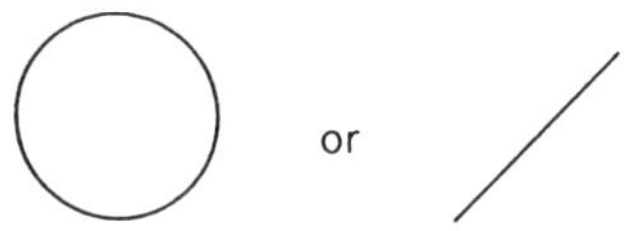
Point	Defining a clear point to rapid to	
Window	Defining one or more contours within a window	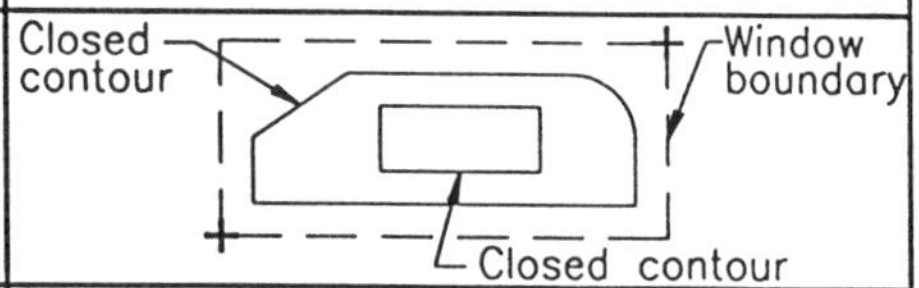
Last	Recalling the last group of chaining operations	
File	Defining one or more contours from a chaining file	
Backup	Backs up to the last contour defined	

7.4 Contour Module

The contour module is used to generate cutter paths along a series of lines and arcs that form the profile of a part. Contouring is normally implemented on 2-D profiles, in which the depth of cut remains constant (Figure 7.18). Mastercam allows us to change the depth of tool motions to generate simple 3-D contouring toolpath by using the step command as shown in Figure 7.19a. The other option is to set the Cplane to 3-d to allow cutting lines and arcs in 3-d space as shown in Figure 7.19b.

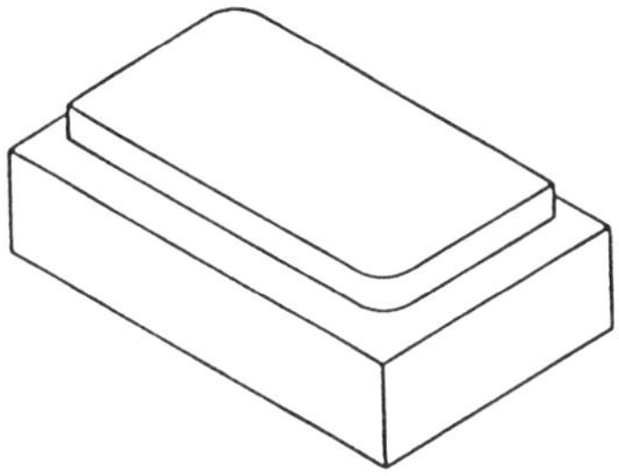

Figure 7.18

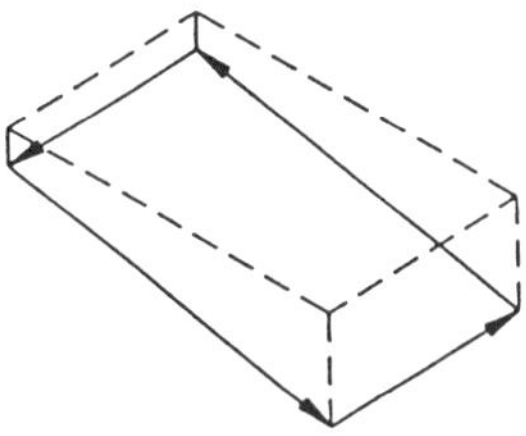

Figure 7.19a Changing depth with step command

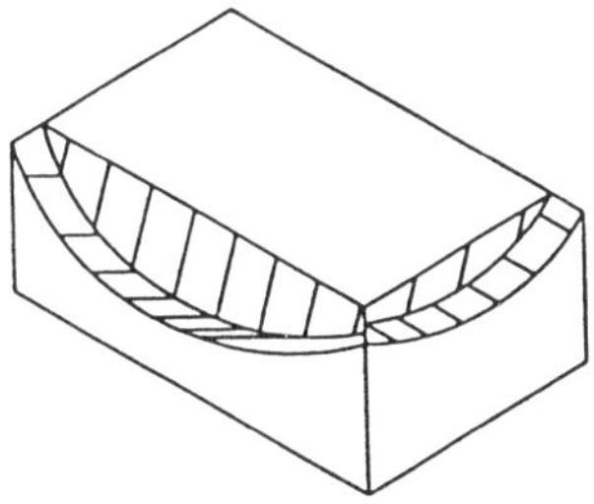

Figure 7.19b 3-D cutting with 3d-Cplane

In addition to the common parameters presented in section 7.2, the contour module uses a set of contour specific parameters to define the toolpaths for contour entry and exit, number of roughing cuts and their spacing, and number of finish passes and their spacing. Contour parameters are listed below:

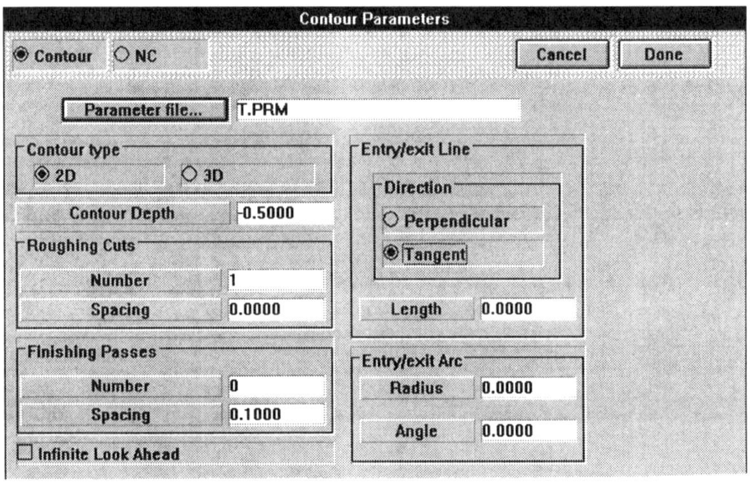

Entry/Exit the Contour Parameters

Mastercam uses three parameters to specify the toolpath pattern for the tool to enter and exit the machining operation for the selected contour. The basic definitions of entry length, entry arc and angle are given in Figure 7.20 . Its main purpose is to prevent gouging and burrs.

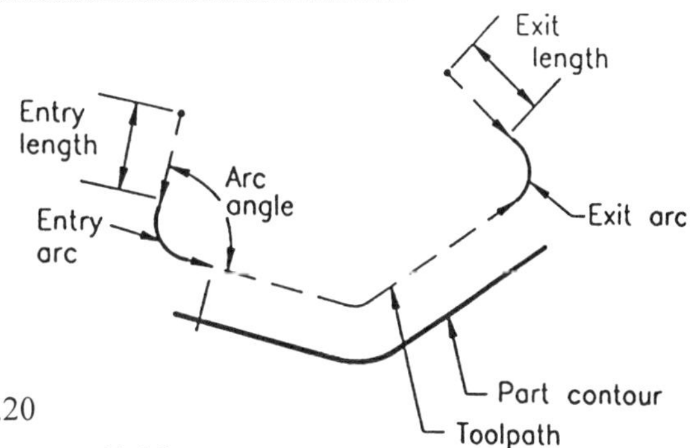

Figure 7.20

Table 7.6 illustrates a variety of combinations of entry/exit length and arc and angle.

Table 7.6 Entry/Exit Length and Arc and Angle

	Line direction	Line length	Arc radius	Arc angle	Illustration
No entry/exit length and arc					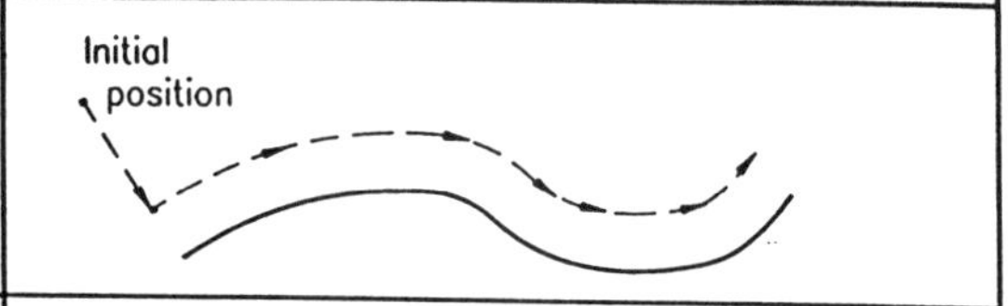
Entry/exit length only	Perpendicular	L	0	–	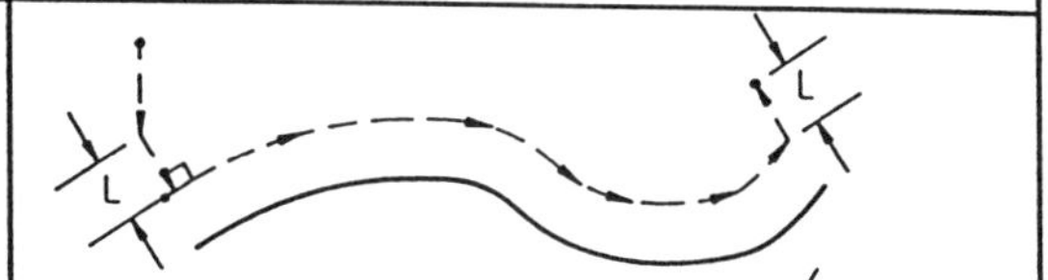
	Tangent	L	0	–	
Entry/exit arc only	–	0	R	45°	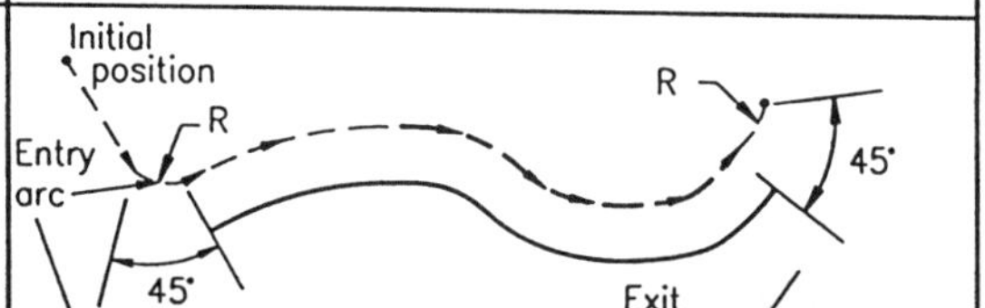
	–	0	R	90°	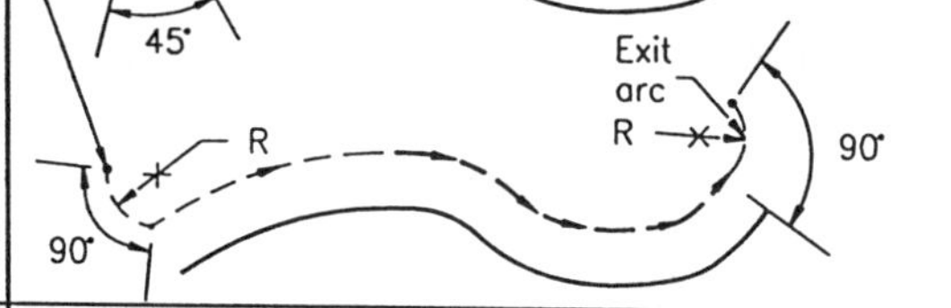
Entry/exit length and arc	Perpendicular	L	R	45°	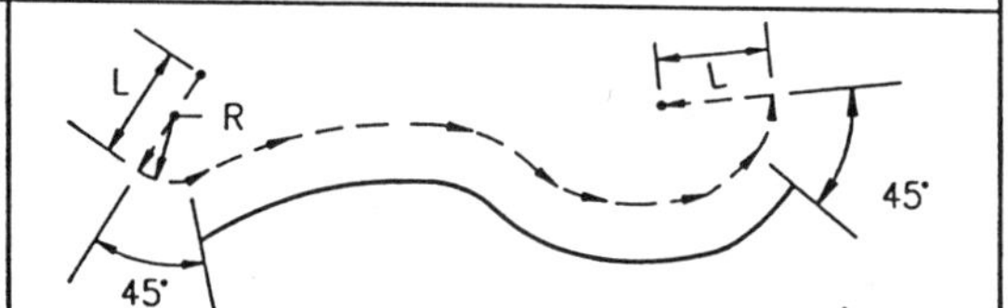
				90°	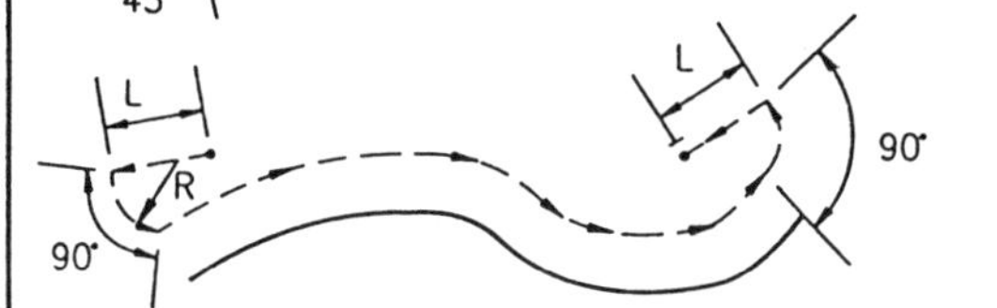
	Tangent	L	R	45°	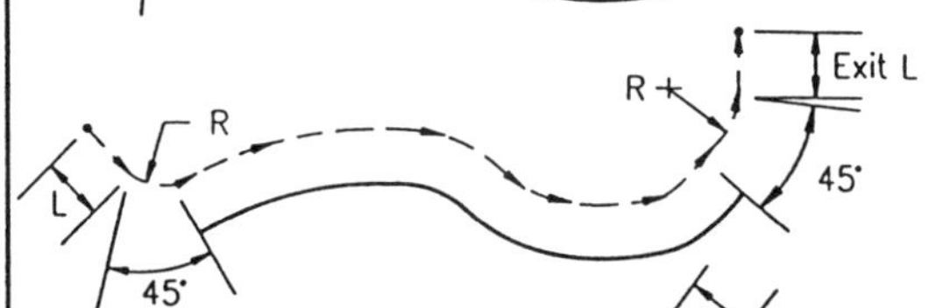
				90°	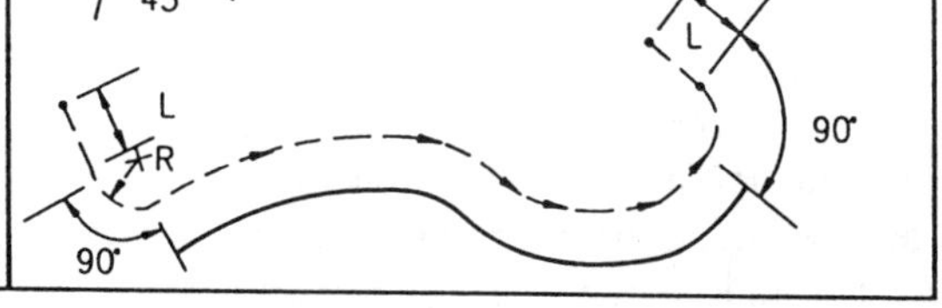

Toolpath Parameters

Four parameters are used to specify the number of roughing and finish cuts to be taken and their stepover distance in the selected cutting plane. The total number of contouring passes to be taken is the sum of the number of roughing cuts and the number of finish passes. The spacing for roughing cuts is determined by the size of cutter diameter. Normally, the roughing spacing is about 60 to 75 percent of the cutter diameter. The required number of roughing cuts is determined by dividing the amount of material to be removed by the roughing spacing. If the amount of material to be removed is 1.25 in. and the roughing cut spacing is 0.7 in. (assuming 1-in. end mill is used), 2 (or 1.25/.7) roughing cuts should be used. Figure 7.21 shows the toolpath pattern for the toolpath parameters having the following setting:

Number of roughing cuts = 2
Roughing cut spacing = 0.25
Number of finish passes = 2
Finishing pass spacing = 0.05

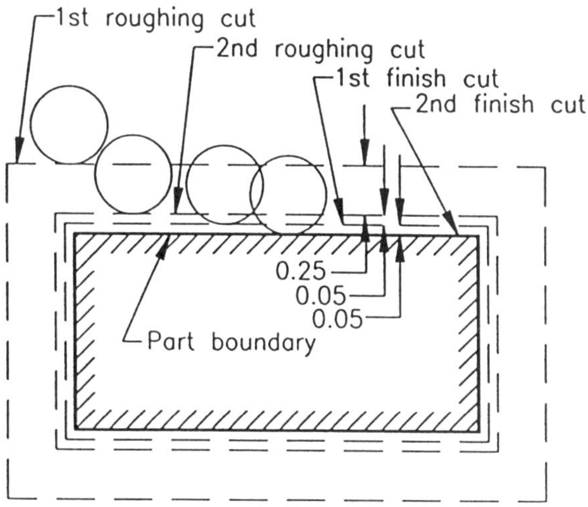

Figure 7.21

Toolpath Around Corners

This parameter determines the toolpath at the corners which are formed by two joined lines. An arc move may be inserted around the corners depending on which mode is selected. The parameter can be toggled to (1) sharp corners, (2) no corners, and (3) all corners.

A sharp corner is defined as an included angle which is less than 180° in the material side (Figure 7.22).

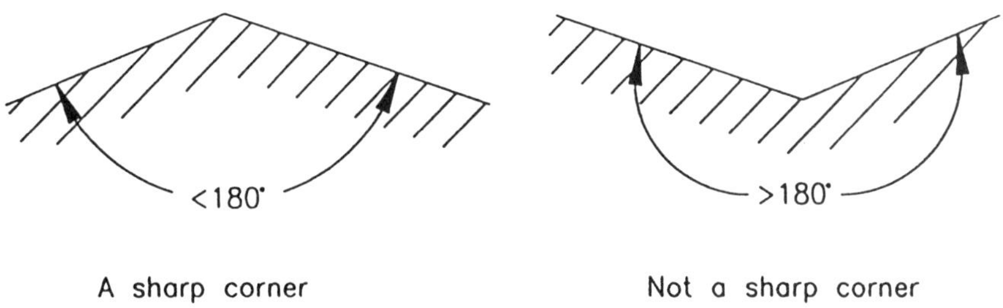

Figure 7.22

Table 7.7 gives typical toolpths around corners for the three modes.

Table 7.7 Toolpath around Corners

Mode	Toolpath
Sharp corners	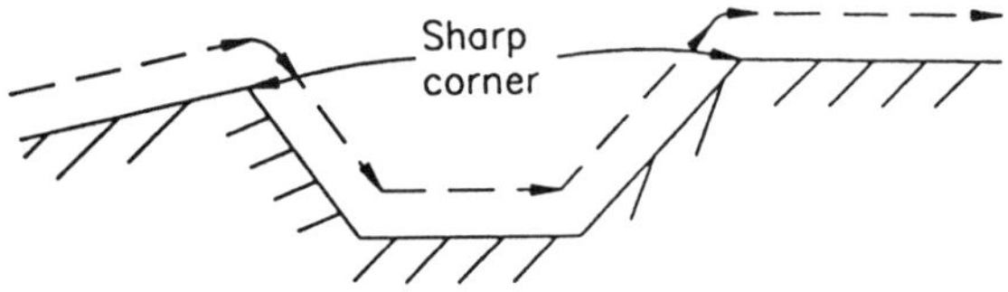
All corners	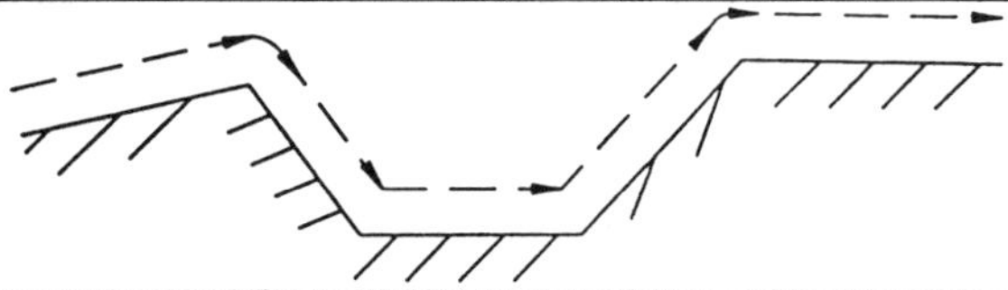
No corner	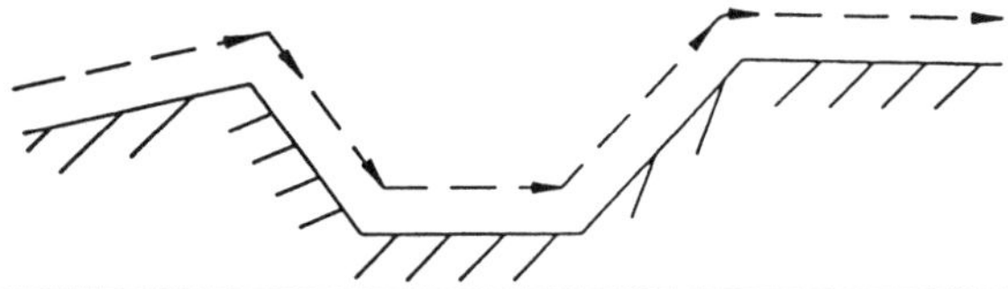

Tips

1. A proper combination of entry/exit length and arc is recommended for cutting a contour. This allows the cutter to smoothly engage the workpiece.
2. The amount of material to be removed in contouring can be determined by subtracting the part profile dimension from the raw material size. This data is then used to determine the number of required roughing cuts and the number of finish passes. The spacing for roughing cuts is recommended as:

   $S = 0.6\ D$ for cutting steels
   $S = 0.75\ D$ for cutting cast iron and other materials

   where S = roughing cut spacing
   D = cutter diameter

3. The toolpath always starts at the end point of the first geometric entity picked to define the contour.
4. Use sharp corners only for the toolpath around corners parameter.
5. There are two ways to linearly change the cutting depth of the profile when the contour module is used: one uses 3-d Cplane and the other uses the ramping move. The advantages and disadvantages of using these two methods are tabulated on the next page.

	Advantages	Restrictions
3-D Cplane	1. Depth can be changed 2. Can cut circular arcs in all three principal planes	1. No cutter compensation 2. No roughing cuts allowed in XY-plane
Ramping move	1. Allow cutter compensation 2. Allow multiple passes of depth cuts in Z direction	1. Can not cut arcs in ZX- and YZ-plane 2. No roughing cuts allowed in XY-plane

Project 1.

1

Part Geometry
Project 1 of Chapter 5 (contour1)

Contouring External Profile

Use the contour module to generate toolpaths to cut an external profile shown in Figure 7.23. The total depth of cut is 1-in. The raw material is the casted workpiece which is about 1/4-in. larger than the finished dimensions in all directions.

We are here ☞ **Go to Toolpath Generation (contour1)**

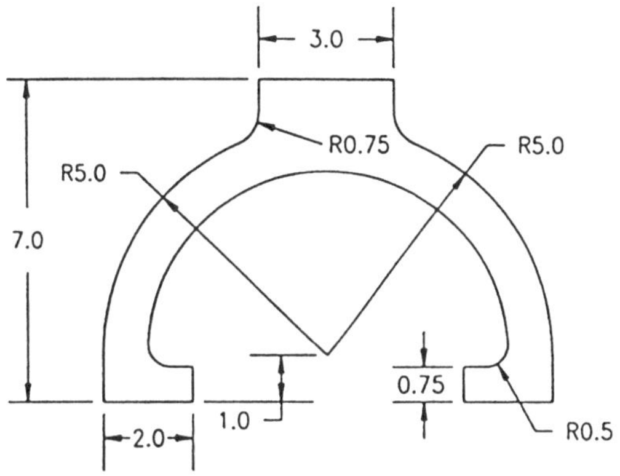

Figure 7.23

Tips 1. Use 3/4-in. end mill.

2. Use one roughing cut and one finish cut for the machining taking place in the XY-plane. The stock for the finish pass is 0.1-in.
3. Use three passes (two roughing cuts and one finish pass) in the depth cut (Z) direction. The two roughing cuts take 0.35-in. each and the finish pass takes 0.3-in.
4. Set the entry/exit length to 0.5-in., the entry/exit arc has a radius of 1-in. and an angle of 90°.
5. Set cutter compensation in control to off and cutter compensation in computer to left center.

Step 1. Load the geometry file (contour1.ge3) or create the geometric model by following the procedure given in project 1 of chapter 5.

Select **MAIN MENU →File → Get**
Enter file name: **contour1 ←**
Select **Yes** to delete the current part (if necessary)

The drawing should appear as Figure 7.24 on the next page.

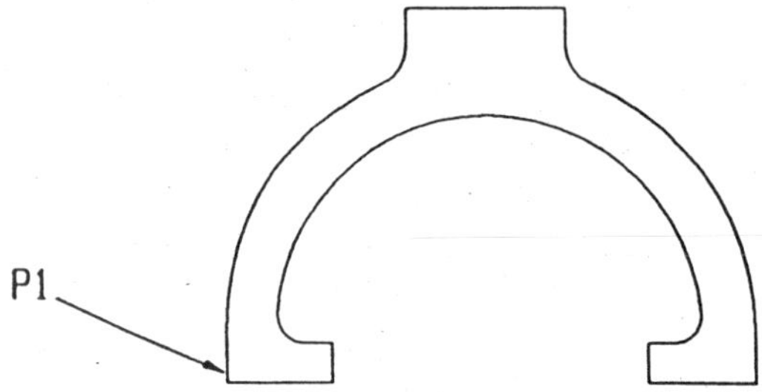

Figure 7.24

Step 2. Set both the construction plane and graphics view to Top.

Select **Cplane** → **Top**
Select **Gview** → **Top**

Step 3. Initiate the contour module.

Select **MAIN MENU** → **Toolpaths** → **Contour**
Enter file name: **contour1** ←

Step 4. Define the contour using the pick point in Figure 7.24.

Select **Chain** from the chaining method menu
Pick at **P1** to select the first entity of the contour
Select **Close** → **End here** → **Done** to complete the contour selection

Step 5. Define the contour parameters.

Select **Params**
Set the contour parameters to the following settings:

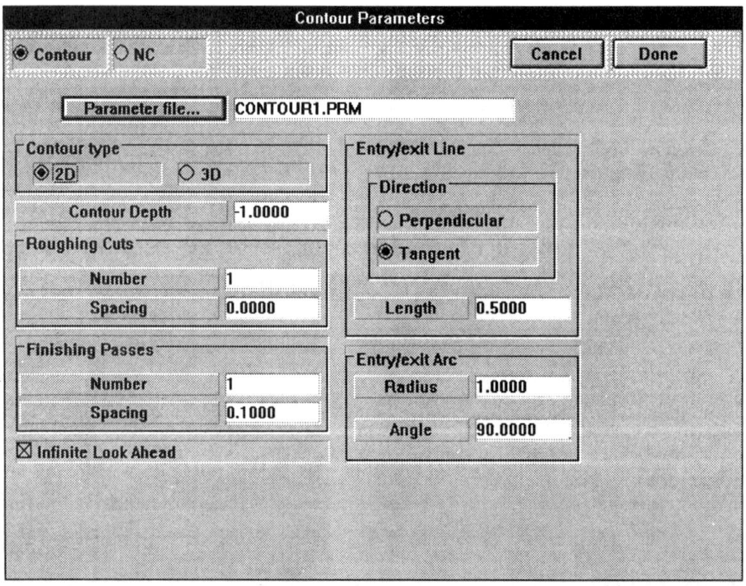

Select the **NC button** to move to the NC parameter page.

Step 6. Define the NC parameters.

Set the NC parameters to the following settings if appropriate for your CNC machine; otherwise, define the settings for your own machine.

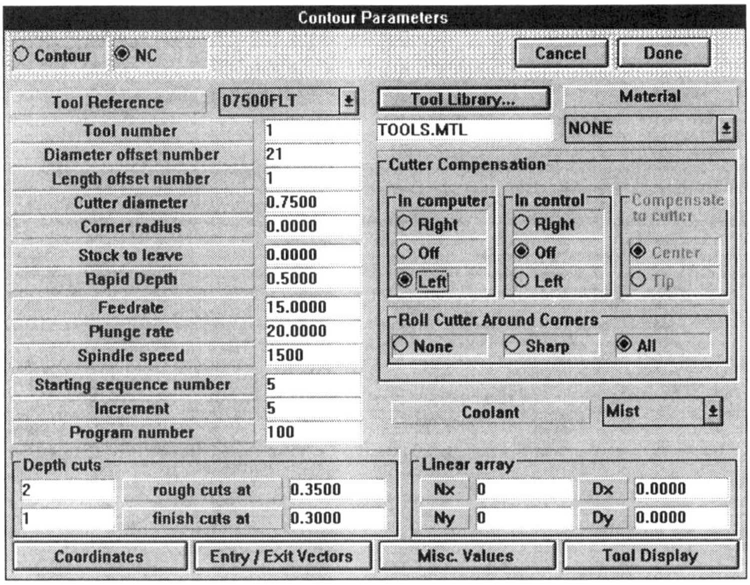

Select the **Done button** to complete the NC parameters settings.

The toolpath should appear as Figure 7.25.

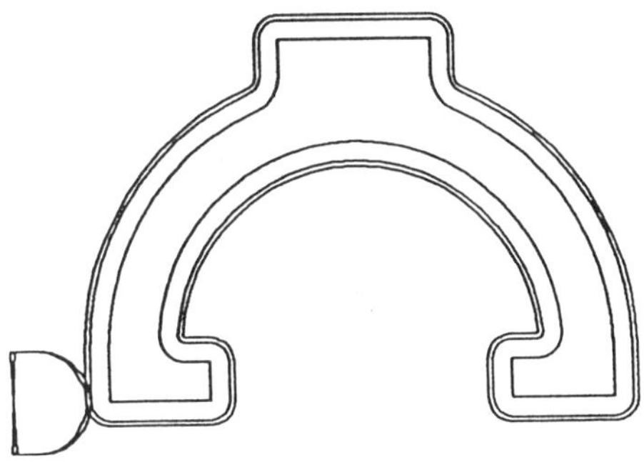

Figure 7.25

Step 7. Change Gview to isometric.

Select **Gview → Isometric**

The drawing shown in an isometric view should resemble Figure 7.26 on page 7-26.

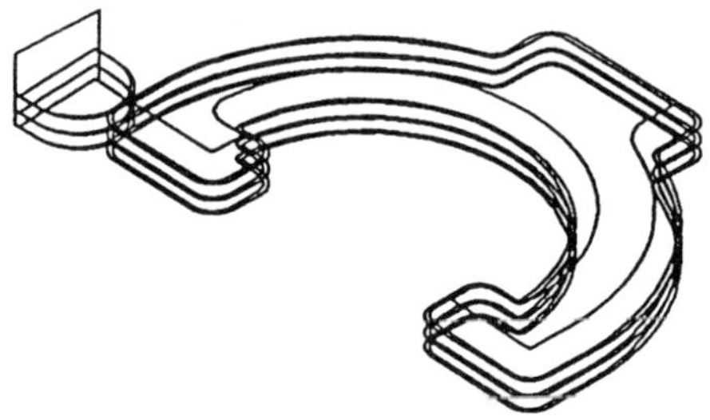

Figure 7.26

TS4

Step 8. Accept the toolpath and run the postprocessor.

Select **Yes** to accept the toolpath
Select **End program** to close the toolpath file
Select **Yes** to run the postprocessor to convert the NCI file to NC file
Enter the file name: **contour1**

The part program should appear on the screen. Double click the button on the upper left corner to return back to graphic mode.

Step 9. Edit the NC file.

Select **MAIN MENU → File → Edit → NC**
Enter file name: **contour1 ←**
The NC file should appear on the screen.

The partial part program is listed below. Your program may look somewhat different from the one listed here because your version may be using a different post processor.

```
O O100
N5 G90 G80 G40 G0
N10 T1 M6
N15 G54 G0 X-6.975 Y-2.
N20 S1500 M3
N25 G43 H1 Z.5 M08
N30 G1 Z-.35 F20.0
N35 X-6.475 F15.0
N40 G3 X-5.475 Y-1. R1.
N45 G1 Y0.
        -
        -
N975 G2 X-2.625 Y-.25 R.375
N980 G1 Y-1.
N985 G2 X-3. Y-1.375 R.375
N990 G1 X-5.
N995 G2 X-5.375 Y-1. R.375
N1000 G3 X-6.375 Y0. R1.
N1005 G1 X-6.875
N1010 G0 Z.5 F0.0
N1015 G91 G28 Z0 M5 M09
N1020 G28 X0 Y0
N1025 M30
%
```

Press **F10 → F9** to return to the graphic mode.

Project 2.

Part Geometry Creation
Project 3 of Chapter 6 (contour2)

We are here ☞ Go to **Toolpath Generation (contour2)**

Contouring internal profile

Use contour module to generate toolpaths to take the cutter along the internal profile of the part shown in Figure 7.27. The workpiece has been casted to its rough size. Therefore, it requires only one finish pass to cut to the desired profile. The depth of cut in Z direction is 0.5-in.

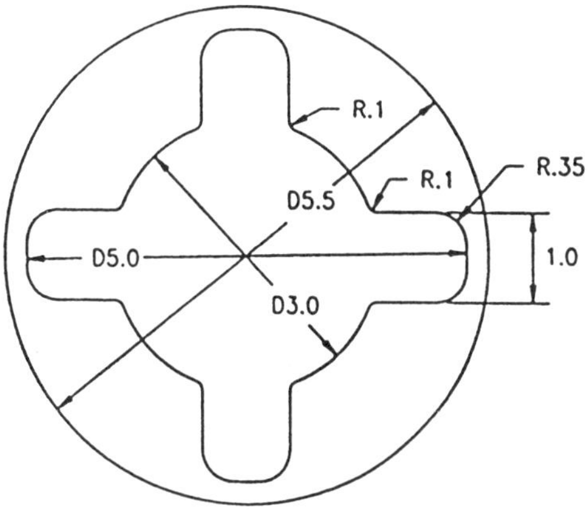

Figure 7.27

Tips 1. Use 0.5-in. end mill.

2. Define the contour direction to be in the counter-clockwise direction to obtain climb milling for a better surface finish.
3. Set entry/exit length to 0 and arc radius to 0.5 and angle to 90°.
4. Set cutter compensation in control to left and cutter compensation in computer to left center.
5. Set rapid depth to 0.3 and contour depth to -0.5.

Step 1. Load the geometry file (contour2.ge3) or create the geometry by following the procedure given in project 3 of Chapter 6.

Select **MAIN MENU →File → Get**
Enter file name: **contour2** ←
Select **Yes** to delete the current part (if necessary)

The drawing should appear as Figure 7.28 .

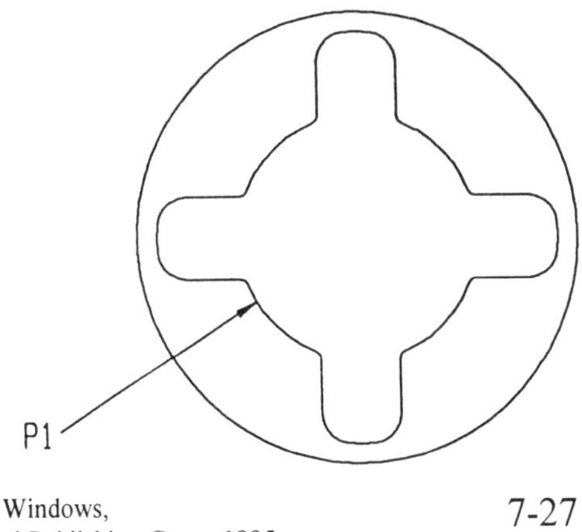

Figure 7.28.

Step 2. Set both Cplane and Gview to Top view if necessary.

Select **Cplane** → **Top**
Select **Gview** → **Top**

Step 3. Initiate the contour module.

Select **MAIN MENU** → **Toolpaths** → **Contour**
Enter file name: **contour2** ←

Step 4. Define the contour using the pick points in Figure 7.28 on page 7-27.

Select **Chain**
Pick at **P1** to select the starting entity of the contour
Select **Close** → **End here** → **Done** → **Params**

Step 5. Define the contour parameters.

Set the contour parameters to the following settings:

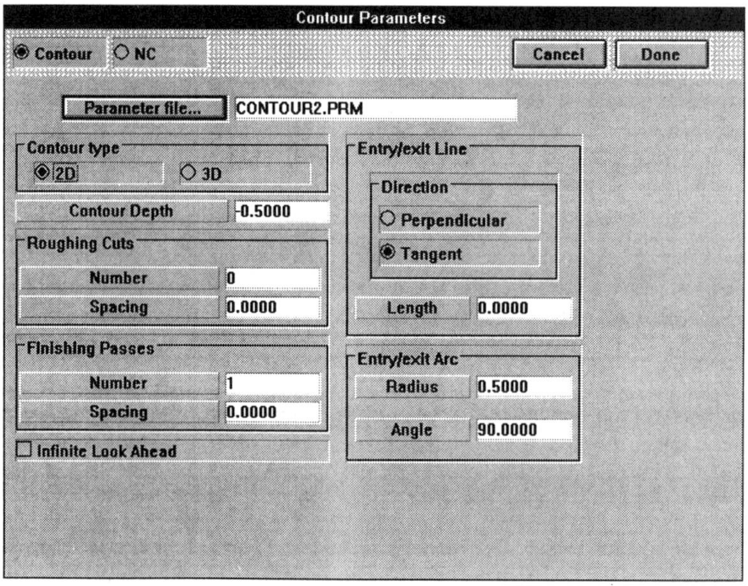

Select the **NC Button** to move to the next NC parameter menu.

Step 6. Define the NC parameters as shown on the next page. The toolpath should appear as in Figure 7.29.

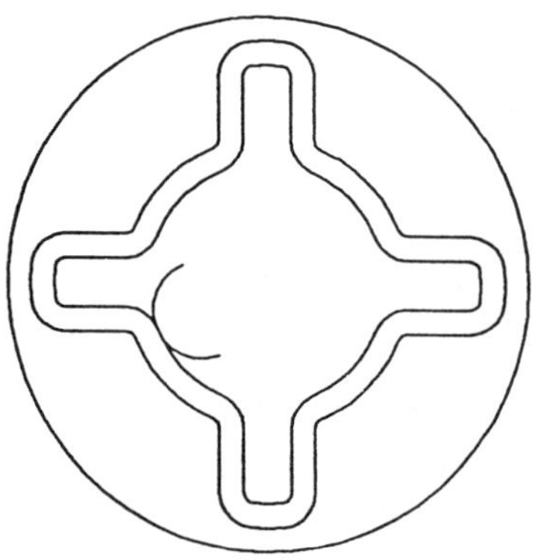

Figure 7.29

Set the NC parameters to the following settings.

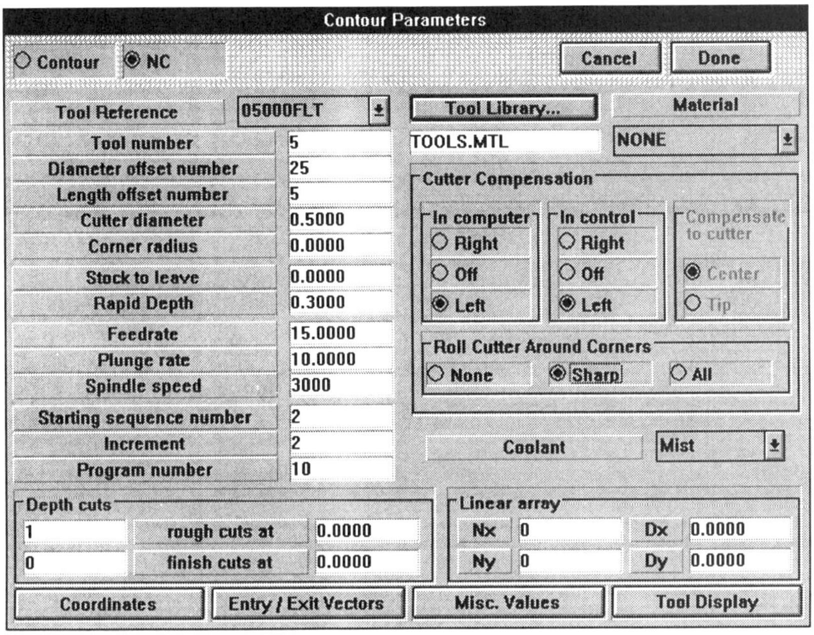

Select the **Done button** to complete the NC parameters setting.

Step 7. Write the toolpath.

Press **F3** to repaint the screen
Select **Write** from the change menu
The drawing with the tool diaplay should resemble that in Figure 7.30.

Figure 7.30.

Step 8. Accept the toolpath and run the post processor.

Select **Yes** to accept the toolpath
Select **End program** to close the NCI file
Select **Yes** to run the postprocessor
Enter file name: **contour2** ←

The part program should appear on the screen. Double click the button at the upper left corner to return to graphic mode.

Project 3.

Contouring an open profile while changing Z-depth

The contour module is used to generate a set of toolpaths to move the cutter along an open contour as shown in Figure 7.31. The Z-depth varies linearly from A to B and from E to F. A ramping move is added at point B and F to change the Z-depth.

Part Geometry Creation
Project 2 of Chapter 5 (contour3)

We are here ☞

Go to ☟
Toolpath Generation
(contour3)

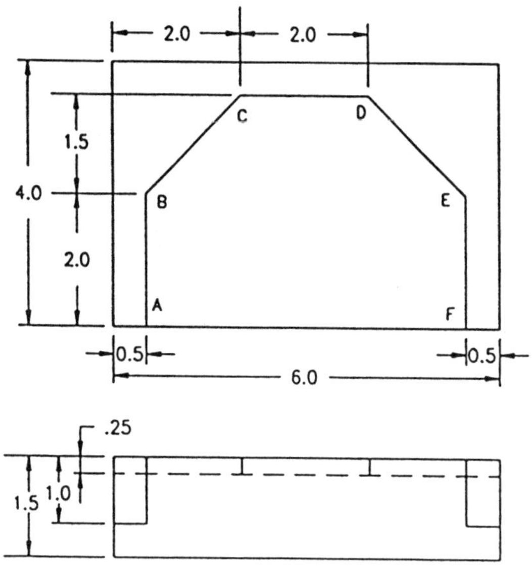

Figure 7.31

Tips 1. Use 1-in. end mill.

2. The contour depth at A is -1.0-in. Use the ramping function to change the depth at B to -0.25-in. and at F to -1.0-in.
3. Take two passes in depth cuts, including one roughing cut and one finish cut. The spacing for a roughing cut is zero becuase there is only one roughing cut. The spacing for the finish pass is 0.2-in.
4. Use isometric Gview to observe the change of depth along the toolpath.
5. Use the backplot function to verify the toolpath for its correctness.

Step 1. Load the part geometry file (contour3.ge3) or create the geometry by following the procedure given in project 2 of Chapter 5. The drawing should appear as in Figure 7.32 on the next page.

Select **MAIN MENU →File → Get**
Enter file name: **contour3**
Select **Yes** to delete the current part if necessary

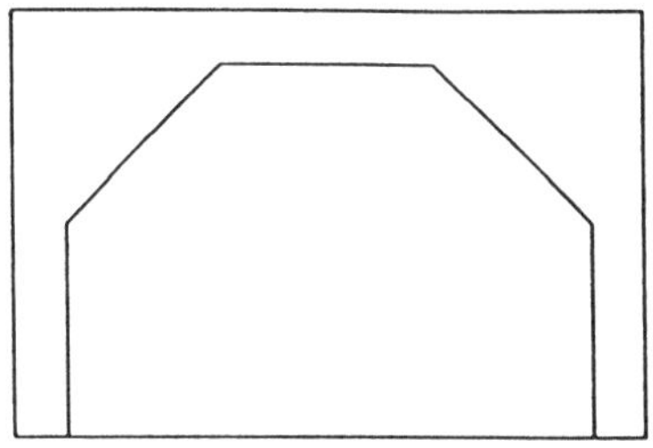

Figure 7.32.

Step 2. Set Gview to isometric and Cplane to top.

Select **Gview→ Isometric→ Cplane →Top**

The drawing shown in isometric view will appear as in Figure 7.33.

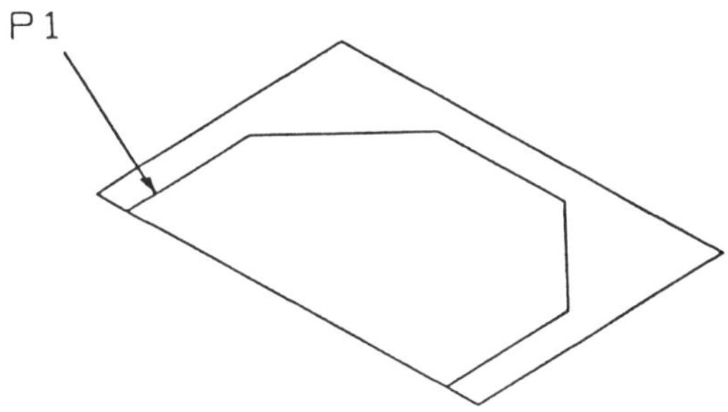

Figure 7.33

Step 3. Initiate the contour module.

Select **MAIN MENU → Toolpaths → Contour**

Enter file name: **contour3** ←

Step 4. Define the contour using the pick point in Figure 7.33.

Select **Chain** from the chaining method menu

Pick at **P1** to select the first entity in the contour

Select **Close → End here → Done → Params**

Step 5. Define the contour parameters.

Set the contour parameters to the following settings:

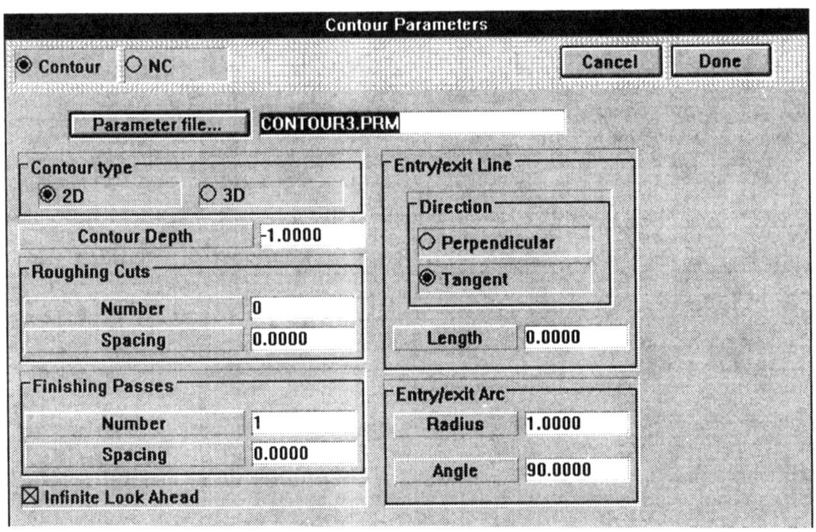

Select the **NC Button** line to move to the NC parameter menu.

Step 6. Define the NC parameters.

Set the NC parameters to the following settings:

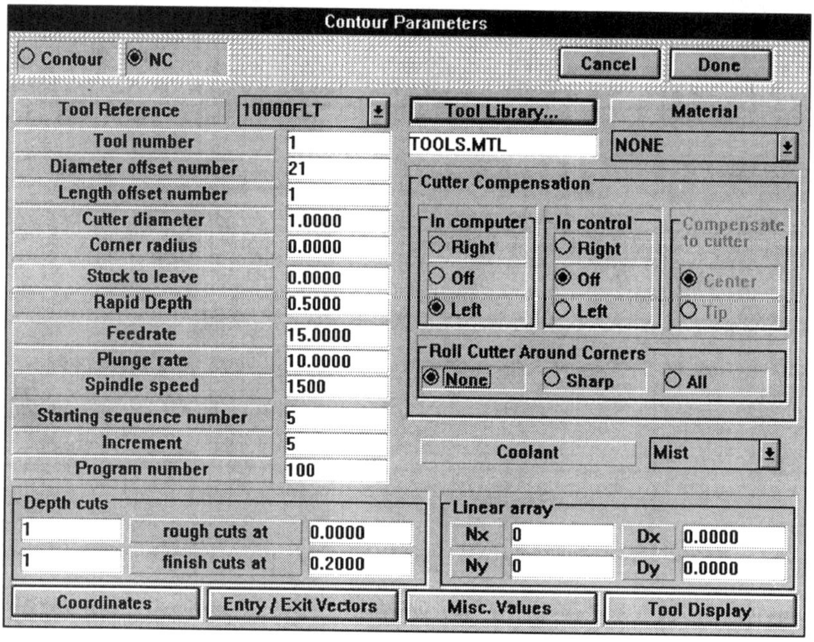

Select the **Done button** to complete the NC parameter settings.

Press **F3** to repaint the screen.

The toolpath should appear as Figure 7.34.

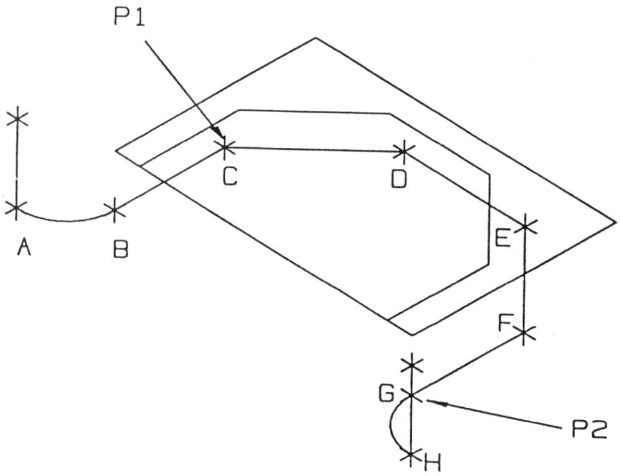

Figure 7.34

Step 7. Change Z-depth at C and G using the pick points in Figure 7.34.

Select **Depth** from the Change menu

Pick at **P1** (point C) then enter **-0.2** for the depth

Select **Ramp** to change the depth at C to -0.2

Select **Depth** again

Pick at **P2** (point G) then enter **-1.0** for the depth

Select **Ramp → Write**

Select **Yes** to accept the toolpath segment

The toolpaths with depth changes should be added to the drawing as shown in Figure 7.35.

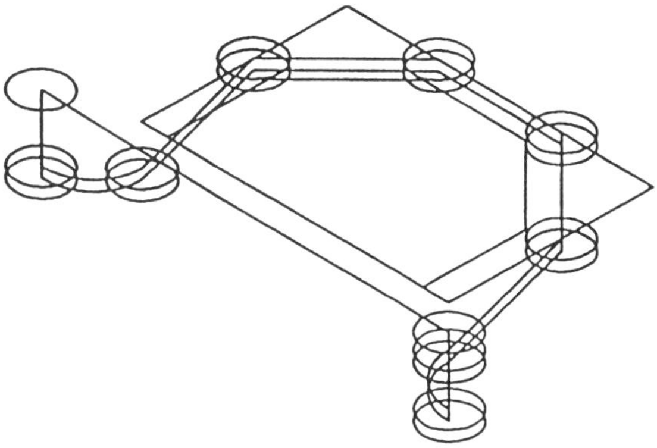

Figure 7.35

Step 8. Close the toolpath(NCI) file.

Select **End program** to end the NCI file
Select **No** to "run the post processor?"

Step 9. Backplot the toolpath.

Select **MAIN MENU →NC utils → Backplot → Display**
Set the display parameters:

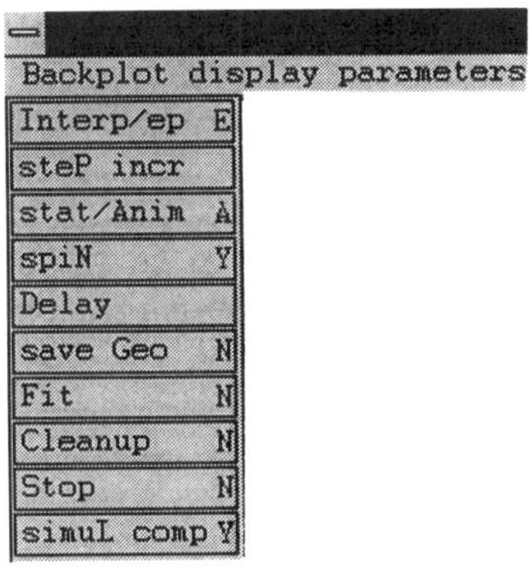

Select **BACKUP**
Set the Backplot parameters as below:

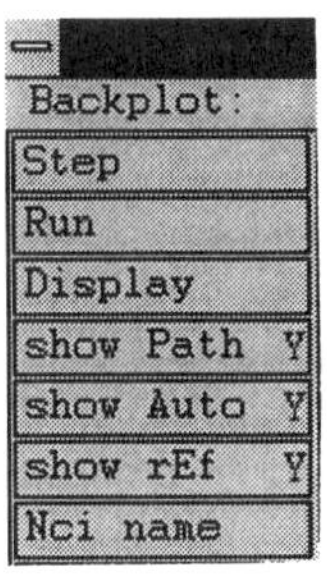

Select **Run**
The toolpaths are animated on the screen.

Step 10. Change Gview to Top.

Select **Gview → Top**

Select **Run** from the Backplot menu.

The geometry and toolpath drawing in the top view should resemble Figure 7.36 .

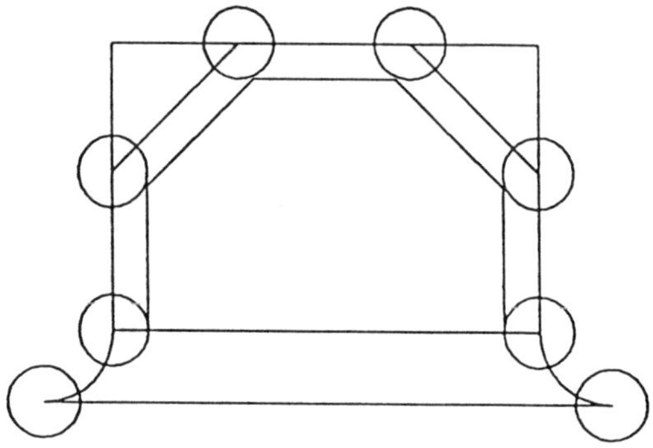

Figure 7.36

Step 11. Run the postprocessor.

Select **MAIN MENU → NC utils → Post proc → Run**

Enter file name of the toolpath: **contour3**

Enter file name of the part program: **contour3**

The partial program appears on screen. Double click the button on the upper left corner to return back to graphic mode.

Step 12. Edit the NC file.

Select **MAIN MENU →File → Edit →NC**

Enter file name: **contour3**

The NC part program should scroll on the screen.

Press **F10 →F9** to return back to graphic mode.

Project 4.

4

3-d Contouring

Mastercam can generate 3-d contouring toolpaths by using the contour module and setting the Cplane to 3-d. This allows lines and arcs to be cut in any plane (YZ-, ZX-, etc.). This project uses the 3-d contour function to create the toolpath along the profiles given in both front and side Cplanes as shown in Figure 7.37.

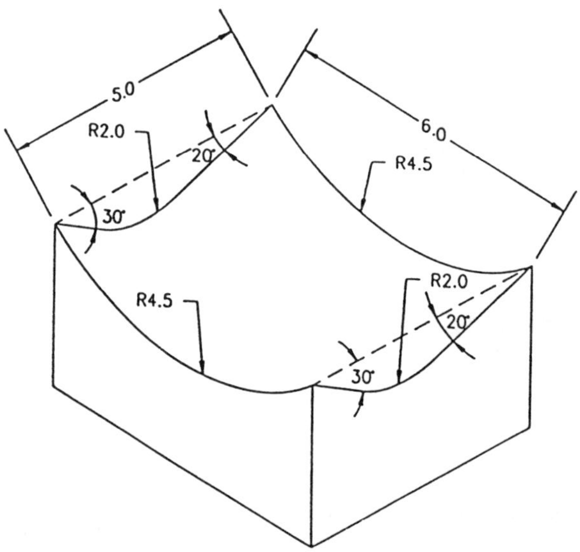

Figure 7.37

⌛**Tips** 1. Set the Cplane to 3-d.

2. Use 0.5-in. ball end mill with a 0.25-in. corner radius. The cutter center coincides with the contour profile. The cutter will cut deeper than the profile because no cutter compensation function is available in 3-d contouring.
3. Use two passes for depth cuts including one roughing cut and one finish cut. Set the finish cut value to 0.1-in.

Step 1. Load the geometry file (contour4.ge3)

Select **MAIN MENU →File → Get**
Enter file name: **contour4** ←
Select **Yes** to delete the current part if necessary

The drawing should look like Figure 7.38.

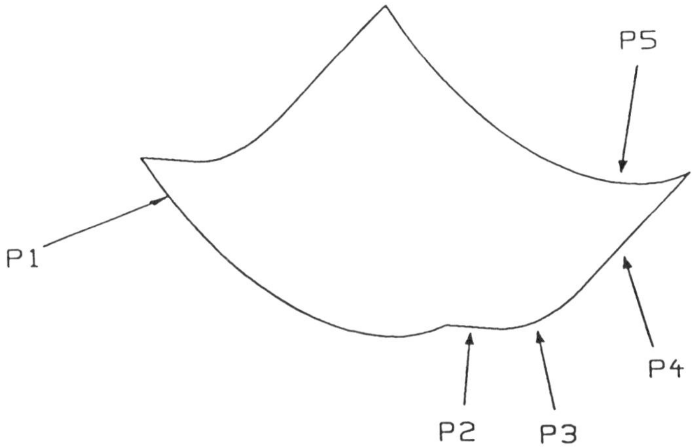

Figure 7.38

Step 2. Set Gview to isometric and Cplane to 3d if necessary.

Select **Gview → Isometric → Cplane → 3d**

Step 3. Initiate the contour module. Use the pick points in Figure 7.38.

Select **MAIN MENU → Toolpaths → Contour**
Enter file name: **contour4** ←
Select **Chain**
Pick at **P1** to select the first entity in the contour
Select **Close → Select nxt**
Sequentially pick at **P2, P3, P4, and P5**
(Note: The diamond shall return back to the start point of the first entity)
Select **End here → Done** to complete the contour
Select **Params**

Step 4. Define the contour parameters.

Set contour type to **3D**
Select the **NC** button

Step 5. Define NC parameters.

Set the NC parameters to the following settings:

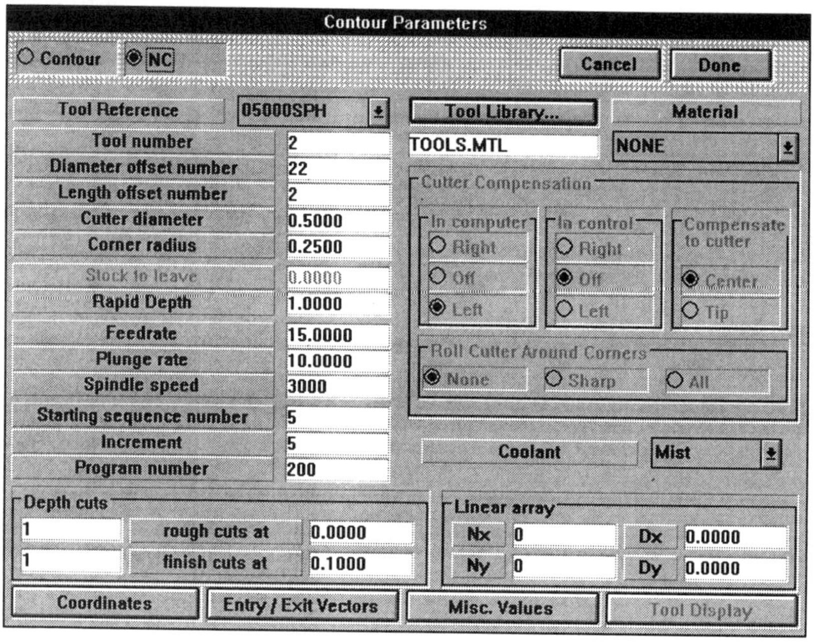

Select the **Done button** to complete the NC parameters settings.

The toolpaths of two passes should appear as seen in Figure 7.39.

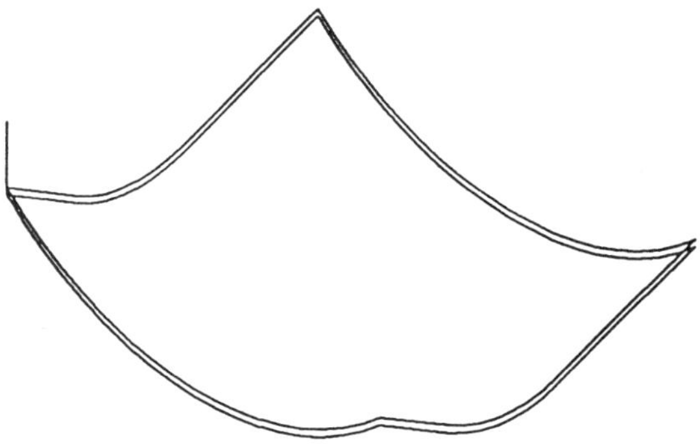

Figure 7.39.

Select **Yes** to accept the toolpaths

Step 5. Run the post processor

Select **End program** to close the NCI file

Select **Yes** to run the post processor

Enter the file name: **contour4**

The partial part program should appear on thescreen. Double click the button on the upper left corner to return back to graphic mode.

Step 6. Edit the NC file.

Select **MAIN MENU → File → Edit → NC**

Enter file name: **contour4 ←**

The NC file should appear on the screen. Do necessary editing, then press **F10 and F10 again** to return back to graphic mode.

7.5 Pocket Module

The pocket module is used to generate a set of toolpaths to (1) remove the material enclosed by a closed contour, (2) face a flat surface and (3) rough cut a local pocket. The following lists are the items the user must know in order to successfully implement the pocket module:

- Pocket parameters
- Cutting method
- Islands and their selection
- Machining sequence
- Pocket depth for finish passes

Pocket Parameters

There are **four** sets of pocket parameters: miscellaneous, roughing, finishing, and additional finish parameters. They are listed next:

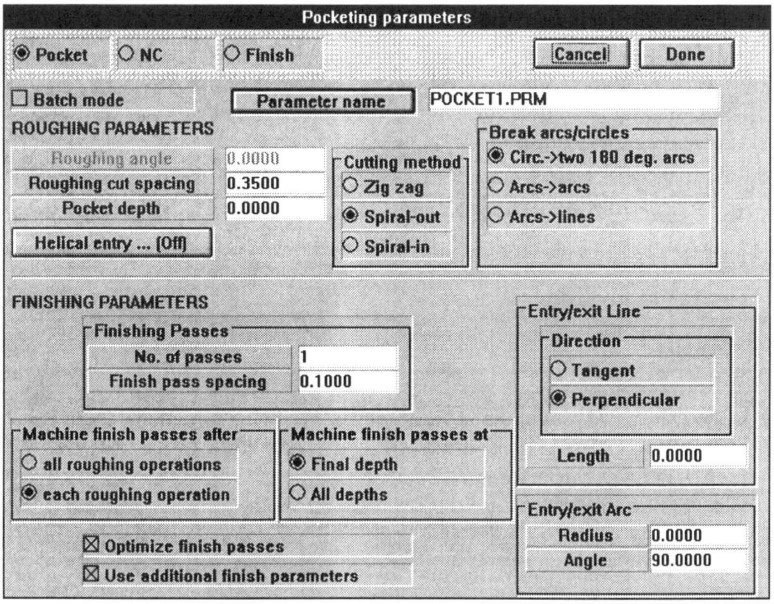

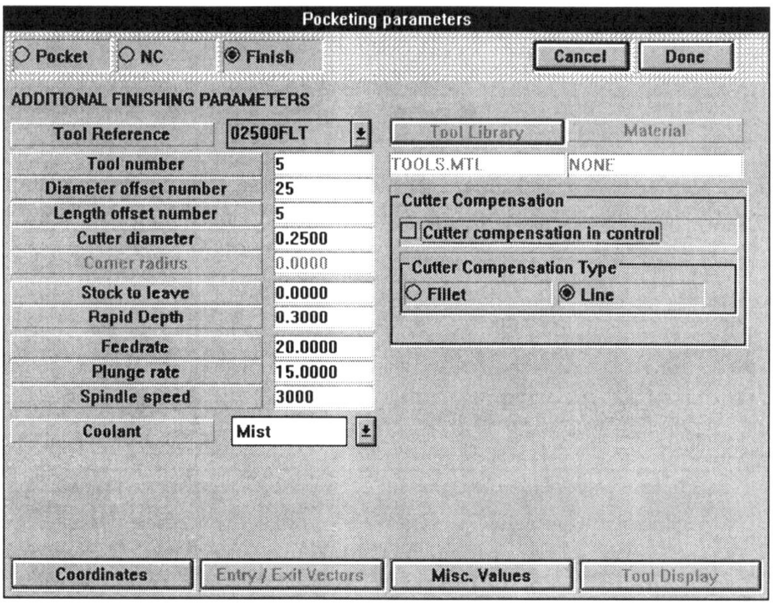

Batch Mode

This parameter allows the use of the same parameter settings for a series of pocketing jobs.

Break Arcs/Circles

This parameter allows a circle or an arc to be broken into more than one segment. It has the following three options:

Circles → two 180-degree arcs: breaks circles in the toolpath into two 180-degree arcs.
Arcs → arcs: breaks arcs in the toolpath into several small arcs. The span angle of these small arcs is determined by the maximum sweep parameter.
Arcs → lines: breaks arcs along the toolpath into a series of lines. The line segments are controlled by the value of chordal deviation.

Helical Entry

This parameter specifies how the cutter enters the part and begins cutting in a helical pattern. The parameters associated with the helical entry function are described below:

Radius	-specifies the maximum radius of the entry helix.
Angle	-specifies the ramp angle of the entry helix.
Error	-specifies the helix approximation error.
XY Clearance	-specifies the minimum clearance between the cutter and the finished pocket wall.
Depth	-specifies the total depth of the helix. It must be a positive value and has a larger value than the pocket depth.
Helix direction	-sets the helix cut direction either clockwise or counter-clockwise.
Helix Start Rate	-defines the feedrate for helix either at the plunge rate or the rapid rate.

Additional Finish Parameters

The purpose of additional finish parameters is to permit the user to define a separate set of NC parameters for finish passes. The parameter " Use additional finish parameters?" in the Pocket finishing parameter menu should be toggled to **yes** (with X mark) when you intend to use additional finish parameters.

When should you use additional finish parameters ?

Additional finish parameters are used in the following **two** applications:

1. A separate cutter is used for finish cuts. In other words, **two cutters** are used for pocketing; one for roughing and the other one for finishing. In this case, the tooling information given in the NC common parameters are for roughing cuts, the information specified in additional finish parameters is used for finish cuts.
2. Use the same tool for roughing and finish cuts but have a different set of feedrate, cutting speed, spindle speed, and cutter compensation for finish passes.

Cutting Methods

Mastercam provides **three cutting methods** for pocketing: zig zag, spiral-out and spiral-in.

Zig Zag Method

This method generates a set of back and forth linear tool paths to rough the pocket (refer to Figure 7.40). The orientation of the toolpath is specified by the roughing angle parameter. The roughing angle also decides the start point of the pocketing toolpath.

The cutting angle is measured from the positive X-axis and has a positive angle in the counter-clockwise direction and a negative angle in the clockwise direction (Figure 7.41).

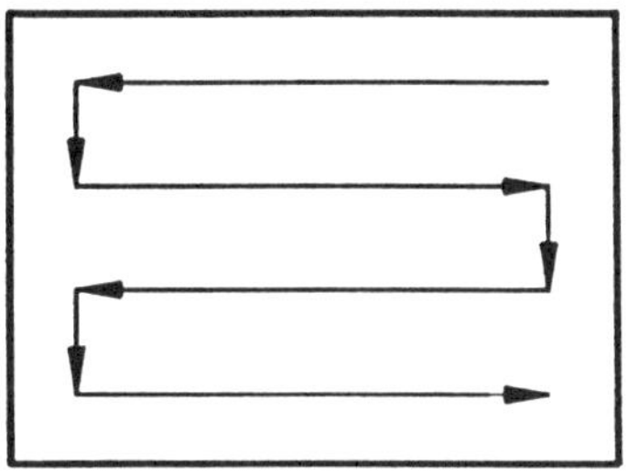

Figure 7.40

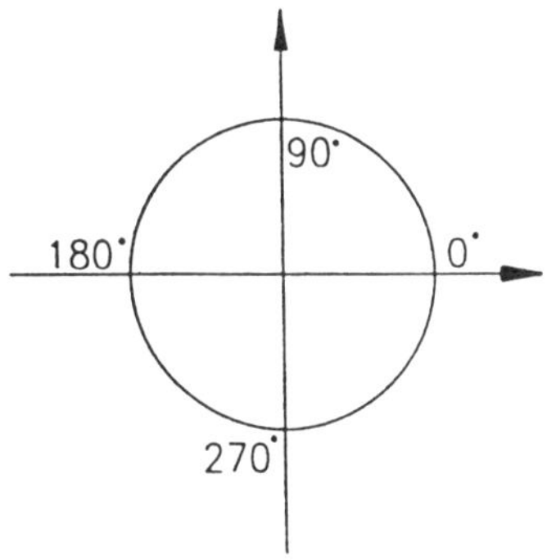

Figure 7.41

Figure 7.42 shows a number of common roughing angles and their toolpaths starting points.

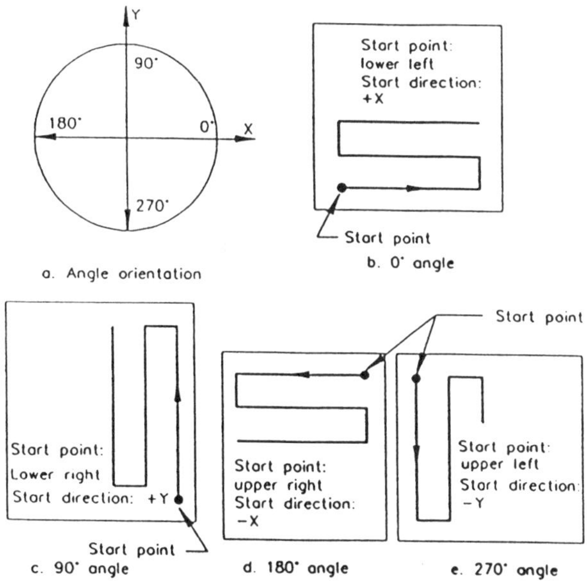

Figure 7.42 (Courtesy of Delmar Publishers, Inc.)

Spiral-out method

The spiral-out method starts the cutter at the pocket center or specified pocket start point and spirals it to the wall of the pocket (Figure 7.43).

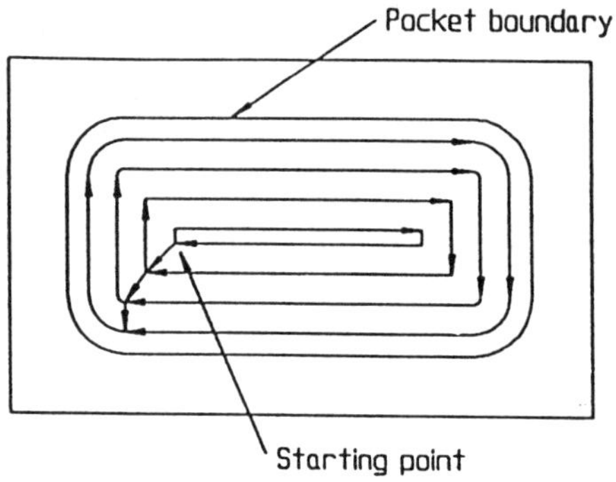

Figure 7.43

Spiral-in method

The spiral-in method spirals the cutter from the outside wall of the pocket to the pocket center (Figure 7.44).

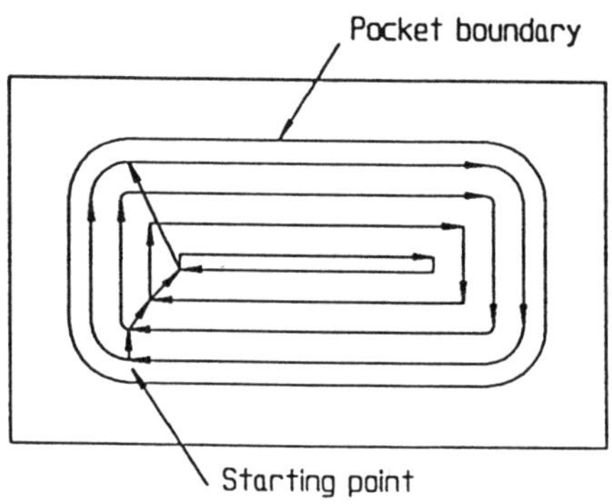

Figure 7.44

Islands

Islands are areas inside the pocket boundary that are not intended to be machined during pocketing (Figure 7.45). The islands must be closed contours.

Mastercam uses the first selected contour as the outside contour for the pocket and all subsequent contours as islands.

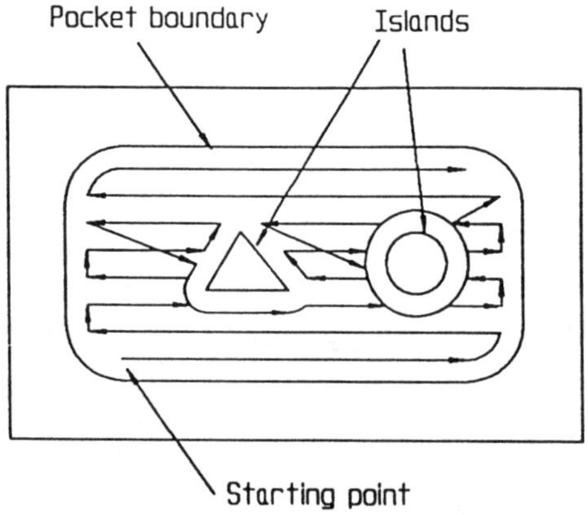

Figure 7.45

Regions

The system may divide the pocketing area into a number of regions when pocketing with islands. More than one region is formed when the gap between the pocket wall and the island is smaller than the cutter diameter. Figure 7.46 shows three regions resulted from two islands that have the gaps with the pocket boundary being less than the designated cutter diameter.

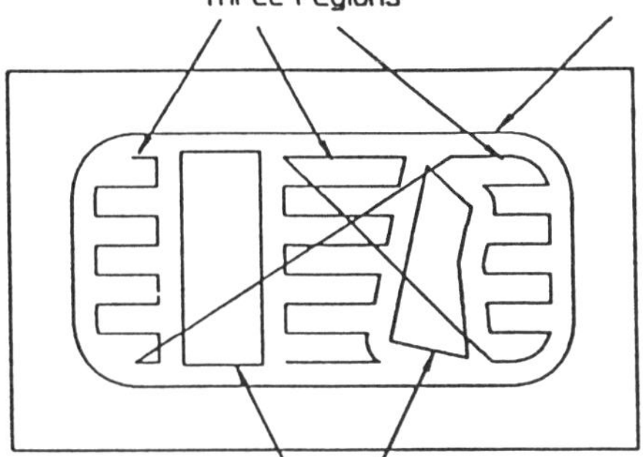

Figure 7.46

Machining sequence

The toolpath pattern for pocketing with islands forming more than one region can be set to either the **all roughing operations mode** or **each roughing operation mode**. In the **each roughing operation mode**, each pocket region is completely machined including rough, finish, depth cuts and linear array before moving to the next region.

In **all roughing operations mode**, the system generates the toolpaths to machine each operation on all pocket regions before performing the next operation. The system will rough all pocket regions before any finish passes or depth cuts are performed.

Figure 7.47 shows a two pocket regions example. In **each roughing operation mode**, the toolpath sequence follows rough region 1 → finish region 1 → rough region 2 → finish region 2. In **all roughing operations mode**, the sequence becomes rough region 1 → rough region 2 → finish region 1 → finish region 2.

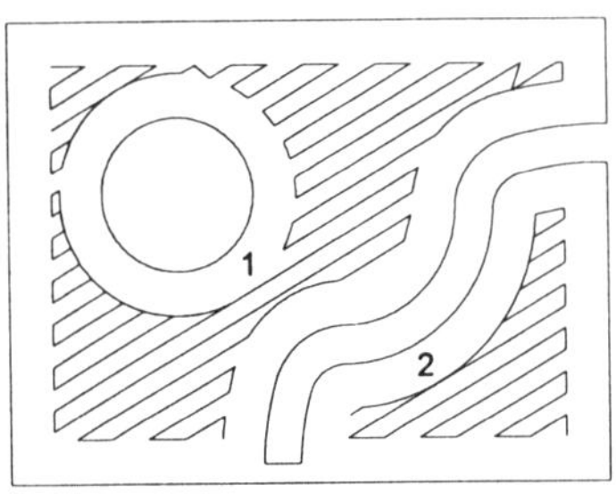

Figure 7.47a All roughing operations

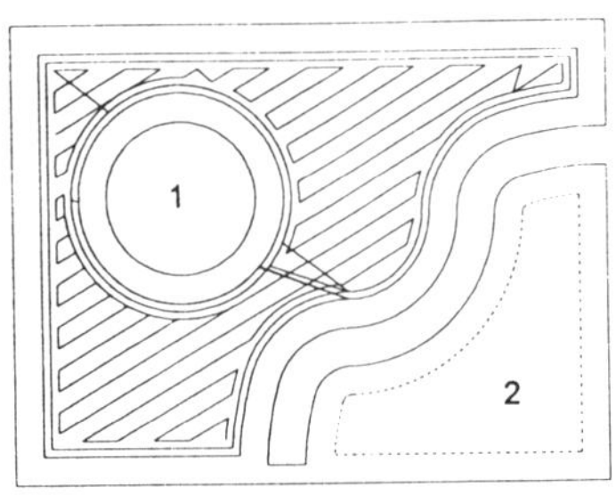

Figure 7.47b Each roughing operation

Depth (Z value) Control

Mastercam uses four parameters to define the depth (Z values) of pocketing operations (refer to Figure 7.48). The values are:

Rapid depth = 0.2 or any value.
Pocket depth = the actual depth of the pocket.
Depth cuts = Rough : _____ cuts at ______
Finish: _____ cuts at ______
Machine finish passes at = final depth/all depths

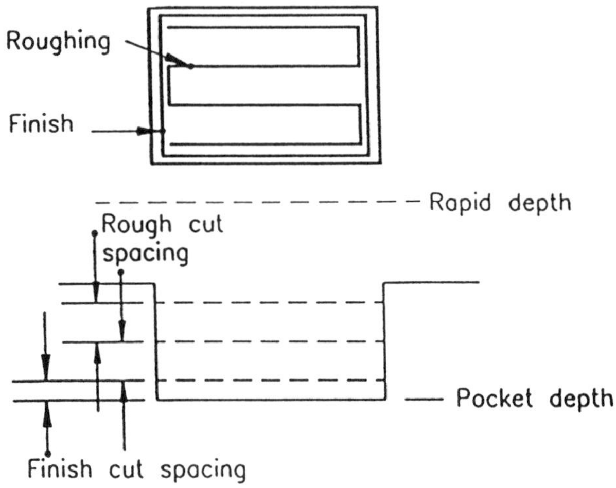

Figure 7.48

The first three parameters have been discussed in previous sections. The parameter of "machine finish passes at" determines the number of finish passes in the Z direction. When this parameter is set to **final depth**, the system will generate the same number of finish toolpaths at the final depth of the pocket as the specified number of finish cuts. When the parameter is set to **all depths**, the system will perform the finish passes after each roughing cut. In other words, the number of finish passes in the Z direction is the sum of rough cuts and finish cuts specified in the depth cuts parameters. Figure 7.49 shows the differences between the finish toolpaths of two finish pass modes.

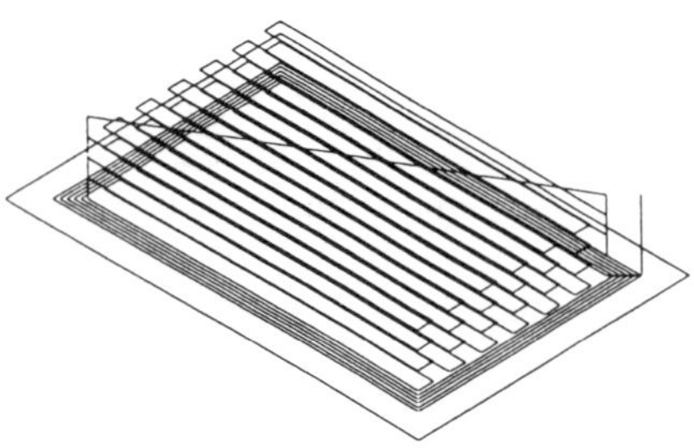

Figure 7.49a Final depth

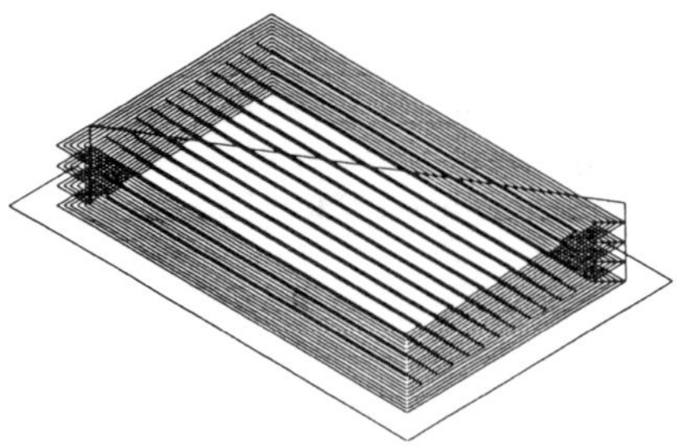

Figure 7.49b All depths

Tips 1. The pocket module is typically used in the following applications:

a. Cut internal pockets without islands.
b. Cut internal pockets with islands.
c. Face flat surfaces.
d. Machine step flat surfaces with islands.

2. Factors to be considered in selecting the cutting method: The selection of a cutting method determines the milling type (conventional milling or climb milling) and program size. With the zig zag cutting method, the cutter engages the workpiece with alternating milling types. It has conventional milling in one direction and changes to climb milling in the other direction as shown in Figure 7.50 on the next page.

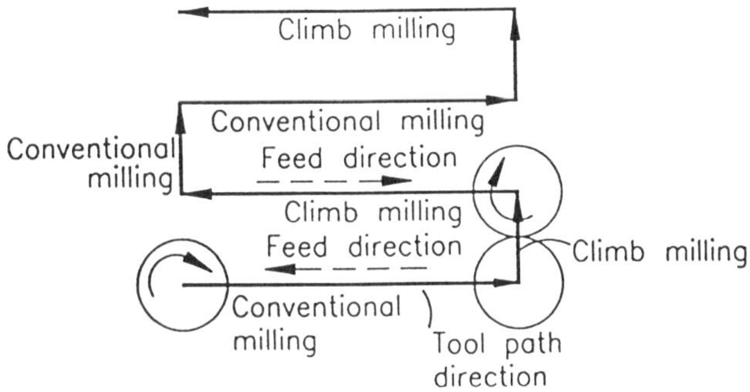

Figure 7.50

In both methods: spiral-out (Figure 7.51) and spiral-in (Figure 7.52), the milling type remains the same througout the profile.

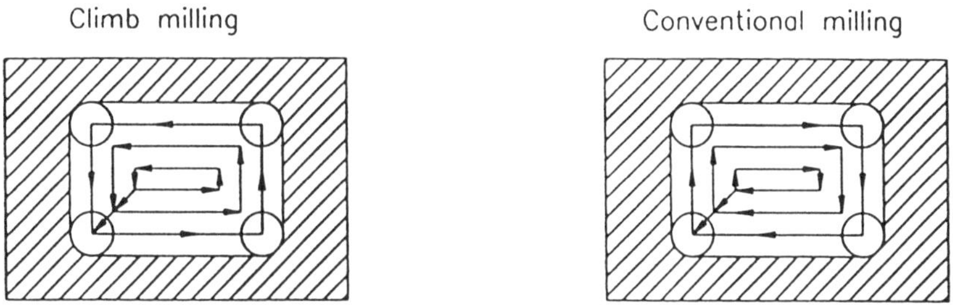

Figures 7.51

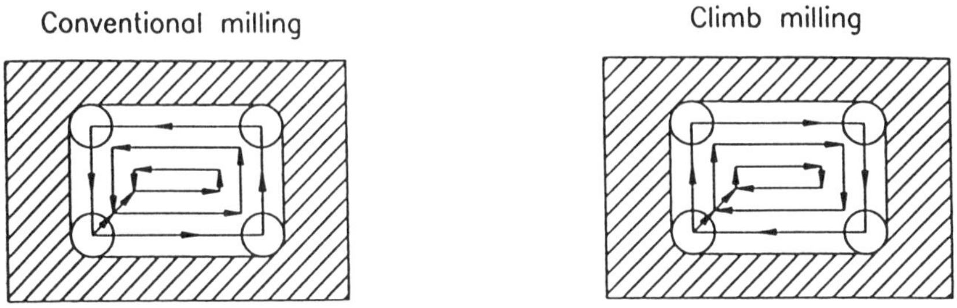

Figure 7.52

Suggestions:

- Use climb milling, if possible, to produce a better surface finish.
- Avoid using the zigzag cutting method if possible. Alternating milling types is undesirable.
- Use the spiral-in method when pocketing with islands that are located near the pocket center.

3. Selecting the start entity of the pocket and the contour direction. The start entity picked during defining the pocket contour determines the start position of the pocketing toolpath and contour direction which is cutting direction being either in clockwise or counter-clockwise (Figure 7.53).

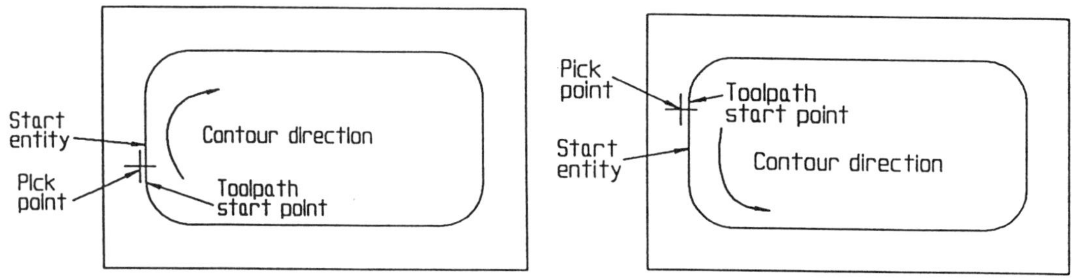

Figure 7.53

4. Selecting machining sequence mode (all roughing operations *or* each roughing operation): The all roughing operations mode should be used when the cutter for finish cuts differs from the roughing tool. This is due to the fact that a tool change is required from each roughing cut to finish cut and from each finish cut to roughing cut. When more than one region boundary is involved, the required number of tool changes is equal to twice of the number of region boundaries in the region mode. Three region boundaries, for example, require 6 (or 2 x 3) tool change actions. With the all roughing operations mode, only one tool change action is required regardless of the number of region boundaries involved.

5. Avoid using entry/exit line and arc in pocketing with islands whenever possible. Improper combination of entry/exit line and arc often results in undesired gouging into the outer boundary or island boundaries (Figure 7.54).

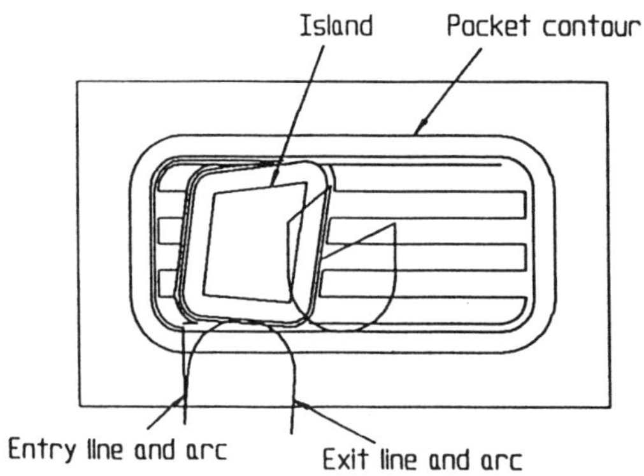

Figure 7.54

Pocketing Projects

Two pocketing projects are presented in this section. The first project generates the toolpaths to cut an internal pocket without having an island. The second project uses the pocket module twice to (1) face the top flat surface and (2) cut the internal pocket with an island.

Project 5.

5

Pocketing an internal pocket

Part Geometry Creation

Project 3 of Chapter 5 (pocket1)

Use the pocket module to generate the toolpaths to cut the internal pocket for the part shown in Figure 7.55.

We are here

Go to

Toolpath Generation (pocket1)

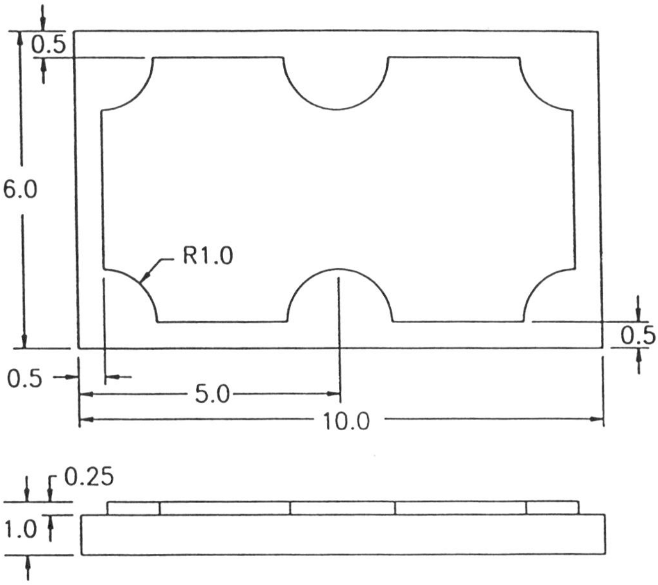

Figure 7.55

Tips 1. Define the contour direction in the counter-clockwise direction to obtain the climb milling operation.

2. Use a spiral-out cutting method because there is no island involved.

3. Use two cutters, 0.5" end mill for roughing cuts and 0.25" end mill for the finish pass.

4. The roughing cut spacing is 0.35" (or 0.7D).

5. The number of the finish pass is 1 and finishing pass spacing is 0.1".

6. Since two cutters are used, the parameter "Use additional finish parameters?" should be set to Yes.

Step 1. Load the part geometry file (pocket1.ge3) or create the geometry by following the instructions given in Project 3 of Chapter 5. The part geometry drawing should appear on screen as Figure 7.56.

Select **MAIN MENU →File → Get**

Enter file name: **pocket1 ←**

Select **Yes** to delete the current part if necessary

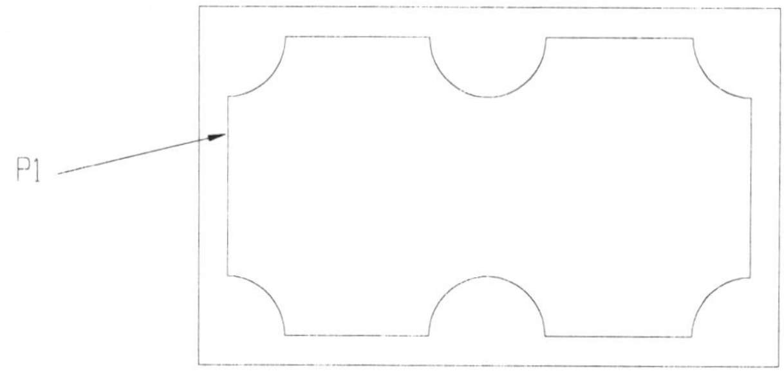

Figure 7.56

Step 2. Initiate the pocket module.

Select **MAIN MENU** → **Toolpaths** → **Pocket**
Enter file name: **pocket1** ←

Step 3. Define pocketing contour using the pick point in Figure 7.53.

Select **Chain** from the Chaining method menu
Pick at **P1** to select the first contour entity
Select **Close** → **End here** → **Done** to complete the contour

Step 4. Define pocketing parameters.

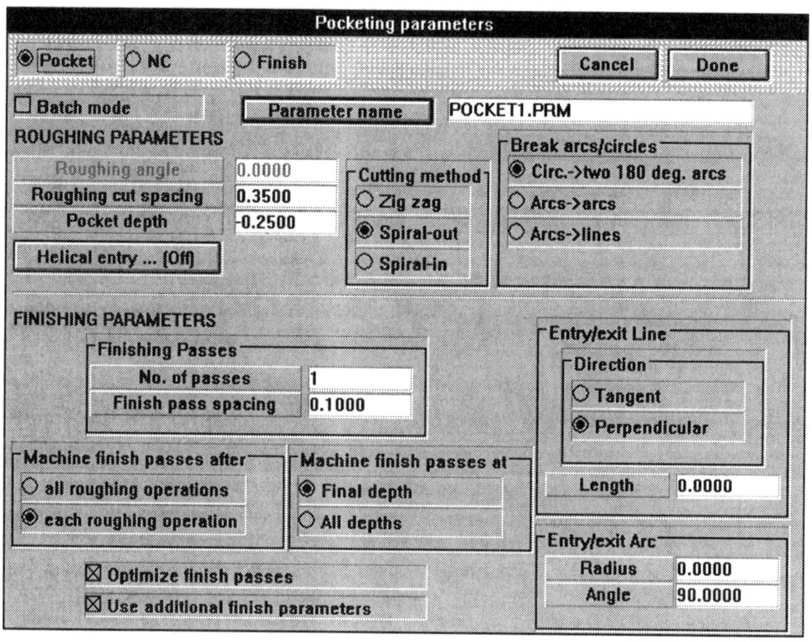

Select the **NC Button** to advance to the NC parameter window.

Step 5. Define the NC Parameters.

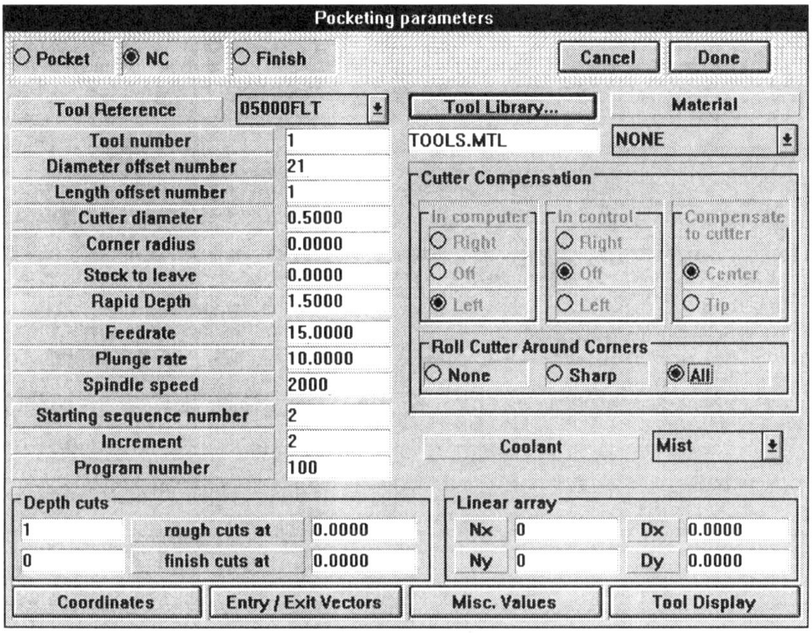

Select the **Finish button** to advance to additional finish parameters menu.

Step 6. Define the additional finish parameters.

Set the additional finish parameters to the following settings:

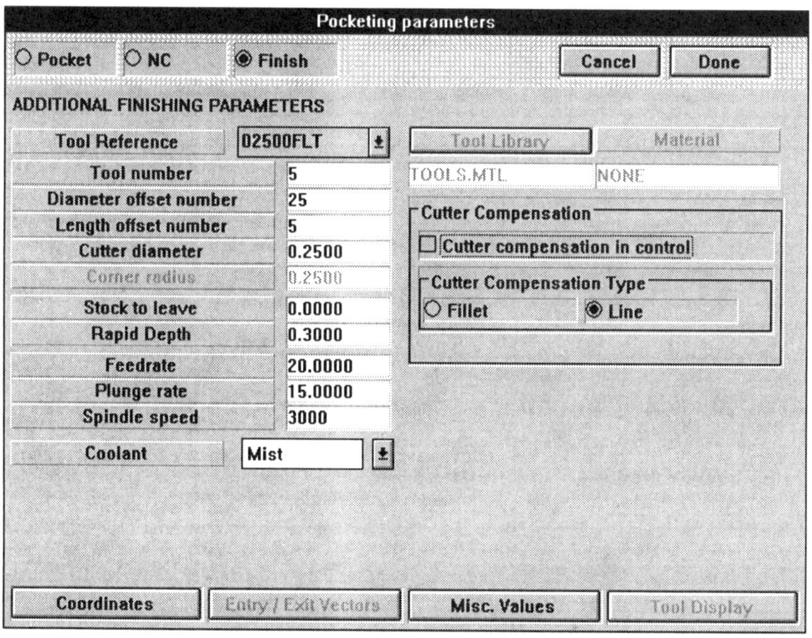

Select the **Done button** to complete the parameter settings.

Step 7. Select command from pocket selection menu.

Press **F3** to repaint the screen
Select **All** to generate pocketing toolpaths
The toolpaths shall resemble Figure 7.57.

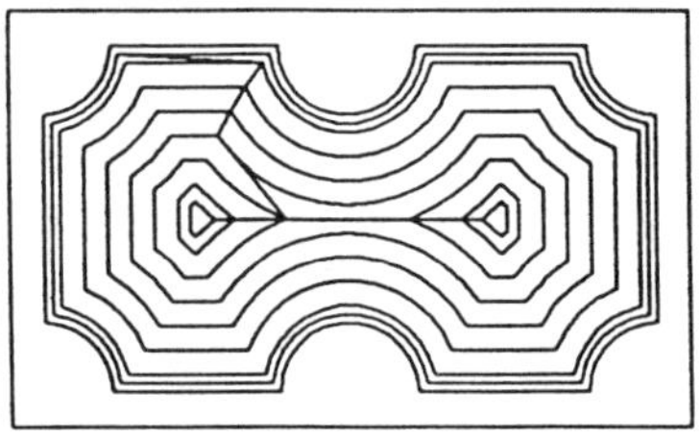

Figure 7.57

Step 8. Accept toolpaths.

Select **Done** from pocket selection menu
Select **Yes** to accept the toolpath segment
Select **End program** to close the toolpath file
Select **No** to "Run the post processor?"

Step 9. Change Gview to isometric.

Select **Gview → Isometric**
The isometric view should look like Figure 7.58.

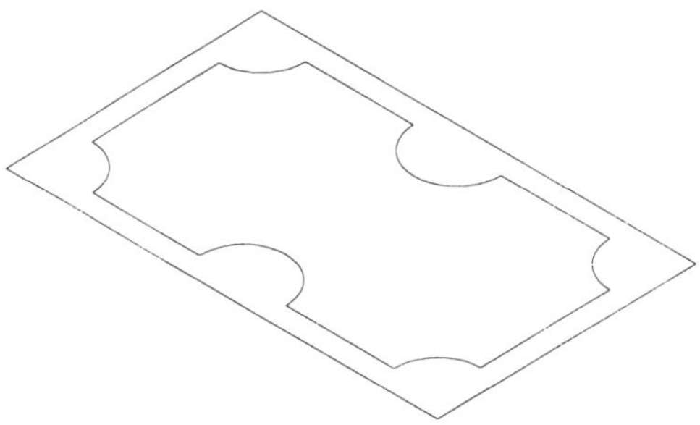

Figure 7.58

Step 10. Initiate the Backplot function.

Select **MAIN MENU → NC utils → Backplot → Display**
Set the Backplot display parameters as shown below:

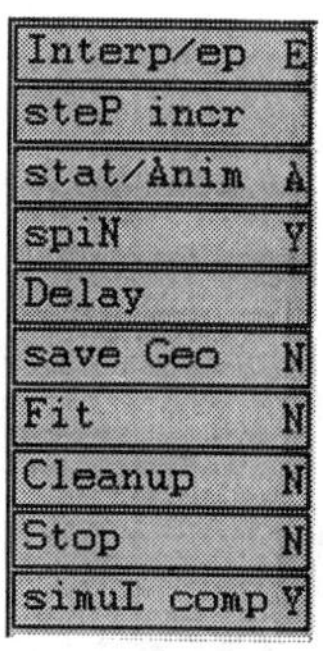

Select **BACKUP**
Set the Backplot parameters as below:

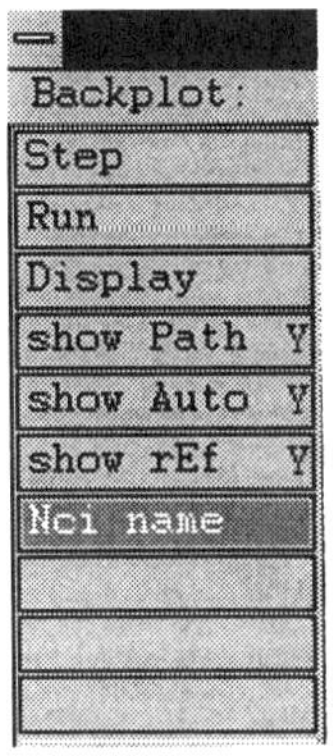

Select **Run**

Note: A 1/2-in. end mill with a tool holder will appear on the screen. The toolpaths will be backplotted with this cutter as in Figure 7.59. A 1/4-in. end mill will appear for the finish cut toolpath.

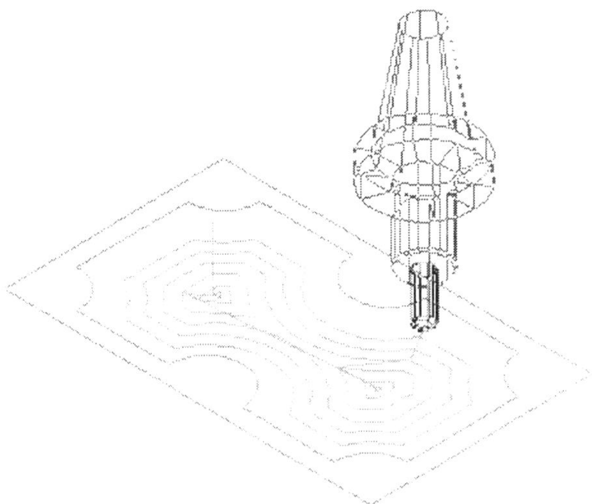

Figure 7.59

Step 11. Run the postprocessor.

Select **BACKUP → Post Proc → Run**
Enter file name: **pocket1 ←**

The part program should appear on the screen. Double click the window button on the upper left corner to return to graphic mode.

MCTV (Mastercam Toolpath Verification) Module

MCTV is a powerful solid-model NC verification tool for Mastercam Mill Version 5. This module uses the NCI file as the input to show the toolpath and the finshed part in solid model form. Toolpath verification is very important in NC programming for the following reasons:

- Detect potential errors in part programs before they are used in tryout run or actual machining on NC machines.
- Simulate graphically the machining of the part programs.
- Eliminate the need for tryout run.

Procedure for Using MCTV

1. Generate toolpath file (.NCI).
2. Initiate the toolpath verification module by using the following commands:

   Select **MAIN MENU → NC utils → mCtv***

3. Define the workpiece stock. Note that the stock you can specify is only rectangular block.
4. Specify the project name (or the NCI file) to be verified.
5. Execute the verification by using the following commands:

   Select **Module → Turbo → Go**

6. Run CMM inspection function to check the coordinate values of the finished part.
7. Exit MCTV module and return back to Mastercam Graphic mode.

Step 12. Initiate the MCTV module.

Select **MAIN MENU → NCutils →mCtv***
Enter file name: **pocket1.nci ←**

Step 13. Define workpiece stock

Set the size of stock to the following values:

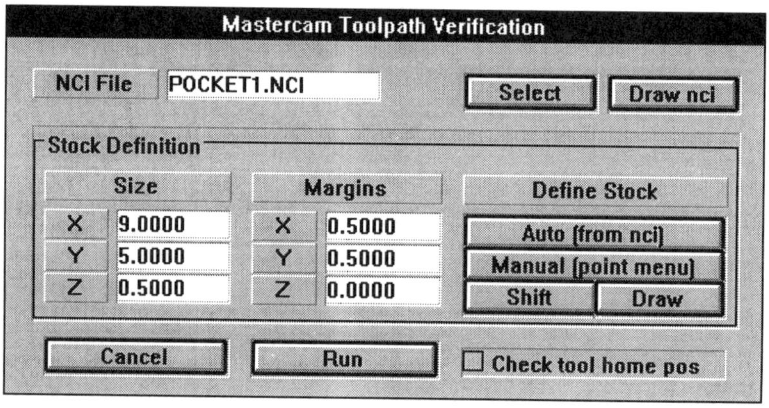

Select **Run**

Step 14. Select the NCI file to be verified.

Select **FILE →PROJECT**
The project name "#\C:\Mill5\NCI\POCKET1.NCI" will appear.
Select **OK**
Select **Yes** to "An old RVP file exists, re-translate?" if necessary.

Step 15. Execute verification module

Select **MODULE → TURBO →Go**

The solid model of a finished part should appear on the screen as shown in figure 7.60 on the following page.

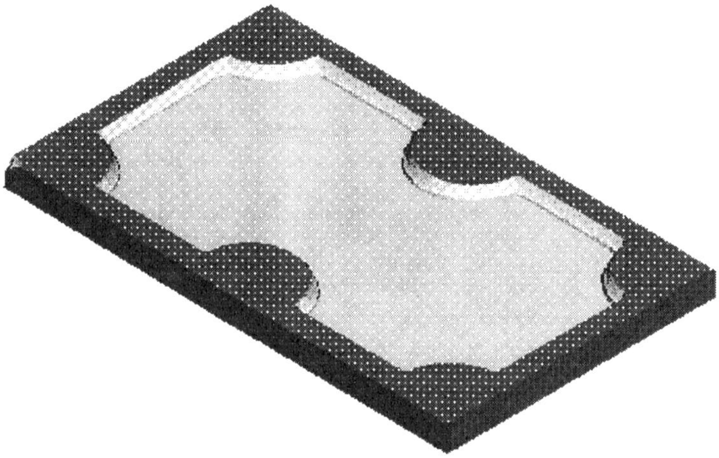

Figure 7.60

Step 16. Execute the CMM inspection function.

Select **EXAMINE → CMM inspection**

Use the mouse to pick the points you want to inspect. The coordinate values of these picked points should be displayed on the screen.

Select **Done**

Step 17. Exit verification module.

Double click the **MCTV window button** in its upper-left corner
Select **Cancel** to return back to the graphic mode

Project 6.

6

Facing top flat surface and pocketing with an island.

In the part shown in Figure 7.61 on the next page, the pocket module is used **three** times to generate the toolpaths to (1) face the top flat surface, (2) pocket the internal profile with a circle island at the center, and (3) pocket a circular profile. The raw material is a solid circular block. The outer circular profile of the block has been premachined to the desired dimension. One face of the block has also been faced. The thickness of the block is about 1.05-in.

Part Geometry Creation

Project 5 of Chapter 6 (pocket2)

Go to

We are here

Toolpath Generation

(pocket2)

Figure 7.61

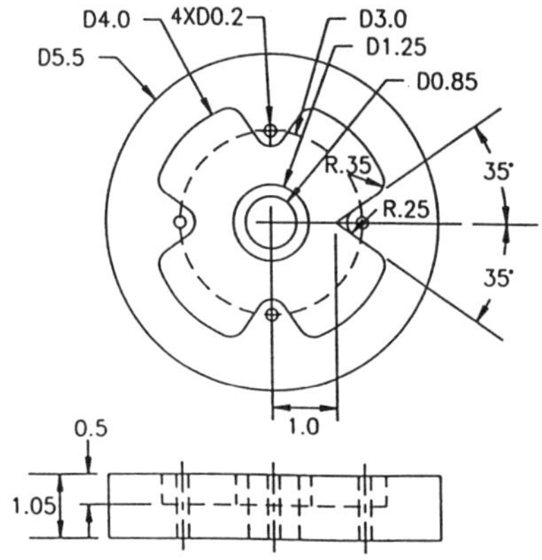

Tips 1. Start the operation sequence with facing the top flat surface followed by pocketing the larger internal profile, and finally pocketing the circular profile.

2. Two cutters are used including:

1-in. end mill for facing the top flat surface
1/2-in. end mill for two pocketing operations

3. A construction circle which has a larger diameter than the outer circle should be added to serve as the outside pocket boundary for facing the top flat surface. If the original outer circle is used as the outside pocketing boundary, several pieces of uncut material may be left around the perimeter of the boundary. The diameter of this construction circle is suggested as 5.7-in.

4. Main pocketing parameters for the facing are:

1 roughing cut and 1 finish cut
Roughing cut spacing = 0.6"
Cutting method = Zig zag

5. Main pocketing parameters for pocketing the larger profile are:

Cutting method: Spiral-out
Roughing cut spacing = 0.35"
Pocket depth = -0.5"
Number of finish passes = 1
Finishing pass spacing = 0.05"
No entry/exit length and arc
Machine finish passes at final depth
Two passes of depth cut: Rough: 1 cut at 0.0 Finish: 1 cut at 0.2"
Do not require additional finish parameters

6. Main pocketing parameters for pocketing the circular profile include:

Cutting method: Spiral-out
Rough cut spacing = 0.35"
Pocket depth = -1.0"
Number of finish passes = 1
Finishing pass spacing = 0.05"
No entry/exit length and arc
Machine finish passes at all depths
Three passes of depth cut: Rough: 2 cuts at 0.4" Finish: 1 cut at 0.2"
No additional finish parameters required

Step 1. Load the part geometry file (pocket2.ge3) or create the geometry by following the instructions given in Project 5 of Chapter 6.

Select **MAIN MENU →File →Get**
Enter file name: **pocket2←**
Select **Yes** to delete the current part

The part geometry drawing should appear on screen as Figure 7.62.

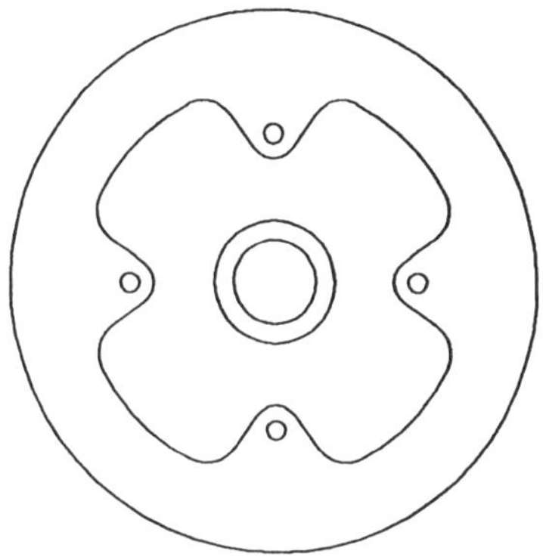

Figure 7.62

Step 2. Create a construction circle.

Select **MAIN MENU → Create → Arc → pt Dia cir**
Enter the center point: **0,0** ←
Enter the diameter: **5.7** ←

The circle should have been added as shown in Figure 7.63.

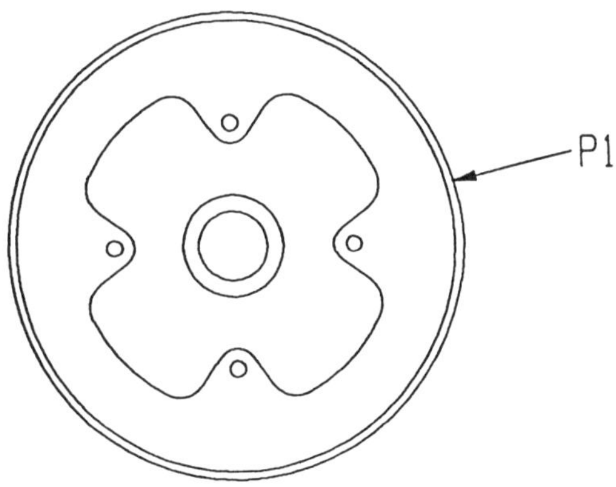

Figure 7.63

Step 3. Initiate the pocket module.

Select **MAIN MENU → Toolpaths → Pocket**
Enter file name: **pocket2** ←

Step 4. Define pocketing contour using the pick point in Figure 7.63.

Select **Single** from the Chaining method menu
Pick at **P1**

Step 5. Define the pocket parameters.

Set the pocket parameters to the following settings:

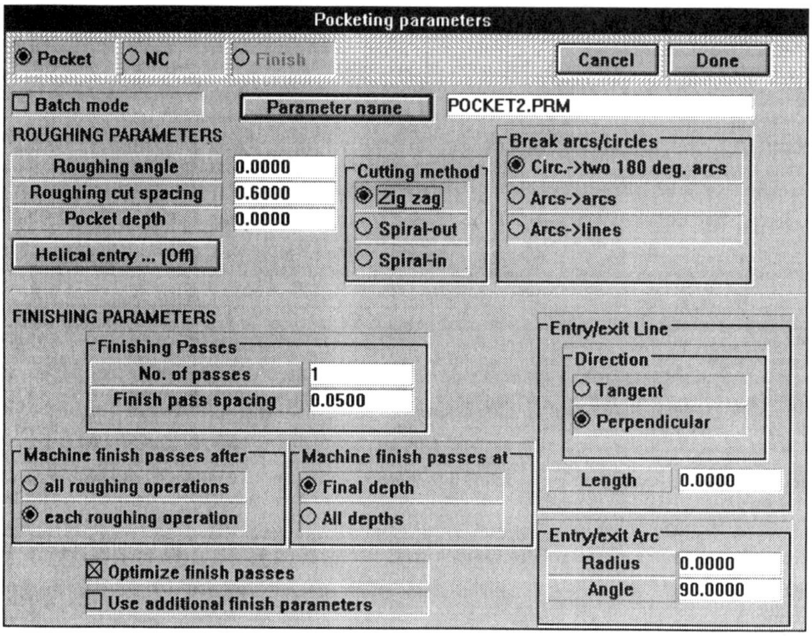

Select the **NC button** to advance to the next parameter screen.

Step 6. Define the NC parameters.

Set the NC parameters to the following settings:

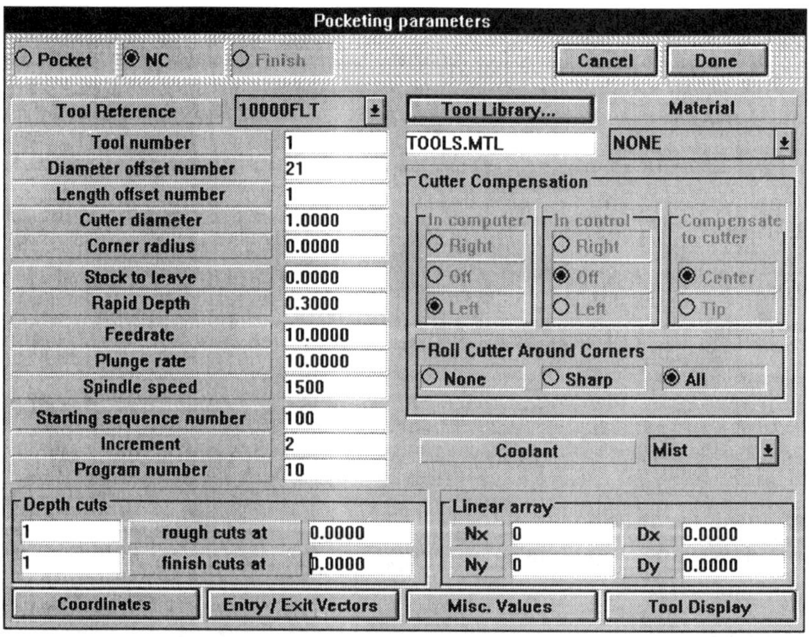

Select the **Done button** to complete the parameter settings.

Step 7. Make pocket selection.

Press **F3** to repaint the screen
Select **All** from the pocket selection menu
Select **Done** to complete the pocketing toolpaths
Select **Yes** to accept the toolpath segment
The toolpaths with the tool should resemble Figure 7.64.

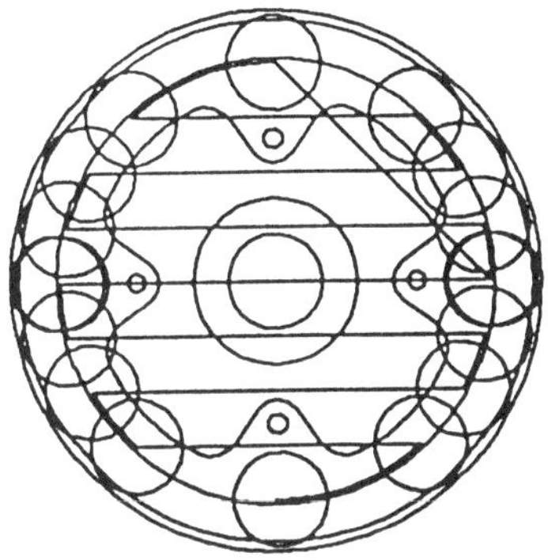

Figure 7.64

Press **Alt + F1** simultanueously to re-display the toolpath as shown in Figure 7.65. Turn tool path off **Alt+T**, **F3**, **Get Back Alt+T**, **F3**, will redisplay until program is ended.

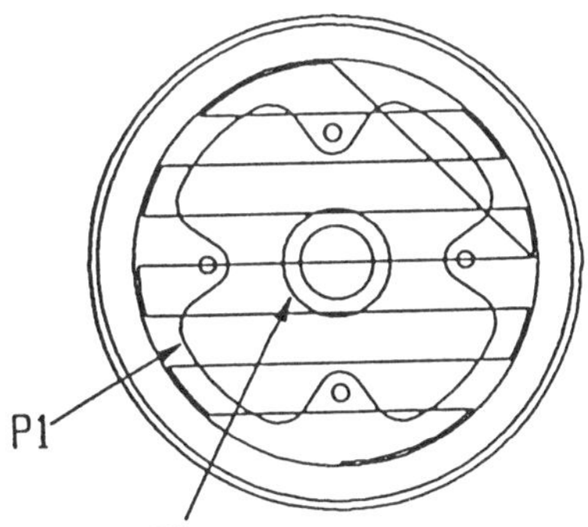

Figure 7.65

Step 8. Initiate pocket module for pocketing the larger internal profile.

Select **MAIN MENU → Toolpaths → Pocket**

Step 9. Define pocketing contour using the pick points in Figure 7.65.

Select **Chain** from the Chaining method menu
Pick at **P1** to select the first entity
Select **Close → End here** to complete the outside contour
Select **Single** from the Chaining method menu for island 1
Pick at **P2** to select the island
Select **Done** to complete the contour selection

Step 10. Define pocket parameters.

Set the pocket parameters to the following settings:

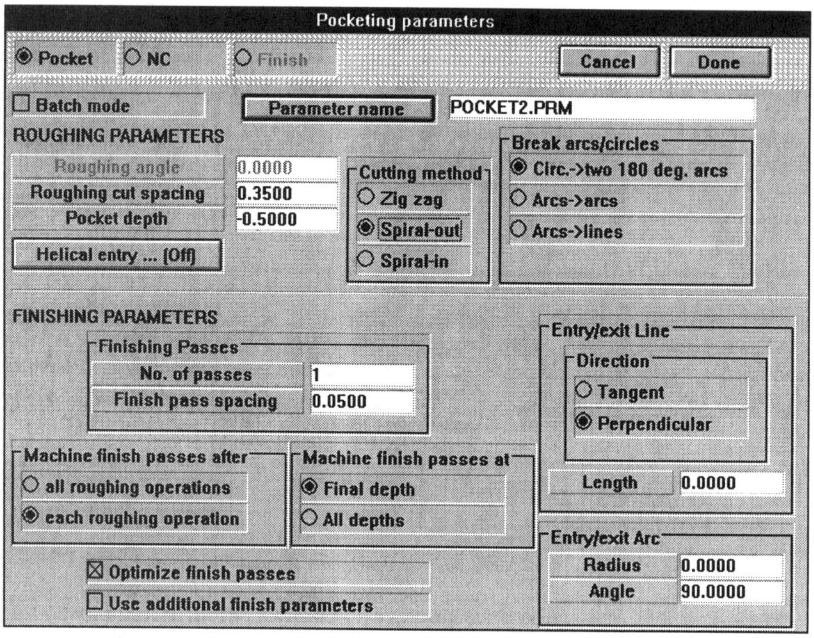

Select the **NC button** to advance to the next parameter screen.

Step 11. Define the NC parameters.

Set the NC parameters to the following settings:

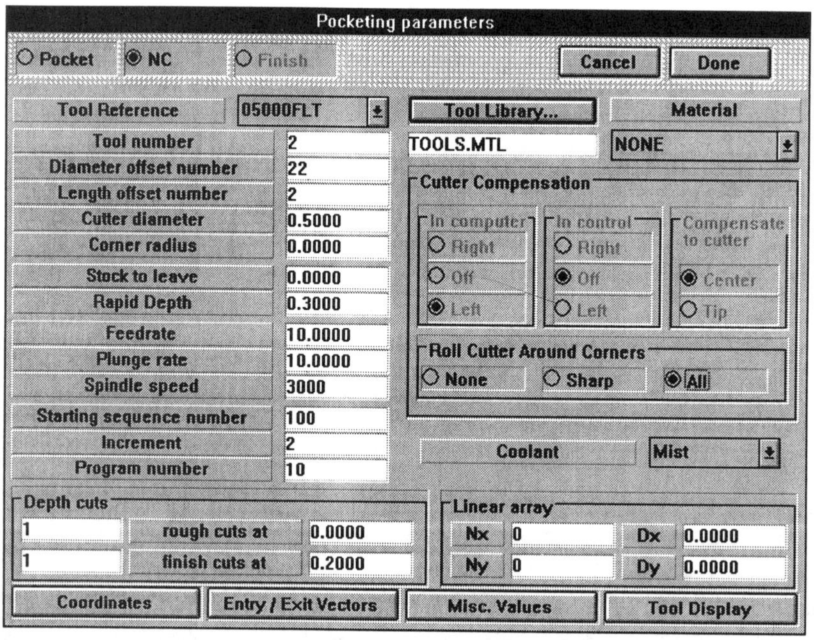

Select the **Done button** to complete the parameter settings.

Step 12. Make pocket selection.

Press **F3** to repaint the screen

Select **All** → **Done** to generate toolpaths

Select **Yes** to accept the toolpath segment

The pocketing toolpaths are added to the drawing as shown in Figure 7.66.

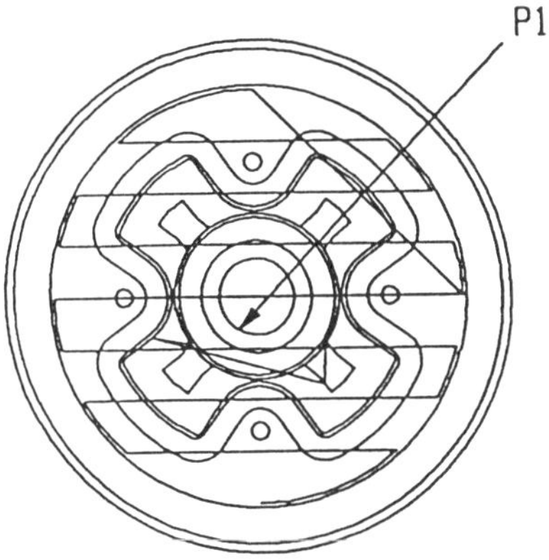

Figure 7.66

Step 13. Initiate the pocket module to cut the circular pocket.

Select **Pocket**

Step 14. Define the pocket boundary using the pick point in Figure 7.66.

Select **Single** from the Chaining method menu

Pick at **P1** to select the inner circle

Select **Done**

Step 15. Define the pocket parameters.

Set the pocket parameters to the following settings:

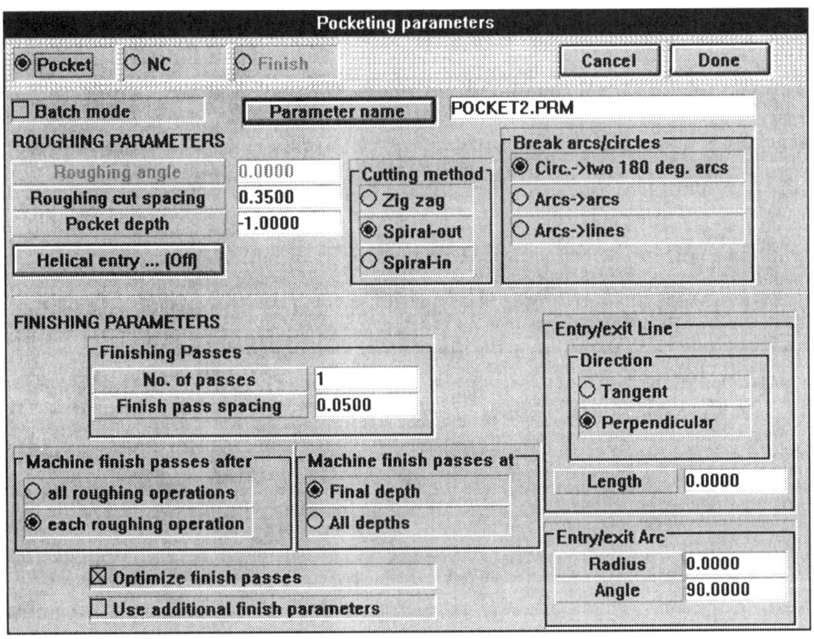

Select the **NC button** to advance to the next parameter screen.

Step 16. Define the NC parameters.

Set the NC parameters to the following settings:

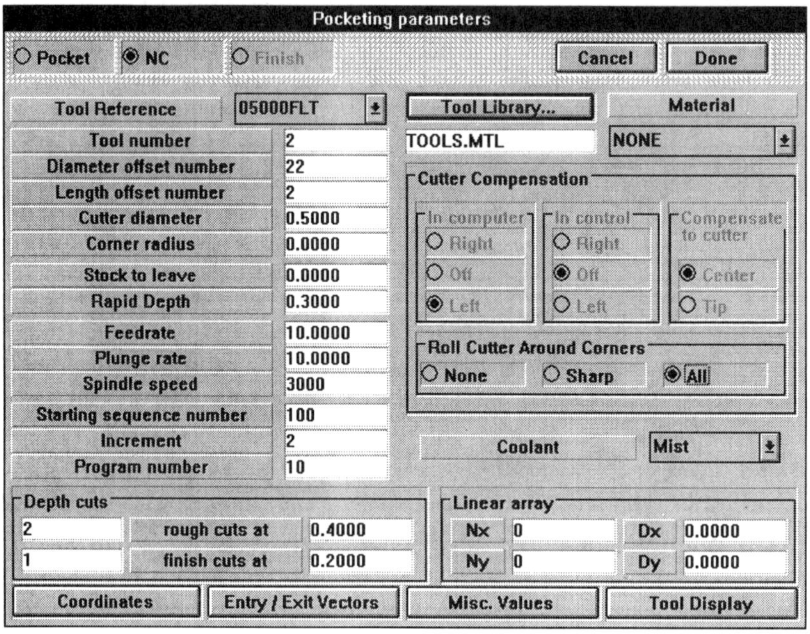

Select the **Done button** to complete the parameter settings.

Step 17. Make pocket selection.

Press **F3** to repaint the screen

Select **All** → **Done** to complete pocketing toolpaths

Select **Yes** to accept the toolpath segment

The complete toolpaths with part geometry should resemble Figure 7.67.

Figure 7.67

Step 18. Change Gview to isometric.

Select **Gview** → **Isometric**

The drawing shown in isometric view shuold look like Figure 7.68.

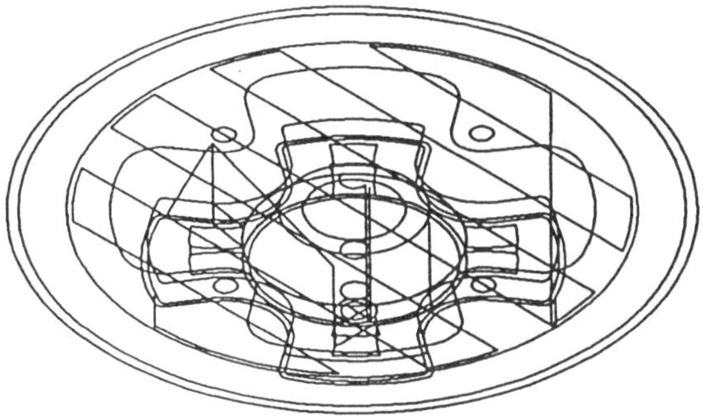

Figure 7.68

Step 19. Run the postprocessor.

Select **End program** to close the toolpath file
Select **Yes** to run the postprocessor
Enter file name: **pocket2** ←

The part program should appear on the screen.

Double click the **Window button** in the upper-left corner to return back to graphic mode.

Step 20. Initiate MCTV module.

Select **MAIN MENU** → **NC utils** → **mCtv***
Enter file name: **pocket2.nci**

Step 21. Define workpiece stock.

Set the size of the stock to the following values:

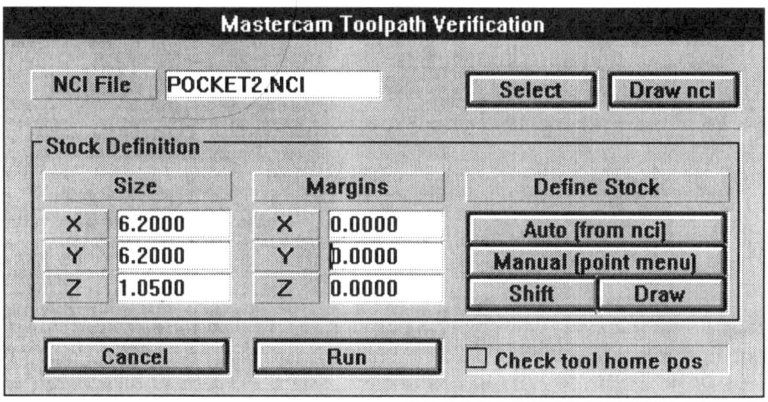

Select **Run**

Step 22. Select the NCI file to be verified.

Select **File → Project**
The project name "#1 c:\MILL5\NCI\pocket2.nci" will appear
Select **OK**
Select **Yes** to "An old RVP file exists, re-translate?" if necessary

Step 23. Execute verification module.

Select **Module → Turbo → Go**

The solid model of finished part should appear on the screen as shown in Figure 7.69

Step 24. Execute CMM inspection function.

Select **Examine → CMM inspection**

Use the mouse to pick the points you want to inspect.
The coordinate values of these particular points should be displayed on the screen

Select **Done**

Step 25. Exit verification module to return back to the Main Menu.

Double-click the MCTV window button in its upper-left corner.

Do not use MCTV's File → eXit feature in the pull-down menu.
Select **Cancel** to return back to graphic mode

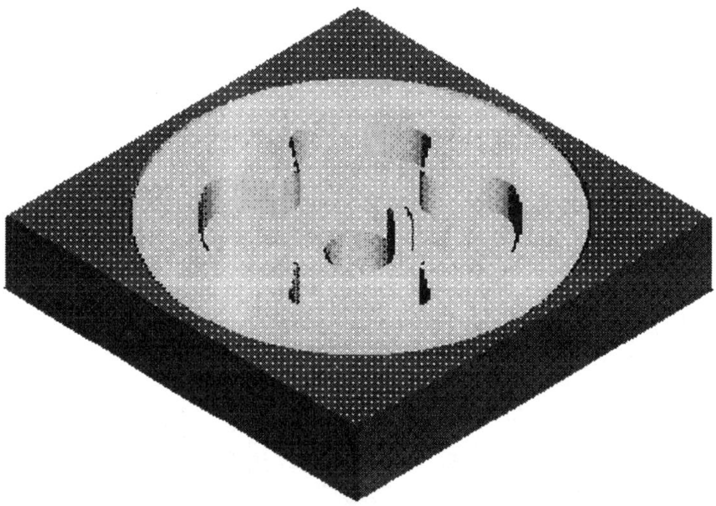

Figure 7.69

7.6 Drill Module

Mastercam's drill module is used to generate toolpaths for drilling, boring, and tapping. Setting drill parameters to proper operating modes and values, and selecting points for the operation to be implemented, are very crucial to the successful execution of the drill module.

Drill Parameters

The drill specific parameters are listed below:

Cycle = drill/peck drill/chip break/tap/bore 1/bore 2/misc.1/misc.2
Initial height = 0.0
Reference height = 0.0
Depth = 0.0
First peck increment = 0.0
Subsequent Peck increment = 0.0
Peck clearance = 0.0
Retraction amount = 0.0
Dwell = 0.0

The previous parameters are divided into three groups: Z-depth, cycle mode and pecking parameters.

Z-depth

Three Z values are involved in cycle operations (Figure 7.70):

Initial height:	The cutter travels at this Z value to the specified hole center.
Reference height:	The cutter moves down in rapid mode to this Z vlaue.
Z-depth:	The cutter feeds down to this Z value in absolute or incremental mode. This is the Z value of the hole bottom.

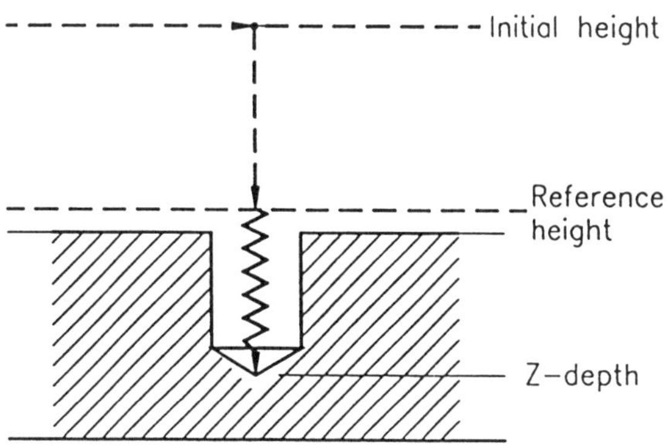

Figure 7.70

Mastercam allows Z values to be specified in either absolute or incremental mode.

The depth is the distance between the selected point position to the bottom of the hole. The sign is determined as negative (-) if the hole bottom is below the selected point (Figure 7.71a) and positive (+) if the hole bottom is above the selected point (Figure 7.71b).

How the specified Z-value is measured depends on whether Incremental or Absolute mode is chosen. When it is set to **Incremental mode**, the Z-value is measured from the Z-coordinate of the selected point to the hole bottom as shown in Figure 7.71. If the selected point has the coordinate of (3,5,1), the following two commands define the Z-depth being at Z=-1.0:

Depth = -2.0 Incremental

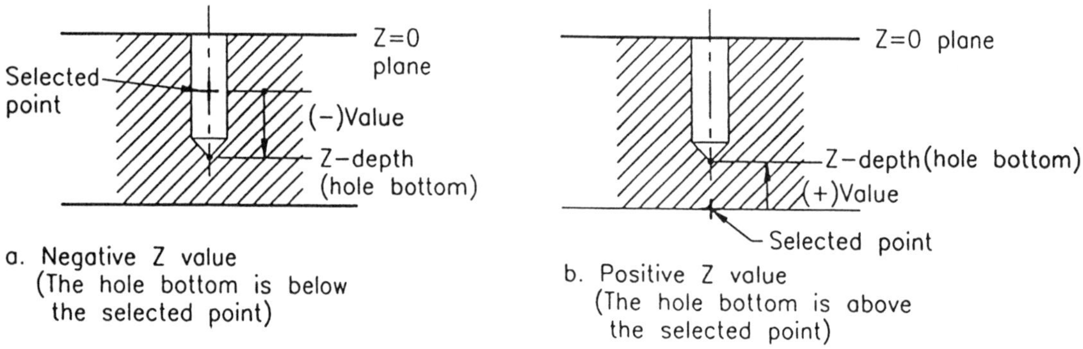

Figure 7.71 Incremental mode

In **absolute mode**, the Z-value is measured always from the Z-zero plane to the hole bottom (Figure 7.72). When this mode is used, the system ignores the Z-coordinate of the selected point and uses the Z-zero plane as the reference to measured the Z-depth.

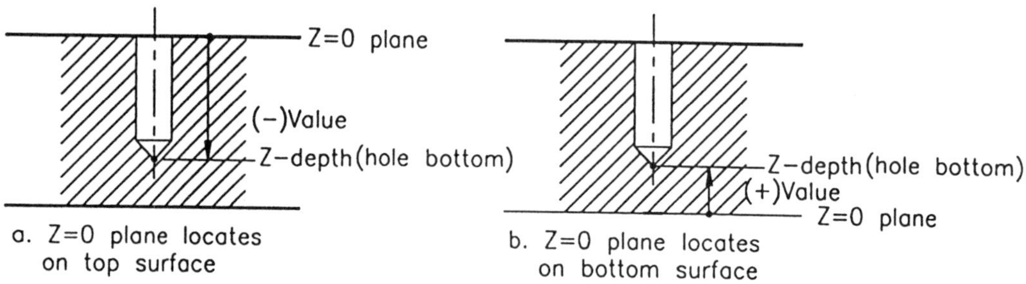

Figure 7.72 Absolute mode

Tip Always use the absolute mode if possible to avoid confusion because you may not know the exact Z-value of those selected points. Use the incremental mode only when the holes having different depths and the selected points have the actual Z-value of the hole bottoms (Figure 7.73). With the incremental mode, the same Z-depth value can be used for all holes although holes may have different depths.

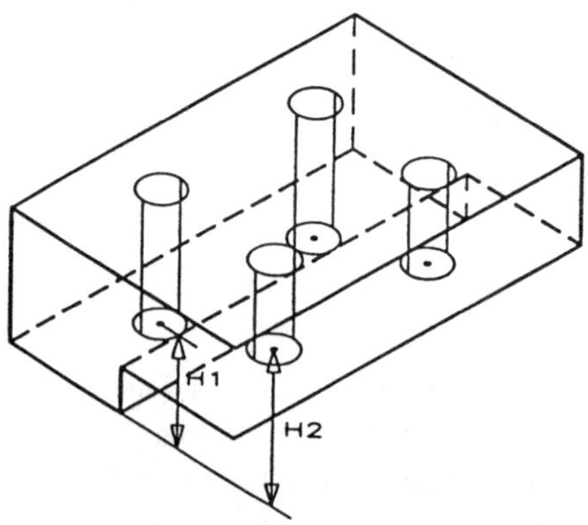

Figure 7.73

Cycle mode

Mastercam provides a total of **eight cycle commands** with six standard types and two optional types. The two optional commands Misc. #1 and Misc. #2 are user defined cycles. They are unique and therefore are not discussed here. The **six standard cycles** are described in table 7.8 below.

Table 7.8 Six standard cycles

Cycle Type	NC Command	Example	Typical Applications
Drill			Drilling or conterboring holes whose depths are shorter than three times of cutter diameter.
1. Dwell = 0	G81	G81 X1.0 Y1.0 Z-1.0 R0.2 F15.0	
2. Dwell ≠ 0	G82	G82 X1.0 Y1.0 Z-1.0 R0.2 P0.5 F15.0	
Peck drill	G83	G83 X1.0 Y1.0 Z-3.0 Q.7 R.2 F15.0	Drilling deep holes whose depths are longer than three times cutter diameter. Especially suited for applications where chips are difficult to remove.
Chip break	G73	G73 X1.0 Y1.0 Z-3.0 Q.7 R.2 F15.0	Drilling deep holes whose depths are longer than three times cutter diameter.
Tap	G84	G84 X1.0 Y1.0 Z-1.0 R0.2 P0.25 F50.0	Tapping right-hand internal threads.
Bore #1			
1. Dwell = 0	G85	G85 X1.0 Y1.0 Z-1.0 R0.2 F15.0	Boring holes with feed-in and feed-out paths.
2. Dwell ≠ 0	G89	G89 X1.0 Y1.0 Z-1.0 R0.2 P0.25 F15.0	
Bore #2	G86	G86 X1.0 Y1.0 Z-1.0 R0.2 P0.25 F15.0	Boring holes with feed-in, spindle stop, rapid-out paths.

The operation sequence of the common drilling or boring operation is listed below (Figure 7.74 on the next page):

1. Rapid to the hole center with Z at the initial height.
2. Rapid Z to the reference height.
3. Feed Z to the Z-depth of the hole bottom.
4. Dwell at the hole bottom for a period of time (if specified).
5. Retract Z to the reference height or initial height.

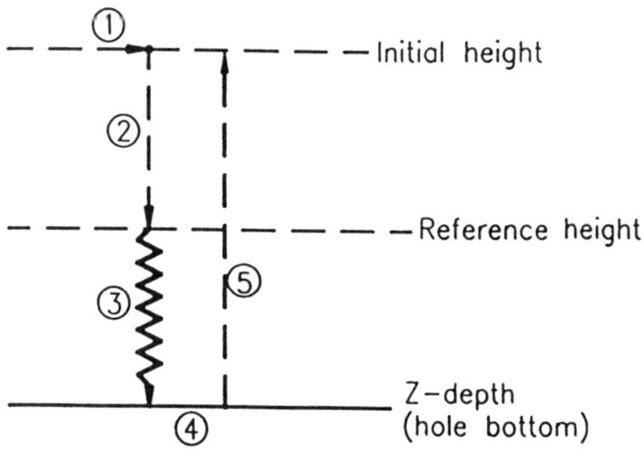

Figure 7.74

Drilling deep holes are normally performed by **two** methods: peck drilling and chip break drilling. They are used when the depth of holes is larger than three times of the cutter diameter. Figure 7.75 illustrates the difference of these two deep hole drilling cycles.

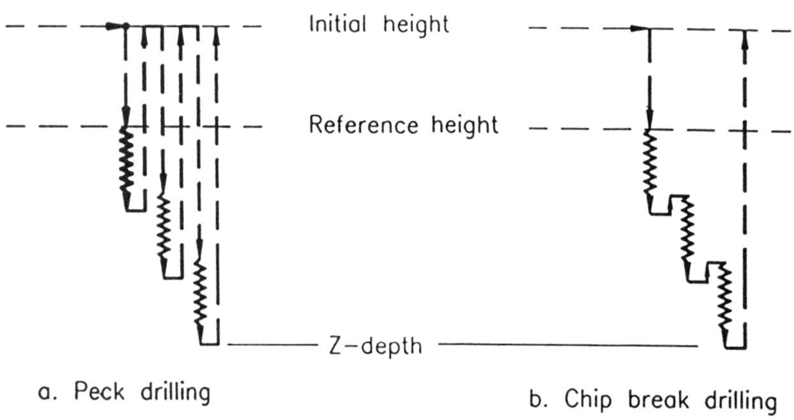

Figure 7.75

The **operation sequence** of the peck drilling cycle is listed below:

1. Rapid to the hole center with Z at initial height.
2. Rapid Z to the reference height.
3. Feed Z down with one peck distance.
4. Rapidly retract Z with the retraction amount.
5. Rapid Z down to one peck clearance up from the previous drilled depth.
6. Feed Z down with one peck distance.
7. Repeat steps 4 - 6 until the hole bottom is reached.

Point selection

There are **three** major options used for selecting the position of the holes to be drilled. They are:

Manual:	manually selects the points to be drilled.
Automatic:	system automatically selects the points to be drilled.
Window:	system selects the points included within the window.

Tips 1. Suggestions for selecting initial height, reference height, and Z depth.

- The initial height must be high enough to clear any interference such as steps, clamping devices, etc.

- Reference height = 0.15" above the part surface to be drilled (for smooth surfaces)
  = 0.3" above the part surface to be drilled (for rough surfaces)

- Z-depth:
  (a) Blind holes: (Figure 7.76a)
  Z-depth = full-diameter depth + 0.3 D
  where D = drill diameter
  (b) Through holes: (Figure 7.76b)
  Z-depth = hole depth + 0.3 D + 0.1
  where 0.1 is the penetration distance

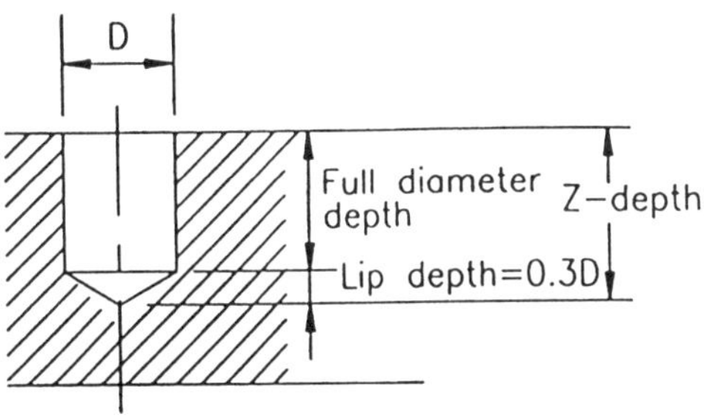

Figure 7.76a Blind hole

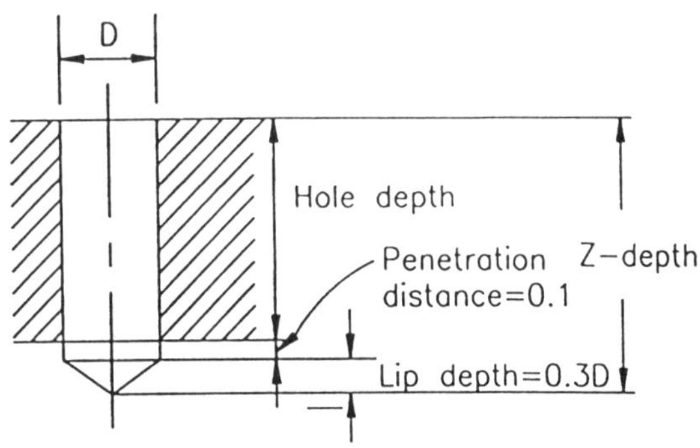

Figure 7.76b Through hole

2. Alway use absolute mode to specify the Z depth (hole bottom) of the holes. The incremental mode is only recommended for drilling holes with different depths with two conditions
   (1) the Z-value of selected points for drilling is specified and must be the exact Z-coordinate of the hole bottom and
   (2) the top surfaces are in the same horizontal plane.
3. When the Z coordinate of selected points is zero, the Z-depth has the same value for both incremental and absolute mode.
4. Use peck or chip break cycle when the depth of hole is longer than three times the cutter diameter. The peck drilling cycle is recommended when the chips are hard to remove from the holes. Using the chip break cycle can shorten the operation time because the drill does not retract back to initial height or reference height. However, its chip removing ability is not as good as the peck cycle.

5. The drilling distance for each peck is about 1.5 times the drill diameter.

6. In the tapping operation, the feedrate and spindle speed must be synchronized to obtain the required thread accuracy. The following formulas can be used to obtain the proper feedrate and spindle speed:

   Feedrate (inch per minute) = Pitch X RPM
   Feedrate (inch per revolution) = Pitch
   where Pitch = 1/number of threads per inch
   RPM = spindle speed

7. When multiple operations such as drilling, boring, and tapping, must be performed in the same set of holes, use the "Repeat with the same points" command to eliminate the need for repeatly selecting points for subsequent operations.

8. Use the "Jump height" command to allow the cutter to be moved between holes at a height higher than the reference plane height. This is especially useful in avoiding interference with clamps or steps as shown in Figure 7.77.

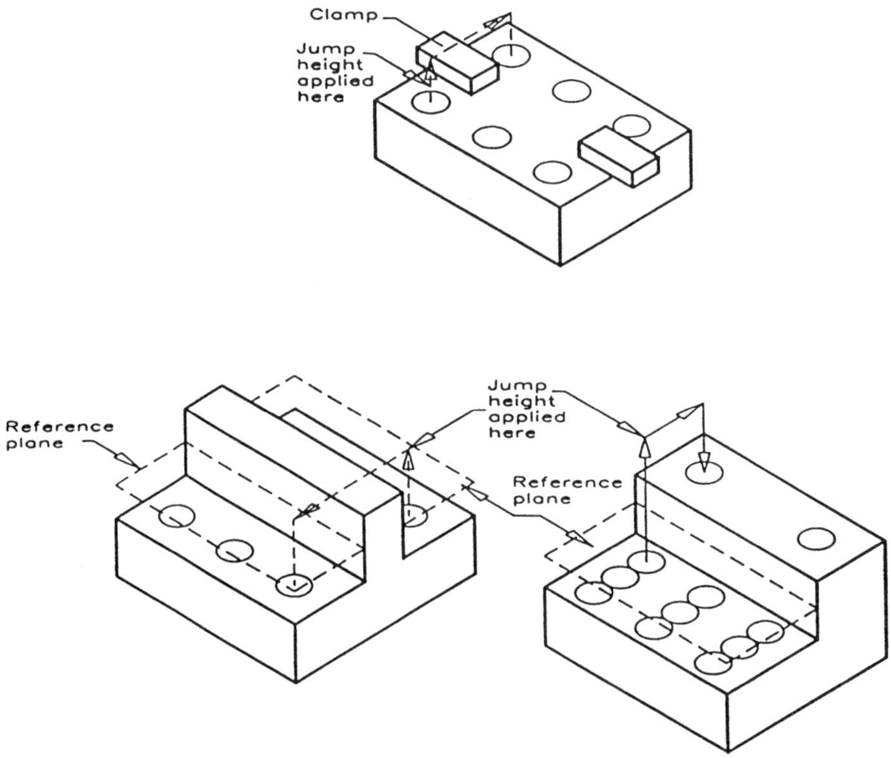

Figure 7.77

Drilling Projects

Three projects are presented in this section. The first one uses the peck cycle to drill 24 deep holes around three circles. The second project requires two operations: drilling and tapping, to produce internal threads in six holes. The last project uses drilling and boring operations to produce a fine surface finish of four holes which have two z-depth sets.

Project 7.

Using the peck cycle to drill 24 deep holes

Part Geometry Creation
Project 8 of Chapter 6 (drill1)

We are here ☞ Go to

Toolpath Generation
(drill1)

The peck drill cycle is used to drill 24 holes around three circles as shown in Figure 7.78. The depth of the holes is 1.75-in. which is longer than 3 times hole diameter.

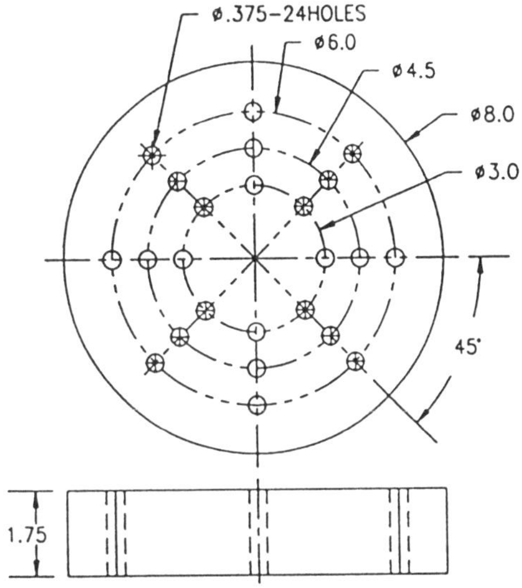

Figure 7.78

Tips 1. Use the peck drill cycle. The main drill parameters are set as below:

Initial height = 1.0
Reference height = 0.2
Depth = Absolute
Depth = -1.8625 (or 1.75 + 0.3 x 3 / 8)
First peck increment = 0.7

2. Use **Window → None** commands to select points to be drilled.

Step 1. Load the part geometry file (drill1.ge3) or create one by following the instructions in Project 8 of Chapter 6.

Select **MAIN MENU →File → Get**
Enter file name: **drill1** ←
Select **Yes** to delete the current part if required
The part drawing should appear as Figure 7.79.

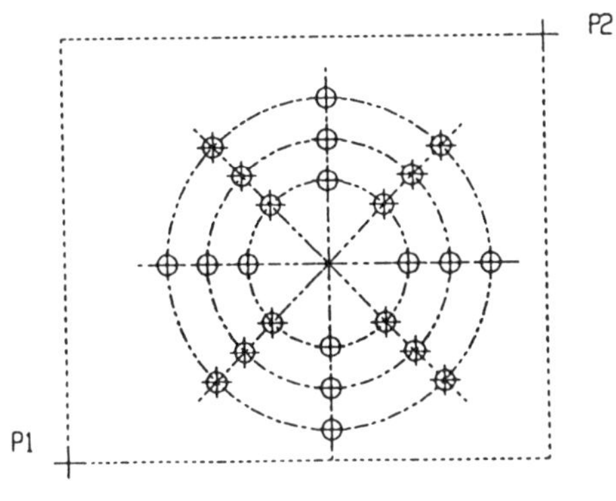

Figure 7.79

Step 2. Initiate the Drill module.

Select **MAIN MENU → Toolpaths → Drill**
Enter file name: **drill1** ←

Step 3. Select points to be drilled. Use the pick points indicated on Figure 7.79 on page 7-67.

Select **Window** from the Select points menu
Pick at **P1** and **P2** to define the Window range
Select **9** from the "Sort points by" menu to select "none" option
Select **Yes** to draw the path between points
Select **Yes** to OK the path

The toolpath path should appear as Figure 7.80.

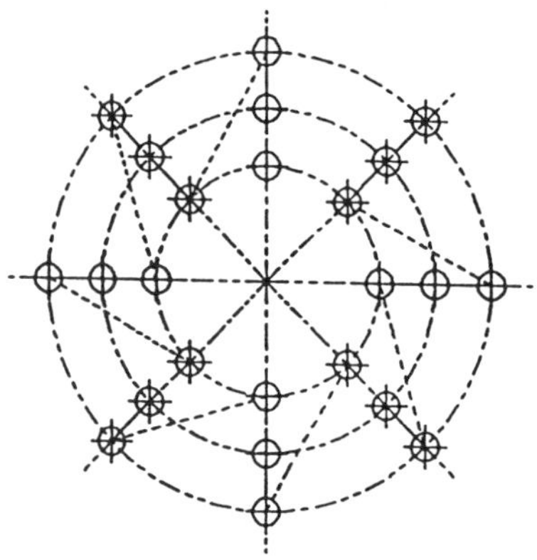

Figure 7.80

Step 4. Define drill parameters.

Set the drill parameters to the following settings:

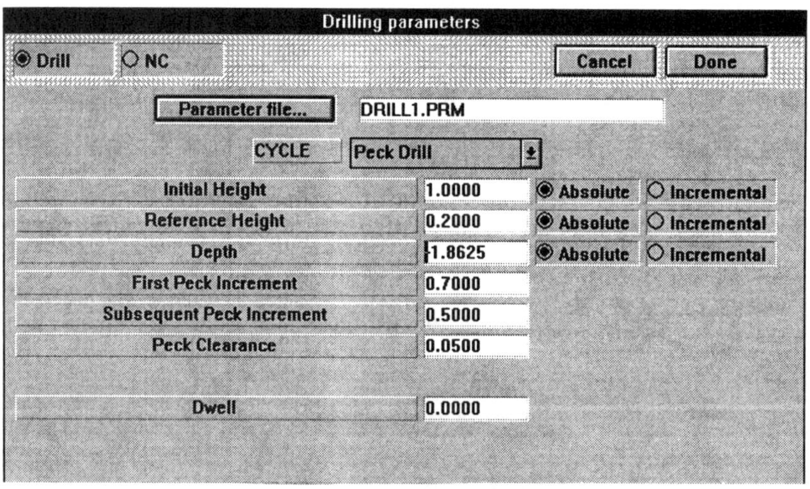

Select the **NC button** to advance to the NC parameters menu.

Step 5. Define NC parameters.

Set your NC parameters to the following settings:

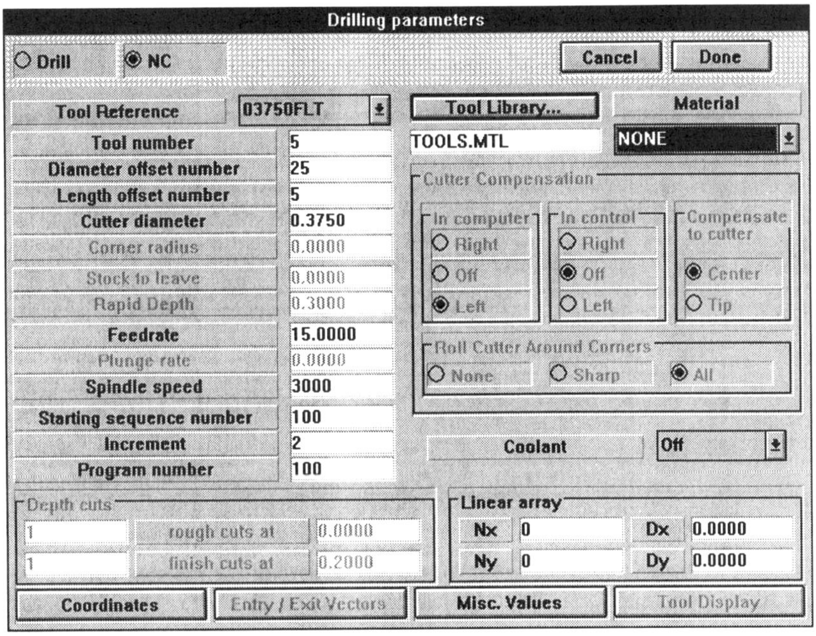

Select the **Done button** to complete the parameter settings.

Step 6. Write the toolpaths.

Press **F3** to repaint the screen
Select **Write** from the Change menu
Select **Yes** to accept the toolpath segment
Select **No** to "Repeat with same points?"

The toolpath should resemble Figure 7.81.

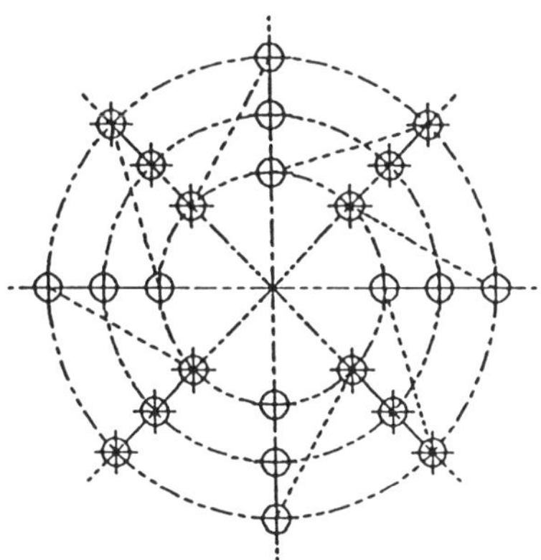

Figure 7.81

Step 7. Run the post processor.

Select **End program** to close the toolpath file
Select **Yes** to run the post processor
Enter file name: **drill1**

The part program should appear on the screen.
Double-click the Window button in the upper-left corner to return back to graphic mode.

Step 8. Change Gview to isometric view.

Select **Gview → Isometric**

Step 9. Backplot the toolpaths.

Select **MAIN MENU →NC utils → Backplot**

Set the Backplot parameters to the following settings:

Select **Run** from the Backplot menu

The drilling toolpath will be plotted on the screen.

You will see the sequence of drilling holes. The toolpaths with part geometry appearing on the screen should resemble Figure 7.82.

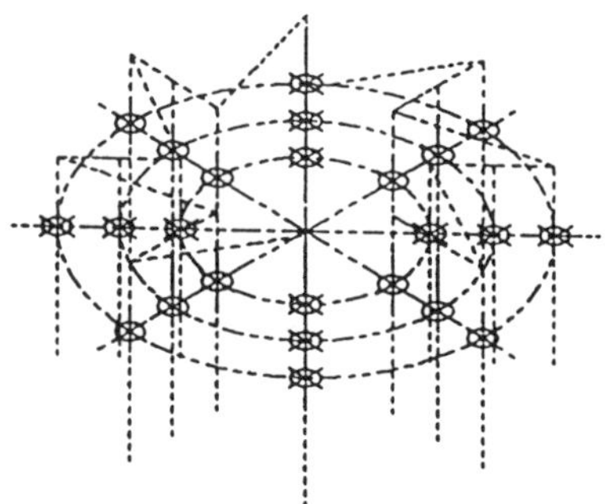

Figure 7.82

Step 10. Edit the part program.

Select **MAIN MENU → File → Edit → NC**

Enter file name: **drill1 ←**

The part program shall appear on the Editor's screen as shown here:

```
%
O100
N100 G90 G80 G40 G0
N102 T5 M6
N104 G54 G0 X1.5 Y0.
N106 S3000 M3 T5
N108 G43 H5 Z1. M08
N110 G0 X1.5 Y0.
N112 G98 G83 X1.5 Y0. Z-1.8625 Q.7 R.2 F12.5
N114 X2.25
N116 X3.
N118 X1.0607 Y1.0607
N120 X1.591 Y1.591
N122 X2.1213 Y2.1213
N124 X0. Y1.5
N126 Y2.25
N128 Y3.
N130 X-1.0607 Y1.0607
N132 X-1.591 Y1.591
N134 X-2.1213 Y2.1213
N136 X-1.5 Y0.
N138 X-2.25
N140 X-3.
N142 X-1.0607 Y-1.0607
N144 X-1.591 Y-1.591
N146 X-2.1213 Y-2.1213
N148 X0. Y-1.5
N150 Y-2.25
N152 Y-3.
N154 X1.0607 Y-1.0607
N156 X1.591 Y-1.591
N158 X2.1213 Y-2.1213
N160 G80
N162 G28 Z1. M09
N164 G28 X0.
N166 M30
```

Note: Your part program may be somewhat different from the one listed here if you use a different post processor.

Step 11. Exit the editor.

Press **F10** → **F10** to return to graphic mode.

Project 8.

Drilling and tapping 6 holes

The part shown in Figure 7.83 has six 9/16-12 internal threads. Producing these six internal threads requires two operations, drilling and tapping. The tap drill size is 31/64 in.

Part Geometry Creation
Project 3 of Chapter 5 (drill2)

We are here

Go to

Toolpath Generation
(drill2)

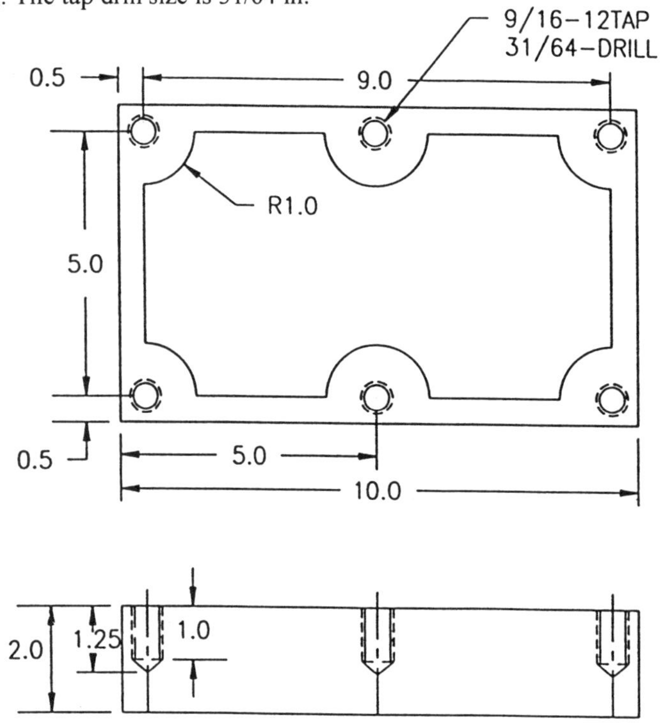

Figure 7.83

Tips 1. The operation sequence starts with drilling all six holes and then is following by tapping.

2. Use the "Automatic "option to select the points to be drilled, then use “Repeat the points” option to select the drilled points for tapping.
3. The drilling depth is calculated as follows:

Drilling depth = Thread depth + 0.3 D + 0.1

or = -(1.0 + 0.3 x (31/64) + 0.1) = -1.25

where D is drill diameter

0.1 is the buffer distance for tapping

Step 1. Load the part geometry file (drill2.ge3) or create one by following the instructions given in Project 3 of Chapter 5 .

Select **MAIN MENU → File → Get**

Enter file name: **drill2** ←

Select **Yes** to delete the current part if necessary

The part drawing should appear as in Figure 7.84 on the next page.

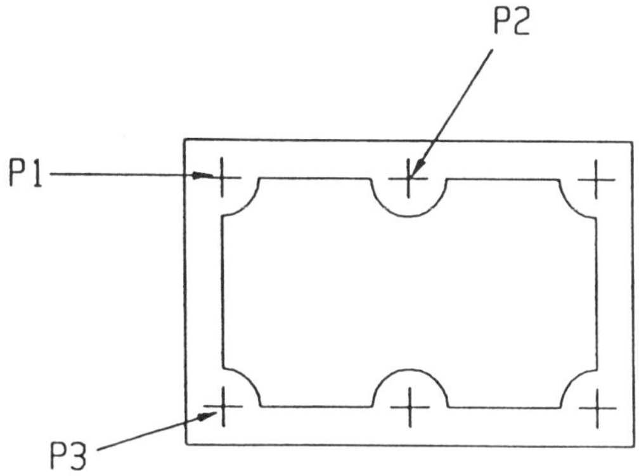

Figure 7.84

Step 2. Initiate the drill module.

Select **MAIN MENU** → **Toolpaths** → **Drill**
Enter file name: **drill2** ←

Step 3. Select points using the pick points in Figure 7.84.

Select **Automatic**
Pick at **P1** for the first point
Pick at **P2** for the second point
Pick at **P3** for the last point
Select **Yes** to draw the path between points
Select **Yes** to OK the path

Step 4. Define the drill parameters for drilling.

Set the drill parameters to the following settings:

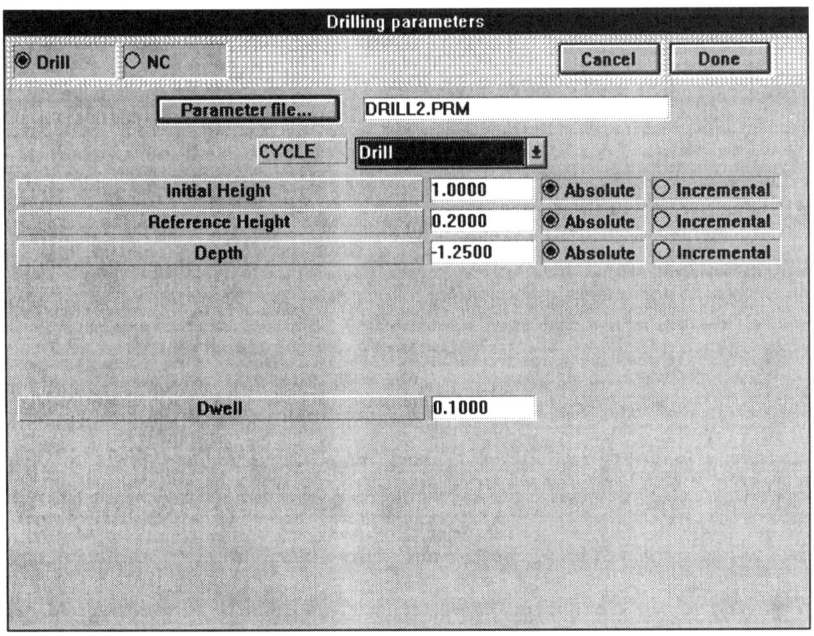

Set the **NC button** to advance to the NC parameter menu.

Step 5. Define NC parameters for drilling.

Set the NC parameters to the following settings:

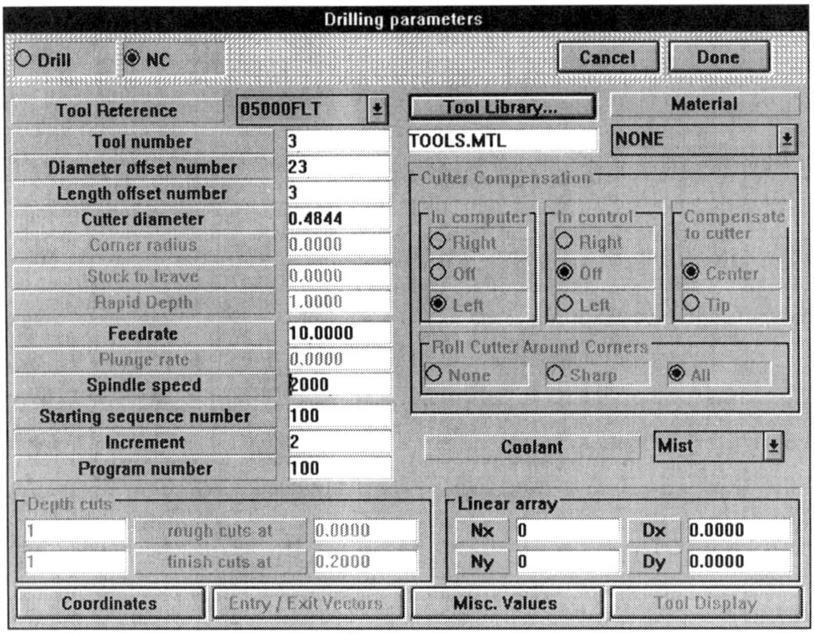

Select the **Done button** to complete the parameter settings.

Step 6. Accept the drilling toolpaths.

Press **F3** to repaint the screen

Select **Write→ Yes** to accept toolpath segment

Select **Yes** to "Repeat with same points"

Step 7. Define tapping parameters.

Set the tapping parameters to the following settings:

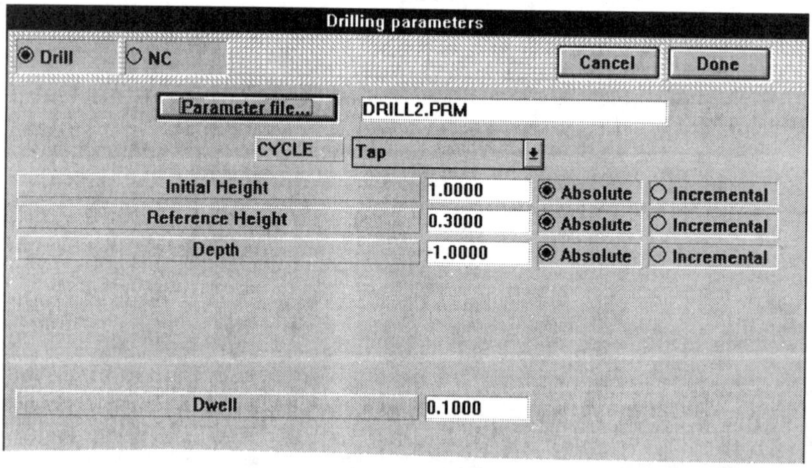

Select the **NC button** to advance to NC parameter menu

Step 8. Define NC parameters for tapping.

Set the NC parameters to the following settings:

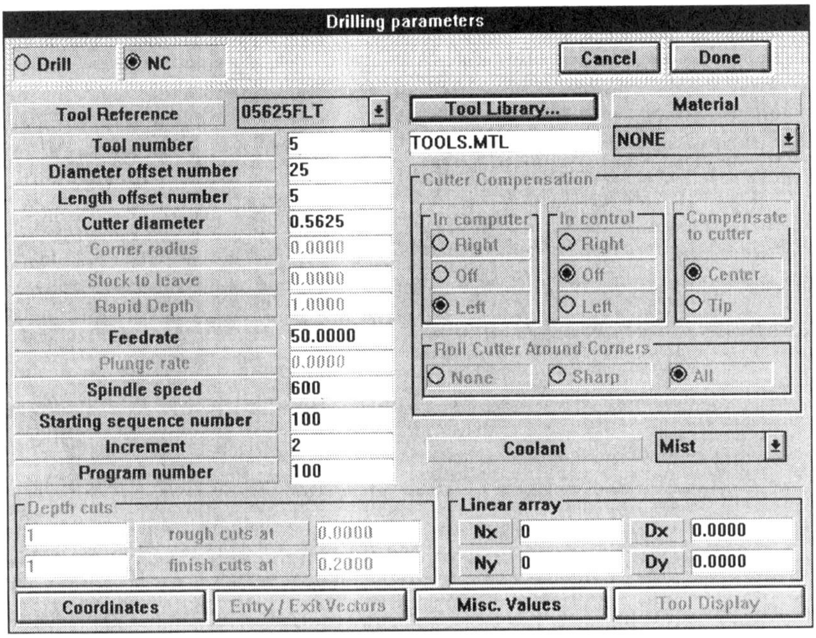

Select the **Done button** to complete the parameter settings.

Step 9. Accept the tapping toolpaths.

Press **F3** to repaint the screen
Select **Write** from the Change menu
Select **Yes** to accept the toolpath segment
Select **No** to "Repeat with same points?"

Step 10. Run the postprocessor.

Select **End program** to close the toolpath file
Select **Yes** to run the postprocessor
Enter file name: **drill2** ←

The part program should appear on the screen.
Double-click the Window button on the upper-left corner to return back to graphic mode.

Step 11. Backplot the toolpaths using Isometric Gview.

Select **Gview** → **Isometric**
Select **MAIN MENU** → **NC utils** → **Backplot**
Select **Step**
Repeatly select **Step** to step through the toolpath segment until you reach the end of the toolpath file.

The toolpaths with part geometry should look like Figure 7.85 on the next page.
Select **OK** to complete the toolpath plotting.

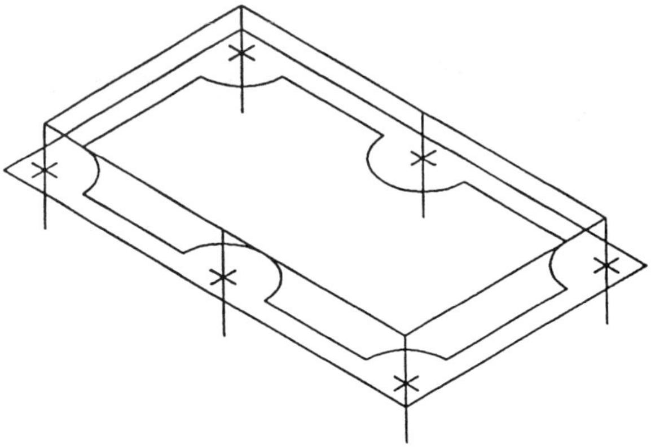

Figure 7.85

Project 9.

Drilling and boring four holes

This project requires you to use drilling and boring operation to produce a fine surface finish for four holes as shown in Figure 7.86. The drill has a diameter of 3/4 in. and the boring tool is 7/8 in. All four holes have the same top surface level (Z=-0.75). The Z-value of the bottom depth for holes A and B is -1.5 in. and for holes C and D is -2.25 in. This is the ideal case for using the incremental mode for defining the drilling depth if the Z coordinate value of the hole depths is included in the point definitions. As can be seen there is a step between the two rows of holes. We can use the **Jump height** command to create the toolpath to retract the tool higher than the step to avoid interference.

Part Geometry Creation

Project 4 of Chapter 5 (drill3)

Go to

We are here **Toolpath Generation (drill3)**

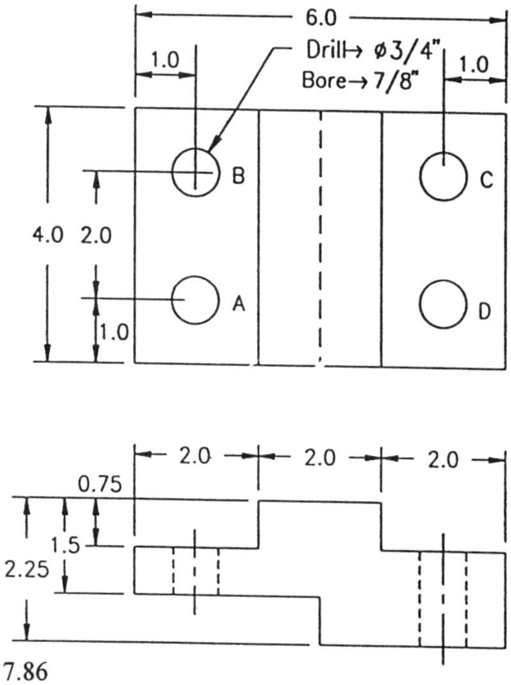

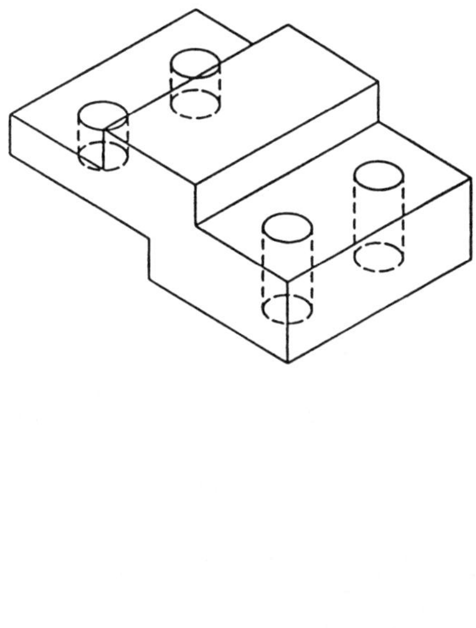

Figure 7.86

Tips 1. The operation sequence starts with drilling and then is followed by boring.

2. Use incremental mode to specify the drilling and boring depth of the holes. The incremental mode is recommended because two different depths are involved. If absolute mode is used, we need to use the drill cycle twice, the first time for drilling holes A and B and the second time for holes C and D.

3. The exact Z coordinate values must be included in defining points to be drilled and bored. The complete point definitions for these four holes are:

   Point A: X1.0 Y1.0 Z-1.5
   Point B: X1.0 Y3.0 Z-1.5
   Point C: X5.0 Y3.0 Z-2.25
   Point D: X5.0 Y1.0 Z-2.25

4. Use the Jump height command at hole B to retract the cutter higher than the step to move to hole C.

Step 1. Load the part geometry file (drill3.ge3) or create one by following the instructions given in Project 4 of Chapter 5.

Select **MAIN MENU →File → Get**
Enter file name: **drill3** ←
Select **Yes** to delete the current part if necessary

The part drawing should appear as in Figure 7.87.

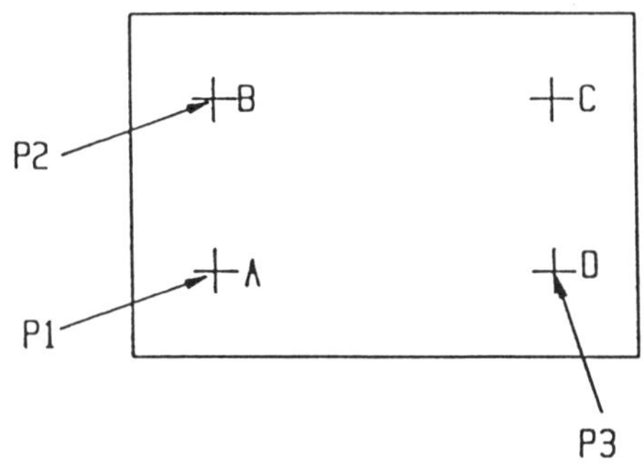

Figure 7.87

Step 2. Initiate the drill module.

Select **MAIN MENU → Toolpaths → Drill**
Enter file name: **drill3** ←

Step 3. Select drilling points using the pick points in Figure 7.87.

Select **Automatic** from the select points menu
Pick at **P1** to select the first point
Pick at **P2** to select the second point
Pick at **P3** to select the last point
Select **Yes** to draw the path between points
Select **Yes** to OK the path

The path should look like Figure 7.88 on the next page.

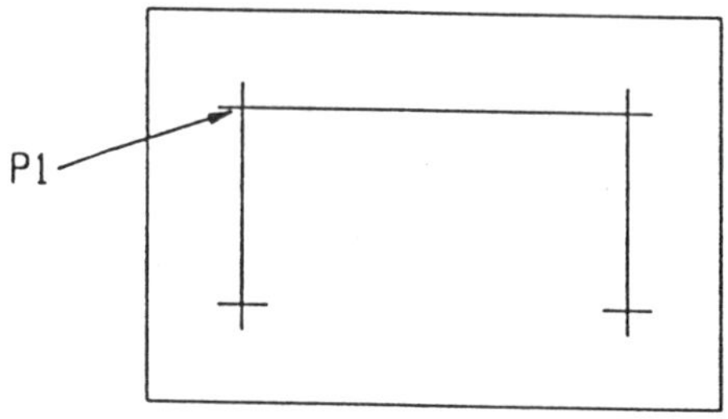

Figure 7.88

Step 4. Define the drill parameters.

Set the drill parameters to the following settings:

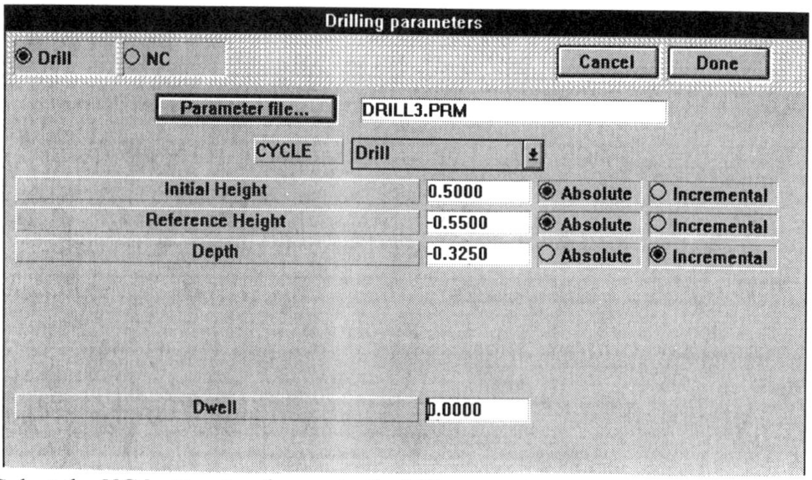

Select the **NC button** to advance to the NC parameter menu.

Step 5. Define NC parameters for drilling.

Set the NC parameters to the following settings:

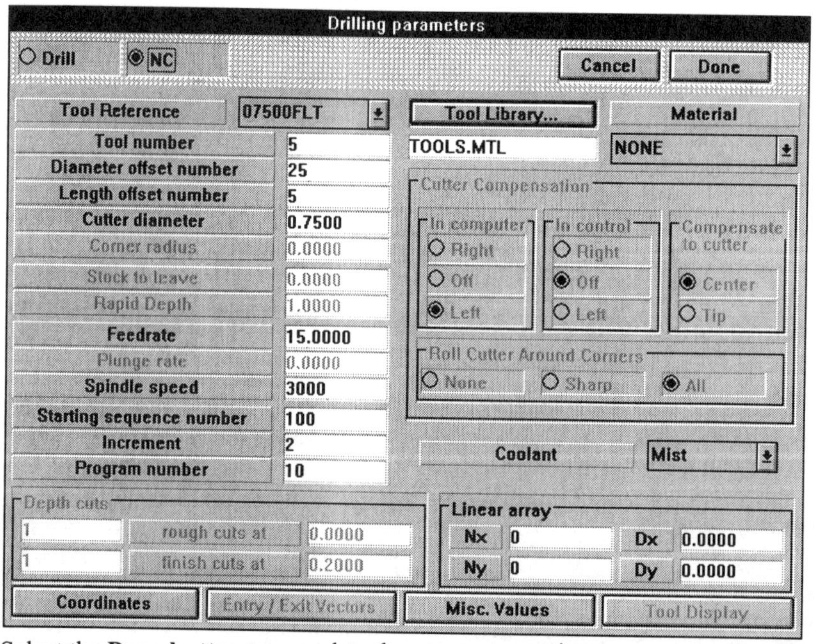

Select the **Done button** to complete the parameter settings.

Step 6. Use jump height command to change the height to retract. Use the pick point in Figure 7.88 on the previous page.

Press **F3** to repaint the screen
Select **Add Jump** from the Change menu
Pick at **P1** to specify the point to change the jump height
Enter the jump height: **1.0** ←
Select **Write** from the Change menu
Select **Yes** to accept the toolpath segment
Select **Yes** to "Repeat with same points?"

Step 7. Define drill parameters for boring.

Set the drill parameters to the following settings:

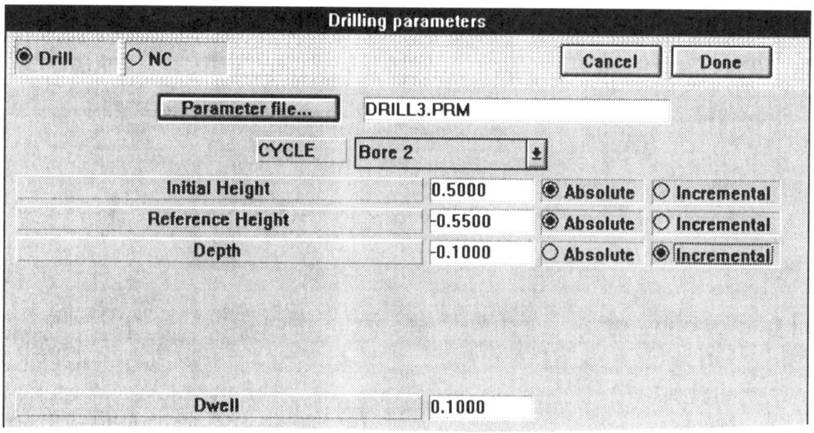

Select the **NC button** to advance to the NC parameter menu.

Step 8. Define NC parameters for boring.

Set the NC parameters to the following settings:

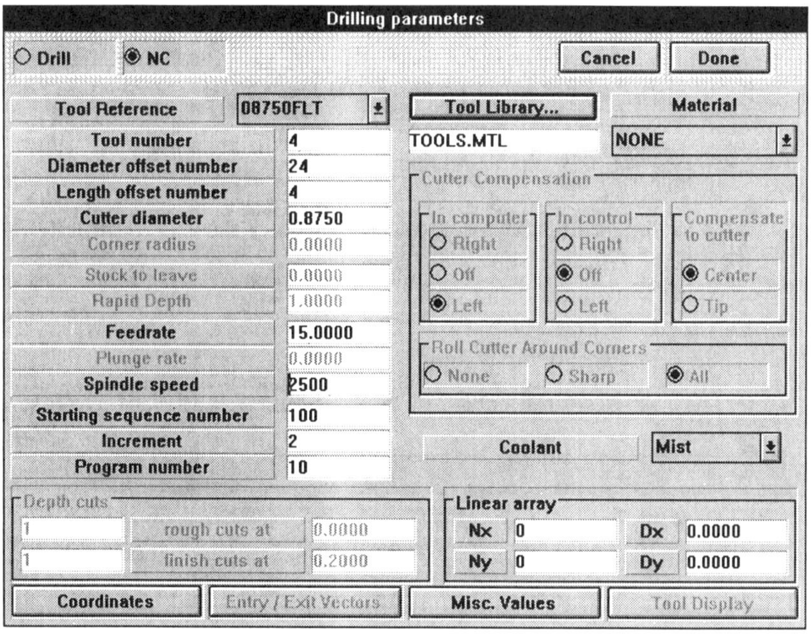

Select the **Done button** to complete the parameter settings.
Press **F3** to repaint the screen

The system returns to graphic mode and the drawing should resemble Figure 7.89.

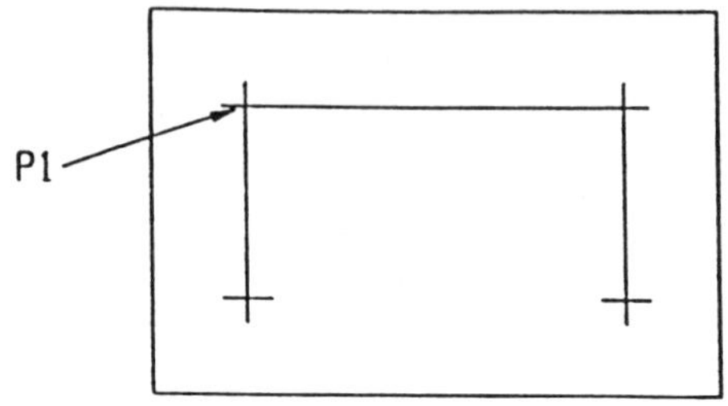

Figure 7.89

Step 9. Use jump height command to change retraction height using the pick point in Figure 7.89.

Select **Add Jump** from the Change menu
Pick at **P1**
Enter the jump height: **1.0** ←
Select **Write** to write the toolpaths
Select **Yes** to accept the toolpath segment
Select **No** to "Repeat with same points?"

Step 10. Run the postprocessor.

Select **End program** to close the toolpath file
Select **Yes** to run the postprocessor
Enter file name: **drill3** ←

The part program should appear on the screen.
Double-click on the Window button in the upper-left corner to return back to graphic mode.

Step 11. Change Gview to isometric.

Select **Gview → Isometric**

Step 12. Backplot the toolpaths. The plotted toolpaths should appear as in Figure 7.90.

Be careful to notice the jump height at the second hole.
Select **MAIN MENU → NC utils → Backplot**
Select **Step**
Repeatly select **Step** to step through the toolpath until you reach the end of the part program.
Select **OK** to complete the plotting.

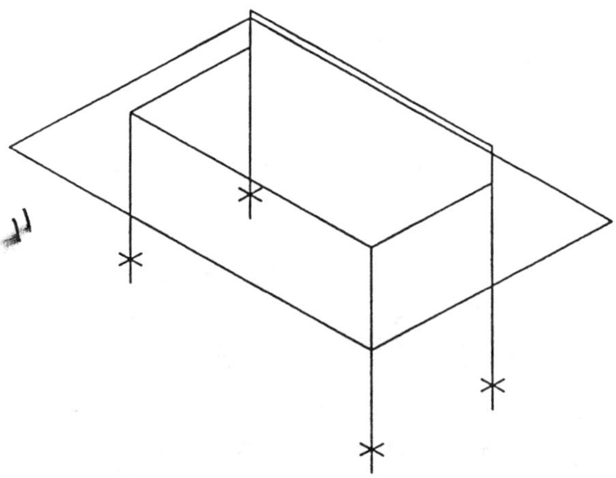

Figure 7.90

7.7 Letters Module

Engraving letters on part surfaces is a common machining application. There are **two** methods to generate lettering toolpaths in Mastercam: lettering geometry method and toolpath module method. For the lettering geometry method, contour or pocket module is used to generate toolpaths from an existing lettering geometry. Lettering geometries can be created in two ways: letters module method and edit note method. These two methods are presented in chapter 5. For the toolpath module method, we use the letters toolpath module to generate toolpaths for engraving letters of various fonts and styles.

This section starts with the discussion of the letters toolpath module, followed by three lettering projects. The first project directly uses the letters toolpath module to generate the toolpaths for cutting two letter strings, both arranged in angular style. The top string uses the box font, and the bottom string uses the block font. The second project uses contour and pocket modules to generate toolpaths for letters in which their geometries have been defined by using Create → Letters commands. The third project involves using the Edit note method to create lettering geometries. These notes are modified to various fonts, sizes, and orientation. Finally the contour toolpath module is used to generate toolpaths for cutting letters.

The letters module can be used to generate toolpaths for engraving letters of various fonts and styles. Mastercam provides **four standard fonts**: box, block, roman, and slant (Figure 7.91). Basically, the letters module uses the contouring principle to generate the toolpath along the letter profiles.

Figure 7.91

Letters Size and Spacing

The letter size is determined by its height and width (Figure 7.92). When using four standard fonts, the ratio of width to height of each letter has been predefined. You can change this ratio in the setup file. The lettering parameters menu only provides for changing the height parameter, the width automatically will be scaled according to the specified height value and the ratio of width to height.

A spacing parameter specifies the spacing distance between letters in the string.

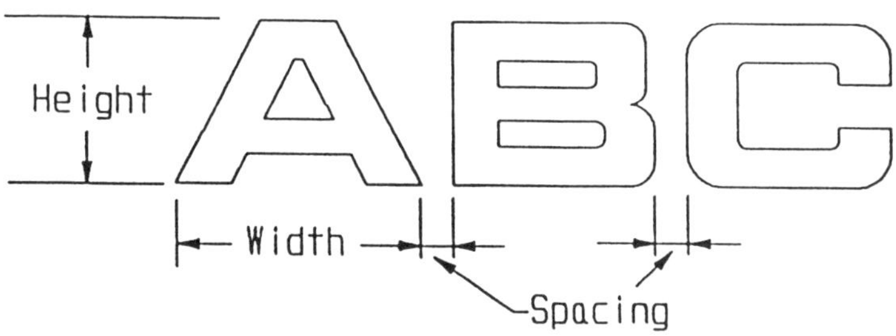

Figure 7.92

Lettering Layout Style

Mastercam provides two lettering layout styles: linear and angular (Figure 7.93).

Figure 7.93

Linear Style

The linear style has the letter strings arranged in a line parallel to the X axis. When using the linear style the user needs to specify the letter's starting point which is the bottom left corner of the letter's string (Figure 7.94).

Figure 7.94

Angular Style

The angular style allows the letter strings to be located along an arc. **Three parameters** are used to define the location of the letter string: arc center, arc radius, and selection of top or bottom arc. When the top arc is specified, the letter string is centered at 90° and arranged in the clockwise direction (Figure 7.95a). In the bottom arc mode, the letters are centered at 270° and arranged in the counter-clockwise direction (Figure 7.95b).

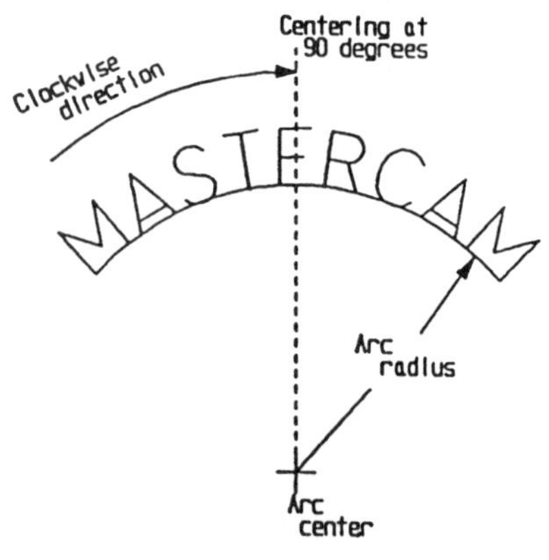

Figure 7.95a Top arc

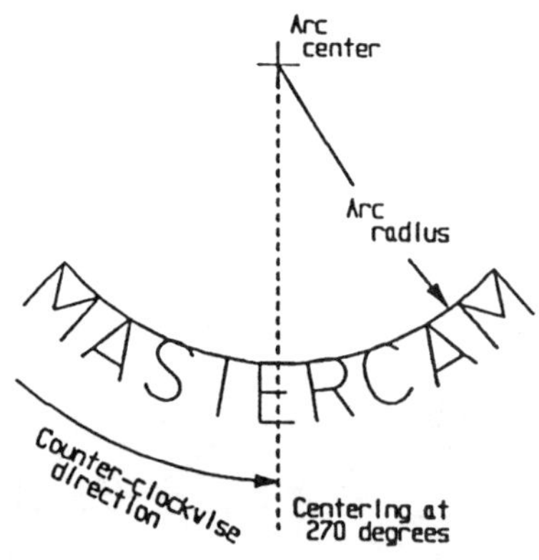

Figure 7.95b Bottom arc

Project 10.

10

Part Geometry Creation

Project 5 of Chapter 5 (letter3)

We are here

Go to

Toolpath Generation

(letter3)

Using letters module to generate lettering toolpaths

A letters module is used to generate the toolpaths for cutting two sets of letter strings Both are arranged in angular style as shown in Figure 7.96. The letter font in the top string is box type and the bottom string is done using block type.

Figure 7.96

Tips

1. No existing geometry is given from previous chapters. Create two rectangles and add four fillets to the corners of the inner rectangle.
2. The upper letter string using the box font is arranged in an arc of 2.75" radius and centers at (3,0). The letters have a height of 0.5" and a spacing of 0.15".
3. The bottom letter string in block font is located around the arc of 2.75" and centers at (3,4). The block letters have a height of 0.4" and a spacing of 0.12".
4. The cutter diameter is 1/16" for cutting both lettering strings.

5. The cutter compensation in computer should be set to **off** for cutting the letters with box font and **left center** for cutting the letters with block font.

Step 1. Create two rectangles.

Select **MAIN MENU** → **Create** → **Rectangle** → **2 points**
Enter the lower left corner: **0,0** ←
Enter the upper right corner: **6,4** ← to complete the first rectangle
Press **Alt** + **F1** simultaneously and then press **F2** to fit the drawing on the screen
Enter the lower left corner: **0.5,0.5** ←
Enter the upper right corner: **5.5,3.5** ← to draw the second rectangle

The two rectangles should appear as Figure 7.97.

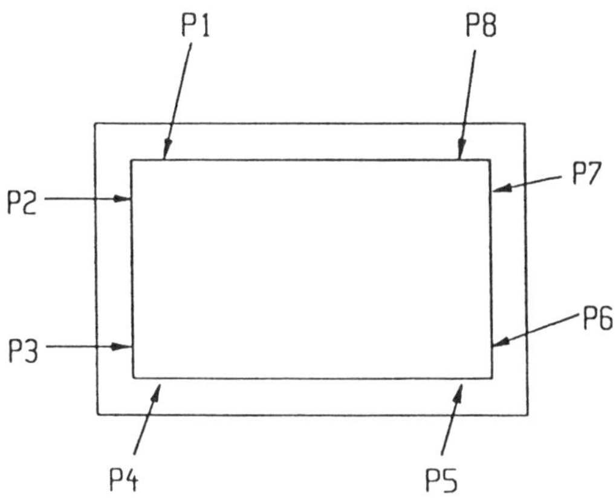

Figure 7.97

Step 2. Add four fillets using the pick points in Figure 7.97 on the previous page.

Select **MAIN MENU** → **Modify** → **Fillet** → **Radius**
Enter the fillet radius: **0.5** ←
Sequentially pick at **P1** - **P8** to complete the four fillets

The new drawing should resemble Figure 7.98.

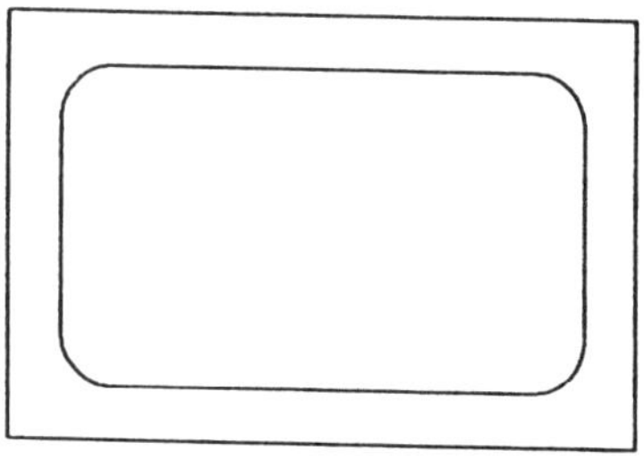

Figure 7.98

Step 3. Initiate letters module.

Select **MAIN MENU** → **Toolpaths** →**mIsc.** → **leTters**
Enter file name: **letters1** ←

Step 4. Define letters to be cut.

Select **Box** from the Letters menu
Enter letter height: **0.5** ←
Enter letter spacing: **0.15** ←
Select **Yes** to write letters on an arc
Enter coordinates of arc center: **3,0** ←
Enter arc radius: **2.75** ←
Enter type of arc: **0** ← for selecting top arc
Enter letters: **EMU IT** ←

Step 5. Define letter parameters.

Select **Params** from the contour menu
Set the parameters to the following settings:

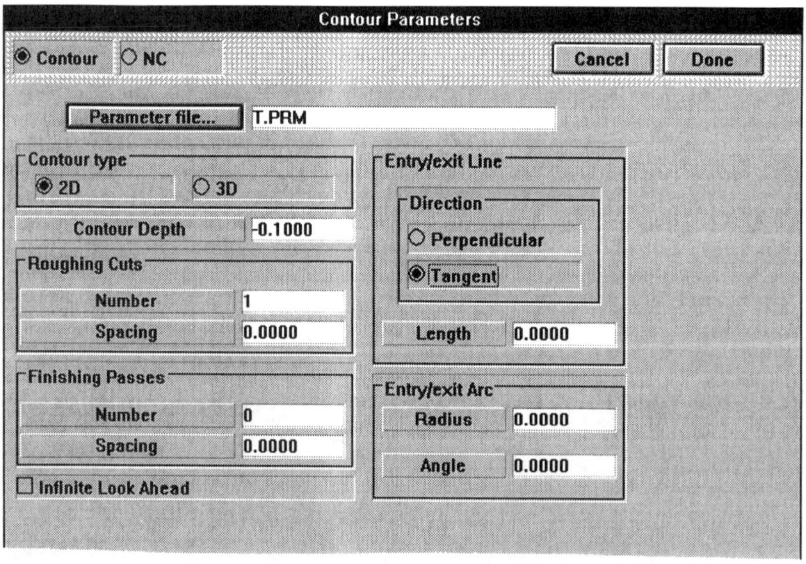

Select the **NC button** to move to the NC parameter menu.

Step 6. Define NC parameters to the following settings.

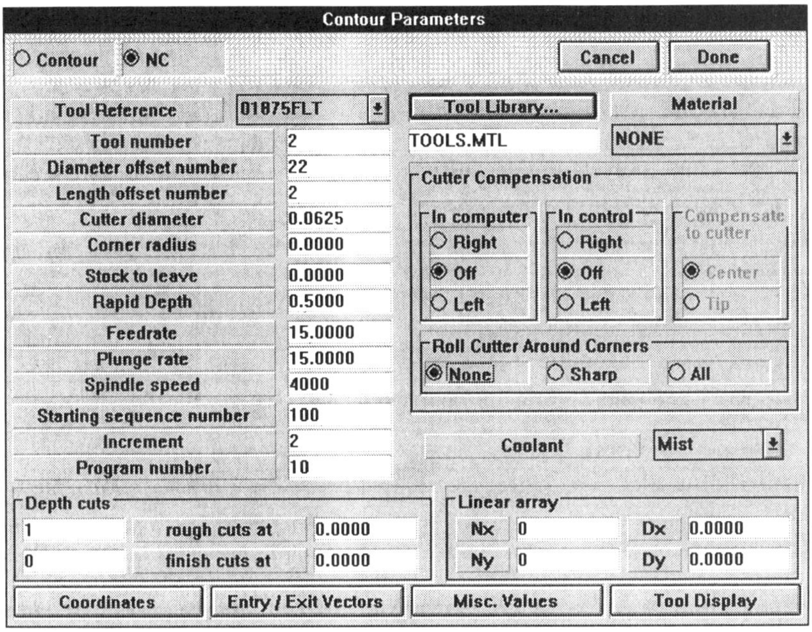

Select the **Done button** to complete the parameters settings.

Step 7. Write the lettering toolpaths.

Press **F3** to repaint the screen
Select **Write** from the Change menu
Select **Yes** to write all remaining contours
Select **Yes** to accept the toolpath segment

The toolpaths should look like Figure 7.99.

Figure 7.99

Step 8. Generate toolpaths for bottom lettering string.

Select **leTters → bLock**
Enter letter geight: **0.4** ←
Enter letter spacing: **0.12** ←
Select **Yes** to write letters on an arc
Enter coordinates of arc center: **3,4** ←
Enter arc radius: **2.75** ←
Enter type of arc: **1** ← to select the bottom arc
Enter letters: **CNC DEMO** ←

Step 9. Define lettering parameters.

Select **Params** from the contour menu

Set the parameters to the following settings:

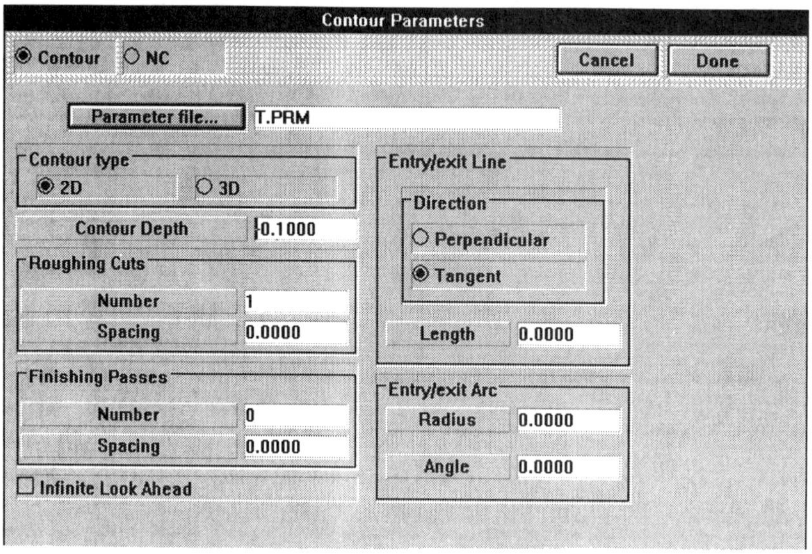

Select the **NC button** to move to the NC parameter menu.

Step 10. Define NC parameters to the following settings.

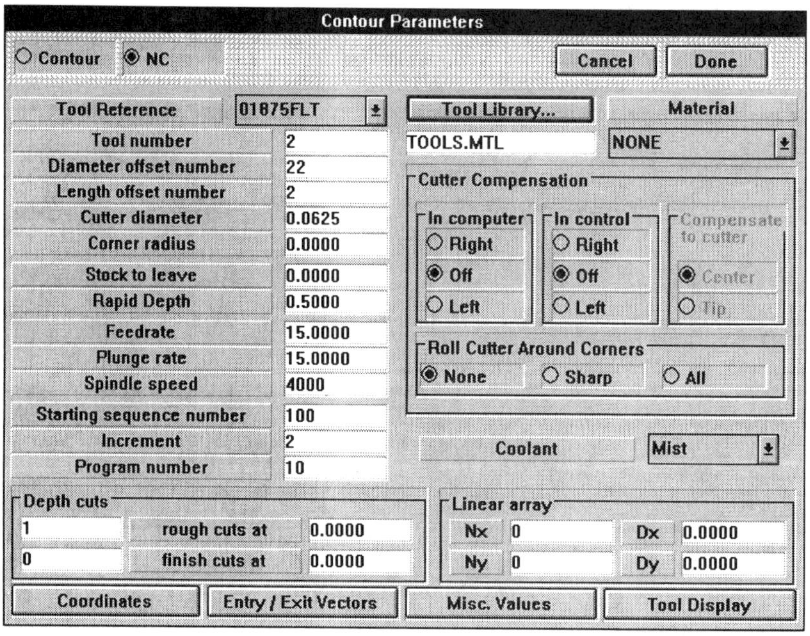

Select the **Done button** to complete the parameters setting.

Step 11. Write the toolpaths.

Press **F3** to repaint the screen

Select **Write** from the Change menu

Select **Yes** to write all remaining contours

Select **Yes** to accept the toolpath segment

The toolpaths should appear as Figure 7.100.

Figure 7.100

Step 12. Close the NCI file.

Select **End program**
Select **No** for running postprocessor

Step 13. Change Gview to isometric.

Select **Gview → Isometric**
Press **Alt** + **F1** simultaneously to fit the drawing on the screen

Step 14. Backplot the toolpath.

Select **MAIN MENU → NC utils → Backplot**
Set the Backplot parameters to the following settings:

Select **Run**

The toolpath file will be backplot on the screen as shown in Figure 7.101.

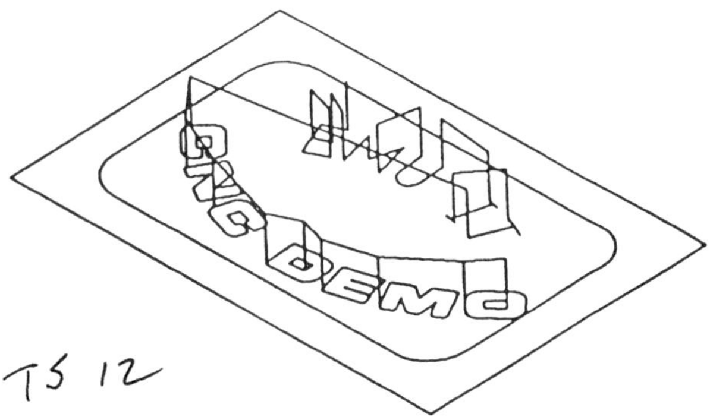

Figure 7.101

Step 15. Run the postprocessor.

Select **MAIN MENU** → **NC utils** → **Post Proc** → **Run**
Enter file name for NCI file: **letters1** ←
Enter file name for NC file: **letters1** ←

The part program should appear on the screen. Double-click the window button to return back to graphic mode.

Project 11.

Using the contour and pocket module to generate toolpaths for cutting existing lettering geometries

Part Geometry Creation
Project 5 of Chapter 5 (letter3)

The letters shown in figure 7.102 have been created by using Create → Letters commands. **Three fonts** are used to create letters as follows:

Box: EASTERN MICHIGAN UNIVERSITY & INDUSTRIAL TECHNOLOGY
Block: CAD CAM & CNC
Roman: YES

We are here ☞

Go to

Toolpath Generation
(letter3)

The box font letters are cut in a concave style, while the other two fonts are machined to the convex form. Note that you may want to change the letters in the box font into your school name and department name instead of EASTERN MICHIGAN UNIVERSITY and INDUSTRIAL TECHNOLOGY.

Figure 7.102

Tips 1. Use the contour module to generate toolpaths for letters with box font.

2. Use the pocket module to generate toolpaths for letters of block and roman fonts. The inner circle is used as the outside contour and profiles of these letters as islands.
3. Make levels 1 and 3 invisible when using the contour module to generate toolpaths for letters of the box font. This allows contours to be easily defined by using the Window command. Use the DB order method to automatically define contouring contours. The number of contours is equal to the number of letters included.

4. Set level 2 to invisible (levels 1 and 3 visible) when using the pocket module to cut letters of block and roman font. Again, this allows letter contours to be readily defined by using the Window command.
5. The cutter diameter must be carefully selected. The cutter for letters contouring should be equal to the width of the letter strokes. In pocketing to form convex letters, the cutter diameter should be slightly smaller than the gaps of letter contours. Otherwise, some pockets will be left uncut. In this project, we use a cutter of 1/16" diameter for contouring and 0.085" for pocketing.
6. Three small closed contours completedly enclosed by an outside contour of the letter will be left uncut. These three letters include two A and one D. We need to use pocket module to separately cut these three pockets.

Step 1. Load the geometry file (letters2.ge3) or create one by following the instructions given in Project 5 of Chapter 5. The part drawing should appear as Figure 7.103.

Select **MAIN MENU → File → Get**
Enter file name: **letters2** ←
Select **Yes** to delete the current part

Figure 7.103

Step 2. Make levels 1 and 3 invisible.

Select **Level → Vis. levels**
Toggle levels 1 and 3 to invisible (dimmed)
Select **OK** → **OK** to return back to graphic mode

The drawing appeared on screen becomes Figure 7.104.

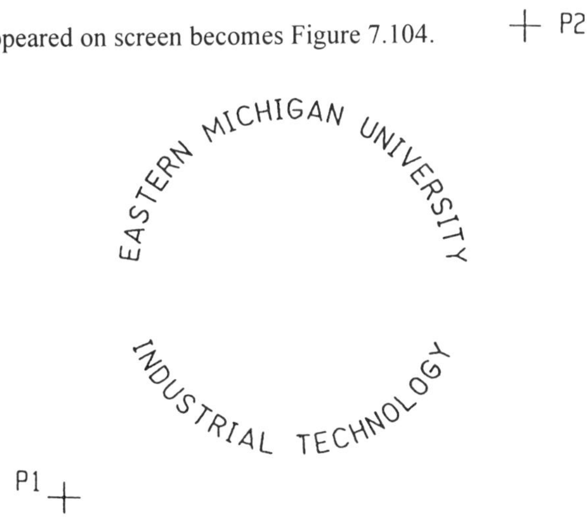

Figure 7.104

Step 3. Initiate the contour toolpath module.

Select **MAIN MENU → Toolpaths → Contour**
Enter file name: **letters2** ←
Select **Yes** to find branch point, if needed

Step 4. Define contours using the pick points in Figure 7.104 on the previous page.

Select **Window** from the Chaining method menu
Pick at **P1** and **P2** to specify the window range
Select **DB order** from the Search by menu
Select **ccW** from the Chaining direction menu
Select **Done** to complete the chaining

Step 5. Define the contour parameters.

Select **Params** from the Contour menu
Set the contour parameters to the following settings:

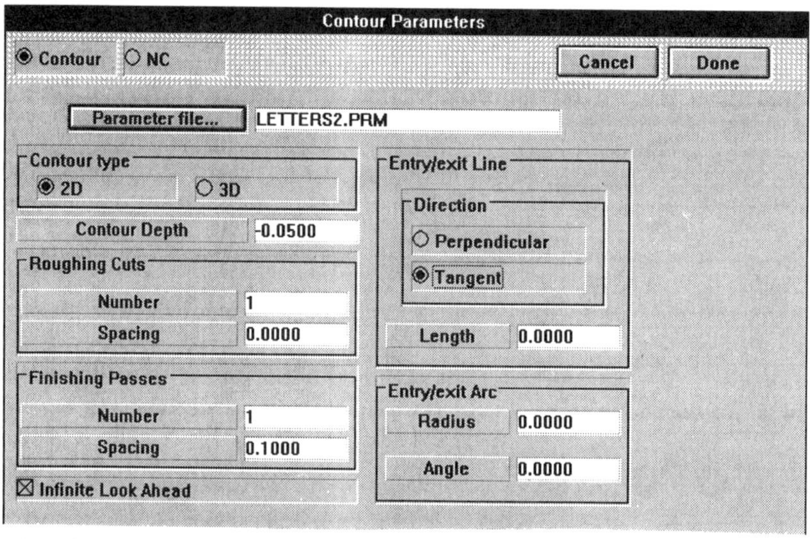

Select the **NC button** to move to the NC parameter menu.

Step 6. Define NC parameters to the following settings.

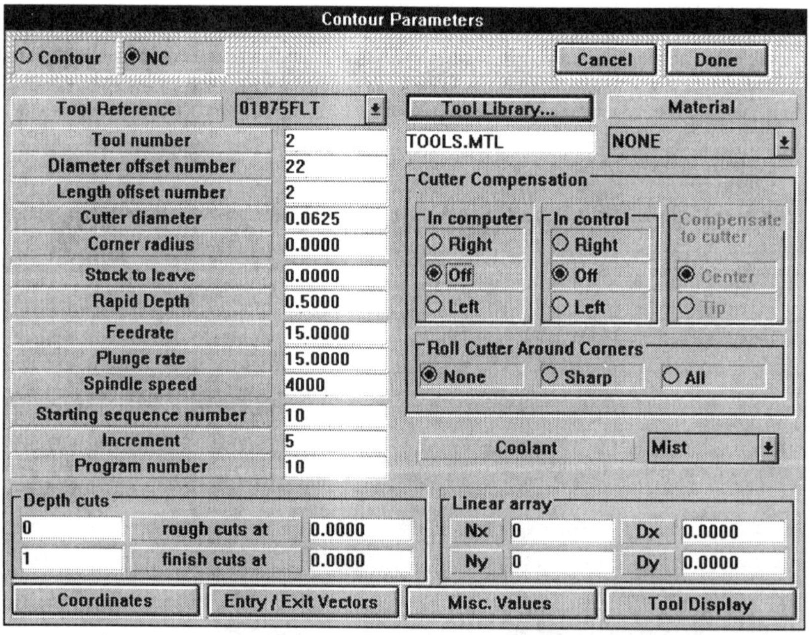

Select the **Done button** to complete the parameters setting.

Step 7. Write the toolpath.

Select **Write** from the Change menu
Select **Yes** to write all remaining contours
Select **Yes** to accept this toolpath segment
The toolpath should appear in blue on screen as Figure 7.105 .

Figure 7.105

Step 8. Make level 2 invisible and levels 1 and 3 visible.

Select **Level → Vis.levels**
Toggle level 1 and 3 to visible(highlighted) and level 2 to invisible (dimmed)
Select **OK** to return back to graphic mode

The new drawing should look like Figure 7.106.

Note: the toolpaths are still visible on the screen.

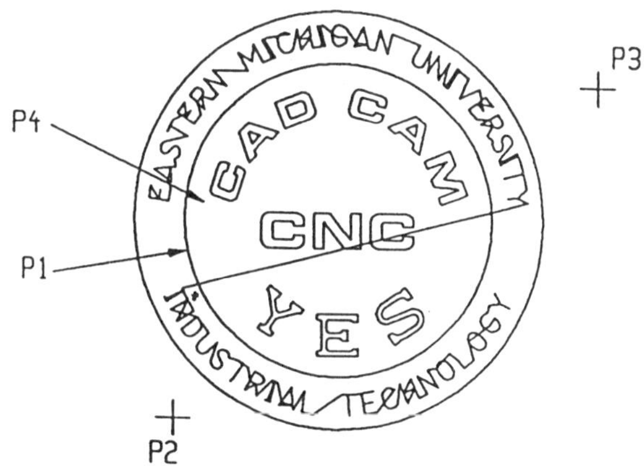

Figure 7.106

Step 9. Initiate pocket module.

Select **MAIN MENU → Toolpaths → Pocket**
Select **Yes** to find branching points, if needed

Step 10. Define contours using the pick points in Figure 7.106.

Select **Single** then pick at **P1** to select the outside contour
Select **Window**
Pick at **P2** and **P3** to define the window range
Select **One way** from Search by menu
Select **CW** from the Chaining direction menu
Pick at **P4** for search point
Select **Done** to complete contours selection

Step 11. Define pocketing parameters.

Set the pocketing parameters to the following settings:

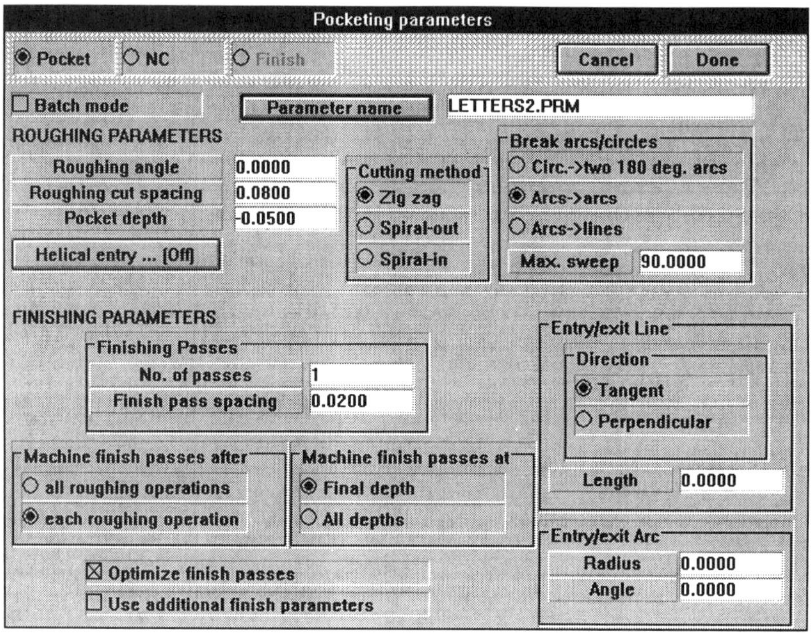

Select the **NC button** to advance to the NC parameters menu.

Step 12. Define NC parameters.

Set the NC parameters to the following settings:

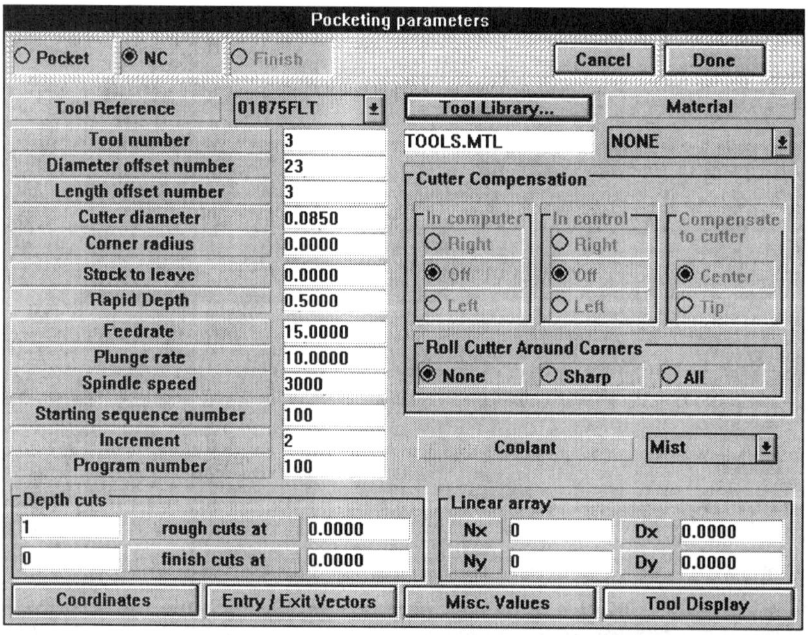

Select the **Done button** to complete the parameters setting

Step 13. Write the pocketing toolpaths.

Select **All** from pocket selection menu to generate roughing toolpaths
Note: It will take a few minutes to generate roughing toolpaths.

Select **Done**
Select **Yes** to accept the toolpath segment

The pocketing toolpath should resemble Figure 7.107.

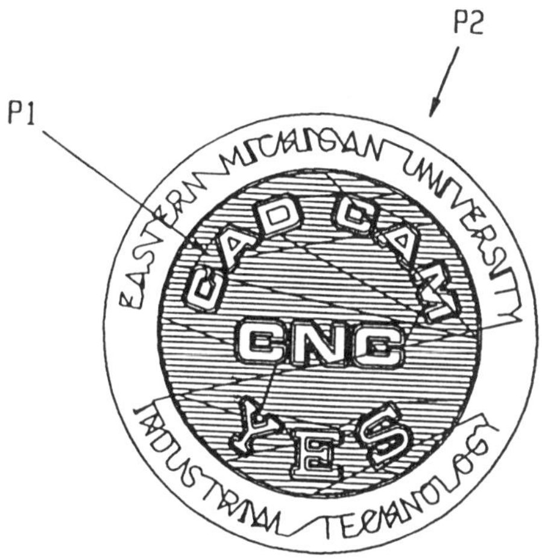

Figure 7.107

Step 14. Zoom the area containing three small uncut pockets. Use the pick points in Figure 7.107.

Press **F1** to initiate Zoom command
Pick at **P1** and **P2** to define the zoom area

The new drawing should resemble Figure 7.108.

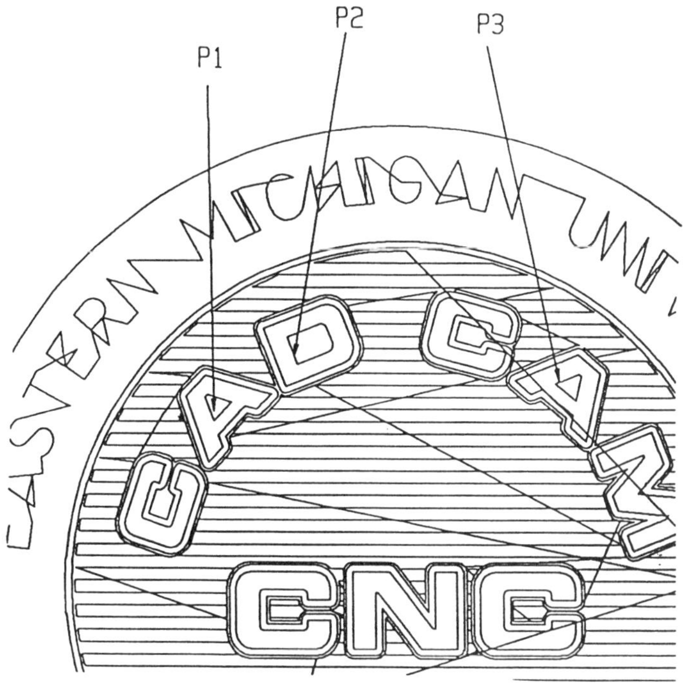

Figure 7.108

Step 15. Initiate pocket module to pocket the first small pocket. Use the pick point in Figure 7.108 on the previous page.

Select **MAIN MENU** → **Toolpaths** → **Pocket**
Select **Chain** from the Chaining method menu
Pick at **P1** to select the first entity
Select **Close** → **End here** → **Done**

Step 16. Define the pocketing parameters to the following settings.

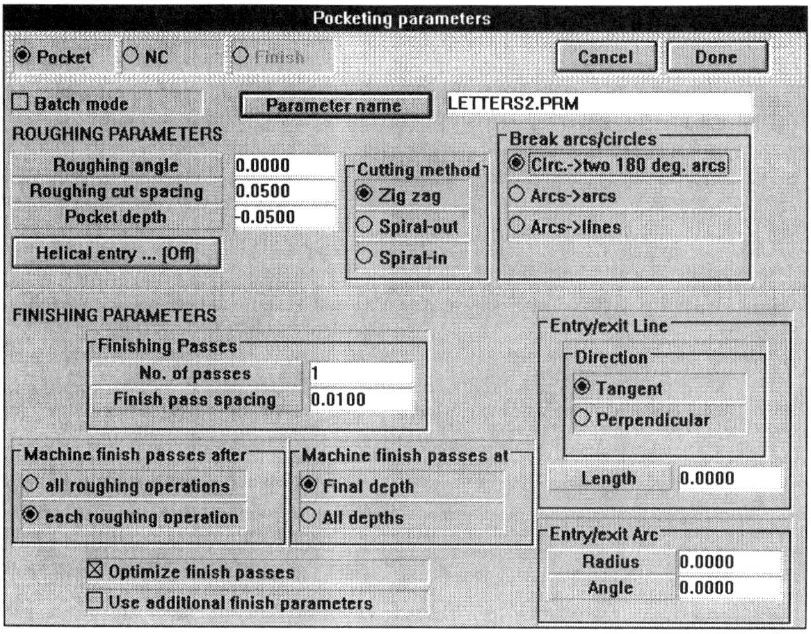

Select the **NC button** to advance to the NC parameter menu.

Step 17. Define the NC parameters to the following settings.

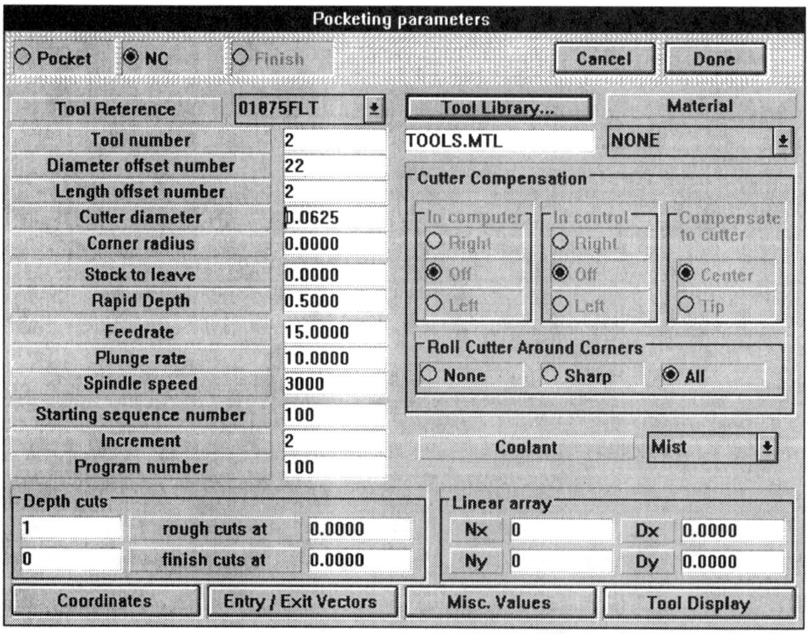

Select the **Done button** to complete the parameters settings.

Step 18. Write the pocket toolpaths.

Select **All** → **Done** → **Yes** to complete the toolpaths

Step 19. Define the boundary for pocketing the second pocket using the pick point in Figure 7.108 on the previous page.

Select **Pocket**
Select **Chain** from the Chaining method menu
Pick at **P2** to select the first entity
Select **Close** → **End here** → **Done** to complete the contour definition

Step 20. Define the pocketing parameters and NC parameters.

Use the parameters setting given in steps 16 - 18 to complete the toolpaths for the second pocket.

Step 21. Define the boundary for pocketing the third pocket using the pick point in Figure 7.108 on the previous page.

Select **Pocket**
Select **Chain** from the Chaining method menu
Pick at **P3** to select the first entity
Select **Close** → **End here** → **Done** to complete the contour definition

Step 22. Define the pocketing parameters and NC parameters.

Use parameters setting in steps 16 - 18 to complete the toolpaths for the third pocket.

Step 23. Close the toolpath file.

Select **End program** to close the toolpath file
Select **No** to "Run the Post Porcessor?"
Press **Alt** + **F1** to fit the drawing

Step 24. Make levels 1 - 3 invisible and change Gview to isometric and backplot the toolpaths.

Select **Level** → **Vis.levels**
Toggle levels 1 - 3 to invisible (dimmed)
then select **OK** to return back to graphic mode
Select **Gview** → **Isometric**
Select **MAIN MENU** → **NC utils** → **Backplot**

Set the Backplot parameters to the following settings:

Select **Run** from the Backplot menu

The toolpaths will be plotted on the screen as shown in Figure 7.109.

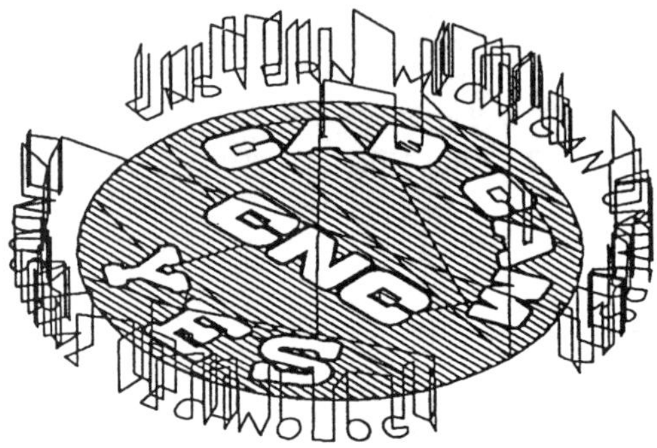

Figure 7.109

Step 25. Make levels 1 - 3 to visible and Gview to top.

Select **Level → Vis.levels**
Toggle levels 1-3 to visible (highlighted)
then select **OK** to return back to graphic mode
Select **Gview → Top**

Select **Run** from the Backplot menu
The final toolpaths
with part geometry
should look like
Figure 7.110.

Figure 7.110

Project 12.

Using the contour module to generate toolpaths for cutting lettering geometries that are converted from notes

This project generates toolpaths to cut three strings of letters that are in different fonts and a combination of upper and lower cases. The lettering geometries must be created by the **edit note method** because lower case letters are involved. The specifications of these three lettering strings are shown in Figure 7.111.

Modern
Font: Old English
Height = 0.4"
Aspect = 0.5
Location = (0.3,1.45)

CNC
Font: Swiss
Height = 0.6"
Aspect = 0.6
Location = (2.25,0.25)

Technology
Font: European
Height = 0.45"
Aspect = 0.5
Location = (0.5,0.1) then
rotate 26.565 degrees

Figure 7.111

Tips 1. Use the edit note method to create lettering geometries. The procedures are:

a. Create three notes using the following commands:
Create → Drafting → Note

b. Edit these three notes to their desired size, font, and orientation using the following commands:
Create → Drafting → Edit → Note

c. Convert these three notes to geometries by using the following commands:
Modify → Break → Note/let → Geometry

2. Use the contour toolpath module to generate toolpaths.

3. The cutter is a 1/16" end mill.

Step 1. Create a rectangle 4" x 2".

Select **MAIN MENU → Create → Rectangle → 2 points**
Enter the lower left corner: **0,0** ←
Enter the upper right corner: **4,2** ←

Press **Alt** + **F1**, then press **F2** to fit the drawing.
The rectangle should appear as in Figure 7.112.

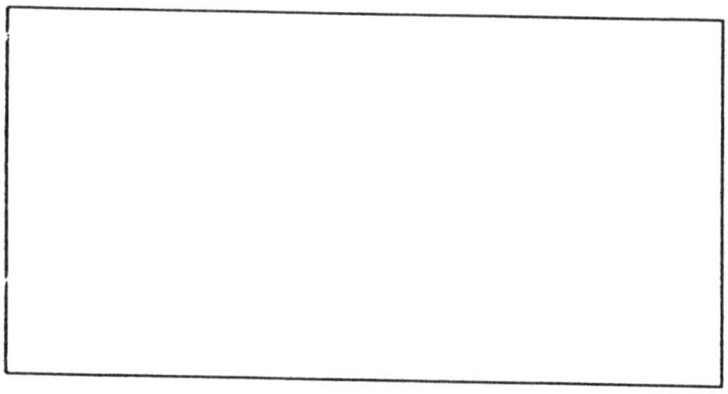

Figure 7.112

Step 2. Set the character height to 0.12" and character aspect to 0.5.

Select **-PM-**
Select button **3**
Select **Note Height** then enter **0.12** ←
Select **Character Aspect** then enter **0.5** ←
Select **Done button** to return back to graphic mode

Step 3. Create three notes.

Select **MAIN MENU → Create → Drafting → Note → Keyin**
Text: **Modern** ←
Press **Enter** to complete note input
Indicate text position: **0.3,1.45** ← for the first note
Select **Keyin** from the menu again
Text: **Technology** ←
Press **Enter** to complete note input
Indicate text position: **0.5,0.1** for the second note
Select **Keyin** from the menu
Text: **CNC** ←
Press **Enter** to complete note input
Indicate text position: **2.25,0.25** ← for the third note

The three notes are added as shown in Figure 7.113.

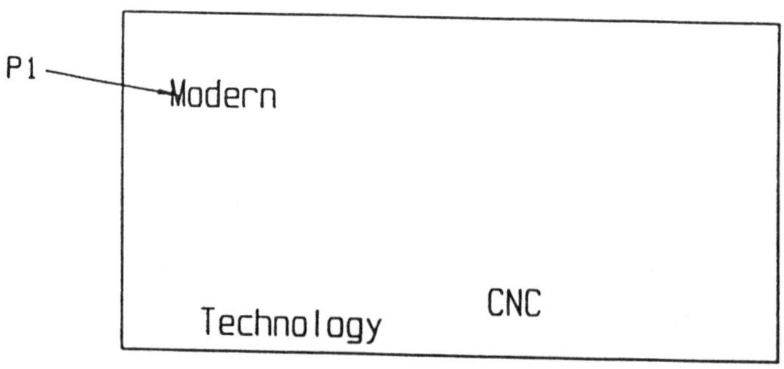

Figure 7.113

Step 4. Edit the first note "Modern" using the pick point in Figure 7.113 from the previous page.

Select **MAIN MENU → Create → Drafting → Edit → Note**
Select note to edit: pick at **P1**
Select **Attribs → Height**
Character height: **0.4** ←
Select **Font**

The initial font is **stick.** Repeatedly select **Next** to select the **Old Englinsh** font

The note "Modern" in the old English font should appear as in Figure 7.114.

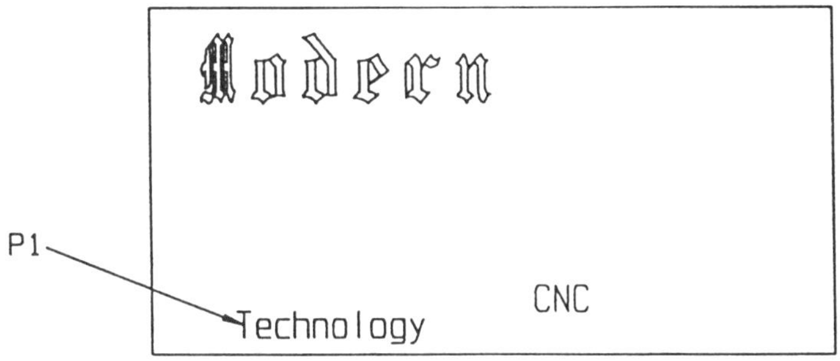

Figure 7.114

Step 5. Edit the second note "Technology" using the pick point in Figure 7.114.

Select **MAIN MENU → Create → Drafting → Edit → Note**
Select note to edit: pick at **P1**
Select **Attribs → Height**
Character height: **0.45** ←
Select **Font**
Toggle **Next** to **European** font
Select **BACKUP → Rotation → String**
Enter string rotation angle: **26.565** ←

The note "Technology" in the European font appears in Figure 7.115.

Figure 7.115

Step 6. Edit the third note "CNC" using the pick point in Figure 7.115 on the previous page.

Select **MAIN MENU → Create → Drafting → Edit → Note**
Select note to edit: pick at **P1**
Select **Attribs → Height**
character height: **0.6 ←**
Select **Aspect**
Character aspect ratio: **0.6 ←**
Select **Font**
Repeatedly toggle **Next** until **sWiss** font appear

The final drawing shall resemble Figure 7.116.

Figure 7.116

Step 7. Convert three notes to geometries using the pick points in Figure 7.116.

Select **MAIN MENU → Modify → Break → Note/let → Geometry → Entity**
Pick at **P1, P2,** and **P3**

Note: These three notes have been converted to geometries. You may not see the difference graphically. The drawing is redrawn in Figure 7.117.

Figure 7.117

Step 8. Initiate the contour toolpath module. Use the pick points in Figure 7.117 on thc previous page.

Select **MAIN MENU** → **Toolpaths** → **Contour**
Enter file name: **letters3** ←
Select **Yes** to "Find branch points?"
Select **Window**
Enter the first corner: pick at **P1**
Enter the second corner: pick at **P2**
Search by: **DB order**
Chaining direction: **ccW**
Select **Done** → **Params**

Step 9. Define contour parameters.

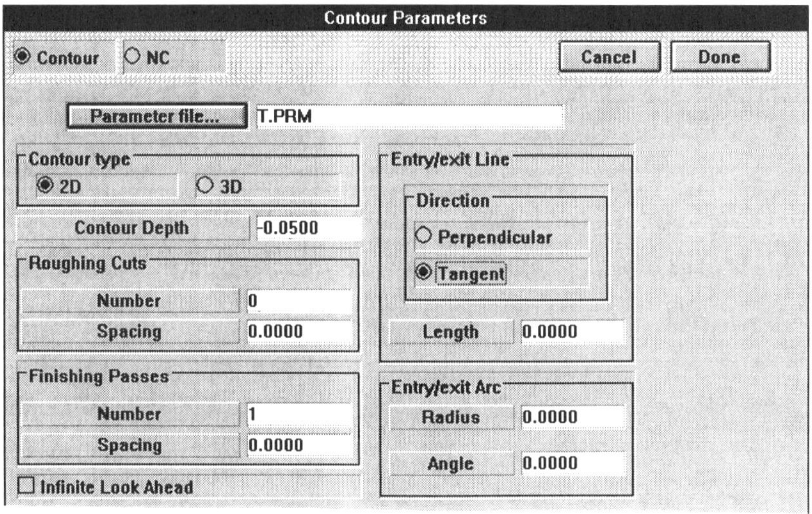

Select the **NC button** to advance to the NC parameters menu.

Step 10. Set the NC parameters to the following settings.

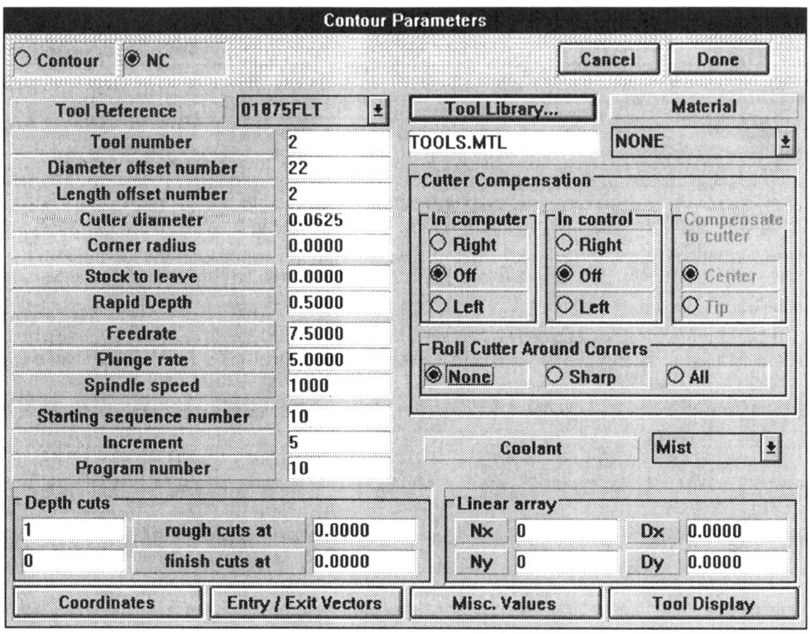

Select the **Done button** to complete the parameters settings.

Step 11. Generate toolpaths.

Select **Write** from the change menu

Select **Yes** to "Write all remaining contours?"

The toolpaths shown in top view shall appear as in Figure 7.118.

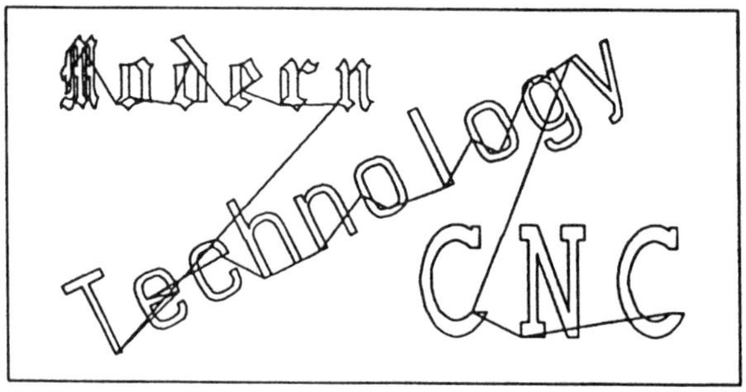

Figure 7.118

Step 12. Show toolpaths in isometric view.

Select **Gview** → **Isometric**

The toolpaths in isometric view are displayed in Figure 7.119

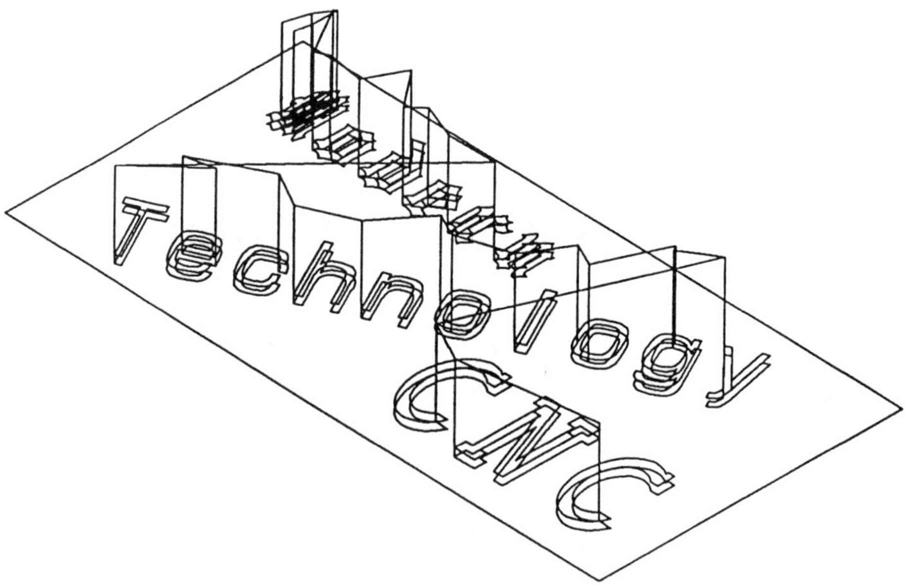

Figure 7.119

Step 13. Close the NCI file.

Select **Yes** to accept this toolpath segment

Select **End progrm**

Select **No** to "Run the post processor?"

Tips 1. This is a **comparison** between the two lettering toolpath methods:

Using the **letters module** to generate lettering toolpaths eliminates the process of creating a letters geometry file. However, this method can only create the toolpaths to move along the lettering profiles. It produces the concave type of letters when the box font is used (Figure 7.120). It will produce letters of the convex or concave style depending on which mode of cutter compensation is used (Figure 7.121 on the next page).

Using the **contour or pocket module** to generate toolpaths from existing letters in a geometry file provides greater flexibility to produce a variety of letters. The contour module is always used for letters of the box font. The pocket or contour module is used for the other three types of fonts depending on the type of application.

2. The cutter compensation in computer should be set to Off when letters are done using the box font. Center left or center right should be used for contouring letters of block, roman, or slant font.

3. Use the window command to define lettering contours when more than one letter is used. When a string of letters is used as pocketing islands for producing convex letters, an out side contour should be defined first to be the outer boundary of the pocketing, then the window command is used to define letters as pocketing islands.
4. When multiple sets of lettering strings are used and they are in different fonts or to be cut in different types, some concave and others convex, assign each set of lettering strings to different levels and colors. This allows the letter strings that are not used for a particular operation to be made invisible.

5. The cutter used in lettering should be carefully selected.

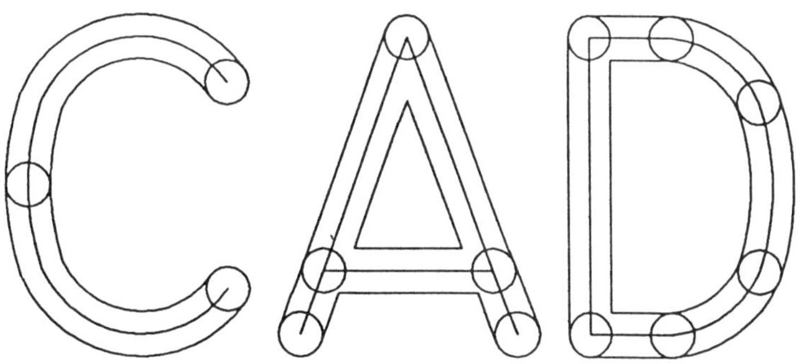

Figure 7.120

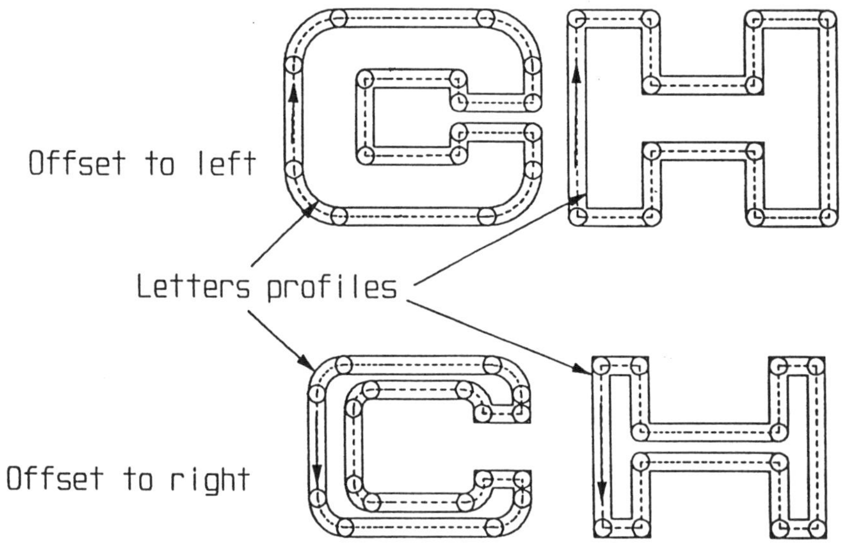

Figure 7.121

7.8 Exercises

7.8.1 Short Answer

1. List the four 2-D toolpath modules in Mastercam and briefly describe what they are.

2. What are common parameters and module specific parameters?

3. Describe the purposes of cutter compensations.

4. Describe the difference between the cutter compensation in control and cutter compensation in computer.

5. Explain how the selection of cutter compensation in computer (left, right, or center) affects the toolpaths.

6. Write the proper NC command codes for the three options (right, left, and off) of cutter compensation in control with the assigned register number for diameter offset.

7. What is the main purpose of stock allowance?

8. Describe the difference between the feedrate and plunge rate.

9. Explain the purpose of rapid depth, and describe its effect on toolpaths.

10. What are depth cuts? Explain how the parameter settings in depth cuts affect the toolpaths.

11. What is the linear array function and when do we use this function?

12. What are the three parameters that can be used to change the coordinate values of a part program?

13. Describe how the settings of home position parameter relates to the reference return point commands in part programs. Also provide a drawing to show the toolpaths generated from the home position parameter.

14. What is the tool origin? How does the setting of the tool origin affect the coordinate values in part programs.

15. What are the three principal tool planes?

16. Give drawings to show how the selected tool plane affects the approaching direction of the cutting tool relevant to the workpiece.

17. What is a contour?

18. Explain why the selection of the first entity in defining a contour is so important.

19. Do a drawing to show how Mastercam determines the contour direction.

20. List the two methods used to change the depth of cutting paths in Mastercam. Briefly compare their advantages and disadvantages.

21. What are entry/exit lines and arcs? List the parameters for entry/exit lines and arcs and use drawings to illustrate the toolpaths caused by these parameters.

22. What are the four parameters used to determine the number of contouring passes?

23. Draw an illustration to show the contouring passes for a rectangular profile having a fillet at four corners under the following toolpath parameters setting:

    Number of roughing cuts = 3
    Roughing cut spacing = 0.5
    Number of finish passes = 1
    Finishing pass spacing = 0.05

24. Explain how to define a sharp corner.

25. Give drawings to illustrate the difference in toolpaths at corners when the toolpath around the corners parameter is toggled to sharp corners and no corners.

26. What is the maximum roughing cut spacing for a 1" end mill to cut a steel workpiece and an aluminum workpiece, respectively? Assume making multiple roughing passes to remove the stock to the desired profile.

27. Determine the four toolpath parameters for using a 3/4" end mill in contouring a profile with a total of 1.5" stock to be removed in all directions. The workpiece material is low-carbon steel.

28. Describe when to use pocket module.

29. Mastercam provides the option for defining additional finish parameters. Explain when to use additional finish parameters.

30. What are the three cutting methods used with the pocket module? Use drawings to illustrate the toolpath patterns of these three cutting methods.

31. Explain why the zig zag cutting method is not recommended in pocketing if possible.

32. Under what conditions should the spiral inside out cutting method be used?

33. Under what conditions is it better to use the spiral outside in cutting method?

34. What are islands in pocketing?

35. Explain how to define outside contours and island contours for pocketing in Mastercam.

36. Describe how regions are formed in pocketing.

37. What are the two modes of machining sequence parameter that can be selected for generating toolpaths sequence in pocketing the pocket having more than one region?

38. Use drawings to show the difference in the toolpaths sequence for the parameter of machining sequence being set to all roughing operations mode oand each roughing operation mode.

39. What is the ideal case of using the all roughingoperations mode for the machining sequence parameter? Explain why.

40. What are the four parameters Mastercam uses to determine the depths of pocketing operations?

41. Explain how the mode of the parameter of "Machine finish passes at" affect the toolpath pattern of finish cuts.

42. Explain why the entry/exit lines and arcs are not recommended in pocketing a pocket with islands.

43. What are the three Z-depths involved in the drill module? Draw an illustration to show these three Z-depths.

44. What are the two parameters Mastercam uses to define the Z-depth?

45. Use drawings to show how the specified Z-value of Z-depth is measured for Absolute mode and Incremental mode, respectively.

46. Explain why the Absolute mode is always recommended in defining the Z-depth.

47. When should you use the Incremental mode in defining the Z-depth?

48. List the seven cycle modes used in drill module and briefly describe their applications.

49. Write the NC fixed cycle command codes for the following cycle type in drill module:

Cycle type	NC command
Drill with dwell = 0	
Drill/counterbore with dwell ≠ 0	
Peck drill	
Chip break	
Tap	
Bore #1 with dwell = 0	
Bore #1 with dwell ≠ 0	
Bore #2	

50. Do a drawing to show the typical operation sequence of a drilling or boring operation.

51. What are two types of deep hole drilling methods? Explain their difference.

52. Explain how to determine the reference height for drilling smooth surfaces and rough surfaces, respectively.

53. Use drawings to show how to determine the Z-depth for drilling blind holes and through holes, respectively.

54. Calculate the Z-depth for drilling a blind hole that has the full-diameter depth of 1.5" and the drill diameter is 0.75". The Z value of the top surface of the hole is Z0.0.

55. Determine the Z-depth for drilling a through hole that has the hole depth of 1.75" and the drill diameter is 1". The Z value of the top surface of the hole is Z0.0.

56. When should you use the peck or chip break drilling cycle.

57. Compare the features of the peck and chip break drilling cycle.

58. What are the four standard fonts for lettering in Mastercam?

59. Describe the two methods of generating toolpaths for engraving letters.

60. What are the three lettering layout styles?

61. What are the three parameters used to specify the location of letters string in angular layout?

62. Describe with a drawing how the letters string is centered along the top arc and bottom arc, respectively.

7.8.2 Problems

63. Use the contour module to generate toolpaths for machining the part shown in Figure 7.122. The raw material is a hollow circular plate with an outside diameter of 6.1" and an inside diameter of 2.5".

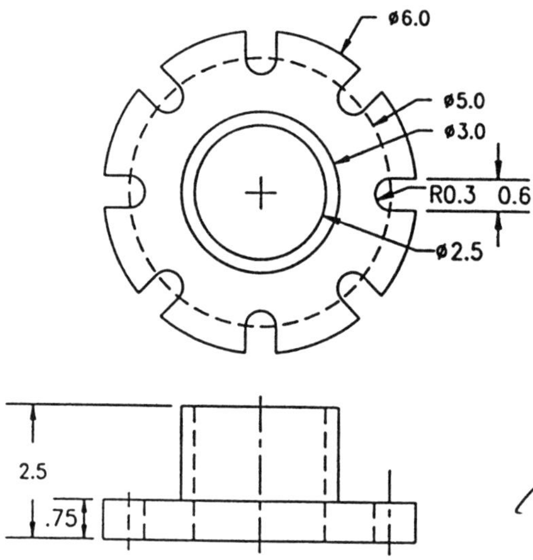

Figure 7.122

Tips 1. The part drawing file uses **contour5** which is created in chapter 6.

2. Use the contour module to cut the upper part from 6.1" diameter to 3" diameter using the following machining data:

   Cutter: 1" end mill
   Number of roughing passes: 2
   Roughing spacing: 0.65"
   Number of finish passes: 1
   Finishing spacing: 0.2"

   Depth cuts: Rough: 3 cuts at 0.5" Finish: 1 cuts at 0.25"

3. Use the contour module to machine the base profile. The machining data is suggested below:

   Cutter: 3/8" end mill
   Number of roughing passes: 0
   Roughing spacing: 0.0
   Number of finish passes: 1
   Finishing spacing: 0.0

   Depth cuts: Rough: 1 cuts at 0.5" Finish: 1 cuts at 0.25"

64. The raw material for the part shown in Figure 7.123 has been casted to its rough shape and size. Cut the internal profile using a 1/2" end mill to produce the profile. Only one finish pass is suggested because the material has been casted to its rough shape. The part geometry file is **contour6** which is constructed in problem 5 of Chapter 6.

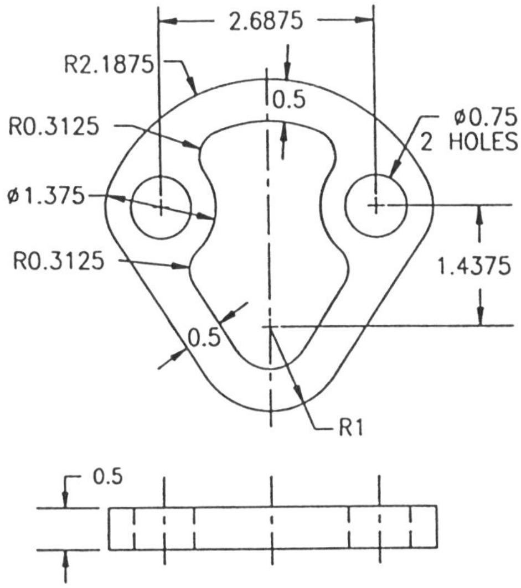

Figure 7.123.

TS 14

65. The raw material for the part shown in Figure 7.124 has been casted to its rough shape. There are four features to be produced, two external profiles and two internal profiles. The contour module is used four times to generate toolpaths for cutting these four features. The part geometry file is **contour7** which is created in problem 16 of Chapter 6. Some hints are given below:

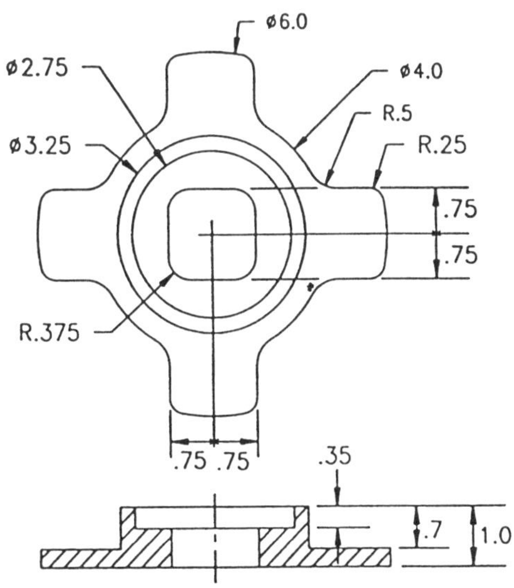

Figure 7.124

TS 15

Tips 1. A 1" end mill can be used to cut both external profiles.

2. Multiple passes should be used for cutting the second external profile (3.25" diameter cylinder) because the flat surface at A must be cut when machining this profile.
3. A 1/2" end mill can be used for both internal profiles.

66. The part shown in Figure 7.125 has two depth changes in the profile. The depth of line profile AB linearly changes from Z-0.1" at point A to Z-0.6" at point B. The depth remains at Z-0.6 from B to E. The depth linearly changes from E (Z-0.6) to F (Z-0.1). The part geometry file name is **contour8** which is created in problem 16 of Chapter 5.

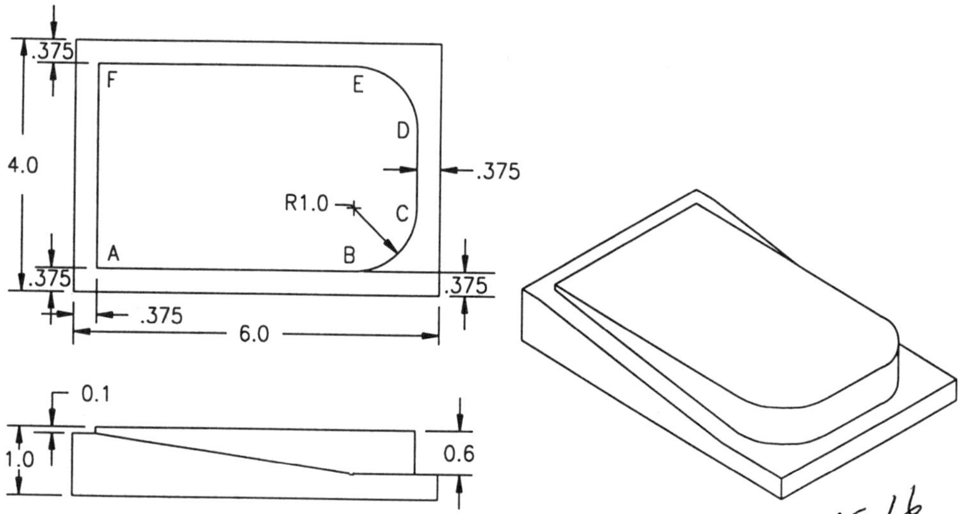

Figure 7.125

Tips 1. The contour modulue is recommended with two passes in depth cuts. One roughing pass and one finish pass with spacing of 0.15". Note that no multiple passes are allowed in the tool plane (XY-plane) when the depth change function is used.

2. Use Depth → Ramp commands to change the depth at points B and F. The depth at B should be -0.6 and at F is -0.1. *Note* that the contour depth should be set to -0.1.
3. Use isometric view to observe the linear change in depth along the line profiles AB and EF.

67. The profile of the part shown in Figure 7.126 has depth change between A and B. The profile has a depth of Z-0.15" except between A and B which has Z-0.5". The part geometry file is **contour9** which is created in problem 17 of Chapter 5.

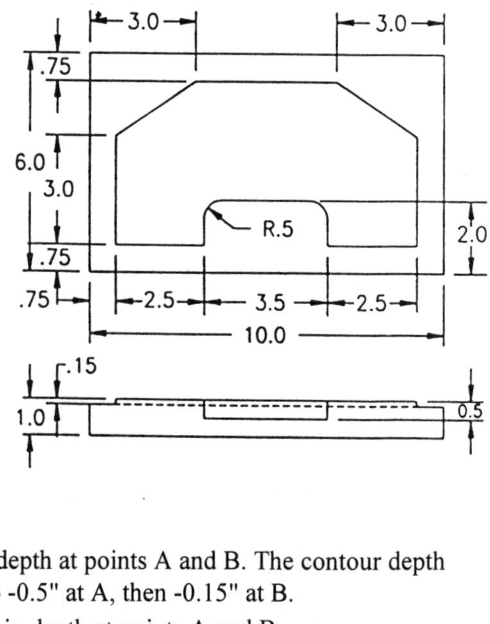

Figure 7.126

Tips 1. Using the contour module is recommended.

2. Use Depth → Step commands to change the depth at points A and B. The contour depth should be set to -0.15. The depth is changed to -0.5" at A, then -0.15" at B.
3. Use isometric view to observe the step change in depth at points A and B.

68. There are two features, top flat surface and internal pocket, to be produced for the part shown in Figure 7.127. Pocket module can be used to produce both features. The part geometry file name is **pocket3** which is created in problem 17 of Chapter 6.

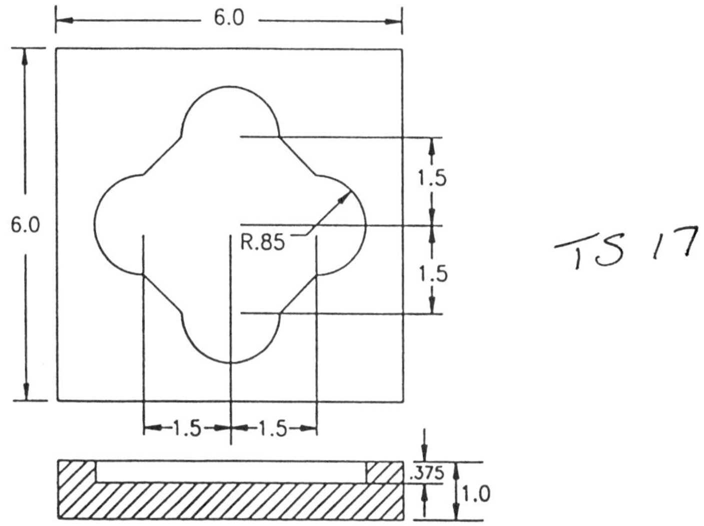

Figure 7.127

Tips 1. Create a construction rectangle (6.5 x 6.5) to serve as the outside contour of pocketing for facing the top surface.

2. A 1" end mill is recommended for facing the top surface. The roughing spacing is 0.75". One finish pass issuggested.
3. Use a 3/4" end mill for cutting the internal pocket.

4. Use the spiral inside out cutting method for cutting the internal pocket.

69. The part shown in Figure 7.128 consists of two internal pockets, one circular pocket in the center and one contourpocket with an island. The part geometry file name is **pocket4** which is created in problem18 of Chapter 6.

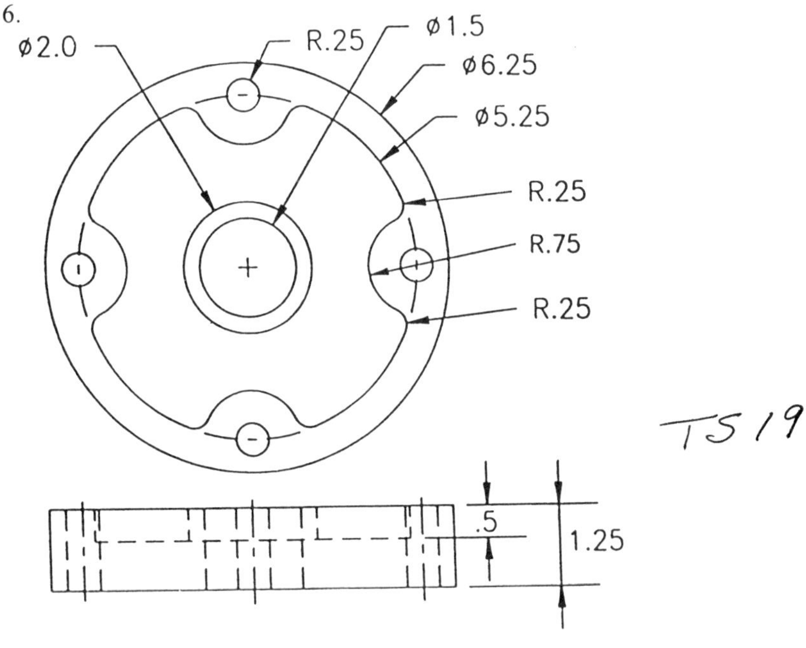

Figure 7.128

69. Continued

Tips 1.Use pocket module to machine both internal pockets. Machine the larger pocket first, then followed by machining the second pocket.

2. The 2.0" diameter circle is used as an island in pocketing the larger pocket.

3. Suggested machining data for pocketing the larger pocket:
   Cutting method: Spiral outside in or zig zag
   Two cutters: 3/4" end mill for roughing passes
   1/2" end mill for the finish pass
   Roughing spacing = 0.5"

4. Suggested machining data for pocketing the second pocket:
   Cutting method: Spiral inside out
   Cutter: 1/2" end mill
   Roughing spacing = 0.35"

70. The part shown in Figure 7.129 consists of one internal pocket with an island. The island and the pocket profile are so close that six pocket regions are formed when a larger roughing cutter is used. The part geometry file is **pocket5** which is created in problem 19 of Chapter 6.

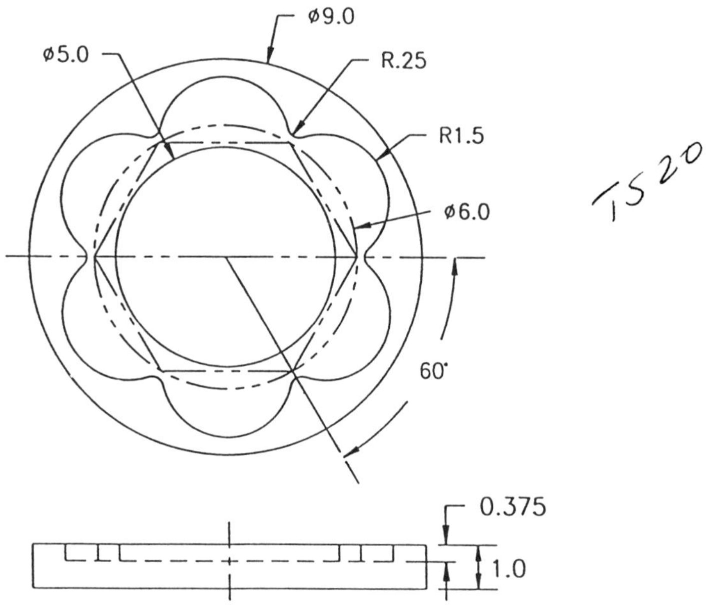

Figure 7.129

Tips Suggested machining data:

Two cutters: 3/4" end mill for roughing passes
1/4" end mill for finish pass

Cutting method = Spiral outside in or Zig zag
Roughing cut spacing = 0.3"
Pocket depth = -0.375"
Number of finish passes = 1
Finishing pass spacing = 0.05"
Machining sequence = operation
Machine finish passes at: final depth
Additional finish parameters = Yes

71. Four fine finish holes are required in the part shown in Figure 7.130. The holes are produced from the solid stock. Various cycle modes of the drill module should be used to produce these holes. The part geometry file is **drill4** which is created in problem 18 of Chapter 5.

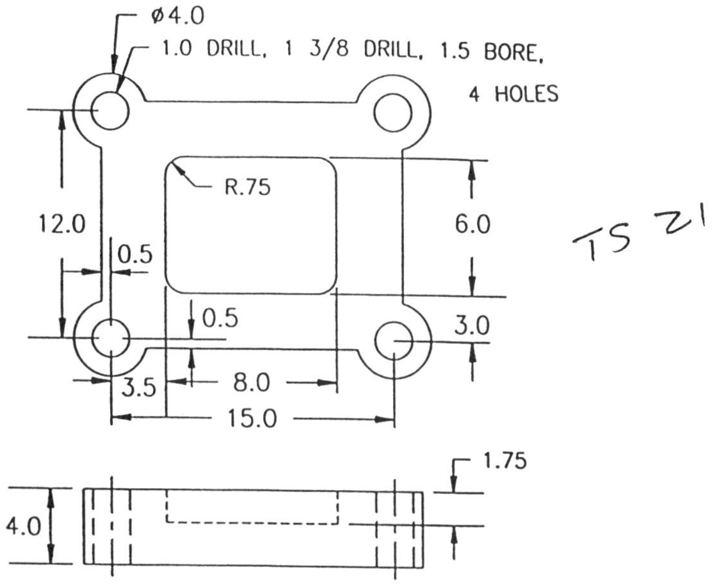

Figure 7.130

Tips 1. The following three processes are suggested:

Pilot drilling with 3/4" drill
Enlarging drilling with 1-3/8" drill
Finish boring with 1-1/2" boring tool

2. Use the peck drilling cycle for both drilling operations. The peck increment is 1.5".

72. Three modules are used to generate toolpaths for machining the part shown in Figure 7.131. The part geometry file name is **comb1** which is created in problem 20 of Chapter 7. Some suggestions are listed on the next page.

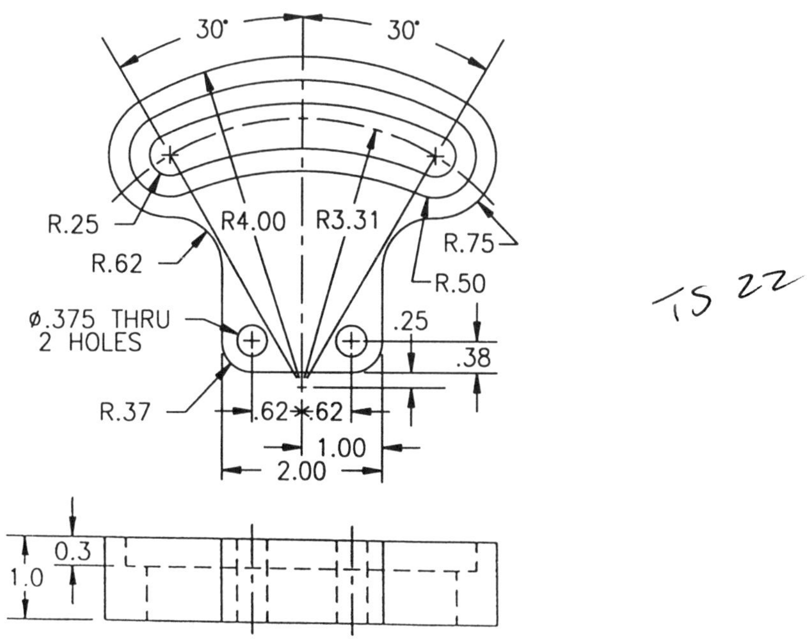

Figure 7.131

72. continued

Tips 1. Suggested machine sequence:

Contour module for cutting the outside profile
Pocket module for pocketing the larger pocket of 0.35" deep
Pocket module for pocketing the smaller pocket of 0.65" deep
Drill module for drilling the two holes

2. Cutting tools:

1" end mill for contouring
1/2" end mill for pocketing both pockets
3/8" drill for drilling two holes

73. Five features are to be produced for the part shown in Figure 7.132. They include the top flat surface, two pockets, four 1/2"-holes, and six 1/4"-holes. Two toolpath modules, pocket and drill, are ` 1 involved in this project. The part geometry file name is **comb2** which is created in problem 19 of Chapter 5.

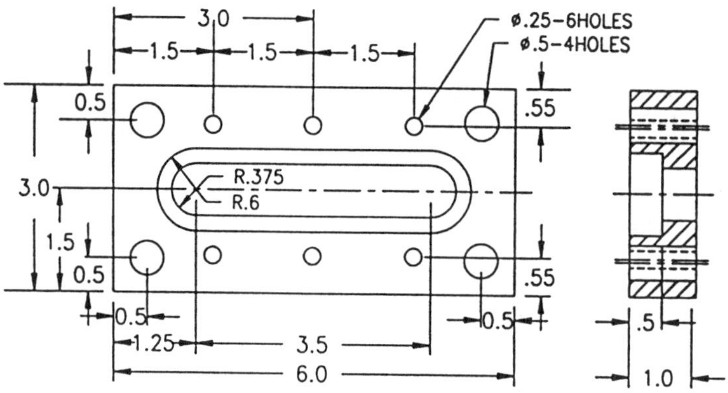

Figure 7.132

Tips 1. Machining sequence and toolpath module to use

Facing top surface by using pocket module
Pocketing the larger pocket by using pocket module
Pocketing the smaller pocket by using pocket module
Drilling four 1/2" holes by using drill module
Drilling six 1/4" holes by using drill module

2. Cutters

1" end mill for facing the top surface
1/2" end mill for pocketing both internal pockets
1/2" drill for drilling 1/2" holes
1/4" drill for drilling 1/4" holes

3. Create a 6.5" x 3.5" rectangle to serve as the outside contour for pocketing a top flat surface.

74. Six features are to be produced for the part shown in Figure 7.133. They include the external profile, two small local profiles, a slot pocket, and two holes of different size. The raw material has been casted to its rough shape. Part geometry file name is **comb3** which is constructed in problem 21 of Chapter 5. Some hints are given below.

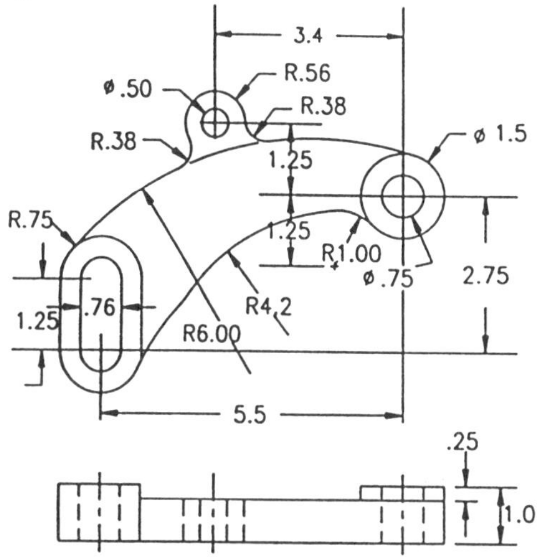

Figure 7.133

Tips 1. Machining sequence and toolpath module to use

Machining outside profile by using contour module
Cutting the larger local profile by using contour module
Cutting the small local profile by using contour module
Cutting the slot pocket by using contour module
Drilling the 3/4" hole by using drill module
Drilling the 1/2" hole by using drill module

2. Cutters

3/4" end mill for machining the outside profile and two local profiles.
1/2" end mill for contouring the profile of the slot pocket
3/4" drill for drilling the 3/4" hole
1/2" drill for drilling the 1/2" hole

75. The part shown in Figure 7.134 consists of five features including the external profile, top flat surface, circular flange, hexagonal pocket, and two holes. The part geometry file name is **comb4** which is constructed in problem 22 of Chapter 5. Some hints are included on the next page.

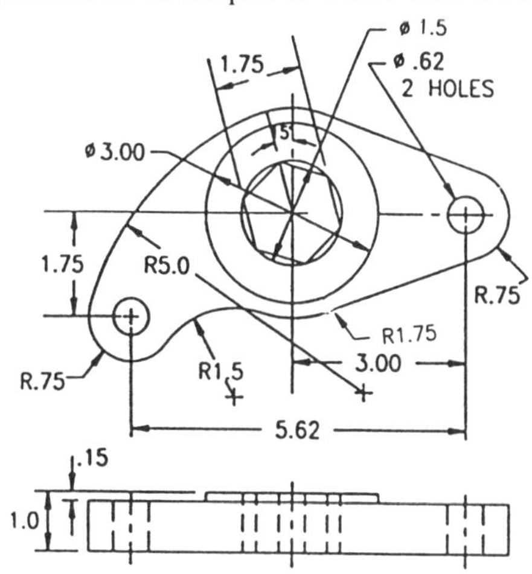

Figure 7.134

75. continued

Tips 1. Use offset function to create a profile which is 0.2" larger than the existing external profile in all directions. This allows the offset profile to be used as the outside contour and the 3" diameter circle as an island for thepocket module to produce the top flat surface and the circular profile in one operation.

2. Use two cutters for cutting the hexagonal pocket. A 1/2" end mill for roughing and a 3/32" end mill for finish pass. Note that the six vertices of the hexagon will have corner arcs of 3/32". This requires a broaching operation to make them straight.

76. Five strings of letters are engraving in a circular plate as shown in Figure 7.135. The part geometry file name is **letters4** which is created in problem 21 of Chapter 5. Replacing the string EMU IT with your school name and department name . Some helpful tips are listed on the next page.

Figure 7.135

Tips: 1. The geometry file is organized by level and color as below:

Two circles:	level 1 and color 10
Box font:	level 2 and color 12
Roman font:	level 3 and color 13
Block font:	level 4 and color 14

77. continued

2. Box font: SOCIETY OF MANUFACTURING ENGINEERING and STUDENT CHAPTER
   Roman font: EMU IT and WELCOME
   Block font: CNC

3. Use the contour module to engraving two letters strings with the box font. Make levels 1, 3, and 4 invisible. This allows you to use Window → DB order → ccW commands to select all letter contours in one operation. The cutter for this operation is 1/16".

4. Use the pocket module to produce three strings of letters of roman and block font. These letters are of the convex style. To do so, we use a circle of 8" diameter as the outside contour and all letters as islands.

5. Make level 2 (which has letters of box font) invisible. This allows the use of Window → One way → CW commands to define all letters as islands.

6. Suggested machining data for pocketing letter strings;

   Two cutters: 3/16" end mill for roughing passes
   1/16" end mill for finish passes

   Roughing spacing = 0.125"
   Number of finish passes = 1

7. The inside pocket for the letter 'O' in the letter string WELCOME is left uncut in pocketing. Therefore we need to use the pocket module again to cut it.

Chapter 8

2-D Toolpath Editing

Objectives:

1. Know the toolpath file structure and determine the number of toolpaths sections for various operations.
2. Delete the toolpath sections from an existing toolpath file.
3. Merge two toolpath files.
4. Know four toolpath editing functions; mirror, rotate, scale, and translate.
5. Understand the features of these toolpath editing functions and know when to apply them.
6. Apply toolpath editing functions to simplify toolpath generation process.

8.1 File Structure of Toolpaths

After toolpaths have been generated from using various toolpath modules, we may need to manipulate these toolpaths. Mastercam provides a variety of ways to modify toolpaths including deleting, merging, and editing. Understanding the file structure of the Mastercam toolpaths is very crucial to successfully implementing these editing features. This chapter starts with the toolpath file structure and follows with the deleting function, four editing functions, and concludes with the linear array. All these functions are very useful in generating proper toolpaths for cutting parts.

Mastercam organizes the toolpaths into sections so that they can be edited. The toolpath sections are assigned according to their generation sequence. The toolpath generated by one operation is normally identified as one operation or section. Therefore, toolpath sections are generated by using the contour, pocket, drill, or surface module. Three operations, for example, are used to machine the part shown in Figure 8.1. The operation sequence starts with using the contour module to contour the outer profile, followed by using the pocket module for pocketing the rectangular pocket and using the drill module to drill the three holes. The toolpaths in this example contain three sections and are organized as below:

Section No.	Toolpaths
Section 1	Contour module
	-
	-
Section 2	Pocket module
	-
	-
Section 3	Drill module
	-
	-
End of file	EOF

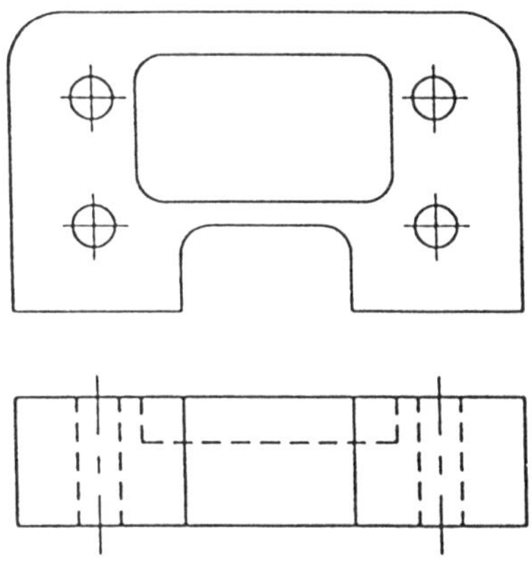

Figure 8.1

Often, more than one section is assigned to the toolpaths generated by one operation. This occurs when the contour module is used when (1) the sum of roughing passes and finish passes is more than one or (2) the sum of rough cuts and finish cuts in depth cut is more than one.

The number of toolpath sections for using the contour module can be calculated as:

$$N_C = (N_R + N_F) \text{ X } (N_{RD} + N_{FD})$$

where N_C = total number of toolpath sections for contouring
N_R = number of rough cuts
N_F = number of finish passes
N_{RD} = number of rough passes in depth cut
N_{FD} = number of finish passes in depth cut

Example 8.1 Number of toolpath sections in contouring

The contour module is used to cut an external profile with these cutting parameters:

Number of rough cuts (N_R) = 1
Number of finish passes (N_F) = 1
Number of rough passes in depth cut (N_{RD}) = 0
Number of finish passes in depth cut (N_{FD}) = 1

The total number of toolpath sections for this particular operation is:

$N_C = (N_R + N_F) \text{ X } (N_{RD} + N_{FD}) = (1 + 1) \text{ X } (1 + 0) = \mathbf{2}$ toolpath sections

Example 8.2 Number of toolpath sections in contouring

Find the total number of toolpath sections for contouring a profile with these cutting parameters:

Number of rough cuts (N_R) = 2
Number of finish passes (N_F) = 1
Number of rough passes in depth cut (N_{RD}) = 2
Number of finish passes in depth cut (N_{FD}) = 1

The total number of toolpath sections in this contouring operation is:

$N_C = (N_R + N_F) \text{ X } (N_{RD} + N_{FD}) = (2 + 1) \text{ X } (2 + 1) = \mathbf{9}$ toolpath sections

In pocketing, the number of toolpath sections is the **sum** of rough cuts and finish cuts in depth cut parameters. The number of finish passes in the XY-plane does not affect the number of toolpath sections. The formula listed below can be used to find the total number of toolpath sections in pocketing:

$$N_P = N_{RD} + N_{FD}$$

where N_P = total number of toolpath sections for pocketing

Example 8.3 Number of toolpath sections in pocketing

Calculate the total number of toolpath sections in pocketing a rectangular pocket under the following cutting parameters:

Number of finish passes (N_F) = 2
Number of rough passes in depth cut (N_{RD}) = 0
Number of finish passes in depth cut (N_{FD}) = 1

The total number of toolpath sections in this pocketing operation is:

$N_P = N_{RD} + N_{FD} = 0 + 1 = \mathbf{1}$ toolpath section

Example 8.4 Number of toolpath sections in pocketing

Calculate the number of toolpath sections in pocketing an enclosed profile under the following cutting parameters:

Number of finish passes (N_F) = 2
Number of rough passes in depth cut (N_{RD}) = 2
Number of finish passes in depth cut (N_{FD}) = 1

The total number of toolpath sections in this pocketing operation is:

$N_P = N_{RD} + N_{FD} = 2 + 1 = \mathbf{3}$ toolpath sections

The number of toolpath segments is always **one** when the drill module is used. When a part program contains the toolpaths generated from using more than one operation (contour, pocket, drill, or surface module), the total number of toolpath sections is the sum of toolpath sections of each operation.

Example 8.5 Number of toolpath sections for multiple operations

A part program consists of the toolpaths generated from three operations (contour, pocket, and drill). Find the number of toolpath sections for the following two sets of cutting parameters:

Case 1:

Contour:	Number of roughing cuts = **0**	
	Number of finish passes = **1**	
	Depth cut: Rough: **0** cuts at **0.0**	Finish: **1** cuts at **0.0**
Pocket:	Number of finish passes = **1**	
	Depth cut: Rough: **0** cuts at **0.0**	Finish: **1** cuts at **0.0**
Drill:	Drilling operation is always one toolpath section.	

The total number of toolpath sections is the sum of these three operations which is

$N = 1 + 1 + 1 = \mathbf{3}$ toolpath sections

The total number of toolpath sections for the operation conditions listed above is 3 (one for contouring, one for pocketing, and one for drilling).

Case 2:

Contour:	Number of roughing cuts = **2**	
	Number of finish passes = **1**	
	Depth cut: Rough: **1** cuts at **0.0**	Finish: **1** cuts at **0.2**
Pocket:	Number of finish passes = **1**	
	Depth cut: Rough: **0** cuts at **0.0**	Finish: **1** cuts at **0.0**
Drill:	Drilling operation is always one toolpath section.	

The contouring operation has 6 toolpath sections. The pocketing has 1 section and drilling 1 section. Therefore, the total number of toolpath sections is **8**.

How to Find the List of Toolpath Sections

Use the following commands to list the toolpath scctions of a toolpath file.

Select **MAIN MENU → NCutils → Edit NCI**

This Edit NCI window should appear.

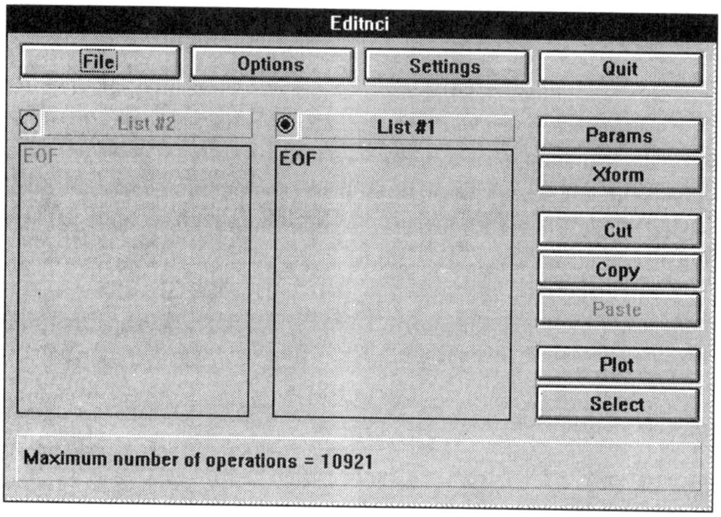

Select **File → Open**
Enter file name: **pocket1** (specify your own file's name)

The toolpath sections should appear under list #1 as shown below.

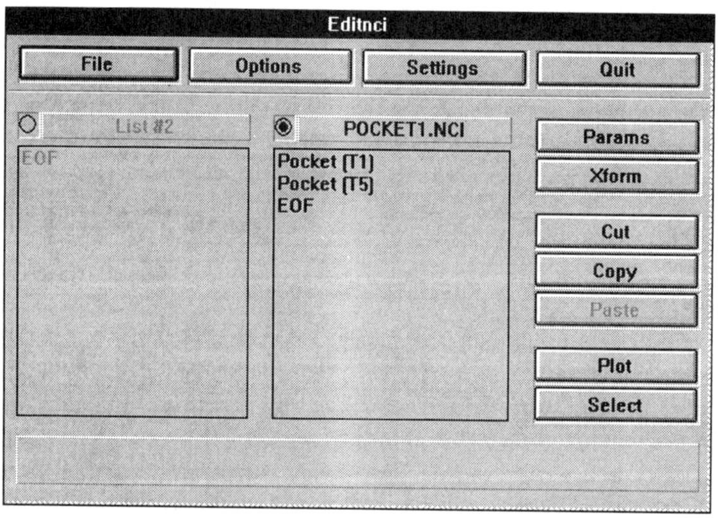

8.2 Deleting Toolpaths

Often we need to delete the toolpaths that have become a part of the toolpath file. Mastercam uses **NC utils → Edit NCI → File → Open (a toolpath file) → Cut** commands to delete the selected toolpath sections.

Project 1. 1

Deleting the roughing toolpaths of the contouring operation

Three operations (contour, pocket, and drill) are used to generate the toolpaths for machining the part in Figure 8.2. The cutting parameters for these three operations are:

Contour:	Number of rough passes = 1 Number of finish cuts = 1 Depth cuts: Rough: 0 cuts at 0.0 Finish: 1 cuts at 0.0
Pocket:	Number of finish passes = 1 Depth cuts: Rough: 0 cuts at 0.0 Finish: 1 cuts at 0.0
Drill:	Always has only one toolpath section.

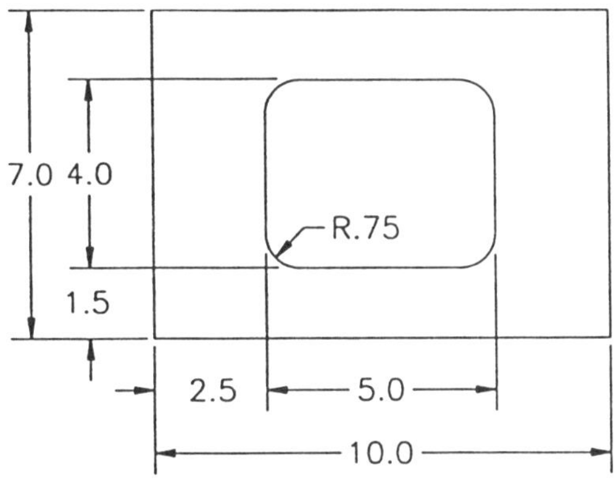

Figure 8.2

Tips 1. Operation sequence starts with contouring, followed by pocketing, and drilling.

2. The toolpath sections for contouring are 2, for pocket is 1, and for drilling is 1.

3. The sequence of toolpath follows:

Toolpath section number	Operation type
1	Rouging pass of contouring
2	Finish pass of contouring
3	Pocketing passes
4	Drilling

4. The toolpath section to be deleted is section 1 which is the roughing pass of contouring.

Step 1. Create two rectangles.

Select **MAIN MENU → Create → Rectangle → 2 points**
Enter the lower left corner: **0,0** ←
Enter the upper right corner: **10,7** ← to complete the first rectangle
Press **Alt** + **F1** simultaneously and then press **F2** to fit the drawing on the screen
Enter the lower left corner: **2.5,1.5** ←
Enter the upper right corner: **7.5,5.5** ← for the second rectangle

The two rectangles should look like Figure 8.3.

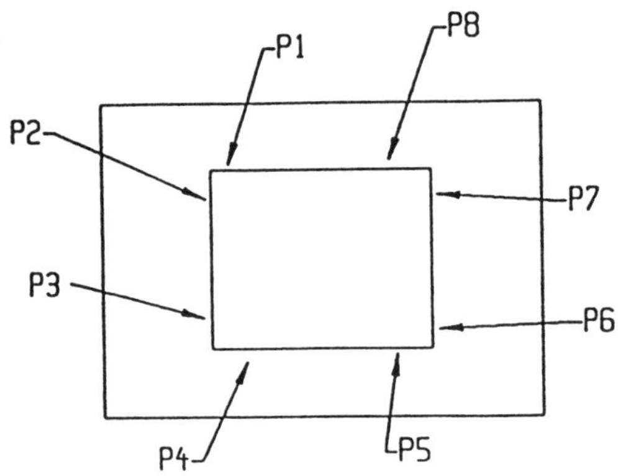

Figure 8.3

Step 2. Add four fillets to the second rectangle using the pick points in Figure 8.3.

The four added fillets are shown in Figure 8.4.
Select **MAIN MENU → Modify → Fillet → Radius**
Enter the fillet radius: **.75** ←
Sequentially pick at **P1** - **P8** to complete four fillets

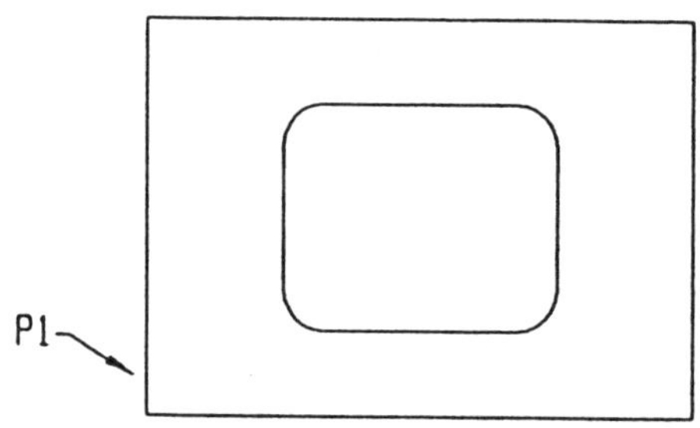

Figure 8.4

Step 3. Initiate the contour module.

Select **MAIN MENU → Toolpaths → Contour**
Enter file name: **delete1** ←

Step 4. Define the contouring contour using the pick point in Figure 8.4.

Select **Chain** from the Chaining method menu
Pick at **P1** to select the first entity in the contour
Select **Close → End here → Done → Params** to complete contour definition

Step 5. Define contour parameters.

Set the contour parameters to the following settings:

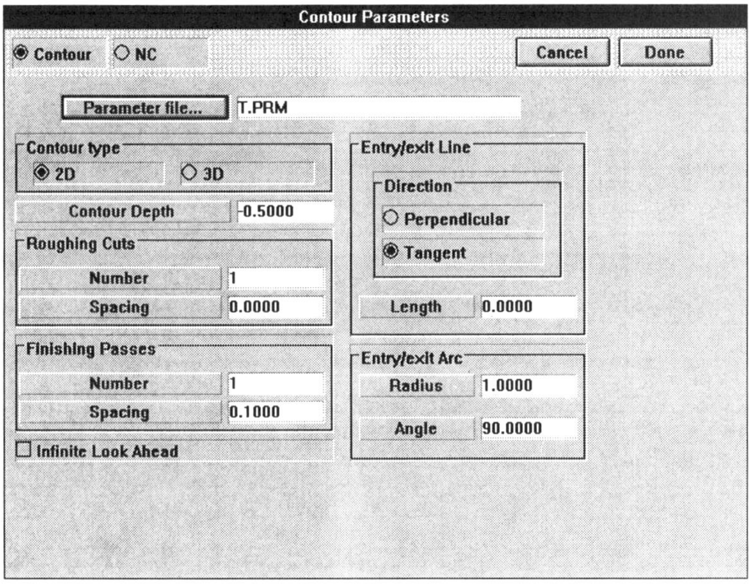

Click the **NC button** to advance to the contour parameters menu.

Step 6. Set the NC parameters to the following settings.

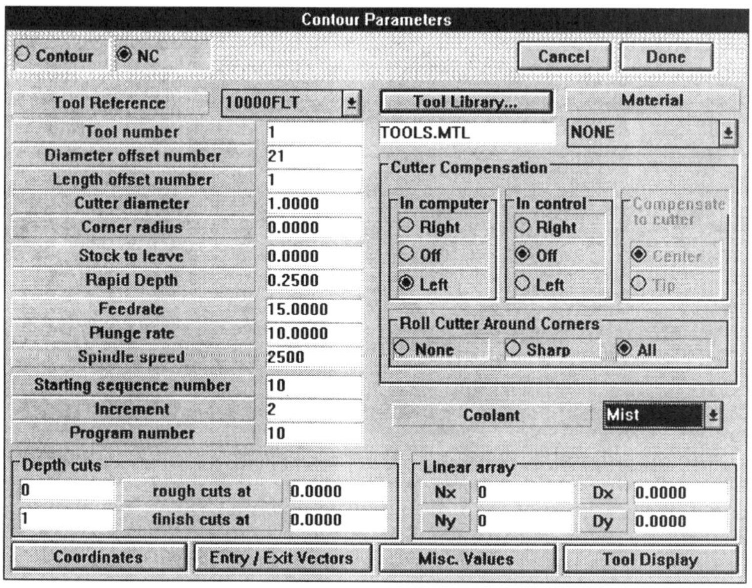

Select the **Done** button on the top of the screen.

Step 7. Accept the toolpath.

Select **Yes** to accept the contouring toolpaths
Press **F3** to remove the parameters menu from the screen

The contouring toolpaths should resemble Figure 8.5

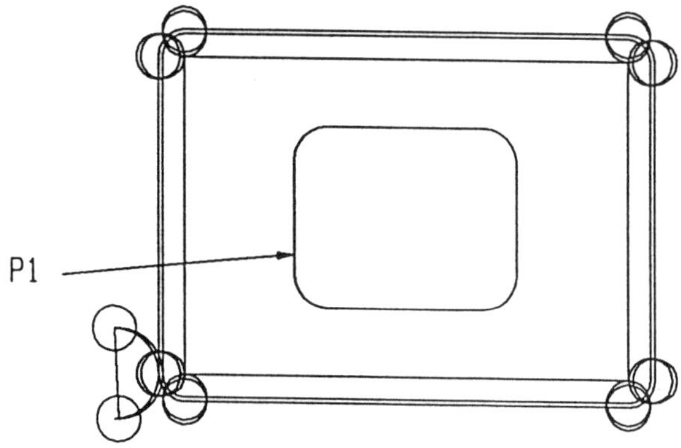

Figure 8.5

Step 8. Initiate the pocket module and define the pocketing contour. Use the pick point in Figure 8.5.

Select **MAIN MENU → Toolpaths → Pocket**
Select **Chain** from the Chaining method menu
Pick at **P1** to select the first entity in the contour
Select **Close → End here → Done** to complete the pocket definition

Step 9. Define pocket parameters to the following settings:

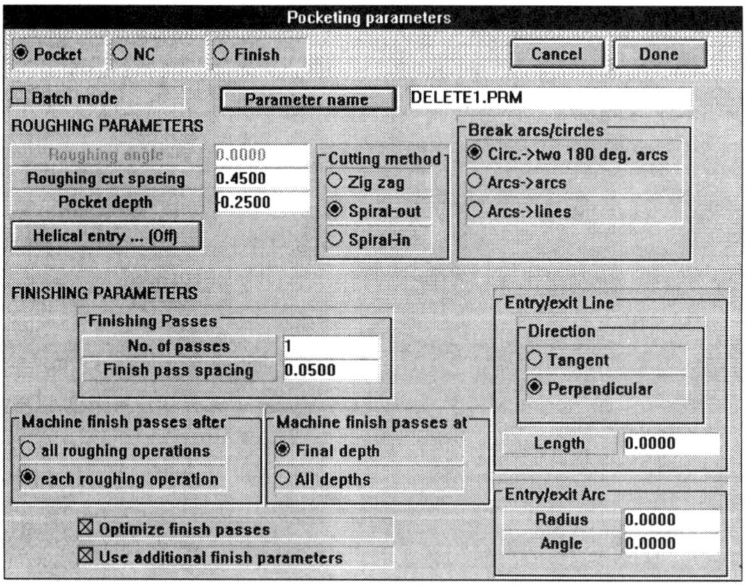

Click the **NC button** to advance to the NC parameters menu.

Step 10. Define the NC parameters to the following settings:

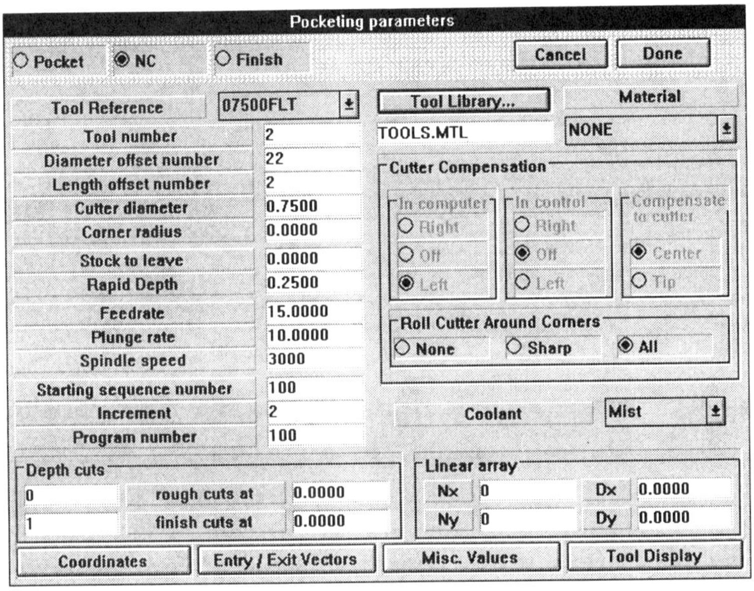

Select the **Done button** to complete the parameters setting.

Step 11. Write and accept the toolpath.

Select **All** from the Pocket selection menu

Select **Done** → **Yes** to accept the toolpath segment

The pocketing toolpaths should appear as Figure 8.6

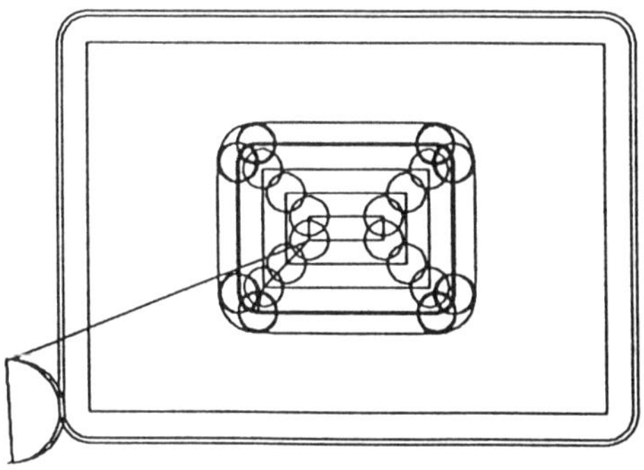

Figure 8.6

Step 12. Initiate the drill module.

Select **Drill** → **Manual**

Enter **1,1** ← for the first drill point

Enter **1,6** ← for the second drill point

Enter **9,6** ← for the third drill point

Enter **9,1** ← for the fourth drill point

Press **Esc** to end defining drilling points

Select **Yes** to draw the path between points

Select **Yes** to OK the path

Step 13. Define the drill parameters to the following settings.

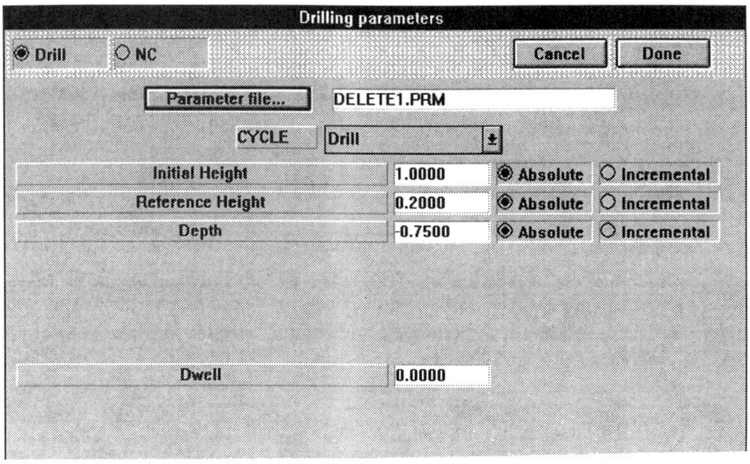

Click the **NC button** to advance to the NC parameters menu.

Step 14. Define the NC parameters to the following settings:

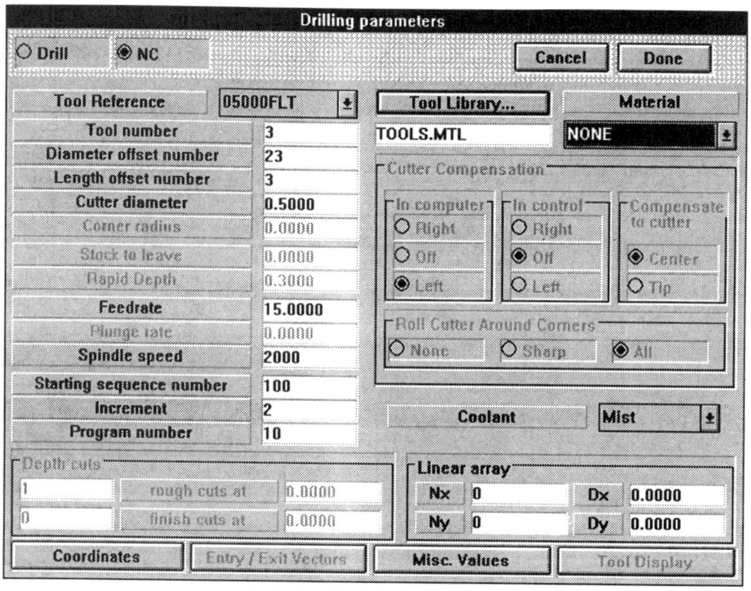

Select the **done button** to complete the parameters setting.

Step 15. Write the toolpaths.

Select **Write** from the Change menu
Select **Yes** to accept the toolpath segment
Select **No** to “Repeat with same point?”
Select **End program**
Select **No** to “Run the post processor?”

The drilling toolpaths should be added as shown in Figure 8.7 on the next page.

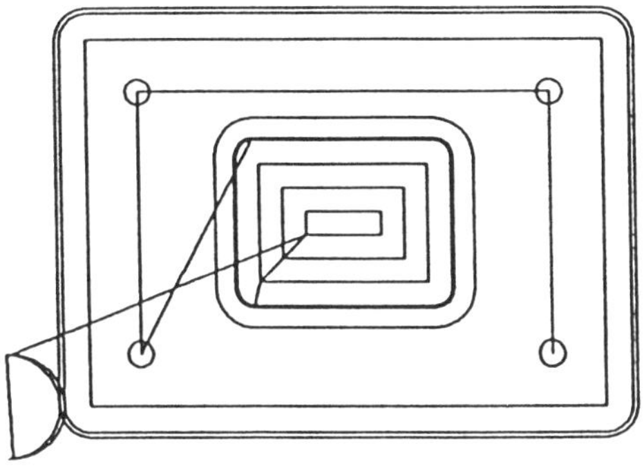

Figure 8.7

Step 16. List the toolpath sections.

Press **F3** to repaint the drawing. Notice that the toolpaths will be clear on the screen.
Select **MAIN MENU →NC utils → Edit NCI**
Click **File → Open** from the Editnci Window
Enter file name: **delete1** ←
Four toolpath sections appear under Delete1.NCI as shown below:

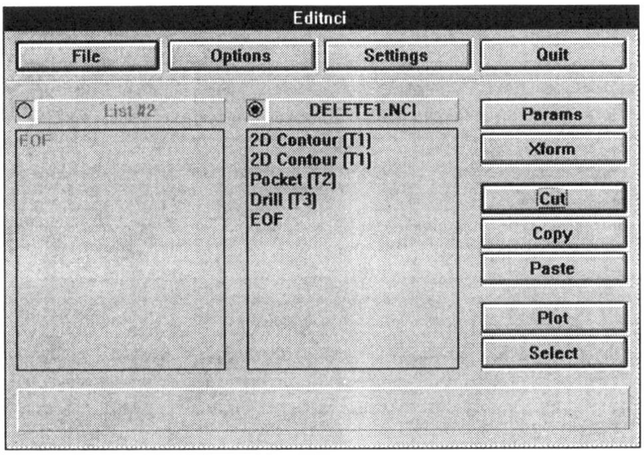

Step 17. Delete the roughing toolpath section (section 1: 2D contour [TI]) from the toolpath file.

Click the first toolpath section (2D Contour [TI])
Note: The selected toolpath section is highlighted in blue. Click the Cut button to delete the highlighted toolpath section. The three remaining sections are shown as below:

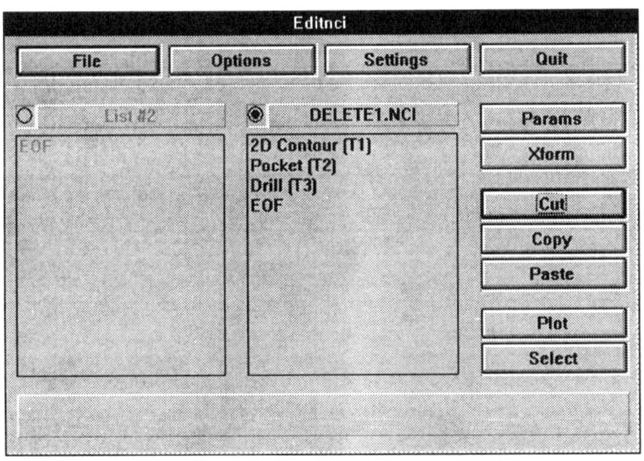

Step 18. Plot the edited toolpaths.

Select **plot**

The edited toolpaths should be plotted on screen as in Figure 8.8.

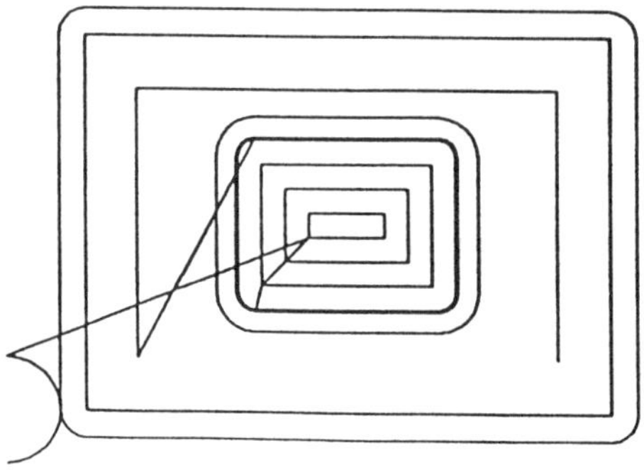

Figure 8.8

Select **Done**

Click **Quit → Save**

Select **yes** to overwrite the existing file.

8.3 Changing the Sequence of Toolpath Sections

Mastercam allows the sequence of toolpath sections to be easily changed.

Project 2.

Changing the sequence of toolpath sections

The toolpaths generated in project 1 of this chapter are used again to demonstrate how to change the sequence of the toolpath sections in this project.

Tips 1. The original toolpath sequence is 2D Contour followed by Pocket and Drill.

2. The new toolpath sequence should start with pocket followed by 2D Contour and Drill.

3. Use the existing toolpath file (delete1) for this project. Follow the procedure in project1 of this chapter to generate the toolpath file to be modified if you have not already done this.

Step 1. List the toolpath sections.

Select **MAIN MENU → NCutils →EditNCI → File → Open**

Enter file name: **delete1**

The three toolpath sections in the delete1 file should appear as below.

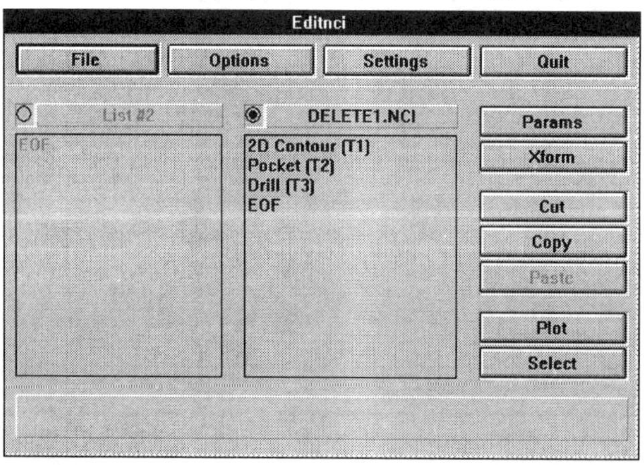

Step 2. Select the toolpath section Pocket[T2] and move it to precede the 2D Contour [T1].

Click **Pocket [T2]**

Select **Cut →Paste**

Select operation to insert before: click on 2D contour[1]

The new toolpath sequence should appear as below:

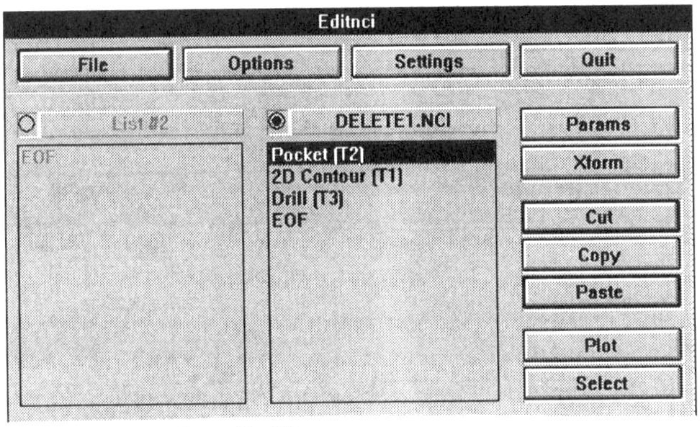

Step 3. Save the new toolpath file.

Select **Quit → Save**

Step 4. Backplot the new toolpath file.

Select **Gview → Isometric**

Press **Alt +F1** then **F2** to fit the drawing on the screen.

Select **NCutils → Backplot → NCI name**

File name: **delete1**

Set the Backplot parameters as shown here ☞.

Select **Run**

Carefully observe the plotting of the toolpath sequence. The pocket toolpath will be plotted first as shown in Figure 8.9 below, followed by 2D Contour and Drill.

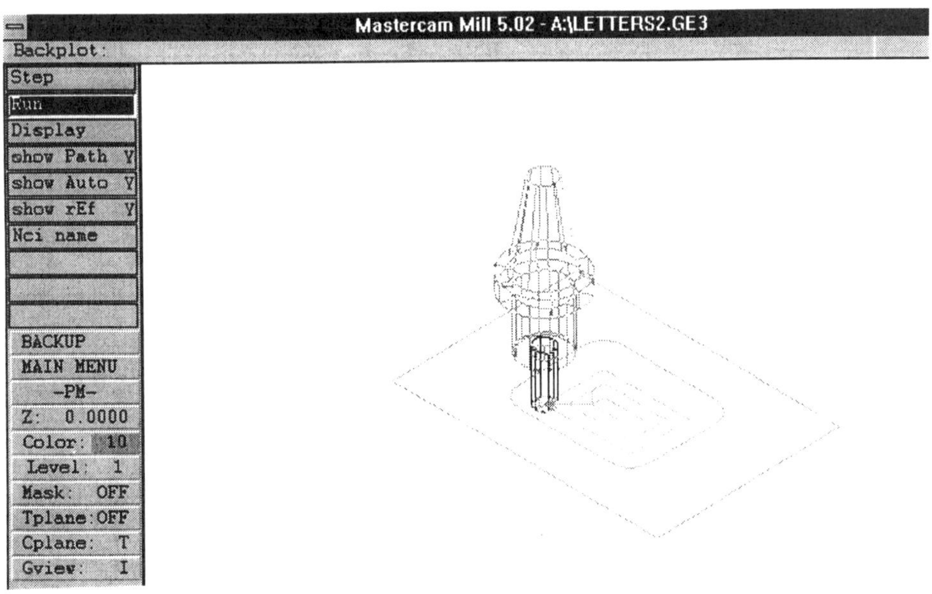

Figure 8.9

8.4 Merging Two Toolpath Files

Mastercam allows the merging of two or more toolpath files. The file name of the merged file can be a new NCI file name, or one of two file names that are to be merged. The table below illustrates how the merged file name of the three possible cases of the merged file is used.

	Use a new file name	**Use File A as the merged file name**	**Use File B as the merged file name**
File A	A	A	A
File B	B	B	B
Merged File	C	A	B

Tips 1. It is suggested that you use a new file name for the merged file. This allows the files to be merged remain unchanged. Later they can be used for other applications.
2. When the file name of one toolpath file to be merged is used, the toolpaths of that particular file will be altered.
3. It is possible to merge more than two toolpath files into one NCI file.
4. It is possible to include only some sections of toolpaths in an NCI file in the merged file.
5. The sequence of the toolpath files being merged determines the sequence of the machining operations. If the toolpaths of a machining operation must be performed first, enter their toolpath file first.

Project 3. 3

Merging two toolpath files

The toolpaths generated in project 1 of this chapter are used to demonstrate the procedure of merging two toolpath files in this project. All three cases of merging NCI files are presented. The contour roughing and finish toolpaths are saved as A.NCI (Figure 8.10a). The pocketing and drilling toolpaths are saved as B.NCI (Figure 8.10b). The merged file is saved as C.NCI, A.NCI, and B.NCI, in the three cases, respectively. Figure 8.10c shows the merged toolpaths.

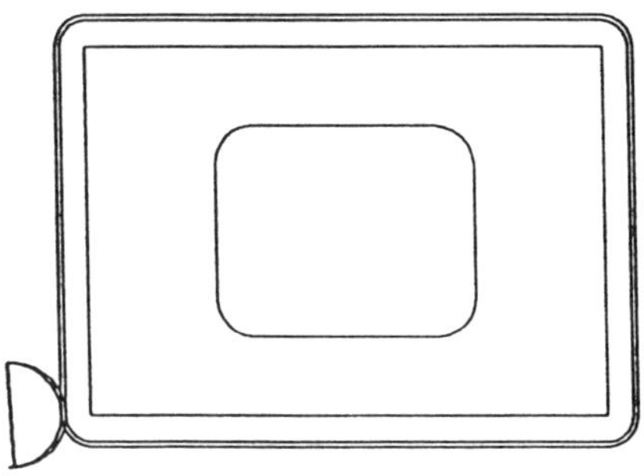

Figure 8.10a

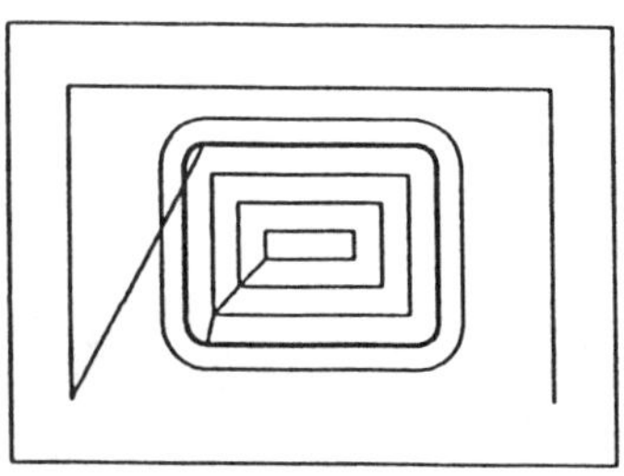

Figure 8.10b

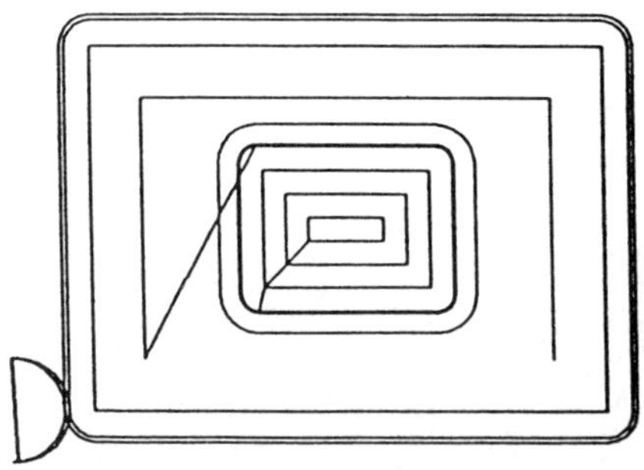

Figure 8.10c

⌛**Tips** 1. Follow the procedures given in steps 1 - 7 of project 1 to generate the roughing and finish contouring toolpaths. Save this file A.NCI in step 3. Add "Select End Program" to step 7 to close the NCI file for file A.NCI.

2. Follow the procedures given in steps 8 - 15 in project 1 to generate the pocketing and drilling toolpaths. Save the file as B.NCI. Add "Enter file name: B" for the new toolpath file in step 8.
3. In case 1, a new file name C.NCI is used as the merged file name.

4. In case 2, the name of the first merged file (A.NCI) is used as the merged file name.

5. Delete the pocketing and drilling toolpaths that are merged into file A.NCI in case 2. This means file A.NCI contains only contouring toolpaths for the case 3.
6. In case 3, the name of the second merged file (B.NCI) is used as the merged file name.

8.4.1 Create two toolpath files to be merged

Step 1. Use the contour module to generate the roughing and finish toolpaths.

Follow Steps 1 - 7 in project 1
Enter file name: **A** (in Step 3 of project 1)
Select **End progrm** to close the A.NCI file (add to Step 7 in project 1)
Select **No** to "Run the post processor?" (add to Step 7 in project 1)

Step 2. Use the pocket and drill modules to generate the pocketing and drilling toolpaths.

Follow Steps 8 - 15 in project 1
Enter file name: **B** (add to Step 8 in project 1)

8.4.2 Case 1: Use a new file name (C.NCI) as the merged file name.

Step 1. Repaint the drawing.

Press **F3** to repaint the screen
Only part geometry appears on the screen as in Figure 8.11.

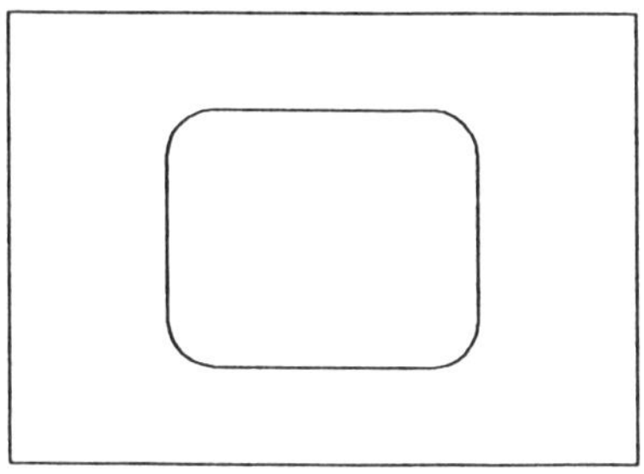

Figure 8.11

Step 2. Initiate the Edit NCI function.

Select **MAIN MENU → NC utils → Edit NCI**
Click on **File → Save As**
Enter the file name: C ←
Note: the filename C now appears at the head of the toolpath list #1.

Step 3. Load the toolpath file A.

Click on **Options → load NCI**

Enter file name: A ←

Note: You should now see two toolpaths sections listed with the identical section name 2D Contour[T1].

Step 4. Load the toolpath file B..

Click on **Options → Load NCI**

Enter file name: **B ←**

Two more toolpath sections are appended to the toolpath file. Their sequence is shown in the figure below.

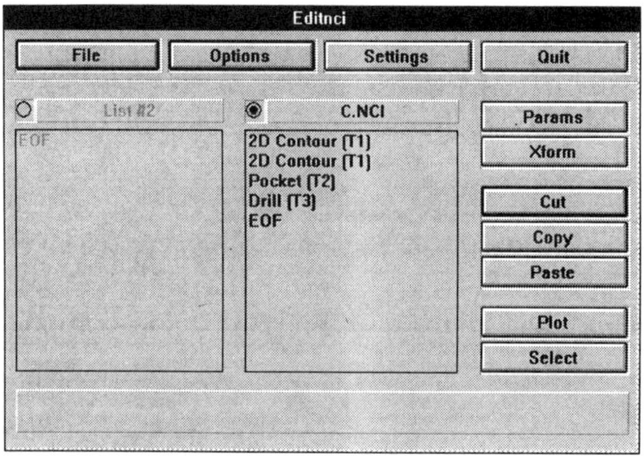

Step 5. Plot the merged toolpath file.

Select **Plot**

Toolpaths should be plotted as in Figure 8.12

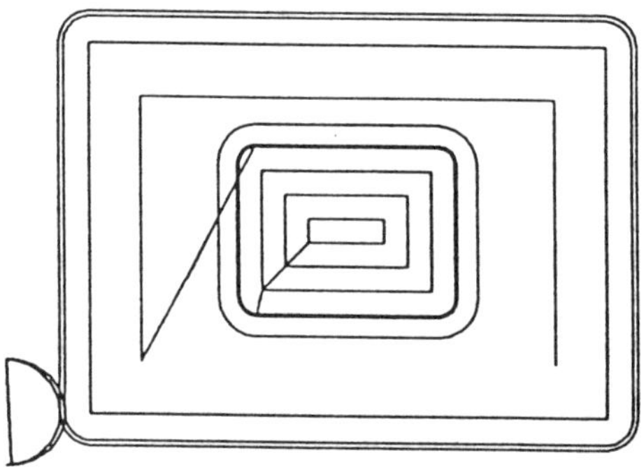

Figure 8.12

Select **Done** to return back to **EditNCI** Window

Select **Quit → Save** to save the file.

8.4.3 Case 2: The file name of the first set of merged toolpath files (A.NCI) is used as the merged file name

Step 1. Repaint the drawing.

Press **F3** to repaint the screen

Step 2. Initiate the Edit NCI command and load the toolpath file A.

Select **MAIN MENU → NC utils → Edit NCI**

Click on **File → Open**

Enter file name: **A** ← (the file name of the first set of merged file)

Two 2D Contour [T1] toolpath sections are read in

Step 3. Load toolpath file B.

Click on **Options → Load NCI**

Enter file name: **B** ←

The two toolpath sections in file B are appended to the file A and appear as the sequence below:

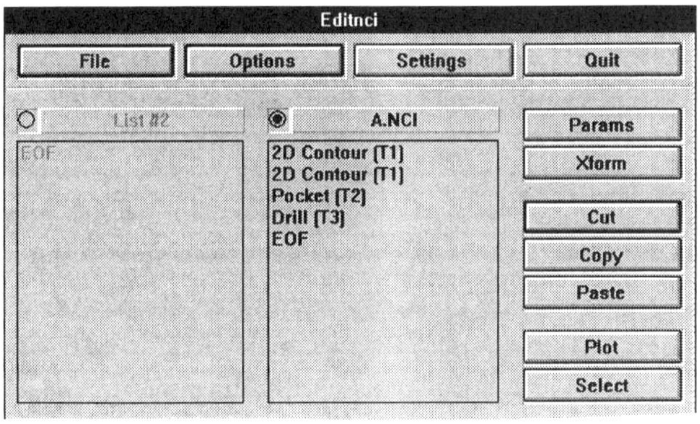

Step 4. Plot the toolpath.

Select **Plot**

The toolpath plots should appear on the screen like figure 8.13.

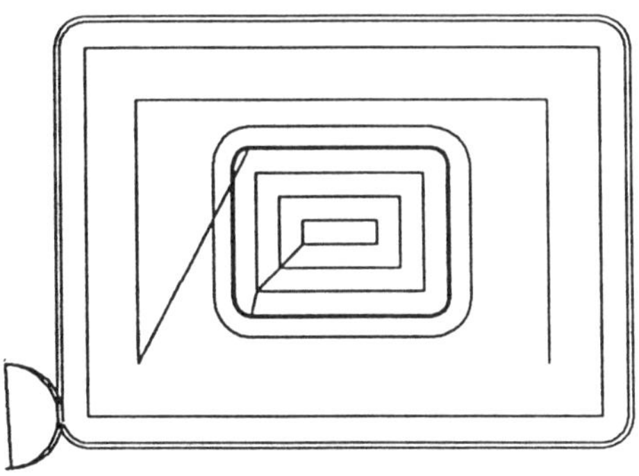

Figure 8.13

Select **Done →Quit → Save** to save the changes into the current file.

Select **Yes** to overwrite the existing file.

8.4.4 Delete the toolpath sections that are added to the first file A.NCI

Step 1. Initiate the Edit NCI command.

Press **F3** to repaint the drawing
Select **MAIN MENU** → **NC utils** → **Edit NCI**

Step 2. Open the A.NCI file.

Select **File** → **Open**
Enter file name: **A**
The four toolpath sections are listed as below.

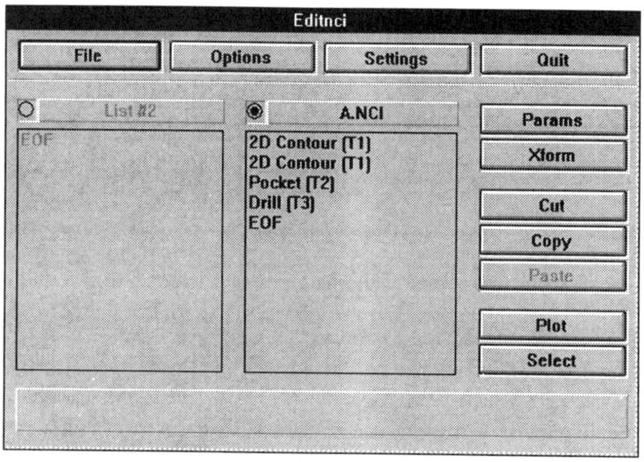

Step 3. Delete Pocket and Drill toolpath sections.

Click on **Pocket[T2]** then select the Cut button
Click on **Drill[T3]** then select the Cut button
Select **Plot** button to plot the remaining two contour sections.
Select **Done** → **Quit** → **Save**
Select **Yes** to overwrite the existing file.

8.4.5 Case 3: The file name of the second set of merged toolpaths file (B.NCI) is used as the merged file name

Step 1. Repaint the drawing on the screen.

Press F3 to repaint the drawing on the screen

Step 2. Initiate the Edit NCI function.

Select **MAIN MENU** → **NC utils** → **Edit NCI**

Step 3. Load the toolpath file A.NCI.

Select **Options** → **Load NCI**
Enter the file name: **A** ←

Step 4. Load the toolpath file B.NCI.

Select **Options** → **Load NCI**
Enter the file name: **B** ←

Step 5. Save the merged files as B.NCI.

Select **File** → **SaveAs**
Enter file name: **B** ←
Select **Yes** to delete old file

Step 6. Plot the merged toolpaths.

Select **Plot**
The merged toolpaths are plotted on the screen
Select **Done** → **Quit** to return back to graphic mode.

8.5 Editing Functions

Mastercam provides four very useful toolpath editing functions to change the position, orientation, and size of exiting toolpaths. These **four functions** are mirror, rotate, scale, and translate which are grouped under the Xform command.

Mirror: mirrors the toolpaths about the X axis, Y axis or any given line.

Rotate: rotates the toolpaths about the origin or any other point relative to the current construction plane.

Scale: increases or decreases the dimensions of toolpaths by a specified scale factor in each of three axes.

Translate: moves or copies the toolpaths to the specified new locations.

The major advantages of using toolpath editing functions are (1) eliminating the need to create the identical or similar feature geometries, and (2) eliminating the need to repeatly use the NC modules to generate toolpaths for machining identical or similar part features.

The procedure for the toolpath editing functions is:

1. Select **MAIN MENU** → **NC utils** → **Edit NCI**
2. Select the toolpath section(s) to be edited
3. Select **Xform**

The following Xform menu should appear:

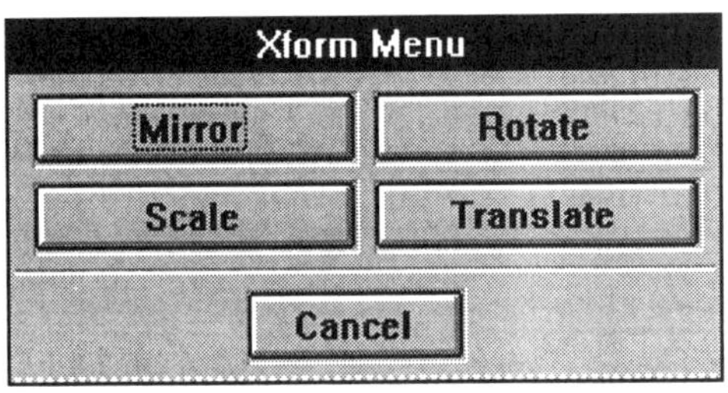

4. Select one of the Xform functions
   Use the **Mirror** function as an example.

5. Define the Xform - Mirror parameters:
The Xform - Mirror menu of parameters should appear:

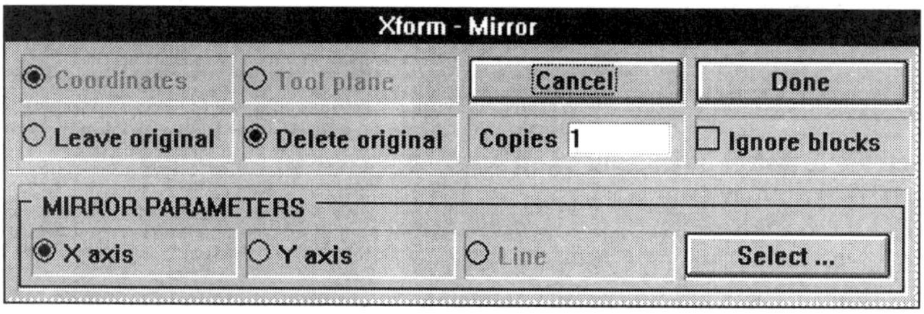

6. Select **Done** to implement the editing

8.6 Mirror

This function mirrors the existing toolpaths about an axis or a line. It is best suited (1) for those parts that have identical features being symmetrical about an axis or a line (Figure 8.14a), and (2) for generating toolpaths to machine multiple workpieces that are symmetrically placed about an axis or a line (Figure 8.14b).

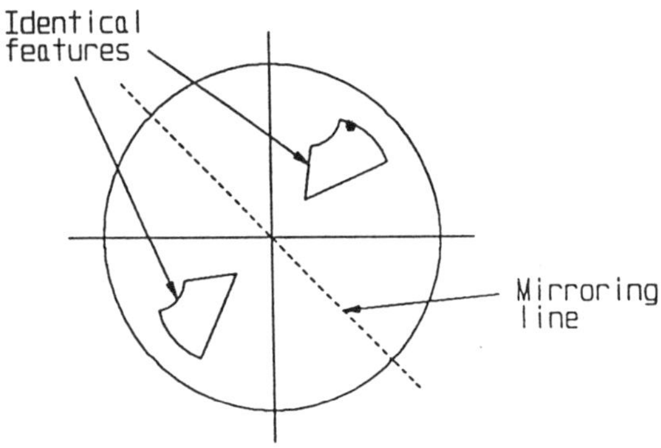

Figure 8.14a

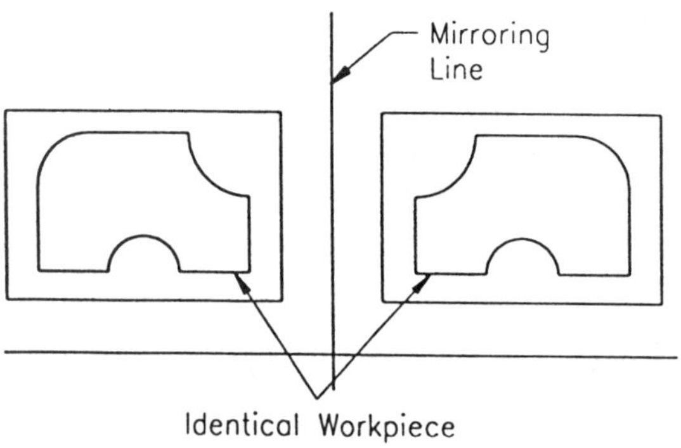

Figure 8.14b

Using the Mirror Function

1. Generate the toolpaths to be mirrored.
   An existing toolpath should be available before using this function.
2. Select **NC utils → Edit NCI** to bring up the Edit NCI menu
3. Select **File → Open**. Then enter the file name:
4. Use the mouse to select the toolpath to be transformed.
5. Select **Xform → Mirror**
6. Define the Xform - Mirror parameters
7. Select **Done → Plot** to show the mirrored toolpaths.

Project 2.

2

Part Geometry Creation

Project 6 of Chapter 6 (Mirror1)

Go to

We are here

Toolpath Generation

(Mirror1)

Mirroring the toolpaths of a feature about X and Y axes to generate the toolpaths for three other locations

The part shown in Figure 8.15 has four features that are symmetrical about the X and Y axes. The Edit NCI Mirror function is best suited for this project. We only need to create the geometry of one feature. Use the pocket module to generate the toolpaths for cutting this feature. This set of toolpaths is then copied to one adjacent side using the mirror function about the X axis. The toolpaths of two features are again copied to the other two locations by mirroring them about the Y axis.

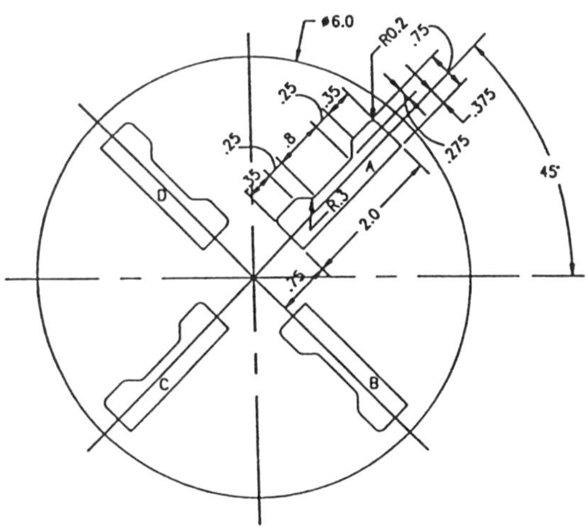

Figure 8.15

Tips 1. Cutter diameter is 0.25".

2. Cutting parameters are:

Roughing cut spacing = 0.2" One finish cut with spacing of 0.05"

3. Use the pocket module to generate toolpaths for feature A.
4. Use Edit NCI → Mirror function to copy the toolpaths to feature B. Mirror about X axis.
5. Mirror the toolpaths of features A and B about the Y axis to produce the other two features C and D.

Step 1. Load the geometry file (mirror1.ge3) or create one by following the instructions given in Project 6 of Chapter 6.

Select **MAIN MENU → File → Get**
Enter file name: **mirror1 ←**
Select **Yes** to delete the current part if necessary

The part drawing should appear as Figure 8.16

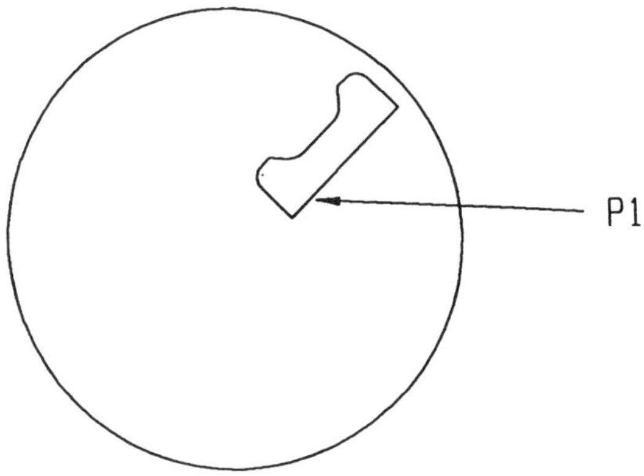

Figure 8.16

Step 2. Initiate the pocket module.

Select **MAIN MENU → Toolpaths → Pocket**
Enter file name: **mirror1 ←**

Step 3. Define pocketing contour using the pick point in Figure 8.19.

Select **Chain** from the Chaining method menu
Pick at **P1** to select the first entity in the contour
Select **Close → End here → Done** to complete contour definition

Step 4. Define pocket parameters to the following settings.

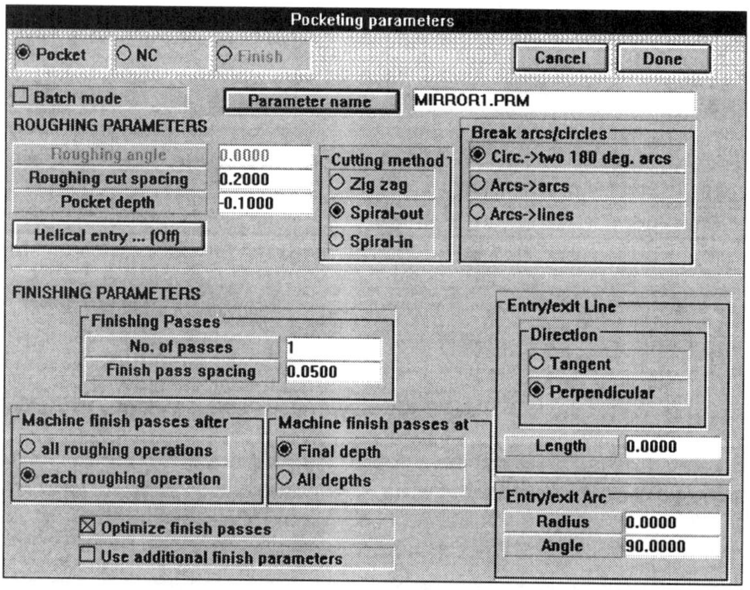

Click the **NC button** to advance to the NC parameters menu

Step 5. Define NC parameters to the following settings.

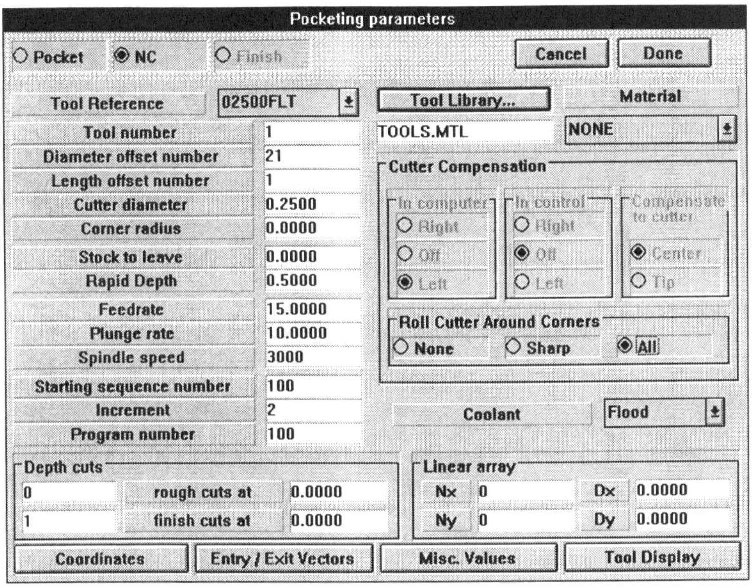

Select the **Done button** to complete the parameters setting

Step 6. Generate toolpaths for roughing and finish cuts.

Select **All** from the pocket selection menu to generate roughing toolpaths
Select **Done** to generate toolpaths for finishing cut
Select **Yes** to accept the toolpath segment

The toolpaths for pocketing the feature A should resemble Figure 8.17.

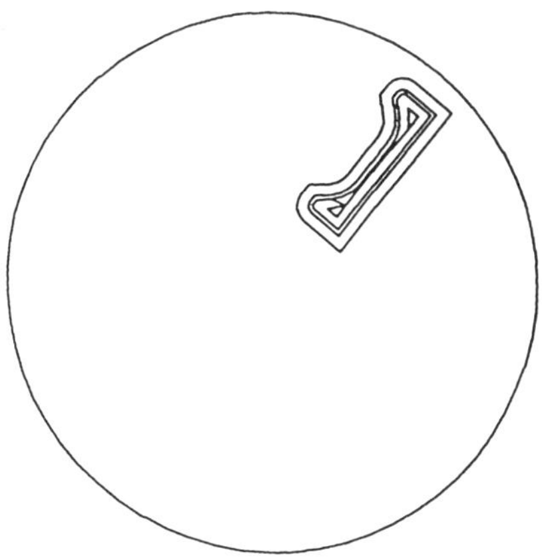

Figure 8.17

Step 7. Close the toolpath file.

Select **End program** to close the NCI file
Select No to "Run the post processor?"

Step 8. Mirror the toolpaths about the X axis.

Select **MAIN MENU → NC utils → Edit NCI**
Click on **File → Open**
Enter file name: **mirror1 ←**
Click the operation(pocket1) to select the toolpath to be mirrored
Select **Xform → Mirror**
Set the Xform - Mirror parameters to the following:

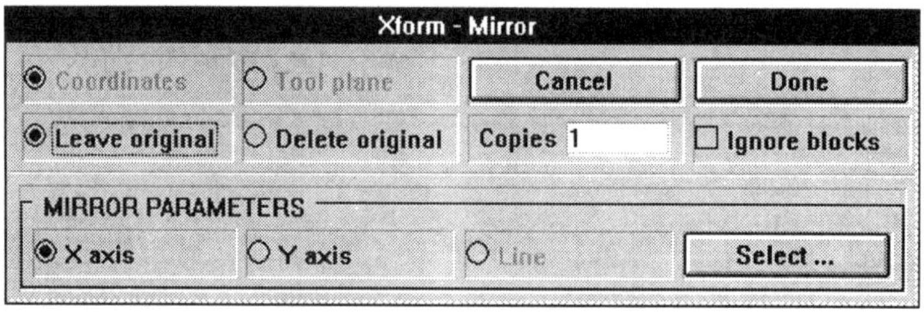

Select **Done**
The plotted toolpaths should look like Figure 8.18.

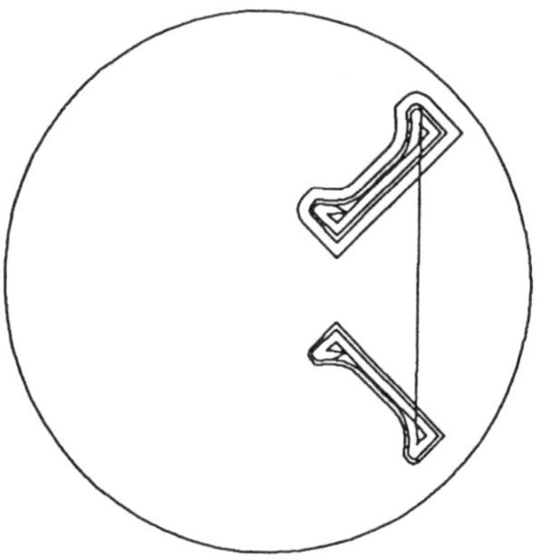

Figure 8.18

Step 9. Mirror the toolpaths in two pockets about the Y axis.

Hold down the **Shift key** and click on the last operation on the list to select both pocket[T1] operations.
Select **Xform → Mirror**
Set the Xform - Mirror parameters as indicated here:

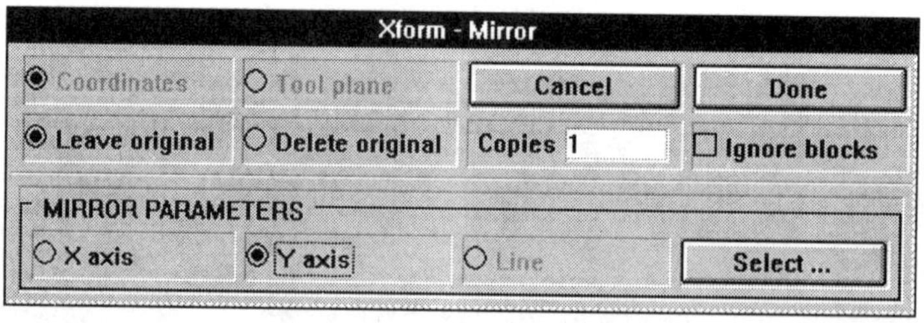

Select **Done** → **Plot** to complete the mirroring
The final toolpaths should resemble Figure 8.19.

Figure 8.19

Select **Done** → **Quit** → **Save**
Select **Yes** to overwrite the existing file.

8.7 Rotate

The rotate function moves (or copies) existing toolpaths of selected operations by rotating them about the origin or any given point. It is best suited to generate the toolpaths for identical patterns or features that are symmetrical about a point (Figure 8.20).

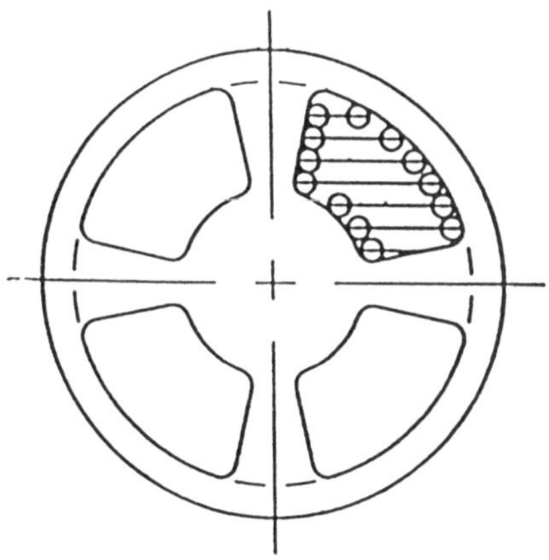

Figure 8.20

Figure 8.21 on the next page illustrates the definition of rotation angle. In Top and Front Cplane, angle is measured from the +X direction and being positive in counter-clockwise direction. In Side Cplane, the angle is measured from +Y axis.

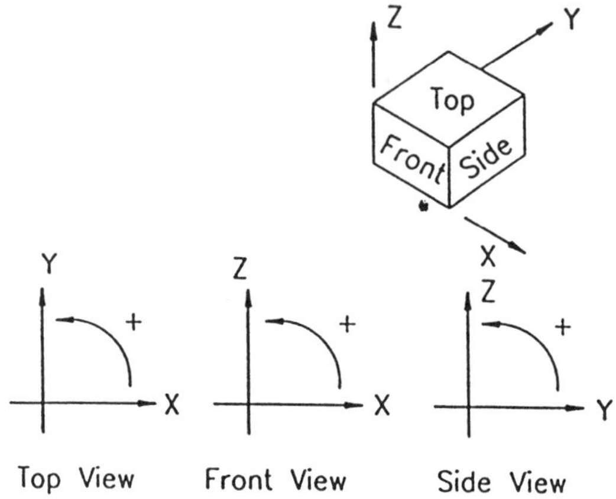

Figure 8.21

Using the Rotate Function

1. Generate the toolpaths for the features to be rotated.

2. Use **NC utils → Edit NCI** to bring up the Edit NCI menu.

3. Select **File →Open** then enter the file name.

4. Use the mouse to select the sections of the toolpath to be transformed.

5. Select **Xform → Rotate**

6. Define the **Xform → Rotate** parameters

7. Select **Done → Plot** to show the rotated toolpaths.

Project 3.

Rotating toolpaths about the origin

The process of generating the toolpaths for cutting the part shown in Figure 8.22 can be significantly simplified by using the Edit NCI → Rotate function. The raw material is a solid circular plate.

Part Geometry Creation

Project 4 of Chapter 6 (rotate1)

Go to

We are here

Toolpath Generation

(Rotate1)

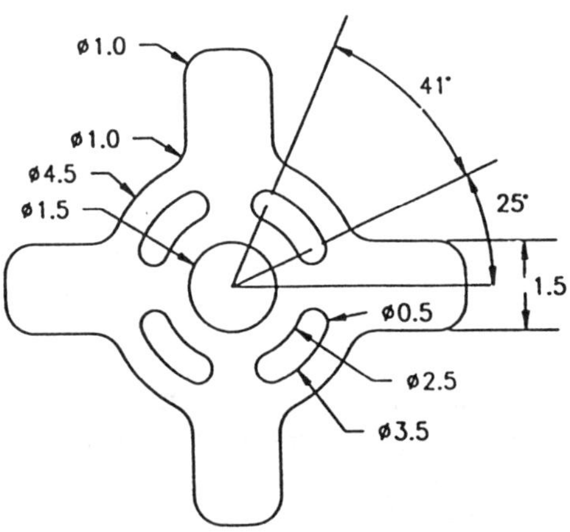

Figure 8.22

Tips 1. Machining sequence:

a. Rough cut four pockets formed between flanges
b. Copy the pocketing toolpaths to other three locations by using rotate function
c. Cut the external profile
d. Pocket one circular groove
e. Copy the grooving toolpaths to the other three locations

2. Use the pocket module to rough cut one of the four pockets. The roughing tolpaths are then copied to the other three locations by the rotate command. This allows the final external profile to be produced by using the contour module in one pass.
3. Use the contour module to cut one of four circular grooves. Cutter diameter for grooving is 3/8". The rotate command is used again to copy the toolpaths to the other three positions.
4. Two separate toolpath (NCI) files are recommended, one for pockets roughing and external profile contouring, the other one for the four circular grooves cutting. This arrangement avoids the confusion of reading the number of toolpath to be edited. Merge two toolpath files to complete the final part program.

Step 1. Load the part geometry file (rotate1.ge3) or create one by following the instructions given in Project 4 of Chapter 6.

Select **MAIN MENU → File → Get**
Enter file name: **rotate1 ←**
Select **Yes** to delete the current part if necessary

The part geometry should appear as Figure 8.23.

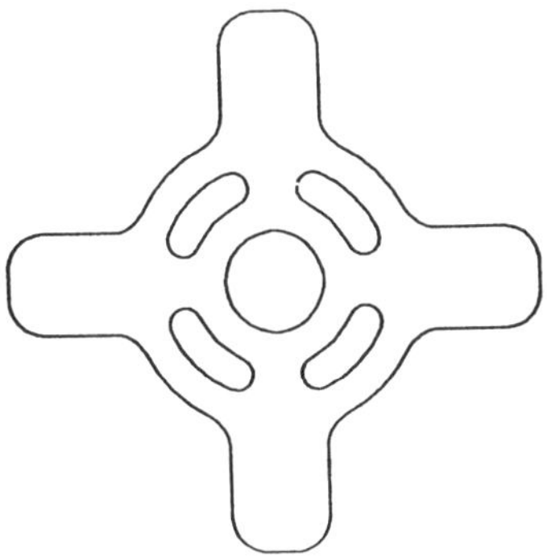

Figure 8.23

Step 2. Create a construction circle.

Select **MAIN MENU → Create → Arc → pt Dia cir**
Enter the center point: **0,0 ←**
Enter the diameter: **8.4 ←**

The new drawing becomes Figure 8.24.

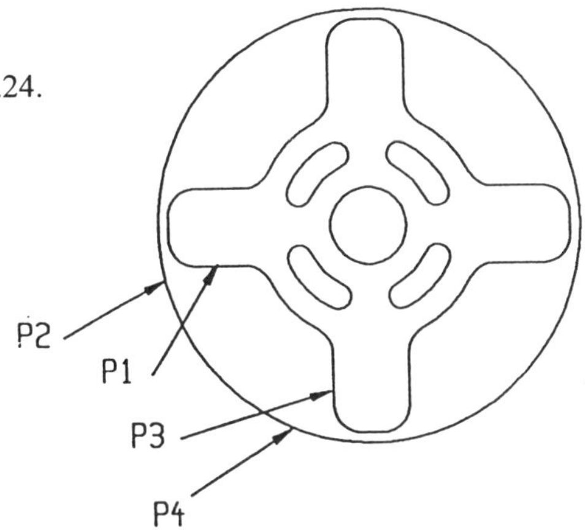

Figure 8.24

Step 3. Extend two lines to form a closed contour for pocketing. Use the pick points in Figure 8.24 on the previous page.

Select **MAIN MENU → Modify → Trim → 1 entity**
Pick at **P1** to select the entity to trim
Pick at **P2** to select the entity to trim to
Pick at **P3** to select the entity to trim
Pick at **P4** to select the entity to trim to

The two extended lines are shown in Figure 8.25.

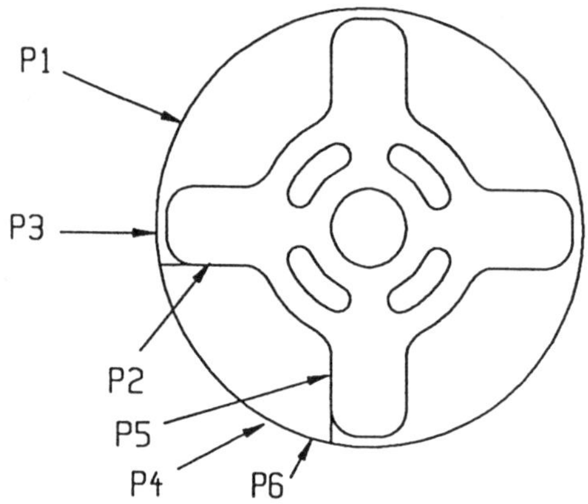

Figure 8.25

Step 4. Break the construction circle into three segments at the two intersection points with the two extended lines. Use the pick points in Figure 8.25.

Select **MAIN MENU → Modify → Break → 2 pieces**
Pick at **P1** to select the entity to break
Select **Intersec** from the Point menu
Pick at **P2** and **P3** to determine the breaking point
Pick at **P4** to select the entity to break
Pick at **P5** and **P6** to determine the breaking point

The drawing appearing on the screen does not change even though the outer circle has been broken into 3 pieces. This drawing is redrawn in Figure 8.26.

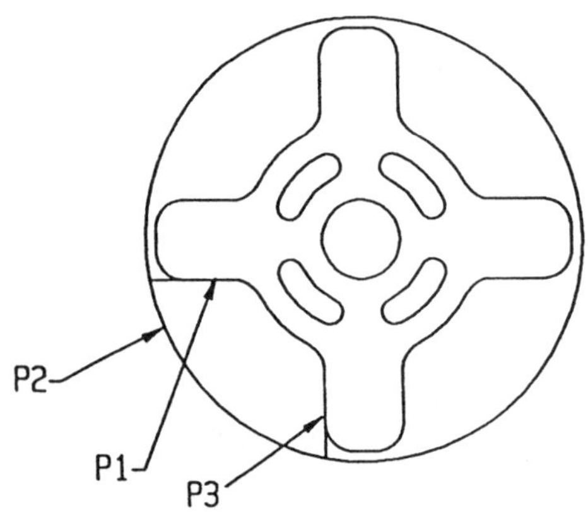

Figure 8.26

Step 5. Initiate the pocket module.

Select **MAIN MENU → Toolpaths → Pocket**
Enter file name: **rotate1**

Step 6. Define the pocketing contour using the pick points in Figure 8.29.

Select **Chain** from the Chaining method menu
Pick at **P1** to select the first entity
Select **Close** → **Select nxt**
Sequentially pick at **P2** and **P3**
Select **End here** → **Done** to complete the contour definition

Step 7. Define the pocket parameters to the following settings

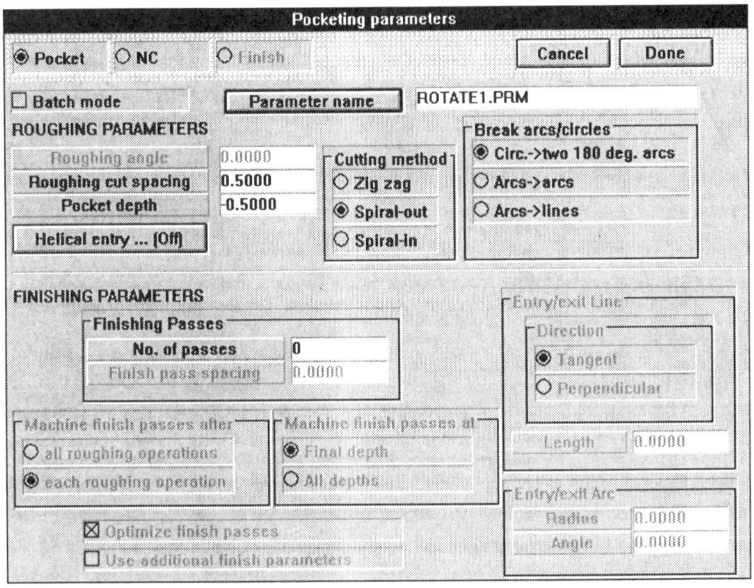

Select the **NC button** to advance to the NC parameters menu.

Step 8. Define NC parameters to the following settings.

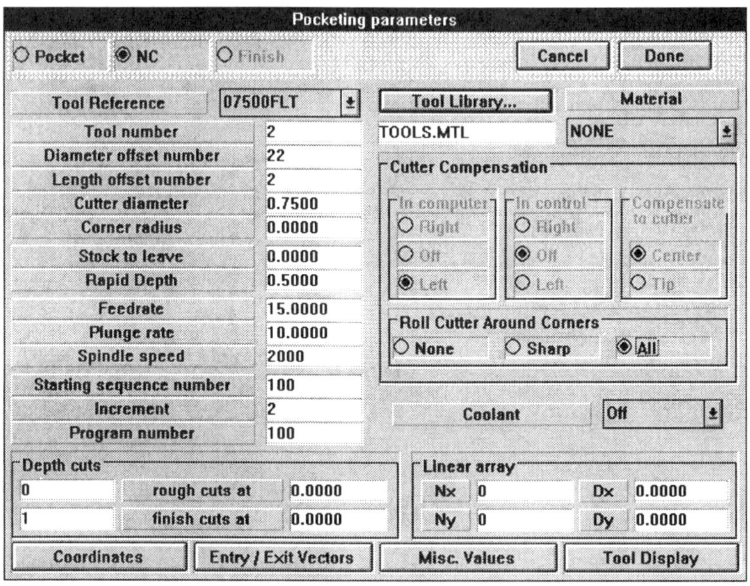

Select the **Done button** to complete the parameters setting

Step 9. Write the toolpaths.

Select **All** in the pocket selection menu to generate roughing toolpaths
Select **Done** → **Yes** to accept the toolpath

The pocketing toolpaths should look like Figure 8.27.

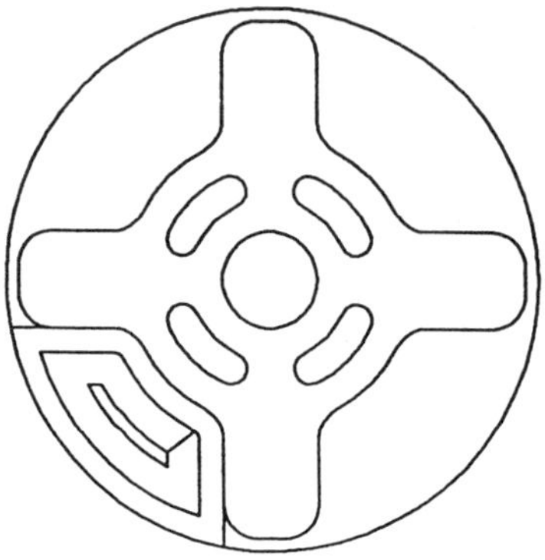

Figure 8.27☞

Step 10. Rotate the roughing toolpaths to three locations.

Select **MAIN MENU** → **NC utils** → **Edit NCI**
Select **File**→ **Open**
Enter file name: **rotate1** ←
Click on the **Pocket [T2]** from the list
Select **Xform** → **Rotate**

Set the Xform →Rotate parameters to the following settings:

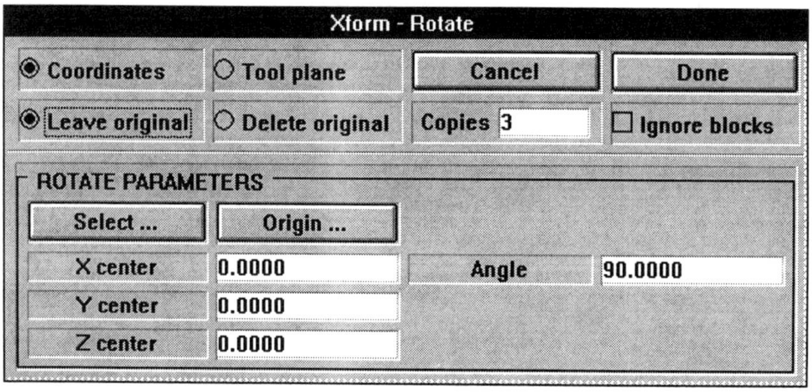

Select **Done**
Three pocket[T2] operations are added to the toolpath file

Select **Plot**
The toolpaths are shown in Figure 8.28

Figure 8.28☞

Step 11. Save the file.

Select **Done → Quit → Save**
Select **Yes** to overwrite the existing file

Step 12. Fit the drawing to the screen.

Press **Alt + F1** simultaneously to fit the drawing

The new drawing should look like Figure 8.29.

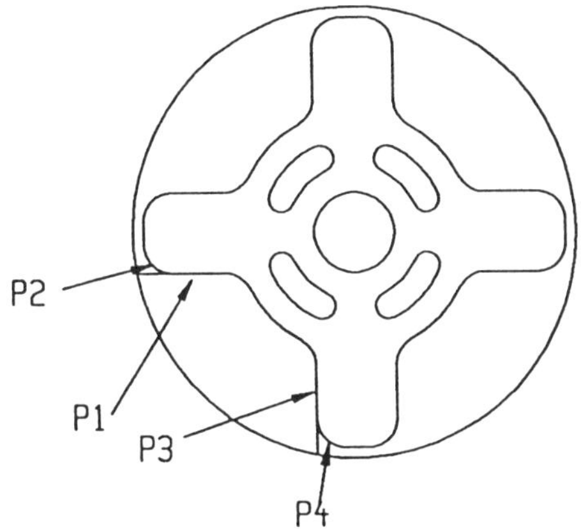

Figure 8.29

Step 13. Trim the two extended lines back to their original length. Use the pick points in Figure 8.29.

Select **MAIN MENU → Modify → Trim → 1 entity**
Pick at **P1** to select the entity to trim
Pick at **P2** to select the entity to trim to
Pick at **P3** to select the entity to trim
Pick at **P4** to select the entity to trim to

The new drawing after trimming becomes Figure 8.30.

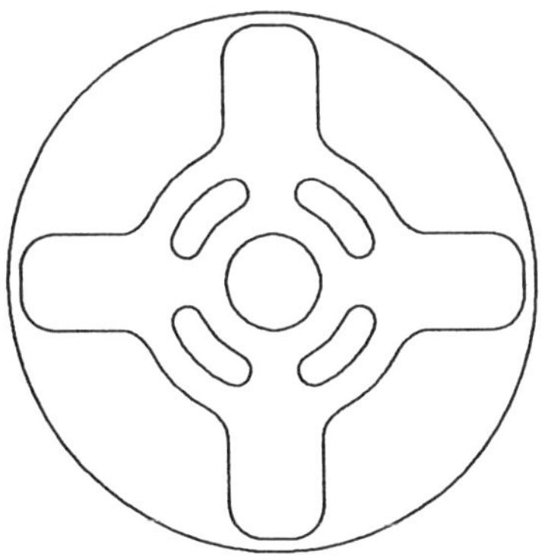

Figure 8.30

Step 14. Initiate the contour module.

Select **MAIN MENU → Toolpaths → Contour**
Enter file name: **rotate1 ←**
Select **Append** to add the succeeding toolpaths to the existing one

The existing toolpaths should appear as Figure 8.31.

Figure 8.31

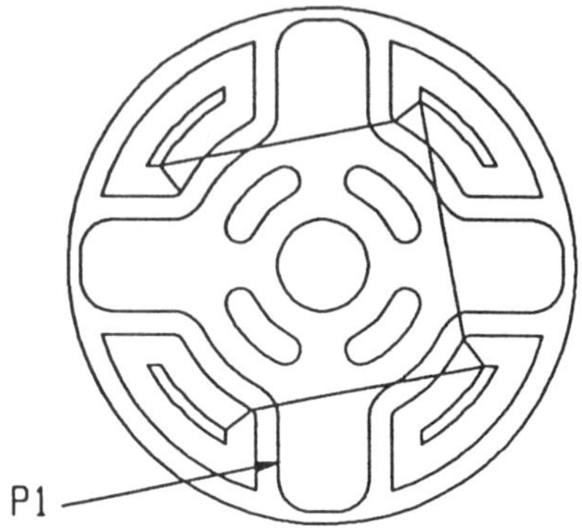

Step 15. Define the contour for contouring.

Use the pick points in Figure 8.31.

Select **Chain** from the Chaining method menu

Pick at **P1** ←

Select **Close** → **End here** → **Done** → **Params**

Step 16. Define the contour parameters to the following settings.

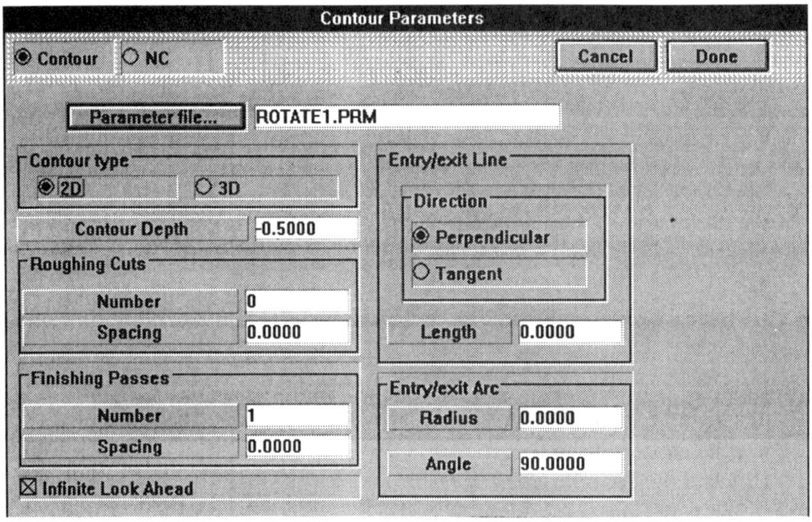

Select the **NC button** to advance to the parameters menu.

Step 17. Define the NC parameters to the following settings.

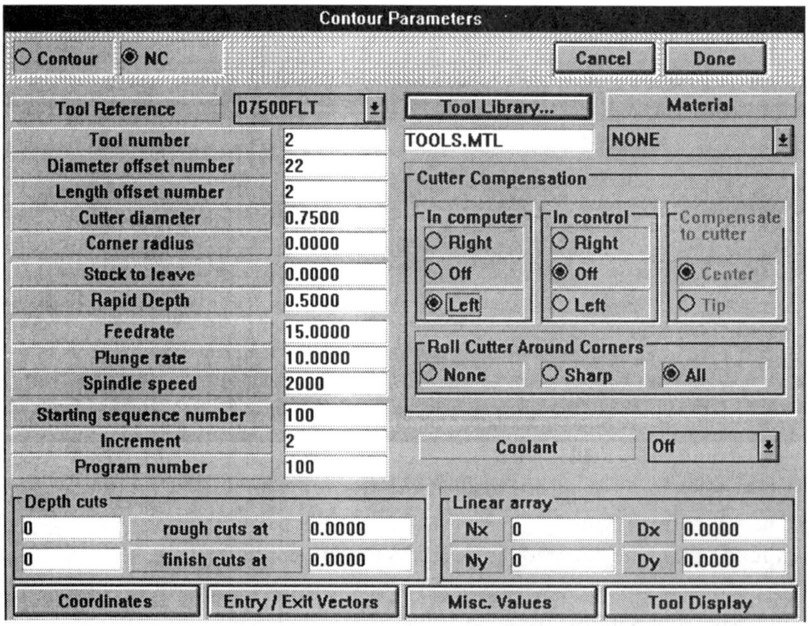

Select the **done button** to complete the parameters setting.

Step 18. Write the toolpaths.

Press F3 to repaint the screen

Select **Write** from the Change menu
Select **Yes** to accept the toolpath segment
Select **End program** to close NCI file
Select **No** to "Run post processor?"
The toolpath should appear as Figure 8.32.

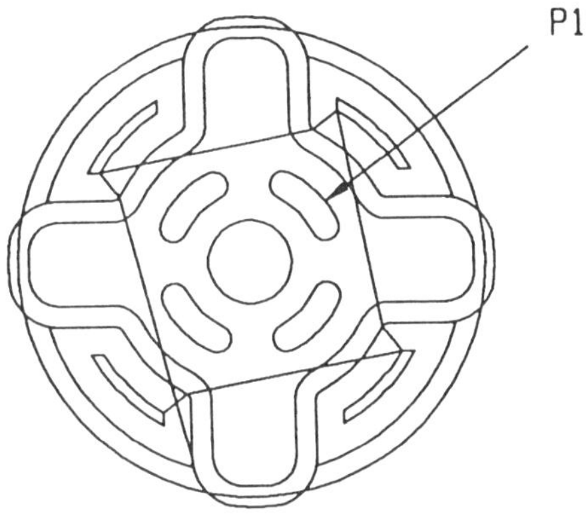

Figure 8.32

Step 19. Initiate the contour module and use a *new* NCI file name.

Press F3 to repaint the screen
Select **MAIN MENU → Toolpaths → Contour**
Enter file name: **rotate2** ←

Step 20. Define the contour using the pick points in Figure 8.35.

Select **Chain**
Pick at **P1** ←
Select **Close → End here → Done → Params**

Step 21. Define the contour parameters.

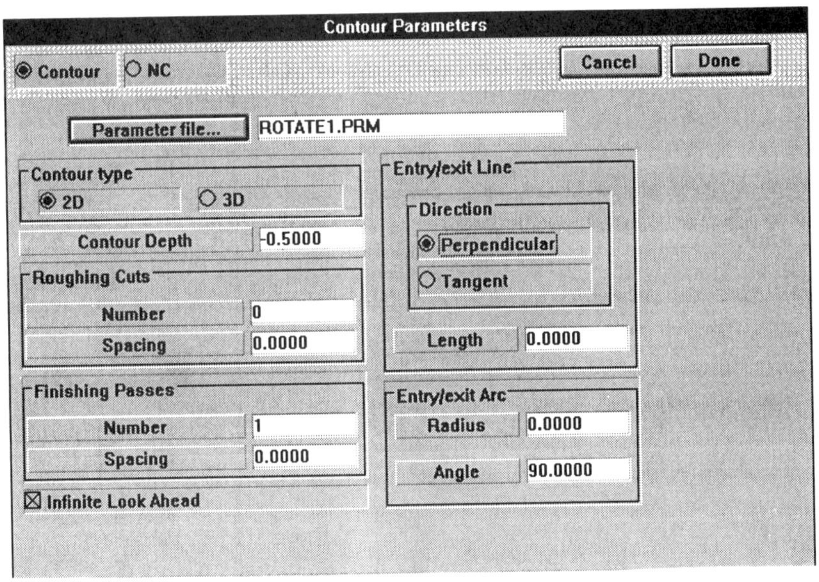

Select the **N C button** to advance the parameters menu

Step 22. Define the NC parameters to the following settings.

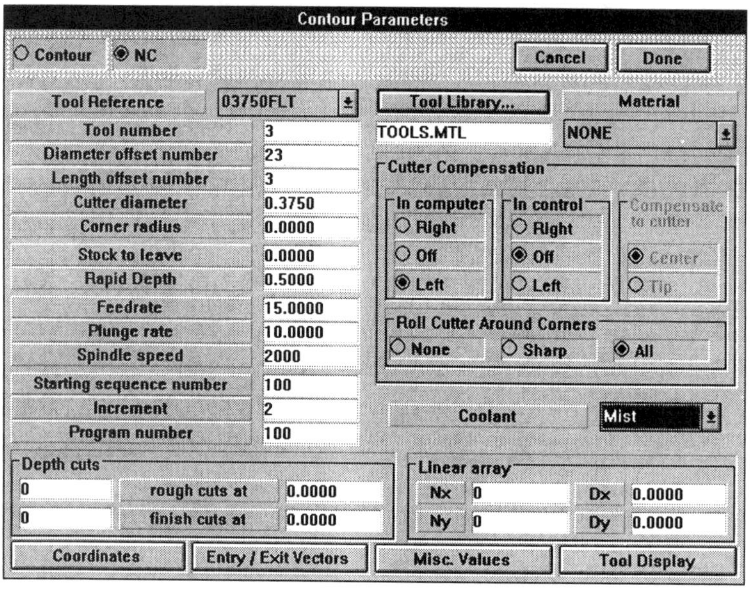

Select the **Done button** to complete the parameters setting

Step 23. Write the toolpath.

Select **Write** from the Change menu
Select **Yes** to accept the toolpath segment

Step 24. Rotate the toolpaths.

Select **BACKUP → NC utils → Edit NCI → File → Open**
Enter file name: **rotate2 ←**
The 2D Contour [T3] toolpath should be listed
Click the Operation 2D contour[T3]
Select **Xform → Rotate**
Define the Xform - Rotate parameters as shown here:

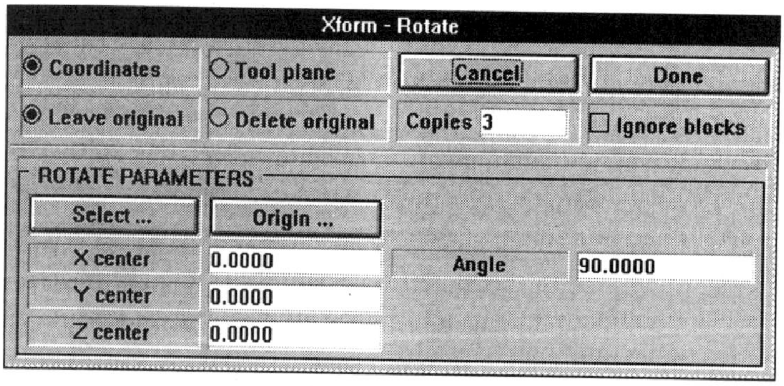

Select **Done**
Three sets of 2D Contour [T3] toolpaths are added to the toolpath file
Select **Plot**

Toolpaths are plotted as shown in Figure 8.33.

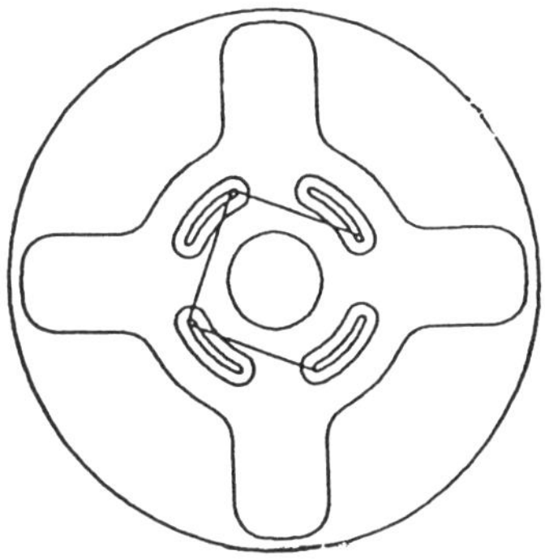

Figure 8.33

Select **Done** to return back to **Edit NCI** menu
Select **Quit → Save**
Select **Yes** to overwrite the existing file.

Step 25. Merge two toolpath files into one.

Press **Alt + F1** simultaneously to fit the drawing on the screen
Select **MAIN MENU → NC utils → Edit NCI → File → Save as**
Enter file name: **rotate ←**
Select **Options → Load NCI**
Enter file name: **rotate1 ←**
Five sections of toolpaths under filename rotate1 should appear as shown here ☞:

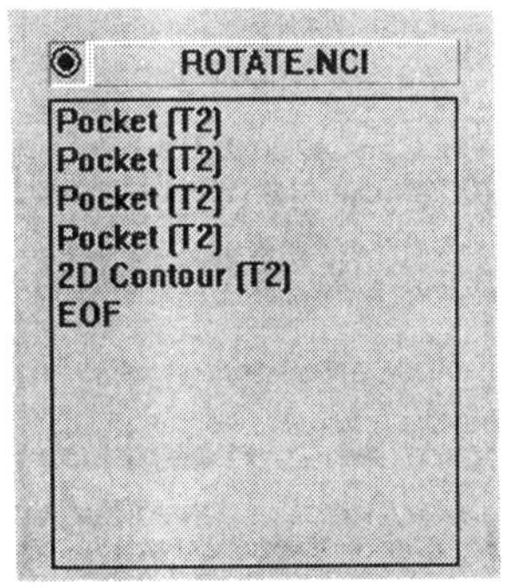

Select **Options → Load NCI**
Enter file name: **rotate2 ←**
Four 2D Contour [T3] toolpath sections should appear as shown here ☞:

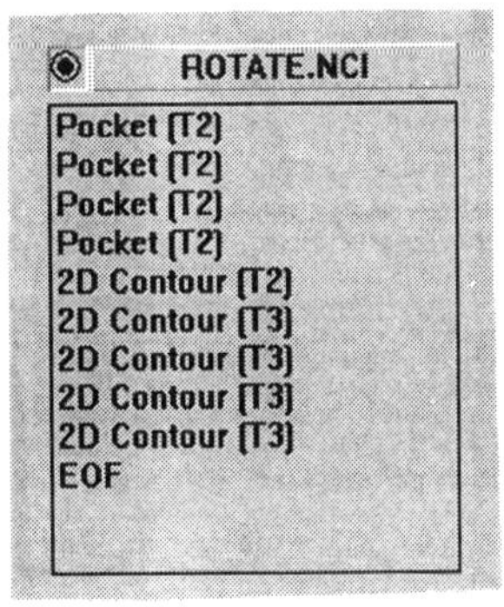

Select **Plot**

The new drawing with the plotted toolpaths should resemble Figure 8.34.

Figure 8.34

Select **Done → Quit → Save**
Select **Yes** to overwrite the file

Step 26. Change Gview to isometric and backplot the merged file (rotate.NCI) to verify toolpaths.

Select **Gview → Isometric**
Select **Backplot → Display**
Set Backplot display parameters to the following settings:

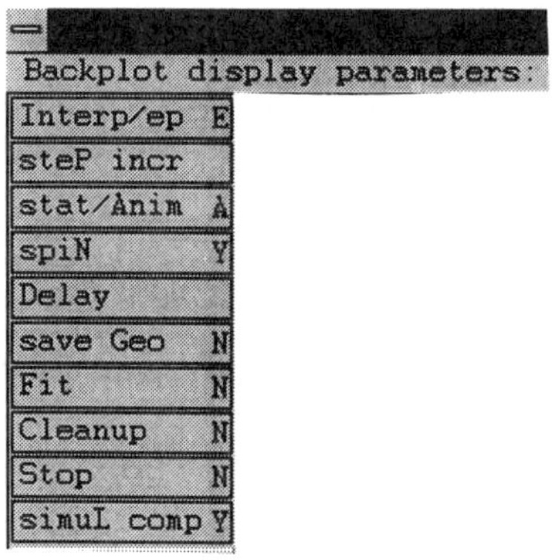

Select **Backup** to return back to Backplot menu
Set Backplot parameters to the following settings:

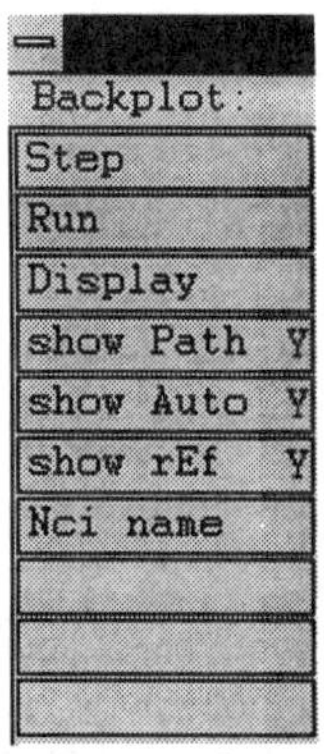

Select **Nci name**
Enter file name: **rotate** ←
Select **Run**

The toolpaths shuold be plotted sequentially and look like Figure 8.35.

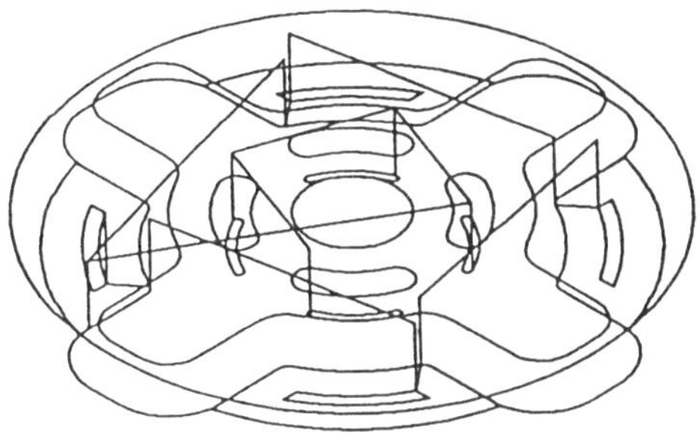

Figure 8.35

8.8 Scale

Scale functions increase or decrease the actual dimensions of toolpaths by a specified scale factor in each of three axes. Two important facts to be determined in scaling are the scaling center and the scaling factor in each of the three axes. The scaling center determines where the toolpaths start. The scaling factor decides which axis coordinates will be scaled and by how much.

SCALE FACTOR: X	Y	Z	
1	≠1	1	X and Z coordinate no change
≠1	1	1	Y and Z coordinate no change

Scaling factor > 1 enlarge the toolpath dimensions
Scaling factor = 1 toolpath dimensions do not change
Scaling factor < 1 reduce the toolpath dimensions

Tips 1. When a value of 1 is given to the scale factor of an axis, the toolpath dimensions in that particular axis do not change.

2. The location of the scaling center drastically affects the locations of the scaled toolpath. The origin and the center of the original toolpath are the two positions which can be used as the scaling center in that the scaled toolpath can be easily predicted (Figure 8.36). Using other positions as the scaling center may result in undesired toolpaths (Figure 8.37 on the next page).

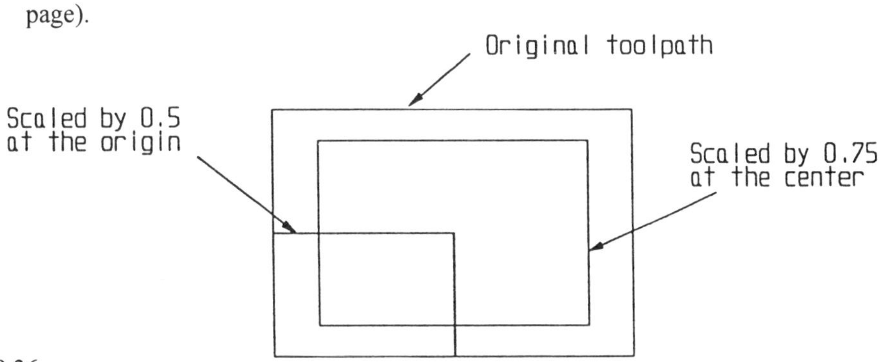

Figures 8.36

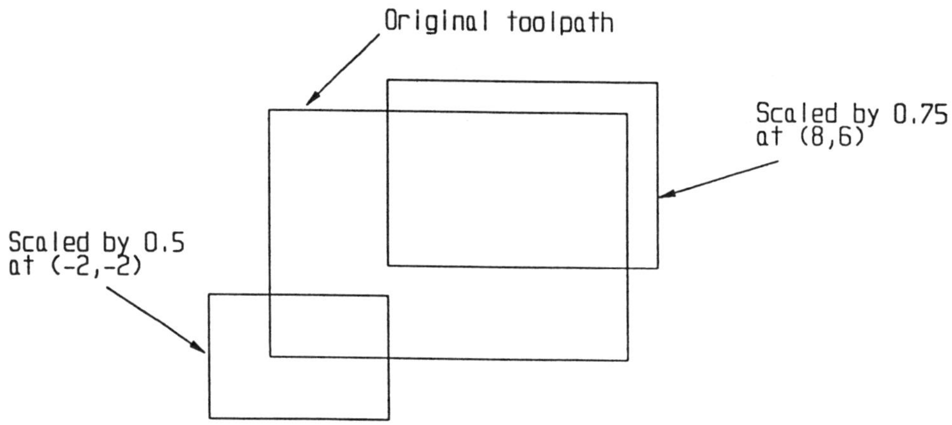

Figure 8.37

3. Do not use the scale function to modify toolpaths unless you know where the exact toolpath locations will be after being scaled.
4. Using the same cutter to cut the scaled toolpaths may result in reduced or enlarged finished parts because the offset values for the scaled toolpaths have been scaled to a larger value or a smaller value.

4

Project 4.

Scaling Project

The part shown in Figure 8.38 has three hexagonal pockets with different depths. The base circle of the outer pocket has a diameter of 6". The X and Y coordinates of the second pocket are scaled down by a scaling factor of 0.75. The third pocket is scaled from the second pocket by the same scaling factor of 0.75. The Z-depth in the second pocket is -0.3" which can be obtained by a scaling factor of 2 from the first pocket depth (Z = -0.15"), and the depth of the third pocket (-0.6") is scaled from the depth of the second pocket by the factor of 2.

Part Geometry Creation

Project 2 of Chapter 6 (scale1)

Go to

We are here

Toolpath Generation

(scale1)

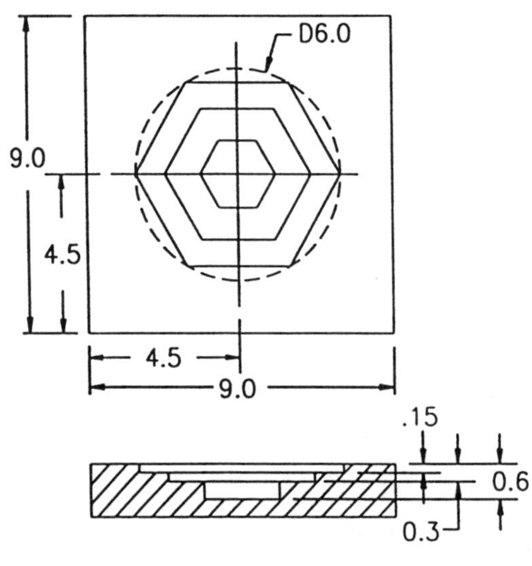

Figure 8.38

Tips 1. Construct a large hexagon to use as the pocketing profile. Use this hexagon to generate pocketing toolpaths. Then scale the pocketing toolpaths for the other two hexagonal pockets.

2. Use **NC utils → Edit NCI → Xform → Scale** commands to scale the pocketing toolpaths. The number of steps should be set to 2. The scaling factors are below:

Axis	Scaling factor	Scaling center
X	0.75	(0,0)
Y	0.75	
Z	2.0	

The depth of the first set of scaled toolpaths is -0.3 (or -.15 x 2) and the second set of scaled toolpaths is -0.6 (or -.3 x 2). Note that the number of steps is more than one. The second set of scaled toolpaths is scaled after the first set by the scaling factor of the axis. When the second set of scaled toolpaths needs to have the same spacing as the first set of scaled toolpaths, set the number of steps to **one** and then repeatedly scale the original toolpaths by changing the scaling factor to the proper value.

In this project we can use two sets of scaling factors to obtain the equally spaced dimensions for the two scaled pockets:

	X	Y	Z
First scaled pocket	0.75	0.75	2.0
Second scaled pocket	0.5	0.5	3.0

3. Use the backplot function to verify the toolpaths. When doing verification of the toolpath coordinates, set the geometry parameter in the Backplot command to "Save the geometry". This allows a set of geometric entities to be created by using the coordinates of toolpaths. We then can use the Analyze → Entity commands to verify the coordinates of the toolpaths.

Step 1. Load the part geometry file (scale1.ge3) or create one by following the instructions given in Project 2 of Chapter 6.

Select **MAIN MENU → File → Get**
Enter file name: **scale1** ←
Select **Yes** to delete the current part

The part drawing should appear as Figure 8.39.

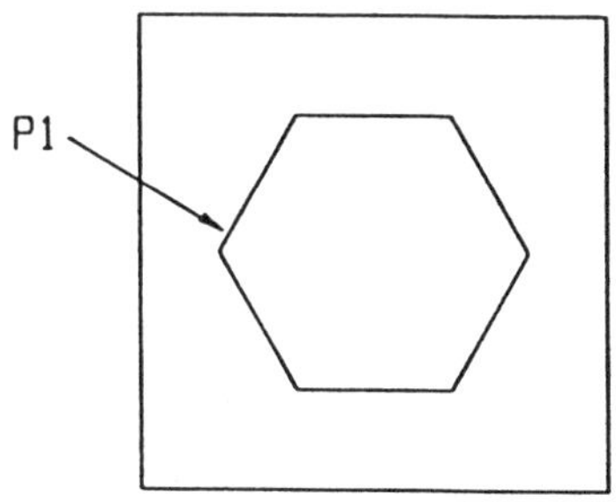

Figure 8.39

Step 2. Initiate the pocket module.

Select **MAIN MENU → Toolpaths → Pocket**
Enter file name: **scale1** ←

Step 3. Define the pocketing boundary use the pick point in Figure 8.39.

Select **Chain**
Pick at **P1**
Select **Close** → **End here** → **Done**

Step 4. Define the pocket parameters to the following settings.

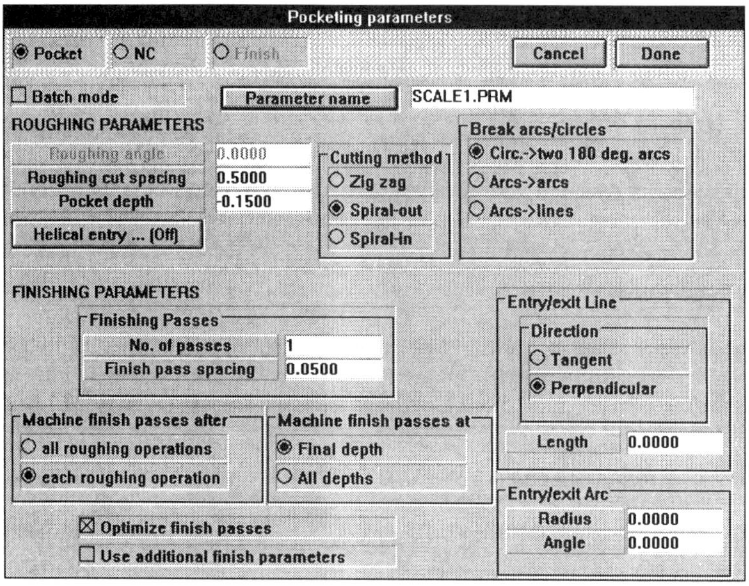

Select the **NC button** to advance to the NC parameters menu.

Step 5. Define NC parameters to the following settings.

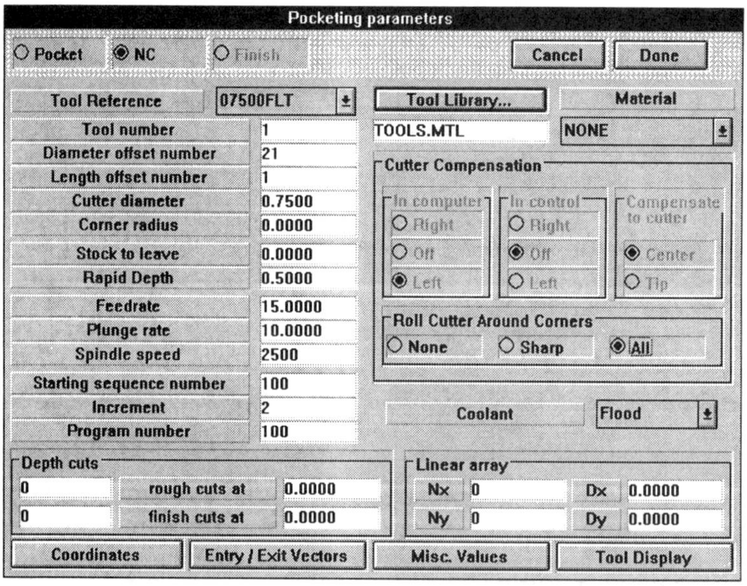

Click the **Done button** to complete the parameters setting

Step 6. Generate toolpaths. The pocketing toolpaths should appear as Figure 8.40.

Press **F3** to repaint the screen

Select **All** → **Done** → **Yes** to accept the toolpath segment

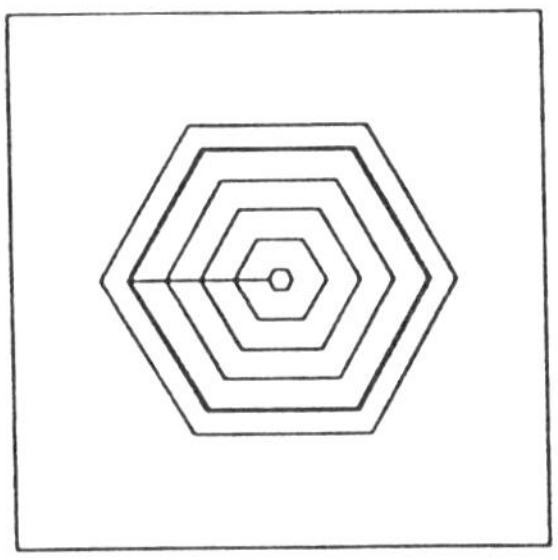

Figure 8.40

Step 7. Scale the toolpaths.

Select **MAIN MENU** → **NC utils** → **Edit NCI** →**Options** → **Load NCI**

Enter file name: **scale1** ←

Click operation **Pocket [T1]** to make it active

Select **Xform** → **Scale**

Set the Xform - Scale parameters to the following settings:

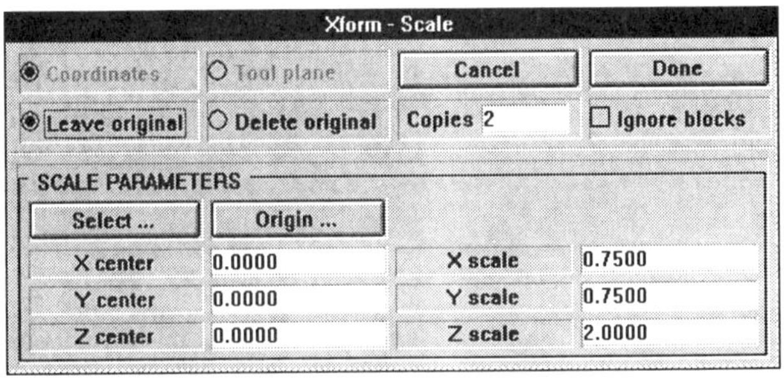

Select **Done**

Two sections of toolpaths are added to the toolpath file

Select **Plot**

The two sets of scaled toolpaths should resemble Figure 8.41

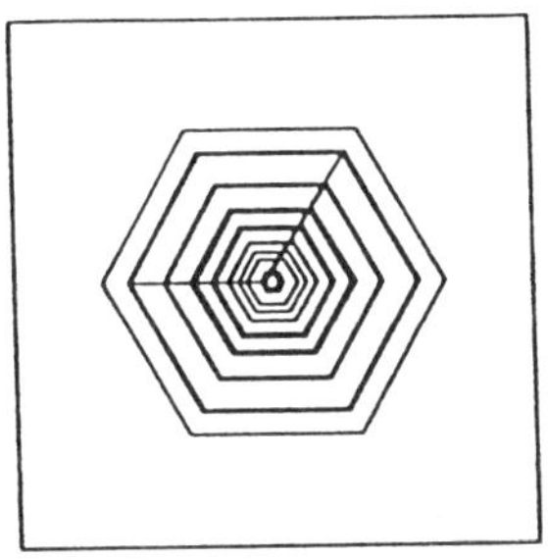

Figure 8.41

Step 8. Change Gview to isometric view and exit Editnci menu.

Select **Gview** → **Isometric**

Press **Alt** + **F1** to fit the drawing on the screen

Select **Done** to return back to Editnci menu

Select **Quit** → **Save**

Enter file name: **scale1** ←

Select **Yes** to delete the old toolpath file

Step 9. Backplot the toolpaths.

Select **Backplot**

Set the **Backplot** parameters to these settings ☞

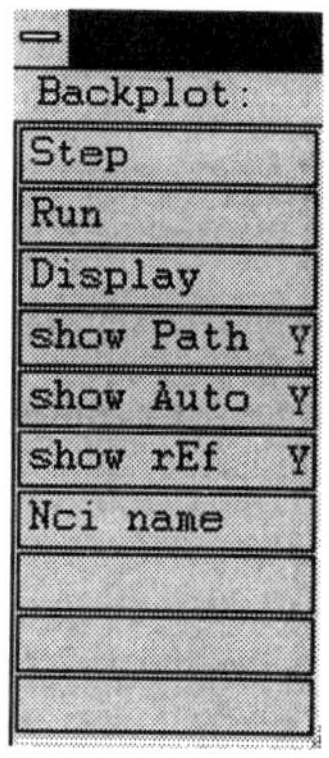

Select **Run**

The toolpaths will be sequentially plotted on the screen. The final toolpaths shown in isometric view appear as in Figure 8.42.

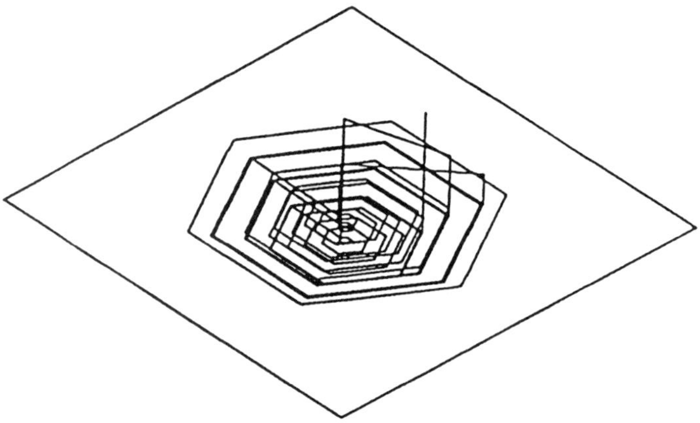

Figure 8.42

8.9 Translate

The translate function moves or copies the toolpath of selected operations to new locations. The locations to be moved can be defined by one of the following four methods:

Rectang:	specifies the incremental distance to be translated in the X, Y, and Z directions.
Polar:	specifies the incremental distance and the desired angle to define the translation position.
Between points:	specifies the translation distances between two points.
Between views:	translates the toolpaths from one view to another.

The translation function can be readily applied in the following **three applications:**

1. **Change coordinate system** (Figure 8.43). When the toolpaths are translated, this can be regarded as an altered coordinate system.

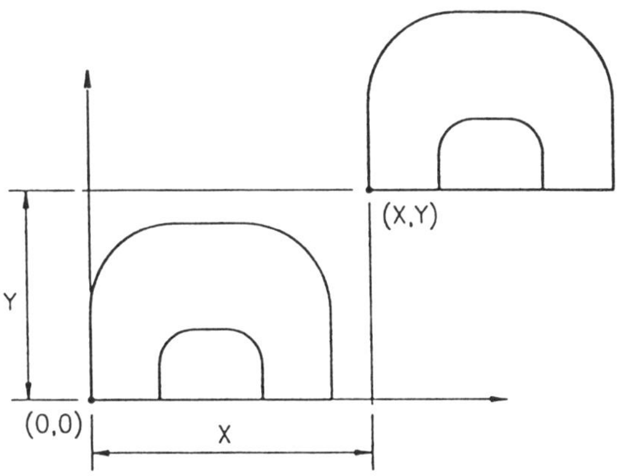

Figure 8.43

2. **Generate toolpaths for identical part features** located at different locations on the same workpiece (Figure 8.44).

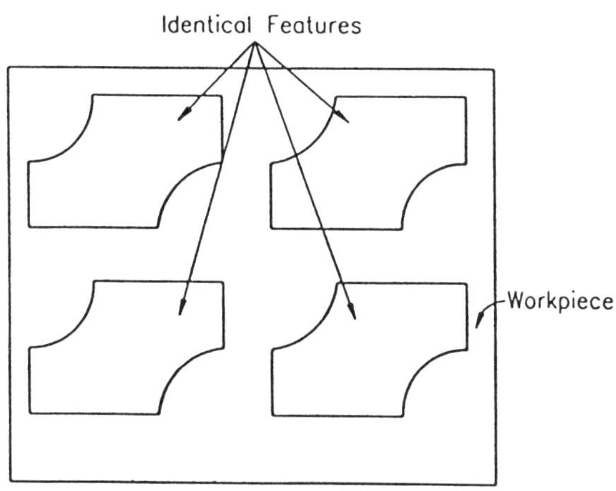

Figure 8.44

3. Generate toolpaths for producing multiple identical workpieces in one part program (Figure 8.45). This facilitates the machining of multiple workpieces in one machine setup.

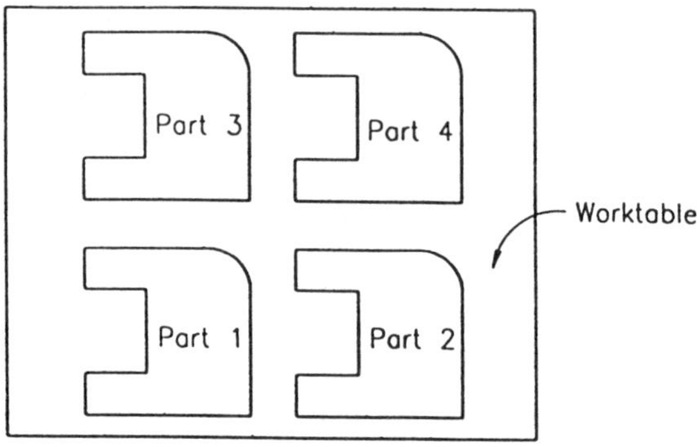

Figure 8.45

Project 5.

Translating Project

5

Part Geometry Creation

Project 7 of Chapter 6 (trans1)

Go to

We are here

Toolpath Generation

(trans1)

The part shown in Figure 8.46 has three identical features. We can generate the toolpaths for one feature and then use Edit NCI → Translate function to copy the toolpaths to the other two locations.

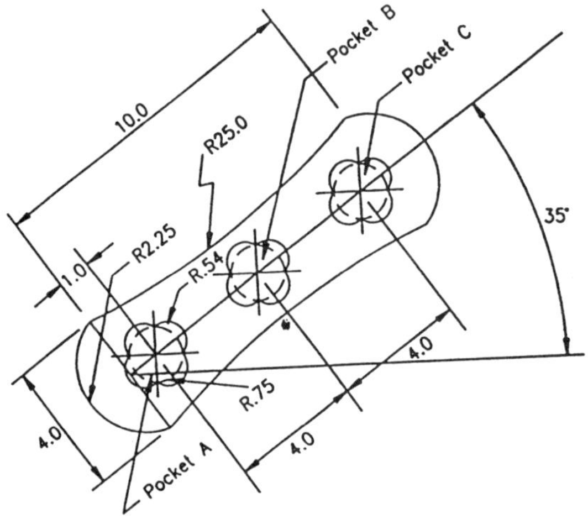

Figure 8.46

Tips 1. Cutter diameter = 0.5".

2. Use the pocket module to generate the toolpaths for cutting the pocket A.

3. Use Edit NCI →Xform→ Translate function to copy the pocketing toolpaths to the other two locations.

Step 1. Load the part geometry file (trans1.ge3) or create one by following the instruction given in Project 7 of Chapter 6 .

Select **MAIN MENU → File → Get**

Enter file name: **trans1 ←**

Select **Yes** to delete the current part if necessary

The part geometry drawing should appear as Figure 8.47.

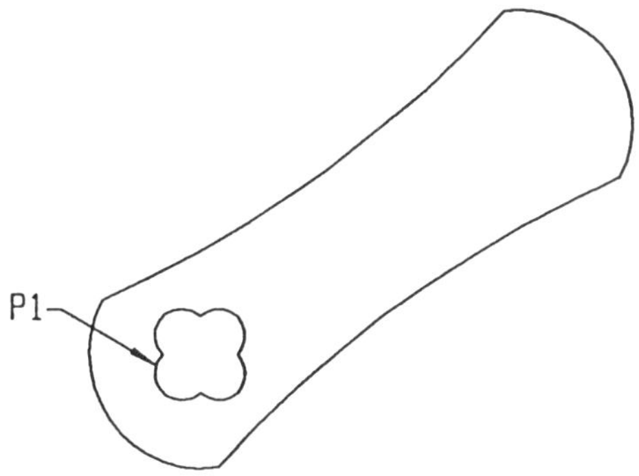

Figure 8.47

Step 2. Initiate the pocket module.

Select **MAIN MENU** → **Toolpaths** → **Pocket**
Enter file name: **trans1** ←

Step 3. Define pocketing contour using the pick point in Figure 8.47.

Select **Chain** from the Chaining method menu
Pick at **P1** to select the first entity in the contour
Select **Close** → **End here** → **Done** to complete contour definition

Step 4. Define pocket parameters to the following settings.

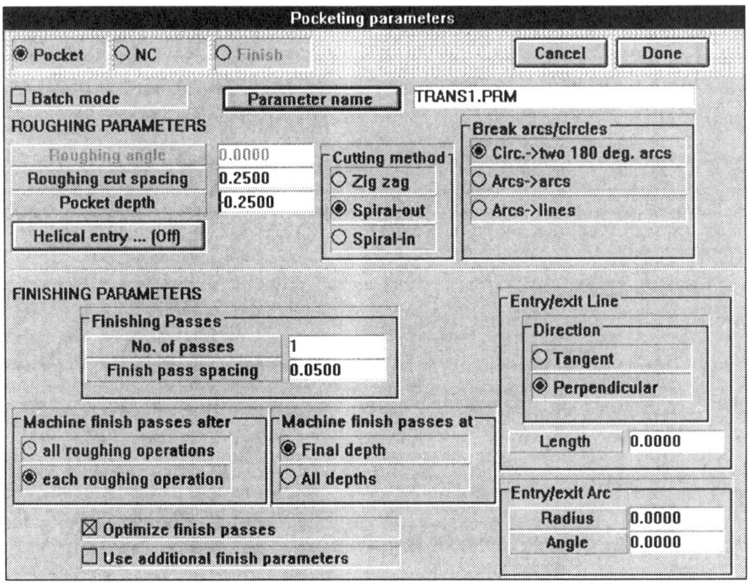

Click the **NC button** to advance to NC parameters menu.

Step 5. Define NC parameters to the following settings.

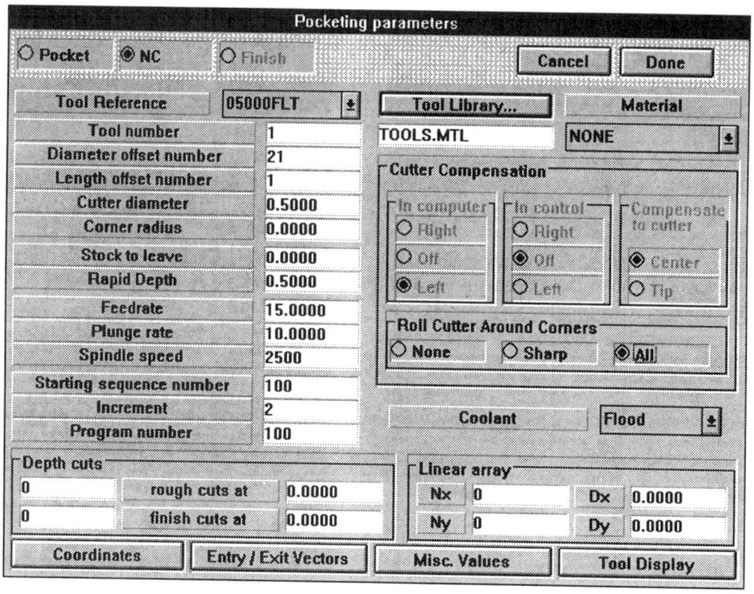

Select the **Done button** to complete the parameters setting.

Step 6. Generate toolpaths for roughing and finish cuts.

Press **F3** to repaint the screen

Select **All** → **Done** to generate toolpaths

Select **Yes** to accept the toolpath segment

The toolpaths for pocketing should look like Figure 8.48.

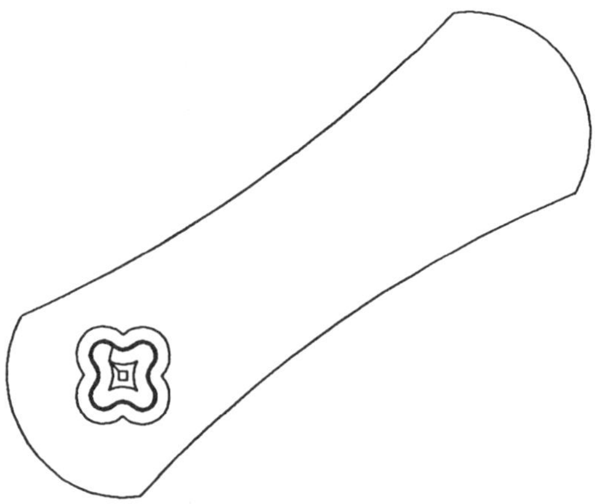

Figure 8.48

Step 7. Translate the toolpaths to two locations.

Select **MAIN MENU** → **NC utils** → **Edit NCI** → **Options** → **Load NCI**
Enter file name: **trans1** ←
Click on the Pocket [T1] operation
Select **Xform** → **Translate**
Set the Xform - Translate parameters to the following settings:

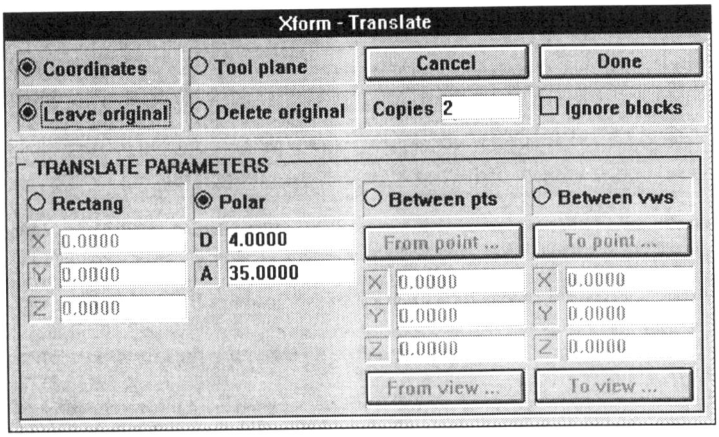

Select **Done**
The toolpaths are plotted as shown in Figure 8.49

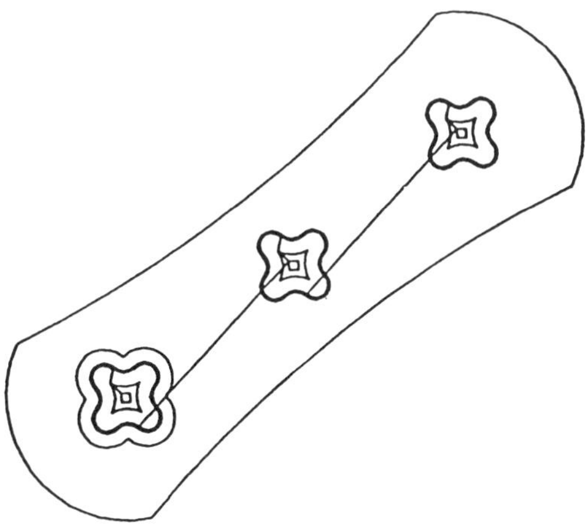

Figure 8.49

Select **Quit** → **Save**
Enter file name: **trans1**
Select **Yes** to delete the old file.

Step 8. Verify the toolpaths.

Select **Gview → Isometric**
Press **Alt** + **F1** to fit the drawing on screen
Select **Backplot**

Set the Backplot parameters to the following settings:

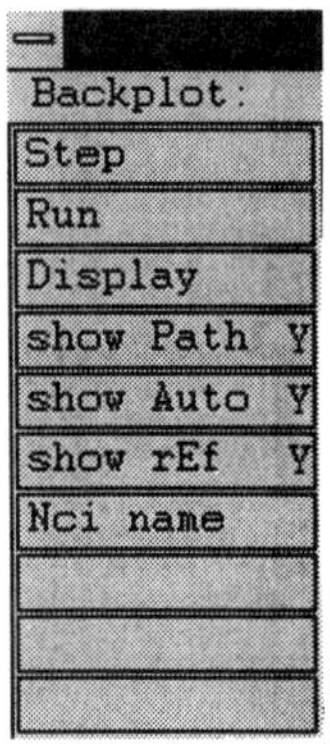

Select **Run**

The toolpaths in isometric view should look like Figure 8.50.

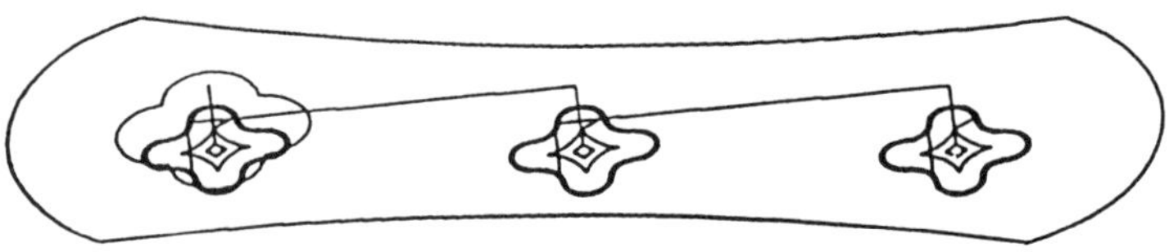

Figure 8.50

8.10 Linear Array

The linear array function allows us to generate a set of duplicate toolpaths to be located at a specified distance along the X and/or Y direction. The linear array function is not one of Edit NCI commands. It is defined in the NC parameters and has the following format:

Linear array: Nx, Ny = _____ _____ Dx, Dy = ______ ______

where Nx = number of times to step and repeat the toolpath along the X axis
Ny = number of times to step and repeat the toolpath along the Y axis
Dx = spacing distance of each step in X direction
Dy = spacing distance of each step in Y direction

The table shown below illustrates how to define the Nx and Ny parameters to generate the duplicate toolpaths.

Table 8.1 Define Nx and Ny Parmeters

Nx	Ny	Description	Illustration
1	1	No duplicated toolpath is generated.	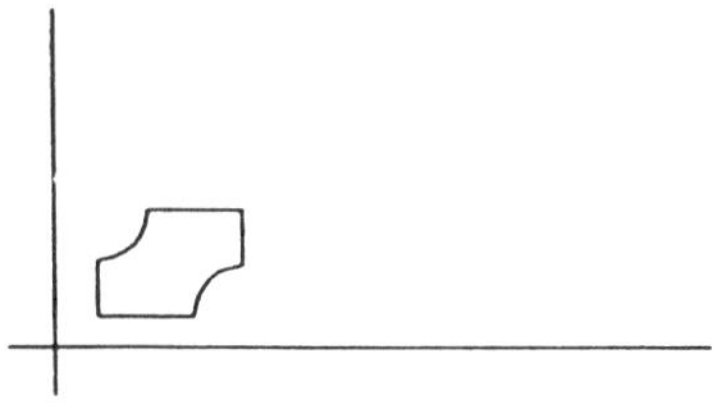
2	1	One duplicated toolpath is generated in X direction.	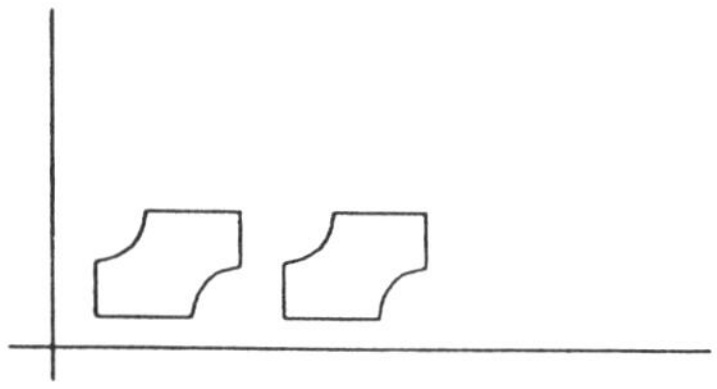
3	1	Two duplicated toolpaths are generated in X direction.	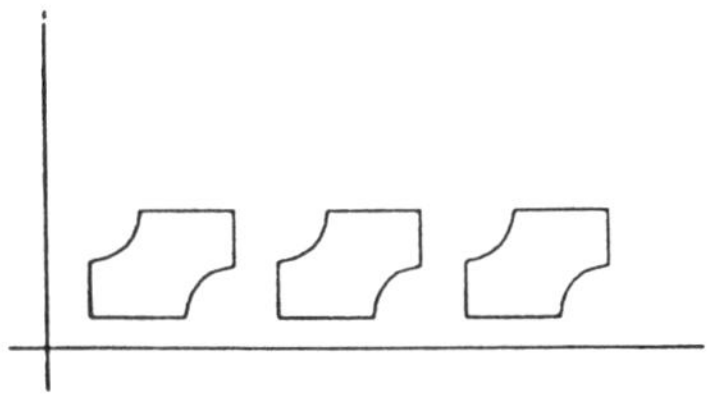
2	2	Three duplicated toolpaths are generated (one in X-direction and two in Y-direction)	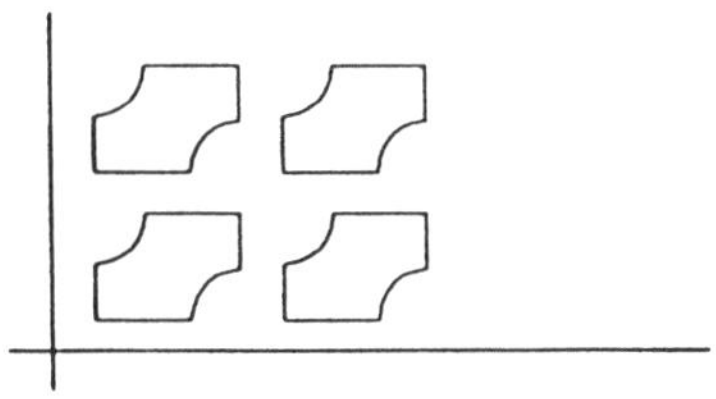
3	2	Five duplicated toolpaths are generated (two in X-direction and three in Y-direction)	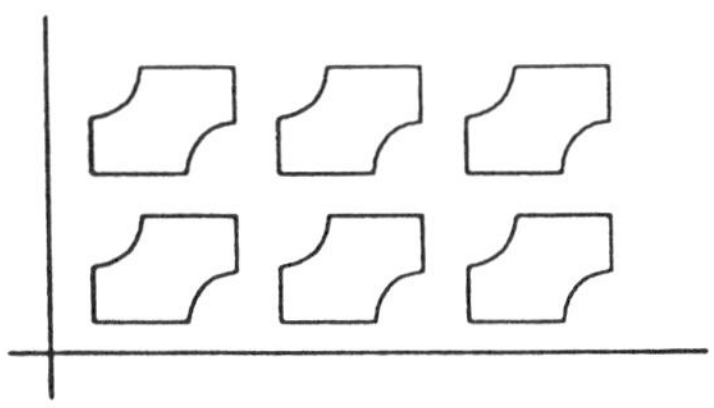

Project 6.

Linear Array Project

The part shown in Figure 8.51 consists of three identical pockets that are equally spaced in the X direction. This is the ideal project for using the linear array function. The pocketing toolpaths for pocket A can be copied to the other two locations.

Part Geometry Creation	6
Project 1 of Chapter 6 (array1)	

Go to

We are here	**Toolpath Generation**
	(array1)

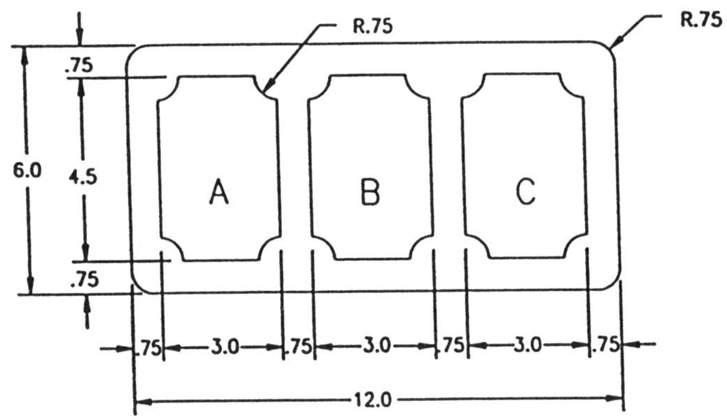

Figure 8.51

Tips 1. The linear array parameters should be set as

Linear array: Nx, Ny = **3 1** Dx, Dy = **3.75 0.0**

2. The system will generate the roughing toolpaths for three pockets first, then will be followed by the finish toolpaths.

Step 1. Load the part geometry file (array1.ge3) or create one by following the instructions given in Project 1 of Chapter 6.

Select **MAIN MENU → File → Get**
Enter file name: **array1 ←**
Select **Yes** to delete the current part if necessary

The part geometry drawing should appear as Figure 8.52.

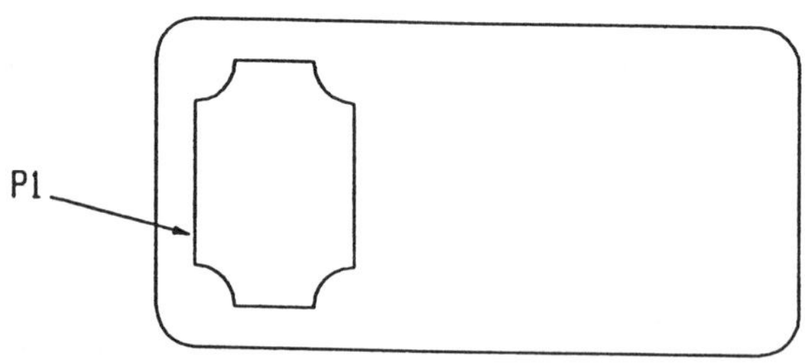

Figure 8.52

Step 2. Initiate the pocket module.

Select **MAIN MENU → Toolpaths → Pocket**
Enter file name: **array1 ←**

Step 3. Define pocketing contour using the pick point in Figure 8.52.

Select **Chain** from the Chaining method menu

Pick at **P1**

Select **Close** → **End here** → **Done** to complete contour definition

Step 4. Set the pocket parameters to the following settings.

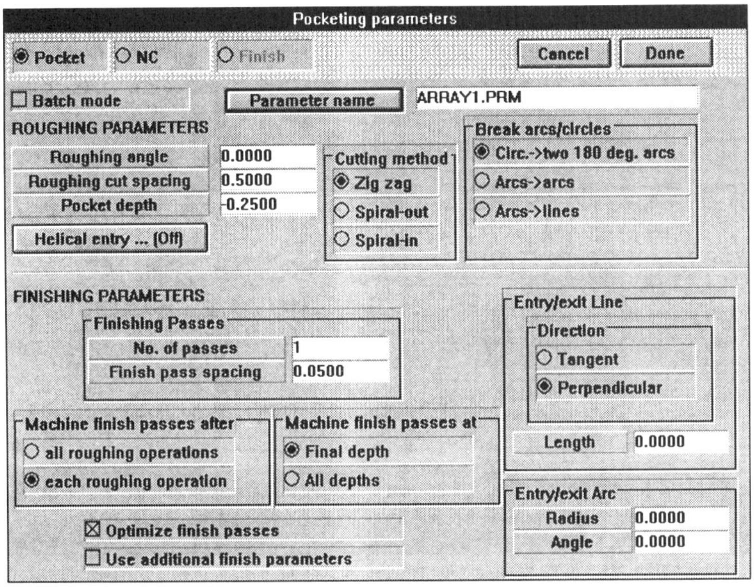

Click the **NC button** to advance to the NC parameters menu

Step 5. Define NC parameters to the following settings.

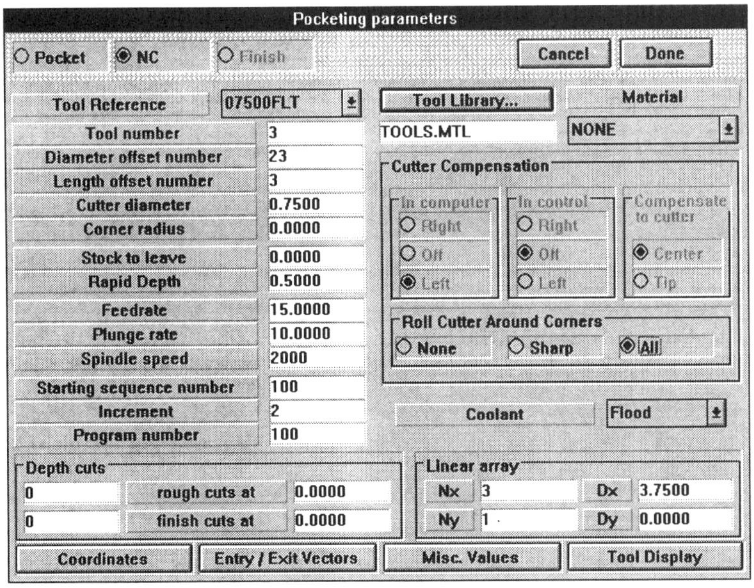

Select the **Done button** to complete the parameters settings.

Step 6. Generate toolpaths.

Press **F3** to repaint the screen

Select **All**

Note: The system will generate roughing toolpaths for all three pockets first, then generate the finish passes.

Select **Done** → **Yes** to accept toolpath segment

The complete toolpaths for these three pockets should resemble Figure 8.53. Below it is Figure 8.54 showing the toolpaths in isometric view.

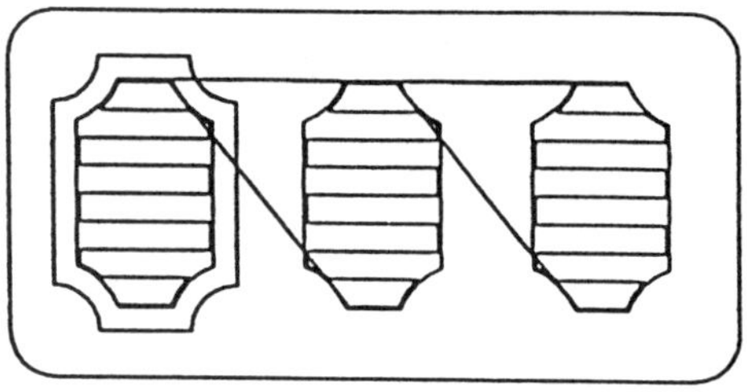

Figure 8.53

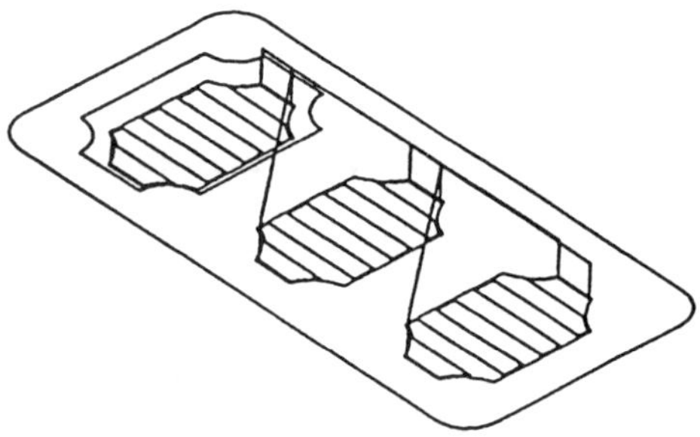

Figure 8.54

Step 7. Finish the process.

Select **End program** to close the toolpath file

Select **Yes** to run the post processor if desired

8.11Exercises

8.10.1 Short Answer

1. Describe how Mastercam organizes its toolpath file structure.

2. Explain how the following four parameters affect the number of toolpath sections generated in using the contour module:

   Number of roughing passes
   Number of finish passes
   Number of rough cuts in depth
   Number of finish cuts in depth

3. Determine the number of toolpath sections for using the contour module to cut an internal profile under the following conditions:

   Number of roughing passes = 2
   Number of finish passes = 1
   Number of rough cuts in depth = 2
   Number of finish cuts in depth = 1

4. What are two main factors determining the number of toolpath sections in using the pocket module?

5. Determine the number of toolpath sections for pocketing under the following conditions:

   Number of finish passes = 1
   Number of rough passes in depth cut = 2
   Number of finish passes in depth cut = 1

6. Explain how an existing toolpath section can be deleted in Mastercam.

7. List the four toolpath editing functions in Mastercam and briefly describe what they are.

8. Describe the advantages of using toolpath editing functions.

9. Explain when to use the mirror function.

10. Explain when to use rotate function.

11. Describe the main features of the scale function.

12. Why is the scale function not recommended for modifying or editing toolpaths?

13. Under what conditions should you use the translation function ?

14. Describe the features of the linear array function and list the four parameters used to define the linear array.

8.10.2 Problems

15. Create the part geometry as shown in Figure 8.55. Use the contour module to generate the toolpaths for the external profile. Purposely generate two roughing passes and one finish pass with the following parameter settings:

Cutter diameter = 1.0"
Number of roughing passes = 2
Rough passes spacing = 0.6"
Number of finish passes = 1
Finish passes spacing = 0.05"
Contour depth = -0.25"

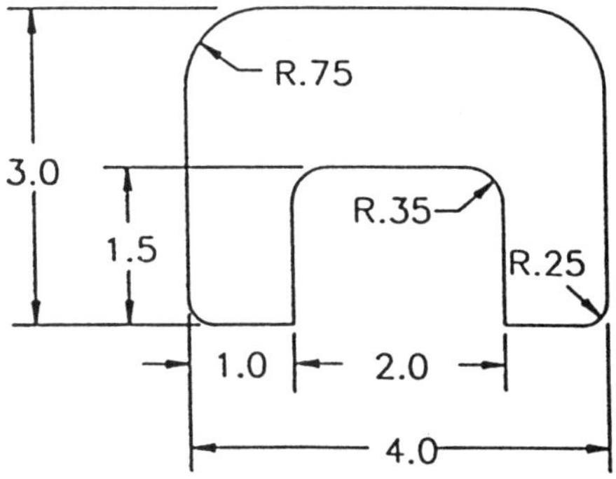

Figure 8.55

After the toolpaths are generated, use End program and Save commands to close the NCI file. This toolpaths file should have three sections. The first roughing toolpaths are the first section of the file. This is one we want to delete. Use NC utils → Edit NCI → File → Open commands to open the toolpath file. Then click the section to be deleted and select the cut command to delete it.

16. The pocket module is used twice to generate toolpaths for pocketing the larger circular pocket and pocketing one of seven small pockets as shown in Figure 8.56. The toolpaths for small pocket are then copied to six locations by using the rotate command. The part geometry file name is **rotate2** which is created in chapter 6. Some helpful tips are given below.

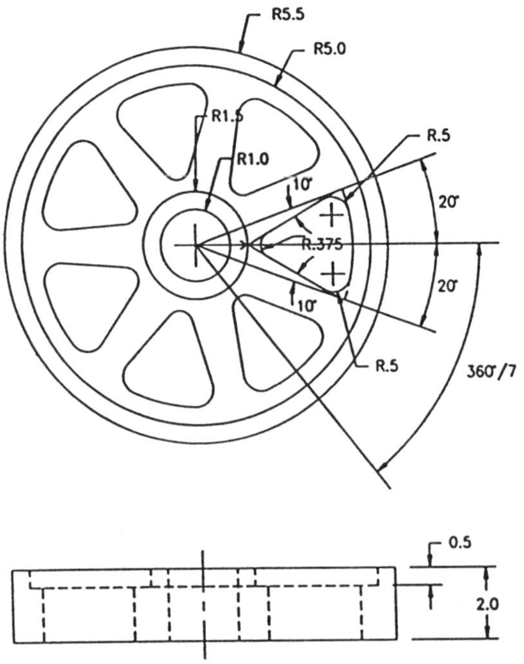

Figure 8.56

Tips 1. Use the pocket module to generate toolpaths for cutting the large pocket of Z-0.5" depth. Use the circle of 10" diameter as the outside contour and the circle of 3" diameter as the island.

2. Use the pocket module to generate toolpaths for cutting one of seven small pockets using the following machining conditions:

   Cutter diameter = 0.5"
   Roughing passes spacing = 0.3"
   Number of finish passes = 1
   Finish passes spacing = 0.05"
   Depth cuts: Rough: 2 cuts at 0.5" Finish: 1 cuts at 0.5"

3. Select End program to close the NCI file for editing.

4. Note that the number of the toolpath sections up to now is 4 and they are assigned as below:

Section number	Operation
1	Pocketing large pocket
2	First rough cut of small pocket
3	Second rough cut of small pocket
4	Finish cut of small pocket

5. Follow the steps given below to copy the toolpaths for the small pocket to six locations by using

   NC utils → Edit NCI → Xform → Rotate commands:

   a. Select NC utils → Edit NCI→ File → Open
   Enter file name: rotate2

   b. Press the Shift key, then click the last three
   toolpath sections to select the toolpaths to be rotated.

   c. Select Xform → Rotate commands
   set the Xform - Rotate parameters to the following settings.

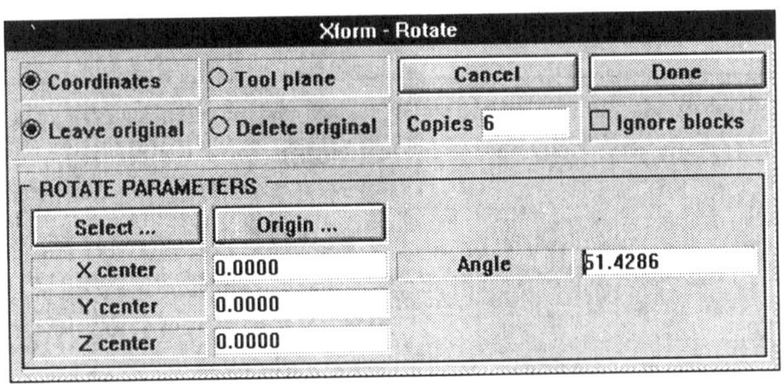

   d. Save the rotated file.

6. Backplot the toolpath to verify the final toolpaths

17. As illustrated in Figure 8.57, two identical parts are machined in one machine setup. These two parts are located symmetrically about a vertical line. This is the ideal case to use the mirror function. Toolpaths for producing one part are generated first, then they are duplicated for the other part by using Edit NCI → Xform → Mirror commands. The part geometry file name is **mirror2.** Assume the part has been pre-machined on the top and bottom surfaces and two holes. Some useful tips are given below.

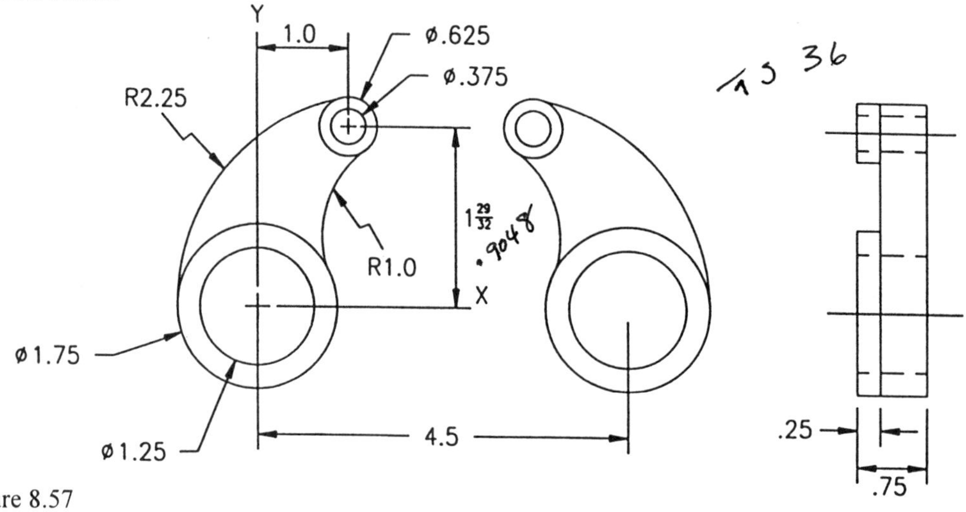

Figure 8.57

Tips 1. Machining processes include contouring two circular flanges and contouring the profile.

2. Use the contour module for all three processes.

3. The two circles that are tangent by two arcs must be broken at the tangent points into several pieces in order to be chained as a contour for profiling.

4. Generate the toolpaths for the part shown at right and then mirror to the left about the vertical line.

5. Backplot the final NCI file to verify the toolpaths.

18. The scale function is used to scale the toolpaths for pocketing a rectangle for cutting two smaller rectangular pockets as shown in Figure 8.58. Some hints are listed below.

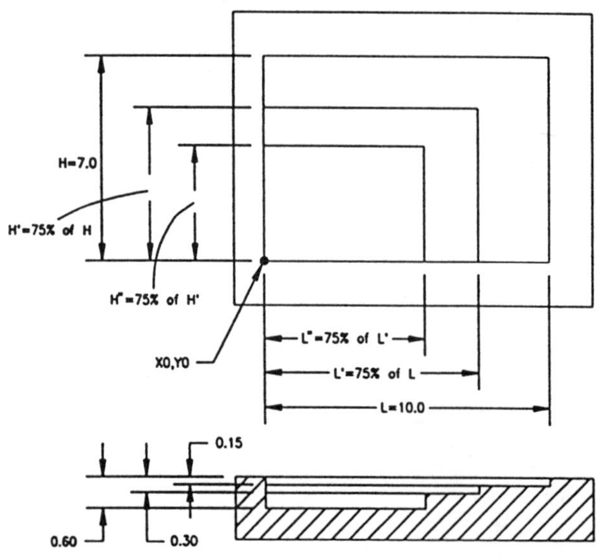

Figure 8.58

Tips 1. Create a 10" x 7" rectangle.

2. Use the pocket module to generate toolpaths to cut the pocket using the following machining data:

Cutter diameter = 0.75"
Cutting method: Spiral inside out
Roughing passes spacing = 0.5"
Number of finish passes = 1
Finish passes spacing = 0.1"
Pocket depth = -0.15"

3. Select End program to close NCI file.

4. Use NCutils → Edit NCI → Xform → Scale commands to scale the original toolpaths and copy to two locations. The scaling data is:

Scale about Origin

Axis	Scaling factor
X	0.75
Y	0.75
Z	2.0

Number of steps = 2
Leave the original entities

5. Use Backplot function to verify the toolpaths.

19. Two identical workpieces are to be produced in one machine setup as shown in Figure 8.59. The set of toolpaths for cutting one part is copied to another location as specified by using translation function. The part geometry file name is **trans2** (which is created in chapter 5.) The generation of toolpaths for machining the part includes using contour, pocket, and drill module. Some hints are given below.

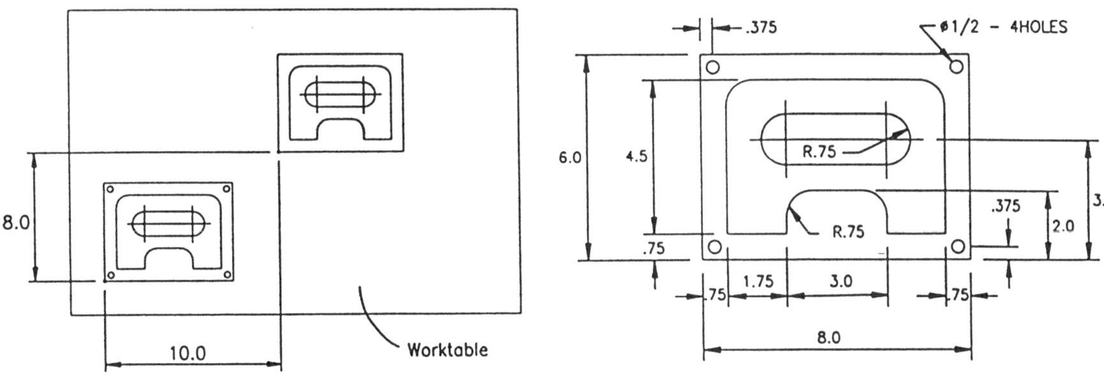

Figure 8.59

Tips 1. The machining sequence starts with the contour module for cutting the external profile, followed by pocket module for pocketing the slot pocket, and finally drill module to drill four holes.

Cutters:
1" end mill for contouring
0.5" end mill for pocketing
1/2" drill for drilling four holes

2. Select End program to close the NCI file.

3. Use NC utils → Edit NCI → Xform → Translate → Rectang commands to copy the toolpaths to the specified location. The incremental distance of translation for the X direction is 10.0" and for the Y direction is 8.0". The Xform parameters should be set to the following settings:

Number of steps = 1
Leave the original entities

20. Use the linear array function to generate the toolpaths for cutting four identical parts in one part program. This allows four parts to be machined in one machine setup. The workholding layout of these four parts is shown in Figure 8.60. The part geometry file name is **trans2** which is identical to the file used in problem 18. Use the instructions given in problem 19 for generating the original toolpaths. The linear array parameters should be set to the following settings:

Linear array: Nx, Ny = 2 2 Dx, Dy = 10.0 8.0

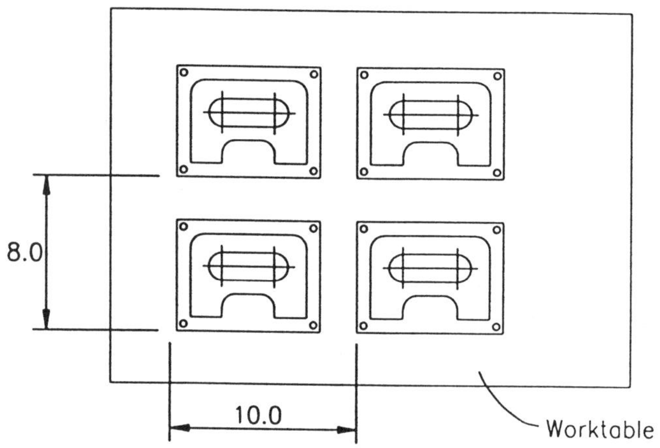

Figure 8.60

Chapter 9
Mastercam Process and Toolpath Planning

Objectives:

1. Understand toolpath generation procedure using Mastercam.
2. Identify part features to be machined from the given part and raw material drawings.
3. Select proper processes and processing sequence to machine features of the part.
4. Select proper toolpath module for the selected process to produce a particular feature.
5. Select proper cutting tools and their machining data.
6. Prepare process plan sheets.

Overview

Mastercam is a very powerful software that can be used to generate toolpaths for machining almost any parts, simple or complex. To effectively use Mastercam's power, the user must have the following knowledge:

- Be familiar with the CAD system to create part geometry
- Know basic CNC programming principles and commands
- Have a good knowledge of machining practices
- Know the CAM system (NC toolpath modules)
- Select proper tooling and machining parameters

In addition, the user must also follow a certain procedure to generate the NC part programs. The process and toolpath planning is the road map for the successful completion of any project. The benefits of good planning include: (1) avoiding errors, (2) eliminating the need for toolpath editing, and (3) serving as a record, reference guide and communication medium. The process and toolpath planning is very useful for beginners who need to follow a logical sequence in completing a project. The planning also is important for experienced users who generate toolpaths for machining complex parts.

Figure 9.1 on the following page is a flow chart that shows the procedure for using the Mastercam system to generate a toolpath to machine a part. This flow chart indicates the input and output relationships of the major tasks in CAD/CAM NC programming.

9.1 Part and Raw Material Drawings

A part drawing describes the shape and size of a part. It provides the following useful information to the part programmer in generating the toolpath:

Part features to be produced
Dimensions, tolerances, and surface roughnesses
Material to be machined
Initial shape and size of the material to be machined
Amount of material to be removed

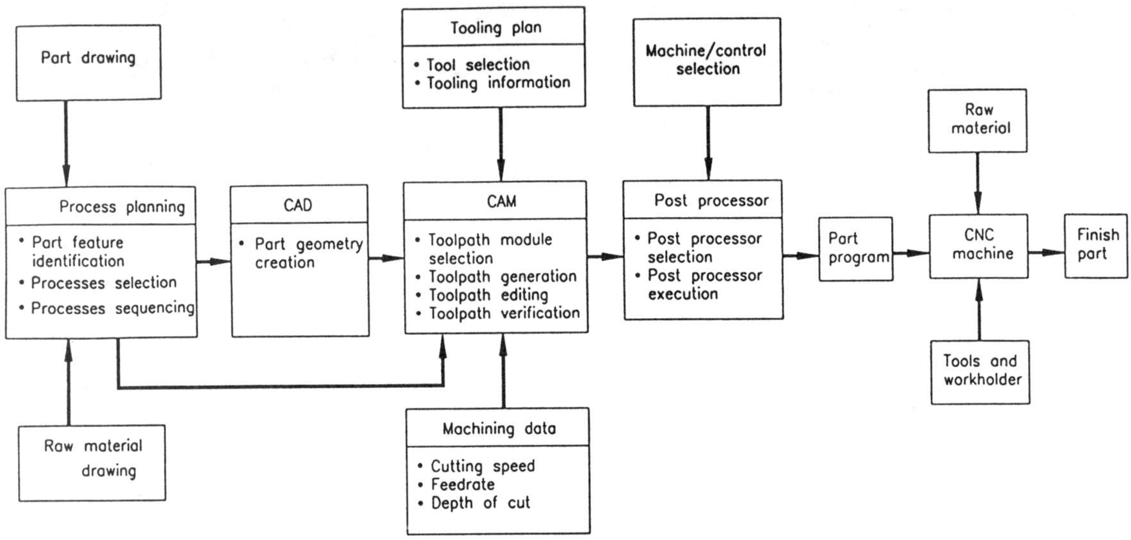

Figure 9.1

Part Features

A part feature is the distinctive shape and size to be produced in a part. Typical part features in milling operations include:

1. Flat surfaces
2. Slots
3. Shoulders or steps
4. Holes
5. Internal threads
6. Profiles (or contours)
7. Letters
8. Spline curves
9. 3-D surfaces

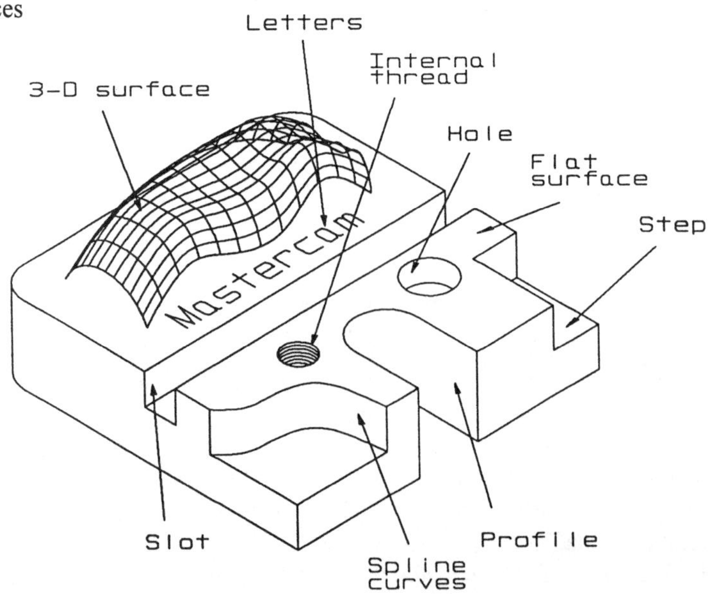

Figure 9.2

Typical part features in turning operations are:
1. End faces
2. External profiles
3. Internal profiles
4. Internal threads
5. External threads
6. Grooves
7. Holes
8. Spline curves
9. Cut-offs

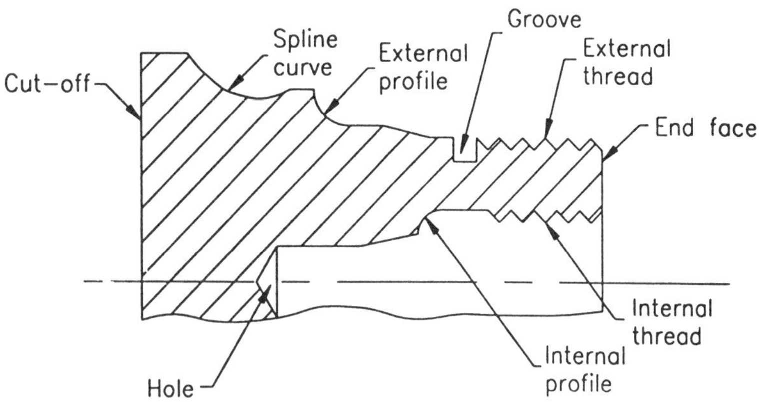

Figure 9.3

Dimensions, Tolerances, and Surface Roughnesses

Selecting a proper process to produce a part feature is dictated by the process capability. Process capability refers to positional accuracy, surface roughness, and amount of material to be removed during a particular machining process. A part drawing should provide the detailed information about dimensions, tolerances and surface roughness of a part feature.

Raw Material Drawing

A raw material drawing depicts the initial shape and size of the workpiece before it is processed. It can be an intermediate form of the part. A comparison of a part drawing and a raw material drawing should reveal the amount of mateiral to be removed to produce a part feature. The information in material removal can be further used to determine (1) the required cutter type and size, and (2) the required number of cutting passes including roughing and finishing.

Processes Selection

After part features have been identified, we need to select the proper processes to produce each feature. The commonly used processes for producing part features in milling and turning operations are listed below:

Milling Operations

Process	**Feature to be produced**
Facing	produce flat surfaces
Profiling	produce external and internal contours
Pocketing	produce internal pockets enclosed by a closed contour
Slot cutting	produce blind and through slots
Shoulder	cutting produce shoulders or steps
Drilling	produce and/or enlarge holes
Boring	enlarge holes
Tapping	produce internal threads
Surface cutting	produce various forms of 3-d surfaces
Lettering	engrave a string of letters

Turning Operations

Process	Feature to be produced
Roughing	produce a rough shape of finished part
Facing	produce a flat end face
Turning	produce external and internal profiles
Grooving	produce grooves
Threading	produce external and internal threads
Drilling	produce and/or enlarge holes
Boring	enlarge holes
Tapping	produce internal threads

Processes Sequencing

The processes required to produce the part features of a piece should be arranged in a proper sequence. Some features must be produced prior to other features. The criteria in sequencing machining processes include:

1. Datum surfaces have precedence. Datum surfaces should be machined first if multiple workholding setups are required.
2. Machine larger surfaces first. Larger surfaces are more adaptable to disturbances resulting from subsequent machining operations.
3. Avoid feature interference. Feature interference happens when the machining of one feature destroys a requirement for the production of other features.
4. Pre-process must be performed first. For example, drilling must be performed before tapping threads in a hole.

Example 1.

Identify the part features to be produced and the machining process(es) to produce each feature for the part shown in Figure 9.4. Also provide the process sequence.

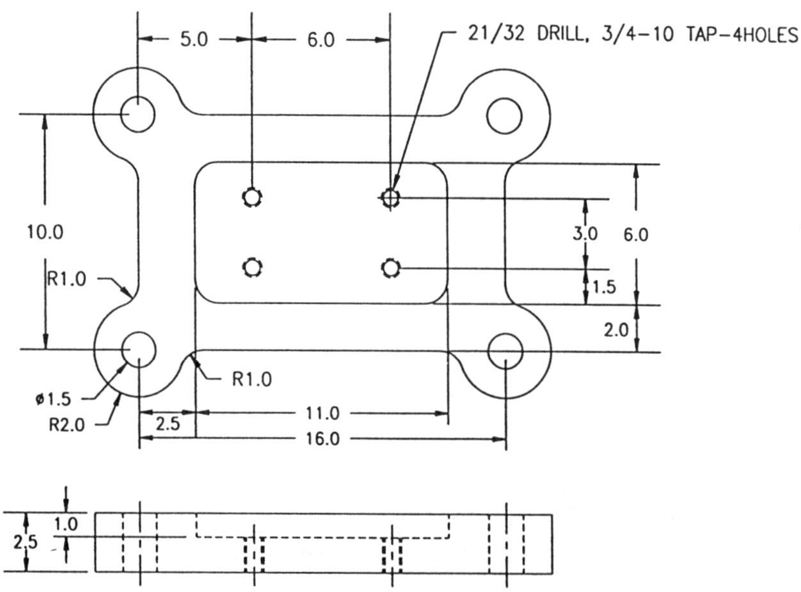

Figure 9.4

Part features:

- Flat top surface
- External profile
- Rectangular pocket
- Four holes
- Internal threads in four holes

Process selection:

Feature	Process(es)
Flat top surface	Facing
External profile	Profiling
Rectangular pocket	Pocketing
Four holes	Drilling and boring
Internal threads in four holes	Drilling and tapping

Processes sequence:

Based on the criteria given above, the suggested process sequence for this part is:

1. Facing the top surface
2. Profiling the external profile
3. Pocketing the internal pocket
4. Drilling four holes
5. Boring four holes
6. Drilling the four holes for threading
7. Tapping threads in four holes

9.2 Part Features Geometry Creation

The geometric entities that describe each part feature should be created. There are **two** types of geometric entities: **true entities and construction entities.** True entities are used to directly define the part features to be produced. They have the true shapes and sizes of the part features. Construction entities are used to help generate toolpaths in machining a part feature. A larger rectangle, for example, is used to define the boundary for generating the toolpaths to face a flat surface that has a smaller size than the rectangle as in Figure 9.5. The geometric entities of this rectangle are construction entities.

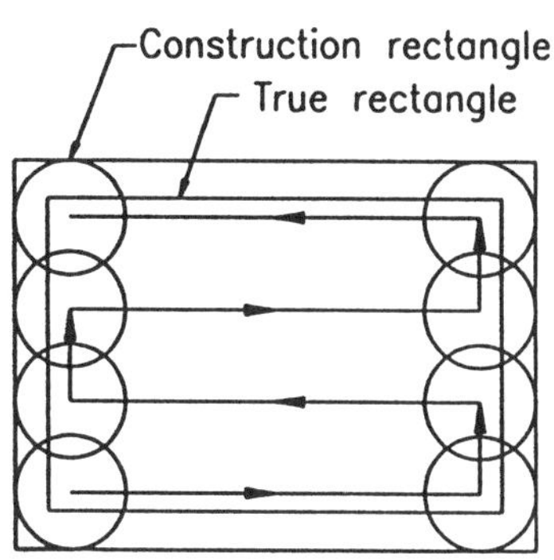

Figure 9.5

9.3 Toolpath Modules Selection

Mastercam provides a variety of toolpath modules for generating the toolpaths to produce part features. The selection of toolpath modules depends on the part feature and the process type. Table 9.3 lists the possible use of toolpath modules for various part features and processes.

Table 9.3 Toolpath Modules

Part Feature	Process	Module	Illustration	Remark
Flat surface	Facing	Pocket	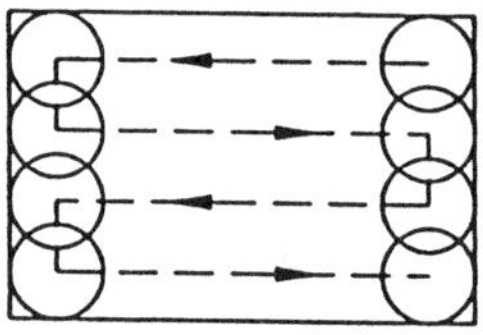	1. Use the larger face mill or end mill to shorten machining time. 2. Create a large pocket boundary to ensure all areas are cut.
Profile/contour	Profiling	Contour	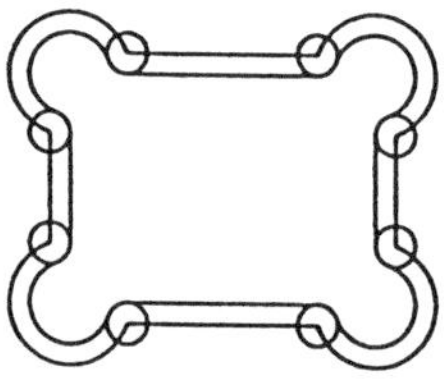	1. Use end mill to move along the part profile 2. Select proper contour direction to obtain climb or conventional milling type.
Pocket	Pocketing	Pocket	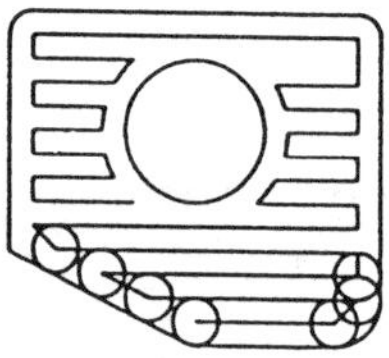	Use end mill to remove the material enclosed by a closed boundary
Slot	Slot cutting	Contour or Pocket	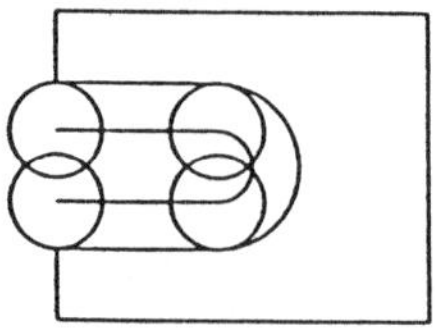	Use end mill to cut open or blind slots.
Shoulder	Shoulder cutting	Contour or Pocket	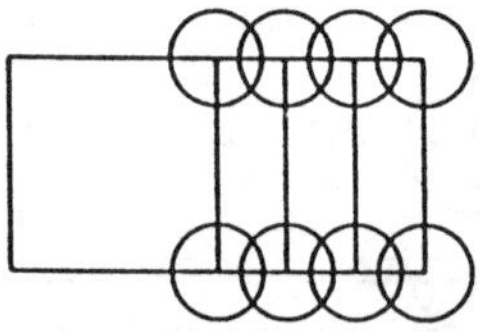	Use end mill to produce steps or shoulders.

Table 9.3 (Continued)

Part Feature	Process	Module	Illustration	Remark
Hole	Drilling and/or boring	Drill/Bore	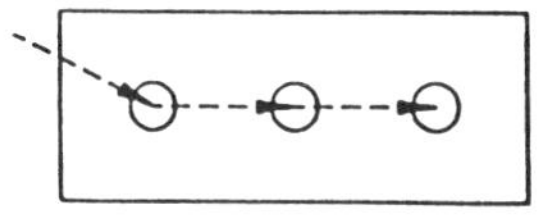	Use drill and/or boring bar to produce holes.
Internal thread	Drilling and tapping	Drill/Tap	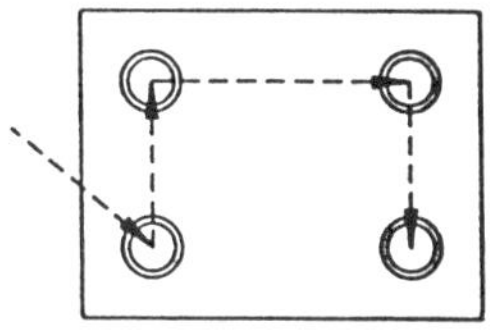	Use tap to produce internal threads of holes.
Letters	Lettering	Letters		Use end mill to engrave letters on part surfaces.
Spline curves	Curve cutting	Profile or Pocket	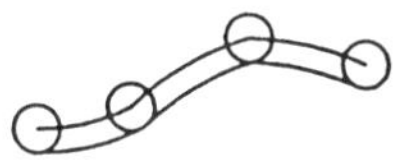	Use end mill to cut along spline curves.
Single 3-D surface	Surface cutting	3-D toolpaths modules such as ruled, loft, swept,coons and flowline	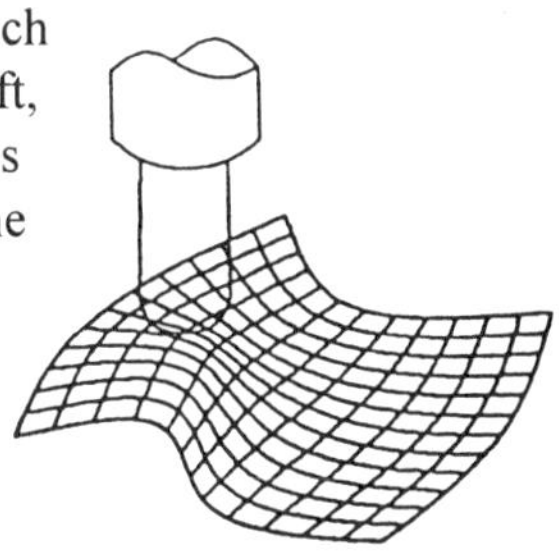	Use ball-end mill to cut 3-D surfaces
Composite surface	Surface cutting	Multisurf	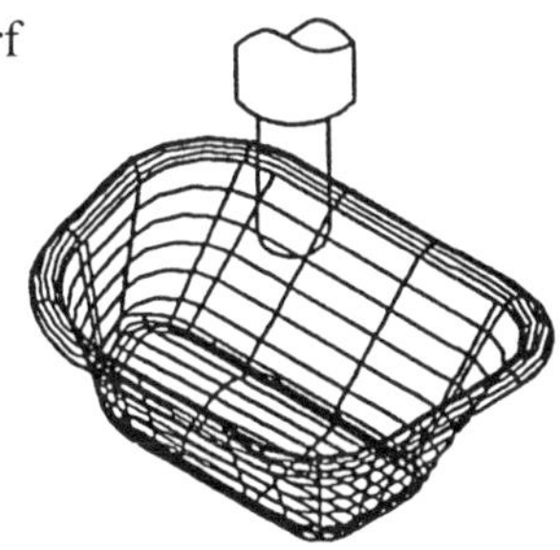	Use ball -end mill to cut multiple surfaces

9.4 Tooling Data and Machining Data

There are **two** types of information that determine the efficiency of CNC machining: **tooling data and machining data.**

- Tooling data includes information related to defining the size of the cutter, the assignment of tool number, tool length offset, and CDC offset.
- Machining data basically consists of **three** components: cutting speed, feedrate, and depth of cut.

Cutting speed, expressed in fpm, normally is not used directly in the milling operations, instead, it is used to calculate the required spindle speed (RPM) using this formula:

$$N = \frac{12 \cdot CS}{\pi \cdot D}$$

CS = cutting speed
N = Spindle speed
D = Cutter diameter

Feedrate refers to the speed of cutter moves along the workpiece. In milling, the feedrate is often expressed in the units of inches/minute.

The proper selection of tooling data and machining data is provided in chapter 2 of this book.

9.5 Process Plan Sheet Preparation

The blank sheet shown in Figure 9.6 can be used to plan the activities for machining a part. This process plan sheet includes the following important information:

Part identification and material
Machine to be used and post processor
Processes and sequencing
Process illustation
Toolpath module used in each machining process
Tools
Machining data

Example 2: Process planning

Use the sheet given in Figure 9.6 on the next page to develop a process plan for the part shown in Figure 9.7 on page 9-10. The raw material is a steel circular plate of D8.1" X 1.55".

PROCESS PLAN	PART NAME:	MATERIAL:	SHEET_________OF_________
MACHINE:	POST PROCESSOR:	PREPARED BY:	DATE:

PROCESS ILLUSTRATION	PROCESS		TOOLPATH MODULE	TOOL		MACHING DATA		
	NO.	DESCRIPTION		NO.	DESCRIPTION	CUTTING SPEED (RPM)	FEED RATE (IPM)	DEPTH OF CUT

Figure 9.6 Blank process plan sheet

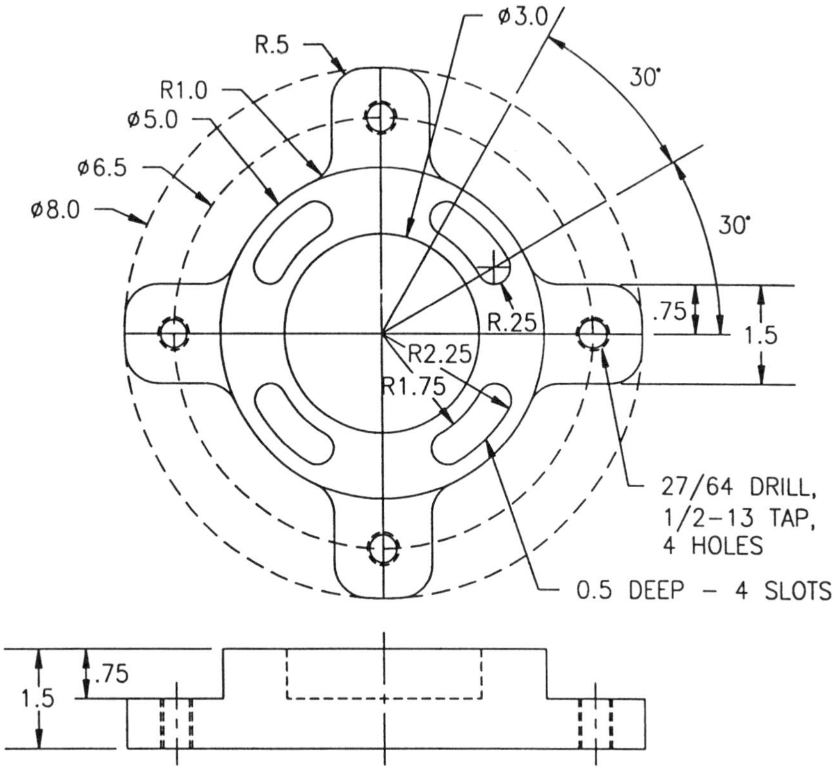

Figure 9.7

Part features:

A study of the part drawing reveals that there are **seven** part features to be produced in this piece:

1. Bottom flat surface
2. Top flat surface
3. Upper circular profile
4. External profile
5. Circular pocket
6. Four circular slots
7. Four holes with internal threads

Process Sequencing:

This project involves **two** workpiece setups. The first setup is to cut the bottom flat surface which is used as the datum for the second setup for the remaining machining operations. Thus, the machining of the bottom flat surface must be the first process. Using the sequencing criteria given in previous section, we can arrange the process sequence as below:

1. Facing the bottom flat surface
2. Facing the top flat surface
3. Cutting the upper circular profile
4. Cutting the external profile
5. Cutting the circular pocket
6. Cutting four circular slots
7. Drilling four holes for threading
8. Tapping internal threads in four holes

Module Selection

The pocket module is used for facing the bottom and top flat surfaces, circular pocket, and four circular slots. The drill module is used to drill four holes and the drill/tap option is used for tapping four holes. A careful consideration must be given to the upper circular profile and the external profile.

We have **two** ways to generate the toolpaths for cutting the upper circular profile. One way is to use the contour module and select the circle as the contour boundary. Since the material to be removed is relatively large, it requires the use of several roughing passes and one finish pass. Another way is to use the pocket module with the circle as the island. A construction circle must be created to serve as the outer pocketing boundary as shown in Figure 9.8. Finally we chose to use the contour module for cutting the upper circular profile.

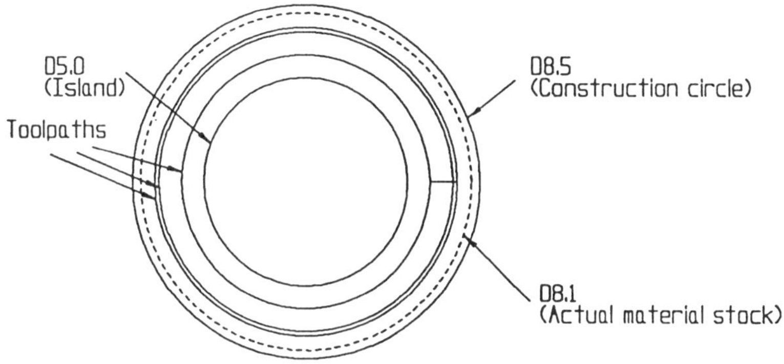

Figure 9.8

There are four local pockets formed between the four ears of the external profile. A more direct way to cut the external profile is to use the contour module with several roughing passes and one finish pass. An alternate way is to use the pocket module to cut one local pocket, then copy the toolpaths onto the other three pockets (Figure 9.9), and finally use the contour module to perform the finish cut as in Figure 9.10. In this project, we use the latter approach for cutting the external profile.

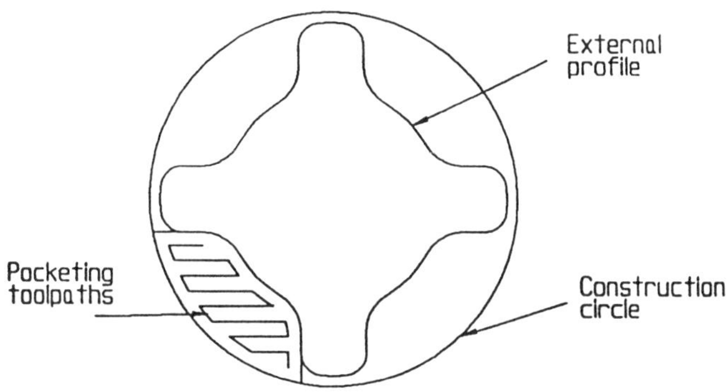

Figure 9.9

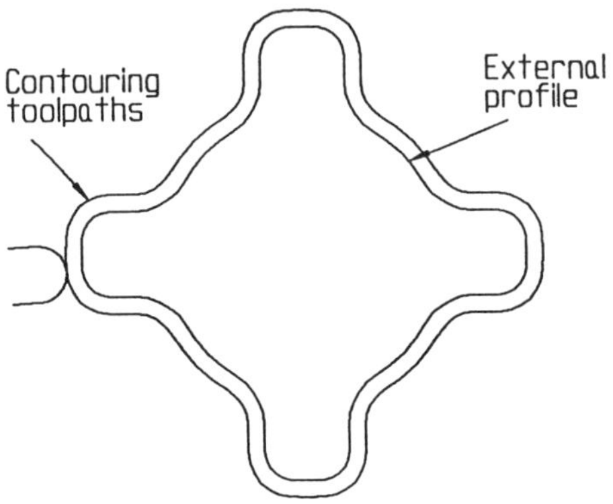

Figure 9.10

Tools and Machining Data

Six cutting tools are used in this project. They are:

- 4" face mill for facing bottom and top flat surface
- 1" end mill for cutting upper circular profile
- 1/2" end mill for cutting pockets and finish profile of the external profile, and to cut the internal circular pocket
- 1/4" end mill to cut the four circular slots
- 17/32" drill to drill four thread holes
- 5/8-11 tap to tap four holes

The machining data for each cutting tool and process is given in Figure 9.11. The completed process plan sheet for this project is given in Figure 9.11 on the next two pages.

9.6 Post Processor Selection

The toolpath file generated from the CAM system is a generic type called an NCI file in Mastercam. T file must be further processed by a software program called a post processor. The main task of a post processor to convert the NCI file into the NC part program. The output from the post processor is the part program that is readable by a CNC controller. Since the CNC controllers of different vendors require different codes and they a used by different machines, there is no one universal post processor that can be used for all machines. In comm practice, one controller/machine combination requires a dedicated post processor. The required post processor will be determined automatically once a CNC machine is chosen to machine a particular project.

Note: It is best to select the post processor you will be using **before** you begin your tool paths.

PROCESS PLAN	PART NAME: Project 5	MATERIAL: Steel	SHEET 1 OF 2
MACHINE: LEAD-M1	POST PROCESSOR: LMC-1	PREPARED BY: J Lin	DATE: 10-8-94

PROCESS ILLUSTRATION	PROCESS		TOOLPATH MODULE	TOOL		MACHING DATA		
	NO.	DESCRIPTION		NO.	DESCRIPTION	CUTTING SPEED (RPM)	FEED RATE (IPM)	DEPTH OF CUT
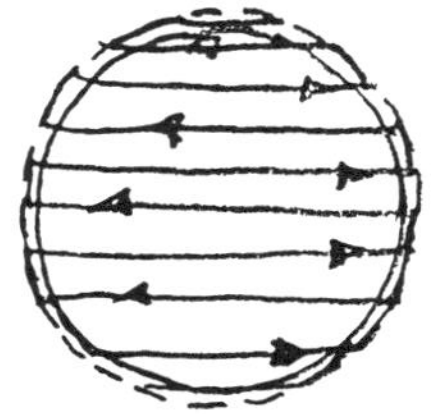	1	Facing bottom flat surface	Pocket	1	2" face mill	150	10	0.15
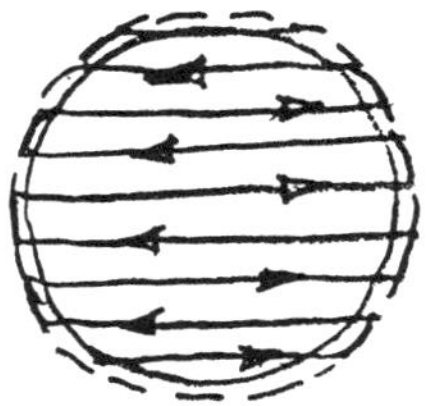	2	Facing the top surface	Pocket	1	2" face mill	150	10	0.15
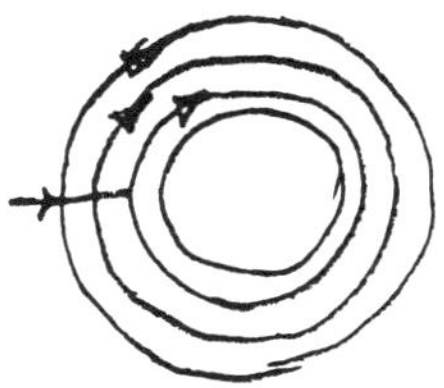	3	Cutting upper circular profile	Contour	2	1" end mill	300	12.5	0.2
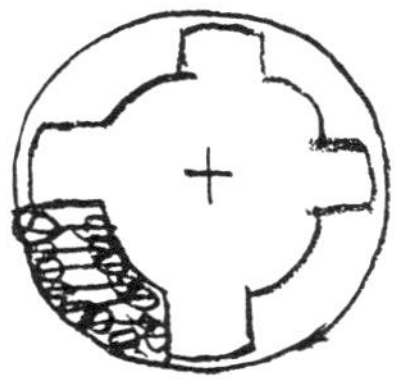	4	Cutting external profile	Pocket and Contour	3	1/2" end mill	600	12.5	0.2

Figure 9.11
Mastercam Book for Windows,
Scholar's International Publishing Corp., 1995

PROCESS PLAN	PART NAME: Project 5		MATERIAL: Steel			SHEET 2 OF 2		
MACHINE: LEAD-M1	POST PROCESSOR: LMC-1		PREPARED BY: J. [illegible]			DATE: 10-8-4		
PROCESS ILLUSTRATION	PROCESS		TOOLPATH MODULE	TOOL		MACHING DATA		
	NO.	DESCRIPTION		NO.	DESCRIPTION	CUTTING SPEED (RPM)	FEED RATE (IPM)	DEPTH OF CUT
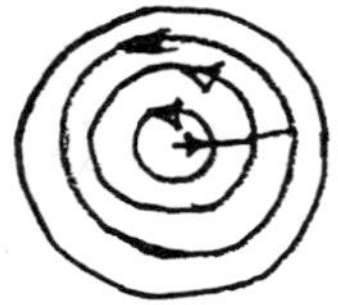	5	Cutting circular pocket	Pocket	3	1/2" end mill	600	12.5	0.2
	6	Cutting four circular slots	Pocket	4	1/4" end mill	1200	10	0.1
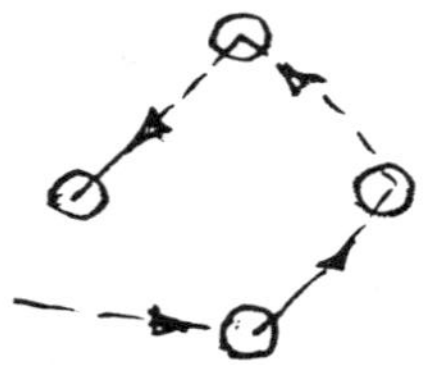	7	Drilling four holes	Drill	5	17/32 drill	500	10	—
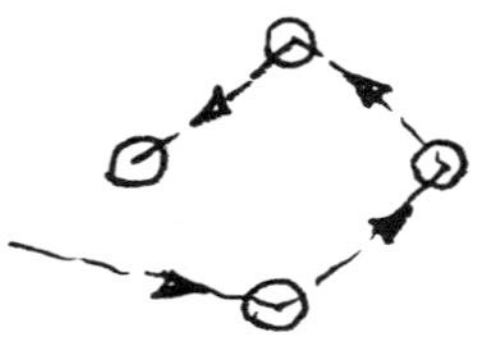	8	Tapping for internal threads	Drill	6	5/8-11 tap	200	18.18	—

Figure 9.11, continued

9.7 Exercises

1. What types of knowledge must a user have in order to effectively use a CAD/CAM system?

2. List the three benefits of good process and toolpath planning.

3. What is a part feature?

4. List at least seven common part features in milling operations.

5. List at least seven common part features in turning operations.

6. Describe how to determine the amount of material removed in producing a part feature.

7. What are the four basic criteria for sequencing machining processes?

8. What are the two types of geometric entitites used to describe part features?

9. What is tooling data?

10. What is machining data?

11. Describe the reasons for using a post processor.

12. Explain the main purpose of a post processor.

13. Use the blank process planning sheet given in Figure 9.6 to develop a process plan for the part shown in Figure 9.12.

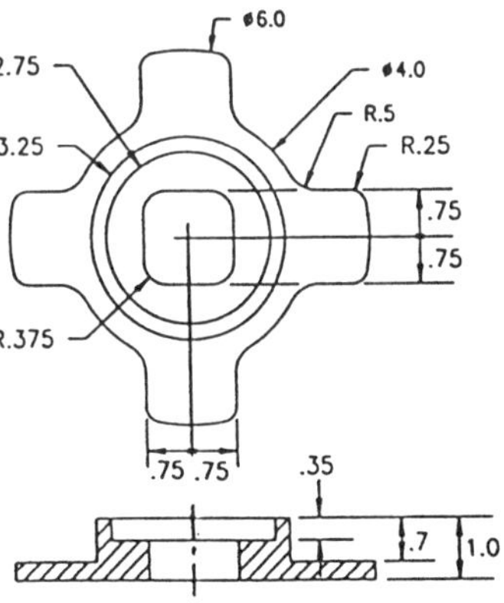

Figure 9.12

14. Use the blank process planning sheet given in Figure 9.6 to develop a process plan for the part shown in Figure 9.13.

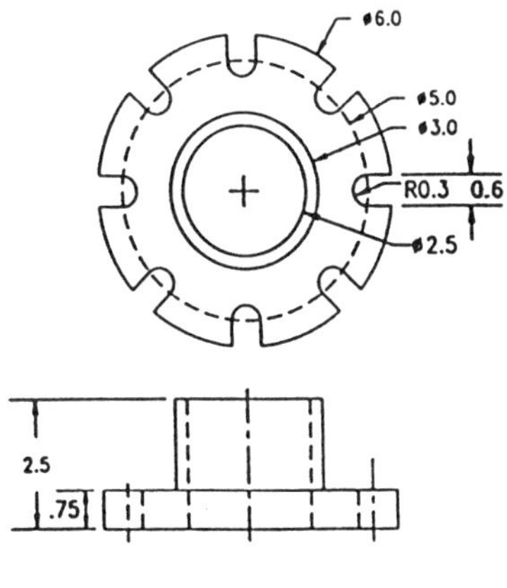

Figure 9.13

Chapter 10

File Conversion

Objectives:

1. Be familiar with the Mastercam file transfer utility.
2. Convert geometry files to and/or from another CAD/CAM system.
3. Convert the files of earlier Mastercam versions to the current version.

Overview

Each CAD/CAM system uses a particular file format to store the drawing data. Normally, the drawing file created in one CAD/CAM system can not be directly used in other CAD/CAM systems. This necessitates a file conversion utility to convert the drawing data from one format to another. For this reason, file conversion has become an important practice in today's design and manufacturing industry. Mastercam provides file conversion facility to allow the geometry models be converted to and/or from a file format that can be used by another CAD/CAM system or earlier Mastercam releases. For most popular 3D CAD/CAM packages, Mastercam can import and export 3D lines, arcs and circles from the exchange format of the package. This exchange format is usually an ASCII file, not the standard binary file created by the package when the model is saved. For example, for AutoCAD, the exchange file has a .DXF extension and the normal drawing file saved has a .DWG extension.

10.1 Mastercam File Conversion

Mastercam uses the menu tree shown in Figure 10.1 to step through the bi-direction file conversion process.

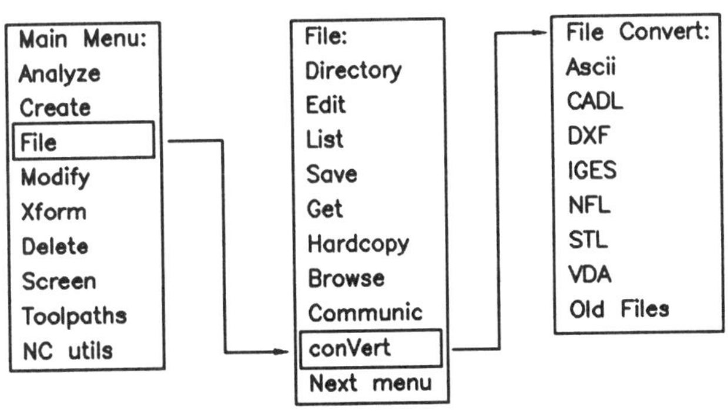

Figure 10.1

There are eight conversion utilities in Mastercam to link with popular CAD/CAM systems. The features of these utilities are summarized in Table 10.1 on the next page.

Table 10.1 Features of Mastercam file conversion facility

Utility Name	CAD/CAM System	Dimension	File Extension	Comment
ASCII	N/A	2D and 3D	.DOC	Converts XY and XYZ coordinates into points, lines or splines
CADL	CADKEY	3D	.CDL	CADL (CADKEY Advanced Design Language) is the format used by CADKEY (CADKEY, Inc.)
DXF	AutoCAD	3D	.DXF	DXF (Drawing Interchange Format File) is used by AutoCAD (Autodesk, Inc.) It is a popular way to exchange geometry files between different CAD/CAM systems.
IGES	Public Standard	3D	.IGS	IGES is a US standard and is used by many full-scale CAD systems.
NFL	Anvil	3D	.NFL	NFL is used by Anvil (MCS, Inc.)
STL	N/A	3D	.STL	Stereolithography files used by rapid prototyping
VDA	German Standard	3D	.VDA	VDA(Verband der Automobilindustrie) is a German standard.
Old Files	Mastercam	(See the following three options)		Old Mastercam file converter for GEO, Old GE3 and 286.
-GEO	Mastercam	2D	.GEO	GEO files are 2D geometry files used by Mastercam prior to V3.00.
-OLD GE3	Mastercam	3D	.GE3	These GE3 files were created by Mastercam prior to V3.21, and can be imported and exported through this function.
-286	Mastercam	3D	.GE3	GE3 files created by a 286 CAM system (CAM3, LATHE, FABRIX,WIRE)

In practice, DXF and IGES files are the most common ways to transfer files from Mastercam to another CAD/CAM system. These two conversion utilities are available in most commercial-based CAD/CAM programs.

Users should be aware that the file conversion between different CAD/CAM systems is not always perfect. In same cases, entities are incorrectly converted or simply lost in the conversion process. For example, **surface information** created by Mastercam might not be transferred to other systems. Therefore, users should verify the results after the conversion. Table 10.2 shows the entity types supported by Mastercam's conversion.

Table 10.2 Entity types supported by Mastercam

Utility Name	Entity types supported by Mastercam conversion
ASCII	Point, line and spline
CADL	Point, line, polyline, arc, circle, spline, conic, view, color, level, array, text, leader and witness
DXF	Point, line, polyline, arc, circle, trace, block, endblk, insert, vertex and seqend. Splines are not supported (use IGES).
IGES	This public standard is considerably more complex than other file formats and is used by many full-scale CAD/CAM/CAE system. Limitation: IGES does not support parametric surfaces and splines with a degree greater than three.
NFL	Point, line and circle
STL	Standard stereolithography file format
VDA	Point, line, circle, curve and SURF as defined in Version 2.0 of VDA. Colors and levels are not supported.
Old Files	(See the following three options)
-GEO	2D point, line and arc
-OLD GE3	Most Mastercam entities. Newer data types, such as Trimmed surfaces, are not supported.
-286	Only read/write the GE3 file from/to Mastercam "286" data path.

10.2 File Conversion Projects

Six projects are presented in this section. They lead you through the step-by-step procedures to transfer drawing files between Mastercam/AutoCAD R.12, and Mastercam/CADKEY 7 using the appropriate file conversion utilities. It is assumed that users already know how to load and save the drawing files in each individual package.

Project 1.

Transfer a 3D drawing file to AutoCAD R.12 using DXF utility

An existing geometry file (CAR.GE3) as shown in Figure 10.2 is used to be converted into DXF file. This file is then used in AutoCAD system.

Note: When working in 3D, IGES is the best conversion utility.

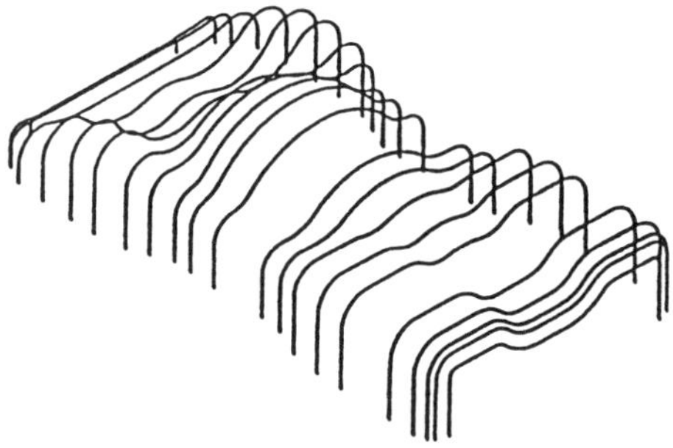

Figure 10.2

To create a DXF file from Mastercam

Step 1. Load the geometry file CAR.GE3.

Select **MAIN MENU → File → Get**
Enter file name: **car ←**
Select **Yes** to delete the current part

The car drawing shall appear on screen as Figure 10.3.

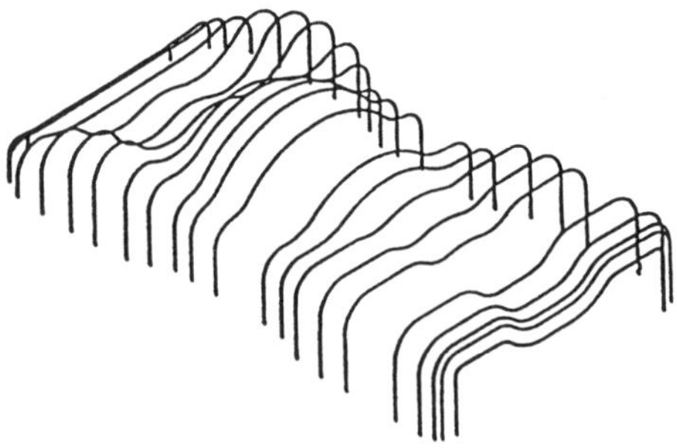

Figure 10.3

Step 2. Initiate the convert utility.

Select **MAIN MENU → File →conVert → DXF → Write file**
Enter file name: **B:\DXFTEST ←** *(or enter a desired file name)*

*Note:*You don't need to enter the file extension. Mastercam will automatically add the file extension DXF to the file.

To receive a DXF file from AutoCAD

In AutoCAD, use the following commands to allow you to read-in an ASCII-format DXF file.

Step 1. Initiate DXFIN function.

After entering AutoCAD, a command prompt should appear.
Command: **DXFIN** ←
(A pop-up dialogue box will ask for the DXF file name.)
File: **B:\DXFTEST** ← *(or enter a desired file name)*

Note: Prior to Release 11, any extension would cancel the command; after Release 11, extensions were acceptable. Here we do not need one. AutoCAD R.12 will use the default file extension as DXF.

The car drawing should appear in the top view as in Figure 10.4.

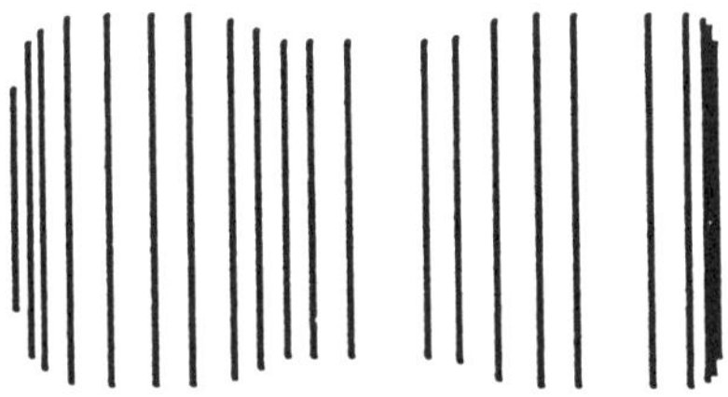

Figure 10.4

Step 2. Display the drawing in isometric view.

Command: **VPOINT** ←
Rotate/(View point): **1,-1,1** ←

The car drawing now is appeared in the isometric view as shown in Figure 10.5.

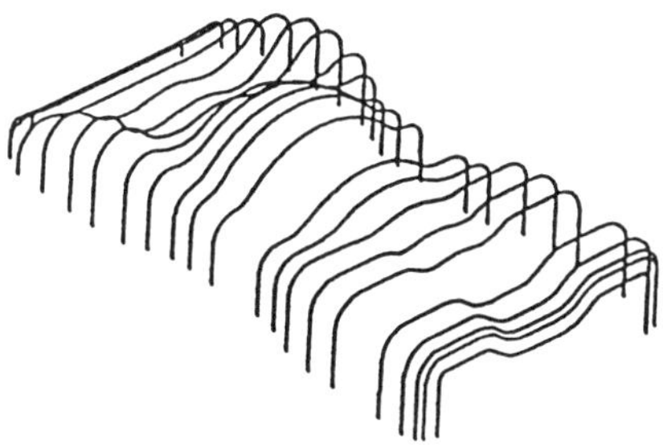

Figure 10.5

Step 3. Save the drawing as CAR.

Command: Save ←

(A pop-up dialogue box will ask for the drawing file name)

File: **CAR** ←

Note: During DXF transfer, parametric splines, NURB and trimmed surfaces, dimensions and notes are not converted.

Project 2. 2

Transfer a 3D drawing file from AutoCAD R.12 to Mastercam using the DXF utility

The car drawing we imported into AutoCAD through the DXFIN command as described in project 1 becomes a DWG file. In this project, we use the same car drawing in AutoCAD but save it to the DXF format. This file is then read into Mastercam.

To create a DXF file from AutoCAD

Step 1. Load the car drawing CAR in AutoCAD.

Command: OPEN ←

(A pop-up dialogue box will ask for the drawing name)

File: **CAR** ←

Step 2. Initiate the DXFOUT function.

Command: **DXFOUT** ←

(A pop-up dialogue box will ask for the DXF file name.)

File name: **B:\DXFTEST** ← *(or enter a desired file name)*

(AutoCAD R.12 will use the default file extension DXF.)

Enter decimal places of accuracy (0-16)/Entities/Binary <6>: **6** ←

(This will allow you to select the accuracy of exported entities. In general, the default of 6 will be accurate enough.)

To receive a DXF file from Mastercam

Step 1. Initiate the convert utility.

Select **MAIN MENU → File → conVert → DXF → Read file**

Enter file name: **B:\DXFTEST** ← *(or enter a desired file name)*

(Mastercam will automatically enter the file extension DXF to the file.)

The car drawing appearing on screen is in the top view as shown in Figure 10.6.

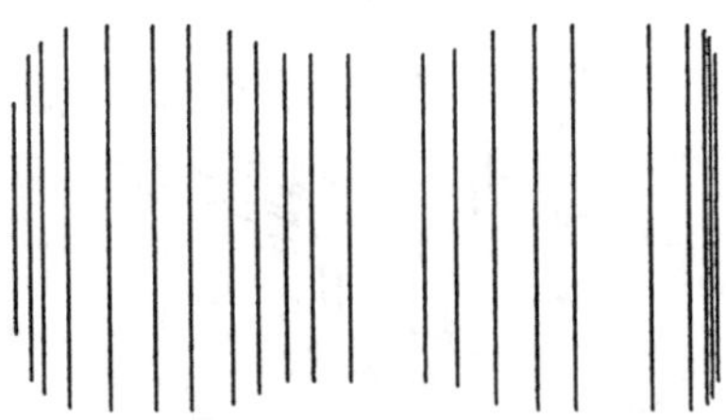

Figure 10.6

Step 2. Change Gview to isometric view.

Select **Gview → Isometric**

Press **Alt + F1** to fit the drawing on screen. The car drawing in isometric view will appear as in Figure 10.7 .

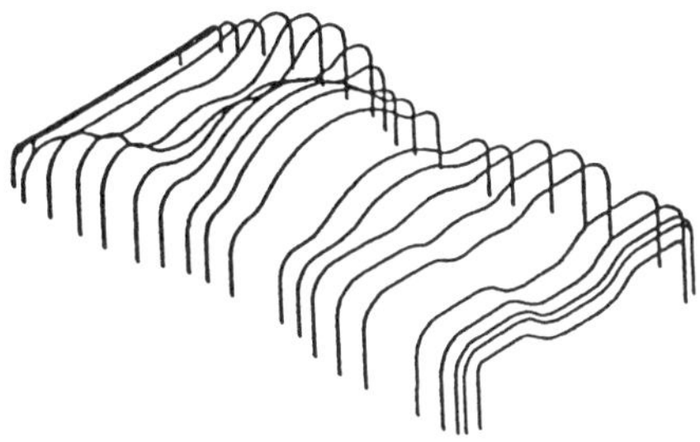

Figure 10.7

Project 3. 3

Transfer a 3D drawing file to AutoCAD R.12 using the IGES utility

An existing geometry file (CALIPER.GE3) as shown in Figure 10.8 will be converted into an IGES file. This file is then imported into AutoCAD.

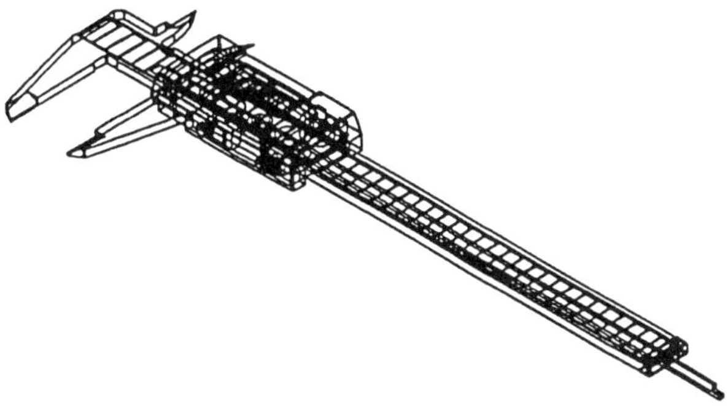

Figure 10.8

<u>To create an IGES file from Mastercam</u>

Step 1. Load the geometry file CALIPER.GE3.

Select **MAIN MENU → File → Get**
Enter file name: **caliper ←**
Select **Yes** to delete the current part

The caliper drawing should appear on screen as Figure 10.9 on the next page.

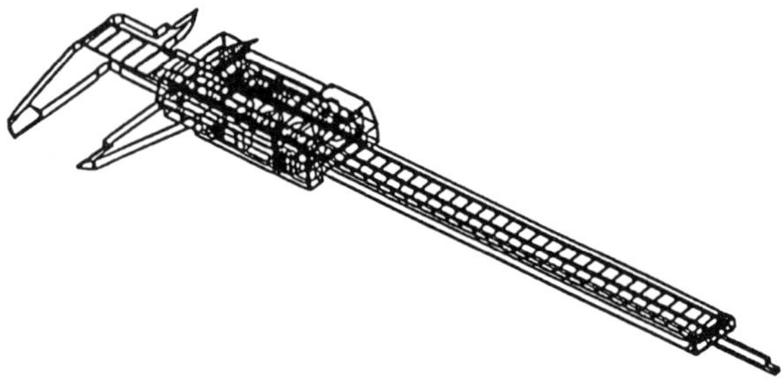

Figure 10.9

Step 2. Initiate the convert utility.

Select **MAIN MENU → File → conVert → IGES → Write file**
Enter file name: **B:\CALIPER ←** *(or enter a desired file name)*
(Mastercam will automatically enter the file extension IGS to the file.)
Enter a comment: ←

<u>To receive an IGES file from AutoCAD</u>

To receive an IGES file in AutoCAD, begin a new drawing. Then execute the IGESIN commands as list below.

Step 1. Initiate IGESIN function.

Command: **IGESIN ←**
(A pop-up dialogue box will ask for the IGES file name.)
File name: **B:\CALIPER ←** *(or enter a desired file name)*
(AutoCAD will use the default file extension as IGS.)

The caliper drawing should appear in the top view as in Figure 10.10.

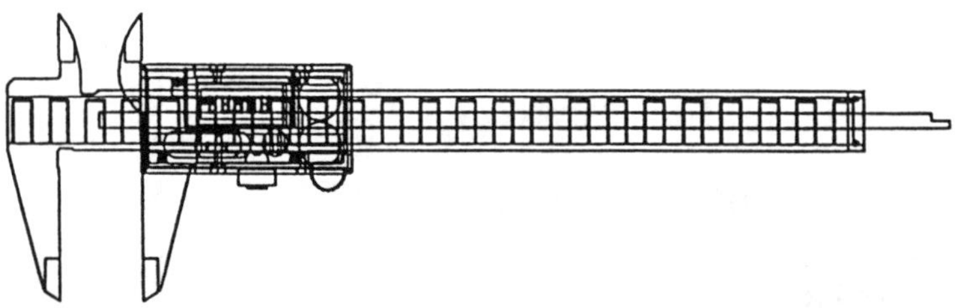

Figure 10.10

Step 2. Display the drawing in isometric view.

Command: **VPOINT** ←
Rotate/(View point): **1,-1,1** ←

The caliper drawing now appears in the isometric view as shown in Figure 10.11.

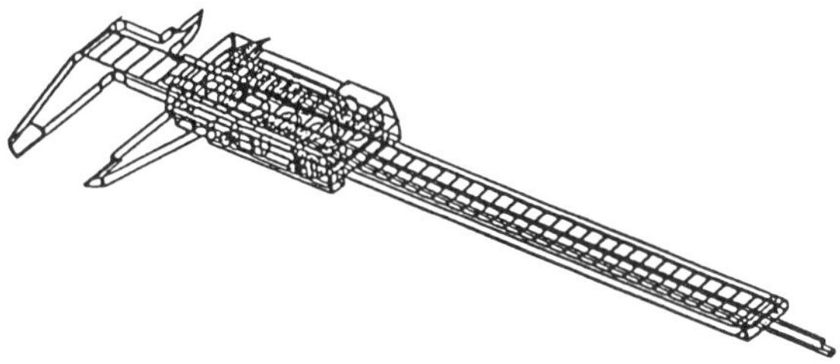

Figure 10.11

Step 3. Save this drawing as CALIPER.

Command: SAVE ←
(A pop-up dialogue box will ask for the drawing file name)
File: **CALIPER** ←

Note: During IGES transfer, NURB and trimmed surfaces are not converted.

Project 4. 4

Transfer a 3D drawing file from AutoCAD R.12 using the IGES utility

The caliper drawing we imported into AutoCAD with the IGESIN command as described in project 3 becomes a DWG file. In this project, we use the same caliper drawing in AutoCAD but save it to an IGES format. This file is then read in Mastercam.

<u>To create an IGES file from AutoCAD</u>

Step 1. Load the caliper drawing CALIPER.

Command: OPEN ←
(A pop-up dialogue box will ask for the drawing file name)
File: **CALIPER** ←

Step 2. Initiate the IGESOUT function.

Command: IGESOUT ←
(A pop-up dialogue box will ask for the IGES file name.)
File name: **B:\IGESTEST** ← *(or enter a desired file name)*
(AutoCAD will enter the default file extension IGS.)

To receive an IGES file from Mastercam

Step 1. Initiate the convert utility.

Select **MAIN MENU → File → conVert → IGES → Read file**
Enter file name: **B:\IGESTEST ←** *(or enter a desired file name)*
(Mastercam will automatically use the file extension IGS for the file.)

The caliper drawing shown in the top view should appear as in Figure 10.12.

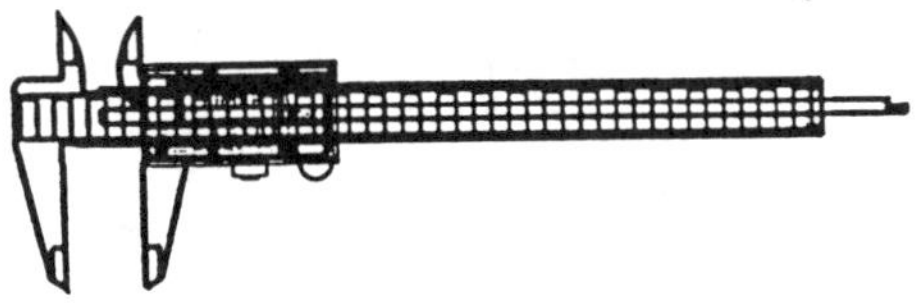

Figure 10.12

Step 2. Change Gview to isometric view.

Select **Gview → Isometric**

Press **Alt** + **F1** to fit the drawing on screen. The drawing shown in isometric view should resemble Figure 10.13.

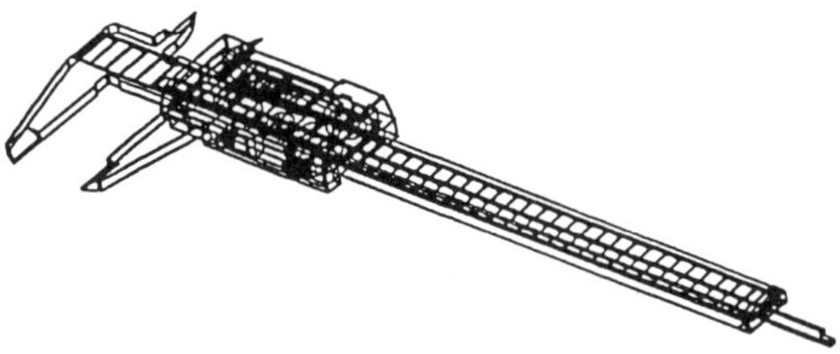

Figure 10.13

Project 5.

Transfer a 3D drawing file to CADKEY 7.0 using CADL utility.

An existing file (DIMENSION.GE3) as shown in Figure 10.14 is used to convert into a CADL file. This file is then used in the CADKEY system. Since the CADL does not transfer dimensions, we need to delete all the dimensions from the drawing.

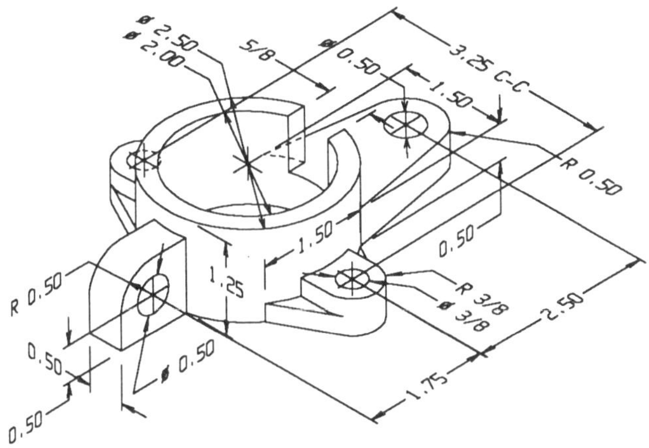

Figure 10.14

To create a CADL file from Mastercam

Step 1. Load the geometry file DIMENSION.GE3.

Select **MAIN MENU → File → Get**
Enter file name: **c:\mill5\ge3\dimension** ←
Select **Yes** to delete the current part

Select **MAIN MENU → Delete → All →Drafting →Dimension**
The part drawing should appear on screen as Figure 10.15.

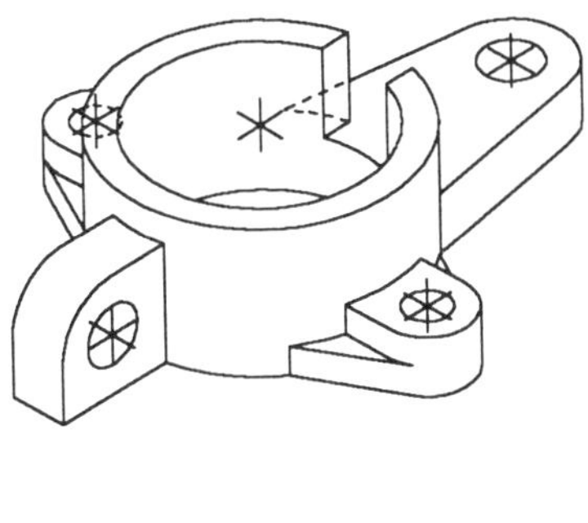

Figure 10.15

Step 2. Initiate the convert utility.

Select **MAIN MENU → File → conVert → CADL → Write file**
Enter file name: **B:\CADLTEST ←** *(or enter a desired file name)*
(Mastercam will automatically enter the file extension CDL to the file.)

To receive a CADL file from CADKEY

In CADKEY, the following commands allow you to read-in an ASCII-format CADL file, stores drawing primitives and entities and execute CADL commands.

Step 1. Initiate CADL function.

Select **FILES → CADL → EXECUTE**
Enter CADL file name: **B:\CADLTEST ←** *(or enter a desired file name)*

Note: If you would like CADKEY to list all the CADL files on the screen and select a particular CADL file for conversion, you can issue the following commands:

Select **FILES → CADL → LIST/EXE**
Enter CADL directory pathname: **B:\ ←** *(or enter a desired pathname)*

The part drawing should appear in the top view. Select **ESCAPE → DISPLAY →ZOOM → AUTO** to see the complete drawing as in Figure 10.16.

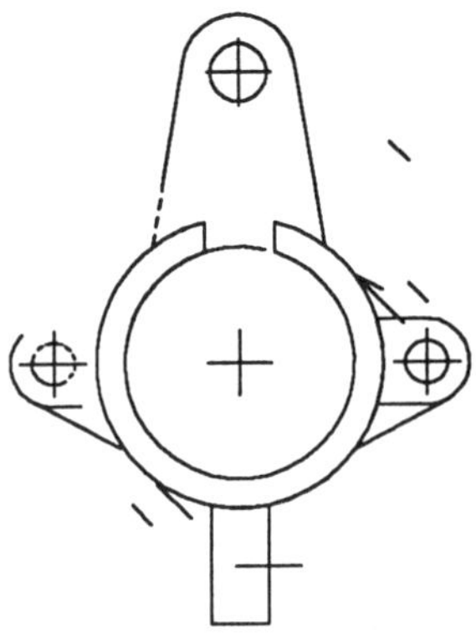

Figure 10.16

Step 2. Display the drawing in isometric view.

Select **VIEW = 1** in the status window
Enter view number or choose menu option (1-10): **7**
Select **ESCAPE →DISPLAY →ZOOM → AUTO**

The part drawing should appear in isometric view as in Figure 10.17 on the next page.

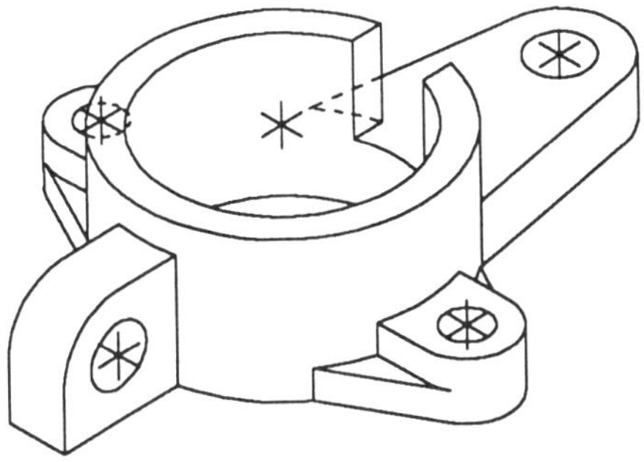

Figure 10.17

Note: During the CADL transfer, NURB and trimmed surfaces, dimensions and notes are not converted.

Step 3. Save this part drawing as CADTEST.

Select **ESCAPE → FILES → PART → SAVE**
Enter part file name to save: **CADTEST**

Project 6. 6

Transfer a 3D drawing file from CADKEY 7.0 using the CADL utility.

The part drawing we imported to CADKEY through CADL commands as described in project 5 becomes a PRT file. In this project, we use the same part drawing in CADKEY but save it to the CADL format. This file is then read into Mastercam.

To create a CADL file from CADKEY

In CADKEY, the following commands allow you to write drawing entities into an ASCII-format CADL file.

Step 1. Load the part drawing file CADTEST.

Select **FILES → PART → LOAD → NO**
Enter part name to load: **CADTEST ←**

Step 2. Initiate the CADL function.

Select **ESCAPE → FILES → CADL → OUTPUT**
Enter CADL file name: **B:\CADLTEST ←** *(or enter a desired file name)*
Select **SELECT → ALL ENT → DONE**

To receive a CADL file from Mastercam

Step 1. Initiate the convert utility.

Select **MAIN MENU → File → conVert → CADL → Read file**
Enter file name: **B:\CADLTEST ←** *(or enter a desired file name)*
(Mastercam will automatically use the default file extension CDL to retrieve the file.)

The part drawing appearing on screen is in the top view as shown in Figure 10.18.

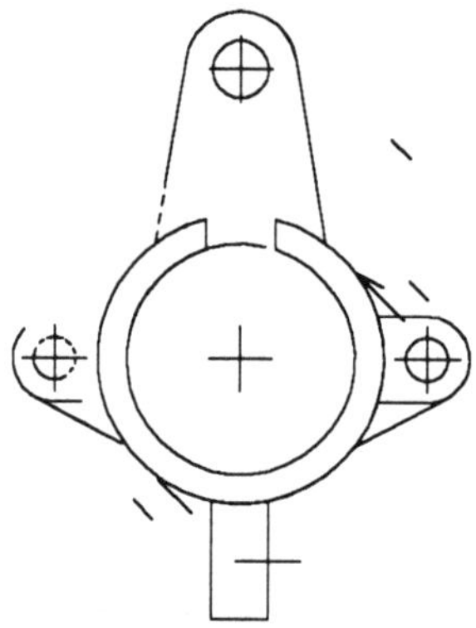

Figure 10.18

Step 2. Change the drawing to isometric view.

Select **Gview → Isometric**

Press **Alt** + **F1** to fit the drawing on screen. The drawing in isometric view should look like Figure 10.19.

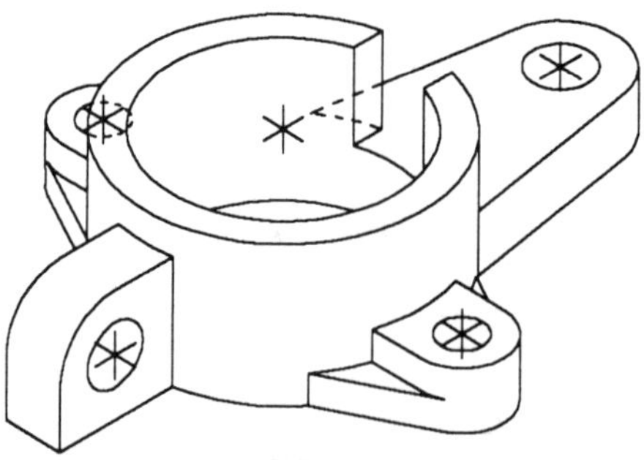

Figure 10.19

10.3 Exercises

1. How many file conversion utilities are available for Mastercam?
2. What is the name of the utility used to transfer files to/from AutoCAD?
3. What is the name of the utility used to transfer files to/from Mastercam?
4. What is the US standard for transfering drawing files between CAD/CAM systems?
5. What are the two most common file formats used to transfer drawings between different CAD/CAM systems?
6. List four entity types that can be transferred between Mastercam and AutoCAD using the DXF utility.
7. List an entity type that cannot be transferred by Mastercam using the IGES utility.

Part II. 3D Toolpaths

Chapter 11

Constructing 3D Wireframe Models

Objectives:

1. Understand the features of wireframe models and surface models.
2. Know the basic elements of the surface edge profiles.
3. Select proper construction planes.
4. Use proper Z depth control.
5. Construct wireframe models.

Overview

This chapter presents important concepts and techniques in constructing wireframe models for 3D surfaces. Features of different wireframe models and surface models are included. The success in constructing a wireframe model depends on the user's ability to create profile elements, use construction planes and Z-depth control. In some cases only a partial wireframe model is needed to generate surfaces.

Sixteen examples are presented to show how the edge profiles of the surfaces are constructed. These examples are arranged in an increasing order of difficulty. They are so designed that new techniques are added in each succeeding example. These examples are used in the later chapters for creating various types of surfaces and the toolpaths to produce the surfaces.

11.1 Wireframe Modeling Fundamentals

Wireframe Models

A wireframe model is normally required to create a surface. Wireframe models represent an object by defining its edges (Figure 11.1). It is impossible to completely define surfaces with wireframe models except for simple flat surfaces. Wireframe models cannot be directly used in generating 3D surface tool paths, however, they are used as surface boundaries and cross-sectional features for developing surface models.

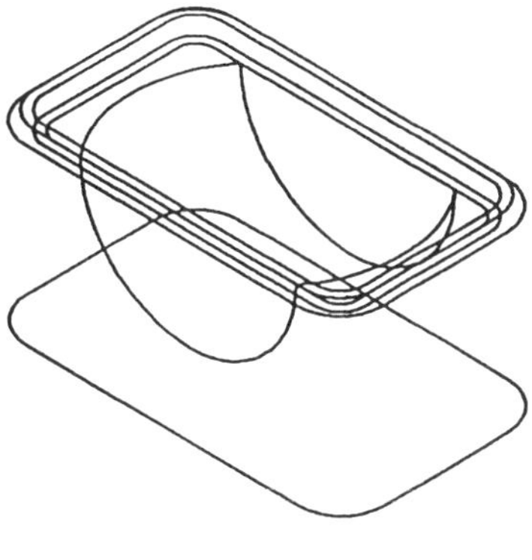

Figure 11.1

Surface Models

Surface models define surfaces, including the edges of each surface. They take the modeling of an object one step further than wireframe models. They show not only the edges of surfaces, but also the shapes. Surface models can be directly used to create a toolpath for machining surfaces. They provide more information, and can be edited and shaded. However, surface models provide no information about the weight of the workpiece. Figure 11.2 shows the surface model of its wireframe counterpart shown in Figure 11.1.

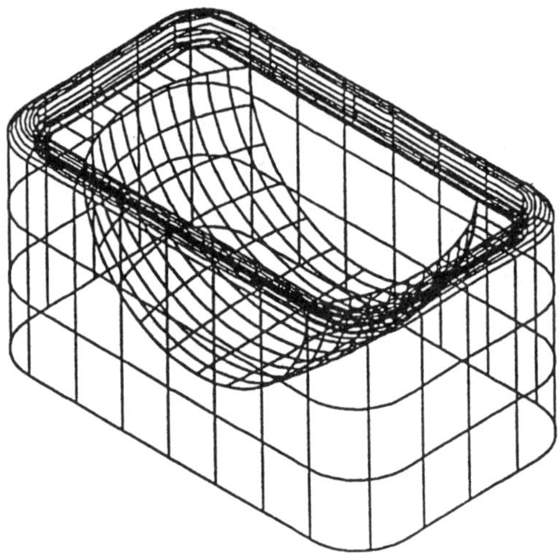

Figure 11.2

Profile Elements of Surfaces

Primitive geometric elements are normally used to form the surface edge profiles or boundaries. They include lines, arcs, splines, and ellipses (Figure 11.3). Figure 11.4 is an example in which wireframe boundaries and cross-sectional features of surfaces are defined by smooth profiles created by using these basic profile elements.

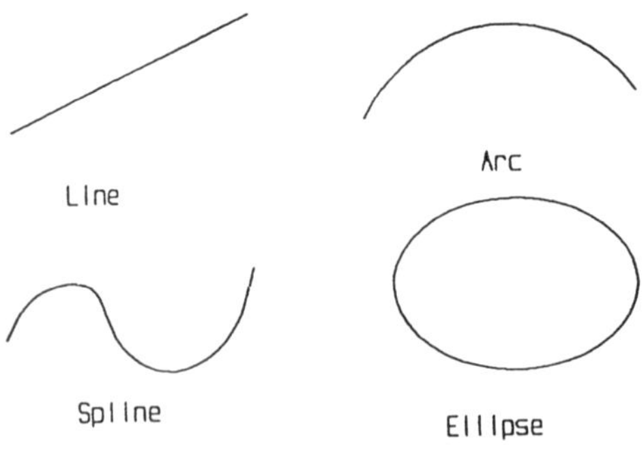

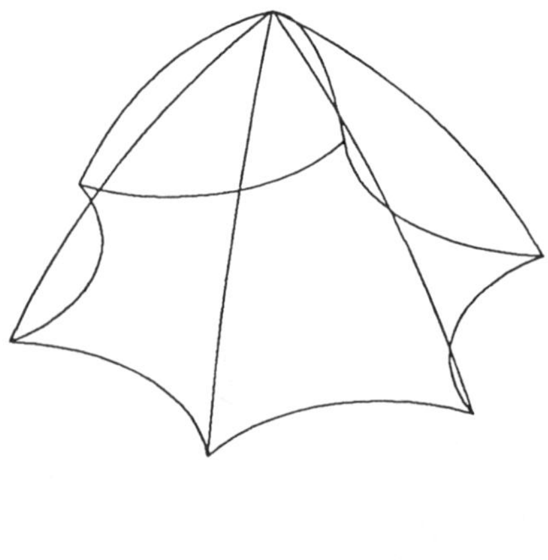

Figure 11.3

Figure 11.4

Construction Plane

A construction plane determines a plane orientation in which a geometric entity is to be placed. An arc, for example, can be constructed on a plane either parallel to the principal XY-, ZX-, or YZ-plane depending on which construction plane is chosen. A construction plane must be specified **before** any geometric entity can be created in a CAD system. Mastercam provides the following **six standard construction planes**:

- Top Cplane
- Front Cplane
- Side Cplane
- 3D Cplane
- 2-Line Cplane
- Normal Cplane

Figure 11.5 shows the axis orientations of the **three** principal construction planes: top, front, and side. The axis orientations for the Top construction plane are the most familiar. Note that the axis assignments are changed when the construction plane is changed to the front or side. The keys to determine the axis orientation for each plane are as follows:

- The X axis is always in the horizontal direction when viewed from the direction normal to the selected plane.
- The Y axis is in the vertical direction on the selected plane.
- The Z axis is perpendicular to both the X and Y axes.

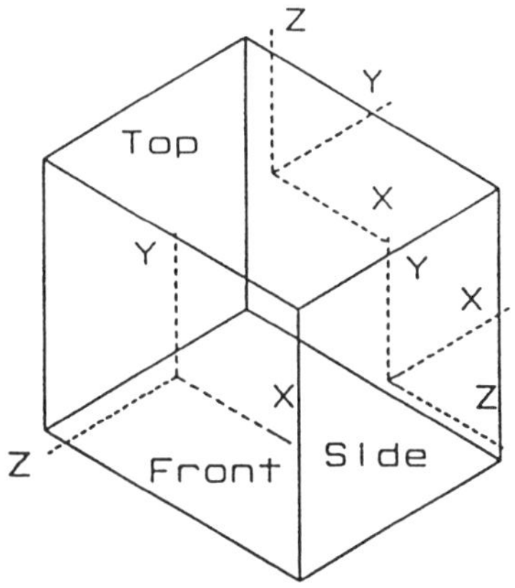

Figure 11.5

The 3D Cplane has similar axis designations to that of the Top plane. The only difference is that it allows lines to be constructed at any two specified endpoints which do not necessarily lie parallel to any one of three principal planes (Figure 11.6).

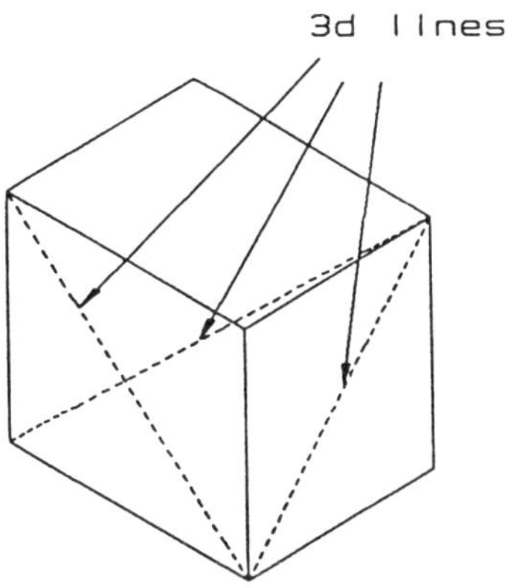

Figure 11.6

2-line Plane

Any two perpendicular lines in the space can be used to define a construction plane. The first line you pick is designated as the X axis and the second picked line becomes the Y axis. The Z axis is perpendicular to both X and Y axes (Figure 11.7).

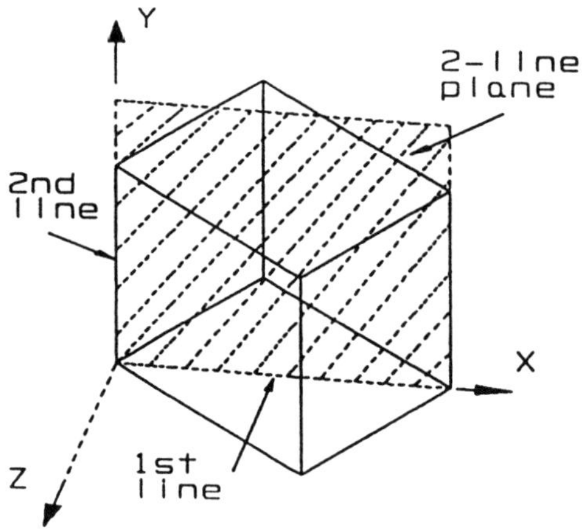

Figure 11.7

Normal Plane

A normal plane is defined by being normal (or perpendicular) to a given line at the selected point (Figure 11.8). An example of using a normal plane is illustrated in Figure 11.9. Two arcs are created using the normal plane which is perpendicular to the given line. These two arcs are located at both ends of the line.

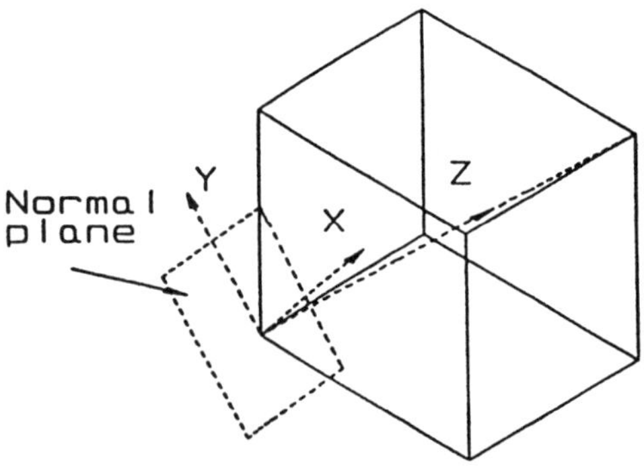

Figure 11.8

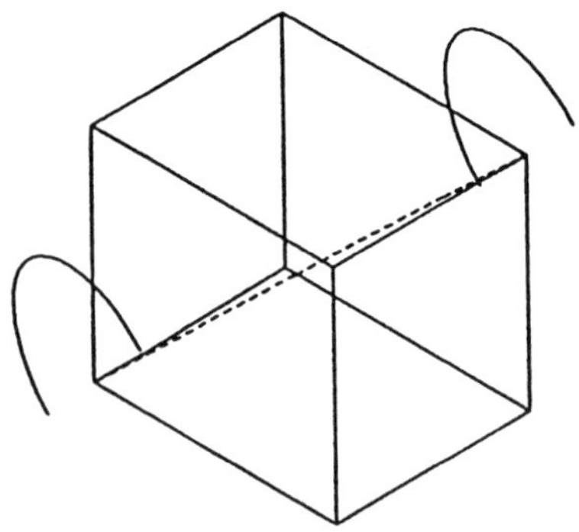

Figure 11.9

Z-Depth Control

The Mastercam system uses the Z command in the Secondary Menu to specify the Z value of the geometric entities. Figure 11.10 illustrates how to specify the Z value to properly place the construction plane in a location.

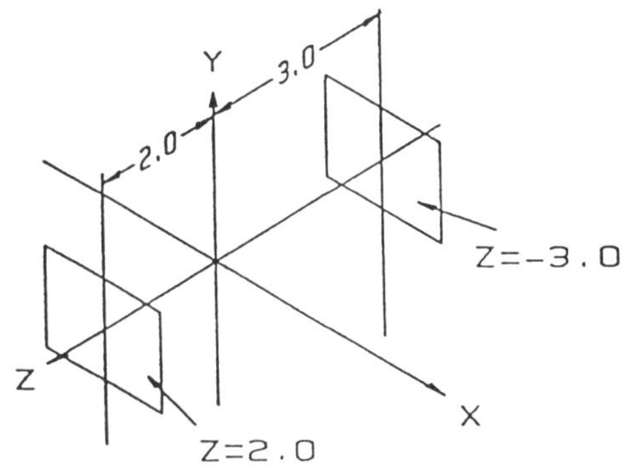

a. Front Cplane

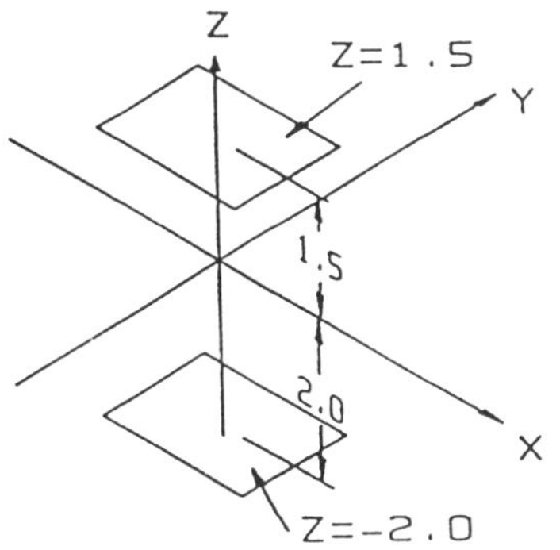

b. Top Cplane

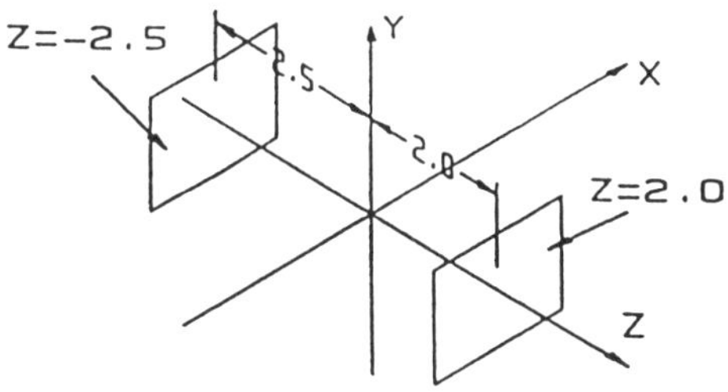

c. Side Cplane

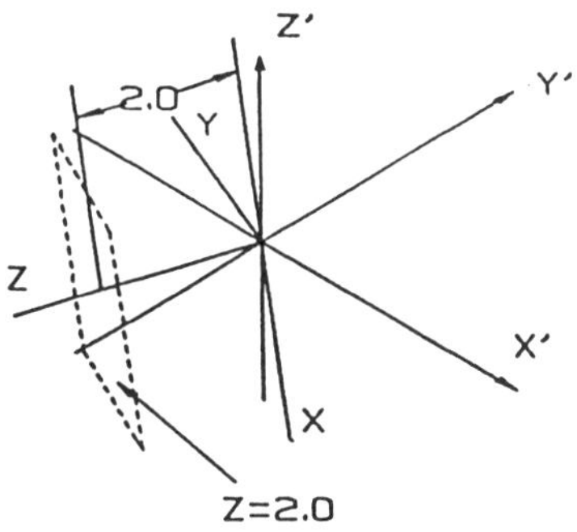

d. Normal Cplane

Figure 11.10

11.2 Wireframe Model Construction Examples

There are sixteen projects presented in this chapter. Each project gives a step-by-step procedure to complete the wireframe model. Only a partial wireframe profile is given in some projects. Useful tips for the edge profiles are provided for most projects. Each wireframe model is used to create the surface model and the toolpath to machine the surface in the following chapters.

Project 1:

In this project, you will learn to use **Front, Side, and 3d** construction planes to create 4 arcs and 2 lines as shown in Figure 11.11. These surface profile entities are then used to create two ruled surfaces and two fillet surfaces in chapters 12 and 13, respectively.

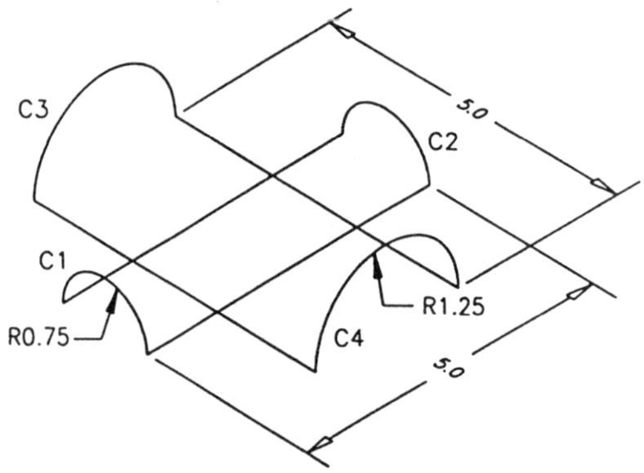

Figure 11.11a. Wireframe model

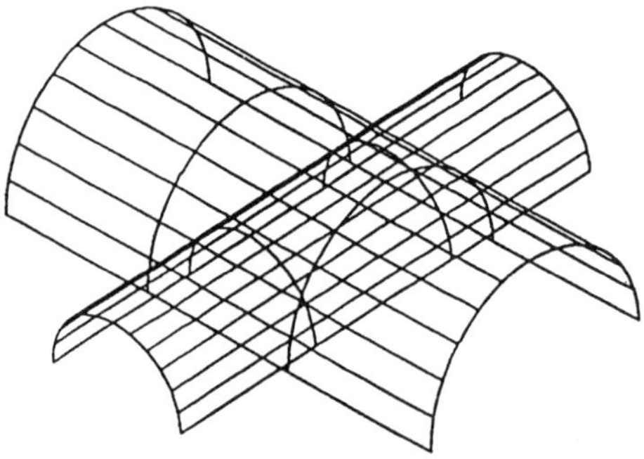

Figure 11.11b. Surface model

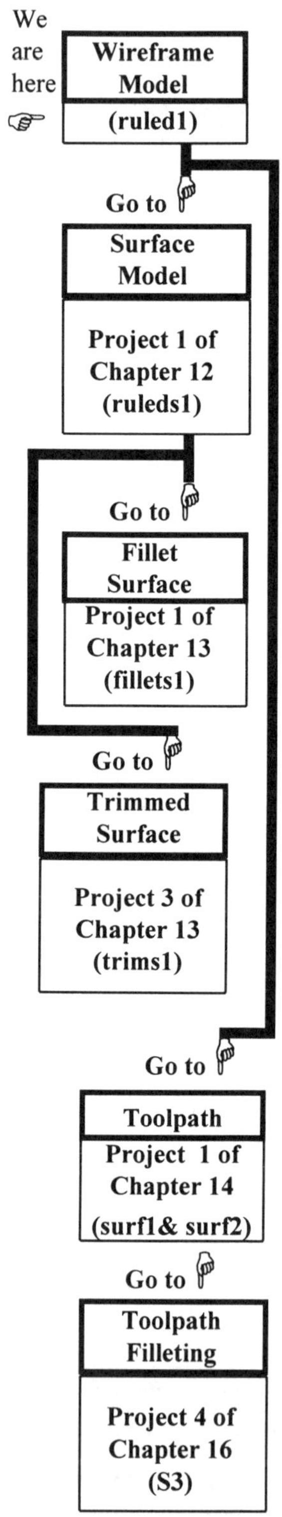

Tips

1. Use the Front Cplane to construct the two arcs of .75-in. radius. The front arc has a Z value of 2.5 and the rear arc has the same Z value of -2.5.
2. Use Side Cplane to create the two arcs of 1.25-in. radius. The right and left arcs have Z values of 2.5 and -2.5 respectively.
3. Use 3d Cplane to construct the four lines connecting the end points of the four arcs.

Step 1. Enter the Mastercam Mill.

Follow the procedure in chapter 3 to enter the Mastercam Mill. Press **F9** to show the coordinate axes on the screen

The screen should look like Figure 11.12, with MAIN MENU on the left side and three coordinate axes in the middle.

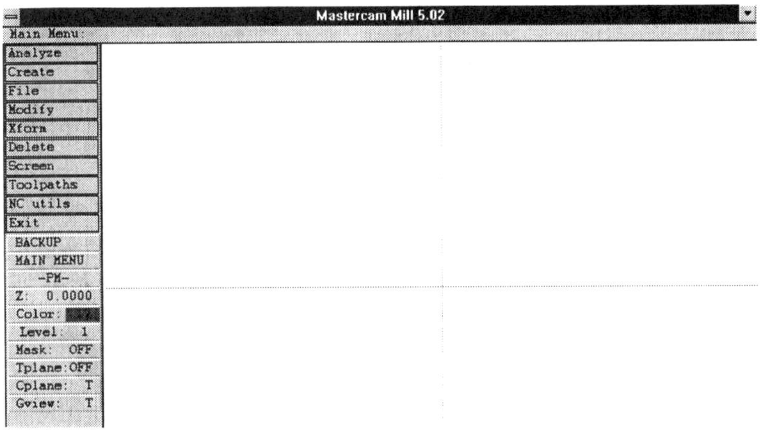

Figure 11.12

Step 2. Select front construction plane and isometric graphics view.

Select **Cplane** from the Secondary Menu,
then pick **Front** from the Cplane Menu
Select **Gview** from the Secondary Menu,
then pick **Isometric** from the Gview Menu

Step 3. Create the circle C1.

Select **Z** from the Secondary Menu, and then enter **2.5**
Select **MAIN MENU** → **Create** → **Arc** → **Polar** → **Ctr point**
Enter the center point: **0,0** ←
Enter the radius (1.0): **0.75** ←
Enter the initial angle (0.0): ← to accept the default
Enter the final angle (0.0): **180** ←

Step 4. Create the circle C2.

Select **Z** from the Secondary Menu, and then enter **-2.5** ←
Select **BACKUP** → **Ctr point**
Enter the center point: **0,0** ←
Enter the radius (0.75): ← to accept the default
Enter the initial angle (0.0): ←
Enter the final angle (180.0): ←

Your drawing should currently look like Figure 11.13.

Figure 11.13

Step 5. Create the circle C3 using the side construction plane.

Select **Cplane** from the Secondary Menu,
then pick **Side** from the Cplane Menu
Enter the center point: **0,0** ←
Enter the radius (0.75): **1.25** ←
Enter the initial angle (0.0): ← to accept the default
Enter the final angle (180.0): ← to accept the default

Step 6. Create the circle C4.

Select **Z** from the Secondary Menu, and then enter **2.5** ←
Enter the center point: **0,0** ←
Enter the radius (1.25): ←
Enter the initial angle (0.0): ← to accept the default
Enter the final angle (180.0): ← to accept the default

The drawing appears as in Figure 11.14.

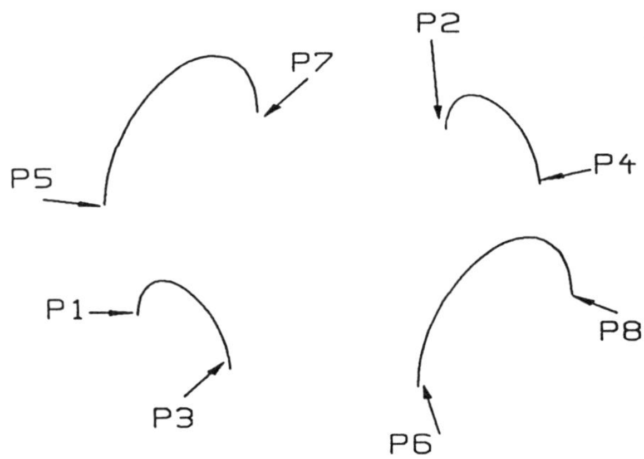

Figure 11.14

Step 7. Create four lines to connect those arcs using 3d construction plane.

Use the pick points in Figure 11.14.
Select **Cplane → 3d**
Select **MAIN MENU → Create → Line → Endpoints → Endpoint**
Specify the first endpoint: pick at **P1**
Specify the second endpoint: pick at **P2** to complete the first line
Sequentially pick at **P3, P4, P5, P6, P7,** and **P8** to complete the remaining three lines.

The complete drawing would look like Figure 11.15.

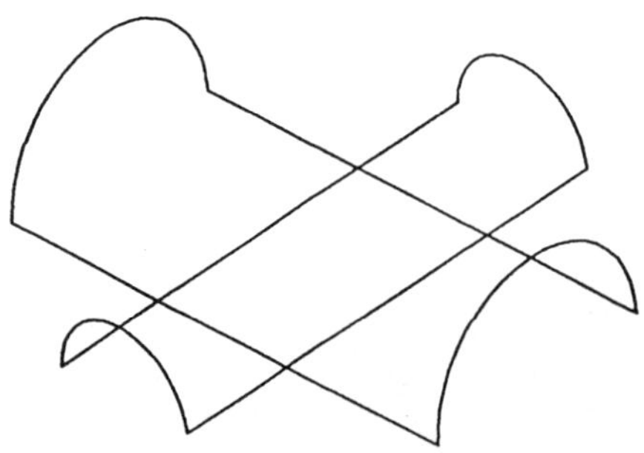

Figure 11.15

Step 8. Save the drawing (ruled1).

Select **MAIN MENU → File → Save**

Enter file name (C:\NC\GE3\T.GE3): **ruled1 ←**

Note: This drawing will be used in the following places:

1. For creating two ruled surfaces and two fillet surfaces in chapter 12.
2. For generating intersecting curves and trimming surfaces in chapter 13.

Project 2:

In this project, a normal construction plane is used to create two arcs that are perpendicular to a line. The drawing to be constructed is shown in Figure 11.16.

We are here ☞ **Wireframe Model (ruled2)** 2

Go to **Surface Model** **Project 2 of Chapter 12 (ruleds2)**

Go to **Fillet Surface** **Project 2 of Chapter 13 (fillets2)**

Go to **Trimmed Surface** **Project 4 of Chapter 13 (trims2)**

Go to **Toolpath** **Project 4 of Chapter 15 (trimst2)**

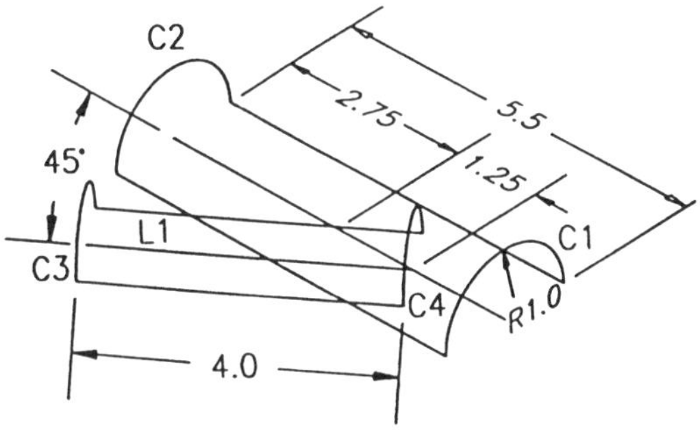

Figure 11.16a. Wireframe model

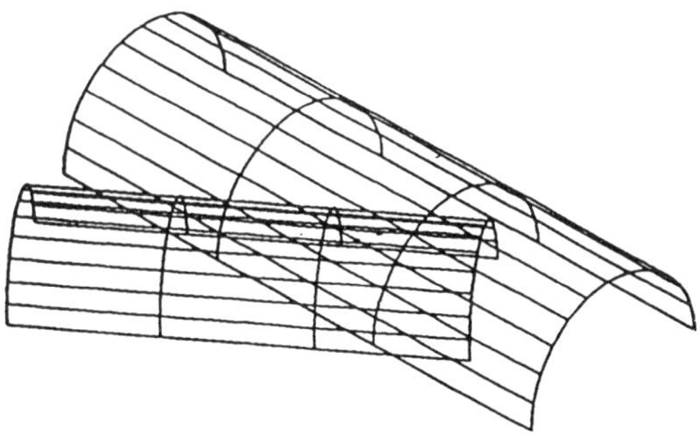

Figure 11.16b. Surface model

Tips 1. Use Side Cplane to construct two arcs of 1-in. radius. The right arc has a Z value of 2.75 and the left arc is located at Z-2.75.

2. Use the Top Cplane to create a line L1 which has a 45 degree angle with the X axis.
3. Define a normal plane which is perpendicular to line L1.
4. Use the Normal Cplane to create the two arcs that are perpendicular to the line L1. Use **Z → Endpoint** commands and pick at the front end of the angle line to obtain the Z value for the center of the arc.
5. Use 3d Cplane to generate four lines connecting the endpoints of the four arcs.

Step 1. Create the arc C1 using the side construction plane. First initialize the screen to begin a new start.

Select **MAIN MENU → Screen → Next Menu → Initialize → Yes**
Select **Cplane → Side**
Select **Gview → Isometric**
Select **Z** and then enter **2.75 ←**
Select **MAIN MENU → Create → Arc → Polar → Ctr point**
Enter the center point: **0,0 ←**
Enter the radius (1.0): **1.0 ←**
Enter the initial angle (0.0): ← to accept the default
Enter the final angle (360.0): **180 ←**

Step 2. Create the arc C2. .

Select **Z** and then enter **-2.75 ←**
Select **BACKUP → Ctr point**
Enter the center point: **0,0 ←**
Enter the radius (1.0): ←
Enter the initial angle (0.0): ←
Enter the final angle (180.0): ←
The drawing of two arcs should appear as in Figure 11.17

Figure 11.17

Step 3. Create line L1 using the top construction plane.

Select **Cplane → Top**
Select **Z**, and then enter **0 ←**
Select **MAIN MENU → Create → Line → Polar**
Specify an endpoint: **1.25,0 ←**
Enter the angle in degrees (0.0): **215 ←**
Enter the line length (1.0): **4 ←**

The drawing now should look like Figure 11.18.

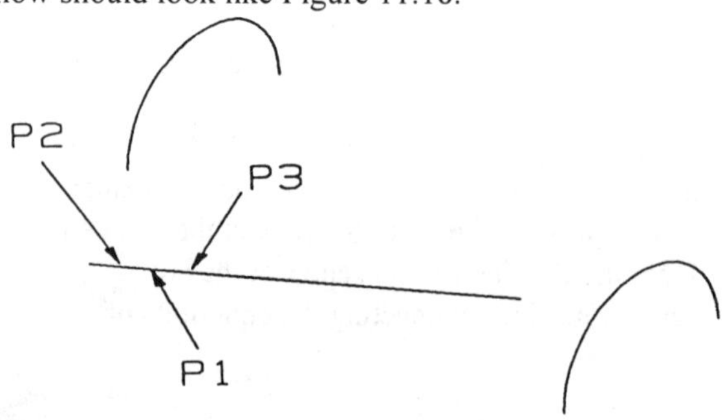

Figure 11.18

Step 4. Create arc C3 using the normal construction plane. Use the pick points labeled in Figure 11.18.

Select **Cplane → nOrmal**
Select the normal line: pick at **P1** ←
Select plane: pick **Save**
Select **Z**, and then select **Endpoint** from the point menu
Pick at **P2** to trap the endpoint
Select **MAIN MENU → Create → Arc → Polar → Ctr point → Endpoint**
Enter the center point: pick at **P3** ←
Enter the radius (1.0): **0.75** ←
Enter the initial angle (0.0): **180** ←
Enter the final angle (0.0): **0** ←

Your drawing should appear as in Figure 11.19.

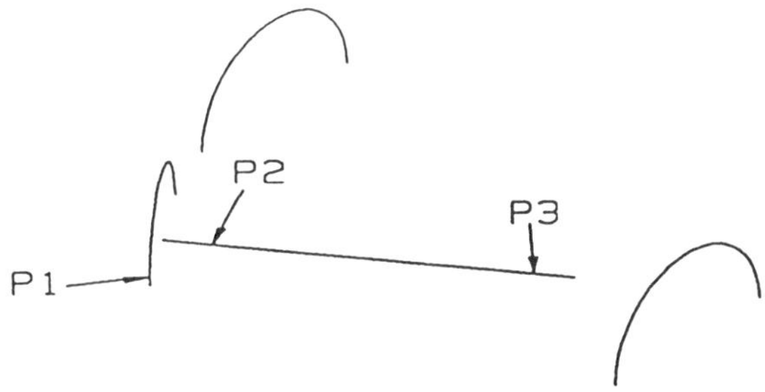

Figure 11.19

Step 5. Create the arc C4 using the transformation command. Use the pick points in Figure 11.19 on the previous page.

Select **Cplane → 3d**
Select **MAIN MENU → Xform → Translate → Entity**
Select an entity: pick at **P1**
Select **BACKUP → Done → Between pts →Endpoint**
Enter the point to translate from: pick at **P2**
Enter the point to translate to : pick at **P3**
Set the parameters as shown in the translate window ☞

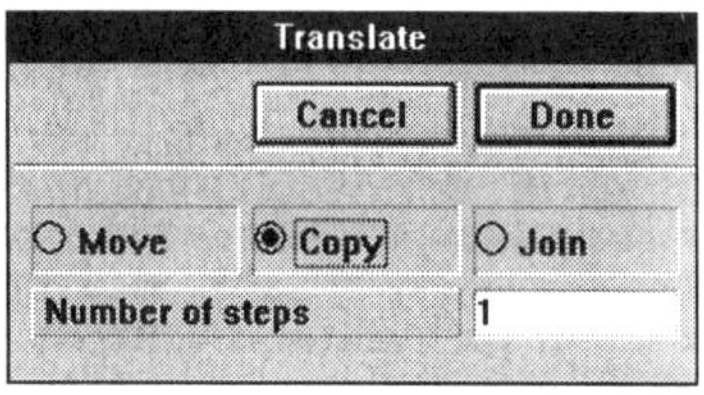

Select **Done**

The drawing with four arcs should look like Figure 11.20.

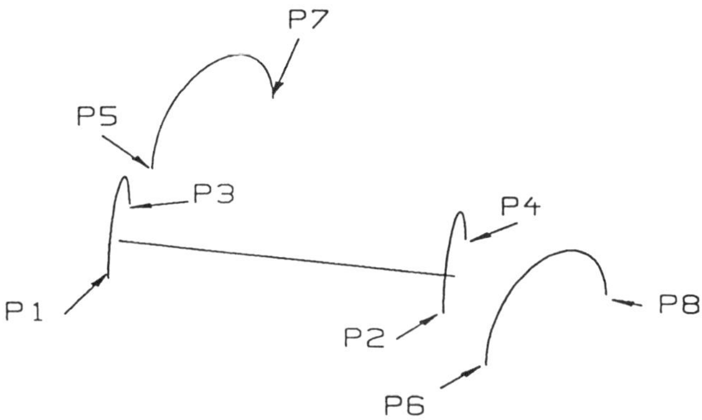

Figure 11.20

Step 6. Construct four lines. Use the pick points in Figure 11.20.

Select **MAIN MENU → Create → Line → Endpoints**
Specify the first end point: pick at **P1**
Specify the second endpoint: pick at **P2** to complete the first line.
Sequentially pick the entities at **P3 - P8** to complete the remaining three lines.

The complete drawing appears in Figure 11.21a.

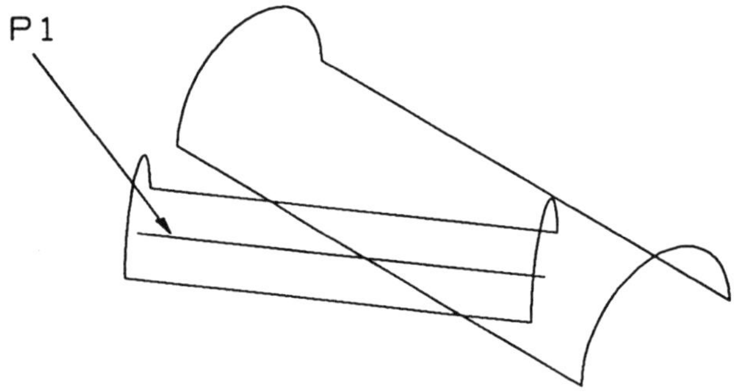

Figure 11.21a

Step 7. Delete the construction line using the pick point in Figure 11.21a.

Select **MAIN MENU → Delete**
Pick at **P1** to delete the construction line.
The complete drawing should look like Figure 11.21b.

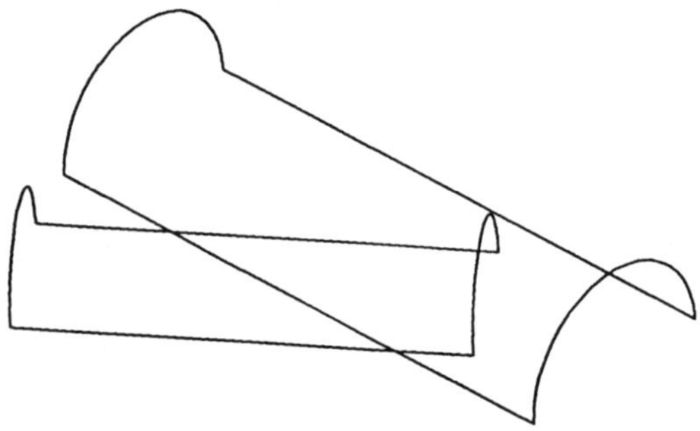

Figure 11.21b

Step 8. Save the drawing ruled2.

Select **MAIN MENU → File → Save**
Enter file name (C:\NC\GE3\T.GE3): **ruled2** ←

Note: This drawing is used to generate ruled surfaces, and fillet surfaces with a 2variable radius in chapter 11.

Project 3:

In this project three entities are constructed at three different Z levels as shown in Figure 11.22. These three entities will be used to create a ruled surface and a loft surface, respectively, in chapter 12.

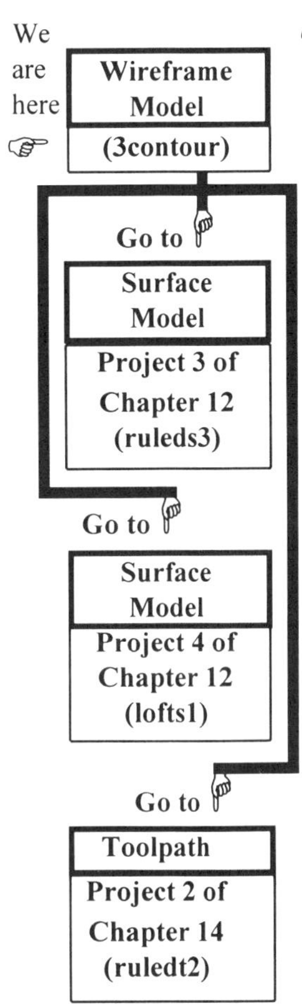

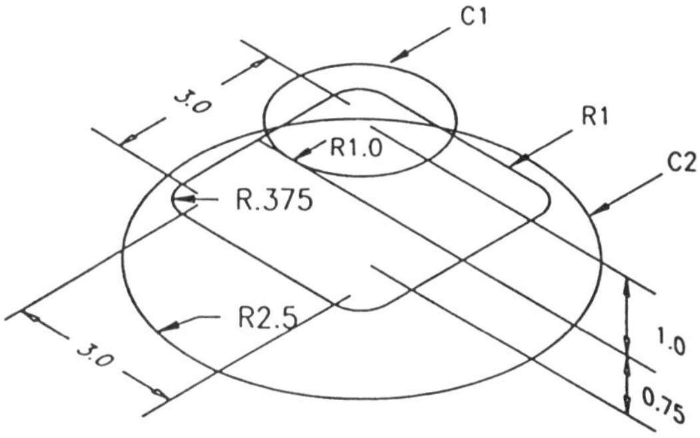

Figure 11.22a. Wireframe model

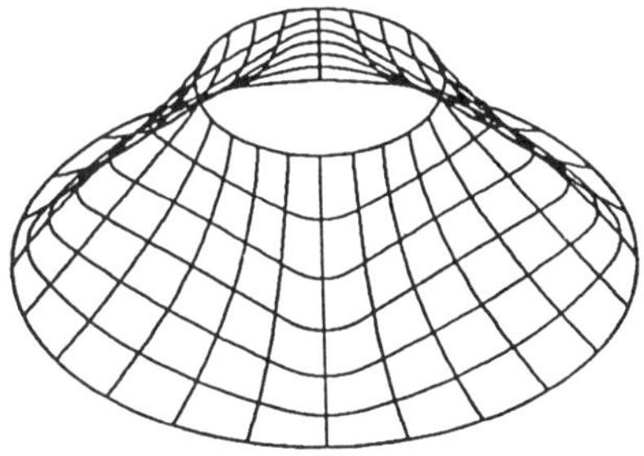

Figure 11.22b. Surface model

Step 1. Create the circle C1 using the Top construction plane.

Initialize the screen if necessary
Select **Cplane** → **Top** to select the top construction plane
Select **Gview** → **Isometric** to select the isometric graphics view
Select **Z**, and then enter **0** ← if necessary
Select **MAIN MENU** → **Create** → **Arc** → **pt Rad cir**
Enter the center point: **0,0** ←
Enter the radius (0.0): **1.0** ←

Step 2. Create the rectangle R1.

Select **Z**, and then enter **-1.0** ←
Select **MAIN MENU** → **Create** → **Rectangle** → **1 point**
Enter the lower left corner: **-1.5,-1.5** ←
Enter the width (2.0): **3** ←
Enter the height (1.0): **3** ←

Your drawing should appear as Figure 11.23.

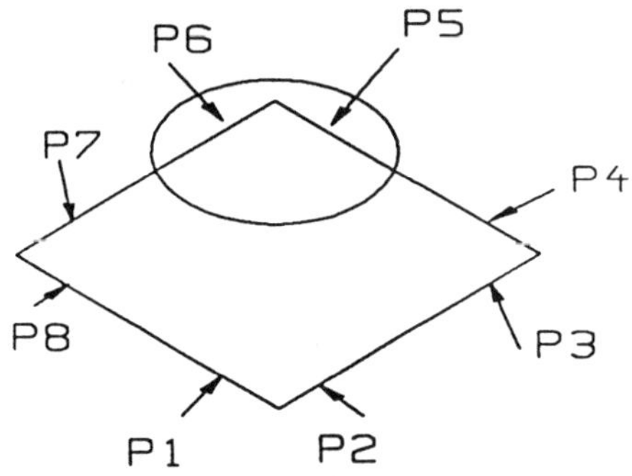

Figure 11.23

Step 3. Add fillets to the four corners of the rectangle. Use the pick points in Figure 11.23.

Select **MAIN MENU → Modify → Fillet**

Pick **Radius** from the parameter menu

Enter the fillet radius: **0.375 ←**

Select an entity: pick the entity sequentially as shown in Figure 11.23.

The four fillets are shown in Figure 11.24.

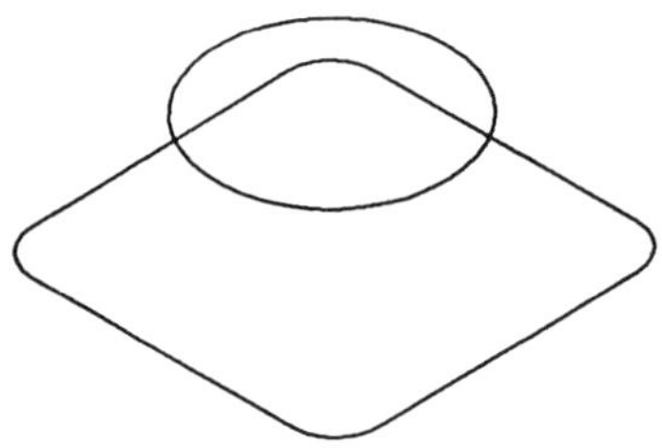

Figure 11.24

Step 4. Create the arc C2.

Select **Z**, and then enter **-1.75 ←**

Select **MAIN MENU → Create → Arc → pt Rad cir**

Enter the center point: **0,0 ←**

Enter the radius (1.0): **2.5 ←**

Your drawing would appear as Figure 11.25.

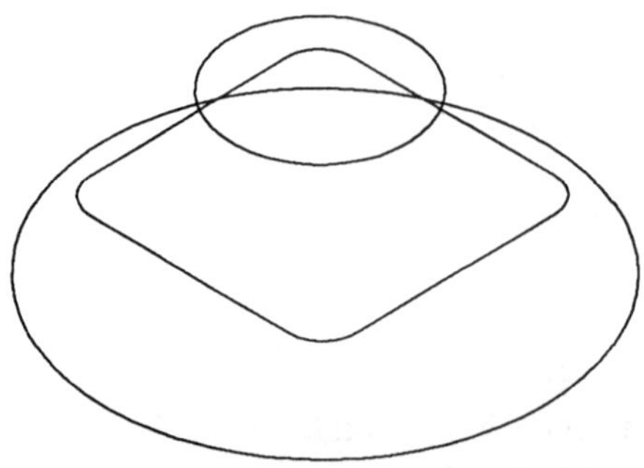

Figure 11.25

Step 5. Save the drawing using the name: 3contour.

Select **MAIN MENU → File → Save**

Enter the file name: **3contour** ←

Note: This drawing is used to create a ruled surface with three defining contours. It is also used to generate a loft surface in chapter 12.

Project 4:

In this example, ninteen elliptical contours are created in the side construction plane (Figure 11.26). The first and the last contours are rotated by 90° and -90°, respectively, about their end points. The rotation of these two contours must be made by using the front construction plane. These cross-sectional contours are the ideal case for creating a **loft surface.**

We are here ☞

Wireframe Model
(loft2)

Go to

Surface Model
Project 5 of Chapter 12 (lofts2)

Go to

Trimmed Surface
Project 5 of Chapter 13 (trims3)

Go to

Toolpath
Project 3 of Chapter 14 (loftt)

4

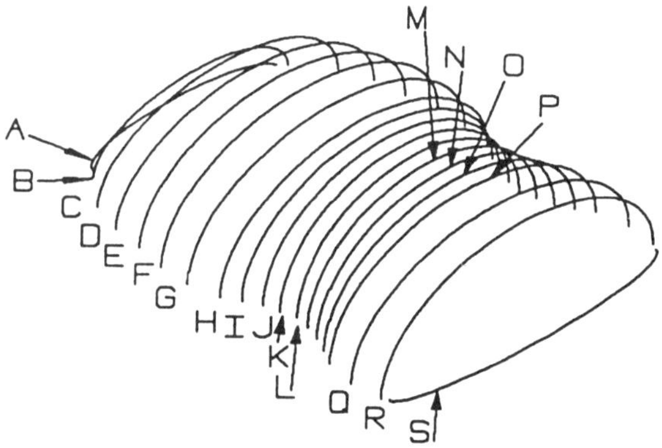

a. Wireframe model

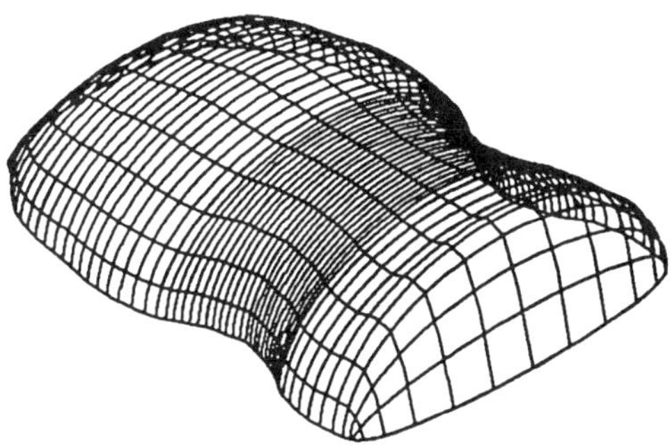

b. Surface model
Figure 11.26

The section position (Z coordinate in the side construction plane) and the axis radii of these elliptical contours at each section are tabulated below.

Section	Z-value	Major axis radius (a)	Minor axis radius (b)
A	0.2	0.8	0.2
B	0.25	0.875	0.375
C	0.5	1.083	0.563
D	0.75	1.167	0.638
E	1.0	1.2	0.7
F	1.25	1.25	0.75
G	1.5	1.25	0.75
H	1.75	1.2	0.75
I	1.875	1.125	0.75
J	2.0	1.063	0.75
K	2.125	1.03	0.75
L	2.25	1.0	0.75
M	2.375	1.03	0.75
N	2.5	1.06	0.75
O	2.625	1.125	0.75
P	2.75	1.2	0.75
Q	3.0	1.25	0.75
R	3.25	1.25	0.75
S	3.3	1.2	0.2

⌛**Tips** 1. Use Side Cplane to construct all ninteen contours.

2. Contours A and S are rotated 90° and -90°, respectively, using the Front Cplane.

Step 1. Enter Mastercam. Set the Secondary Menu to the following settings:

Initialize the screen if necessary
Select **Z**, and then enter **0.2** ←
Select **Cplane** → **Side**
Select **Gview** → **Isometric**

Step 2. Construct the first contour A.

Select **MAIN MENU** → **Create** → **Curve** → **Ellipse**
Enter a (X axis radius) (2.00): **0.8** ←
Enter b (Y axis radius) (1.00): **0.2** ←
Enter the starting angle (0.00): to accept the default
Enter the final angle (360.00): **180** ←
Enter the rotation angle (0.00): ← to accept the default
Enter the center: **0,0** ←

The drawing with the contour A should appear as in Figure 11.27.

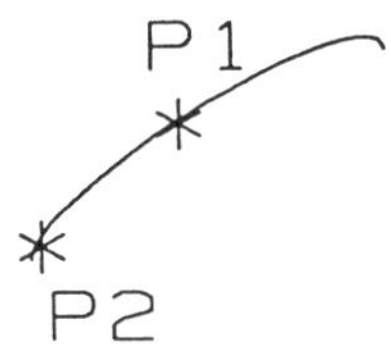

Figure 11.27

Step 3. Rotate the contour A by 90° using the Front construction plane.

Use the pick points of Figure 11.27.
Select **Cplane** → **Front**
Select **MAIN MENU** → **Xform** → **Rotate** → **Entity**
Pick at **P1** to select the entity
Select **BACKUP** → **Done** → **Point** → **Endpoint**
Pick at **P2** to select the endpoint of the ellipse
Set the Rotate parameters as below.

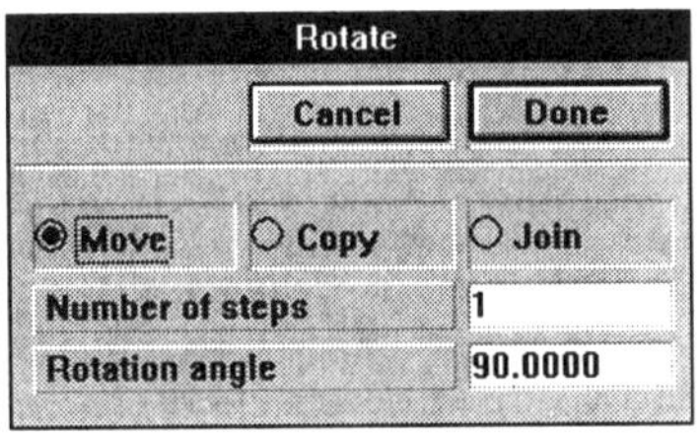

Select **Done**
The rotated ellipse contour should resemble Figure 11.28.

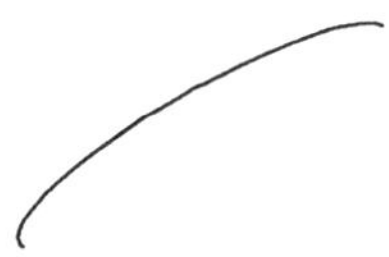

Figure 11.28

Step 4. Construct the second contour B using the side construction plane.

Select **Cplane** → **Side**
Select **Z**, and then enter **0.25** ←
Select **MAIN MENU** → **Create** → **Curve** → **Ellipse**
Enter a: **0.875** ←
Enter b: **0.375** ←
Enter the starting angle (0.00): → to accept the default
Enter the final angle (180.00): ← to accept the default
Enter the rotation angle (0.00); ← to accept the default
Enter the center: **0,0** ←

Step 5. Construct the remaining seventeen contours.

Repeat step 4 by using the Z value, X axis radius (a), and Y axis radius (b) given in the table on page 11-16 to complete the remaining contours.

The nineteen contours should appear as Figure 11.29.

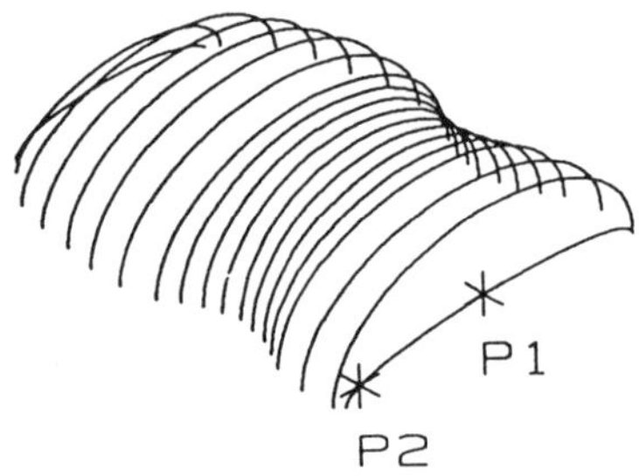

Figure 11.29

Step 6. Rotate the last contour S by -90° using the front construction plane. Use the pick points in Figure 11.29.

Select **Cplane → Front**
Select **MAIN MENU → Xform → Rotate → Entity**
Pick at **P1** to select the last contour **S** for rotation
Select **BACKUP → Done → Point → Endpoint**
Pick at **P2** to select the end point of the contour
Set the Rotate parameters as below:

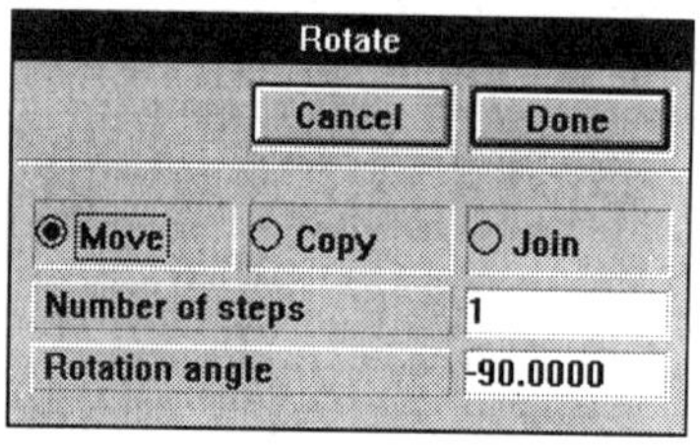

Select **Done** to complete the rotation.

Your final drawing should appear as Figure 11.30.

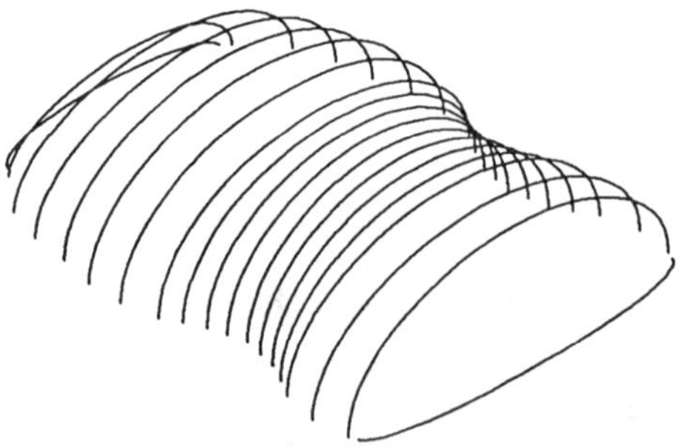

Tom 47

Figure 11.30

Step 7. Save the drawing using the filename loft2.

Select **MAIN MENU → File → Save**
Enter the file name: **loft2 ←**
Note: This drawing will be used to generate a loft surface in chapter 12.

Project 5:

A wireframe model consisting of four contours as shown in Figure 11.31 are created in this example. A rectangular box is constructed first in the top plane. Arcs C1 and C2 are created using the front plane, and the other two contours are generated using the side plane.

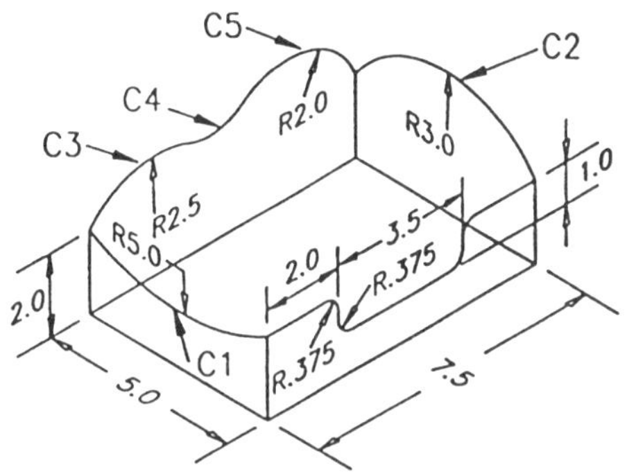

Figure 11.31a. Wireframe model

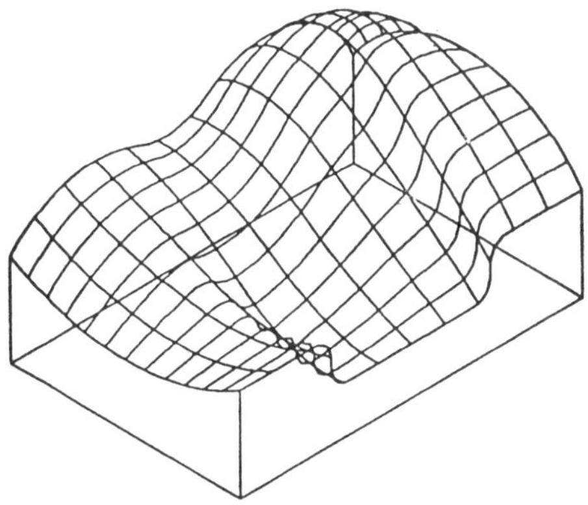

Figure 11.31b. Surface model

Tips 1. Create a rectangular box using Top Cplane.

2. Use Front Cplane to create arcs C1 and C2. Both arcs are defined by endpoints and radius.
3. Use Side Cplane to create the other two contours.

4. Generate three construction lines for creating the right contour.

5. Create a vertical construction line to help determine the endpoints of two base arcs in the left contour.

We are here

Wireframe Model
(coons1)

Go to

Surface Model
Project 7 of Chapter 12 (coonss1)

Go to

Toolpath
Project 4 of Chapter 14 (coonst1)

Go to

Surface Model
Project 8 of Chapter 12 (coonsst2)

Go to

Roughing Toolpath
Project 9 of Chapter 15 (rough)

Go to

Toolpath and Gouge Checking
Project 7 of Chapter 16 (GCF)

Step 1. Enter Mastercam Mill and set the Secondary Menu to the proper settings. Initialize the screen if necessary.

Select **Z**, and then enter **0** ← if necessary
Select **Cplane** → **Top** if necessary
Select **Gview** → **Isometric**

Step 2. Create a rectangular box.

Select **MAIN MENU** →**Create** → **Rectangular** → **2 points**
Enter **0,0** ← for the lower left corner
Enter **5,7.5** ← for the upper right corner
Press **Alt** + **F1** then **F2** to fit the drawing.
Select **MAIN MENU** → **Xform**
Select **Translate** → **All** → **Lines** → **Done** → **Rectang**
Enter the translation vector: **Z-2** ←
Set the parameters as below:

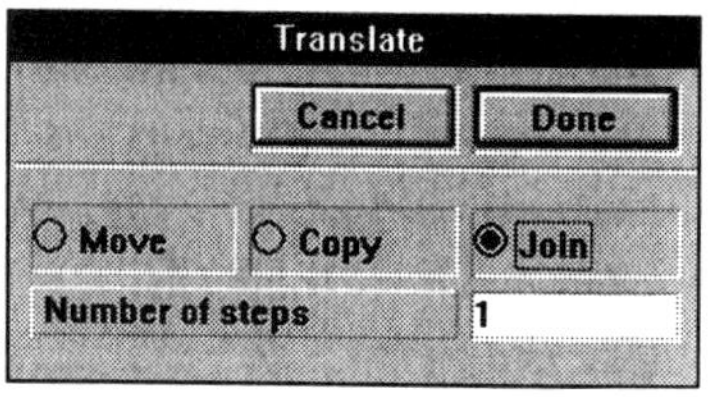

Select **Done**

The rectangular box should appear as Figure 11.32.

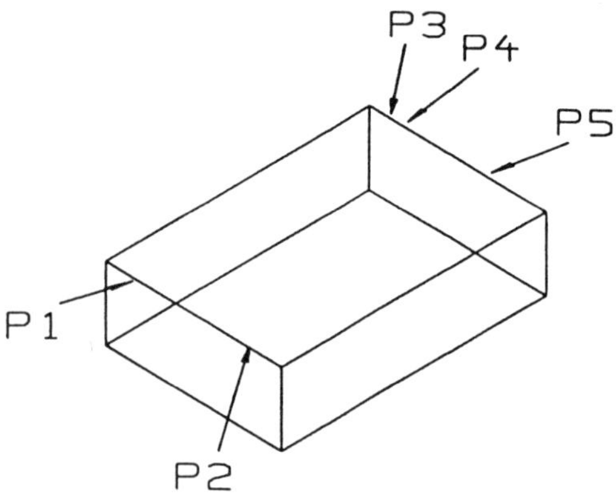

Figure 11.32

Step 3. Create the two arcs C1 and C2 using the front construction plane.

Use the pick points in Figure 11.32.
Select **Cplane** → **Front**
Select **MAIN MENU** →**Create** → **Arc** → **Endpoints** → **Endpoint**
Pick at **P1** and **P2**
Enter the radius (1.00): **5** ←
Four arc segments shall appear on the screen.
Use the mouse to pick the desired arc for C1 (3rd arc from the top).
Select **Z** → **Endpoint**
Pick at **P3** to trap to the endpoint of the selected line
Pick at **P4** and **P5** to trap the end points for the second arc
Enter the radius (5.00): **3** ←
Pick the desired arc (2nd arc from the top) to complete the arc C2

The drawing should look like Figure 11.33.

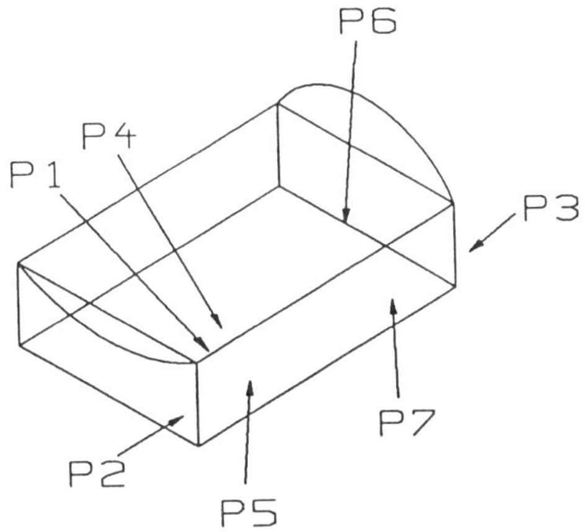

Figure 11.33

Step 4. Create three construction lines using pick points in Figure 11.33.

Select **Cplane → Side**
Select **Z → Endpoint**
Pick at **P1** to obtain the Z value of the picked line (Z5.00 should appear)
Select **MAIN MENU → Create → Line → Horizontal**
Pick at **P2** and **P3**, then enter **-1.0** for the Y coordinate
Select **BACKUP → Vertical**
Pick at **P4** and **P5**, then enter **2.0** for the X coordinate
Pick at **P6** and **P7**, then enter **5.5** for the X coordinate

The drawing should resemble Figure 11.34.

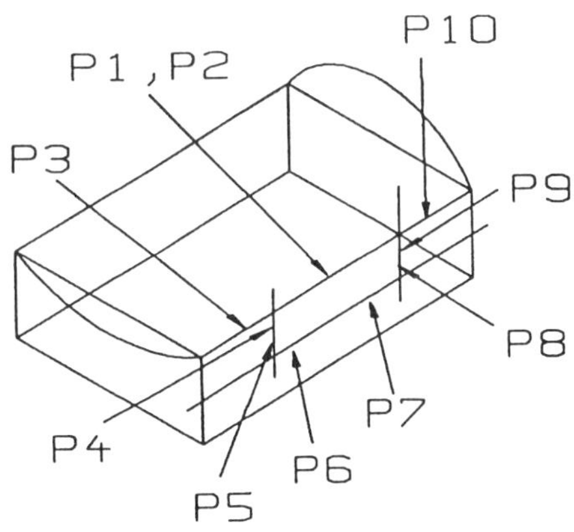

Figure 11.34

Step 5. Add four fillets. Use the pick points in Figure 11.34.

Select **MAIN MENU → Modify → Break → 2 pieces**
Pick at **P1** to select the entity to break
Pick at **P2** to enter the breakpoint
Select **MAIN MENU → Modify → Fillet → Radius**
Enter the fillet radius (0.25): **0.375** ←
Sequentially pick at **P3, P4, P5, P6, P7, P8, P9,** and **P10** to complete the four fillets.

The drawing should appear as Figure 11.35.

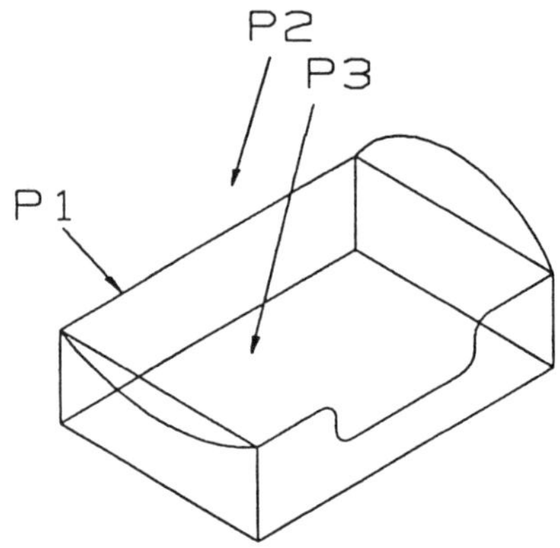

Figure 11.35

Step 6. Create a vertical construction line for creating the three arcs; C3, C4, and C5. Use the pick points in Figure 11.35.

Select **Z → Endpoint**
Pick at **P1** to set Z value (Z=0 should appear)
Select **MAIN MENU → Create → Line → Vertical**
Pick at **P2** and **P3**
Enter **3.75 ←** for the X coordinate

The vertical construction line should appear as Figure 11.36.

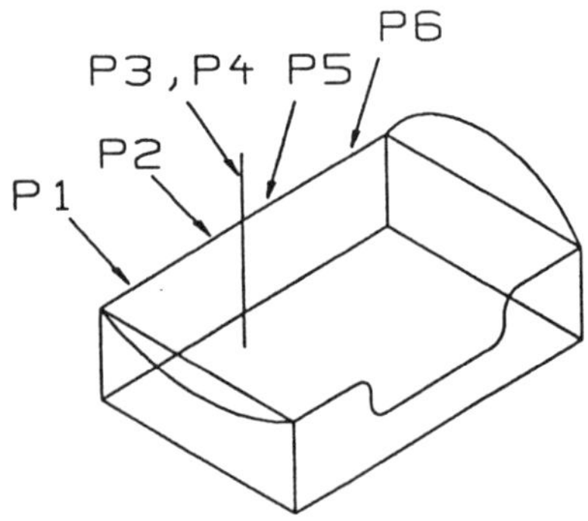

Figure 11.36

Step 7. Create two arcs C3 and C4. Use the pick points from Figure 11.36 .

Select **MAIN MENU → Create → Arc →Endpoints → Endpoint**
Pick at **P1** for the first point
Select **Intersec** from the point menu
Pick at **P2** and **P3** to determine the second point
Enter **2.5 ←** for the radius (Four arc segments will appear.)
Use the mouse to pick the desired arc (2nd from the top) for C3
Pick at **P4** and **P5** for the first point of arc C4
Select **Endpoint** from the point menu, than pick at **P6** for the second point
Enter **2.0 ←** for the radius
Pick the desired arc (2nd arc from the top) from the given four arc segments

The two arcs C3 and C4 should appear as in Figure 11.37.

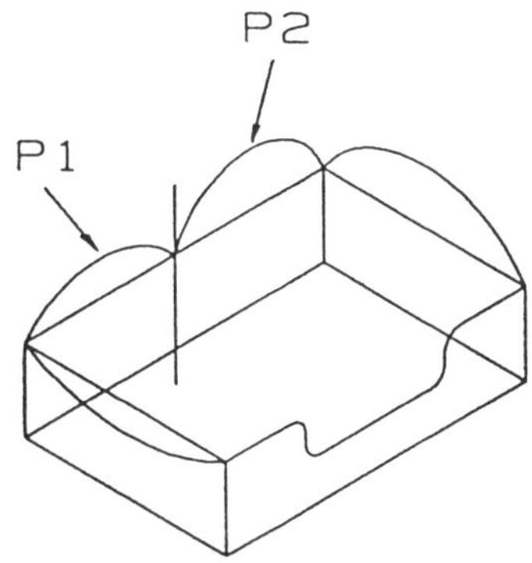

Figure 11.37

Step 8. Create a fillet C5 that is tangent to two arcs C3 and C4. Use the pick points in Figure 11.37.

Select **MAIN MENU → Modify → Fillet → Radius**
Enter **1.5 ←** for the radius
Pick at **P1** and **P2** to complete the fillet
The drawing should look like Figure 11.38.

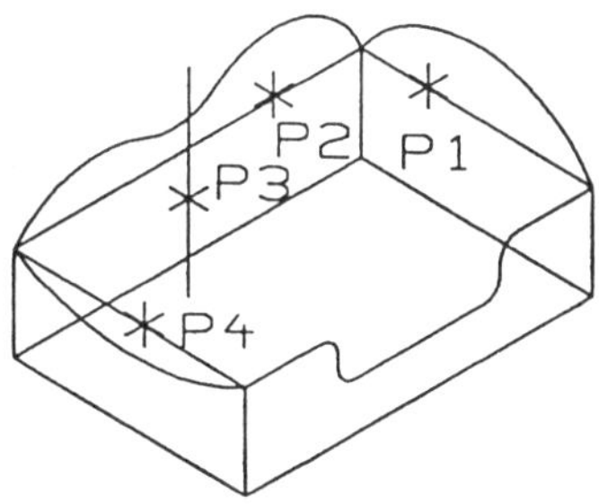

Figure 11.38

Step 9. Delete construction lines. Use the pick points in Figure 11.38.

Select **MAIN MENU → Delete**
Pick at **P1, P2, P3,** and **P4** to delect four lines

The final drawing should appear as Figure 11.39.

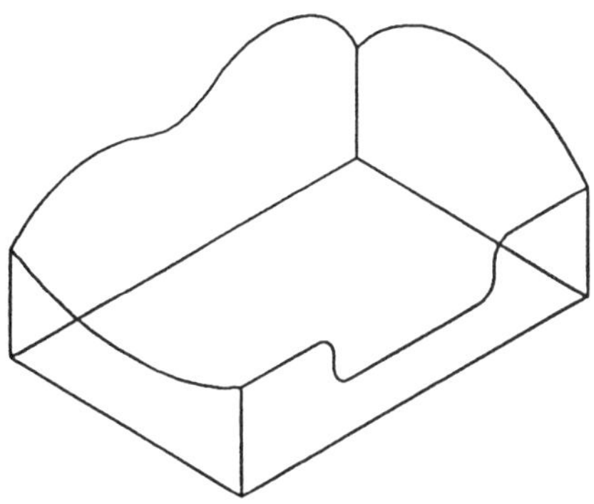

Figure 11.39

Step 10. Save the drawing in the filename coons1.

Select **MAIN MENU → File → Save**
Enter **coons1** for the file name

Project 6:

We are here ☞

Wireframe Model
(coons3)

Go to

Surface Model
Project 9 of Chapter 12 (coonss3)

A wireframe model as shown in Figure 11.40a is constructed in this example. It is used to generate a surface shown in Figure 11.40b.

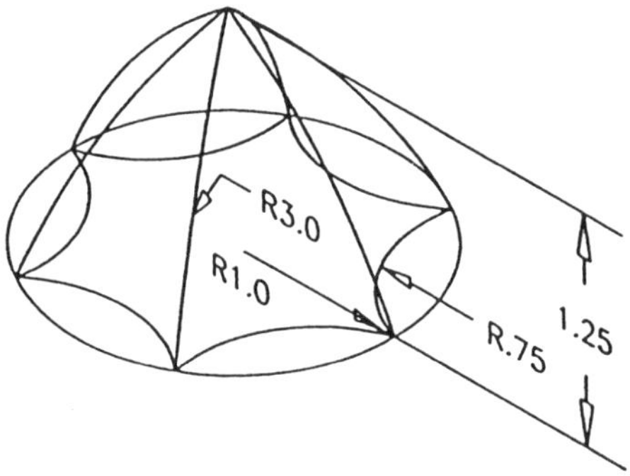

Figure 11.40a. Wireframe model

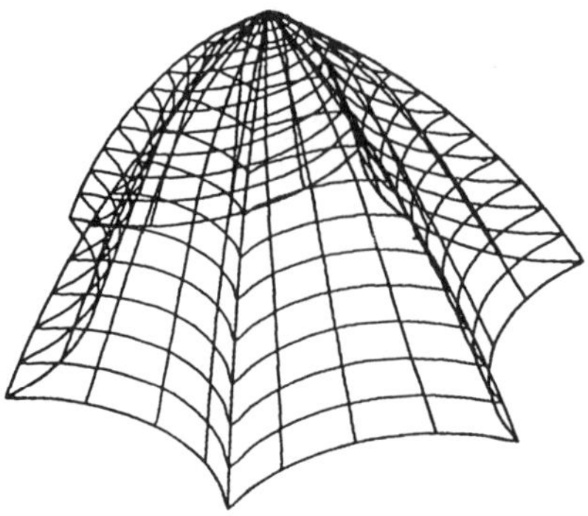

Figure 11.40b. Surface model

Tips 1. Create a base circle and a line that starts from the origin and is parallel to the X axis in the Top Cplane. Copy this line 5 times by rotating about the origin.

2. Use the intersection points between the base circle and the six lines as the endpoints to create six arcs.
3. Use Front Cplane to create a profile arc. This profile arc is then copied 5 times by rotating about the origin in Top Cplane.

Step 1. Enter the Mastercam Mill and set the Secondary Menu to the following settings if necessary:

Z = 0 Cplane: Top Gview: Top

Step 2. Create one circle and two lines.

Select **MAIN MENU →Create → Arc → pt Rad cir**
Enter the center point: **0,0** ←
Enter the radius (1.00): **1.0** ← (A circle will appear on the screen.)
Select **MAIN MENU → Create → Line → Polar**
Specify an endpoint: **0,0** ←
Enter the angle in degrees (0.00): **0** ←
Enter the line length (1.00): **1.5** ←
Specify an endpoint: **0,0** ←
Enter the angle in degrees: **60** ←
Enter the line length: **1.5** ←

The drawing should appear as Figure 11.41.

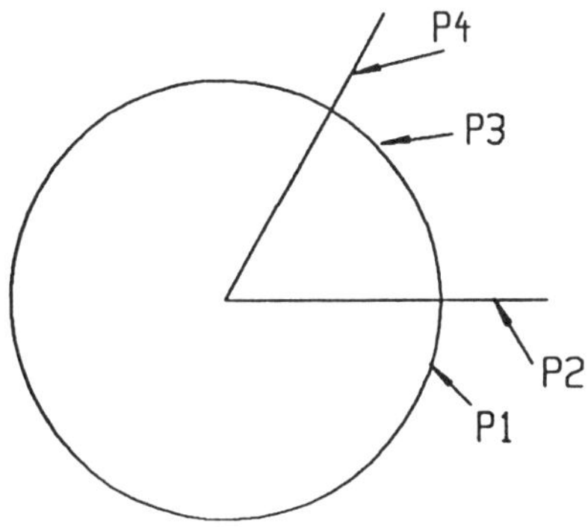

Figure 11.41

Step 3. Create an arc. Use the pick points in Figure 11.41 on the previous page.

Select **MAIN MENU → Create → Arc → Endpoints → Intersec**
Enter the first point: pick at **P1** and **P2**
Enter the second point: pick at **P3** and **P4**
Enter the radius (1.00): **0.75** ← (Four arc segments should appear.)
Pick at the desired arc (3rd arc from the right) to complete the selection.
The arc is added as shown in Figure 11.42 as shown at the top of the next page.

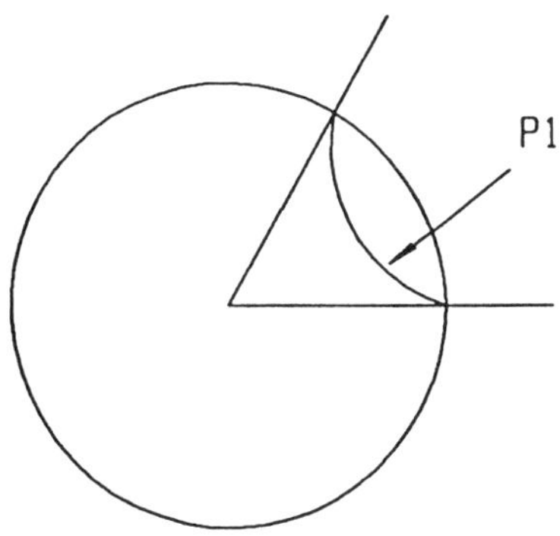

Figure 11.42

Step 4. Create the remaining five arcs. Rotate the arc five times, at 60° intervals each.

Use the pick point in Figure 11.42.

Select **MAIN MENU → Xform → Rotate → Entity**

Pick at **P1** to select the arc to rotate

Select **BACKUP → Done → Origin**

Set the Rotate parameters as below:

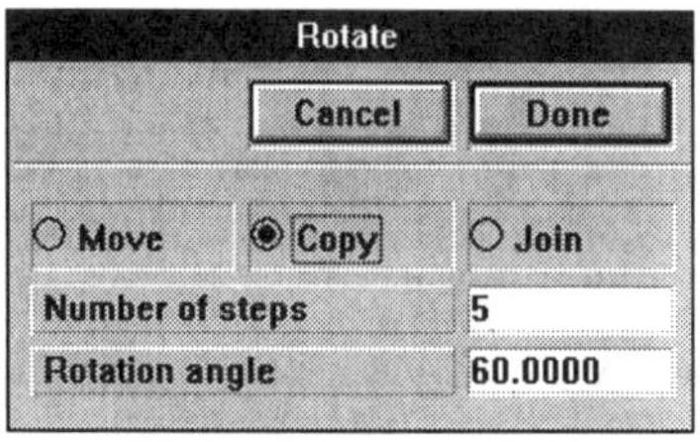

Select **Done**

Your drawing should look like Figure 11.43.

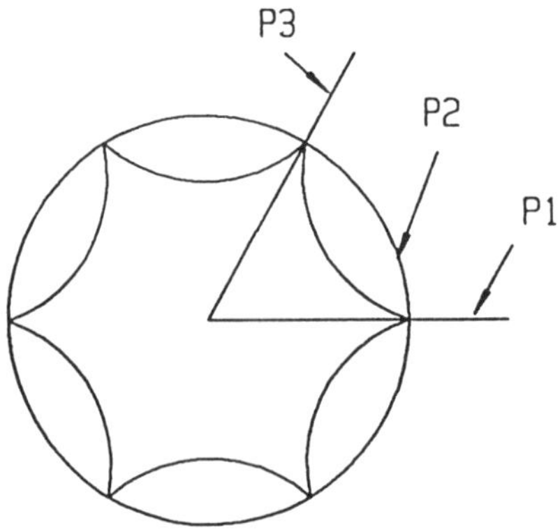

Figure 11.43

Step 5. Delete the construction lines and arc. Use the pick points in Figure 11.43.

Select **MAIN MENU → Delete**

Sequentially pick at **P1 - P3** to erase 2 lines and 1 arc

Select **Gview → Isometric**

The drawing should resemble Figure 11.44.

Figure 11.44

Step 6. Create the profile arc using the Front construction plane. Use the pick points in Figure 11.44.

Select **Cplane → Front**
Select MAIN MENU →Create → Arc → Endpoints → Endpoint
Enter the first point: pick at **P1**
Enter the second point: enter **0,1.25** ←
Enter the radius (.75): **3** ←
Select an arc: pick at the desired arc (the small convex arc)

The drawing should look like Figure 11.45.

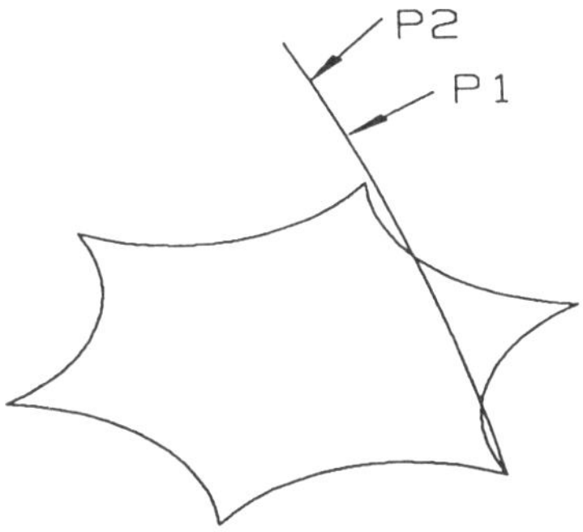

Figure 11.45

Step 7. Copy the arc profile to the other five locations using the Top construction plane. Use the pick points in Figure 11.45.

Select **Cplane → Top**
Select **MAIN MENU → Xform → Rotate → Entity**
Select an entity: pick at **P1**
Select **BACKUP → Done → Point → Endpoint**
Pick at **P2** to select the point to rotate about
Set the rotate parameters as shown here:

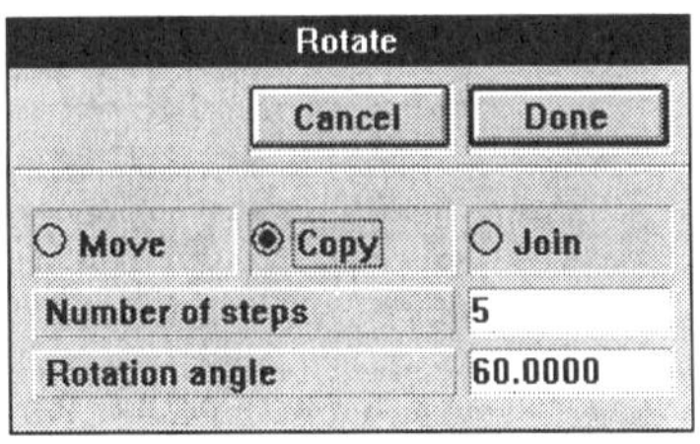

Select **Done**
The final drawing should resemble Figure 11.46.

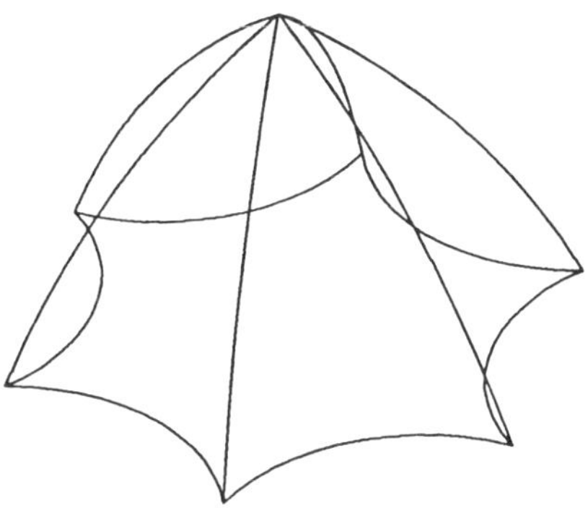

Figure 11.46

Step 8. Save the drawing (coons3).

Select **MAIN MENU → File → Save**
Enter file name: **coons3** ←

Note: This drawing is an ideal case for creating a coons surface.

Project 7:

The wireframe model of an object with 26 faces, Figure 11.47, is presented in this example.

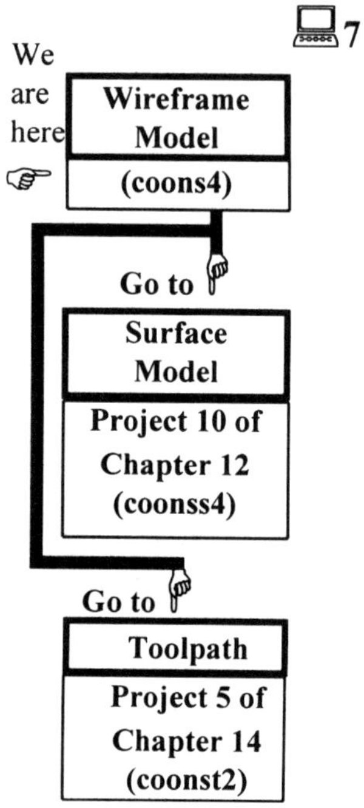

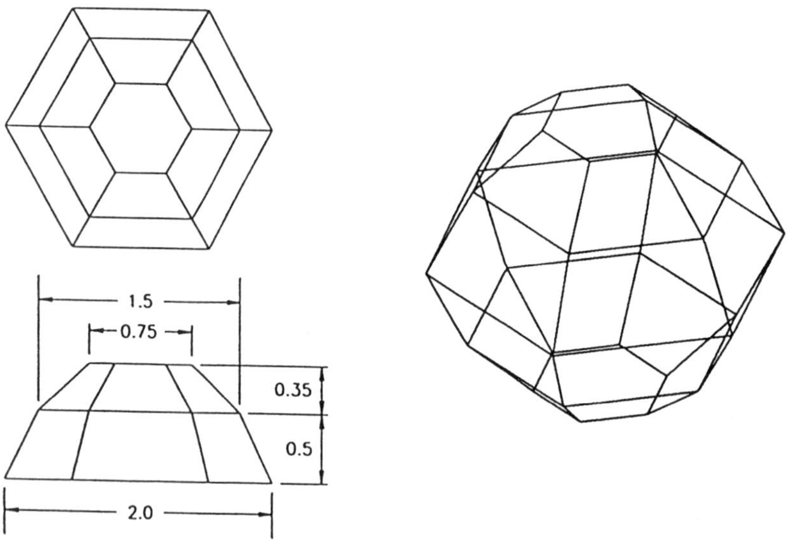

Figure 11.47

Tips 1. Create 3 construction circles and six lines to find the vertices of the three hexagons.

2. The two smaller hexagons are then translated to the proper Z positions, Z0.5 and Z0.85, respectively.
3. Use the Top Gview and the 3-d construction plane to connect the lines between the vertices. The use of the Top Gview helps in picking the right vertices which are not so easily seen in the isometric view.
4. Rotate the upper half model by 180° about the origin using the Front construction plane.

Step 1. Create three construction arcs using the Top construction plane.

Select **MAIN MENU →Create → Arc → pt Rad cir**
Enter **0,0** ← for the center point
Enter **0.375** ← for the radius to complete the first arc
Enter **0,0** ← for the center point
Enter **0.75** ← for the radius of the second arc
Enter **0,0** ← for the center point
Enter **1** ← for the radius of the third arc

Press **Alt** + **F1**, and then **F2** to fit the drawing.

The drawing with three arcs should resemble Figure 11.48.

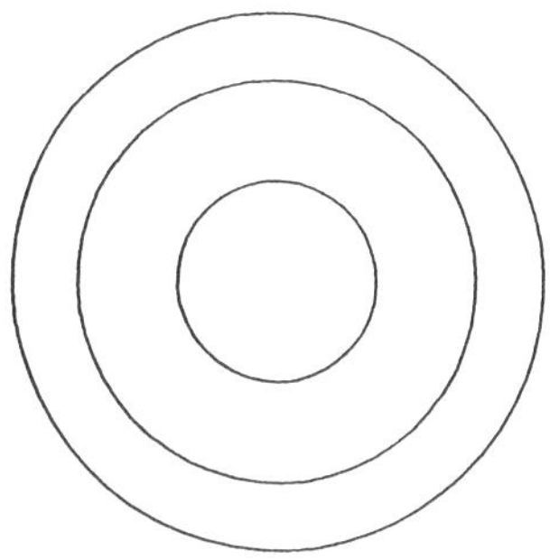

Figure 11.48

Step 2. Create six construction lines. Use the pick point in Figure 11.48.

Select **MAIN MENU → Create → Line → Polar**
Enter **0,0** ← for an endpoint
Enter **0** ← for the angle
Enter **1.25** ← for the line length to complete the first line

The new drawing should look like Figure 11.49.

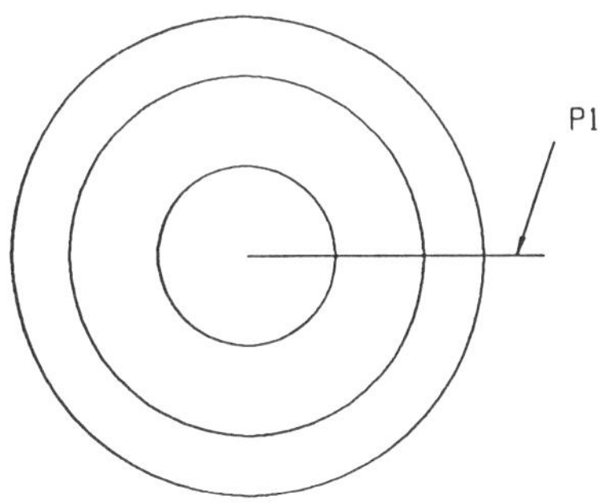

Figure 11.49

Select **MAIN MENU → Xform → Rotate → Entity**
Pick at **P1** to select the line to rotate from Figure 11.49
Select **BACKUP → Done → Origin**
Set the Rotate parameters as below:

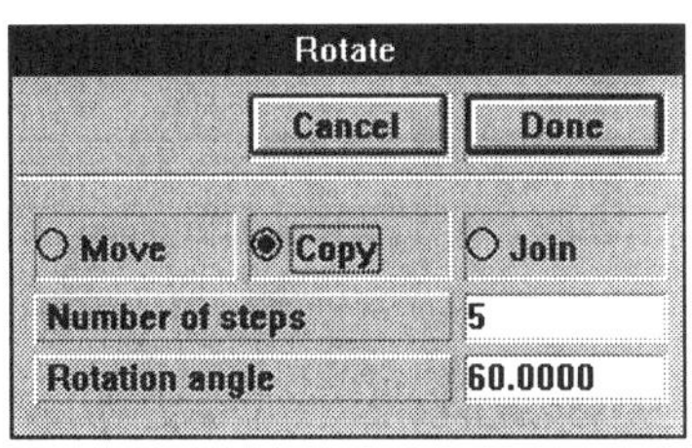

Select **Done**

The drawing should appear as Figure 11.50.

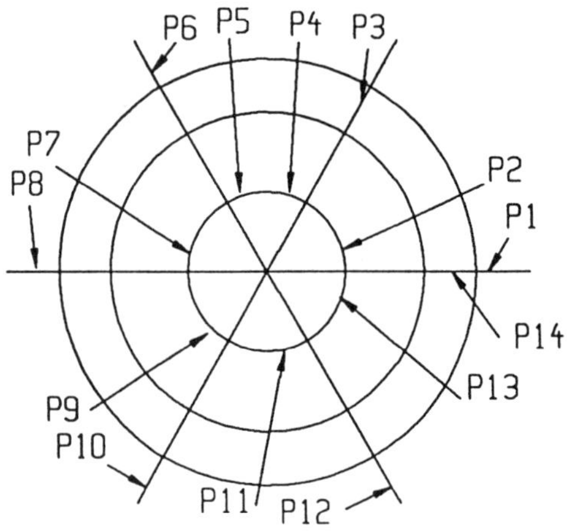

Figure 11.50

Step 3. Construct the first polygon around the smallest circle. Use the pick points in Figure 11.50 above.

Select **MAIN MENU → Create → Line → Multi → Intersec**

Sequentially pick at **P1 - P14** to complete the polygon around the smallest circle.

The first polygon should resemble Figure 11.51.

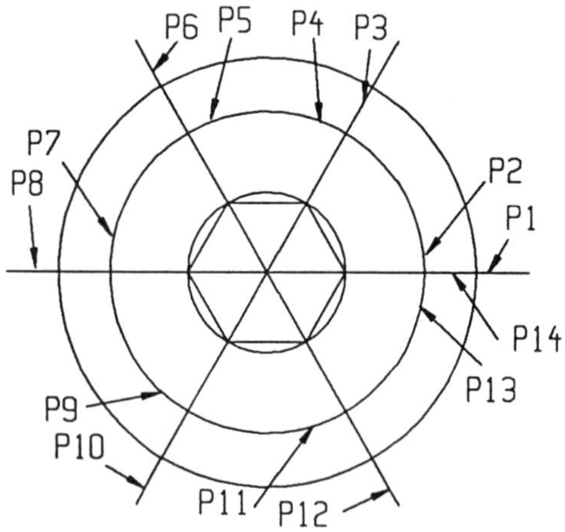

Figure 11.51

Step 4. Construct the second polygon around the mid-sized circle. Use the pick points in Figure 11.51 on the prevoius page.

Select **BACKUP → Multi → Intersec**

Sequentially pick at **P1 - P14** to complete the polygon

The new drawing should appear as Figure 11.52.

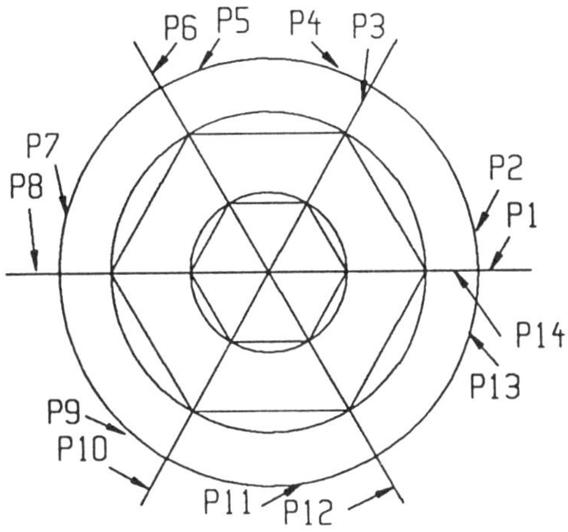

Figure 11.52

Step 5. Create a third polygon around the largest circle. Use pick points in Figure 11.52.

Select **BACKUP → Multi → Intersec**

Sequentially pick at **P1 - P14** to complete the polygon

The drawing now should look like Figure 11.53.

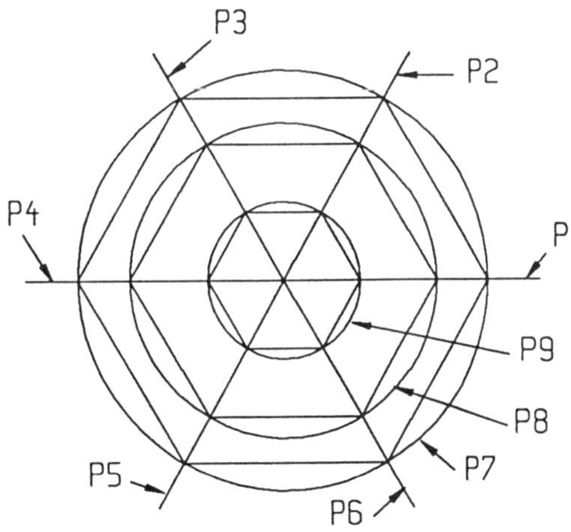

Figure 11.53

Step 6. Delete construction lines and arcs. Use the pick points in Figure 11. 53.

Select **MAIN MENU → Delete**

Pick at **P1 - P9** to delete the six construction lines and three construction circles

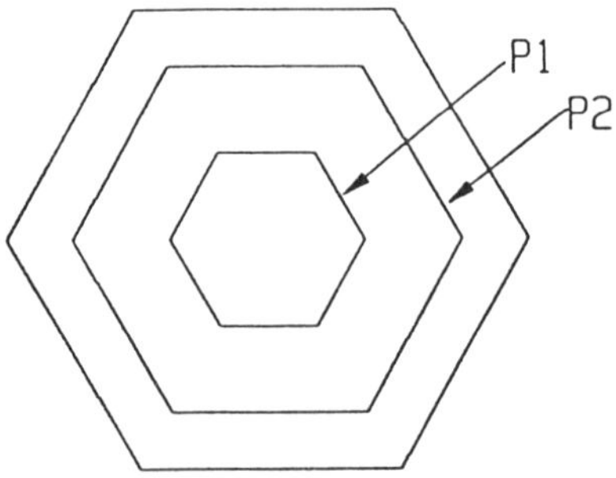

Figure 11.54

Step 7. Translate the smallest polygon to Z.85. Use the pick points in above Figure 11.54.

Select **MAIN MENU → Xform → Translate → Chain**
Pick at **P1**, then select **Close → End here → Done → Rectang**
Enter the translation vector: **Z.85 ←** to complete the translation
Set the Translate parameters as below:

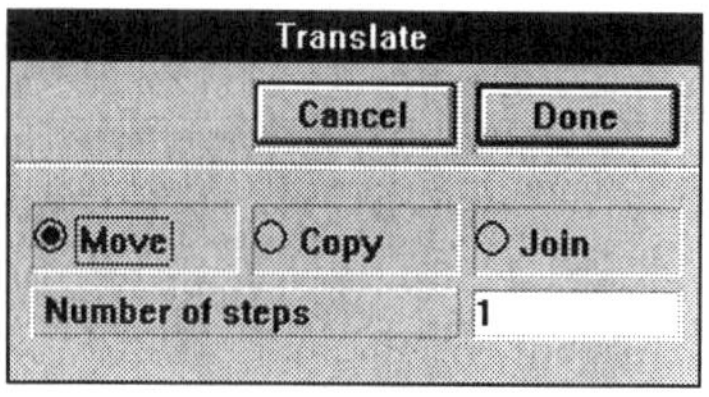

Select **Done**

Note: Your translated polygon may disappear from the screen. It will come back when you change the Gview to isometric.

Step 8. Translate the mid-sized polygon to Z.5. Use the pick point in previous Figure 11.54.

Select **Chain**, and then pick at **P2**
Select **Close → End here → Done → Rectang**
Enter the translation vector: **Z.5 ←**
Select **Gview → Isometric**
Set the Translate parameters as below:

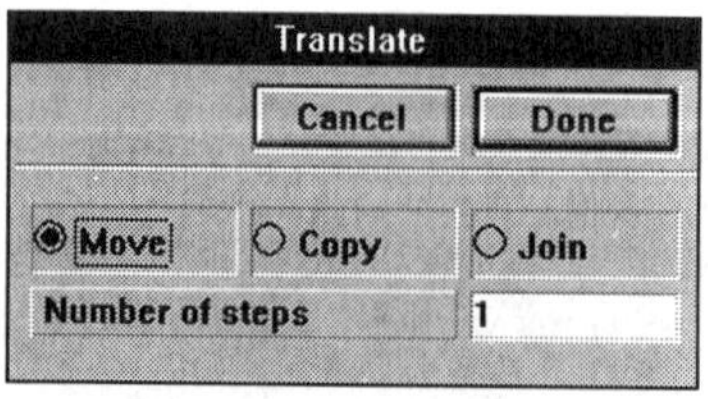

Select **Done**
The three polygon should appear as Figure 11.55.

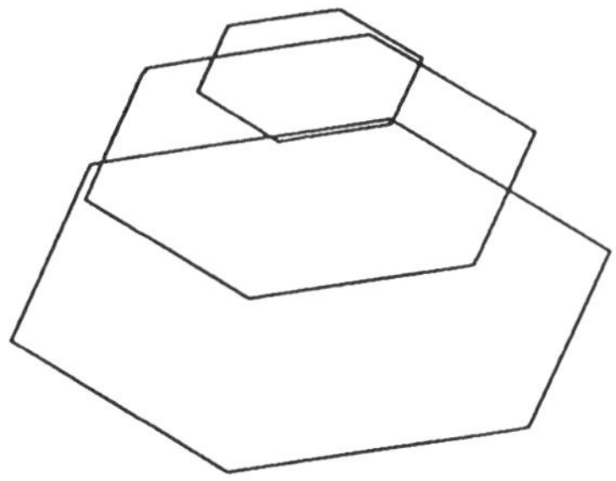

Figure 11.55

Step 9. Return the drawing to Top view to make it easier to connect the lines between the vertices.

Select **Gview → Top**

The drawing displayed in the top view should look like Figure 11.56.

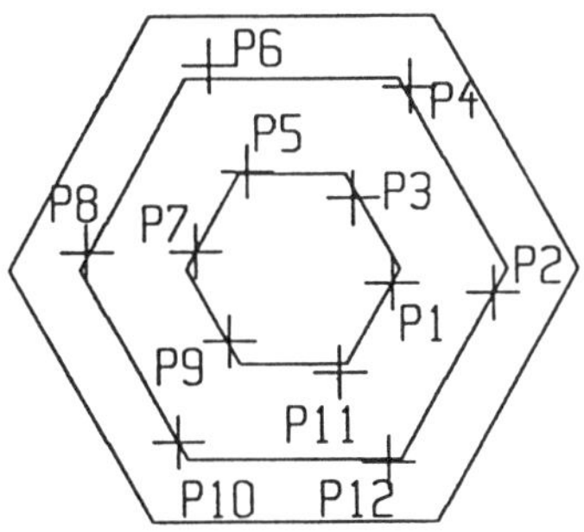

Figure 11.56

Step 10. Connect two inner polygons with lines using the 3-d construction plane.

Use the pick points in Figure 11.56.
Select **Cplane → 3d**
Select **MAIN MENU → Create → Line → Endpoints → Endpoint**
Sequentially pick at **P1 - P12** to complete the connecting lines
Select **Gview → Isometric**

The drawing now should look like Figure 11.57.

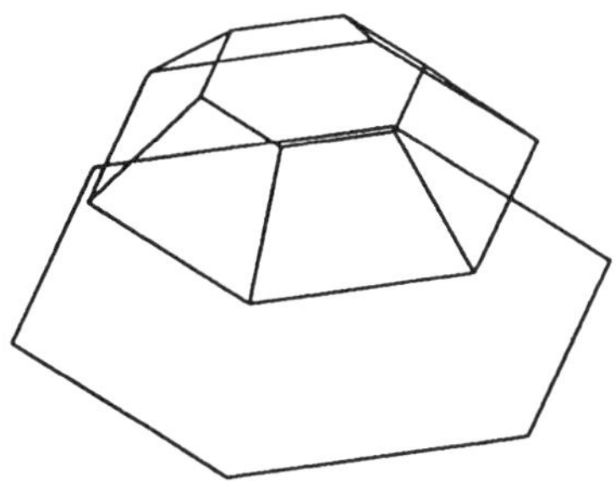

Figure 11.57

Again, change the Gview back to Top view to make picking the points easy for connecting the lines between the two outer polygons.

Select **Gview → Top**

The top view of the drawing should resemble Figure 11.58.

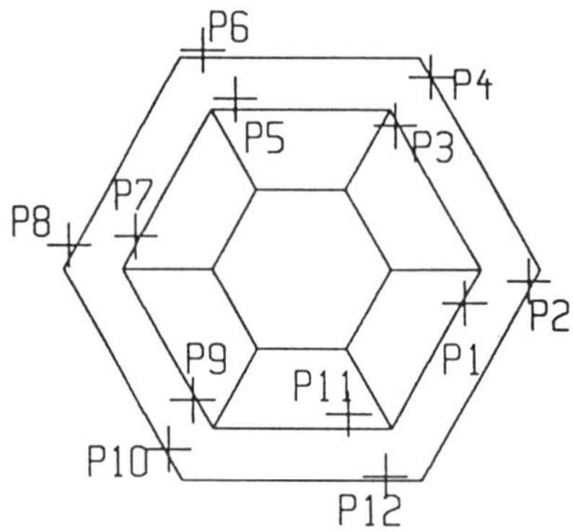

Figure 11.58

Step 11. Connect two outer polygons with lines. Use the pick points in above Figure 11.58.

Select **BACKUP → Endpoints → Endpoint**

Sequentially pick at **P1 - P12** to complete the connecting lines

Select **Gview → Isometric**

The upper half of the wireframe is done and shall look like Figure 11.59. Actually, for modeling purposes, the upper half of the model is all we need since the object is symmetrical. For visualization purposes, the entire model can be obtained by rotating the upper half of the model by 180° about the origin using the Front construction plane.

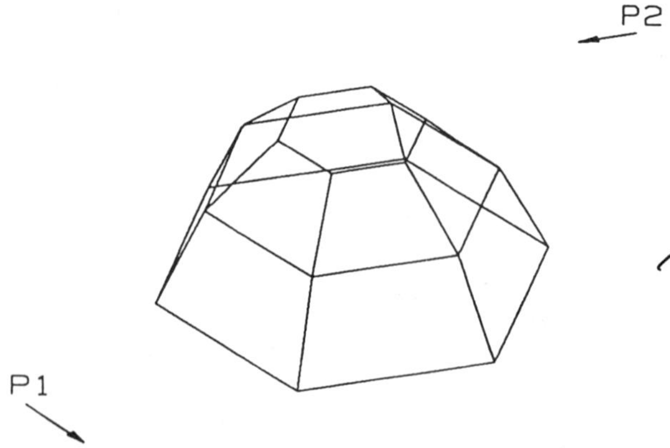

Tom 50

Figure 11.59

Step 12. Save the drawing coons4.

Select **MAIN MENU → File → Save**
Enter **coons4** for the file name

Step 13. Copy the upper half model to the lower half using the Front construction plane.

Use the pick points in Figure 11.59.
Select **Cplane → Front**
Select **MAIN MENU → Xform → Rotate → Window**
Pick at **P1** and **P2** to completely include the entire drawing
Select **Done → Origin**
Set the Rotate parameters as below:

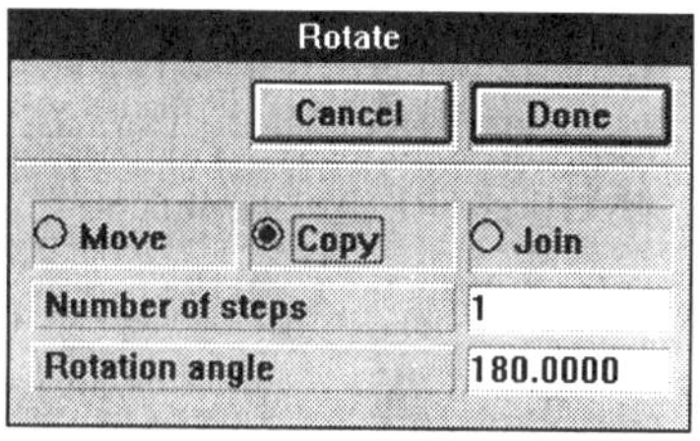

Select **Done**

The complete wireframe model is shown in Figure 11.60.

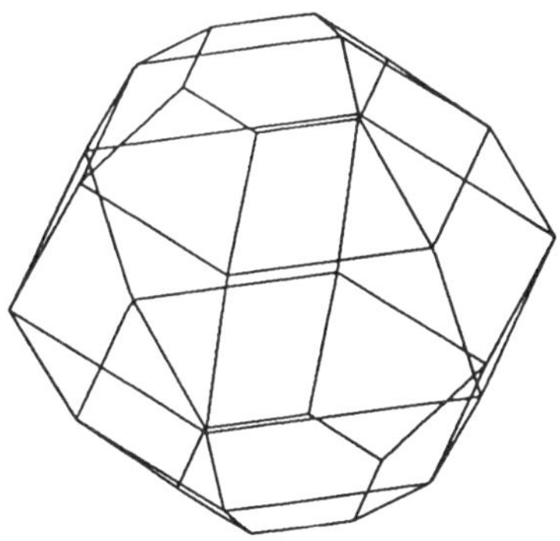

Figure 11.60

Note: This wireframe model will be used to generate two coons surfaces in the next chapter.

Project 8:

This example illustrates how to construct the wireframe surface profile for a cup shown in Figure 11.61.

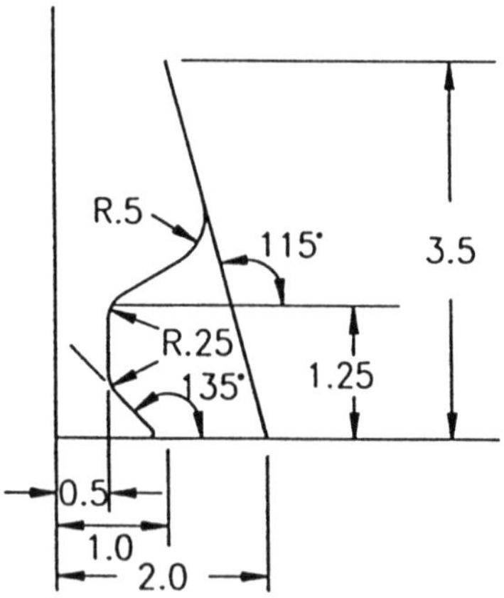

Figure 11.61a. Wireframe profile

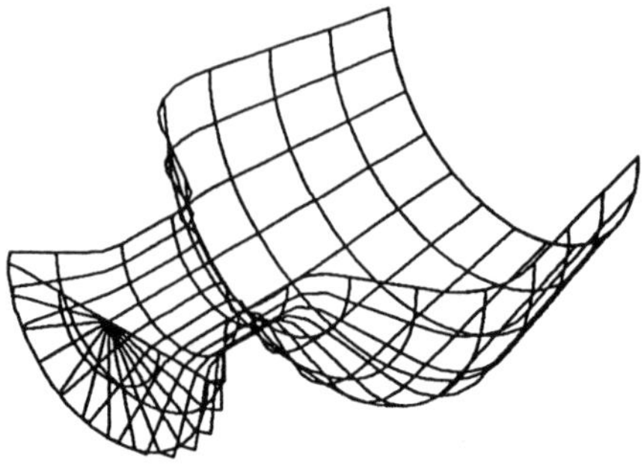

Figure 11.61b. Surface model

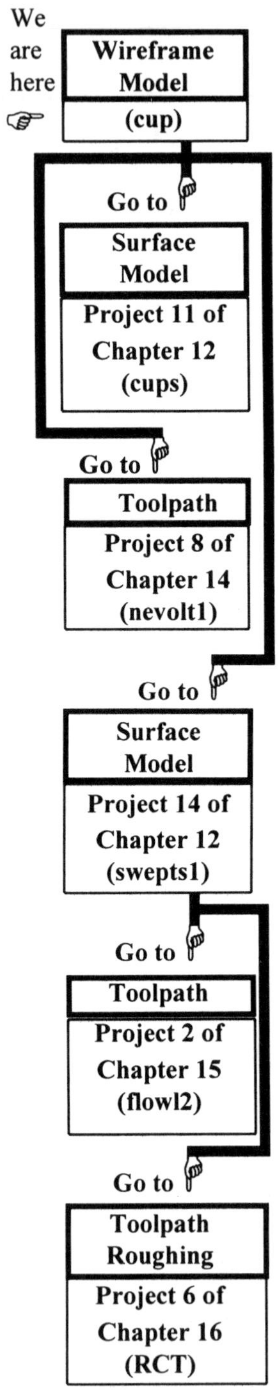

Tips
1. Create two slope lines using the polar method in the top construction view.
2. Create three horizontal lines and two vertical lines.
3. Create another slope line using the polar method with one intersection point as the end point.
4. Create four fillets.
5. Delete the construction entities.

Step 1. Enter the Mastercam Mill. Set the Secondary Menu to the following settings if necessary:

Z: **0**
Cplane: **Top**
Gview: **Top**

Step 2. Create two slope lines.

Select **MAIN MENU →Create → Line → Polar**
Enter **1.0,0** ← for an endpoint
Enter **135** ← for the angle
Enter **1.5** ← for the line length to complete the first line
Enter **2.0,0** ← for an endpoint
Enter **105** ← for the angle
Enter **5** ← for the line length

Press **Alt** + **F1**, and then **F2** to fit the drawing

The drawing appears as in Figure 11.62.

Figure 11.62

Step 3. Create three horizontal lines and two vertical lines.

Select **BACKUP → Endpoints → Endpoint**

Sequentially enter the following five pairs of point data to complete the five lines:

First end point	Second end point
0,0	1,0
0,1.25	2,1.25
0,3.5	2.5,3.5
0,-0.5	0,4
0.5,0.2	0.5,2

The drawing now should look like Figure 11.63.

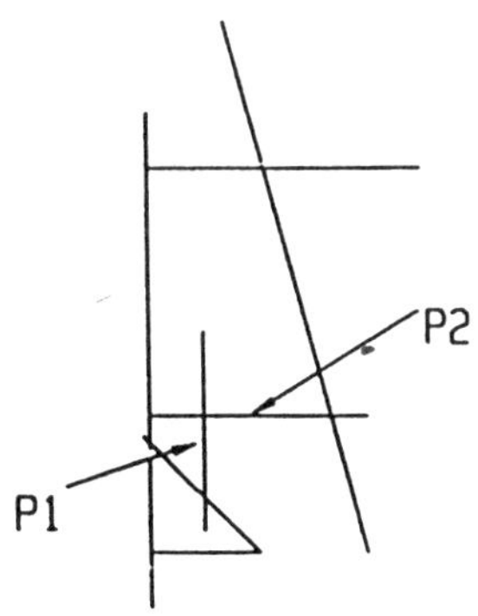

Figure 11.63

Step 4. Create another slope line that is passing through the intersection point of two lines.

Use the pick points in Figure 11.63.

Select **BACKUP → Polar → Intersec**

Pick at **P1** and **P2** to trap at the intersection point

Enter **30** ← for the angle

Enter **1.5** ← for the line length

The drawing now should resemble Figure 11.64.

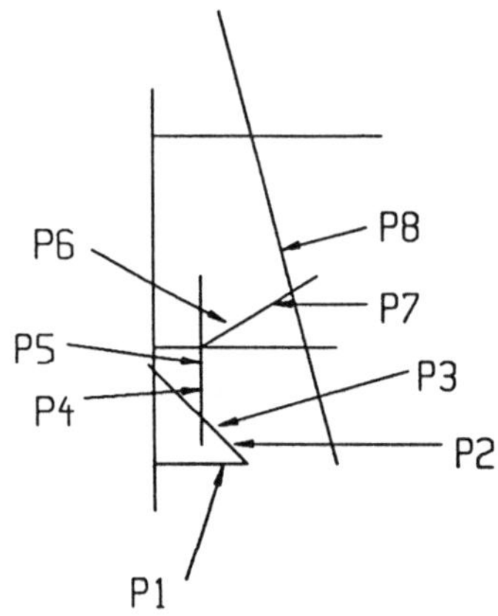

Figure 11.64

Step 5. Add four fillets. Use the pick points in Figure 11.64.

Select **MAIN MENU → Modify → Fillet → Radius**
Enter **0.05 ←** for the fillet radius
Pick at **P1** and **P2** to complete the first fillet
Select **Radius**
Enter **.25 ←** for the fillet radius
Pick at **P3, P4, P5,** and **P6** to complete the two fillets having .25 radius
Select **Radius**
Enter **0.5 ←** for the fillet radius
Pick at **P7** and **P8** to complete the fillet of **.5** radius

The drawing should appear as Figure 11.65.

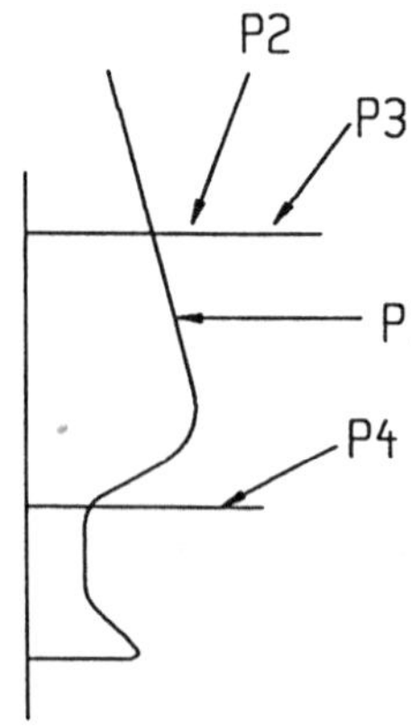

Figure 11.65

Step 6. Trim the slope line and delete two construction lines. Use the pick points in Figure 11.65.

Select **MAIN MENU → Modify → Trim → 1 entity**
Pick at **P1** and **P2** to trim the slope line
Select **MAIN MENU → Delete**
Pick at **P3** and **P4** to delete the two construction lines

The final drawing should appear as Figure 11.66.

Figure 11.66

Step 7. Save the drawing. Use the file name: **cup**.

Select **MAIN MENU** → **File** → **Save**
Enter the file name: **cup**

Note: This wireframe model can be used to create the surface by using the revolved or swept command.

Project 9:

9

We are here ☞ **Wireframe Model** **(swept2)**

Go to **Surface Model** **Project 15 of Chapter 12 (swepts2)**

In this example, the surface profiles for a channel surface model are constructed. The cross section of the channel varies from a rectangular shape down to a circle as shown in Figure 11.67.

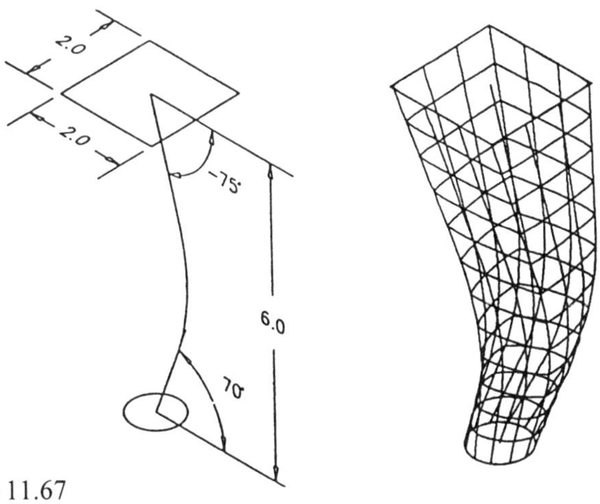

Figure 11.67

Tips 1. Use Front Cplane to construct the profile consisting of two lines and a fillet.

2. Use Top Cplane to create the rectangle and the circle.

Step 1. Construct two slope lines using Front Cplane.

Select **Cplane** → **Front**
Select **Gview** → **Isometric**
Select **Z** then enter **0** ← if necessary
Select **MAIN MENU** → **Create** → **Line** → **Polar**
Specify and endpoint: **0,0** ←
Enter the angle in degrees: **-75** ←
Enter the line length: **5** ← to complete the first line
Specify an endpoint: **0,-6** ←
Enter the angle in degrees: **70** ←
Enter the line length: **5** ← for the second line

The drawing of the two lines should appear as in Figure 11.68.

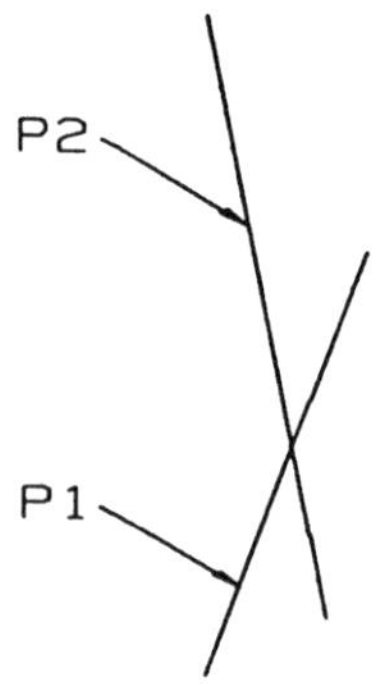

Figure 11.68

Step 2. Add a fillet using the pick points in Figure 11.68.

Select **MAIN MENU** → **Modify** → **Fillet** → **Radius**
Enter the fillet radius: **4** ←
Pick at **P1** and **P2** to complete the fillet

The new drawing becomes Figure 11.69.

Figure 11.69

Step 3. Create a rectangle using Top Cplane.

Select **Cplane** → **Top**
Select **MAIN MENU** → **Create** → **Rectangle** → **1 point**
Enter the lower left corner: **-1,-1** ←
Enter the width: **2** ←
Enter the height: **2** ←

The drawing should look like Figure 11.70.

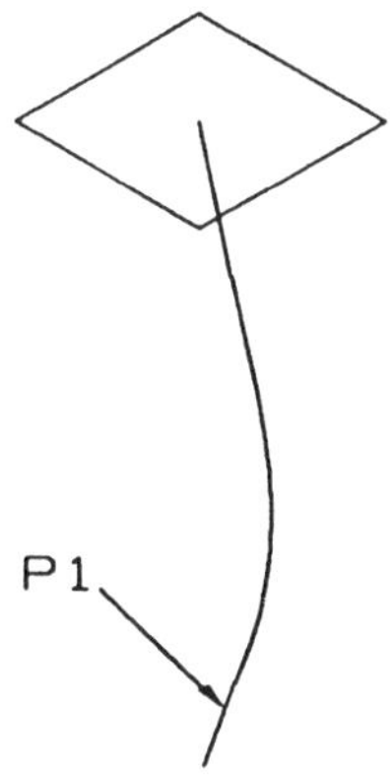

Figure 11.70

Step 4. Create a circle using the pick point in Figure 11.70.

Select **Z** → **Endpoint**

Pick at **P1** to trap the Z value (Z-6.0 shall appear in the Secondary Menu)

Select **MAIN MENU** → **Create** → **Arc** → **pt Dia cir**

Enter the center point: **0,0** ←

Enter the diameter: **1** ←

The complete wireframe model appears in Figure 11.71.

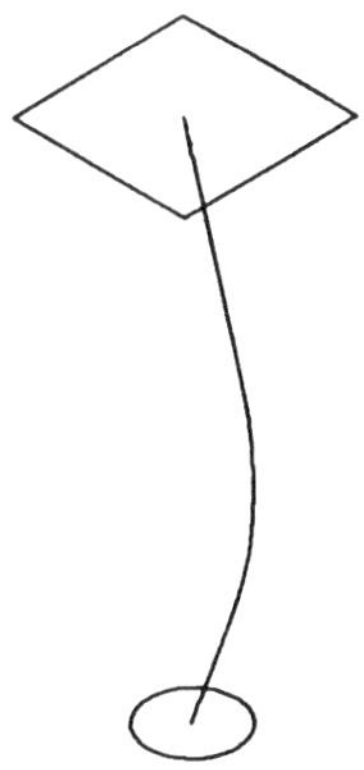

Figure 11.71

Step 5. Save the drawing. Use the file name: **Swept2**.

Select **MAIN MENU** → **File** → **Save**

Enter the file name **Swept2**

Note: This wireframe model will be used to generate a surface model using swept modeling technique in chapter 12.

Project 10:

This example creates a wireframe model, Figure 11.72a, of the swept surface (Figure 11.72b).

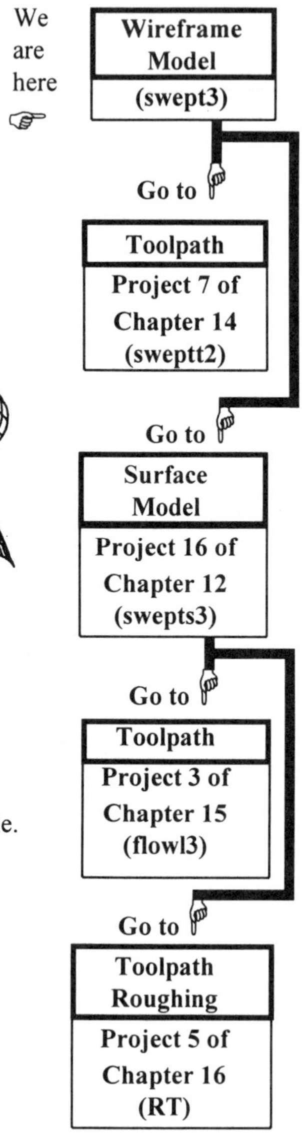

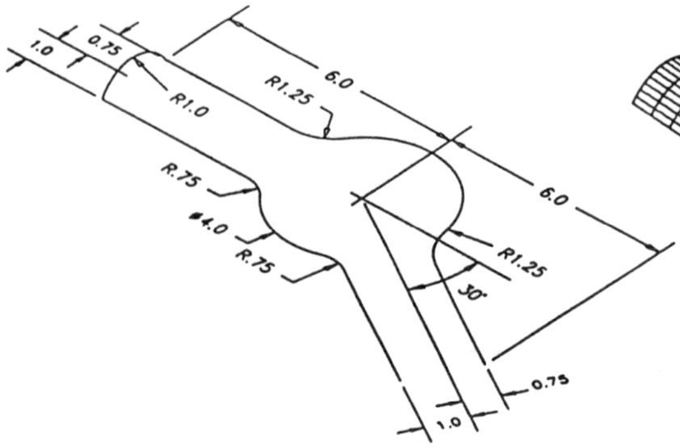

Figure 11.72a. Wireframe model

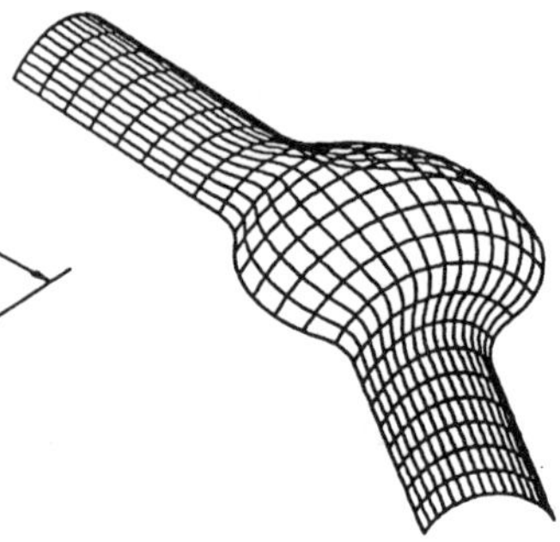

Figure 11.72b. Surface model

Tips
1. Create two construction lines that start from the center of the circle. These two lines are then offset to the two sides by 0.75-in. and 1-in., respectively.
2. The circle must be broken into four pieces in order to add four fillets with proper trimming.
3. Create the across arc using the Side Cplane.

Step 1. Create an arc using Top Cplane.

Select **Cplane → Top**
Select **Z** then enter **0** ← if necessary
Select **Gview → Top**
Select **MAIN MENU → Create → Arc → pt Dia cir**
Enter the center point: **0,0** ←
Enter the diameter: **4** ←

Step 2. Create two construction lines.

Select **MAIN MENU → Create → Line → Polar**
Specify an endpoint: **0,0** ←
Enter the angle in degrees: **-30** ←
Enter the line length: **6** ← to complete the first line
Specify an endpoint: **0,0** ←
Enter the angle in degrees: **180** ←
Enter the line length: **6** ←

The drawing should look like Figure 11.73.

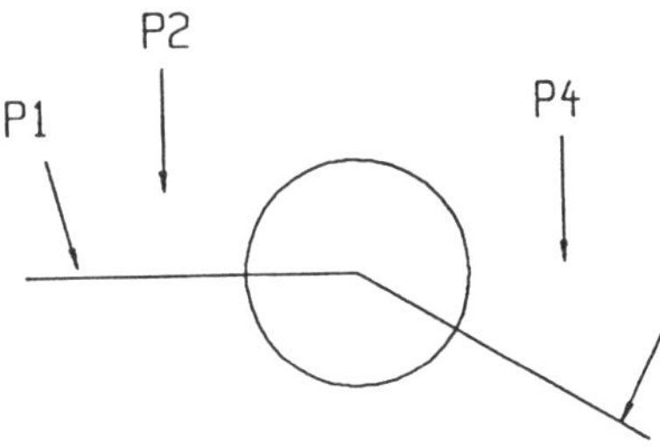

Figure 11.73

Step 3. Offset the two construction lines to the specified side by 0.75-in. using the pick points in Figure 11.73.

Select **MAIN MENU → Xform →Offset**
Set the parameters for Offset as below:

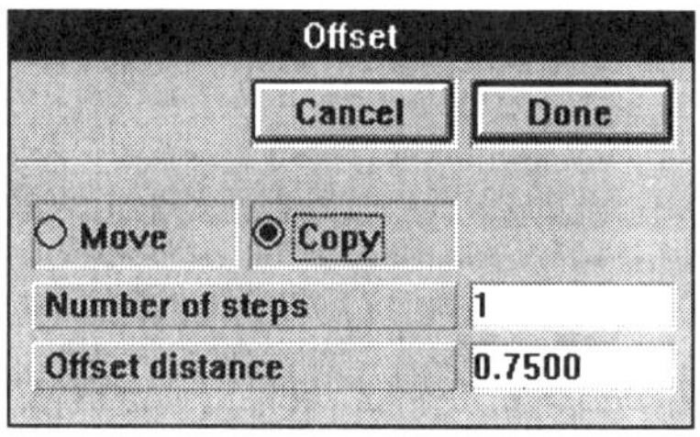

Select **Done**

Select the line or arc to offset: pick at **P1**
Indicate the offset direction: pick at **P2**
Select the line or arc to offset: pick at **P3**
Indicate the offset direction: pick at **P4**

Two offset lines will be added to the drawing as in Figure 11.74.

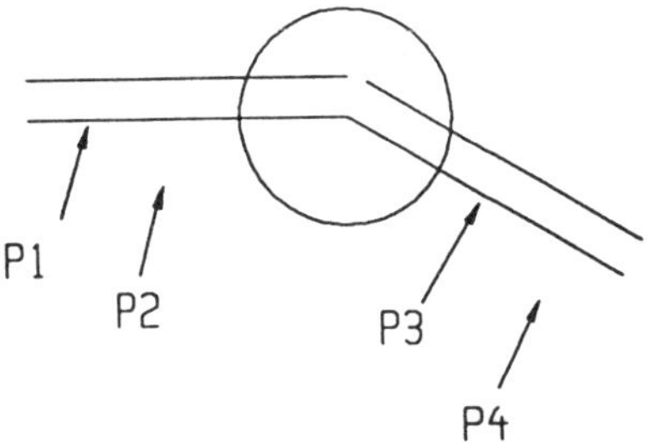

Figure 11.74

Step 4. Offset the two construction lines to the other side by 1-in. Use the pick points in Figure 11.74.

Select **BACKUP → Offset**

Set the Offset parameters as below:

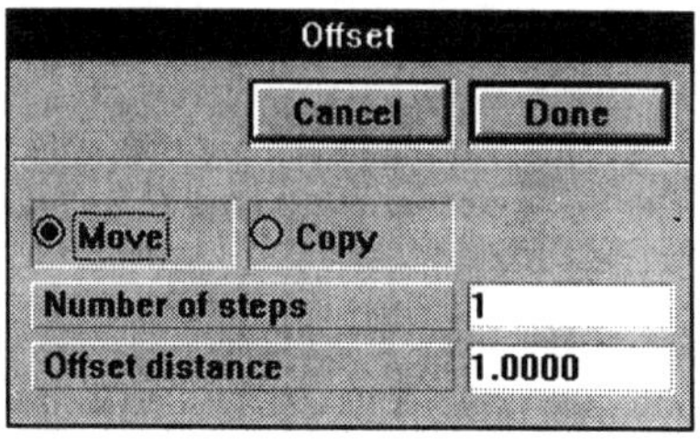

Select **Done**

Select the line or arc to offset: pick at **P1 ←**

Indicate the offset direction: pick at **P2**

Select the line or arc to offset: pick at **P3**

Indicate the offset direction: pick at **P4**

The four offset lines should resemble Figure 11.75.

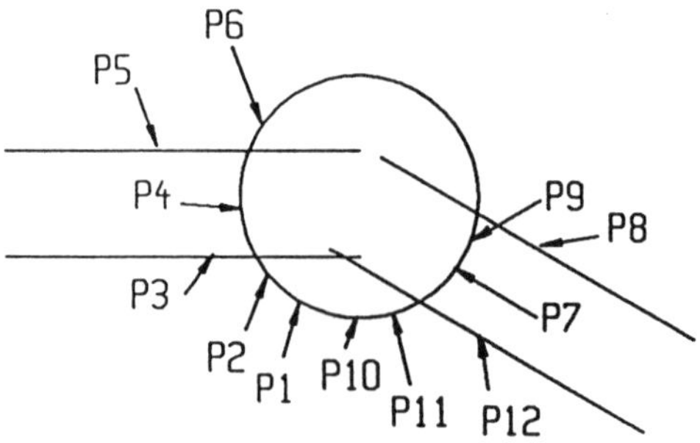

Figure 11.75

Step 5. Break the arc into four pieces using the pick points in above Figure 11.75.

Select **MAIN MENU → Modify → Break → 2 pieces**

Select an entity: pick at **P1**

Select **Intersec** from the Point menu and then pick at **P2** and **P3** to break the arc

Sequentially pick at **P4 - P6** to break the second time

Sequentially pick at **P7 - P9** to break the third time

Sequentially pick at **P10 - P12** to break the fourth time

Note: The broken arc does not look different before breaking. The drawing reappears in Figure 11.76 to show the pick points for next step.

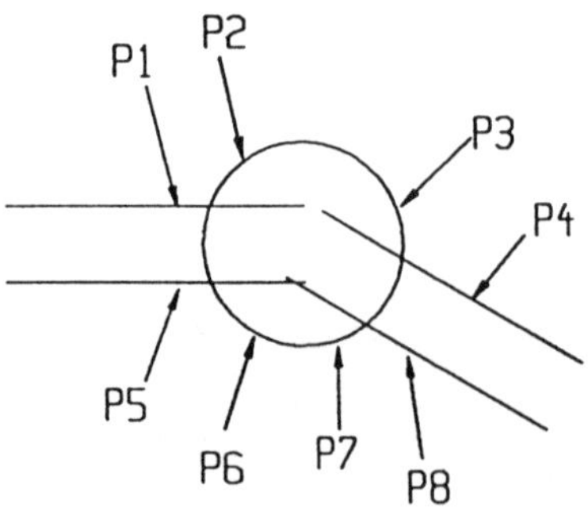

Figure 11.76

Step 6. Add four fillets using the pick points in Figure 11.76.

Select **MAIN MENU → Modify → Fillet → Radius**
Enter the fillet radius: **1.25** ←
Pick at **P1** and **P2** to complete the 1st fillet
Pick at **P3** and **P4** to complete the 2nd fillet
Select **Radius** from the Fillet menu
Enter the fillet radius: **.75** ←
Pick at **P5** and **P6** for the 3rd fillet
Pick at **P7** and **P8** for the 4th fillet

The new drawing should resemble Figure 11.77.

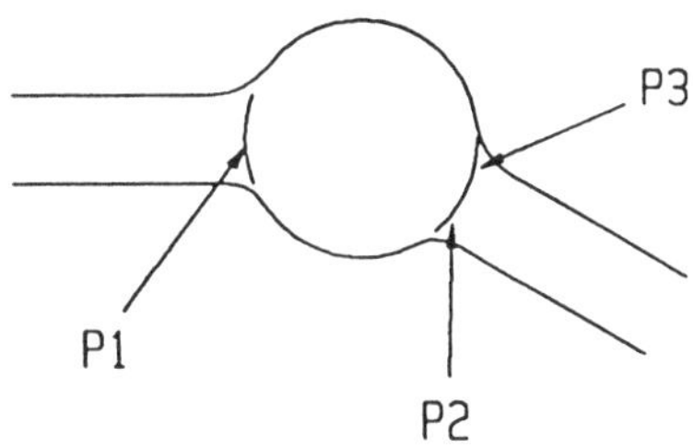

Figure 11.77

Step 7. Delete three unwanted arc segments using the pick points in Figure 11.77.

Select **MAIN MENU → Delete**
Pick at **P1, P2** and **P3** to complete the deletion

The drawing becomes Figure 11.78.

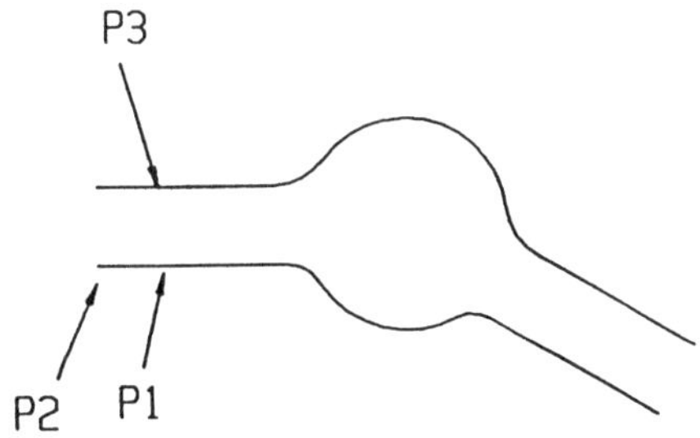

Figure 11.78

Step 8. Create an across arc using Side Cplane. Use the pick points from Figure 11.78.

Select **Cplane → Side**
Select **Gview → Isometric**
Select **Z → Endpoint**, then pick at **P1**

Z-6.0 shall appear in the Secondary Menu.

Select **MAIN MENU → Create → Arc → Endpoints → Endpoint**
Pick at **P2** and **P3** to select two endpoints
Enter the radius: **1** ←
Select an arc: pick the desired arc (2nd from the top)

The wireframe model should resemble Figure 11.79 .

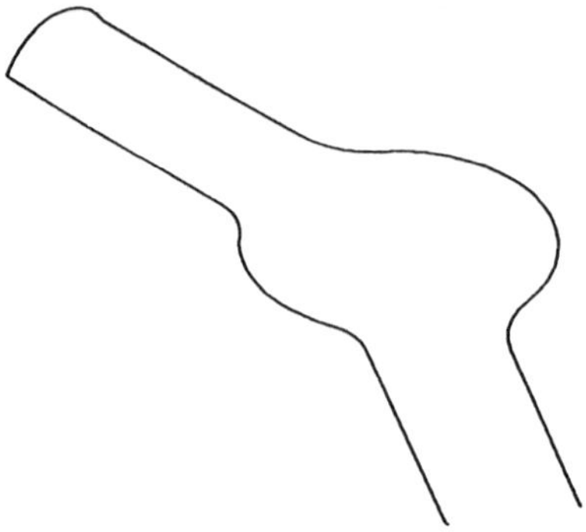

Figure 11.79

Step 9. Save the drawing. Use the file name: **Swept3**.

Select **MAIN MENU → File → Save**

Enter the file name: **Swept3**

Project 11:

The part shown in Figure 11.80 consists of **four** surfaces: a flat surface at the bottom, a wall surface, a fillet surface between the wall and the bottom, and a rim surface. The required wireframe model for these four surfaces is given in Figure 11.80a.

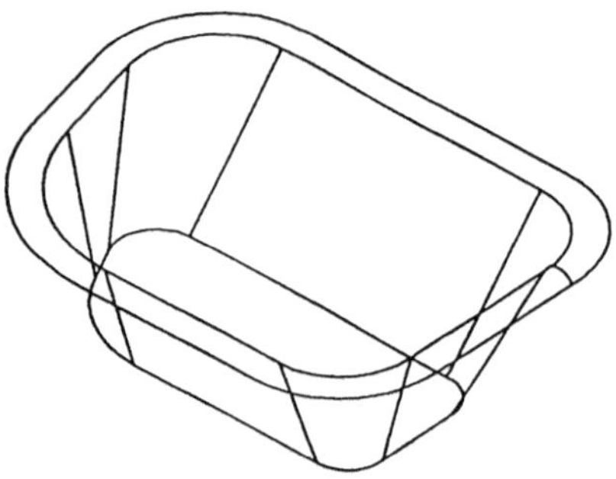

a. Wireframe model

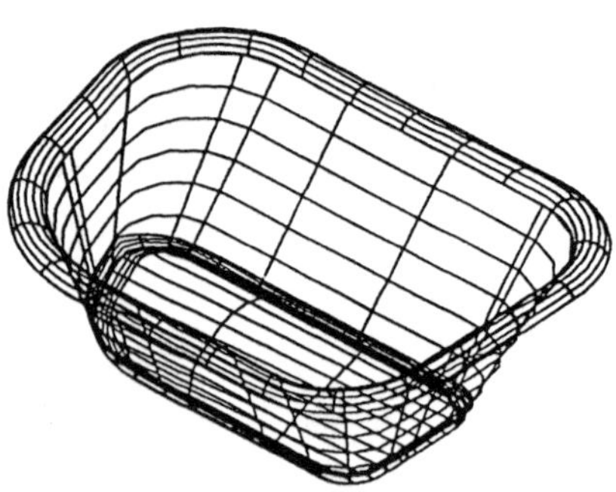

b. Surface model

Figure 11.80

Tips 1. Use the Top construction plane to construct the top and the bottom frames of the part.

2. Use the 3d construction plane to create the connecting lines between the top and the bottom frame. The connecting points of these lines are trapped at the end points of each arc.

3. Use the side construction plane to create the sweeping arc of the rim.

11

We are here ☞ **Wireframe Model (basket)**

Go to **Surface Model** — **Project 8 of Chapter 13 (baskets)**

Go to **Toolpath** — **Project 5 of Chapter 15 (basket)**

Go to **Toolpath Trimming** — **Project 2 of Chapter 16 (Trim1)**

Step 1. Enter the Mastercam Mill. Set the Secondary Menu to the proper settings if necessary.

Select **Cplane** → **Top**

Select **Gview** → **Top**

Select **Z** and then enter **0** ←

Step 2. Construct a rectangle.

Select **Create** → **Rectangle** → **1 point**

Enter **0,0** ← for the lower left corner

Enter **6** ← for the width of the rectangle

Enter **4** ← for the height of the rectangle

Press **Alt** + **F1** then **F2** to fit the drawing.

A rectangle should appear as Figure 11.81.

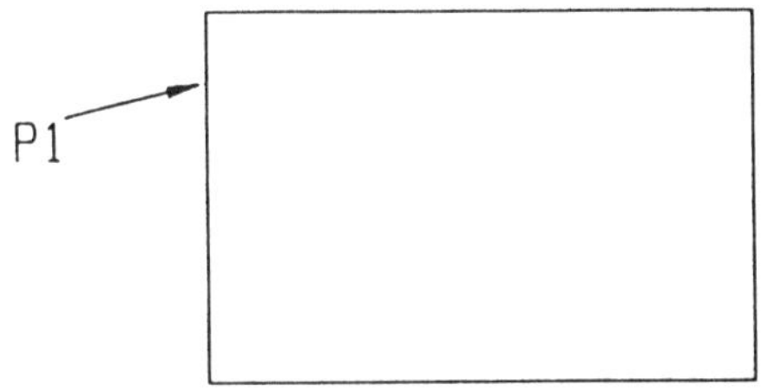

Figure 11.81

Step 3. Construct a slope line to the rectangle. Use the pick point in Figure 11.81.

Select **MAIN MENU** → **Create** → **Line** → **Endpoints** → **Endpoint**

Pick at **P1** for the first point

Enter **1,0** ← for the second point

The drawing should look like Figure 11.82.

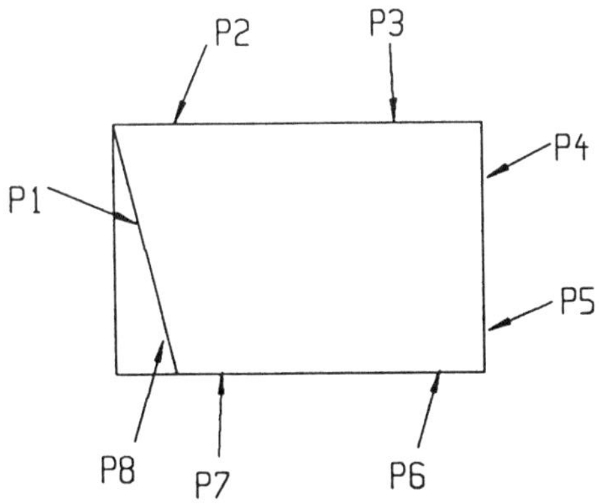

Figure 11.82

Step 4. Add four arcs at corners. Use the pick points in Figure 11.82.

Select **MAIN MENU** → **Modify** → **Fillet** → **Radius**

Enter **1.0** ← for the radius value

Sequentially pick at **P1 - P6** to complete the three fillets

Select **Radius**, and then enter **2.0** ← for the radius value

Pick at **P7** and **P8** to complete the larger fillet

The drawing now should resemble Figure 11.83.

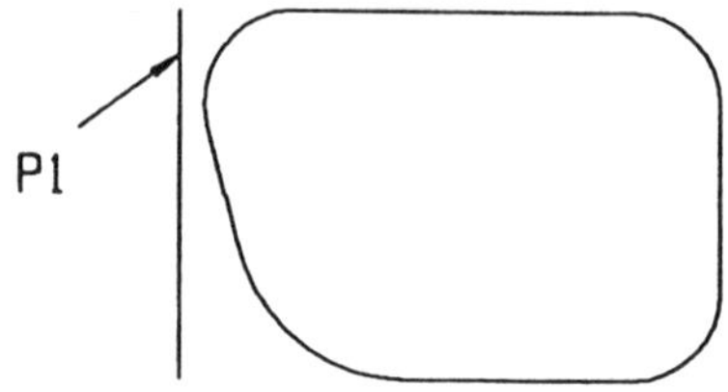

Figure 11.83

Step 5. Delete a line. Use the pick point in Figure 11.83.

Select **MAIN MENU → Delete**

Pick at **P1**

The top frame appears as in Figure 11.84.

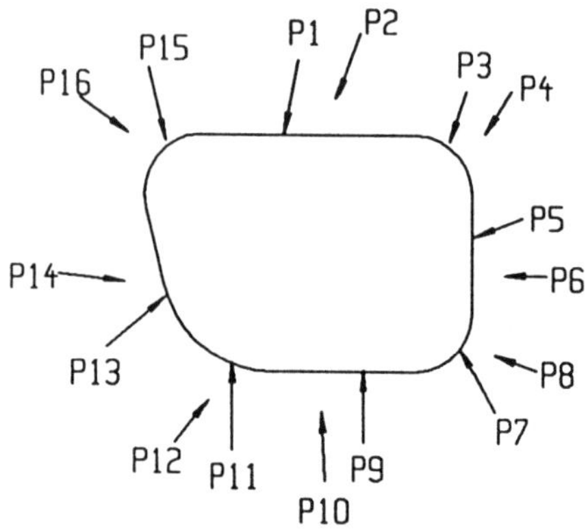

Figure 11.84

Step 6. Create the outer contour by offseting the top frame just created.

Use the pick points in Figure 11.84.

Select **MAIN MENU → Xform → Offset**

Set the Offset parameters as below:

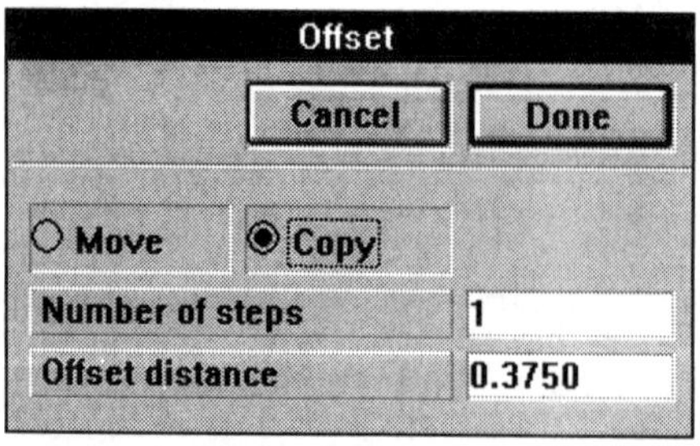

Select **Done**

Sequentially pick at **P1 - P16** to complete the outer contour

The drawing now should look like Figure 11.85.

Figure 11.85

Step 7. Create the rectangle for the bottom frame.

Select **Z** and then enter **-1.5** ←
Select **MAIN MENU** → **Create** → **Rectangle** → **1 point**
Enter **0.5,0.5** ← for the lower left corner
Enter **5** ← for the width
Enter **2** ← for the height

The drawing appears as Figure 11.86.

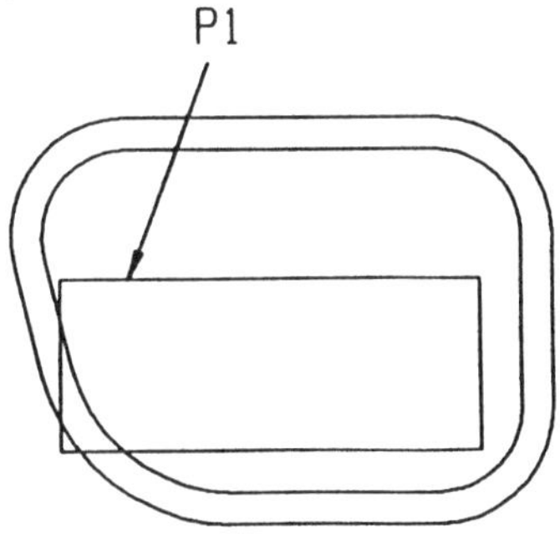

Figure 11.86

Step 8. Create a slope line to the rectangle. Use the pick point In Figure 11.86.

Select **MAIN MENU** → **Create** → **Line** → **Endpoints** → **Endpoint**
Pick at **P1** to define the first point
Enter **1.5,0.5** ← for the second point

Now the drawing should look like Figure 11.87.

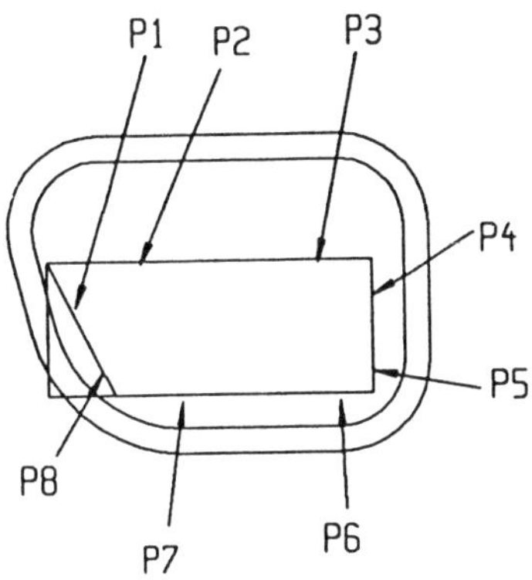

Figure 11.87

Step 9. Add fillets to four corners. Use the pick points in Figure 11.87.

Select **MAIN MENU → Modify → Fillet → Radius**
Enter **0.5 ←** for the fillet radius
Sequentially pick at **P1 - P6** to complete three three fillets
Select **Radius**, and then enter **1.5 ←**
Pick at **P7** and **P8** to complete the fourth fillet

The drawing should resemble Figure 11.88.

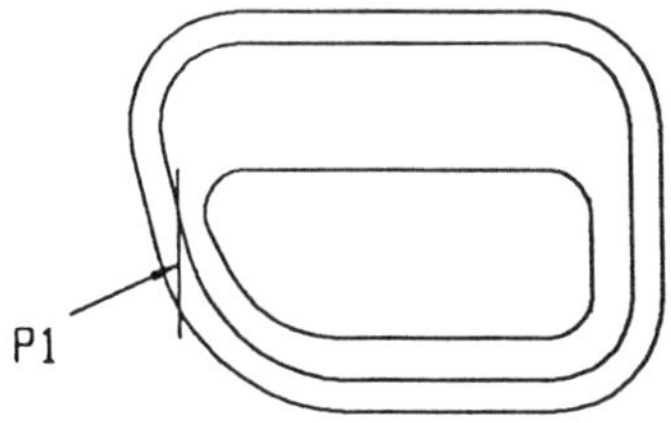

Figure 11.88

Step 10. Delete one line. Use the pick point in Figure 11.88.

Select **MAIN MENU → Delete**
Pick at **P1** to delete the line

The new drawing appears as Figure 11.89.

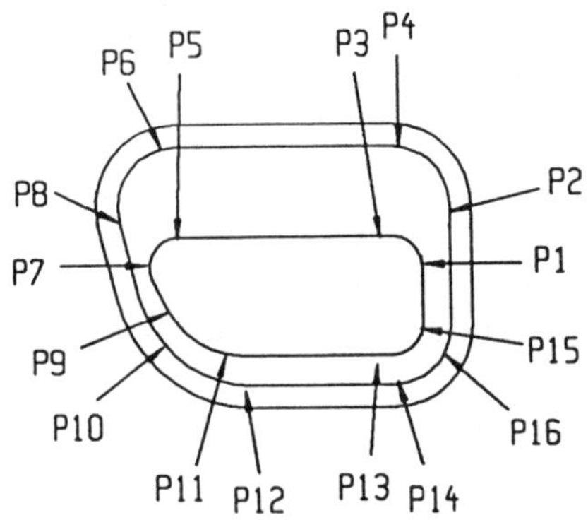

Figure 11.89

Step 11. Connect the top and bottom frames with straight lines using the 3D construction plane. Use the pick points in Figure 11.89.

Select **Cplane → 3d**
Select **MAIN MENU → Create → Line → Endpoints → Endpoint**
Sequentially pick at **P1 - P16**
Select **Gview → Isometric**

Press **Alt** + **F1** and then **F2** to fit the drawing.

The new drawing should resemble Figure 11.90 on the following page.

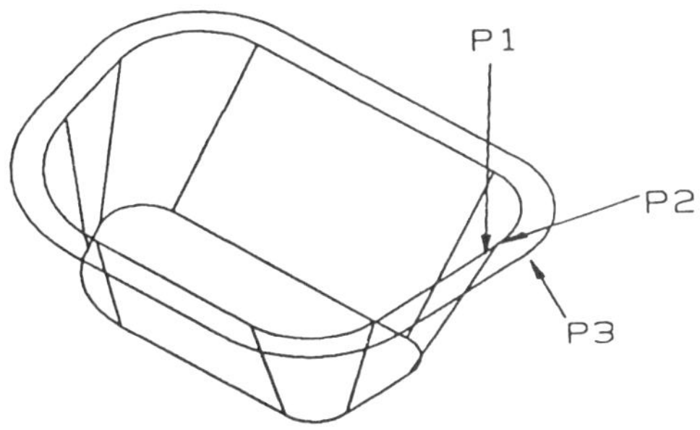

Figure 11.90

Step 12. Create the sweeping arc of the rim using the front construction plane.

Use the pick points in Figure 11.90.
Select **Cplane** → **Front**
Select **Z** → **Endpoint**
Pick at **P1** to find the Z depth of the entity endpoint

Z-3.0 shall appear in the Secondary Menu.
Select **MAIN MENU** → **Create** → **Arc** → **Endpoints** → **Endpoint**
Pick at **P2** and **P3** to define the two endpoints
Enter **0.2** ← for the rac radius
Pick at the desired arc (the second from the top)
The final drawing should resemble Figure 11.91.

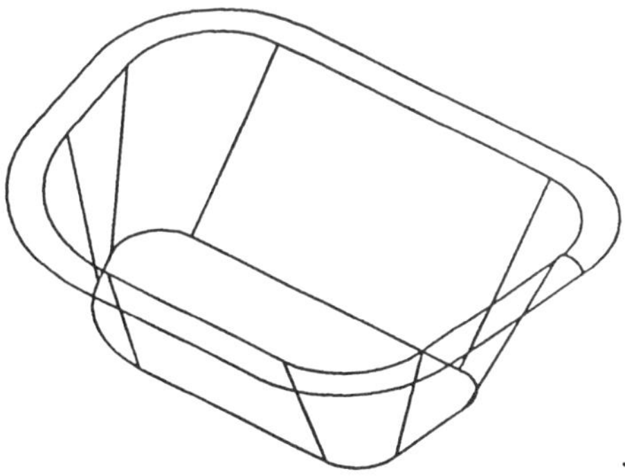

Figure 11.91

Step 13. Save the drawing.

Use the file name: **basket**.
Select **MAIN MENU** → **File** → **Save**
Enter the file name: **basket**

Project 12:
Flashlight

We are here ☞ **Wireframe Model (flash)**

Go to **Surface Model** Project 9 of Chapter 13 (flashs)

Go to **Toolpath** Project 6 of Chapter 15 (flash)

Construct the wireframe model of the flash light shown in Figure 11.92. The surface model consists of six surfaces: an outer frame surface, a top rim surface, a vertical wall surface, an inner top flat surface, a curved surface, and a fillet surface between the vertical wall surface and the inner top flat surface.

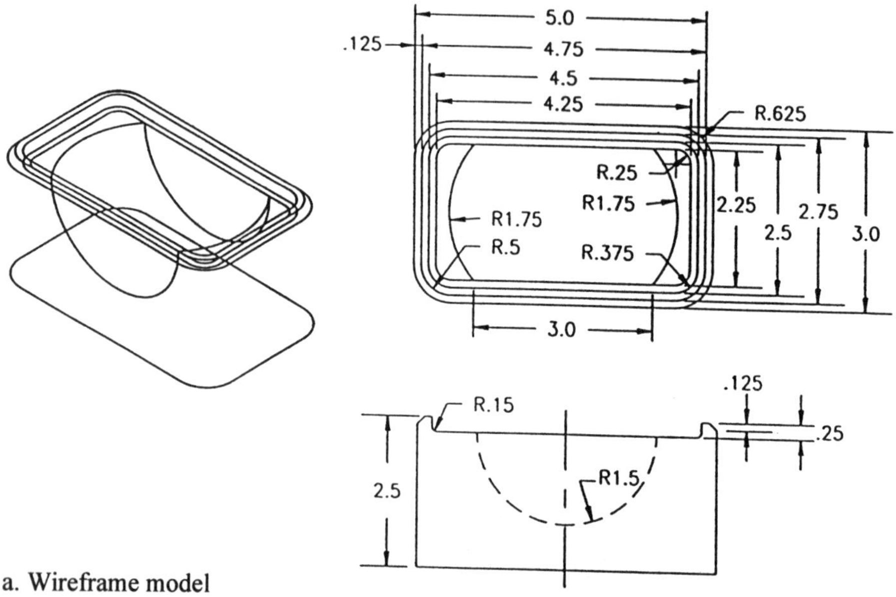

a. Wireframe model

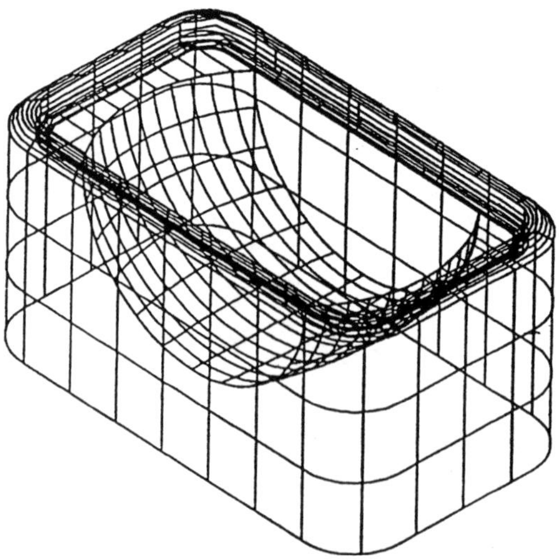

b. Surface model

Figure 11.92

Tips 1. Create four rectangles with corner arcs at the specified Z depth in the top view.

2. Translate the outer porfile in the negative Z direction to form the bottom profile of the outer frame surface.
3. Construct two arcs in the top view and another two arcs in the front view to define the edge profile for the recessed surface.

Step 1. Enter the Mastercam Mill. Set the Secondary Menu to these settings:

Cplane:	**Top**
Gview:	**Top**
Z:	**-0.125**

Step 2. Create the first rectangle.

Select **MAIN MENU →Create → Rectangle → 1 Point**
Enter the lower left corner: **-2.5, -1.5←**
Enter the width: **5←**
Enter the height: **3** ←

The rectangle will appear on the screen like Figure 11.93.

Figure 11.93

Step 3. Add four filletts using the pick points from Figure 11.93.

Select **MAIN MENU → Modify → Fillet → Radius**
Enter the fillet radius: **0.625** ←
Select **Chain**
Select the first entity in the contour: pick at **P1**
Select **Close → End here** to complete the four fillets.

Now the drawing should look like Figure 11.94

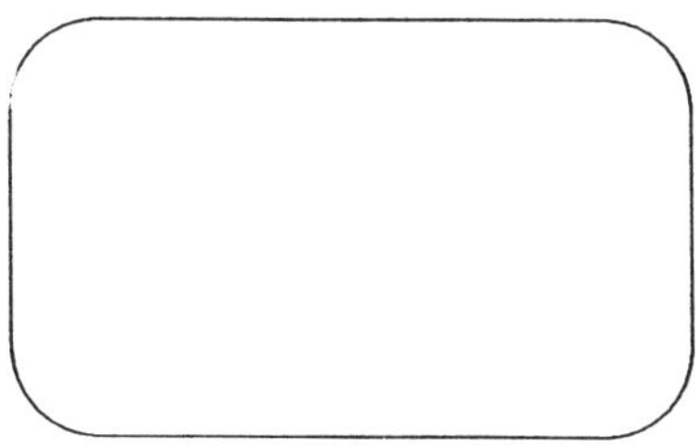

Figure 11.94

Step 4. Create the second rectangle.

Select **Z** from the Secondary Menu and then enter **0**
Select **MAIN MENU → Create → Rectangle → 1 point**
Enter the lower left corner: **-2.375,-1.375** ←
Enter the width: **4.75** ←
Enter the height: **2.75** ←

The drawing should resemble Figure 11.95.

Figure 11.95

Step 5. Add four fillets to the second rectangle. Use the pick points from Figure 11.95 on the previous page.

Select **MAIN MENU → Modify → Fillet → Radius**
Enter the fillet radius: **0.5** ←
Select **Chain**
Pick at **P1**
Select **Close → End here** to complete the four fillets.

The drawing should look like Figure 11.96.

Figure 11.96

Step 6. Create the third rectangle.

Select **MAIN MENU → Create → Rectangle → 1 point**
Enter the lower left corner: **-2.25,-1.25** ←
Enter the width: **4.5** ←
Enter the height: **2.5** ←

The drawing now should appear as in Figure 11.97.

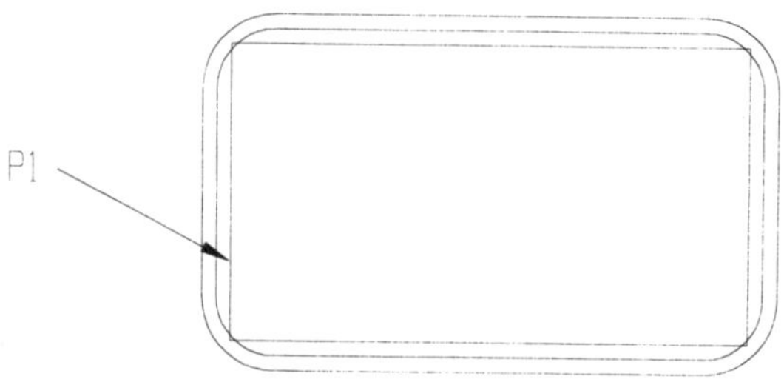

Figure 11.97

Step 7. Add four fillets to the third rectangle. Use the pick points in Figure 11.97.

Select **MAIN MENU → Modify → Fillet → Radius**
Enter the fillet radius: **0.375** ←
Select **Chain**
Pick at **P1**
Select **Close → End here** to complete the four fillets.

Now the drawing should look like Figure 11.98.

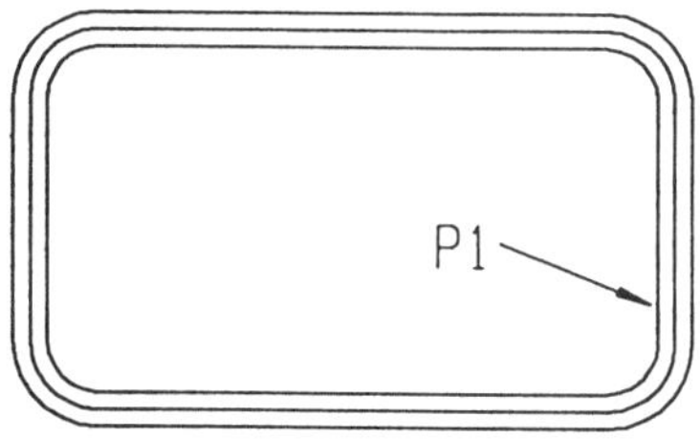

Figure 11.98

Step 8. Translate the third rectangle with fillets to Z-0.25. Use the pick points in Figure 11.98.

Select **MAIN MENU → Xform → Translate → Chain**
Select the first entity in the contour: pick at **P1←**
Select **Close → End here → Done → Rectang**
Enter the translation vector: **Z-0.25 ←**
Set the Translate parameters as below:

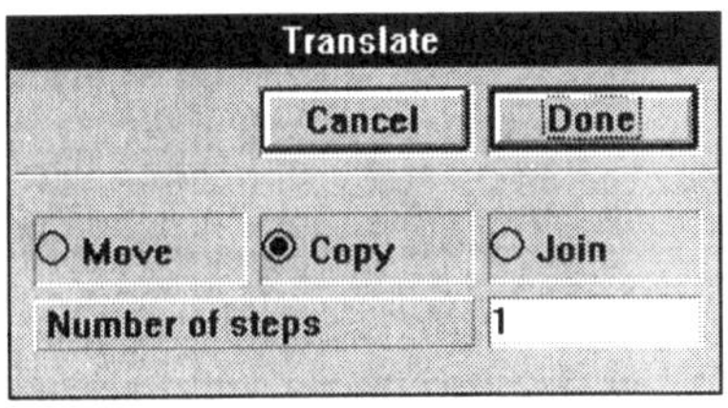

Select **Done**
Select **Gview → Isometric**

The drawing should resemble Figure 11.99.

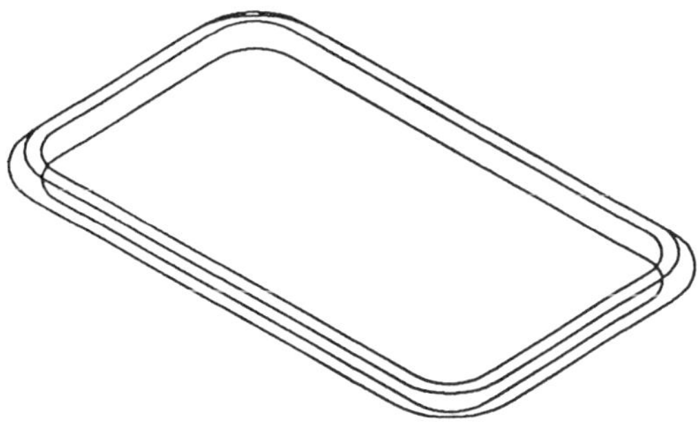

Figure 11.99

Select **Gview → Top**
Now the drawing in the top view should look like Figure 11.100.

Figure 11.100

Step 9. Create the fourth rectangle.

Select **Z** and then enter **-0.25** ←
Select **MAIN MENU → Create → Rectangle → 1 point**
Enter the lower left corner: **-2.125,-1.125** ←
Enter the width: **4.25** ←
Enter the height: **2.25** ←

The drawing now appears as in Figure 11.101.

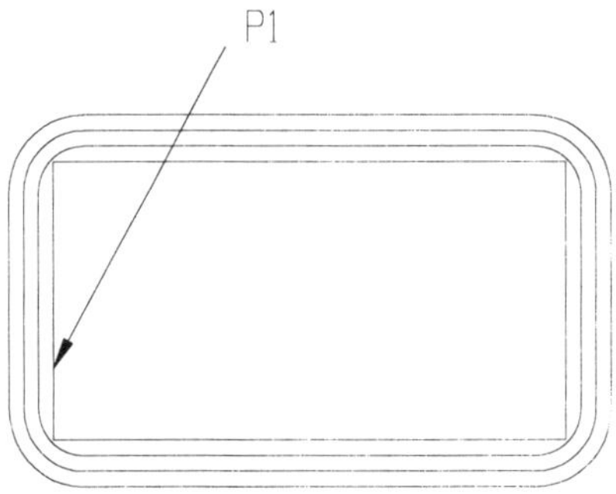

Figure 11.101

Step 10. Add four fillets to the fourth rectangle. Use the pick points shown in Figure 11.101.

Select **MAIN MENU ← Modify ← Fillet ← Radius**
Enter the fillet radius: **0.25** ←
Select **Chain**
Pick at **P1**
Select **Close → End here** to complete the four fillets.

The drawing should look like Figure 11.102.

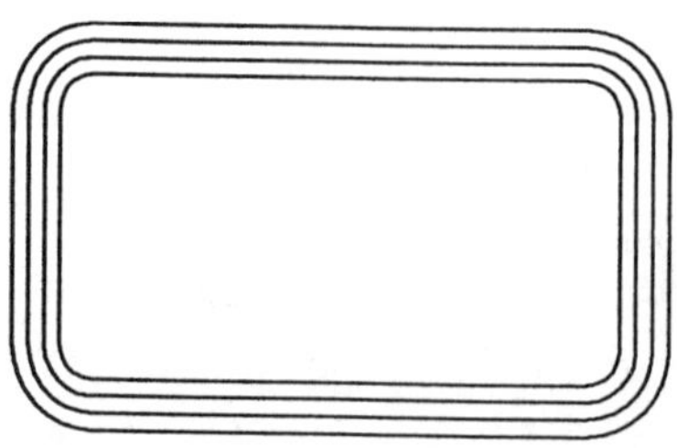

Figure 11.102

Step 11. Create two arcs on the top construction plane.

Select **MAIN MENU → Create → Arc → Endpoints**
Enter the first point: **-1.5,-1.125 ←**
Enter the second point: **-1.5,1.125 ←**
Enter the radius: **1.75 ←**
Select an arc: pick the desired arc (3rd arc from the right)
Enter the first point: **1.5,-1.125 ←**
Enter the second point: **1.5,1.125 ←**
Enter the radius: **1.75 ←**
Select an arc: pick the desired arc (2nd arc from the right)
Select **Gview → Isometric**
The drawing should resemble Figure 11.103.

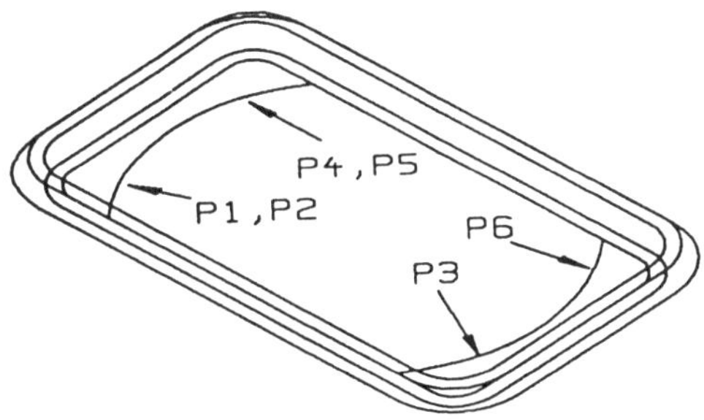

Figure 11.103

Step 12. Create the other two arcs using the front construction plane. Use the pick points in Figure 11.103.

Select **Cplane → Front**
Select **Z → Endpoint**
Pick at **P1** to obtain the Z value of the picked endpoint

Z1.125 should appear in the Secondary Menu.

Select **MAIN MENU → Create → Arc → Endpoints → Endpoint**
Pick at **P2** and **P3** for the first and second point, respectively
Enter the radius: **1.5 ←**
Select an arc: pick the lower half of the arc to complete the first arc
Select **Z → Endpoint**
Pick at **P4** to obtain the Z value of the picked endpoint

Z-1.125 should appear in the Secondary Menu.

Pick at **P5** and **P6** for the first and second point, respectively
Enter the radius: **1.5 ←**
Select an arc: pick the desired arc

The drawing will appear as in Figure 11.104 on the next page.

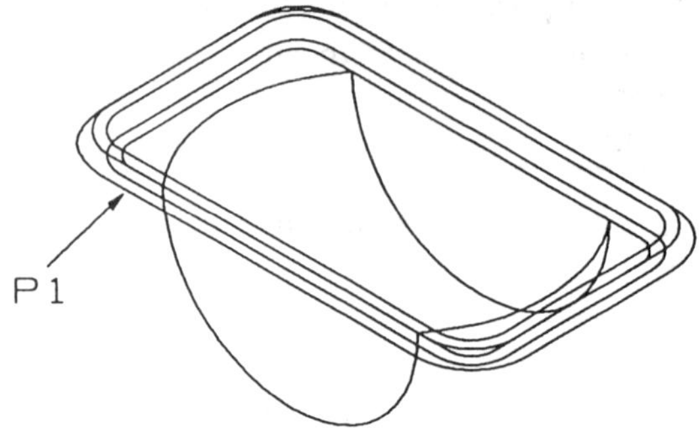

Figure 11.104

Step 13. Translate the outer rectangle to form a rectangular box. Use the pick points in Figure 11.104.

Select **Cplane** → **Top**
Select **MAIN MENU** → **Xform** → **Translate** → **Chain**
Selete the first entity in the contour: pick at **P1** ←
Select **Close** → **End here** → **Done** → **Rectang**
Enter the translation vector: **Z-2.375** ←
Set the Translate parameters as below:

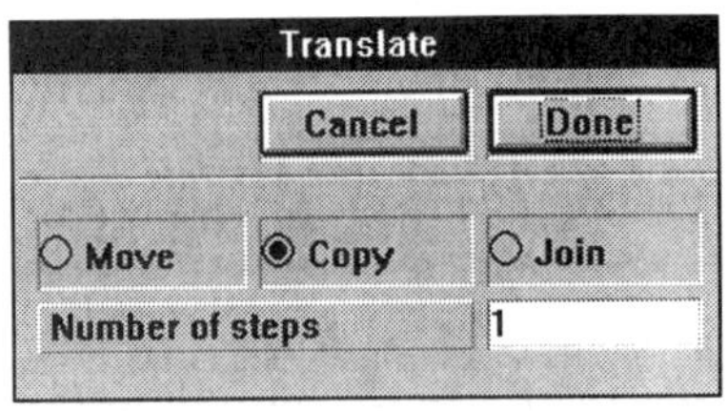

Select **Done**
The final drawing should look like Figure 11.105.

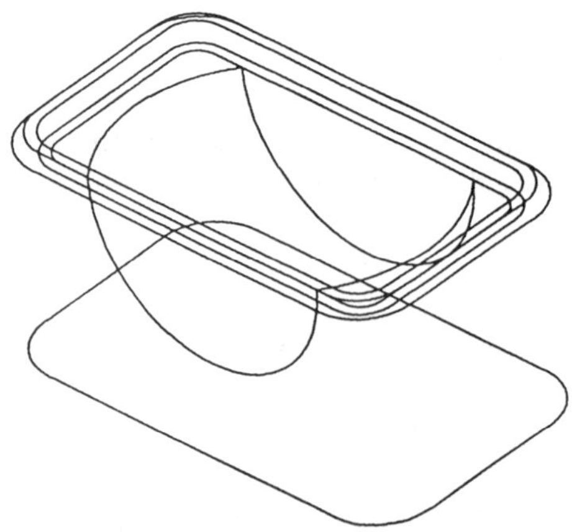

Figure 11.105

Step 14. Save the drawing. Use the file name: **flash**.

Select **MAIN MENU** → **File** → **Save**
Enter the file name: **flash**

Project 13:
Hair dryer

The hair dryer consists of three segments: handle, frame, and tube. The wireframe model is shown in Figure 11.106.

We are here ☞ **Wireframe Model** (dryer)

Go to ☞ **Surface Model** — Project 10 of Chapter 13 (dryers)

Go to ☞ **Toolpath** — Project 7 of Chapter 15 (dryer)

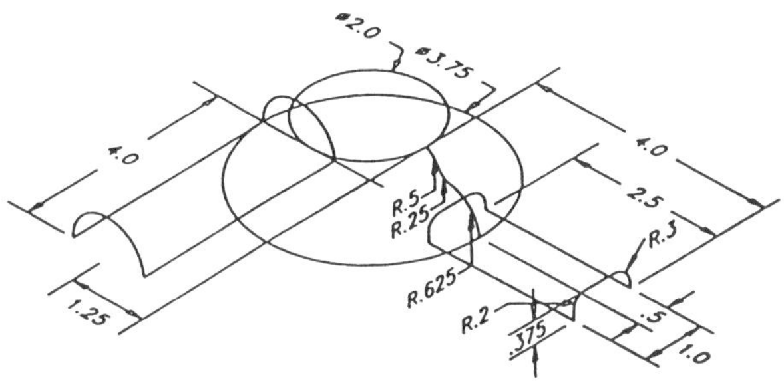

a. Wireframe model

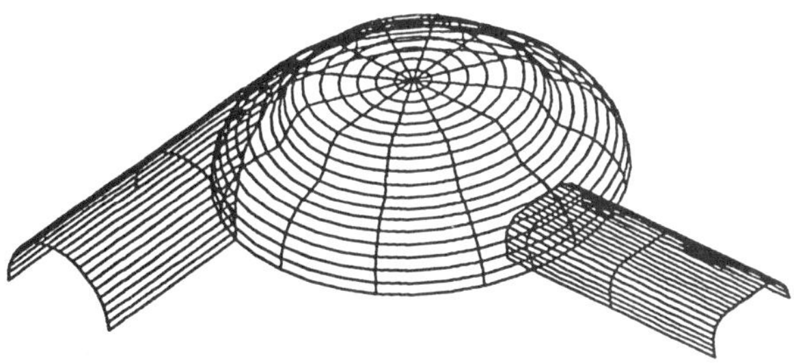

b. Surface model
Figure 11.106

Tips 1. Create three circles in the top construction plane.

2. Construct the edge profile of the frame which is formed by three tangent arcs in the front construction view.
3. Create two semi-circles for making the tube in the front construction view.
4. Construct the handle profile using the top construction view.
5. The edge profiles for the tube and the handle are made longer than needed to ensure that the surfaces intersect.

Step 1. Enter the Mastercam Mill. Set the Secondary Menu to the following settings:

Z: **1.0**
Cplane: **Top**
Gview: **Top**

Step 2. Create three construction circles using the top construction plane.

Select **MAIN MENU →Create → Arc → pt Rad cir**
Enter the center point: **0,0** ←
Enter the radius: **1** ←
Select **Z**, and then enter **0.625** ←
Enter the center point: **0,0** ←
Enter the radius: **1.25** ←
Select **Z**, and then enter **Z0** ←
Enter the center point: **0,0** ←
Enter the radius: **1.875** ←
Select **Gview → Isometric**
The drawing of these three circles should look like Figure 11.107.

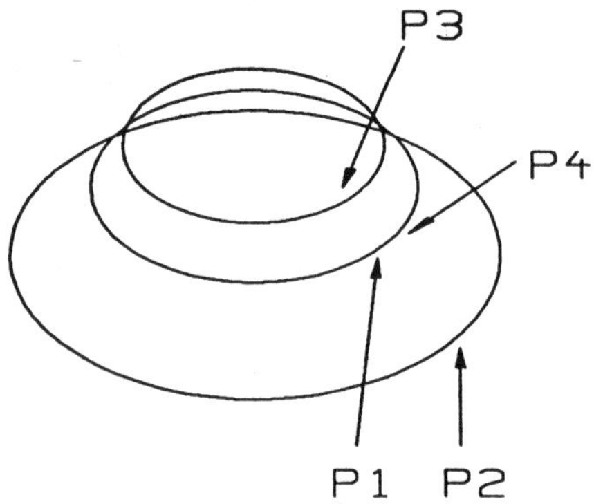

Figure 11.107

Step 3. Create the edge profile of the frame using the front consturction plane.

Use the pick points in Figure 11.107.
Select **Cplane → Front**
Select **Z** and then enter **0** ← if necessary
Select **MAIN MENU → Create → Arc → Endpoints → Endpoint**
Pick **P1** and **P2** for the first point and second point
Enter the radius: **0.625** ←
Select an arc: pick the desired arc segment (2nd from the right)
Enter the first point: pick at **P3**
Enter the second point: pick at **P4**
Enter the radius: **0.5** ←
Select an arc: pick the desired arc segment (2nd from the right)

The drawing should look like Figure 11.108.

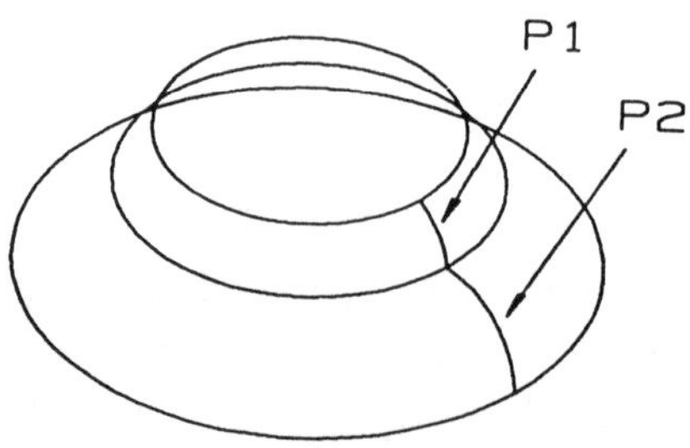

Figure 11.108

Step 4. Create an arc tangent to the two arcs. Use the pick points from Figure 11.108.

Select **MAIN MENU → Modify → Fillet → Radius**
Enter the fillet radius: **0.25** ←
Select an entity: pick at **P1**
Select another entity: pick at **P2**

Now the drawing should appear as in Figure 11.109.

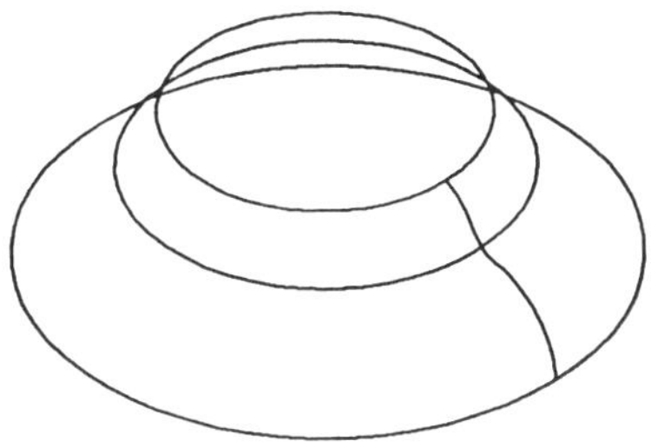

Figure 11.109

Step 5. Create two arcs for the tube.

Select **MAIN MENU → Create → Arc → Polar → Ctr point**
Enter the center point: **-1.25,0** ←
Enter the radius: **0.625** ←
Enter the initial angle: **0** ←
Enter the final angle: **180** ←
Select **Z** and then enter **3.5** ←
Enter the center point: **-1.25,0** ←
Enter the radius: **0.625** ←
Enter the initial angle: **0** ←←
Enter the final angle: **180** ←

The drawing should appear as in Figure 11.110.

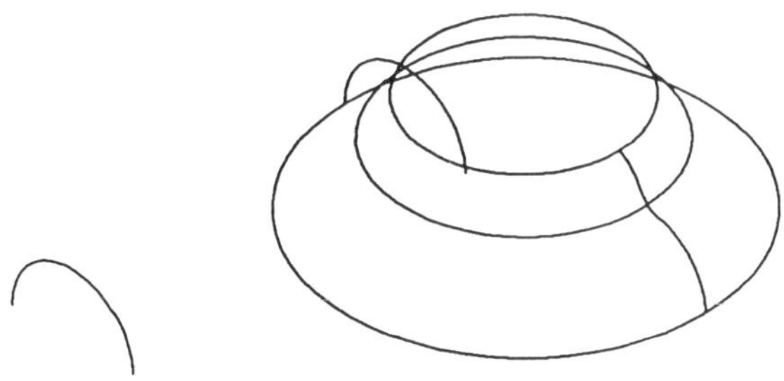

Figure 11.110

Step 6. Create the edge profile of the handle using the side construction view.

Select **Cplane → Side**
Select **Z** and then enter **4.0** ←
Select **MAIN MENU → Create → Rectangle → 2 points**
Enter the lower left corner: **-0.5,0** ←
Enter the upper right corner: **0.5,0.375** ←

The drawing should resemble Figure 11.111.

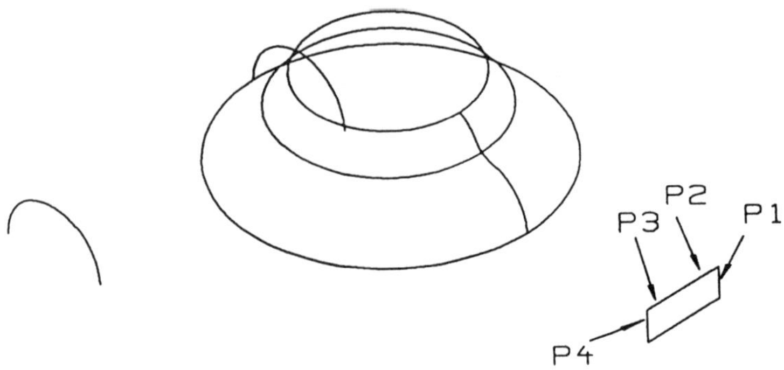

Figure 11.111

Step 7. Add two arcs. Use the pick points in Figure 11.111.

Select **MAIN MENU → Modify → Fillet → Radius**
Enter the fillet radius: **0.3** ←
Select an entity: pick at **P1** ←
Select another entity: pick at **P2** ←
Select **Radius**
Enter the fillet radius: **0.2** ←
Select an entity: pick at **P3**
Select another entity: pick at **P4**

The drawing should appear as Figure 11.112.

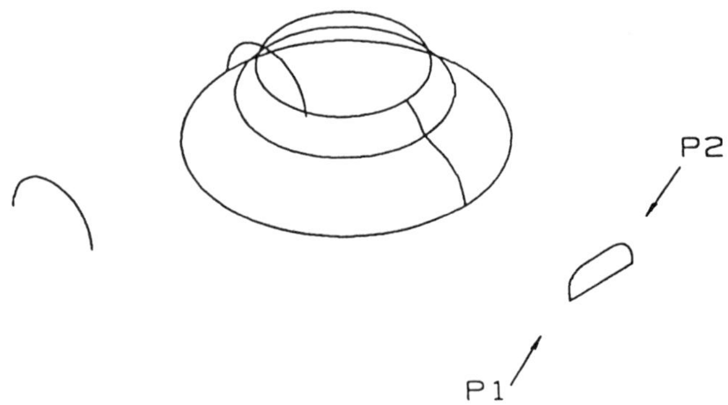

Figure 11.112

Step 8. Translate the handle profile. Use the pick points in Figure 11.112.

Select **MAIN MENU → Xform → Translate → Window**
Enter the first corner: pick at **P1**
Enter the second corner: pick at **P2**
Select **Done → Rectang**
Enter the translation vector: **Z-2.5** ←
Set the Translate paramenters as below:

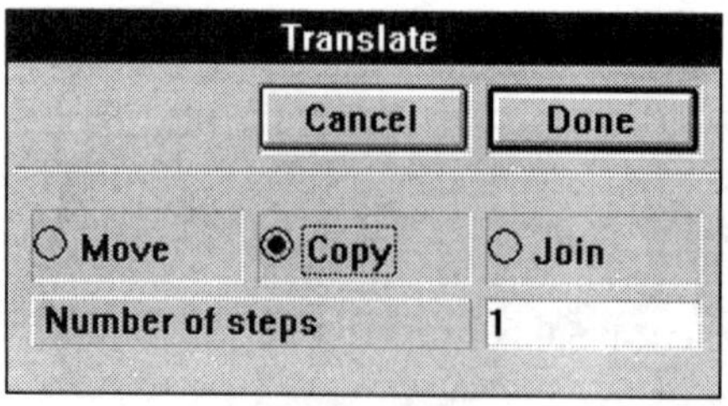

Select **Done**

The drawing should resemble Figure 11.113.

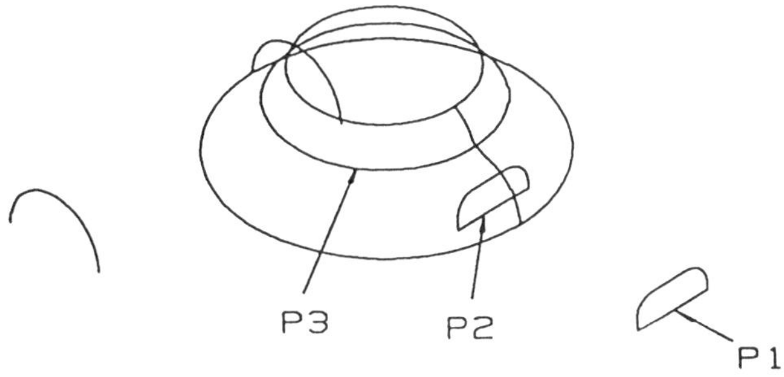

Figure 11.113

Step 9. Delete construction lines. Use the pick points in Figure 11.113.

Select **MAIN MENU** → **Delete**

Pick at **P1, P2,** and **P3**

The new drawing appears as Figure 11.114.

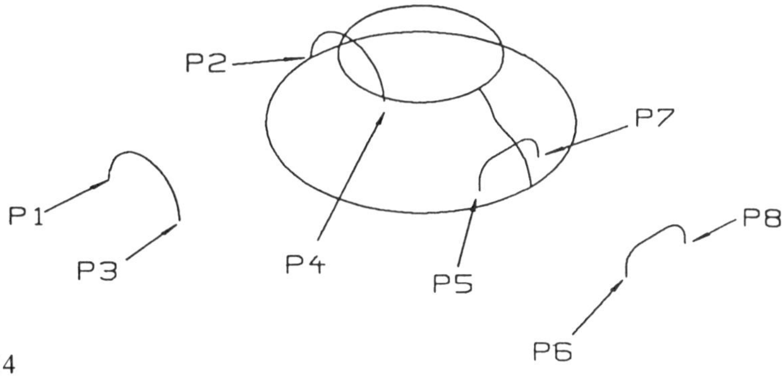

Figure 11.114

Step 10. Construct four lines to join two arcs and two handle profiles using the 3D construction plane. Use the pick points in Figure 11.114.

Select **Cplane** → **3d**

Select **MAIN MENU** → **Create** → **Line** → **Endpoints** → **Endpoint**

Sequentially pick at **P1 - P8** to complete the four lines

The final drawing should resemble Figure 11.115.

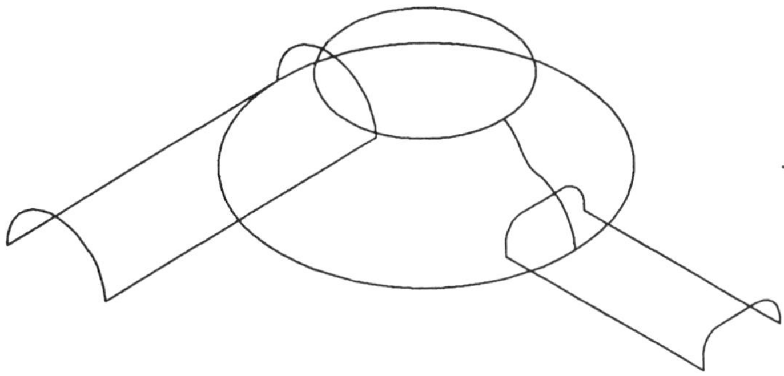

Tom 57

Figure 11.115

Step 11. Save the drawing: Use the filename: dryer.

Select **MAIN MENU → File → Save**

Enter the file name: **dryer**

Project 14:

We are here ☞ **Wireframe Model (loft3)**

Go to ☞ **Surface Model** **Project 6 of Chapter 12 (lofts3)**

Go to ☞ **Toolpath** **Project 1 of Chapter 15 (flowl1)**

Go to ☞ **Toolpath Trimming** **Project 1 of Chapter 16 (lofts3)**

The surface shown in Figure 11.116 is defined by **five** contours including one circle at one end, one line-profile at the other end, and three ellipses. These three ellipses are obtained by rotating a circle at a specified angle and then projecting it onto a vertical plannar surface as shown in Figure 11.117. Since the part is symmetrical about the axis, only one half of the part profile contours is required. The other half is obtained by mirroring the profile contours about the X axis. The plannar surface used for the curves to be projected onto in obtaining a surface curve can be generated as a ruled surface.

Ruled surfaces are covered in chapter 12.

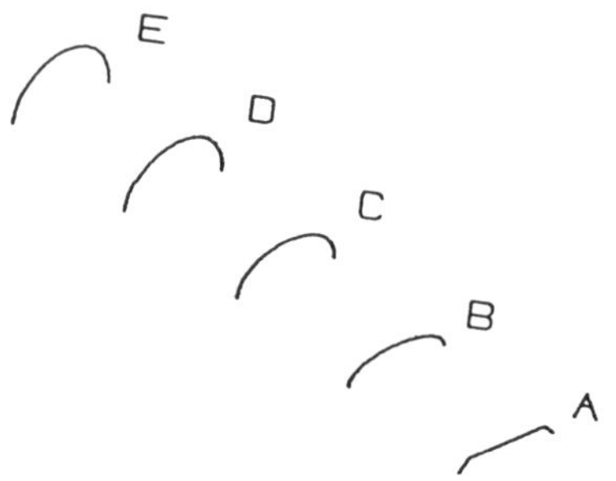

Figure 11.116a. Wireframe model

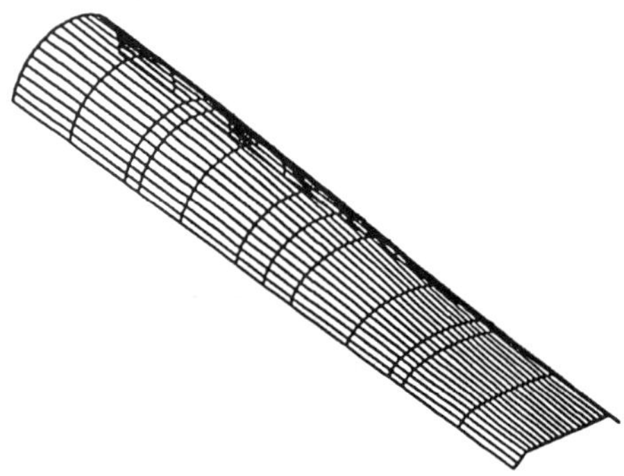

Figure 11.116b. Surface model

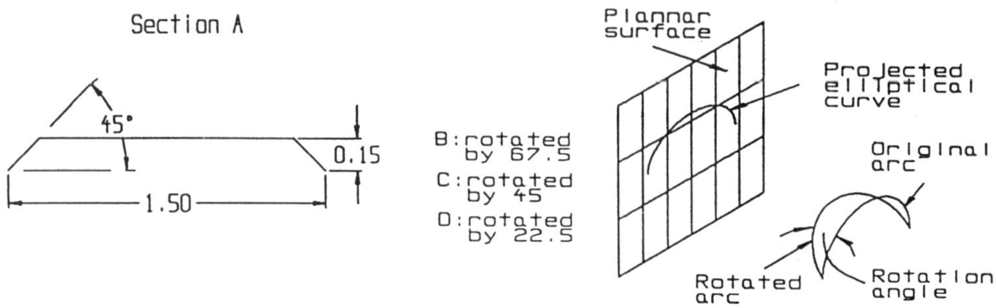

Figure 11.117

Step 1. Enter the Mastercam Mill. Set these values: Cplane to side plane, Gview to Isometric, and Z value to 3.0.

Select **Cplane → Side → Gview → Isometric**

Select **Z** and then enter **3.0** ←

Step 2. Create a semi-circle.

Select **MAIN MENU →Create → Arc → Polar → Ctr point**
Enter the center point: **0,0** ←
Enter the radius: **0.75** ←
Enter the initial angle: **0** ←
Enter the final angle: **180** ←

The drawing should resemble Figure 11.118.

Figure 11.118

Step 3. Create two horizontal lines for generating a ruled surface.

Select **Z** and then enter **0.5** ←
Select **MAIN MENU → Create → Line → Endpoints**
Enter the first endpoint: **-1.5,1.5** ←
Enter the second endpoint: **1.5,1.5** ←
Enter the first endpoint: **-1.5,-1.5** ←
Enter the second endpoint: **1.5,-1.5** ←

These two lines now appear as in Figure 11.119.

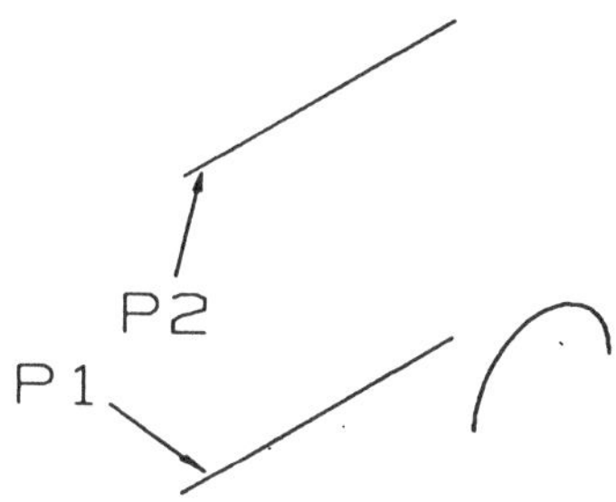

Figure 11.119

Step 4. Create a ruled surface. Use the pick points in Figure 11.119.

Select **MAIN MENU → Create → sUrface → rUled → Nurbs**
Select **Single** from the chaining method menu,
then pick at **P1** for contour 1
Select **Single** again and pick at **P2** for contour 2
Select **Done** to complete the selection
Select **Done** from the ruled surface parameters menu

The ruled surface should appear as in Figure 11.120.

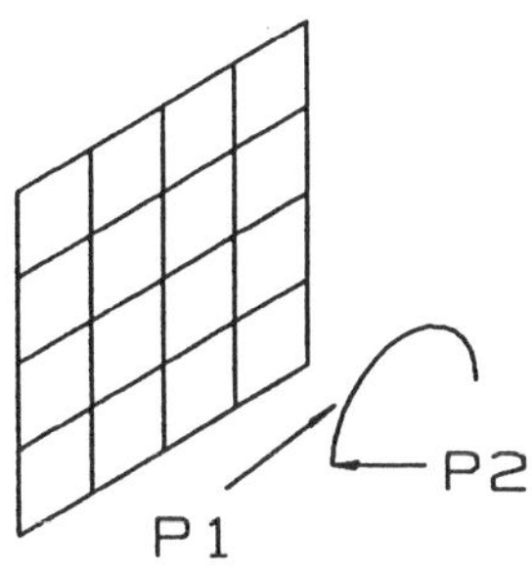

Figure 11.120

Step 5. Rotate the semi-circle by 22.5° using the Front construction plane.

Use the pick points in Figure 11.120.
Select **Cplane** → **Front**
Select **MAIN MENU** → **Xform** → **Rotate** → **Entity**
Pick at **P1** to select the entity
Select **BACKUP** → **Done** → **Point** → **Endpoint**
Pick at **P2** to trap the endpoint of the entity
Set the Rotate parameters as below:

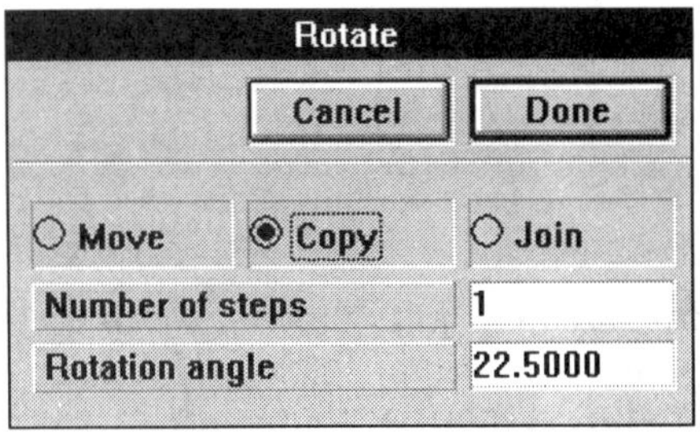

Select **Done**

The drawing with the first rotated arc is shown in Figure 11.121.

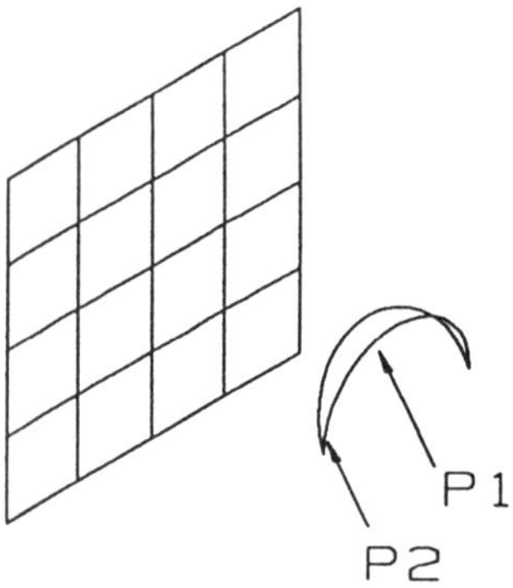

Figure 11.121

Step 6. Rotate the semi-circle by 45°. Use the pick points in Figure 11.121.

Select **Entity** from the Rotate Menu
Pick at **P1** to select the entity
Select **BACKUP** → **Done** → **Point** → **Endpoint**
Pick at **P2**
Set the Rotate parameters as below:

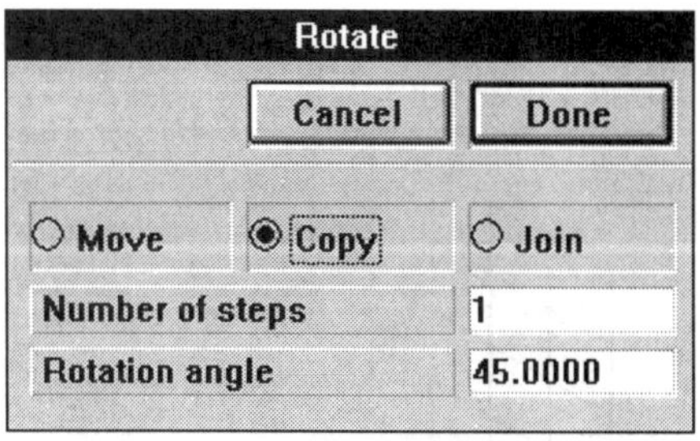

Select **Done**

The drawing now should resemble Figure 11.122.

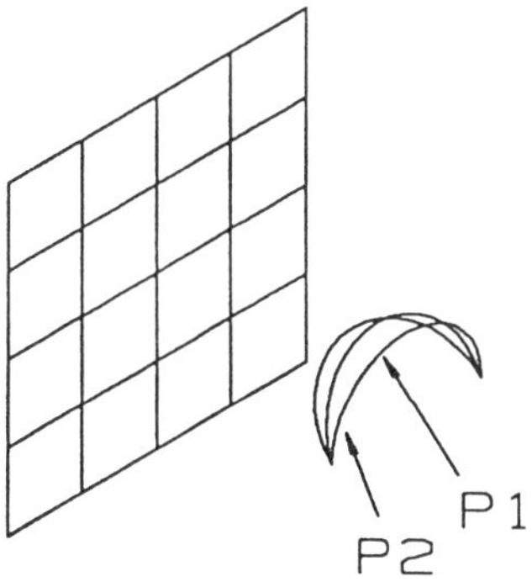

Figure 11.122

Step 7. Rotate the semi-circle by 67.5°. Use the pick points in Figure 11.122.

Select **Entity** from the Rotate Menu
Pick at **P1** to select the entity
Select **BACKUP** → **Done** → **Point** → **Endpoint**
Pick at **P2**
Set the Rotate parameters as below:

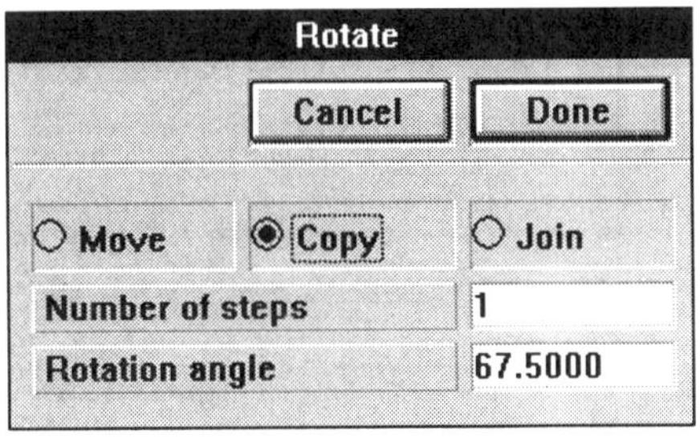

Select **Done**

The drawing should appear as Figure 11.123 .

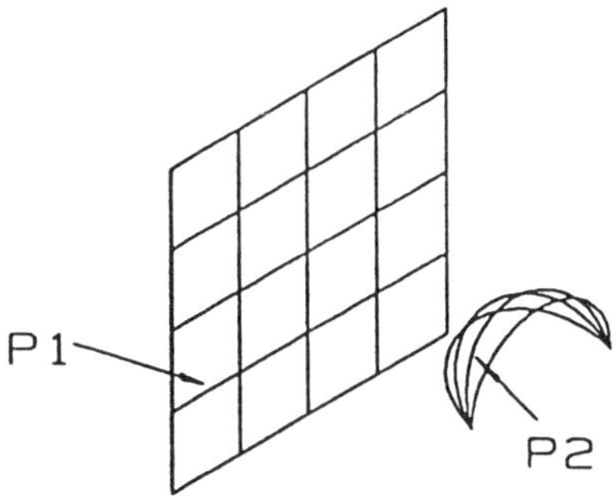

Figure 11.123

Step 8. Project the first arc onto the plannar plane using the Side construction plane. Use the pick points in Figure 11.123 on the previous page.

Select **Cplane → Side**
Select **MAIN MENU → Create → Curve → Project**
Set the Project Curve parameters
to the following settings ☞

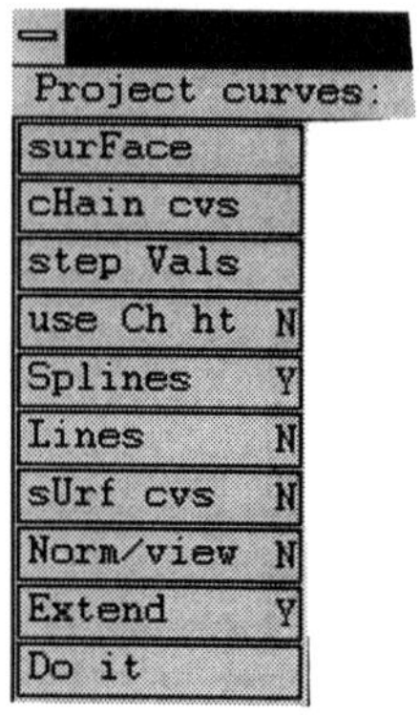

Pick at **P1** to select the ruled surface
Select **Single** from the chaining method menu
Pick at **P2** to select the arc rotated by 22.5°
Select **Done → Do it**

The new drawing becomes Figure 11.124.

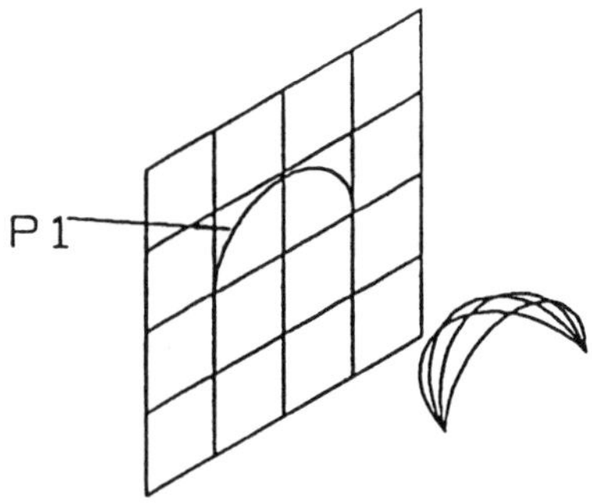

Figure 11.124

Step 9. Translate the curve to the proper position. Use the pick points labeled above in Figure 11.124.

Select **MAIN MENU → Xform → Translate → Entity**
Pick at **P1** to select the entity
Select **BACKUP → Done → Rectang**
Enter the translation vector: **Z-6.5** ←
Set the Translate parameters as shown here:

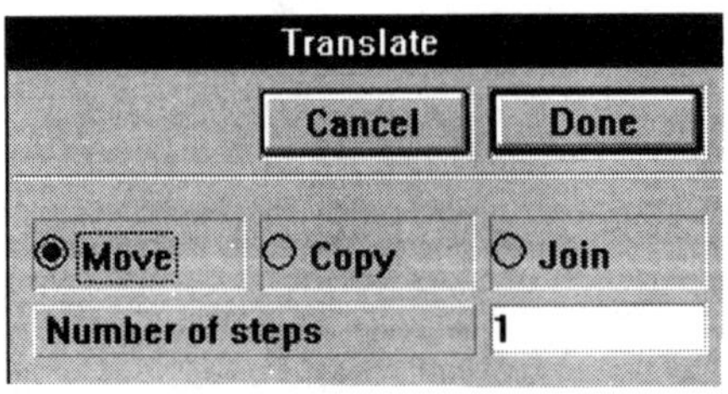

Select **Done**
Press Alt and F1 simultaneously to fit the drawing
The drawing should resemble Figure 11.125 on the next page.

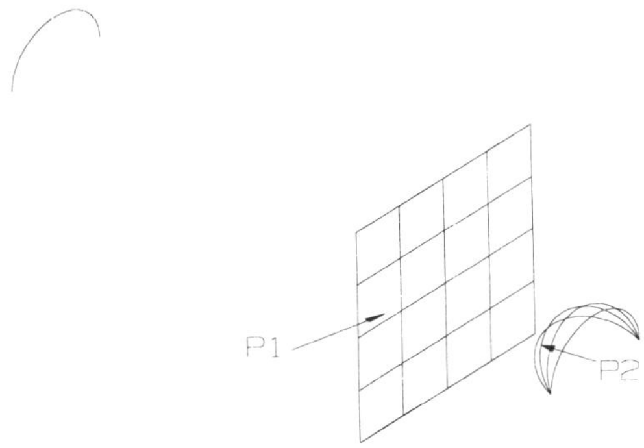

Figure 11.125

Step 10. Project the second curve. Use the pick points in Figure 11.125.

Select **MAIN MENU → Create → Curve → Project**
Pick at **P1** to select the surface
Select **Single** from the chaining method menu
Pick at **P2** to select the second curve
Select **Done → Do it**

The projected curve appears as in Figure 11.126.

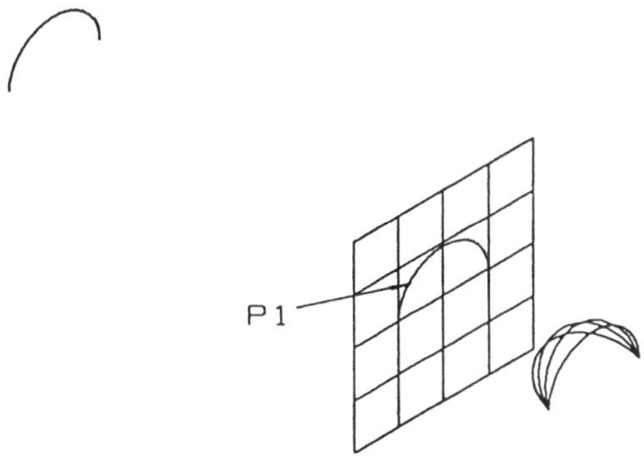

Figure 11.126

Step 11. Translate the second curve. Use the pick points in Figure 11.126.

Select **MAIN MENU → Xform → Translate →Entity**
Pick at **P1**
Select **BACKUP → Done → Rectang**
Enter the translation vector: **Z-4.5** ←
Select **Done** from the Translate parameters menu
The new drawing becomes Figure 11.127.

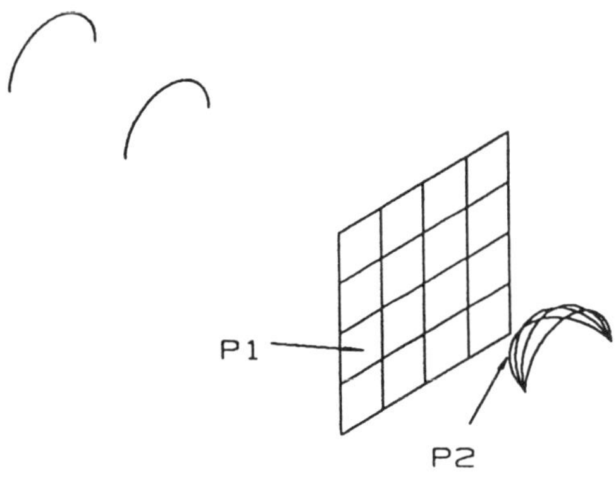

Figure 11.127

Step 12. Project the third curve. Use the pick points in Figure 11.127.

Select **MAIN MENU → Create → Curve → Project**
Pick at **P1** to select the ruled surface
Select **Single** from the chaining method menu
Pick at **P2** to select the third curve
Select **Done → Do it**

The drawing now should look like Figure 11.128.

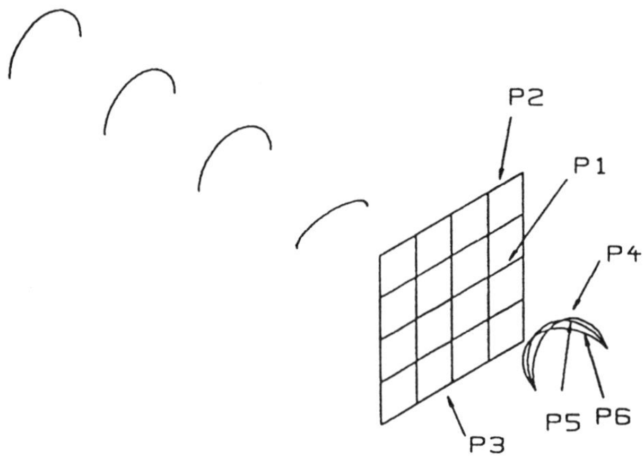

Figure 11.128

Step 13. Translate the third curve. Use the pick points in Figure 11.128.

Select **MAIN MENU → Xform → Translate → Entity**
Pick at **P1**
Select **BACKUP → Done → Rectang**
Enter the translation vector; **Z-2.5 ←**
Select **Done** from the Translate parameters menu

Step 14. Translate the original arc. Continue to use the pick points in Figure 11.128.

Select **Entity** from the menu
Pick at **P2** to select the arc
Select **BACKUP → Done → Rectang**
Enter the translation vector: **Z-11 ←**
Select **Done** from the Translate parameters menu
Press **Alt** & **F1** simultaneously to fit the drawing

The new drawing should resemble Figure 11.129.

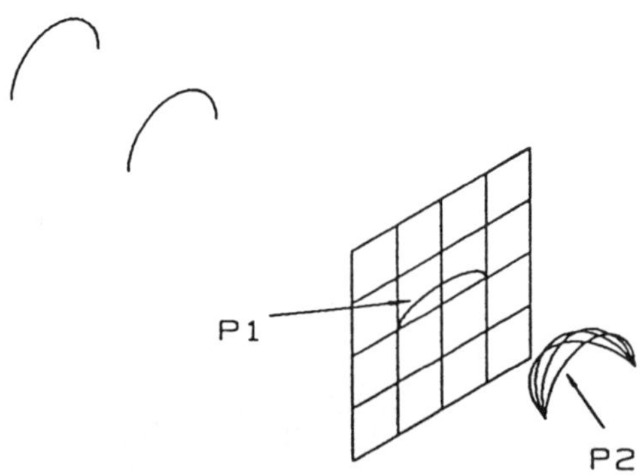

Figure 11.129

Step 15. Delete the construction entities. Use the pick points in Figure 11.129.

Select **MAIN MENU → Delete**

Pick at **P1, P2, P3, P4, P5** and **P6** to delete the three curves, one surface and two lines.

The drawing becomes Figure 11.130.

Figure 11.130

Step 16. Construct the sectional profile at A.

Select **Z** and then enter **0** ←

Select **MAIN MENU → Create → Line → Multi**

Specify point 1: **-0.75,0** ←

Specify point 2: **-0.6,0.15** ←

Specify point 3: **0.6,0.15** ←

Specify point 4: **0.75,0** ←

The final drawing should resemble Figure 11.131.

Figure 11.131

Step 17. Save the drawing. Use the Filename: loft2.

Select **MAIN MENU → File → Save**

Enter the file name: **loft3**

Project 15

We are here ☞ **Wireframe Model (fan)**

Go to **Surface Model** — **Project 11 of Chapter 13 (fans)**

A fan, shown in Figure 11.132, consists of seven blades that are evenly spaced around the hub. The two ends of each blade have the same cross section profile (Figure 11.133). The inside end is rotated 15° with the horizontal line and the outside end is rotated 40° with respect to the line. The end profile is curved along the hub profile.

Figure 11.132

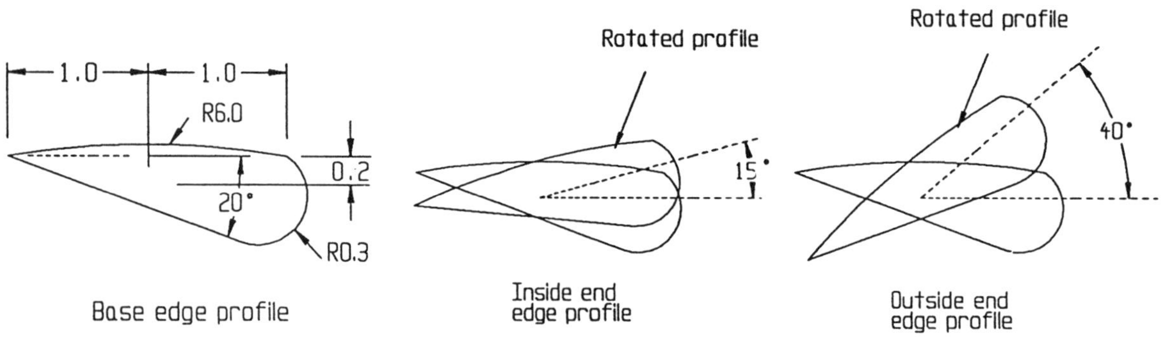

Figure 11.133

Tips 1. Create the edge profile for the hub using the Front Cplane.

2. Construct the cross section profile of the blade in the Front Cplane.

3. Create a swept surface for the outer rim which is a cylinder. This surface is used to obtain the surface curves by projecting the cross section profile onto this surface.
4. Rotate the blade edge profile by 15° with the horizontal axis, and then project it onto the outer rim surface to obtain a curved edge profile for the inside end.
5. Rotate the blade profile by 40° with the horizontal axis and then project it onto the outer rim surface to obtain the outside edge profile of the blade. This edge profile is then translated to the specified position.
6. Use different levels and colors to facilitate the creation of the wireframe model.

Step 1. Create three lines using Front Cplane. Initialize the screen if necessary.

Select **Cplane → Front**
Select **Gview → Front**
Select **MAIN MENU → Create → Line → Multi**
Specify endpoint 1: **0,1** ←
Specify endpoint 2: **0.625,1** ←
Specify endpoint 3: **0.625,0** ←
Specify endpoint 4: **2.5,1** ←

The drawing with three lines should appears as Figure 11.134.

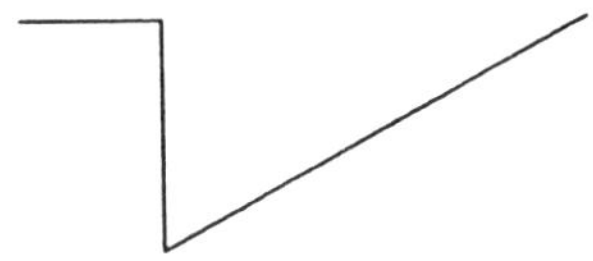

Figure 11.134

Step 2. Create a horizontal line and a vertical line.

Select **BACKUP → Endpoints**
Specify the first endpoint: **1,1** ←
Specify the second endpoint: **4,1** ←
Specify the first endpoint: **3,1.5** ←
Specify the second endpoint: **3,-1** ←

The new drawing should look like Figure 11.135.

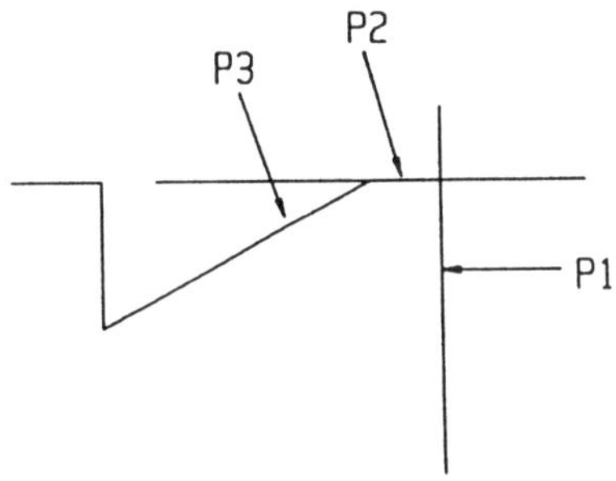

Figure 11.135

Step 3. Create an arc using the pick points in Figure 11.135.

Select **MAIN MENU → Create → Arc → Tangent → 3 entities**
Pick at **P1, P2,** and **P3** to select the three entities

The arc added to the drawing now appears as Figure 11.136.

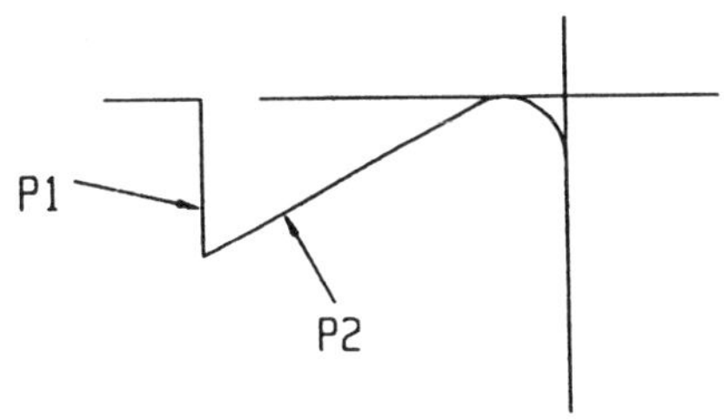

Figure 11.136

Step 4. Create a fillet using the pick points in Figure 11.136.

Select **MAIN MENU → Modify → Fillet → Radius**
Enter the fillet radius: **0.25 ←**
Pick at **P1** and **P2**

The fillet is added to the drawing as shown in Figure 11.137.

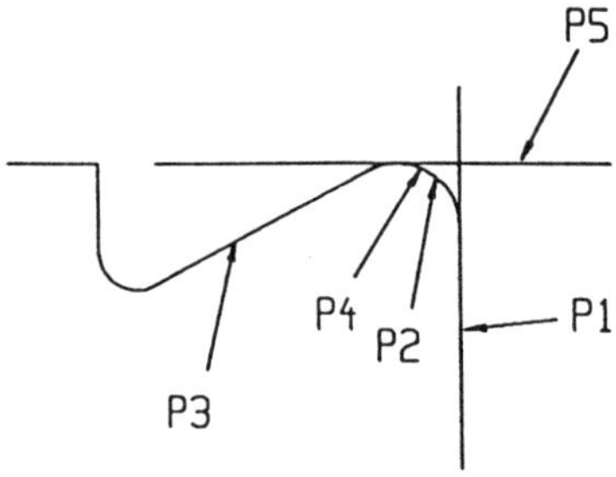

Figure 11.137

Step 5. Trim the vetical line and the slope line. Then delete the horizontal line using the pick points in Figure 11.137 above.

Select **BACKUP → Trim → 1 entity**
Pick at **P1** and **P2** to trim the vertical line
Pick at **P3** and **P4** to trim the slope line
Select **MAIN MENU → Delete**
Pick at **P5** to delete the horizontal line

The hub profile should look like Figure 11.138.

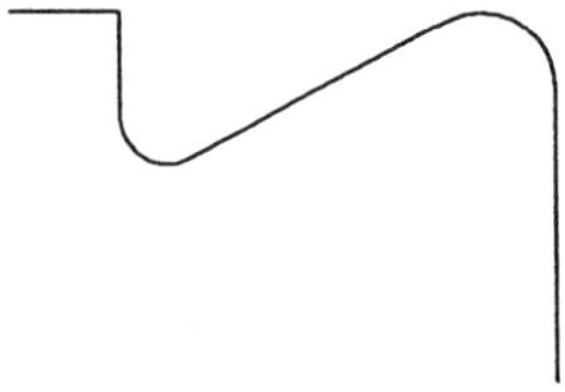

Figure 11.138

Step 6. Create a circle using Top Cplane. Change Gview to Isometric.

Select **Cplane → Top**
Select **Gview → Isometric**
Select **Z** then enter **1 ←**
Select **MAIN MENU → Create → Arc → pt Rad cir**
Enter the center point: **0,0 ←**
Enter the radius: **0.625 ←**

The hub profile should resemble Figure 11.139.

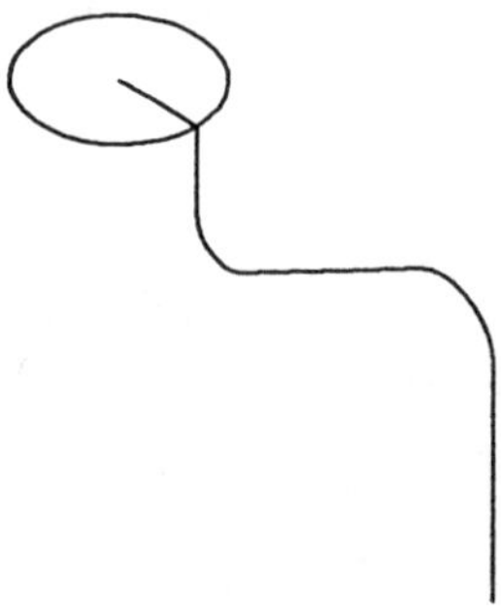

Figure 11.139

Step 7. Create the blade edge profile using Front Cplane.

Change the level to 2 and the color to 11.
Select **Level → Main Level**, then enter **2 ←**
Select **Color** then **11 ←**
Select **Cplane → Front**
Select **Z** then enter **6 ←**
Select **MAIN MENU → Create → Arc → Endpoints**
Enter the first point: **-1,0.2 ←**
Enter the second point: **1,0.2 ←**
Enter the radius: **6 ←**
Select an arc: pick at the desired arc segment (smaller concave arc)

The arc appears on the screen as Figure 11.140.

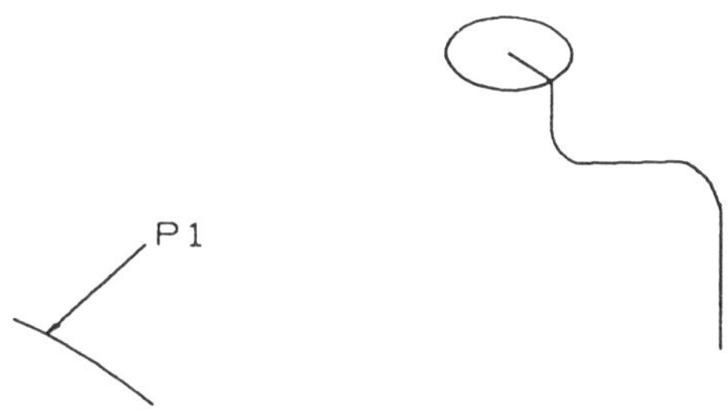

Figure 11.140

Step 8. Create a slope line using the pick points in Figure 11.140.

Select **MAIN MENU → Create → Line → Polar → Endpoint**
Pick at **P1**
Enter the angle in degrees: **-20 ←**
Enter the line length: **3 ←**

The drawing now becomes Figure 11.141.

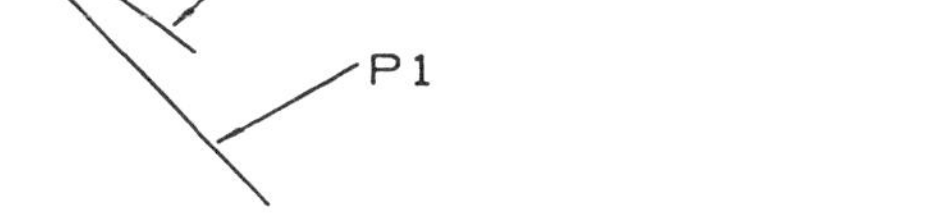

Figure 11.141

Step 9. Create an arc tangent to the slope line. Use pick points from Figure 11.141.

Select **MAIN MENU → Create → Arc → Tangent → Point**
Pick at **P1** for the arc to be tangent to
Enter the thru point: select **Endpoint** from the Point Menu
Pick at **P2**
Enter the radius: **.35 ←**
Select an arc: pick at the desired arc segment (2nd arc from right)

The new drawing should look like Figure 11.142.

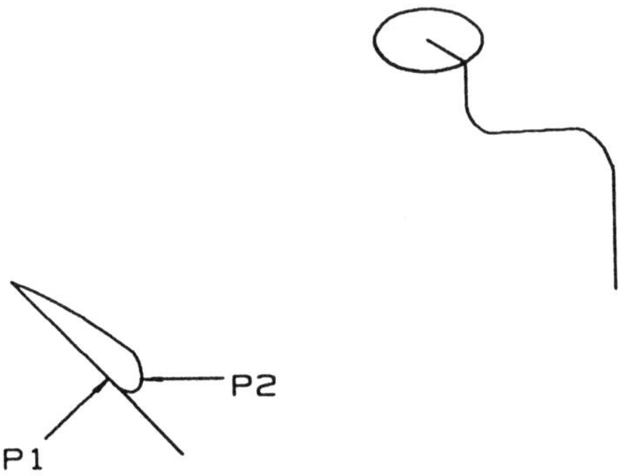

Figure 11.142

Step 10. Trim the slope line using the pick points in Figure 11.142.

Select **MAIN MENU → Modify → Trim → 1 entity**
Sequentially pick at **P1** and **P2** to complete the trimming

The trimmed profile should appear as Figure 11.143.

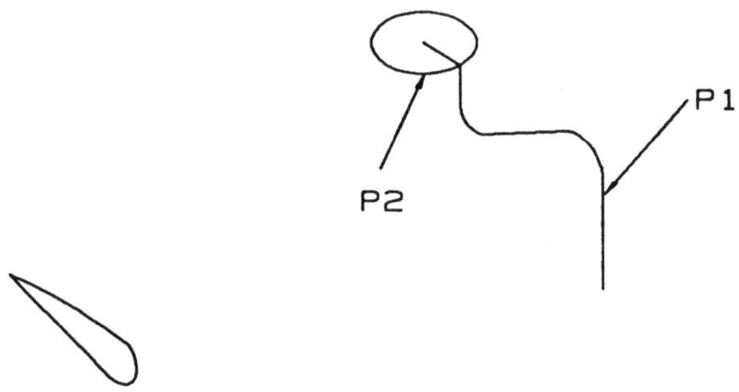

Figure 11.143

Step 11. Create a swept surface using the pick points in Figure 11.143.

Change level to 3 and color to 12.
Select **Level** then enter **3** ←
Select **Color** then enter **12** ←
Select **MAIN MENU → Create → sUrface → Swept → Nurbs**
Enter the number of across contours: **1** ←
define the across contour: select **Single** then pick at **P1**
define the along contour 1: select **Single** then pick at **P2**
Select **Done**
Set the Swept surface parameters to the following settings:

Along cut distance = **0.15**
Across cut distance = **0.15**
Rotate the across contour

Select **Done** to complete the surface

The swept surface appears as Figure 11.144.

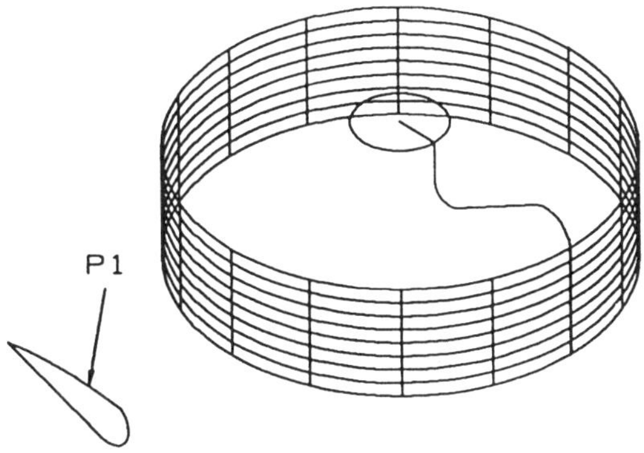

Figure 11.144

Step 12. Rotate the blade edge profile by 15°, use the pick points in Figure11.144.

Change level to 4 and color to 13.
Select **Level** then enter **4** ←
Select **Color** then enter **13** ←
Select **MAIN MENU** → **Xform** → **Rotate** → **Chain**
Pick at **P1**
Select **Close** → **End here** → **Done** → **Origin**
Set the Rotate parameters below:

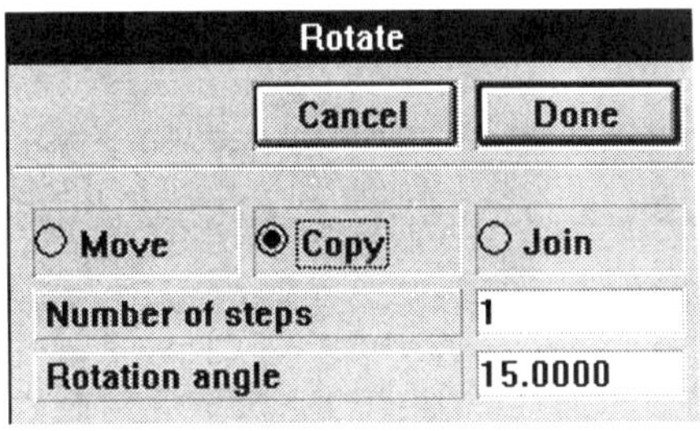

Select **Done**

The rotated profile is shown in Figure 11.145.

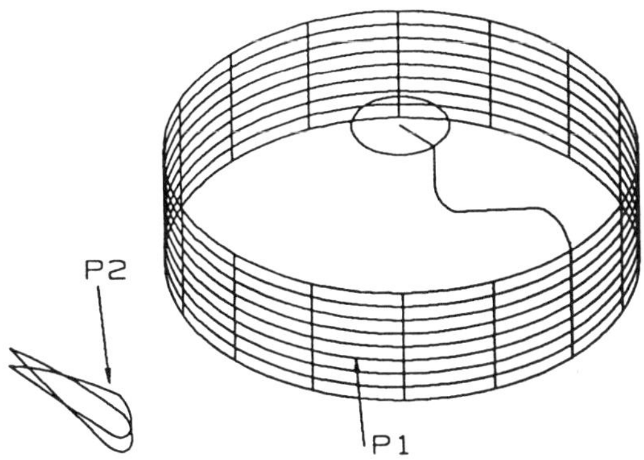

Figure 11.145

Step 13. Project the rotated profile onto the swept surface using the pick points in Figure 11.145.

Select **MAIN MENU → Create → Curve → Project**

Set the Project curves menu

to the following settings ☞

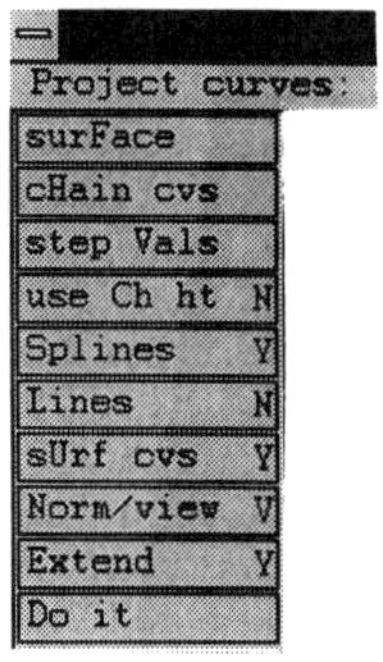

Pick at **P1** to select a surface

Select **Chain** then pick at **P2**

Select **Close → End here → Done → Do it** to complete the surface curve

The surface curve on the swept surface is shown in Figure 11.146.

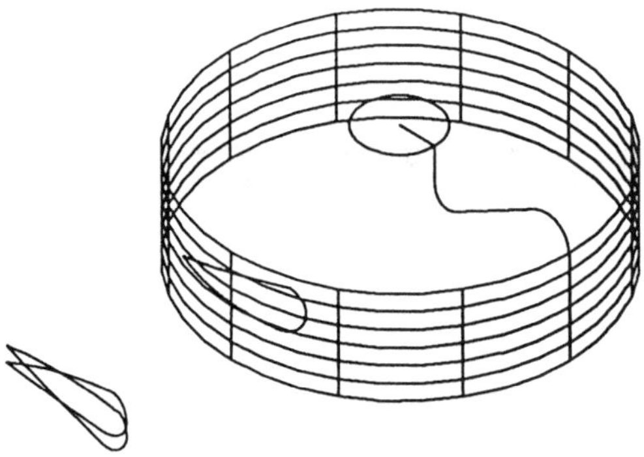

Figure 11.146

Step 14. Make level 4 invisible.

Select **Level → Vis. levels**

Click on **level 4** button,

then **OK → OK** to return back to graphic mode

The drawing becomes Figure 11.147.

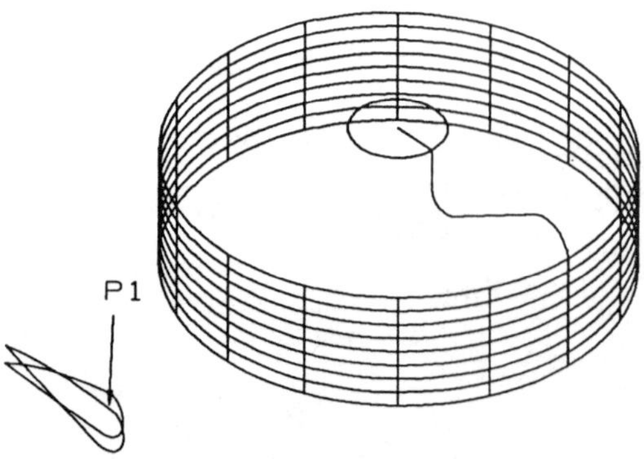

Figure 11.147

Step 15. Rotate the edge profile by 40°. Use the pick points in Figure 11.147 on the previous page. Change level to 5.

Select **Level →Main Level,** then enter **5** ←

Select **MAIN MENU → Xform → Rotate → Chain**

Pick at **P1**

Select **Close → End here → Done → Origin**

Set the Rotate parameters as below:

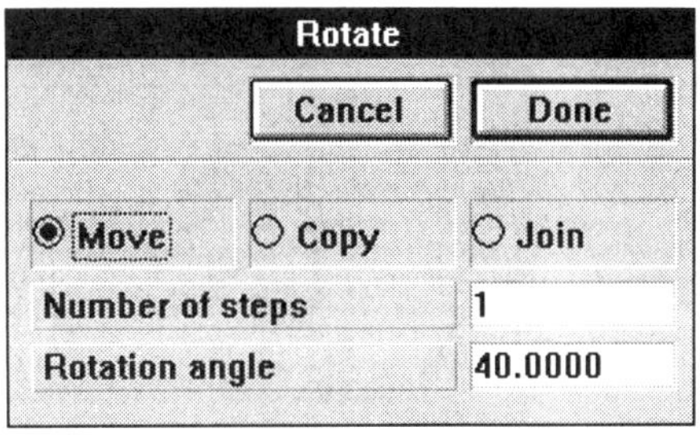

Select **Done**

The rotated profile is shown in Figure 11.148.

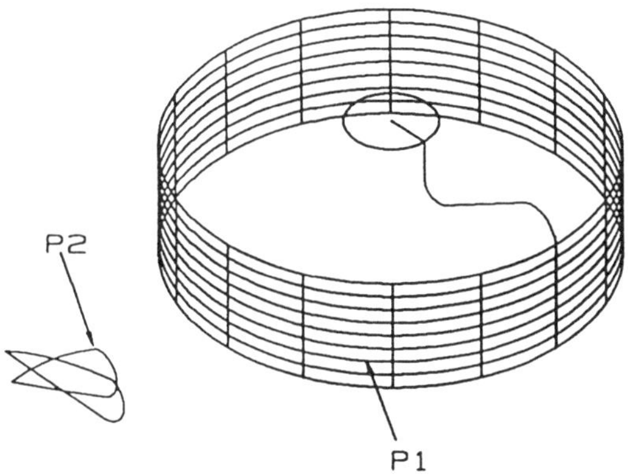

Figure 11.148

Step 16. Project the profile onto the surface using the pick points in Figure 11.148.

Select **MAIN MENU → Create → Curve → Project**

Pick at **P1** to select the surface

Select **Chain** then pick at **P2**

Select **Close → End here → Done → Do it**

The drawing should resemble Figure 11.149.

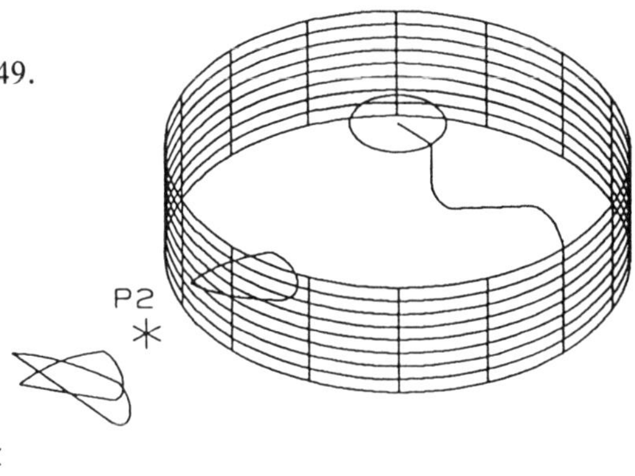

Figure 11.149

Step 17. Delete the rotated profile using the pick points in Figure 11.149.

Select **MAIN MENU → Delete →Window**
Pick at **P1** and **P2** to delete 2 entities

The new drawing should look like Figure 11.150.

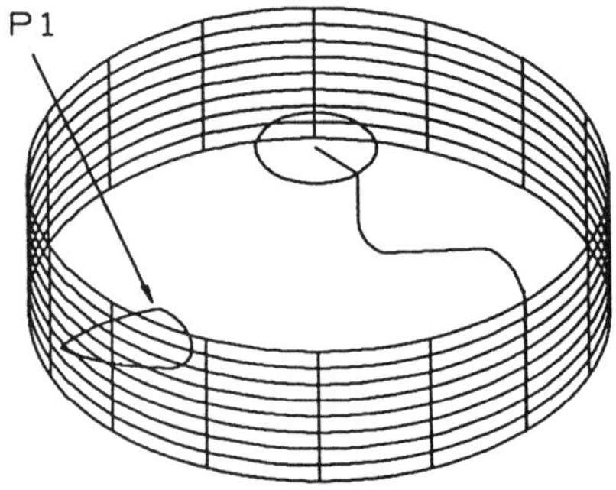

Figure 11.150

Step 18. Translate the projected curve back to the desired position using the pick points in Figure 11.150.

Select **MAIN MENU → Xform → Translate → Chain**
Pick at **P1**
Select **Close → End here → Done → Rectang**
Enter the translation vector: **Z3 ←**
Set the Translate parameters as below:

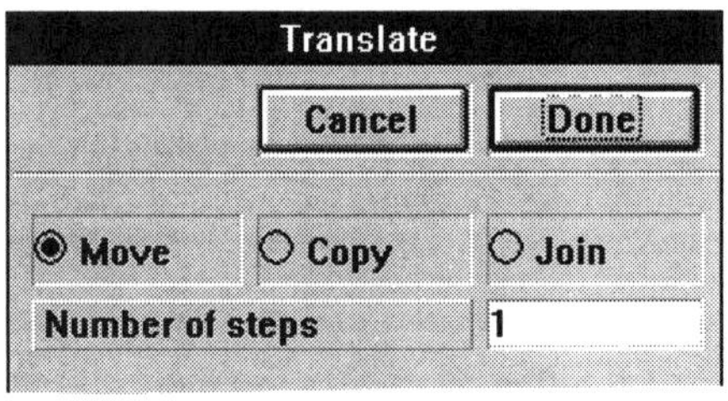

Select **Done**

The drawing becomes Figure 11.151.

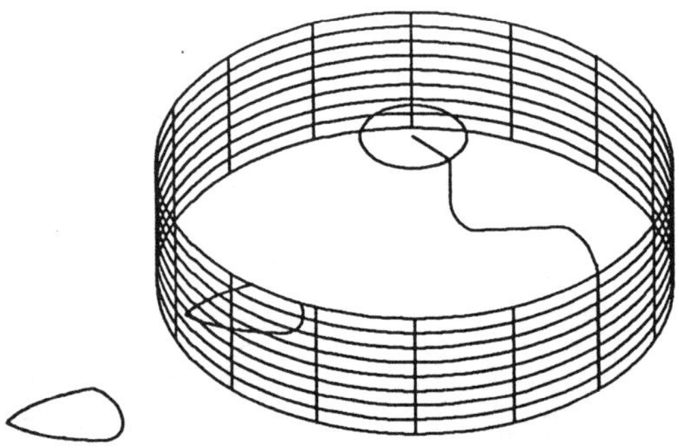

Figure 11.151

Step 19. Make level 4 visible.

Select **Level→ Vis. levels**
Click on the level 4 button (highlighted)
Click on the **OK** to return back to graphic mode

The new drawing should resemble Figure 11.152.

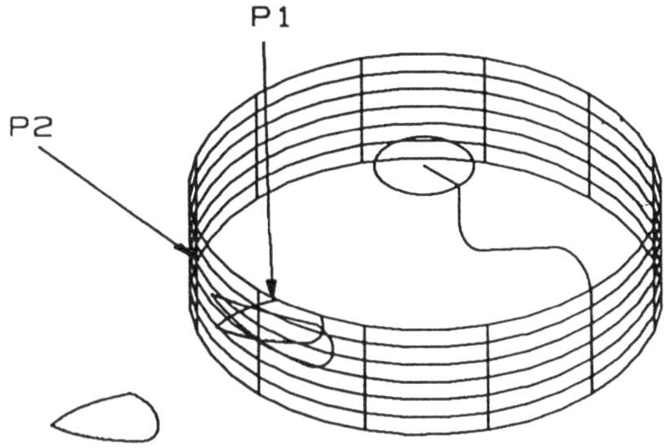

Figure 11.152

Step 20. Delete the surface curve and the swept surface using the pick points in Figure 11.152.

Select **MAIN MENU → Delete**
Pick at **P1** and **P2**
Select **Yes** to delete the associated entities
Press **F3** to repaint the screen

The drawing should look like Figure 11.153.

Figure 11.153

Step 21. Make level 1 invisible.

Select **Level → Vis. levels**
Click on the level 1 button to dim the lines
Select **OK** to return back to graphic mode

The drawing becomes Figure 11.154 on the next page.

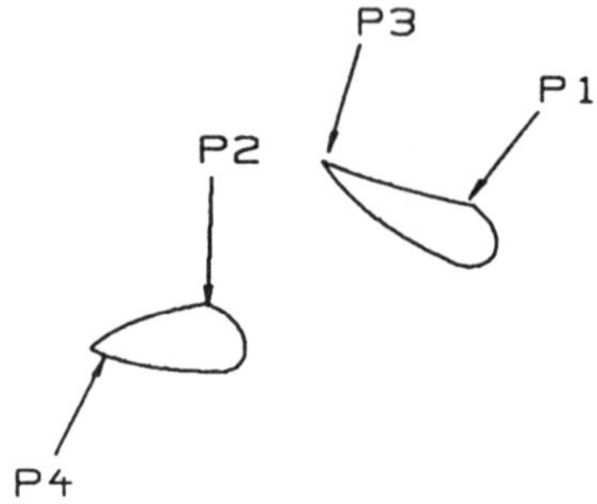

Figure 11.154

Step 22. Create two lines connecting the two profiles using the pick points in Figure 11.154. Use the 3d Cplane.

Select **Cplane → 3d**
Select **MAIN MENU → Create → Line → Endpoints → Endpoint**
Pick at **P1** and **P2** for the first line
Pick at **P3** and **P4** for the second line

The wireframe model needed of the blade should resemble Figure 11.155.

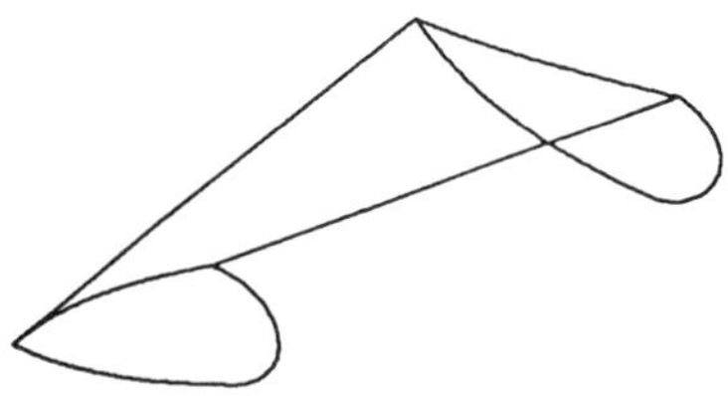

Figure 11.155

Step 23. Toggle level 1 back to visible.

Select **Level**
Click on the level 1 button to highlight
Select **OK** to return back to graphic mode

The final wireframe model should look like Figure 11.156.

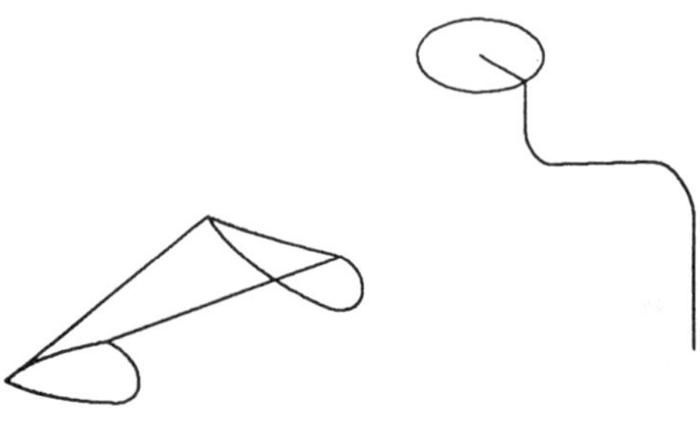

Figure 11.156

Step 24. Save the drawing file as fan.

Select **MAIN MENU → File → Save**
Enter file name: **fan ←**

Project 16.

Construct a wireframe model for the surface model of a car wheel (Figure 11.157b & c). The model consists of a hub, a rim, and six pockets. The two edge curves of the pockets are shown in Figure 11.157a. The coordinate values of critical points for hub and rim edge profiles are tabulated below:

We are here ☞ **Wireframe Model** (wheel)

Go to **Surface Model** Project 12 of Chapter 13 (wheels)

Go to **Toolpath** Project 8 of Chapter 15 (wheels)

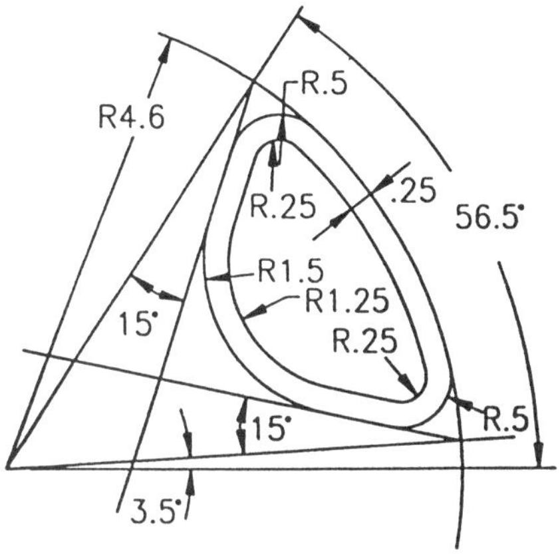

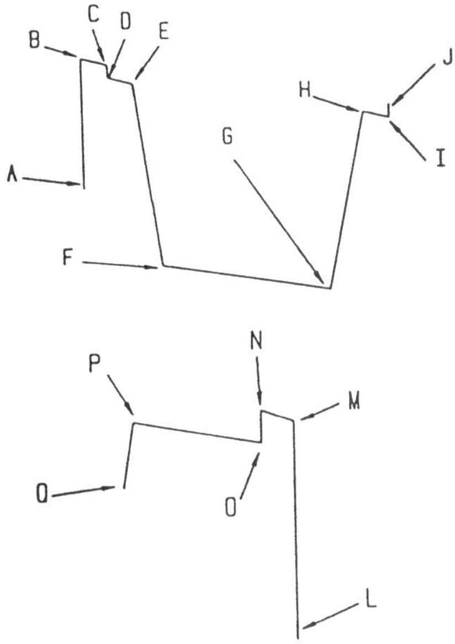

a. Pocket profile

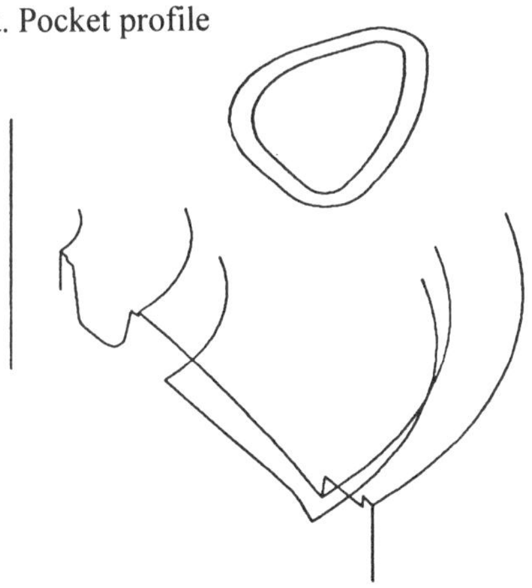

b. Wireframe model

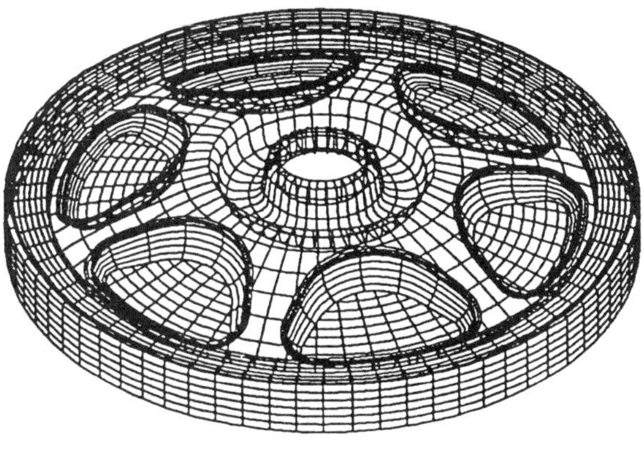

c. Surface model

Figure 11.157

Point	X-coord	Y-coord
A	0.8	1.4
B	0.8	1.9
C	0.9	1.875
D	0.9	1.825
E	1.0	1.8
F	1.1	1.1
G	1.75	1.0
H	1.9	1.675
I	2.0	1.65
J	2.0	1.7
L	5.65	0
M	5.65	1.0
N	5.5	1.05
O	5.5	0.9
P	4.9	1.0
Q	4.85	0.7
R	4.7	0.3
S	2.4	1.0

Tips 1. Use Front Cplane to construct the edge profiles of the hub, rim, and frame, as well as two upper and lower surfaces.

2. Use Top Cplane to create two of the contours for the pocket surface. The outer contour is created first. The six entities in the outer contour are then offset by a distance of 0.25-in. to obtain the inner contour. Note that these two contours are projected onto the two surfaces to obtain two surface curves for defining the pocket surface in chapter 13.

Step 1. Construct a series of lines for the hub profile using the Front construction plane.

Select **Cplane → Front**
Select **Gview → Front**
Select **MAIN MENU → Create → Line → Multi → Endpoint**
Specify endpoint 1: **0.8,1.4** ←
Specify endpoint 2: **0.8,1.9** ←
Specify endpoint 3: **0.9,1.875** ←
Specify endpoint 4: **0.9,1.825** ←
Specify endpoint 5: **1,1.8** ←
Specify endpoint 6: **1.1,1.1** ←
Specify endpoint 7: **1.75,1.0** ←
Specify endpoint 8: **1.9,1.675** ←
Specify endpoint 9: **2,1.65** ←
Specify endpoint 10: **2,1.7** ←

Your drawing will appear as Figure 11.158.

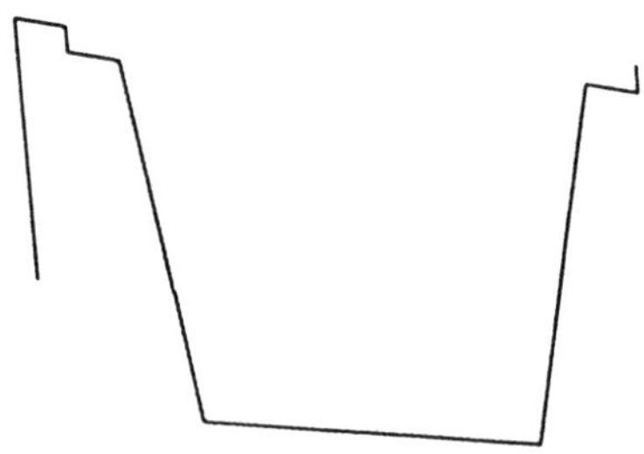

Figure 11.158

Step 2. Create another set of lines for the outer rim.

Select **BACKUP → Multi → Endpoint**
Specify endpoint 1: **5.65,0** ←
Specify endpoint 2: **5.65,1** ←

Press **Alt + F1** and then **F2** to fit the drawing in the screen

Specify endpoint 3: **5.5,1.05** ←
Specify endpoint 4: **5.5,0.9** ←
Specify endpoint 5: **4.9,1.0** ←
Specify endpoint 6: **4.85,0.7** ←

The drawing should look like Figure 11.159.

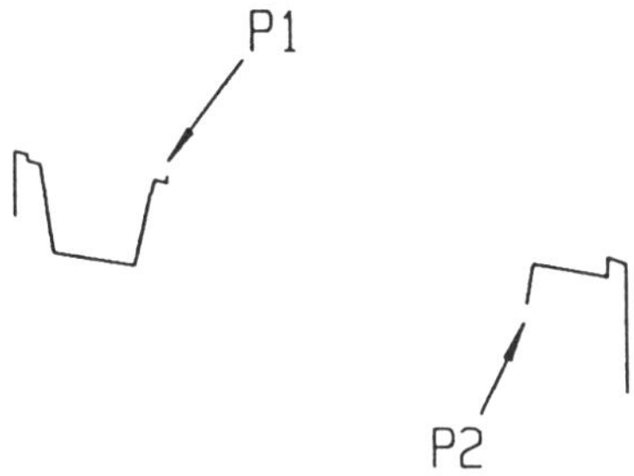

Figure 11.159

Step 3. Construct the arc for creating the top surface. Use the pick points in Figure 11.159.

Select **MAIN MENU → Create → Arc → Endpoints → Endpoint**
Enter the first point: Pick at **P1**
Enter the second point: Pick at **P2**
Enter the radius: **10** ←
Select an arc: Pick the upper arc to complete the arc selection.

Your drawing should appear as Figure 11.160.

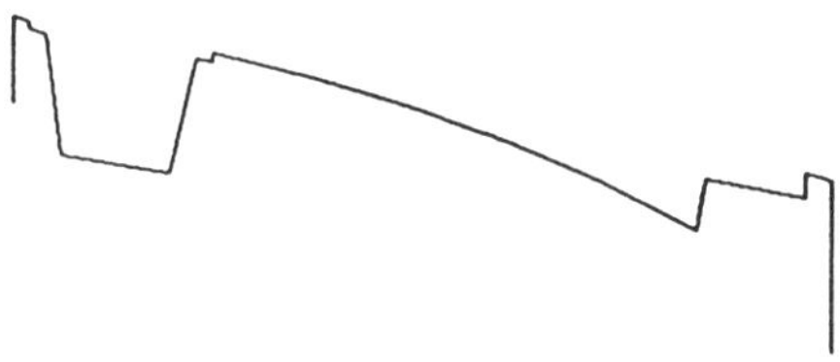

Figure 11.160

Step 4. Construct the edge profile for the lower surface.

Select **MAIN MENU → Create → Line → Polar**
Specify an endpoint: **2.4,1** ←
Enter the angle in degrees (0.00): **-12.5** ←
Enter the line length (1.00): **3** ←

The drawing should look like Figure 11.161.

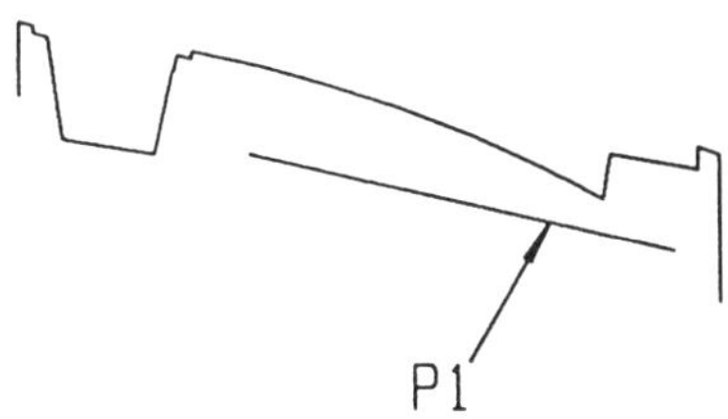

Figure 11.161

Step 5. Create the arc tangent to the line. Use the pick points in Figure 11.161.

Select **MAIN MENU → Create →Arc → Tangent → Point**
Pick at P1 to select the entity that the arc is to be tangent to
Enter the thru point: **4.7,0.3** ←
Enter the radius: **0.8** ←
Select the right arc to complete the arc

The drawing will appear as Figure 11.162.

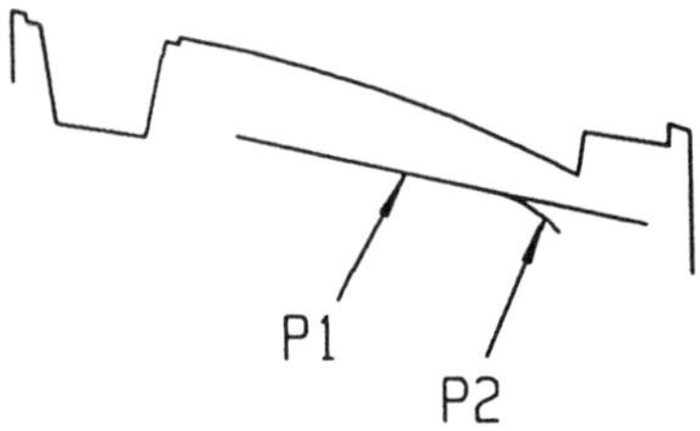

Figure 11.162

Step 6. Trim the line to the tangent point. Use the pick points in Figure 11.162.

Select **MAIN MENU → Modify → Trim → 1 entity**
Select the entity to trim: pick at **P1**
Select the entity to trim to: pick at **P2**

The resulted drawing is shown in Figure 11.163.

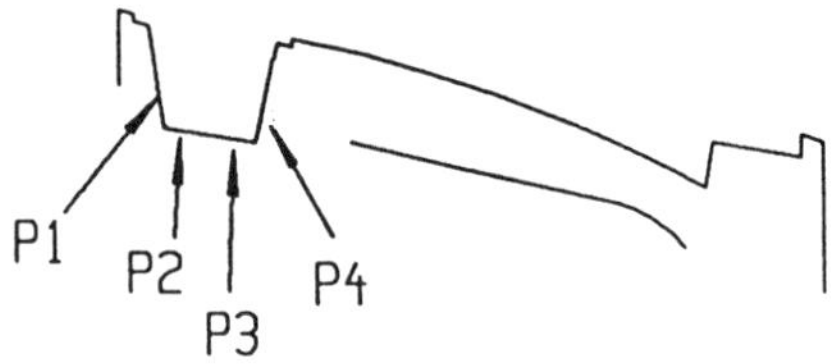

Figure 11.163

Step 7. Add two fillets. Use the pick points in Figure 11.163.

Select **MAIN MENU → Modify → Fillet**
Pick **Radius**, and then enter **0.1** ←
Pick at **P1** to select an entity
Pick at **P2** to select another entity to complete the first fillet
Pick **Radius**, and then enter **0.3** ←
Pick at **P3** to select an entity
Pick at **P4** to select another entity to complete the second fillet

The drawing will appear as Figure 11.164.

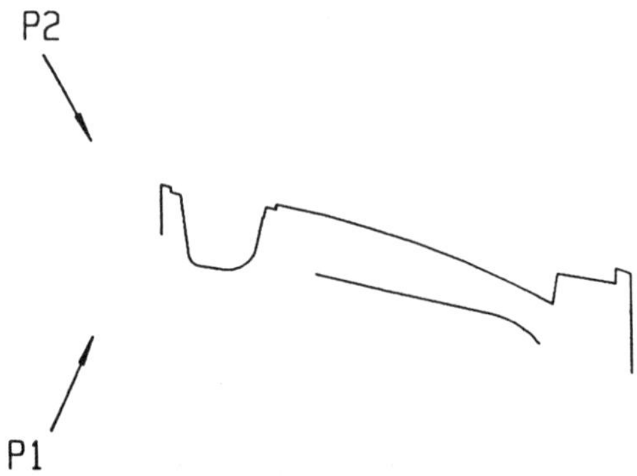

Figure 11.164

Step 8. Create a vertical line. Use the pick points in Figure 11.164.

Select **MAIN MENU → Create → Line → Vertical**
Pick at **P1** and **P2**, and then enter **0** ← for X coordinate
Press Alt + F1 to fit the drawing if necessary.

The drawing should appear as Figure 11.165.

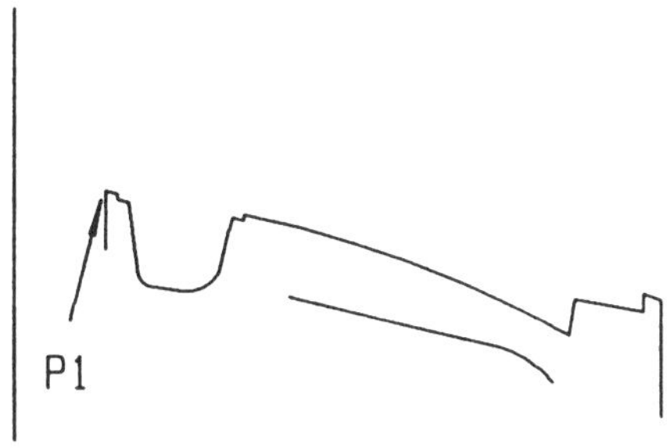

Figure 11.165

Step 9. Create six arcs using the top construction plane. Use the pick points labeled in Figure 11.165.

Select **Cplane → Top**
Select **Gview → Isometric**
Select **Z → Endpoint** and then pick at **P1** to set the Z value

Z1.9 should appear in the secondary menu

Select **MAIN MENU → Create → Arc → Polar → Ctr point**
Enter the center point: **0,0** ←
Enter the radius (1.00): **0.8** ←
Enter the initial angle (0.0): press ← to accept the default value
Enter the final angle (360.0): **60** ←

The drawing now becomes Figure 11.166.

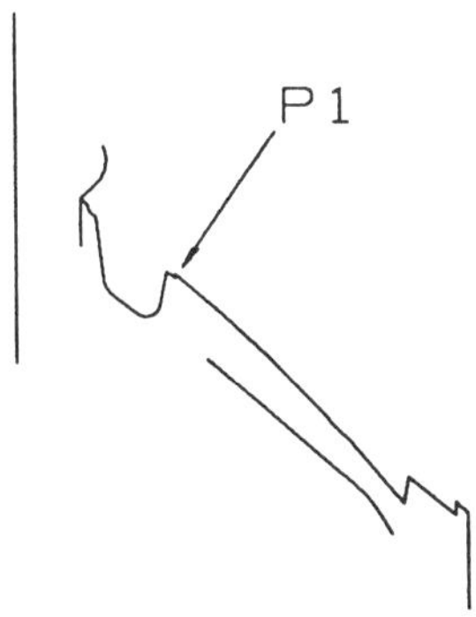

Figure 11.166

Step 10. Create the second arc using the pick points in Figure 11.166.

Pick **Z → Endpoint** and then pick at **P1**

Z1.7 should appear in the Secondary menu

Select **MAIN MENU → Create → Arc → Polar → Ctr point**
Enter the center point: **0,0** ←
Enter the radius (0.8): **2** ←
Enter the initial angle (0.0): ←
Enter the final angle (60.0): ←

The drawing will appear as Figure 11.167.

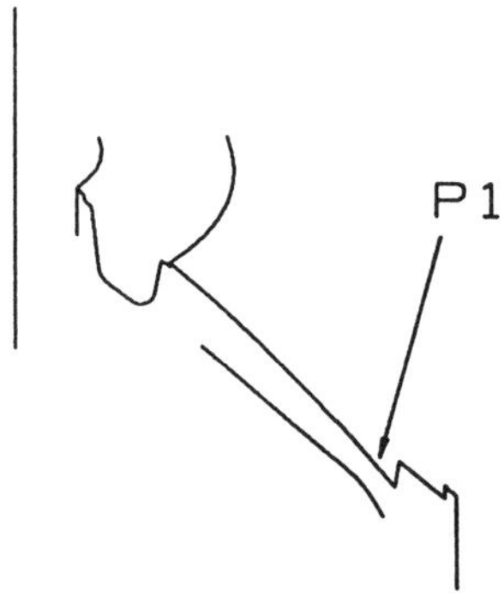

Figure 11.167

Step 11. Create the third arc. Use the pick point in Figure 11.167.
Select **Z → Endpoint** and then pick at **P1**

Z0.7 should appear in the Secondary menu

Select **MAIN MENU → Create → Arc → Polar → Ctr point**
Enter the center point: **0,0** ←
Enter the radius: **4.85** ←
Enter the initial angle (0.0): ←
Enter the final angle (60.0): ←

The drawing should resemble Figure 11.168.

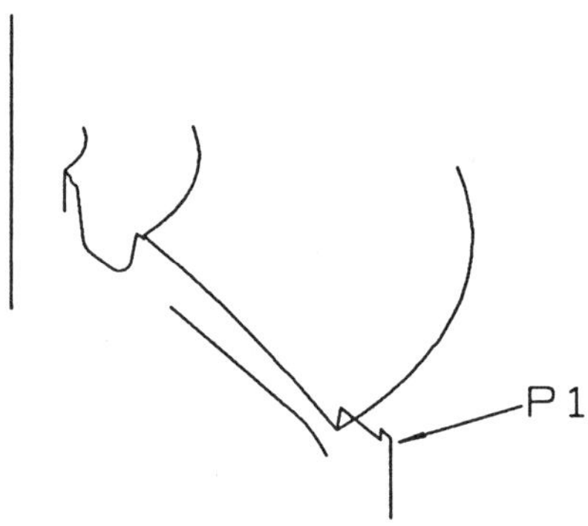

Figure 11.168

Step 12. Create the fourth arc using the pick point in Figure 11.168.
Pick **Z → Endpoint** and then pick at **P1**

Z1.0 should appear in the Secondary menu

Enter the center point: **0,0** ←
Enter the radius: **5.65** ←
Enter the initial angle (0.0): ←
Enter the final angle (60.0): ←

Your drawing should appear as Figure 11.169.

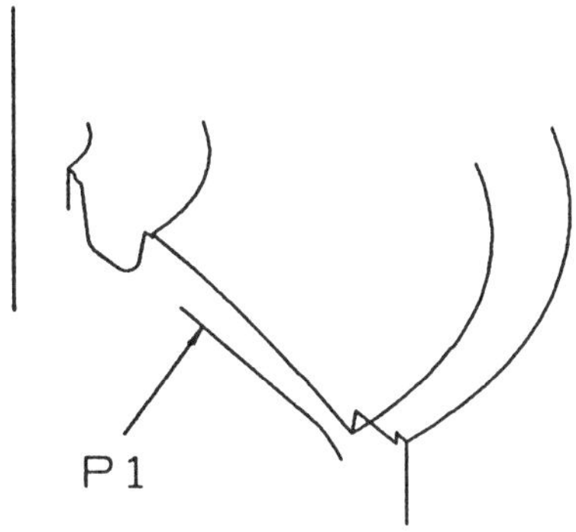

Figure 11.169

Step 13. Create the fifth arc. Use the pick point in Figure 11.169.

Pick **Z → Endpoint** and then pick at **P1**

Z1.0 should appear in the Secondary menu

Enter the center point: **0,0** ←
Enter the radius: **2.4** ←
Enter the initial angle (0.0): ←
Enter the final angle (60.0): ←

The drawing should resemble Figure 11.170.

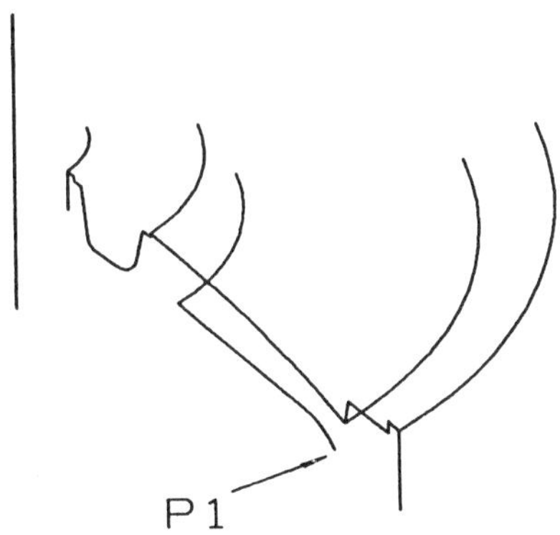

Figure 11.170

Step 14. Create the sixth arc using the pick point in Figure 11.170.

Pick **Z → Endpoint** and then pick at **P1**

Z0.3 should appear in the Secondary menu

Enter the center point: **0,0** ←
Enter the radius: **4.7** ←
Enter the initial angle (0.0): ←
Enter the final angle (60.0): ←

The drawing now should look like Figure 11.171.

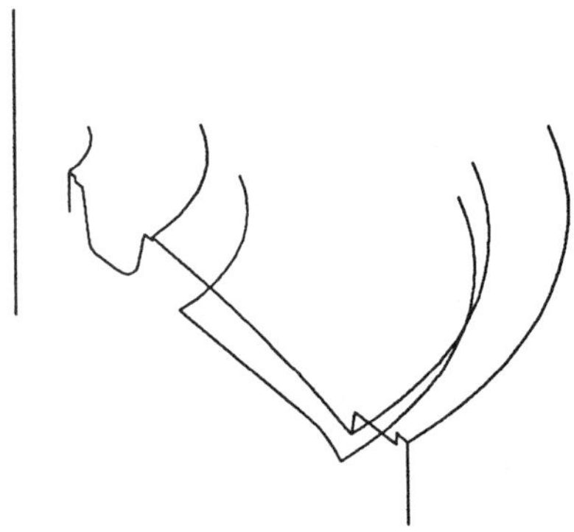

Figure 11.171

Step 15. Make level 1 invisible. Set the Secondary menu parameters to the following settings:

Select **Level → Vis. levels**
Click on the level 1 button (dimmed)
Select **OK → OK** to return back to graphic mode
Select **Level → Main Level** and then enter **2** ←
Select **Color** and then enter **12** ←
Select **Z** and then enter **4** ←
Select **Gview → Top**

Step 16. Create an arc.

Select **MAIN MENU → Create → Arc → Polar → Ctr Point**
Enter the center point: **0,0** ←
Enter the radius: **4.6** ←
Enter the initial angle: **-10** ←
Enter the final angle: **70** ←

Step 17. Create two construction lines.

Select **MAIN MENU → Create → Line → Polar**
Specify an endpoint: **0,0** ←
Enter the angle in degrees (0.0): **3.5** ←
Enter the line length (3.0): **5.5** ←
Specify an endpoint: **0,0** ←
Enter the angle in degrees (0.0): **56.5** ←
Enter the line length (5.5): press ← to accept the default value

The drawing now will look like Figure 11.172.

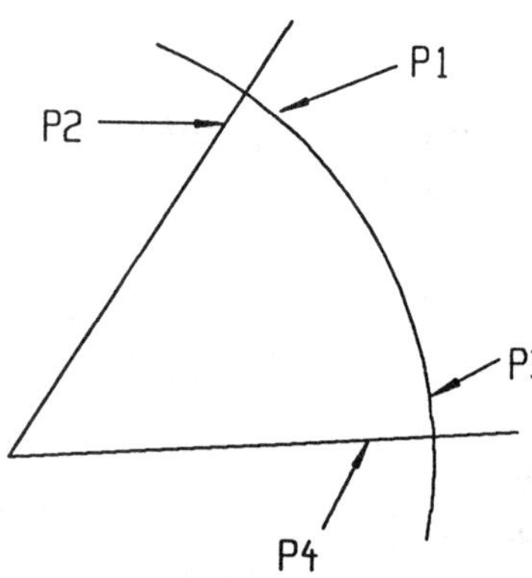

Figure 11.172

Step 18. Create another two construction lines using the pick points in Figure 11.172 on the previous page.

Select **Intersec** then pick at **P1** and **P2**
Enter the angle in degrees: **-108.5 (or 180 - 56.5 - 15)** ←
Enter the line length: **4.5** ← for the first line
Pick at **P3** and **P4**
Enter the angle in degrees: **168.5 (or 180 - 15 + 3.5)** ←
Enter the line length: **4.5** ← to complete the second line

The drawing now should resemble Figure 11.173.

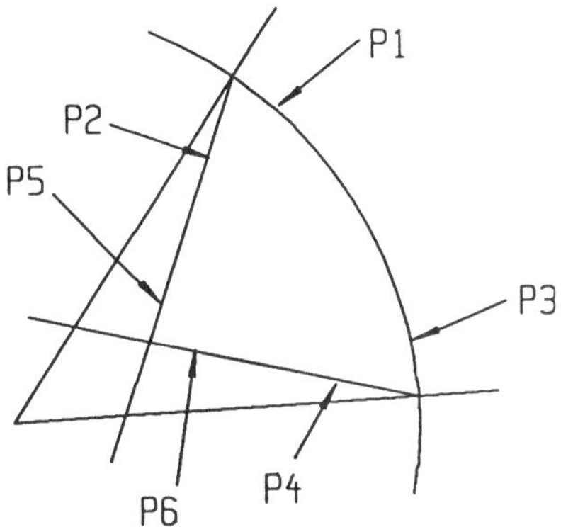

Figure 11.173

Step 19. Add three fillets. Use the pick points in Figure 11.173.

Select **MAIN MENU → Modify → Fillet**
Select **Radius** from the parameter menu, and then enter **0.5** ← for fillet radius
Select an entity: pick at **P1**
Select another entity: pick at **P2** for the first fillet
Select an entity: pick at **P3**
Select another entity: pick at **P4** for the second fillet
Select **Radius** then enter **1.5** ←
Pick at **P5** and **P6** to complete the third fillet

The new drawing will appear as Figure 11.174.

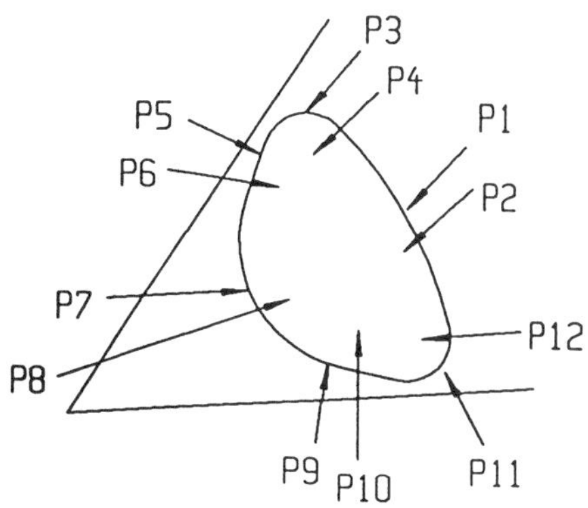

Figure 11.174

Step 20. Create the inner pocket using the offset command. Use the pick points in Figure 11.174 on the previous page.

Select **MAIN MENU → Xform → Offset**

Set the Offset parameters as below:

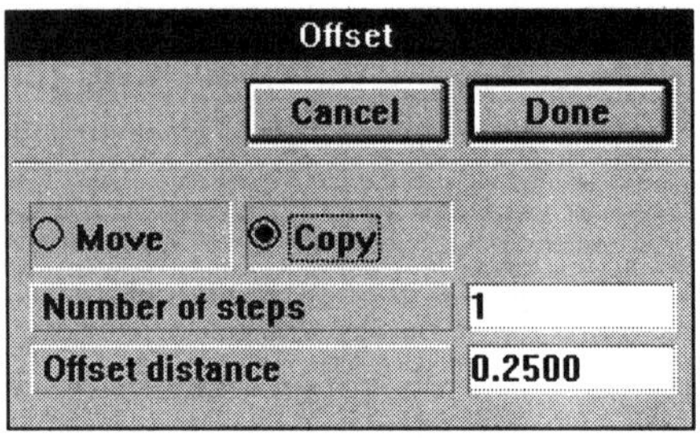

Select **Done**

Select the line or arc to offset: pick at **P1**

Indicate the offset direction: pick at **P2**

Sequentially pick at **P3 - P12** to complete the selection

The resulted inner pocket shows in Figure 11.175.

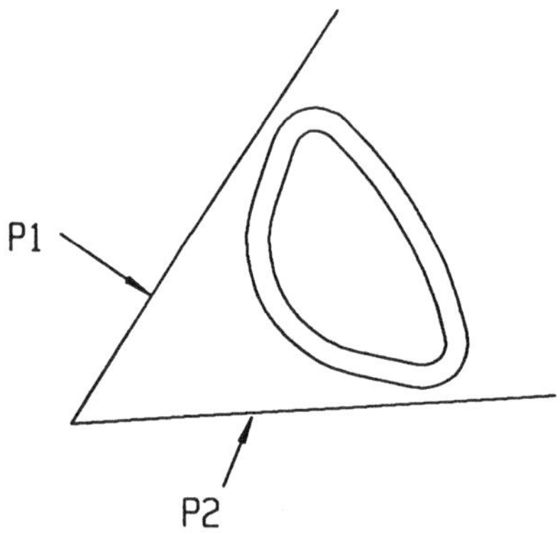

Figure 11.175

Step 21. Delete two construction lines using the pick points in Figure 11.175.

Select **MAIN MENU → Delete**

Pick at **P1** and **P2**

The final drawing in Top Gview should resemble Figure 11.176.

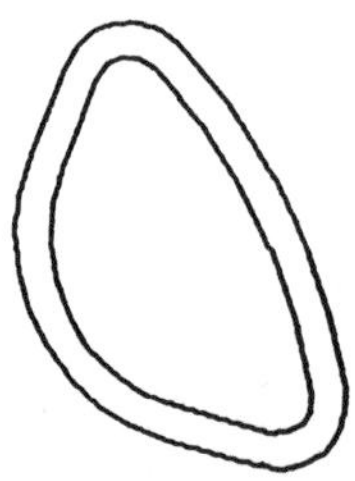

Figure 11.176

Step 22. Make level 1 visible and change Gview to isometric.

Select **Level → Vis. Levels**
Click on the level 1button to highlight
Select **OK** to return back to graphic mode
Select **Gview → Isometric**

The final drawing should look like Figure 11.177.

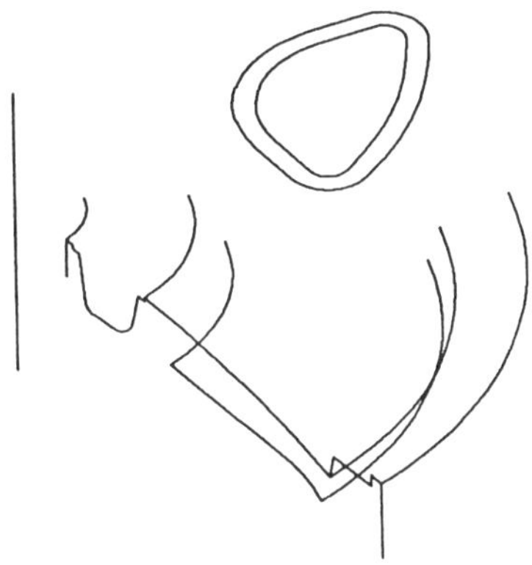

Figure 11.177

Step 23. Save the wireframe model file. Use the filename: wheel

Select **MAIN MENU → File → Save**

Enter file name: **wheel** ←

11.3 Exercises

11.3.1 Short answer

1. Explain how a wireframe model describes an object.

2. What additional information does a surface model provide over a wireframe model?

3. What is construction plane?

4. What are the three principal construction planes? Use a drawing to illustrate the definition of these three principal planes.

5. What are the six Mastercam construction planes?

6. Give the reasons we use a 3d construction plane.

7. Use a drawing to show how to define a 2-line construction plane. Explain when to use a 2-line construction plane.

8. Use a drawing to show how to define a normal construction plane; and explain when to use a normal construction plane.

9. Use drawings to show how to specify Z-depth in various construction planes.

11.3.2 Problems

10. Construct a wireframe model as shown in Figure 11.178. The model consists of two semi-circles, two profiles, and four lines. Save the drawing in the file name **E1**. This model can be used to generate two ruled surfaces and two fillet surfaces in chapter 12. Some helpful hints are given below.

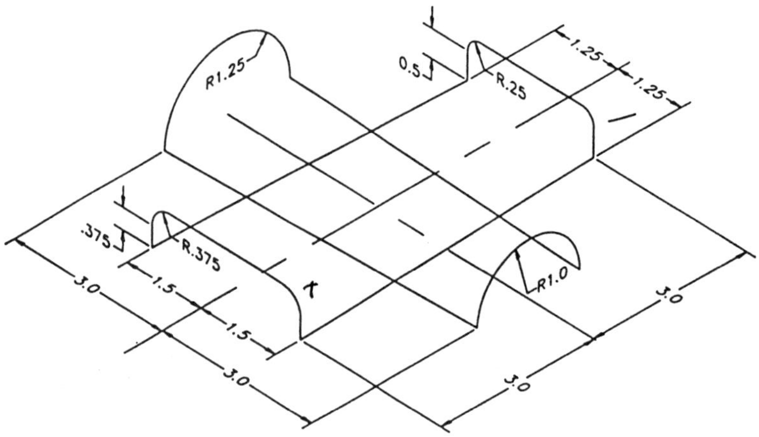

Figure 11.178

Tips 1. Follow the instructions in project 1.

2. Create two semi-circles using the side construction plane. The Z-depth is 3.0 and -3.0 for the two semi-circles, respectively.
3. Create two profiles using the front construction plane. The Z-depth is 3.0 and -3.0 for the two profiles, respectively.
4. Create four lines connecting the end points of the entities. Use the 3d construction plane.

11. Construct the wireframe model shown in Figure 11.179. This model consists of four arcs and one rectangular box. It can be used to create two ruled surfaces, generate a fillet surface, and trim the smaller ruled surface to the fillet surface. Save the file name as **E2**. Tips are suggested below.

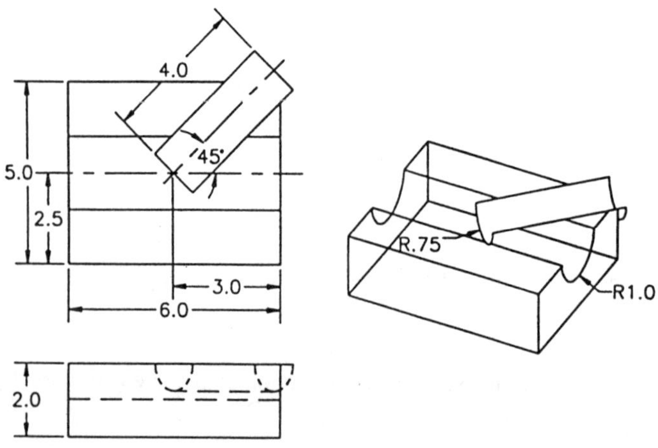

Figure 11.179

Tips 1. Study the instructions from project 2.

2. Construct a rectangular box using the top Cplane.
3. Create the two arcs of 1.0" radius using the side Cplane.
4. Create a slope line that has a 45° with the X axis.
5. Define a normal Cplane which is perpendicular to the slope line.
6. Create two arcs of 0.75" radius using the normal Cplane.
7. Break the two upper side lines of the rectangular box into two pieces. This allows these two lines to be trimmed to the two arcs.
8. Connect four lines using 3d Cplane.

12. Construct the wireframe model consisting three cross-section profiles and four lines as shown in Figure 11.180. This model can be used to create a ruled surface, a loft surface, or a Coons surface. Save the file name as **E3**.

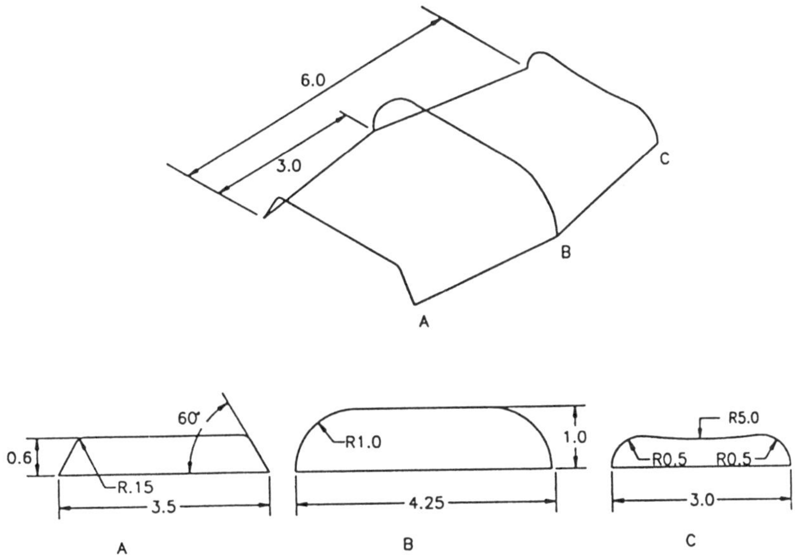

Figure 11.180

Tips 1. Construct three profiles using Front Cplane.

2. Use the Endpoints command to create the two 0.5" radius arcs. Then use Modify → Fillet commands to create the tangent arc of 8" radius.
3. There are two ways you can place profiles B and C in the proper Z loaction. One is set Z-3.0 for profile B and Z-6.0 for profile C. The other method is to create the profile at Z0.0, then use Xform → Translate commands to move the profile to correct position.
4. Connect the four lines using the 3d Cplane.

13. Construct a wireframe model consisting of four arcs as shown in Figure 11.181. This model is used to create a Coons surface. Save the file name as **E4**. Some helpful tips are listed below.

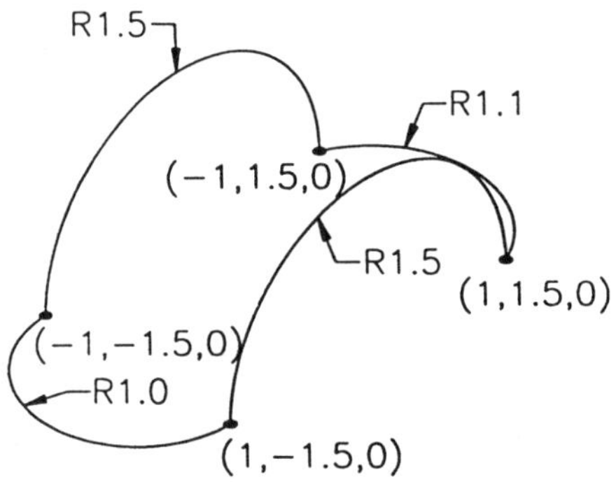

Figure 11.181

Tips 1. Create two arcs of 1.5" radius using the Side Cplane and the other two arcs in Top Cplane.

2. Use Arc → Endpoints command to construct these four arcs.

14. Construct the wireframe model shown in Figure 11.182. The model consists of four profiles set in four sides of a rectangular box. This model is used to create a Coons surface. Save the file as **E5**. Hints are provided on the next page.

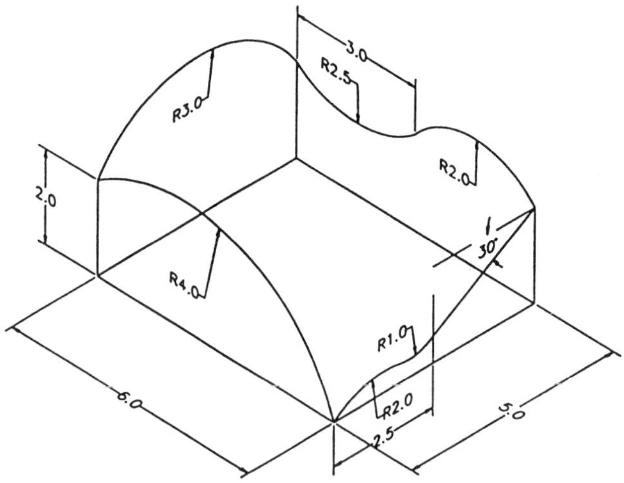

Figure 11.182

Tips 1. Study the instructions given in project 5.

2. Use Arc → Endpoints commands to construct four arcs C1, C3, C5, and C6.

3. Use Arc → Tangent commands to with Point option to create arc C2.

4. Use Modify → Fillet commands to construct arc C4.

5. Construct arcs C1, C2, and C5 using Front Cplane, and Arcs C3, C4, and C6 in Side Cplane.

15. Construct a wireframe model as shown in Figure 11.183. The model consists of eight triangular slope surfaces whose vertices joined at one point. The model can be used to create a Coons surface connecting the eight lines and the eight-sided polygon and a ruled surface on the top flat surface. Save the file as **E6**. Hints are given on below.

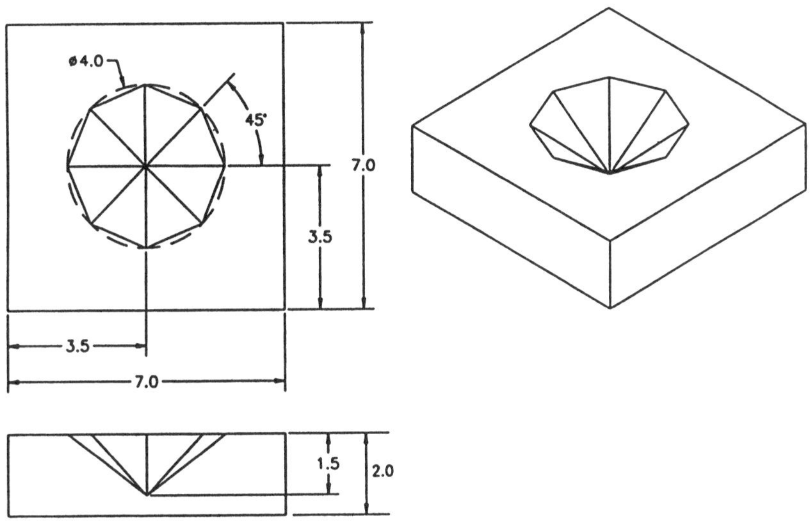

Figure 11.183

Tips 1. Study the instructions given in projects 6 and 7.

2. Create a rectangle and an octagon using Top Cplane.

3. Create eight lines connecting the eight vertices of the octagon and the common joined point using 3d Cplane.

16. Create the wireframe model for a multiple-faced part shown in Figure 11.184. The model has two octagons at different Z levels. A total of 16 faces are formed in the upper half of the part. The bottom half also has 16 faces that can be created from the upper half by using the mirror function. Save the file as **E7**. Useful tips are given below.

Tips 1. Study the instructions given in project 7.

2. Create two construction circles and eight lines to find the vertices of the two octagons.

3. Use Top Gview and 3d Cplane to connect the lines between vertices, and between the vertices and the common join point.

4. Save the drawing of the upper half of the model.

5. Rotate the upper half model by 180° about the origin using Front Cplane to complete the entire wireframe model.

Note: Do not use the complete wireframe model for surfacing. This makes picking correct entities more difficult in surfacing because the one entity appearing in Top Gview may represent two or more entities in the model.

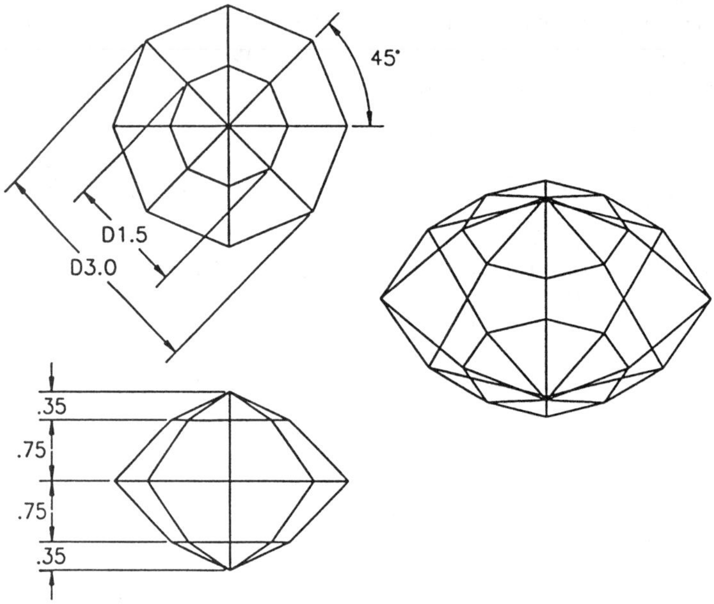

Figure 11.184

17. Construct the wireframe profile for a cup shown in Figure 11.185. The model can be used to generate a revolved surface or a swept surface. Save the file as **E8**. Tips are listed below.

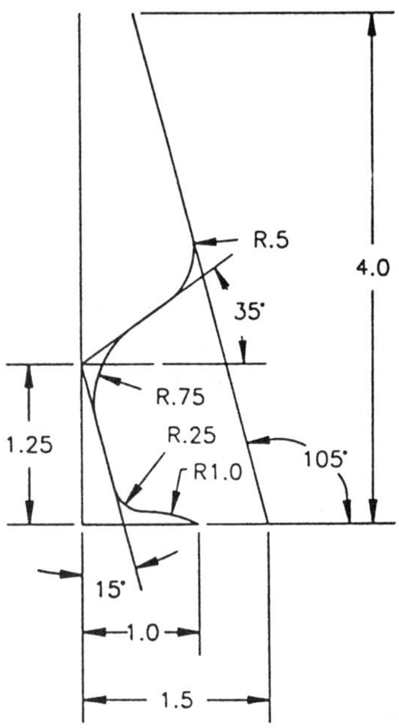

Figure 11.185

Tips 1. Study the instructions given in project 8.

2. Construct five lines, one vertical, one horizontal, and three sloped.

3. Add three fillets.

4. Use Arc → Tangent → Point commands to create the arc near the base.

18. Construct the wireframe profile for a cup shown in Figure 11.186. The model can be used to generate a revolved surface or a swept surface. Save the file as **E9**. Tips are listed below.

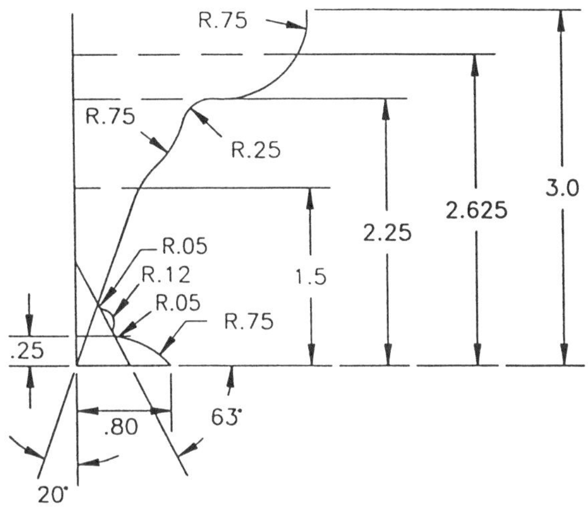

Figure 11.186

Tips 1. Study the instructions given in project 8.

2. Create necessary construction lines to help determining the end points of arcs.

3. Use Arc → Endpoints to create most of the arcs.

19. Create a wireframe model for the fly disk as shown in Figure 11.187. This model can be used to create a revolved surface or a swept surface. Save the file as **E10**. Hints are listed below.

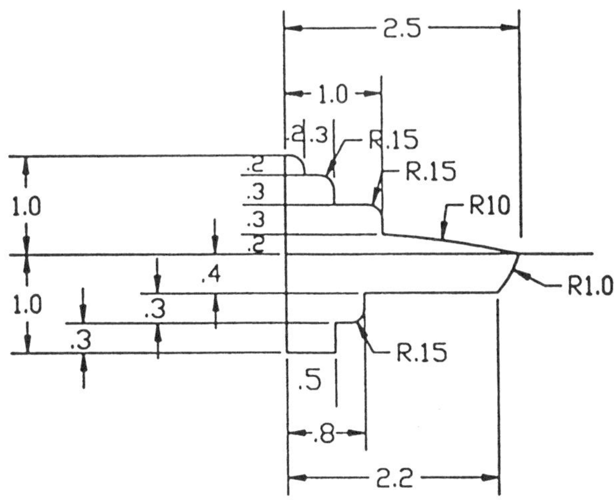

Figure 11.187

Tips 1. Create necessary construction lines to help determining the end points of arcs.

2. Use Arc → Endpoints commands to create arcs.

20. Construct the wireframe model for the part shown in Figure 11.188. The model consists of two rectangles with fillets at four corners and a section profile. One larger rectangle is located on the top to define the outer boundary of the top rim, and the smaller rectangle defines the shape of the part bottom. The section profile defines the wall and the top rim. This model is used to create a composite surface model in which multiple surfaces are blended together. Save the file as **E11**. Some hints are given below.

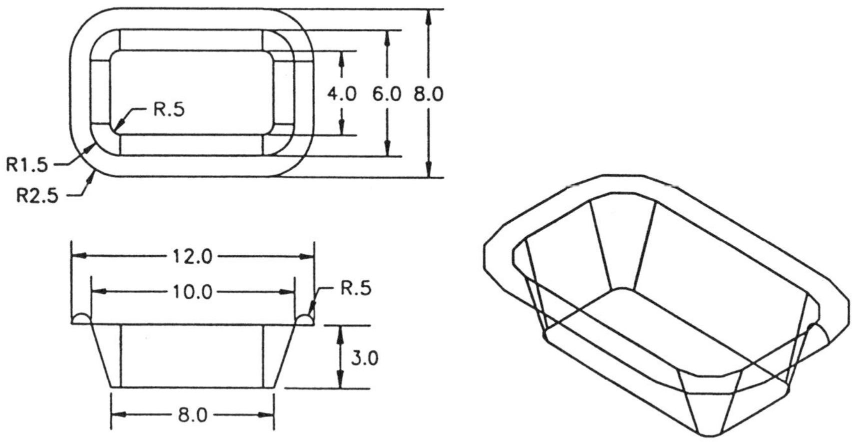

Figure 11.188

Tips 1. Use Top Cplane to construct the two rectangles with fillets. Note that the two rectangles have different Z depths.

2. Create the section profile in Front Cplane.

21. Create the wireframe model for the part shown in Figure 11.189. The model consists of two circles, one profile arc, eight identical edge profiles, and eight lines connecting end points of eight edge profiles. This model is used to create a composite surface model. Save the file as **E12**. Hints are given on the next page.

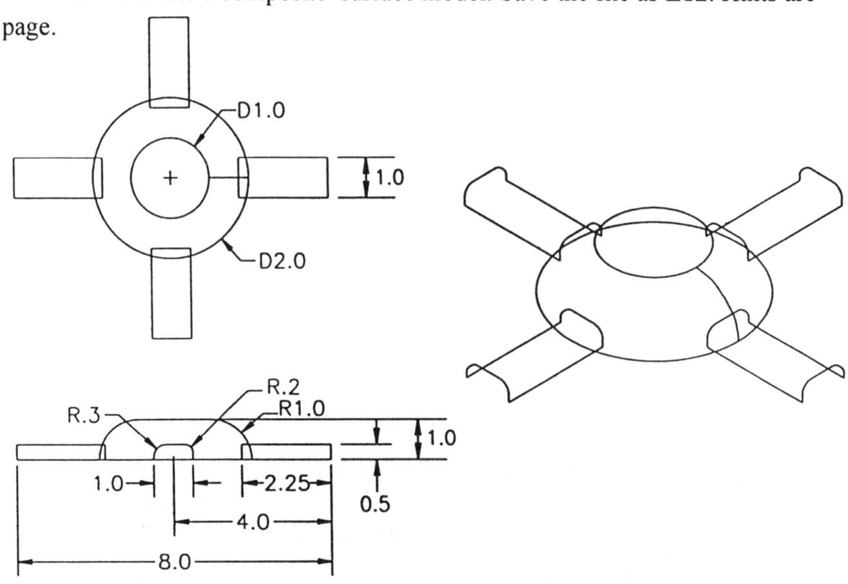

Figure 11.189

⌛**Tips** 1. Construct two circles in the Top Cplane with different depths.

2. Create four edge profiles and an arc profile which connects two circles in Front Cplane.

3. Construct the other four edge profiles in Side Cplane.

4. Create eight connecting lines between eight profiles in 3d Cplane.

Chapter 12
Surfaces Modeling (I): Fundamentals and Creation

Objectives:

1. Know surfaces and their applications.
2. Understand surface mathematics.
3. Identify surface types.
4. Use Mastercam surface modules to create surfaces.
5. Know what works, and what doesn't, in creating surfaces.

Overview

This chapter covers important surfacing mathematics and techniques. Four surface mathematics styles and a comparison of their features are described. Sixteen projects are presented to show how to create primitive surfaces and free-form surfaces from the wireframe models in Mastercam. Useful tips are provided to help in your understanding of the principles and procedures of each surfacing technique. Derived surfacing techniques and their examples as well as several composite surface models are presented in chapter 13.

12.1 Surfaces

A surface is the shape representation of a part's skin defined by mathematical equations. A surface normally consists of many sections or patches that are smoothly blended together to form an entity. Due to the increased computer power and the new surface modeling techniques, today's surface modeling in CAD/CAM systems can accurately and completely describe a complex part shape. In addition the multiple surfaces found in many complex parts, can be blended together to form a single surface model for design analysis and NC tool path generation. This kind of multi-surfaces model is often called the **composite surface.**

Surface modeling is widely used to describe complex objects such as a car, ship, and airplane body, as well as their dies and molds. The information of surface models can be used to perform the following engineering, design, and manufacturing functions:

- Part geometric design and representation
- Mass properties calculation
- Interference checking between mating parts
- Cross-sectioned views generation
- Finite element meshes generation
- NC tool paths generation

12.2 Surface Mathematics

All surfaces are created by using one of the following four mathematical methods: Coons surface, Bezier surface, B-spline surface, and NURBS surface. They are briefly described in this section.

Coons Surface

A Coons surface is often referred to as the **Coons patch**. A single Coons patch is a surface patch constructed by blending four boundary curves (Figure 12.1). The multiple-patches Coons surface is generated from several individual patches smoothly blended together (Figure 12.2). The blending functions used in Coons surfaces could be either bi-linear or bi-cubic.

a. Wireframe model

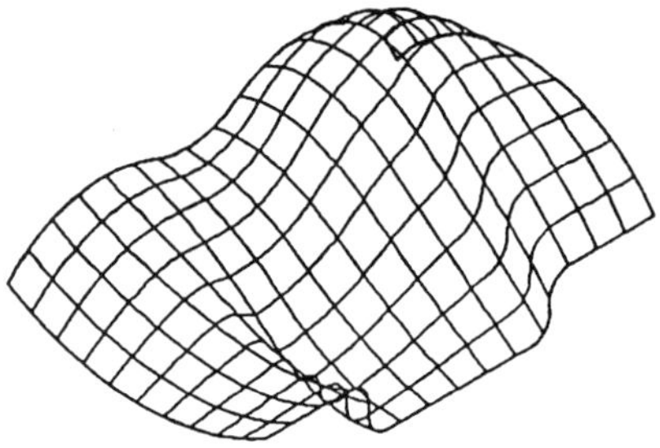

b. Surface model

Figure 12.1

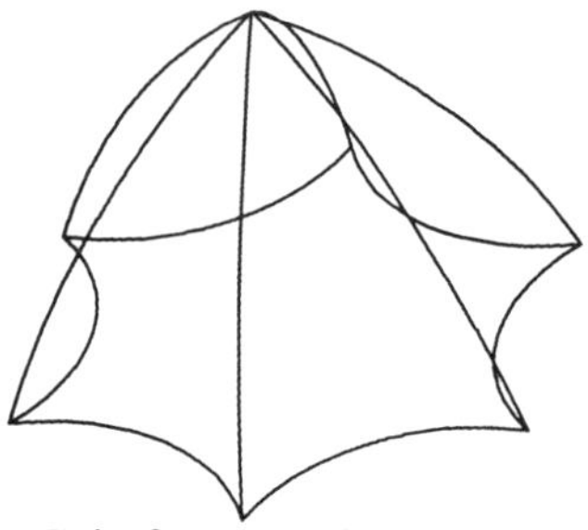

a. Wireframe model

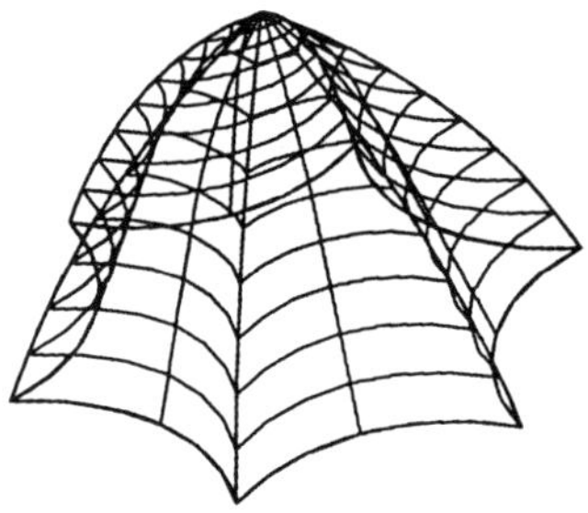

b. Surface model

Figure 12.2

The strength of the Coons surfaces is their ability to fit a smooth surface precisely throughout the wireframe curves or digitized point data. In other words, the surface must pass through all control points. The weakness is that a change of a shape of a surface requires that the control curves be altered.

Bezier Surface

A Bezier surface is created by blending all the connecting lines or facets formed by a grid of control points (Figure 12.3). Multiple-patches Bezier surfaces are formed in a way similar to Coons surfaces that smoothly blend individual Bezier patches together.

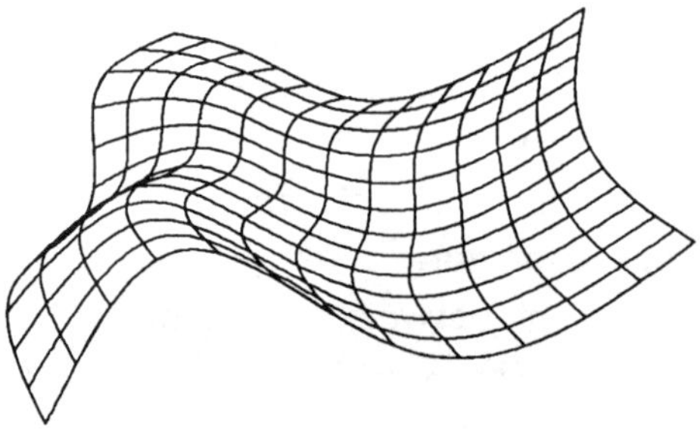

Figure 12.3

The advantage of using Bezier surfaces lies in their ability to reshape the surface by manipulating the control points. Control points can be pulled to create a new design. The weakness of Bezier surfaces is that the entire surface shape is affected simply by moving any one of the control points. They produce approximated surfaces in which specific cross-sectional shapes in particular positions are hard to obtain (if not impossible to obtain.)

B-Spline Surface

A B-spline surface possesses the combined strong features of both Coons and Bezier surfaces. Similar to the Coons patch, B-spline surfaces can be formed from a set of cross-sectional curves, and like the Bezier patch, it also has control points which can be manipulated to alter the surface texture.

A multiple-patches B-spline surface is possible and the continuity between adjacent patches can be guaranteed regardless of how the control points are moved.

The weakness of using B-spline surfaces is that primitive surfaces such as cylinders, spheres, and cones cannot be represented precisely. These surfaces can only be approximated, therefore, unacceptable dimensional errors may occur when machining these simple surfaces.

NURBS Surface

The term NURBS is an acronym for **Non-Uniform Rational B-Spline**. A rational surface is a surface in which each point described has a weight associated with it. A non-rational surface is a surface whose mathematical equations are not a rational number. NURBS surfaces are rational. They have all of B-spline surface abilities. In addition, they provide a weighting function to change the effect of the control points on the surface texture. When the weight function has a constant value of one, the NURBS surface is equivalent to a B-spline surface.

NURBS surfaces overcome the problem of the B-spline in modeling primitive surfaces. Surfaces based on conics, arcs, or spheres can be precisely represented by a NURBS surface. NURBS surface modeling is the most advanced technique of surface mathematics.

12.3 Surface Types

Surfaces can be classified into the following **three** categories: geometrical surfaces, free-form surfaces, and derived surfaces.

Geometrical Surfaces

Geometrical surfaces have constant geometrical shapes such as spheres, cones, and cyliners as well as draft surfaces and surfaces of revolution. They are generated with entities like lines, arcs, splines, and cones. Thus, there is little ambiguity in the definitions of these surfaces. Mastercam provides **two** surfacing techniques to create geometrical surfaces: draft surface modeling and revolved surface modeling. Table 12.1 on the following page summarizes these two geometrical surfacing techniques.

Table 12.1 Geometrical Surfaces

Surface type	Description	Applications	Example
Draft surface (Extruded)	A surface created by extruding a sectional shape straight along a line. The line is defined by a length and an angle.	Used to create cones, cylinders. Draft angles on molds, and tabulated cylinders.	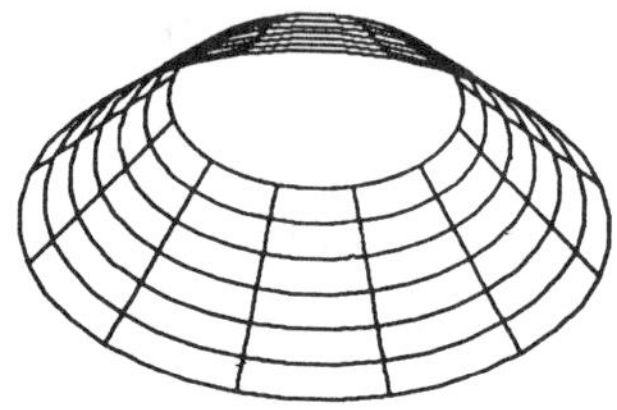
Revolved surface	A surface created by rotating a sectional shape around an axis or a line.	Used on any part that requires surfaces with arc or circular cross sections.	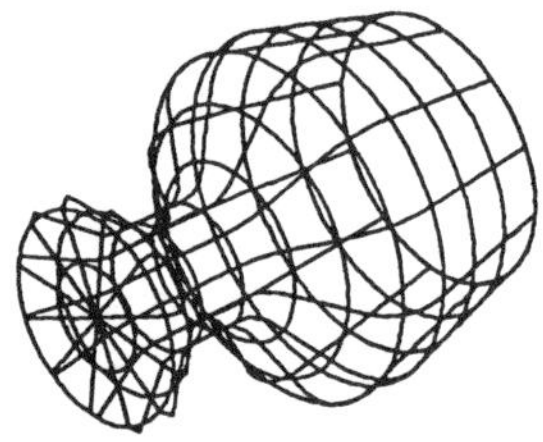

Free-Form Surfaces

Free-form surfaces follow no set geometric pattern and are normally generated from arbitrarily shaped lines and curves. These surfaces require more sophisticated surface mathematics such as Coons patches, Bezier patches, B-spline surfaces, and NURBS surfaces.

Free-form surfaces may be classified further into **two kinds** by their use: constrained surfaces and unconstrained surfaces. **Constrained surfaces** are restricted to existing data sets that may be in the form of sections or cross sections. In other words, the surfaces must pass through the given sections exactly. Coons patches is a typical constrained surface because of its direct relationship to the geometry.

Unconstrained surfaces are not restricted to pre-existing sets of data points or curves. They use control points to create the surface shape that is not necessarily passed through all pre-defined data points or curves. They are mainly used in conceptual designs. Bezier, B-spline, and NURBS surfaces are unconstrained surface types. Table 12.2 summarizes surface types, their desription, typical applications, and examples of free-form surfaces.

Derived Surfaces

Derived surfaces are surfaces that are generated from existing surfaces. They are also called edited surfaces. Table 12.3 on the next page shows **four** commonly used derived surfaces; offset, trimmed, fillet and blend.

Table 12.2 Free-form surfaces

Surface Type	Description	Applications	Example
Ruled surface	A surface created by connecting straight lines between two or more lines or curves.	Used any time a surface must be fit between two or more curves.	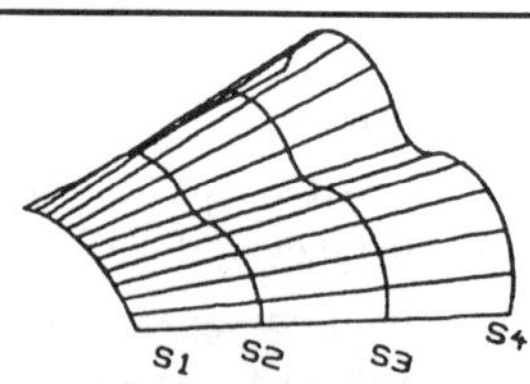
Lofted surface	A surface created by fitting through a set of cross sectional curves.	Used when a surface must be parabolically blended through more than two curves.	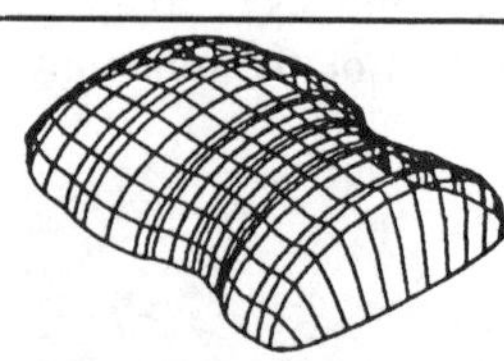

Table 12.2 Continued

Drag surface (2-D swept)	A surface created by translating or rotating a sectional profile along a drive curve.	Used when the cross section of the surface at any point remain constant.	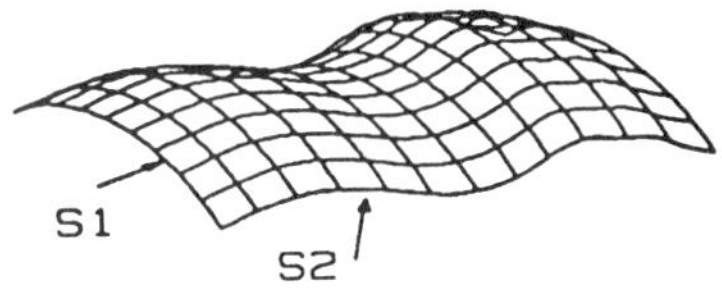
3-D swept surface (Drag with blending)	A surface created by (1) translating a sectional profile along two drive curves, (2) translating two sectional profiles along a drive curve	Used when the across sections at any section is not constant.	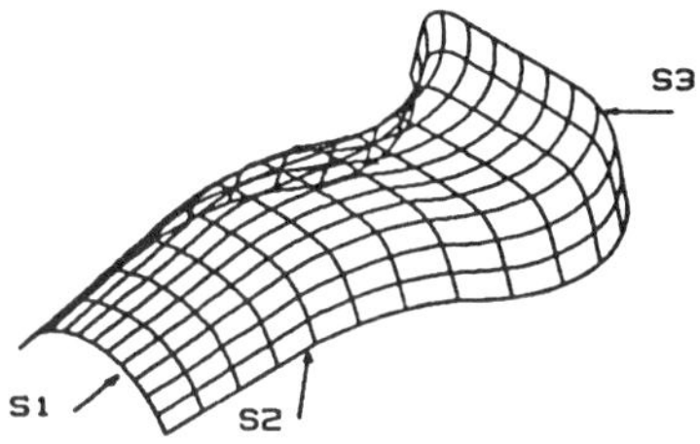
Coons surface	A surface created by blending a number of patches that have four prescribed intersecting curves which form a closed boundary.	Used when a surface is formed by a set of patches.	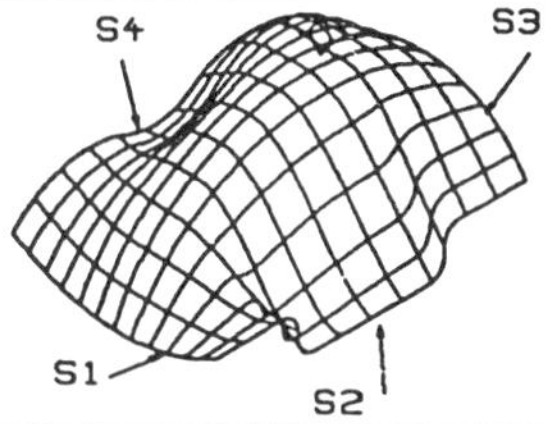

Table 12.3 Derived surfaces

Surface Type	Description	Applications	Example
Offset surface	A surface created by offsetting an existing surface by a distance. The offset is applied normal (perpendicular) to the original surface.	Used to create a new surface that is offset from the original surface.	
Trimmed surface	A surface created by trimming an existing surface to a specified boundary.	Used to redefine the borders of the existing surfaces.	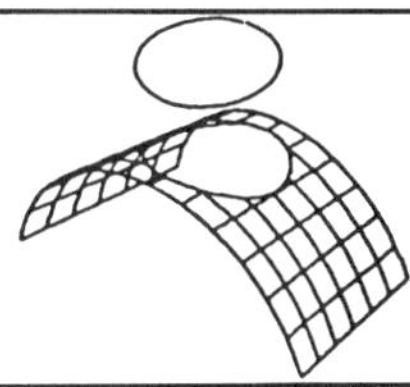
Fillet surface	A surface created by generating arc cross sections that are tangent to two surfaces.	Used to smooth sharp edges.	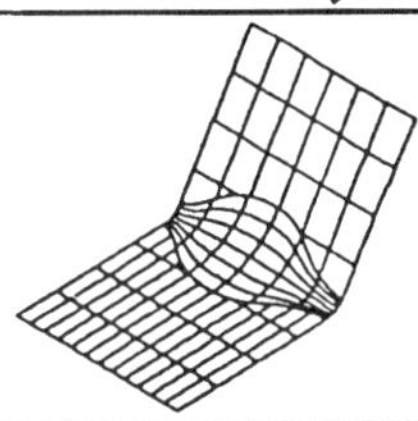
Blend surface	A surface created by joining two existing surfaces, and is tangent to each parent surface.	Used to join two surfaces with a smooth surface.	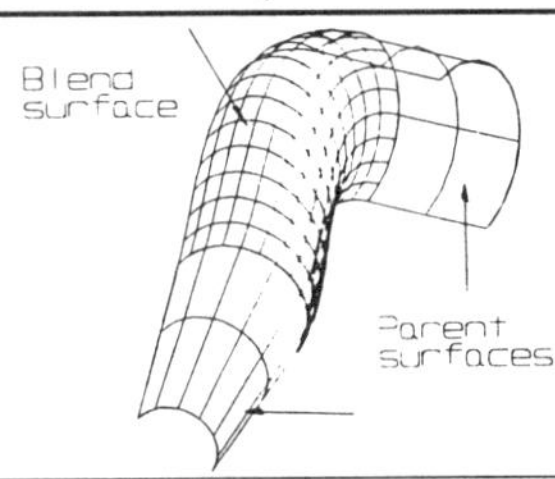

12.4 Mastercam Surfaces

The Mastercam software provides a series of very powerful surfacing techniques including:

> **two geometric** surface models: revolved and draft
> **four free-form** surface models: ruled, loft, Coons, and swept
> **four derived** surface models: fillet, offset, trimmed and blend.

These free-form and derived surfaces are primarily based on three surfacing mathematics principles: blend, parametric, and NURBS. Table 12.4 gives the available surfacing methods for **four** types of free-form surfaces in Mastercam.

Blend: approximates a surface by blending between the boundaries of piecewise surface contours.

Parametric: uses bi-cubic approximation to create parametric splines along and across an array of points that lie on the surface. The parametric bi-cubic surface patch connects four corner data points and utilize a bi-cublic equation.

NURBS: interpolates a surface by weighting the effect of the control points on the surface skin.

Table 12.4 Surfacing methods of free-form surfaces in Mastercam

Surface Types	Surface Methods		
	Blend	Parametric	NURBS
Loft	Yes	Yes	Yes
Coons	No	Yes	Yes
Ruled	Yes	Yes	Yes
Swept	No	Yes	Yes

Surfacing Projects

The examples given in this chapter use the wireframe models constructed in chapter 11. They are arranged in such a way that each surface modeling method begins with important tips which outline what to do for the sussessful completion of the surface model. Additional examples are used to re-enforce the use of each modeling method. The derived surfaces and composite surfaces are presented in chapter 13.

12.5 Ruled Surfaces Modeling

Mastercam's ruled surfaces modeling allows two or more contours to be linearly blended to form a surface.

Tips 1.The first pick position of each contour affects the shape of the surface (Figure 12.4). Make each contour start from the same orientation.

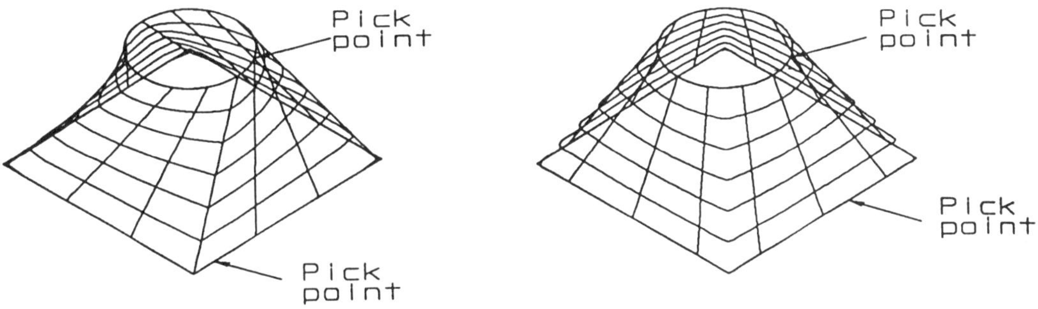

Figure 12.4a. Twisted surface shape Figure 12.4b. Correct surface shape

2. An entity sometimes has to be broken into two entities in order to allow the contours to start from the same orientation. The right vertical line in Figure 12.5, for example, is broken into two segments to permit the alignment of starting point.

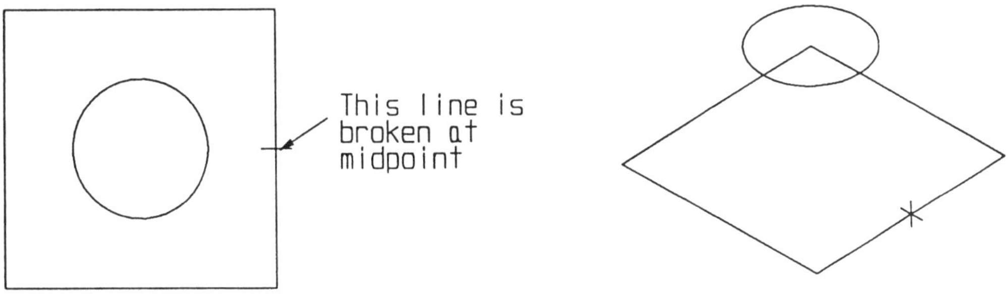

Figure 12.5a. Top view Figure 12.5b. Isometric view

3. Contours must be orderly selected. Any misplace of the picking order may result in a unacceptable surface (Figure 12.6).

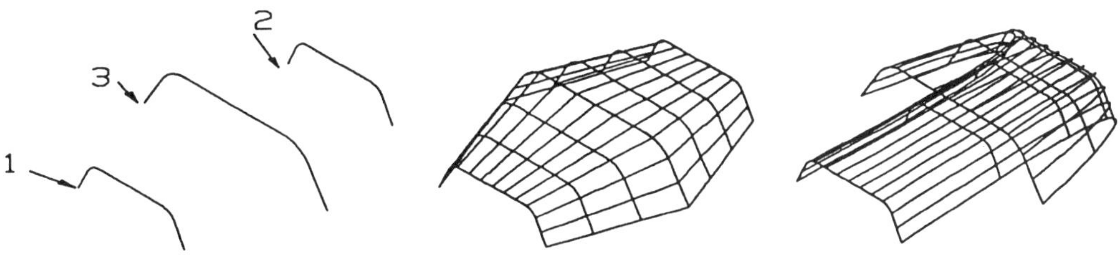

Figure 12.6a. Pick order Figure 12.6b. Proper surface Figure 12.6c. Twisted surface

4. Use the Top Gview to pick the contours as the number of contours increases. Isometric Gview tends to cause confusion when the wireframe model becomes complicated. Use the Window command to automatically define the order of contours.
5. Have the same chaining direction for all contours. Reversing the chaining direction of one entity results in an improper surface (Figure 12.7).

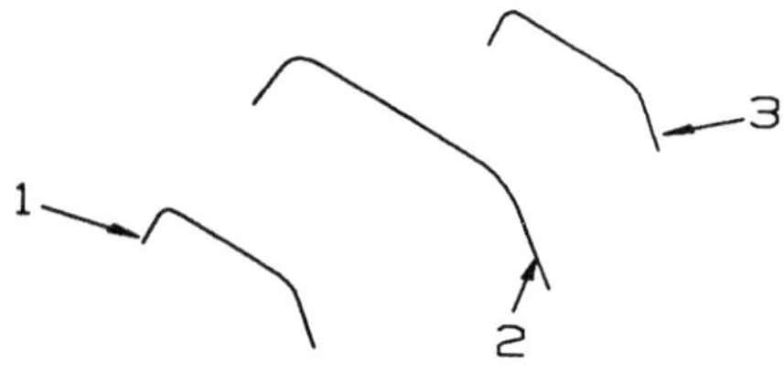

a. Contour directions

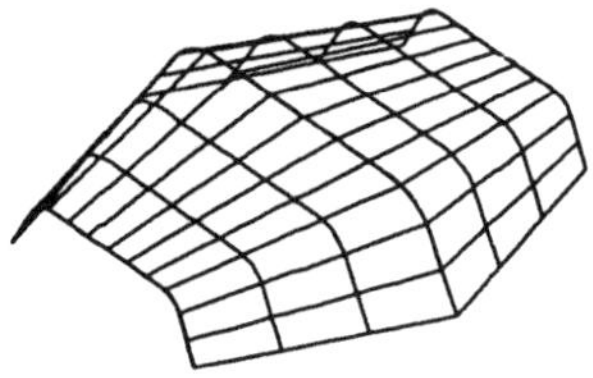

b. Proper surface

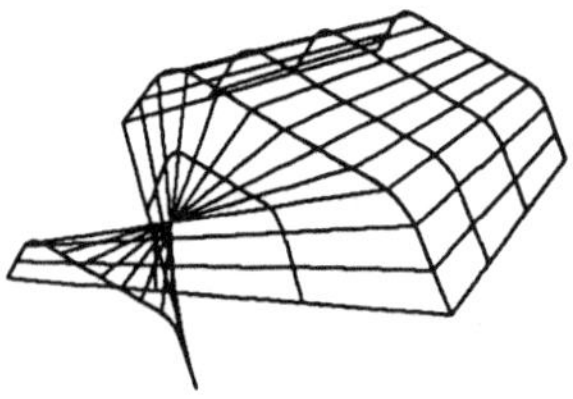

c. Twisted surface

Figure 12.7

Project 1.

Creating two ruled surfaces, both formed by two contours

This example uses the wireframe model constructed in project 1 of chapter 11 to generate two ruled surfaces. The contour profiles is shown in Figure 12.8a and the finished ruled surfaces in Figure 12.8b.

Wireframe Model
Project 1 of Chapter 11 (ruled1)

1

Go to

We are here **Surface Model (ruleds1)**

Go to

Fillct Surface
Project 1 of Chapter 13 (fillets1)

Go to

Trimmed Surface
Project 3 of Chapter 13 (trims1)

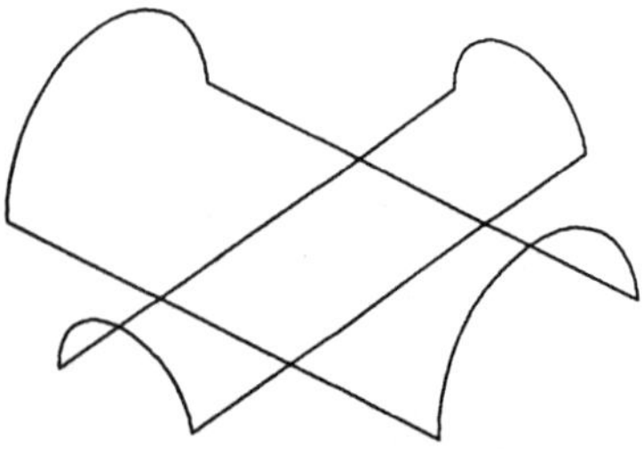

Figure 12.8a. Wireframe model

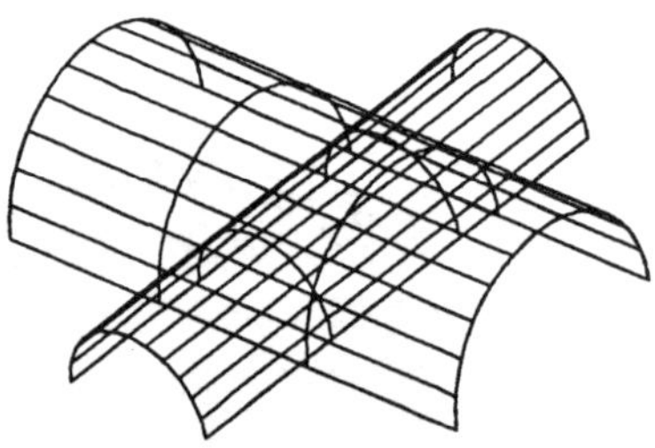

Figure 12.8b. Surface model

Step 1. Enter the Mastercam Mill and load the drawing file (ruled1). If the wireframe model is not available yet, follow the step-by-step procedure given in the project 1 of chapter 11 to create the drawing.

Select **MAIN MENU → File → Get**
Enter file name (C:\NC\GE3\T.GE3): **ruled1 ←**
Pick **Yes** to select the current part
The drawing should appear as Figure 12.9.

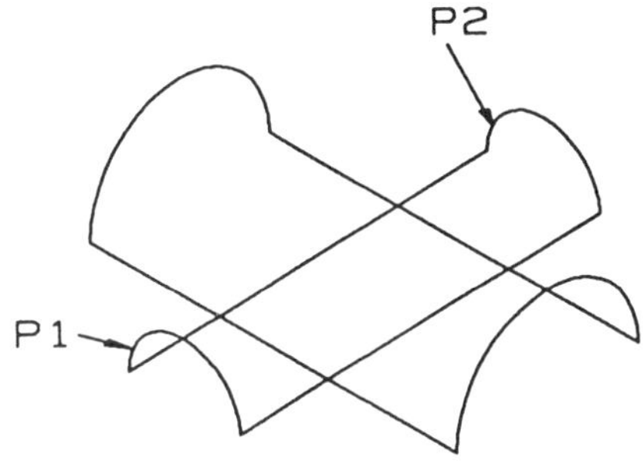

Figure 12.9

Step 2. Create the first ruled surface. Use the pick points in Figure 12.9.

Select **MAIN MENU → Create → sUrface → rUled → Blend**
define contour 1: pick **Single** from the chaining method menu
Pick at **P1** to select the first contour
define contour 2: pick **Single** from the chaining method menu
Pick at **P2** to select the second contour
define contour 3: pick **Done** from the chaining method menu to complete the selection of the first ruled surface

The drawing with the first ruled surface should resemble Figure 12.10.

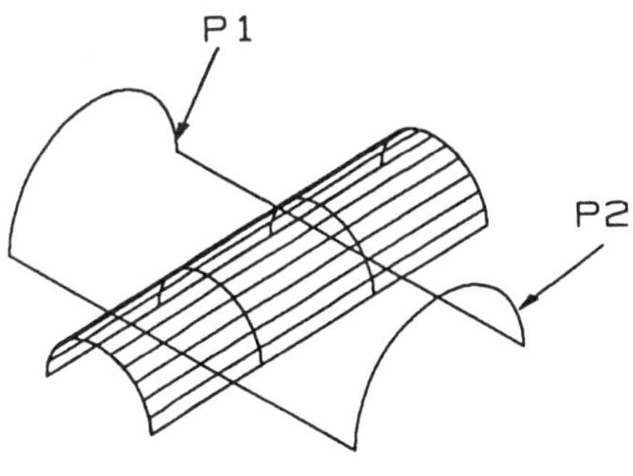

Figure 12.10

Step 3. Create the second ruled surface. Use the pick points in Figure 12.10.

Select **rUled** from the surface menu
Select **Blend** from the surfacing method menu
define contour 1: select **Single** and then pick at **P1**
define contour 2: select **Single** and then pick at **P2**
define contour 3: select **Done** to complete the selection of the second ruled surface

The two ruled surfaces should look like Figure 12.11.

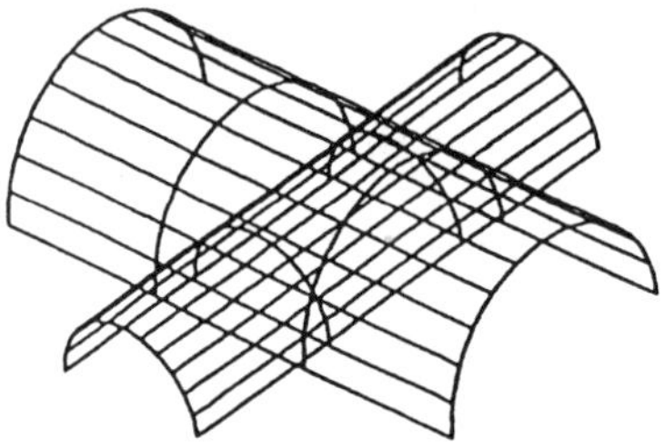

Figure 12.11

Step 4. Shade two-surfaces

Select **MAIN MENU →Screen → shAde** from the Surface menu

Set the selected Shade parameters to the following settings:

Size of each facet (in pixels): **4**
Output will go on the screen

Select **Do it**

Note: for the Size of each facet, increase the size of each facet for rough shade and decrease the size for smooth shade.

The shaded surfaces will appear on the screen as shown in Figure 12.11a.

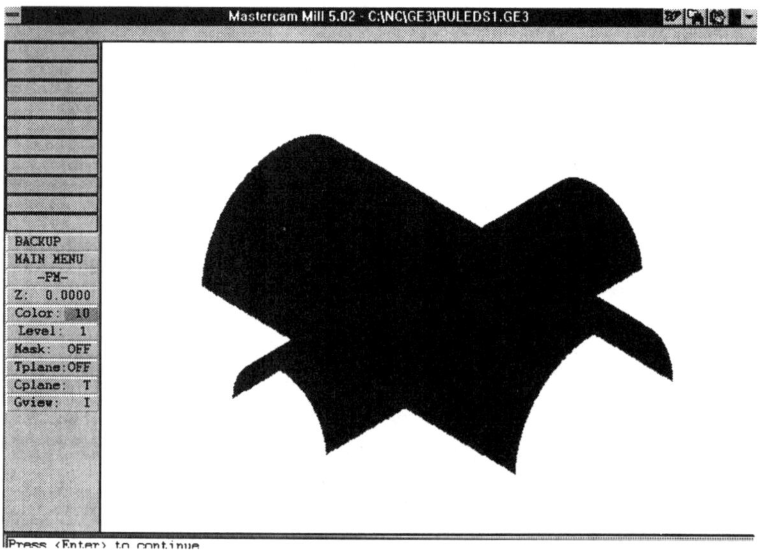

Figure 12.11a

Press **Enter** to return to graphic mode.

Step 5. Save the surfaces (ruleds1).

Select **MAIN MENU → File → Save**

Enter file name: **ruleds1**

Note: This surface file is used to generate intersecting curves, fillet surfaces and trimmed surfaces in the preceeding chapters.

Project 2.

2

Creating two ruled surfaces

In this example, we use the wireframe model constructed in the project 2 of chapter 11 to create two ruled surfaces. These two surfaces intersect forming an angle. The wireframe model is redrawn in Figure 12.12a, and the completed surface model is in Figure 12.12b.

Wireframe Model
Project 2 of Chapter 11 (ruled2)

Go to

We are here

Surface Model
(ruleds2)

Go to

Fillet Surface
Project 2 of Chapter 13 (fillets2)

Go to

Trimmed Surface
Project 4 of Chapter 13 (trims2)

Go to

Toolpath
Project 4 of Chapter 15 (trimst2)

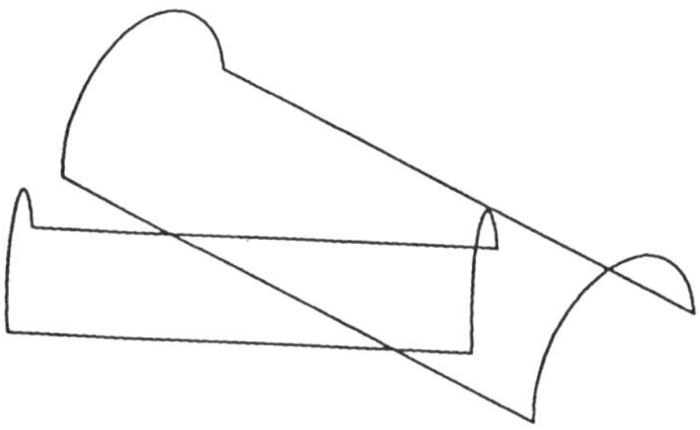

Figure 12.12a. Wireframe model

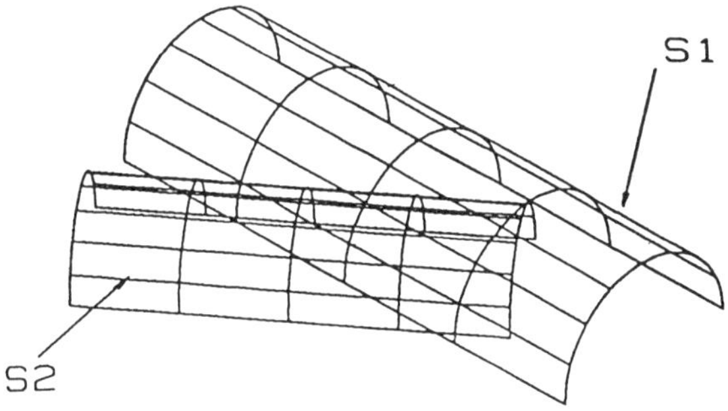

Figure 12.12b. Surface model

Step 1. Load the drawing file, or create the contour profiles by following the instructions in project 2 of chapter 11.

Select **MAIN MENU → File → Get**
Enter file name: **ruled2**
Pick **Yes** to delect the current part if necessary

The drawing on the screen should look like Figure 12.13.

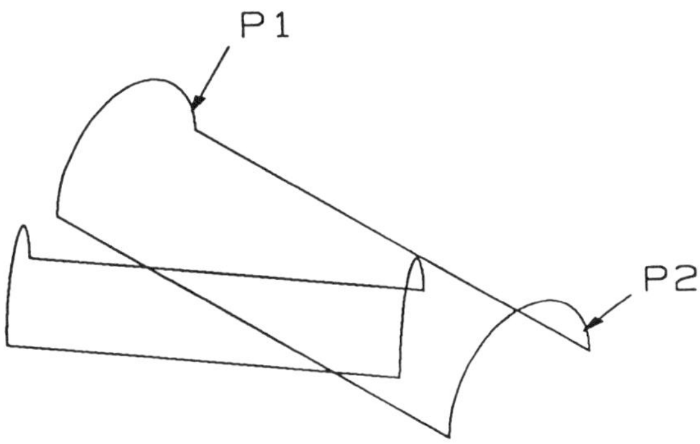

Figure 12.13

Step 2. Create the first ruled surface S1. Use the pick points in Figure 12.13.

Select **MAIN MENU → Create → sUrface → rUled →Parametric**
define contour 1: select **Single** and then pick at **P1**
define contour 2: select **Single** and then pick at **P2**
define contour 3: select **Done→Done** to complete the contour selection

The first ruled surface should appear as Figure 12.14.

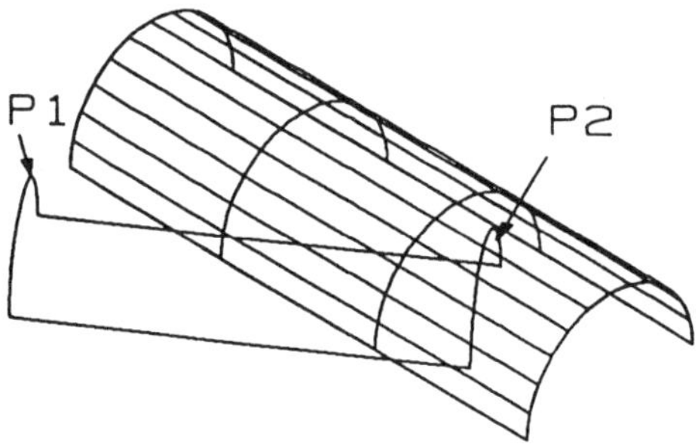

Figure 12.14

Step 3. Create the second ruled surface S2. Use the pick points in Figure 12.14.

Select **rUled → Parametric**
define contour 1: select **Single** and then pick at **P1**
define contour 2: select **Single** and then pick at **P2**
define contour 3: select **Done** to complete the contour selection

The two ruled surfaces appear as Figure 12.15.

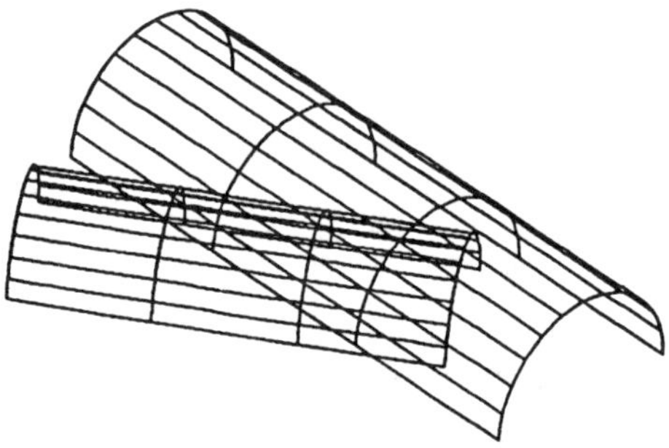

Figure 12.15

Step 4. Save the surfaces (ruleds2).

Select **MAIN MENU → File → Save**
Enter file name: **ruleds2**

Note: These two ruled surfaces are used to create two fillet surfaces with a variable radius in chapter 13.

Project 3.

3

Creating a ruled surface formed by three contours

In this project, three contours are used to construct a ruled surface. The wireframe profiles are constructed in project 3 of chapter 11 which is redrawn in Figure 12.16a. The completed ruled surface is shown in Figure 12.16b.

Wireframe Model
Project 2 of Chapter 11 (3contour)

We are here

Go to

Surface Model
(ruleds2)

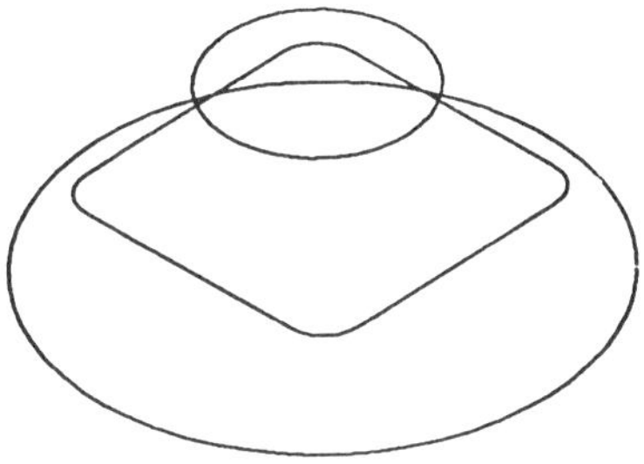

Figure 12.16a. Wireframe model

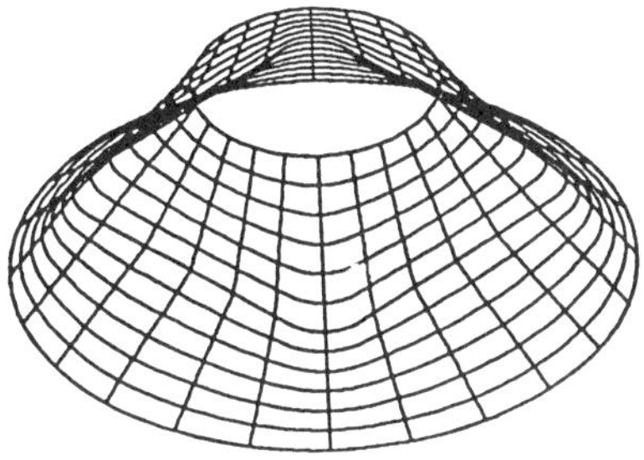

Figure 12.16b. Surface model

The keys to successfully create a ruled surface based on these three contours are:

Tips 1. Use the Top Gview to give a better view of picking at entities.

2. Break the right vertical line of the rectangular contour into two pieces. This allows each contour to start at the same orientation.
3. The pick points at each contour should be placed on the position that make contours going the same direction.

Step 1. Load the wireframe model file (3contour) or create one according to the instructions given in project 3 of chapter 11.

Select **MAIN MENU → File → Get**

Enter file name: **3contour**

Select **Yes** to delete the current part

The wireframe drawing should appear as Figure 12.17.

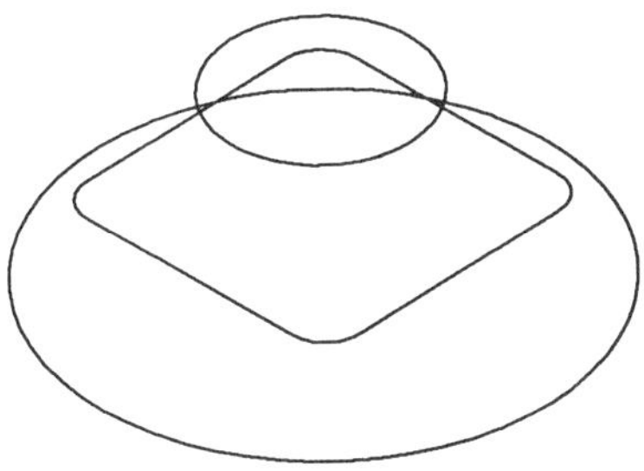

Figure 12.17

Step 2. Change to Top Gview.

Select **Gview → Top**

The drawing in Top Gview should resemble Figure 12.18.

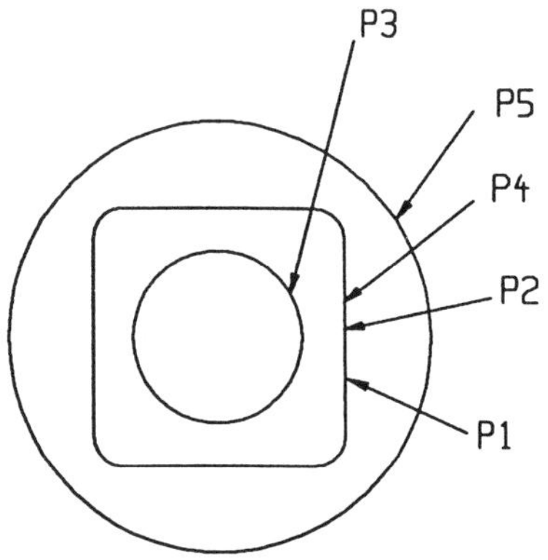

Figure 12.18

Step 3. Break the right vertical line of the rectangular contour into two pieces. Use the pick points of Figure 12.18.

Select **MAIN MENU → Modify → Break → 2 pieces**
Pick at **P1** to select the entity to break
Select **Midpoint** from the Point Menu
Pick at **P2** to complete the breaking of the line

Step 4. Create a ruled surface. Continue to use the pick points in Figure 12.18.

Select **MAIN MENU → Create → sUrface → rUled → Nurbs**
define contour 1: Select **Single** and then pick at **P3** on the inside circle
define contour 2: Select **Chain** and then pick at **P4**
Select **Close → End here** to complete the selection of the rectangular contour
define contour 3: Select **Single** and then pick at **P5** on the outside circle
Select **Done → Done** to complete the surface
Select **Gview → Isometric** to change drawing to isometric view

The surface drawing should resemble Figure 12.19 .

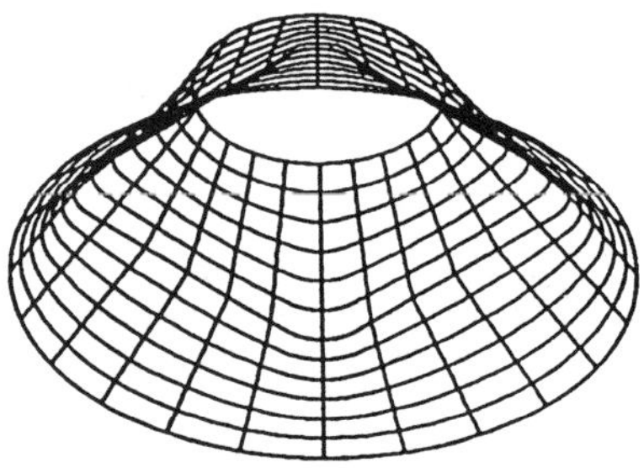

Figure 12.19

Step 5. Save the surface drawing (ruleds3).

Select **MAIN MENU → File → Save**
Enter file name: **ruleds3**

12.6 Loft Surfaces Modeling

Mastercam's loft surfaces modeling permits three or more sectional contours to be parabolically blended to form a smooth surface.

Keys to the successful completion of loft surfaces include:

Tips 1. The number of sectional contours must be more than two. When the number of contours is equal to two, the resulted surface is a ruled surface.
2. Break an entity into two pieces to allow the alignment of starting points for all contours when a contour has more than one entity. See the example in Figure 12.5.
3. Contours must be orderly selected.
4. Have the same chaining direction for all contours.
5. When the number of contours is relatively large and no contours are connected, use **Window → one way** commands to select the contours. This drastically reduces the time and the number of picking at entities and reduces the errors.

Project 4.

4

Wireframe Model

Project 3 of Chapter 11 (3contour)

Creating a loft surface formed by three contours

The three-contour wireframe model (3contour) is used again in this example to generate a loft surface. The contour profiles and the finished loft surface are shown in Figure 12.20.

Go to

We are here **Surface Model** **(lofts1)**

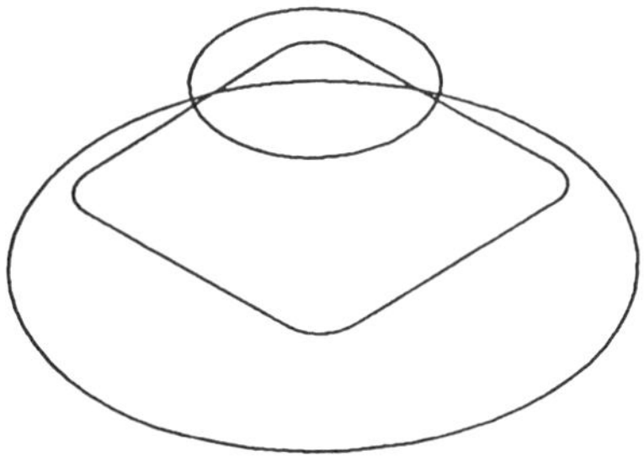

Figure 12.20a. Wireframe model

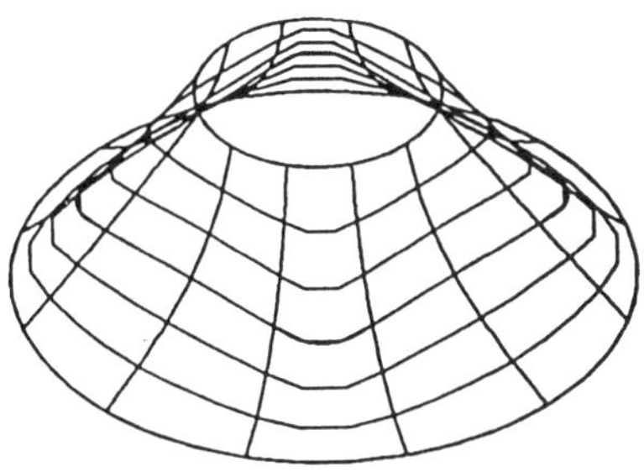

Figure 12.20b. Surface model

Tip The right vertical edge of the rectangular contour must be broken into two pieces at the midpoint.

Step 1. Load the wireframe model file (3contour) or follow the instructions given in project 3 of chapter 11 to create one.

Select **MAIN MANU → File → Get**
Enter file name: **3contour**
Select **Yes** to delete the current part
Select **Gview → Top** to change the Gview to Top view

The wireframe model on the screen appears as Figure 12.21.

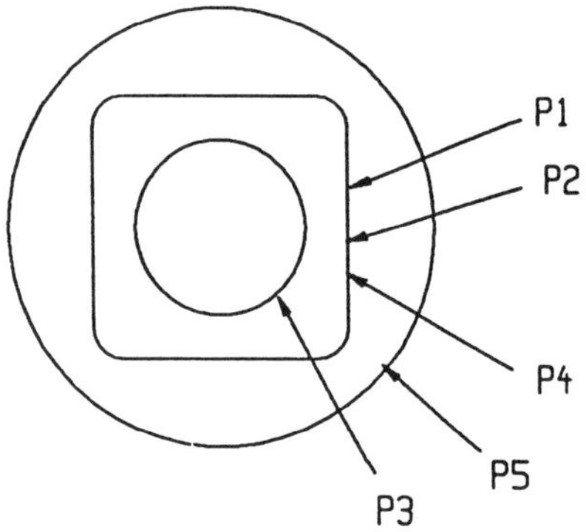

Figure 12.21

Step 2. Break the right vertical line of the rectangular contour into two pieces at the midpoint. Use the pick points in Figure 12.21.

Select **MAIN MENU → Modify → Break → 2 pieces**
Select an entity: pick at **P1**
Enter the breakpoint: select **Midpoint** from the point menu and then pick at **P2**

Step 3. Create the loft surface. Continue to use the pick points in Figure 12.21.

Select **MAIN MENU → Create → sUrface → Loft → Blend**
define contour 1: select **Single** and then pick at **P3** on the inside circle
define contour 2: select **Chain** and then pick at **P4**
Select **Close → End here** to complete the selection of the rectangular contour
define contour 3: select **Single** and then pick at **P5**
Select **Done** to complete the surface

The drawing in the Top Gview should appear on the screen as Figure 12.22.

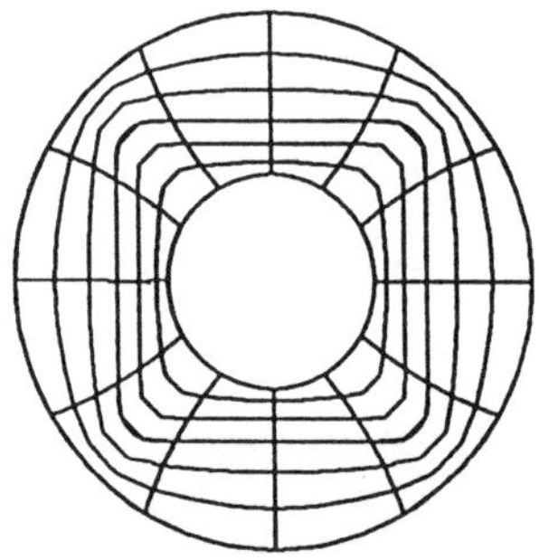

Figure 12.22

Step 4. Change the Gview to isometric.

Select **Gview → Isometric**

The final surface drawing should resemble Figure 12.23.

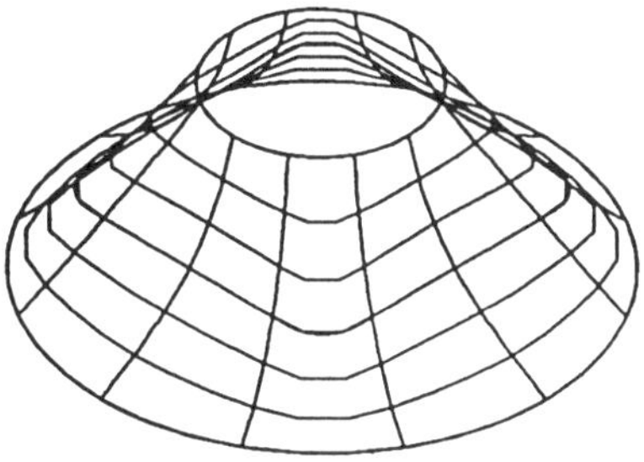

Figure 12.23

Step 5. Save the drawing file (lofts1).

Select **MAIN MENU → File → Save**

Enter file name: **lofts1**

5

Project 5.

Creating a loft surface of ninteen sectional contours

The nineteen sectional contours created in the project 4 of chapter 11 are used to generate a loft surface. The wireframe model and the finished surface model are shown in Figure 12.24.

Wireframe Model
Project 4 of Chapter 11 (loft2)

Go to

We are here

Surface Model
(lofts2)

Go to

Trimmed Surface
Project 5 of Chapter 13 (trims3)

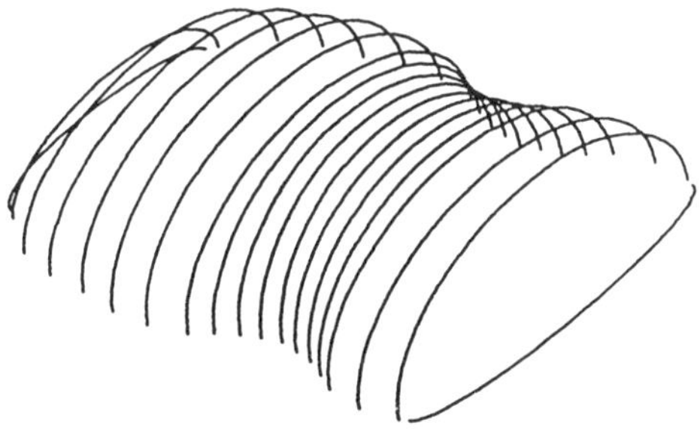

Figure 12.24a. Wireframe model

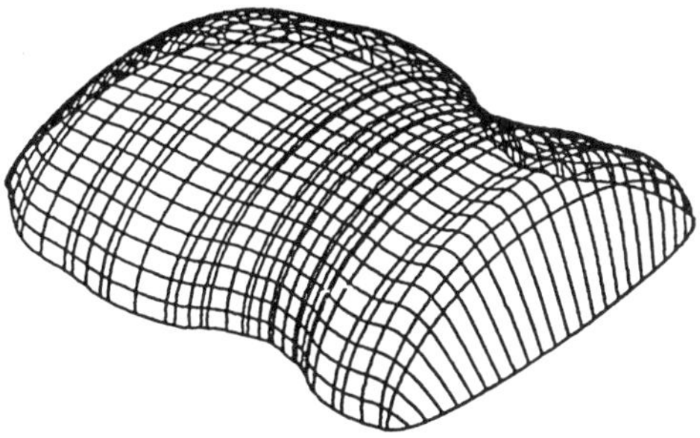

Figure 12.24b. Surface model

Tip: The Window chaining menu is used in this example to reduce the picking of contours.

Step 1. Load the wireframe model file (loft2) or follow the instructions in project 4 of chapter 11 to create one.

Select **MAIN MENU** → **File** → **Get**
Enter file name: **loft2**
Select **Yes** to delete the current part
The wireframe model should appear as Figure 12.25.

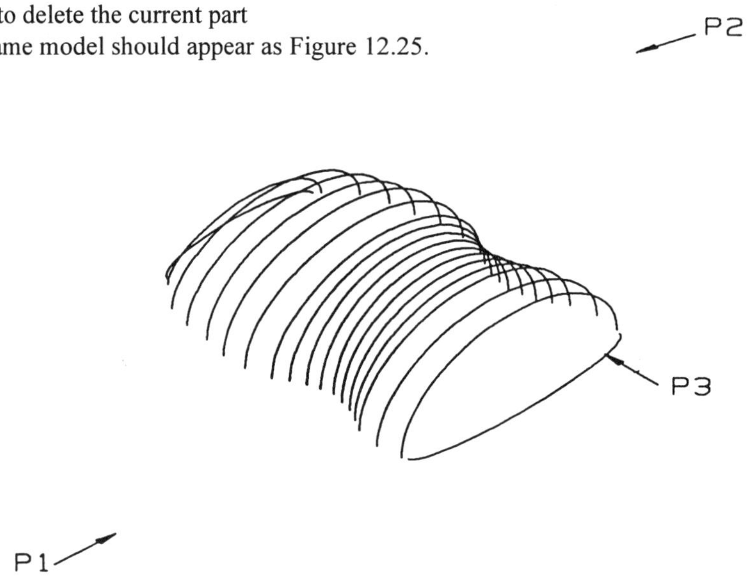

Figure 12.25

Step 2. Create the loft surface. Use the pick points in Figure 12.25.

Select **MAIN MENU** → **Create** → **sUrface** → **Loft** → **Nurbs**
Select **Window** from the chaining method menu
Enter the first corner: pick at **P1**
Enter the second corner: Pick at **P2** to ensure all contours are included in the window
Select **One way** in the Search by Menu
Select **ccW** in the Chaining direction Menu
Enter search point: select **Endpoint** from the Point Menu and then pick at **P3**
Select **Done** from the Chaining method Menu
Select **Done** from the Lofted surface parameters Menu

The loft surface should resemble Figure 12.26.

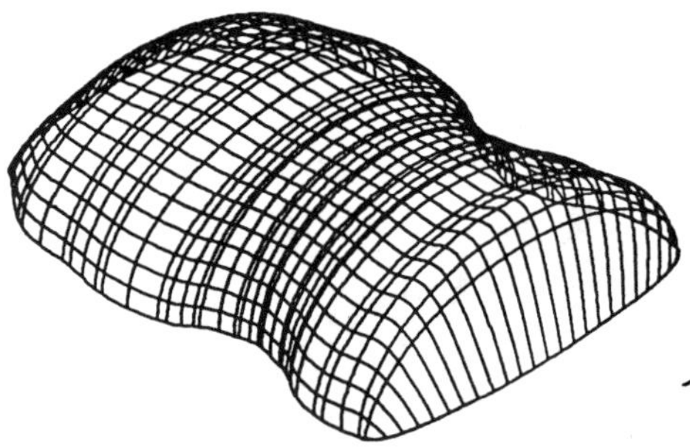

Figure 12.26

Step 3. Save the surface model file (lofts2).

Select **MAIN MENU** → **File** → **Save**
Enter file name: **lofts2**

Note: This surface model is used to create a trimmed surface in chapter 13.

Project 6.

Creating a loft surface using five sectional contours

The five sectional contours constructed in the project 14 of chapter 11 are used to create a loft surface. The contours are redrawn in Figure 12.27a and the finished loft surface is in Figure 12.27b.

Figure 12.27a. Wireframe model

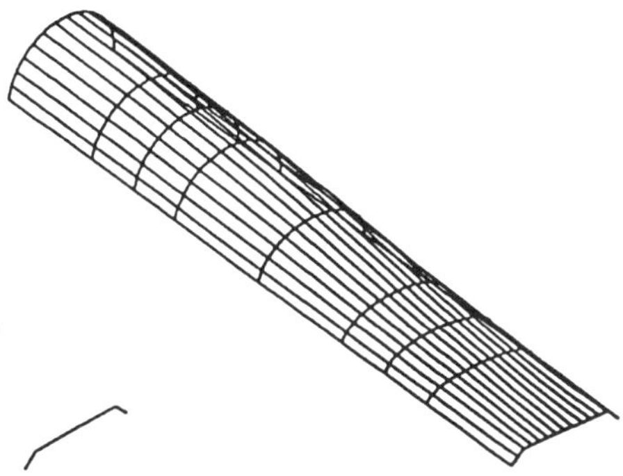

Figure 12.27b. Surface model

Tips 1. Create a loft surface based on the five sectional profiles.

2. Mirror the loft surface about the X axis to create the lower surface section. Note that the Cplane needs to be either Front or Side view.

Step 1. Load the wireframe model profiles (loft3) or create one by following instructions in project 14 of chapter 11.
Select **MAIN MENU → File → Get**
Enter file name: **loft3**
Select **Yes** to delete the current part
The five contours should look like Figure 12.28.

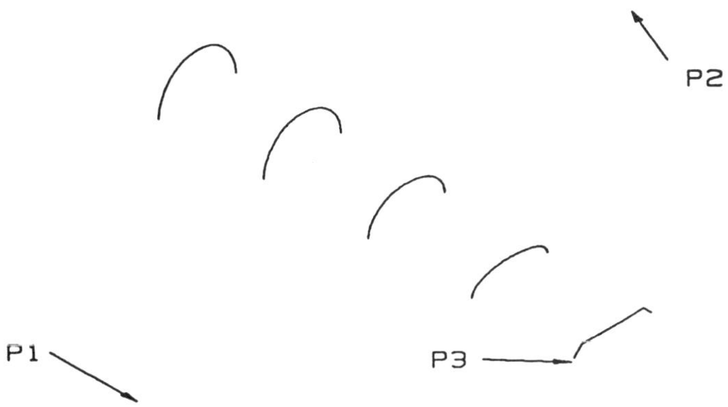

Figure 12.28

6

Wireframe Model
Project 14 of Chapter 11 (loft3)

We are here

Go to
Surface Model
(lofts3)

Go to
Toolpath
Project 1 of Chapter 15 (flow1)

Go to
Toolpath Trimming
Project 3 of Chapter 16 (lofts3)

Step 2. Create a loft surface. Use the pick points in Figure 12.28.

Select **MAIN MENU → Create → sUrface → Loft → Nurbs → Window**
Pick at **P1** and **P2** to specify the window range
Select **One way → ccW → Endpoint**
Pick at **P3** to trap the endpoint for the search point
Select **Done**
Change the following Lofted surface parameters:

> Select **aCross** then enter **0.1** ← for the Across cut distance
> Select **Error chk** to toggle the selection to **On**
> Select **Done** to complete the surface

The system will show the maximum error between theoretical and parametric surface = 0.0033
Press **Enter** to continue

The loft surface should appear as Figure 12.29.

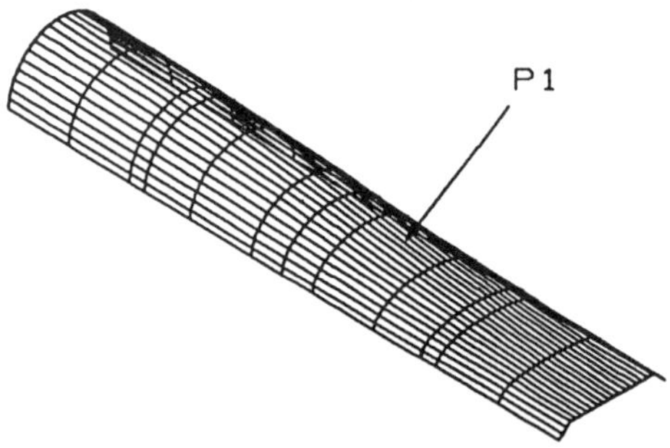

Figure 12.29

Step 3. Save the surface model file (lofts3).

Select **MAIN MENU → File → Save**
Enter file name: **lofts3**

Step 4. Mirror the surface about the X axis to create the lower surface section.

Use either Front or Side Cplane. Use the pick points in Figure 12.29.
Select **Cplane → Front**
Select **MAIN MENU → Xform → Mirror → Entity**
Select an entity: pick at **P1**
Select **BACKUP → Done → X axis**
Select **Copy →** **Done** from the Mirror parameters menu

The entire surface model now should appear as Figure 12.30.

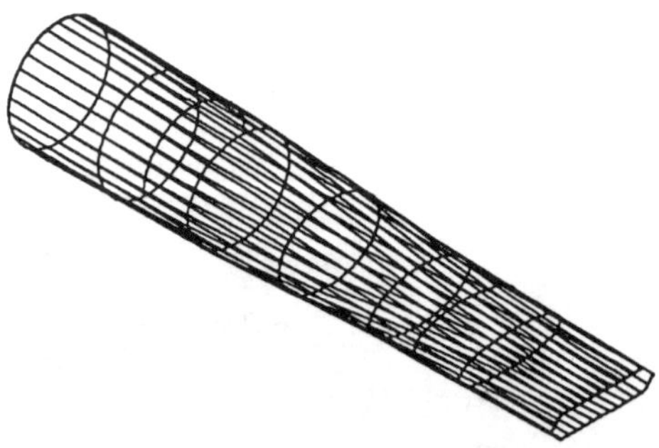

Figure 12.30

12.7 Coons Surfaces Modeling

A Coons surface is created by blending a set of surface patches, each formed by four edge curves. Defining contours for Coons surfaces is a rather difficult process because they involve many more contours than other surface modeling techniques. The instructions given below should help in successfully completing a Coons surface.

Tip 1. Select the start point. The start point is normally chosen at a join point of two contours. One of these two join contours becomes the first **along** contour, and the other is the first **across** contour. Figure 12.31 shows an example of selecting the start point of defining a Coons surface.

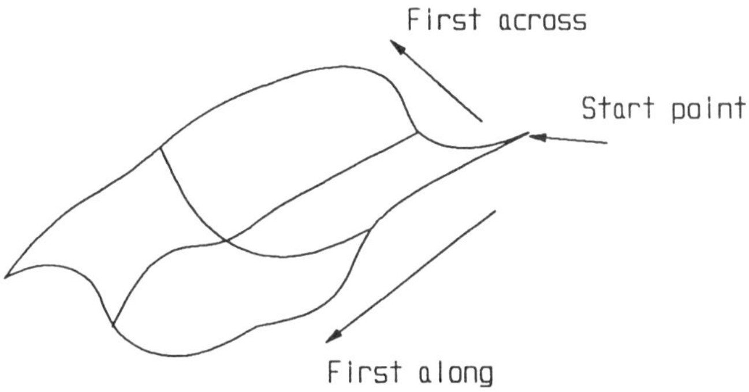

Figure 12.31

Tip 2. Determine the number of patches in the along direction and the number of patches in the across direction.

In the case of an open boundary where the first and the last contour are not connected as shown in Figure 12.32.

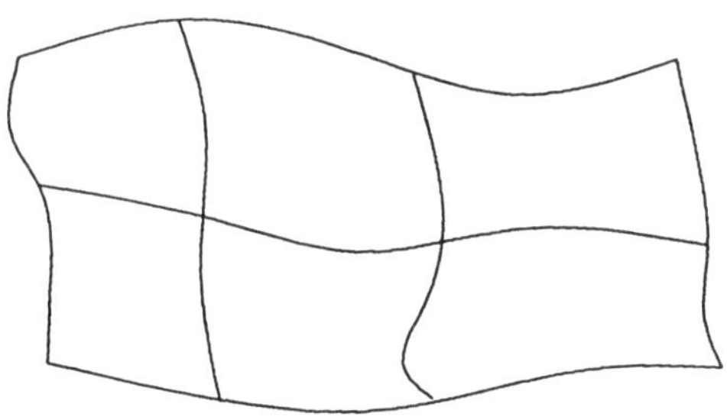

Figure 12.32

$P_L = N_C - 1$
$P_C = N_L - 1$
$P_T = P_L \times P_C$

where P_L = number of patches in along direction
P_C = number of patches in across direction
P_T = total number of patches
N_L = number of along contours
N_C = number of across contours

Example 12.1:

Find the numbers of patches in along and across direction for the surface contours given in Figure 12.33.

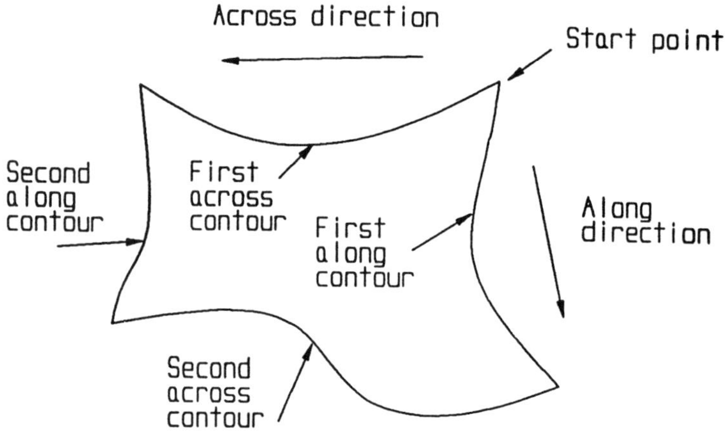

Figure 12.33

Solution:

Number of along contours $N_L = 2$
Number of across contours $N_C = 2$
Number of patches in along direction $P_L = N_C - 1 = 2 - 1 = 1$
Number of patches in across direction $P_C = N_L - 1 = 2 - 1 = 1$
Total number of patches $P_T = P_L \text{ X } P_C = 1 \text{ X } 1 = 1$

Example 12.2:

Find the numbers of patches in along and across direction for the surface contours given in Figure 12.34.

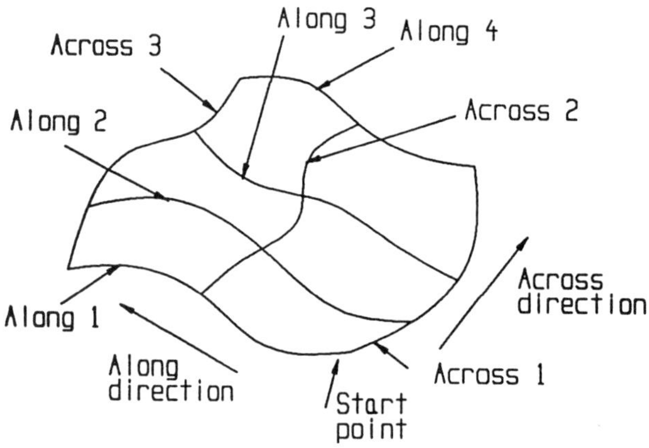

Figure 12.34

Solution:

$N_L = 4$
$N_C = 3$
$P_L = N_C - 1 = 3 - 1 = 2$
$P_C = N_L - 1 = 4 - 1 = 3$
$P_T = P_L \text{ X } P_C = 2 \text{ X } 3 = 6$

In the case of a close boundary where the first and the last contour are connected. Actually they are the identical contour (Figure 12.35 on the following page).

The number of patches in along direction $P_L = N_C$
The number of patches in across direction $P_C = N_L - 1$

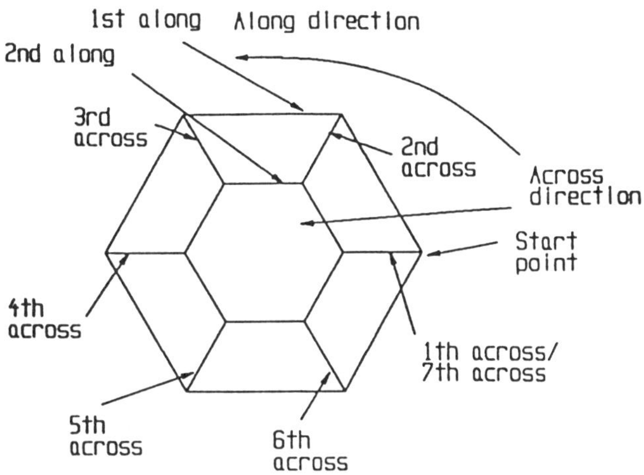

Figure 12.35

Example 12.3:

Determine the number of patches in the along and across direction for the surface shown in Figure 12.36.

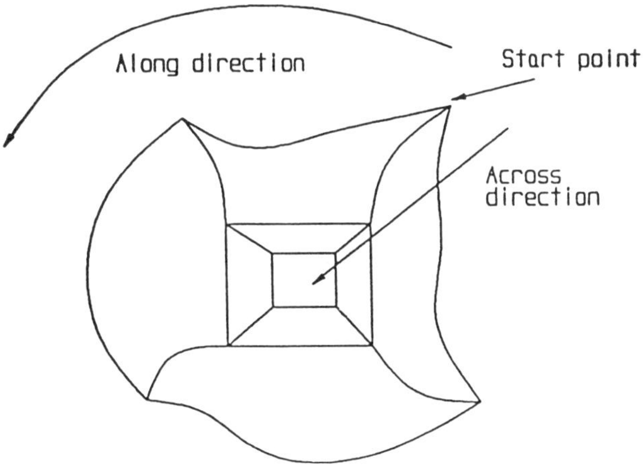

Figure 12.36

$N_L = 3$
$N_C = 4$
$P_L = N_C = 4$
$P_C = N_L - 1 = 3 - 1 = 2$
$P_T = P_L \text{ X } P_C = 4 \text{ X } 2 = 8$

Tip 3. Assignment of along rows and across columns.

The surface patch boundaries are laid out in a grid. Along contours are assigned in rows and across contours in columns. Each contour in the grid is identified by an along row number and an across column number (Figure 12.37).

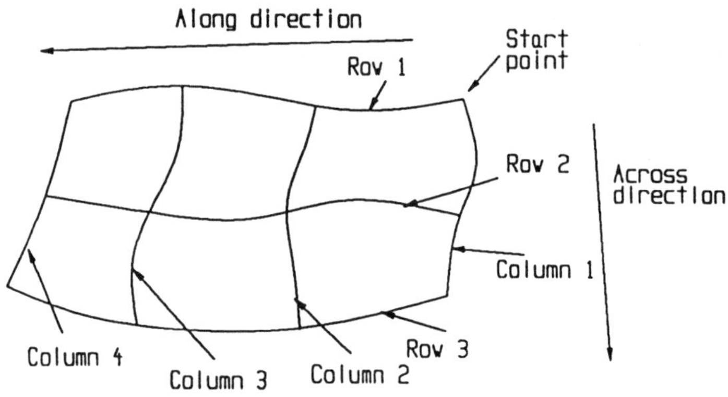

Figure 12.37

Tip 4. The order of contours selection.

The contours selection must follow a predetermined order that is along contours are sequentially selected first, followed by the across contours as follows:

Selection order	entity to be picked
1st selection	along row 1 - across column 1
2nd selection	along row 1 - across column 2
-	-
-	-
nth selection	along row 1 - across column n
n+1 selection	along row 2 - across column 1
n+2 selection	along row 2 - across column 2
-	-
-	-
2n selection	along row 2 - across column n
-	-
-	-
mn selection	along row m - across column n

Example 12.4:

This example shows the contours selection sequence for the patches having an open boundary (Figure 12.38).

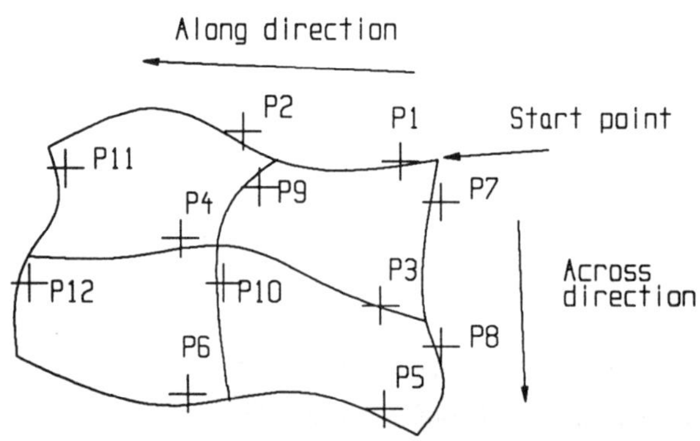

Figure 12.38

Example 12.5:

In this example the contours selection sequence for the surface patches having a closed boundary is illustrated (Figure 12.39).

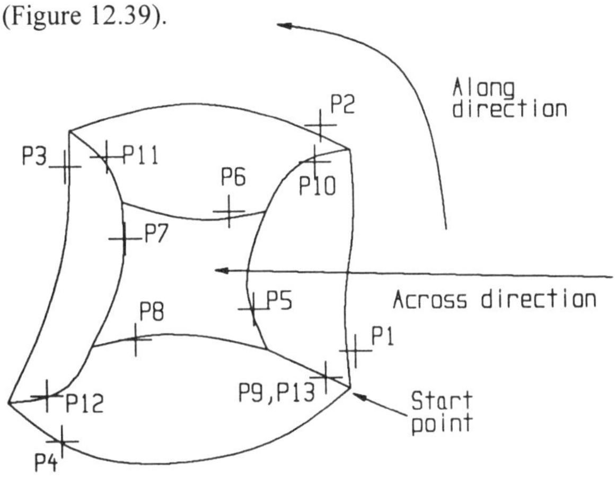

Figure 12.39

Example 12.6:

Figure 12.40 shows an example where six lines are joined in one point. The patch grid layout requires two along contours and six across contours. The first along contour consists of the six sides of the hexagon. The second along contour is a point which is the common point the six lines joined.

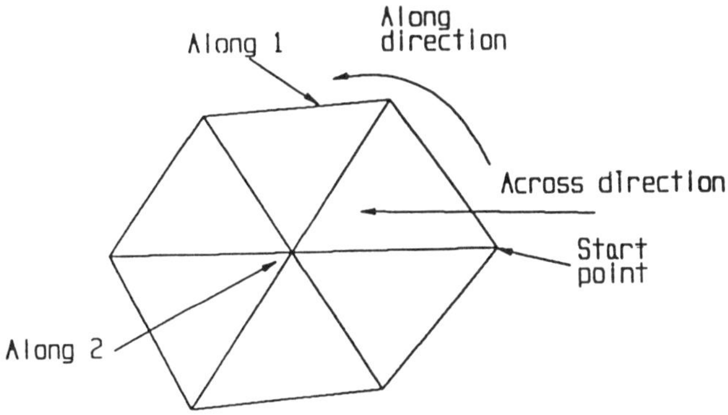

Figure 12.40

Tip 5. Selection of the blending method

There are four blending methods for generating a Coons surface:

Linear: used when surfaces are fairly flat Parabolic: used when surfaces have greater curvatures Cubic: used when surfaces have greater curvatures Cubic with slope matching: used when parabolic or cubic produces flat spots on the surfaces

Figure 12.41 compares the effect of these four blending methods on a surface.

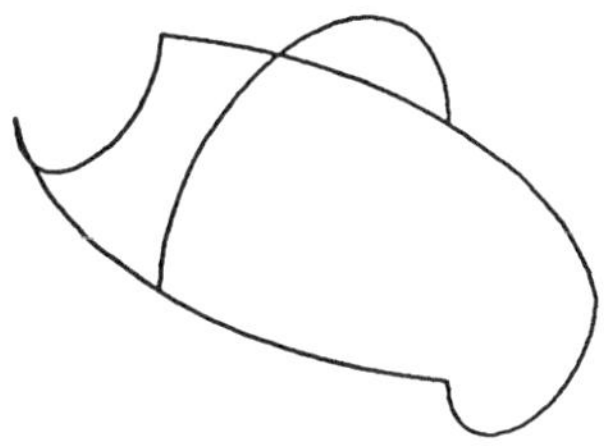

a. Wireframe model

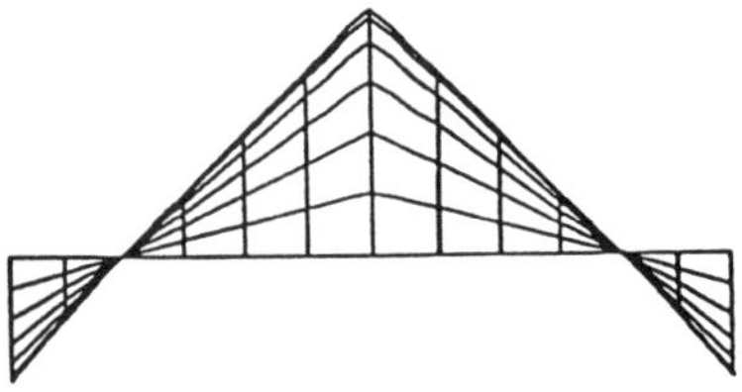

b. Linear

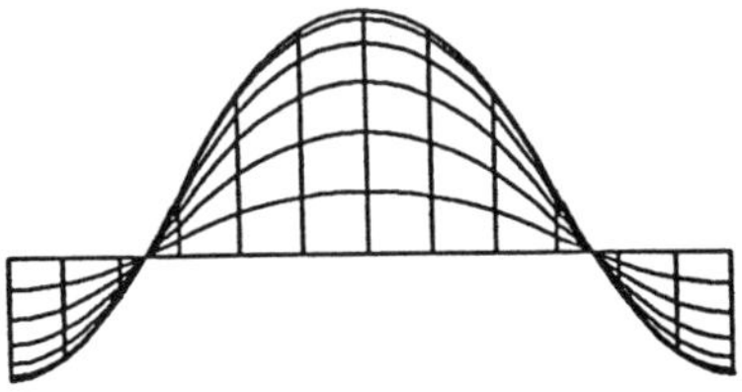

c. Parabolic

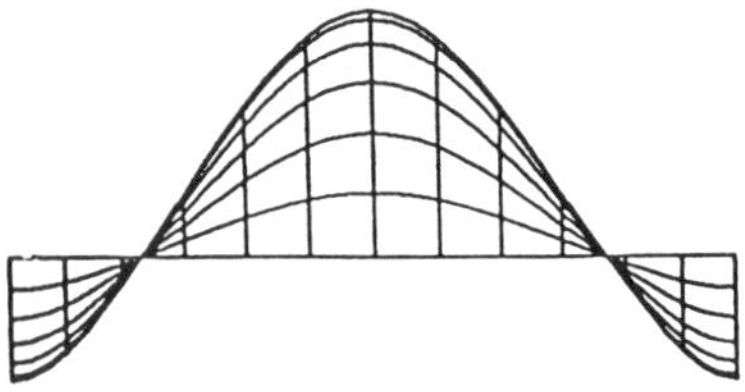

d. Cubic

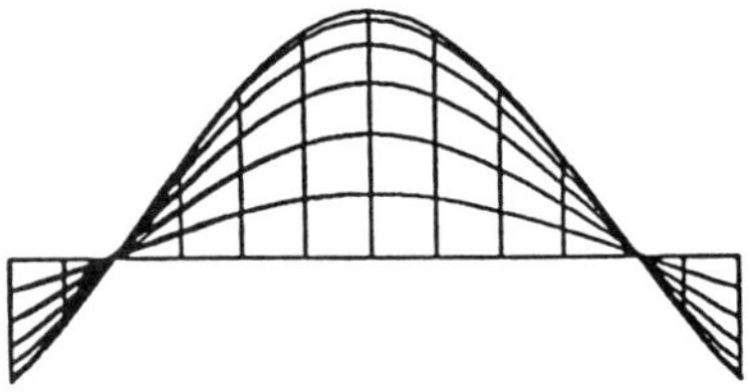

e. Cubic with slope matching

Figure 12.41

Project 7.

7

Creating a Coons surface of one patch

This example uses the wireframe model of project 5 in chapter 11 to generate a Coons surface. The wireframe model and the final surface model are shown in Figure 12.42.

Wireframe Model

Project 5 of Chapter 11 (coons1)

Go to

We are here

Surface Model

(coonss1)

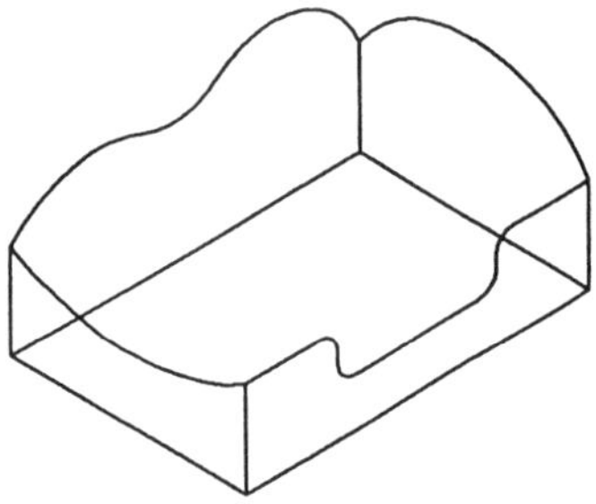

Figure 12.42a. Wireframe model

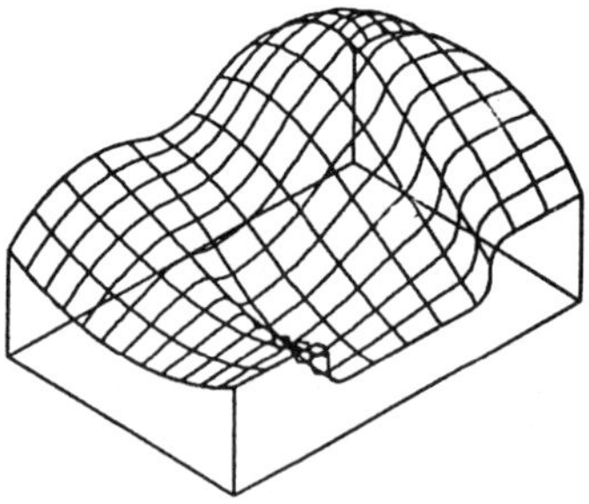

Figure 12.42b. Surface model

Tips 1. This is a single path surface.

2. The number of patches in the along direction is 1.

3 The number of patches in the across direction is 1.

Step 1. Load the wireframe model (coons1) or create one by following the instructions given in project 5 of chapter 11.

Select **MAIN MENU →File → Get**
Enter file name: **coons1**
Select **Yes** to delete the old drawing if necessary

The wireframe model on the screen should resemble Figure 12.43.

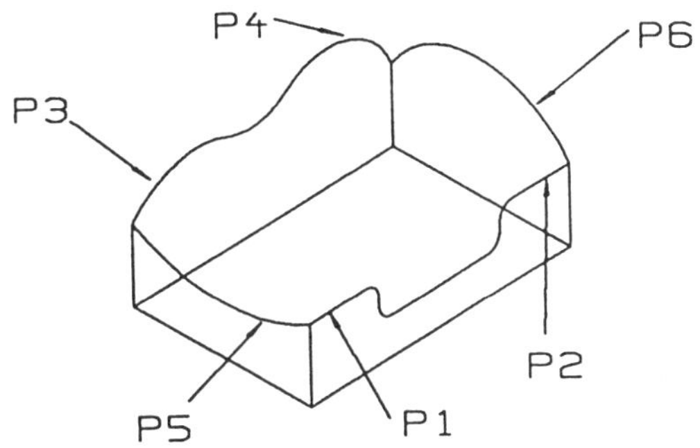

Figure 12.43

Step 2. Create the Coons surface. Use the pick points in Figure 12.43.

Select **MAIN MENU → Create → sUrface → Coons → Nurbs**
Enter number of patches in the along direction: **1** ←
Enter number of patches in the across direction: **1** ←

Define along countour 1 of row 1: select **Chain** from the Chaining method Menu and then pick at **P1** and **P2**, then select **End here** to complete the selection

Define along contour 1 of row 2: select **Chain** from the Chaining method Menu and then pick at **P3** and **P4**, then select **End here** to complete the selection

Define across contour 1 of column 1: select **Single** from the Chaining method Menu and then pick at **P5**

Define across contour 1 of column 2: select **Single** from the Chaining method Menu and then pick at **P6**

Select **Done** from the Chaining method Menu

Toggle **Blending** from the Coons surface parameters to **Parabolic** and select **Done** to compete the surface

The newly created Coons surface should look like Figure 12.44.

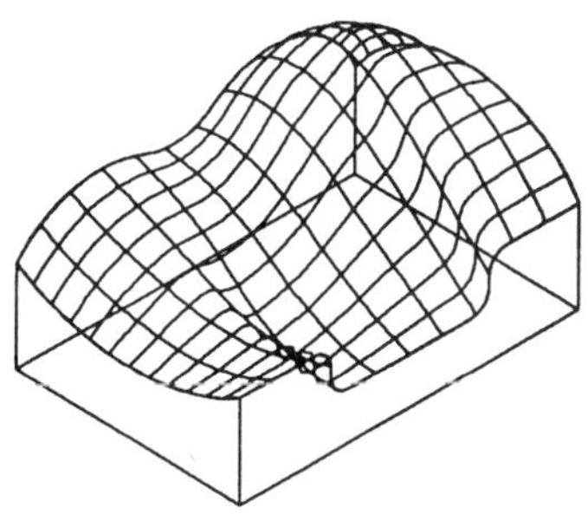

Figure 12.44

Step 3. Save the surface model file (coonss1).

Select **MAIN MENU → file → Save**
Enter file name: **coonss1**

Project 8.

Creating a Coons surface of two patches

In this project, we still use the wireframe model of project 5 in chapter 11 except that we add an arc to form a three-along-contours surface. It is intended to show how the added contour changes the skin of the surface. The new wireframe model and the resulted surface are illustrated in Figure 12.45.

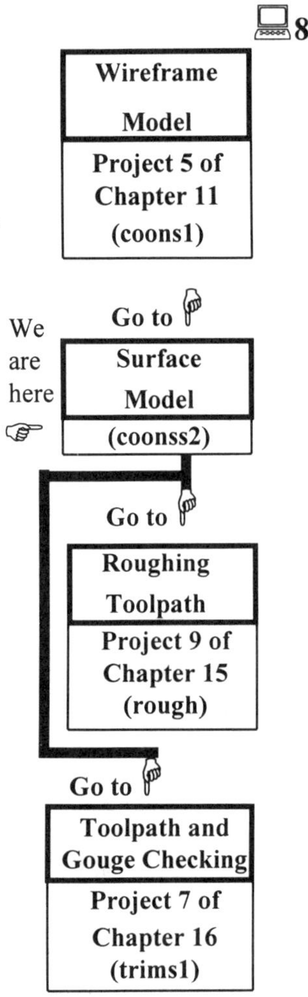

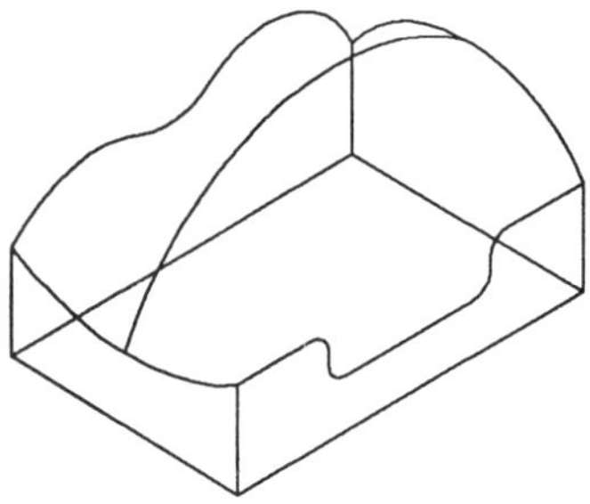

Figure 12.45a Wireframe model

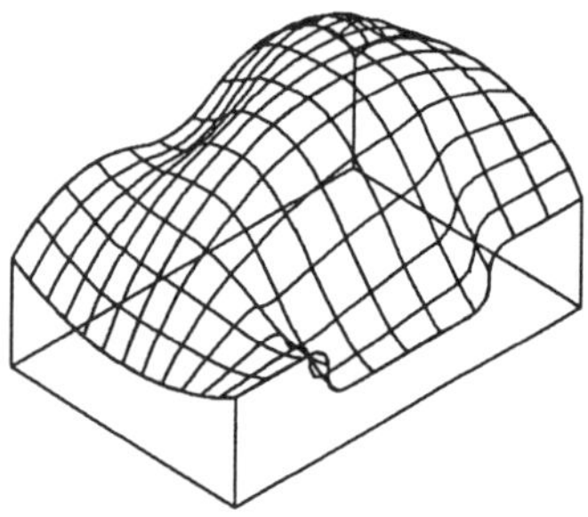

Figure 12.45b. Surface model

Tips 1. Use the Side Cplane to add an arc between the midpoint of the two arcs in the across direction.

2. The number of patches in the along direction is 1.
3. The number of patches in the across direction is 2.
4. Each of two across arcs must be broken into two entities at the midpoints because an along contour is added to the profile.

Step 1. Load the wireframe model file (coons1).

Select **MAIN MENU → File → Get**
Enter file name: **coons1 ←**
Select **Yes** to delete the old drawing if necessary

The wireframe model should appear as Figure 12.46.

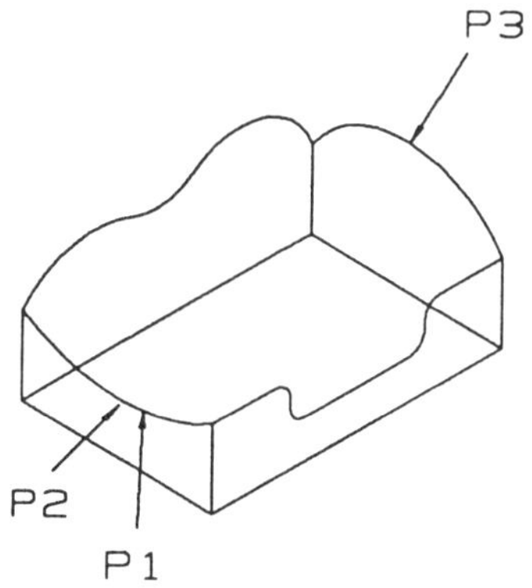

Figure 12.46

Step 2. Add an arc using the Side Cplane. Use the pick points in Figure 12.46.

Select **Cplane → Side**
Select **Z → Midpoint** and then pick at **P1**

Z2.5 should appear in the Secondary menu.

Select **MAIN MENU → Create → Arc → Endpoints → Midpoint**
Pick at **P2** and **P3**
Enter the radius: **5** ←
Pick the second arc segment from the top to complete the arc

The new wireframe model should resemble Figure 12.47.

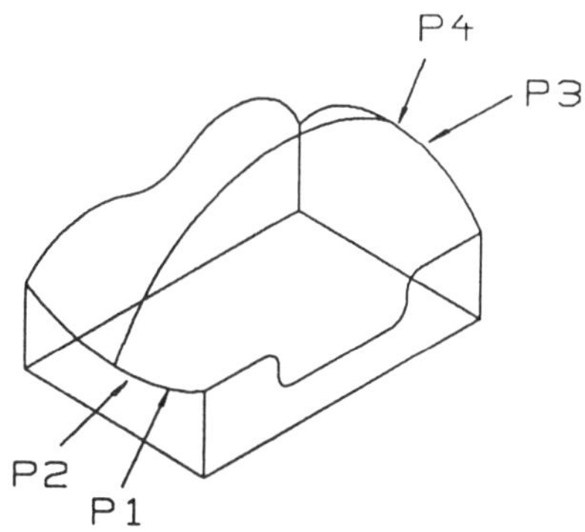

Figure 12.47

Step 3. Break the two arcs into two pieces each, using the Front Cplane.

Use the pick points in Figure 12.47.
Select **Cplane → Front**
Select **MAIN MENU → Modify → Break → 2 pieces**
Select an entity: pick at **P1**
Enter the breakpoint: select **Midpoint** from the Point Menu
then pick at **P2** to complete the breaking of the first arc
Select an entity: pick at **P3**
Enter the breakpoint: pick at **P4** for the breaking of the second arc

The new drawing looks identical to the one before breaking the two arcs. The drawing is redrawn in Figure 12.48.

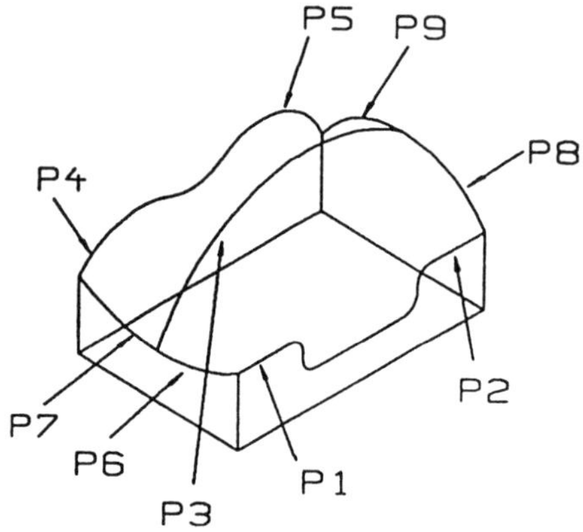

Figure 12.48

Step 4. Create the Coons surface using the pick points in Figure 12.48.

Select **MAIN MENU → Create → sUrface → Coons → Nurbs**
Enter the number of patches in the along direction: **1** ←
Enter the number of patches in the across direction: **2** ←

Define along contour 1 of row 1: select **Chain**
then pick at **P1** and **P2** and then select **End here**
Define along contour 1 of row 2: select **Single**, then pick at **P3**
Define along contour 1 of row 3: select **Chain**,
then pick at **P4** and **P5**, then select **End here**
Define across contour 1 of column 1: select **Single** then pick at **P6**
Define across contour 2 of column 1: select **Single** then pick at **P7**
Define across contour 1 of column 2: select **Single** then pick at **P8**
Define across contour 2 of column 2: select **Single** then pick at **P9**
Select **Done** to complete the chaining

Change the Coons surface parameters to the following settings:

aLong = 0.15	(select aLong then enter 0.15 ←)
aCross = 0.15	(select aCross then enter 0.15 ←)
Blending = Parabolic	(toggle Blending to parabolic)
Error chk = Y	(toggle Error to Y)

Select **Done** to complete the surface

The surface model should resemble Figure 12.49.

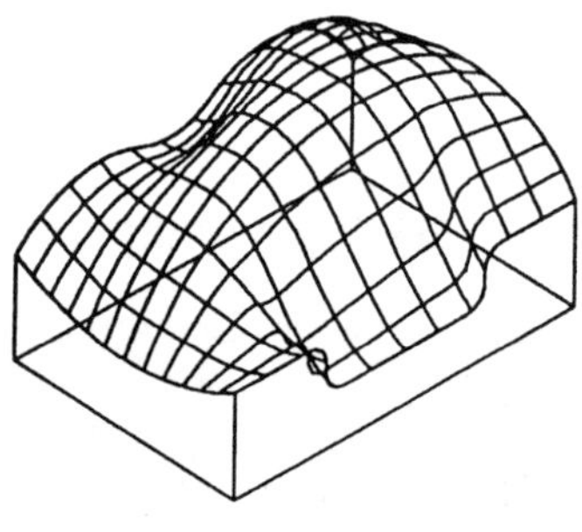

Figure 12.49

Step 5. Save the surface model file (coonss2).

Select **MAIN MENU → File → Save**
Enter file name: **coonss2**

Project 9. 9

Creating a Coons surface with a joint point being along contours

This project uses a common join point as an along contour. The wireframe model is constructed in project 6 of chapter 11. The wireframe model and the final surface model are shown in Figure 12.50.

Wireframe Model
Project 6 of Chapter 11 (coons3)

We are here → **Go to** **Surface Model** **(coonss3)**

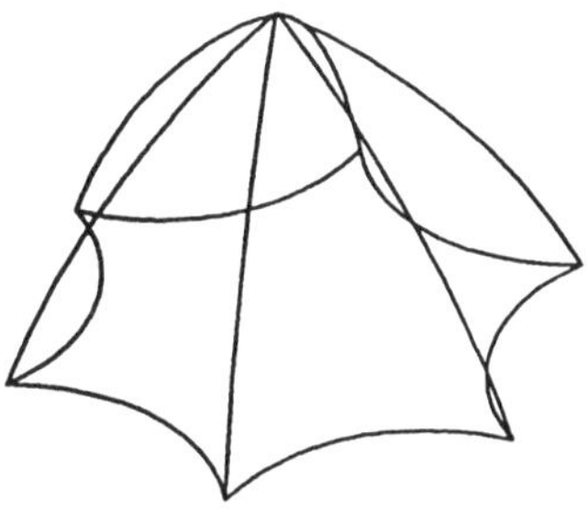

Figure 12.50a. Wireframe model

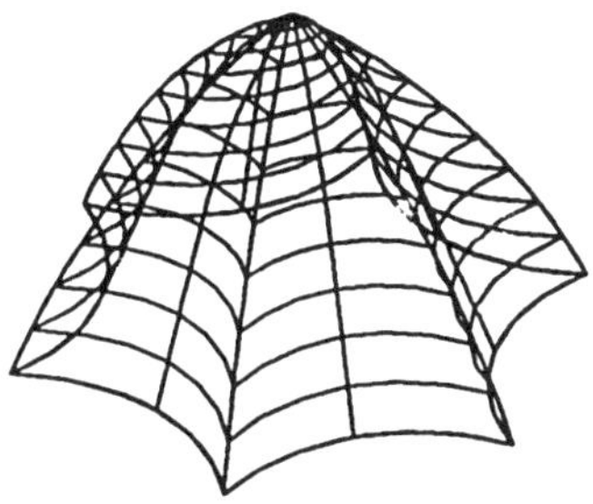

Figure 12.50b. Surface model

Tips 1. Use Top Gview to facilitate the picking at the contours.

2. Use the common join point as one of along contour.

3. Number of patches in the along direction is 6.

4. Number of patches in the across direction is 1.

Step 1. Load the wireframe model file (coons3) or create one by following the instructions in project 6 of chapter 11. The drawing should appear as Figure 12.51.

Select **MAIN MENU→ File → Get**
Enter file name: **coons3**
Select **Yes** to delete the current

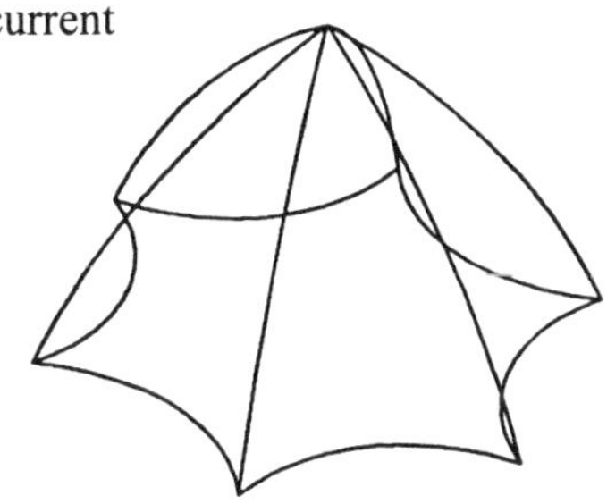

Figure 12.51

Step 2. Change the Gview to Top.

Select **Gview → Top**

The drawing becomes Figure 12.52.

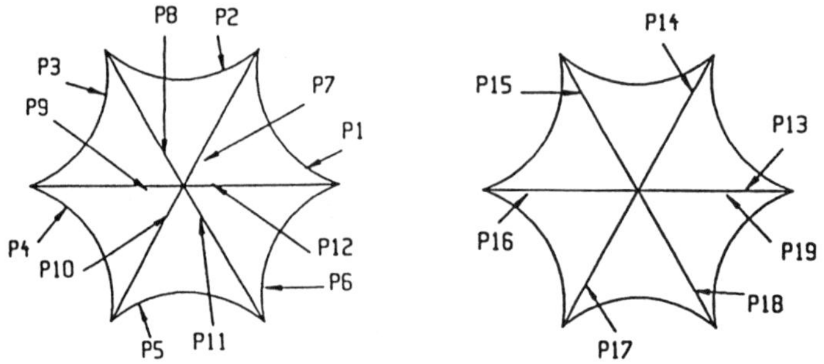

Figure 12.52

Step 3. Create the Coons surface using the pick points in Figure 12.52.

Select **MAIN MENU → Create → sUrface → Coons →Nurbs**
Enter the number of patches in the along direction: **6** ←
Enter the number of patches in the across direction: **1** ←
Sequentially pick at **P1 - P6** to complete the along contour of row 1.
Pick **Single** from the Chaining method Menu before picking at each entity.
Sequentially pick at **P7 - P12** for completing along contour of row 2
after selecting **Point** from the Chaining method menu and **Endpoint** from
the Point menu.
Sequentially pick at **P13 - P19** with selecting **Single** from the Chaining method menu before each picking at the entity. This is to complete the across contour.

Select **Done** to complete the selection
Change the Coons surface parameters to the following settings:

aLong = 0.1
aCross = 0.1
Blending = Parabolic
Error chk = Y

Select **Done** to complete the surface

The surface model in Top Gview should appear as Figure 12.53.

Figure 12.53

Step 4. Change Gview to isometric.

Select **Gview → Isometric**

The surface model shown in isometric view should resemble Figure 12.54.

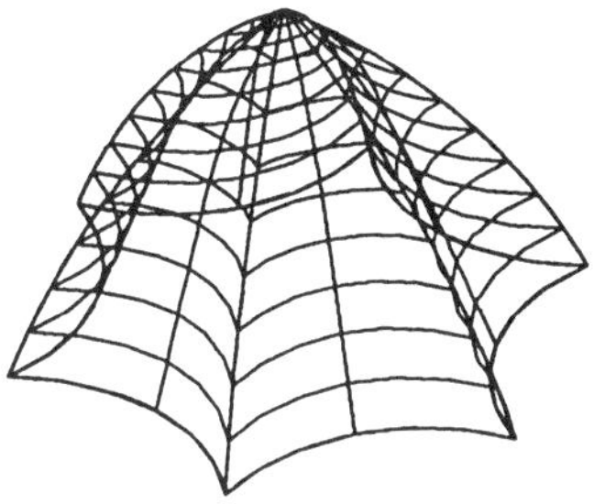

Figure 12.54

Step 5. Save the surface model file (coonss3).

Select **MAIN MENU → File → Save**

Enter file name: **coonss3**

Project 10.

10

Wireframe Model
Project 7 of Chapter 11 (coons4)

Go to

We are here

Surface Model
(coonss4)

Creating a Coons surface of multiple faces

This project uses a wireframe model with thirteen faces to create a Coons surface. The wireframe model is shown in Figure 12.55a and the resultant Coons surface is illustrated in Figure 12.55b.

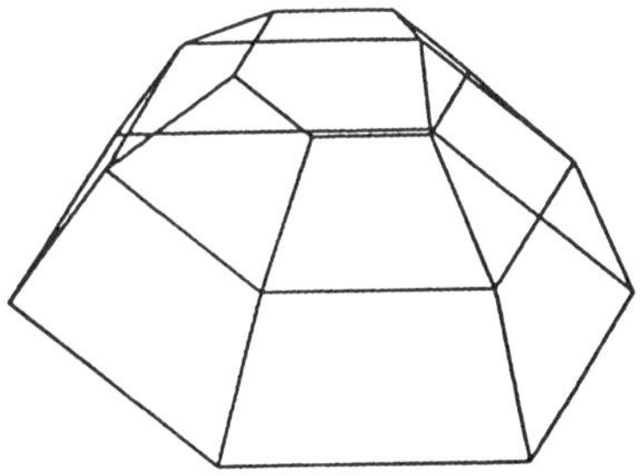

Figure 12.55a. Wireframe model

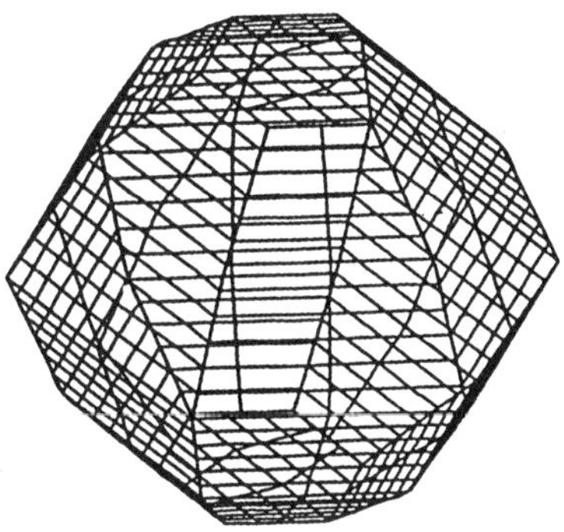

Figure 12.55b.Surface model

Tips 1. Use the Top Gview to facilitate the picking of contours.

2. Create a Coons surface based on the twelve faces.

3. The number of patches in the along direction is 6.

4. The number of patches in the across direction is 2.

5. Create a ruled surface for the top face.

6. Use separate levels and different colors for these two surfaces.

7. Mirror the two surfaces about the X axis using the Front Cplane to complete the surface model.

Step 1. Load the wireframe model file (coons4) or create one by following the instructions in the project 7 of chapter 11.

Select **MAIN MENU → File → Get**
Enter file name: **coons4**
Select **Yes** to delete the current part

The wireframe model drawing of thirteen faces should appear on your screen as it is shown in Figure 12.56.

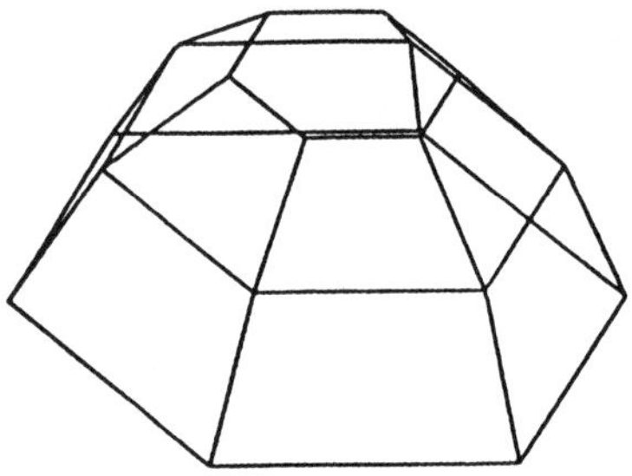

Figure 12.56

Step 2. Change the drawing to Top Gview.

Select **Gview → Top**

The drawing in Top Gview appears as in Figure 12.57.

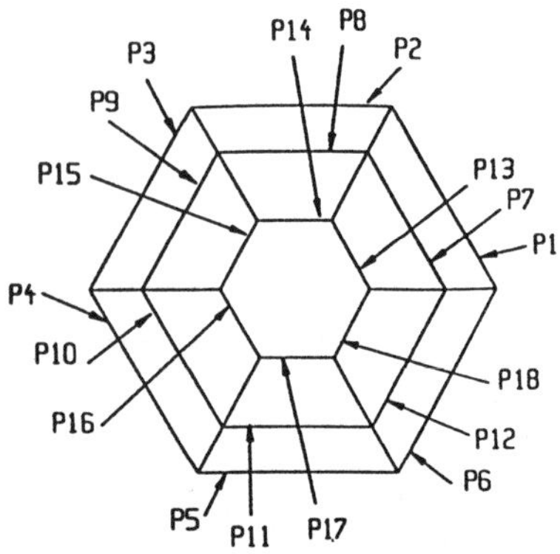

Figure 12.57a

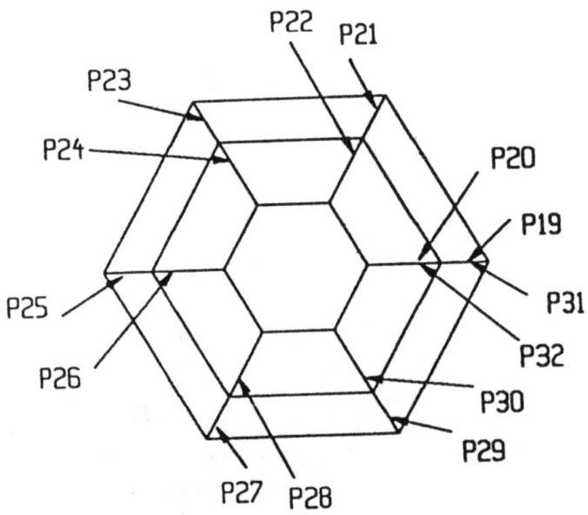

Figure 12.57b

Step 3. Create the Coons surface using the pick points in Figure 12.57.

Change the level to 2 and the color to 12.
Select **Level → Main Level**, click at **2** then select **OK**
Select **Color** than enter **12**
Select **MAIN MENU → Create → sUrface → Coons → Nurbs**
Enter the number of patches in the along direction: **6** ←
Enter the number of patches in the across direction: **2** ←

Sequentially pick at **P1 - P18** in Figure 12.57a and then
pick **P19-P32** in Figure 12.57b to complete the selection of contours
Select **Single** from the Point Menu before picking at each contour entities.
Select **Done**
Set the Coons surface parameters to the following settings:

aLong = 0.15
aCross = 0.15
Blending = Linear
Error chk = Y

Select **Done** to complete the surface
Select **Gview → Isometric** to display the surface in isometric view

The Coons surface should look like Figure 12.58.

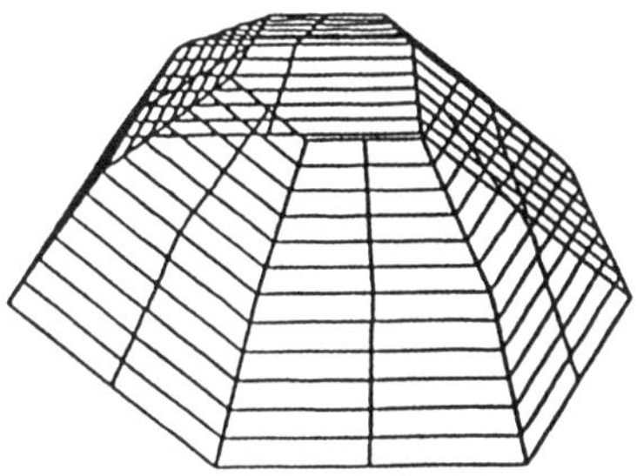

Figure 12.58

Step 4. Save the surface model file (coonss4).

Select **MAIN MENU → File → Save**
Enter file name: **coonss4**

Step 5. Make the Coons surface in Level 2 invisible.

Select **Level → Vis levels**
then toggle the # **2** button to dimmed (invisible),
select **OK → OK** to return back to the graphic mode.

Step 6. Change to Top Gview.

Select **Gview → Top**

The drawing on the screen should resemble Figure 12.59 on the next page.

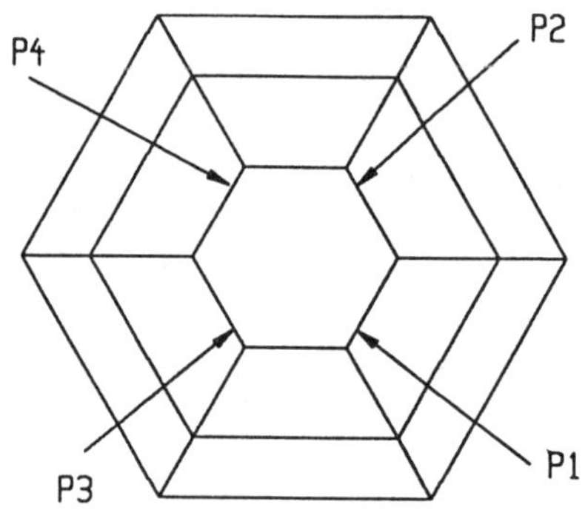

Figure 12.59

Step 7. Create a ruled surface for the top face using the pick points marked in Figure 12.59. Change to Level 3 and Color 13.

Select **Level → Main Level**
Click the **#3** button, then select **OK**
Select **Color** then enter **13** ←
Select **MAIN MENU → Create → sUrface → rUled → Blend**

define contour 1: select **Chain** from the Chaining method Menu, then pick at **P1**, and then select **Close** → **Select nxt** and pick at **P2**, and finally select **End here** to complete the first contour

define contour 2: select **Chain** from the Chaining method Menu, then pick at **P3**, and then select **Close** → **Select nxt** and pick at **P4**, and finally select **End here** → **Done** to complete the surface

Step 8. Change Gview to Isometric and make Level 2 visible.

Select **Gview → Isometric**
Select **Level → Vis. levels**
then click on the **#2** button to make the level visible
Select **OK** to return to the graphic mode.

The drawing with two surfaces should appear as in Figure 12.60.

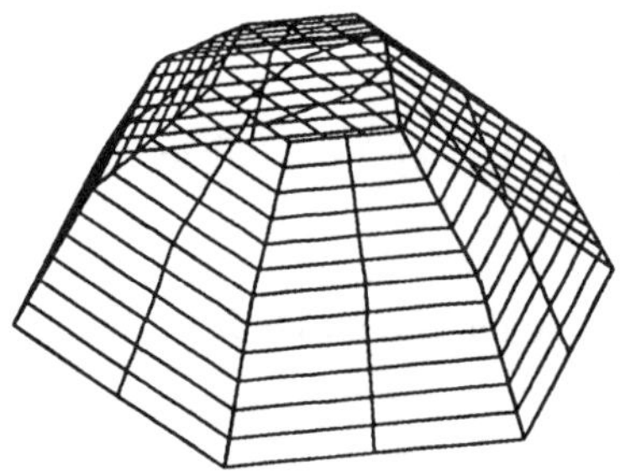

Figure 12.60

Step 9. Mirror the two surface about X axis to generate the bottom half of the surface model. Use Front or Side Cplane.

Select **Cplane → Front**

Select **MAIN MENU → Xform →Mirror → All → surFaces→ All → Lines→ Done**

Select the **X axis**

Select **Copy → Done** from the Mirror Parameters menu to complete the Surface model.

The complete surface model should appear as Figure 12.61.

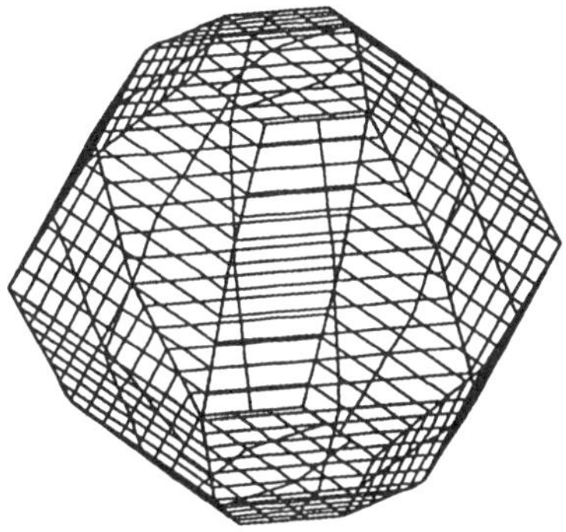

Figure 12.61

12.8 Revolved Surfaces Modeling

A revolved surface is created by revolving a geometric entity about an axis or a line. The geometric entity to be revolved is referred to as the **generating curve**, and the axis or line to be revolved about is called **revolving axis** or **line.** The resulting surface is perpendicular to the revolving line.

Tips
1. The revolved modeling technique in Version 5 has been significantly improved. Its generating curve can consist of more than one entity. You can use the Chain command to connect all entities together as a single generating curve. However, the number of resultant surfaces is equal to the number of entities included in the chained generating profile.

2. The rotation angle direction is determined by which end of the revolving axis is chosen when the user uses the mouse to pick the axis or line. A zero degree angle is assigned to the orientation of the generating curve currently identified. Negative angles are invalid. The angle can rotate in either direction about the revolving axis. Figure 12.62 on the following page shows how the direction of the rotation angle is determined. The rotation direction is always in the clockwise direction when viewed from the selected end of the revolving axis toward the other end.

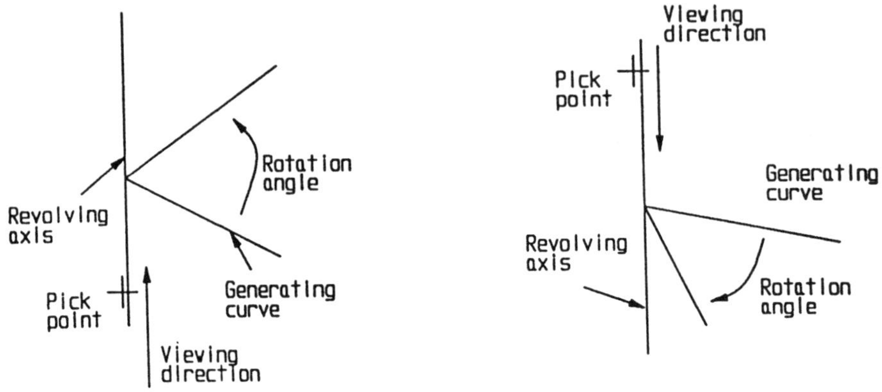

Figure 12.62

Project 11.

Creating revolved surfaces to form a cup

The revolved surface of a cup is created by using the wireframe model in project 8 of chapter 11. The wireframe model and the surface is shown in Figure 12.63.

11

Wireframe Model
Project 8 of Chapter 11 (cup)

Go to

We are here

Surface Model
(cups)

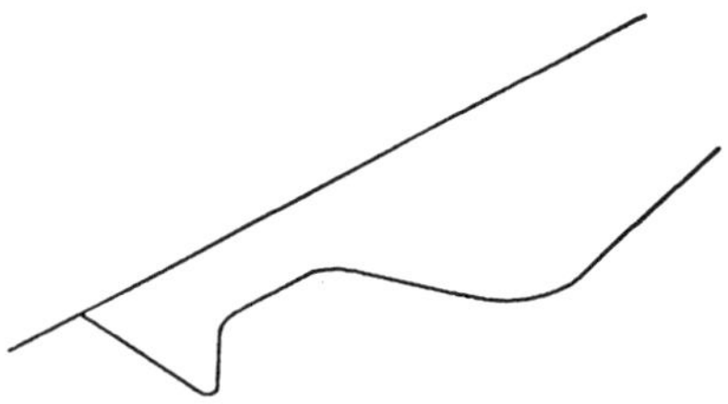

Figure 12.63a. Wireframe model

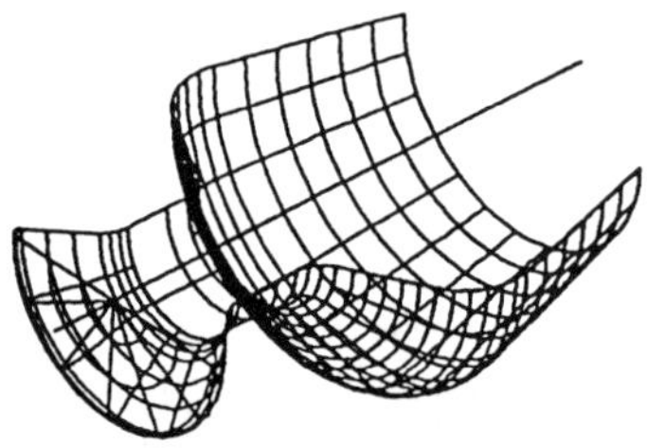

Figure 12.63b. Surface model

Tips 1. This surface model consists of nine revolved surfaces.

2. Each revolved surface is rotated 180° to form one-half of the surface model, or rotated 360° to form the complete surface model. In a manufacturing point of view, the cup mold requires one-half of the surface model.
3. The picking point on the revolving axis should be placed at the lower half segment of the line to create the correct revolving angle.

Step 1. Load the wireframe model file (cup) or create one by following the instructions given in project 8 of chapter 11.
Select **MAIN MENU →File → Get**
Enter file name: **cup**
Select **Yes** to delete the current part

The wireframe model drawing should resemble Figure 12.64.

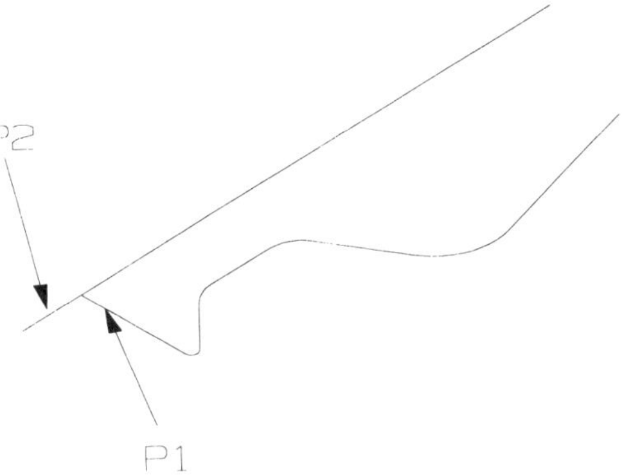

Figure 12.64

Step 2. Create the first revolved surface of the cup using the pick points from Figure 12.64.

Select **MAIN MENU → Create → sUrface → Revolved**
Select the profile entities: select **Chain** then pick at **P1**
Select **Close →** **End here →** **Done**
Select the axis of rotation: pick at **P2**
Enter the starting angle: **0** ←
Enter the final angle: **180** ←

The drawing with all nine revolved surfaces appears as Figure 12.65.

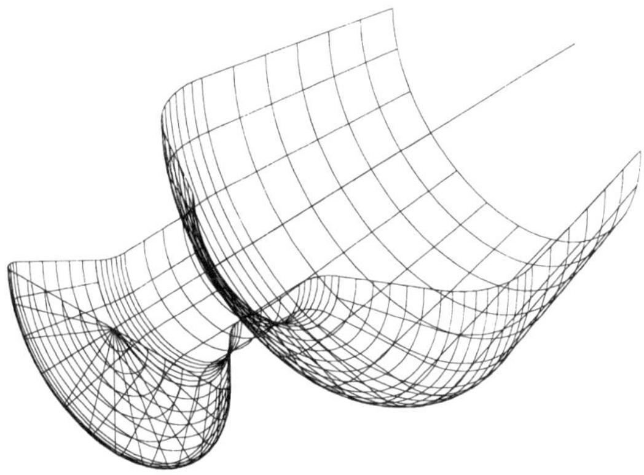

Figure 12.65

Step 3.Save the surface model file (cups).

Select **MAIN MENU → File → Save**
Enter file name: **cups**

Tom 113

12.9 Draft Surfaces Modeling

A draft surface is created by extruding a sectional shape (or base curve) straight along a line (Figure 12.66). This line is defined by a length and an angle. The length is referred to as the draft length and the angle as the draft angle.

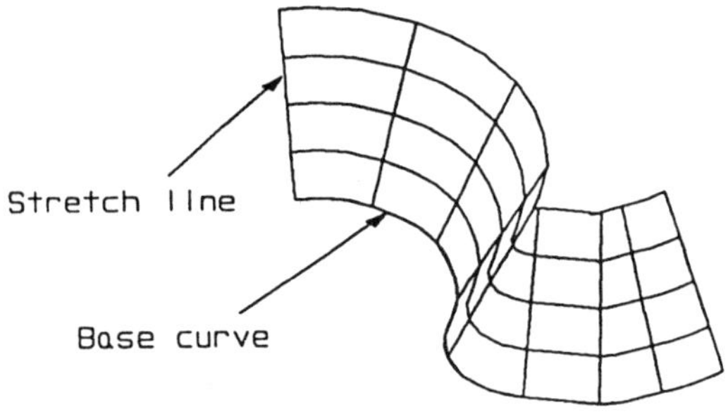

Figure 12.66

Tips 1. The base curve can be a line, an arc, a parametric spline, or a curve.

2. The draft modeling technique in Version 5 can chain more than one entity to create multiple draft surfaces. However, the number of draft surfaces is equal to the number of chained entities.
3. The draft length indicates how far the surface is to be stretched. It is measured in the direction perpendicular to the current Cplane. An arrow will appear to indicate the positive direction of the length (Figure 12.67). Entering a positive value will stretch the surface in the direction the arrow is pointing. Likewise, a negative value extends the surface in the opposite direction of the arrow.

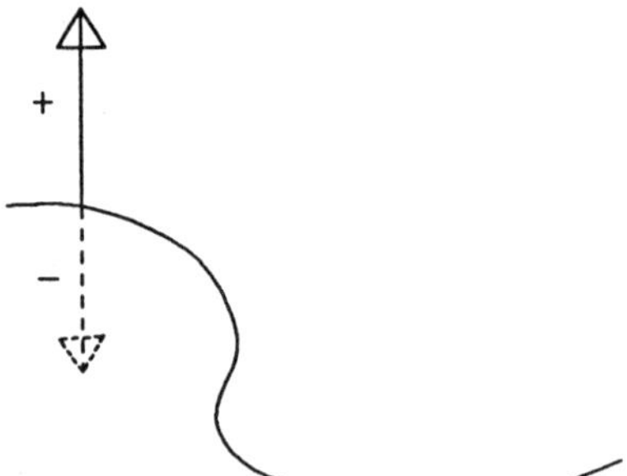

Figure 12.67

4. The draft angle specifies the orientation of the surface which in turn determines the shape of the surface. An arrow will appear to indicate the angle direction (Figure 12.68 on the next page). A positive angle will extend the surface in the direction of the angle arrow, while a negative angle value will extend the surface in the opposite direction of the indicator arrow.

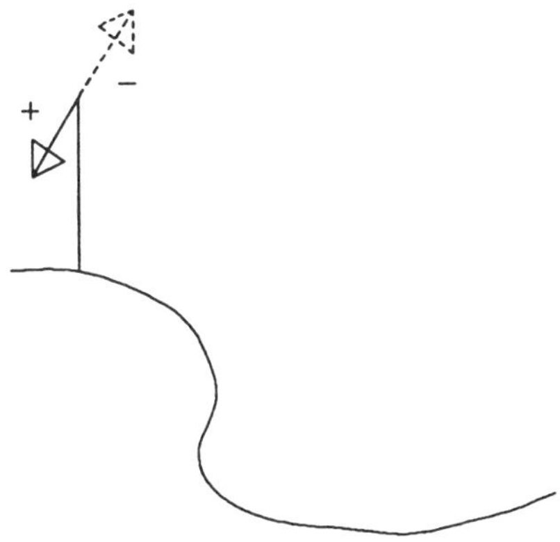

Figure 12.68

Project 12.

12

Creating the draft surfaces to form a tabulated cylinder

This example creates a set of draft surfaces to form a tabulated cylinder based on a rectangle with a fillet at four corners as shown in Figure 12.69.

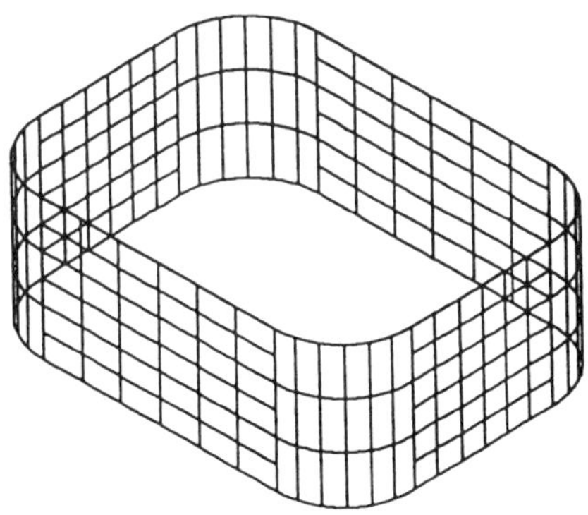

Figure 12.69

Tips 1. The base profile is a rectangle with a fillet at four corners. It is constructed in the Top Cplane.

2. The draft length is -1.5 in. and the draft angle is 0.

3. The surface model consists of eight draft surfaces.

Step 1. Create a rectangle using the Top Cplane.

Select **MAIN MENU → Screen → Next Menu → Initialize → Yes** to initialize the screen
Select **Gview → Isometric**
Select **MAIN MENU → Create → Rectangle → 1 point**
Enter the lower left corner: **0,0** ←
Enter the width: **4** ←
Enter the height: **3** ←

The rectangle should appear on the screen as Figure 12.70.

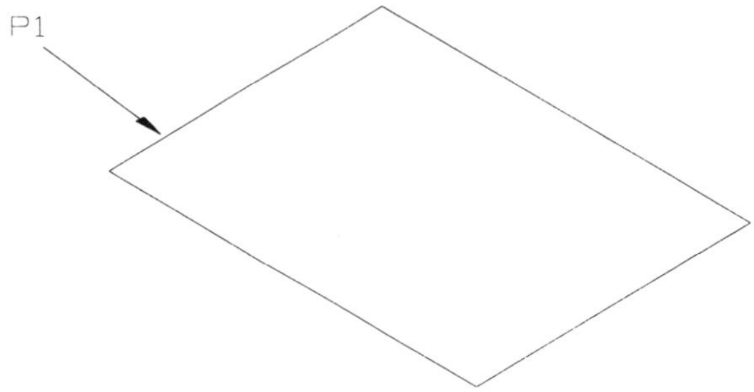

Figure 12.70

Step 2. Add four corner fillets using the pick points in Figure 12.70.

Select **MAIN MENU → Modify → Fillet → Radius**
Enter the fillet radius: **0.75** ←
Select **Chain**
Pick at **P1**
Select **Close → End here** to complete the four fillets

The new drawing should look like Figure 12.71.

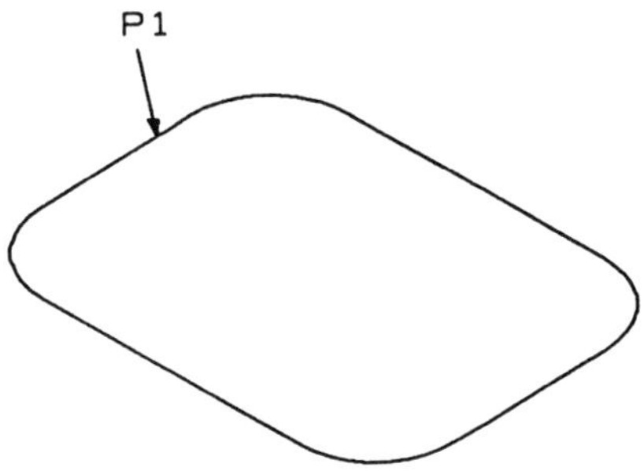

Figure 12.71

Step 3. Create eight draft surfaces using the pick points in Figure 12.71.

Select **MAIN MENU → Create → sUrface → Draft**
Select the profile entities: Select **Chain** then pick at **P1**
Select **Close → End here → Done**
Specify the length: **-1.5** ←
Specify the draft angle: **0** ←

The first draft surface should resemble Figure 12.72.

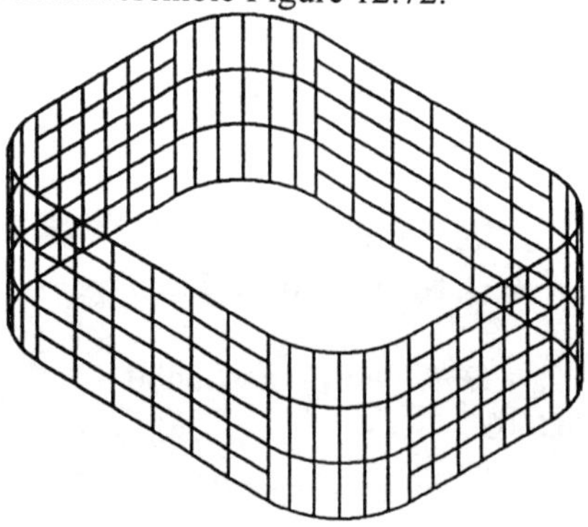

Figure 12.72

Step 4. Save the surface model (drafts1).

Select **File → Save**
Enter file name: **drafts1**

Project 13. 13

This example uses the draft surface modeling technique to create a cone surface, a spline surface, and a rectangular draft surface with four corner fillets as shown in these Figures 12.75a, b and c.

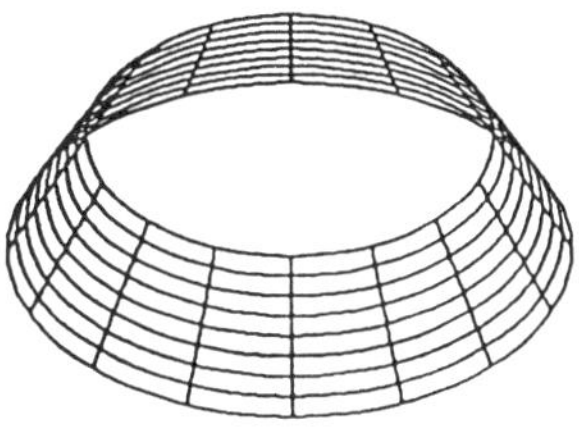

a. Cone surface

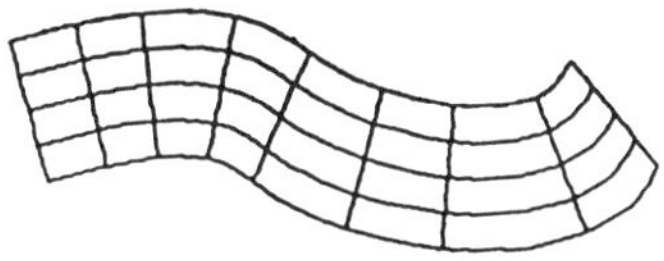

b. Spline surface

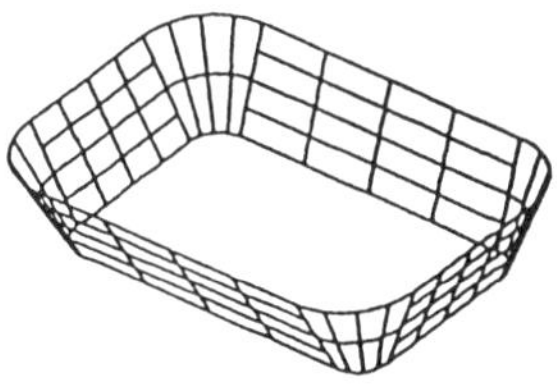

c. Rectangular draft surface
Figure 12.73

Cone Surface

The cone surface has a basic circle with a 3-in. diameter. The draft length is 1-in in the downward direction and the draft angle is 30° in the outward direction.

Step 1. Create the base circle. Initialize the system if necessary.

Select **Z** then enter **0** if necessary
Select **Cplane → Top** if necessary
Select **Gview → Isometric** if necessary
Select **MAIN MENU → Create → Arc → pt Rad cir**
Enter the center point: **0,0** ←
Enter the radius: **1.5** ←

The circle should look like Figure 12.74.

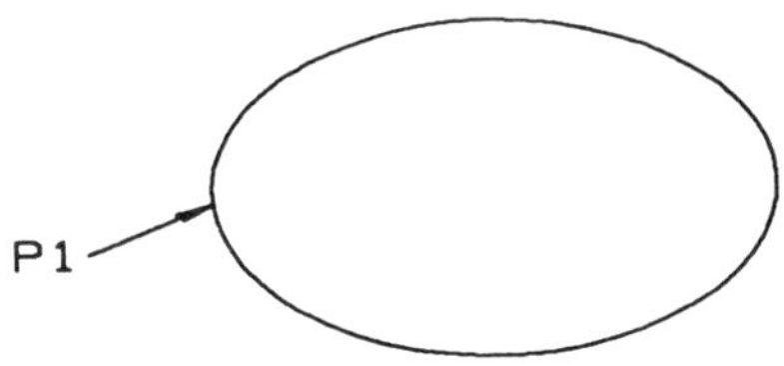

Figure 12.74

Step 2. Create the draft surface using the pick point in Figure 12.74.

Select **MAIN MENU → Create → sUrface → Draft**
Select the profile entities: pick at **P1,** then select **Done**
Specify the length: **-1** ←
Specify the draft angle: **-30** ←

The cone surface should resemble Figure 12.75.

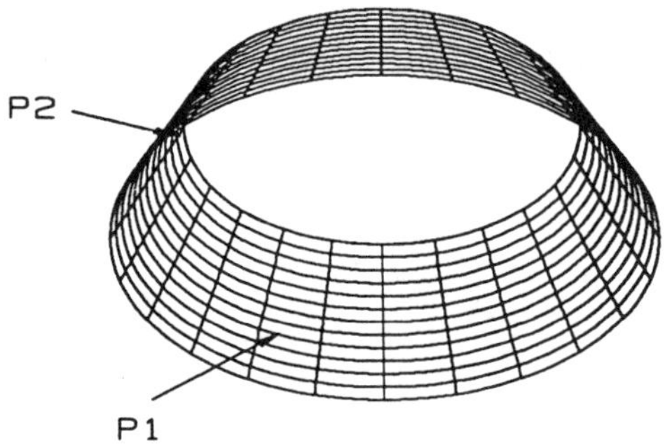

Figure 12.75

Step 3. Delete the circle and the surface using the pick points from Figure 12.75.

You may want to save the cone surface drawing for later use.
Select **MAIN MENU → Delete**
Pick at **P1** and **P2**

This should give you a **clean screen** to work with.

Spline Surface

The base curve of the spline surface is a spline formed by nine points. The draft length is 1-in. in the downward direction and the draft angle is 35° in the inward direction.

Step 4. Create a spline using a set of point data.

Select **MAIN MENU → Create → Spline**
Toggle the spline type to **Nurbs**
Select **Manual**
Sequentially enter the following sets of point data:

0,0 ←
0.25,0.48 ←
0.5,0.85 ←
1,1.32 ←
1.75,1.5 ←
2.5,1.4 ←
3.25,1.5 ←
3.75,1.72 ←
4.15,2.25 ←
4,2.75 ←

Press **Esc** to terminate the point data entry

The spline should resemble Figure 12.76.

Figure 12.76

Step 5. Create a draft surface using the pick point in Figure 12.76.

Select **MAIN MENU → Create → sUrface → Draft**
Select the base curve: pick at **P1,** then select **Done**
Specify the length: **-1** ←
Specify the draft angle: **-35** ←

The draft surface should look like Figure 12.77.

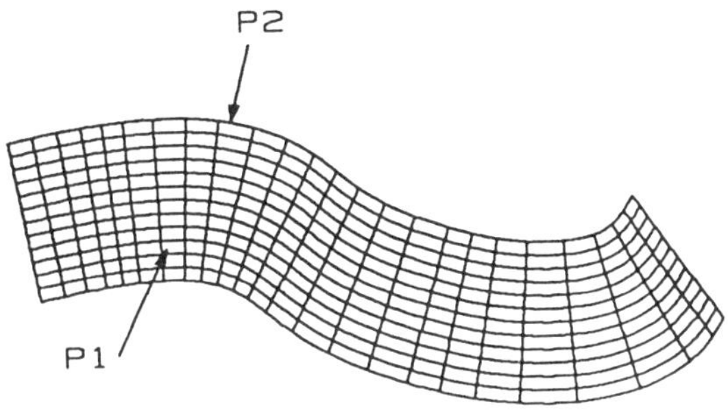

Figure 12.77

Step 6. Save the spline surface (drafts2).

Select **MAIN MENU → File → Save**
Enter file name: **drafts2**

Step 7. Delete the spline curve and the spline surface using the pick points in Figure 12.77.

Select **MAIN MENU → Delete**
Pick at **P1** and **P2**

This should give you a clean screen to work with.

Rectangular Draft Surfaces with four Corner Fillets

This surface model consists of eight draft surfaces which are extended in the downward direction by 1.25-in. and have a 25° draft angle in the inward direction.

Step 8. Create a rectangle.

Select **Main Menu →Create → Rectangle → 1 point**
Enter the lower left corner: **0,0** ←
Enter the width: **6** ←
Enter the height: **4** ←

The rectangle should appear like Figure 12.78.

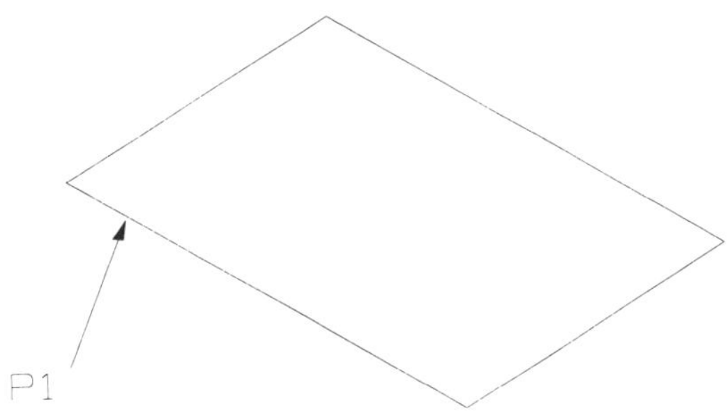

Figure 12.78

Step 9. Add four fillets using the points in Figure 12.78 on the previous page.

Select **MAIN MENU → Modify → Fillet → Radius**
Enter radius value: **1** ←
Select **Chain**, then pick at **P1**
select **Close → End Here**

The new drawing should resemble Figure 12.79.

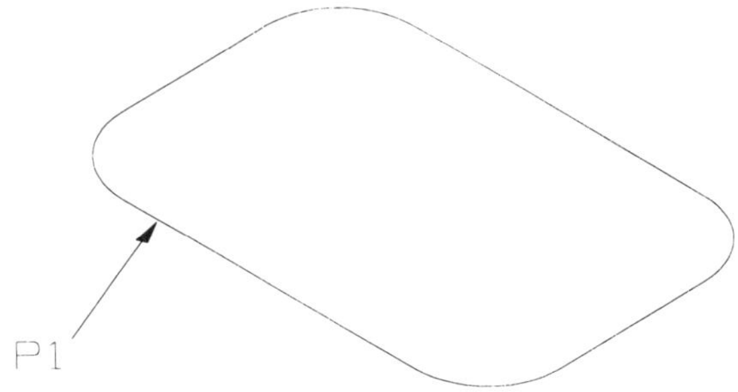

Figure 12.79

Step 10. Create eight draft surfaces. Use the pick point in Figure 12.79.

Select **MAIN MENU → Create → sUrface → Draft**
Select the profile entities: Select **Chain,** then pick at **P1**
Select **Close → End here → Done**
Specify the length: **-1.25** ←
Specify the draft angle: **-25** ←

The eight draft surfaces should appear as Figure 12.80 .

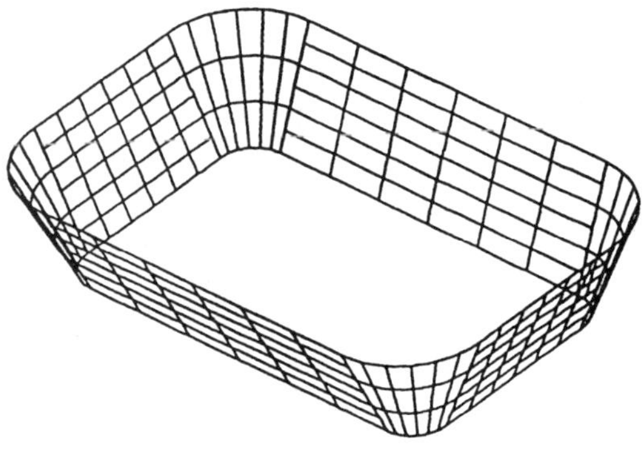

Figure 12.80

Step 11. Save the drawing (drafts3).

Select **MAIN MENU → File → Save**
Enter file name: **drafts3**

12.10 Swept Surfaces Modeling

A swept surface is created by either translating **a** sectional profile along one or two drive curves or translating **two** sectional profiles along a drive curve. Mastercam provides **three** types of swept surfaces: one across/one along, one across/two along, and two across/one along. Their descriptions and applications are given in Table 12.5 on the next page.

Table 12.5 Swept surfaces modeling techniques

Surface type	Description	Application	Illustration
One across/ one along	Translate or rotate an across contour while following the along contour.	Used for a surface in which cross sections remain constant along a driving profile.	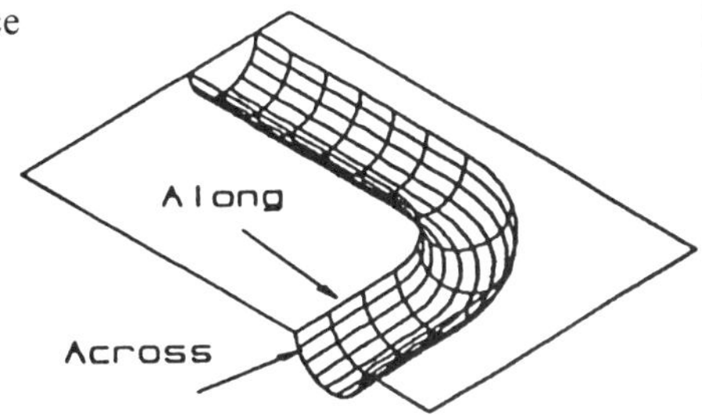
One across/ two along	Proportionally scale the across contour between the two along contours.	Used when cross sections are scaled along two driving profiles.	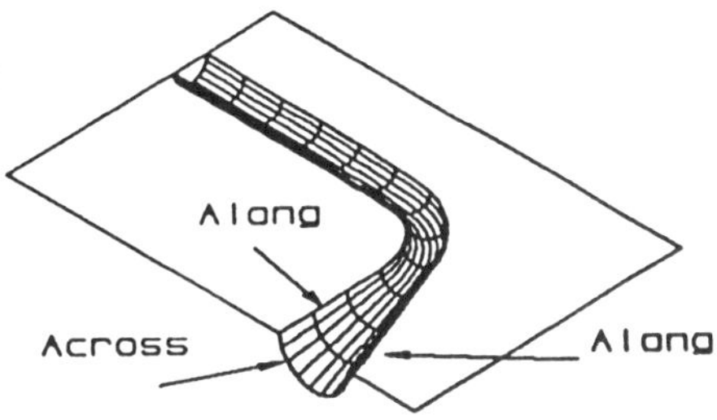
Two across/ one along	Perform a linear blend between the two across contours while following the along contour.	Used when two cross sections are linearly scaled along a driving profile.	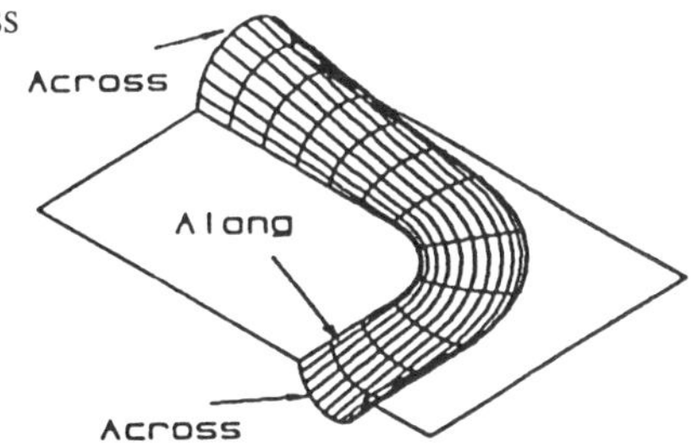

Project 14.

The swept surface modeling technique is used to create a surface model from the wireframe model of the cup given in project 8 of chapter 11. The advantage of modeling this cap with the swept method is that the entire surface profile can be chained as one entity to be swept along an arc which in turn generates all surfaces but is regarded only as a single surface entity. The wireframe model and the surface model of this cup are shown in Figure 12.81.

Wireframe Model
Project 8 of Chapter 11 (cup)

Go to

We are here

Surface Model
(swepts1)

Go to

Toopath
Project 9 of Chapter 15 (rough)

Go to

Toolpath Roughing
Project 6 of Chapter 16 (RCT)

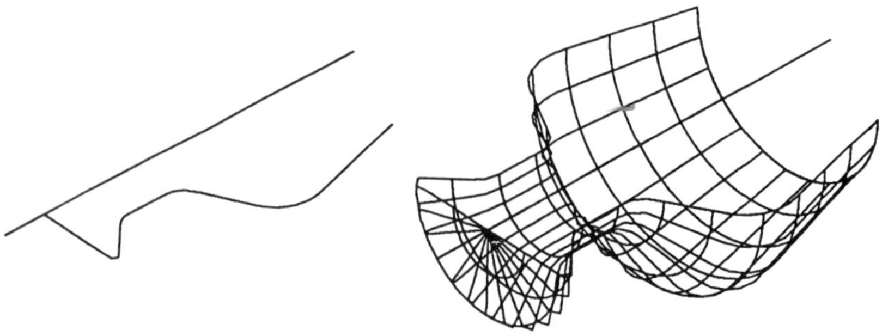

Figure 12.81

Tips 1. A semi-circle has to be created in the Front Cplane to serve as the along contour in surface modeling.
2. Use one across/one along method using the edge profile of the cup as the across contour.

Step 1. Load the wireframe model file (cup) or create one by following the instructions given in example 8 of chapter 11.
Select **MAIN MENU → File → Get**
Enter file name: **cup**
Select **Yes** to delete the current part
The wireframe drawing appears on the screen as Figure 12.82.

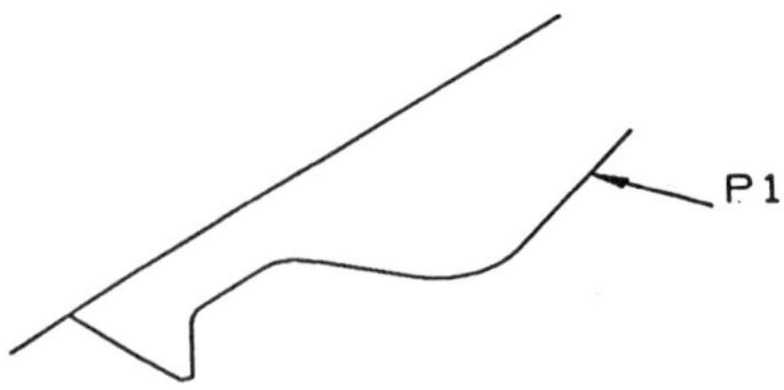

Figure 12.82

Step 2. Create an arc (semi-circle) using the Front Cplane. Use the pick points in Figure 12.82 on the previous page.

Select **Cplane → Front**
Select **Z → Endpoint**,
then pick at **P1** to obtain the Z coordinate of the trapped endpoint

Z-3.5 should appear in the Secondary Menu

Select **MAIN MENU → Create → Arc → Polar → Ctr point**
Enter the center point: **0,0** ←
Enter the radius: **1.062** ←
Enter the initial angle: **180** ←
Enter the final angle: **0** ←

The added arc should appear on the screen as Figure 12.83.

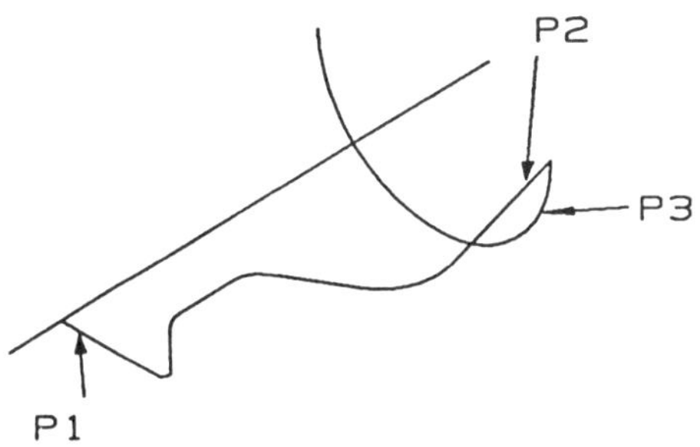

Figure 12.83

Step 3. Create a swept surface using the pick points in Figure 12.83.

Select **MAIN MENU → Create → sUrface → Swept → Nurbs**
Enter the number of across contours: **1** ←
define the across contour: select **Chain** from the Chaining method menu,
then pick at **P1** and **P2**
Select **End here**

define along contour 1: select **Single** from the Chaining method menu,
then pick at **P3**

Select **Done** to complete contours selection

Set the Swept surface parameters to the following settings:

Along cut distance = 0.1
Across cut distance = 0.1
Rotate the across contour
Error measurement = on

Select **Done** to compute the surface

Press Enter to display the surface model as shown here in Figure 12.84.

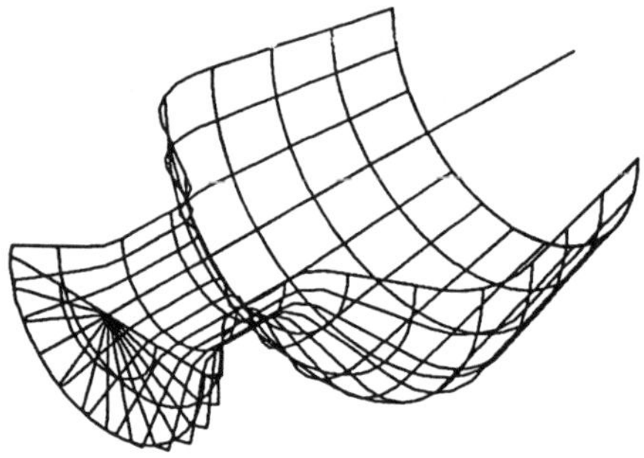

Figure 12.84

Step 4. Save the surface model (swepts1).

Select **MAIN MENU → File → Save**
Enter file name: **swepts1**

Project 15.

The wireframe model of project 9 in chapter 11 is used to create a swept surface. **Two** across contours are given, a rectangle on the top and a circle in the bottom. The along contour consists of two slope lines and a fillet in between. The wireframe model and surface model are illustrated in Figure 12.85.

Wireframe Model
Project 9 of Chapter 11 (swept2)

Go to

We are here **Surface Model**
(swepts2)

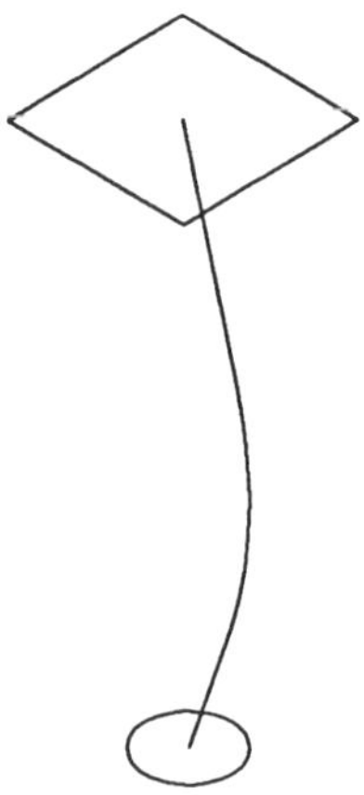

Figure 12.85a. Wireframe model

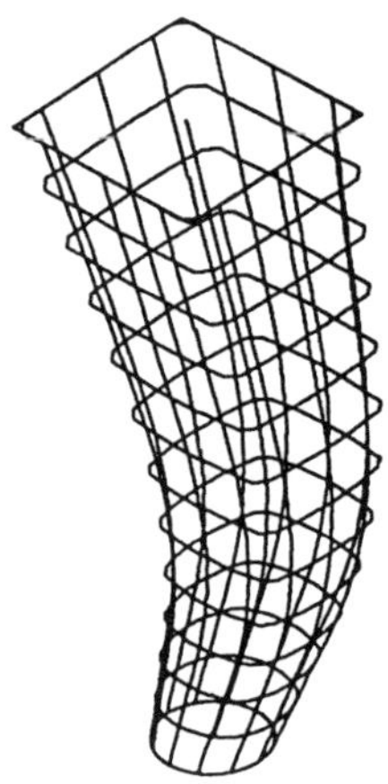

Figure 12.85b. Surface model

Tip The right vertical line of the rectangle must be broken into two pieces to obtain the orientation alignment of the two across contours. In other words, these two contours start at the same orientation to prevent the surface from twisting.

Step 1. Load the wireframe model file or create one following the instructions given in project 9 of chapter 11.

Select **MAIN MENU → File → Get**
Enter file name: **swept2**
Select **Yes** to delete the current part

The wireframe model is shown in Figure 12.86.

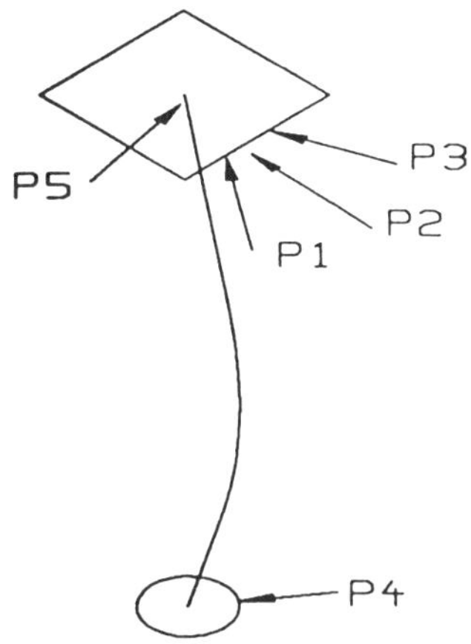

Figure 12.86

Step 2. Break the right vertical line of the rectangle into two segments using the pick points in Figure 12.86.

Select **MAIN MENU → Modify → Break → 2 pieces**
Select an entity: pick at **P1**
Enter the breakpoint: select **Midpoint** from the Point Menu, and then pick at **P2**

Step 3. Create the swept surface still use the pick points in Figure 12.86.

Select **MAIN MENU → Create → sUrface → Swept → Nurbs**
Enter the number of across contours: **2** ←
define across contour 1: select **Chain** from the Chaining method menu, then pick at **P3**
Select **Close → End here**
define across contour 2: select **Single** from the Chaining method menu, then pick at **P4**
define the along contour: select **Chain** from the Chaining method menu, then pick at **P5**
Select **Close → End here → Done** to complete the contours selection
Set the Swept surface parameters to the following settings:

Along cut distance = 0.15
Across cut distance = 0.15
Translate the across contour
Error measurement = off

Select **Done** to complete the surface

The surface model should look like Figure 12.87.

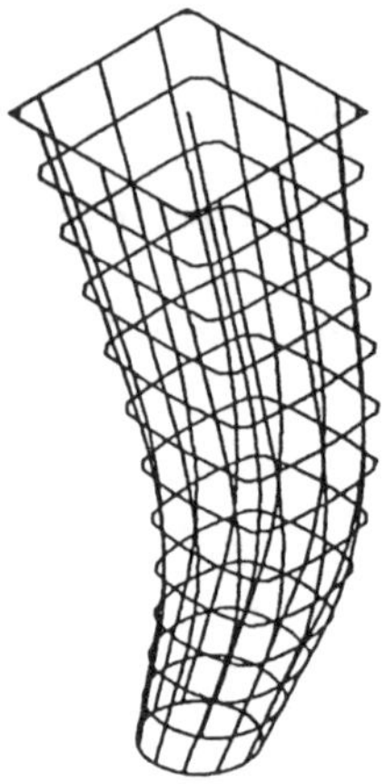

Figure 12.87

Step 4. Save the surface file (swepts2).

Select **MAIN MENU → File → Save**
Enter file name: **swepts2**

Project 16.

16

This example uses the wireframe model of project 10 in chapter 11 to create a swept surface. The model consists of two along contours and one across contour. The wireframe and surface model are given in Figure 12.88.

Wireframe Model
Project 10 of Chapter 11 (swept3)

Go to

We are here

Surface Model (swepts3)

Go to

Toopath
Project 3 of Chapter 15 (flowl3)

Go to

Toolpath Roughing
Project 5 of Chapter 16 (RT)

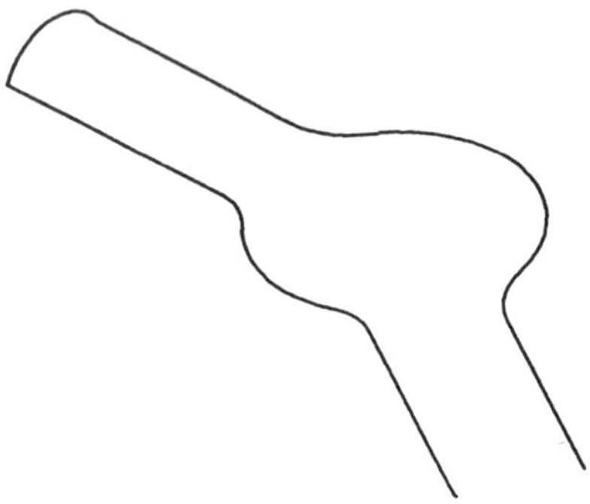

Figure 12.88a. Wireframe model

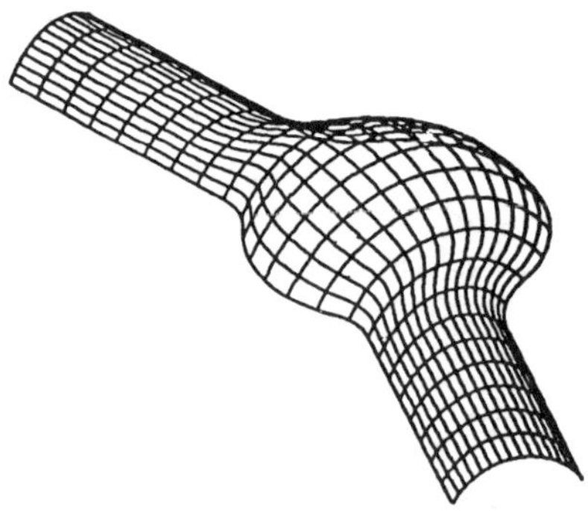

Figure 12.88b. Surface model

Step 1. Load the wireframe model file (swept3) or create one by following the instructions of example in chapter 11.

Select **MAIN MENU → File → Get**
Enter file name: **swept3**
Select **Yes** to delete the current part

The wireframe model drawing should appear as Figure 12.92.

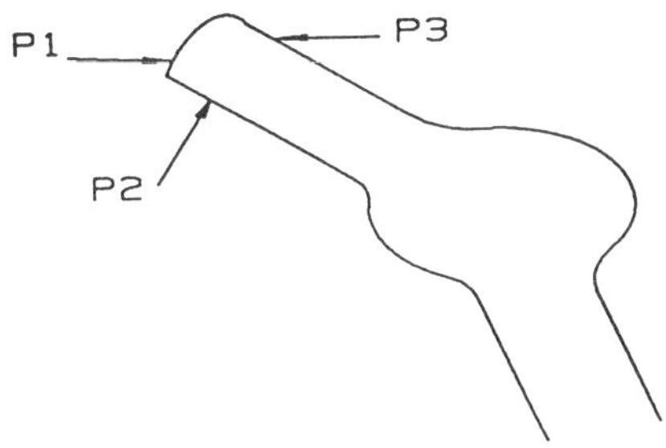

Figure 12.89

Step 2. Create a swept surface using the pick points in Figure 12.89.

Select **MAIN MENU → Create → sUrface → Swept → Nurbs**
Enter the number of across contours: **1** ←
define the across contour: select **Single** from the Chaining method menu, then pick at **P1**

define along contour 1: select **Chain**, then pick at **P2**
Select **Close → End here**
define along contour 2: select **Chain**, then pick at **P3**
Select **Close → End here → Done** to complete contours selection

Define the Swept surface parameters to the following settings:

Along cut distance = 0.15
Across cut distance = 0.15
Error measurement = off

Select **Done** from the parameters menu to complete the surface

The swept surface should resemble Figure 12.90.

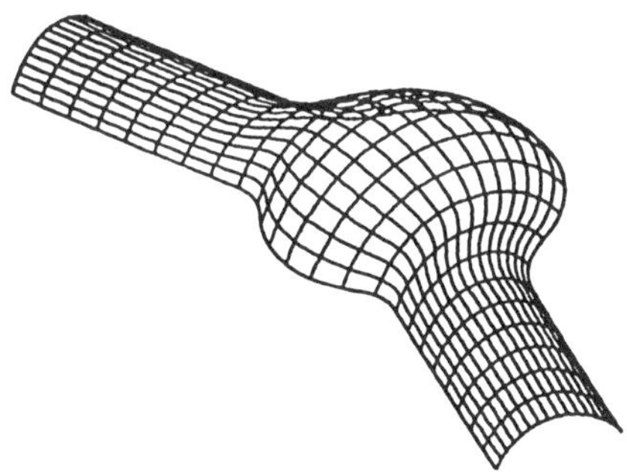

Figure 12.90

Step 3. Save the surface file (swepts3).

Select **MAIN MENU → File → Save**
Enter file name: **swepts3**

12.11 Exercises

12.11.1 Short Answer

1. What is a surface?

2. What is a composite surface model?

3. What are the four mathematical methods of modeling surfaces?

4. How is a Coons surface defined? Explain the strengths and weaknesses of a Coons surface.

5. Describe the strengths and weaknesses of Bezier surfaces.

6. Explain the strengths and weaknesses of B-spline surfaces.

7. What is NURBS surface?

8. Describe the major difference between the B-spline surface and NURBS surface.

9. List the three types of surfaces.

10. What are the two surface modeling techniques Mastercam provides to create geometrical surfaces?

11. What are free-form surfaces?

12. What are the two kinds of free-form surfaces? Describe their differences.

13. What are the four types of free-form surfaces that Mastercam provides?

14. What are derived surfaces?

15. List the three types of derived surfaces in Mastercam.

16. What are the three surfacing mathematics Mastercam uses to generate free-form and derived surfaces?

12.11.2 Problems

17. Use the wireframe model created in problem 11.10 to generate two ruled surfaces. The wireframe profile and the finished ruled surfaces are shown in Figure 12.91. The wireframe file is **E1**. Save the surface model file as **ES1**. Project 1 in this chapter is a similar example.

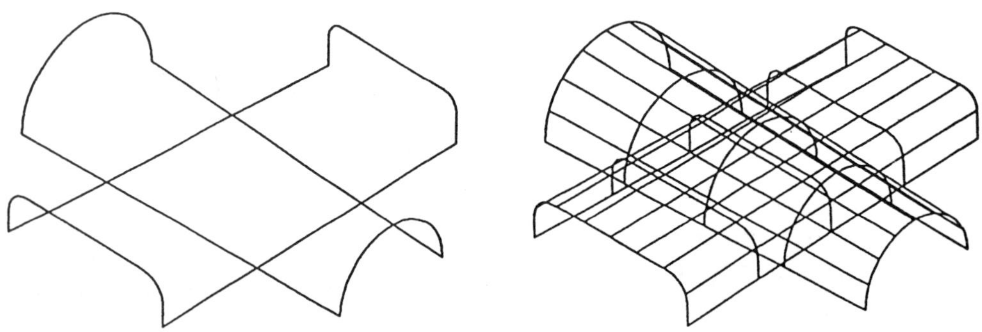

Figure 12.91

18. Use the wireframe model created in problem 11.11 to generate two ruled surfaces which intersect at an angle of 45°. The wireframe profile and the finished ruled surfaces look like Figure 12.92. The wireframe file is **E2**. Save the surface model file as **ES2**. A similar example is project 2 of this chapter.

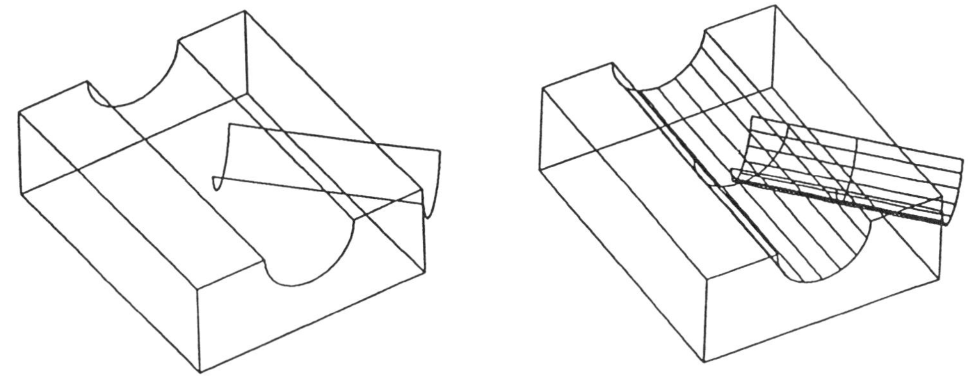

Figure 12.92

19. The three contours in problem 11.12 are used to create a ruled surface. The wireframe and finished surface model are shown in Figure 12.93. The wireframe model file is **E3**. Save the surface model file as **ES3**. A similar example in this chapter is project 3.

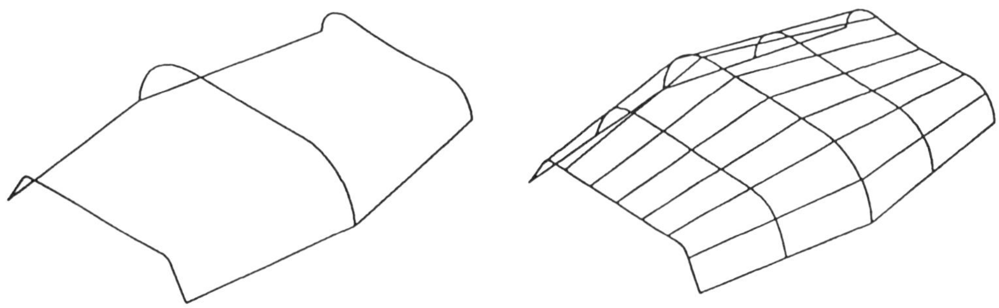

Figure 12.93

20. Use the three contours in problem 11.12 to create a loft surface. The wireframe and finished loft surface model resemble Figure 12.94. The wireframe model file is **E3**. Save the surface model file as **ES4**. A similar example is project 4 of this chapter.

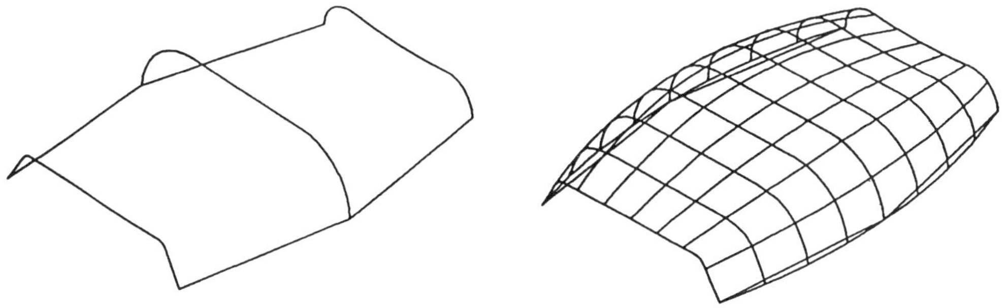

Figure 12.94

21. Use the four arcs in problem 11.13 to create a single-patch Coons surface. Both wireframe and surface models are illustrated in Figure 12.95. The wireframe model file is **E4**. Save the surface model file as **ES5**. A similar example is project 7 of this chapter.

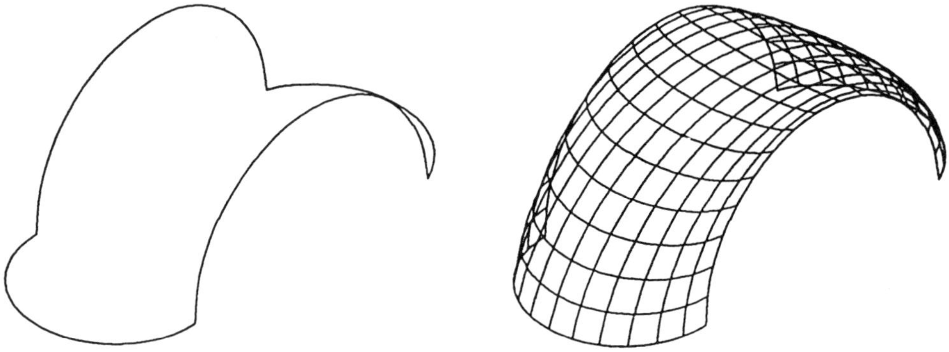

Figure 12.95

22. Create a single-patch Coons surface from the wireframe model of problem 11.14. The wireframe model file is **E5**. Save the surface model file as **ES6**. Both wireframe and surface models are given in Figure 12.96. A similar example is project 7 in this chapter.

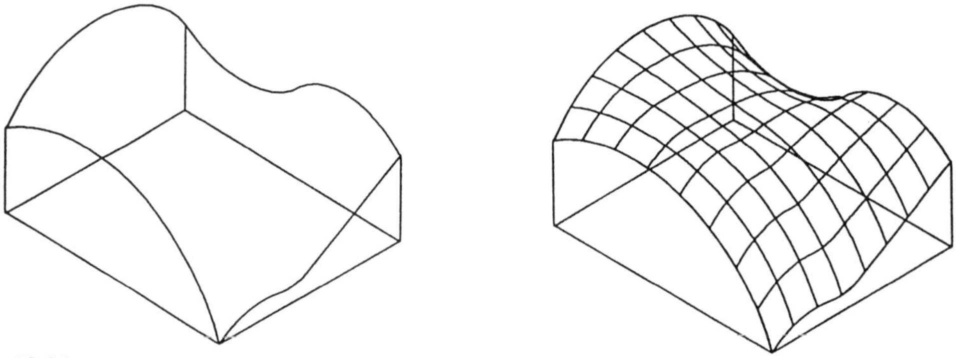

Figure 12.96

23. Use the wireframe model in problem 11.15 to create a multi-patch Coons surface. The wireframe model file is **E6**. Figure 12.97 shows both wireframe model and finished surface model. Save the surface model file as **ES7**. A similar example is project 9 of this chapter.

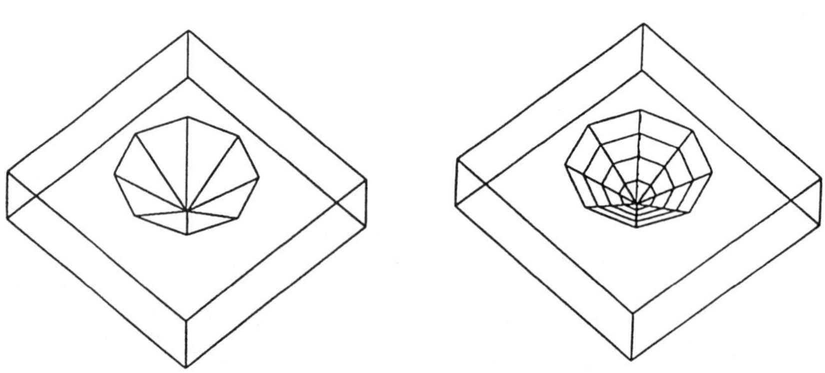

Figure 12.97

24. Use the multi-faced wireframe model given in problem 11.16 to generate a Coons surface of multiple patches. The wireframe model file is **E7**. Save the surface model file as **ES8**. A similar example is project 10 in this chapter. Both wireframe and surface models should look like Figure 12.98.

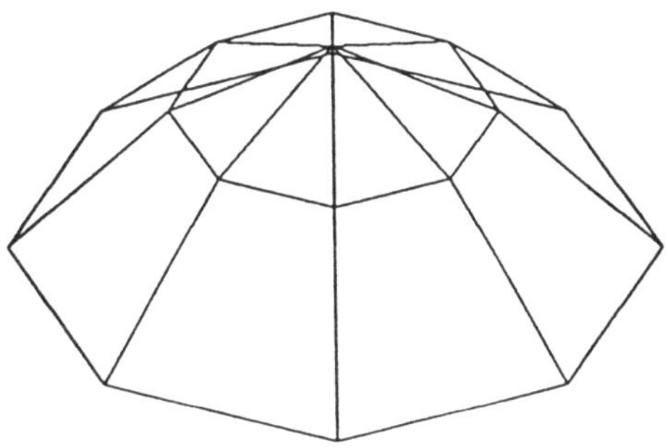

Figure 12.98a. Wireframe model

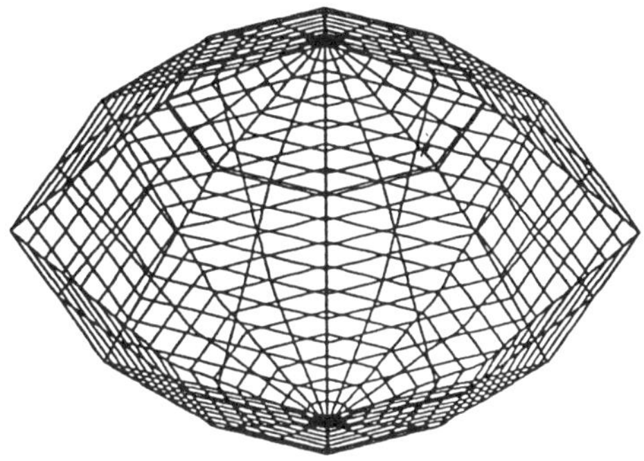

Figure 12.98b. Surface model

25. Use the revolved surfacing technique to creat a surface model from the wireframe model in problem 11.17. The wireframe model file is **E8**. Save the surface model file as **ES9**. Both models are illustrated in Figure 12.99. A similar example is project 11 of this chapter.

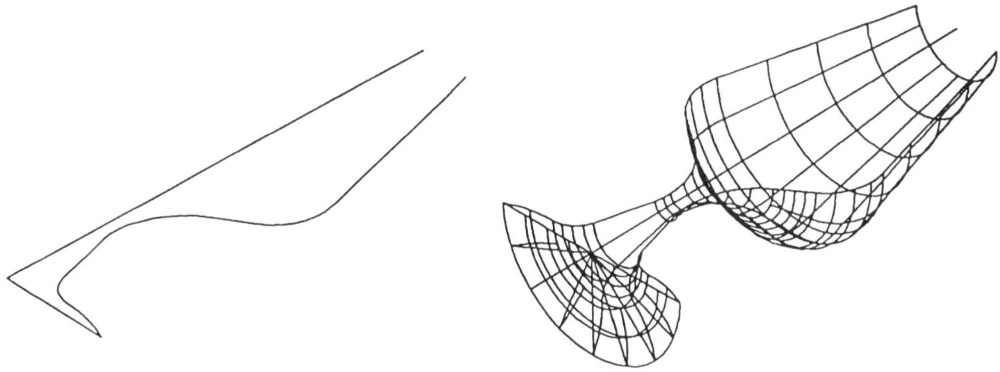

Figure 12.99

26. Use the revolved surfacing technique to create a surface model of a cup from the wireframe profiles in problem 11.18. The wireframe model file is **E9**. Save the surface model file as **ES10**. The wireframe and finished surface models are shown in Figure 12.100. A similar example is project 11 in this chapter.

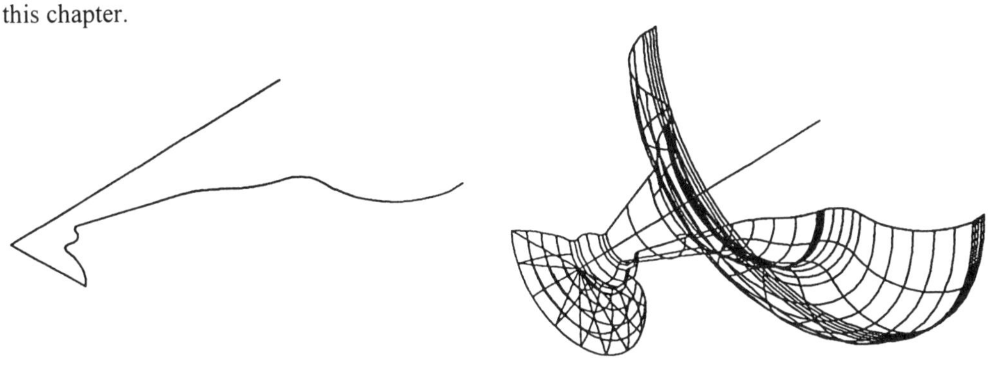

Figure 12.100

27. The wireframe model of a fly disk given in problem 11.19 is used to create a surface model by using the swept surfacing technique. The wireframe model file is **E10**. Both wireframe and surface models in front view are illustrated in Figure 12.101. Save the surface model file as **ES11**. A similar example is project 11 of this chapter.

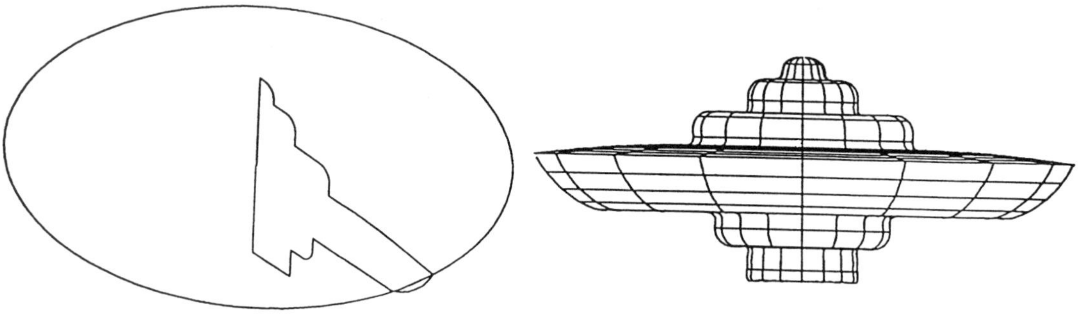

Figure 12.101

28. Create a draft surface using an 8" x 6" rectangle with a 1" fillet at four corners as the base profile. The draft length is -2" and the draft angle is 15° in the outward direction. The base profile and finished draft surfaces should resemble Figure 12.102.

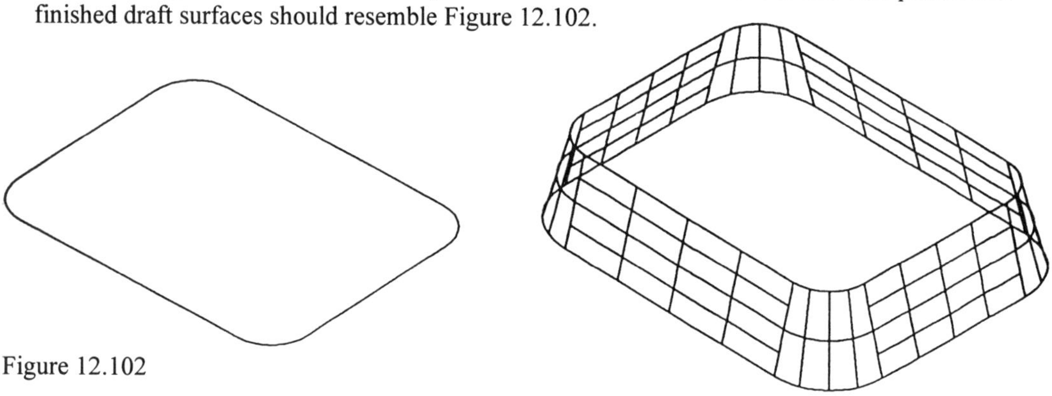

Figure 12.102

29. Create a draft surface from a spline which is defined by thc the set of points given below. The draft length is 1.5" and the draft angle is 20° in the outward direction. The base spline and the finished draft surfaces are shown in Figure 12.103.

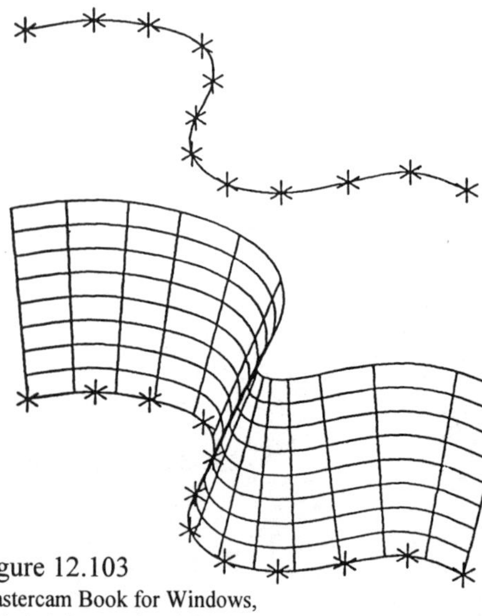

X	Y	Z
0.0	0.0	0.0
0.3	0.5	0.0
0.67	0.77	0.0
1.18	0.89	0.0
1.59	0.61	0.0
1.85	0.14	0.0
2.18	-0.24	0.0
2.69	-0.32	0.0
3.08	-0.08	0.0
3.36	0.42	0.0
3.62	0.89	0.0
4.11	1.05	0.0

Figure 12.103

Chapter 13

Surfaces Modeling (II): Derived and Composite Surfaces

Objectives:

1. Use Mastercam to create derived surfaces from existing surfaces.
2. Create composite surface models.

Overview:

Six basic surface modeling techniques and examples have been presented in chapter 12. In this chapter, four derived surfacing techniques are covered, followed by five composite surface modeling examples. Each of these five composite surface examples consists of several surfaces that are modeled by more than one surface modeling technique. They are arranged in increasing order of difficulty. Useful tips that lead to successful completion of the surface model are given in each example.

13.1 Derived Surfaces Modeling

Derived surfaces are those surfaces that are generated from existing surfaces. They are used to modify or edit the existing surfaces, and because of this, they are also called edited surfaces. Mastercam provides **four derived surface modeling techniques:** fillet surface modeling, trimmed surface modeling, offset surfaces modeling and blend surface modeling.

13.1.1 Fillet Surfaces Modeling

A fillet surface is created between two existing surfaces. Fillet surfaces are mainly used in
(1) adding a smooth fillet between two intersecting surfaces (Figure 13.1); and
(2) adding a fillet at the end of object (Figure 13.2).

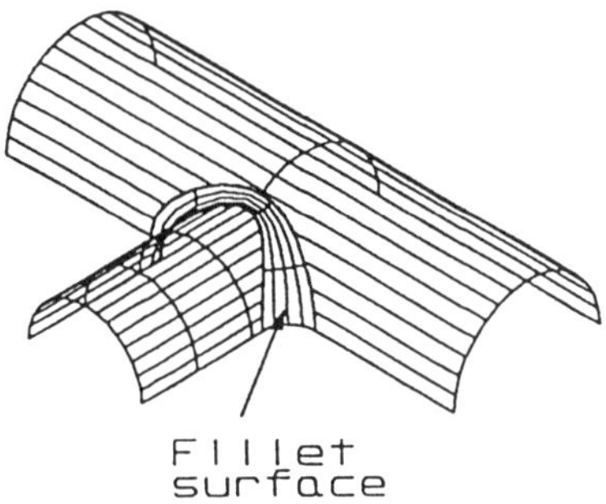

Figure 13.1

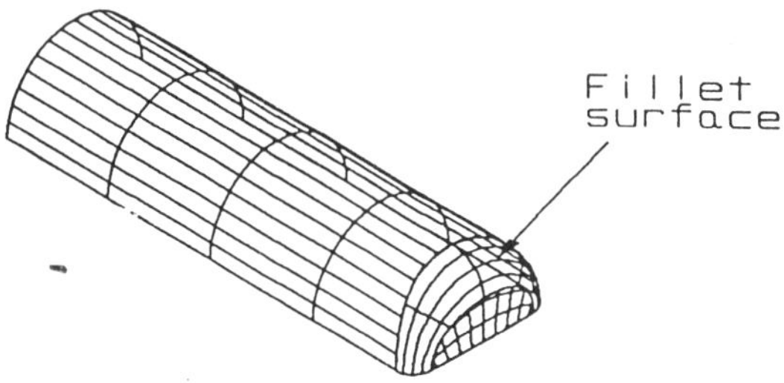

Figure 13.2

Types of Fillet Surfaces

There are **two** categories of fillet surfaces: fillet surfaces with a constant radius and fillet surfaces with a variable radius. The radius of the variable radius fillet surfaces can vary in one of six patterns: linear, parabolic, cubic, sine, horn, and middle. Table 13.1 on the next page summaries the characteristics and illustration of each radius pattern.

Table 13.1 Fillet surfaces modeling types

Radius type	Description	Illustration
A. Constant	The fillet radius remains constant throughout the surface intersecting boundary.	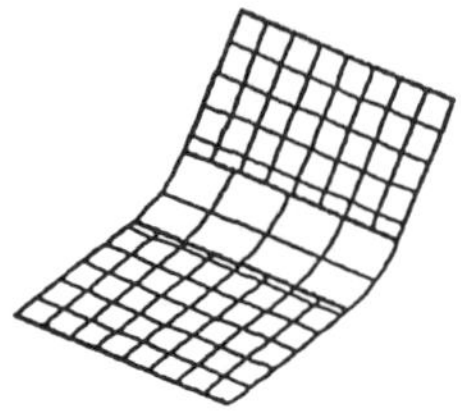
B. Variable	Radius varies along the surface intersecting boundary.	
1. Linear	Radius varies linearly from the start to the end of surface boundary.	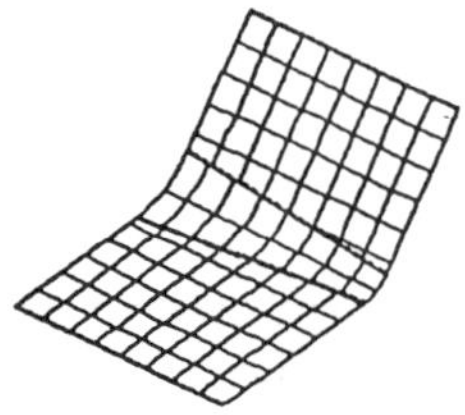
2. Parabolic	Radius varies in a curve of the second degree order.	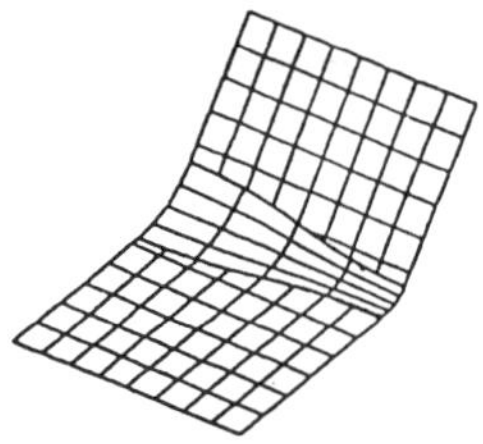
3. Cubic	Radius changes in a curve of the third degree order.	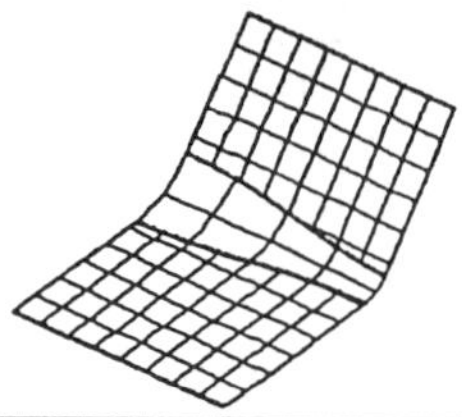
4. Sine	Radius varics in a sinusoidal curve.	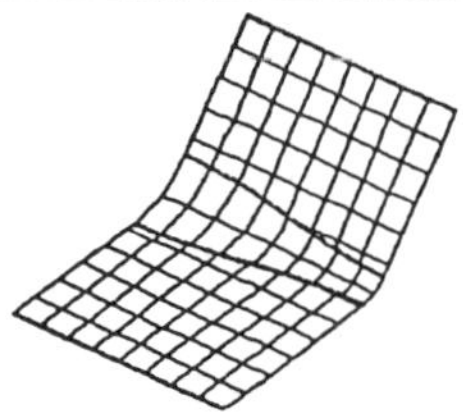
5. Horn	Radius changes in a curve of the horn shape.	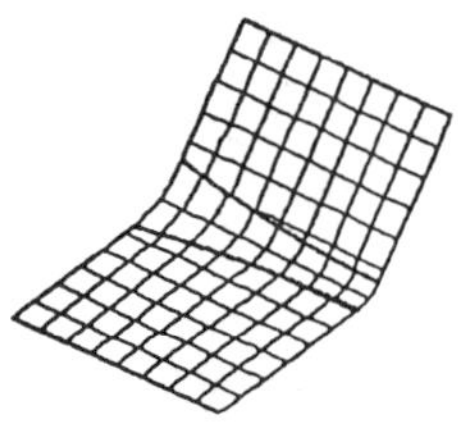
6. Middle	Radius varies parabolically from the start to the middle of the surface intersection, and is symmetrical about the middle.	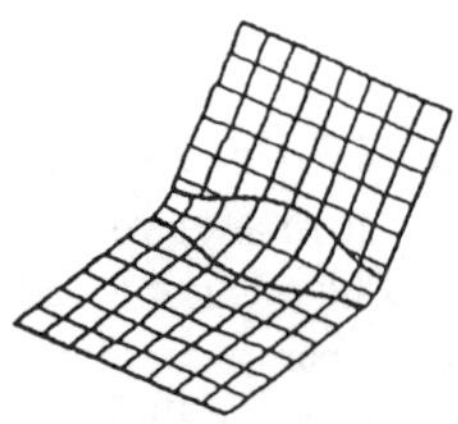

Stepping Parameters

The stepping distance of the surface can be specified by **two stepping methods**: step distance and chord deviation. Toggle the **use Ch ht** parameter to select one. The chordal deviation method is used when the use Ch ht parameter is toggled to Y (Yes). If this parameter is toggled to N (No), the step distance is selected. The step distance is the only variable defined for constructing the surface with the step distance method. When using the chord deviation method, the value of the stepping chord height and the maximum step must be specified. In Version 5, the step Vals parameter is used to set the stepping distances for both step distance and chord deviation method.

Use smaller values for these parameters to tighten the accuracy of the surface. However, this will take the computer a longer amount of time to process the surface and will make the surface file bigger.

Splines, Surface Curves, Fillets and Trim Surfaces to Be Generated

While creating a fillet surface, the system can generate **four** types of information:

- •Two parametric splines (one at each surface)
- •Two surface curves (one at each intersecting surface)
- •Fillet surface (blend, parametric or NURBS type)
- •Trimmed surfaces (one at each intersecting surface)

Mastercam uses the the following **Fillet Menus** ☞ to select the type of curves and surface you want to create:

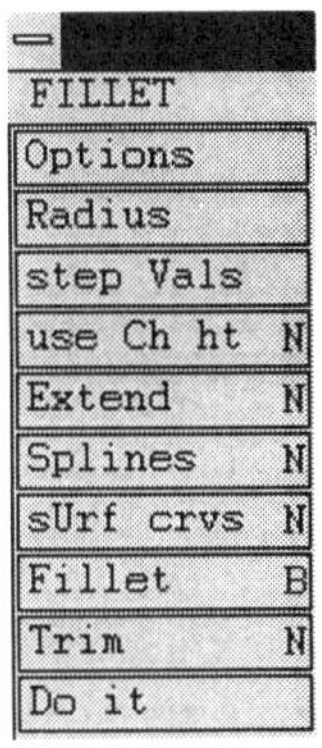

Fillet parameters are described below:

Extend (Y/N) :extends beyond surface edges

Splines (1/2/B/N):creates a spline for
1: surface 1
2: surface 2
B: both surfaces
N: None

sUrf crvs (1/2/B/N) : Creates a surface curve for
1: one surface
2: surface 2
B: both surfaces
N: None

Fillet (B/N/P/O) :Creates a fillet surface of this type:
B: blend surface
N: Nurbs surface
P: parametric surface
O: nOne

Trim (1/2/B/N) : trims the surfaces to a boundary of:
1: surface 1
2: surface 2
B: both surfaces
N: none

The selection of the Option parameter in the Fillet menu brings up Fillet options/types submenu as shown here ☞ This submenu is used to define the type of fillet radius.

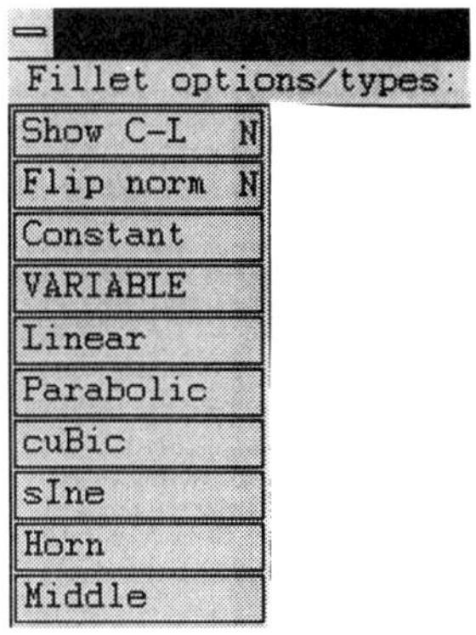

Tips For successful surfaces, use these procedures:

1. Check the surface normal of both surfaces. The two surface normals must point to the directions that intersect each other (Figure 13.3). If not, use **Modify → Normal** to set to the proper normal direction.

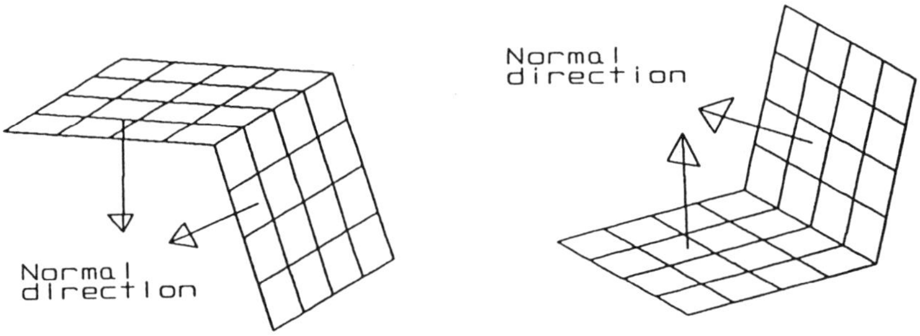

Figure 13.3

2. Use the mouse to select the first surface. Then move the arrow to the starting position of the surface. The start radius always begins at one end of the surface and follows the surface direction.
3. Select the second surface. The start point of the second surface must be positioned near the point at the base of the first arrow.

Notes: a. Three common problems in creating fillet surfaces are
(1) the surface normals are not in the proper direction,
(2) the start position of the surface is not proper, and
(3) the fillet radius may be too large to fit the two surfaces.

When a fillet surface can not be successfully generated, check the surface normals first. If the surface normals are correct and the problem still exists, try to pick different locations for the start point of the surface. Finally, check to see if the fillet radius is too big to fit the surfaces.

b. When filleting a cylindrical (or closed) surface to a plannar surface,the the cylindrical surface should be selected first (Figure 13.4).

c. The surface which resembles the shape of the desired fillet surface should always be selected first.

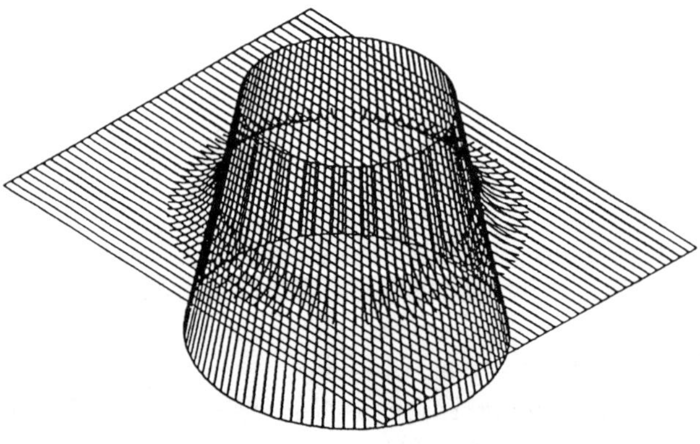

Figure 13.4

Project 1.

Two fillet surfaces with a constant radius

Two fillet surfaces are created at the intersection of two ruled surfaces (Figure 13.5). The two perpendicularly intersected ruled surfaces are created in project 1 of chapter 12. These two fillet surfaces have a constant radius of 0.25-in.

1

Wireframe Model
Project 1 of Chapter 11 (Ruled1)

Go to

Surface Model
Project 1 of Chapter 12 (ruleds1)

Go to

We are here

Fillet Surface
(fillets1)

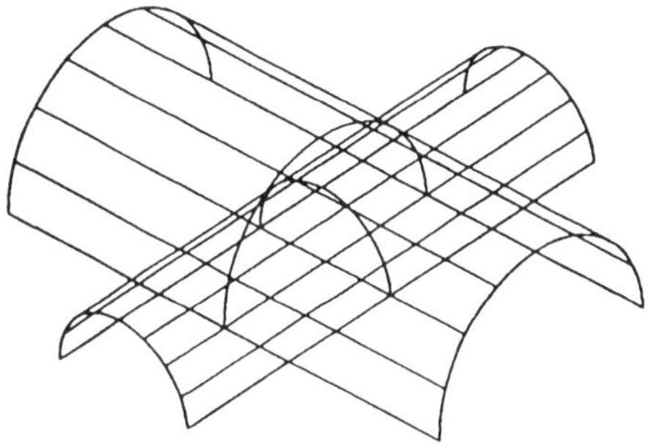

Figure 13.5a. Without fillet surface

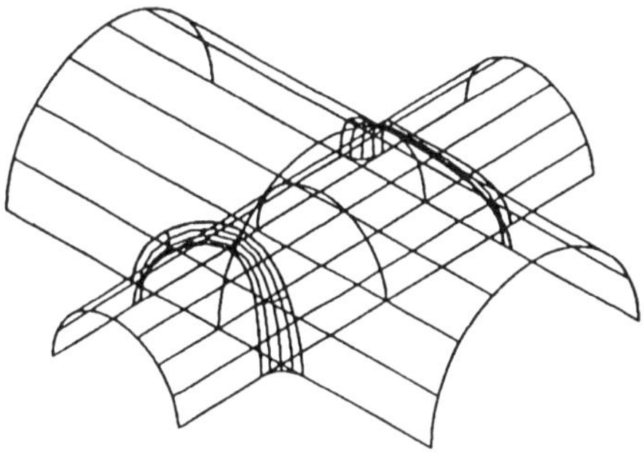

Figure 13.5b. With fillet surface

Step 1. Load the surface model file (ruleds1).

Select **MAIN MENU → File → Get**
Enter file name: **ruleds1**

The drawing of two ruled surfaces should appear as Figure 13.6.

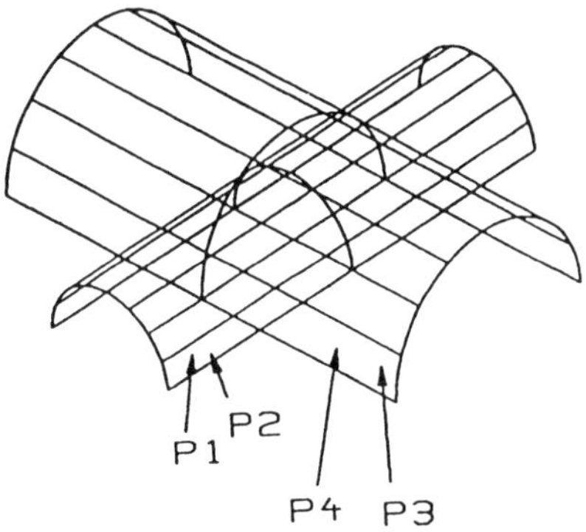

Figure 13.6

Step 2. Create the first fillet surface using the pick points in Figure 13.6.

Select **MAIN MENU →Create → sUrface → Fillet →Option→ Constant→Radius**
Enter the start fillet radius: **0.25** ←

Set the stepping parameters to the following settings:

Use Ch ht = **Y**
Step Vals:
Maximum step distance = **0.1**
Stepping chord height = **0.005**

Pick at **P1** to select the first surface
Move arrow to **P2** and click the mouse to start the fillet
Pick at **P3** to select another surface
Move arrow to **P4** and click the mouse to start the fillet

Set the Fillet Menu to the following settings:

Extend	= **N**
Splines	= **B**
sUrf crvs	= **B**
Fillet	= **N**
Trim	= **N**

Select **Do it** from the Menu to complete the first fillet surface
The first fillet surface is added as shown in Figure 13.7.

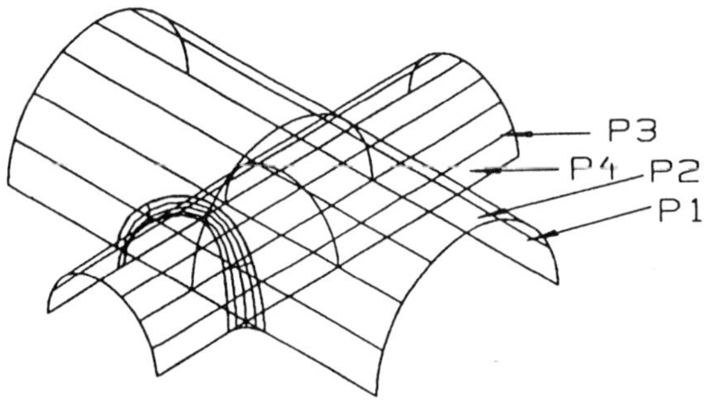

Figure 13.7

Step 3. Create another fillet surface using the pick points in Figure 13.7.

Select **BACKUP → Fillet**
Enter the start fillet radius: **0.25** ←
Pick at **P1** on the first surface
Move arrow to **P2** and click the mouse to start a fillet
Pick at **P3** to select another surface
Move arrow to **P4** and click the mouse
Select **Do it** to complete the surface

The final drawing should look like Figure 13.8 on the next page.

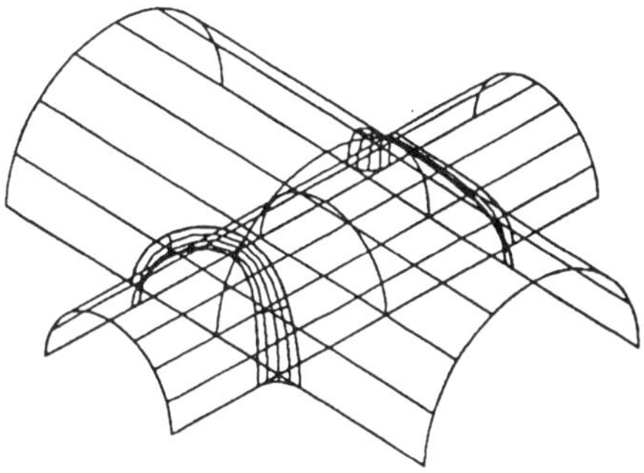

Figure 13.8

Step 4. Save the two fillet surfaces with two ruled surfaces.

Select **MAIN MENU** → **File** → **Save**

Enter file name: **fillets1**

Project 2.

Two fillet surfaces with a variable radius

Create two fillet surfaces based on the two ruled surfaces generated in Project 2 of chapter 12. Both two fillet surfaces have a variable radius. The radius of the fillet surface at the intersection of the two ruled surfaces varies in a linear pattern. The other fillet surface is added at the right end of the larger ruled surface. The radius of the second fillet surface changes in the Middle pattern. A ruled surface must be constructed at the right end before the fillet surface can be generated. Figure 13.9 shows both surface models before and after fillet surfaces are added.

2

Wireframe Model
Project 2 of Chapter 11 (Ruled2)

Go to

Surface Model
Project 2 of Chapter 12 (ruleds2)

Go to

We are here

Fillet Surface
(fillets2)

Go to

Trimmed Surface
Project 4 of Chapter 13 (Trims2)

Go to

Toolpath
Project 4 of Chapter 15 (trimst2)

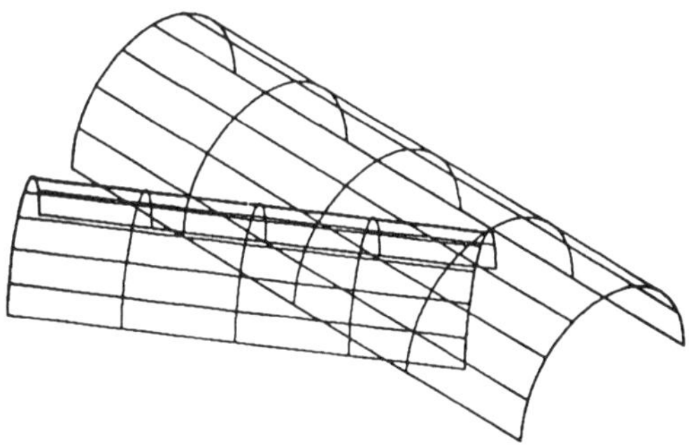

Figure 13.9a

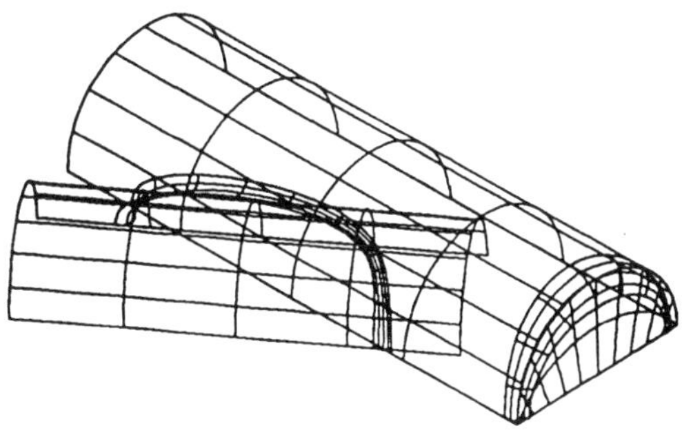

Figure 13.9b

Tips 1. Use different colors to display each surface.

2. The start fillet radius is 0.3-in and end fillet radius is 0.15-in for the linear pattern.

3. Use the step distance method to control the surface stepping pattern.

4. In the Fillet Menu, toggle Splines and sUrf crvs to **B** (both). The two surface curves can be used to form the trimming boundary for trimming the surface in project 4 of this chapter.
5. A line should be added to the two endpoints at the right end of the larger ruled surface. This line is used with the arc to create a ruled surface.
6. The radius of the end fillet surface varies in the Middle pattern. The radius starts with 0.15 in. from one end and increases to 0.3-in. in the middle and then decreases to 0.15 in. at the other end.
7. The surface normals of both ruled surfaces for creating end fillet surface must point toward the surfaces. Use **Modify → Normal** command to change the surface normals if necessary.

Step 1. Load the surface model file (ruleds2).

Select **MAIN MENU → File → Get**
Enter file name: **ruleds2**

The two ruled surfaces should appear as Figure 13.10.

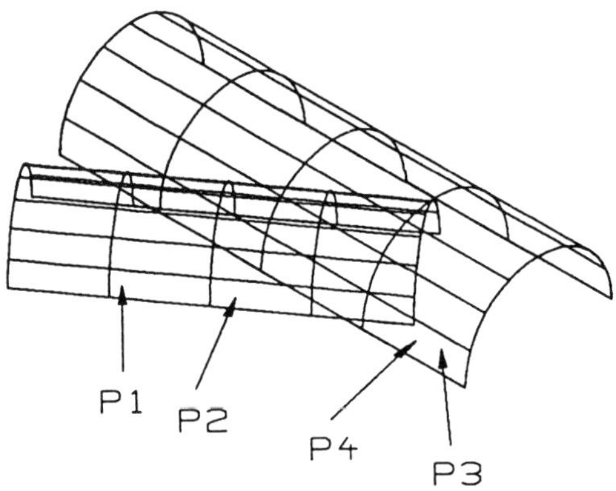

Figure 13.10

Step 2. Change color to 12.

Select **Color** from the Secondary menu, then enter **12**

Step 3. Create the first fillet surface between the two ruled surfaces. Use the pick points in Figure 13.10.

Select **MAIN MENU → Create → sUrface → Fillet → Options → Linear → Radius**
Enter the start fillet radius: **0.3** ←
Enter the end fillet radius: **0.15** ←

Set the stepping method menu to the following settings:

Use Ch ht = **N**
Step Vals :
Stepping distance = **0.05**

Pick at **P1** to select the first surface
Move arrow to **P2** and click the mouse to start a fillet
Pick at **P3** to select another surface
Move arrow to **P4** and click the mouse to start a fillet

Set the Fillet Menu to following settings:

Extend	= **N**
Splines	= **B**
sUrf crvs	= **B**
Fillet	= **B**
Trim	= **N**

Select **Do it** to complete the fillet surface

The isometric and top Gview of the drawing are shown in Figure 13.11.

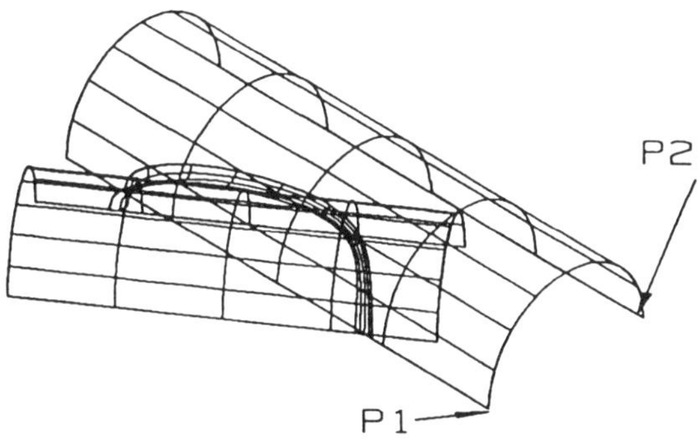

Figure 13.11a. Isometric view

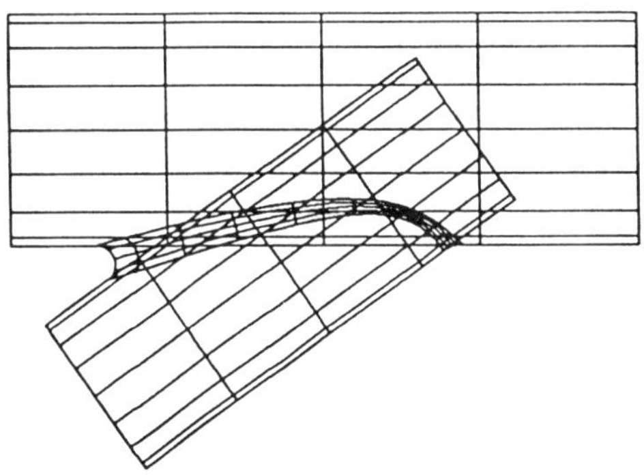

Figure 13.11b. Top view

Step 4. Add a line to the right face of the larger ruled surface using 3d Cplane.

Use the pick points in Figure 13.11.
Select **Cplane → 3d**
Select **MAIN MENU → Create → Line → Endpoints → Endpoint**
Pick at **P1** and **P2** to complete the line

The line is added as shown in Figure 13.12.

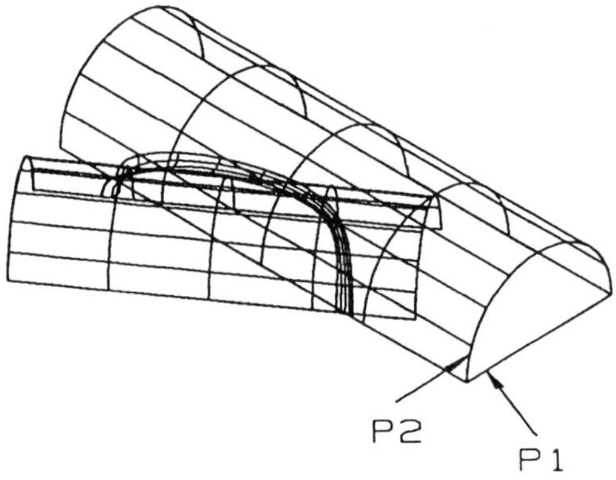

Figure 13.12

Step 5. Create a ruled surface at the right end of the semi-cone. Use the pick points in Figure 13.12.

Select **MAIN MENU → Create → sUrface → rUled → Blend**
define contour 1: select **Single** then pick at **P1**
define contour 2: select **Single** then pick at **P2**
Select **Done** to complete the surface

The new ruled surface should appear on the screen as Figure 13.13.

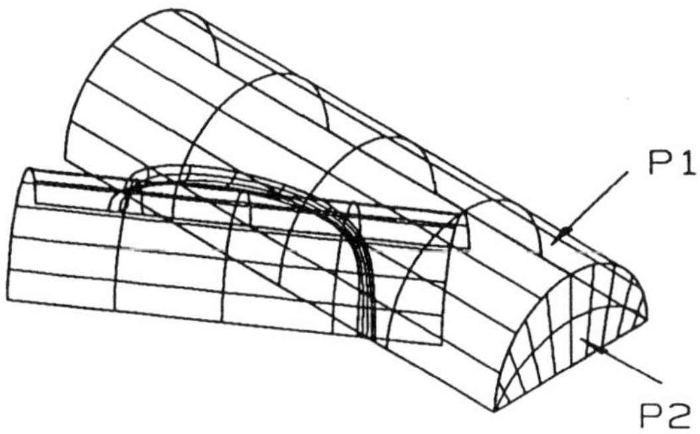

Figure 13.13

Step 6. Change the normal direction of the surfaces by using the pick points in Figure 13.13.

Select **MAIN MENU → Modify → Normal → Reverse**
Pick at **P1** to select a surface

Note: the surface curves are dimed when the surface normal is changed to pointing in the inward direction.

Pick at **P2** to select the end surface to change the normal direction of the second surface
Note: Surface curves on both surfaces should appear dimmed.

The drawing on the screen should look like Figure 13.14.

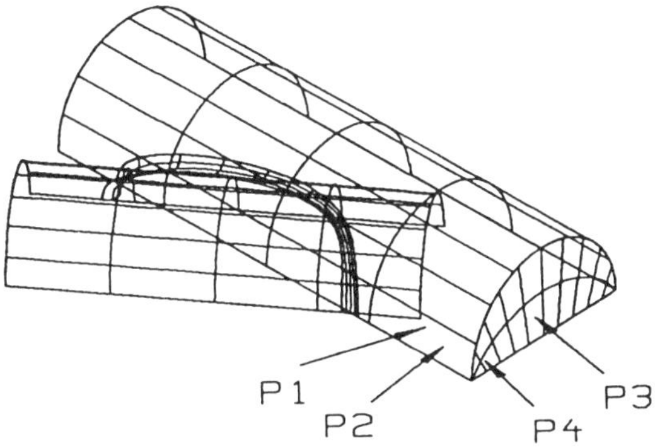

Figure 13.14

Step 7. Create a fillet with a variable radius which varies in the Middle pattern.

Use the pick points in Figure 13.14. Change color to 14.
Select **Color** from the Secondary menu and then enter **14**
Select **MAIN MENU → Create → sUrface →Fillet →Options → Middle→ Radius**
Enter the fillet radius for the ends: **0.15** ←
Enter the fillet radius for the middle: **0.3** ←

Set the Step Meth menu to the following settings:

Use Ch ht = **N**
Step Vals:
Stepping distance = **0.005**

Pick at **P1** to select a surface
Move arrow to **P2** and click the mouse
Pick at **P3** to select another surface
Move arrow to **P4** and click the mouse

Set the Keep Menu to the following settings:

Extend	= **N**
Splines	= **B**
sUrf crvs	**= B**
Fillet	= **B**
Trim	= **N**

Select **Do it** to complete the surface

The drawing should look like Figure 13.15.

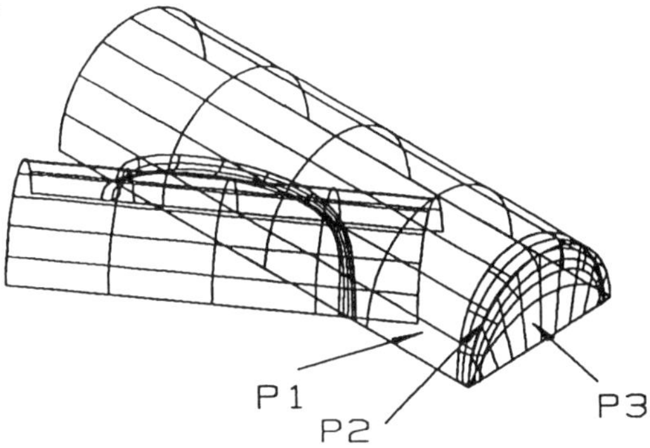

Figure 13.15

Step 8. Change three surface normals. Use the pick points in Figure 13.15.

Select **MAIN MENU → Modify → Normal → Reverse**

Pick at **P1** , **P2** and **P3** to select three surfaces to change their normal direction to outward.

The final drawing should resemble Figure 13.16.

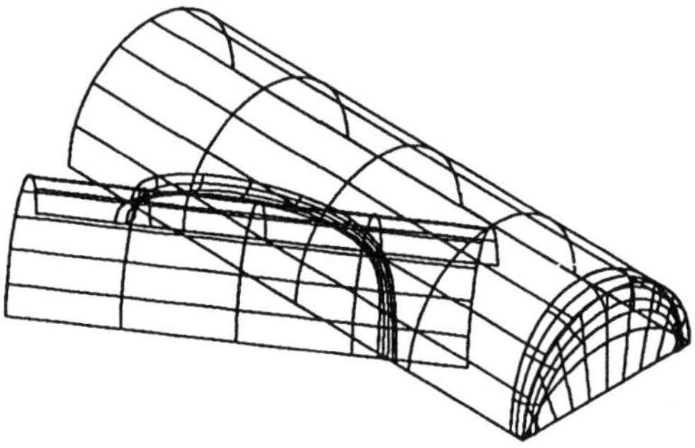

Figure 13.16

Step 9. Save the surface model file (fillets2).

Select **MAIN MENU → File → Save**

Enter file name: **fillets2**

13.1.2 Trimmed Surfaces Modeling

The trimmed surface modeling technique is used to create a trimmed surface from an existing surface (Figure 13.17). It requires an existing surface and at least one trim boundary.

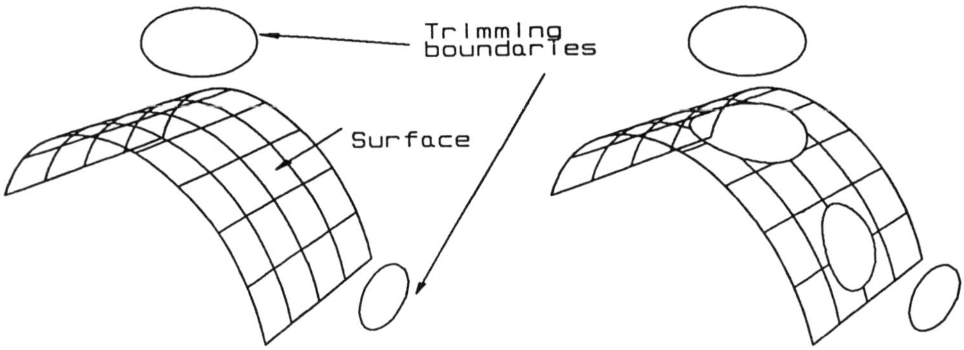

Figure 13.17a Before trimming Figure 13.17b After trimming

Trimming surface Commands in Version 5 are:

MAIN MENU → Create→ sUrface → Trimmed

The trim surface functions in Version 5 are significantly improved and more user-friendly than its predecessor Version 4. Table 13.2 summaries the surface trimming methods in Version 5.

Table 13.2 Trimmed surfaces modeling methods in Version 5.

Method	Description	Illustration
To curves	Trim surface(s) to given curves.	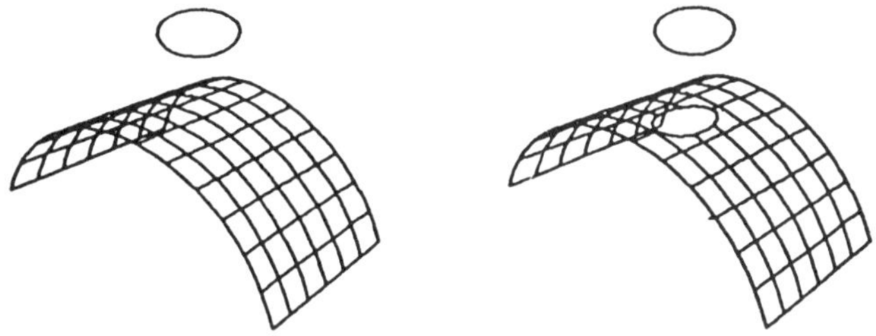
To a surface	Trim surface(s) to a surface.	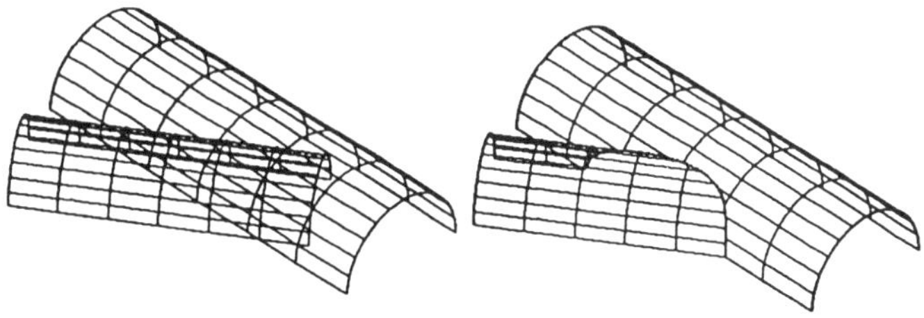
Flat bndy	Create a flat surface to the specified boundary.	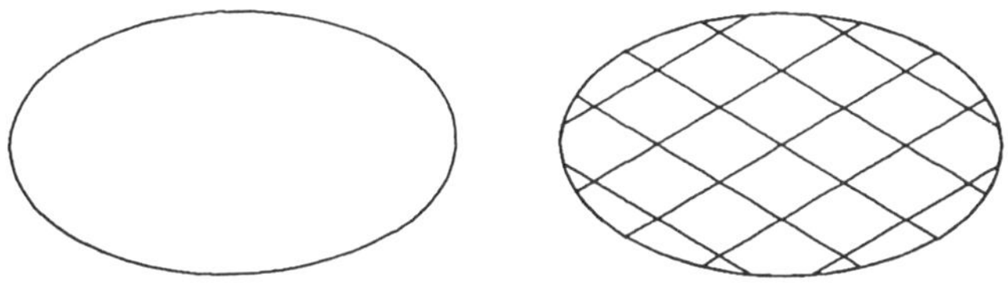
Untrim	Untrim the trimmed surfaces.	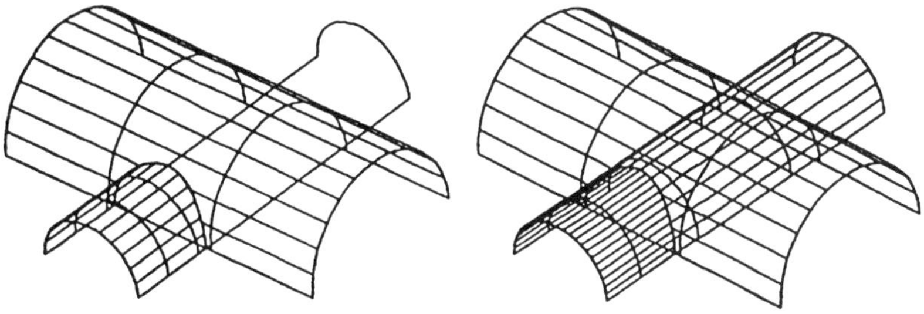

Project 3.

Trimming two ruled surfaces to their intersection boundary

Two intersecting ruled surfaces are trimmed to their intersecting boundaries. Surface curves are not required to trim surfaces in Version 5. Both surface models before and after trimming are shown in Figure 13.18.

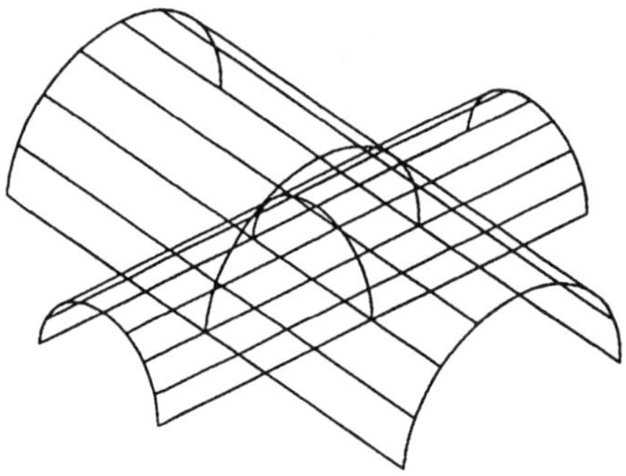

Figure 13.18a. Before trimming

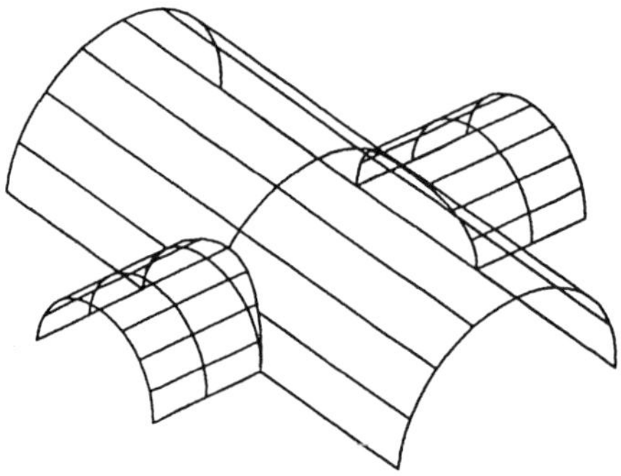

Figure 13.18b After trimming

Tips 1. The surface file to be trimmed is **ruleds1.**

2. Use the **to a surf** method to trim both surfaces to their intersection boundaries.

3. These two ruled surfaces are intersected at two locations. Therefore, they need to be trimmed twice. After trimming at one end, the smaller surface must be recovered to its original shape by using the untrim function. This will produce two surfaces; one is the short trimmed surface and the other is the original surface. The original surface is then used with the trimmed larger surface to trim each other at the other end.

Step 1. Load the surface file (ruleds1).

Select **MAIN MENU → File → Get**
Enter file name: **ruleds1**
Select **Yes** to delete the current part

The two ruled surfaces should appear as in Figure 13.19.

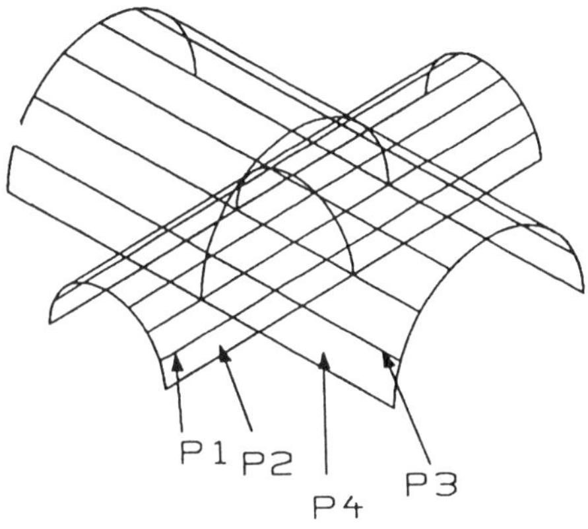

Figure 13.19

Step 2. Initiate the trimmed surface module.

Select **Level** → **Main level** then enter **2**
Select **MAIN MENU** → **Create** → **sUrface** → **Trimmed** → **to a surf**

Step 3. Define the Trim Surf parameters to the following settings.

Dispose	= **D**
Both	= **Y**
Step Vals	= **0.1**
Use ch Ht	= **N**

Step 4. Select the surfaces to be trimmed using the pick points in Figure 13.19.

Pick at **P1** to select a surface
Move arrow to **P2** and click the mouse to indicate the Area to keep after trimming
Pick at **P3** to select another surface
Move arrow to **P4** and click the mouse indicate the area to keep after trimming
Select **Do it**

Both surfaces are trimmed at one side as shown in Figure 13.20.

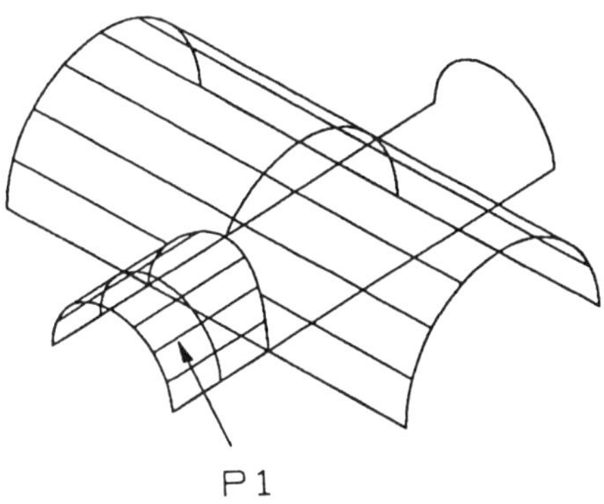

Figure 13.20

Step 5. Untrim the smaller surface. Use the pick point in Figure 13.20.

Select **BACKUP → Untrim**
Toggle disPose parameter to **K** (Keep)
Pick at **P1** to select a surface
The trimmed surface is recovered as shown in Figure 13.21.
Note: two surfaces are produced.

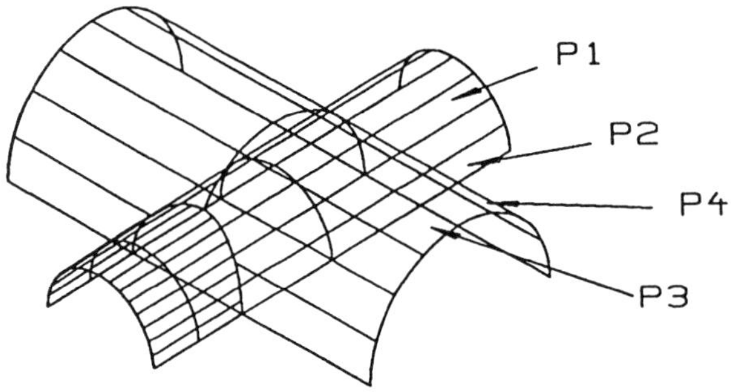

Figure 13.21

Step 6. Trim both surfaces to their intersection boundary at the other end.

Use the pick points in Figure 13.21.
Select **BACKUP → to a surf**

Use the same parameter settings as in Step 3.

Pick at **P1** to select a surface
Move arrow to **P2** and click the mouse to indicate the kept area
Pick at **P3** to select another surface
Move arrow to **P4** and click the mouse to indicate the kept area
Select **Do it**
Select **Level** from the secondary menu
Pick **Vis. Levels**
Click level #1 to invisible (dimmed)
Select **OK**

The trimmed surface should look like Figure 13.22.

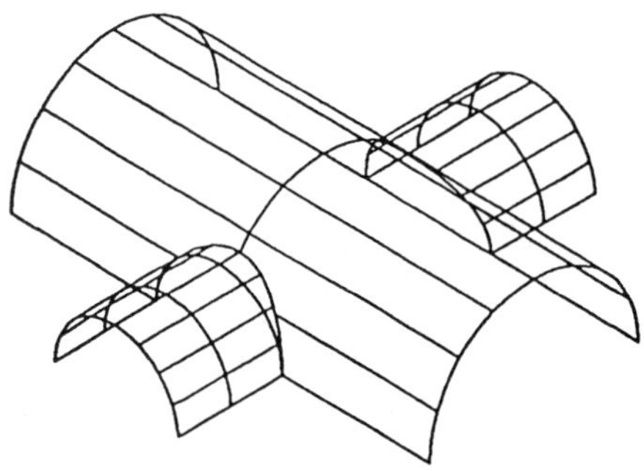

Figure 13.22

Step 7. Save the trimmed surfaces as trims1.

Select **MAIN MENU → File → Save**
Enter file name: **trims1**

Project 4.

Trimming three surfaces to their surface boundaries

In this example, three trimmed surfaces are generated based on the surface model of project 2 in this chapter. These three ruled surfaces are trimmed to their surface boundary. The surface models before and after trimming are shown in Figure 13.23.

4

Wireframe Model
Project 2 of Chapter 11 (ruled2)

Go to

Surface Model
Project 2 of Chapter 12 (ruleds2)

Go to

Fillet Surface
Project 2 of Chapter 13 (fillets2)

Go to

We are here

Trimmed Surface
(Trims2)

Go to

Toolpath
Project 4 of Chapter 15 (trimst2)

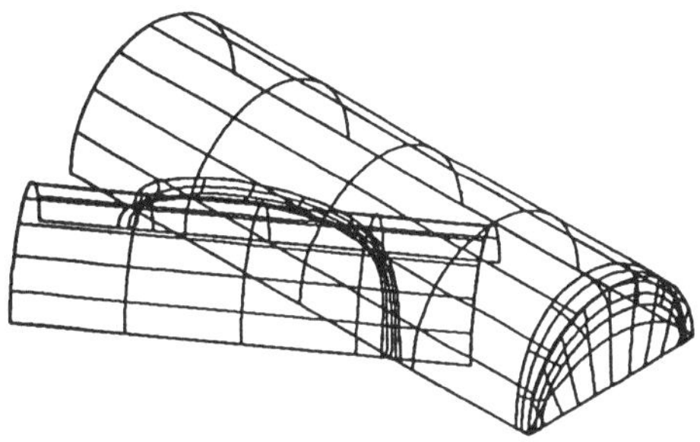

a. Before trimming

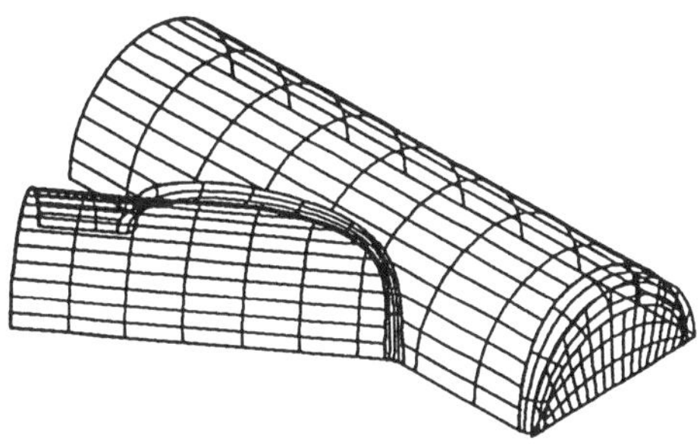

b. After trimming
Figure 13.23

Tips 1. Use the surface model file fillets2.

2. Use a different level and color for each trimmed surface.

3. Trim all three surfaces to the surface curve.

Step 1. load the surface model file (fillets2).

Select **MAIN MENU → File → Get**
Enter file name: **fillets2**
Select **Yes** to delete the current part

The drawing should resemble Figure 13.24.

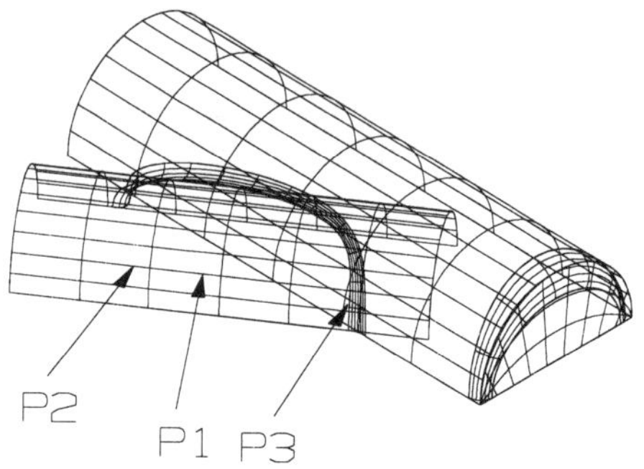

Figure 13.24

Step 2. Change to level 2 and color 11.

Select **Level →** **Main Level** then enter **2**
Select **Color** then enter **11**

Step 3. Trim the smaller ruled surface using the pick points in Figure 13.24

Select **MAIN MENU → Create → sUrface →Trimmed →to Curves**
Set the Trim Surf Parameters to the following settings:

Constr Vw	= **N**
Dispose	= **D**
Step Vals:	
Maximum Step distance= **0.2**	
Stepping chord height = **0.05**	
Use ch Ht	= **Y**

Pick **P1** to select a surface
Move the arrow to **P2** and click the mouse to indicate the area to be retained.
Select **Single** then pick at **P3** to select the surface curve
Select **Done → Do it** to trim the surface

The trimmed surface should appear as in Figure 13.25.

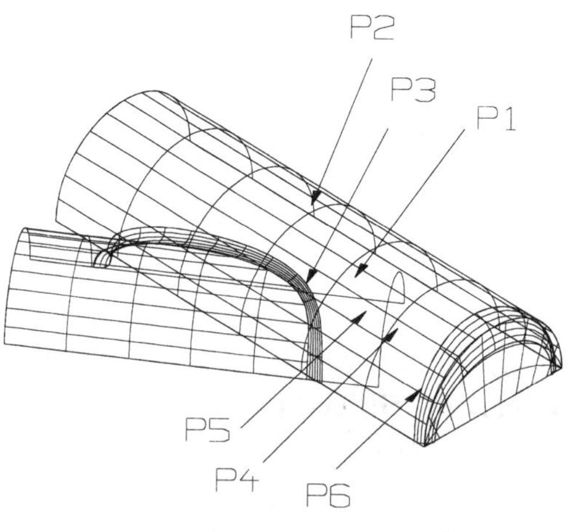

Figure 13.25

Step 4. Trim the larger ruled surface to two surface curves.

Use the pick points labeled in Figure 13.25 Change Level to 3 and Color to 14.
Select **Level → Main level**, then enter **3 ←**
Select **Color** then enter **14 ←**
Pick at **P1** to Select a surface
Move the arrow to **P2** and click the mouse to select the retained region.
Select **Single** then pick at **P3** to select the surface curve
Select **Done → Do it** to trim the surface

Pick at **P4** to select the same surface to be trimmed
Move the arrow to **P5** and click the mouse to indicate the kept area
Pick at **P6** to select the surface curve
Select **Done → Do it** to trim the end of the surface

The newly trimmed surface should look like Figure 13.26.

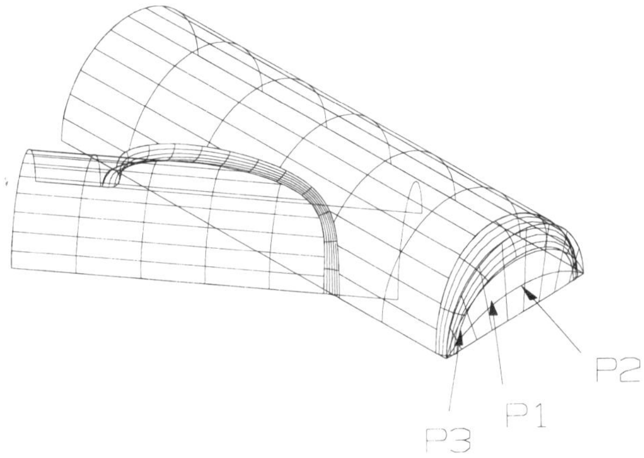

Figure 13.26

Step 5. Trim the ruled surface at the end face using the pick points in Figure 13.26.

Change the level to 4 and the color to 15.
Select **Level → Main level** then enter **4 ←**
Select **Color** and enter the number **15←**
Pick at **P1** to select the surface to be trimmed
Move the arrow to **P2** and click the mouse to select the area to be retained
Select **Single** then pick at **P3**

Select **Done →Do it** to trim the surface
The drawing now resembles Figure 13.27

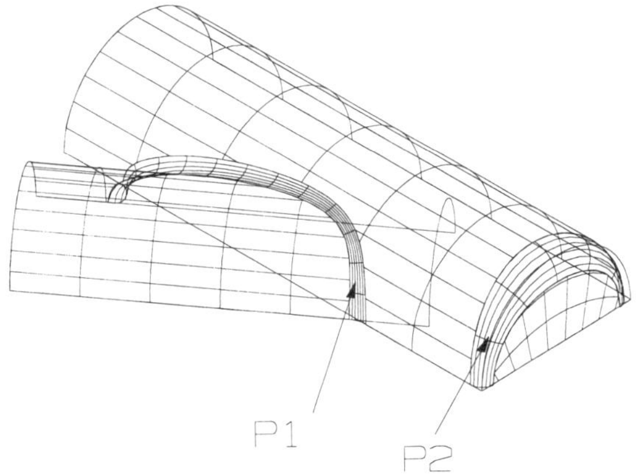

Figure 13.27

Step 6. Change two fillet surfaces to level 5 using the pick points in Figure 13.27.

Finally, make the surfaces visible.
Select **Level → Main level** then enter **5 ←**
Select **MAIN MENU → Screen → Chg leVels → Entity**
Pick at **P1** and **P2** to select the two fillet surfaces
Select **Level → Vis. levels** then toggle **Level 1** to invisible (dimmed).
Select **OK** to return back to graphic mode.
The trimmed surfaces should resemble Figure 13.28

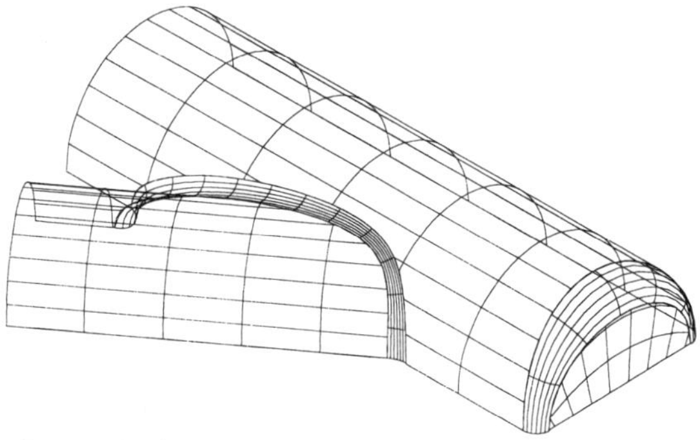

Figure 13.28

Step 7. Save the trimmed surfaces (trims2).

Select **MAIN MENU → File → Save**
Enter the file name: **trims2**

Project 5.

5

Wireframe Model
Project 4 of Chapter 11 (loft 2)

Go to

Surface Model
Project 5 of Chapter 12 (lofts2)

Go to

We are here

Trimmed Surface (trims3)

This project trims a loft surface to a curve which is a circle of 1.5" diameter. Its center is located at (1.6,0). The surface models before and after trimming are shown in Figure 13.29.

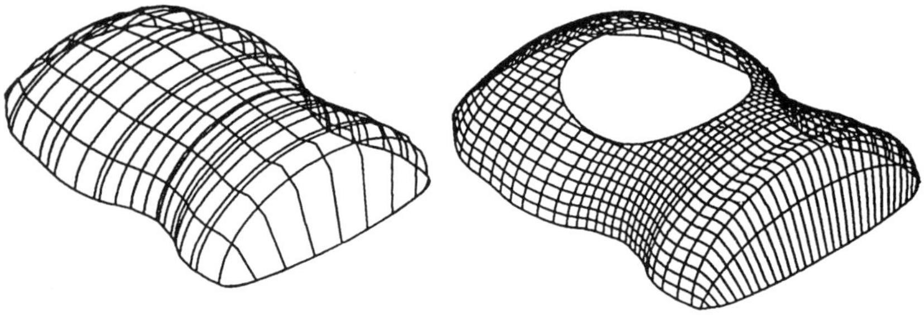

Figure 13.29

Tips 1. Create a circle to be used as the trimming curve. The curve does not necessarily have to be on the surface to be trimmed.
2. Use the trim to curves method.

3. Select the "Project normal to the construction plane" mode. The construction plane should be in the Top Cplane. If project normal to the surface mode is used, the trimmed area will be altered.

Step 1. Load the surface file (lofts2).

Select **MAIN MENU → File → Get**

Enter file name: **lofts2**

Select **Yes** to delete the current part

The loft surface should appear as in Figure 13.30.

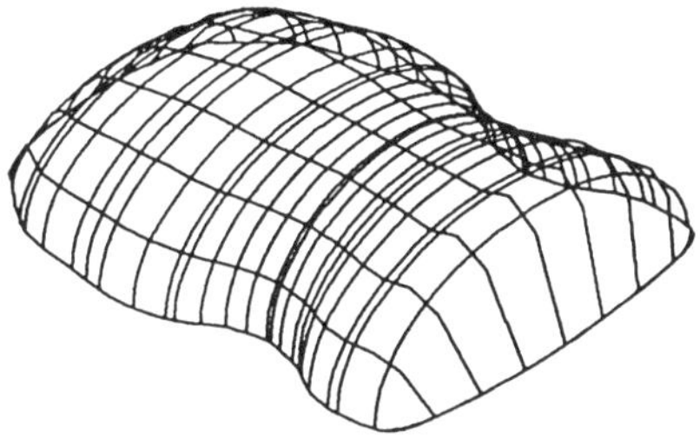

Figure 13.30

Step 2. Create a circle using Top Cplane. The circle center is located at (1.6,0). Its radius is 0.75-in. Put the circle in level 2.

Select **Level**, toggle the **Main level** button, then enter **2** ←

Select **Color** then enter **14**←

Select **Cplane → Top** if necessary

Select **Z** then enter **2.5** ←

Select **MAIN MENU → Create → Arc → pt Rad Cir**

Enter the center point: **1.6,0** ←

Enter the radius: **0.75** ←

The circle is added to the drawing as shown in Figure 13.31.

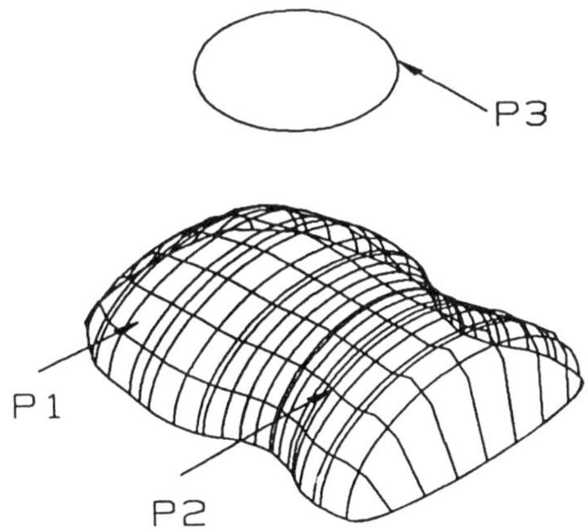

Figure 13.31

Step 3. Initiate the trim surface module.

Select **Level** then enter **3** ←

Select **MAIN MENU → Create → sUrface → Trimmed → to Curves**

Step 4. Set the parameters to following settings.

Constr Vw	= **Y**
Dispose	= **D**
Step Vals:	
Stepping distance	= **0.05**
Use ch Ht	= **N**

Step 5. Select the surface to be trimmed using the pick points in Figure 13.31 on the previous page.

Pick at **P1** to select a surface
Move arrow to **P2** to indicate the area you want to keep, then click the mouse
Select **Single** from the menu
Pick at **P3** to select the curve to trim to
Select **Done** → **Do it**

The trimmed surface should appear as Figure 13.32.

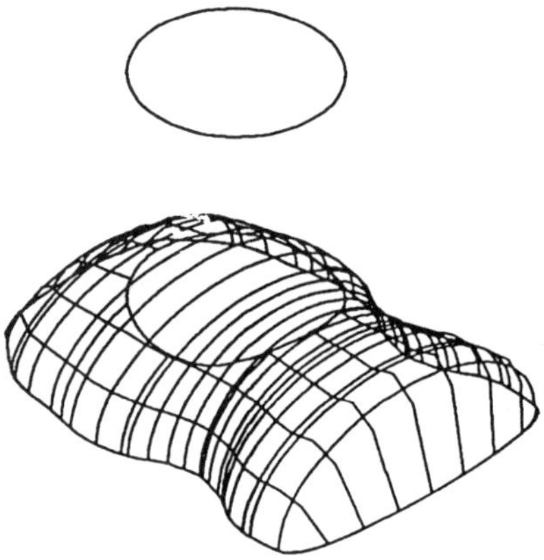

Figure 13.32

Step 6. Make levels 1 and 2 invisible.

Select **Level** → **Vis. levels**
Toggle levels 1 and 2 to invisible (dimmed)
Select **OK** to return back to graphic mode
The trimmed surface is displayed as in Figure 13.33.

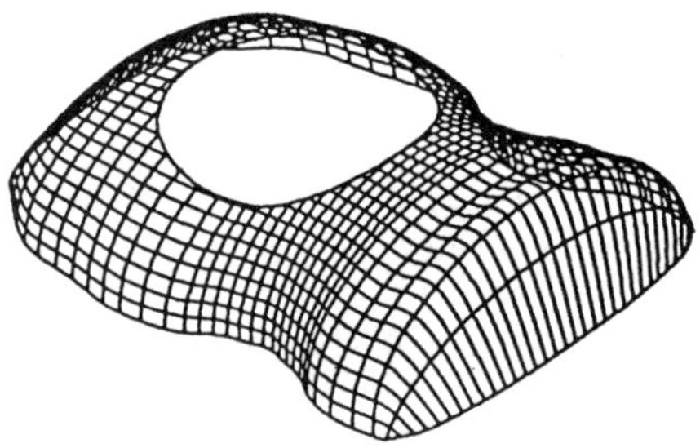

Figure 13.33

Step 7. Save the trimmed surface.

Select **MAIN MENU** → **File** → **Save**
Enter file name: **trims3**

13.1.3 Offset Surface Modeling

This technique creates a surface that is offset to a distance from an existing surface in the normal direction (Figure 13.34). It requires two inputs: an existing surface and an offset distance. The offset distance value can be either positive or negative. A positive offset distance value will offset the surface to the surface normal direction, while a negative value will offset to the opposite of the surface normal direction (Figure 13.35).

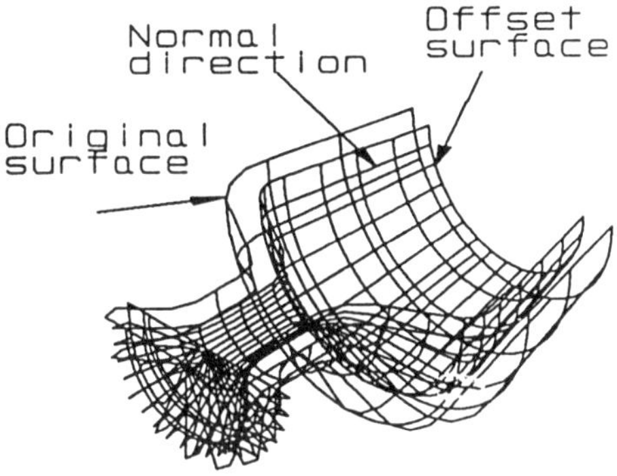

Figure 13.34

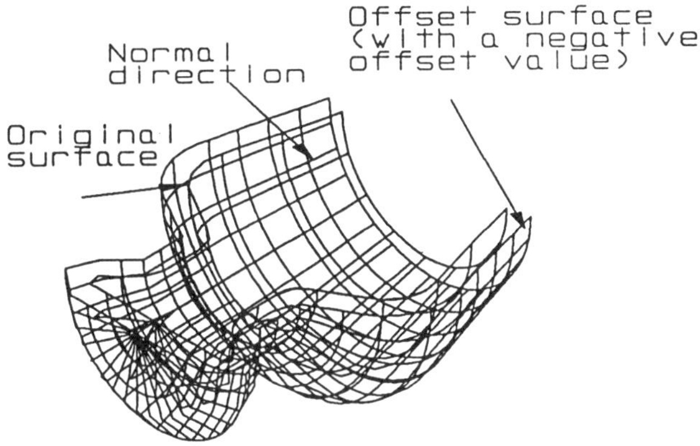

Figure 13.35

Tips 1. The trimmed surfaces can not be used to produce an offset surface. Only original surfaces can be used.

2. The surface normal direction and the sign of offset value determine the offset direction. You can use **Modify → Normal** command to change the surface normal direction if necessary.

Project 6.

6

Creating two offset surfaces

Create two offset surfaces from the two ruled surfaces generated in project 1 of chapter 12. Both ruled surfaces are offset by 0.5-in. in the outward direction. The offset surfaces are shown in Figure 13.36.

Wireframe Model
Project 1 of Chapter 11 (Ruled1)

Go to

Surface Model
Project 1 of Chapter 12 (ruleds1)

Go to

We are here

Trimmed Surface
(trims1)

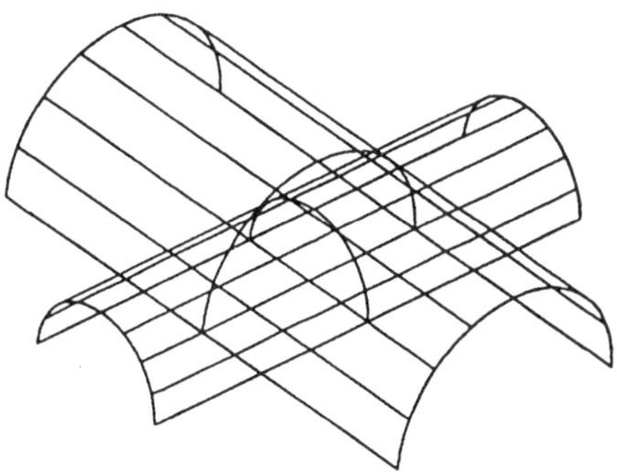

Figure 13.36a. Before offsetting

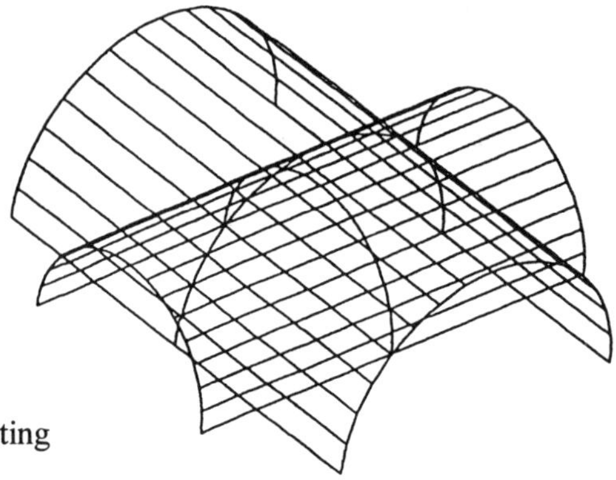

Figure13.36b. After offsetting

Step 1. Load the existing surface model file (ruleds1).

Select **MAIN MENU → File → Get**
Enter file name: **ruleds1**

The two ruled surfaces should appear on screen as Figure 13.37.

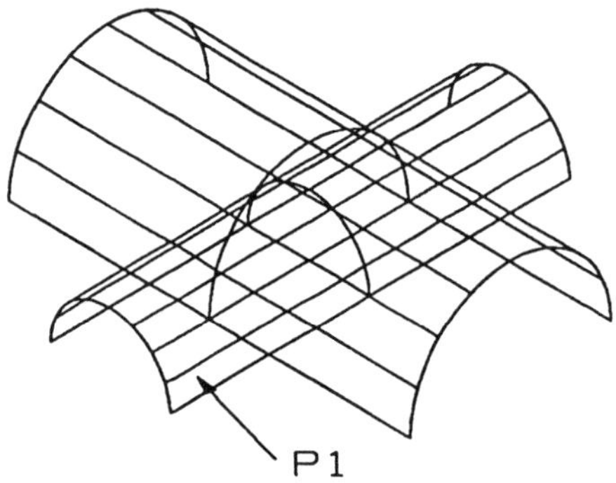

Figure 13.37

Step 2. Create the first offset surface using the pick point in Figure 13.37.

Change level to 2 and color to 12.
Select **Level → Main Level** then enter **2** ←
Select **Color** then enter **12** ←
Select **MAIN MENU → Create → sUrface → Offset**
Enter the offset distance: **0.5** ←
Select a surface: pick at **P1**

The first offset surface is added as shown in Figure 13.38.

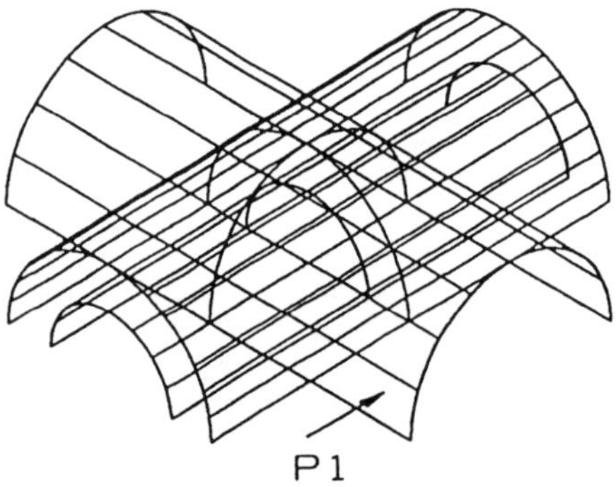

Figure 13.38

Step 3. Create the second offset surface using the pick point in Figure 13.38.

Select a surface: pick at **P1** to select the second surface

The drawing becomes Figure 13.39.

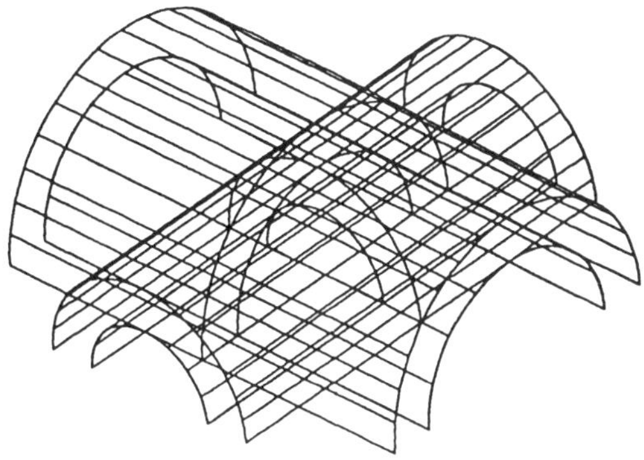

Figure 13.39

Step 4. Make level 1 invisible.

Select **Level → Vis. levels**
Toggle button 1
Select **OK** to return to graphic mode

The two offset surfaces should look like Figure 13.40.

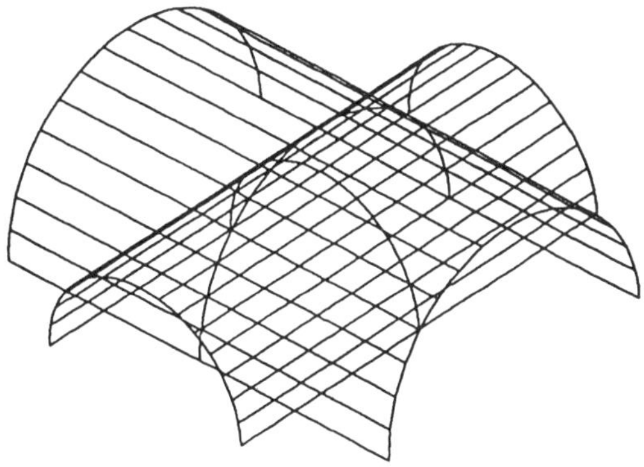

Figure 13.40

Step 5. Save the offset surface file (offsets).

Select **MAIN MENU → File → Save**
Enter file name: **offsets**

Tom 206

13.1.4 Blend Surface Modeling

Blend surface modeling is a new feature in version 5 that allows us to create a surface that smoothly joins two existing surfaces and is tangent to each parent surface. Figure 13.41 shows an example of adding a surface to join two intersected ruled surfaces. The two parent ruled surfaces are trimmed to the blending boundaries.

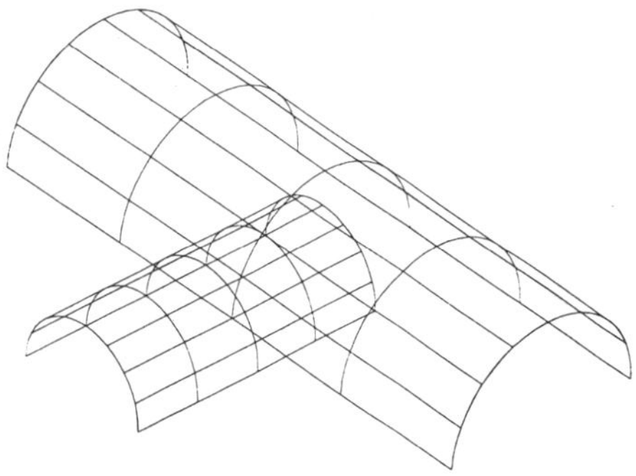

Figure 13.41a. Before blending and trimming

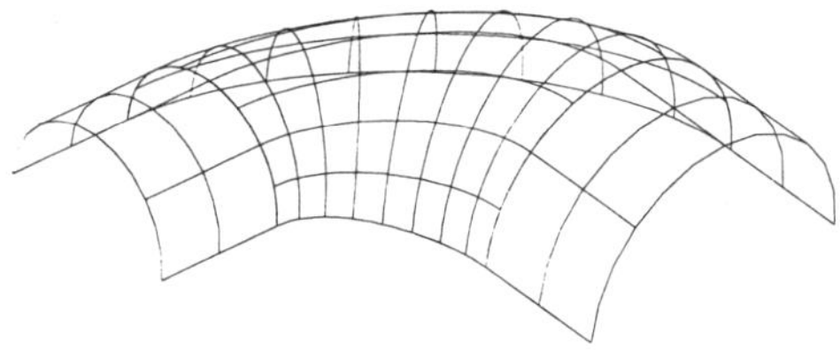

Figure 13.41b. After blending and trimming

To Create Blend Surfaces, use these commands:

MAIN MENU → Create → sUrface → Blend

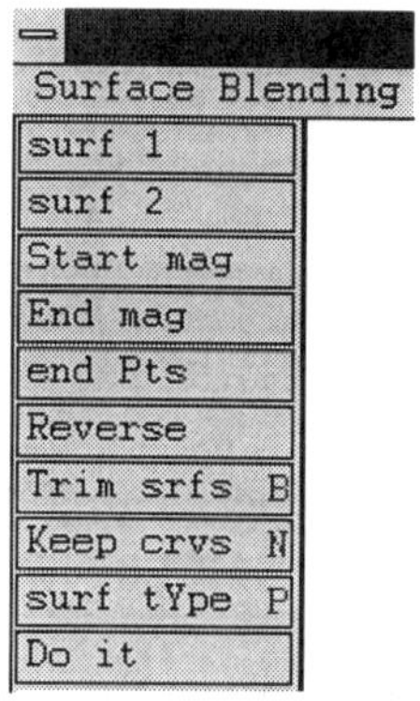

The surface blending parameters are shown here ☞.

Surf 1:	The first picked surface to be blended onto
Surf 2:	The second picked surface to be blended onto
Start mag:	Start blending magnitude on Surf 1 and Surf 2
End mag:	End blending magnitude on Surf 1 and Surf 2
end pts:	Indicate an end of one of blend location splines
Reverse:	Manually reverse the blending curve directing
Trim srfs:	Select the surface(s) to be trimmed to blending boundaries.
Keep crvs:	Select the blending curve(s) to be kept
surf tYpe:	Specify the blending surface to be created being parametric or Nurbs type.

Tips 1. Theoretically, it requires two parent surfaces to create a blend surface. However, a single surface can be used to create a blend surface. This is done by carefully picking the surface twice and selecting the position to start blending. Figure 13.42 on the next page shows a blend surface created from a single ruled surface.

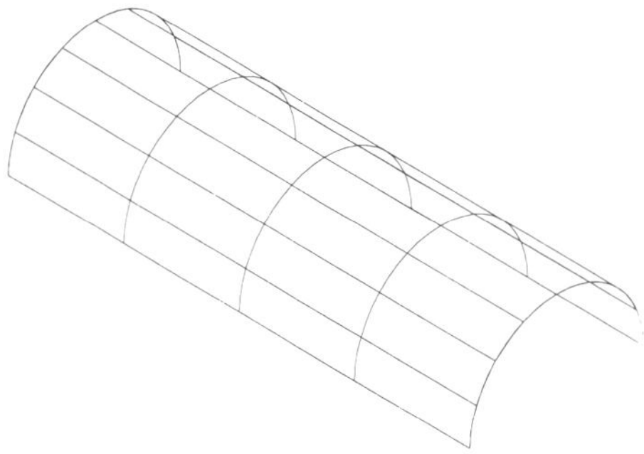

Figure 13.42a Ruled surface before blending

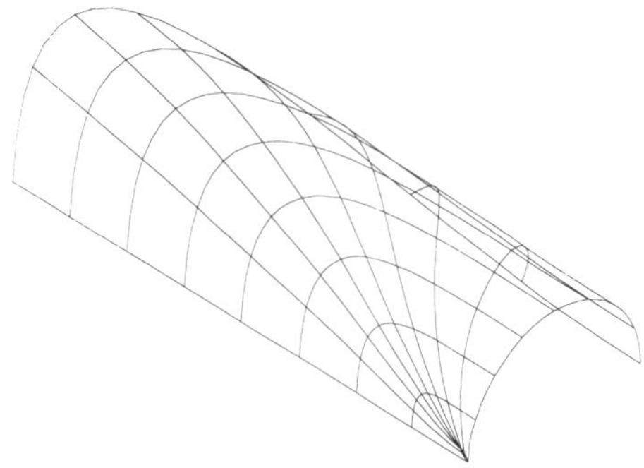

Figure 13.42b. Blend surface

2. The position you pick to blend onto determines where the blend surface will be started. It also determines the size of the blend surface. Figures 13.43 and 13.44 illustrate the effect of picked positions on the blended surface.

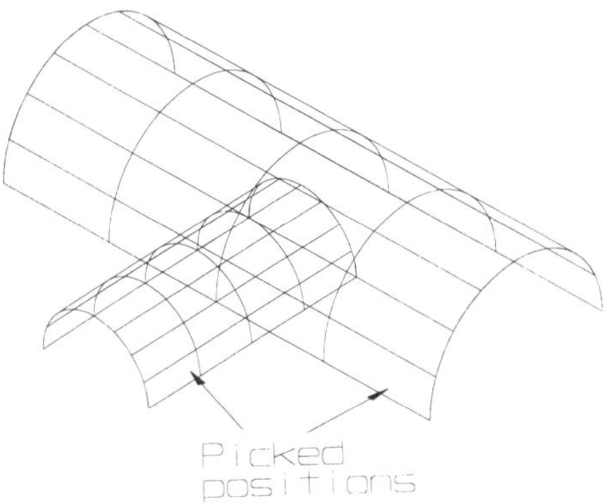

Figures 13.43a Picked positions

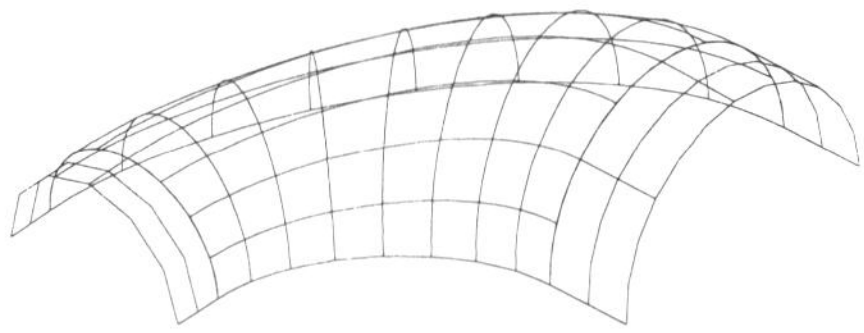

Figure 13.43b Blend surface

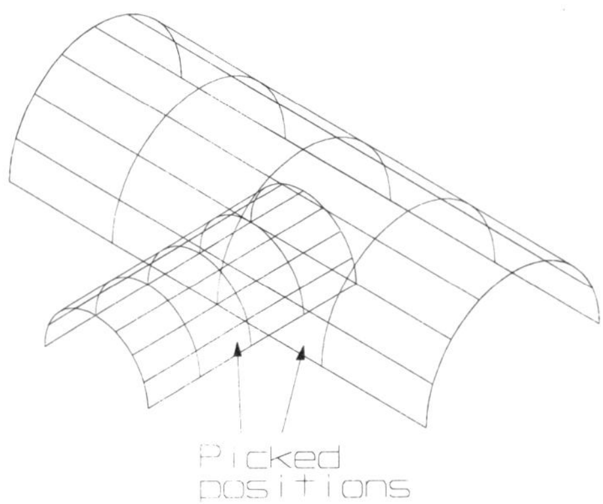

Figures 13.44a Picked positions

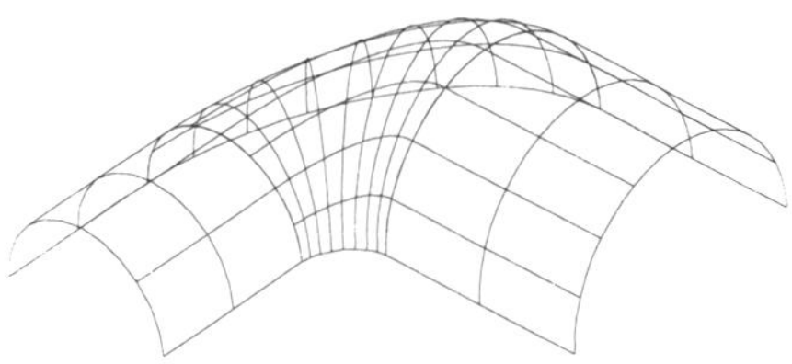

Figure 13.44b Blend surface

3. The spline direction determines the orientation of the blend surface. The spline direction can be toggled to the along or across direction. The blend surface is normal (perpendicular) to the spline direction. Table 13.3 on the following page illustrates the effect of spline direction on blend surfaces.

Table 13.3 Effects of spline direction on blend surface

Surf 1	Surf 2	Spline Direction	Resulted Blend Surface
Across	Across	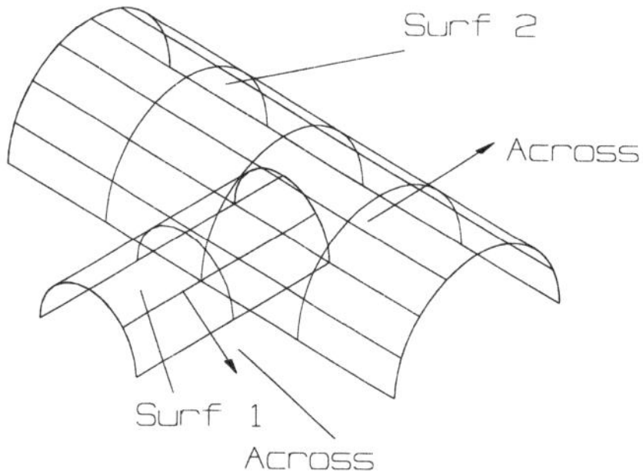	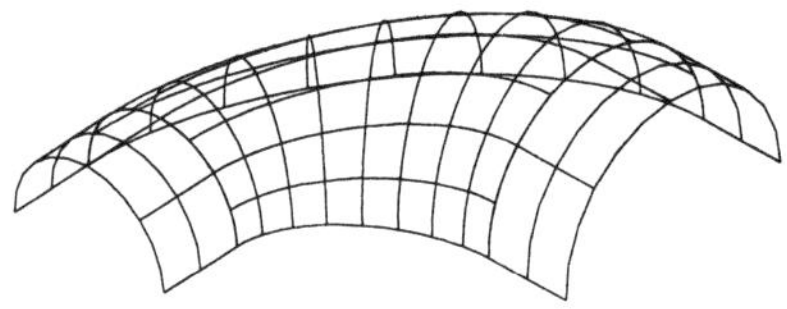
Across	Along	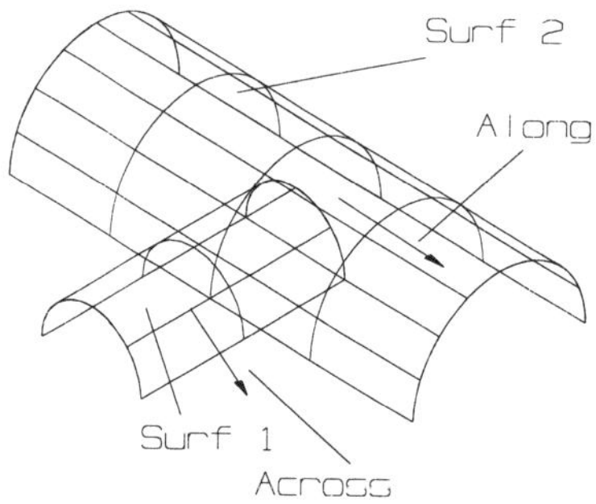	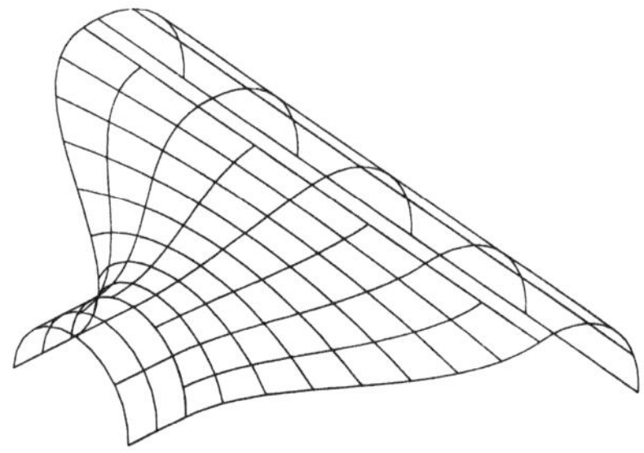
Along	Along	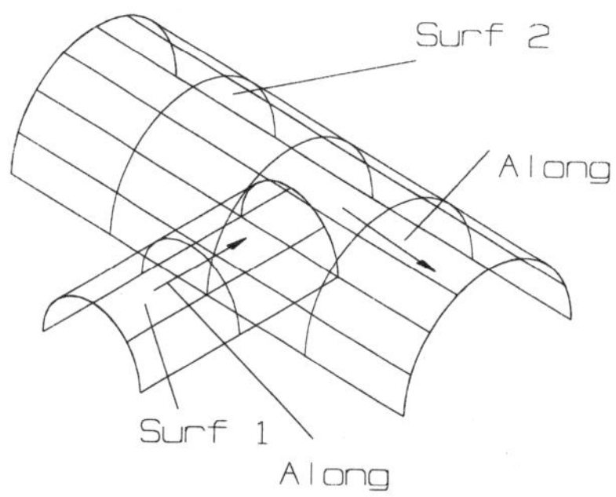	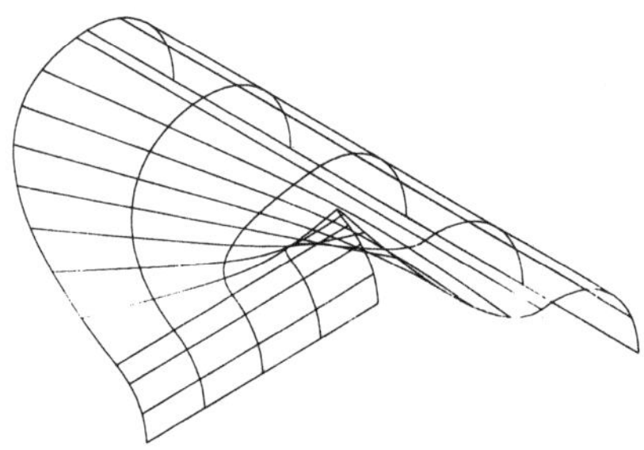

4. Blending magnitude values

There are two blending magnitude parameters for each surface to define the blend surface shape: **Start blending magnitude** and **end blending magnitude**. The blending magnitude value can be regarded as the order of the curve that determines the skin form of the surface.

Magnitude Value	Surface Order
0	a plane (1st order)
1	1st order
2	2nd order
3	3rd order

Figure 13.45 shows how the magnitude value affects the blend surface.

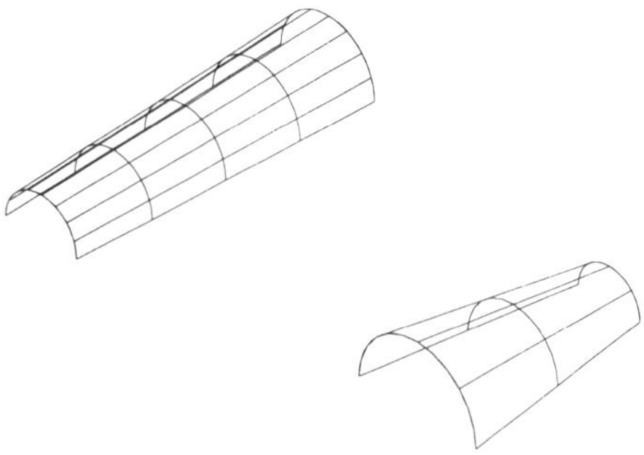

Figure 13.45a

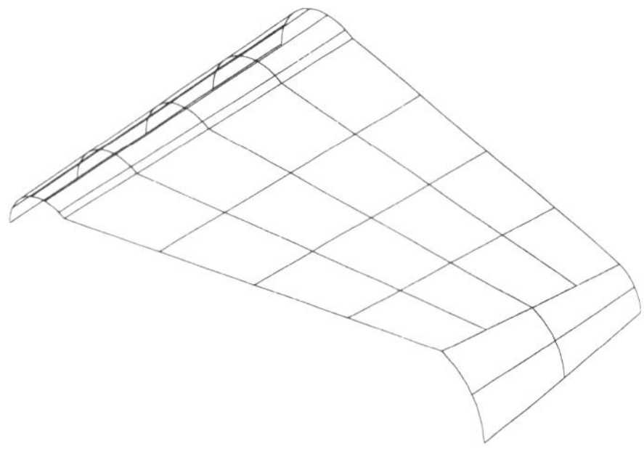

Figure 13.45b Start and End magnitudes are 0

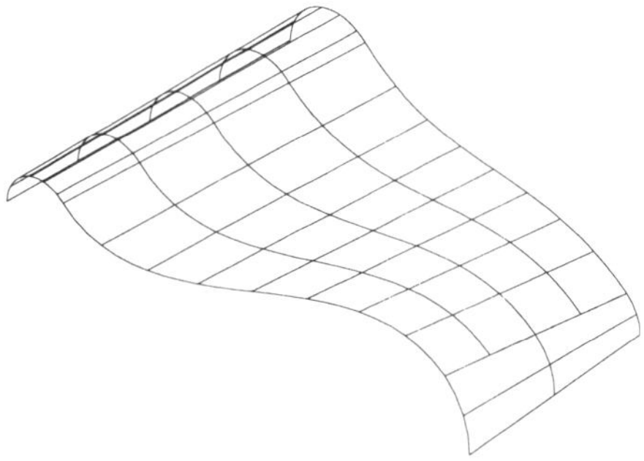

Figure 13.45c Start and End magnitudes are 1

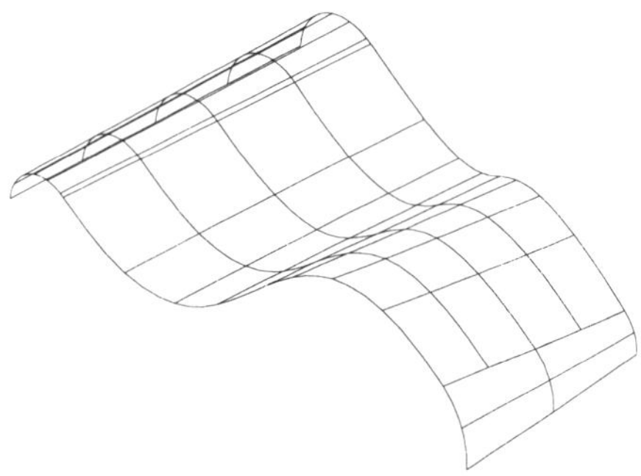

Figure 13.45d Start and End magnitudes are 2

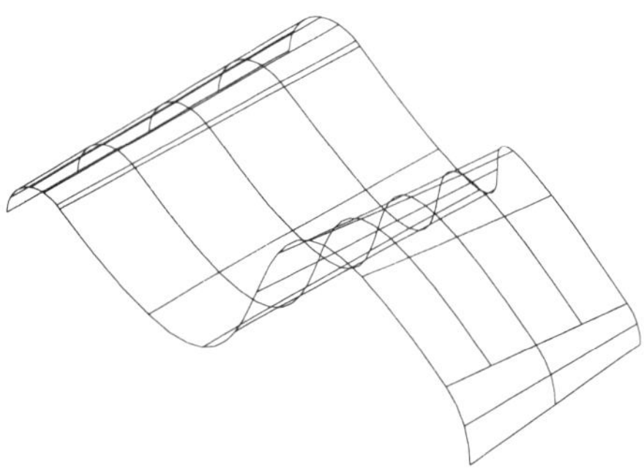

Figrure 13.45e Start and End magnitudes are 3

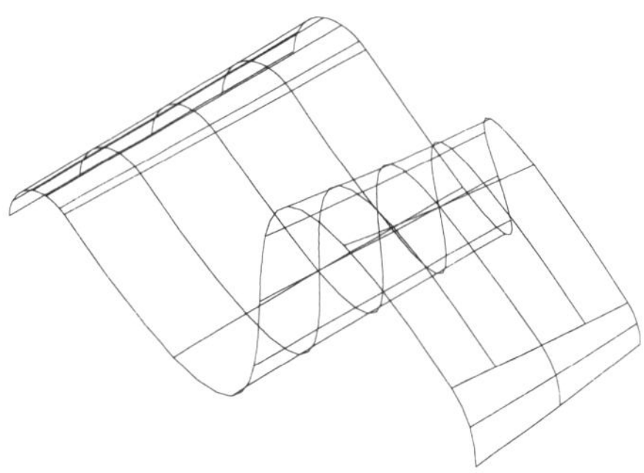

Figure 13.45f Start and End magnitudes are 4

It is possible to have **different values** for start and end magnitude as shown in Figure 13.46. The blend surface in Figure 13.46a has a value of 2 for start magnitude and 1 for end magnitude in both parent surfaces. In Figure 13.46b the start magnitude for surf 1 is 3 and the remaining three magnitudes are 1.

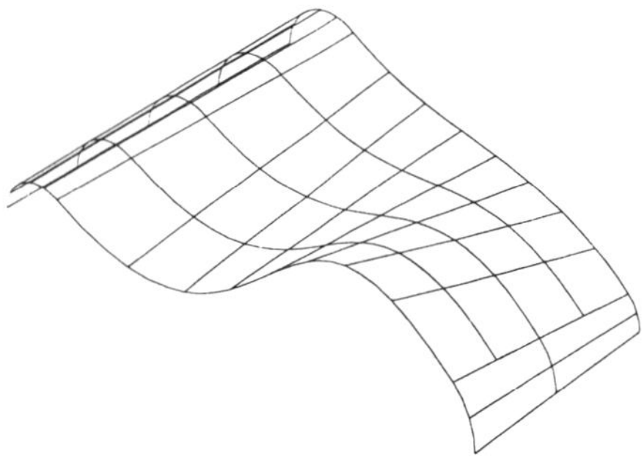

Figure 13.46a

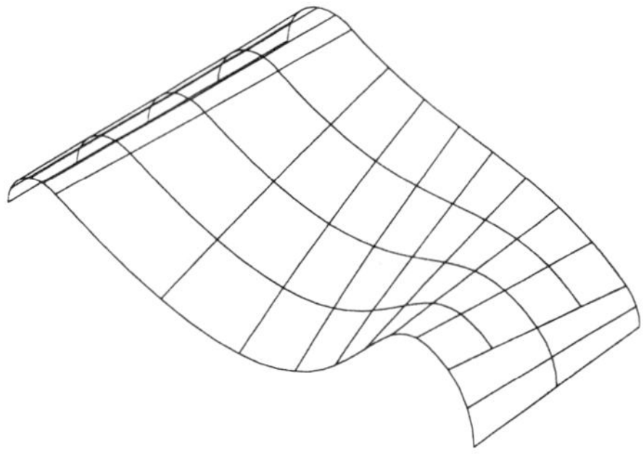

Figure 13.46b

5. The selection of surface and the kept section

Case 1: Spline orientation is in a cross direction for both surfaces. The direction of the blend surface and the kept section of the two parent surfaces are decided by the relationship between the two picked points located on two surfaces. The blending directions on the two parent surfaces are always opposed to each other (Figure 13.47a & a', b & b').

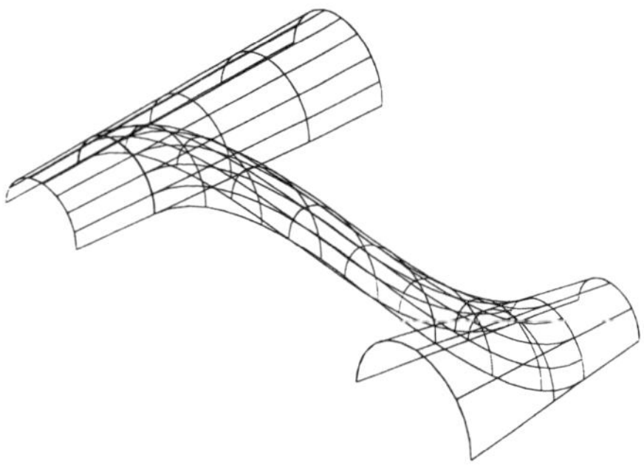

Figure 13.47a

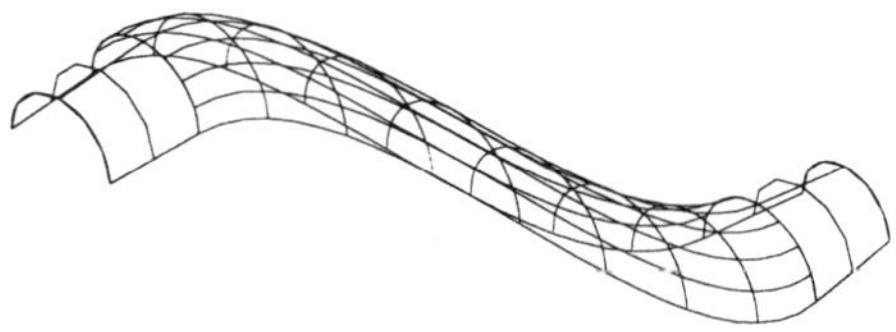

Figure 13.47a'

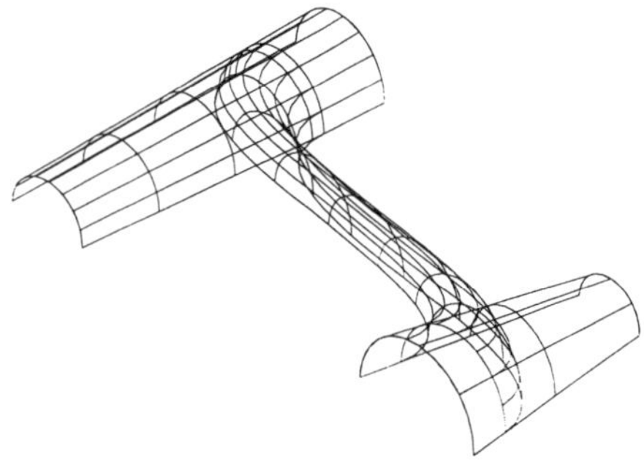

Figure 13.47b

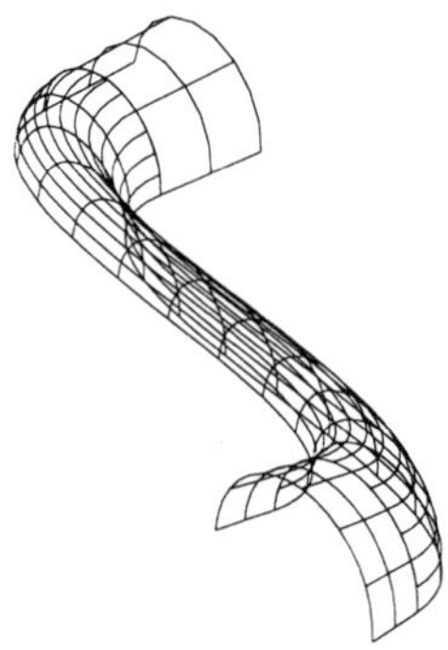

Figure 13.47b'

If the trim parameter is set for one surface or both surfaces, the kept section is the one opposite to the blend surface direction.

Case 2: Spline orientation of one surface is in along and the other in across.

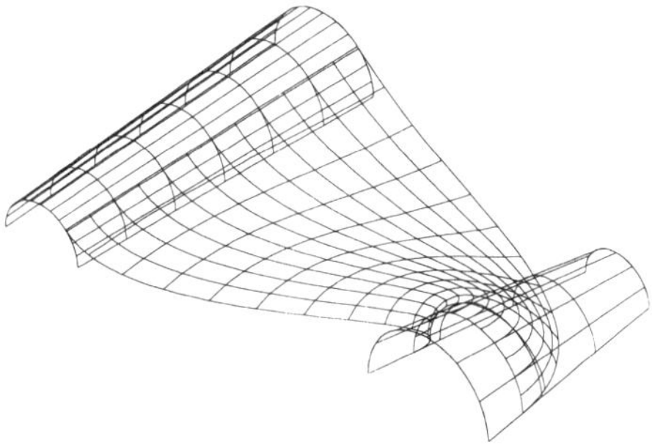

Figure 13.48a

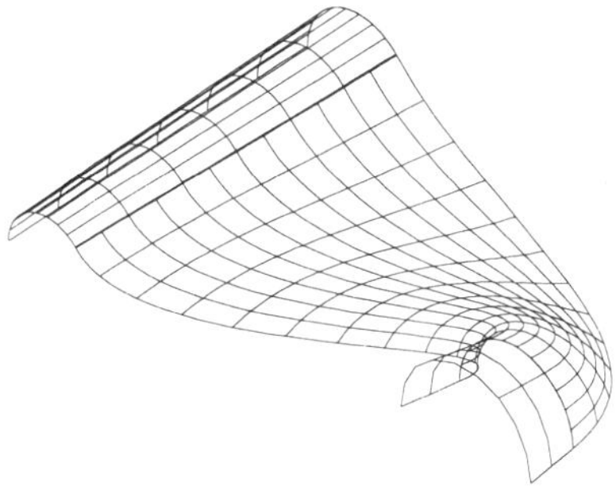

Figure 13.48a'

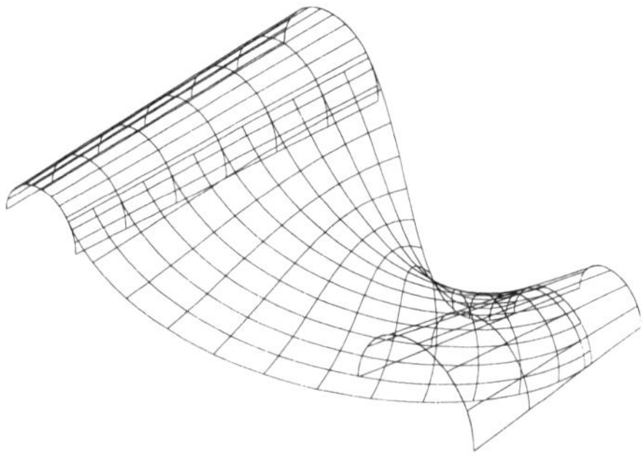

Figure 13.48b

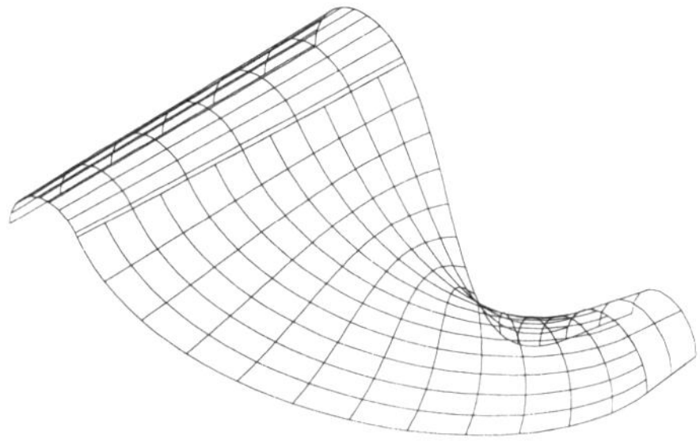

Figure 13.48b'

Case 3: Spline orientation in the along direction for both surfaces

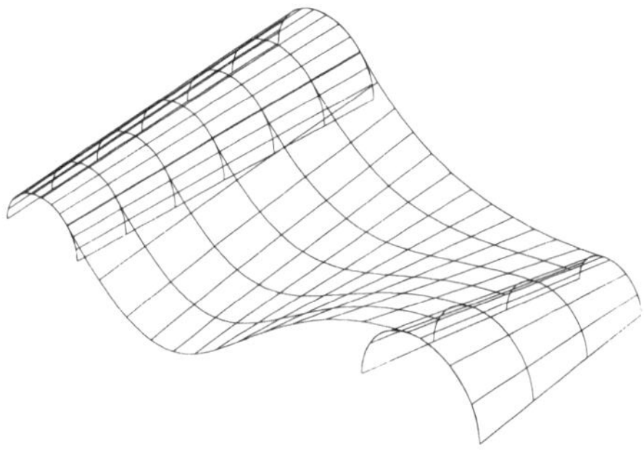

Figure 13.49a

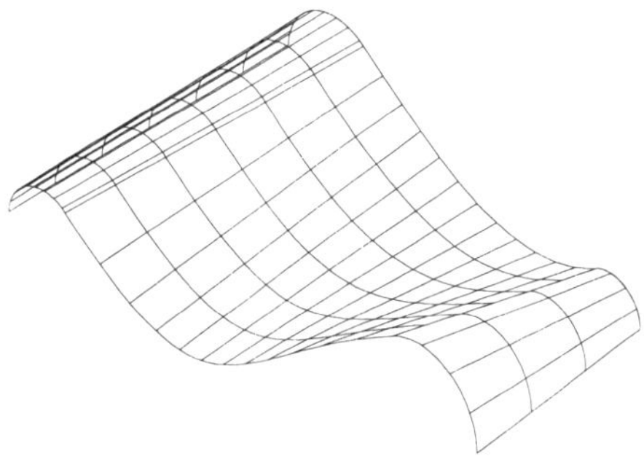

Figure 13.49b

6. Use the **Reverse function** to change the mating ends of the blend surface on the two parent surfaces.

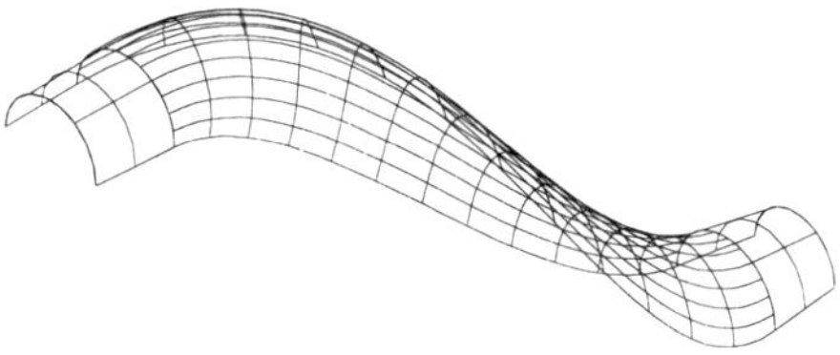

Figure 13.50a Before reverse

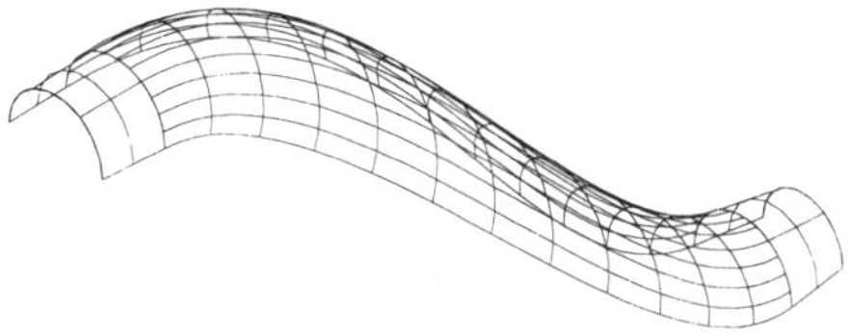

Figure 13.50a' after reverse

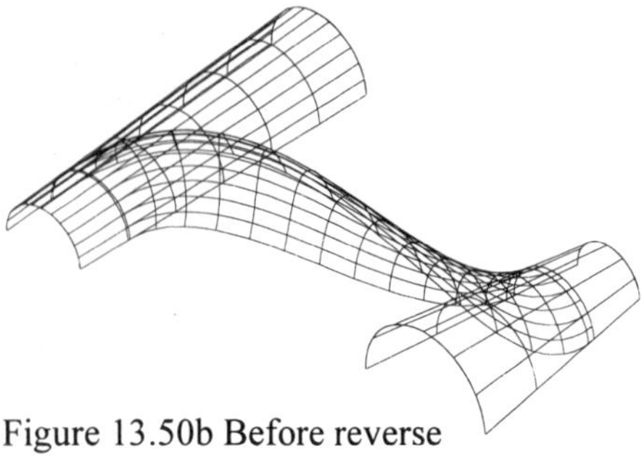

Figure 13.50b Before reverse

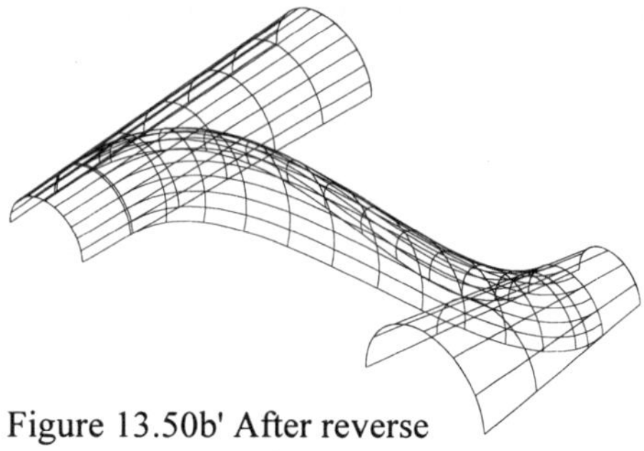

Figure 13.50b' After reverse

Project 7. Blend surfaces between two intersected surfaces

Create three blend surfaces based on the two intersected ruled surfaces generated in project 2 of chapter 12.

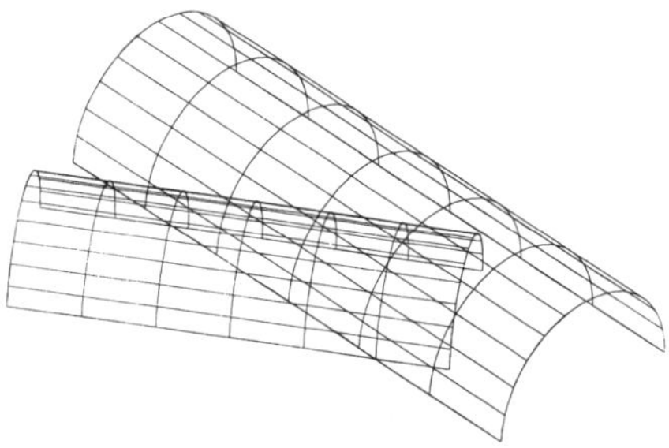

Figure 13.51a

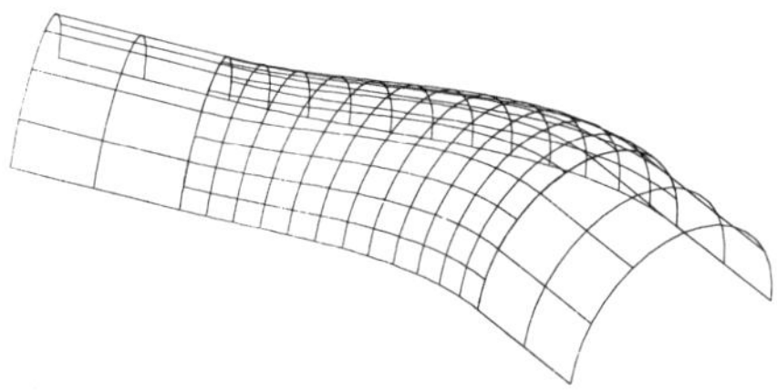

Figure 13.51b

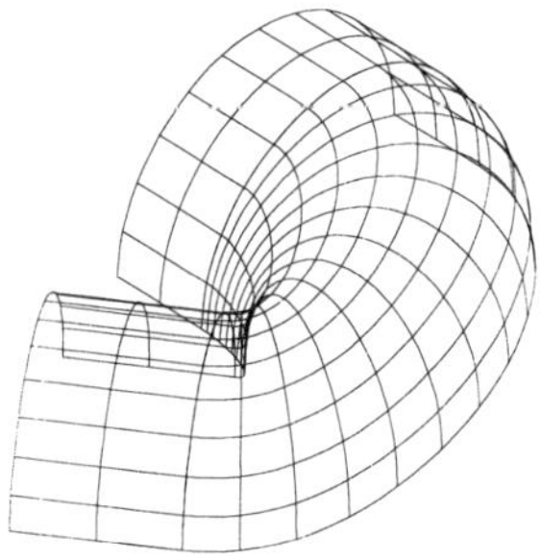

Figure 13.51c

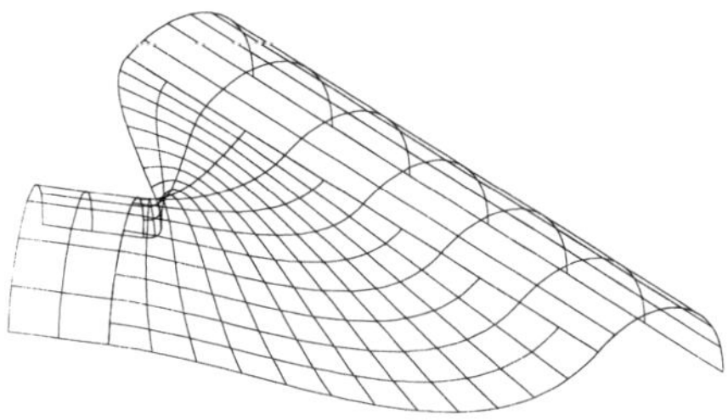

Figure 13.51d

Tips 1. The spline orientation of both parent surfaces should be set to the *across* direction for the first blend surface (Figure 13.51b) and second blend surface (Figure 13.51c). The third blend surface (Figure 13.51d) has the *along* direction in the main surface and the *across* direction in the other surface.

2. Set all blending magnitude values to 1.

3. Set the Trim srfs parameter to B (both) to trim both parent surfaces to the spline curves.

4. Set surf type parameter to N (nurbs).

Case 1.

Step1. Load the surface file ruleds 2 and set level to 2

Select **MAIN MENU** → **File** → **Get**
File name: **ruleds2**
Select **Yes** to delete the current part if necessary.
Select **Level** → **Main level**, then enter 2
The two ruled surfaces should appear as Figure 13.52.

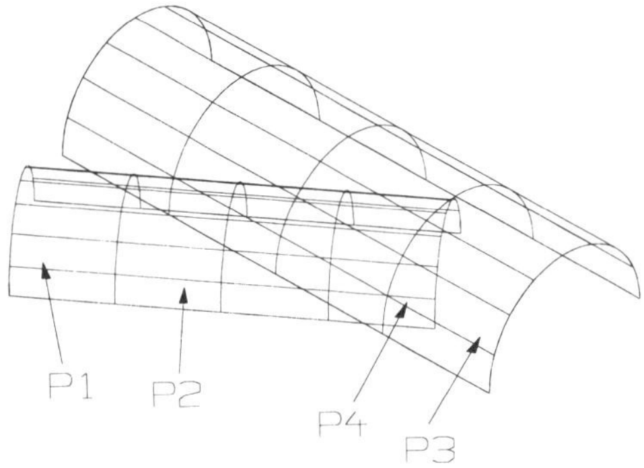

Figure 13.52

Step 2. Initiate the blend surface function. Set the start and end magnitude values.

Select **MAIN MENU** → **Create** → **sUrface** → **Blend** → **Start mag**
Enter Start Blending magnitude on Surf 1: **1**
Enter Start Blending magnitude on Surf 2: **1**
Select **End mag**
Enter End Blending magnitude on Surf 1: **1**
Enter End Blending magnitude on Surf 2: **1**
Note: Actually the default value for all four blending magnitude is 1.

Step 3. Use the pick points in Figure 13.52.

Pick at **P1** to select a surface to blend onto
Move the arrow to **P2** and click the mouse to indicate the position of the spline curve
An arrow should appear to indicate the default spline orientation (in the across direction)
Select **OK** to accept the across direction
Pick at **P3** to select the other Surface to blend onto
Move arrow to **P4** and click the mouse to select the position of the spline curve
Select **OK** to accept the default spline orientation in the across direction
The blend surface mesh should appear as in Figure 13.53.

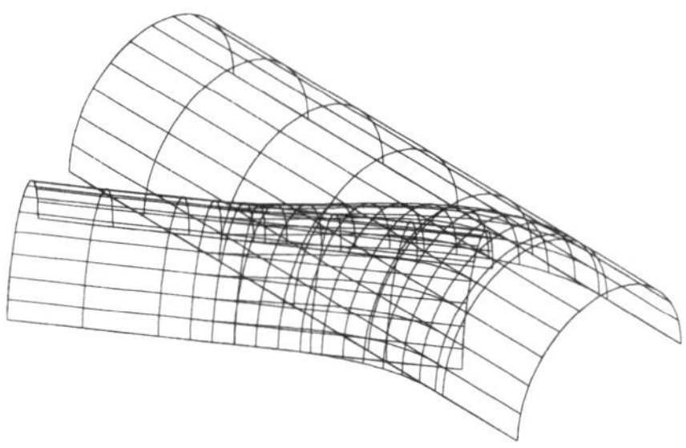

Figure 13.53

Surf Blending parameters.

Step 4. Def nding parameters as below.

Set

Trim srfs	= **B**
Keep crVs	= **N**
Surf tYpe	= **N**

Select **Do it**
The blend surface should appear as Figure 13.54

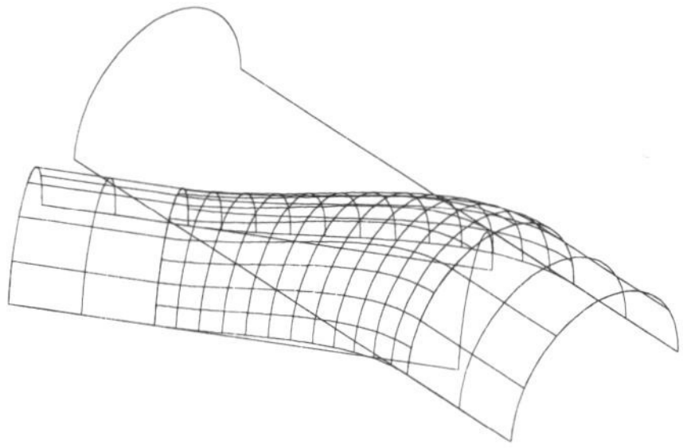

Figure 13.54

Step 5. Make level 1 to invisible.

Select **Level → Vis. levels**
Toggle **level 1** button to invisible (dimmed)
Select **OK** to return back to graphic mode
The blend surface with two kept surface sections of parent surfaces are shown in Figure 13.55

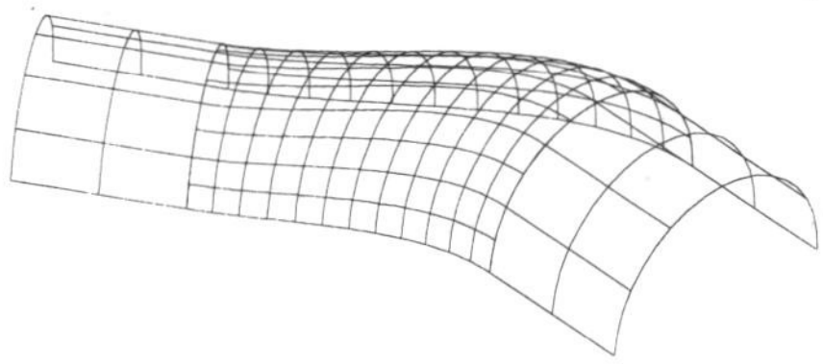

Figure 13.55

Step 6. Save the surface as blends1.

Select **MAIN MENU → File → Save**
Enter file name : **blends1**

<u>**Case 2:**</u>

Step 1. Load the surface file ruleds2.

Select **Get**←
Enter file name: **ruleds2**←
Select **Yes** to delete the current part

The surface model appears as Figure 13.56

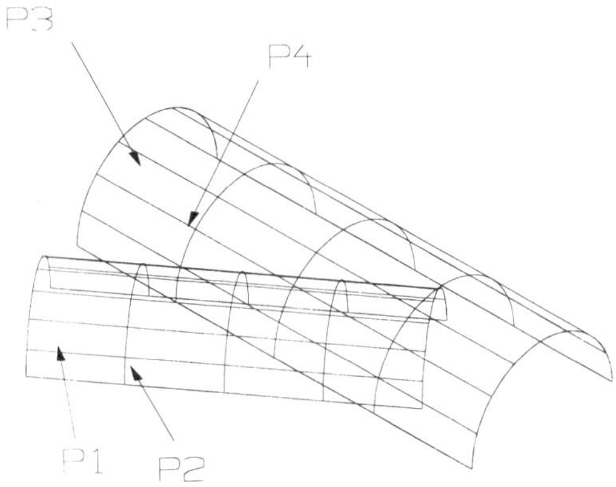

Figure 13.56

Step 2. Initiate the blend surface function. Use the pick points in Figure 13.56.

Select **MAIN MENU** → **Create** → **sUrface** → **Blend**
Pick at **P1** to select a surface to blend onto
Move arrow to **P2** and click the mouse to indicate the spline location
Select **OK** to accept the default spline direction (across)
Pick at **P3** to select another surface
Move arrow to **P4** and click the mouse to decide the spline location
Select **OK** to accept the default across spline direction

Step 3. Define the Surf Blending parameters as below

Trim srfs	= **B**
Keep crvs	= **N**
Surf type	= **N**

Select **Do it**
The blend surface should be added as in Figure 13.57.

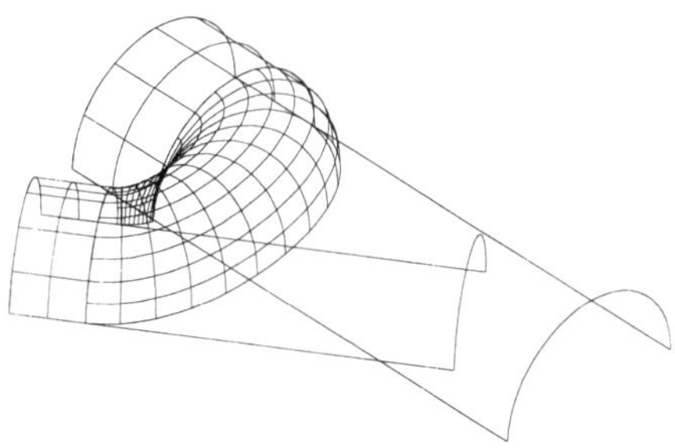

Figure 13.57

Step 4. Make level 1 to invisible.

Select **Level → Vis. levels**
Toggle **level 1** button to invisible (dimmed)
Select **OK** to return to graphic mode.

The final blend surface should appear as in Figure 13.58.

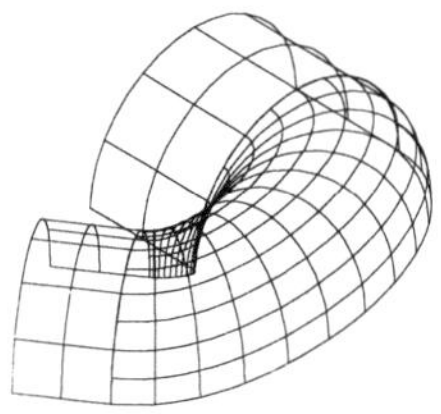

Figure 13.58

Step 5. Save the surface as blends2.

Select **MAIN MENU → File → Save**
File name: **blends2**

__Case 3:__

Step 1. Load the surface file ruleds2.

Select **Get**
Enter file name: **ruleds2**
Select **Yes** to delete the current part

The surface model appears as Figure 13.59

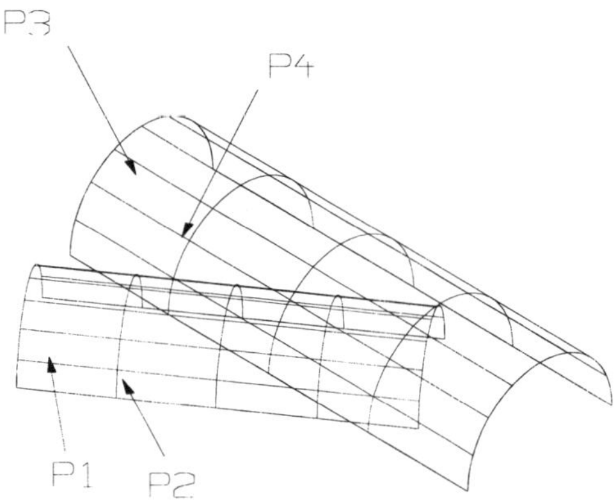

Figure 13.59

Step 2. Initiate the blend surface function and pick surfaces and spline locations.

Use the pick points in Figure 13.59.
Select **MAIN MENU → Create → sUrface → Blend**
Pick at **P1** to select a surface to blend onto
Move arrow to **P2** and click the mouse to determine the spline location
Select **OK** to accept the default spline direction (across)
Pick at **P3** to select another surface
Move the arrow to **P4** and click the mouse to indicate the spline location
Toggle the **Flip** command to change the spline direction to along, then select **OK**

Step 3. Define the Surf Blending parameters as below.

Trim srfs	= **B**
Keep crvs	= **N**
Surf type	= **N**

Select **Do it**

The blend surface is added as in Figure 13.60

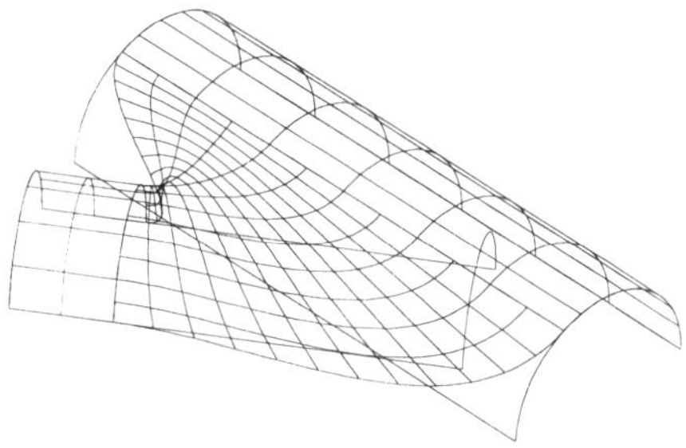

Figure 13.60

Step 4. Make level 1 invisible.

Select **Level → Vis. Levels**, then toggle **level 1** button to invisible (dimmed)
Select **OK** to return to graphic mode
The final surface model should resemble Figure 13.61

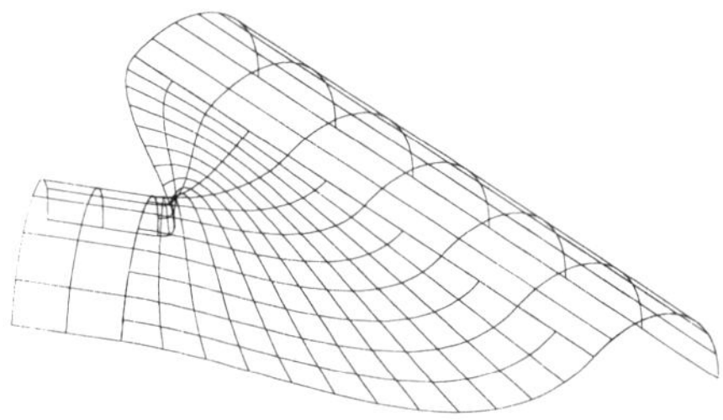

Figure 13.61

Step 5. Save the surface as blends3.

Select **MAIN MENU → File → Save**
Enter file name: **blends3**

13.2. Composite Surfaces Models

Composite surfaces models use more than one surfacing technique to create multiple surfaces in representing an object. In fact, most surface modeling of objects today are of the composite type. Five composite surface models are presented in this section. They are arranged in an increasing order of difficulty. Their wireframe models were presented in chapter 11.

Project 8.

8

Basket surfaces model

The surface model of a basket shown in Figure 13.62 consists of four surfaces: top rim surface, wall surface, bottom flat surface, and fillet surface at the intersection between the wall surface and the bottom flat surface.

Wireframe Model
Project 11 of Chapter 11 (basket)

We are here

Go to
Surface Model
(baskets)

Go to
Toolpath
Project 5 of Chapter 15 (basket)

Go to
Toolpath Trimming
Project 2 of Chapter 16 (trim1)

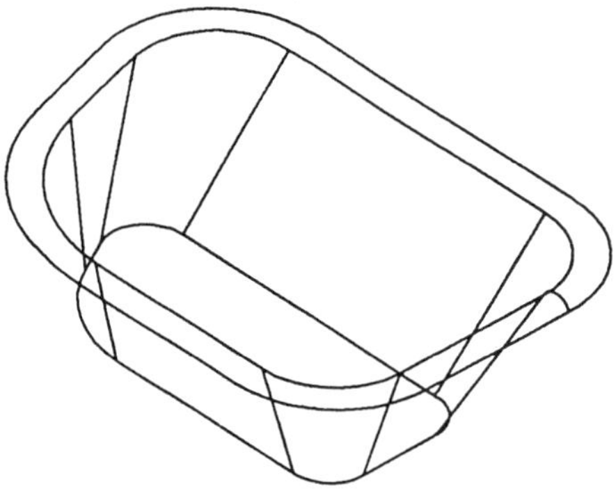

a. Wireframe model

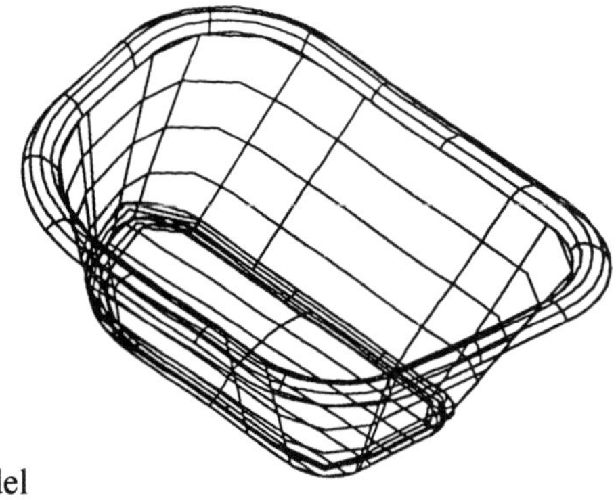

b.Surface model
Figure 13.62

Tips
1. Use two along/one across swept surfacing technique to create the top rim surface. The two along contours are the two outer profiles. The across contour is the arc that encompasses these two profiles.
2. Use the Coons surfacing technique to generate the wall surface. The number of patches in the along direction is 8 and the number of patches in the across direction is 1.
3. The bottom flat surface can be modeled as a ruled surface.
4. The start point of the fillet surface between the wall surface and the bottom flat surface must be placed near the start point of the Coons surface and the ruled surface.
5. Use a different level and color for each surface.

Step 1. Load the wireframe model file (basket).

Select **MAIN MENU → File → Get**
Enter file name: **basket**
Select **Yes** to delete the current part

The wireframe model should appear as Figure 13.63.

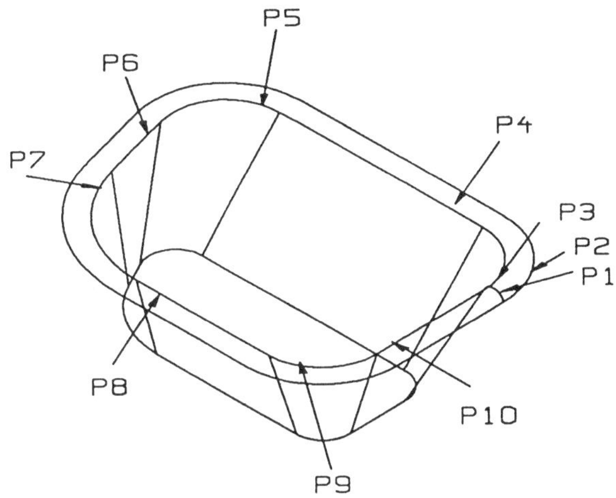

Figure 13.63

Step 2. Create the top rim surface using swept surfacing technique. Use the pick points in Figure 13.63. Change level to 2 and color to 12.

Select **Level → MAIN Level** then enter **2** ←
Select **Color** then enter **12** ←
Select **MAIN MENU → Create → sUrface → Swept → Nurbs**
Enter the number of across contours: **1** ←
define the across contour: select **Single** then pick at **P1**
define along contour 1: select **Chain** then pick at **P2**,
select **Close → End here** to complete along contour 1
define along contour 2: select **Chain** then pick at **P3**,
Select **Close → Select nxt**, then sequentially pick at **P4 - P10**,
then select **End here → Done** to complete the contours selection

Set the Swept surface parameters to the following settings:

Along cut distance = **0.15** Across cut distance = **0.05** Error measurement = **off**

Select **Done** to complete the swept surface

The swept surface appearing on screen should look like Figure 13.64 on the next page.

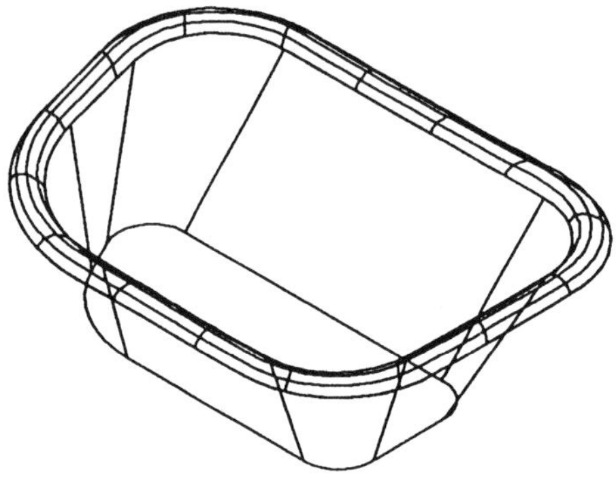

Figure 13.64

Step 3. Make level 2 invisible and change to Top Gview.

Select **Level→ Vis. levels**
Click on button 2 to set invisible (dimmed)
Select **OK → OK** to return the screen back to graphic mode
Select **Gview → Top**

Press Alt + F1, then F2 to fit the drawing, if necessary
The drawing becomes Figure 13.65.

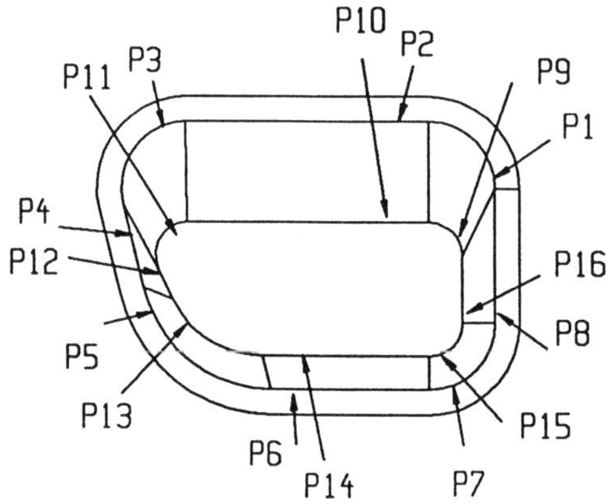

Figure 13.65a

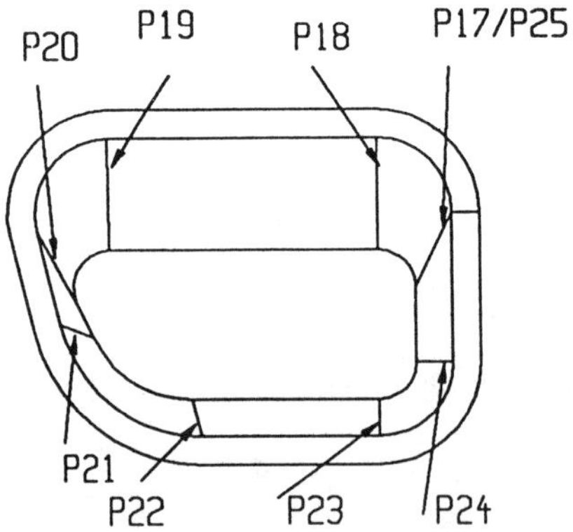

Figure 13.65b

Step 4. Create a Coons surface using the pick points in Figure 13.65 on the previous page.

Use level 3 and color 13.

Select **Level → Main Level** then enter **3** ←
Select **Color** then enter **13** ←
Select **MAIN MENU → Create → sUrface → Coons → Nurbs**
Enter number of patches in the along direction: **8** ←
Enter number of patches in the across direction: **1** ←
define along contour 1 of row 1: sequentially pick at **P1 to P8** to complete the row 1.
Select **Single** in the Chaining method menu before picking at the entities

Sequentially pick at **P9 to P16** to complete the row 2

Sequentially pick at **P17 to P25** to complete the across contour of column 1
Select **Done** to complete the chaining

Set the Coons surface parameters to the following settings:

Along cut distance: **0.15**
Across cut distance: **0.15**
Blending = **Linear**

Select **Done** to complete the Coons surface

The new Coons surface appears in Top Gview as in Figure 13.66.

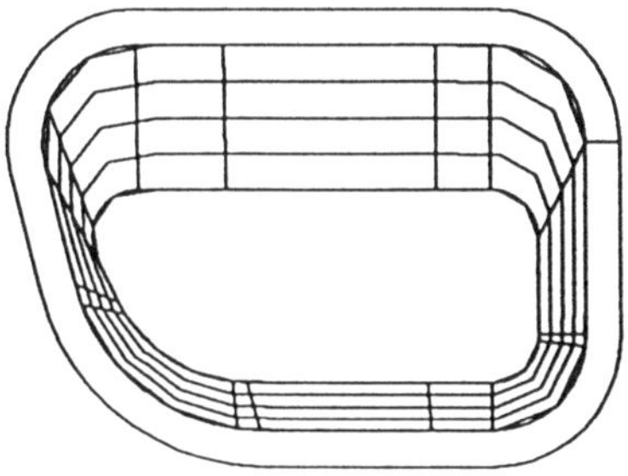

Figure 13.66

Step 5. Make level 3 invisible.

Select **Level → Vis. levels**
Click on button 3 to set invisible (dimmed)
then select **OK → OK** to return back to graphic mode

The drawing now should look like Figure 13.67.

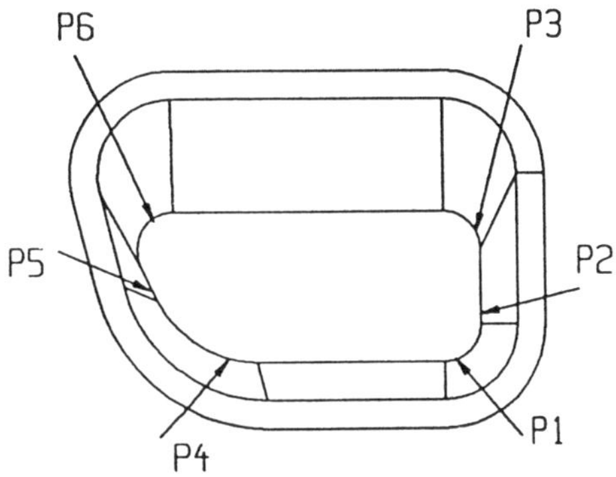

Figure 13.67

Step 6. Create a ruled surface at the bottom using the pick points labeled in Figure 13.67 on the previous page. Change level to 4 and color to 14.

Select **Level → Main Level,** then enter **4 ←**
Select **Color** then enter **14 ←**
Select **MAIN MENU → Create→ sUrface → rUled → Blend**
define contour 1: select **Chain** then pick at **P1**
Select **Close → Select nxt**, then pick at **P2** and **P3**
Select **End here** to complete the contour 1
define contour 2: select **Chain** then pick at **P4**
Select **Close → Select nxt**, then pick at **P5** and **P6**
Select **End here** to complete the contour 2
Select **Done** to complete contour selection

The ruled surface should resemble Figure 13.68

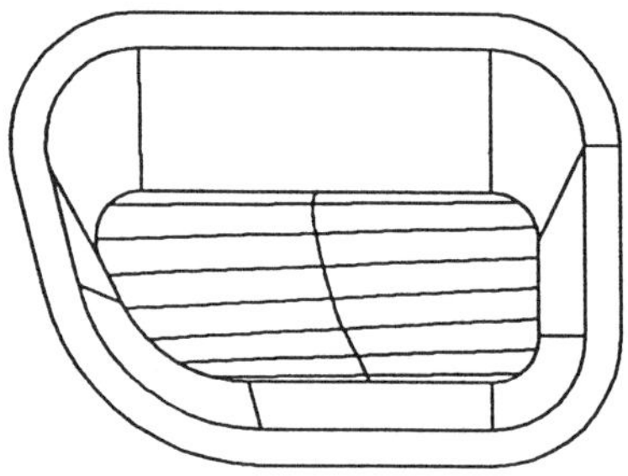

Figure 13.68

Step 7. Toggle level 3 to visible and change the level to 5.

Select **Level → Vis. levels**
Click on button 3 to set visible (highlighted)
Select **Main Level**, the enter **5**

The drawing now should look like Figure 13.69.

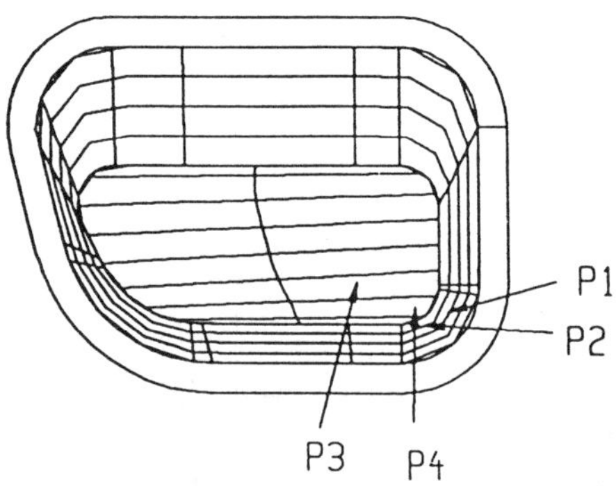

Figure 13.69

Step 8. Create a fillet surface at the intersection between the wall surface and the bottom surface. Use the pick points in Figure 13.69. Change color to 15.

Select **Color** then enter **15** ←
Select **MAIN MENU → Create → sUrface → Fillet → Options→ Constant → Radius**
Enter the fillet radius: **0.25** ←
Set the Surface fillet parameters to the following settings:

Use Ch ht	= **Y**
Step Vals:	
Maximum step distance	= **0.02**
Stopping chord height	= **0.005**
Extend	=**Y**
Splines	=**B**
sUrf crvs	=**B**
Fillet	=**N**
Trim	=**B**

Pick at **P1** to select the wall surface
Move arrow to **P2** and click the mouse to start a fillet
Pick at **P3** to select the bottom surface
Move arrow to **P4** and click the mouse (The position you pick indicates the kept portion of the surface after trimming.)
Select **Do it** to complete the fillet surface
The fillet surface should add to the drawing as shown in Figure 13.70 ☞

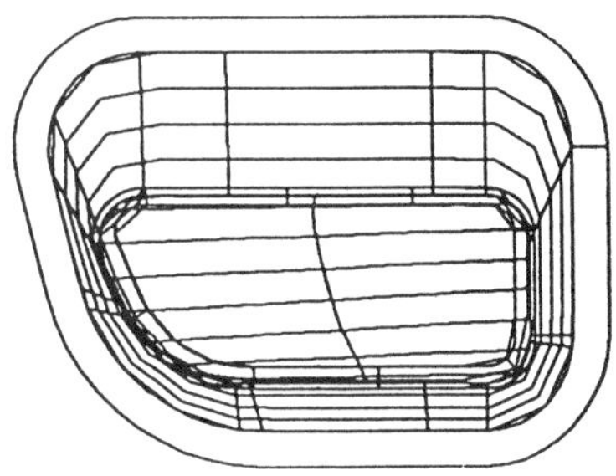

Figure 13.70

Step 9. Make all surface levels to visible and change to isometric Gview.

Select **Level → Vis. levels**
Toggle level 2 to set visible (highlighted)
then select **OK** to return back to graphic mode

Select **Gview → Isometric**
The final surface model is shown in Figure 13.71 ☞

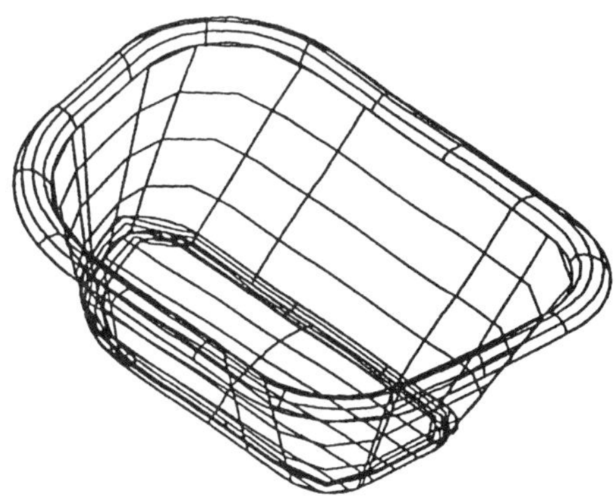

Figure 13.71

Step 10. Save the surface model (baskets).

Select **MAIN MENU → File → Save**
Enter file name: **baskets**

Project 9.

Flash light surface model

The flash light surface model (Figure 13.72b) consists of four ruled surfaces, one coons surface and one fillet surface. The wireframe model (Figure 13.72a) is presented in project 12 of chapter 11.

Wireframe Model
Project 12 of Chapter 11 (flash)

Go to

We are here **Surface Model**
(flashs)

Go to

Toolpath
Project 6 of Chapter 15 (flash)

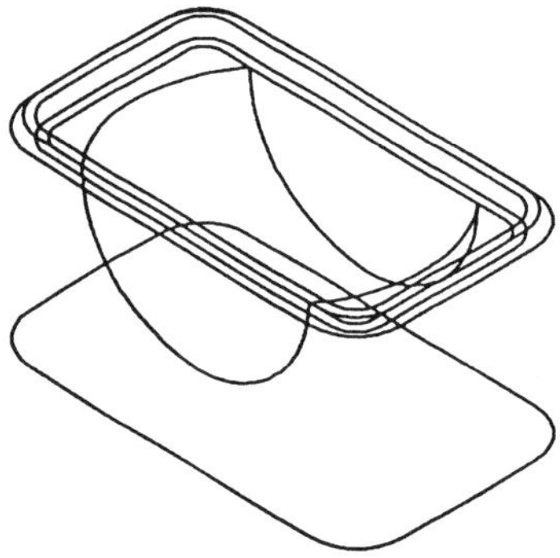

Figure 13.72a. Wireframe model

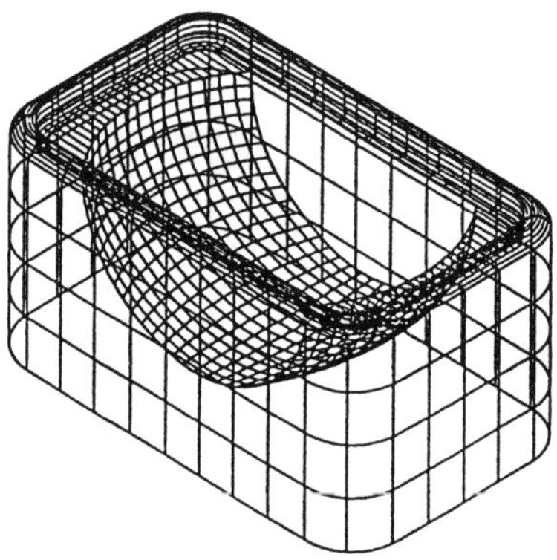

Figure 13.72b. surface model

Tips 1. Use two outer rectangular profiles to create a ruled surface for the outer frame.

2. Use three rectangular profiles to create a ruled surface for the top rim.

3. Create a vertical ruled surface for the inside wall.

4. The inner flat surface can be created as a ruled surface using the inner rectangular profile.

5. The curved surface is generated as a single-patch Coons surface.

6.The fillet surface is generated between the vertical ruled surface and the inner flat ruled surface.

7. The inner flat surface is trimmed by the surface curve created by projecting the Coons patch profile onto the inner flat ruled surface.

8. Use a different level and color for each surface.

Step 1. Load the wireframe model file "flash".

Select **MAIN MENU → File → Get**
Enter file name: **flash**
Select **Yes** to delete the current part if necessary

The wireframe model drawing should appear on screen as Figure 13.73.

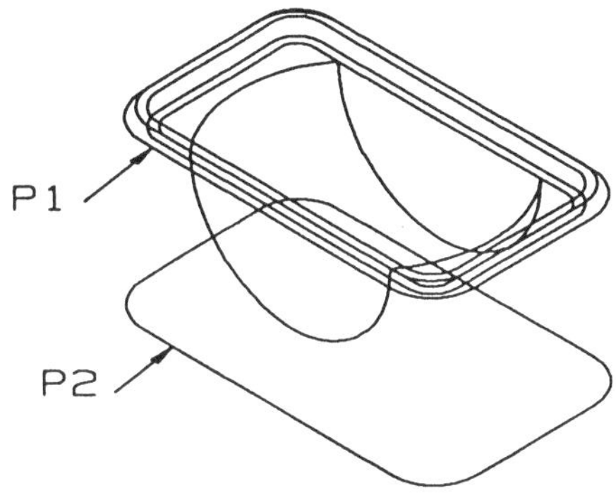

Figure 13.73

Step 2. Create a ruled surface for the outer frame using the pick points labeled in Figure 13.78. Change to level 2 and color 11.

Select **Level → MAIN Level**, then enter **2** ←
Select **Color** then enter **11** ←
Select **MAIN MENU → Create → sUrface → rUled → Blend → Chain**
Pick at **P1** to select the first entity
Select **Close → End here** to complete the first contour
Select **Chain**
Pick at **P2**
Select **Close → End here → Done** to complete the surface

The added ruled surface should look like Figure 13.74.

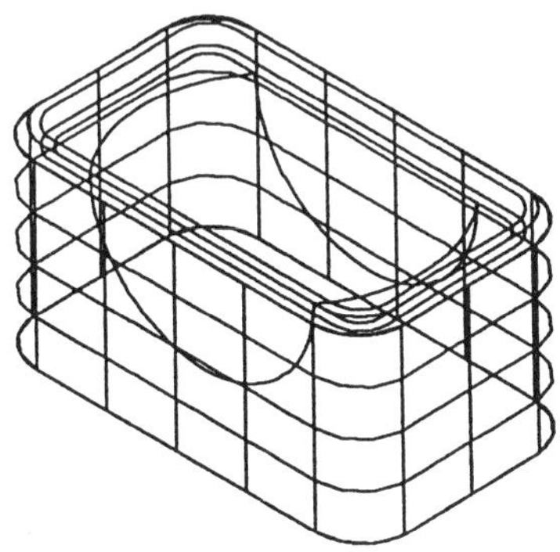

Figure 13.74

Step 3. Make level 2 invisible. Change to Top Gview.

Select **Level → Vis. levels**
Click on the level 2 button to set invisible (dimmed)
then select **OK → OK** to return back to graphic mode
Select **Gview → Top**

The drawing in Top Gview should resemble Figure 13.75.

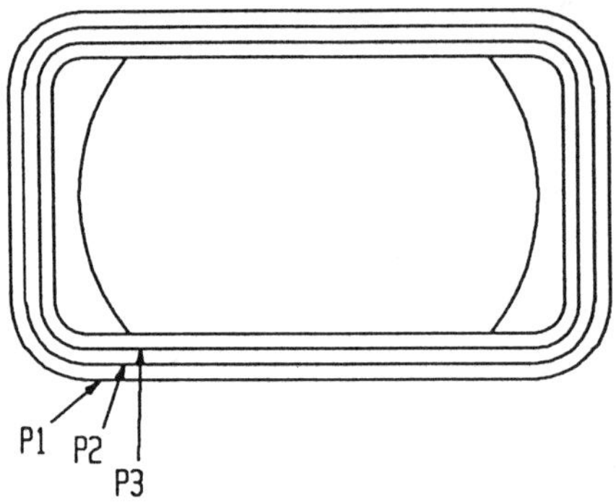

Figure 13.75

Step 4. Create a ruled surface on the top ring using the pick points labeled in **Figure 13.80.** Change to level 3 and color 12.

Select **Level → Main level,** then enter **3** ←
Select **Color** then enter **12** ←
Select **MAIN MENU → Create → sUrface → rUled → Blend → Chain**
Pick at **P1**
Select **Close → End here**
Select **Chain**
Pick at **P2**
Select **Close → End here**
Select **Chain**
Pick at **P3**
Select **Close → End here → Done** to complete the surface.
Select **Gview → Isometric**

The new ruled surface is shown in Figure 13.76

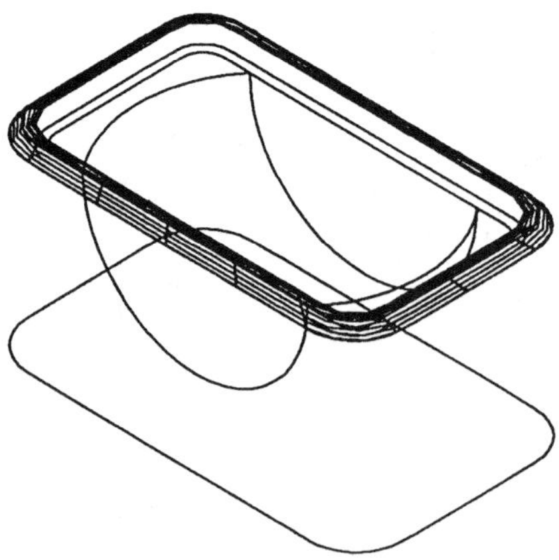

Figure 13.76

Step 5. Make level 3 invisible.

Select **Level → Vis. levels**
Click on the level 3 button to set invisible (dimmed)
Select **OK → OK** to return back to graphic mode

The drawing on the screen should resemble Figure 13.77.

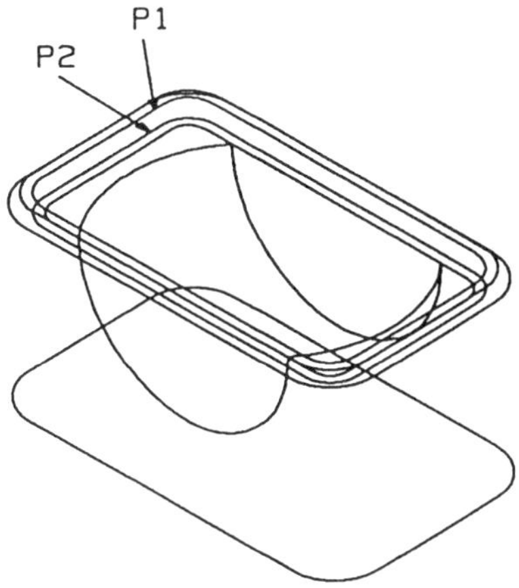

Figure 13.77

Step 6. Create a vertical ruled surface using the pick points in Figure 13.77.

Change level to 4 and color 13.
Select **Level → MAIN Level,** then enter **4** ←
Select **Color** then enter **13** ←
Select **MAIN MENU →Create→ sUrface → rUled → Blend**
Select **Chain**
Pick at **P1**
Select **Close → End here**
Select **Chain**
Pick at **P2**
Select **Close → End here → Done**

The drawing should resemble Figure 13.78.

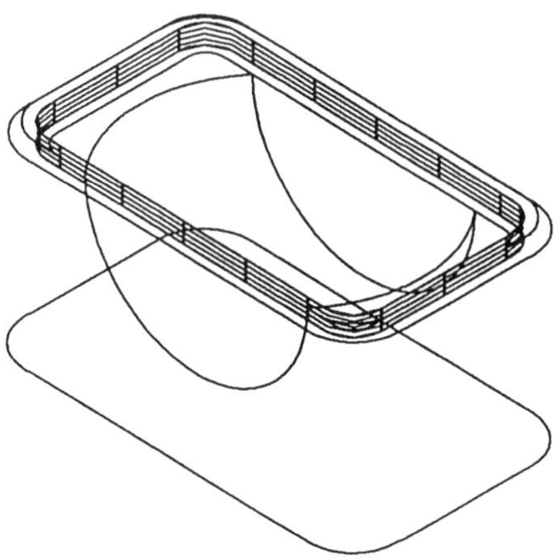

Figure 13.78

Step 7. Make level 4 invisible.

Select **Level → Vis. levels**
Click on the level 4 button to set to invisible (dimmed)
Select **OK → OK** to return back to graphic mode

The drawing now appears as Figure 13.79 on the next page.

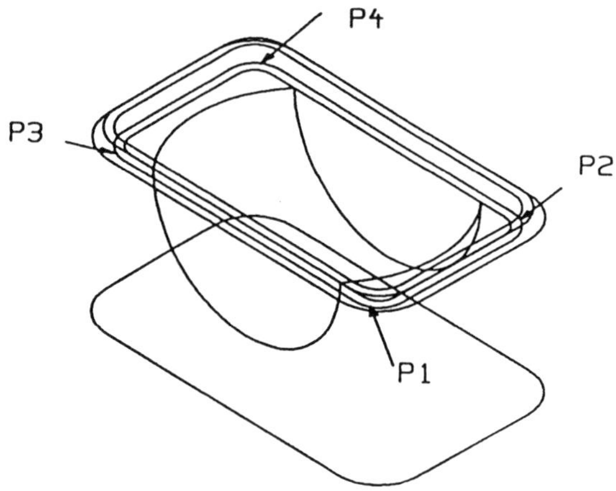

Figure 13.79

Step 8. Create a ruled surface for inner flat surface using the pick points labeled in Figure 13.79.

Change level to 5 and color to 14.

Select **Level → Main level,** then enter **5** ←
Select **Color** then enter **14** ←
Select **MAIN MENU → Create → sUrface → rUled → Blend → Chain**
Pick at **P1** and **P2** then select **End here** to complete contour 1
Select **Chain**
Pick at **P3** and **P4**
Select **End here → Done** to complete the surface

The surface model appears as Figure 13.80.

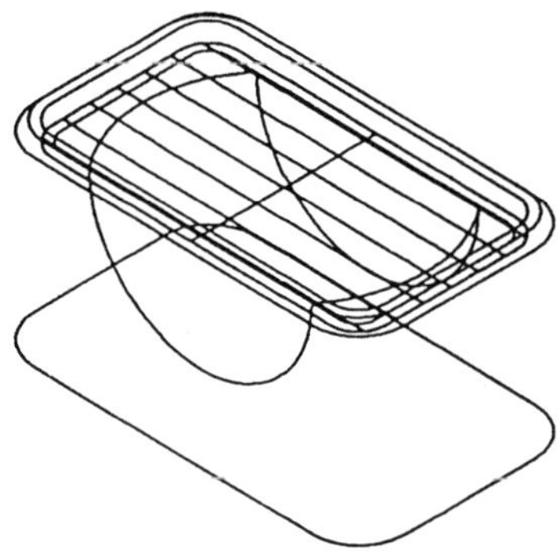

Figure 13.80

Step 9. Make level 5 invisible.

Select **Level → Vis. levels**
Click on the level 5 button to set to invisible (dimmed)
Select **OK → OK** to return back to graphic mode

The drawing now should resemble Figure 13.81 on the following page.

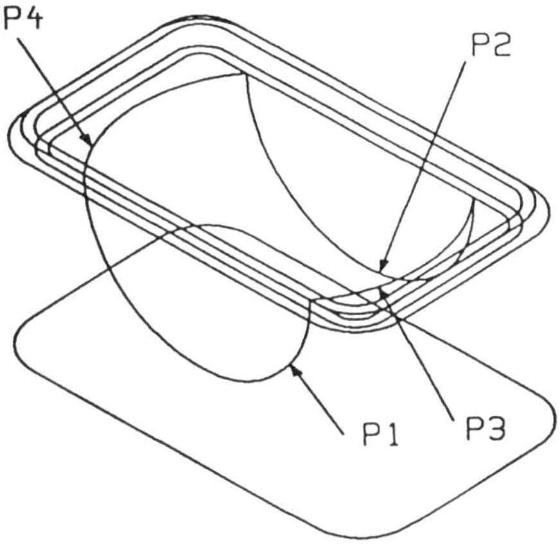

Figure 13.81

Step 10. Create a Coons surface using the pick points in Figure 13.81.

Change **Level** → **Main level**, then enter **6** ←
Select **Color** then enter **15** ←
Select **MAIN MENU** → **Create** → **sUrface** → **Coons** → **Nurbs**
Enter number of patches in the along direction: **1** ←
Enter number of patches in the across direction: **1** ←
define along contour 1 of row 1: select **Single** then pick at **P1**
define along contour 1 or row 2: select **Single** then pick at **P2**
define across contour 1 of column 1: select **Single** then pick at **P3**
define across contour 1 of column 2; select **Single** then pick at **P4**
Select **Done** to complete chaining

Set the Coons surface parameters to the following settings:

Along cut distance = **0.15**
Across cut distance = **0.15**
Error measurement = **on**
Blending = **Parabolic**

Select **Done** to complete the surface
Press **Enter** to continue

The Coons surface should appear as Figure 13.82.

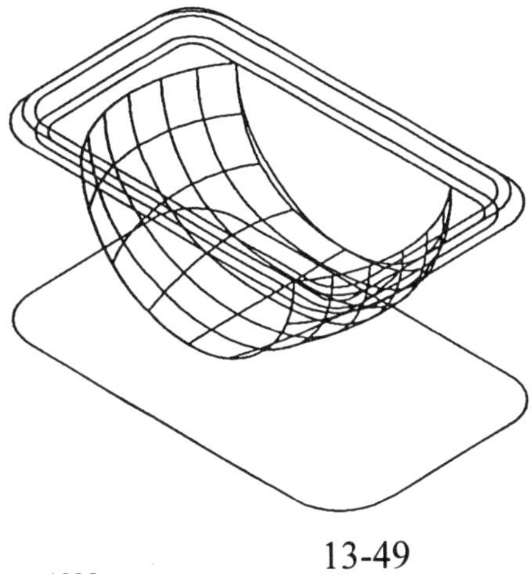

Figure 13.82

Step 11. Make level 6 invisible and levels 4 and 5 visible.

Select **Level → Vis. levels**
Toggle the level 6 to invisible (dimmed)
Toggle levels 4 and 5 to visible (highlighted)
Select **OK → OK** to return back to graphic mode

The new drawing on the screen should resemble Figure 13.83.

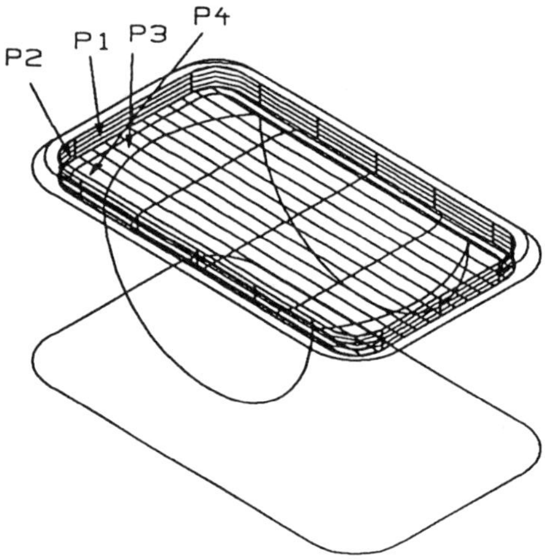

Figure 13.83

Step 12. Create a fillet surface at the intersection between the inner flat surface and the vertical wall surface.

Use the pick points in Figure 13.83
Change level to 7 and color to 12.
Select **Level → Main Level**, then enter 7
Select **Color** then enter **12**
Select **MAIN MENU → Create → sUrface → Fillet → Radius**
Enter the start fillet radius: **0.1**
Set the Surface fillet menu to the following settings:

Use Ch ht	= **Y**
Step Vals:	
Maximum step distance	= **0.1**
Stopping chord height	= **0.005**
Extend	=**Y**
Splines	=**B**
sUrf crvs	=**B**
Fillet	=**N**
Trim	=**N**

Note: The normal direction of the vertical wall needs to be in the inward direction. Use **Modify →Normal** commands to check and change if necessary.

Pick at **P1** to select the vertical wall surface
Move arrow to **P2** and click the mouse to start a fillet
Pick at **P3** to select the inner flat surface
Move arrow to **P4** and click the mouse
Select **Do it** to complete the surface

The fillet surface should appear as Figure 13.84 on the next page.

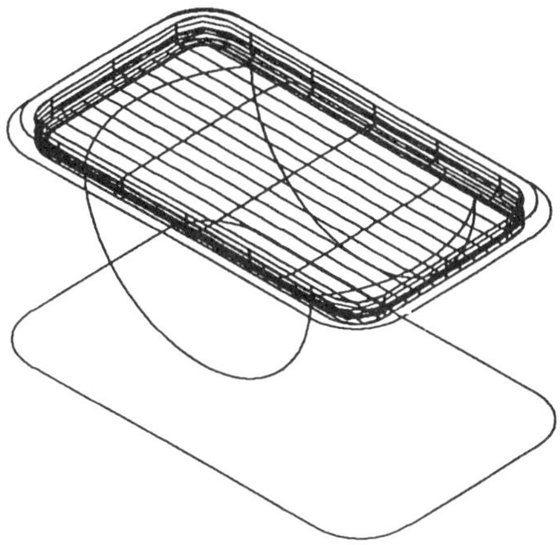

Figure 13.84

Step 13. Make levels 2, 3, 4, 6, and 7 invisible.

Select **Level → Vis. levels**
Toggle only levels 1 and 5 to visible (highlighted)
Select **OK → OK** to return back to graphic mode

The drawing should resemble Figure 13.85.

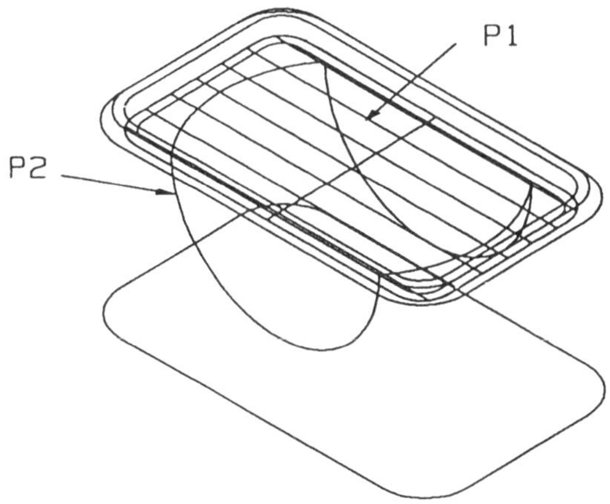

Figure 13.85

Step 14. Create the surface curve for trimming the inner flat ruled surface. Use the pick points in Figure 13.85.

Change level to 8 and color to 13.
Select **Level → Main level**, then enter **8** ←
Select **Color** then enter **13** ←
Select **MAIN MENU → Create → Curve → Project**

Set the project curve parameters to the following settings:

Use Ch ht	=**N**
Step Vals:	
Stepping distance = **0.015**	
Splines	**N**
Lines	**N**
sUrf cvs	**Y**
Norm/view	**N**
Extend	**N**

Step 14, continued.

Pick at **P1** to select the ruled surface
Select **Chain**
Pick at **P2** to select the first entity
Select **Close** → **End here** to complete the selection of contour to be projected
Select **Done** → **Do it** to complete the surface curve

The surface curve appearing on screen should look like Figures 13.86.

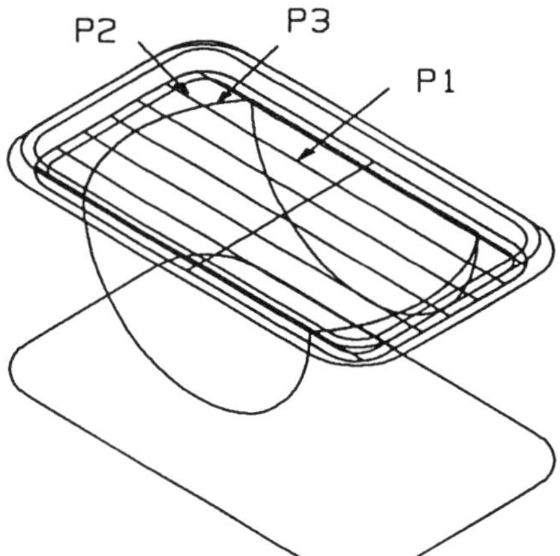

Figure 13.86

Step 15. Trim the inner flat ruled surface using the pick points in Figure 13.86.

Select **Level** → **Main level**, then enter **9** ←
Select **Color** then enter **12** ←
Select **MAIN MENU** → **Create** → **sUrface** → **Trimmed** → **to Curves**
Pick at **P1** to select the surface to be trimmed
Move arrow to **P2,** click the mouse to indicate the area on the surface to keep after trimming
Select **chain** then pick at **P3**
Select **close** → **End here** → **Done**
Set the trimming parameters to the following settings:

constr Vw	=**N**
dispose	=**D**
Step Vals:	
Stepping distance = **0.1**	
Use Ch ht	=**N**

Select **Do it**

The trimmed surface should look like Figure 13.87.

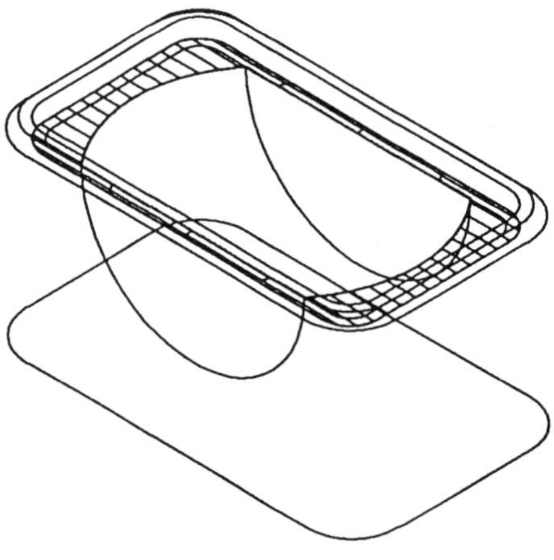

Figure 13.87

Step 16. Display all necessary surfaces.

Select **Select Level → Vis. levels**
Toggle every level to visible beside level 5
Press **OK** to return back to graphic mode

The final surface model should look like Figure 13.88.

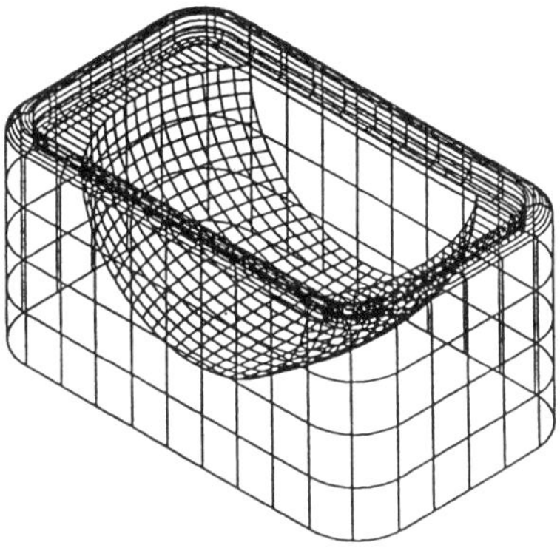

Figure 13.88

Step 17. Save the surface model (flashs).

Select **MAIN MENU → File → Save**
Enter file name: **flashs**

10

Project 10.

Hair dryer surface model

The hair dryer surface model consists of **four** surfaces; two swept surfaces and two ruled surfaces (Figure 13.89). The two swept surfaces are the top surface and the frame surface. The two ruled surfaces include the tube surface and the handle surface. The two ruled surfaces are trimmed to the frame surface. These four surfaces are mirrored about the X axis in the Front Cplane to complete the surface model.

Wireframe Model
Project 13 of Chapter 11 (dryer)

Go to

We are here

Surface Model (dryers)

Go to

Toolpath
Project 7 of Chapter 15 (flash)

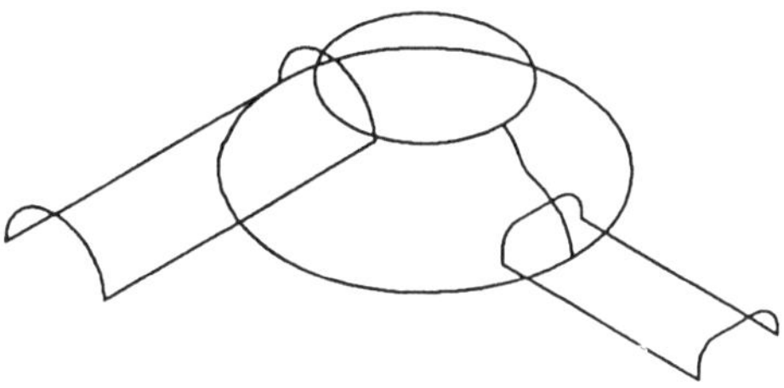

Figure 13.89a. Wireframe model

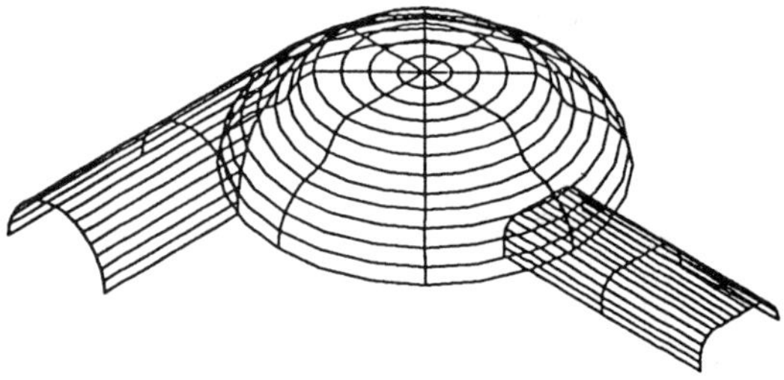

Figure 13.89b. Surface model

Tips 1. The top flat face and the frame can be formed as a single swept surface. In this case we purposely create it as two separate swept surfaces because the top flat surface can be easily machined by using a flat end mill instead of ball end cutter.

2. In this surface model, the two ruled surfaces are constructed long enough to extrude into the frame surface. Therefore, they should be trimmed.
3. Two surface curves should be created at the intersection boundary between the frame surface and the tube surface, and between the frame surface and the handle surface. These two surface curves are then used to trim the two ruled surfaces.
4. Trimming both ruled surfaces requires us to redefine the outer boundary.

5. Use the Front Cplane to mirror the upper composite surface model about the X axis to complete the modeling of the object.

Step 1. Load the wireframe model file (dryer).

Select **MAIN MENU → File → Get**
Enter file name: **dryer**
Select **Yes** to delete the current part if necessary

The wireframe model of hair dryer appears as Figure 13.90.

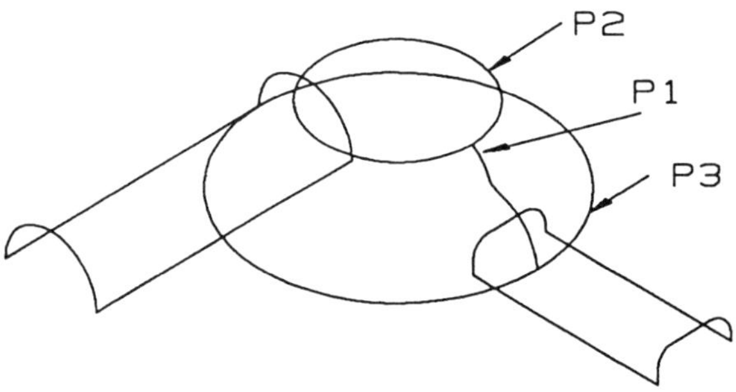

Figure 13.90

Step 2. Create a swept surface using the pick points in Figure 13.90.

Change level to 2 and color to 11.
Select **Level** → **Main level**, then enter **2** ←
Select **Color** then enter **11** ←
Select **MAIN MENU** → **Create** → **sUrface** → **Swept** → **Nurbs**
Enter the number of across contour: **1** ←
define the across contour: select **Chain** from the Chaining method menu
Pick at **P1** to select the starting entity
Select **Close** → **End here**
define along contour 1: select **Single**, then pick at **P2**
define along contour 2: select **Single**, then pick at **P3**
Select **Done** to complete contour selection

Set the Swept surface parameters to the following settings:

Along cut distance = **0.15**
Across cut distance = **0.15**

Select **Done** to complete the swept surface

The swept surface should appear as Figure 13.91.

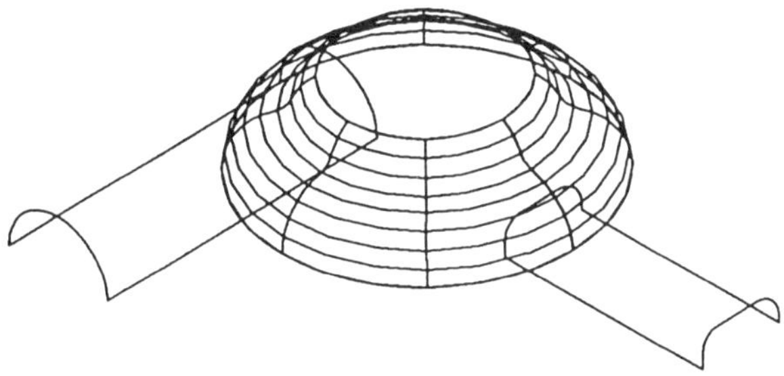

Figure 13.91

Step 3. Make level 2 invisible.

Select **Level** →**Vis. levels**
Toggle level 2 to invisible (dimmed)
Select **OK** → **OK** to return back to graphic mode

The drawing becomes Figure 13.92.

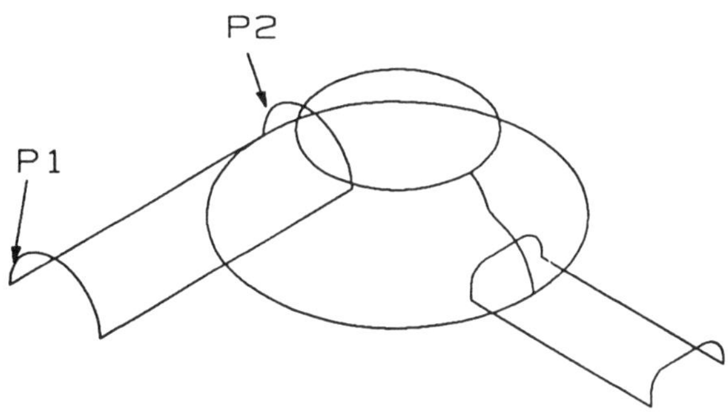

Figure 13.92

Step 4. Create a ruled surface for the tube using the pick points in Figure 13.92.

Change level to 3 and color to 12.
Select **Level → Main Level**, then enter **3 ←**
Select **Color** then enter **12 ←**
Select **MAIN MENU → Create → sUrface → rUled → Blend**
define contour 1: select **Single** then pick at **P1**
define contour 2: select **Single** then pick at **P2**
Select **Done** to complete the ruled surface

The ruled surface should resemble Figure 13.93.

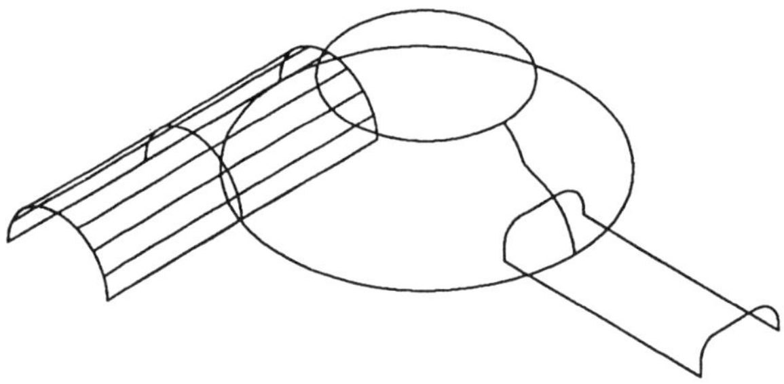

Figure 13.93

Step 5. Make level 3 invisible.

Select **Level → Vis. levels**
Toggle level 3 to invisible (dimmed)
Select **OK → OK** to return back to graphic mode

The drawing now should appear as Figure 13.94.

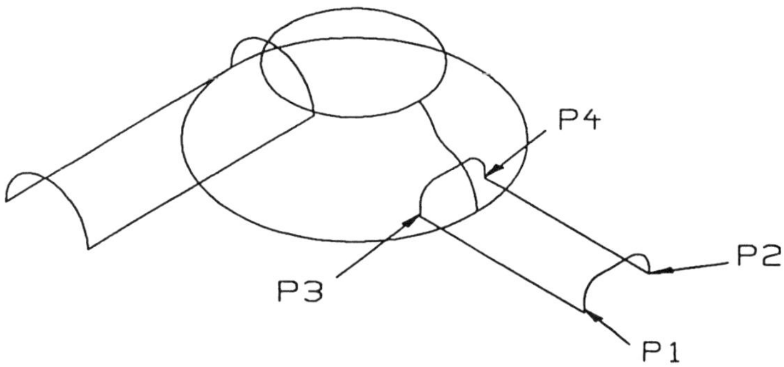

Figure 13.94

Step 6. Create a ruled surface for the handle using the pick points in Figure 13.94.

Change level to 4 and color to 13.
Select **Level → Main level,** then enter **4 ←**
Select **Color** then enter **13 ←**
Select **MAIN MENU → Create → sUrface → rUled → Blend**
define contour 1: select **Chain**, then pick at **P1** and **P2**
Select **End here** to complete contour 1
define contour 2: select **Chain**, then pick at **P3** and **P4**
Select **End here → Done** to complete the surface

The new ruled surface should resemble Figure 13.95.

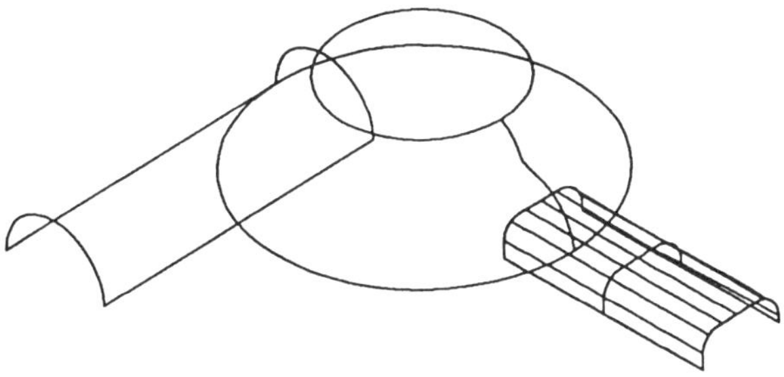

Figure 13.95

Step 7. Make levels 2 and 3 visible.

Select **Level → Vis. levels**
Toggle levels 2 and 3 to visible (highlighted)
Select **OK** to return back to graphic mode

The new drawing becomes Figure 13.96.

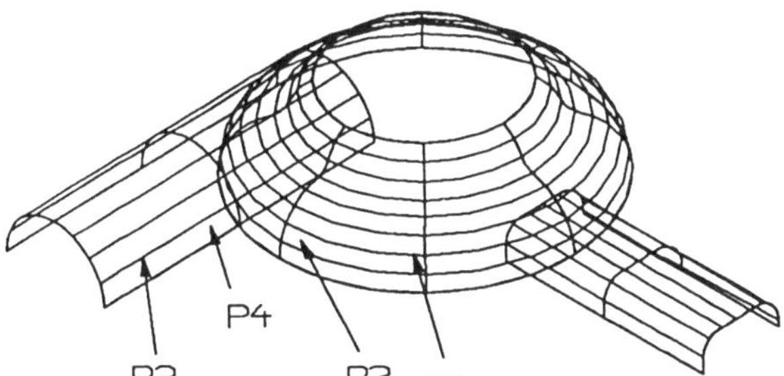

Figure 13.96

Step 8. Create a surface curve at the intersection between the frame surface and the tube surface. Use the pick points in Figure 13.96.

Change level to 5 and color to 14
Select **Level → Main Level**, then enter **5** ←
Select **Color** then enter **14** ←
Select **MAIN MENU →Create → Curve → Intersect**
Set the Surface intersection menu to the following settings:

Use Ch ht	= **Y**
Step Vals:	
Maximum step distance	= **0.05**
Stopping chord height	= **0.005**
Extend	=**N**
Splines	=**N**
sUrf crvs	=**B**
Trim	=**N**

Step 8, continued.

Pick at **P1** to select the frame surface
Move arrow to **P2** and click the mouse to start an intersection
Pick at **P3** to select the tube surface
Move arrow to **P4** and click the mouse

Select **Do it** to complete the surface curve

The surface curve should appear as Figure 13.97.

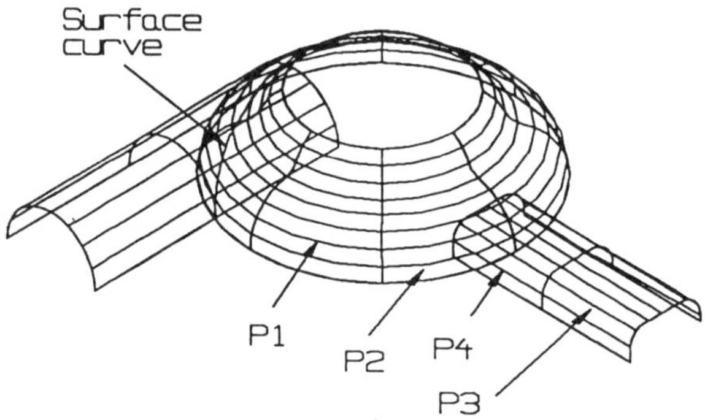

Figure 13.97

Step 9. Create a surface curve at the intersection between the frame surface and the handler surface. Use the pick points in Figure 13.97.

Set Extend ? to **Yes** in the Surface intersection menu
Pick at **P1** to select the frame surface
Move the arrow to **P2** and click the mouse to start an intersection
Pick at **P3** to select the handler surface
Move arrow to **P4** and click the mouse
Select **Do it** to complete the surface curve

Both surface curves should appear as Figure 13.98.

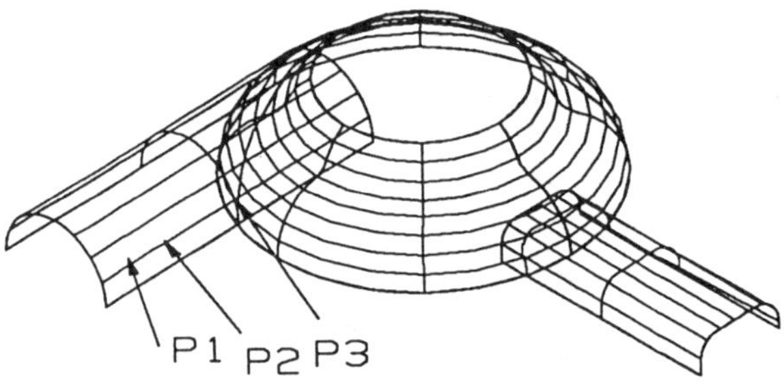

Figure 13.98

Step 10. Trim the tube surface using the pick points in Figure 13.98.

Change level to 6 and color to 15.
Select **Level → Main level,** then enter **6** ←
Select **Color** then enter **15** ←
Select **MAIN MENU → Create → sUrface → Trimmed → to Curves**

Step 10, continued.

Set the parameters to the following settings:

constr Vw	=**N**
dispose	=**D**
use Ch ht	=**N**
Step Vals:	
Stepping distance = **0.005**	

Pick at **P1** to select the surface to trim
Move arrow to **P2** and then click the mouse to indicate the surface area to keep
Select **Single,** then pick at **P3**
Select **Done → Do it** to complete the surface trimming
The trimmed surface is shown in Figure 13.99.

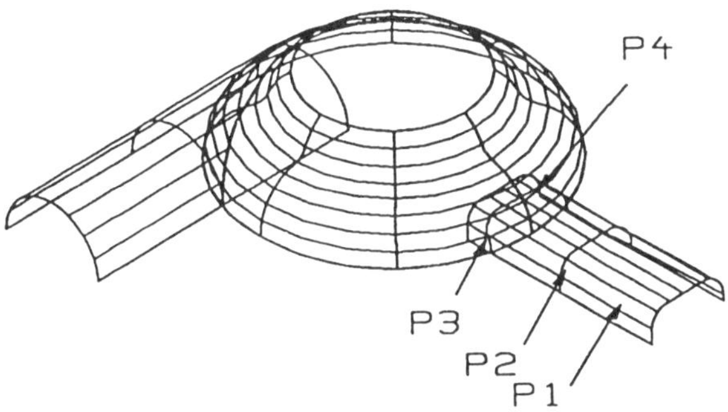

Figure 13.99

Step 11. Trim the handle surface using the pick points in Figure 13.99.

Pick at **P1** to select the surface to trim
Move arrow to **P2** and then click the mouse to indicate the surface area to keep
Select **Single** then pick at **P3**
Select **Single** then pick at **P4**
Select **Done → Do it**
The trimmed surfaces should appear as in Figure 13.100.

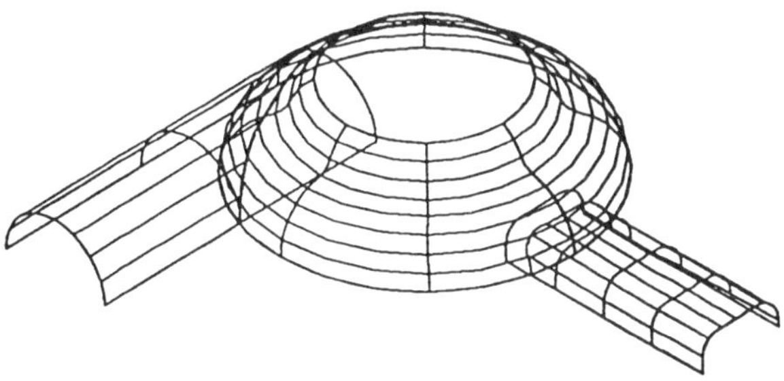

Figure 13.100

Step 12. Make levels 2 to 6 invisible.

Select **Level → Vis. levels**
Toggle levels 2 to 6 invisible (dimmed)
Select **OK → OK** to return back to graphic mode

The new drawing appears as Figure 13.101.

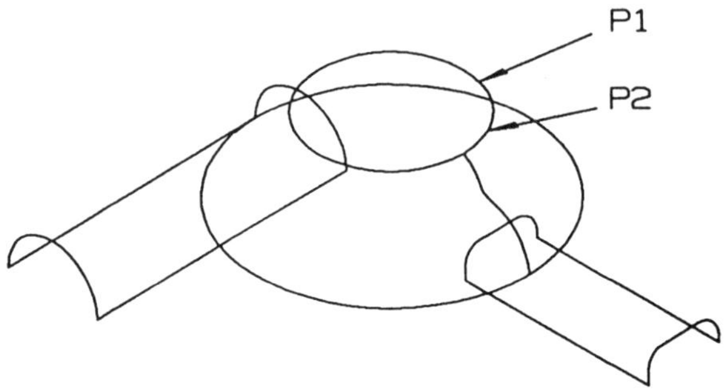

Figure 13.101

Step 13. Add a line to the top of the frame using the pick points in Figure 13.101.

Change level to 7 and color to 12. Use Top Cplane.
Select **Level** → **Main level**, then enter **7** ←
Select **Color** then enter **12** ←
Select **Cplane** → **Top** if necessary
Select **Z** → **Endpoint**
Pick at **P1** to obtain Z value

Z1.0 should appear in the Secondary menu

Select **MAIN MENU** → **Create** → **Line** → **Endpoints**
Specify the first endpoint: **0,0** ←
Specify the seond endpoint: select **Endpoint** then pick at **P2**

The line is added to the drawing as shown in Figure 13.102.

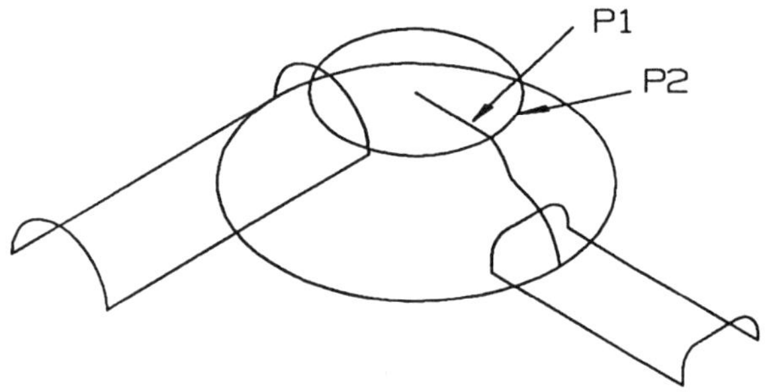

Figure 13.102

Step 14. Create a swept surface on the top frame using the pick points in Figure 13.102.

Select **MAIN MENU** → **Create** → **sUrface** → **Swept** → **Nurbs**
Enter the number of across contour: **1** ←
define the across contour: select **Single** then pick at **P1**
define along contour 1: select **Single** then pick at **P2**
Select **Done** to complete contour selection

Step 14, continued.

Set the Swept surface parameters to the following settings:

> Along cut distance = **0.15**
> Across cut distance = **0.15**
> **Rotate** the across contour

Select **Done** to complete the surface
Press **Enter** to continue

The top swept surface should look like Figure 13.103.

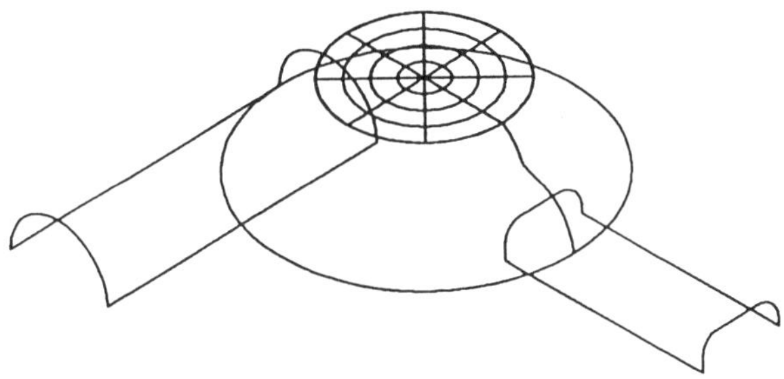

Figure 13.103

Step 15. Make levels 2, 6, and 7 visible.

Select **Level→ Vis. levels**
Toggle levels 2, 6, and 7 to visible (highlighted)
Select **OK** to return back to graphic mode

The drawing now appears as Figure 13.104.

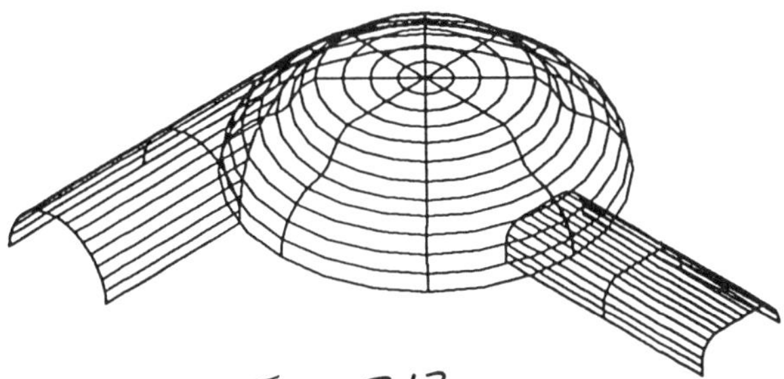

Figure 13.104

Step 16. Save the surface model.

Select **MAIN MENU → File → Save**
Enter file name: **dryers**

Step 17. Mirror the surface model about the X axis.

Use the Front Cplane. Change level to 8 and color to 13.
Select **Cplane → Front**
Select **Level → Main level**, then enter **8** ←
Select **Color** then enter **13** ←
Select **MAIN MENU → Xform → Mirror → All → surFaces → Done → X axis**
Set the Mirror parameters to **Copy**
Select **Done**

The complete surface model should appear as Figure 13.105.

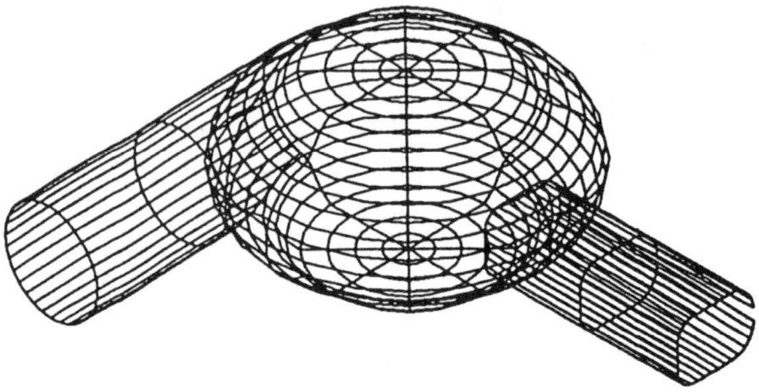

Figure 13.105

Project 11.

Fan surface model

This surface model consists of **six** basic surfaces: one flat surface of the hub, one inner rim surface, one outer rim surface, and three surfaces for the blade. The three surfaces of the blade are copied to six locations to generate the surfaces of the other six blades. The wireframe model and surface model are shown in Figure 13.106a and Figure 13.106b.

1

Wireframe Model

Project 15 of Chapter 11 (fan)

We are here

Go to

Surface Model

(fans)

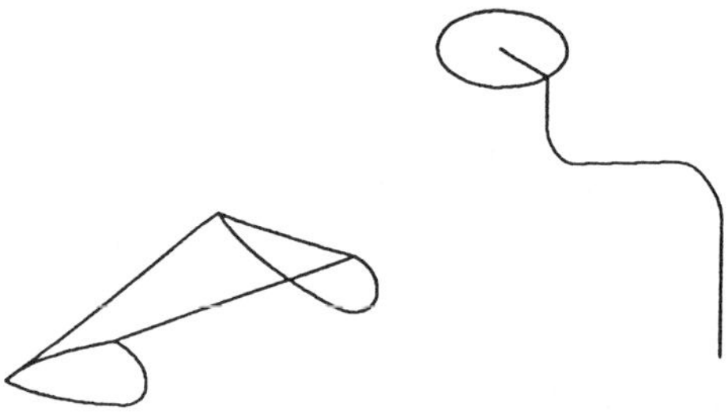

Figure 13.106a. Wireframe model

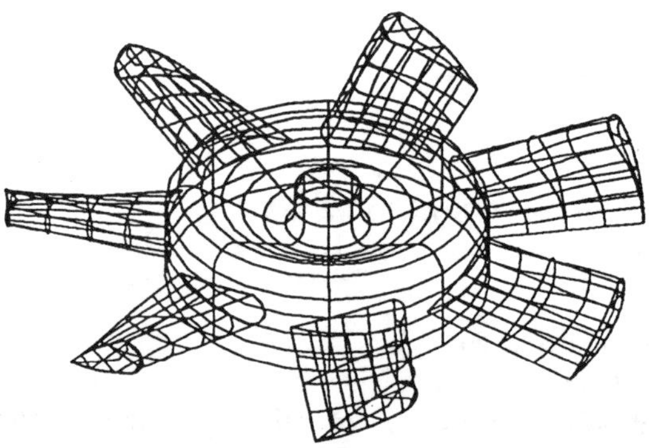

Figure 13.106b. Surface model

⌛**Tips** 1. The hub, rim and outer rim can be modeled as a single surface entity. However, we use three surface entities to model them to facilitate the generation of the toolpath.

2. The flat surface of the hub is created as a swept surface.

3. The inner rim surface of the hub is created as a swept surface. The across contour consists of four entities.

4. The outer rim surface can be modeled as a swept surface.

5. Both top and bottom surfaces of the blade are modeled by Coons surfacing technique. The number of patches in both along direction and across direction is one for both surfaces.

6. The outer end edge surface is modeled by the ruled surfacing technique.

7. Use Xform → Rotate commands to copy the three surfaces of the blade to six locations.

8. Use a different level and color for each surface.

Step 1. Load the wireframe model file (fan).

Select **MAIN MENU** → **File** → **Get**
Enter file name: **fan**
Select **Yes** to delete the current part if necessary
The wireframe model of the fan should look like Figure 13.107.

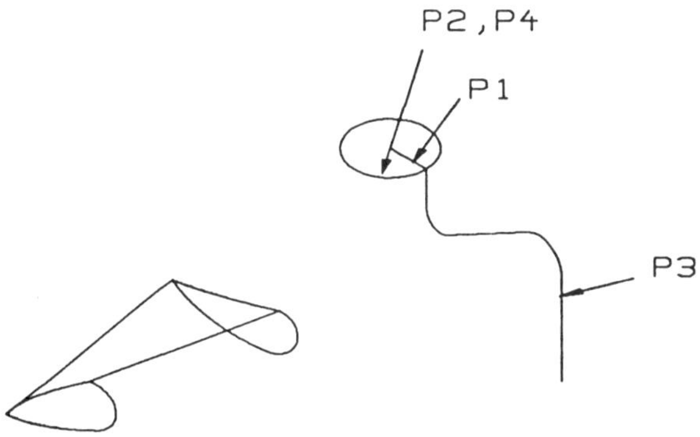

Figure 13.107

Step 2. Create two swept surfaces for the flat surface of the hub and the outer rim surface.

Use the pick points in Figure 13.107.
Change level to 6 and color to 14.
Select **Level** → **Main level** then enter **6** ←
Select **Color** then enter **14** ←
Select **MAIN MENU** → **Create** → **sUrface** → **Swept** → **Nurbs**
Enter the number of across contours: **1** ←
define the across contour: select **Single** then pick at **P1**
define along contour 1: select **Single** then pick at **P2**
Select **Done** to complete contours selection

Set the Swept surface parameters to the following settings;

Along cut distance	= **0.15**
Across cut distance	= **0.15**
Rotate the across contour	
Error measurement:	**off**

Select **Done** to complete the flat surface
Select **Swept →Nurbs**
Enter the number of across contours:**1**
define the across contour: Select **Single** and pick at **P3**
define the along contour1: select **Single** then pick at **P4**
Select **Done → Done** to complete the outer rim surface

The flat swept surface and the outer rim surface are shown in Figure 13.108.

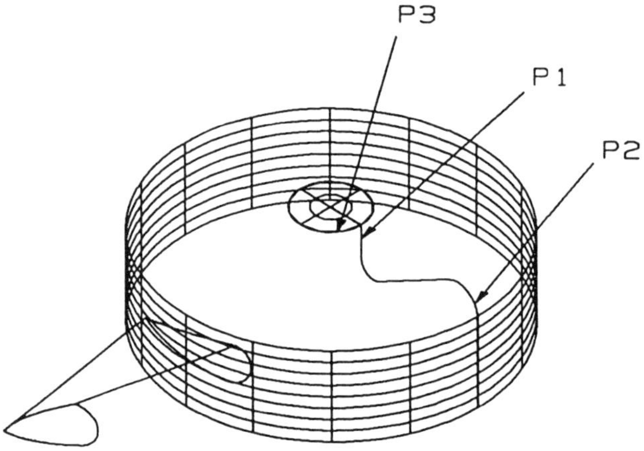

Figure 13.108

Step 3. Create a swept surface for the rim using the pick points in Figure 13.108.

Next, change color to 15.
Select **Color** then enter **15** ←
Select **Swept → Nurbs**
Enter the number of across contours: **1** ←
define the across contour: select **Chain** then pick at **P1** and **P2**
Select **End here**
define along contour 1: select **Single** then pick at **P3**
Select **Done** to complete contours selection

Set the Swept surface parameters to the following settings:

Along cut distance	= **0.2**
Across cut distance	= **0.2**
Rotate the across contour	
Error measurement:	**off**

Select **Done** to complete the surface

The surface should resemble Figure 13.109.

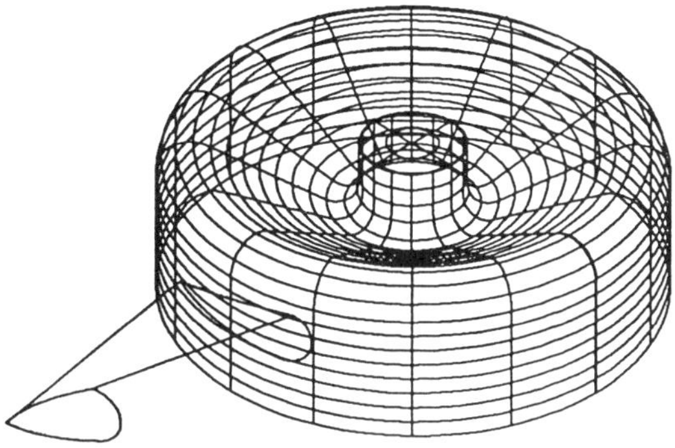

Figure 13.109

Step 4. Make levels 3 and 6 invisible.

Select **Level** → **Vis. levels**
Toggle levels **3** and **6** to invisible (dimmed)
Select **OK** → **OK** to return back to graphic mode

The drawing should look like Figure 13.110.

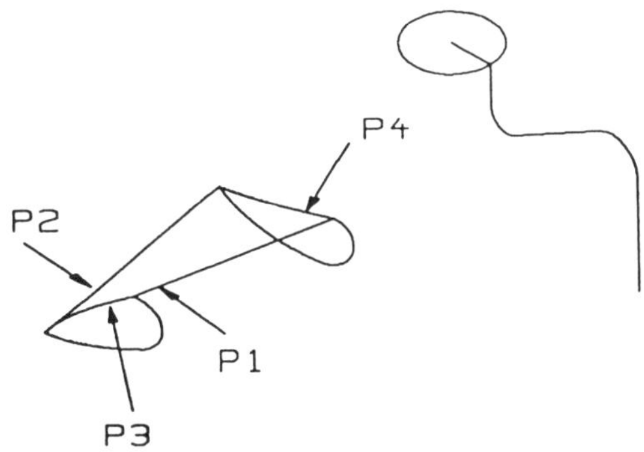

Figure 13.110

Step 5. Create a Coons surface for the top blade face using the pick points in Figure 13.110. Change level to 7 and color to 11.

Select **Level** → **Main level** then enter **7** ←
Select **Color** then enter **11** ←
Select **MAIN MENU** → **Create** → **sUrface** → **Coons** → **Nurbs**
Enter number of patches in the along direction: **1** ←
Enter number of patches in the across direction: **1** ←
define along contour 1 of row 1: select **Single** then pick at **P1**
define along contour 1 of row 2: select **Single** then pick at **P2**
define across contour 1 of column 1: select **Single** then pick at **P3**
define across contour 1 of column 2: select **Single** then pick at **P4**
Select **Done** to complete contours selection

Step 5, continued.

Set the Coons surface parameters to the following settings:

Along cut distance	= **0.2**
Across cut distance	= **0.2**
Error measurement	= **off**
Blending	= **Parabolic**

Select **Done** to complete the surface

The surface should resemble Figure 13.111.

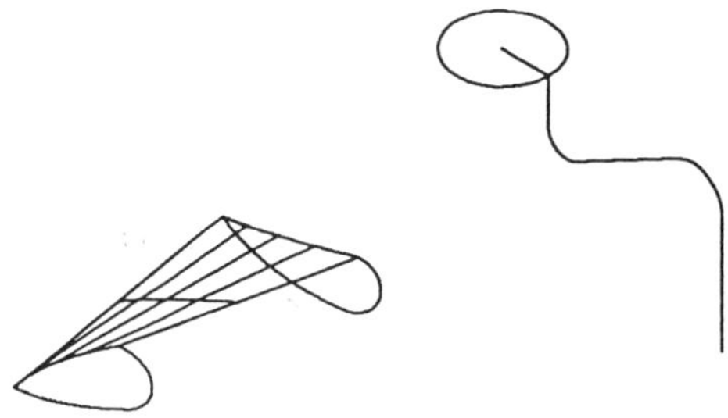

Figure 13.111

Step 6. Make level 7 invisible.

Select **Level→ Vis. levels**
Toggle level 7 to invisible (dimmed)
Select **OK → OK** to return back to graphic mode

The drawing appears as Figure 13.112

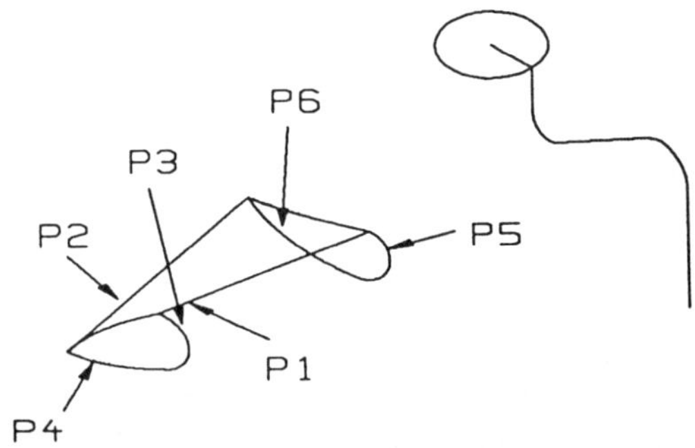

Figure 13.112

Step 7. Create a Coons surface for the bottom blade face. Use the pick points in Figure 13.112. Change level to 8 and color to 12.

Select **Level → Main level,** then enter **8** ←
Select **Color** then enter **12** ←
Select **MAIN MENU → Create → sUrface → Coons → Nurbs**
Enter number of patches in the along direction: **1** ←
Enter number of patches in the across direction: **1** ←
define along contour 1 of row 1: select **Single** then pick at **P1**
define along contour 1 of row 2: select **Single** then pick at **P2**
define across contour 1 of column 1: select **Chain** then pick at **P3** and **P4**
Select **End here**
define across contour 1 of column 2: select **Chain** then pick at **P5** and **P6**
Select **End here → Done** to complete contours selection

Set the Coons surface parameters to the following settings:

Along cut direction:	**0.2**
Across cut direction:	**0.2**
Error measurement:	**off**
Blending	= **Parabolic**

Select **Done** to complete the surface

The bottom Coons surface should appear as Figure 13.113.

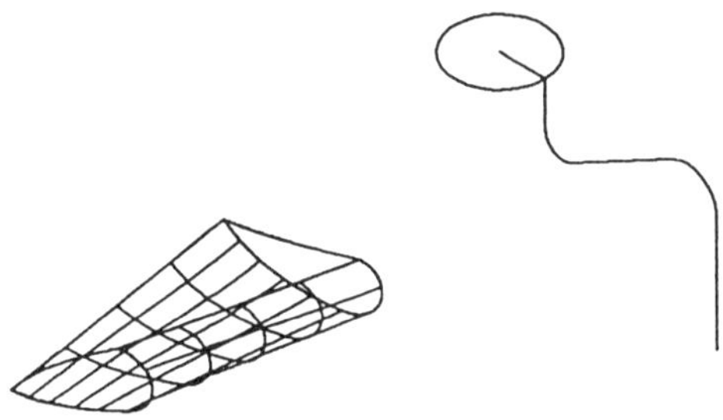

Figure 13.113

Step 8. Make level 8 invisible.

Select **Level → Vis. levels**
Toggle level 8 to invisible (dimmed)
Select **OK → OK** to return back to graphic mode

The drawing now appears as Figure 13.114.

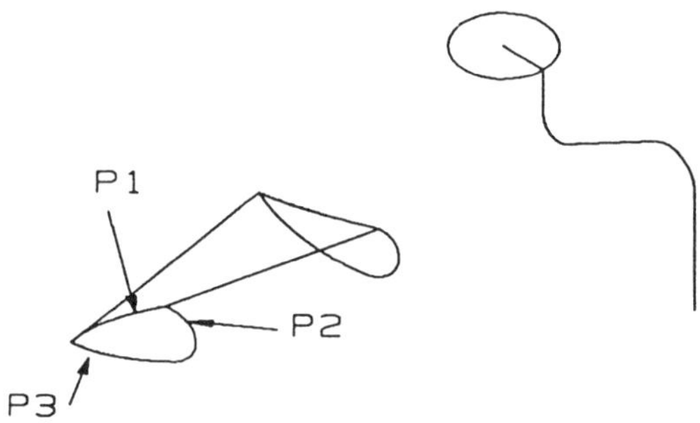

Figure 13.114

Step 9. Create a ruled surface for the outer end edge of the blade using the pick points labeled in Figure 13.114 on the previous page.

Change level to 9 and color to 14.
Select **Level→ Main level**, then enter **9** ←
Select **Color** then enter **14** ←
Select **MAIN MENU → Create → sUrface → rUled → Blend**
define contour 1: select **Single** then pick at **P1**
define contour 2: select **Chain** then pick at **P2** and **P3**
Select **End here → Done** to complete the ruled surface

The end edge surface should look like Figure 13.115.

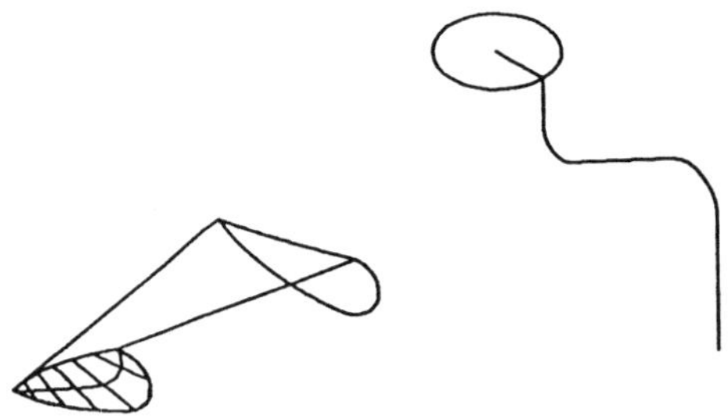

Figure 13.115

Step 10. Make levels 7 and 8 back to visible.

Select **Level→ Vis. levels**
Toggle levels 7 and 8 to visible (highlighted)
Select **OK** to return back to graphic mode

The three blade surfaces should resemble Figure 13.116.

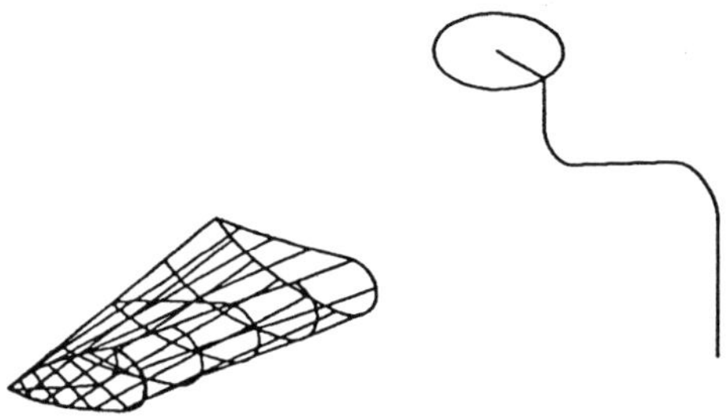

Figure 13.116

Step 11. Copy the blade surfaces to six locations using the Xform → Rotate commands.

Change level to 10 and color to 15.
Select **Level → Main level**, then enter **10** ←
Select **Color** then enter **15** ←
Select **MAIN MENU → Xform → Rotate → All → surFaces → Done → Origin**
Set the Rotate parameters as below.

Copy
Number of Steps = **6**
Rotation angle = **360/7**

Select **Done**

The three surfaces are copied to six locations as shown in Figure 13.117.

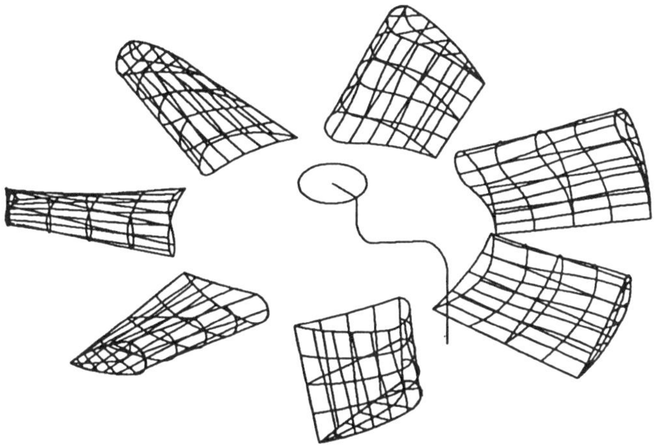

Figure 13.117

Step 12. Make levels 3 and 6 back to visible.

Select **Level** → **Vis. levels**
Toggle levels 3 and 6 to visible (highlighted)
Select **OK** to return back to graphic mode

The complete surface model should resemble Figure 13.118.

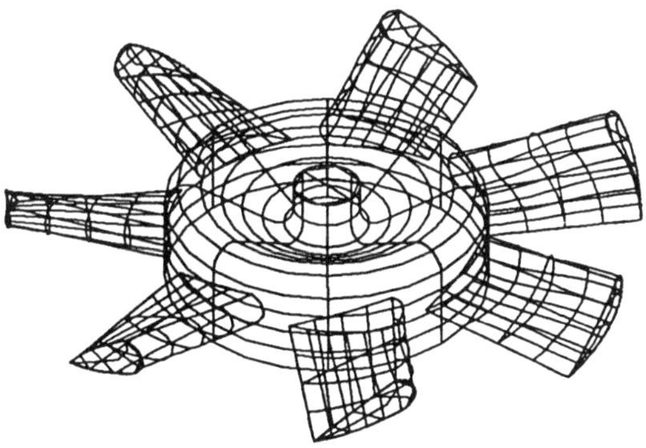

Figure 13.118

Step 13. Save the surface model (fans).

Select **MAIN MENU** → **File** → **Save**
Enter file name: **fans**

Project 12.

Car wheel hub

This example creates a surface model of a car wheel from the wireframe model of project 16 in chapter 11. The wireframe model and the completed surface model are shown in Figure 13.119. This is a rather complicated surface model which consists of many surfaces. The tips given on this page should help to complete the surface model:

Wireframe Model
Project 16 of Chapter 11 (wheel)

Go to

We are here ☞

Surface Model
(wheels)

Go to

Toolpath
Project 8 of Chapter 15 (wheels)

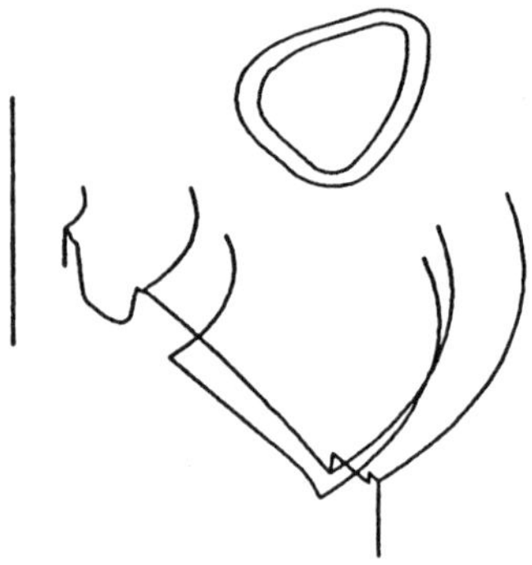

a. Wireframe model

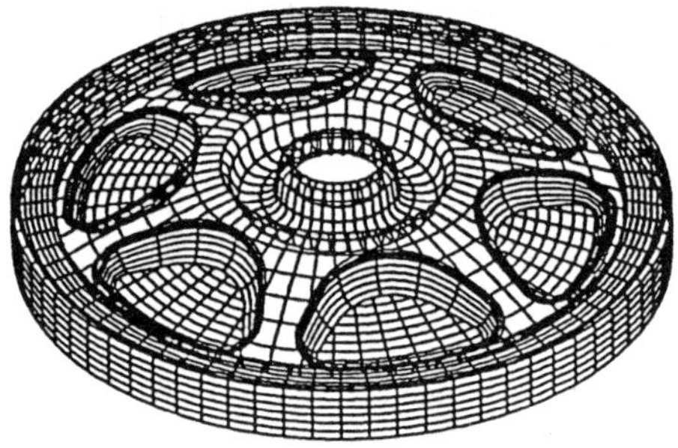

b. Surface model

Figure 13.119

Tips
1. Create the upper and the lower surface using the swept surfacing technique.
2. The outer pocket profile projects onto the upper swept surface to generate a surface curve.
3. The inner pocket profile is projected onto the lower swept surface to generate another surface curve.
4. Create two construction lines for defining a Cplane using the "2 lines" command. This Cplane is used to create an arc as the across contour for the pocket surface.
5. Create the pocket surface using the two surface curves as the two along contours and an arc as the across contour.
6. Create a fillet surface between the pocket surface and the upper swept surface.
7. Trim the upper surface to the fillet surface boundary.
8. Trim the lower surface to the pocket surface boundary.
9. Create two swept surfaces, one for the hub and the other for the rim.
10. Create two revolved surfaces, one for the inner hole and the other for the outer profile.
11. Copy all surfaces to five locations by using Xform → Rotate commands to complete the surface model.

Step 1. Load the wireframe model (wheel).

Select **MAIN MENU → File → Get**
Enter file name: **wheel**
Select **Yes** to delete the current part if necessary
The wireframe model drawing should appear as Figure 13.120.

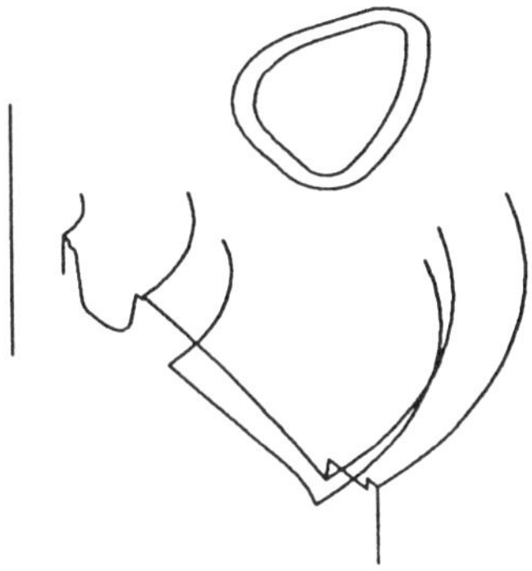

Figure 13.120

Step 2. Make level 2 invisible. Change level to 3 and color to 13.

Select **Level → Vis. levels**
Toggle level 2 to invisible (dimmed)
Select **Main Level,** then enter **3** ←
Select **Color** then enter **13** ←

The drawing should look like Figure 13.121.

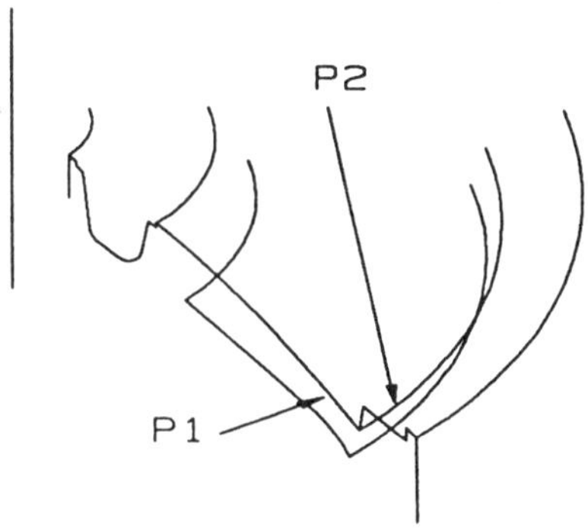

Figure 13.121

Step 3. Create the upper surface using the pick points in Figure 13.121.

Select **MAIN MENU → Create → sUrface → Swept → Nurbs**
Enter the number of across contours: **1** ←
define the across contour: select **Single** then pick at **P1**
define along contour 1: select **Single** then pick at **P2**
Select **Done** to complete contours selection
Set the Swept surface parameters to the following settings:

Along cut distance	= **0.25**
Across cut distance	= **0.25**
Rotate the across contour	

Select **Done** to complete the surface

The surface should appear as Figure 13.122.

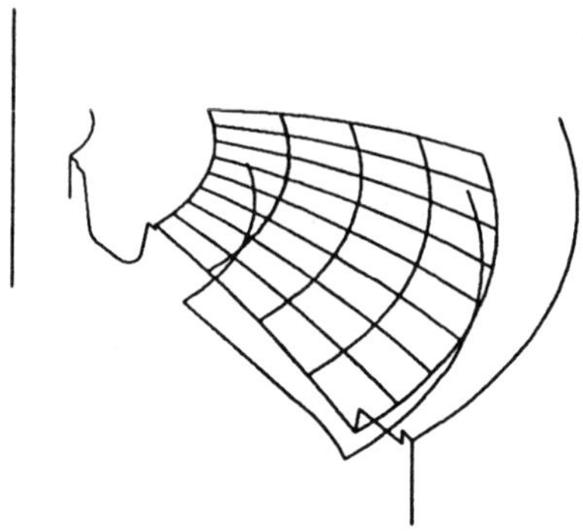

Figure 13.122

Step 4. Make level 3 invisible. Change level to 4 and color to 14.

Select **Level → Vis. levels**
Toggle level 3 to invisible (dimmed)
Select **Main Level,** then enter **4** ←
Select **Color** then enter **14** ←

The drawing becomes Figure 13.123.

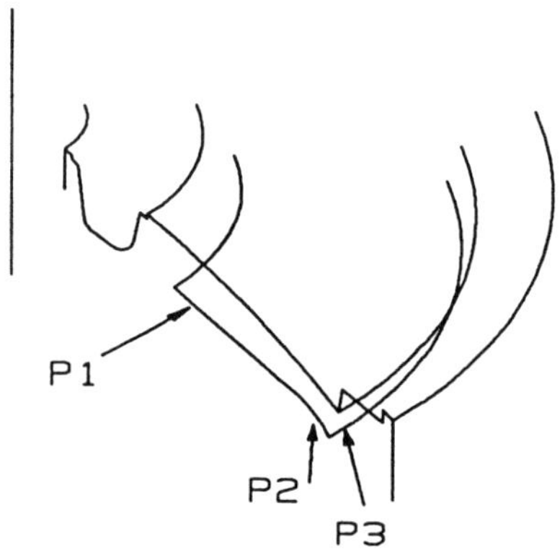

Figure 13.123

Step 5. Create the lower surface using swept surfacing technique. Use the pick points in Figure 13.123.

Select **MAIN MENU → Create → sUrface → Swept → Nurbs**
Enter the number of across contour: **1** ←
define the across contour: select **Chain** then pick at **P1** and **P2**
Select **End here**
define along contour 1: select **Single** then pick at **P3**
Select **Done** to complete the contour selection
Select **Done** to complete the surface

The new created surface should resemble Figure 13.124.

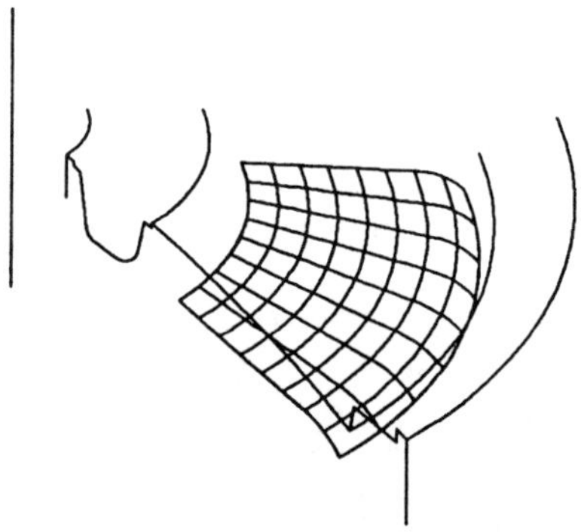

Figure 13.124

Step 6. Make level 2 visible. Change level to 5 and color to 15.

Select **Level → Vis. levels**
Toggle level 2 to visible
Select **Main Level,** then enter **5** ←
Select **color** then enter **15** ←

The drawing now should look like Figure 13.125.

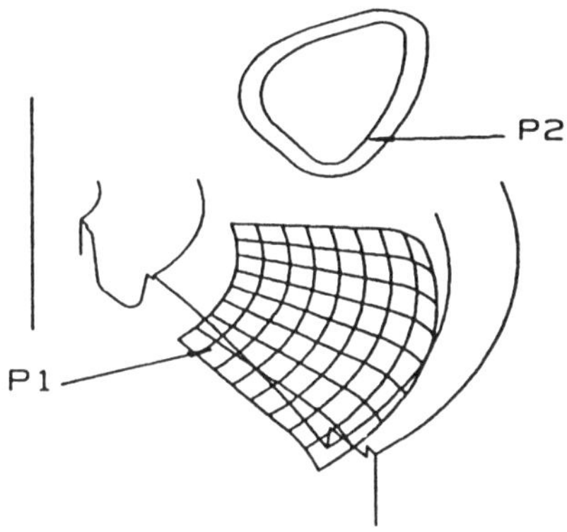

Figure 13.125

Step 7. Project the inner pocket profile to the lower surface to generate a surface curve. Use the pick points in Figure 13.125.

Select **MAIN MENU → Create → Curve → Project**
Set the Project curves parameters to the following settings:

Use Ch ht	=**N**
Step Vals:	
Stepping distance	=**0.03**
Splines	=**Y**
Lines	=**N**
sUrf cvs	=**Y**
Norm/view	=**V**
Extend	=**Y**

Pick at **P1** to select the surface
Select **Chain** then pick at **P2**
Select **Close → End here → Done → Do it** to complete the surface
The first surface curve should appear as in Figure 13.126.

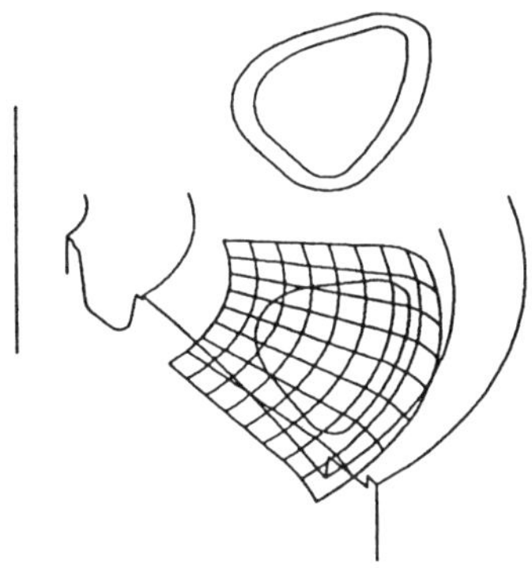

Figure 13.126

Step 8. Make level 4 invisible and level 3 visible.

Select **Level → Vis. levels**
Toggle level 4 to invisible (dimmed) and level 3 to visible (highlighted)
Select **OK** to return back to graphic mode

The drawing now should look like Figure 13.127.

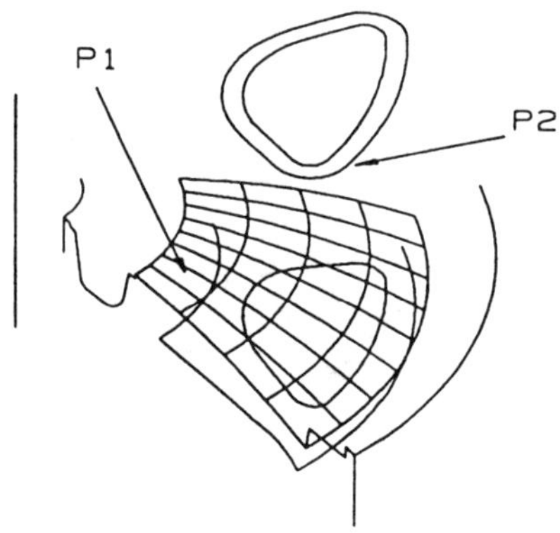

Figure 13.127

Step 9. Project the outer pocket profile to the supper surface to generate the second surface curve. Use the pick points in Figure 13.127.

Select **Surface**
Pick at **P1** to select the surface
Select **cHain CVS →Chain,** then pick at **P2**
Select **Close → End here → Done → Do it**

The second surface curve is added as shown in Figure 13.128.

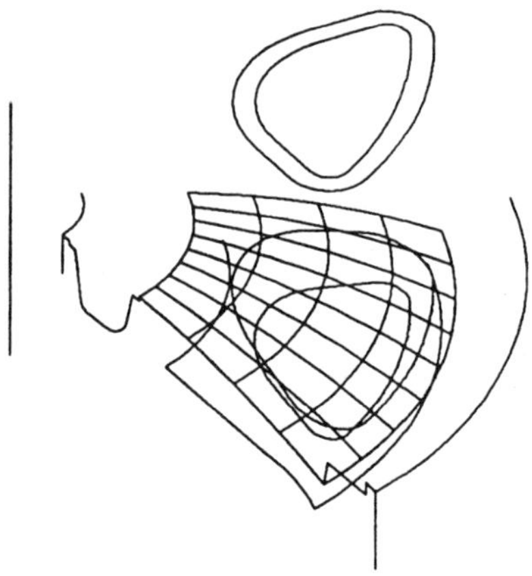

Figure 13.128

Step 10. Make levels 1, 2, and 3 invisible.

Select **Level → Vis. levels**
Toggle levels 1, 2 and 3 to invisible (dimmed)
Select **OK** to return back to graphic mode

The drawing appeared on the screen should now become Figure 13.129.

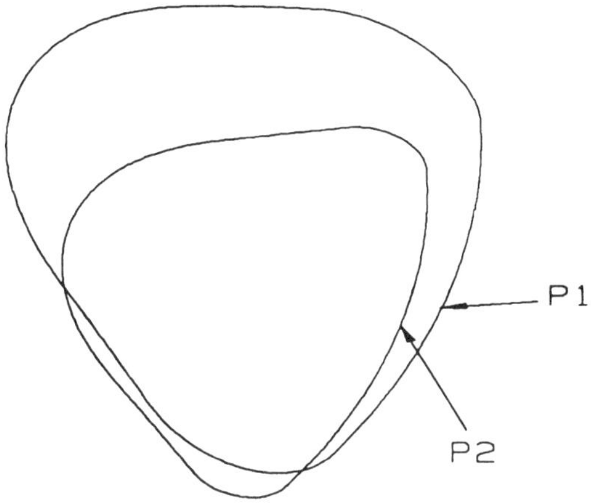

Figure 13.129

Step 11. Create a construction line using the pick points in Figure 13.129. Use the 3d Cplane.

Select **Cplane → 3d**

Select **MAIN MENU → Create → Line → Endpoints → Midpoint**

Pick at **P1** and **P2** to construction a line

Note: Both splines and surface curves should have appeared and cannot be distinguished from each other on the screen. You need to pick the splines to construct the line. If the line does not appear as in Figure 13.130, undo it (alt + U) and try again until you get it right.

The line is added as shown in Figure 13.130.

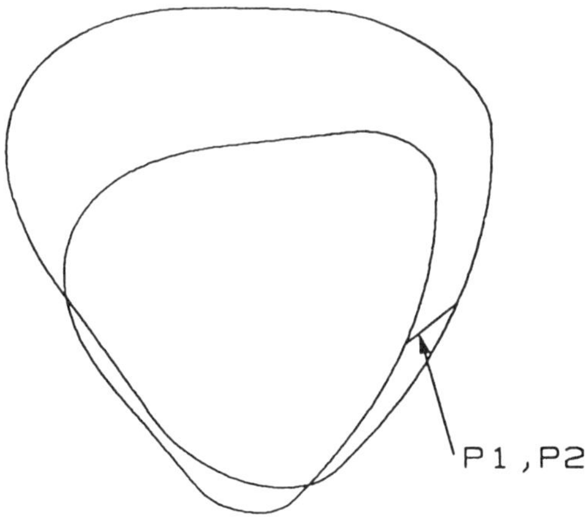

Figure 13.130

Step 12. Create another construction line using the pick points marked in Figure 13.130. Use Top Cplane.

Select **Cplane → Top**

Select **Z → Endpoint** then pick at **P1**

(Z0.5589 should appear in the Secondary menu)

Select **MAIN MENU → Create → Line → Endpoints → Endpoint**

Specify the first point: pick at **P2**

Specify the second point: **0,0 ←**

The drawing should appear as Figure 13.131.

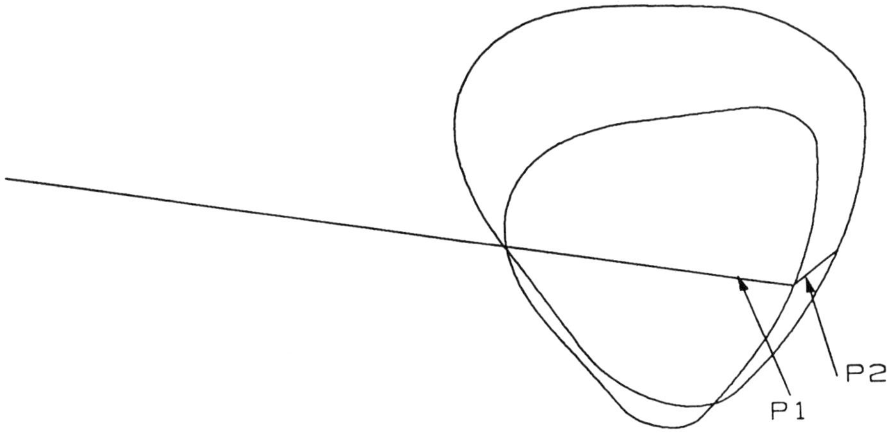

Figure 13.131

Step 13. Use the two construction lines to define a Cplane using the pick points labeled in Figure 13.131.

Select **Cplane → 2 lines**
Pick at **P1** and **P2** to select the two lines
Select **Save** to accept the new Cplane

The drawing should look like Figure 13.132 (*Note:* the same as Figure 13.131).

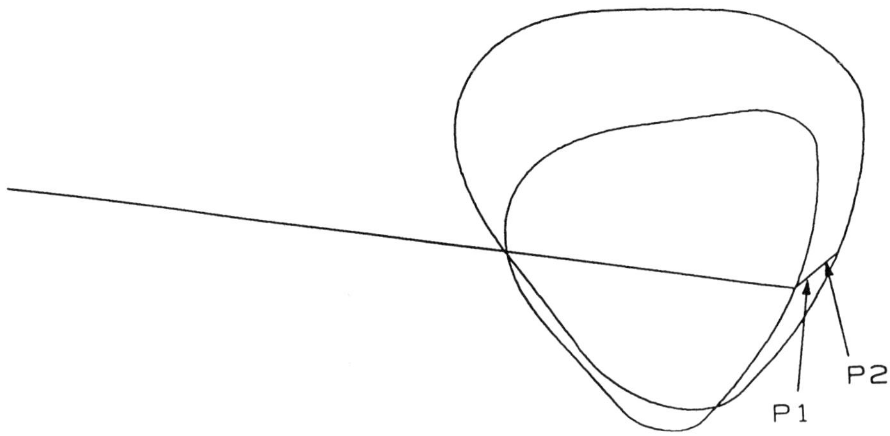

Figure 13.132

Step 14. Create an arc between two surface curves. Use the pick points in Figure 13.132.

Select **MAIN MENU → Create → Arc → Endpoints → Endpoint**
Pick at **P1** and **P2**
Enter the radius: **.25 ←**
Pick the desired arc (2nd arc from right)

The arc is added as shown in Figure 13.133.

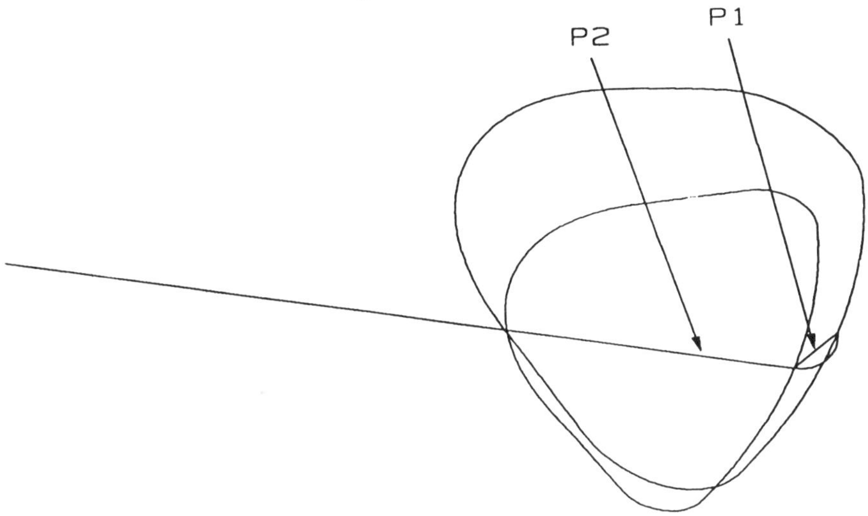

Figure 13.133

Step 15. Delete two construction lines using the pick points in Figure 13.133.

Select **MAIN MENU → Delete**
Pick at **P1** and **P2**

The drawing now should resemble Figure 13.134.

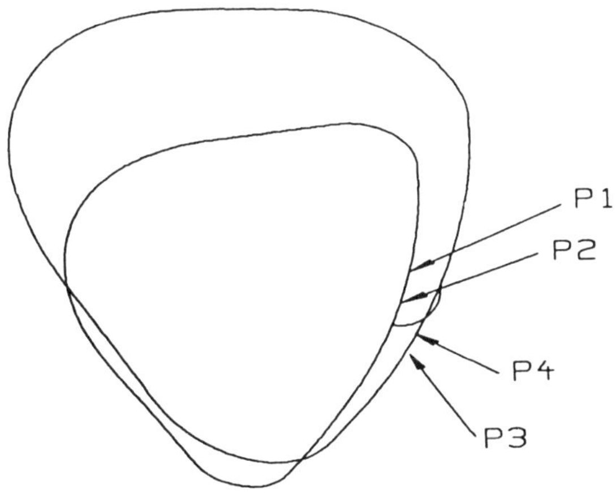

Figure 13.134

Step 16. Break two arcs into two pieces using the pick points in Figure 13.134.

Then change Cplane to Top.
Select **Cplane → Top**
Select **MAIN MENU→ Modify →Break→ 2 pieces**
Pick at **P1** to select an entity
Select **Midpoint** then pick at **P2** to break the entity
Pick at **P3** to select another entity
Select **Midpoint** then pick at **P4** to break the entity

The drawing should appear on the screen as Figure 13.135 .

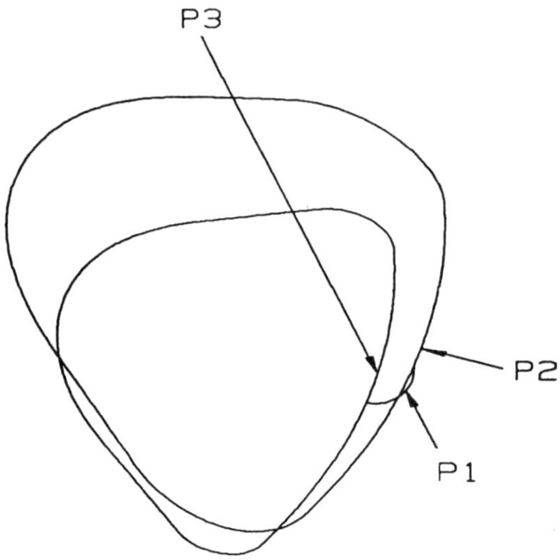

Figure 13.135

Step 17. Create the pocket surface by sweeping the arc along two surface curves.

Use the pick points in Figure 13.135.
Select **Color** then enter **14** ←
Select **MAIN MENU** → **Create** → **sUrface** → **Swept** → **Nurbs**
Enter the number of across contours: **1** ←
define the across contour: select **Single** then pick at **P1**
define along contour 1: select **Chain** then pick at **P2**

Note: If the chaining direction is not in the counter-clockwise direction, press the ESC key to try again.

Select **Close** → **End here**
define along contour 2: select **Chain** then pick at **P3**
Select **Close** → **End here** → **Done**
Set the Swept surface parameters to the following settings:

Along cut distance	= **0.25**
Across cut distance	= **0.1**

Select **Done** to complete the surface
The pocket surface should look like Figure 13.136.

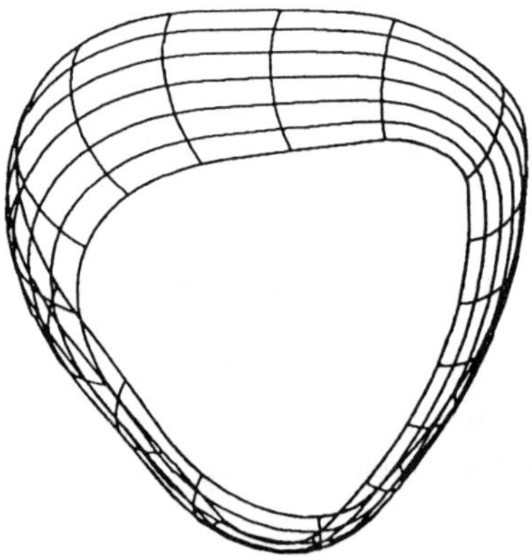

Figue 13.136

Step 18. Make level 3 visible.

Select **Level → Vis. levels**
Toggle level 3 to visible (highlighted)
Select **OK** to return back to graphic mode
The drawing now becomes Figure 13.137.

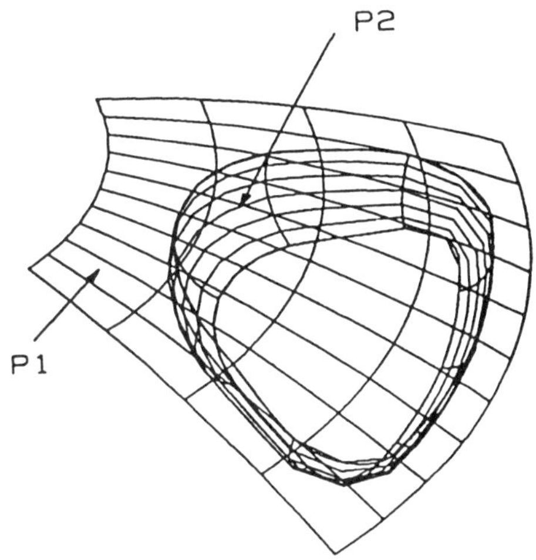

Figure 13.137

Step 19. Change the normal direction of the upper surface and the pocket surface using the pick points in Figure 13.137.

Select **MAIN MENU → Modify → Normal → Dynamic**
Pick at **P1** and click the mouse to locate the arrow
Select **Flip** (the arrow should point downward)
Select **OK** for the normal direction for the upper surface
Pick at **P2** to select the pocket surface and click the mouse to locate the arrow
Select **Flip** (the arrow should point outward)
Select **OK** for the normal direction for the pocket surface

The isometric drawing now should look like Figure 13.138a.
Select **Gview → Top**

The top view of the drawing should resemble Figure 13.138b.

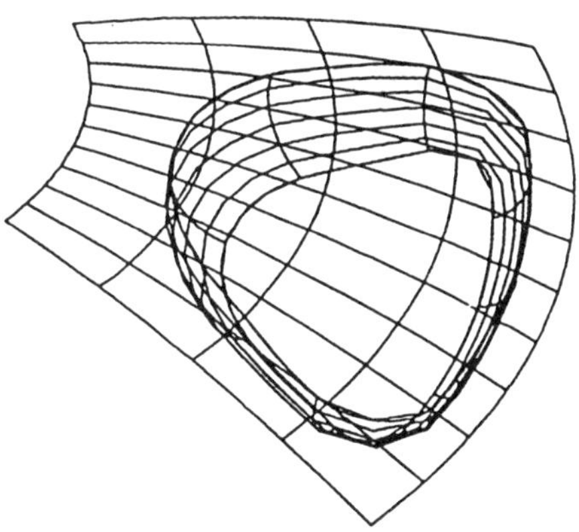

Figure 13.138a. Isometric view

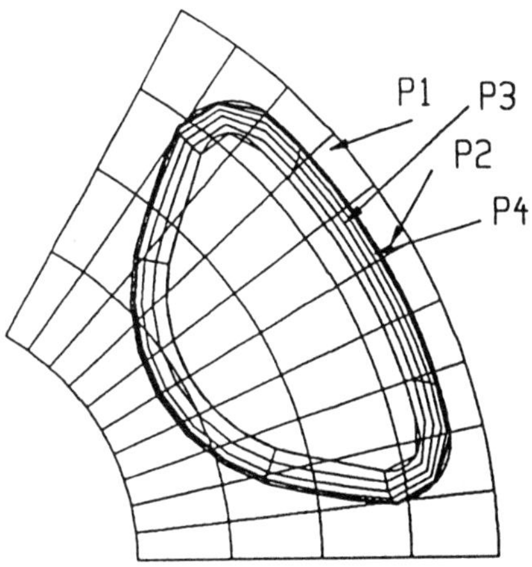

Figure 13.138b. Top view

Step 20. Create a fillet surface between the upper surface and the pocket surface.

Use the pick points in Figure 13.138b. Change level to 6 and color to 11.
Select **Level → Main level**, then enter **6 ←**
Select **Color** then enter **11 ←**
Select **MAIN MENU → Create → sUrface → Fillet → Radius**
Enter the start fillet radius: **0.1**
Set the surface fillet parameters to the following settings:

Use Ch ht	=Y
Step Vals:	
Maximum step distance = **0.1**	
Stepping chord height = **0.005**	
Extend	=**N**
Spline	=**B**
sUrf crvs	=**B**
Fillet	=**N**
Trim	=**2**

Pick at **P1** on the upper surface
Move arrow to **P2** and click the mouse to start a fillet
Pick at **P3** to select the pocket surface
Move arrow to **P4** and click the mouse

Select **Do it** to complete the fillet surface

Select **Gview → Isometric**

The fillet surface should appear as Figure 13.139.

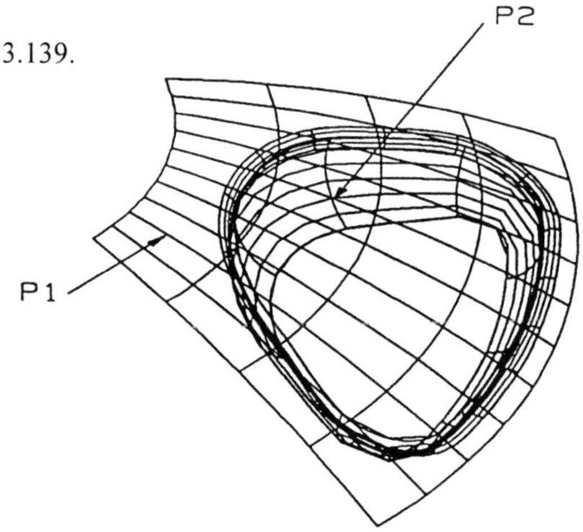

Figure 13.139

Step 21. Change the normal direction of the two surfaces using the pick points in Figure 13.139.

Select **MAIN MENU → Modify → Normal → Dynamic**
Pick at **P1** to select the upper surface
Click the mouse at the point near the pick point **P1**
Select **Flip** (the arrow should point upward)
Select **OK** to accept the surface outward direction
Note: The surface color should turn to purple
Pick at **P2** to select the pocket surface and
click the mouse at the point near the pick point P2
Select **Flip** (the arrow should point inward) then click the mouse
Select **OK** to accept the surface outward direction
Note: The surface color should turn to yellow

The new drawing becomes Figure 13.140.

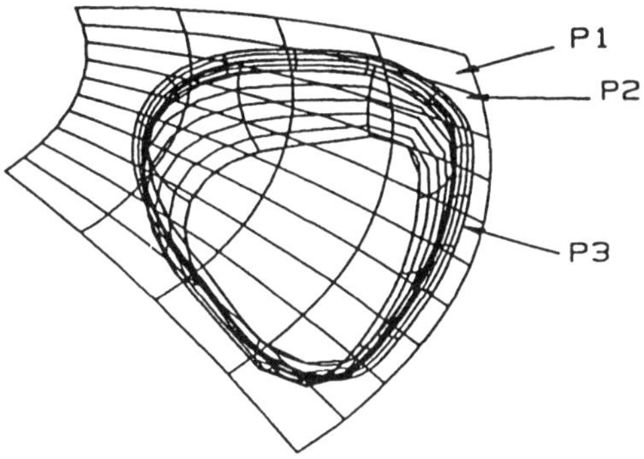

Figure 13.140

Step 22. Trim the upper surface to the fillet surface boundary. Use the pick points in Figure 13.140. Change level to 7 and color to 15.

Select **Level → Main level,** then enter **7** ←
Select **Color** then enter **15** ←
Select **MAIN MENU → Create → sUrface → Trimmed → to Curves**

Set the parameters to the following settings:

Constr Vw	=**N**
Dispose	=**D**
Use Ch ht	=**N**
Step Vals:	
Stepping distance = **0.1**	

Pick at **P1** to select the surface to trim
Pick at **P2** to indicate the surface area to keep
Select **Single** then pick at **P3**
Select **Done → Do it**

The trimmed surface should appear as Figure 13.141.

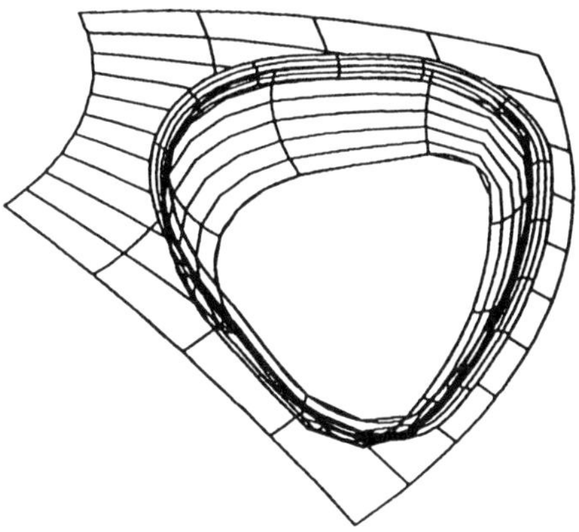

Figure 13.141

Step 23. Make only levels 4 and 5 visible. Change level to 8 and color to 12.

Select **Level → Vis. levels**
Toggle levels 4, 5 and 6 only to visible (highlighted)
Note: levels 1, 2, 3 and 7 are visible (dimmed)
Select **Main level**, then enter 8 ←

The new drawing becomes Figure 13.142.

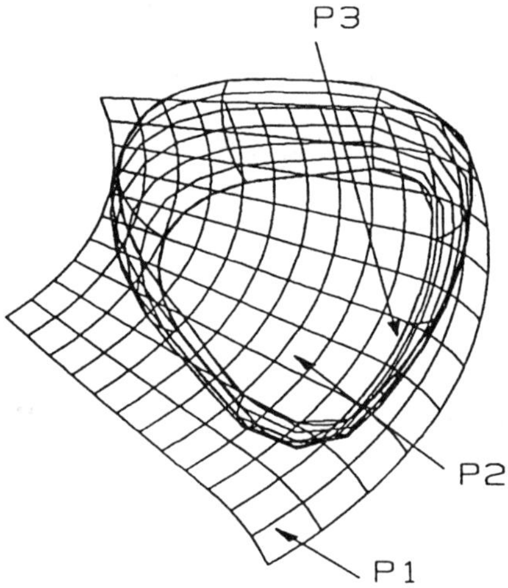

Figure 13.142

Step 24. Trim the lower surface to the pocket surface boundary using the pick points in Figure 13.142.

Select **MAIN MENU → Create → sUrface → Trimmed→ to Curves**
Pick at **P1** to select the lower surface to be trimmed
Move arrow to **P2** and click the mouse to indicate the portion to keep
Select **Chain** then pick at **P3**
Select **Close → End here → Done → Do it**
The trimmed lower surface should appear as Figure 13.143.

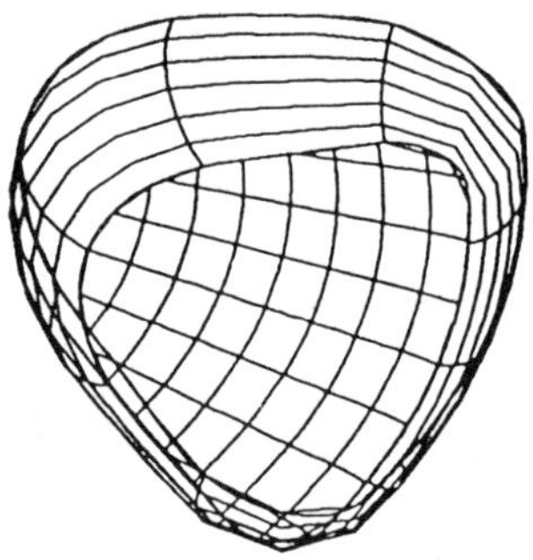

Figure 13.143

Step 25. Make levels 5, 6, 7, and 8 to visible to show trimmed surfaces.

Select **Level → Vis. levels**
Toggle levles 5, 6, 7, and 8 to visible (highlighted)
Note: levels 1, 2, 3 and 4 are invisible
Select **OK** to return back to graphic mode

The new drawing should resemble Figure 13.144.

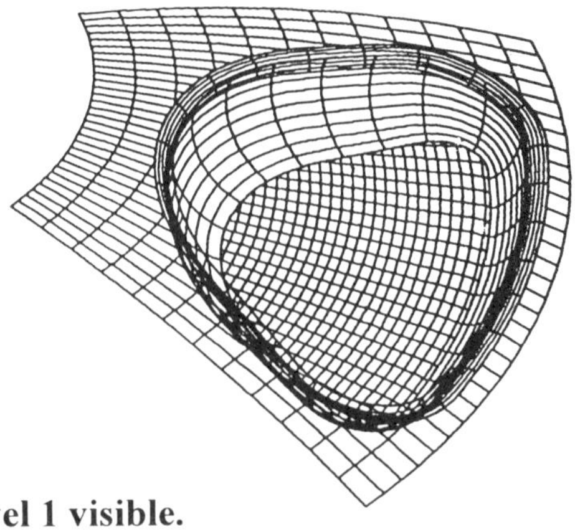

Figure 13.144

Step 26. Make only level 1 visible.

Select **Level → Vis. levels**
Toggle level 1 to visible (levels 2 - 8 are invisible)
Select **OK → OK** to return back to graphic mode

The drawing should look like Figure 13.145

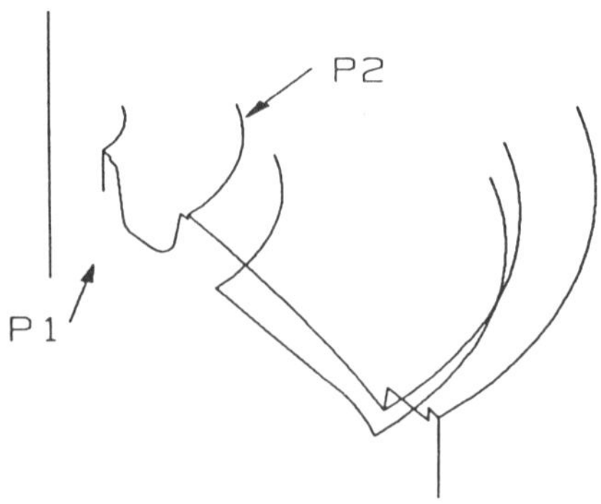

Figure 13.145

Step 27. Zoom the section profile for the hub. Use the pick points in Figure 13.145.

Press **F1** to select the Zoom command
Pick at **P1** and **P2** to zoom the hub profile

The zoomed drawing should appear as Figure 13.146.

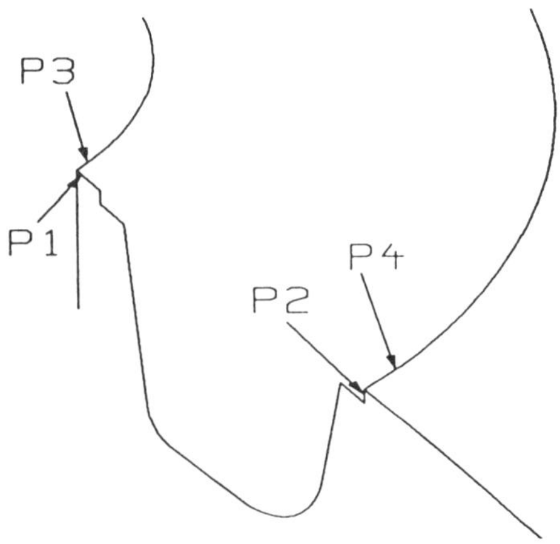

Figure 13.146

Step 28. Create a swept surface for the hub using the pick points in Figure 13.146 on the previous page. Change level to 9 and color to 14.

Select **Level → Mail level**, then enter **9** ←
Select **Color** then enter **14**←
Select **MAIN MENU → Create → sUrface → Swept → Nurbs**
Enter the number of across contours: **1** ←
define the across contour: select **Chain** then pick at **P1** and **P2**
Select **End here** to complete the across contour
define along contour 1: select **Single** then pick at **P3**
define along contour 2: select **Single** then pick at **P4**
Select **Done** to complete contours selection
Set the Swept surface parameters as follows:

Along cut distance = **0.25**
Across cut distance = **0.1**

Select **Done** to complete the surface
Press **Alt + F1** to fit the drawing

The new hub surface should look like Figure 13.147.

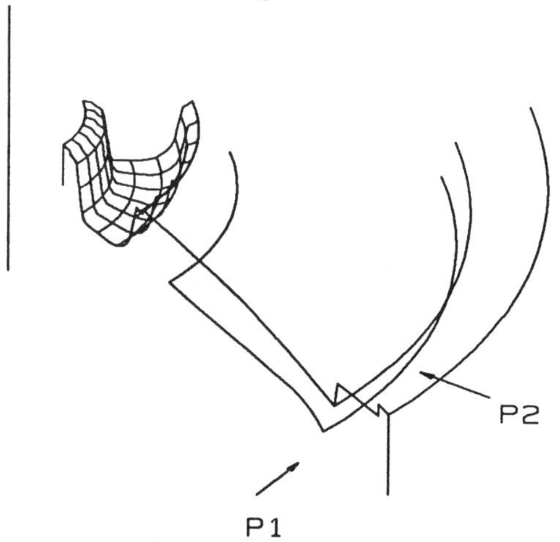

Figure 13.147

Step 29. Zoom the rim profile using the pick points in Figure 13.147.

Press **F1** to select the Zoom command
Pick at **P1** and **P2** to define the zoom area

The zoomed drawing should resemble Figure 13.148.

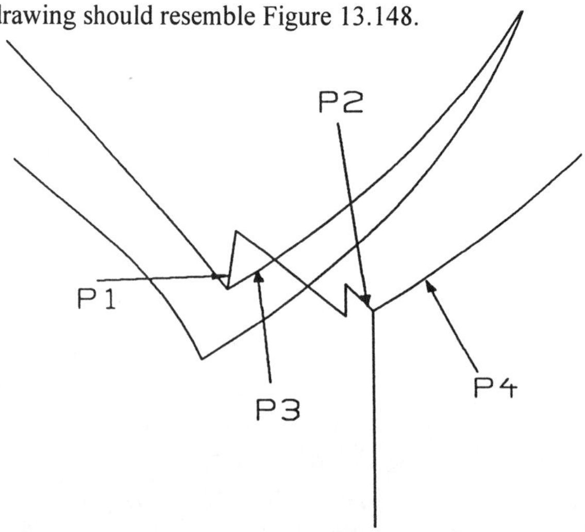

Figure 13.148

Step 30. Create a swept surface for the rim using the pick points in Figure 13.148 on the previous page.

Select **MAIN MENU → Create → sUrface → Swept → Nurbs**
Enter the number of across contours: **1** ←
define the across contour: select **Chain** then pick at **P1** and **P2**
Select **End here**
define along contour 1: select **Single** then pick at **P3**
define along contour 2: select **Single** then pick at **P4**
Select **Done → Done**
Press **Alt** + **F1** to fit the drawing

The rim surface should appear as Figure 13.149.

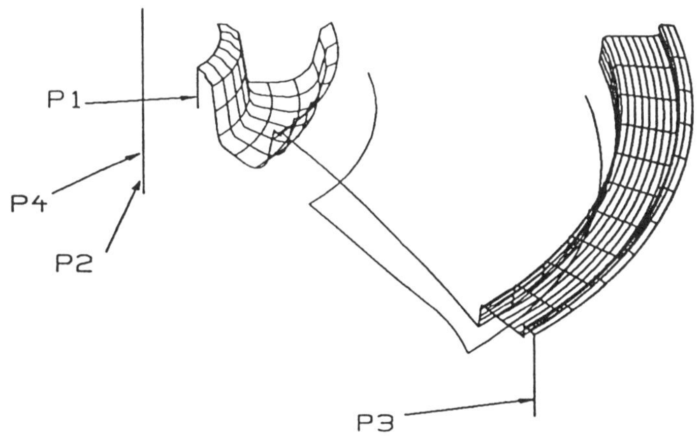

Figure 13.149

Step 31. Create two revolved surfaces using the pick points in Figure 13.149. Change level to 10 and color to 15.

Select **Level → Main level**, then enter **10** ←
Select **Color** then enter **15** ←
Select **MAIN MENU → Create → sUrface → Revolved**
Select the profile entities: pick at **P1**
Select **Done**
Select the axis of rotation: pick at **P2**
Enter the starting angle: **0** ←
Enter the final angle: **60** ← to complete the first surface
Select **Revolved**
Select the profile entities: pick at **P3**
Select **Done**
Select the axis of rotation: pick at **P4**
Enter the starting angle: **0** ←
Enter the final angle: **60** ← to complete the second surface

The two surfaces should resemble Figure 13.150 on the following page.

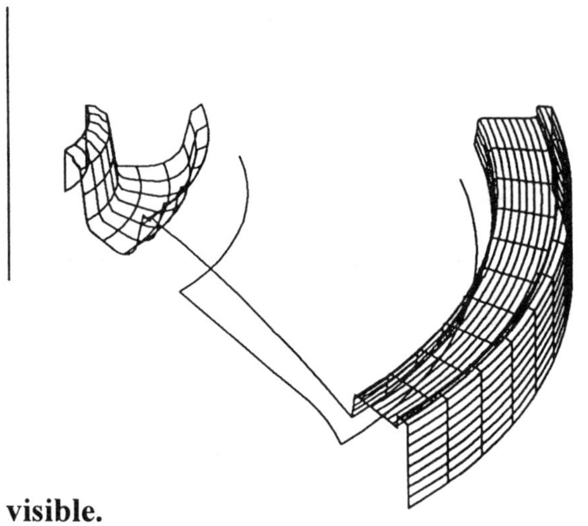

Figure 13.150

Step 32. Make levels 5, 6, 7, 8, 9, and 10 visible.

Select **Level→ Vis. levels**
Toggle levels 5 - 10 to visible (highlighted)
Select **OK** to return back to graphic mode

The complete sectional surfaces should look like Figure 13.151.

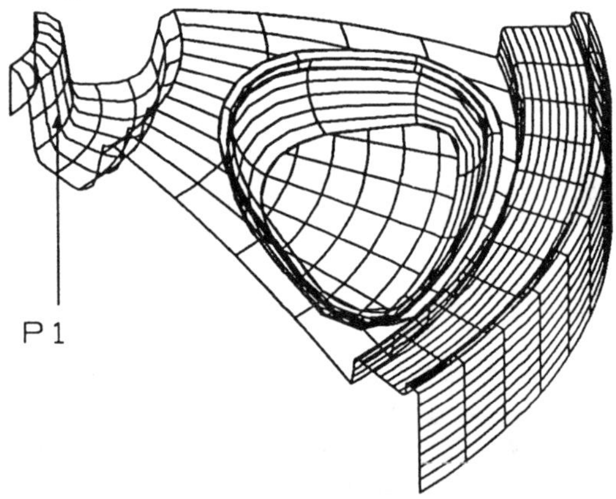

Figure 13.151

Step 33. Change the surface normal direction of the hub surface, if necessary. Use the pick points in Figure 13.151.

Select **MAIN MENU → Modify → Normal → Dynamic**
Pick at **P1** to select the surface and then click the mouse to locate the arrow
Select **Flip** (the arrow should point outward) and click the mouse again
Select **OK** to accept the outward direction

The drawing now becomes Figure 13.152

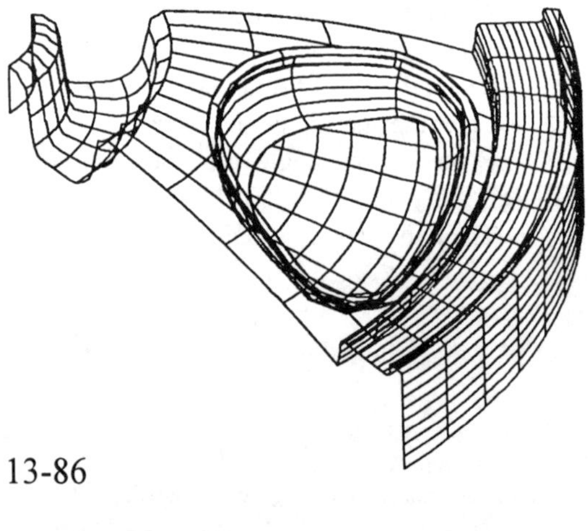

Figure 13.152

Step 34. Save the surface file (wheels).

Select **MAIN MENU → File → Save**
Enter file name: **wheels**

Step 35. Copy the surfaces to five locations using Xform → Rotate commands.

Select **MAIN MENU → Xform → Rotate → All → surFaces → Done → Origin**
Set the Rotate parameters as below:

Copy Number of steps = **5** Rotation angle = **60** ←

Select **Done** to complete the surface model

The final drawing should resemble Figure 13.153.

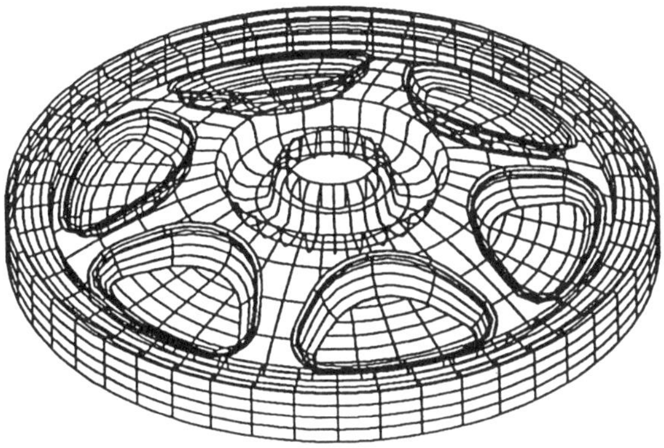

Figure 13.153

13.3 Exercises

13.3.1 Short Answer

1. What are derived surfaces?
2. What are the three derived surface modeling techniques available in Mastercam?
3. Explain when to use fillet surfaces.
4. What are the two types of fillet surfaces?
5. What are the six patterns of variable radius fillet surfaces?
6. List the two stepping methods for specifying the stepping distance of the surface.
7. What are the three types of information to be generated during the creation of a fillet surface?
8. What is a trimmed surface?

9. Under what conditions does surface trimming require you to redefine the outer boundary?

10. What is an offset surface?

11. What are composite surface models?

13.3.2 Problems

12. Create two fillet surfaces from the surface model created in problem 12.17. The original surface model file is **ES1**. Save the fillet surface model as **ES14**. The two fillet surfaces have a constant radius of 0.25". The fillet surfaces with the base surfaces are shown in Figue 13.154. A similar example is project 1 of this chapter.

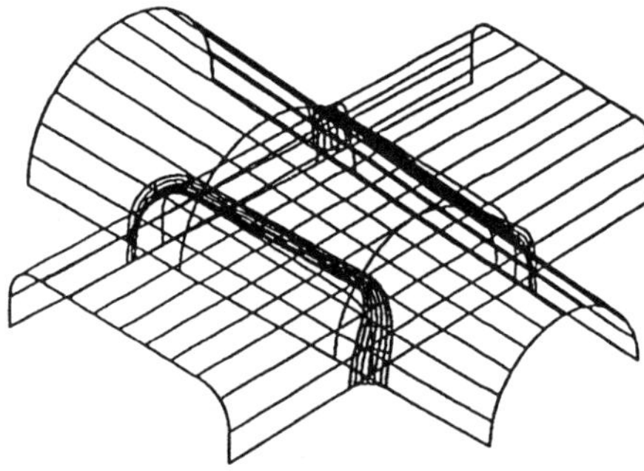

Figure 13.154

13. Create a fillet surface at the intersection of two ruled surfaces created in problem 12.18. The radius of the fillet surface varies in a linear pattern which starts at 0.5" at the right end to 0.35" at the other end. The fillet surface with the two base surfaces are shown in Figure 13.155. The original surface model file is **ES2**. Save the fillet surface model **ES15**. A similar example is project 2 in this chapter.

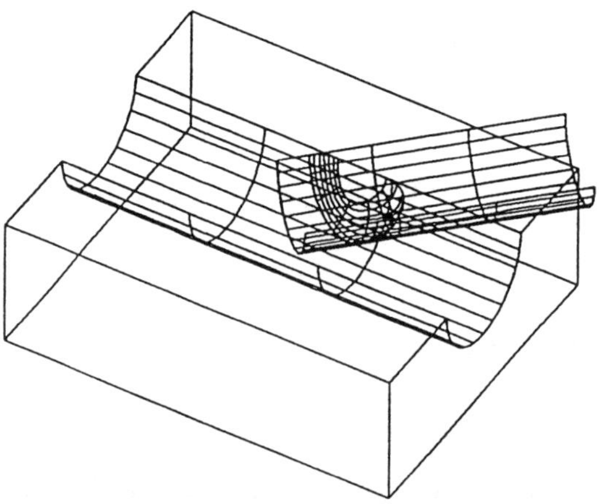

Figure 13.155

14. Create two trimmed surfaces from the surface model created in problem 12. The original surface model is **ES1**. Two surface curves should be created at the intersection between two ruled surfaces. These two surface curves are then used as the trimming boundary to trim the two ruled surfaces. The trimmed surfaces are shown in Figure 13.156. Save the trimmed surfaces as **ES16**. A similar example is project 3 of this chapter.

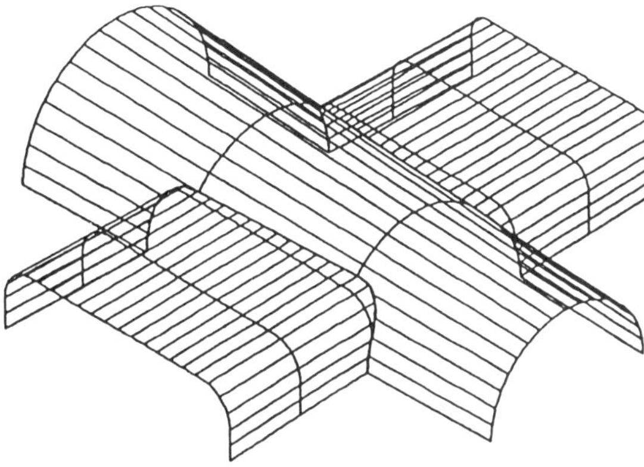

Figure 13.156

15. Create two trimmed surfaces from the surface model created in problem 13 of this chapter. The surface curves of the fillet surface are used as the trimming boundary. The base surface model file is **ES15**. Save the trimmed surfaces as **ES17**. The trimmed surfaces should look like Figure 13.157. A similar example is project 4 in this chapter.

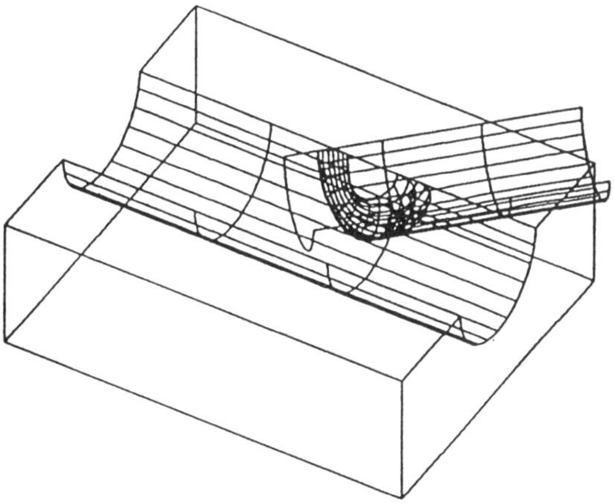

Figure 13.157

16. Generate an offset surface from the surface model created in problem 12.21. The original surface model file is **ES5**. The Coons surface is offset by 0.375" in the outward direction. The offset surface should resemble Figure 13.158. Save the offset surface as **ES18**. A similar example is project 6 of this chapter.

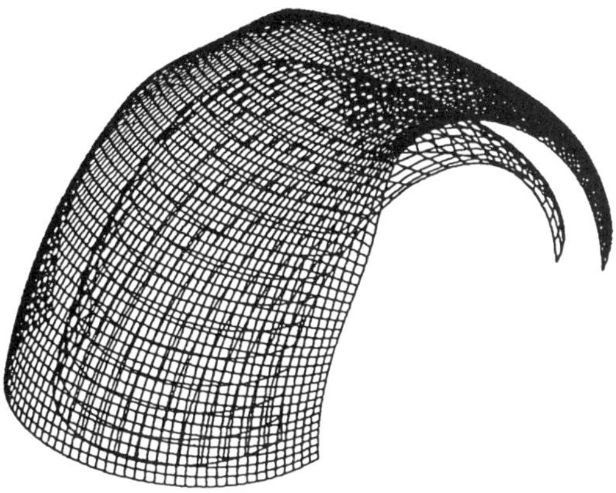

Figure 13.158

17. Create a composite surface model from the wireframe model given in problem 11.20. The wireframe model file is **E11**. The surface model consists of **four** surfaces: a ruled surface at the bottom, a swept surface for wall and top rim, and a fillet surface between the two surfaces as shown in Figure 13.159. Save the surface model as **ES19**. A similar example is project 7 in this chapter.

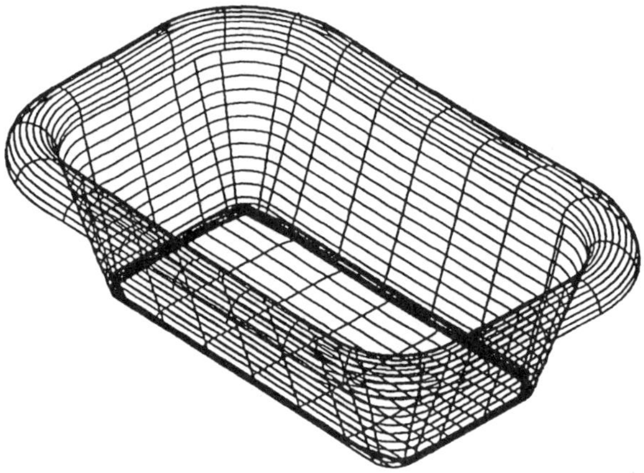

Figure 13.159

18. Create a composite surface model from the wireframe model given in problem 11.21. The wireframe model file is **E12**. This surface model consists of **four** surfaces including one swept surface on the top, one swept surface of the middle frame, and four ruled surfaces for the handles. Save the surface model file as **ES20**. The surface model should look like Figure 13.160. A similar example is project 9 in this chapter.

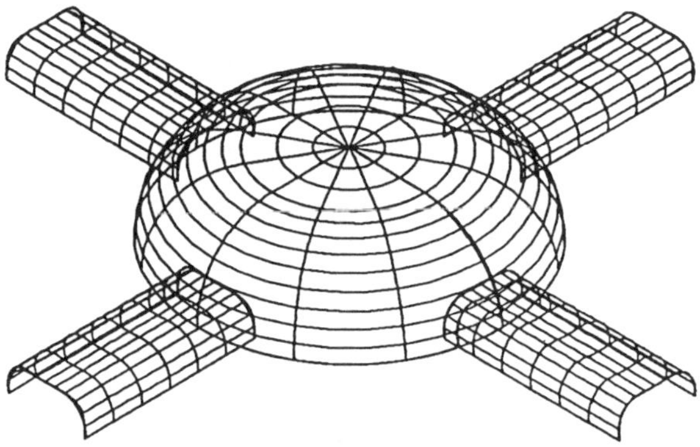

Figure 13.160

Chapter 14

3-D Toolpaths (I): Generated from Wireframe Models

Objectives:

1. Know two methods of generating toolpaths to cut surfaces.
2. Understand 3-d toolpath common parameters.
3. Know 3-d toolpath modules used to generate toolpaths from wireframe models.
4. Apply 3-d toolpath modules.

14.1 Two Surface Toolpath Generation Methods

Mastercam provides **two** methods to generate toolpaths for machining various forms of surfaces: wireframe and surface. Using the wireframe method, the wireframe model is used in a 3-d toolpath module to generate the toolpaths which machine the surface. In the surface method, it takes an extra step to generate the surfacing toolpaths. The wireframe model is used to create the surface model first, then this surface model is used to generate the toolpaths by the flowline or multisurf toolpath module. Figure 14.1 shows a flow chart of these two methods of generating toolpaths for machining surfaces.

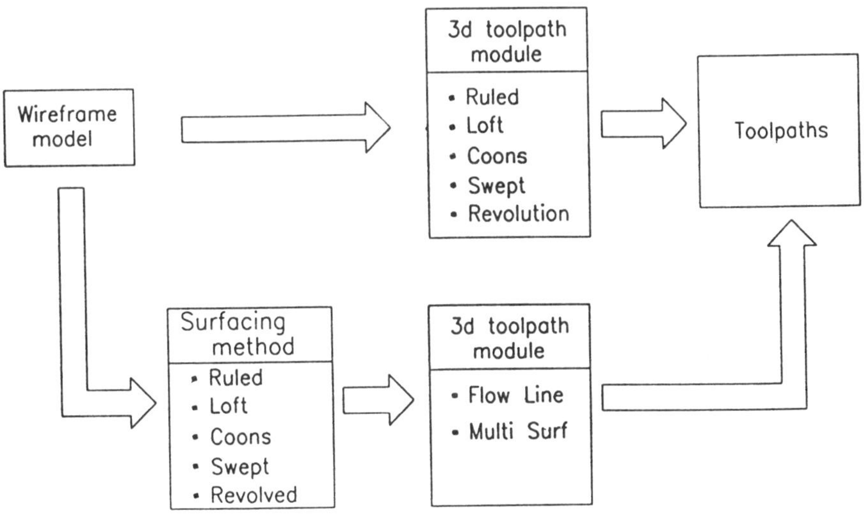

Figure 14.1

At the first glance, the wireframe method seems more straight forward and easy to use. However, we recommend using the surface method except for machining very simple surfaces. The reasons are elaborated in Table 14.1 which compares the two methods of generating surfacing toolpaths.

Table 14.1 Comparing two methods of generating 3-d surfacing toolpaths

Method	Advantages	Disadvantages
Wireframe method	1. Do not require creating a surface before generating toolpaths.	1. Can generate toolpaths for only a single surface. 2. Do not give the surface skin before toolpaths are created. 3. No surface model to be analyzed before generating toolpaths. 4. Required to define more parameters.
Surface method	1. Can generate toolpaths for multiple surfaces simultaneously. 2. Has the surface to be analyzed, examined, and edited before generating toolpaths. 3. Fewer parameters to define. 4. More flexible and easier to be edited.	1. Require an existing surface model to generate the toolpaths.

The wireframe method in generating surfacing toolpaths is presented in this chapter and the surface method is in chapter 15.

14.2 3D Toolpaths Common Parameters

As indicated in chapter 7, Mastercam uses two groups of parameters, common and module specific, to define machining and tooling data. Most common parameters presented in chapter 7 are applicable to 3-d cases. However, a number of additional parameters should be added for 3-d toolpath modules including; *along* and *across*, cutting method, stepping over distances (along cut distance, across cut distance), cutting direction, and cutter compensation.

Along and Across

Surfaces are defined by a series of joined or non-connected contours. These contours are arranged into two groups, along and across, according to their orientations. In other words, along and across are used to indicate the direction of a group of contours (Figure 14.2). Normally, the *along* direction follows the longer contours of the two directions. The *across* direction is the shorter contours.

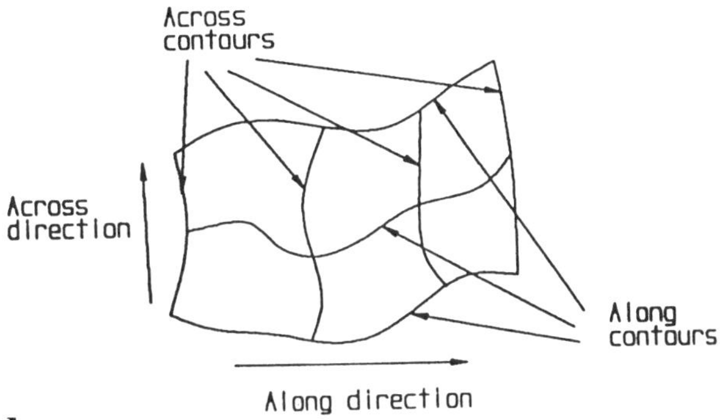

Figure 14.2

Cutting Methods

The cutting method determines the toolpath pattern Mastercam used to generate toolpaths in cutting a surface. There are **three** cutting methods: zig zag, one way and circular. Each method has its unique features and uses. Table 14.2 summaries the features of each cutting method.

Table 14.2 Cutting methods in 3-d surfacing

Type	Features	Illustration
Zig zag	• Cutter moves back and forth across the part to cut the surface. The cutter makes constant contact with the surface. • Takes shorter time. • Conventional milling in one direction and climb milling in the other direction. This alternate milling pattern is not desirable.	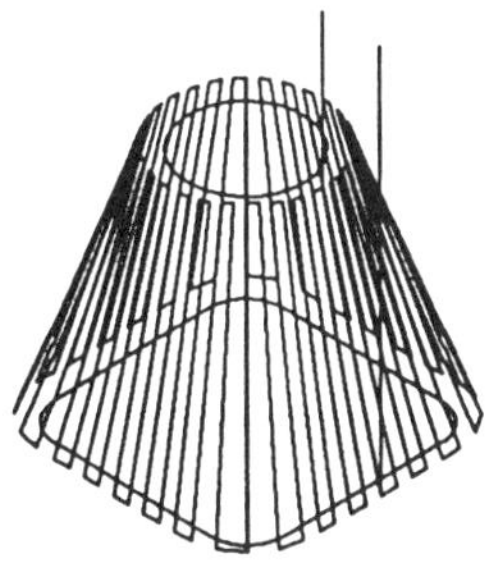
One way	• Cutter takes all passes on the surface in the same direction. It makes a pass, then retracts in Z direction, rapids to another starting point, takes another pass in the specified direction. Repeat the toolpath patern until completing the surface cutting. • Keep the same milling type (climb or conventional) • Take longer time due to retracting and plunging for each cutting pass.	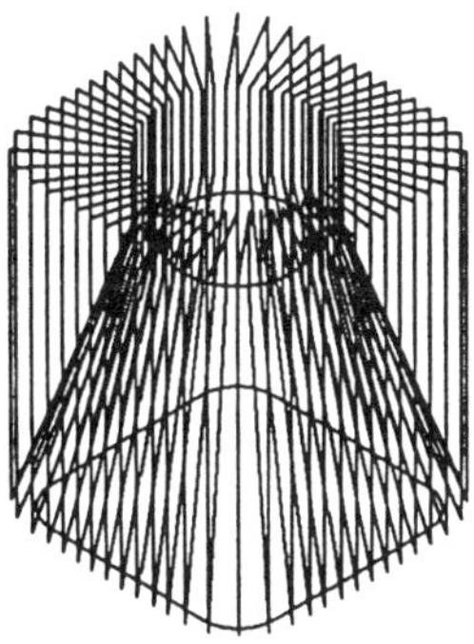
Circular	• Cutter moves along a spiral pattern to machine a surface. • Circular should only be used when closed contours are used. This means that the first and last contour are idential.	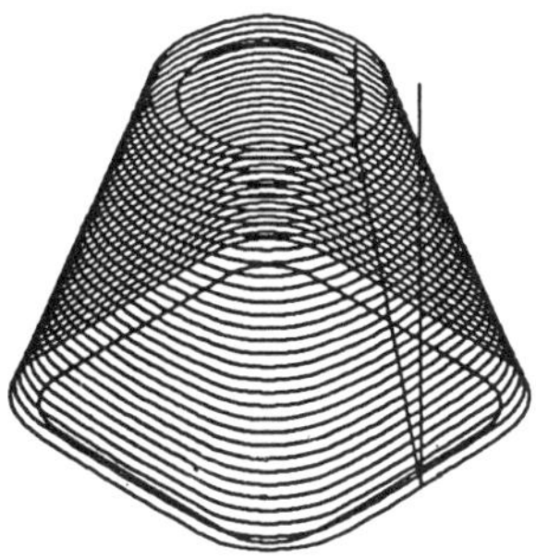

Cutting Direction

This parameter can be toggled to along or across which specifies the cutting direction of the toolpaths. In the **along** mode, the cutter cuts in the along direction while stepping over in the across direction as shown in Figure 14.3 . In the **across** mode, the cutter cuts in the across direction while stepping over in the along direction (Figure 14.4).

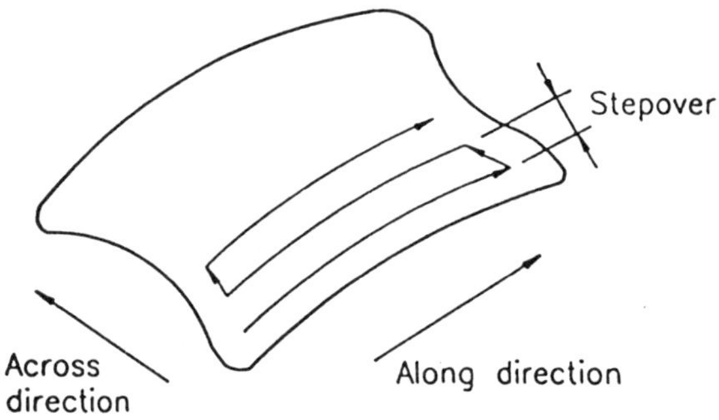

Figure 14.3

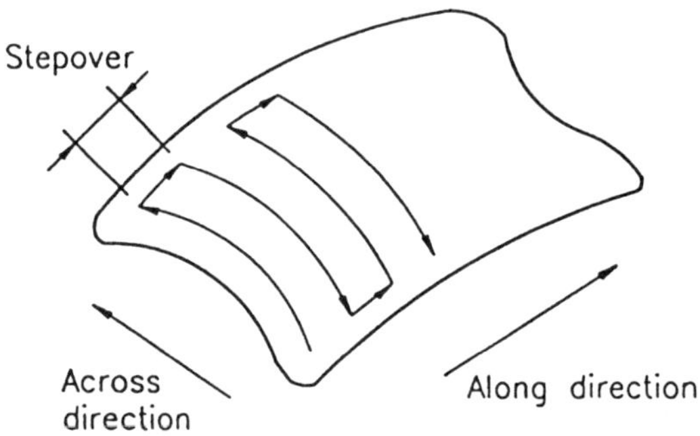

Figure 14.4

Stepping Over Distances

Surface cuttings are normally implemented in linear interpolation mode. In fact, the surface is approximated by a set of linear interpolation motion commands which step over the surface skin. Therefore, the system requires two stepping over values, one in along direction and the other in the across direction, to determine the actual coordinates of toolpaths. Mastercam uses two terms, along cut distance and across cut distance, to indicate these two stepping over values. The **along cut distance** is the cutter step-over distance in each along pass. The **across cut distance** is the cutter step-over distance between each along cut. Figure 14.5 illustrates the use of along cut distance and across cut distance in surface cutting. It should be noted that these two distances determine the cutting accuracy and the program size. The larger the distance, the bigger the surface positional error and the shorter the program size. Conversely, the smaller the distance, the smaller the surface positional error and the larger the program size.

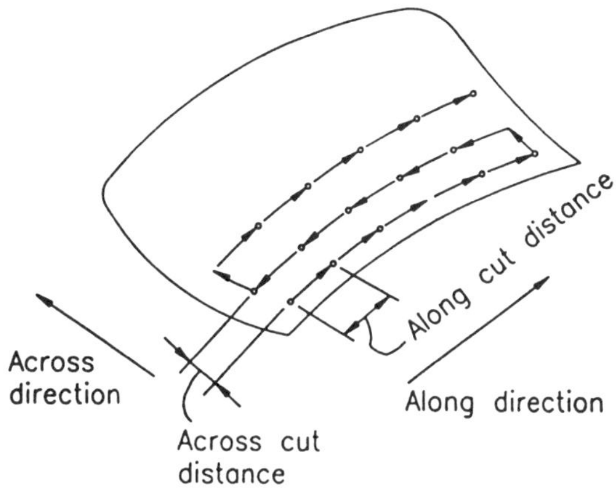

Figure 14.5

Cutter Compensation

Cutter compensation in a 3-d machining is more difficult to be determined than those in 2-d machining. The "cutter compensation in computer" parameter can be toggled to one of **five modes**: left center, left tip, right center, right tip, and off. It should be noted that ball-end mills or bull-nose mills are normally used in 3-d machining. The definition of cutter tip and cutter center for ball-end, bull-nose, and straight-end mills are illustrated in Figure 14.6. The selection of tip and center of the cutter has a significant effect on the toolpaths as shown in Figure 14.7.

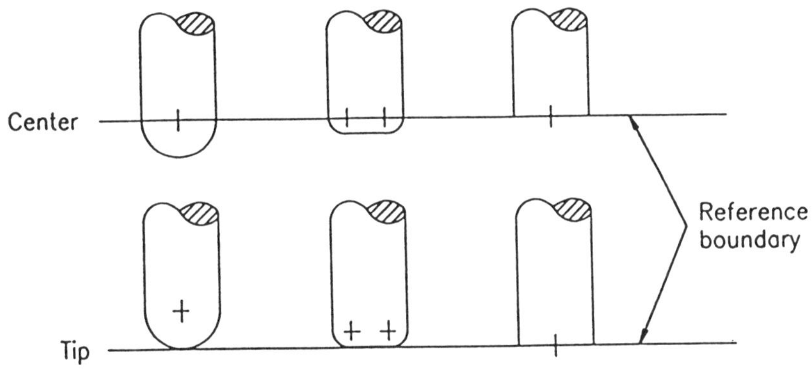

Figures 14.6

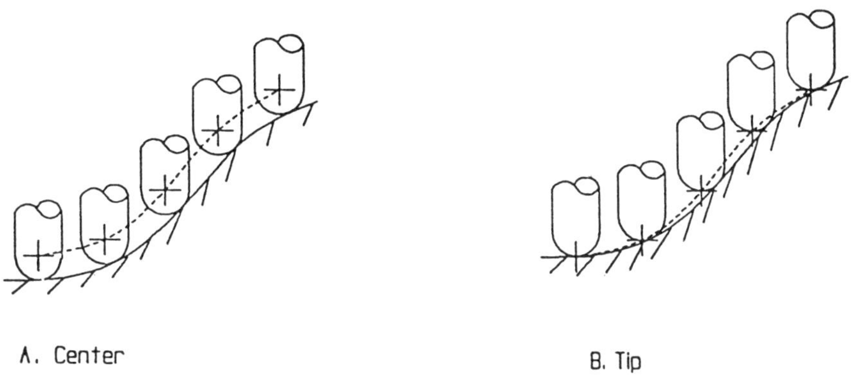

Figure 14.7

Tip Mastercam actually calculates for a sphere when you specify a ball end mill so one could use a special shaped cutter if necessary.

The direction of cutter compensation can be left, right, or off. The offset direction is determined as followed:

Viewing from the first contour toward the last contour in the along direction:

Left:	The contrours used to define the surface are located at the left side of the toolpaths (Figure 14.8a).
Right:	The contours used to define the surface are located at the right side of the toolpaths (Figure 14.8b).

Note: the cutter compensation in Figure 14.8b produces undercut throughout the surface.

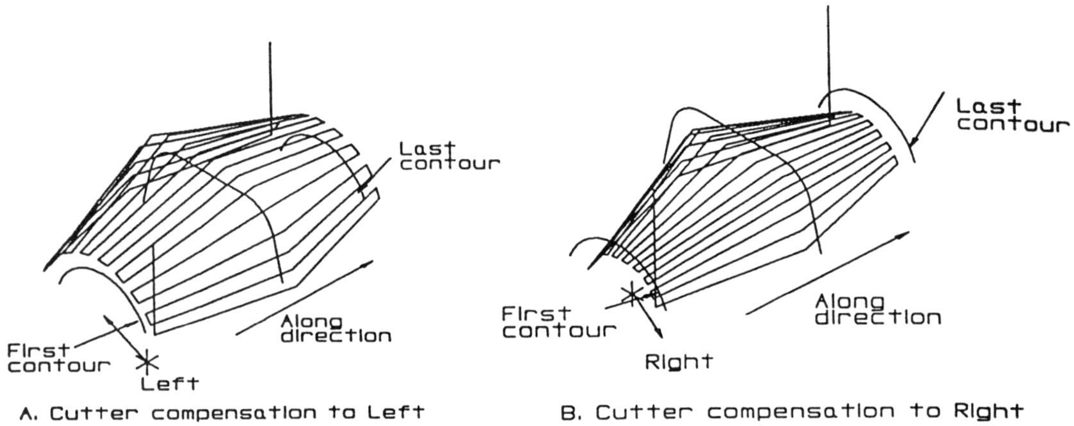

Figure 14.8

Figure 14.9 shows an example of picking the contour order reversed from that in Figure 14.8.

Note: when the picking order of the contours is reversed, the direction for cutter compensation should be changed accordingly.

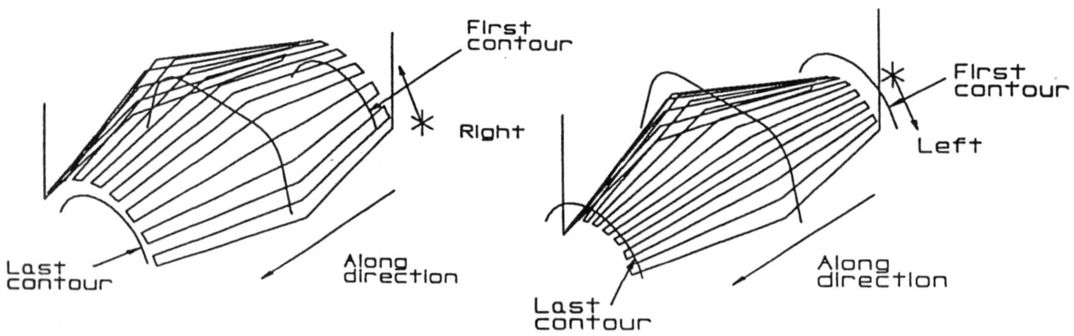

Figure 14.9

When cutter compensation is applied to the across direction, the viewing direction follows the across contour from the picking end to the other end. Then the direction of left and right is determined with the same principle as in the along direction. Figure 14.10 shows an example of cutter compensation in the across direction.

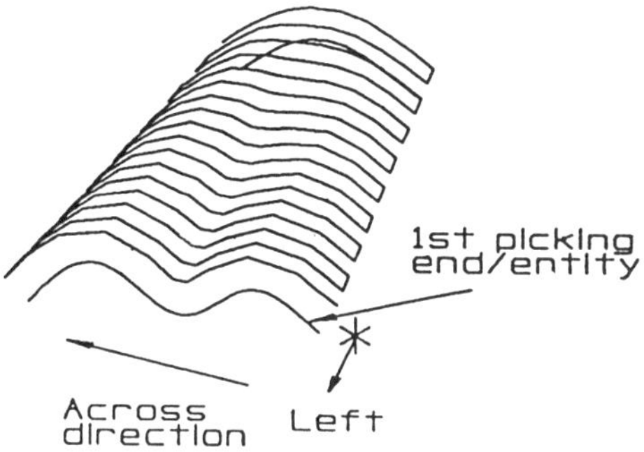

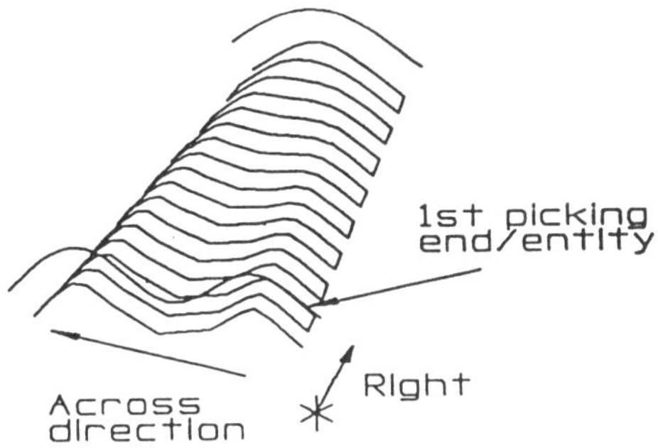

Figure 14.10a Cutter compensation to **left**   Figure 14.10b Cutter compensation to **right**

14.3 3D Toolpath Modules

Mastercam has two groups of 3-d toolpath modules. The **first group** has **five** toolpath modules which are used to generate toolpaths for cutting a single surface from a wireframe model. The **second group** has **two** toolpath modules that are used to generate toolpaths to cut a single surface or multiple surfaces from an existing surface model. In this chapter we only present the first group. The second group is covered in chapter 15.

The **five 3-d toolpath modules** for working with wireframe models include ruled, loft, Coons, swept, and revolution. The selection of a proper 3-d toolpath module mainly depends on the nature of the surface to be cut and the type and number of surface profiles avilable in the wireframe model. On the next page, Table 14.3 summarizes the features of these five modules.

These five toolpath modules are presented in the following five sections. Each section begins with a brief discussion of the features of the module, module specific parameters, and concluded with one or two examples.

14.4 Ruled Toolpath Module

This ruled module is used for blending two to one hundred contours to produce a linear 3D surface as shown in Figure 14.11.

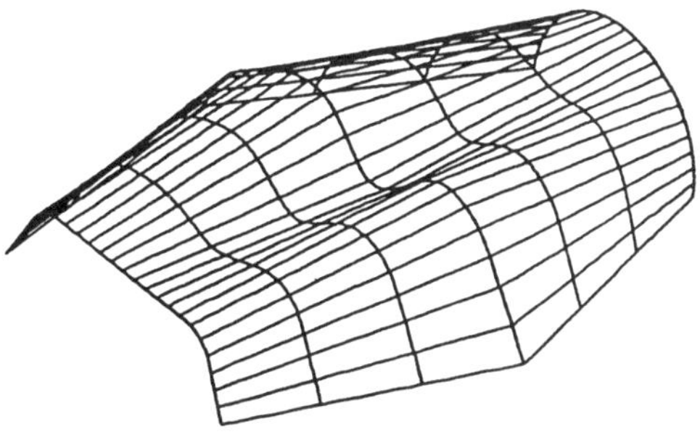

Figure 14.11

Table 14.3 3-d toolpath modules for machining surfaces from a wireframe model

Module type	Description	Illustration
Ruled	Creates the toolpaths to produce a surface formed by linearly blending at least two contours.	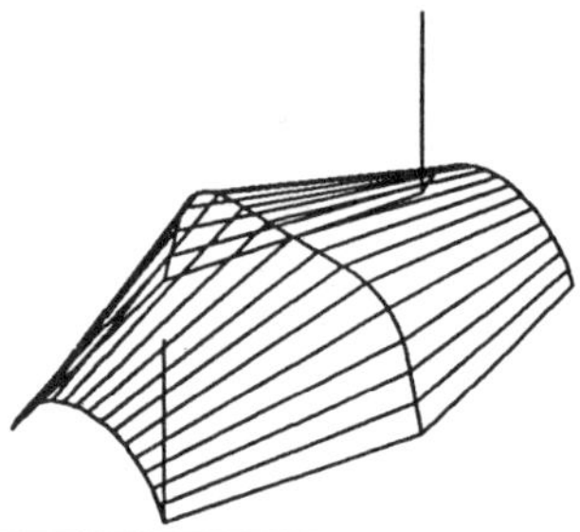
Loft	Creates the toolpaths to produce a surface formed by blending parabolically more than two contours.	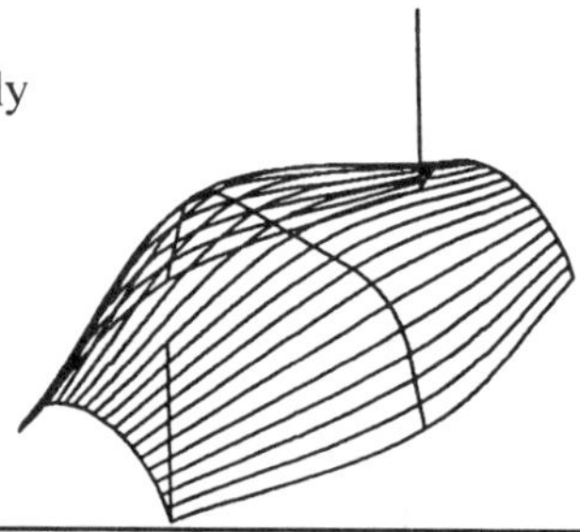
Coons	Creates the toolpaths to produce a surface that is formed by blending a grid of closed boundaries (patches).	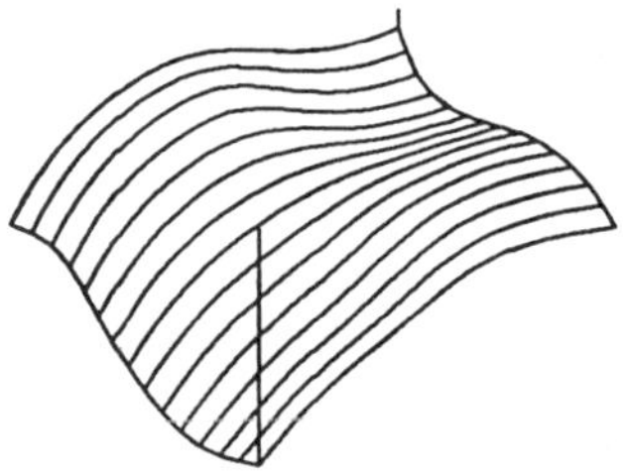
Swept 3D	Creates the toolpaths to cut a surface that is formed by sweeping one or two across contours along one or two rails (along contours).	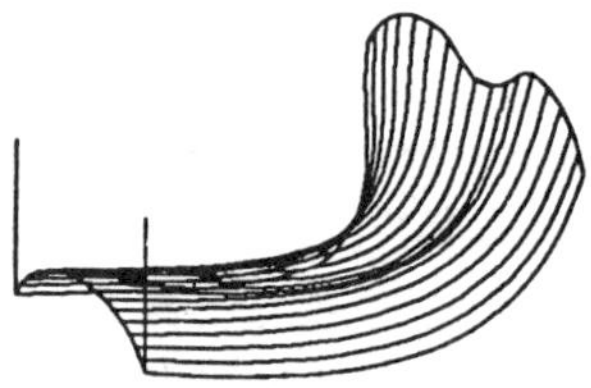
Revolution	Creates the toolpaths to produce a surface by rotating a contour about an axis of rotation.	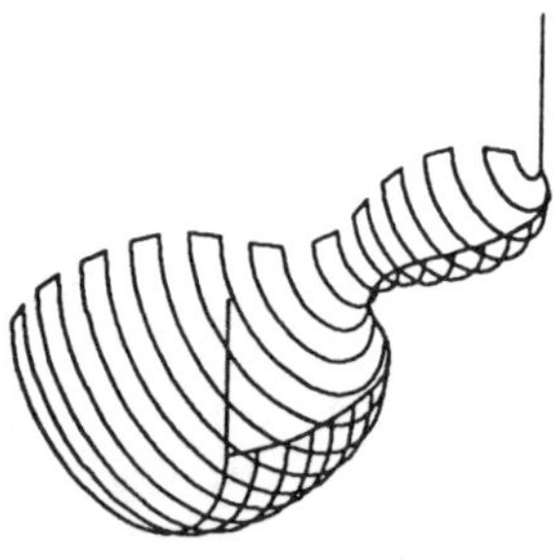

Ruled Parameters

The ruled parameters appear as below:

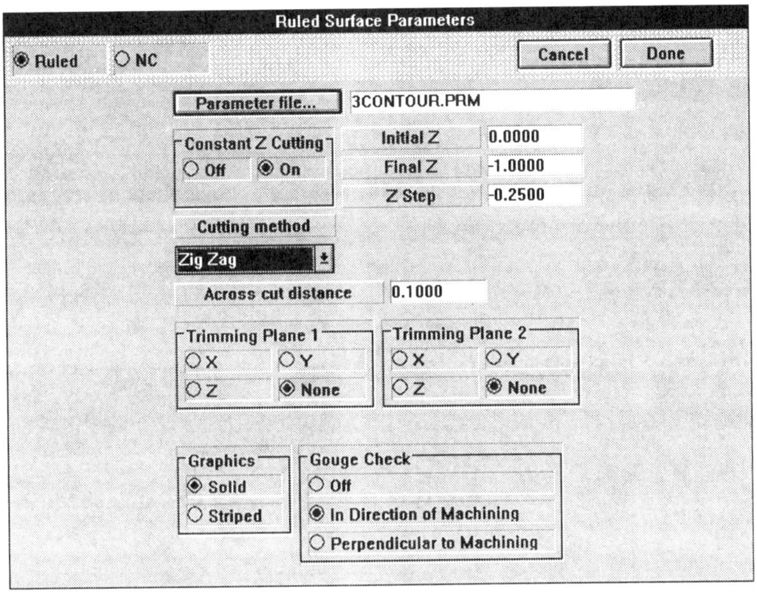

Constant Z Cutting

This parameter can be set to On or Off. When set to On, the cutter will be kept at a constant Z depth for each cut pass. The following three parameters will appear when the Constant Z cutting is set to On:

Initial Z:	specifies the Z value of top boundary
Final Z:	specifies the Z value of bottom boundary
Z step:	specifies the stepover value in Z direction of each pass

The initial Z and final Z define the constant Z cutting boundaries. These boundaries can be used to extend the toolpath beyond the defined surface or cut only a portion of the defined surface. Figure 14.12 illustrates the three parameters in constant Z cutting.

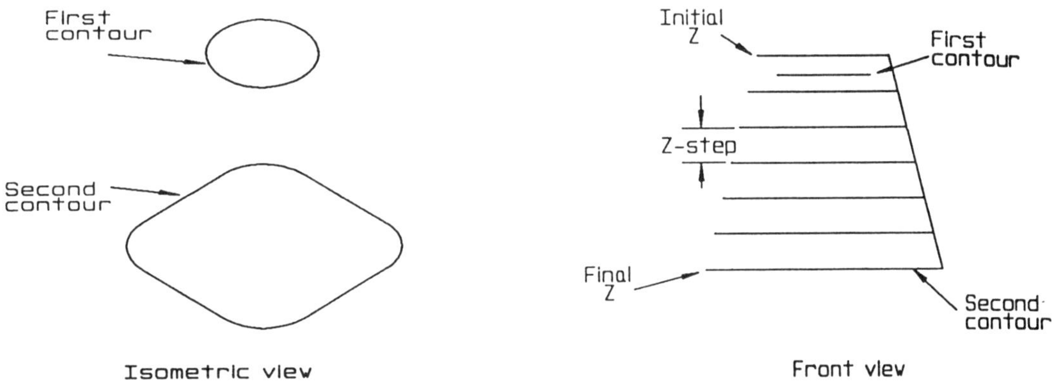

Figure 14.12

Taper Angle

This parameter specifies the angle of the surface slope for the cutting tool. It is only available for 5 axis cutting.

Trimming Planes

The ruled module allows to define two trimming planes. These trimming planes can be used to (1) extend the cut to the specified boundaries (Figure 14.13) and (2) limit the cut to pass the specified boundaries (Figure 14.14). When the trimming planes are located outside the surface boundaries, the toolpaths are extended. When the trimming planes fit inside the surface boundaries, the toolpaths are trimmed.

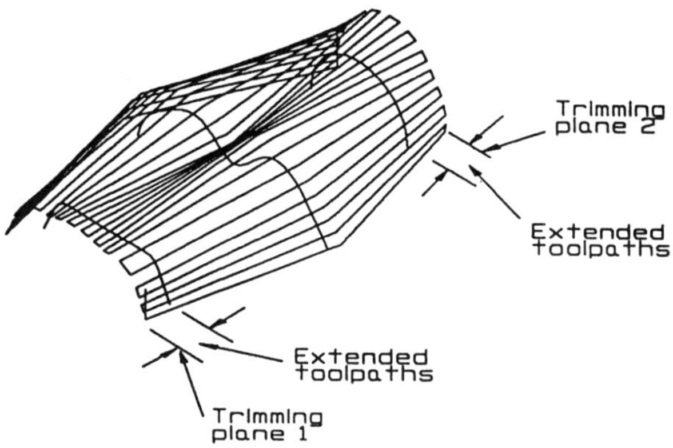

Figure 14.13 Extending

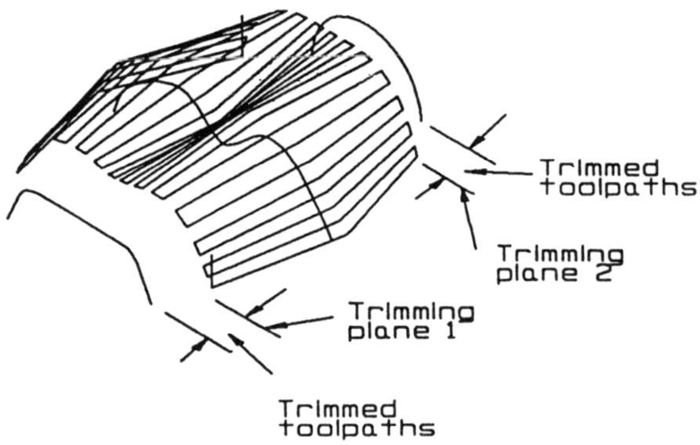

Figure 14.14 Trimming

Gouge Check Direction

This parameter can be toggled to one of three modes to determine whether the gouge check is to be performed, and in what direction. Gouge checking is ignored when off mode is selected. Gouge checking is performed in the *along* direction if the parameter is set to "Mainly in direction of machining" and is carried out in the *across* direction when the "Mainly perpendicular to machining" mode is selected.

Project 1.

1

Machining a ruled surface formed by two contours

Wireframe Model
Project 1 of Chapter 11 (Ruled1)

Go to

Toolpath
(Surf1 & Surf2)

We are here

The ruled toolpath module is used to generate toolpaths for machining two ruled surfaces as shown in Figure 14.15. The wireframe model file is **ruled1** which is created in chapter 11. These two ruled surfaces intersect in the middle. Therefore, their toolpaths can not be used without modification. Actually, we can not machine these two ruled surfaces using the toolpaths generated from this project because the toolpath in one surface cuts into the other surface. In this project we can only illustrate generating toolpaths for machining ruled surfaces. We also assume that two fillet surfaces are to be added at the two places where the ruled surfaces intersect. This is done in chapter 15. Here we create two sets of toolpaths to machine two ruled surfaces. One file is saved as Surf1 and the other as Surf2.

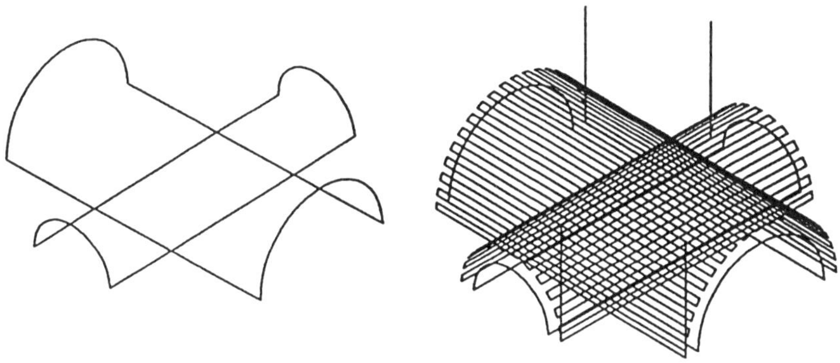

Figure 14.15

Tips 1. Cutter compensation in computer is set to **left** center for the first ruled surface and set to **right** center for the second ruled surface.

2. Cutter is 0.5" ball-end mill.

3. Save the toolpaths for each surface in a separate file, **surf1** for the first ruled surface and **surf2** for the second. These two toolpaths files can not be used without modification. They will cut through each other in the middle.

Step 1. Load the wireframe model file (ruled1.ge3) or create one by following the instructions in project 1 of chapter 11. The wireframe model should appear as in Figure 14.16.

Select **MAIN MENU → File → Get**

Enter file name: **ruled1** ←

Select **Yes** to delete the current part

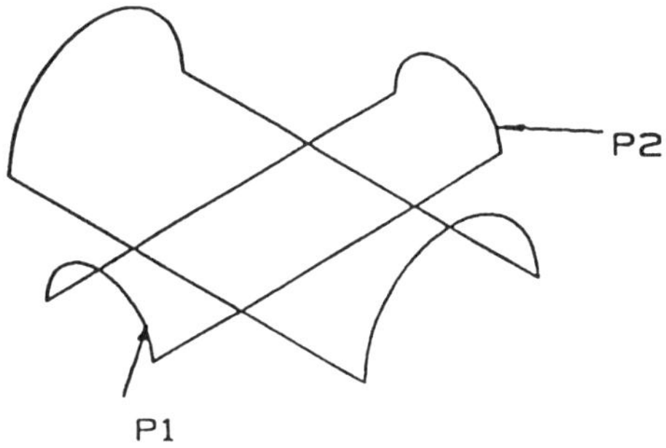

Figure 14.16

Step 2. Initiate ruled toolpath module.

Select **MAIN MENU** → **Toolpaths** → **mIsc.** → **rUled**

Enter file name: **surf1** ←

Step 3. Define the contours.
Use the pick points in Figure 14.16 on the previous page .

Select **Single** then pick at **P1**

Select **Single** then pick at **P2**

Select **Done**

Step 4. Set the ruled parameters to the following settings.

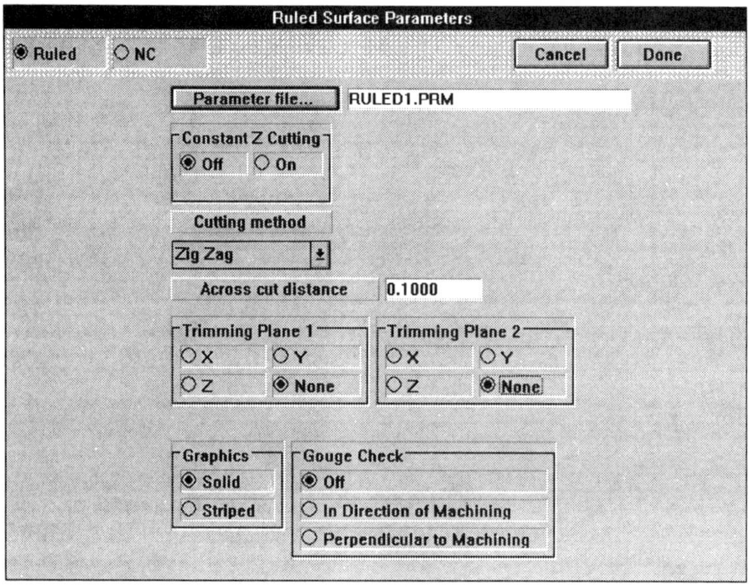

Click the **NC botton** to advance to the NC parameters menu.

Step 5. Define NC parameters to the following settings.

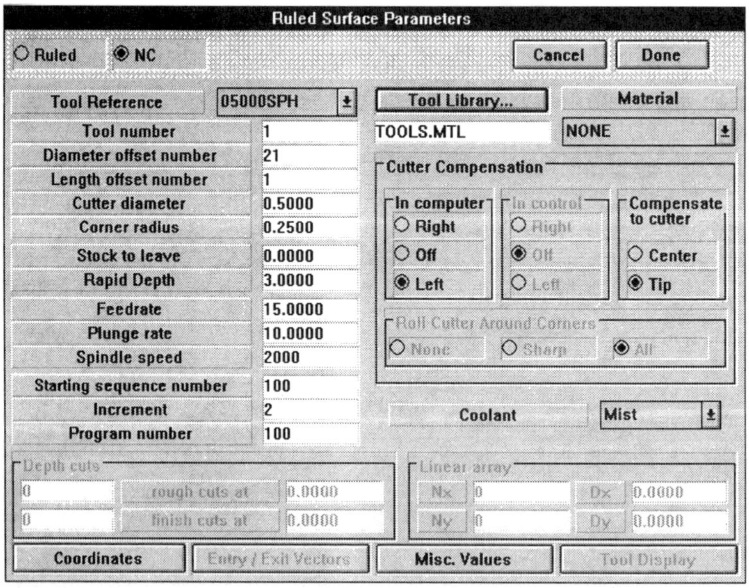

Click on the **Done button** to complete the parameter settings.

Step 6. Write and save the toolpaths.

The toolpaths should display on the screen as Figure 14.17.

Select **Yes** to accept the toolpath
Select **End program** to close the NCI file
Select **No** to "Run the post processor?"

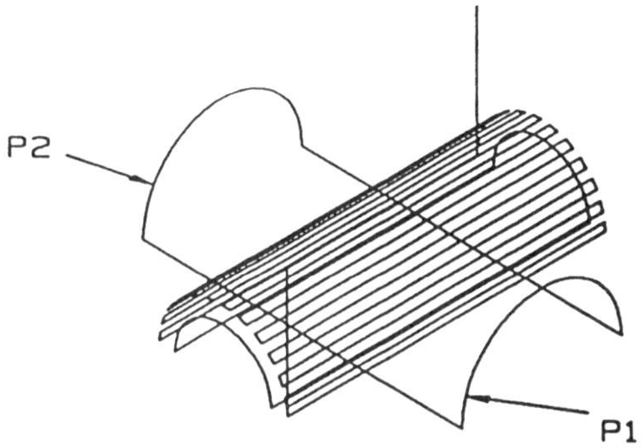

Figure 14.17

Step 7. Initiate ruled toolpath module again to generate toolpaths for the second ruled surface.

Select **rUled**
Enter file name: **surf2** ←

Step 8. Define ruled surface contours using the pick points (Figure 14.17).

Select **Single** then pick at **P1**
Select **Single** then pick at **P2**
Select **Done**

Step 9. Define the ruled toolpath parameters to the following settings.

The Ruled parameters for this surface are the same as those in step 4.
Click the **NC** to advance to the NC parameters menu.

Step 10. Define NC parameters to the following settings.

Set the NC parameters as those given in step 5, with the exception of
Set Cutter Compensation to ☞

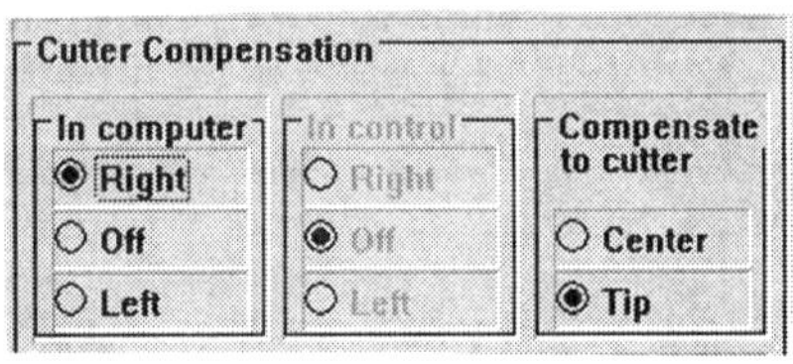

Select the **Done button** to complete the parameter settings.

Step 11. Write and accept the toolpaths.

Select **Yes** to accept the toolpaths
Select **End program** to close NCI file

The toolpaths should resemble Figure 14.18.

Select **No** to “Run the post processor?”

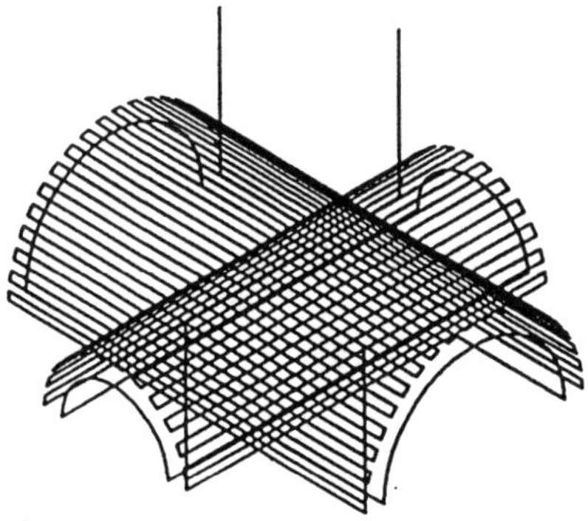

Figure 14.18

Project 2.

Machining a ruled surface formed by three contours

A ruled surface is defined by a wireframe model of three contours as created in project 3 of chapter 11. The wireframe model and finished toolpaths are illustrated in Figure 14.19.

2

Wireframe Model
Project 3 of Chapter 11 (3Contour)

We are here

Go to

Toolpath
(ruledt2)

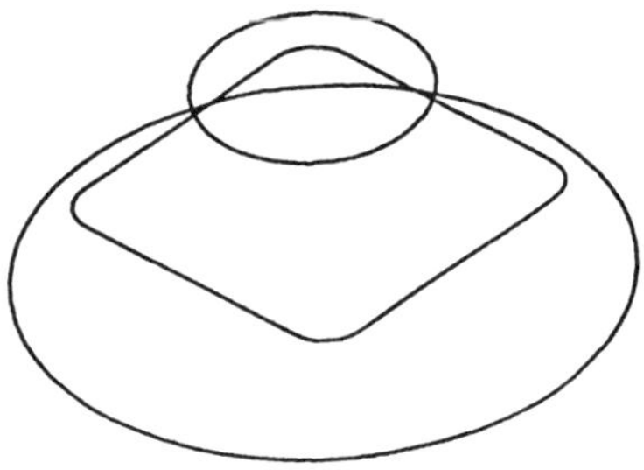

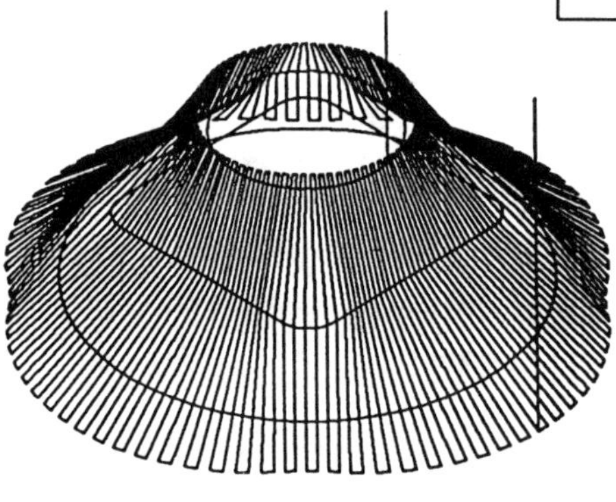

Figure 14.19

Tips 1. Use trimming planes to extend the cutting paths. The first trim plane is Z0.25 and the second plane Z-2.0.

2. The right vertical line of the rectangular contour must be broken into two pieces at the middle. This allows the alignment of the start points of three contours.
3. Picking sequence of the contours starts from the top downward. This determines the direction of toolpaths to go from top to bottom.

Step 1. Load the wireframe model file (3contour.ge3) or create one by following the instructions in project 3 of chpater 11.

Select **MAIN MENU → File → Get**
Enter file name: **3contour ←**
Select **Yes** to delete the current part

The wireframe model should appear as Figure 14.20.

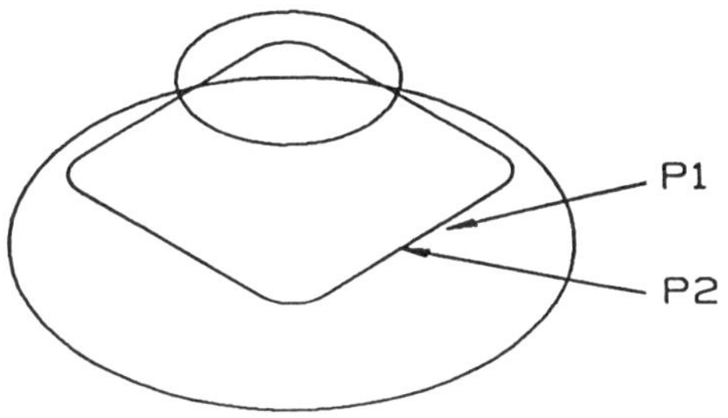

Figure 14.20

Step 2. Break the right vertical line of the rectangular contour into two pieces in the middle. Use the pick points in Figure 14.20.

Select **MAIN MENU → Modify → Break → 2 pieces**
Pick at **P1** to select the entity to break
Select **Midpoint** from the Point menu
Pick at **P2** to break the entity

The drawing does not look different before and after breaking. The drawing is redisplayed as in Figure 14.21.

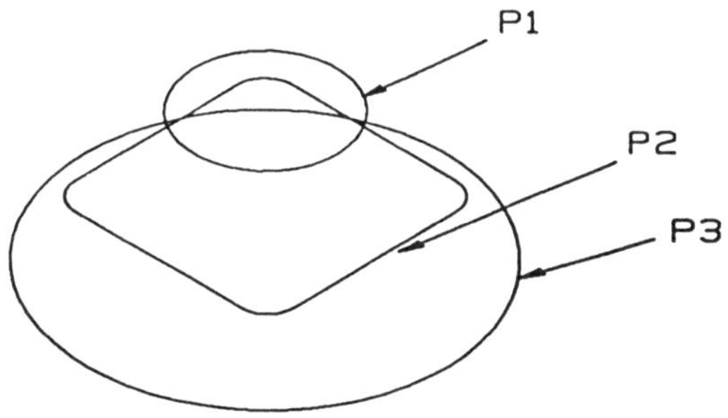

Figure 14.21

Step 3. Initiate ruled toolpath module.

Select **MAIN MENU → Toolpaths → mIsc. → rUled**
Enter file name: **ruledt2 ←**

Step 4. Define the contours using the pick points in Figure 14.21.

Select **Single** then pick at **P1** for contour 1
Select **Chain** then pick at **P2**
Select **Close → End here** for the rectangular contour
Select **Single** then pick at **P3** for contour 3
Select **Done** to complete defining contours

Step 5. Define ruled parameters to the following settings.

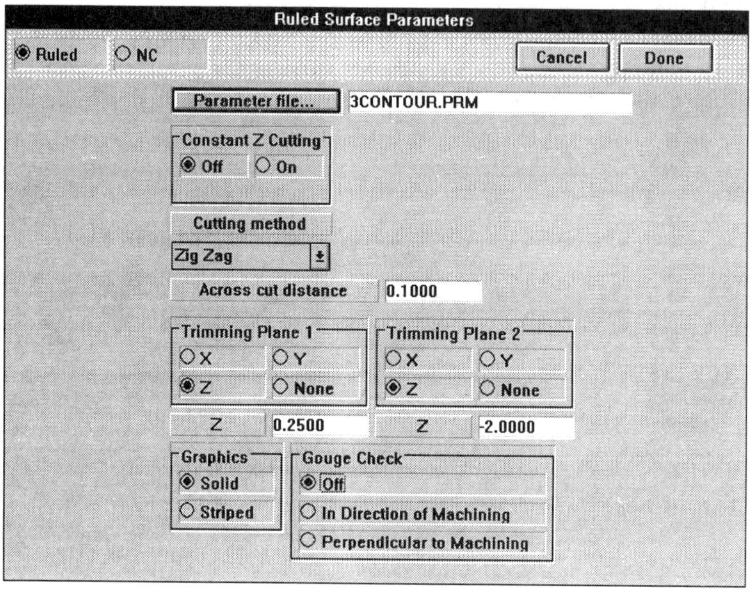

Select the **NC botton** to advance to the NC parameters menu.

Step 6. Define NC parameters to the following settings.

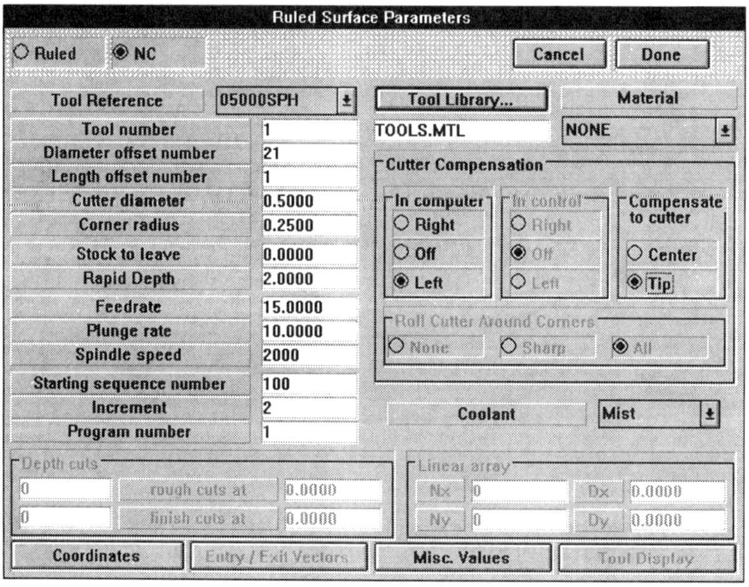

Select the **Done botton** to complete the parameter settings.

Step 7. Write and save the toolpaths.

The toolpaths should display on the screen as in Figure 14.22.

Select **Yes** to accept the toolpaths
Select **End program** to close the NCI file
Select **Yes** to "Run the post processor?"
Enter file name: **ruled2** ←
The partial part program should appear on the screen
Double click the Window button in the upper left corner to return back to graphic mode.

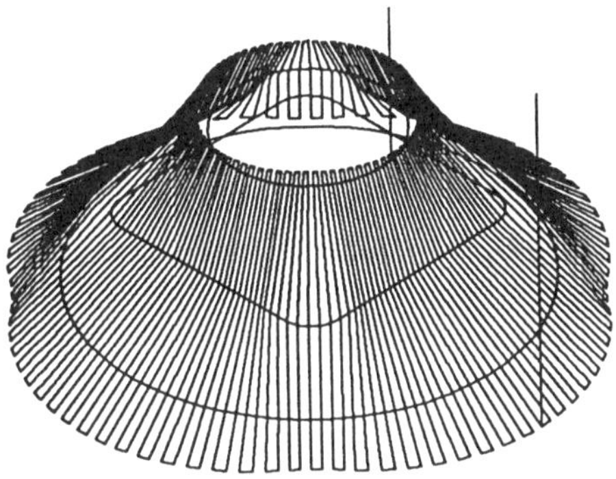

Figure 14.22

14.5 Loft Toolpath Module

This module is used to blend parabolically up to 100 contours which can be points, lines, arcs and splines or any combination of entity types. Figure 14.23 shows an example of the toolpaths generated by using the loft toolpath module.

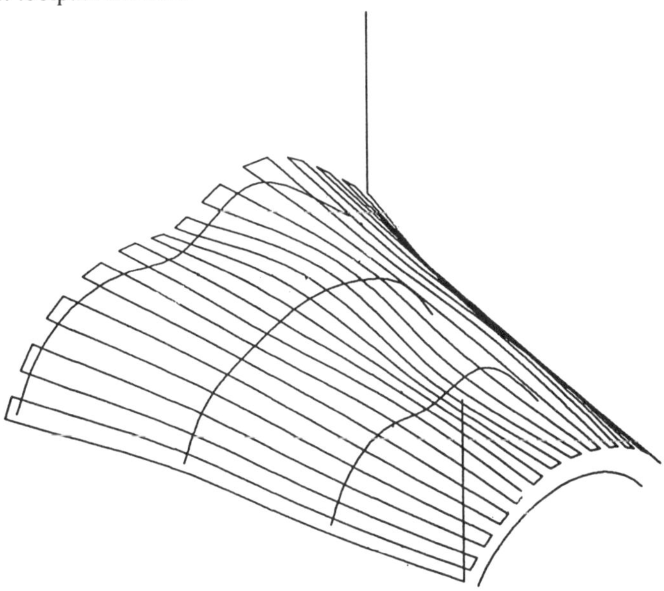

Figure 14.23

Loft Parameters

The five loft parameters are listed below:

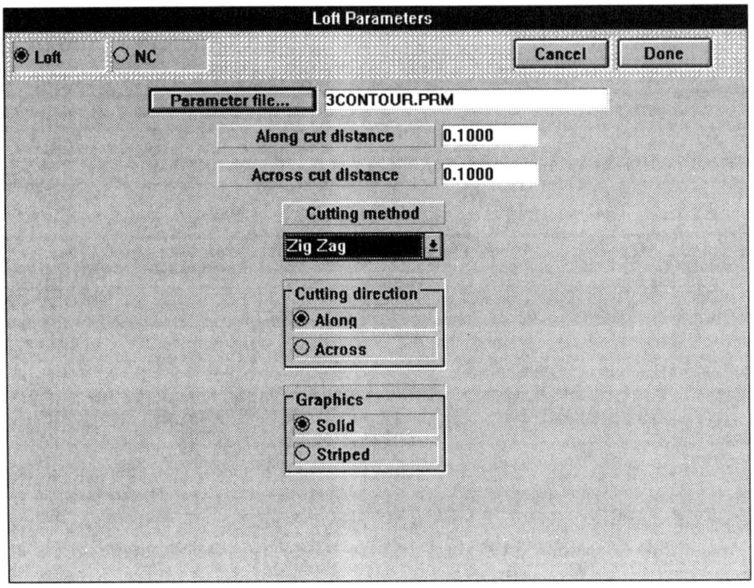

These five parameters have been discussed in previous sections.

Project 3.

Machining a loft surface

The loft toolpath module is used to generate a set of toolpaths to machine a loft surface defined by 19 contours. The wireframe model for this surface is the file loft2 created in chapter 11. Figure 14.24 shows both the wireframe model and the toolpaths to cut this surface.

3

Wireframe Model

Project 4 of Chapter 11 (loft2)

We are here

Go to

Toolpath

(loftt)

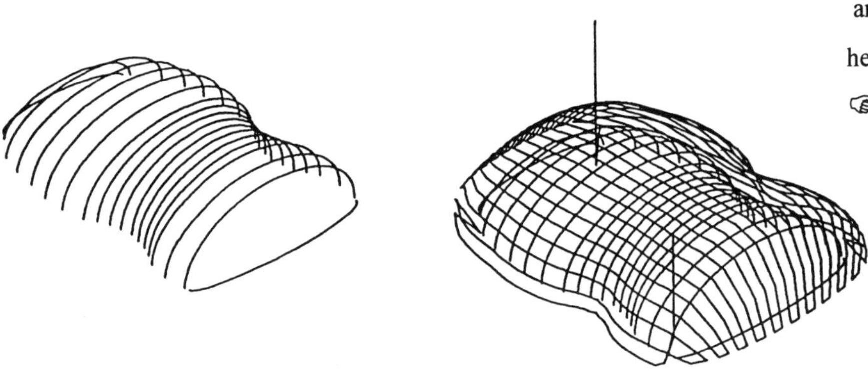

Figure 14.24

Tips 1. Wireframe model file is loft2.ge3.

2. Use Window → One Way → CW commands to orderly select contours.

3. Cutter compensation in computer should be set to right center.

Step 1. Load the part wireframe model file (loft2.ge3) or create one by following the instructions in project 4 of chapter 11.

Select **MAIN MENU → File → Get**
Enter file name: **loft2** ←
Select **Yes** to delete the current part if necessary

The wireframe model should appear as Figure 14.25.

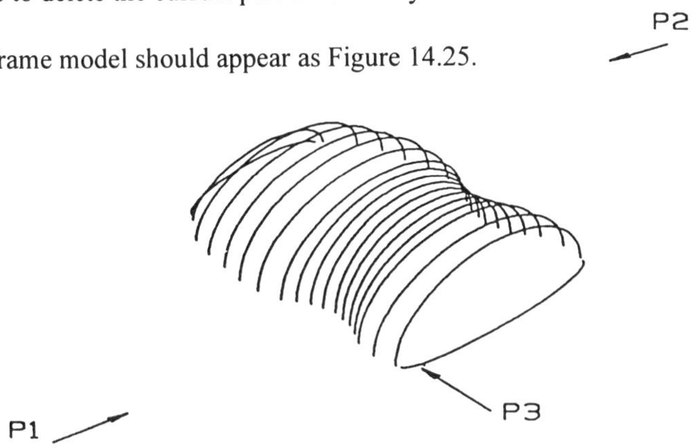

Figure 14.25

Step 2. Initiate loft toolpath module.

Select **MAIN MENU → Toolpaths → mIsc. → Loft**
Enter file name: **loftt** ←

Step 3. Define the contours using the pick points in Figure 14.25.

Select **Window** from the Chaining method menu
Pick at **P1** and **P2** to include all contours in the window
Select **One way** in the Search by menu
Select **CW** in the Chaining direction menu
Select **Endpoint** then pick at **P3**
Select **Done** to complete contours selection

Step 4. Define loft parameters to the following settings.

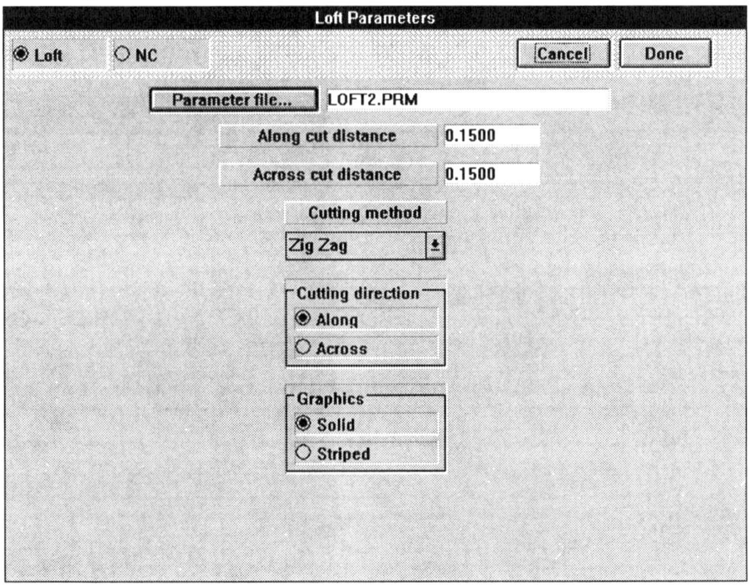

Select the **NC button** to advance to the NC parameters menu.

Step 5. Define NC parameters to the following settings.

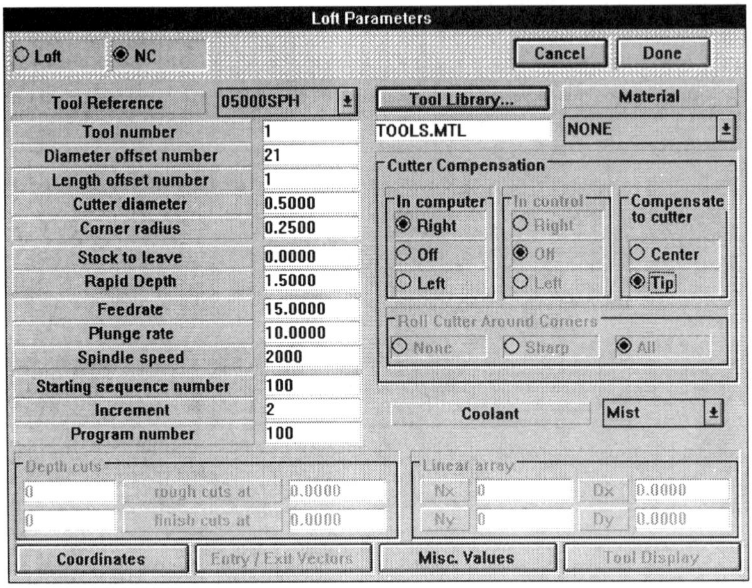

Select the **Done button** to complete the parameter settings.

Step 6. Write and save the toolpath file.

Note: The system will issue a warning to indicate that there is an undercut on 14 of 1815 points, and the largest undercut = -0.25.

Press **Enter** to display the toolpaths
Select **Yes** to accept the toolpaths
Select **End program** to close the NCI file
Select **No** to "Run the post processor ?"

The toolpaths should resemble Figure 14.26.

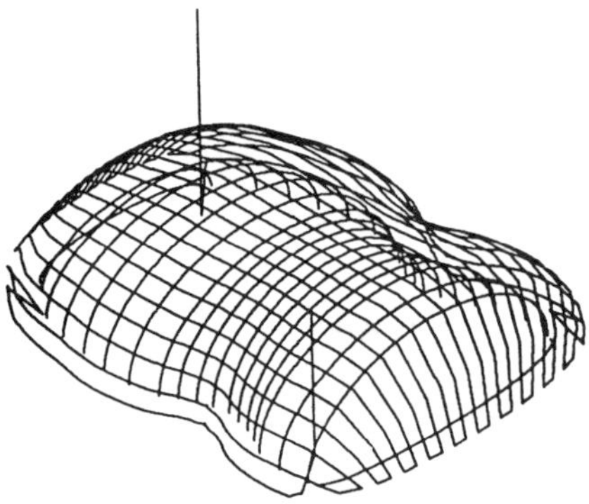

Figure 14.26

14.6 Coons Toolpath Module

The Coons module is used to generate a series of toolpaths to machine a surface defined by a single patch or multiple-patch model. Each patch normally consists of four contours. Figure 14.27 shows a surface produced by the toolpaths generated from Coons module.

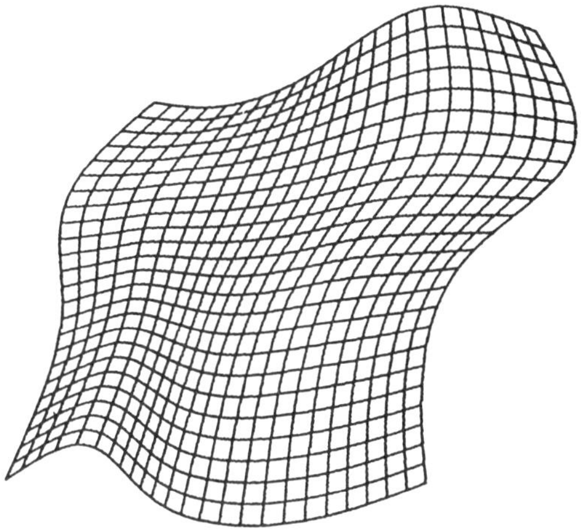

Figure 14.27

Coons Parameters

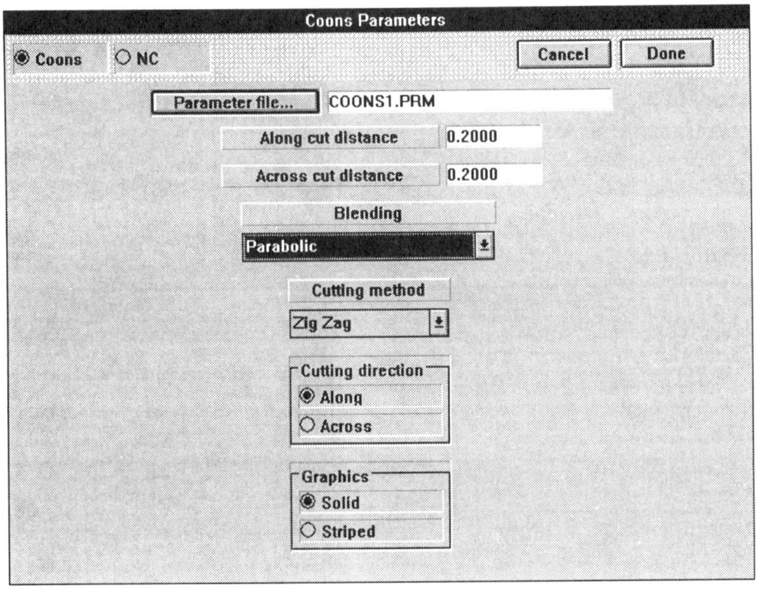

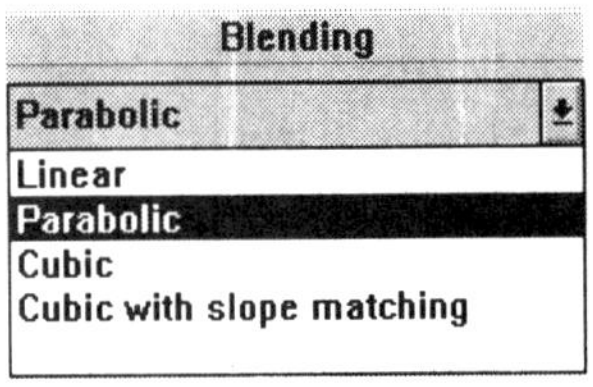

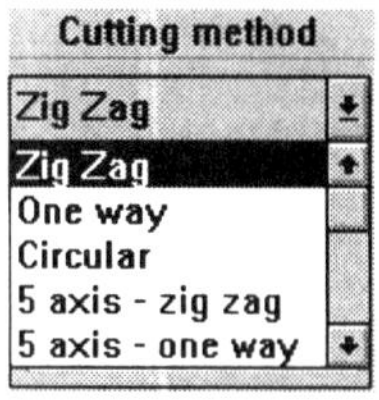

All parameters listed above, excepting the blending method, have been discussed in previous sections. Table 14.4 on the following page summarizes the features and applications of four blending methods used in Coons surfaces.

Tips 1. Refer to the instructions given for Coons surfaces in section 12.7 of chapter 12.

2. Select the starting point, along direction, and across direction.

3. Determine the number of along contours and the number of across contours.

4. Determine the number of along patches and the number of across patches.

5. Observe the picking order of selecting contours.

Table 14.4 Blending methods of Coons surfaces

Blending	Description	Application	Illustration
Linear	Patch contours are blended linearly to form a surface.	Use in single patch surfaces.	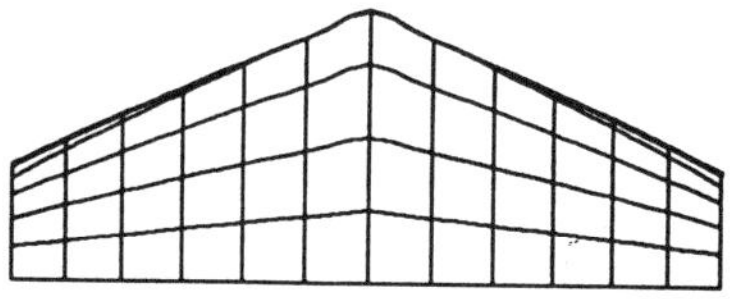
Parabolic	Patch contours are blended parabolically (2nd order) to form a surface.	Used in multiple-patch surfaces. These surfaces tend to produce flat spots on the surface.	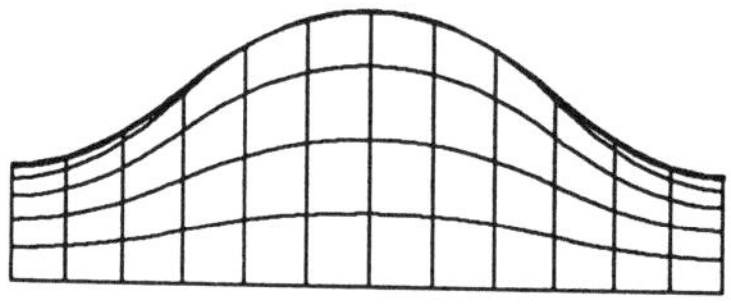
Cubic	Patch contours are blended cubically (3rd order) to form a surface.	Used in multiple-patch surfaces. These surfaces tend to produce flat spots on the surface.	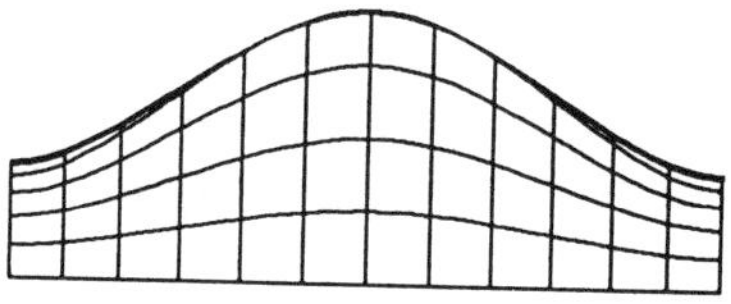
Cubic with slope matching	Patch contours are blended cubically (3rd order) with matching slope at the boundaries.	Used in multiple-patch surfaces whenever possible. The flat spots are eliminated.	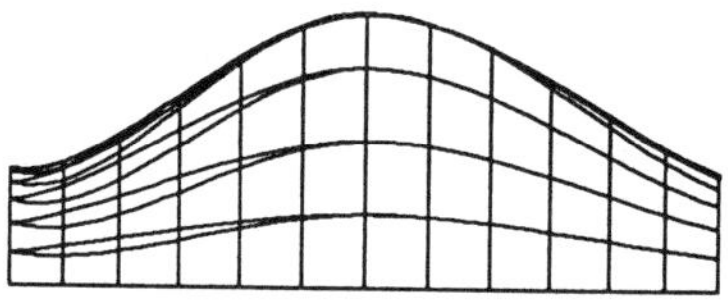

Row and Column

Mastercam uses rows and columns to identify the patch boundary grid. Along contours are assigned in rows and across contours in columns. Each contour in the grid is identified by an *along* row number and an *across* column number as shown in Figure 14.28.

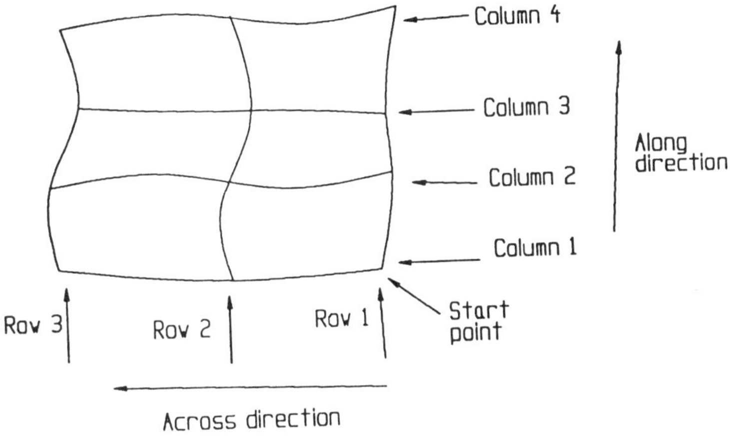

Figure 14.28

Number of Patches in Along and Across Directions

The system will ask you to enter the number of patches in the along and across directions, respectively. Whether the boundaries are closed affects your counting the number of patches. In open boundary cases, where the first and the last contour are not connected, the number of patches in the along direction is the number of across contours minus 1 and the number of patches in across direction is the number of along contours minus 1.

Figure 14.29 shows the contour profiles having an open boundary for defining a Coons surface. In this model, the start point is selected at point A and the along and across direction are as shown in the figure.

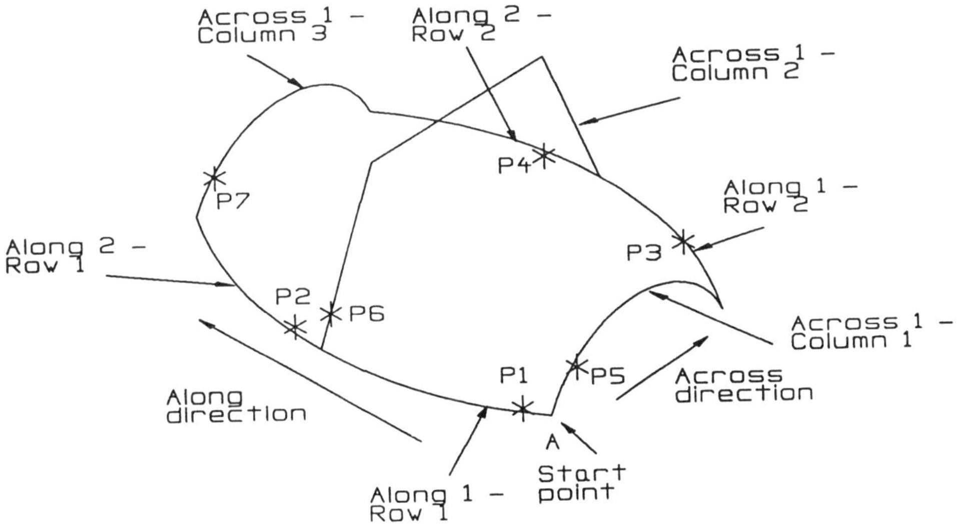

Figure 14.29

The number of along contours = 2 The number of across contours = 3 The number of along patches = The number of across contours - 1 = 3 - 1 = 2 The number of across patches = The number of along contours - 1 = 2 - 1 = 1

In close boundary cases where the first and the last contours are connected, the number of patches in the along direction is equal to the number of the across contours and the number of patches in the across direction is the number of along contours minus 1. Figure 14.30 shows an example of a closed boundary Coons surface.

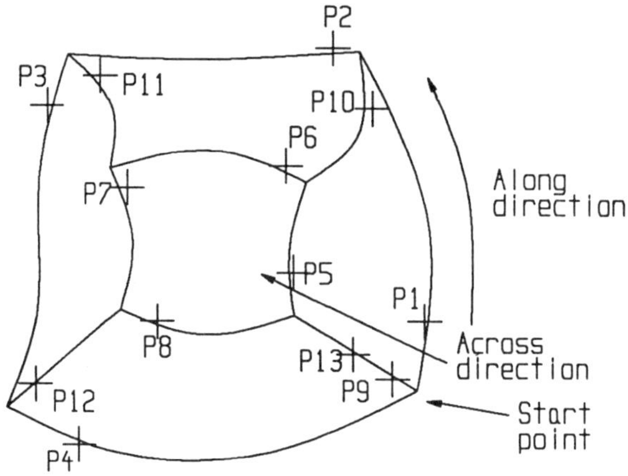

Figure 14.30

Number of along contours = 2
Number of across contours = 4
The number of patches in along direction = number of across contours = 4
The number of patches in across direction = number of along contours - 1 = 2 - 1 = 1

The Order of Contour Selection

The contours selection must follow a predetermined order that is along contours that are sequentially selected first, followed by the across contours as follows:

Selection order	Entity to be picked
1st selection	along row 1 - across colunm 1
2nd selection	along row 1 - across column 2
-	-
-	-
nth selection	along row 1 - across column n
n+1 selection	along row 2 - across column 1
n+2 selection	along row 2 - across column 2
-	-
-	-
2n selection	along row 2 - across column n
-	-
-	-
mn selection	along row m - across column n

Figure 14.29 on the previous page shows the contours selection sequence for an open boundary case and Figure 14.30 shows a closed boundary case.

Project 4.

Machining a Coons surface of a single patch

The Coons toolpath module is used to generate the toolpaths for machining a surface defined by a single patch of four contours. The wireframe model and the toolpaths are illustrated in Figure 14.31.

Wireframe Model
Project 5 of Chapter 11 (Coons1)

We are here

Go to

Toolpath
(coonst1)

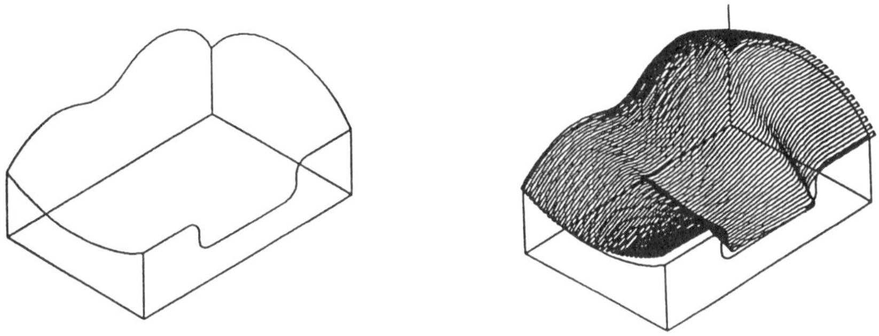

Figure 14.31

Tips 1. Use wireframe model file (coons1.ge3).

2. This is an open boundary case. The number of *along* contours is 2 and the number of *across* contours is 2. The number of patches in both along and across directions is 1 (or 2 - 1).
3. Use linear blending method because this is a single patch surface.

4. Cutter compensation in computer = left tip.

Step 1. Load the wireframe model file (coons1.ge3) or create one by following the instructions in project 5 of chapter 11.

Select **MAIN MENU → File → Get**
Enter file name: **coons1 ←**
Select **Yes** to delete the current part

The wireframe model should appear as Figure 14.32.

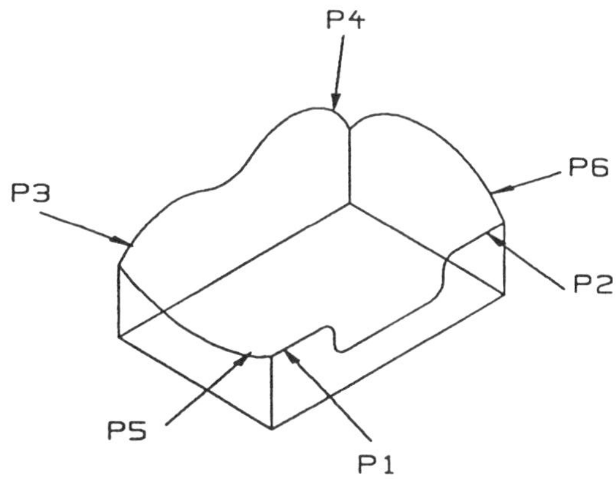

Figure 14.32

Step 2. Initiate the Coons toolpath module.

Select **MAIN MENU → Toolpaths →mIsc.→ Coons**
Enter file name: **coonst1 ←**

Step 3. Specify number of patches in along and across direction.

Enter **1** for the number of patches in the along direction
Enter **1** for the number of patches in the across direction

Step 4. Define contours using the pick points in Figure 14.32.

Select **Chain** then pick at **P1** and **P2**
Select **End here** to complete along contour 1 of row 1
Select **Chain** then pick at **P3** and **P4**
Select **End here** to complete along contour 1 of row 2
Select **Single** then pick at **P5** to define across contour 1 of column 1
Select **Single** then pick at **P6** to define across contour 1 of column 2
Select **Done**

Step 5. Define Coons parameters to the following settings.

Along cut distance = 0.1
Across cut distance = 0.1
Blending = Linear
Cutting method = Zig Zag
Cutting direction = Along
Graphics = Solid

Select the **NC button** to advance to the NC parameters menu.

Step 6. Define NC parameters to the following settings.

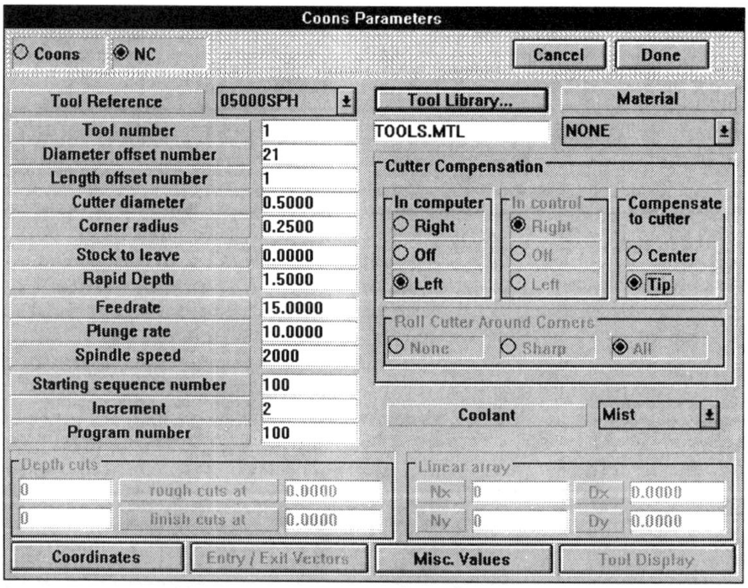

Select the **Done button** to complete the parameter settings.

Step 7. Write and save the toolpaths.

The toolpaths should appear on screen as in Figure 14.33.

Select **Yes** to accept this toolpath segment
Select **End program** to close the NCI file
Select **No** to "Run the post processor?"

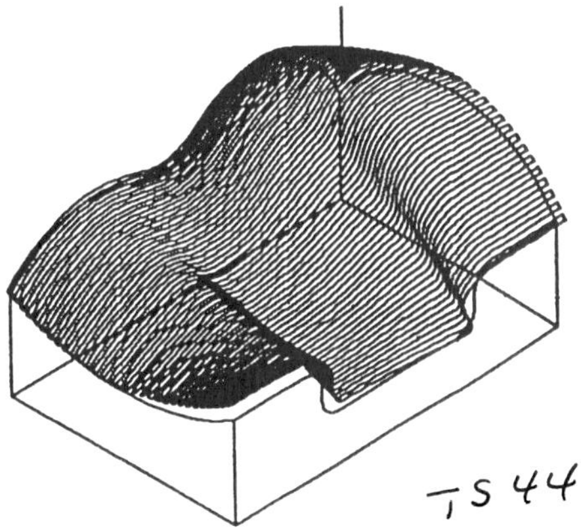

Figure 14.33

Project 5. 5

Machining a Coons surface formed by multiple-patch

Wireframe Model
Project 7 of Chapter 11 (Coons4)

We are here — Go to

Toolpath
(coonst2)

The Coons module is used to generate toolpaths to machine a Coons surface defined by a total of 12 patches. The wireframe model file is **coons4.ge3** created in project 7 of chapter 11. Figure 14.34 shows both the wireframe model and the toolpaths.

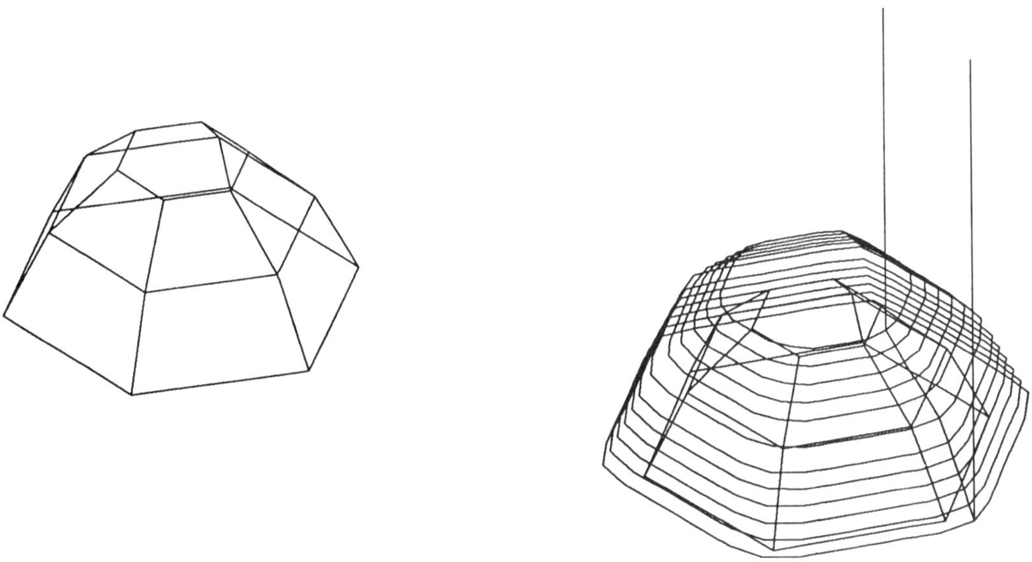

Figure 14.34

Tips 1. Use top Gview to facilitate the picking of contours.

2. The number of along contours = 3
   The number of across contours = 6
   The number of patches in along direction = 6
   The number of patches in across direction = 3 - 1 = 2
3. Use circular cutting method to reduce the part program size.

4. Set the cutting direction to along mode.

5. Cutter compensation in computer = left tip

6. Use the filter function to significantly reduce the toolpath points.

Step 1. Load the wireframe model file (coons4.ge3) or create one by following the instructions in project 7 of chapter 11.

Select **MAIN MENU → File → Get**

Enter file name: **coons4 ←**

Select **Yes** to delete the current part

The wireframe model should appear as in Figure 14.35.

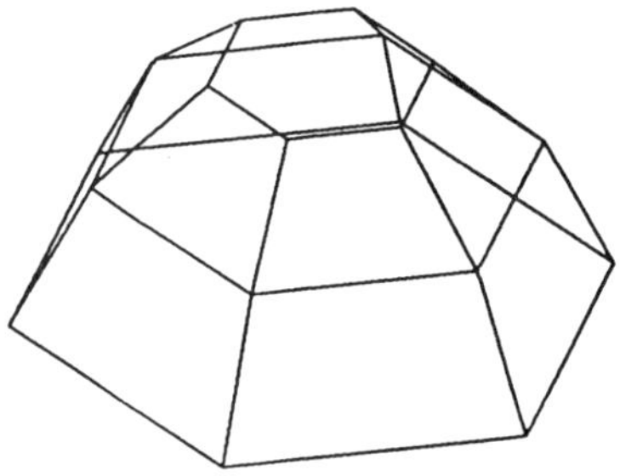

Figure 14.35

Step 2. Change Gview to top view.

Select **Gview → Top**

The wireframe model in the top view looks like Figure 14.36.

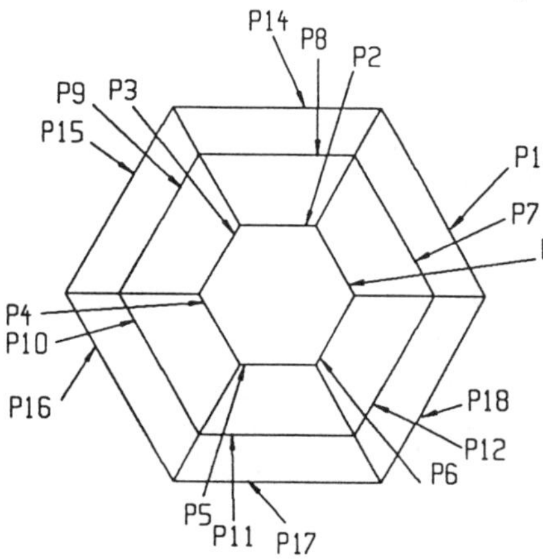

Figure 14.36a Along

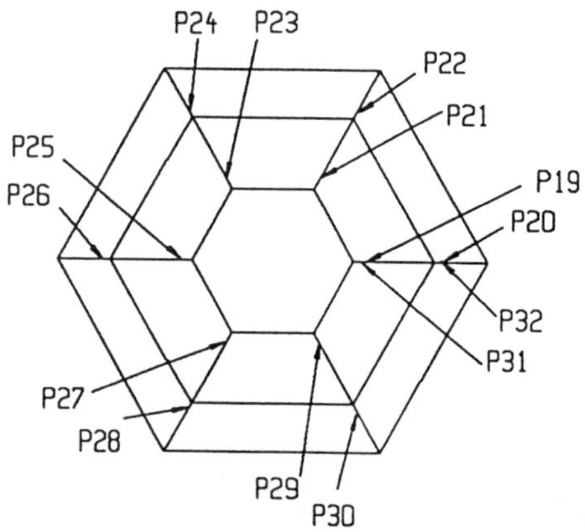

Figure 14.36b Across

Step 3. Initiate the Coons toolpath module.

Select **MAIN MENU** → **Toolpaths** →**mIsc.** → **Coons**
Enter file name: **coonst2** ←

Step 4. Specify the number of patches in along and across directions.

Enter **6** for the number of patches in the along direction
Enter **2** for the number of patches in the across direction

Step 5. Define the contours using the pick points in Figure 14.36.

Select **Single** then pick at **P1**
Sequentially pick at **P2 - P32**, select **Single** before each entity picking
Select **Done** to complete the contour definition

Step 6. Define Coons parameters to the following settings.

Along cut distance = 0.1 Across cut distance = 0.1 Blending = Linear Cutting method = Circular Cutting direction = Along Graphics = Solid

Select the **NC button** to advance to the NC parameters menu.

Step 7. Define NC parameters to the following settings.

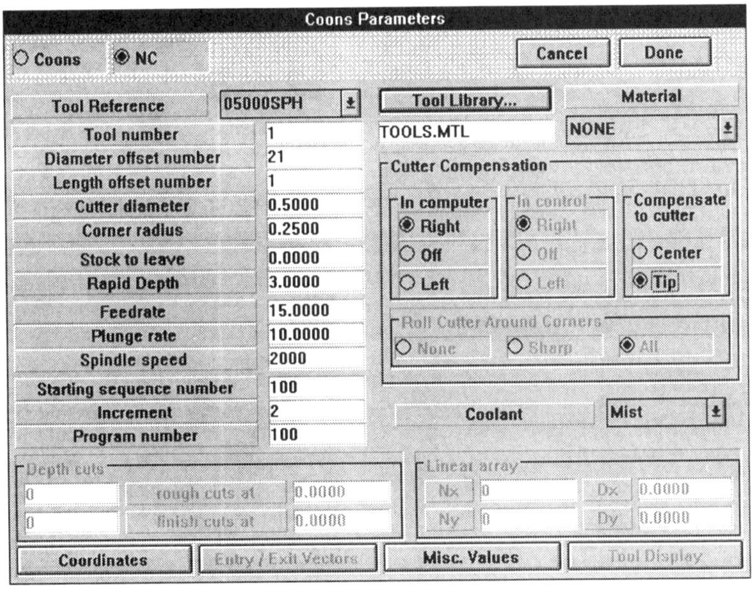

Select the **Done button** to complete the parameters settings.

Step 8. Accept and save the toolpaths.

Select **Yes** to accept this toolpath segment

The toolpaths shown in top Gview should look like Figure 14.37.

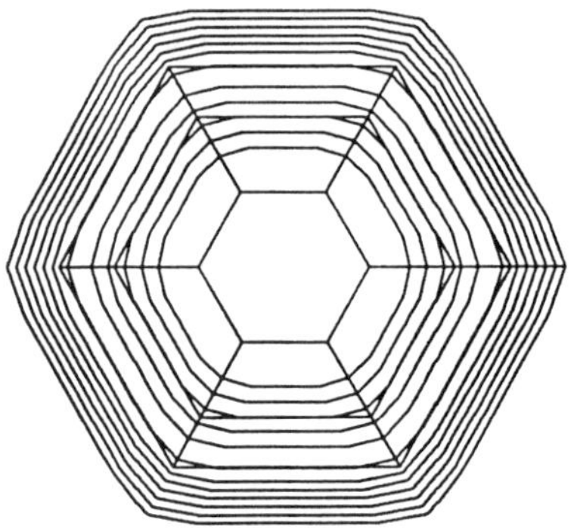

Figure 14.37

Step 9. Change Gview to Isometric.

Select **Gview** → **Isometric**

The toolpaths are shown in isometric view as in Figure 14.38.

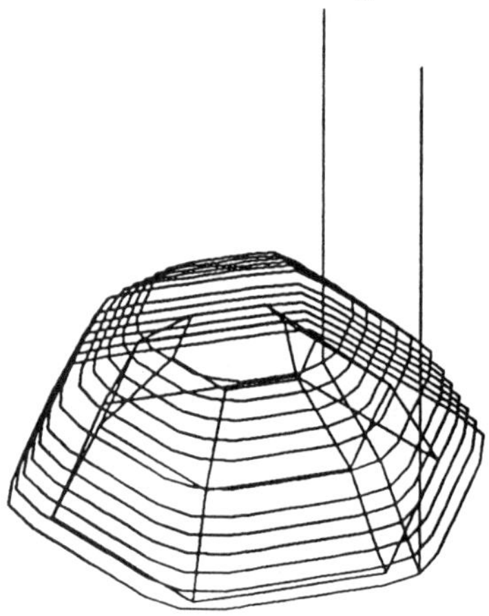

Figure 14.38

Step 10. Close NCI file.

Select **End program** to close the NCI file

Step 11. Run the post processor.

Select **Yes** to "Run the post processor?"
Enter file name: **coonst2** ←

Step 12. List the NC file.

Select **MAIN MENU** → **File** → **List**
Enter file name: **coonst2** ←

The part program will be listed on the screen. The last line is N1760 M30. This part program has a total of 830 lines.

Double click the button at the upper left corner of the window to return to graphic mode.

Step 13. Run the filter function.

Select **MAIN MENU** → **NC utils** → **Filter**
Enter file patter: **C:\mill5\NCI\coonst2.nc** ←
Enter maximum error: **0.001** ←
Enter maximum number of points to look ahear (100): ←

The system will perform the filtering to remove those unwanted program blocks. The system will indicate that **572** of **819** points were discarded.

Press Enter to continue
Select **Yes** to save changes

Step 14. Repost process the filtered file

Select **Post proc** → **Run**
Filename: **coonst2.nci** for the NCI file
Filename: **coonst2.nc** for the NC file
Select **Yes** to delete the old NC file
Double-click the button on the upper left corner to return back to graphic mode.

Step 15. Edit the filtered NC file.

Select **MAIN MENU** → **File** → **Edit** → **NC**
Enter file pattern: **coonst2** ←

The filtered program should be listed on the screen and the last line of the file is **N616**. This file contains a total of **255** lines (or blocks).

Step 16. Press F10 → F9 to exit the Edit utility.

14.7 Swept Toolpath Module

The swept module is used to generate toolpaths for cutting surfaces that are formed by either translating a sectional profile along one or two rail contours or translating two sectional profiles along a rail contour. Mastercam provides the following three modes of swept toolpath module:

One across/ one along:	translate or rotate an across contour while following the along contour.
One across/ two along:	proportionally scale the across contour between the two along contours.
Two across/ one along:	perform a linear blend between the two across contours while following the along contour.

The one across/one along mode is referred to as **2d swept** in Mastercam. In 2d mode, the along contour must lie parallel or perpendicular to the current tool plane if a tool plane is defined. Otherwise, it must parallel or perpendicular to the XY-plane. Any cross section taken normal to any part of the along contour remains constant (Figure 14.39).

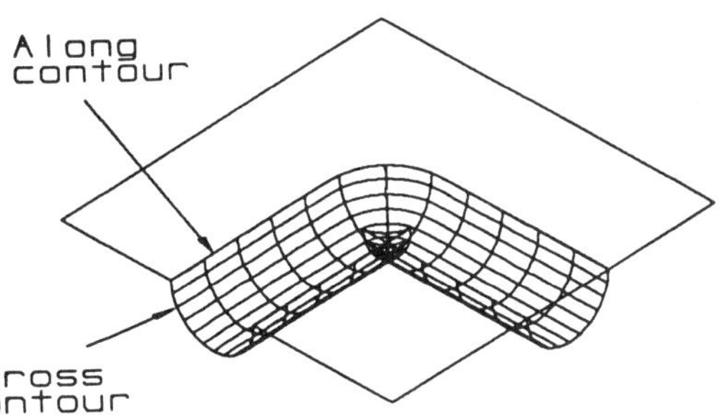

Figure 14.39

The other two modes (two across/ one along and one across/ two along) are refered to as **3d swept**. In 3d mode, contours can be in any plane, and in any orientation. Figures 14.40 and 14.41 illustate one across/two along, and two across/one along swept surface, respectively.

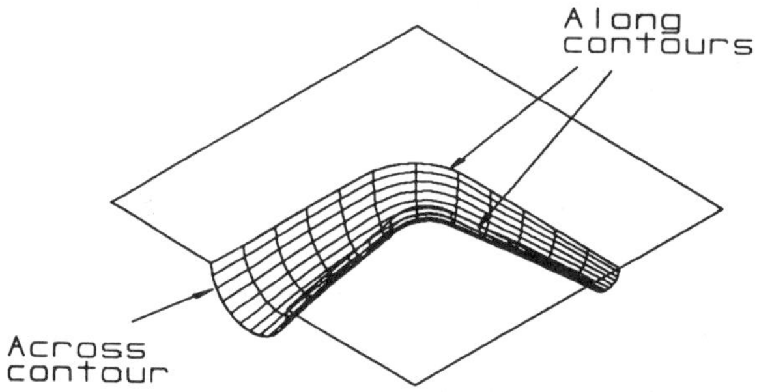

Figures 14.40

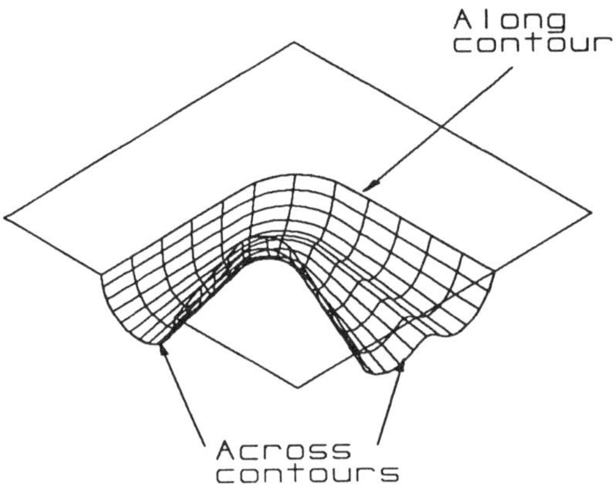

Figure 14.41

Project 6. 6

Machining a 2D swept surface

Use a 2D swept module to generate toolpaths for cutting a swept surface. Figure 14.42 shows both the wireframe model and the toolpaths.

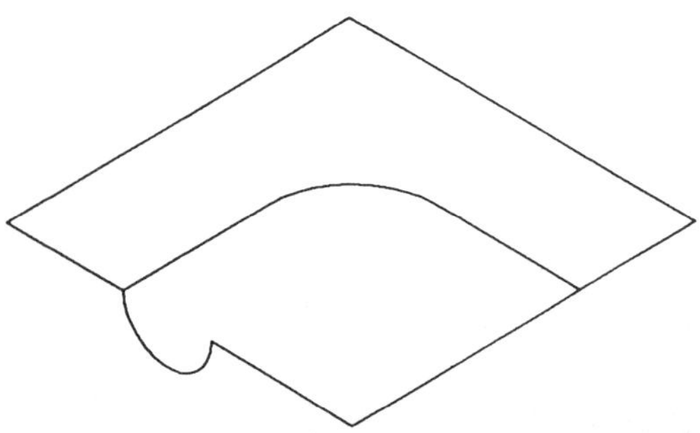

Figure 14.42a Wireframe

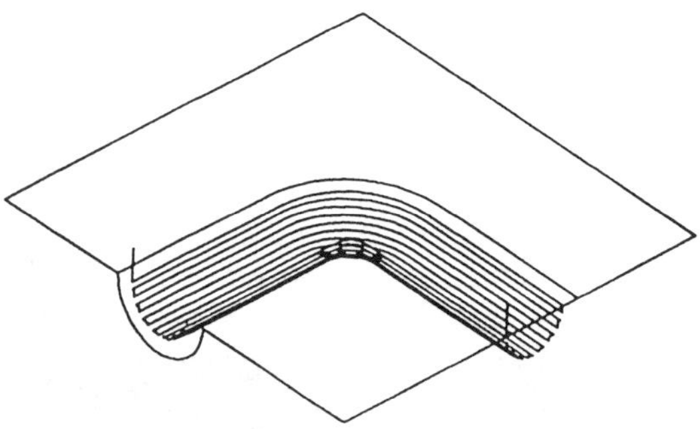

Figure 14.42b Toolpaths

Tips 1. Construct a wireframe model as shown in Figure 14.42.

2. Use the Front Cplane to create an arc for across contour.

3. The front horizontal line must be broken into two pieces in the middle. This allows the line to be trimmed to the two intersection points with the arc.

Step 1. Create a rectangle using the isometric Gview.

Select **Gview → Isometric**
Select **Cplane → Top** if necessary
Select **MAIN MENU → Create → Rectangle → 1 point**
Enter the lower left corner: **0,0** ←
Enter the width: **6** ←
Enter the height: **6** ←
Press **Alt** + **F1** simultaneously then press **F2** to fit the drawing on the screen

The rectangle should appear as Figure 14.43.

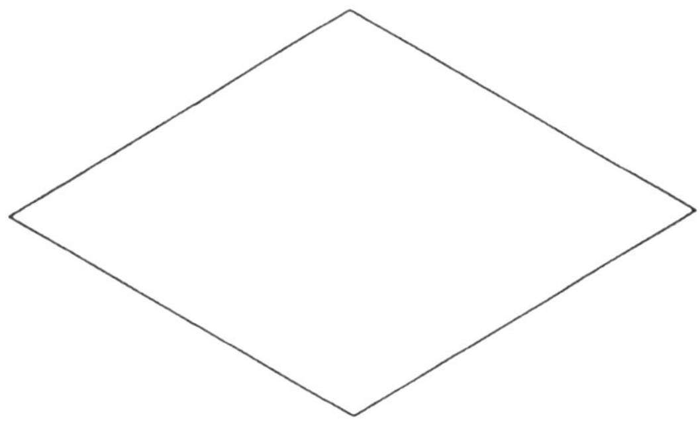

Figure 14.43

Step 2. Create two lines.

Select **MAIN MENU → Create → Line → Endpoints**
Specify the first endpoint: **2,0** ←
Specify the second endpoint: **2,5** ← for the vertical line
Specify the first endpoint: **6,4** ←
Specify the second endpoint: **1,4** ← for the horizontal line

The two lines are added as shown in Figure 14.44.

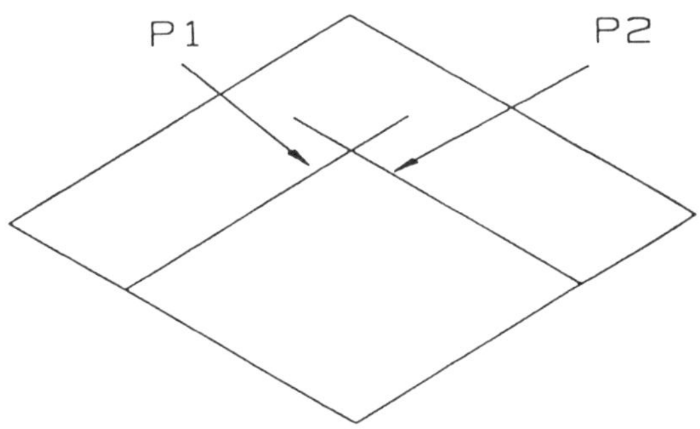

Figure 14.44

Step 3. Add a fillet to the two lines using the pick points in Figure 14.44.

Select **MAIN MENU → Modify → Fillet → Radius**
Enter radius: **1.5** ←
Pick at **P1** and **P2**

The fillet is added to the drawing as shown in Figure 14.45.

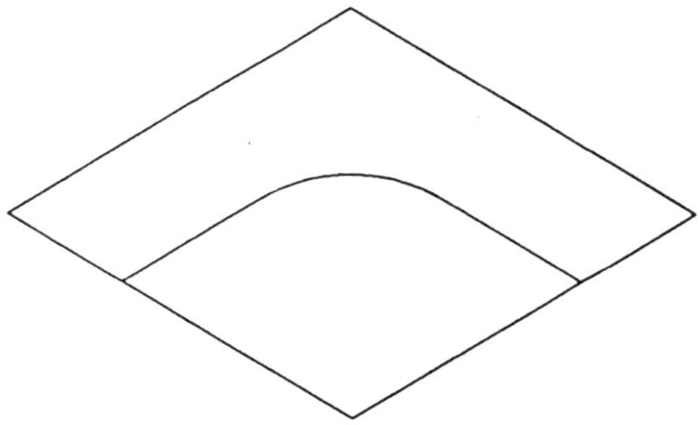

Figure 14.45

Step 4. Create an arc using the Front Cplane.

Select **Cplane → Front**
Select **MAIN MENU → Create → Arc → Endpoints**
Enter the first point: **2,0** ←
Enter the second point: **3.5,0** ←
Enter the radius: **0.75** ←
Select arc: pick at the lower arc of the two

The arc is added to the drawing as shown in Figure 14.46.

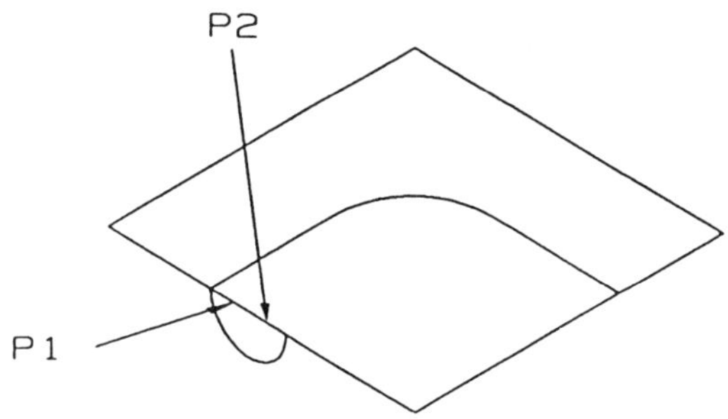

Figure 14.46

Step 5. Break the front line of the rectangle into two pieces using the pick points in Figure 14.46.

Select **MAIN MENU → Modify → Break → 2 pieces**
Pick at **P1** to select an entity
Pick at **P2** to enter the breakpoint

The front line is broken into two pieces but the drawing does not look different. The drawing is redrawn in Figure 14.47.

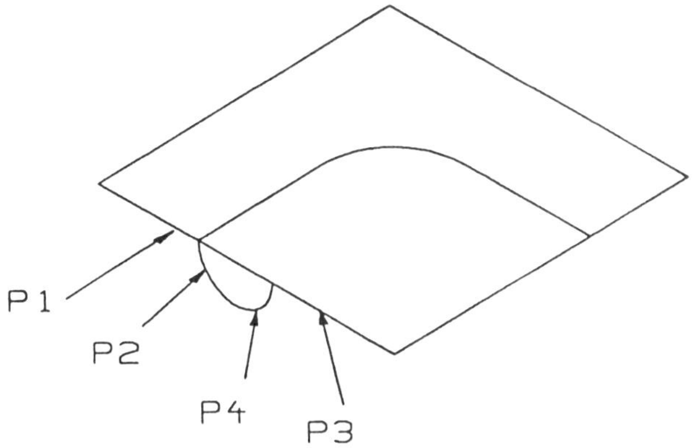

Figure 14.47

Step 6. Trim the front line using the pick points in Figure 14.47.

Change Cplane to 3d.
Select **Cplane → 3d**
Select **MAIN MENU → Modify → Trim → 2 entities**
Pick at **P1** to select the entity to trim
Pick at **P2** to select the entity to trim to
Pick at **P3** to select the entity to trim
Pick at **P4** to select the entity to trim to

The new drawing becomes Figures 14.48.

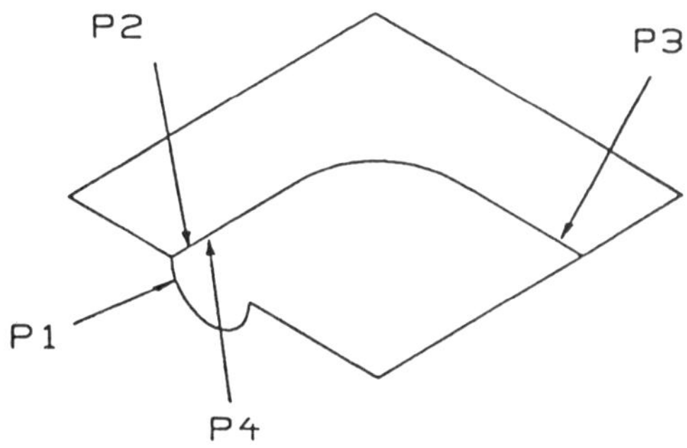

Figure 14.48

Step 7. Initiate swept toolpath module.

Select **MAIN MENU → Toolpaths →mIsc. → Swept**
Enter file name: **swepttl ←**
Select **2d** from compensation method menu

Step 8. Define contours using the pick points in Figure 14.48.

Select **Single** then pick at **P1** to define the across contour
Select **Chain** then pick at **P2** and **P3**
Select **End here** to define the along contour
Select **Done** to complete contour selection
Select **Endpoint** then pick at **P4** to enter the intersection of the across and along contours

Step 9. Define 2d swept parameters to the following settings.

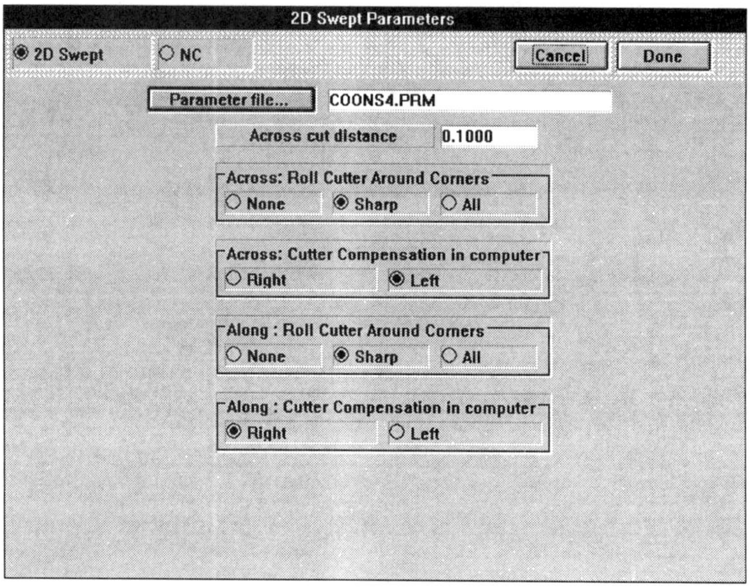

Select the **NC button** to advance to the NC parameters menu.

Step 10. Define NC parameters to the following settings.

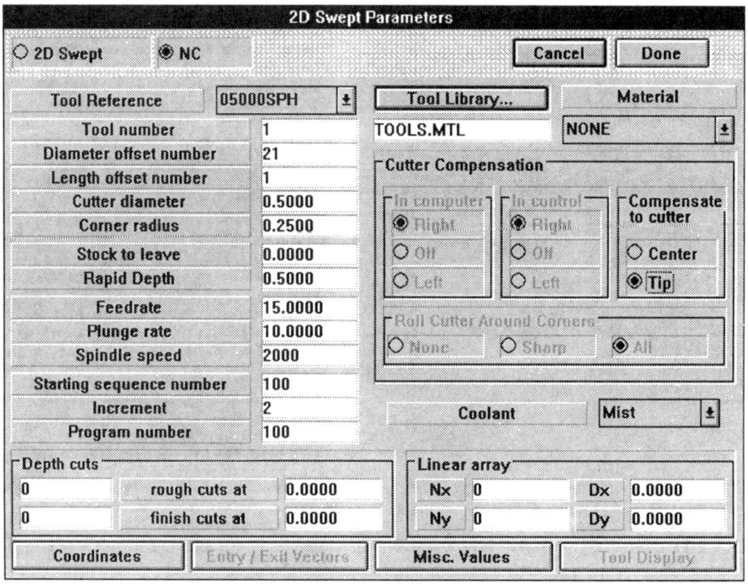

Select the **Done button** to complete the parameter settings.

Step 11. Accept and save the toolpaths.

Select **Yes** to accept this toolpath segment

Select **End program**

Select **No** to "Run the post processor?"

The toolpaths for cutting the swept surface are shown in Figure 14.49.

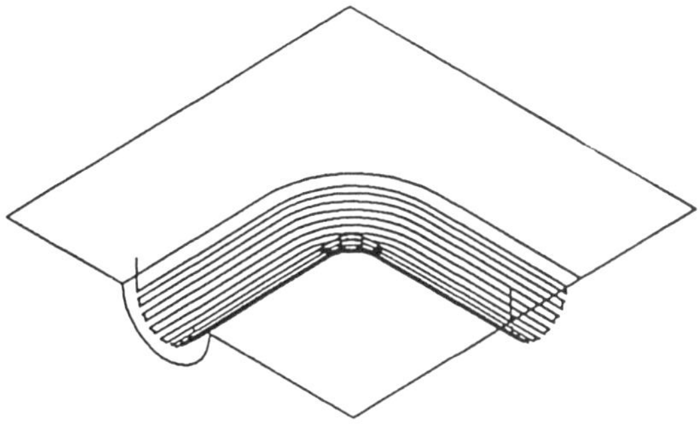

Figure 14.49

Project 7.

Machining a swept surface defined by one across contour and two along contours

Use the swept toolpath module to generate a set of toolpaths to machine a swept surface defined by an across contour and two along contours. The wireframe model and the toolpaths are shown in Figure 14.50.

7

Wireframe Model
Project 10 of Chapter 11 (swept3)

We are here

Go to

Toolpath
(sweptt2)

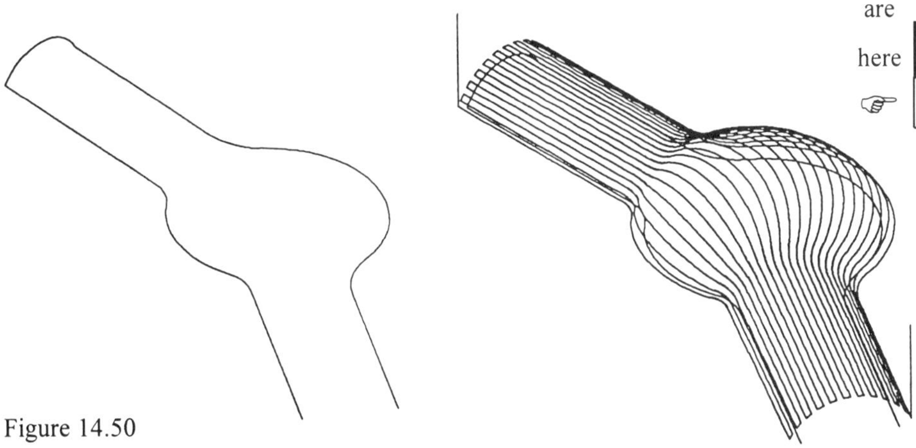

Figure 14.50

Tips 1. Use the wireframe model file swept3.ge3.

2. Use 3d swept with one across/ two along commands.

3. The syncs command is used to change the density of cutting steps of the two fillets in the first along contour. The cutting density is a ratio used to determine the step from one sync to another. One sync should be designated as the reference sync. This reference sync is defined with a cutting density of 1. Other syncs are determined by the value given to the cutting density. The section with a cutting density of 2, for example, has twice the density of the reference sync. In this project, we assign a cutting density of 5 to the two fillets, and all other sections have the density of 1.

4. Cutter compensation in computer should be set to right tip.

Step 1. Load the wireframe model file (swept3.ge3) or create one by following the instructions in project 10 of chapter 11.

Select **MAIN MENU → File → Get**
Enter file name: **swept3 ←**
Select **Yes** to delete the current part

The wireframe model should look like Figure 14.51.

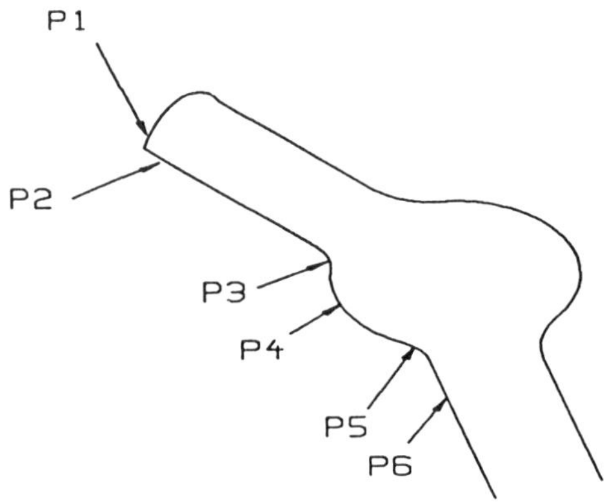

Figure 14.51

Step 2. Initiate swept toolpath module.

Select **MAIN MENU → Toolpaths → mIsc.→ Swept**
Enter file name: **sweptt2 ←**
Select **3d**
Enter the number of across contours: **1 ←**

Step 3. Define the across contour using the pick points in Figure 14.51.

Define the across contour: Select **Single** then pick at **P1**

Step 4. Define the along contour one using syncs command. Still use the pick points in Figure 14.51.

Define the along contour 1: Select **sYnc** from the Chaining method menu
Define section 1 of along contour 1:
Select **Single** then enter **1** for the cutting density
Pick at **P2** for section 1

Define section 2 of along contour 1:
Select **Single** then enter **5** for the cutting density
Pick at **P3** for section 2

Define section 3 of along contour 1:
Select **Single** then enter **1** for the cutting density
Pick at **P4** for section 3

Define section 4 of along contour 1:
Select **Single** then enter **5** for section 4
Pick at **P5** for section 4

Define section 5 of along contour 1:
Select **Single** then enter **1** for section 5
Pick at **P6** for section 5
Select **Done** to complete along contour 1

The drawing is redisplayed in Figure 14.52 .

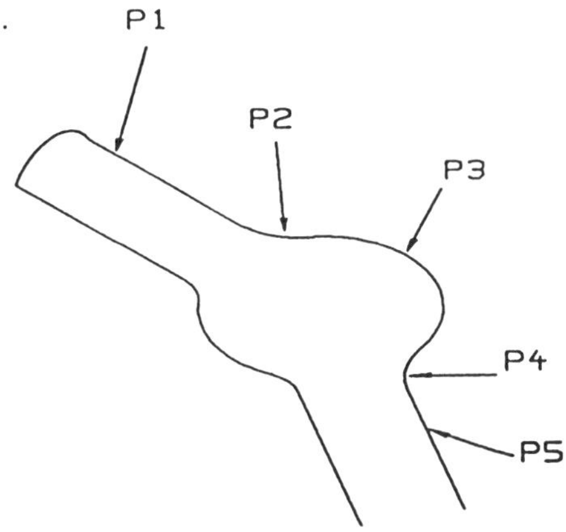

Figure 14.52

Step 5. Define the along contour two. Use the pick points in Figure 14.52.

Define section 1 of the along contour 2:
Select **Single** then pick at **P1**

Define section 2 of the along contour 2:
Select **Single** then pick at **P2**

Define section 3 of the along contour 2:
Select **Single** then pick at **P3**

Define section 4 of the along contour 2:
Select **Single** then pick at **P4**

Define section 5 of the along contour 2:
Select **Single** then pick at **P5**

Select **Done** to complete the along contour 2

Step 6. Define swept parameters to the following settings.

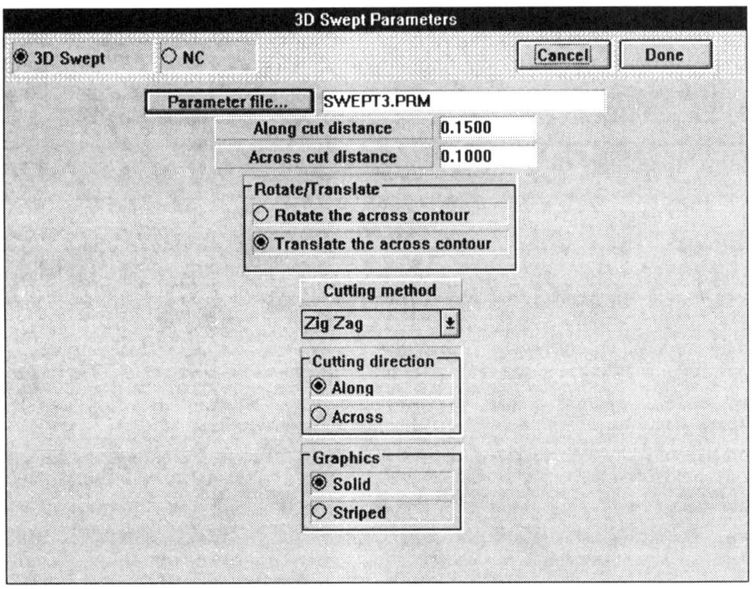

Select the **NC button** to advance to the NC parameters menu.

Step 7. Define NC parameters to the following settings.

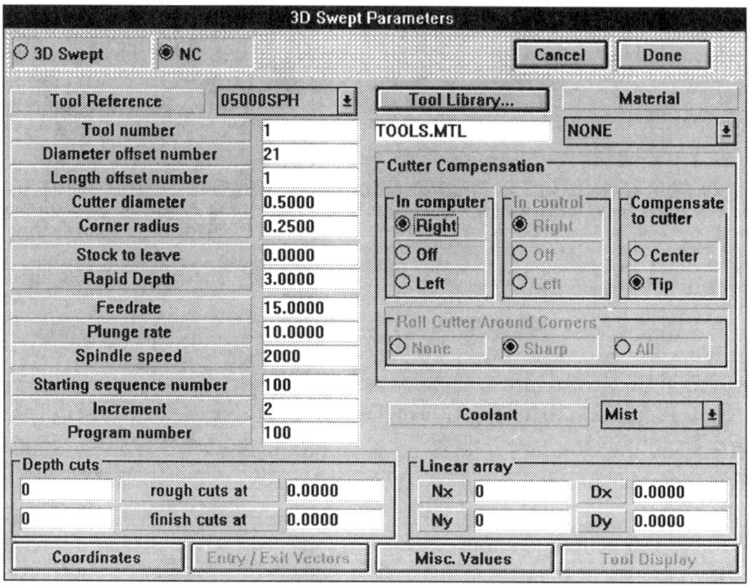

Select the **Done button** to complete the parameter settings.

Step 8. Write and save the toolpaths.

The system will take a while to generate toolpaths.

Select **Yes** to accept the toolpath segment
Select **End program**
Select **No** to "Run the post processor?"

The toolpaths should resemble Figure 14.53.

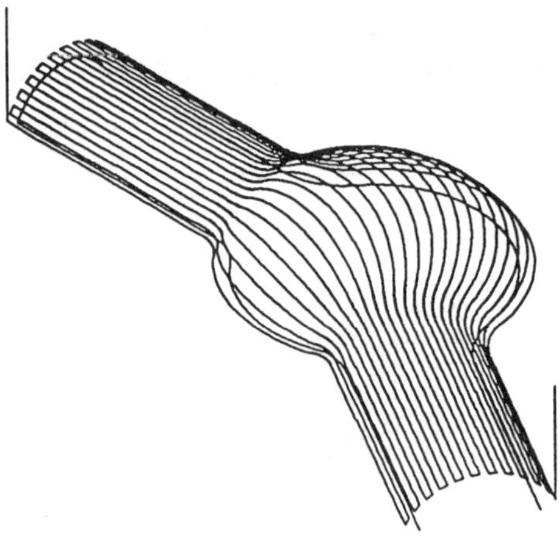

Figure 14.53

14.8 Surface of Revolution Toolpath Module

The surface of a revolution toolpath module is used to generate toolpaths to machine a surface that is defined by revolving a geometric contour about an axis. This is a very powerful tool for cutting any surface that is symmetrical about an axis. The surface of revolution parameters are listed below.

Step size = 0.1 Axial depth = 0.0 Shape = Concave/Convex Retract to nothing Trim toolpath to nothing

Step size

This parameter specifies the distance between cuts in the current construction plane.

Axis depth

This parameter specifies the Z-coordinate of the axis of rotation. This Z value automatically determines the depth of the plane at which the toolpath starts being generated. Figures 14.54a and 14.54b show how the axial depth affects the toolpaths.

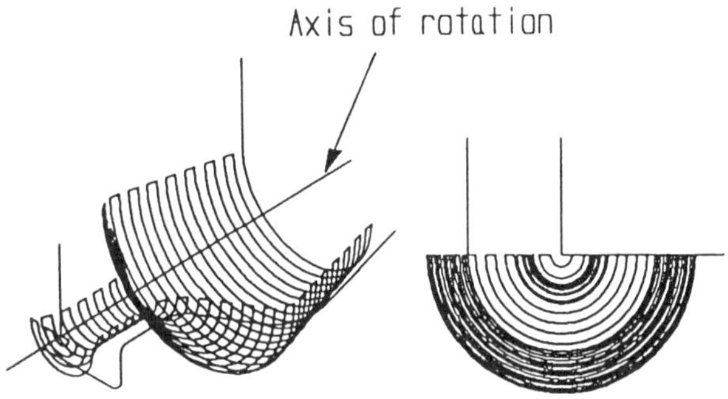

Figure 14.54a Axial depth = 0.0

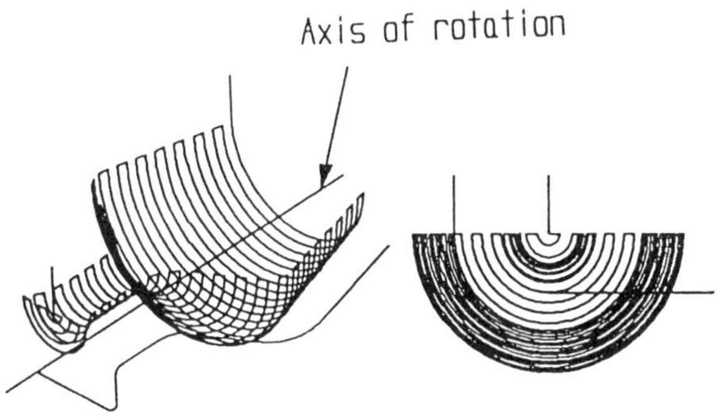

Figure 14.54b Axial depth= 0.5

Shape

This parameter allows us to select the shape of the revolved surface to be the concave or convex type. Figure 14.55 shows the toolpaths for cutting a cup in concave and convex shape.

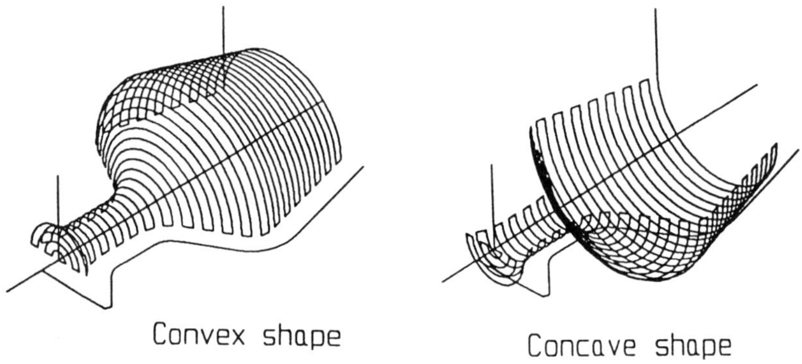

Figure 14.55

Retract to

This parameter adds a vertical wall to the surface. The system will generate a series of extended toolpaths normal to the current construction plane at surface's endpoints. At each of the surface endpoints, the tool retracts to the level specified by the Retract to parameter, then moves a stepover distance, moves down to the surface endpoint, and moves over the surface.Figure 14.56 shows the toolpath pattern of rectract to parameter.

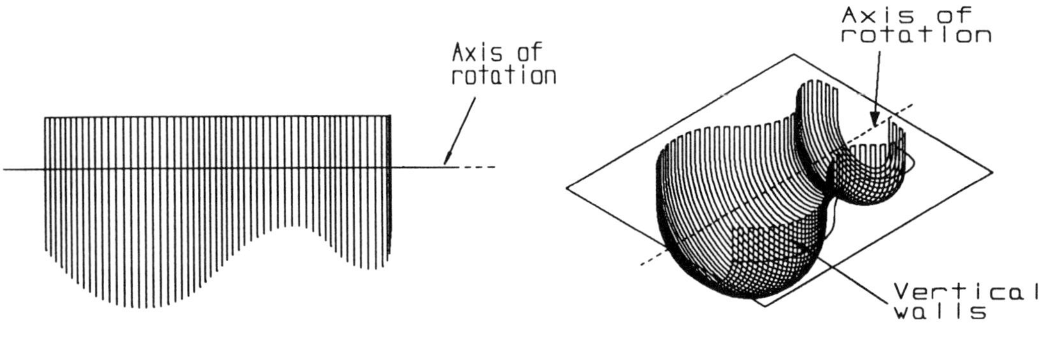

Figure 14.56

Trim to

This parameter allows the toolpaths to be trimmed or extended to a specified plane or boundary. There are two trim to modes: height and width. In trim to height mode, the toolpaths are extended to the specified height if this height is above the axis depth (axis of rotation) shown on the next page in Figure 14.57a, or the toolpaths are trimmed to the specified height if this height is below the axis depth shown in Figure 14.57b.

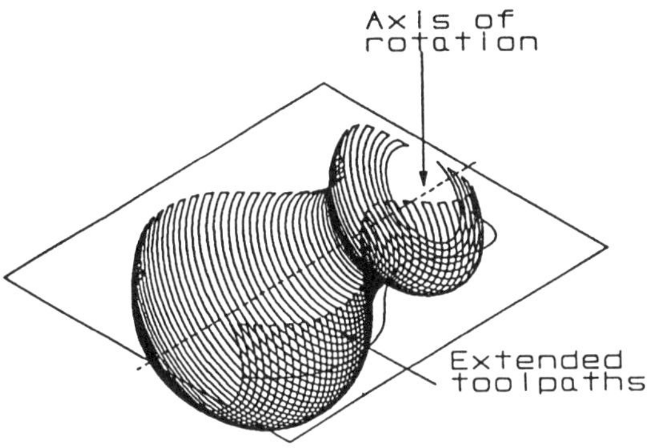

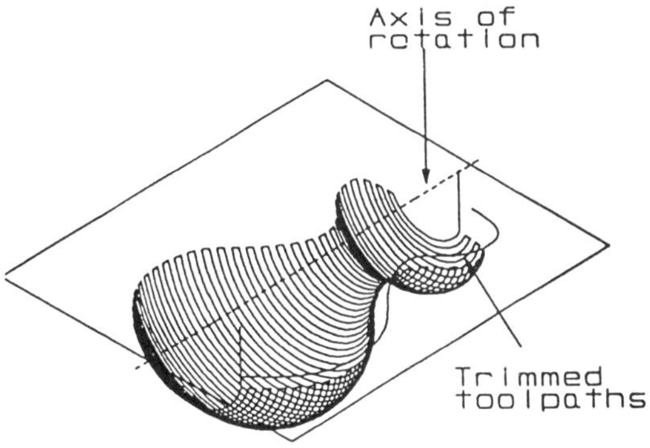

Figure 14.57a

Figure 14.57b

Note: When the toolpaths are extended above the axis depth, undercuts may occur in most cases.

In the **convex cases,** the toolpaths will be trimmed when the trimming height is above the axis of rotation (Figure 14.58a), or the toolpaths will be extended when the trimming height is below the axis of rotation (Figure 14.58b).

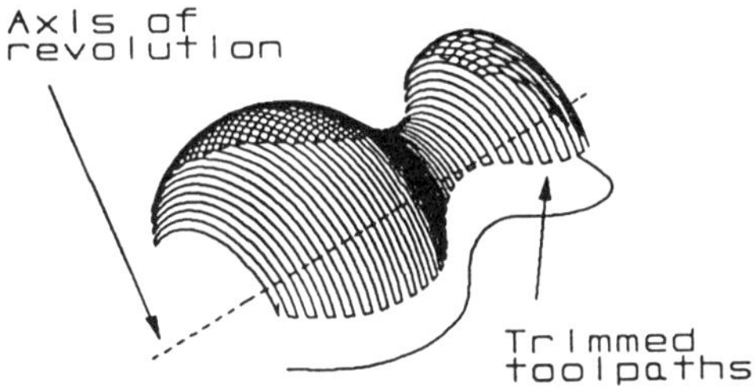

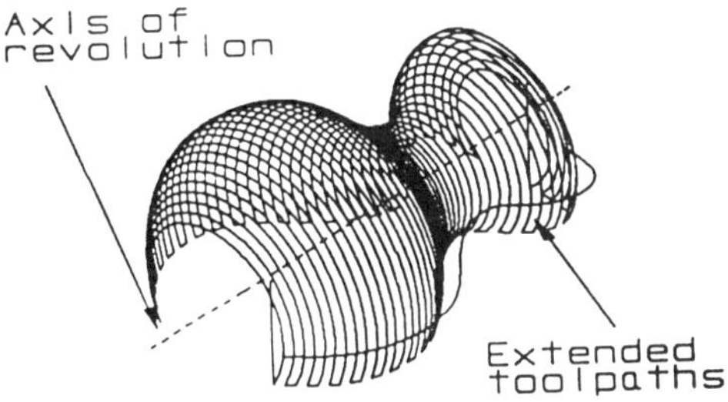

Figure 14.58a

Figure 14.58b

In trim to width mode, the toolpaths are to be trimmed to a fixed width specified by two parallel lines. Note that the toolapths are trimmed to the tool center instead of the edge. Figure 14.59 shows a trim to width example.

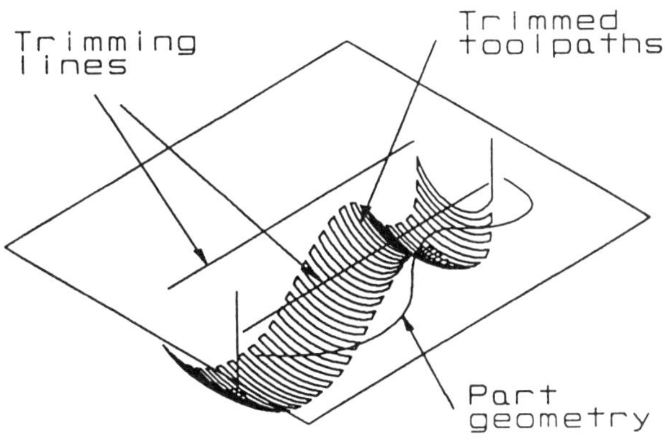

Figure 14.59

Project 8.

Machining a surface of revolution

The revolution module is used to generate toolpaths to machine a cup with a convex shape. The wireframe model file is cup.ge3 created in project 8 of chapter 11. The wireframe model and the toolpaths are shown in Figure 14.60.

Wireframe Model
Project 8 of Chapter 11 (Cup)

We are here

Go to

Toolpath
(revolt1)

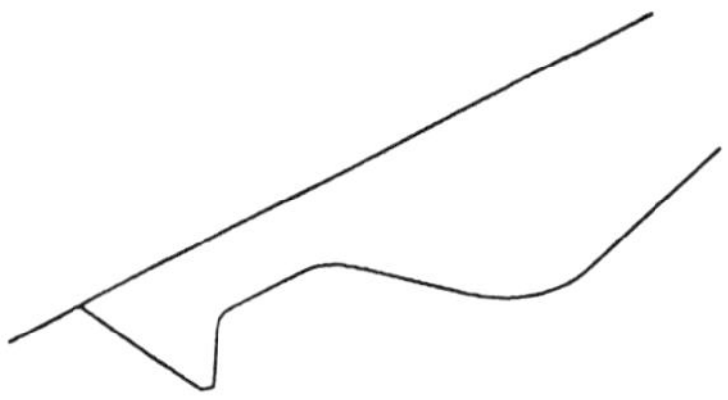

Figure 14.60a Wireframe model

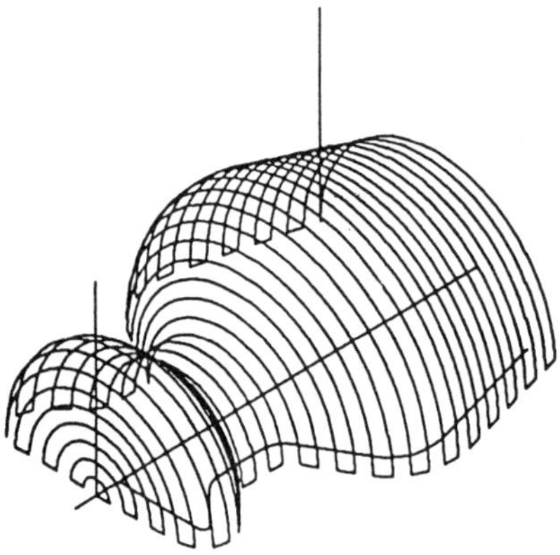

Figure 14.60b Toolpaths

Tips 1. Wireframe model file is cup.ge3.

2. Axis of rotation is Y axis.

3. Shape = Convex

Step 1. Load the wireframe model file (cup.ge3) or create one by following the instructions in project 8 of chapter 11.

Select **MAIN MENU** → **File** → **Get**
Enter file name: **cup** ←
Select **Yes** to delete the current part

The wireframe model of the cup should appear as Figure 14.61.

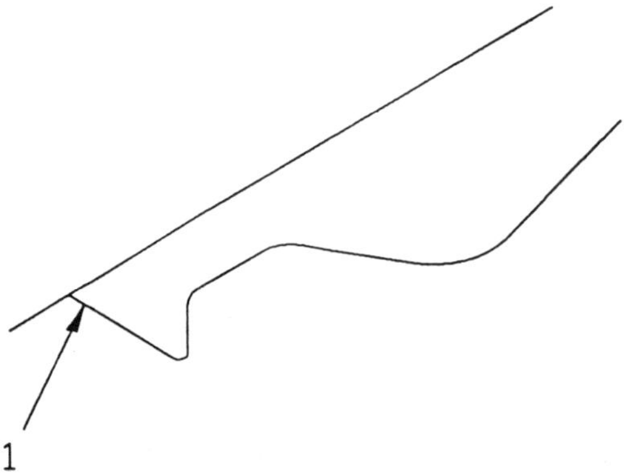

Figure 14.61

Step 2. Initiate the revolution toolpath module.

Select **MAIN MENU** → **Toolpaths** → **mIsc.**→ **Revolution**
Enter file name: **revolt1** ←

Step 3. Define the contours using the pick point in Figure 14.61.

Select the edge of the surface: Select **Chain** then pick at **P1**
Select **Close** → **End here**
Select **Y** for the axis of rotation

Step 4. Define the surface of revolution parameters to the following settings.

Step size = 0.1
Axis depth = 0.0
Shape = Convex
Retract to nothing
Trim toolpath to nothing

Select the **NC button** to advance to the NC parameters menu.

Step 5. Define the NC parameters to the following settings.

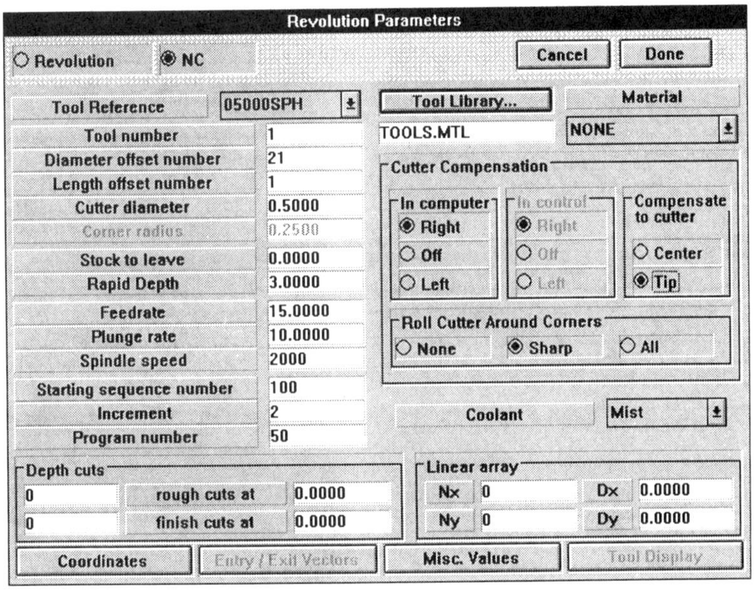

Select the **Done button** to complete the parameters settings.

Step 6. Save and close the toolpath file.

Select **Yes** to accept this toolpath segment
Select **End program** to close the toolpath file
Select **No** to run the post processor.

The toolpaths should resemble Figure 14.62.

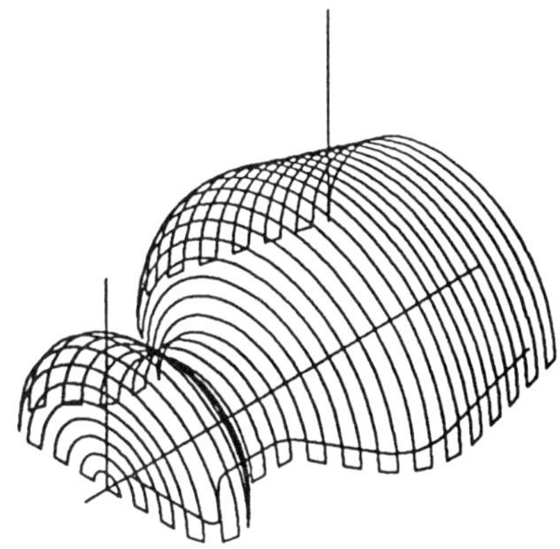

Figure 14.62

14.9 Exercises

14.9.1 Short Answer

1. What are the two methods used to generate toolpaths to cut surfaces in Mastercam? Describe the advantages and disadvantages of using these two methods, respectively.

2. Define along and across directions.

3. What are the four cutting methods in 3d surfacing?

4. Describe, with a drawing, the main features of the Zig zag cutting method.

5. Describe, with a drawing, the main features of the one way cutting method.

6. Describe, with a drawing, the main features of the circular cutting method.

7. What are the two modes of cutting direction?

8. What are the two stepping over distances used in surfacing cutting? Use drawings to illustrate these two distances.

9. Describe how the stepping over distances affects the dimensional accuracy and part program size of surface machining.

10. What are the five modes of cutter compensation in computer?

11. What are two common types of cutters used in cutting surfaces?

12. Use drawings to show how the selection of cutter tip and cutter center affect the toolpaths?

13. Describe the two groups of 3d toolpath modules in Mastercam. Explain their differences.

14. List the five 3d toolpath modules that generate toolpaths from a wireframe model.

15. What is constant Z cutting in ruled module?

16. What do initial Z and final Z parameters perform in setting constant Z cutting?

17. Describe the functions of trimming planes in ruled module.

18. What are the four blending methods used in Coons module?

14.9.2 Problems

19. Use the ruled toolpath module to generate the toolpaths for machining two ruled surfaces from the wireframe model created in problem 11.10. The wireframe model file is **E1.** The wireframe model and the toolpaths are illustrated in Figure 14.63.

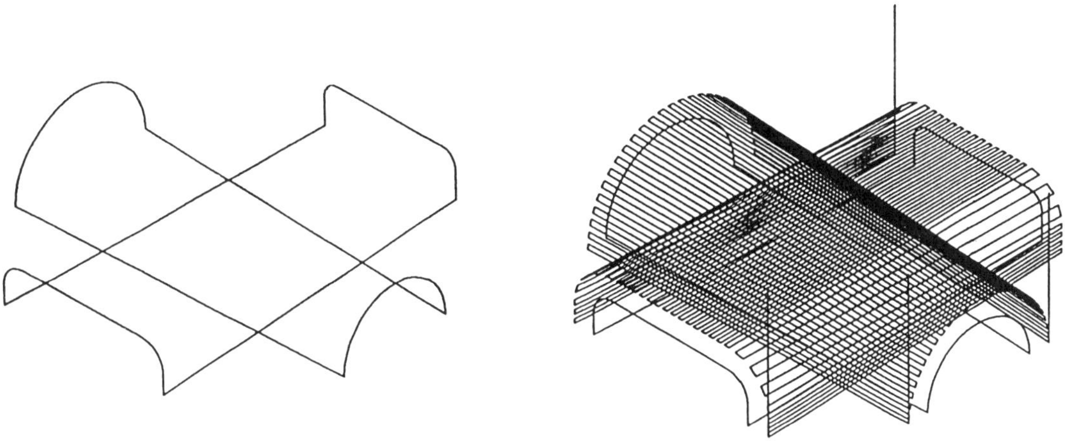

Figure 14.63

Tips 1.Wireframe model file is E1.

2. Save the toolpaths for cutting two ruled surfaces in two separate files ET1 and ET2.

3.. Cutter is 0.75" ball-end mill.

4. Cutting method = Zig zag

20. Use the loft toolpath module to generate toolpaths for cutting a loft surface defined by the wireframe model created in problem 11.12. The wireframe model file is **E3.ge3**. Both the wireframe model and toolpaths are illustrated in Figure 14.64.

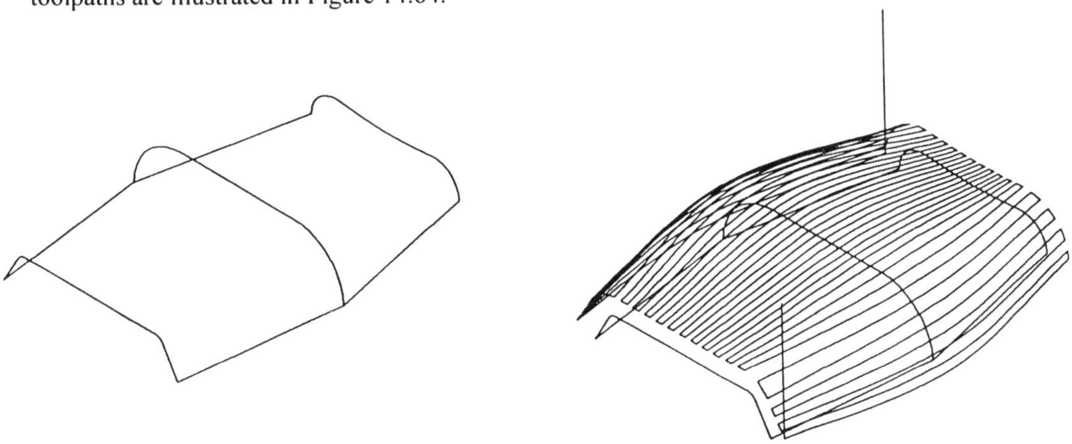

Figure 14.64

Tips 1. Wireframe model file is **E3.ge3.**

2. Pick the contours at the right end and start at contour A.

3. Set cutter compensation in computer to left tip.

21. Use the Coons toolpath module to generate toolpaths to cut the surface created from the wireframe model given in problem 11.14. This is a single patch Coons surface. The wireframe model file is **E5**. Both the wireframe model and toolpaths are shown in Figure 14.65.

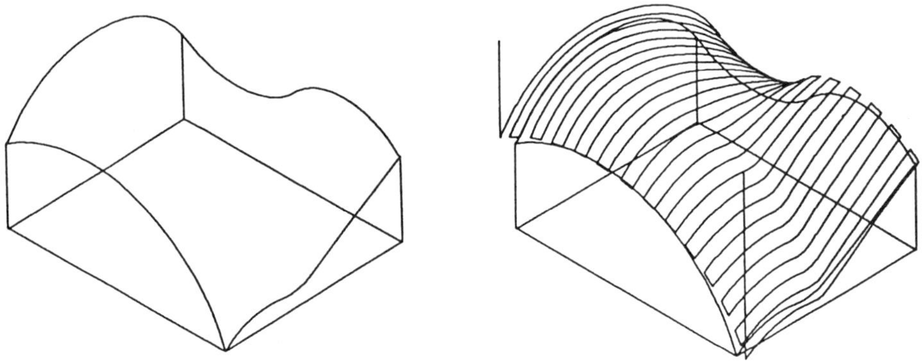

Figure 14.65

Tips 1. Wireframe model file is **E5.ge3.**

2. The number of patches in the along direction is 1.
   The number of patches in the across direction is 1.
3. Use the linear blending method because this is a single patch surface.

22. The Coons toolpath module is used to generate the toolpaths for machining a multiple-patch Coons surface. The wireframe model is created in problem 11.15 and has the name **E6.ge3**. Figure 14.66 shows both the wireframe model and the toolpaths.

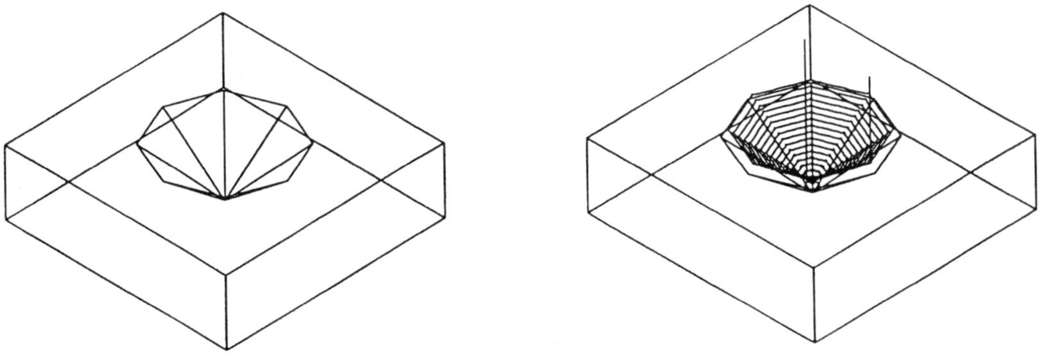

Figure 14.66

Tips 1. Wireframe model file is **E6.ge3.**

2. The number of patches in the along direction is 8.
   The number of patches in the across direction is 1.
3. The second along contours are a common point. This point serves as the contours for the second along contour rows.
4. Use linear blending method because all patches are flat surfaces.

23. The revolution toolpath module is used to generate the toolpaths for machining the cup defined by the wireframe model **E8** in problem 11.17. The cup model is made using the concave shape. Figure 14.67 shows both wireframe model and toolpaths.

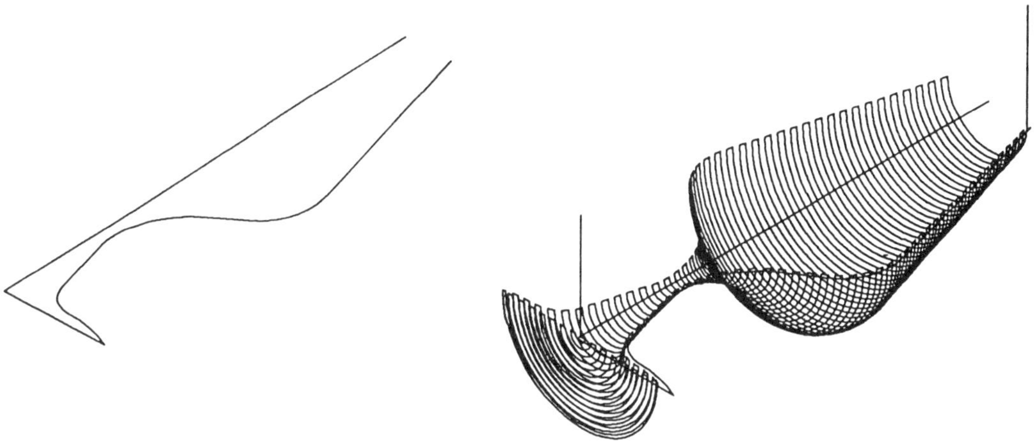

Figure 14.67

Tips 1. Wireframe model file name is **E8.ge3.**

2. The axis of rotation is Y axis.

3. Surface shape is concave.

4. Set both *retraction to* and *trim to* parameters to nothing.

24. Use the swept toolpath module to generate the toolpaths to cut a fly disk as shown in Figure 14.68. The wireframe model file is **E10**. The toolpaths for cutting the upper section of the model can be obtained by revolving the upper section profile about the Z axis. However, the bottom half of the model can not be machined in the same machine setup as the upper half. We need to flip the workpiece over and has the second setup for machining the bottom half. Therefore, it requires two toolpath files, one for the upper half and the other for the bottom half.

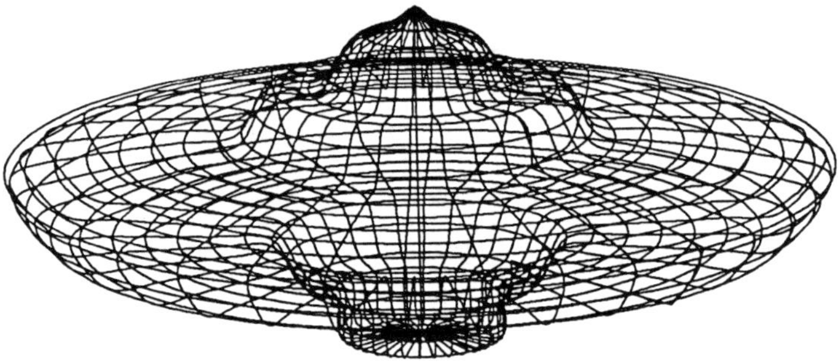

Figure 14.68

Tips 1. Use the contour profile of the upper half in the swept module to generate toolpaths and save it under one file name.

2. Change the contour profile in the bottom half to level 2. This allows the upper half contour (level 1) to be made invisible.
3. Rotate the contours in the bottom half about the X axis by 180°.

4. Use swept module to generate toolpaths for the bottom half and save under another file name.

Chapter 15

3-D Toolpaths (II): Generated from Surface Models

Objectives:

1. Generate toolpaths from existing surface models.
2. Use the flowline module to generate toolpaths for single surfaces.
3. Use the multisurf module to generate toolpths for composite surfaces.

Overview

Mastercam provides **two modules** to generate toolpaths from existing surface models: flowline and multisurf. The flowline module is used to generate the toolpath for a single surface only. The multisurf module allows the toolpaths for more than one surface to be generated simultaneously. The flowline module can also be used in composite surfaces models, but it has to be used as many times as the number of surfaces since it generates the toolpaths for a single surface only.

15.1 Flowline Module

The flowline toolpath module is used to generate the toolpaths to produce a single surface that is already existed in the database. For a surface model that has more than one surface, the toolpaths for machining each surface entity must be generated separately with the flowline module. In other words, the flowline module must be repeatedly used as many times as the number of surface entities.

Flowline Parameters

The flowline parameters menu is shown here:

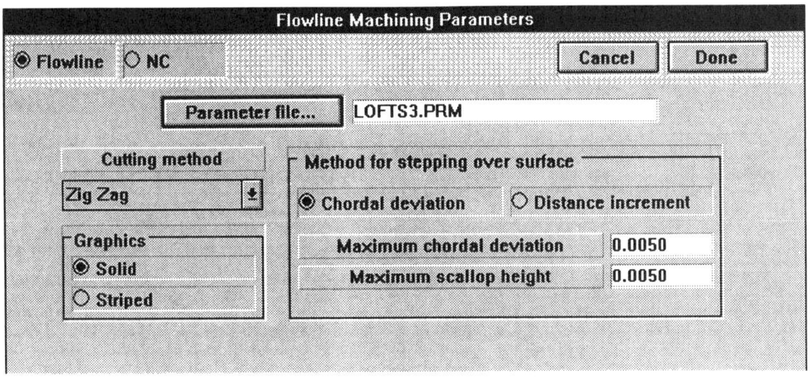

Cutting Method

The user can select one of the six cutting methods shown below to generate toolpaths.

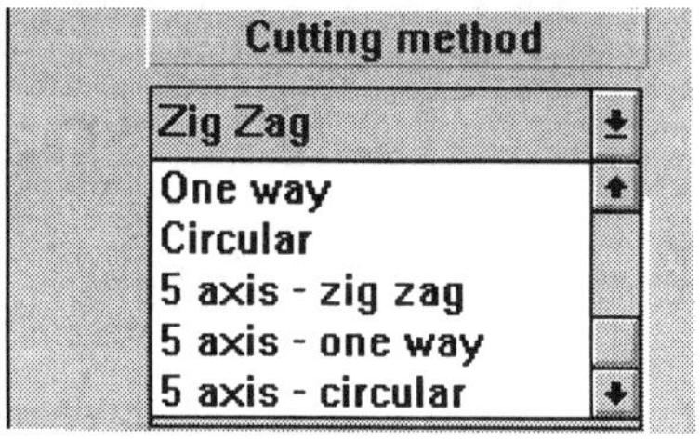

The first three methods; zig-zag, one way, and circular, are used for 3-axis machines. The last three methods; 5axis-zig zag, 5axis-one way, and 5axis-circular, are for wire EDM applications.

Stepping Over Surface Method

There are **two** methods in determining the stepping distance of the toolpath over the surface: distance increment method, and chordal deviation method.

Distance Increment Method

Two cut distance increment values should be specified in this method: along cut incremental distance and across cut incremental distance. The along cut distance is the step-over interval between two adjacent paths in the along direction. The across cut incremental distance is the step-over interval in the across direction. Figure 15.1 shows the surface toolpaths generated by using distance increment method.

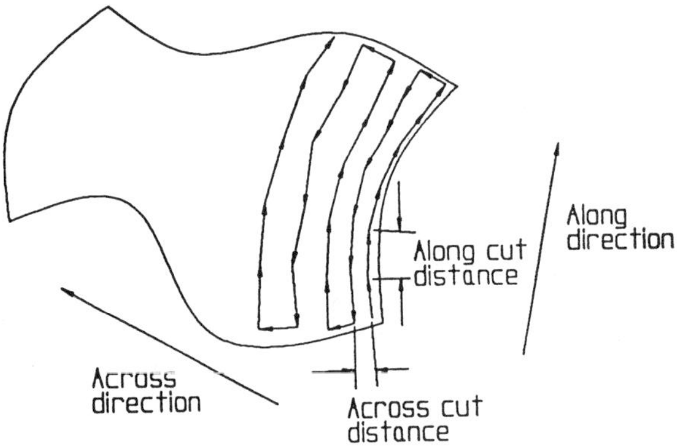

Figure 15.1

Chordal Deviation Method

Chordal deviation is the distance between the actual toolpath and the true surface (Figure 15.2). Two variables in Mastercam, maximum chordal deviation and maximum scallop height, are used to determine the stepping distance over surfaces. The maximum chordal deviation value is the maximum allowable dimensional error between the toolpath and the surface. Chordal deviation is used to calculate the cutting increment in the along direction.

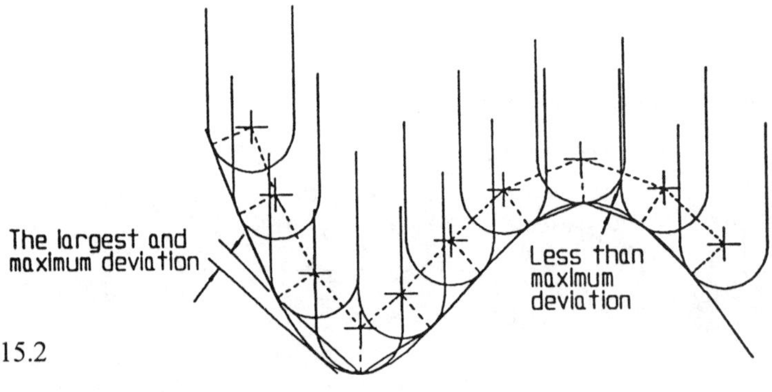

Figure 15.2

When a cutter with a non-flat end, such as a ball end mill, is used to cut a surface in a zigzag pattern, an uncut strip results between the two adjacent cutting passes as shown in Figure 15.3. The height of these undesirable strips is called scallop height. The larger the step-over value between the two cutting passes, the bigger the scallop height. The given maximum scallop height value is used to calculate the cutter step-over distance in the across direction (or between each along cut).

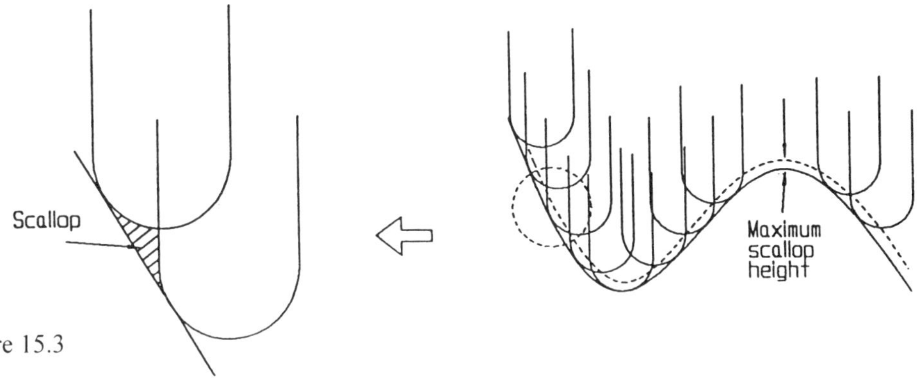

Figure 15.3

Suggestions are given below for selecting the Stepping Over method:

Step 1. Use the distance increment method when the surface has relatively large curvature radii, has no sharp shapes, or does not require a close dimensional accuracy (Figure 15.4).

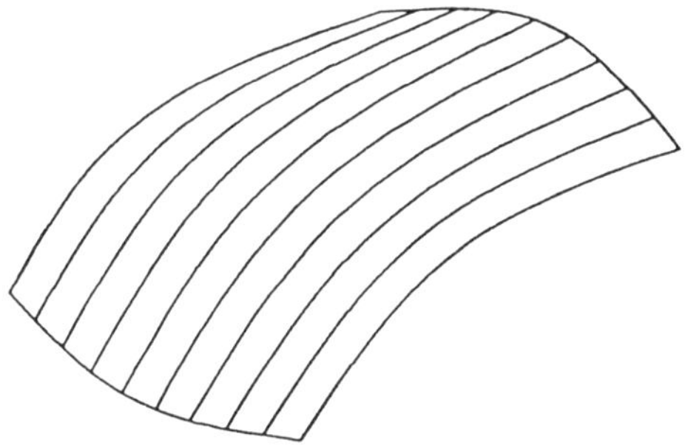

Figure 15.4

Step 2.. Use chordal deviation method for those surfaces that have small curvature radii, have sharp shapes, or require a close dimensional tolerance (Figure 15.5). This method can accurately produce the surface within the specified dimensional accuracy.

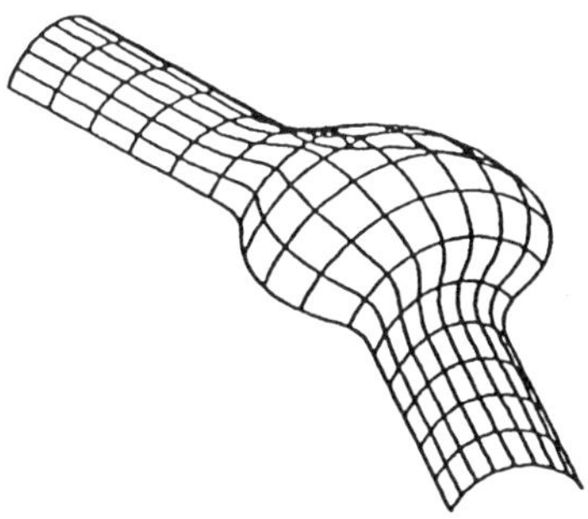

Figure 15.5

Step 3. Computer processing time is significantly shorter when using the distance increment method than with the chordal deviation method.

⌛**Tip** 1. **Selection of the toolpath direction:** after the desired surface to be machined is selected, the system will prompt the user to select the toolpath direction either in the along direction or in the across direction. An arrow indicates the toolpath direction (Figure 15.6). You can toggle the arrow direction by using the Flip command.

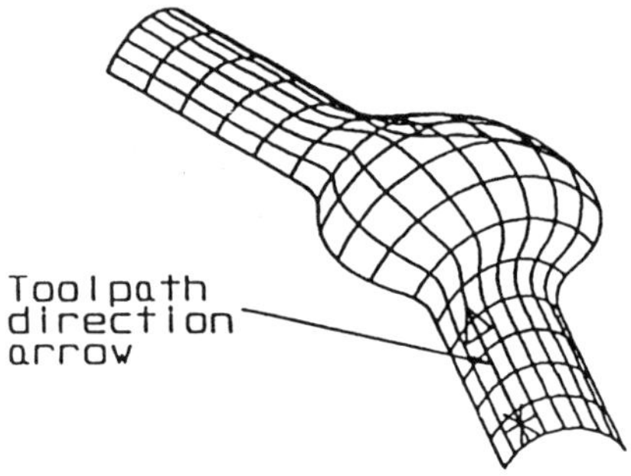

Figure 15.6

⌛**Tip** 2. **Selection of the cutter offset direction:** an arrow indicates which direction the cutter is offset (Figure 15.7). The initial offset direction is in the surface normal direction. You can use the Flip command to change the cutter offset direction.

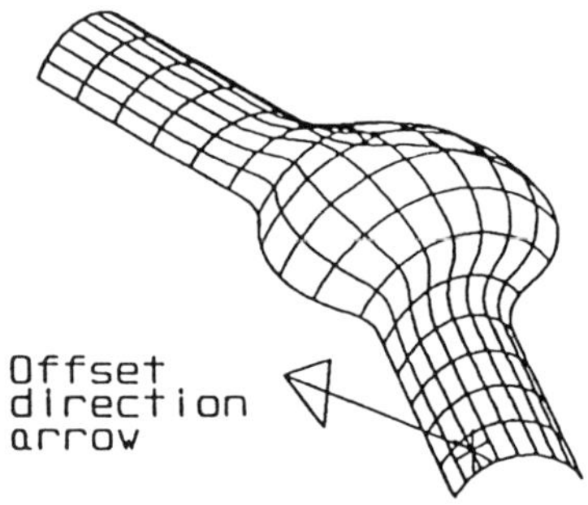

Figure 15.7

Three projects that use the flowline module to generate toolpaths for cutting a single surface are presented in this section. The first project machines a loft surface model consisting of five contours. The second project is a cup modeled as a swept surface. The third project is also cutting a swept surface that is formed by one across contour and two along contour.

Project 1.

1

Generating toolpaths for a loft surface model

Use the flowline module to generate the toolpaths for machining a loft surface defined by five contours. The loft surface model is lofts3 created in project 6 of chapter 12. The surface model and the toolpaths are shown in Figure 15.8.

Wireframe Model
Project 14 of Chapter 11 (loft3)

Go to

Surface Model
Project 6 of Chapter 12 (lofts3)

We are here

Go to

Toolpath
(flowl1)

Go to

Toolpath Trimming
Project 3 of Chapter 16 (lofts3)

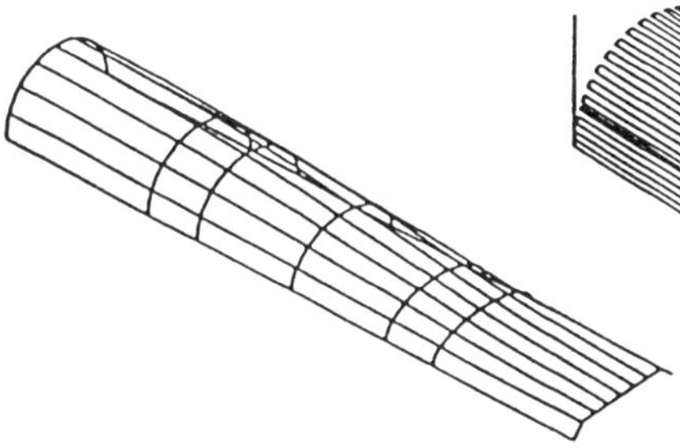

Figure 15.8a Surface model

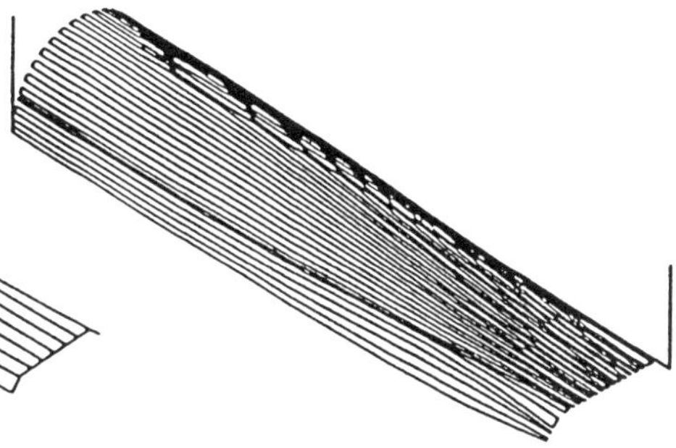

Figure 15.8b Toolpaths

Tips 1. Surface model file is **lofts3.ge3.**

2. Set the toolpath to the along direction and the cutter offset to the outward direction.

3. A ball end mill (0.5" diameter and 0.25" corner radius) is used.

Step 1. Load the surface model file lofts3.

Select **MAIN MENU → File → Get**
Enter file name: **lofts3**
Select **Yes** to delete the current part

The surface model will appear as Figure 15.9.

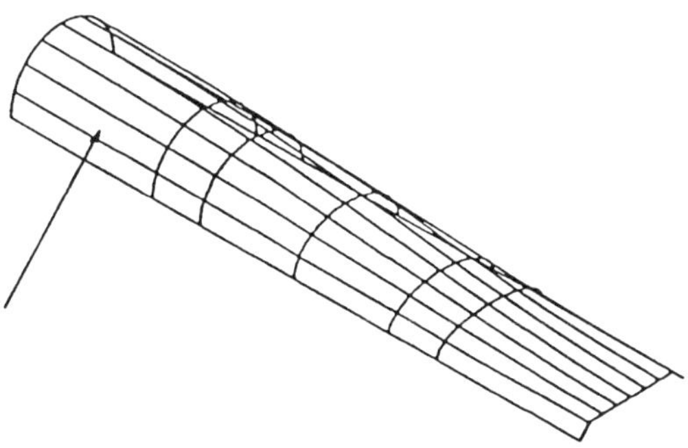

Figure 15.9

Step 2. Initiate the flowline module using the pick point in Figure 15.9.

Select **MAIN MENU → Toolpaths → Flowline**
Enter file name: **flowl1** ←
Select a surface: pick at **P1**

Step 3. Select the toolpath direction.

An arrow indicator will appear on the surface to indicate the toolpath direction as shown in Figure 15.10.

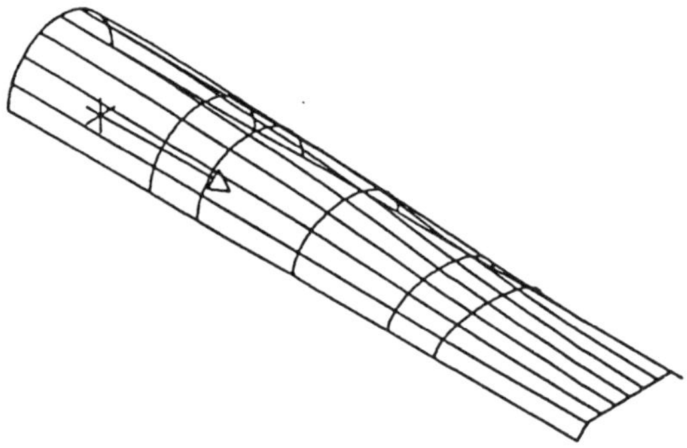

Figure 15.10

Toggle the indicator by selecting the **Flip** command to the desired direction (along), then select **OK**

Step 4. Select the cutter offset direction.

An arrow indicator for cutter offset direction will appear on the surface as shown in Figure 15.11.

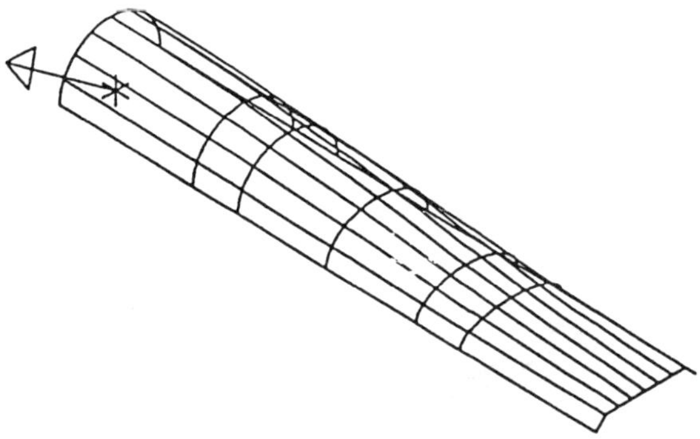

Figure 15.11

Toggle the indicator by selecting **Flip** command to the desired direction (outward), then select **OK**

Step 5. Set the flowline parameters to the following settings.

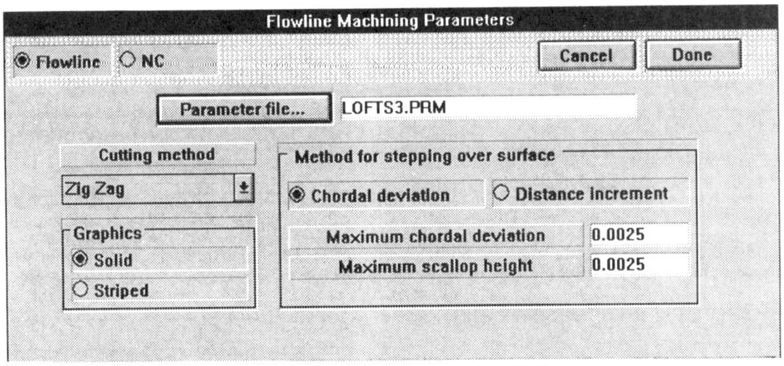

Select the **NC button** of the screen to advance to the NC parameters menu.

Step 6. Set the NC parameters to the following settings.

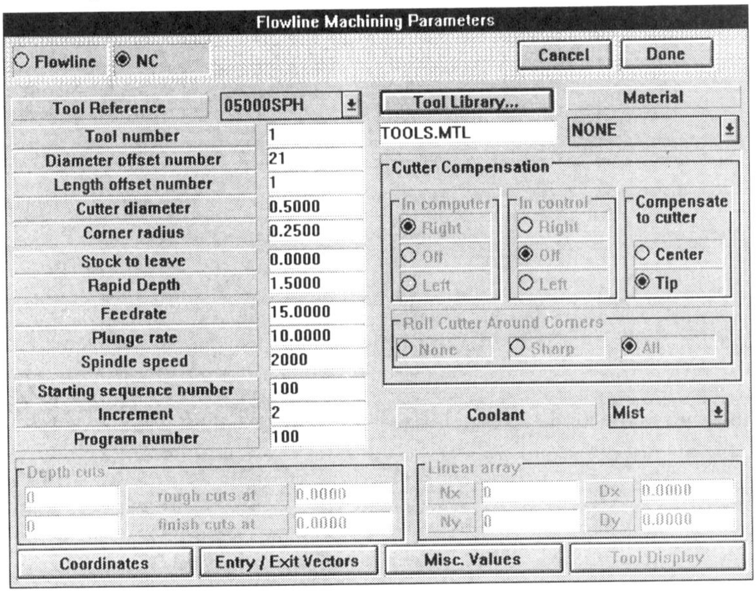

Select the **Done button** of the screen to complete the parameters settings.

Step 7. Accept the toolpaths.

Press **F3** to make the NC Parameters window removed from the screen.
The toolpaths should appear as Figure 15.12.

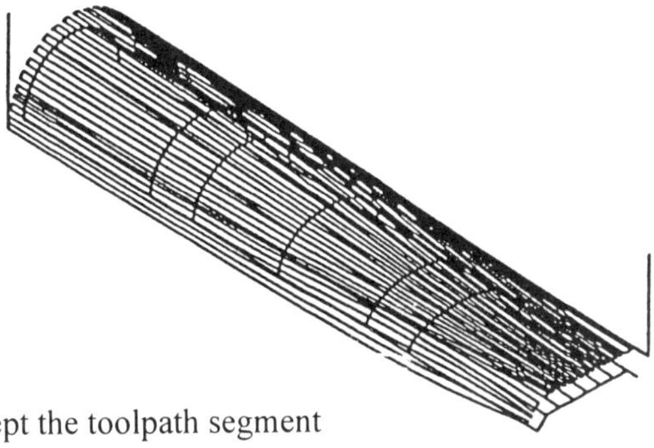

Figure 15.12

Select **Yes** to accept the toolpath segment
Select **End program** to close NCI file
Select **Yes** to run the post processor
Enter file name: **flow1**

Project 2.

Generating toolpaths for cutting a cup

The flowline module is used to generate the toolpaths for cutting a mold of the cup as shown in Figure 15.13. The surface model is generated by using the swept function and has the filename **swepts1.**

Wireframe Model
Project 8 of Chapter 11 (cup)

Go to

Surface Model
Project 14 of Chapter 12 (swepts1)

Go to

Toolpath
(flowl2)

We are here

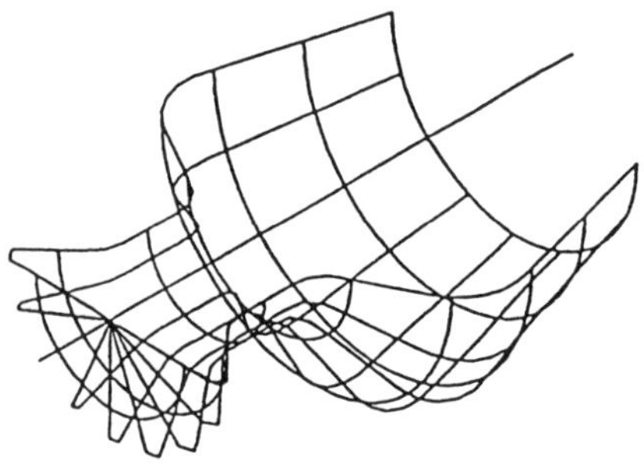

Figure 15.13a Surface Model

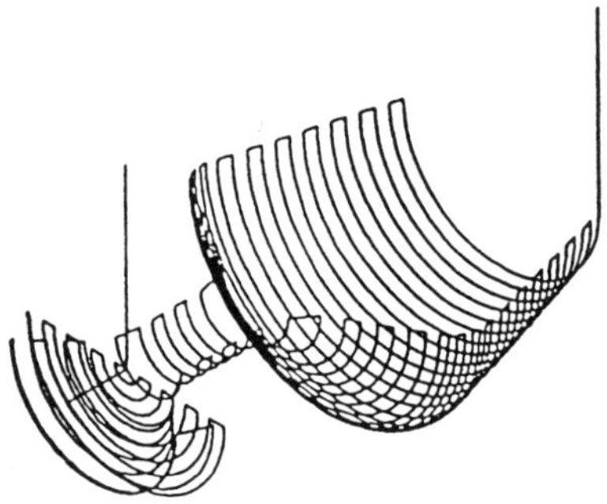

Figure 15.13b Toolpaths

Tips 1. The surface model file name is **swepts1.ge3.**

2. Set the toolpath to the along direction which is in the orientation of the arc. Set the cutter offset to the inward direction.
3. The cutter is a 0.5" ball end mill with 0.25" of corner radius.

Step 1. Load the surface file swepts1 or create one by following the instructions in project 14 of chapter 12.
Select **MAIN MENU → File → Get**
Enter file name: **swepts1**

Select **Yes** to delete the current part
The surface model should resemble Figure 15.14.

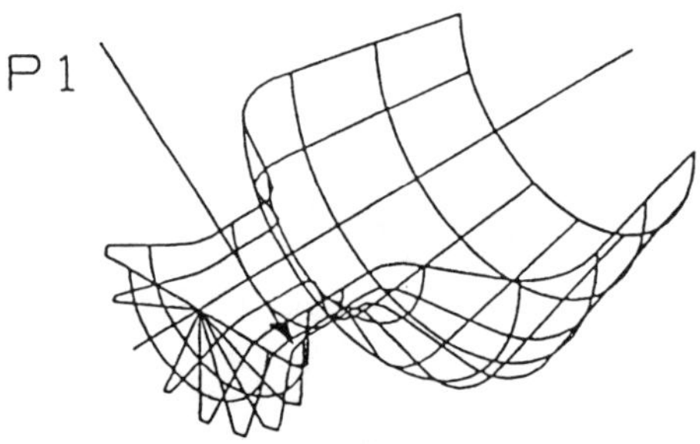

Figure 15.14

Step 2. Initiate the flowline module using the pick point in Figure 15.14.

Select **MAIN MENU** → **Toolpaths** → **Flowline**

Enter file name: **flowl2** ←

Select a surface: pick at **P1**

Step 3. Select the toolpath direction.

An arrow indicator should appear to indicate the toolpath direction in the across direction as shown in Figure 15.15.

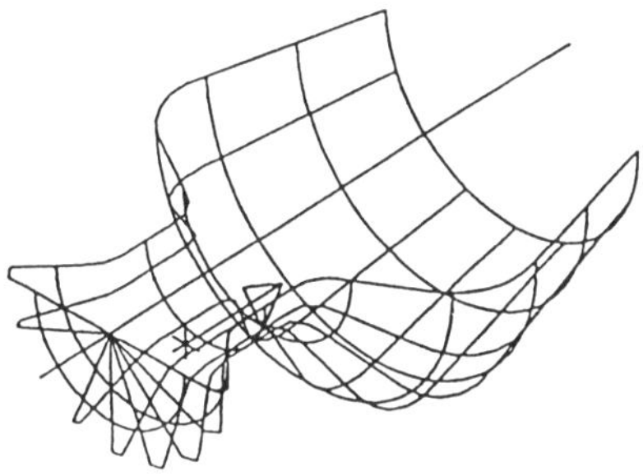

Figure 15.15

Toggle to the other direction (in the along direction) by selecting the **Flip** command, then select **OK**

Step 4. Select the cutter offset direction.

An arrow indicator should appear to indicate the cutter offset direction as shown in figure 15.16.

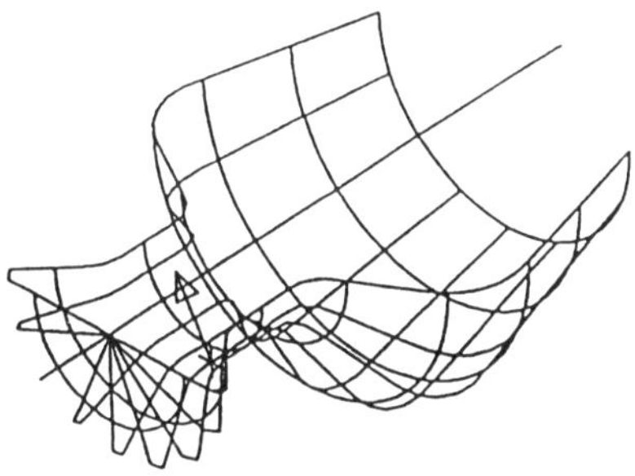

Figure 15.16

Select **OK** to accept the current offset direction (inward direction)

Step 5. Set the flowline parameters to the following setting.

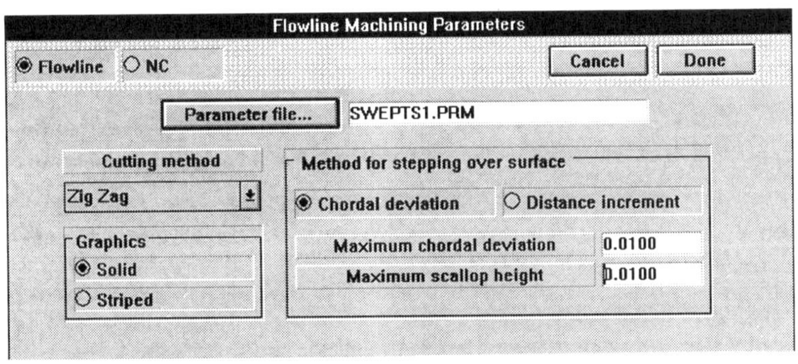

Select the **NC button** of the screen to advance to the NC parameters menu.

Step 6. Set the NC parameters to the following settings.

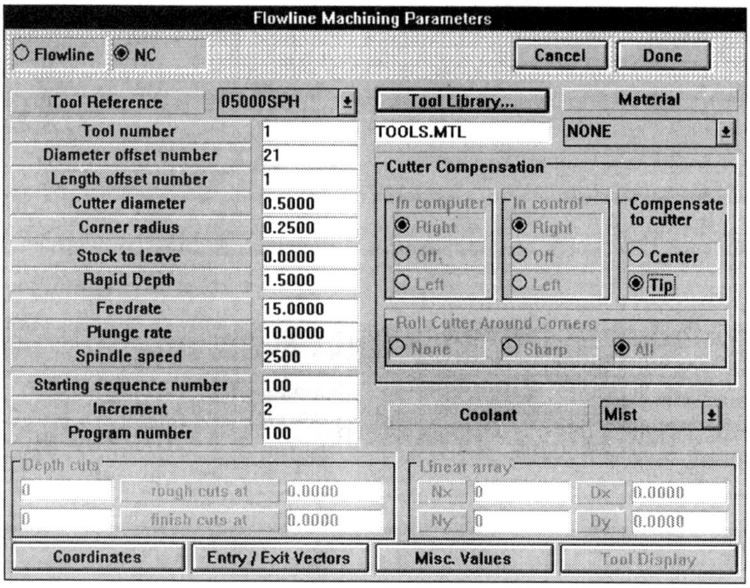

Select the **Done button**of the screen to complete the parameters settings.

Step 7. Generate the toolpaths.

Enter name of surface disk file: **flowl2** ←

The toolpaths should resemble Figure 15.17.

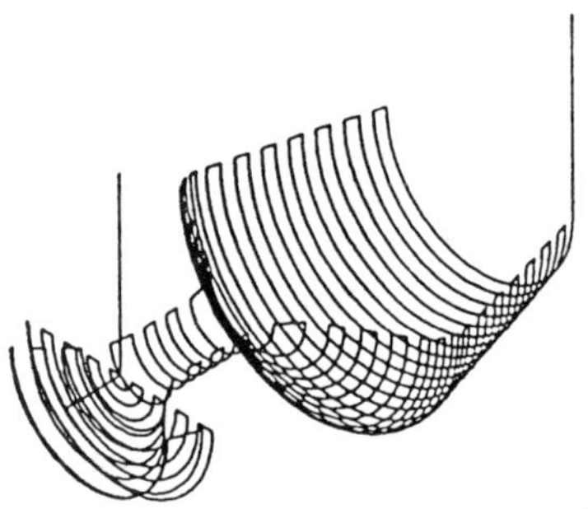

Figure 15.17

Select **Yes** to accept the toolpath segment
Select **End program** to close NCI file
Select **No** to "Run the post processor?"

Project 3.

Generating toolpaths for cutting a swept surface

The flowline module is used to generate a set of toolpaths to cut a swept surface defined by one across contour and two along contours. The surface model file is **swepts3** created in project 16 of chapter 12. The surface model and the toolpaths are shown in Figure 15.18.

Wireframe Model
Project 10 of Chapter 11 (swept3)

Go to

Surface Model
Project 16 of Chapter 12 (swepts3)

Go to

We are here

Toolpath
(flowl3)

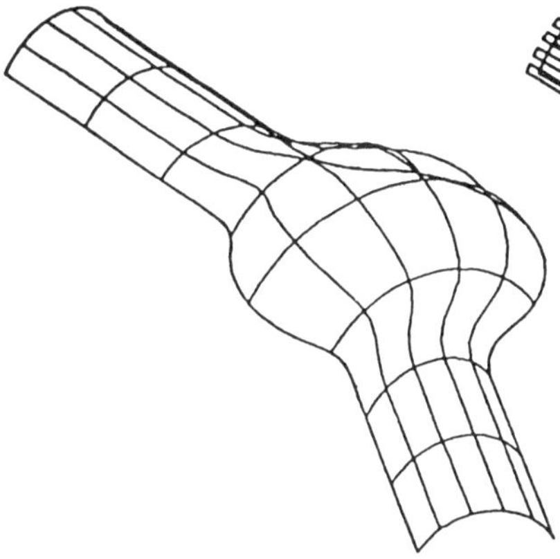

Figure 15.18a Surface model

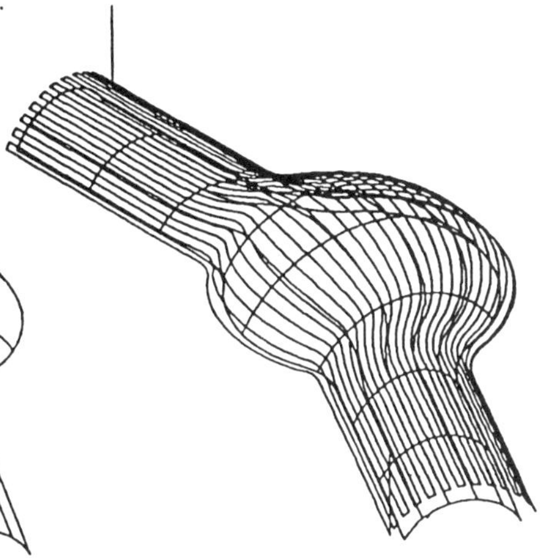

Figure 15.18b Toolpaths

Tips 1.The surface model file name is **swepts3.ge3.**

2. Set the toolpath to the along direction and the cutter offset to the outward direction.

3. Set the chordal deviation and scallop height to 0.03" to reduce the program size.

Step 1. Load the surface model swepts3 or create one by following the instructions in project 16 of chapter 12.

Select **MAIN MENU** → **File** → **Get**
Enter file name: **swepts3** ←
Select **Yes** to delete the current part

The surface model should appear as Figure 15.19.

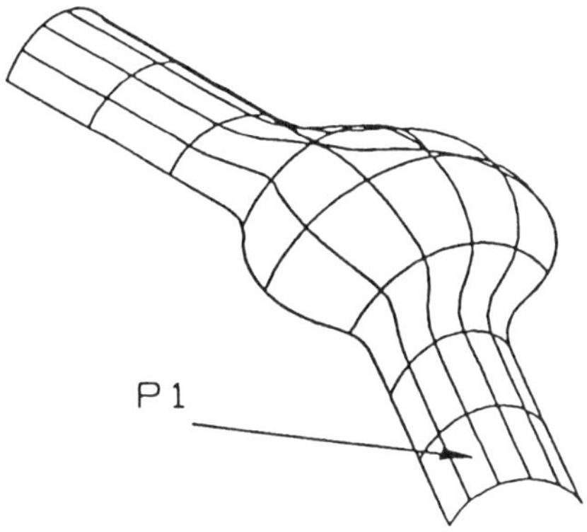

Figure 15.19

Step 2. Initiate the flowline module. Use the pick point in Figure 15.19 on the previous page.

Select **MAIN MENU → Toolpaths→ Flowline**
Enter file name: **flowl3** ←
Select a surface: pick at **P1**

Step 3. Set the toolpath direction.

An arrow indicating the toolpath direction will appear on the surface as shown in Figure 15.20.

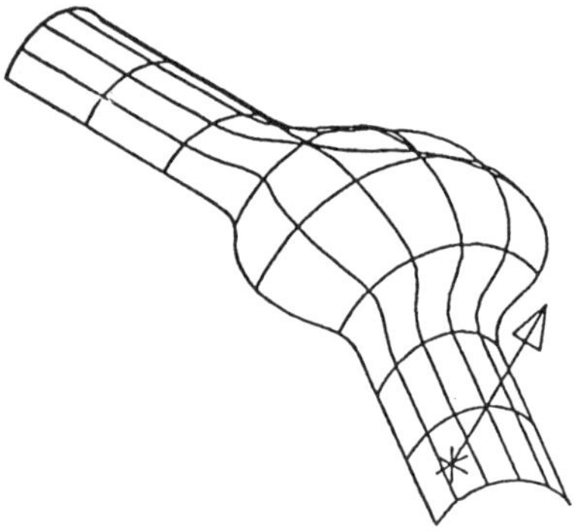

Figure 15.20

Toggle the indicator by picking the **Flip** command to the along direction then select **OK**

Step 4. Set the cutter offset direction.

An arrow indicator for cutter offset direction should appear as shown in the next Figure 15.21.

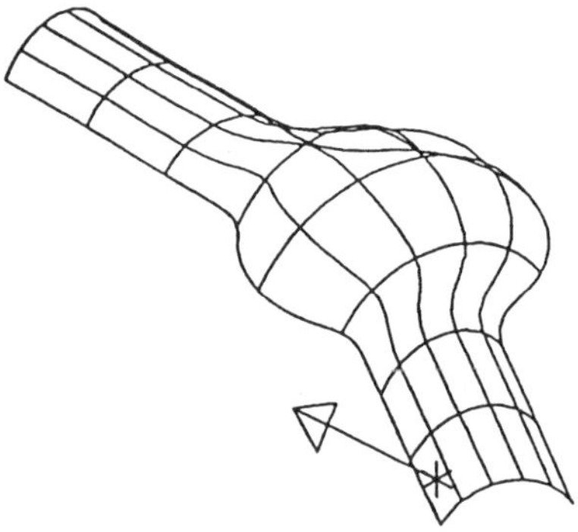

Figure 15.21

Toggle the indicator by picking the **Flip** command to outward direction if necessary, then select **OK**

Step 5. Define the flowline parameters.

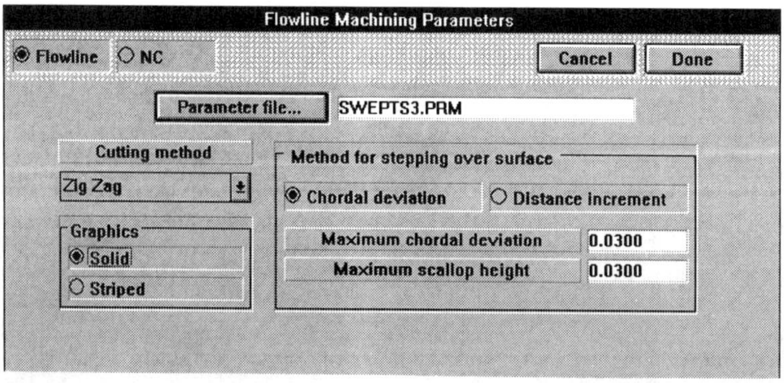

Select the **NC button** of the screen to advance to the NC parameters menu.

Step 6. Set the NC parameters.

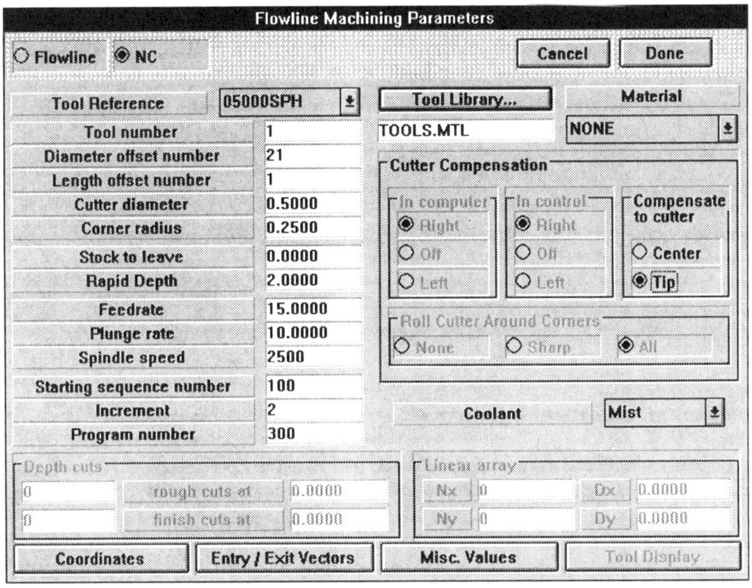

Select the **Done button** of the screen to complete the parameters settings.

Step 7. Accept the toolpath.

The toolpaths should resemble Figure 15.22.

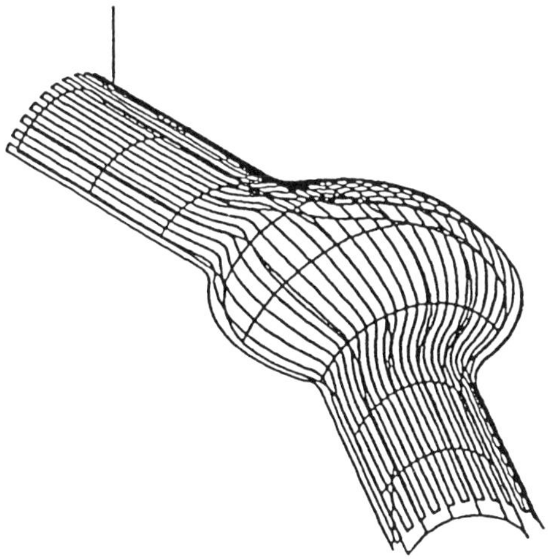

Figure 15.22

Select **Yes** to accept the toolpath segment
Select **End program**
Select **No** to "Run the post processor?"

15.2 Multisurf Module

This toolpath module is used to generate the continuous toolpaths to simultaneously machine multiple surfaces. The maximum number of surfaces is determined by the toolpath allocation set by using Screen → Configure → Allocations window. This is a very powerful tool in machining composite surfaces. The Multisurf module has three functions which are described in the table below.

Table 15.1 The Msurf menu

Function	Description
Set norms	Sets the normal of the selected surfaces to the desired direction.
Finish	Generates toolpaths for finish cutting surfaces.
Rough	Generates toolpaths for rough cutting surfaces.

Multisurf-Finish Parameters

It is very important to know the multisurf-finish parameters in order to effectively use the multisurf module. The multisurf parameters are listed below:

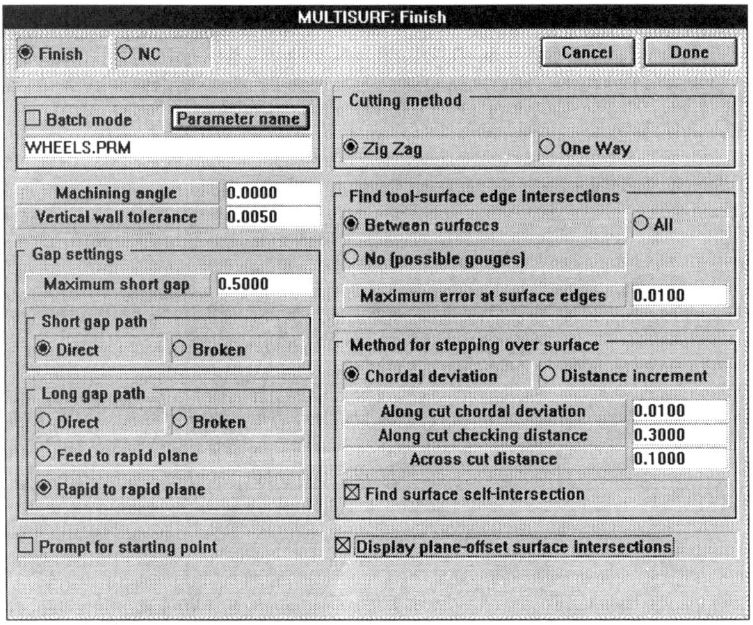

The above multisurf parameters consist of at least **five groups** including gouge check, method of stepping over, gap step method, cutting method, and compensate to cutter. They are explained on the following pages.

Gouge Check

Gouging in machining means the cutter scooping out certain material that is not intended to be cut while moving along the toolpaths for producing a part feature (Figure 15.23). The act of producing gouges is referred to as gouging. Gouging can occur in most machining especially in pocketing and surface cutting. Fortunately, Mastercam provides useful gouging check functions to allow gouges to be removed from the toolpaths.

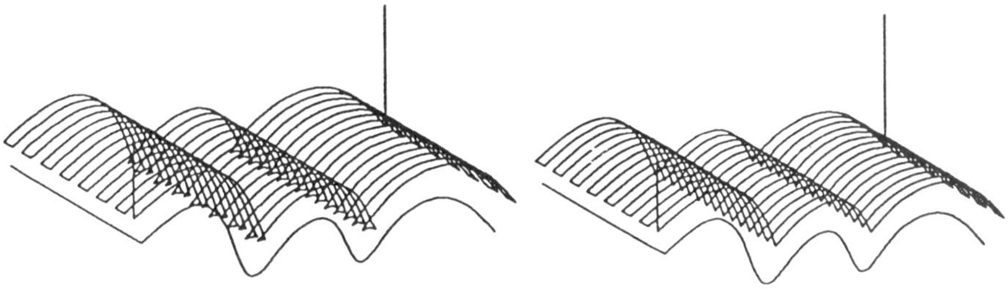

Figure 15.23a Top view

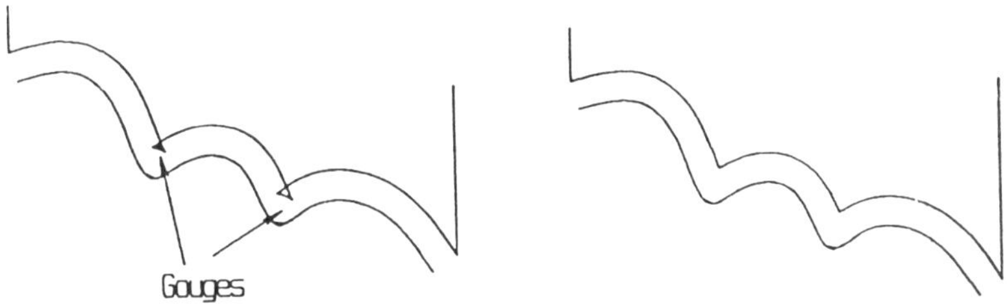

Figure 15.23b Side view

Three gouge check parameters that are specifically used in the multisurf module include: tool-surface edge intersections, maximum error at surface edges, and surface self-intersection.

Tool-Surface Edge Interaction

In composite surface models, some surfaces may have open edges in which the surface skin is not fully extended to cover the edges of the surfaces. Mastercam classifies the surface open edges into **two** categories: open edges between surfaces and open edges in single surfaces (Figure 15.24). In between surfaces group, the open edges are located at the intersection of two surfaces. In a single surface group, the open edges are on a surface that is not intersected with other surfaces at the open edge boundaries.

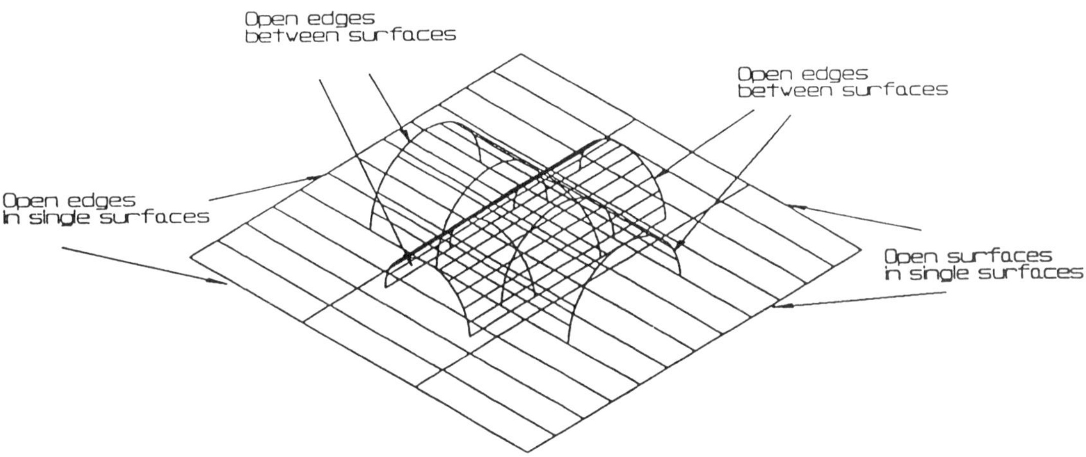

Figure 15.24

Mastercam uses a "Find tool-surface edge intersections" parameter to select the gouge check option. This parameter can be toggled to **no, between surfaces,** and **all.** Table 15.2 below illustrates the effect of selection mode on the toolpaths and gouges.

Table 15.2 Selection Modes

Selection mode	Effects on open edges	Illustration
No	No offset in all open edges. The cutter center lies at the open edges of all surfaces. Edge gouging occurs at all open edges.	See Figure 15.25
Between surfaces	Edge gougings will be removed in surfaces that are intersected with other surfaces. However, the cutter center lies at the open edges of single surfaces.	See Figure 15.26
All	Edge gougings will be removed in all surfaces including between surfaces and single surfaces.	See Figure 15.27

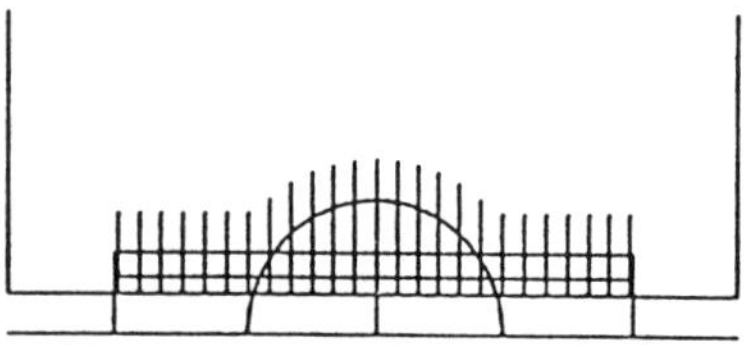

Side View

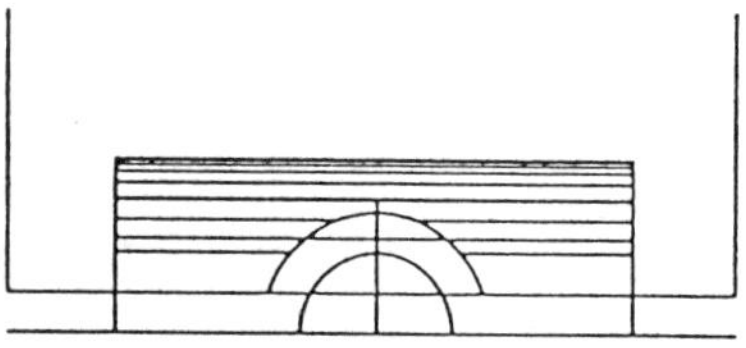

Front View

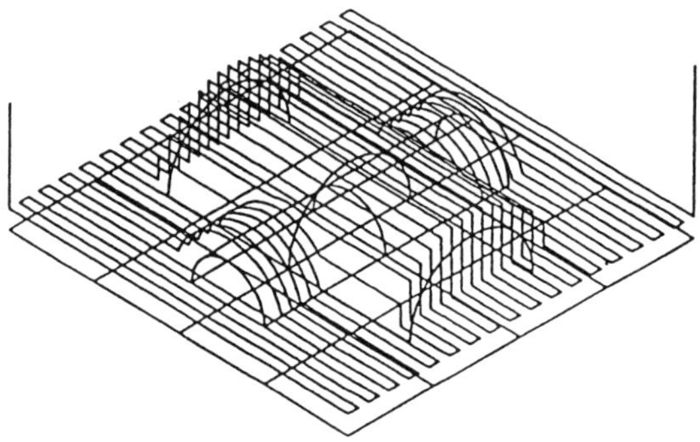

Isometric View

Figures 15.25 No Surface

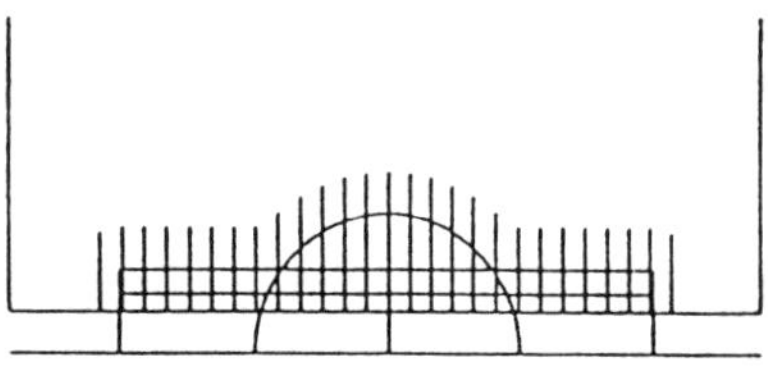

Side View

Front View

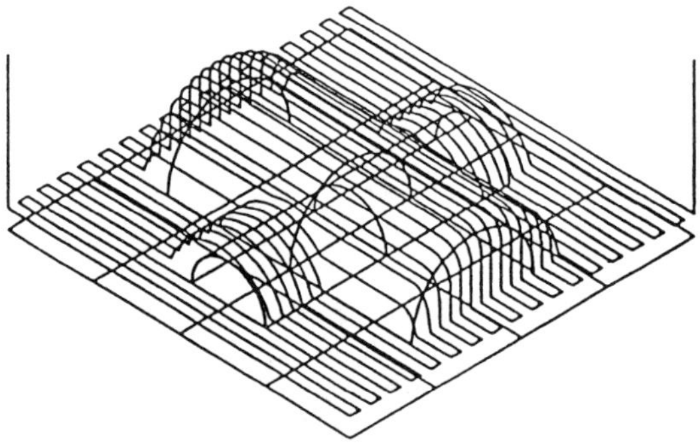

Isometric View

Figure 15.26 Between surfaces

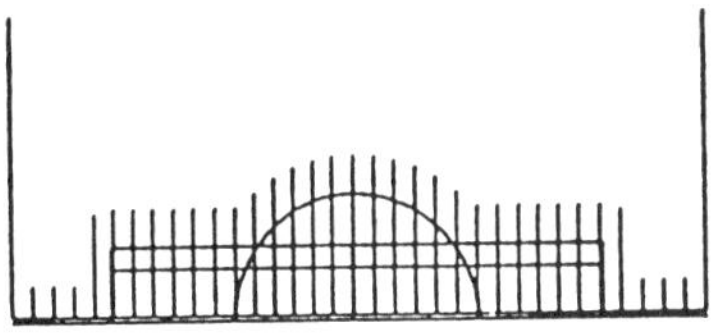

Side View

Front View

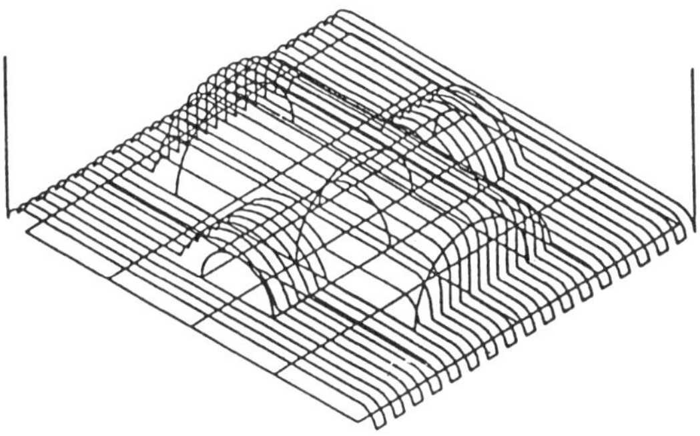

Isometric View

Figure 15.27 All surfaces

Selecting the gouge checking parameter:

⌛**Tips** 1. Do not use **No** mode because it may produce gouges.

2. Always select **Between surfaces** mode if possible.

3. Use **All** mode only when the open edges of the single surfaces must be cut.

Maximum Error at Surface Edges

This parameter specifies the maximum allowable tolerance for cutting the surface open edges.

Surface Self-Intersection

Surfaces may curve in such a way that gouging into itself may occur while cutting a surface. Mastercam refers to this type of gouging as surface self-intersection. Figure 15.28 shows a surface that has the feature of self-intersection. The "Find surface self-intersection" parameter can be toggled to **yes(** ☒ **)** or **no(** ☐ **)**. When **yes** is selected, the self gougings will be removed as in Figure 15.29a. With **no** mode, the cutter will gouge into the surface as indicated in Figure 15.29b. *Note:* Always set this parameter to **yes** to remove the self-gougings of surfaces.

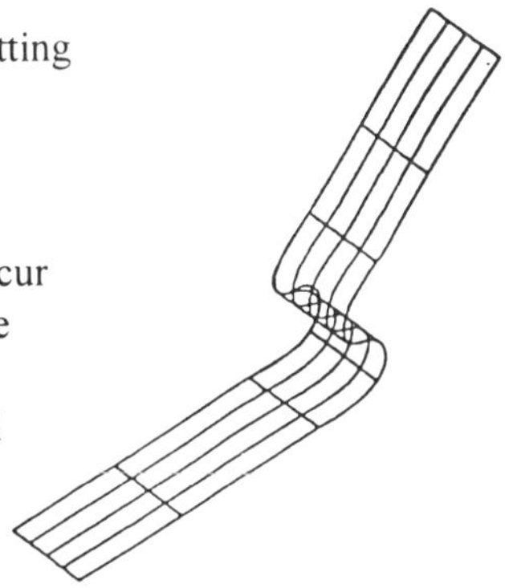

Figure 15.28

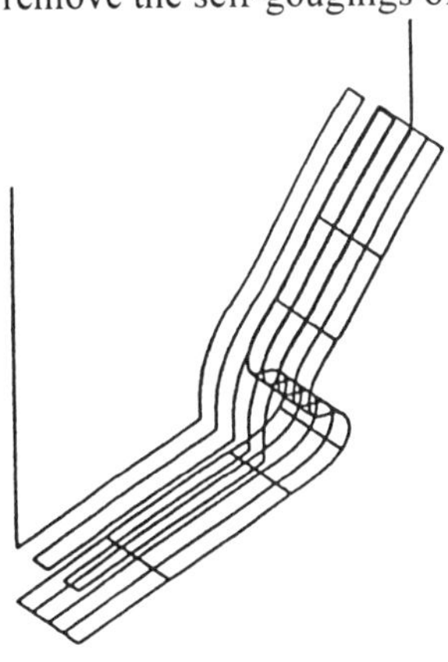

Figure 15.29a

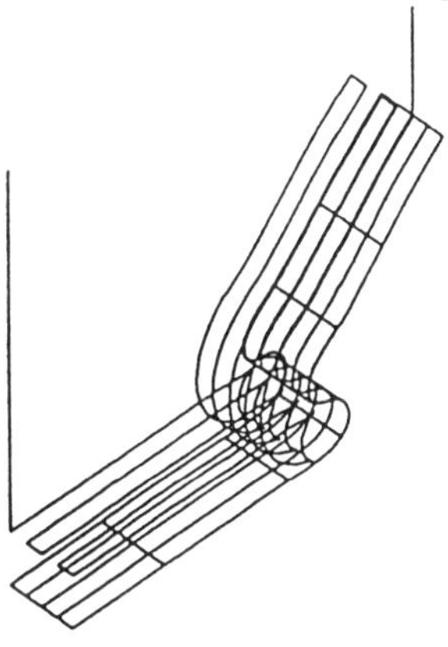

Figure 15.29b

Method for Stepping Over Surface

Two methods are available: distance increment and chordal deviation. In the chordal deviation method, the following **three** parameters are used to determine the stepover distance in the along and across direction:

Along cut chordal deviation = 0.001
Along cut checking distance = 0.1
Across cut distance = 0.05

When using the distance increment method, the along cut distance is used to replace the along cut choral deviation, the other two parameters remain the same. See the flowline module for detail.

Gap Step Method

Gaps are any opening or any break in the continuity of surfaces. Gaps are normally caused by :

(1) adjacent surfaces that are not directly connected (Figure 15.30)
(2) trimmed areas where gaps are produced (Figure 15.31)
or gouge removed areas (Figure 15.32).

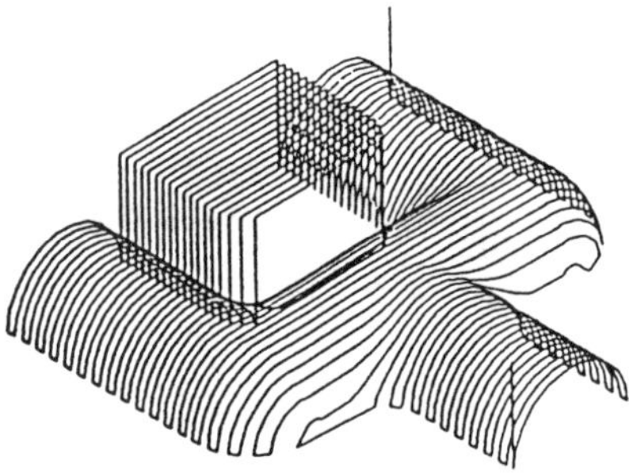

Figures 15.30

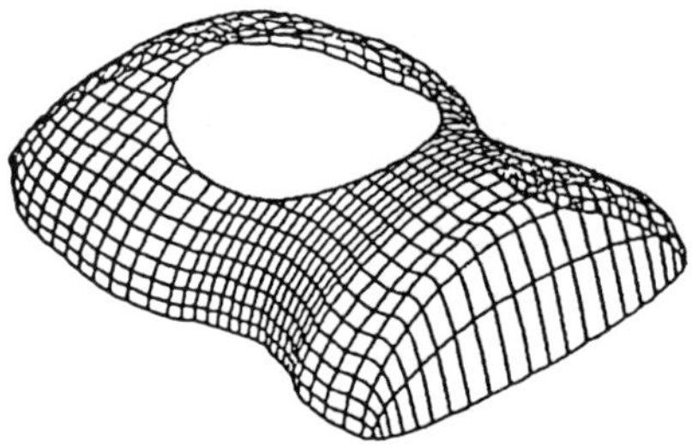

Figure 15.31

Gaps are classified into **two** groups, short gaps and long gaps, based on their length. The gap length is defined as the separating distance between two surfaces in the toolpath direction. The parameter "maximum short gap" is used to determine if the gap in a particular toolpath is a short gap path or a long gap path. A long gap occurs when the gap length is greater than the specified maximum short gap value. A short gap exists when the gap length is equal to <u>or</u> shorter than the specified maximum short gap value.

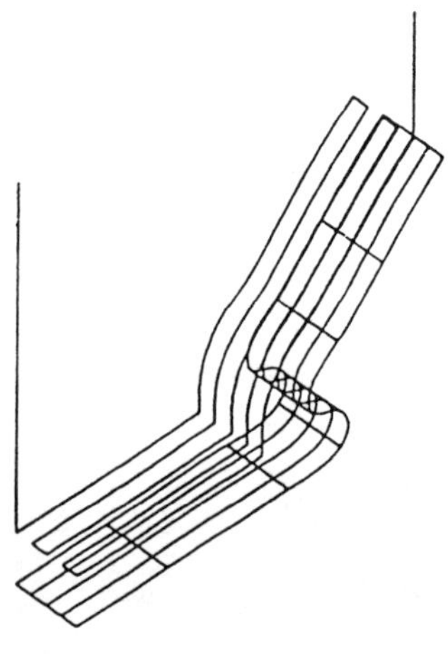

Figure 15.34

Toolpath pattern for Short gaps

The parameter "short gap path" can be toggled to **either** direct or broken mode to specify the toolpath pattern for short gaps. In the direct mode, the cutter moves straight over the gaps in feed speed (Figure 15.33). In other words, the cutter moves from the end point of the toolpath on one surface to the start point of the toolpath on the adjacent surface.

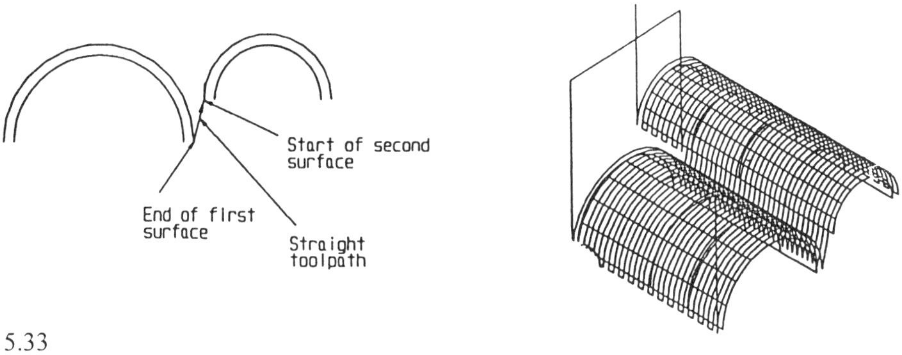

Figure 15.33

In broken mode, the toolpaths which move over gaps are broken into two segments; one with Z movement only and the other with movement in the X and/or Y direction
(Figure 15.34).

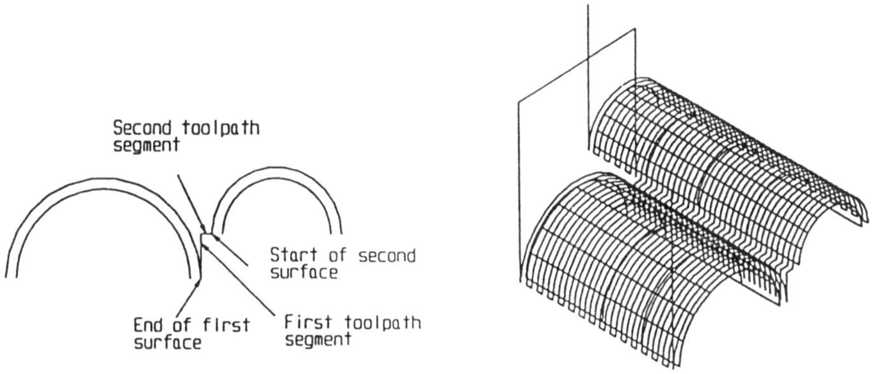

Figure 15.34

Toolpath pattern for Long gaps

There are **four** toolpath patterns for long gaps: direct, broken, rapid to rapid plane, and feed to rapid plane. The toolpath pattern for both direct and broken mode in long gaps are identical to those of short gaps. Figure 15.35 illustrates the toolpath pattern of rapid to rapid plane mode which consists of the following steps:

1. Cut over the first surface to one end in the specified direction
2. Rapidly retract to the rapid plane
3. Rapidly move over the gap to the start end of the second surface
4. Plunge to the start point of the second surface
5. Cut the second surface in the specified direction

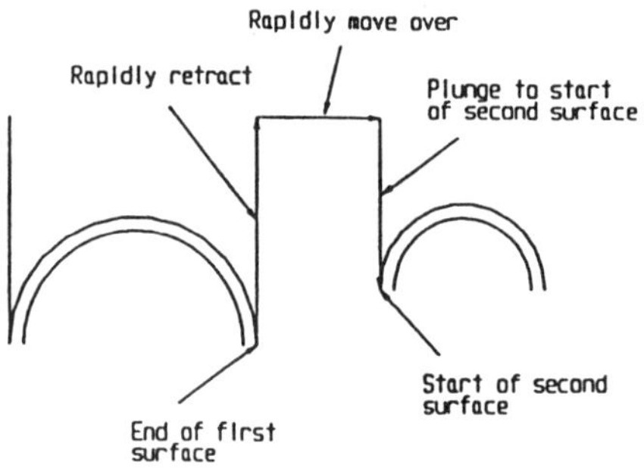

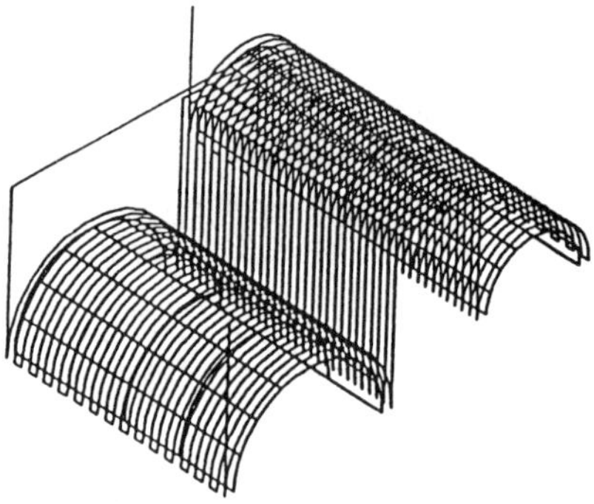

Figure 15.35

In feed to rapid plane mode, the toolpath pattern is identical to that of rapid to rapid plane mode when the tool motions for retraction and move over the gap are in feed mode.

Selection of Gap Step method:

1. Use direct mode if gaps between surfaces or within surfaces are connected with flat planes, or have no interferences in between. This mode has the simplest toolpath pattern and probably is the most efficient way for cutting the composite surface models.

2. The broken mode is used when there are interferences in between that are lower than the surfaces.

3. The rapid to rapid plane mode is recommended when there are interferences in between that are taller than the surfaces. This mode allows the cutter to clear from these interferences yet does not sacrifice too much machining time.

4. The feed to rapid plane mode is not recommended unless justified. This mode will take a much longer time to machine the surface model because it takes time to retract to the rapid plane and move over the gaps. This is true especially for cutting surfaces involving many gaps.

Cutting Methods

Two cutting methods are available in multisurf module: zig zag and one way. Figure 15.36 shows the difference between these two cutting methods using the same surface model.

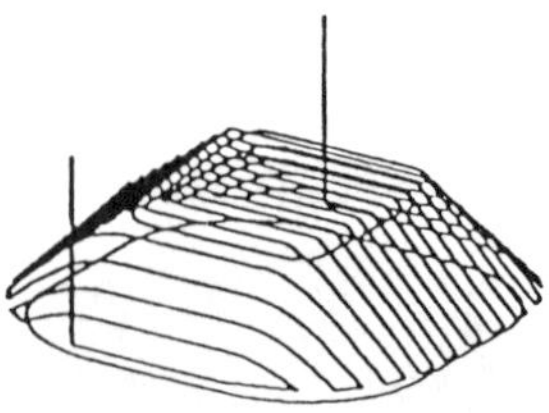

Figure 15.36a Zig Zag

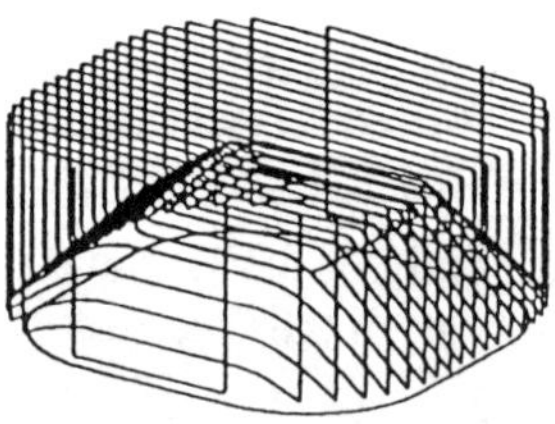

15.36b One way

Machining angle

The machining angle parameter determines the orientation of the toolpath in the along direction. This angle can be set to any value between 0 and 360 degrees. The angle is measured from the +X axis and is positive in the counterclockwise direction. Figure 15.37 shows an example of machining angles of 0°, 45°, and 90°.

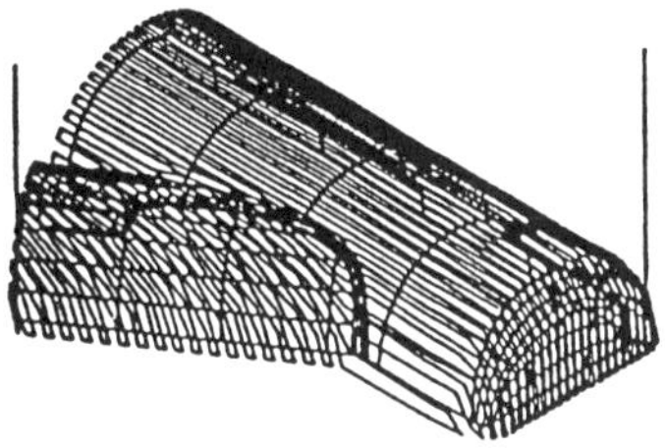

Figure 15.37a 0°

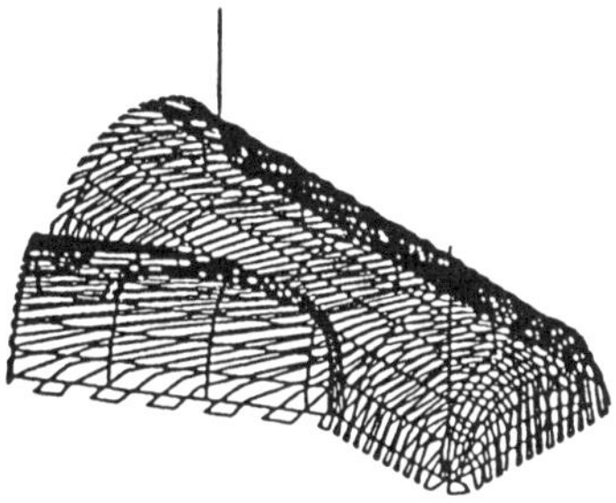

Figure 15.37b 45°

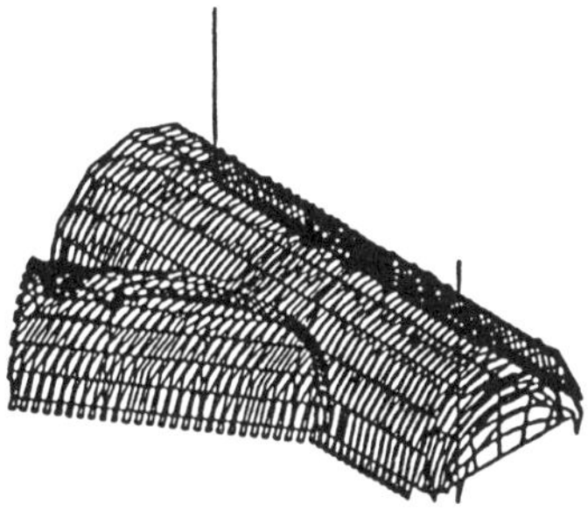

Figure 15.37c 90°

Compensate to Cutter

This parameter in the NC parameters window allows you to select the reference point on the cutter for cutter compensation. It can be toggled to either center or tip. In the center mode, the reference point for cutter compensation is the center of the cutter, the tip of the cutter becomes the reference point when the tip mode is used. Figure 15.38 shows how the toolpaths are affected by these two modes.

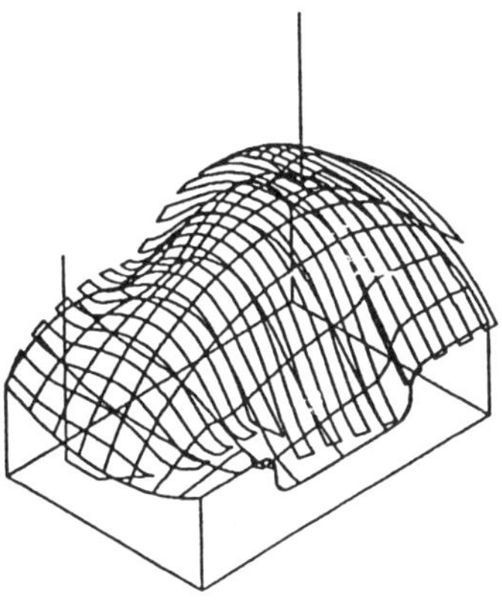

Figure 15.38a Center

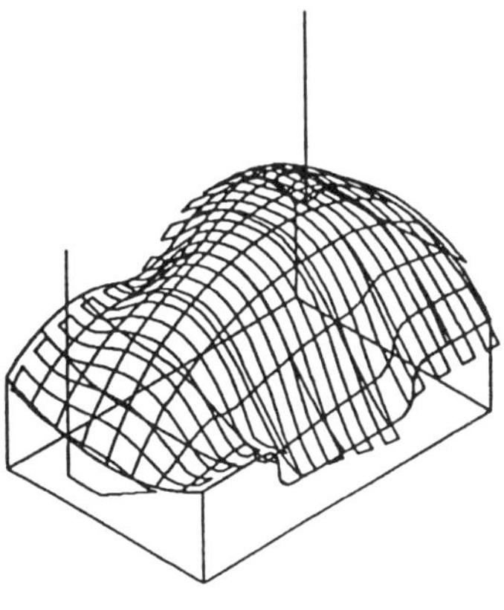

Figure 15.38b Tip

Tips 1. The surface normal direction of all surfaces must be consistent in the appropriate direction because the system determines the cutter offset direction based on the normal direction of each surface. Figure 15.39 shows one example with correct surface normal direction and one example with incorrect surface normal direction.

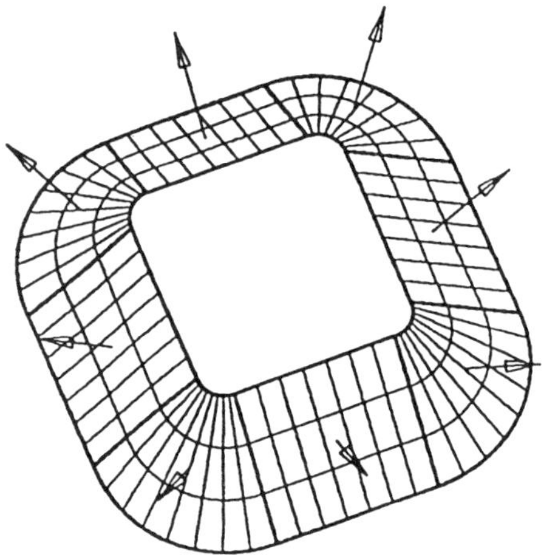

Figure 15.39a Correct normal direction

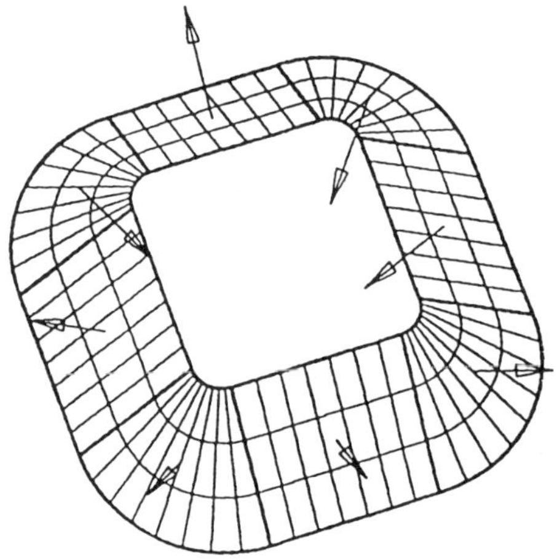

Figure 15.39b Incorrect normal direction
(Courtesy of CNC Software Inc.)

2. Use the Modify → Normal commands to change the normal direction of surfaces or use the Set norms command which is located in the Multi-surface machining menu to change the normal direction of selected surfaces.

3. Use All → Surfaces to select surfaces if all surfaces are to be included. Otherwise, use the mouse to pick those surfaces to be machined.

Five projects that use Multisurf module to generate toolpaths for cutting a composite surface model are presented next in this section. The creation of all four composite surface models is detailed in chapter 13.

Project 4.

Generating toolpaths to machine a trimmed surface model

The Msurf module is used to generate toolpaths for the trimmed surface model (trims2) created in project 4 of chapter 13. The surface model and toolpaths are shown in Figure 15.40.

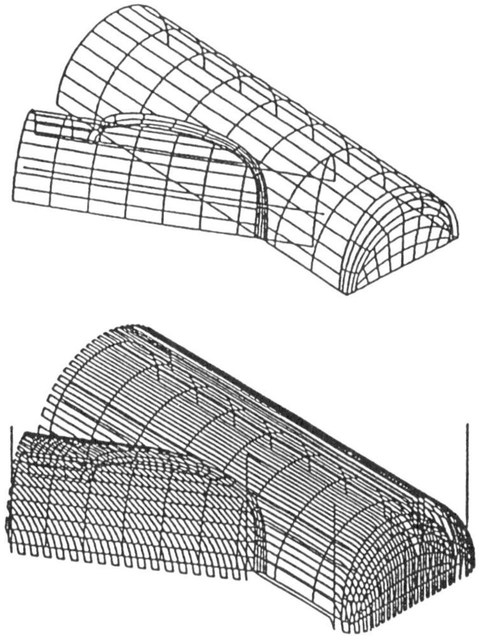

Figure 15.40

Wireframe Model Project 2 of Chapter 11 (ruled2)

Go to

Surface Model Project 2 of Chapter 12 (ruleds2)

Go to

Fillet Surface Project 2 of Chapter 13 (fillets2)

Go to

Trimmed Surface Project 4 of Chapter 13 (trims2)

Go to

We are here

Toolpath (trimst2)

Tips 1. The surface model file is **trims2.ge3.**

2. Make level 1, containing wireframe model, invisible. This allows five surfaces to be clearly displayed on the screen.
3. Set the gouge check parameters to the following settings:

Find tool-surface edge intersections? between surfaces Maximum error at surface edges = 0.005 Find surface self-intersection? yes

4. Use the chordal deviation method for stepping over a surface to obtain required surface accuracy.
5. Set the short gap path to direct and long gap path to rapid to rapid plane.

6. Cutter is 0.5" ball end mill.

Step 1. Load the trimmed surface model (trims2).

Select **MAIN MENU → File → Get**
Enter file name: **trims2 ←**
Select **Yes** to delete current part

The surface model should appear as Figure 15.41on the next page.

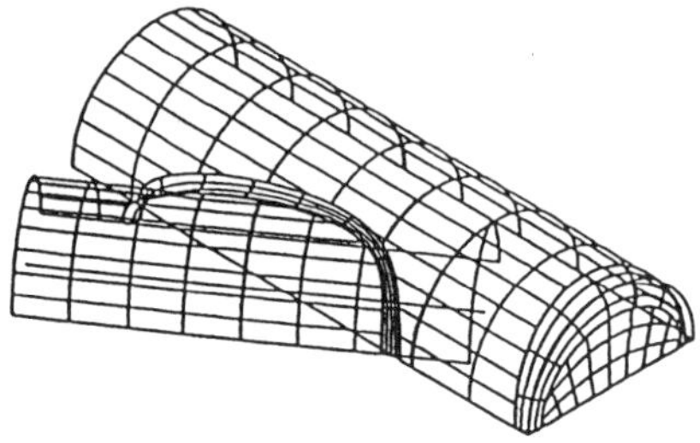

Figure 15.41

Step 2. Make level 1 to invisible and Set Cplane to Top if necessary.

Select **Level → Vis. levels**
Click on the level 1 button (dimmed)
Select **OK → OK** to return back to graphic mode

The drawing becomes Figure 15.42.

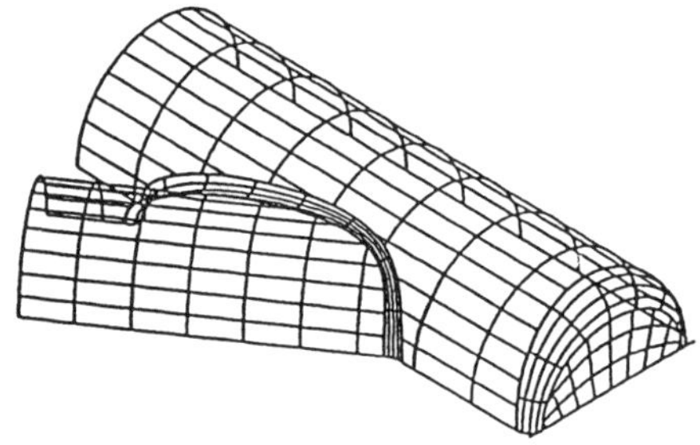

Figure 15.42

Step 3. Initiate the Multisurf module.

Select **MAIN MENU → Toolpaths → Multisurf → Finish**
File name: **trims2**

Step 4. Select surfaces to machine.

Select **All → surFaces → Done**

Step 5. Define the Msurf parameters to the following settings.

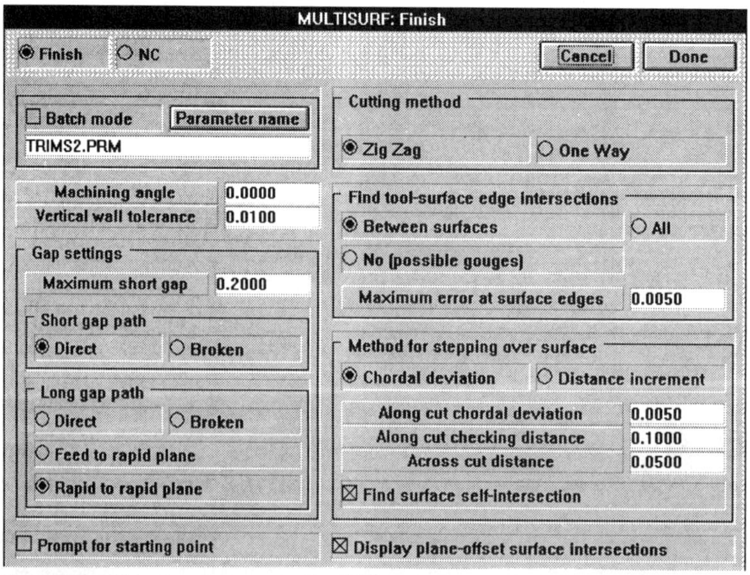

Select the **NC button** to advance to the NC parameters menu.

Step 6. Define NC parameters to the following settings.

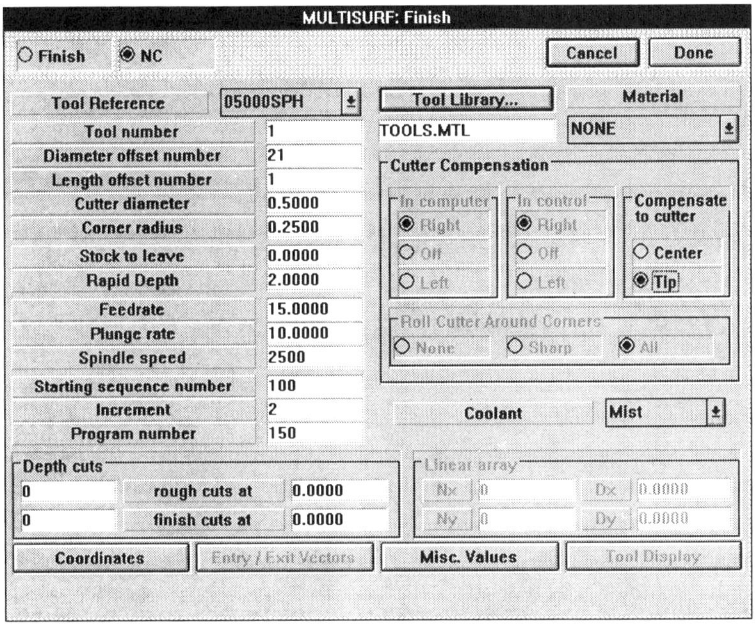

Select the **Done button** to complete the parameters settings.

Step 7. Accept and save the toolpaths.

The system will take a few minutes to generate toolpaths to cut this surface model. The complete toolpaths should look like Figure 15.43.

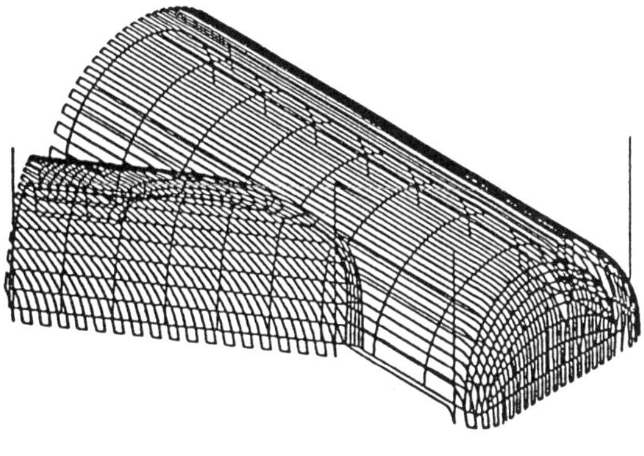

Figure 15.43

Select **Yes** to accept the toolpath segment
Select **End progrm** to close NCI file
Select **No** to "Run the post processor?"

Project 5.

Generating toolpaths for machining the basket surface model

Use the Msurf module to generate the toolpaths to finish cut the basket surface model created in project 7 of chapter 13. The surface model file name is **baskets.** The surface model and the toolpaths are shown in Figure 15.44.

Wireframe Model
Project 11 of Chapter 11 (basket)

Go to

Surface Model
Project 8 of Chapter 13 (baskets)

We are here

Go to

Toolpath
(basket)

Go to

Toolpath Trimming
Project 2 of Chapter 16 (trim1)

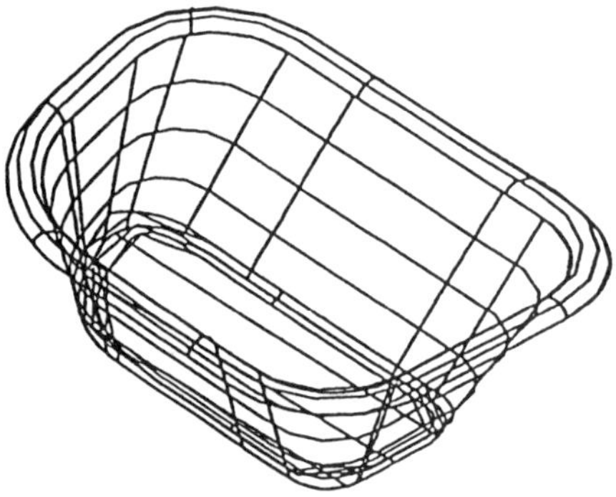

Figure 15.44a

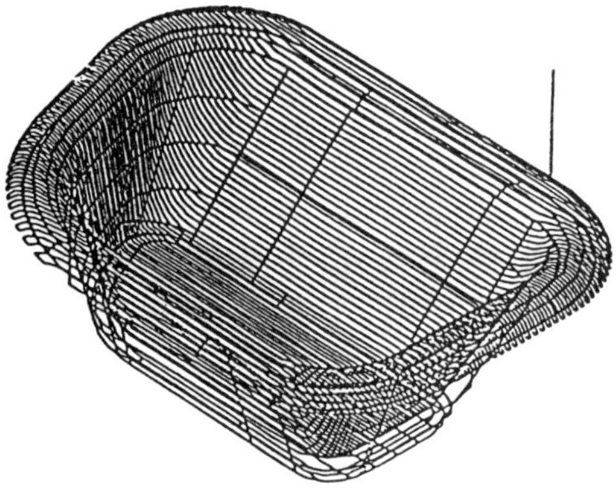

Figure 15.44b

Tips 1. The surface model file is **baskets.ge3.**

2. Set the gouge check parameters to the following settings:

Find tool-surface edge intersections? between surfaces Maximum error at surface edges = 0.005 Find surface self-intersection? Yes

3. Use the chordal deviation method for stepping over the surface to obtain the required surface accuracy.
4. Set both short gap and long gap path mode to direct.

5. Cutter is 3/8" ball end mill with 3/16" corner radius.

Step 1. Load the basket surface model (baskets.ge3) or create one by following the instructions in project 7 of chapter 13.

Select **MAIN MENU → File → Get**
Enter file name: **baskets** ←
Select **Yes** to delete the current part if necessary

The surface model should appear as Figure 15.45.

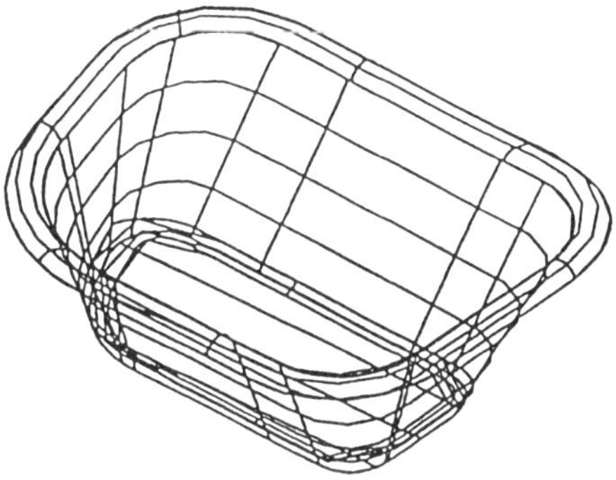

Figure 15.45

Step 2. Initiate the multisurf module.

Select **MAIN MENU** → **Toolpaths** → **Multisurf**

Step 3. Test surface normals.

Select **Set norms** → **All** → **surFaces** → **Done**

Note: It will take a while for the system to test surfaces. The system will indicate "The surface normal has been reversed on 0 surfaces". Press **Enter** to continue

Select **Finish**

Enter file name: **basket** ←

Step 4. Select surfaces to machine.

Select **Yes** to "Reuse the last set of surfaces ?"

Step 5. Define multisurf parameters to the following settings.

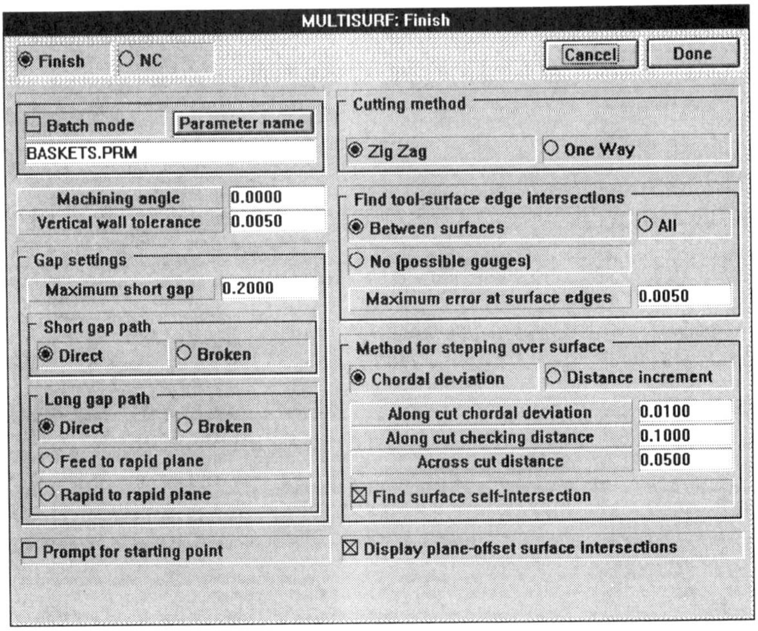

Select the **NC button** to advance to the NC parameters menu.

Step 6. Define NC parameters to the following settings.

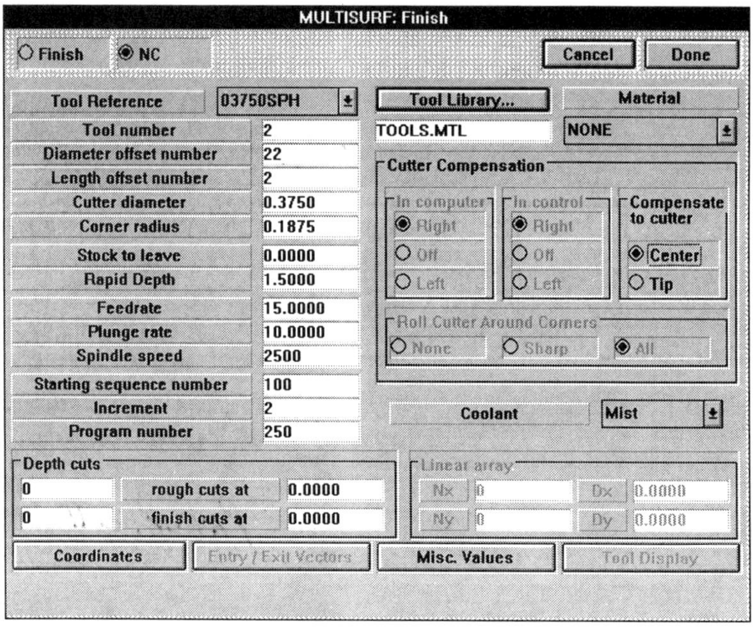

Select the **Done button** to complete the parameter settings.

Step 7. Generate the toolpaths.

It will take several minutes for the system to generate toolpaths. The toolpaths should look like Figure 15.46

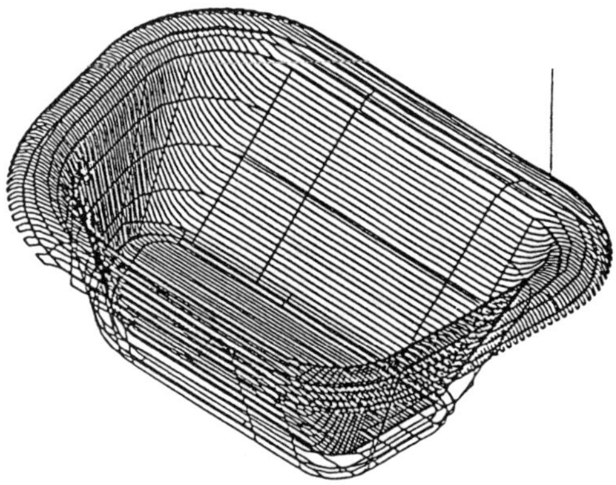

Figure 15.46

Select **Yes** → **End program** to accept the toolpath segment
Select **no** to "Run the post processor?"

Project 6.

6

Wireframe Model
Project 12 of Chapter 11 (flash)

Go to

Surface Model
Project 9 of Chapter 13 (flashs)

We are here

Go to

Toolpath
(flash)

Generating toolpaths for machining the flash light surface model

The Msurf module is used to generate toolpaths for machining the surface model of the flash light. The surface model and the toolpaths are shown in Figure 15.47.

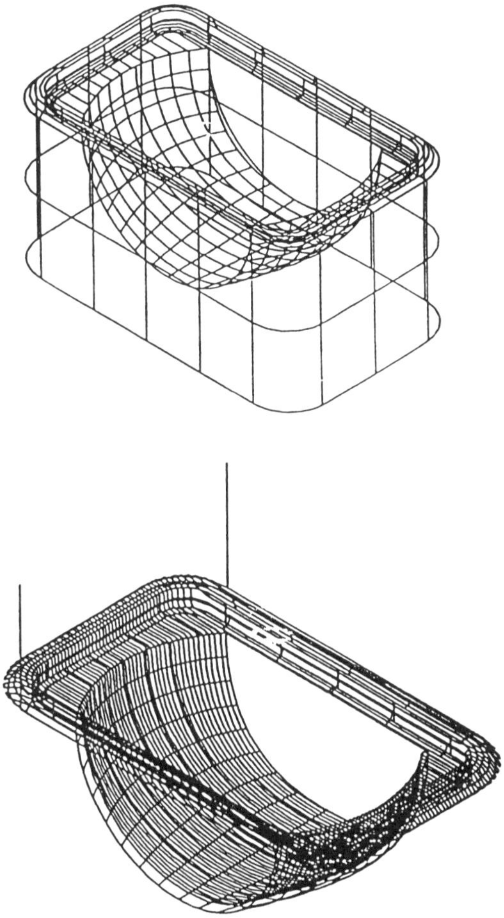

Figure 15.47

Tips 1. The surface model file is **flashs.ge3.**

2. Set the gouge check parameters to the same setups as in project 5.

3. Use the chordal deviation method for stepping over surface .

4. Cutter is 1/8" ball end mill.

Step 1. Load the surface model (flashs.ge3). Also, set levels 1 and 2 to invisible.

Select **MAIN MENU** → **File** → **Get**
Enter file name: **flashs** ←
Select **Yes** to delete the current part
Select **Level** → **Vis. Levels**
Toggle levels 1 and 2 to invisible (dimmed)
Select **OK** → **OK** to return to graphic mode

The partial surface model of the flash light should look like Figure 15.48.

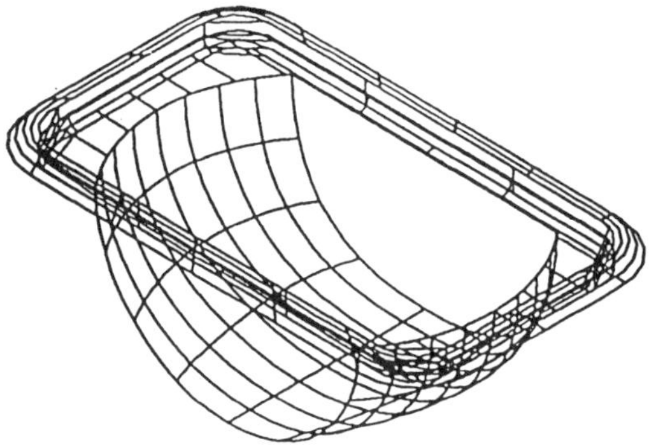

Figure 15.48

Step 2. Initiate Multisurf module.

Select **MAIN MENU** → **Toolpaths** → **Multisurf** → **Finish**
Enter file name: **flash** ←

Step 3. Select surfaces.

Select **All** → **surFaces** → **Done**

Step 4. Define Msurf parameters to the following settings.

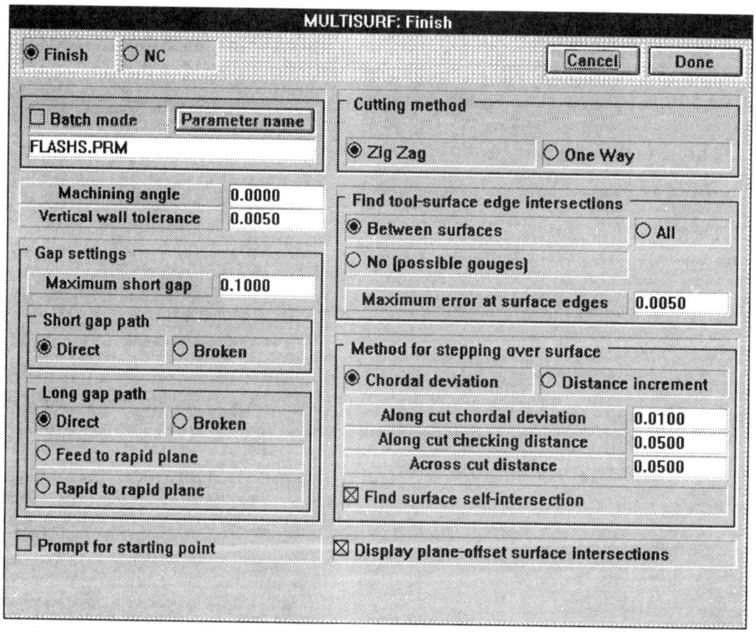

Select the **NC button** to advance to the NC parameters menu.

Step 5. Define NC parameters to the following settings.

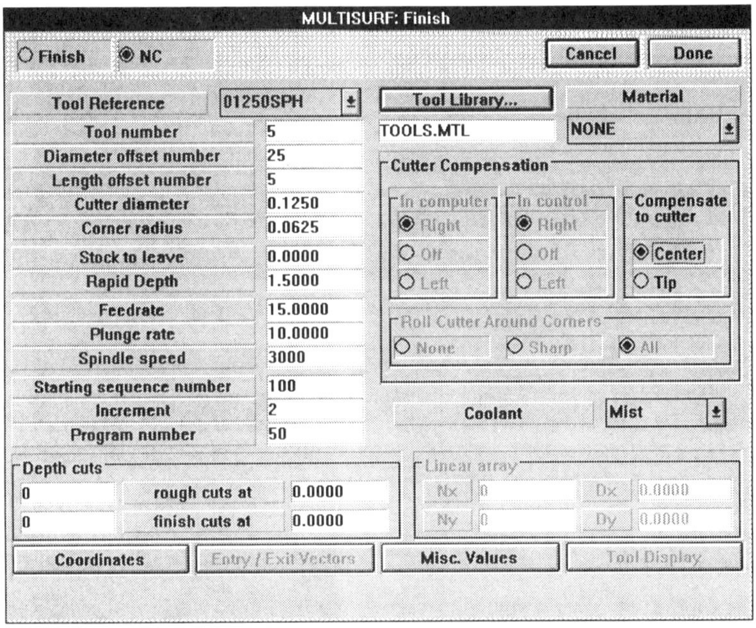

Select the **Done button** to complete the parameter settings.

Step 6. Generate and save the toolpaths.

The system will take several minutes to generate the toolpaths that resemble Figure 15.49.

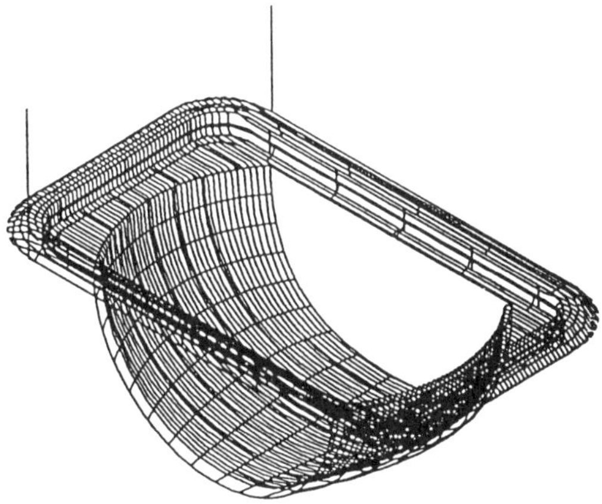

Figure 15.49

Select **Yes** to accept the toolpath segment
Select **End program** to close NCI file
Select **No** to "Run the post processor?"

TS 54

Project 7.

Generating toolpaths for cutting the dryer surface model

Use the Msurf module to generate a set of toolpaths for cutting the hair dryer surface model. The surface model consists of four surfaces. Both surface model and toolpaths are shown in Figure 15.50.

Wireframe Model
Project 13 of Chapter 11 (dryer)

Go to

Surface Model
Project 10 of Chapter 13 (dryers)

Go to

We are here

Toolpath
(dryer)

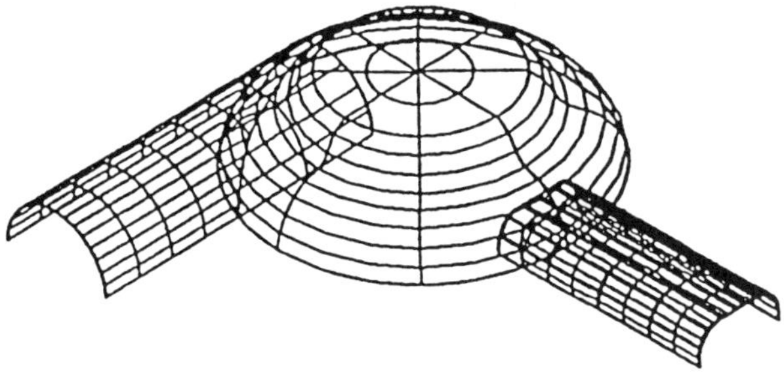

Figure 15.50a. Surface model

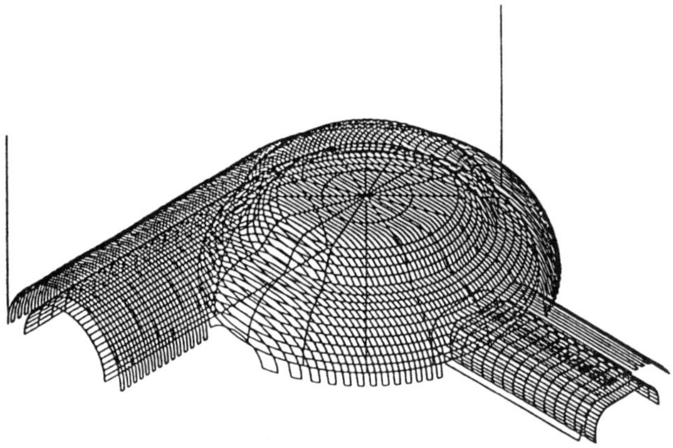

Figure 15.50b Toolpaths

Tips 1. Surface model file is dryers.ge3.

2. Make levels 1, 4, and 5, which contain geometry and surface entities not used, to invisible.

3. Use Test surfs → Normals → All → surFaces → Done commands to test the normal direction of surfaces.
4. Use the chordal deviation method for stepping over surface.

5. Cutter is 0.5" ball end mill.

Step 1. Load the surface model dryers.ge3.

Select **MAIN MENU → File → Get**
Enter file name: **dryers**
Select **Yes** to delete the current part

The surface model should appear as Figure 15.51.

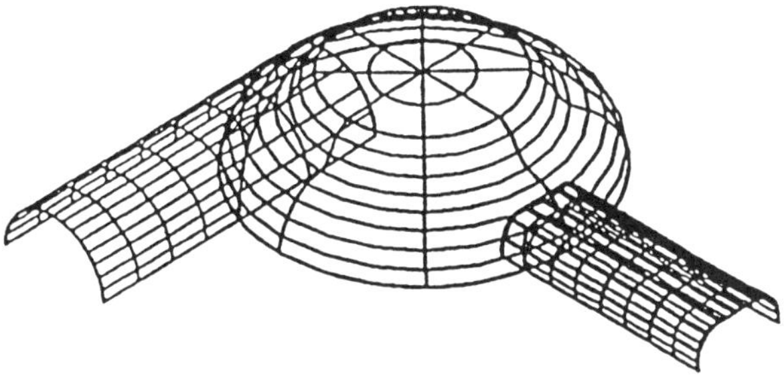

Figure 15.51

Step 2. Make levels 1, 4, and 5 invisible.

Select **Cplane** → **Top** if necessary
Select **Level** → **Vis. levels**
Toggle levels **1**, **4**, and **5** to invisible (dimmed)
Select **OK** → **OK** to return to graphic mode

The four surfaces should appear as Figure 15.52.

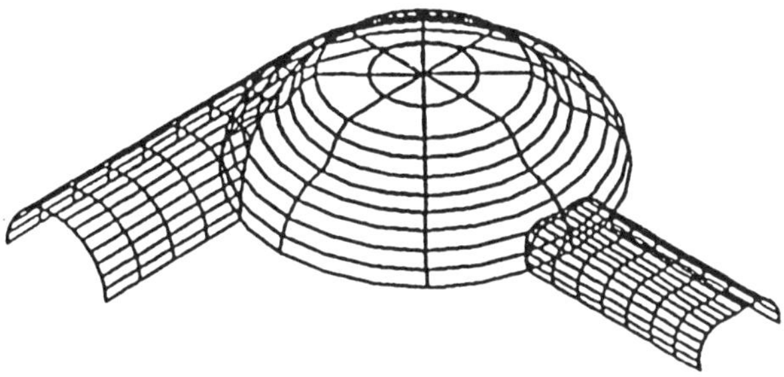

Figure 15.52

Step 3. Initiate Multisurf module.

Select **MAIN MENU** → **Toolpaths** → **Multisurf** → **Set norms** →**All** → **surFaces** → **Done**
The system will indicate "The surfaces normal has been reversed on 0 surfaces"

Note: a bad surface indicates a possible problem area exists in a surface. A bad surface normally can be machined correctly but slowly.

Press **Enter** to continue
Select **Finish**
Enter File name: **dryer**

Step 4. Select surfaces to be machined.

Select **Yes** to "Reuse the last set of surfaces ?"

Step 5. Define Multisurf parameters to the following settings.

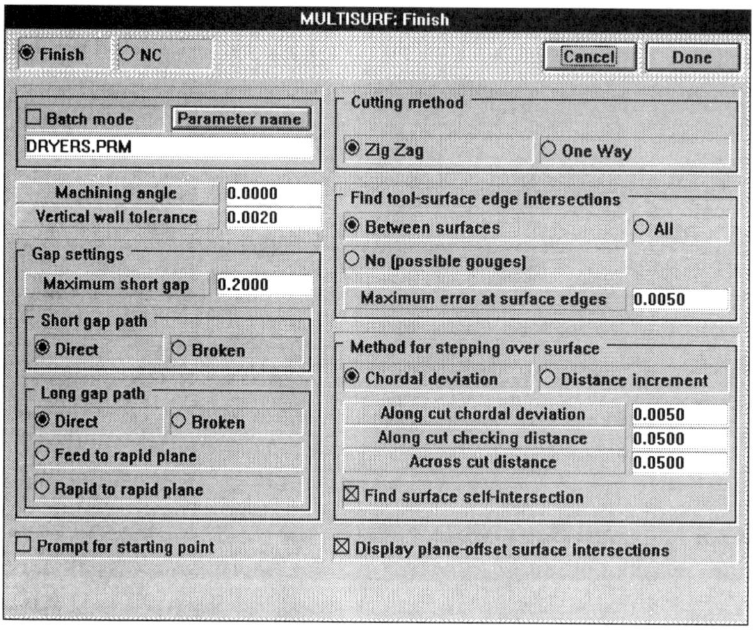

Select the **NC button** to advance to the NC parameters menu.

Step 6. Define NC parameters to the following settings.

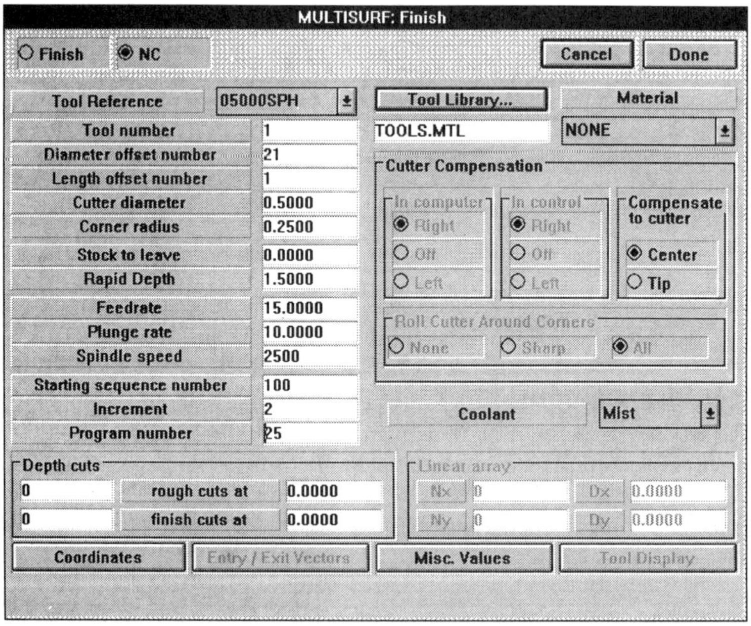

Select the **Done button** to complete the parameters setting.

Step 7. Generate and save toolpaths.

The system will take several minutes to generate toolpaths to cut the model. The toolpaths should resemble Figure 15.53.

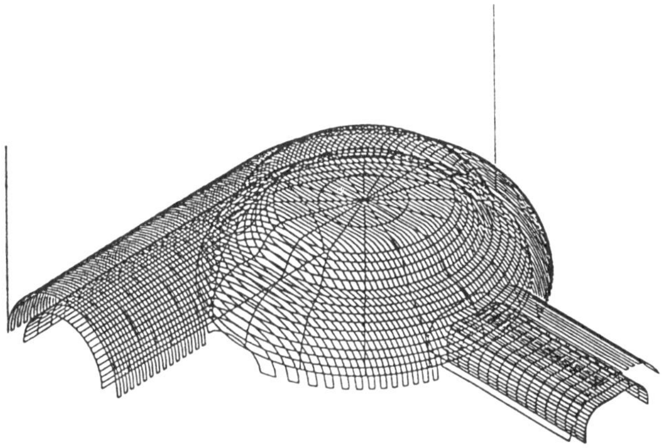

Figure 15.53

Select **Yes** to accept the toolpaths
Select **End program** to close NCI file
Select **Yes** to "Run the post processor?"

Project 8.

8

Generating toolpaths for machining the car wheel model

To generate a set of toolpaths to cut the car wheel surface model is a challenge for Mastercam users. The complete surface model consists of 60 surfaces (some surfaces are hidden in the model.) If the Msurf module is used to generate the toolpaths for the entire surface model, it may take a 486-66 system more than one day to complete the process of generating toolpaths. The approach we use here is to generate the toolpaths for a partial surface model consisting of only six surfaces. This set of toolpaths is then copied to the other five locations. By doing so, the system may need less than 20 minutes to complete the toolpaths for the entire model. The partial surface model and the complete toolpaths are shown in Figure 15.54.

Wireframe Model
Project 16 of Chapter 11 (wheel)

Go to

Surface Model
Project 12 of Chapter 13 (wheels)

Go to

We are here

Toolpath
(wheels)

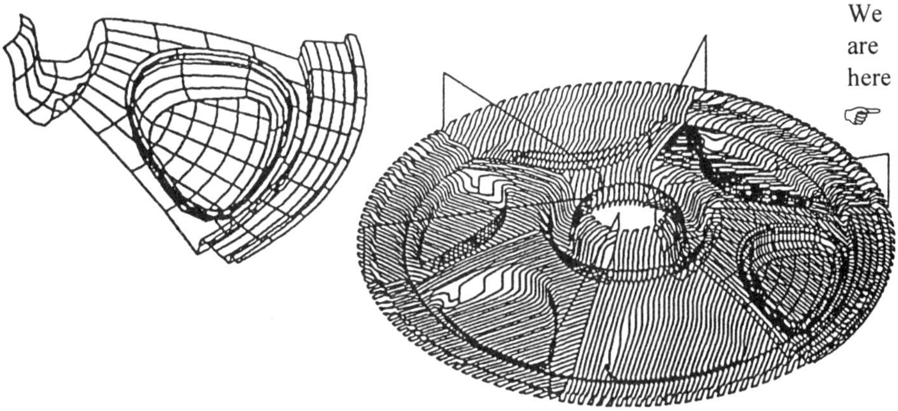

a. Complete toolpaths
b. Partial surface model

Figure 15.54

Tips 1. Use only a section of the surface model to generate toolpaths. This set of toolpaths is used to copy to five locations by using NC utils → Edit NCI → Xform → Rotate commands.

2. The inner and outer rim surfaces can be cut by using a 2d toolpath module such as contour or pocket. They are not included in using Msurf module. This significantly shortens the part program and processing time.
3. The surface model file is **wheels.ge3**.
4. Make levels 1, 2, and 10 invisible. This allows only those surfaces to be included in machining to appear on the screen.
5. Use chordal deviation method.
6. Cutter is 3/8" ball end mill.
7. Use Edit NCI → Xform → Rotate commands with the following parameters to copy the toolpaths to five locations:

Rotation angle: 60° Number of steps = 5 Leave the original entities

Step 1. Load the surface model file (wheels.ge3).

Select **MAIN MENU** → **File** → **Get**
Enter file name: **wheels** ←
Select **Yes** to delete current part

The partial surface model should appear on screen as Figure 15.55.

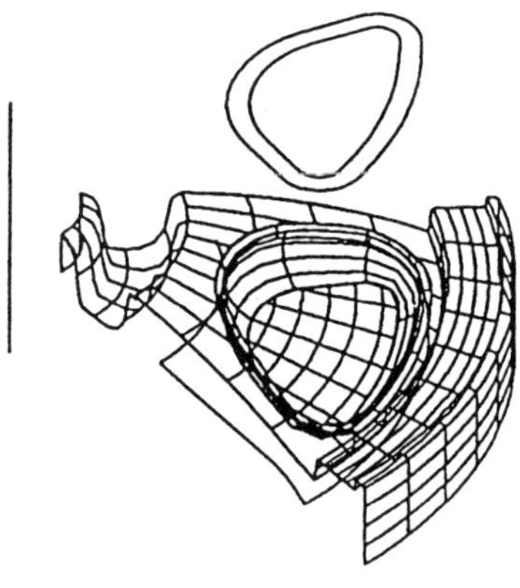

Figure 15.55

Step 2. Make levels 1, 2, and 10 invisible (no asterisk).

Select **Level** → **Vis. levels**
Toggle levels 1, 2, and 10 to invisible (dimmed)
Press **OK** → **OK** to return to graphic mode

The surfaces to be included should resemble Figure 15.56 on the next page.

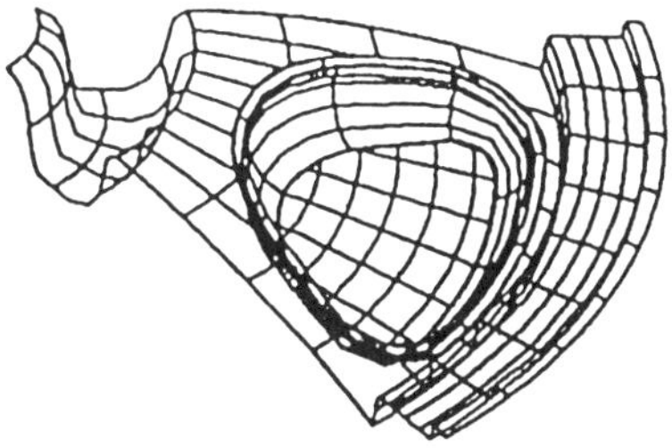

Figure 15.56

Step 3. Set Cplane to Top if necessary.

Select **Cplane** → **Top**

Step 4. Initiate the Multisurf module.

Select **MAIN MENU** → **Toolpaths** → **Multisurf** → **Finish**
Enter file name: **wheels**

Step 5. Select surfaces to be included.

Select **All** → **surFaces** → **Done**

Step 6. Define the Msurf parameters to the following settings.

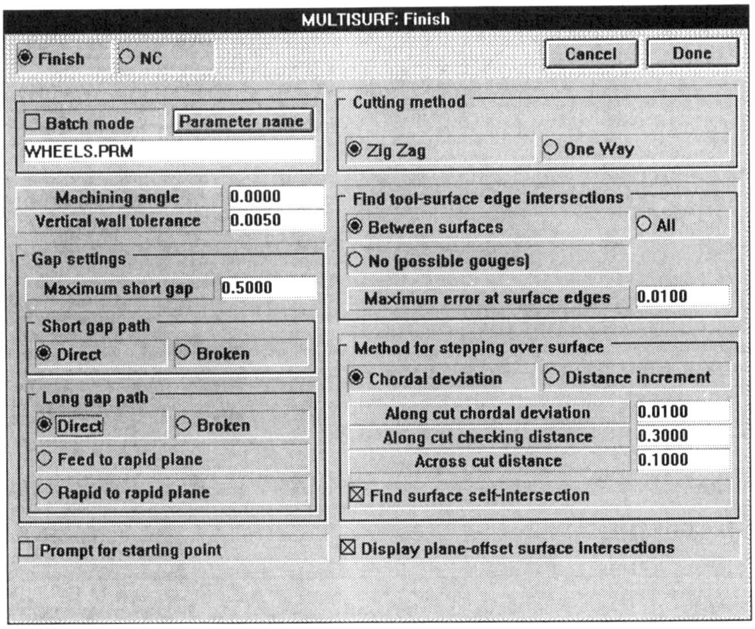

Select the **NC button** to advance to the NC parameters menu.

Step 7. Define NC parameters to the following settings.

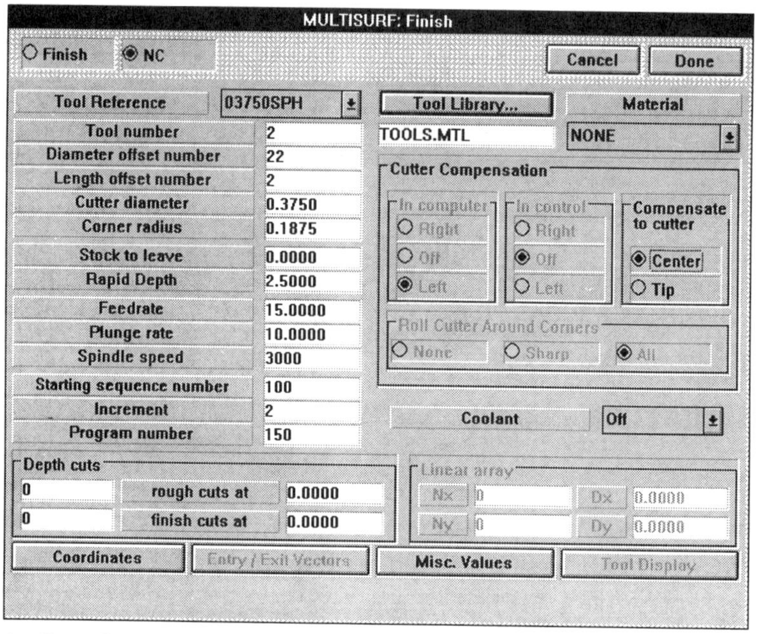

Select the **Done button**to complete the parameters settings.

Step 8. Generate and save toolpaths.

The system will take several minutes to generate toolpaths. The toolpaths should appear on screen as Figure 15.57.

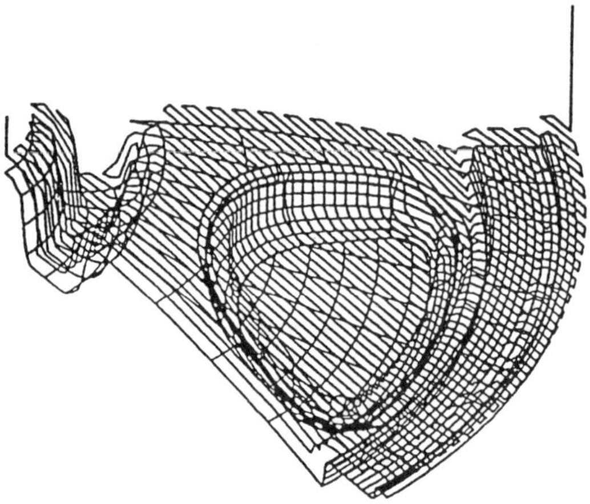

Figure 15.57

Select **Yes** to acccept the toolpath segment
Select **End program** to close the NCI file
Select **No** to "Run the post processor?"

Step 9. Copy the toolpaths to the other five locations by using the Edit NCI → Xform → Rotate commands.

Select MAIN MENU → NCutils → Edit NCI
Select File → Open
Enter file name: **wheels** ←
Click the **Multisurf finish [T2]** to select the toolpath to be rotated.
Select **Xform → Rotate**
Set the **Xform → Rotate** parameters as below:

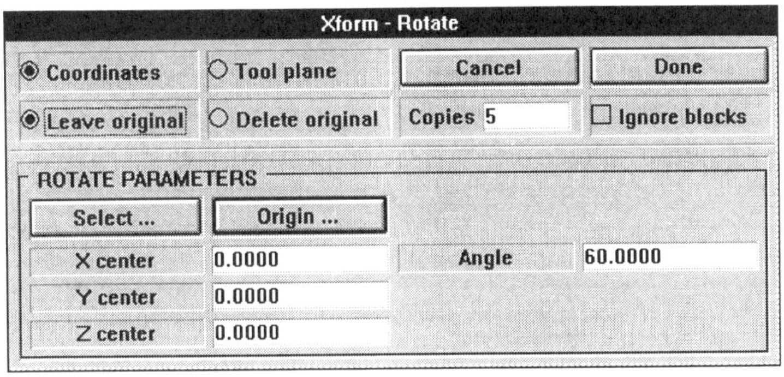

Select **Done** to copy the toolpaths to five locations
Select **Quit**
Select **Save** to save changes to the current file
Select **Yes** to delete the current file

The toolpaths for the complete surface model should resemble Figure 15.58.

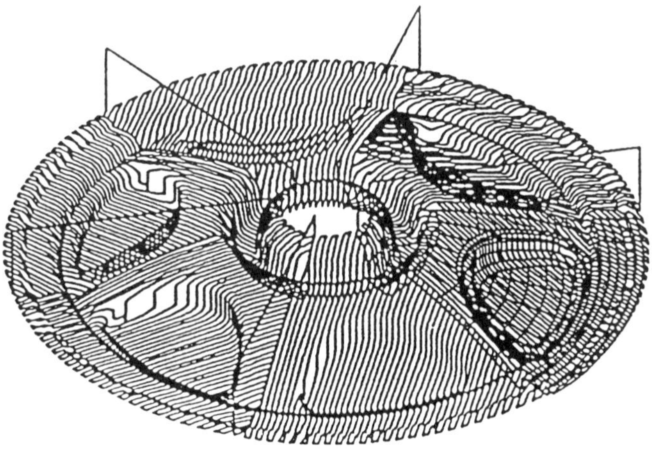

Figure 15.58

Note: We suggest the use of the contour module to cut the outer rim of the wheel. A full-circle should be constructed to serve as the contour of the outer rim. Use the pocket module to machine the hole in the center. These two operations are not included in this project.

15.3 Rough Function

The rough function in the Multisurf module is used to generate a set of toolpaths for roughing a surface model. The surface model can consist of a single surface or mutiple surfaces. This function is used prior to the finish function.

Note: The rough function in the current Version is still under development. It can only successfully implement simple single surface models. Be aware of problem areas when using this function.

⌛Tips: Procedure steps for Using Rough Function successfully

1. Load the surface model and create the outer boundary contour if necessary.
2. Use the following commands to initiate the rough function:
   MAIN MENU → Toolpaths → 3d toolpth → Multisurf → Rough
3. Select the surfaces to be included in roughing.
4. Define the rough parameters.
5. Define the outside boundary contour if necessary.
6. Generate roughing toolpaths.

Rough Parameters

The rough parameters are listed below:

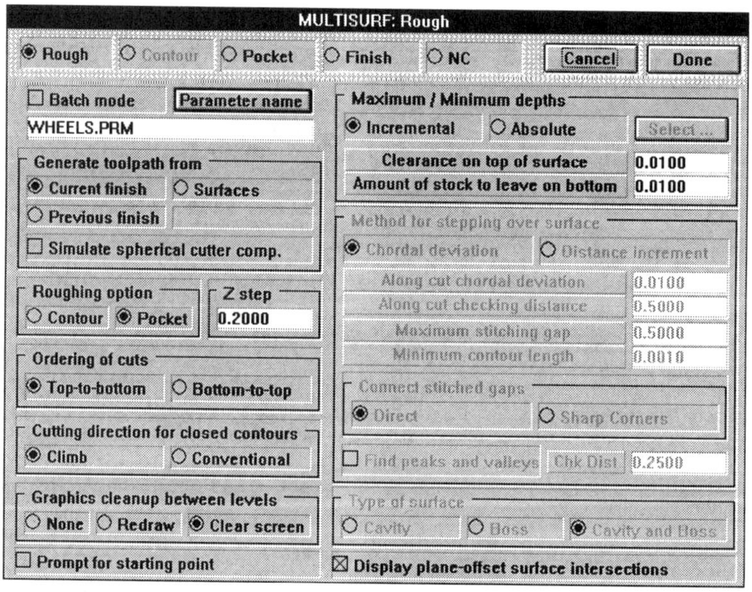

For Pocket Roughing

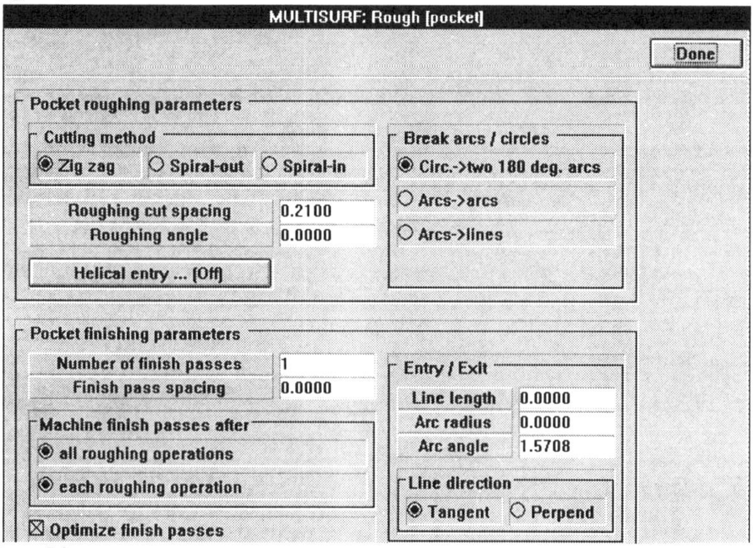

For Contour Roughing

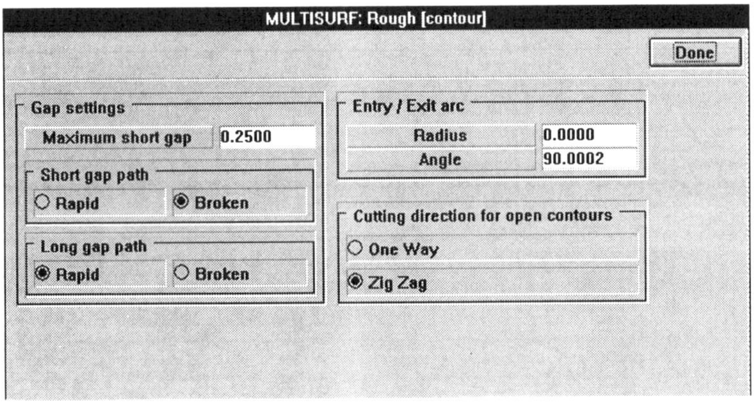

The following parameters are unique to the rough function and should be discussed: Z-depth control, roughing option, surface type, ordering of cuts, and graphics cleanup between levels.

Z-depth Control

The following **four** parameters are used to specify the number of roughing passes and the Z-depth for each roughing passes:

Maximum/minimum depth: Incremental/ Absolute
Clearance on top of surface = 0.01 (Incremental mode)
Amount of stock to leave on bottom = 0.05 (Incremental mode)
Maximum depth = 0.0 (Absolute mode)
Minimum depth = -2.0 (Absolute mode)
Distance between constant-Z levels = 0.1

Figure 15.59 shows the parameters used in incremental mode. The number of roughing passes is determined by:

$$\text{No. of Roughing passes} = \frac{\text{Surface height - Top clearance - Stock to leave}}{\text{Initial constant-Z value}}$$

Round up the number of roughing passes to the next integer if the computed No. of roughing passes is not an integer.

The system will compute the actual constant-Z value using the formula given below:

$$\text{Constant-Z value} = \frac{\text{Surface height - Top clearance - Stock to leave}}{\text{No. of roughing passes}}$$

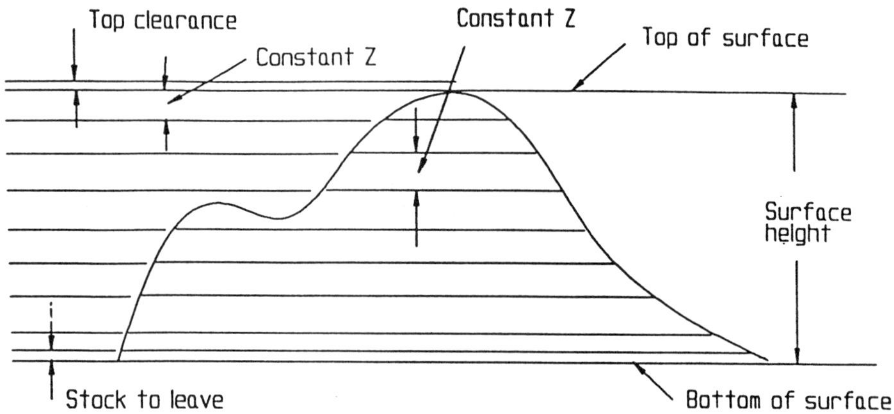

Figure 15.59

Figure 15.60 shows the parameters used in absolute mode. The No. of roughing passes can be found from

$$\text{No. of roughing passes} = \frac{\text{Maximum depth - minimum depth}}{\text{Initial constant-Z value}}$$

Round up the No. of roughing passes to next integer if the computed No. of roughing passes is not an integer.

The system will compute the actual constant-Z value using the foumula given below.

$$\text{Constant-Z value} = \frac{\text{Maximum depth - Minimum depth}}{\text{No. of roughing passes}}$$

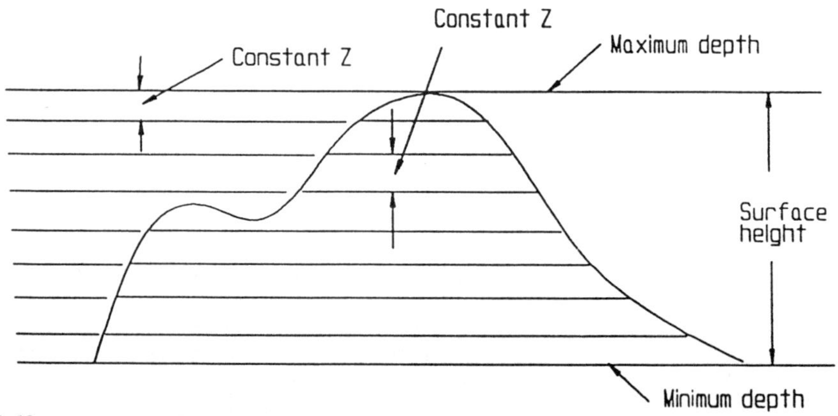

Figure 15.60

Roughing Option

This parameter specifies the type of roughing to be performed. The parameter can be toggled to pocket or contour. With the pocket mode, the system roughs the surface by pocketing between an inner contour and a outer boundary (Figure 15.61a). In contour mode, the system roughs the surface by contouring along the surface (Figure 15.61b).

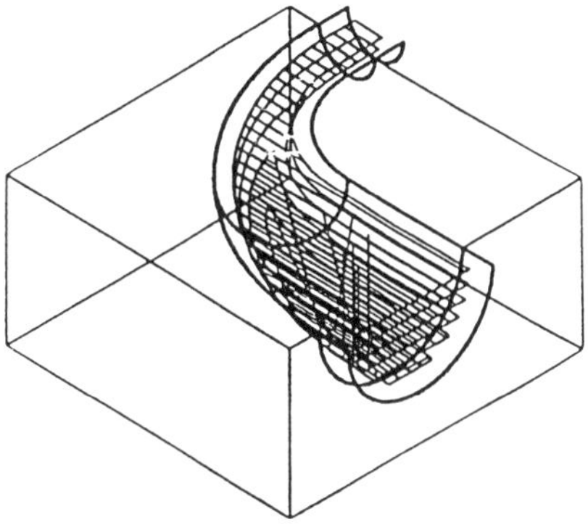

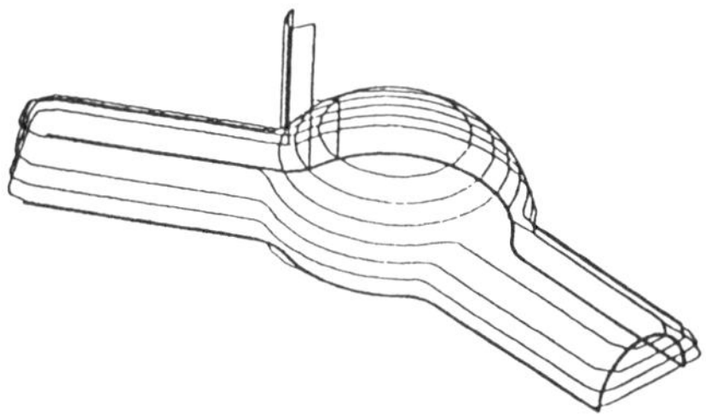

a. Pocketing mode

b. Contour mode

Figure 15.61

Surface Type

This parameter indicates the form of the surface either to be boss type, cavity type or combination of cavity and boss type. The parameter should be set to boss, cavity or cavity and boss depending on the surface type; the parameter is set to boss if the surface is a convex type (Figure 15.62a), and cavity if the surface is a concave type (Figure 15.62b).

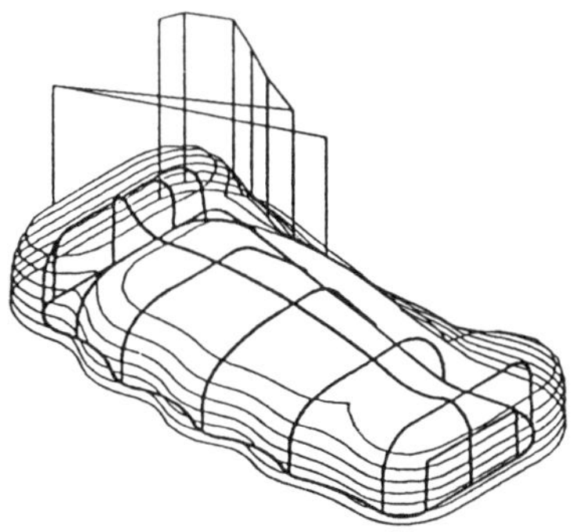

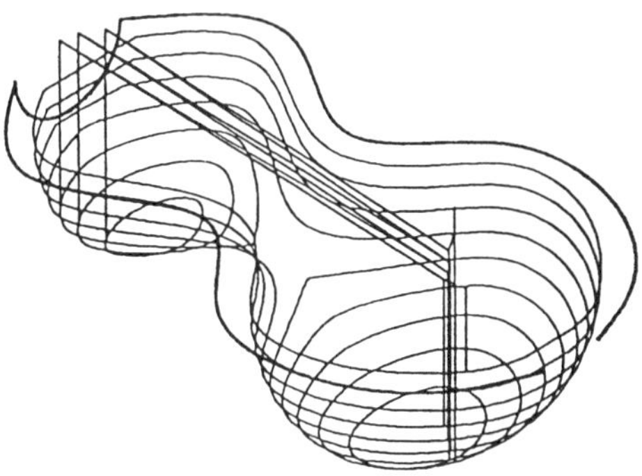

a. Boss/convex type

b. Cavity/concave type

Figure 15.62

Ordering of Cuts

This parameter specifies the cutting direction in the Z axis. The parameter can be toggled to one of the following two modes:

Top-to-bottom:	cuts from the **highest** Z coordinate on the surface to the lowest.
Bottom-to-top:	cuts from the **lowest** Z coordinate on the surface to the height.

Characteristics associated with climb milling include the following:

1. The cutting forces tend to pull the workpiece into the cutter. If there is a significant amount of backlash in the machine, the use of climb milling may result in a broken tool, a damaged workpiece or possible injury from flying metal. It is recommended that climb milling be avoided for machines that have backlash.

2. The cutter tooth starts with a chip of maximum thickness and ends with one of zero thickness. The scraping action between the tool and machine surface is eliminated, and chips are not swept back through the cut. Because of this, climb milling can produce a better surface finish if a light cut is used.

Machining in the clockwise {CW} direction or counterclockwise {CCW} direction in roughing will be determined by two parameters: type of surface {cavity or boss} and cutting direction for closed {climb or conventional}. Refer to the table shown below:

Table 15.3 Machining directions for roughing

Type of Surface for	Cutting Direction Closed Contour	Machining Direction
Cavity	Climb	CCW
Cavity	Conventional	CW
Boss	Climb	CW
Boss	Conventional	CCW

Cutting Direction for Closed Contours

The parameter "Cutting direction for closed contours" can be selected to either Climb or Conventional milling. The operation you choose depends on the following factors:

1. Whether backlash is encountered in the machine drive mechanisms
2. Required surface finish
3. Types of material to be cut
4. Surface condition of raw material

Some characteristics of conventional milling are given below:

1. The cutter tooth starts with a chip of zero thickness and ends with a chip of maximum thickness.

2. The cutting forces tend to lift the workpiece up from the holding vise and push it away from the tool, eliminating backlash in the driving mechanism. Conventional milling should be used for machining where backlash may be encountered.

3. Conventional milling has a tendency to produce rough surfaces compared with down milling.

4. The use of conventional milling to cut a workpiece with a hard or dirty surface may result in increased tool life.

5. Conventional milling is recommended for cutting soft ferrous materials, cast iron, and other ductile metals such as brass and bronze, as well as for roughing cuts on aluminum.

Graphics Cleanup between Levels

This parameter selects the graphics display mode for each of the roughing passes. It can be toggled to one of the following three modes:

None: displays all roughing passes with geometric entities.

Redraw: in each roughing pass, the system redisplays geometric entities, intersection contours and toolpaths of the roughing cut.

Clear screen: in each roughing pass, the system only displays the intersection contours and toolpaths of the roughing cut.

Project 9.

9

Generating roughing toolpaths for rough cutting a surface

The rough function in the Msurf module is used to generate toolpaths for roughing a surface. The surface model file name is **coonss2.ge3.** The surface model and roughing toolpaths are shown in Figure 15.63.

Wireframe Model
Project 5 of Chapter 11 (coons1)

Go to

Surface Model
Project 8 of Chapter 12 (coonss2)

Go to

We are here

Roughing Toolpath
(rough)

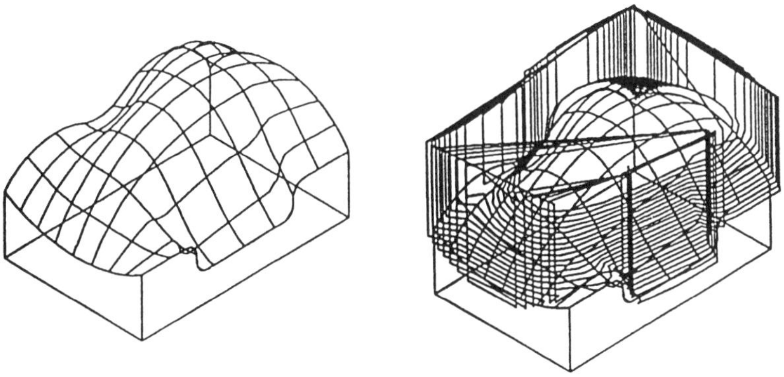

Figure 15.63

Tips 1. The surface model file name is **coonss2.ge3.**

2. Use contour roughing option.

3.The surface type is boss.

4. Set the Z-depth control parameters to the following settings:

Maximum/minimum depth: Incremental
Clearance on top of surface = 0.01
Amount of stock to leave on bottom = 0.01
Z Step = 0.1

5. Cutter is 0.75" end mill.

Step 1. Load the surface file coonss2.ge3.

Select **MAIN MENU → File → Get**
Enter file name: **coonss2**
Select **Yes** to delete current part

The surface model should appear as Figure 15.64.

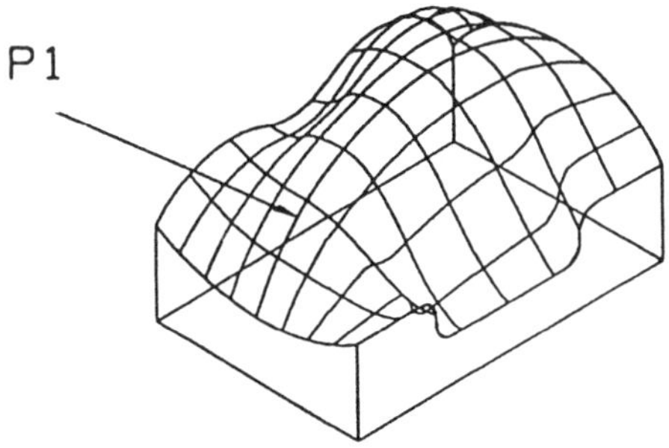

Figure 15.64

Step 2. Change Cplane to top view if necessary.

Select **Cplane → Top**

Step 3. Initiate rough function.

Select **MAIN MENU → Toolpaths → Multisurf → Rough**
Enter file name: **rough**

Step 4. Select surfaces for roughing using the pick point in Figure 15.66.

Select **Entity**, then pick at **P1** to select the surface
Select **BACKUP → Done** to complete selecting surface

Step 5. Define rough parameters to the following settings.

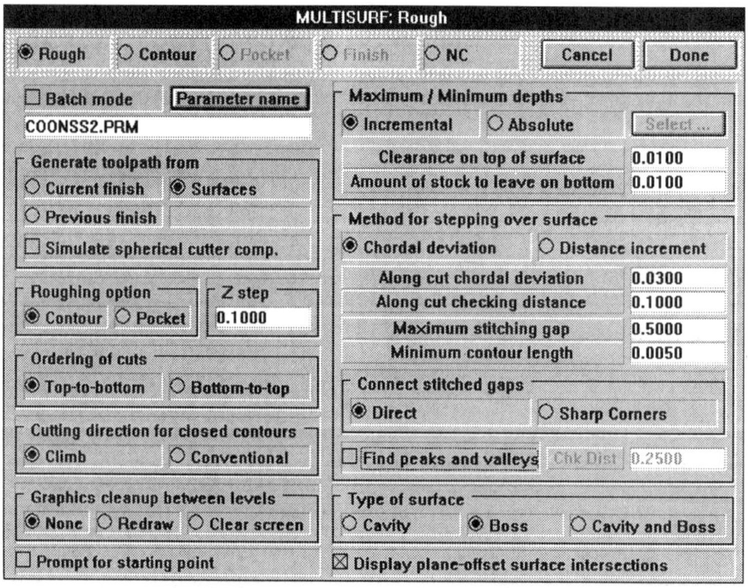

Select the **NC button** to advance to the next parameter menu.

Step 6. Define NC parameters to the following settings.

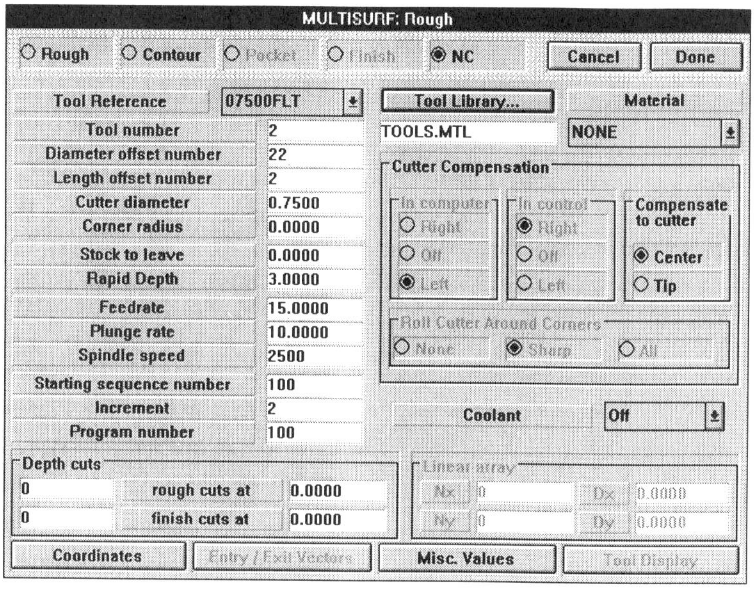

Select the **Done button** to complete the parameters setting.

Step 7. Generate and accept roughing toolpaths.

The system will take a few minutes to generate the roughing toolpaths shown in Figure15.65.

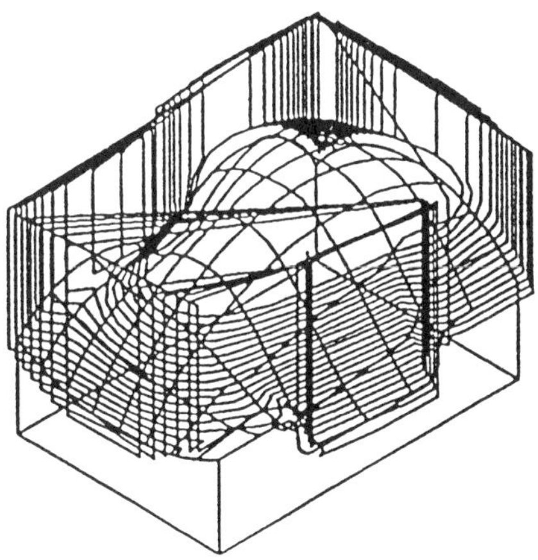

Figure 15.65

Select **Yes** to accept the toolpath segment
Select **End progm** to close toolpath file
Select **No** to "Run the post processor?"

15.4 Exercises

15.4.1 Short answer

1. What are the two modules used to generate toolpaths from existing surface models?
2. When should you use the flowline module?
3. When is it better to use the multisurf module?
4. What are the two stepping over surface methods?
5. Define, with a drawing, the chordal deviation.
6. Define, with a drawing, the scallop height.
7. When should you use the distance increments method?
8. When should you use chordal deviation and scallop height method?
9. Define the following two terms: Gouges: Gouging:
10. What are the three gouge check parameters used in the Multisurf module?
11. What are open edges of surfaces? What are the two groups of open edges?
12. List the three modes of "Find tool-surface edge intersections" parameters. Describe the effect of these three modes on the open edges.
13. What is surface self-intersection?
14. What are gaps between surfaces?
15. Describe how to determine whether a gap is a short gap or long gap.
16. What are the two modes of toolpath patterns for short gaps?
17. Illustrate, with a drawing, the toolpath pattern for the direct mode.
18. Illustrate, with a drawing, the toolpath pattern for the broken mode.
19. List the four modes of toolpath patterns for long gaps.
20. Describe, with a drawing, the toolpath pattern of rapid to rapid plane mode.
21. Explain the difference in toolpaths between rapid to rapid plane mode and feed to rapid plane mode.
22. Define, with a drawing, the machining angle.
23. Illustrate the effect on toolpaths when the compensate to cutter is set to center and tip, respectively.

15.4.2 Problems

24. Use the flowline module to generate the toolpaths for cutting the surface created in problem 19 of chapter 12. The surface file name is **ES3.** The surface model is shown in Figure 15.66.

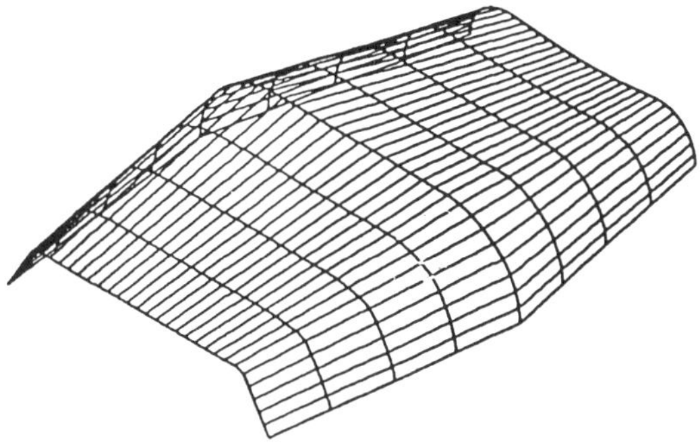

Figure 15.66

25. Use the flowline module to generate the toolpaths for cutting the surface created in problem 22 of chapter 12. The surface file name is **ES6**. The surface model looks like Figure 15.67.

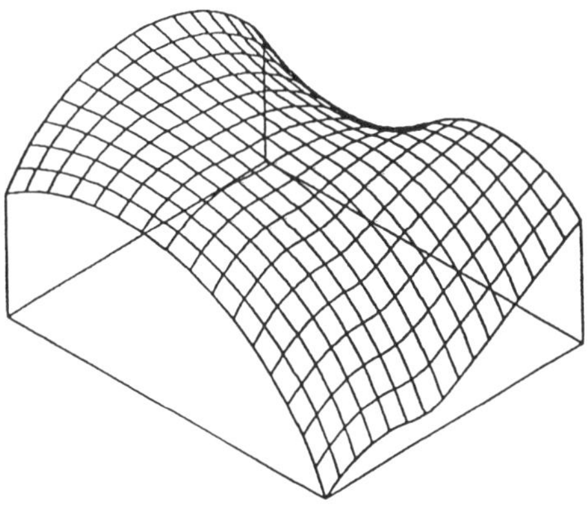

Figure 15.67

26. Use the flowline module to generate the toolpaths for cutting a Coons surface of multiple patches. The surface is created in problem 24 of chapter 12. The surface file name is **ES8**. The surface model is shown in Figure 15.68.

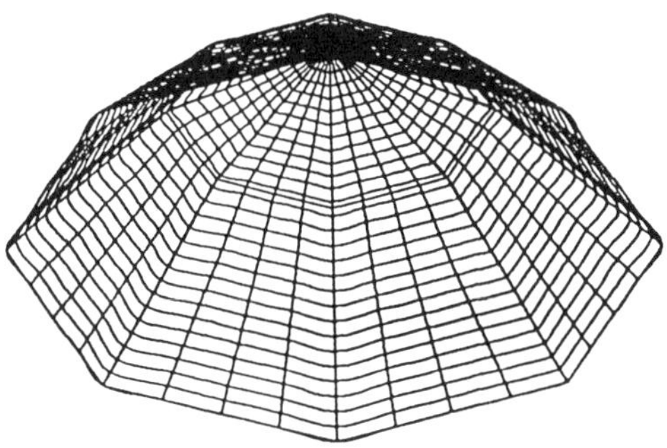

Figure 15.68

27. Use the Msurf module to generate the toolpaths for the fillet surface model created in problem 12 of chapter 13. The surface model file is **ES14.** The surface model is shown in Figure 15.69.

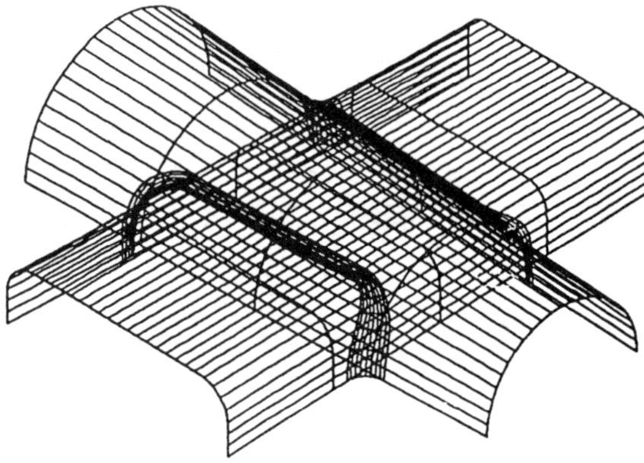

Figure 15.69

28. Generate the toolpaths for the surface model created in problem 13 of chapter 13. The surface model is shown in Figure 15.70 and has the file name **ES15**.

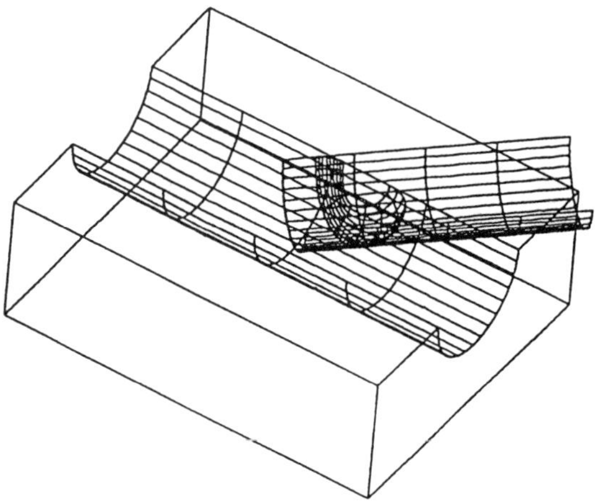

Figure 15.70

29. Generate a set of toolpaths to machine the trimmed surface model created in problem 14 of chapter 13. The surface file name is **ES16**. Figure 15.71 shows the surface model. Msurf module is recommended.

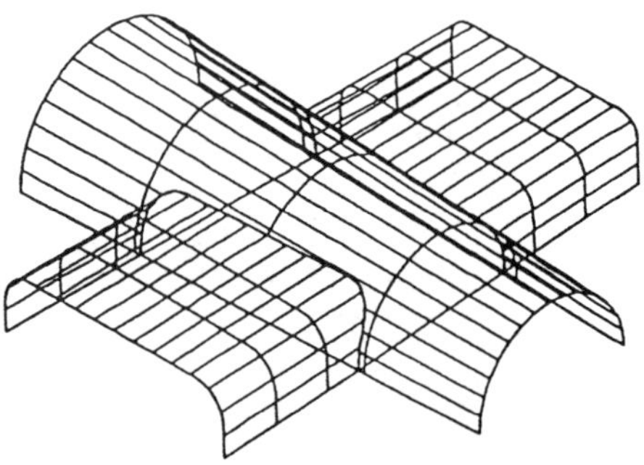

Figure 15.71

30. Use Msurf module to generate toolpaths for cutting a composite surface model created in problem 17 of chapter 13. The surface file name is **ES19.** The surface model is shown in Figure 15.72.

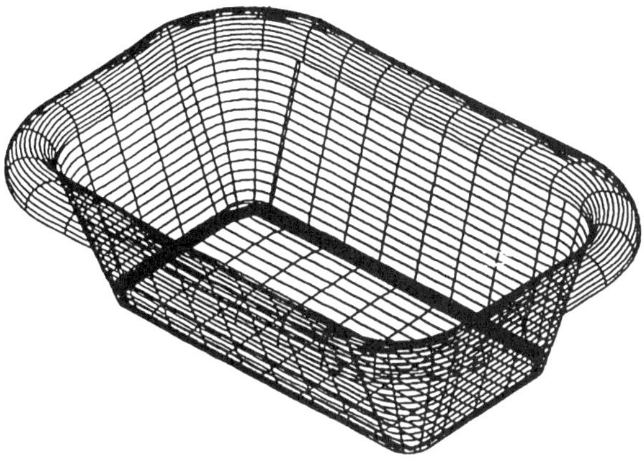

Figure 15.72

31. Generate a set of toolpaths to cut a composite surface model created in problem 18 of chapter 13. The surface model file is **ES20.** The surface model looks like Figure 15.73.

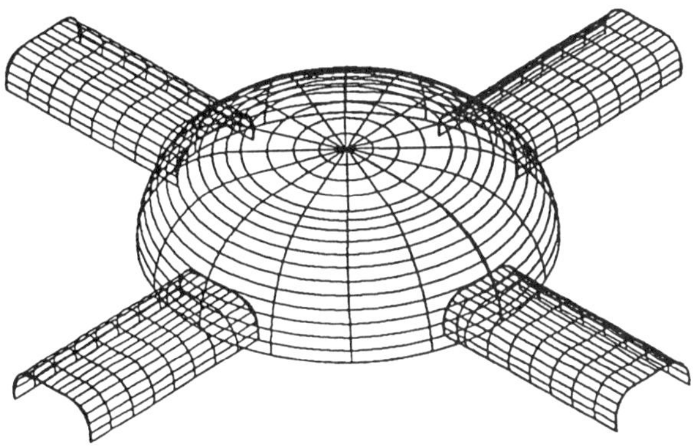

Figure 15.73

Chapter 16

3-D Toolpath Editing

Objectives:

1. Know two toolpath editing functions to modify toolpaths for machining 3d surfaces: project and trim.
2. Understand the features of these toolpath editing functions and know when to apply them.
3. Apply these editing functions to 3d surfacing toolpath projects.

Overview

Toolpaths for cutting some surface models can be significantly simplified by using toolpath editing functions. Those toolpath editing functions given in chapter 8 are applicable to editing 3d surfacing toolpaths. **Two** additional editing functions that are particularly designed for 3d surfacing toolpaths are presented in this chapter. They are project and trim.

16.1 Project Function

Project function allows toolpaths to be projected onto a plane, cylinder, cone, sphere, cross section or 3d surface. The projected toolpaths only change the depth (Z-coordinate) of the original toolpaths; both X and Y coordinates remain the same (Figure 16.1).

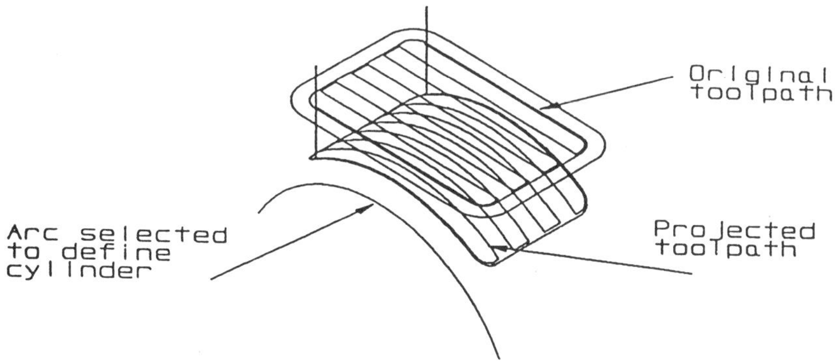

Figure 16.1

The following toolpath types can **not** be projected:

1. Drilling, boring, and taping.
2. Five axis moves.
3. Arcs in the ZX-plane and YZ-plane.

Note that arcs in the ZX-plane or YZ-plane are normally generated from surface of revolution, 2-D contouring and 2-D swept surface. Table 16.1 on the next page illustrates the six types of toolpath projection.

Table 16.1 Six Types of Toolpath Projection

Project type	Description	Illustration
Plane	Project a toolpath file onto any 3d plane defined by the construction plane.	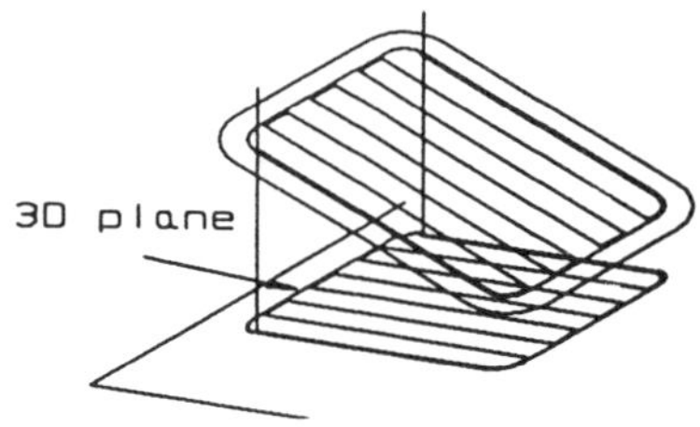
Cylinder	Project a toolpath file onto any cylinder that is defined by an arc. The axis of cylinder must be parallel to XY-plane. Concave or convex cylinders can be selected.	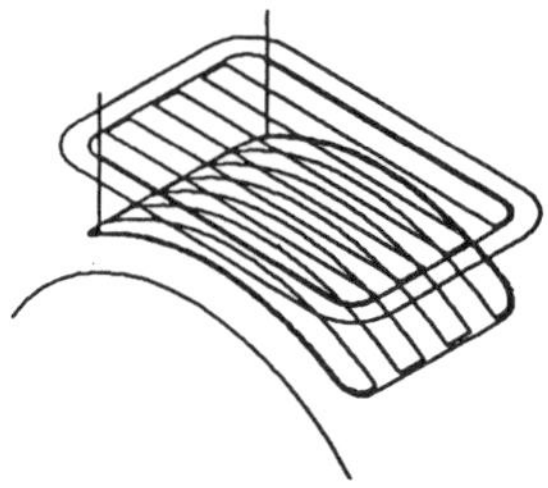
Sphere	Project a toolpath file onto any sphere. The sphere is defined by an arc. Concave or convex sphere is possible.	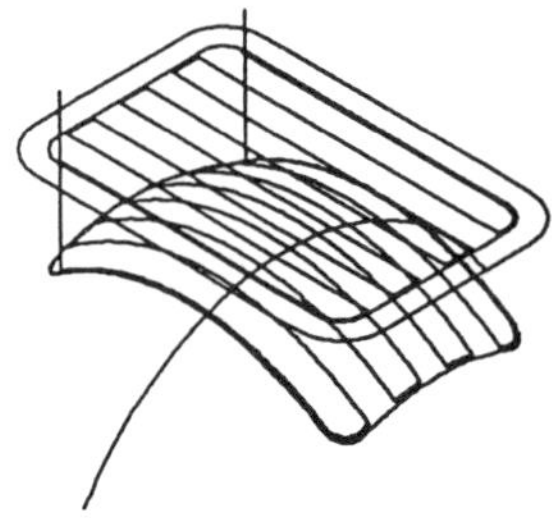
Cone	Project a toolpath file onto any cone. The cone is defined by two lines, one for the axis and the other for edge of the cone.	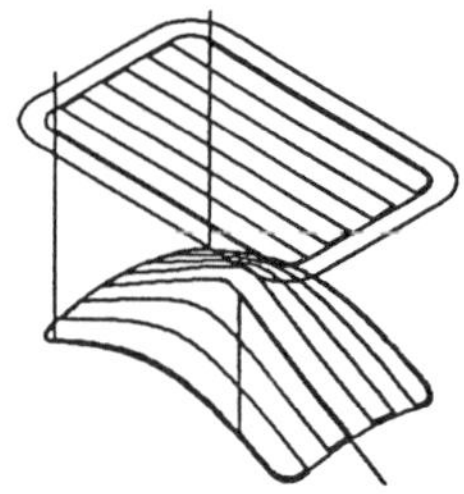
X-section	Project a toolpath file onto any cross section which is perpendicular to XY-plane or the current tool plane.	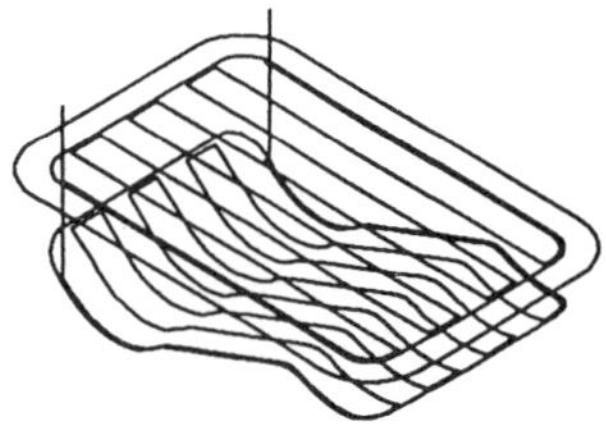
Surface	Project a toolpath file onto any surface.	

Steps for Implementing Toolpath Projects:

1. Create the profile or surface for defining the shape onto which the toolpaths are to be projected.
2. Generate the original toolpath file.
   (1) This file defines the X and Y coordinates of the toolpaths
   (2) Also the boundaries in the X and Y directions of the final toolpaths.
   (3) End program
   (4) Make sure the geometry to be projected fits on the surface.
3. Initiate the project function. Give a new name for projected path file.
4. Define the project parameters.
5. Accept the projected toolpaths.

Project 1. 1

Projecting a set of lettering toolpaths to a surface

The toolpaths of a letter string which is arranged in an angular form are projected onto a swept surface as shown in Figure 16.2.

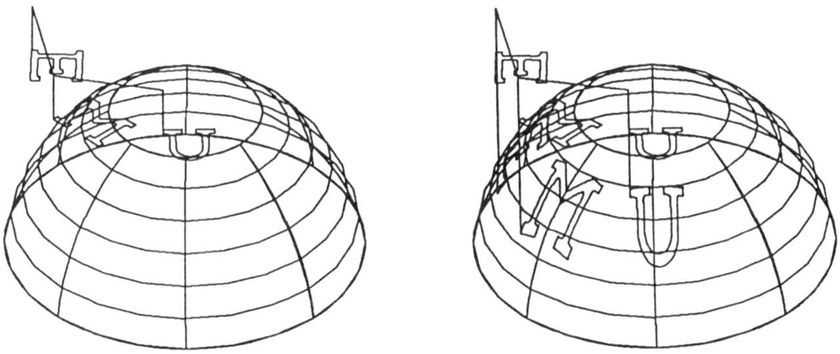

a. Before projection b. After projection
Figure 16.2

Tips 1. Create three circles to form the wireframe model of the swept surface.

2. Create the swept surface.

3. Use the Letters module to generate the toolpaths for engraving letters.

4. Use the project module to project the lettering toolpaths onto the swept surface.

Step 1. Create two circles using the top Cplane.

Select **Gview → Isometric**
Select **MAIN MENU → Create → Arc → pt Dia cir**
Enter the center point: **0,0 ←**
Enter the diameter: **3.5 ←**
Select **Z** from the Secondary menu
Enter **Z1.5 ←**
Z1.5 should appear in the Secondary menu
Enter the center point: **0,0 ←**
Enter the diameter: **1.5 ←**

The two circles are shown in Figure 16.3.

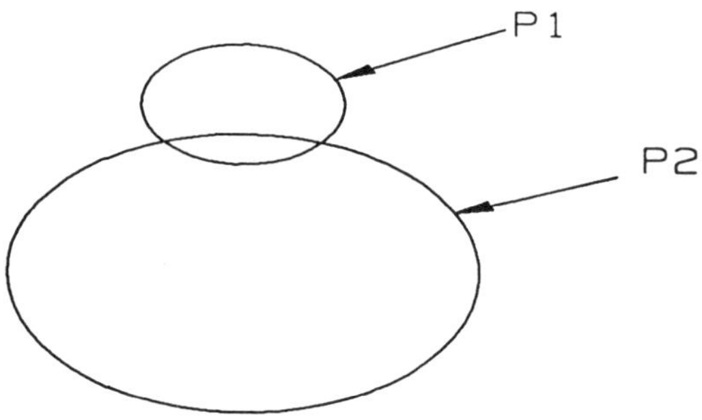

Figure 16.3

Step 2. Create an arc using the front Cplane. Set Z = 0. Use the pick points in Figure 16.3.

Select **Cplane → Front**
Select **Z**, then enter **Z0 ←**
Select **BACKUP → Endpoints → Endpoint**
Enter the first point: pick at **P1**
Enter the second point: pick at **P2**
Enter the radius: **2 ←**
Pick the second arc from the right

The wireframe model should look like Figure 16.4.

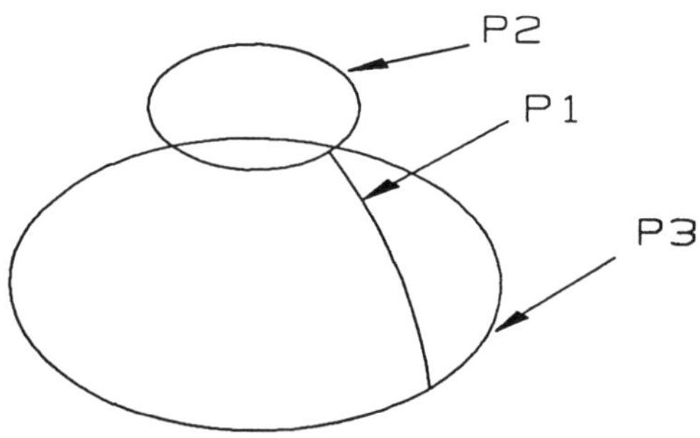

Figure 16.4

Step 3. Create a swept surface using the pick points in Figure 16.4.

Change Cplane to top.
Select **Cplane → Top**
Select **MAIN MENU → Create → sUrface → Swept → Nurbs**
Enter the number of across contour: **1 ←**
define the across contour: select **Single**, then pick at **P1**
define along contour 1: select **Single**, then pick at **P2**
define along contour 2: select **Single**, then pick at **P3**
Select **Done** to complete the contour selection
Set the Swept surface parameters to the following settings:

Along cut distance = 0.15 Across cut distance = 0.15

Select **Done**
The swept surface should appear as in Figure 16.5.

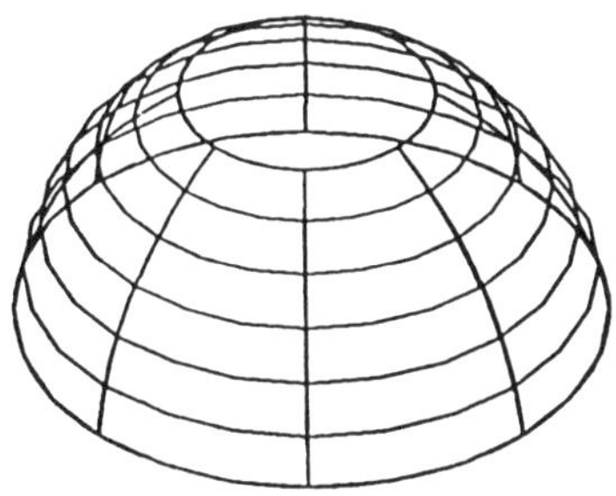

Figure 16.5

Step 4. Generate the lettering toolpaths.

Select Z then enter **Z2.0 ←**
Select **MAIN MENU → Toolpaths → mIsc. → leTters**
Enter file name: **T1 ←**
Select **bLock** from the Letters menu
Enter letter height: **0.5 ←**
Enter letter spacing: **0.13 ←**
Select **Yes** to "Write letters on an arc?"
Enter coordinates of arc center: **0,0 ←**
Enter arc radius: **1 ←**
Enter type of arc: **1 ←**
Enter letters: **EMU**

Select **Params** to define contour parameters

Step 5. Define the contour parameters.

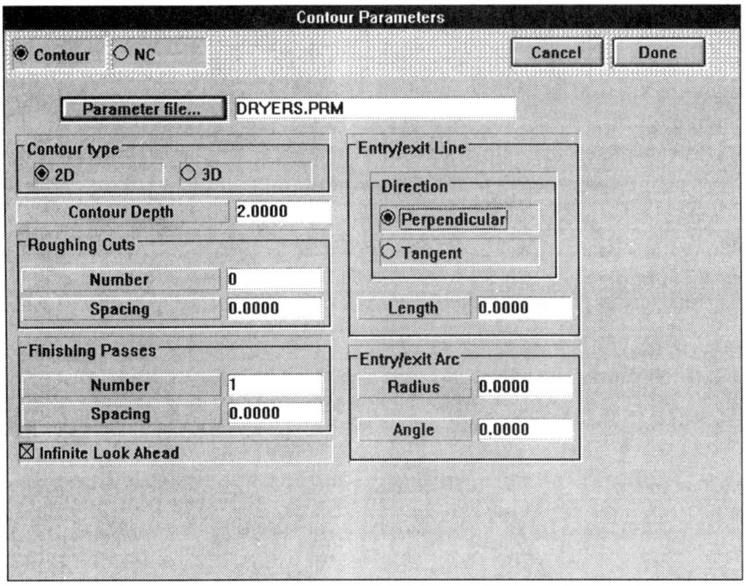

Select the **NC button** to advance to THE NC parameters menu.

Step 6. Define the NC parameters.

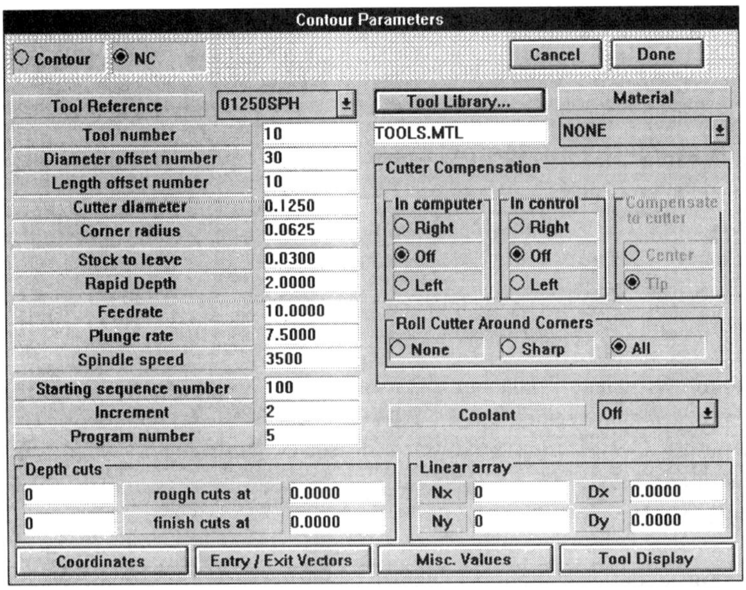

Select the **Done button** to complete the parameter settings.

Step 7. Write the toolpaths.

Select **Write** from the Change menu

Select **Yes** to write all remaining contours

The toolpaths appear as in Figure 16.6 on the next page.

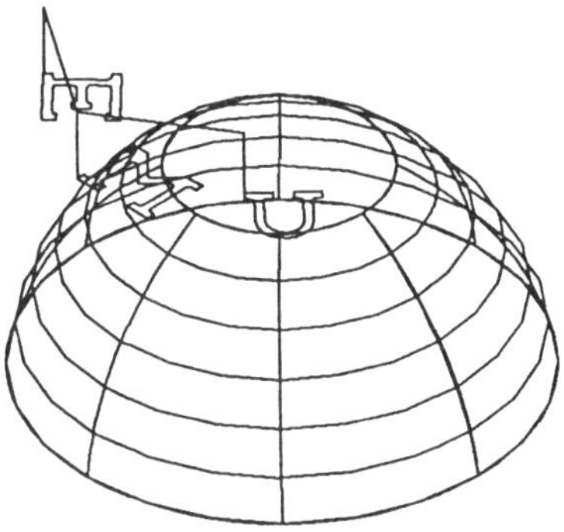

Figure 16.6

Select **Yes** to accept this toolpath segment
Select **End progrm** to close the NCI file
Select **No** to "Run the post processor?"

Tip Record your NCI file names and define them in projection. These names can get confusing when doing multiple projections.

Step 8. Initiate the project module.

Select **MAIN MENU → Toolpaths → Project**
Enter file name: **TP1 ←**
Select **surFace** from the Project onto menu
Pick at any point on the surface to pick that surface

Step 9. Define the project parameters to the following settings.

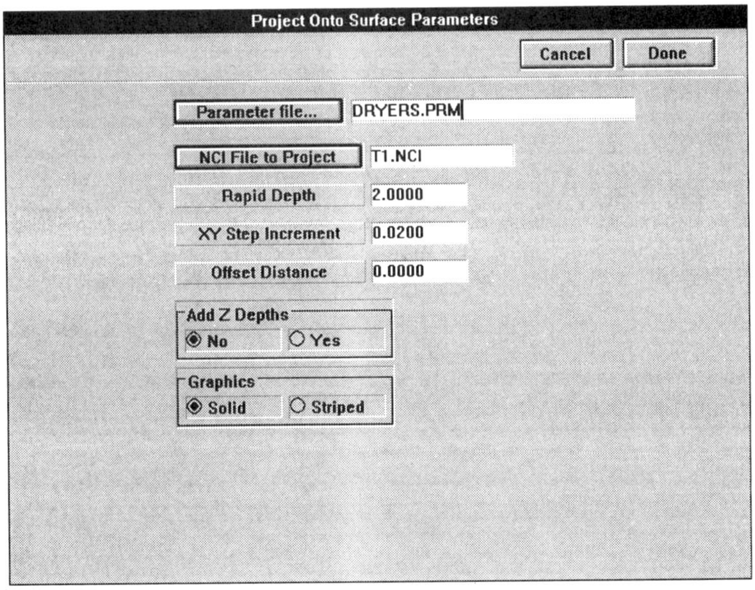

Select the **Done button** to complete the parameter settings.

Step 10. Accept the toolpaths.

The projected toolpaths should appear as Figure 16.7.

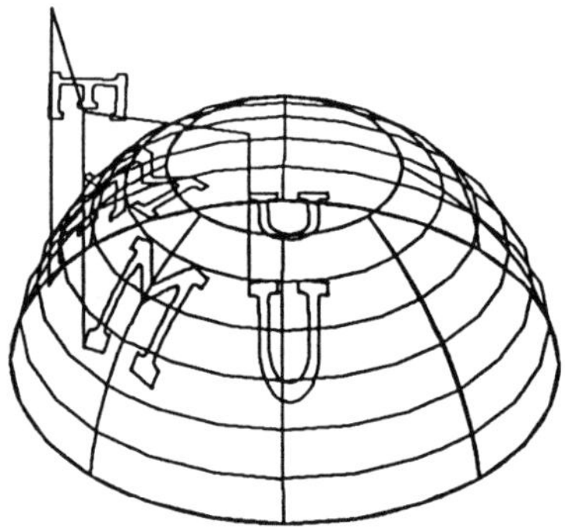

Figure 16.7

Select **Yes** to accept this toolpath segment
Select **BACKUP → End progrm**
Select **No** to "Run the post processor?"

Step 11. Backplot the toolpaths.

Press **Alt** + **F1** to fit the drawing
Select **MAIN MENU → NC utils → Backplot**
Set the Backplot parameters to the following settings:

Show Path	= Y
Show Auto	= Y
Show rEf	= N

Select **Run** from the Backplot menu

The projected toolpaths should be backploted as in Figure 16.8.

Figure 16.8

16.2 Trim Function

The trim function is used to create a new set of toolpaths file by trimming an existing toolpath file to the specified boundaries (Figure 16.9). The original toolpath remains unchanged.

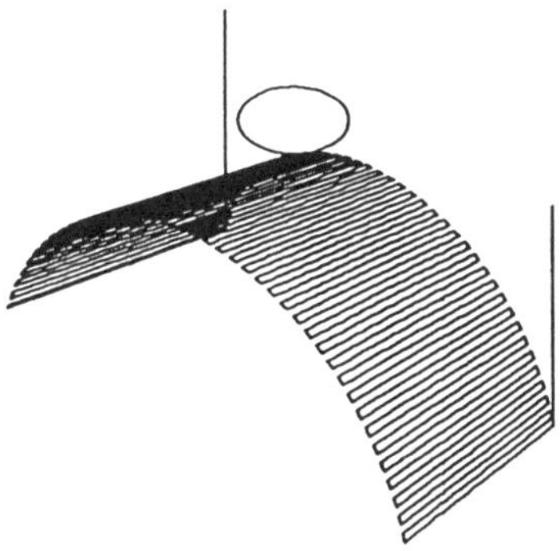

Figure 16.9 Before trimming

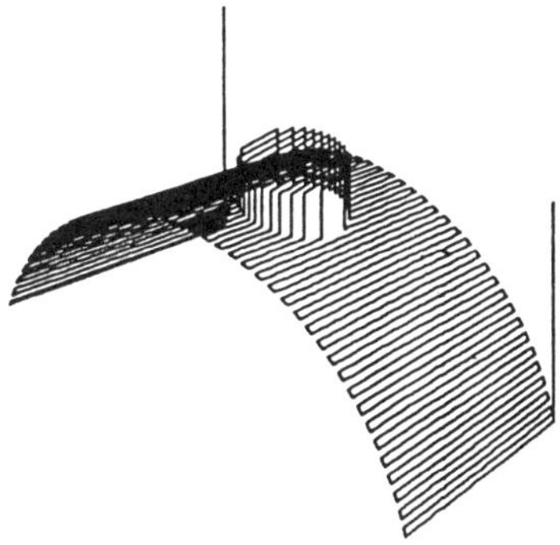

Figure 16.9b After trimming

Trimming is normally used in the following two applications:

1. To avoid islands or interferences (boss avoidance). This is especially useful in pocketing and surfacing.
2. To trim irregular boundaries at outside edges.

Trimming Boundaries

Mastercam allows us to use multiple trimming boundaries. The maximum number of boundaries is 50. The trimming boundaries must be **closed contours.** The trimming boundaries can be any shape and size and it is not necessary that they completely fall inside the toolpath range. **The trim function does not incorporate any cutter compensation. Therefore, the trimming contours should be created to reflect the center line of the cutter.**

Trimming Procedure

1. Generate the toolpath file to be trimmed and create the trimming boundaries. The toolpath (.NCI) file to be trimmed must exist before entering the Trim function.

2. Initiate the Trim function using the following commands:
   MAIN MENU → Toolpaths → Trim

3. Enter a new name for the trimmed file name. The system issues a prompt "Enter file name:" to specify the file name for storing the trimmed toolpath.

4. Define trimming boundaries using the chain option.

5. Specify a point to indicate the side of the toolpath to keep.

6. Indicate whether the tool is up or down in the trimmed areas.

7. Enter the name of the toolpath file to trim.

8. Accept the trimmed toolpath segment.

9. Select End program to close the NCI file.

Project 2.

Trimming an existing toolpath file

This project trims the toolpaths for a basket which is a composite surface model. The trimming boundary is a 2" diameter circle. The trimmed area include the bottom surface and the sloped wall surface as shown in Figure 16.10.

Wireframe Model
Project 11 of Chapter 11 (basket)

Go to

Surface Model
Project 8 of Chapter 13 (baskets)

Go to

Toolpath
Project 5 of Chapter 15 (basket)

We are here — Go to

Toolpath Trimming
(trim1)

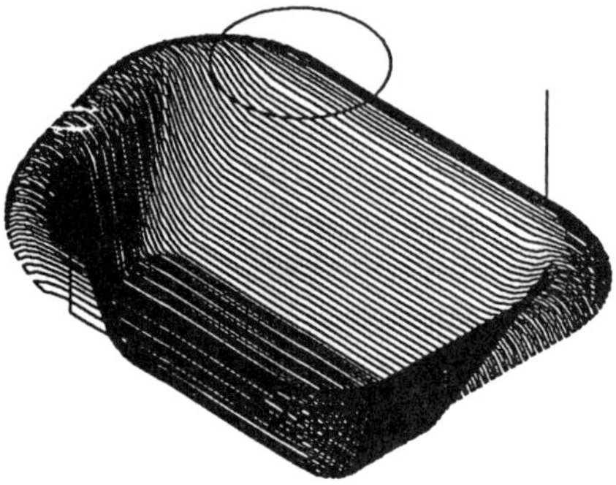

Figure 16.10 Before trimming

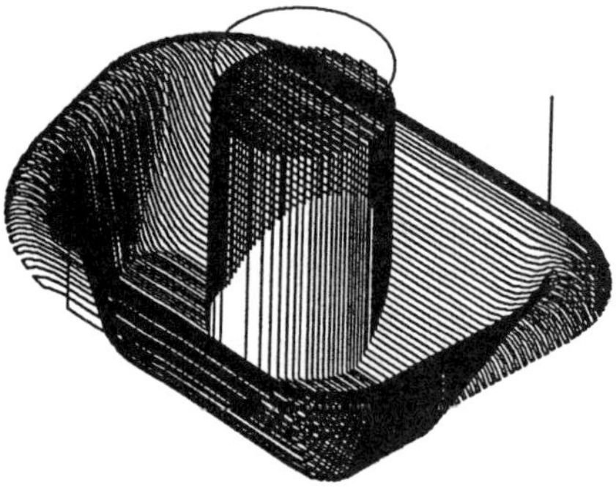

Figure 16.10 After trimming

Tips 1. Create an arc of 2" diameter as the trimming boundary. The circle is centered at (3,2.5).

2. Initiate the trim function and retrieve the toolpath file (basket).

3. Backplot the trimmed toolpaths.

Step 1. Create an arc as the trimming boundary.

Select **Z** from the Secondary menu
Enter **Z2.0** ←
Select **Gview** then pick **Isometric**
Select **MAIN MENU → Create → Arc → pt Dia cir**
Enter the center point: **3,2.5** ←
Enter the diameter: **2** ←

The arc appears as in Figure 16.11.

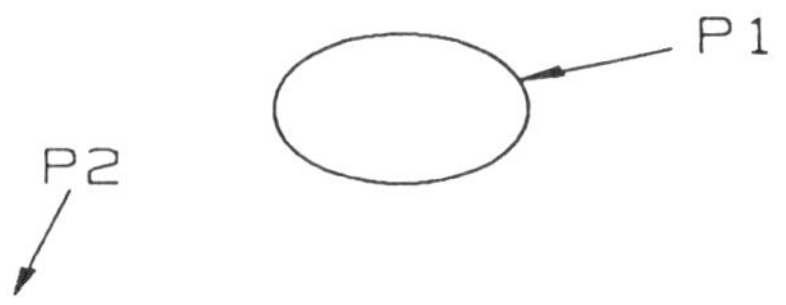

Figure 16.11

Step 2. Initiate the trim function using the pick point in Figure 16.11.

Select **MAIN MENU → Toolpaths → Trim**
Enter file name: **trim1 ←**
Define trimming boundary 1: select **Single** then pick at **P1**
Select **Done** to complete the selection of the trimming boundary
Enter a point on the side to keep: pick at **P2**
Keep the tool: select **Up**
Enter file pattern: **basket ←**

The trimmed toolpaths should appear as in Figure 16.12.

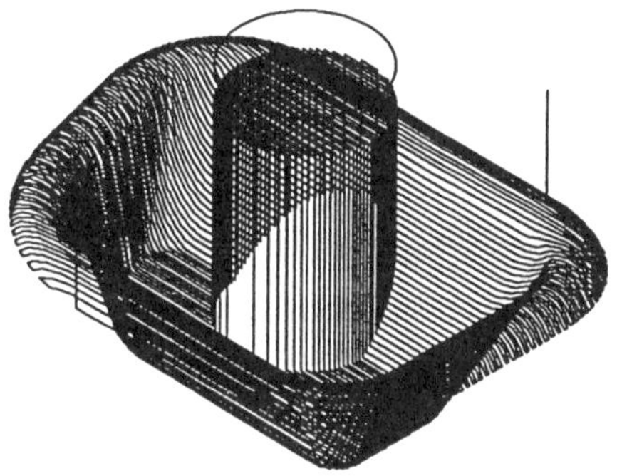

Figure 16.12

Step 3. Save the toolpaths.

Select **Yes** to accept this toolpath segment
Select **End progrm** to close the NCI file
Select **No** to "Run the post processor?"

Step 4. Backplot the trimmed toolpaths.

Select **MAIN MENU → NC utils → Backplot**

Set the Backplot parameters to the following settings.

Show Path = Y
Show Auto = Y
Show rEf = N

Select **Run**

The trimmed toolpaths should be plotted on the screen.

Project 3.

Generating toolpaths for a surface and trimming the toolpaths to a rectangular boundary

The intent of this project is to trim the surfacing toolpaths to avoid an island of a rectangle as shown in Figure 16.13. The toolpaths are generated by using the flowline module.

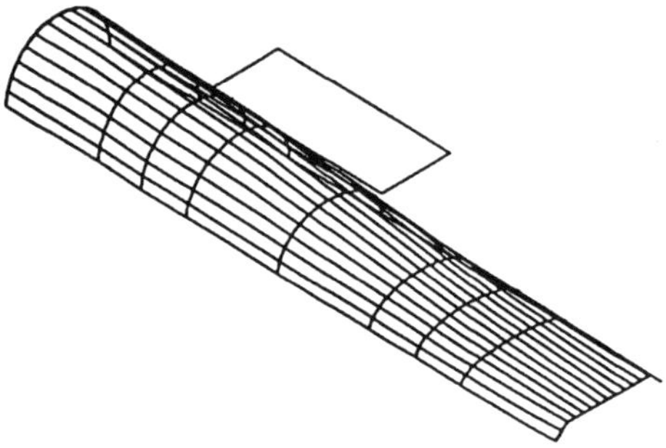

Figure 16.13a Before trimming

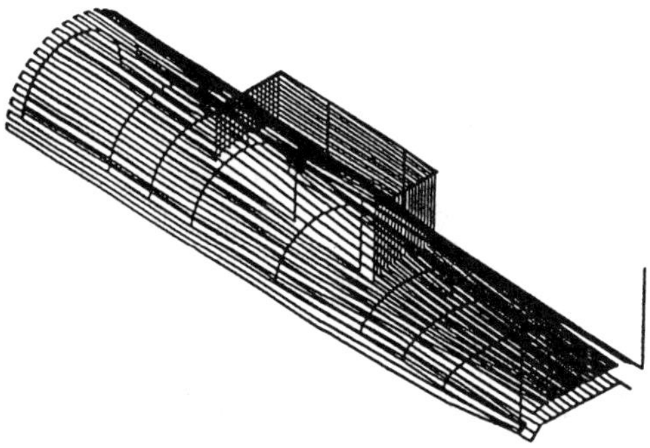

Figure 16.13b After trimming

3

Wireframe Model
Project 14 of Chapter 11 (loft3)

Go to

Surface Model
Project 6 of Chapter 12 (lofts3)

Go to

Toolpath
Project 1 of Chapter 15 (flowl1)

Go to

We are here

Toolpath Trimming
(lofts3)

Tips 1. The surface model used in this project is **lofts3.**

2. The island is a rectangle of 2"x 0.5". The trimming boundary for this rectangle should be 2.5"x1" because no cutter compensation is allowed in trimming. Therefore, we need to add the dimension of one-half of the cutter diameter to all sides of trimming boundary. The rectangle is centered at (-4,0) and has a height of Z1.5".
3. Use the flowline 3d toolpath module to generate the toolpaths for cutting the loft surface with a 0.5" ball end mill.
4. Initiate the trim function to trim the toolpaths to the rectangular boundary.

Step 1. Load the surface model file lofts3.

Select **MAIN MENU → File → Get**
Enter file pattern: **lofts3 ←**
Select **Yes** to delete the current part

The surface model should appear on screen as in Figure 16.14 on the next page.

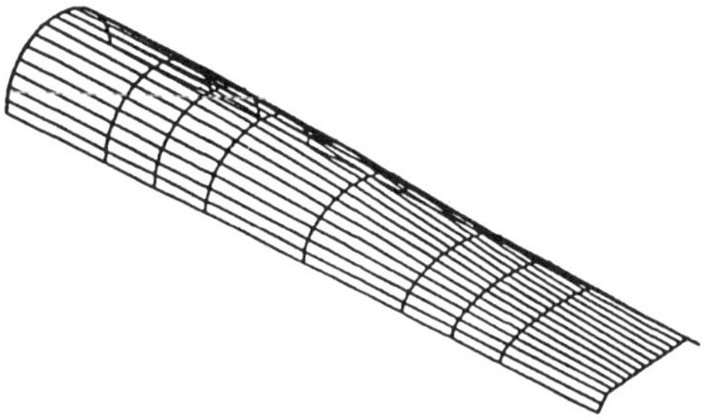

Figure 16.14

Step 2. Create a rectangle as the trimming boundary.

Select **Cplane → Top**
Select **Z** then enter **Z1.5 ←**
Select **MAIN MENU → Create → Rectangle → 2 points**
Enter the lower left corner: **-5.25,-0.5 ←**
Enter the upper right corner: **-2.75,0.5 ←**

The rectangle is added to the drawing as shown in Figure 16.15.

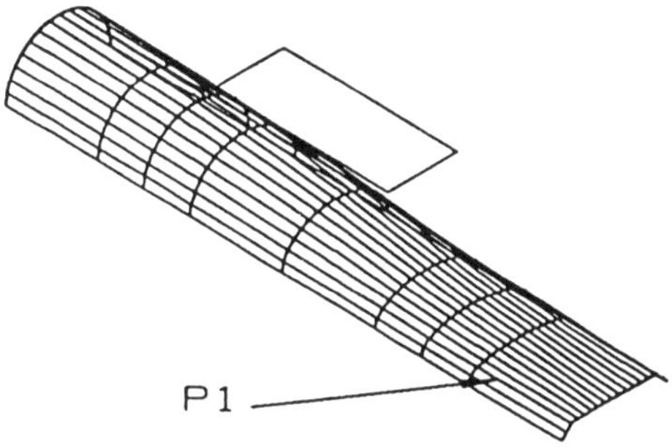

Figure 16.15

Step 3. Initiate the flowline toolpath module. Use the pick points in Figure 16.15.

Select **MAIN MENU → Toolpaths → Flowline**
Enter file name: **lofts3 ←**
Select a surface: pick at **P1**
Select TOOLPATH direction: select **OK** (in along direction)
Select CUTTER OFFSET direction: select **OK** (in outward direction)

Step 4. Define the flowline parameters to the following settings.

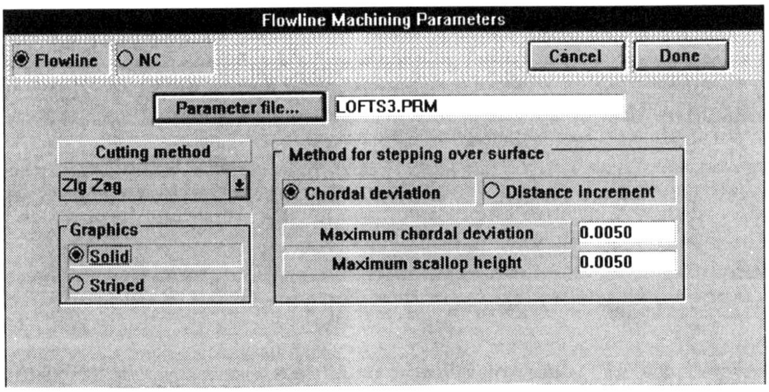

Select the **NC button** to advance to the NC parameters menu.

Step 5. Set the NC parameters to the following settings.

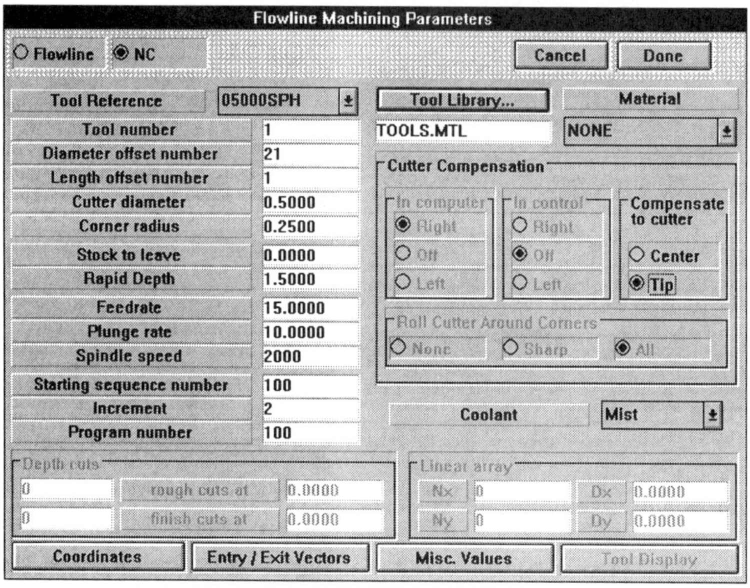

Select the **Done button** to complete the parameters settings.

Step 6. Accept the toolpaths.

The toolpaths are shown in Figure 16.16 below.
Select **Yes** to accept this toolpath segment
Select **End progrm** to close the NCI file
Select **No** to "Run the post processor?"

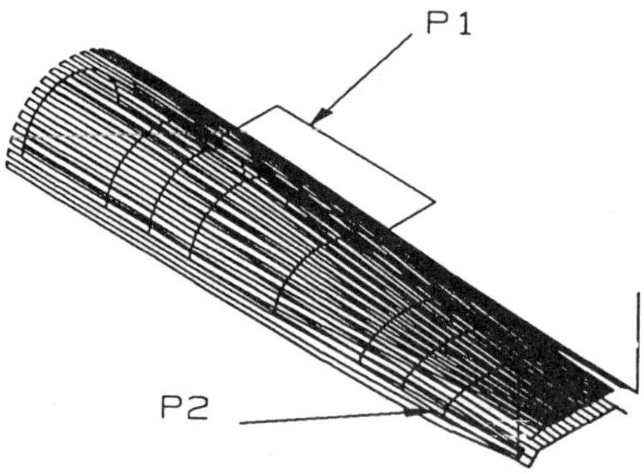

Figure 16.16

Step 7. Initiate the trim function. Use the pick points in Figure 16.16.

Select **MAIN MENU → Toolpaths → Trim**
Enter file name: **trim2 ←**
Define trimming boundary 1: select **Chain** then pick at **P1**
Select **Close → End here → Done**
Enter a point on the side to keep: pick at **P2**
Keep the tool: select **Up**
Enter file name: **lofts3 ←**

The trimmed toolpaths should resemble Figure 16.17.

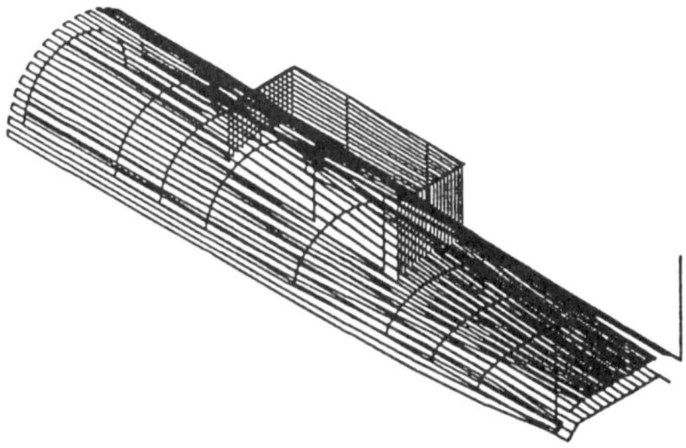

Figure 16.17

TS61

Step 8. Accept the trimmed toolpaths.

Select **Yes** to accept this toolpath segment
Select **End progrm** to close the NCI file
Select **No** to "Run the post processor?"

16.3 Exercises

1. What are the two toolpath editing functions commonly used in editing 3d surfacing toolpaths?
2. How does the project function affect the X, Y, and Z coordinate values of the toolpath?
3. List three types of toolpaths that can not be projected.
4. Explain the main features of the trim function.
5. Identify two typical applications of the trim function.
6. What is the requirement of a trimming boundary?

Chapter 17

3-D Toolpath Planning

Objectives:

1. Understand the toolpath generation procedure for 3-D surfaces.
2. Identify features and surfaces of the parts.
3. Determine the edge and skin profiles of the wireframe model for a surface model.
4. Select the surface modeling module and toolpath module for each surface.
5. Select proper tooling and machining parameters.

Overview

The procedure of process planning for 2d projects is presented in chapter 9. Most of the material covered in chapter 9 is applicable to 3d surfacing projects. However, there are unique features in 3d surfacing toolpath planning that warrant the discussion of this topic in a separate chapter. This chapter focuses on surface identification, wireframe model construction, surfacing module selection, toolpath generation, toolpath editing, tools and machining data selection, and NC files management. The flow chart for planning 3d surfacing toolpaths is illustrated in Figure 17.1 on the following page.

17.1 Features and Surfaces Identification

A part feature is the distinctive shape and size to be produced in a part. Part features can be generalized as 2d features or 3d features. Flat surfaces, external and internal profiles, pockets, holes, etc., are typical 2d features. Surfaces are 3d features. It is very common to have a combination of both 2d features and 3d features in a part. In this case, we need to treat 2d features and 3d features separately.

The 3d features are identified according to their surface types; geometric surfaces or free-form surfaces, and single surface or composite surfaces. The surface type dictates the complexity of the required wireframe model. Some surface models require a single patch edge profile, while some need multiple patches or multiple profile sections. Geometric surfaces provide exact surface skin, while the free-form surfaces furnish approximated surface texture. In most cases, a surface can be modeled by more than one surfacing technique. The answer to the following questions should help in selecting proper surfacing techniques which in turn determines the required wireframe model:

Is the surface aesthetic or toleranced ?
Is a single surface model or a composite surface model ?
How accurate is the surface skin required ?

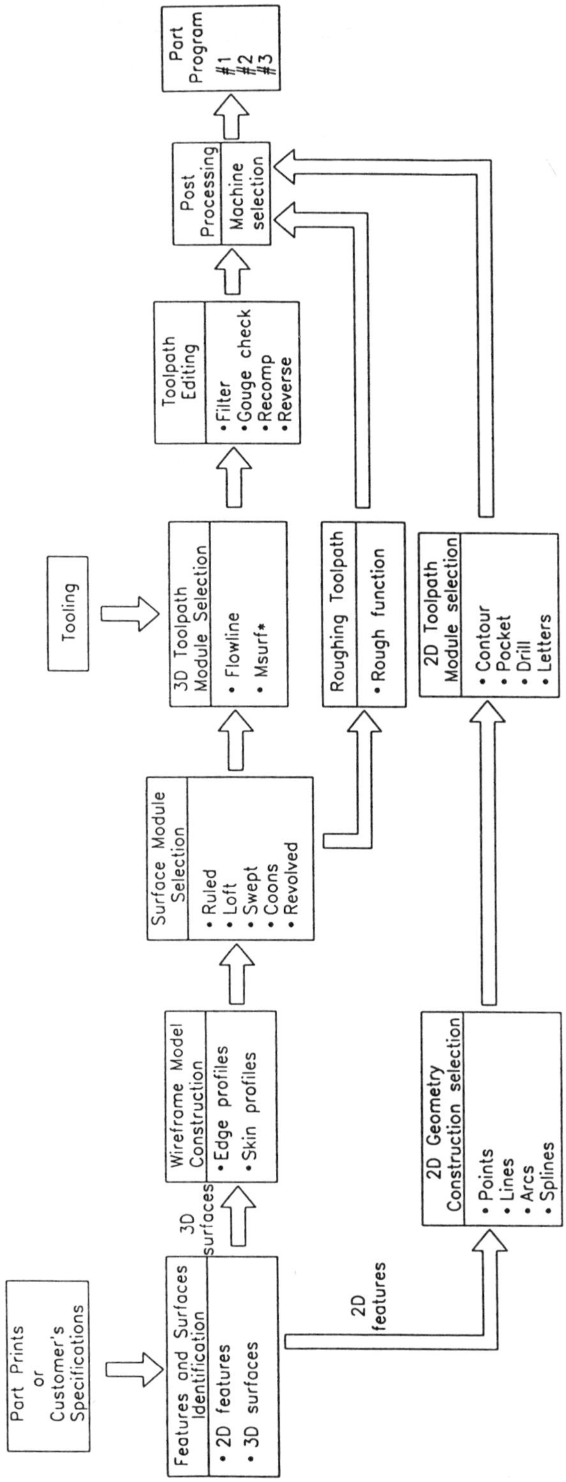
Part Prints
or
Customer's
Specifications
Features and Surfaces
Identification
• 2D features
• 3D surfaces
3D
surfaces
2D
features
Wireframe Model
Construction
•Edge profiles
•Skin profiles
2D Geometry
Construction selection
• Points
• Lines
• Arcs
• Splines
Surface Module
Selection
• Ruled
• Loft
• Swept
• Coons
• Revolved
Tooling
3D Toolpath
Module Selection
• Flowline
• Msurf*
Roughing Toolpath
• Rough function
2D Toolpath
Module selection
• Contour
• Pocket
• Drill
• Letters
Toolpath
Editing
•Filter
•Gouge check
•Recomp
•Reverse
Post
Processing
Machine
selection
Part
Program
#1
#2
#3

Figure 17.1

17.2 Wireframe Model Construction

A CAD system uses a set of edge and skin profiles to create a surface. The complete set of edge and skin profiles for a part is often referred to as the wireframe model. Actually, in most surface modeling cases only a partial wireframe model is required. The following two guidelines should help to determine how many edge and skin profiles are needed and where they are located:

- Edge profiles should be defined at the outer boundaries in all sides
- Skin profiles should be used to represent significant features in the surface skin

The edge profiles define the shape of the surface outer boundaries. They are definitely required. The skin profiles define the detailed texture of the surface skin. The more the skin profiles used, the more accurate the surface produced.

The typical elements of edge profiles and skin profiles are points, lines, arcs, splines, and surface curves.

17.3 Surface Module Selection

Choosing proper surface modeling methods is very crucial for successfully defining surfaces. The analysis of surface features should reveal the proper surface modeling techniques to be used. The **seven** surface modeling modules Mastercam provides to create various forms of surfaces are:

Ruled surface	• at least two profiles • created by connecting straight lines between profiles
Lofted surface	• at least three profiles • created by fitting parabolically through a set of cross sectional curves
Revolved surface	• a sectional profile and a line to revolve about • created by rotating a sectional shape around an axis or a line
Draft surface	• a sectional shape • created by extruding a sectional shape straight along a line
Drag surface (2-D swept)	• an along contour and an across contour • create by translating or rotating a sectional profile along a drive curve
Swept surface	• three profiles (two along and one across, or one along and two across) • created by (1) translating an across profile along two drive curves (2) translating two across profiles along a drive curve
Coons surface	• a single patch of four profiles or multiple patches • created by blending a patch of three or four prescribed intersecting curves or points which form a close boundary, or multiple patches

There are **four** secondary surfacing techniques used to generate surfaces from existing surfaces. They are:

Offset surface	• an existing surface • created by offsetting an existing surface by a distance
Trimmed surface	• an existing surface • created by trimming an existing surface to a specified boundary
Fillet surface	• two existing surfaces • created by generating arc cross sections that are tangent to two existing surfaces
Blend surface	• two existing surfaces • created by blending a smooth surface between two existing surfaces

17.4 Toolpath Modules Selection

There are **two** ways of generating toolpaths to cut surfaces. One is directly using 3D surfacing toolpath modules to generate the toolpath from the wireframe model. The other method is to define the surface model first, then use the flowline or multisurf module to generate the toolpaths from the surface model. It is recommended that the toolpaths be generated from the surface models.

Flowline module:	generating toolpaths for cutting a single surface
Multisurf module:	generating toolpaths for cutting multiple surfaces

17.5 Toolpath Planning

The toolpaths used to machine the part having 3D surfaces, normally, consist of **three** types: 2D toolpaths, roughing toolpaths for surfaces, and finishing toolpaths for surfaces. These three types of toolpaths should be handled separately.

1. Use 2-D toolpath modules whenever possible.

The 2D toolpath modules are often used in the following operations:

contours/profiles
pockets
holes
horizontal and vertical flat surfaces

Note: Many flat planes can be defined as surfaces. But their toolpaths should be generated from 2d modules such as pocket or contour. Sloped flat planes should be treated as surfaces in generating their toolpaths.

2. Roughing toolpaths for surfaces

The roughing toolpaths for cutting surfaces normally are 2d in nature. Therefore, their part programs are relatively much shorter than the finishing toolpaths. The workpiece should be cut to approximate size and shape by the roughing toolpaths. This allows to use one single pass of finishing toolpaths to complete the surface(s). Consequently, it helps to reduce part program size and machining time.

3. Finishing toolpaths for surfaces

- Make one single pass if possible.

- Use the largest ball end mill that the surface curvature allows.

- When the surface features are symmetrical, generate the toolpaths based on the selected surface segments, then use toolpath editing functions such as mirror, rotate, and translate to simplify the process. The larger the number of the surfaces included in using the multisurf function, the longer the time needed by the system to generate toolpaths. It may take two days for the system to generate the finishing toolpaths for cutting a composite surface model of 60 surfaces that are formed by 10 symmetrical segments about the center. The processing time can be reduced to merely 20 minutes if the primary toolpaths for cutting one of ten surfacing segments is generated, and then rotated to the other nine locations.

The machining sequence for surface(s) starts with 2d machining, then is followed by roughing and finishing.

17.6 Tooling

Two types of cutters that are used extensively in machining 3d surfaces are: ball-end mills and bull-corner mills. The radius of ball-end mills is one-half of the cutter diameter. The radius of the corner arc for bull-corner mills is smaller than one-half of the cutter diameter. The following tips can be used to select proper tools for machining 3d surfaces:

- **Use the larger cutter.** The larger cutter reduces the cusp height, allows bigger stepover values, and shortens program size.

- The largest cutter usable is limited by the size of the surface curvatures and surface gaps. The cutter radius must be at least slightly smaller than the smallest surface curvature or its diameter should be smaller than the smallest surface gap in the model. A gouging or undercut may occur when the cutter size is too large.

- Cusp height is one of the main factors determining the roughness and tolerance of the machined surfaces. The formula given below can be used to calculate the cusp height:

$$H_C = R - [R^2 - (S/2)^2]^{1/2}$$

or

$$S = 2[R^2 - (R-H_C)^2]^{1/2}$$

where H_C = cusp height
R = tool nose radius
S = stepover value between two cutting passes

Note: The cutting speed and feedrate for cutting surfaces are the same as that used in 2d cases.

17.7 Accuracy Requirement

Surface roughness and tolerance are the two major factors to be considered in determining the accuracy requirement. The tips given below can be used to obtain the required surface quality:

- Use increment mode when dimensional accuracy is not crucial or surfaces are rather flat (large curvature radius).

- Use chordal mode when the dimensional accuracy is important or surfaces are irregular.

- When chordal mode is used, the value for chordal deviation should be somewhat smaller than the required dimensional accuracy.

Use a smaller stepover value or chordal deviation value to generate the toolpaths for cutting surfaces. Then use the filter function to remove those unnecessary toolpath points. The filter function allows settting the allowed deviation or error. Any two adjacent toolpath segments that do not deviate by a value that is larger than the allowed value will be combined to one segment. This significantly shortens the part program while meeting the accuracy and tolerance requirements.

17.8 Toolpath File Management

Here are two guidelines:

- Do not combine 2D toolpaths, roughing toolpaths, and finishing toolpaths altogether in one part program.

- The memory size of the controller needs to be known. The program size can not be larger than the available memory size of the controller. Divide the part program into several subprograms if the part program is larger than the controller memory.

17.9 3-D Toolpath Planning Projects

Two projects are given in this section to show how to perform toolpath planning for cutting 3-D surfacing models.

Project 1.

1

Prepare a toolpath plan for cutting a composite surface model as shown in Figure 17.2. This surface model is the project 7 of chapter 13.

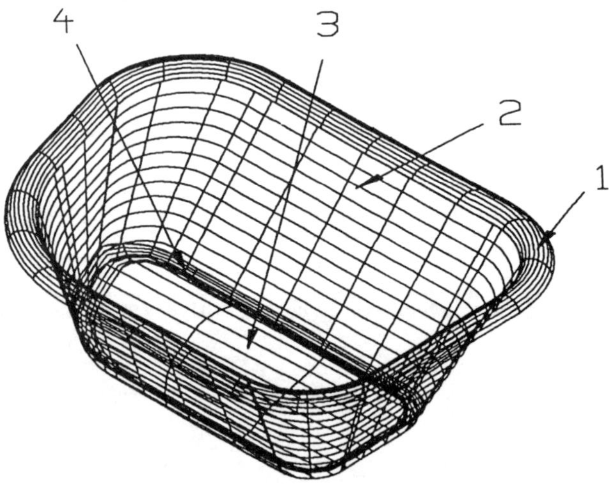

Figure 17.2

Step 1. Identify part features and surfaces to be machined.

The following four surfaces can be identified in this model; together they form a composite surface model that can be used to generate roughing toolpaths and finish toolpaths

1. Top rim surface
2. Wall surface
3. Bottom flat surface
4. Fillet surface.

Step 2. Select surface modeling techniques for each surface.

The surface modeling techniques used for the four surfaces are:

1. Top rim surface:	swept surface module with 2 along and 1 across
2. Wall surface:	coons surface module or ruled surface module
3. Bottom flat surace:	ruled surface module
4. Fillet surface:	fillet surface module

Step 3. Construct the wireframe model.

The complexity of the required wireframe model dictates the type of modeling techniques used and the required accuracy on the surface skin. The edge profiles and skin profiles of each surface are listed below and indicated in the Figure 17.3.

Top rim surface:	Edge profiles: contours 1 and 2 as well as arc 4 Skin profiles: arc 4
Wall surface:	Edge profiles: contours 2 and 3 Skin profile: lines 5 - 12
Bottom flat surface:	Edge profile: contour 3 Skin profile: none
Fillet surface:	No profile is required. Use two existing surfaces (wall surface and bottom flat surface)

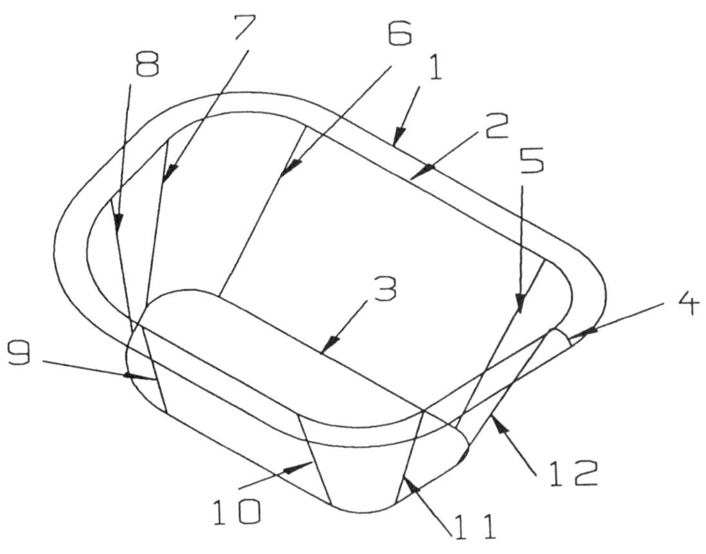

Figure 17.3

Step 4. Select toolpath modules.

The toolpaths required to machine this project consist of two parts, roughing toolpaths and finish toolpaths. Since this is a model with multiple surfaces, the best toolpath module is the Multisurf toolpath module. Use the rough function of the Multisurf module to generate the roughing toolpaths and the finish function of Multisurf module to generate the finishing toolpaths. Figures 17.4 and 17.5 show the roughing toolpaths and finish toolpaths for the surface model, respectively.

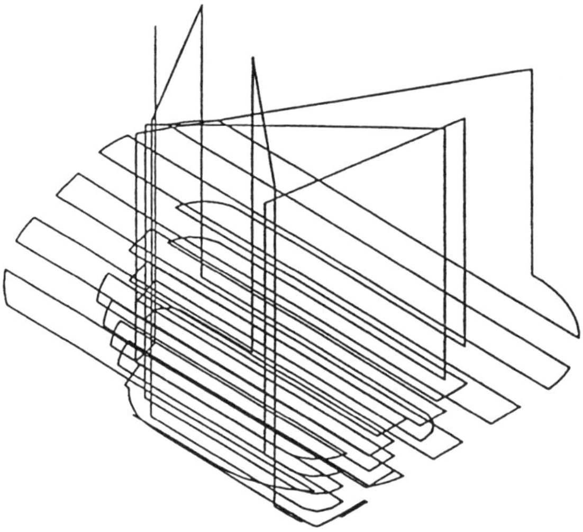

Figure 17.4

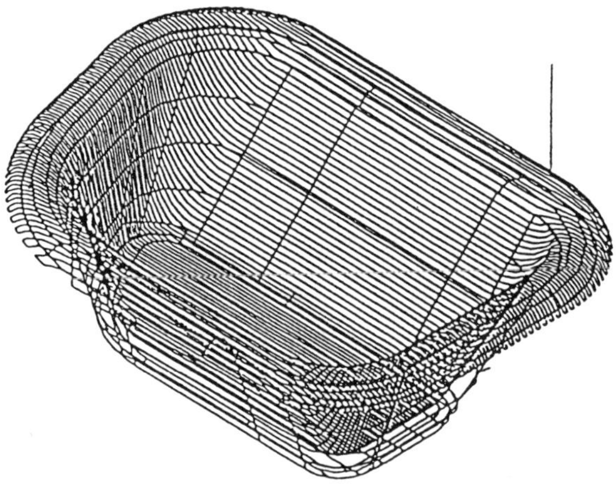

Figure 17.5

Step 5. Select the tooling and machining information.

Cutters:	Roughing:	3/4" end mill
	Finishing:	3/8" ball end mill
Machining data:	Roughing:	Cutting speed = 350 fpm or (1780 RPM) Feedrate = 10 inches/min Depth of cut = 0.15 inches/pass
	Finishing:	Cutting speed = 250 fpm or (2500 RPM) Feedrate = 15 inches/minute Chordal deviation = 0.01 inches

Project 2.

Prepare a toolpath plan for cutting a very complicated surface model as shown in Figure 17.6. This surface model is project 11 of chapter 13. The finish toolpaths for the surface model is given in project 8 of chapter 15.

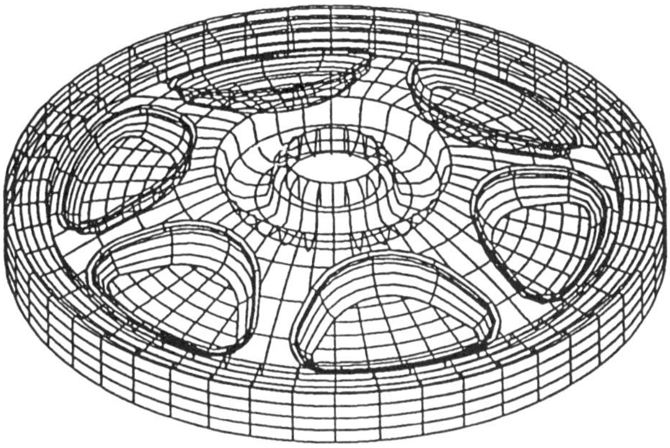

Figure 17.6

Step 1. Identify part features and surfaces.

The complete surface model consists of 48 surfaces that are formed by six segments that are symmetric about the origin. This model can be generated by modeling a surface segment as shown in Figure 17.7 and then copying this surface segment to five locations by rotating about the origin. Therefore, we need to define only the following eight surfaces:

1. Inner hole surface (straight circular surface)
2. Hub surface
3. Upper surface
4. Lower surface (pocket bottom surface)
5. Pocket wall surface
6. Fillet surface
7. Rim surface
8. Outer surface (straight circular surface)

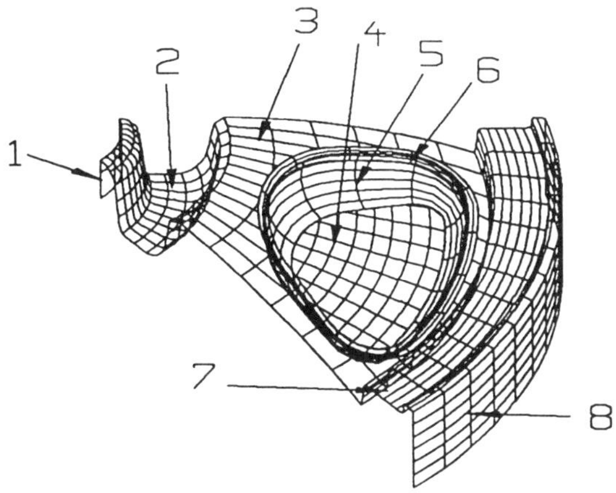

Figure 17.7

Note: The upper and lower surfaces are the trimmed surfaces.

Step 2. Select surface modeling techniques for each surface.

The surface modeling techniques used for the eight surfaces are listed below. Some surfaces can be modeled by more than one technique.

1. Inner hole surface: revolved or swept surface module
2. Hub surface: swept surface module (2 along and 1 across)
3. Upper surface: swept surface module (2 along and 1 across) and trim function (trimmed to fillet surface)
4. Lower surface: swept surface module (2 along and 1 across) and trimfunction (trimmed to pocket wall surface)
5. Pocket wall surface: swept surface module (2 along and 1 across)
6. Fillet surface: fillet surface module (between the upper surface and the pocket wall surface)
7. Rim surface: swept surface (two along and 1 across)
8. Outer surface: revolved surface module

Step 3. Construct the wireframe model.

The required wireframe model consists of lines and arcs that are used to model the surface segment. The two defining along contours for the pocket wall surface are the two surface curves that are obtained by projecting the inner and outer pocket profiles onto the upper and lower surfaces. The required wireframe model for the basic surface segment is shown in Figure 17.8.

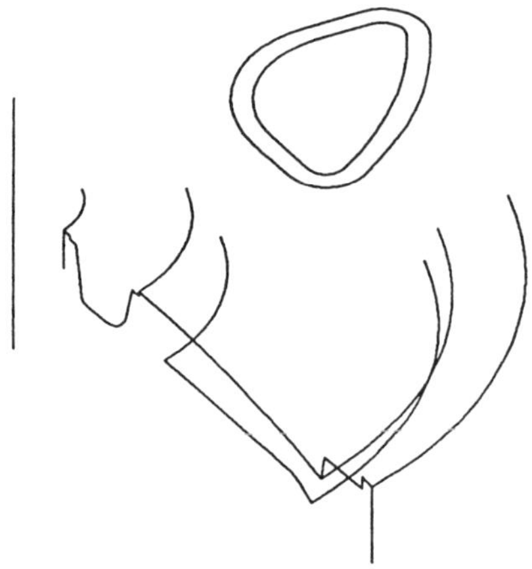

Figure 17.8

Step 4. Select toolpath modules.

2-D toolpaths: 2d pocket module to cut the inner hole surface
2d contour module to cut the outer surface

Roughing: Use the Multisurf → Rough commands to generate toolpaths for roughing the following three surfaces:
1. hub surface 2. upper surface 3. pocket surface

Note that the roughing toolpaths for the three surfaces listed above are copied to five locations by using the rotating function.

Finishing: Use Multisurf→ Finish commands to generate toolpaths for finish cutting the composite surface model that consists of six surfaces as shown in Figure 17.9 on the next page.

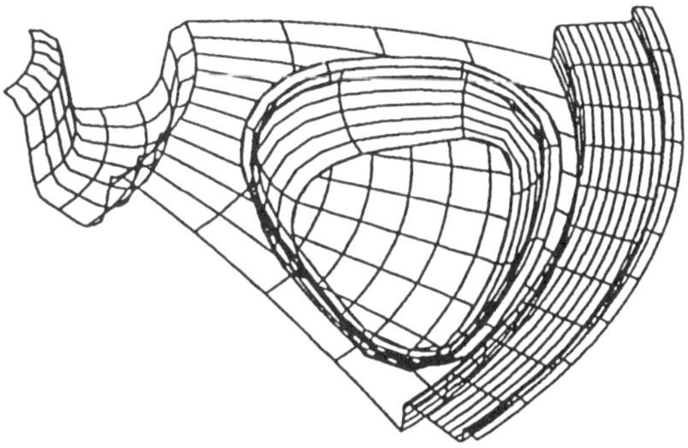

Figure 17.9

The finish toolpaths for the six surfaces should look like Figure 17.10. These finish toolpaths are then copied to five locations by using the rotating command. The finish toolpaths for the complete model are shown in

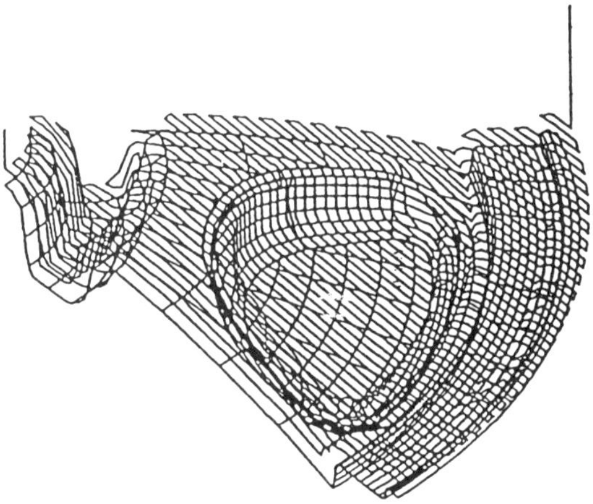

Figure17.10

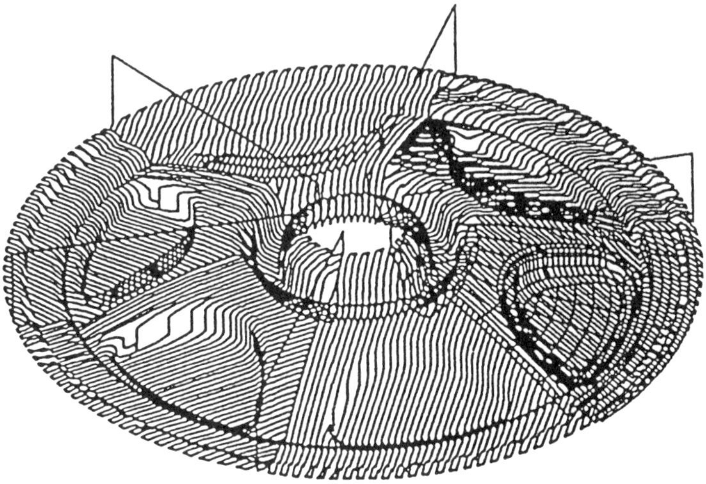

Figure 17.11

Note: It is possible to include all surfaces in a composite model to generate the finish toolpaths. However, it may take up to 2 days for the system to generate the toolpaths because it involves many more surfaces in the model.

Step 5. Select the tooling and machining information.

Cutters:	Roughing:	1/2" end mill
	Finishing:	3/8" ball end mill
Machining data:	Roughing:	Cutting speed = 350 fpm or (2670 RPM) Feedrate = 10 inches/min Depth of cut = 0.15 inches/pass
	Finishing:	Cutting speed = 250 fpm or (2500 RPM) Feedrate = 15 inches/minute Chordal deviation = 0.01 inches

17.10 Exercises

1. What are the two types of part features? Describe their differences.

2. What is the difference between the geometric surfaces and the free-form surfaces in terms of the accuracy of surface skin?

3. What is the prime factor in determining the number of skin profiles needed in a surface model?

4. What are the typical elements of edge profiles and skin profiles?

5. List the seven surface modeling modules of Mastercam. What is the required or minimum number of profiles for each surface modeling module?

6. List the three secondary surfacing techniques.

7. Describe the two ways to generate the toolpaths for cutting surfaces.

8. Explain when to use the flowline module and the multisurf module, respectively.

9. Explain why the 2D toolpaths, roughing toolpaths for surfaces, and finishing toolpaths for surfaces should be generated separately and stored in separate files.

10. What are the two types of cutters that are extensively used in machining 3D surfaces?

11. Why is the larger cutter recommended in cutting surfaces? What are the limiting factors for the largest size of the cutters?

12. What are the two major factors to be considered in determining the accuracy of surfaces?

Chapter 18
Milling Tools Construction and Definition

Objectives:

1. Understand the tool assembly for CNC mills and machining centers.
2. Know two common toolholder systems used in CNC mills and machining centers.
3. Define tools.
4. Generate tool setup sheets.

Overview

Many types of operation can be performed with a CNC mill or machining center. They include: **facing, milling, slot cutting, grooving, drilling, boring, tapping and surfacing**. Each operation requires a particular kind of cutting tool. A facing tool, for example, is required to perform facing, an end mill is used for contouring, a drill for drilling, and a tap for tapping. These commonly used cutting tools should be defined in the tool database so they can be retrieved when needed. Mastercam provides a **Define Tools utility** for users to create a tool database and geometry. This allows the tool to be correctly displayed on the screen so that gouging checking can be observed.

This chapter presents important information about the tooling system for CNC milling machines. It includes the style and specifications of toolholders as well as the shape and size of cutters. Tips for naming the tool reference for a particular tool are covered. Examples show how to define three tool assemblies. The content and use of the setup sheet are followed by an example which generates a setup sheet for a machining project.

18.1 Milling Tool Assembly

The milling tools used in CNC mills and machining centers normally consist of three components; holder, adaptor, and cutter as shown in Figure 18.1 on the next page. Normally the holder and adaptor are made in one assembly, and are called the toolholder. A holder consists of two components; taper shank and flange. Adaptors are designed with various configurations to allow for the use of different types of cutting tools. Toolholders are often named according to their adaptor type. Some commonly used toolholders are; end mill holders, face mill holders, tap holders, collet holders, Morse taper holders, boring bar holders, Jacob taper holders, and straight shank holders.

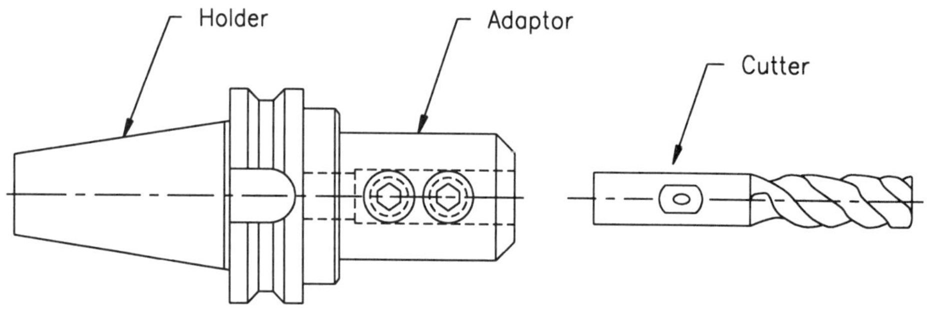

Figure 18.1

Holder Styles

The two common holder styles used in CNC mills and machining centers are the **V-flange and BT-flange** type. V-flange holders are normally used in machines made in North America. They use inch-based threads for the retention knob and hold cutting tools dimensioned in inches. BT-flange holders are used by imported machines with BT-style automatic tool changers. They have metric threads for the retention knob, but their adaptors are designed to accommodate a wide range of inch-dimensioned cutting tools.

The size of holders is specified by the taper number of the shank. The ANSI standard defines **six** basic taper shank sizes: #30, #35, #40, #45, #50, and #60. The shank with the #50 taper is the most commonly used for machining centers with a power capacity of 10 to 50 HP. Very large machines use the #60 taper shank, and very small machines adopt the #30 shank.

18.2 Define Holders in Mastercam

Mastercam uses a group of variables to define the toolholers. These variables include top length, top diameter, taper angle, flange length, flange diameter, end (adaptor) length, end (adaptor) diameter, and end (adaptor) chamfer (Figure 18.2 on the following page). Tables 18.1 and 18.2 give typical dimensions of holder variables for various taper shank sizes for V-flange and BT-flange, respectively.

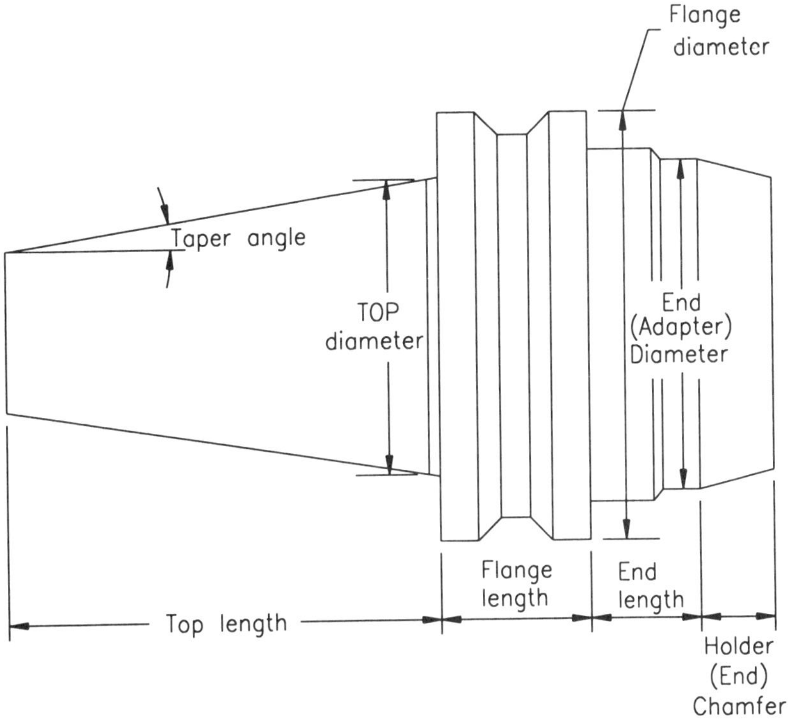

Figure 18.2

Table 18.1 Dimensions of various V-flange taper sizes

(diminsioned in inches)

	V30	V40	V45	V50	V60
Top length	1.875	2.687	3.25	4.0	6.375
Top diameter	1.25	1.75	2.25	2.75	4.25
Taper angle	8.13°	8.13°	8.13°	8.13°	8.13°
Flange length	-	-	-	-	-
Flange diameter	1.812	2.5	3.25	3.875	5.5
End (adaptor) length		Adaptor dependent			
End (adaptor) diameter		Adaptor dependent			
End (adaptor) chamfer		Adaptor dependent			

Table 18.2 Dimensions of various BT-flange taper sizes

(dimensioned in inches)

	BT-30	BT-40	BT-45	BT-50
Top length	1.906	2.575	3.26	4.008
Top diameter	1.25	1.75	2.25	2.75
Taper angle	8.13°	8.13°	8.13°	8.13°
Flange length	0.866	1.062	1.299	1.496
Flange diameter	1.811	2.479	3.345	3.937
End (adaptor) length		Adaptor dependent		
End (adaptor) diameter		Adaptor dependent		
End (adaptor) chamfer		Adaptor dependent		

Cutters

A wide variety of cutters are used in machining centers. They include flat end mills, ball end mills, face mills, drills, taps, and boring tools. Mastercam uses the following six variables to describe a cutter (Figure 18.3):

Shape:	selects cutter shape to be Flat/ Spherical/ Bull nose
Length:	specifies cutter length
Shaft diameter:	specifies cutter diameter
Taper angle:	defines cutter taper angle measured from the cutter center line
Tip diameter:	sets the cutter's tip diameter
Corner radius:	specifies the cutter tip's corner radius

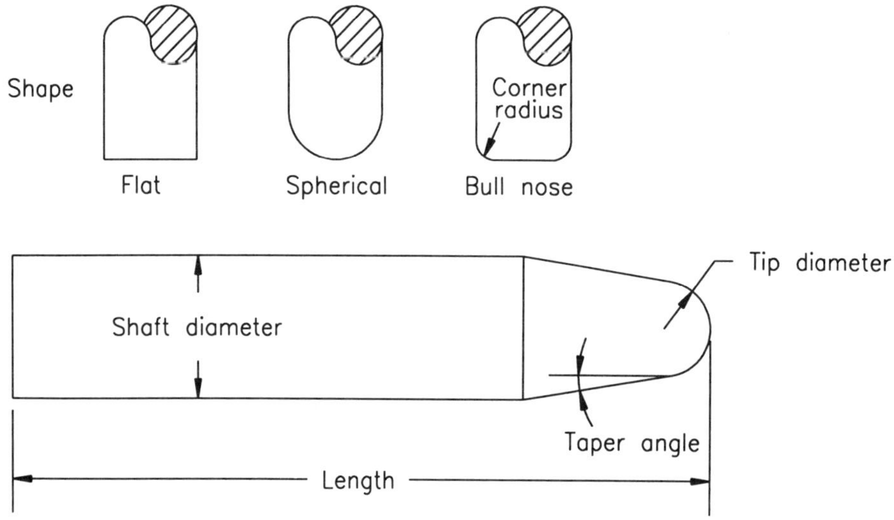

Figure 18.3

Define Tool Commands: **NC utils → Def. tools**

Tips 1. Tool reference

A tool must be defined by using the Def. tools utility before it can be used in generating toolpaths. Use a number to indicate the diameter of the tool. Mastercam provides a list of default tools. They use the 044 (without a decimal point) input format which means that four places are allowed before the decimal point and four places after the decimal point. For example, 5000 is equivalent to 0.5, and 12500 is equivalent to 1.25.

Use this legend to indicate the cutter shape:

FLT :	flat end cutter
SPH:	spherical (ball end) cutter
DRL:	drill
TAP:	tap
FAC:	face mill

Examples:

1250FLT:	1/8" flat end cutter
10000FLT:	1" flat end cutter
5000SPH:	1/2" ball end mill
7500DR L:	3/4" drill

2. Material file

Mastercam provides a material file that contains a set of default cutting speed and chip load for cutting various materials for **two** kinds of cutting tool materials; high speed steel (s) and carbide (c). The material file is listed below. The user can modify the material table to fit the application.

(Milling material table - material name shown in quotes - up to 20 characters) (SFM and Chip load per tooth are shown next)

"ALUM-S"	600	0.005	(Aluminum and Magnesium - HSS cutter)
"ALUM-C"	1000	0.005	(Aluminum and Magnesium - Carbide cutter)
"BRASS1-S"	250	0.005	(Brass and Bronze, Soft - HSS cutter)
"BRASS1-C"	1000	0.010	(Brass and Bronze, Soft - Carbide cutter)
"BRASS2-S"	150	0.003	(Brass and Bronze, Hard - HSS cutter)
"BRASS2-C"	400	0.005	(Brass and Bronze, Hard - Carbide cutter)
"COPPER-S"	150	0.005	(Copper - HSS cutter)
"COPPER-C"	1000	0.005	(Copper - Carbide cutter)
"CAST1-S"	75	0.005	(Cast Iron, Soft - HSS cutter)
"CAST1-C"	250	0.010	(Cast Iron, Soft - Carbide cutter)
"CAST2-S"	50	0.003	(Cast Iron, Hard - HSS cutter)
"CAST2-C"	200	0.005	(Cast Iron, Hard - Carbide cutter)
"100BHN-S"	25	0.004	(Steel - HSS cutter)
"100BHN-C"	450	0.005	(Steel - Carbide cutter)
"200BHN-S"	70	0.004	(Steel - HSS cutter)
"200BHN-C"	350	0.005	(Steel - Carbide cutter)
"300BHN-S"	40	0.003	(Steel - HSS cutter)
"300BHN-C"	250	0.005	(Steel - Carbide cutter)
"400BHN-S"	20	0.001	(Steel - HSS cutter)
"400BHN-C"	100	0.004	(Steel - Carbide cutter)
"500BHN-S"	10	0.001	(Steel - HSS cutter)
"500BHN-C"	75	0.004	(Steel - Carbide cutter)
"STAINLESS1-S"	35	0.003	(Stainless steel, Hard - HSS cutter)
"STAINLESS1-C"	250	0.003	(Stainless steel, Hard - Carbide cutter)
"STAINLESS2-S"	70	0.003	(Stainless steel, free machining - HSS cutter)
"STAINLESS2-C"	250	0.003	(Stainless steel, free machining - Carbide cutter)
"TITANIUM1-S"	35	0.003	(Titanium, under 100K PSI - HSS cutter)
"TITANIUM1-C"	150	0.004	(Titanium, under 100K PSI - Carbide cutter)
"TITANIUM2-S"	25	0.002	(Titanium, 100K - 135K PSI - HSS cutter)
"TITANIUM2-C"	120	0.003	(Titanium, 100K - 135K PSI - Carbide cutter)
"TITANIUM3-S"	15	0.001	(Titanium, 135K PSI and over - HSS cutter)
"TITANIUM3-C"	80	0.002	(Titanium, 135K PSI and over - Carbide cutter)
"FERR-H"	40	0.002	(Ferritic Low Alloys - HSS cutter)
"FERR-C"	150	0.003	(Ferritic Low Alloys - Carbide cutter)
"AUSTEN-H"	20	0.001	(Austenitic Alloys - HSS cutter)
"AUSTEN-C"	100	0.002	(Austenitic Alloys - Carbide cutter)
"NICKEL-H"	5	0.001	(Nickel Base Alloys - HSS cutter)
"NICKEL-C"	50	0.002	(Nickel Base Alloys - Carbide cutter)
"COBALT-H"	5	0.001	(Cobalt Base Alloys - HSS cutter)
"COBALT-C"	50	0.002	(Cobalt Base Alloys - Carbide cutter)

Project 1. 1

Three tool assemblies

In this project we are going to define three tool assemblies with the following information;

Holder type and shank size: BT-40

Three tools:

1" end mill
1/2" ball end mill
3/8" drill

Tooling Information

Tool type	Tool reference	Tool number	Diameter offset no.	Length offset no.	Cutter diameter	Corner radius	No. of flutes
1" end mill mill	10000FLT	1	21	1	1.0	0	2
1/2" ball end mill	5000SPH	5	25	5	0.5	0.25	3
3/8" drill	3750DRL	7	27	7	0.375	0	2

Define Tool Parameters

	T1	T5	T7
Top length	2.653	2.653	2.653
Top diameter	1.75	1.75	1.75
Taper angle	8.13°	8.13°	8.13°
Flange length	0.984	0.984	0.984
Flange diameter	2.479	2.479	2.479
End (adaptor) length	1.5	2.0	1.5
End (adaptor) diameter	1.75	2.25	1.5
End (adaptor) chamfer	0.375	0.0	0.0

Step 1. Initiate the define tool function.

Select **MAIN MENU → NC utils → Def. tools**

The Define Tools window should appear as below.

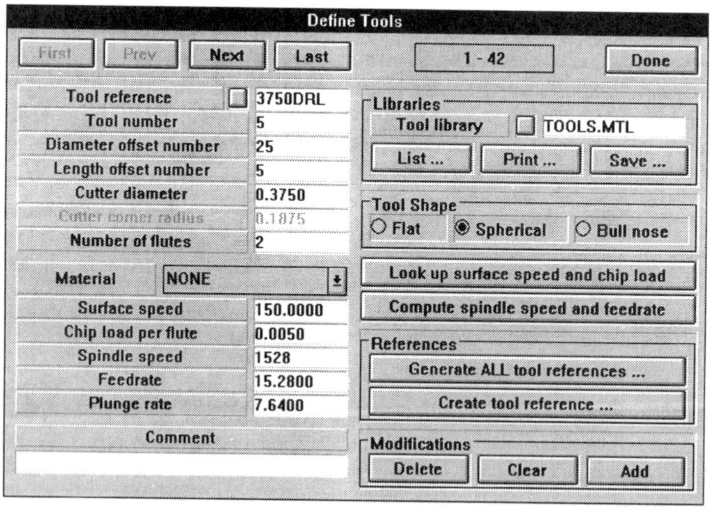

Step 2. Set the tooling parameters for the first tool (1" end mill).

Click on the **Add** button at the bottom of the right column of the Define Tools window
Set the tooling parameters as below.

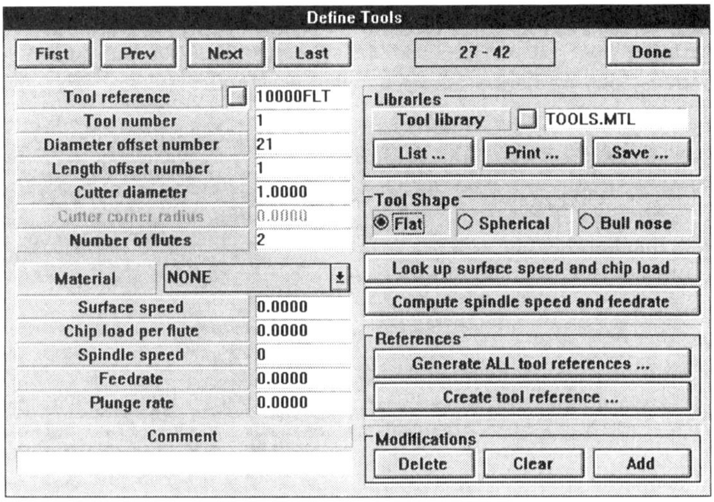

Step 3. Define machining parameters for the first tool.

Click on the button next to the **Material** button to get the material list to choose from
Select **ALUS-S**
You will see the default value for surface speed and chip load per flute automatically appear
Click on the **"Compute spindle speed and feedrate"** button in the middle of the right column to compute the spindle speed and feedrate

The machining parameters should resemble these.

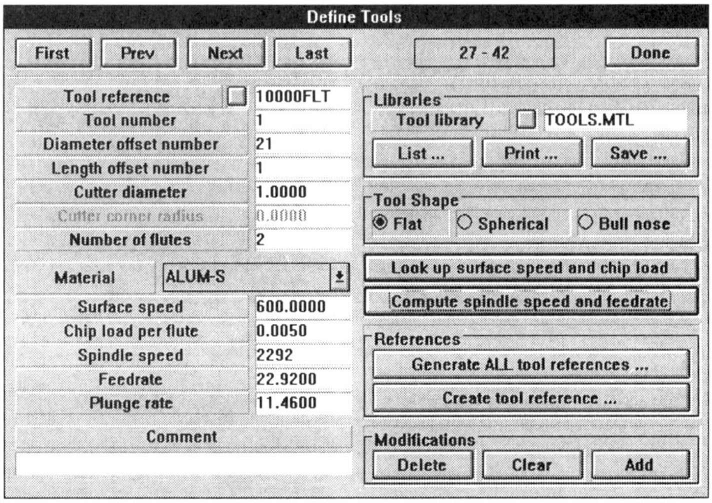

Step 4. Initiate tool reference menus.

Click on the **"Create tool reference"** button in the lower right corner of the window
Select **Gview → Isometric**
Press **Alt + F1** simultaneously and then press **F2** to fit the initial tool assembly on the screen

Step 5. Define the toolholder.

Select **Holder** from the Create tool reference menu
Set the toolholder parameters as below.

Top:	length = 2.653	diam.= 1.75	Taper angle = 8.13
Flange:	length = 0.984	diam.= 2.479	Lines drawn = 11
End:	length = 1.50	diam.= 1.75	chamfer length = 0.375

Step 6. Define the cutter.

Select **BACKUP → Tool**
Set the Tool Parameters menu as below:

Tool shape = Flat	
Tool length = 1.5	Shaft diam = 1.0
Taper angle = 0.0	Tip diameter = 0.0
Corner radius = 0.0	Lines drawn = 11

The new tool assembly appears as Figure 18.4.

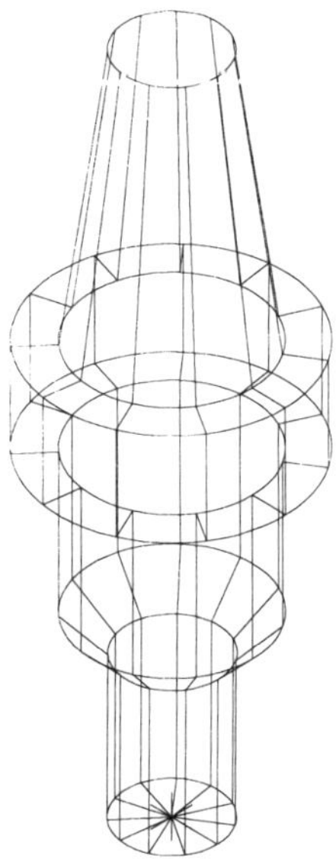

Figure 18.4 ☞

Step 7. Save the tool file.

Select **BACKUP → Save**
File name: **10000flt.ge3**
Select **OK** to save the tool geometry file
Click on **Yes** to delete the old file
Select **OK** to return back to the Define Tools menu

Step 8. Set the tooling parameters for the second tool (0.5" ball end mill).

Select **Add** in the bottom of the right column in the Define Tools window
Set the tooling parameters as below.

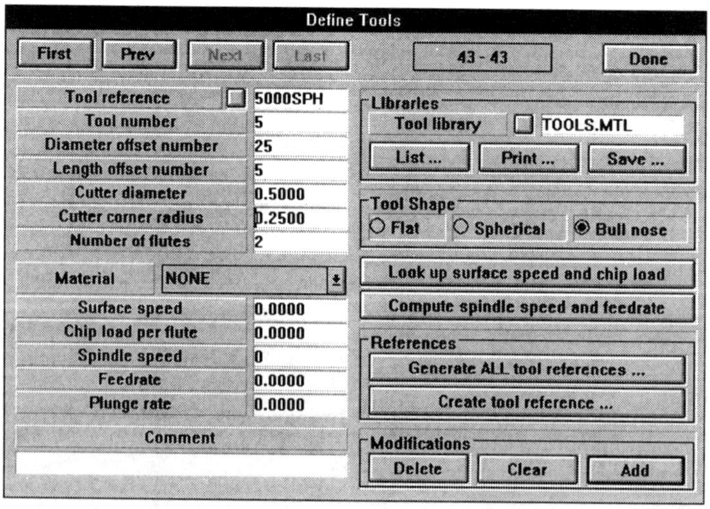

Step 9. Define the machining parameters.

Click on the button next to the **Material** button to get the material list to choose from
Select **ALUM-S**
Click on the **"Compute spindle speed and feedrate"** button in the middle of the right column to compute the spindle speed and feedrate

The machining parameters should be automatically set as below.

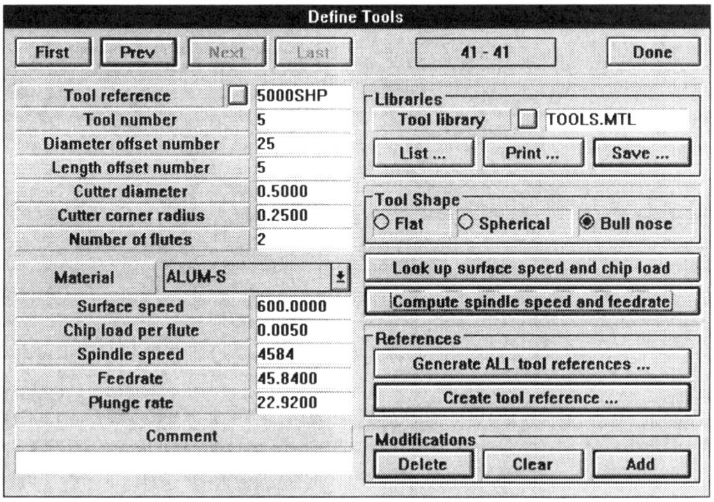

Step 10. Initiate create tool reference menus.

Click on the **"Create tool reference"** in the lower right corner of the window
Select **Gview → Isometric**
Press **Alt + F1** simultaneously
then press **F2** to fit the initial tool assembly drawing on the screen

Step 11. Define the toolholder.

Select **Holder** from the create tool reference menu
Set the toolholder parameters as below.

Top:	length = 2.653	diam.= 1.75	Taper angle = 8.13
Flange:	length = 0.984	diam.= 2.479	Lines drawn = 11
End:	length = 1.50	diam.= 1.75	chamfer length = 0.375

Step 12. Define the cutter.

Select **BACKUP → Tool**
Set the tool parameters as below.

Tool shape = Bull nose	
Tool length = 1.75	Shaft diam. = 0.5
Taper angle = 0.0	Tip diam. = 0.5
Corner radius = 0.25	Lines drawn = 11

The new tool assembly appears as Figure 18.5.

Figure 18.5 ☞

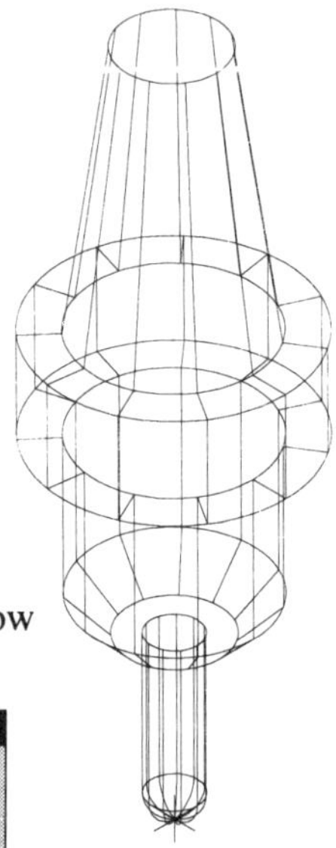

Step 13. Save the tool geometry.

Select **Save** from the create tool reference menu
Enter file name: **5000sph.ge3**
Select **yes** to delete the old file if necessary

Step 14. Define the third tool and set its tooling parameters.

Select **Add** in the bottom of right column in the Define Tools window
Set the tooling parameters as below.

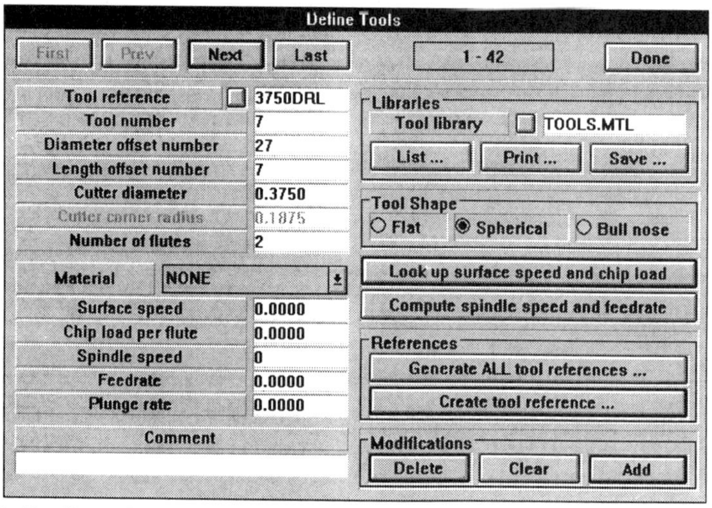

Step 15. Define the machining parameters.

Click on the button next to the **Material** button to get the material list to choose from
Select **ALUM-S**
Click on the **"Compute spindle speed and feedrate"** button in the middle of the right column to compute the spindle speed and feedrate
The machining parameters should be automatically set as below.

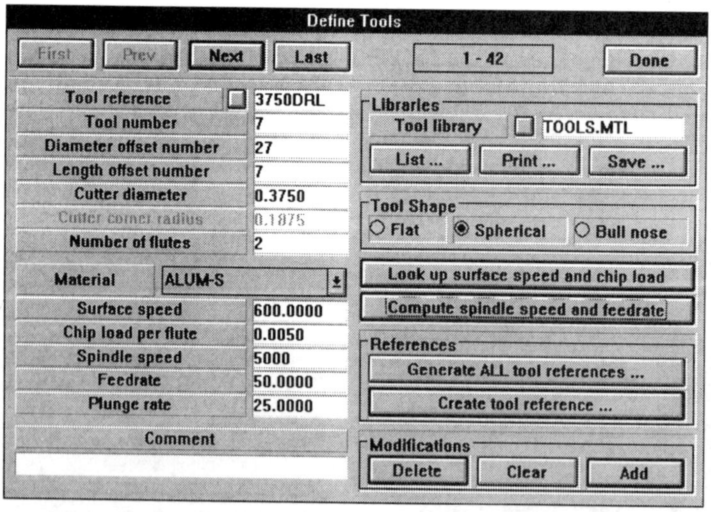

Step 16. Define the toolholder

Click on the **"Create tool reference"** in the lower right corner of the window
Select **Gview → Isometric**
Press **Alt + F1** simultaneously and
then press **F2** to fit the initial tool assembly drawing on the screen
Select **Holder** from the Create tool reference menu

Set the toolholder parameters as below.

Top:	length = 2.653	diam.= 1.75	Taper angle = 8.13
Flange:	length = 0.984	diam.= 2.479	Lines drawn = 11
End:	length = 1.50	diam.= 1.75	chamfer length = 0.375

Step 17. Define the cutter.

Select **BACKUP → Tool**
Set the tool parameters as below.

Tool shape = Spherical
Tool length = 3.0 Shaft diam. = 0.375
Taper angle = 0.0 Tip diameter = 0.375
Corner radius = 0.1875 Lines drawn = 11

The new tool assembly appears as Figure 18.6.

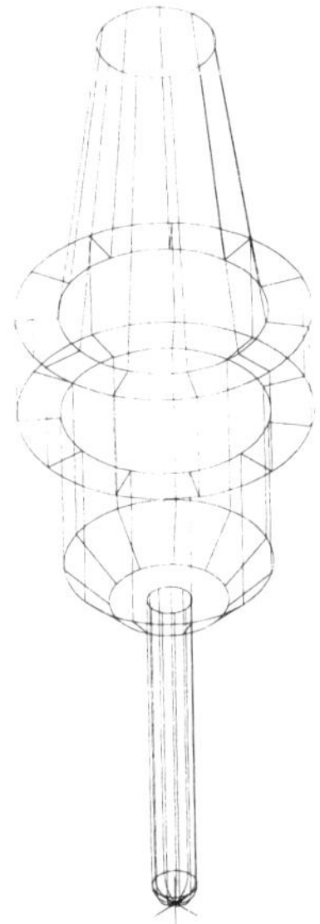

Figure 18.6 ☞

Step 18. Save the tool geometry file.

Select **BACKUP → Save**
enter file name: **3750drl.ge3**
Select **Yes** to delete the old file if necessary

Step 19. Save the tool library file.

Select **OK** to return back to the Define Tools window
Select **Save** from the Define Tools window
Enter file name: **tools.mtl**
Select **Yes** to delete the old file

Step 20. Return back to the NC utilities menu.

Select **Done** to return back to the NC utilities menu.

18.3 Setup Sheet

The toolpath (NCI) files contain cutter location data as well as tooling and machining information to machine a part. Mastercam uses **NC utils → Setup sh.** commands to extract tooling and machining information from the NCI file to generate setup sheets as a reference for machine setup persons and machine operators. A setup sheet consists of the following data:

- Tool number
- Diameter offset number
- Length offset number
- Tool diameter
- Feedrate
- Spindle speed
- Cutter compensation in control
- Total time for a particular tool
- Total time for the entire NCI file

A sample setup sheet is given below.

```
CUSTOMIZABLE MILL SETUP SHEET - MILL.SET

DATE PROCESSED = 02-17-95
PROGRAM NAME = CONTOUR2
PROGRAM NUMBER = 10

OPERATION = 2D-CONTOUR
TOOL REF = 05000FLT
TOOL NO = 5
TOOL DIA = .5
DIA OFFSET = 25
LEN OFFSET = 5
SPINDLE = 3000
FEEDRATE = 15.
CUTTER COMP = ON
**********************
TOOL FEED CUT LENGTH = 17.4487
TOOL RAPID TRAVERSE LENGTH = 2.0014
**********************
TOTAL TOOL TIME = 0 HOURS, 1 MINUTES, 11.8 SECONDS
**********************

TOTAL PART TIME = 0 HOURS, 1 MINUTES, 17.8 SECONDS
```

Project 2. 2

Generating a setup sheet

In this project we develop the procedure to generate a setup sheet from an NCI file created in project 6 of chapter 7. This project involves using two cutters to machine the part shown in Figure 18.7. The first cutter is a 1-in. end mill for facing the top flat surface and the second cutter is a 1/2-in. end mill for two pocketing operations.

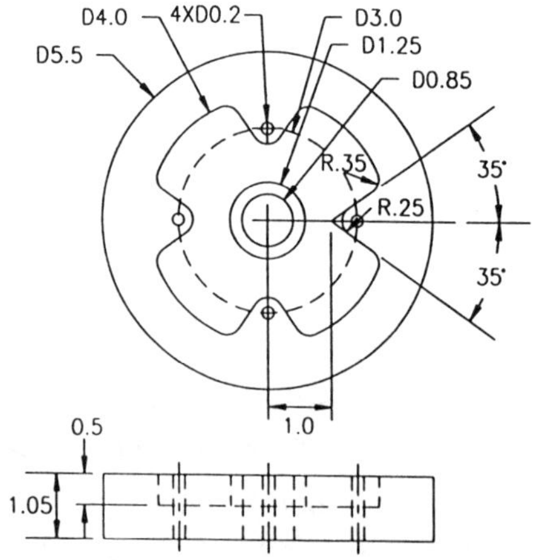

Figure 18.7

Step 1. Initiate Setup sh. commands.

Select **NC utils → Setup sh.**

Enter file name: **pocket2.nci** for NCI file

Enter file name: **pocket2.doc** for the setup file name to write

The system generates a setup sheet as below.

```
PROGRAM NAME = POCKET2
PROGRAM NUMBER = 10

OPERATION = POCKET....
TOOL REF = 10000FLT
TOOL NO = 1
TOOL DIA = 1.
DIA OFFSET = 21
LEN OFFSET = 1
SPINDLE = 1500
FEEDRATE = 10.
CUTTER COMP = OFF
**********************
TOOL FEED CUT LENGTH = 117.212
TOOL RAPID TRVERSE LENGTH = 7.8
**********************
TOTAL TOOL TIME = 0 HOURS, 11 MINUTES, 44.83 SECONDS
**********************

OPERATION = POCKET....
TOOL REF = 05000FLT
TOOL NO = 2
TOOL DIA = .5
DIA OFFSET = 22
LEN OFFSET = 2
SPINDLE = 3000
FEEDRATE = 10.
CUTTER COMP = OFF
**********************
TOOL FEED CUT LENGTH = 101.5014
TOOL RAPID TRAVERSE LENGTH = 30.139
**********************
TOTAL TOOL TIME = 0 HOURS. 10 MINUTES. 15.04 SECONDS
```

Step 2. Return to the NC utility menu.

Double-click the window button at the upper left corner, then press **Enter** to return to the NC utilities menu

Step 3. Print the setup sheet.

Select **File → Next menu → Print → Doc**

File name: **pocket2.doc**

Enter a comment:

Select **Ok** from the print window to print the setup sheet

The printed setup sheet should appear as below.

CUSTOMIZABLE MILL SETUP SHEET - MILL.SET
DATE PROCESSED = 02-17-95
PROGRAM NAME = POCKET2
PROGRAM NUMBER = 10

OPERATION = POCKET....
TOOL REF = 10000FLT
TOOL NO = 1
TOOL DIA = 1.
DIA OFFSET = 21

OFFSET = 1
SPINDLE = 1500
FEEDRATE = 10.
CUTTER COMP = OFF
****
TOOL FEED CUT LENGTH = 117.212
TOOL RAPID TRVERSE LENGTH = 7.8
****
TOTAL TOOL TIME = 0 HOURS, 11 MINUTES, 44.83 SECONDS
****
OPERATION = POCKET....
TOOL REF = 05000FLT
TOOL NO = 2
TOOL DIA = .5
DIA OFFSET = 22
LEN OFFSET = 2
SPINDLE = 3000
FEEDRATE = 10.
CUTTER COMP = OFF
****
TOOL FEED CUT LENGTH = 101.5014
TOOL RAPID TRAVERSE LENGTH = 30.139
****
TOTAL TOOL TIME = 0 HOURS, 10 MINUTES, 15.04 SECONDS
****

TOTAL PART TIME = 0 HOURS, 22 MINUTES, 11.87 SECONDS

18.4 Exercises

1. What are the three components of milling tools used in CNC mills and machining centers?

2. What are the two main components of a toolholder?

3. Explain how a toolholder is named.

4. What are the two common holder styles?

5. List the six shank taper numbers and describe their use.

6. Use a sketch to identify those variables Mastercam uses to define a toolholder.

7. What are the six variables Mastercam uses to define a cutter?

8. Define three tool assemblies with the following information:

Holder type and shank size: V-50

Three tools:

3/16" end mill

7/8" ball end mill

17/32" drill

Tooling Information:

Tool type	Tool reference	Tool number	Diameter offset no.	Length offset no.	Cutter diameter	Corner radius	No. of flutes
3/16" end mill	1875FLT	15	35	15	0.1875	0	3
7/8" ball end mill	8750SPH	16	36	16	0.5	0.4375	2
17/32" drill	5313DRL	10	30	10	0.5313	0	2

Define Tool Parameters

Use the information given in Table 18.1 to complete the required data below.

	T15	T16	T10
Top length			
Top diameter			
Taper angle			
Flange length			
Flange diameter			
End (adaptor) length			
End (adaptor) diameter End (adaptor) chamfer	1.75 0.375	2.25 0.0	1.5 0.0

9. What is the purpose of a setup sheet?

10. List the information contained in a setup sheet.

Chapter 19

Lathe Programming

Objectives:

1. Know lathe basics of coordinate systems, program zero, radius and diameter dimensioning.
2. Create part geometry for lathes.
3. Understand the features of five toolpath modules of lathes and know when to use each one.
4. Be familiar with common lathe parameters.

Overview

Many machining operations can be performed in a CNC lathe. These operations include facing, turning, profiling, grooving, drilling, boring, threading, chamfering, cutting off, and milling (in mill-turn machines). Chapters 1 and 2 presented essential information about CNC programming, machining, and operation. This chapter shows how to generate part programs for cutting parts with CNC lathes. It begins with lathe basics, and is followed by part geometry creation, toolpath modules, common parameters, and several examples of using various toolpath modules.

19.1 Lathe Basics

Coordinate Systems

Most CNC controls for lathes provide for controlling two basic axes. The axis and direction designations for a two-axis lathe are illustrated in Figure 19.1. The Z axis is parallel to the spindle axis and represents the carriage travel in the longitudinal direction. The X axis is perpendicular to the Z axis and represents the cross slide travel. The direction designations for the Z and X axes are given below.

+Z	Tool carriage moves away from the spindle head
- Z	Tool carriage moves toward the spindle head
+X	Cross slide moves away from the spindle axis
- X	Cross slide moves toward the spindle axis

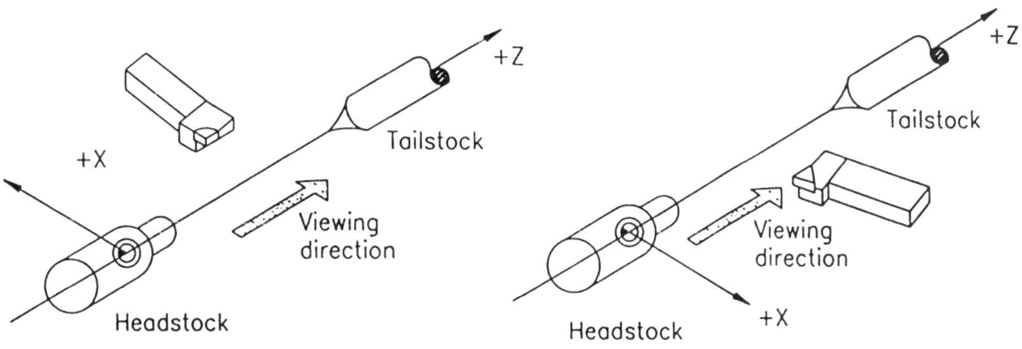

a. Left-handed (slant bed) b. Right-handed (Standard)

Figure 19.1 Coordinate Systems of CNC lathes

The coordinate system of a lathe can be either right-handed or left-handed, depending on which side of the spindle axis the turret is located.

Left-Handed Coordinate System

The turret is located to the left of the spindle center line (Z axis) when viewing the spindle axis from the headstock toward the tailstock (Figure 19.1a) in the left-handed coordinate system. Slant bed lathes use the left-handed coordinate system. Most CNC lathes use this left-handed coordinate system.

Right-Handed Coordinate System

The turret is located to the right of the spindle center line when observing from the headstock toward the tailstock (Figure 19.1b) in the right-handed coordinate system. Standard bed lathes use the right-handed coordinate system. Most desktop CNC lathes have the right-handed coordinate system.

Selection of Program Zero (Origin)

The program origin must be chosen before the part geometry can be created. There are **two** common ways to select program zeros for lathe works: located at right end face of the part (Figure 19.2a) and located at the chuck face (Figure 19.2b). The common practice in most shops is to use the right end face of the part as the program origin.

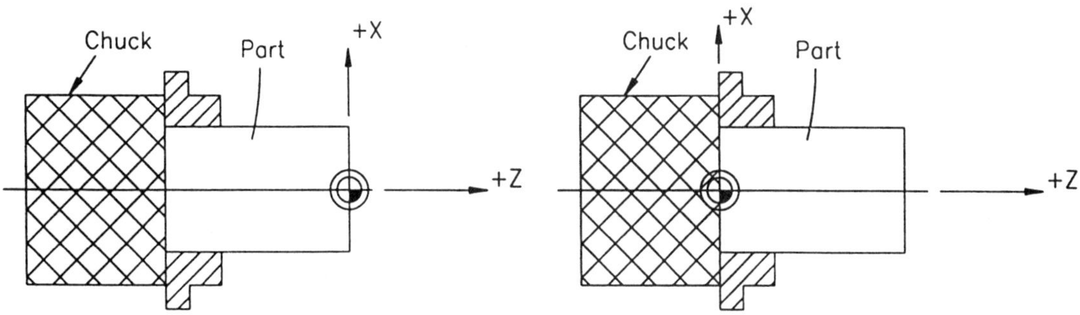

a. At Right face of the part b. At the chuck face

Figure 19.2 Selection of Program Zero

Radius and Diameter Dimensioning

The dimensions in the X direction can be specified in **two** ways: radius and diameter dimensioning. Mastercam uses the prefix letter **X** to indicate the radius value input and the letter **D** to specify the diameter value input. Table 19.1 shows the coordinate values of the significant points for the part shown in Figure 19.3 on the next page. Both radius and diameter values of X coordinates are given.

Table 19.1. Radius and diameter dimensioning

Point	X-coordinate		Z-coordinate
	Radius input	Diameter input	
O	0	0	0
A	X0.5	D1.0	0
B	X0.5	D1.0	-1.0
C	X0.75	D1.5	-1.0
D	X0.75	D1.5	-2.0
E	X1.25	D2.5	-2.0
F	X1.25	D2.5	-3.0

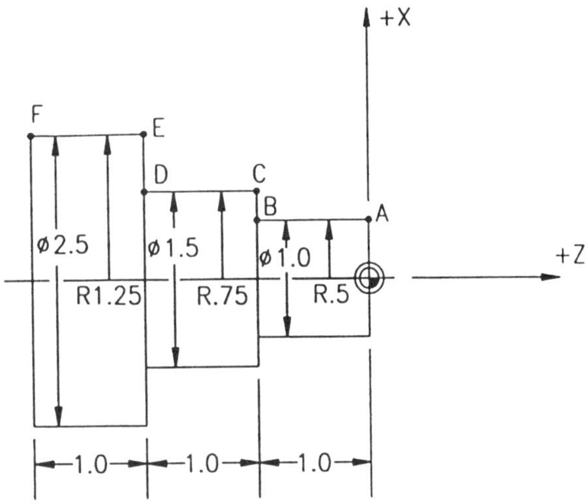

Figure 19.3 Radius and Diameter dimensioning

19.2 Creating Part Geometry

Most parts machined on a CNC lathe are symmetrical about the Z axis. Therefore, they require only one-half of the part geometry to be created. The techniques used in previous chapters for creating and editing part geometries for milling parts are applicable for turning except for the following two differences:

- Only two axes (X and Z) are used
- Horizontal direction represents the Z axis and the vertical direction is the X axis

Three projects with step-by-step instructions are presented in this section.

Project 1. 1

The part to be machined is shown in Figure 19.4a. Assume that the raw material has the size of ϕ4.0 x 4.05. The part geometry to be used to generate the toolpath is given in Figure 19.4b.

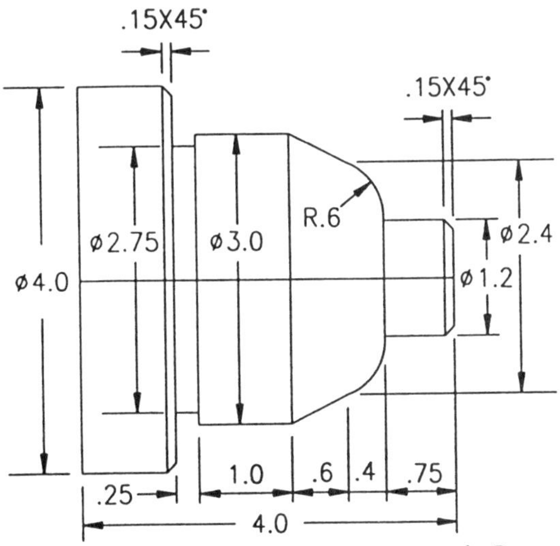

a. Dimensioned part

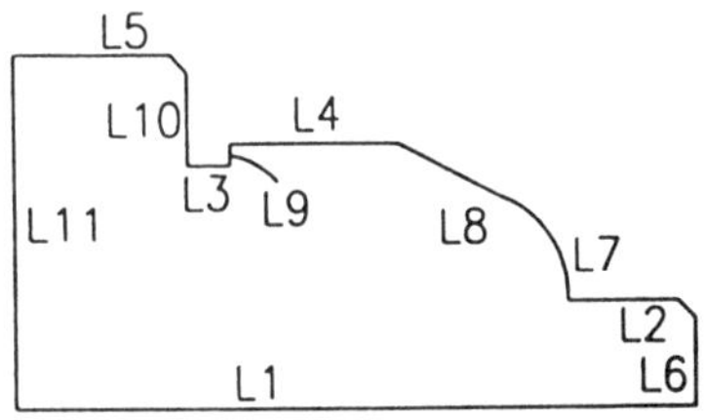

b. Part geometry

Figure 19.4 Lathe example 1

Step 1. Enter Mastercam lathe.

Type **Win** to enter Windows
Double-click the **Mastercam** lathe icon
Press **F9** to display the coordinate axes on the screen

The screen should look like Figure 19.5, with the MAIN MENU on the left side and two coordinate axes in the middle. In the following example we will rough sketch the appropriate horizontal and vertical lines. Then we will trim them back to their required lengths. This method is very efficient when working from a print.

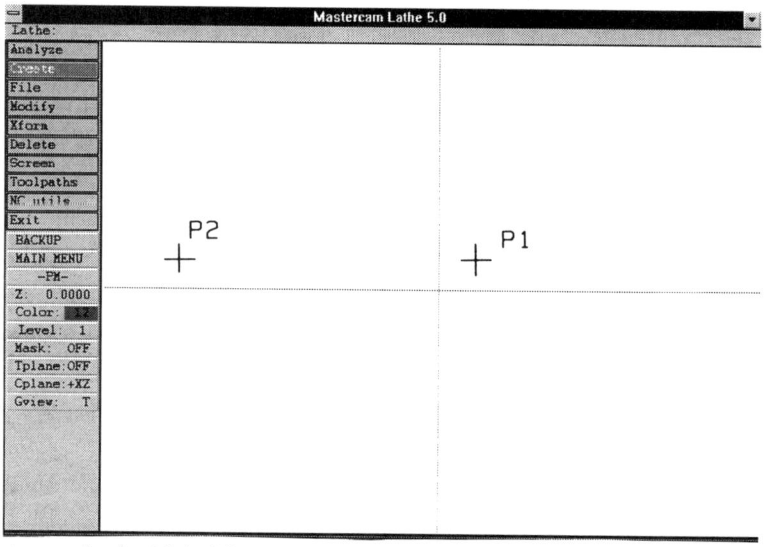

Figure 19.5 Mastercam Lathe Main Menu

⌛**Tips** 1. The system will prompt you to enter two points which are used to decide the length of the line. Pick these two points at the approximate positions of the two ends of the line. Do not be concerned with the X-position of the point.

2. Next a temporary horizontal line will appear on the screen. You are then prompted to enter the X coordinate value of the line. The value you enter at this prompt must be the exact X value of the line.

Step 2. Create the first horizontal line.
Use the pick points in Figure 19.5.

Select **Create → Line → Horizontal**
Respond to the following three prompts to complete line L1:
Specify the first endpoint: pick at **P1**
Specify the second endpoint: pick at **P2**
Enter the X coordinate (x.x): **0** ←
Press **F3** to remove the two axis lines.
The line L1 now appears on the screen like Figure 19.6.

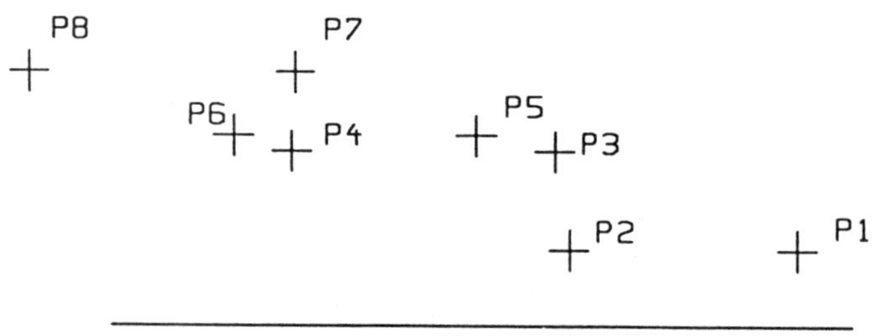

Figure 19.6

Step 3. Create the remaining four horizontal lines using pick points in Figure 19.6.

Pick at **P1** and **P2** then enter **0.6** ← for L2
Pick at **P3** and **P4** then enter **1.375** ← for L3
Pick at **P5** and **P6** then enter **1.5** ← for L4
Pick at **P7** and **P8** than enter **2.0** ← for L5

The drawing with five horizontal lines should look like Figure 19.7.

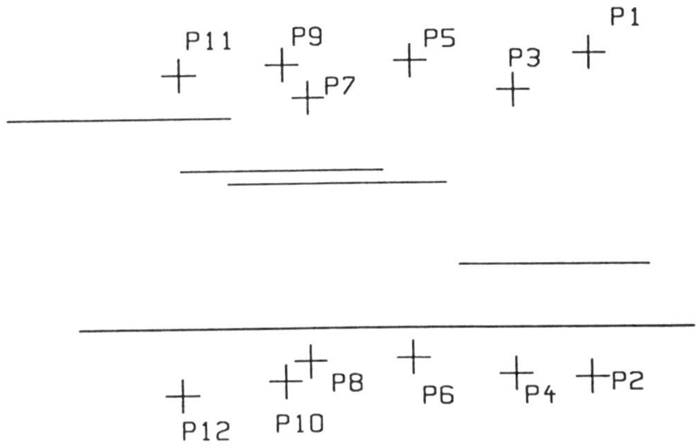

Figure 19.7

Step 4. Create six vertical lines. Use the pick points in Figure 19.7.
Select **BACKUP → Vertical**

Note: The hints given in step 2 are applicable to constructing vertical lines except that the system will prompt for a Z value for the line instead of an X value.

Respond to the following three prompts to complete line L6:

Specify the first endpoint: pick at **P1**
Specify the second endpoint: pick at **P2**
Enter the Z coordinate (x.x): **0** ←

To complete the remaining five vertical lines, pick at two points for each entry of the following Z values:

Pick at **P3** and **P4** and then enter **-0.75** ← for L7
Pick at **P5** and **P6** and then enter **-1.75** ← for L8
Pick at **P7** and **P8** and then enter **-2.75** ← for L9
Pick at **P9** and **P10** and then enter **-3.0** ← for L10
Pick at **P11** and **P12** and then enter **-4.0** ← for L11

Your drawing should appear as Figure 19.8 on the following page.

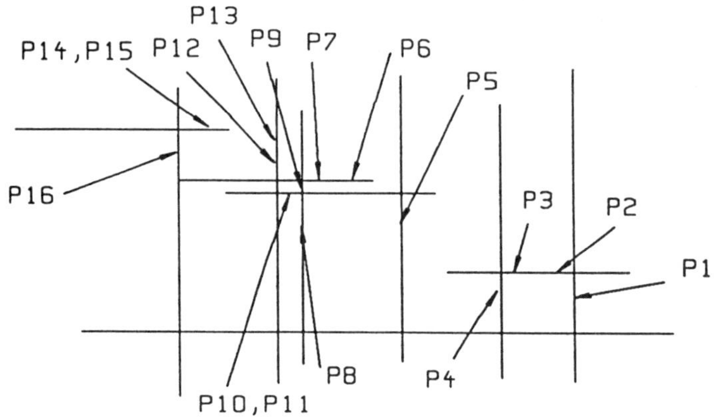

Figure 19.8

Step 5. Trim lines using the pick points in Figure 19.8.

Select **MAIN MENU → Modify → Trim → 2 entities**

Note: Pick the segment of the line you want to keep.

Sequentially pick at the points shown in Figure 19.8 to complete the trimming selection. The trimmed drawing should look like Figure 19.9.

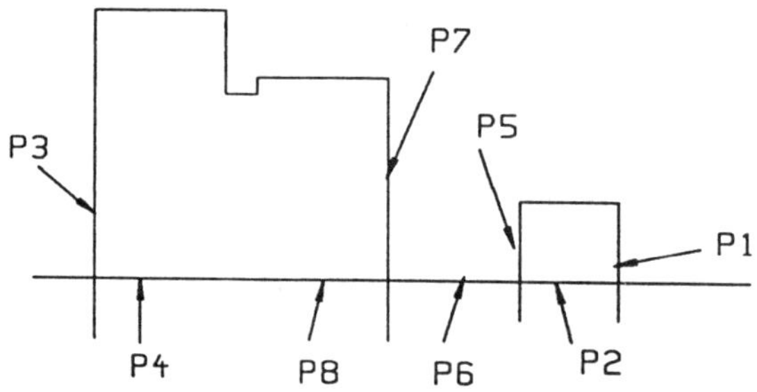

Figure 19.9

Step 6. Trim the lower half of the verical lines. Use the pick points in Figure 19.9.

Select **BACKUP → 1 entity**

Sequentially pick at the points to complete the trimming selection.

The final trimmed lines should appear as Figure 19.10.

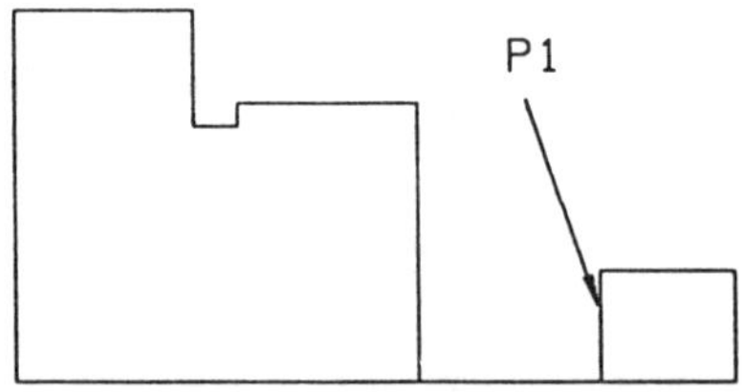

Figure 19.10

Step 7. Create an arc. Use the pick point in Figure 19.10 on the previous page.

Select **MAIN MENU → Create → Arc → Endpoints → Endpoint**
Pick at **P1** for the first point
Enter **1.2,-1.15** for the second point
Enter **0.6** for the arc radius

Pick the second arc from the right that appears on the screen.

The arc appears as shown in Figure 19.11.

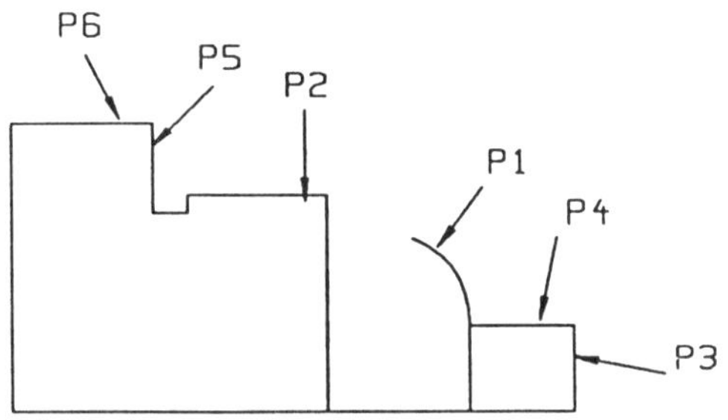

Figure 19.11

Step 8. Create a line using the pick points in Figure 19.11.

Select **MAIN MENU → Create → Line → Endpoints → Endpoint**
Pick at **P1** and **P2** to complete the line

Step 9. Create two chamfers. Still use the pick points in Figure 19.11.

Select **MAIN MENU → Create → Next Menu → Chamfer → Distance**
Enter the first distance (0.25): **0.15** ←
Enter the second distance (0.25): **0.15** ←
Pick at **P3** and **P4** to complete the first chamfer
Pick at **P5** and **P6** to complete the second chamfer

The drawing with two chamfers appears in Figure 19.12.

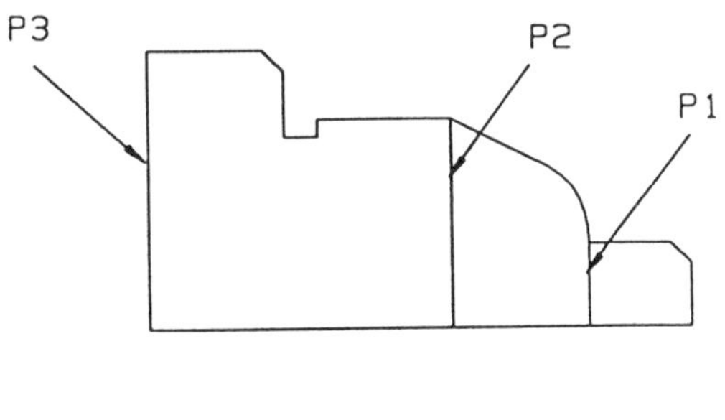

Figure 19.12

Step 10. Delete three vertical lines. Use the pick points in Figure 19.12 on the previous page.

Select **MAIN MENU → Delete**
Pick at **P1**, **P2**, and **P3**

The final drawing should look like Figure 19.13.

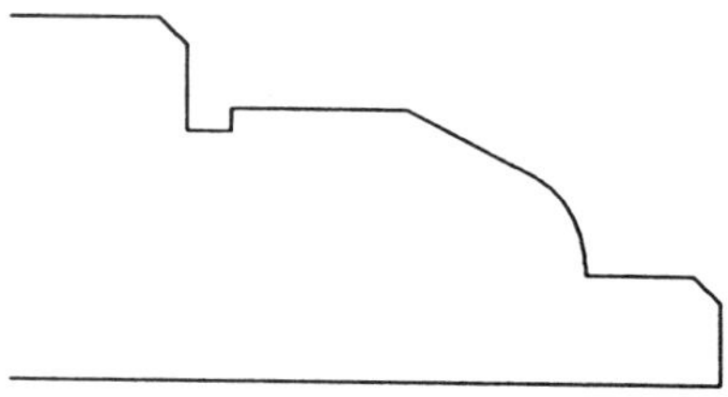

Figure 19.13

Step 11. Save the drawing. Use the file name **LATHE1**.

Select **MAIN MENU → File → Save →Geometry**
Enter a file name: type **lathe1** ←

Project 2. 2

Construct a part geometry for machining the part shown in Figure 19.14a. The part geometry to be used to generate the toolpath is illustrated in Figure 19.14b. In this example we will use a different construction method to build the contour of the part. The line profile is constructed by using the multi-line command.

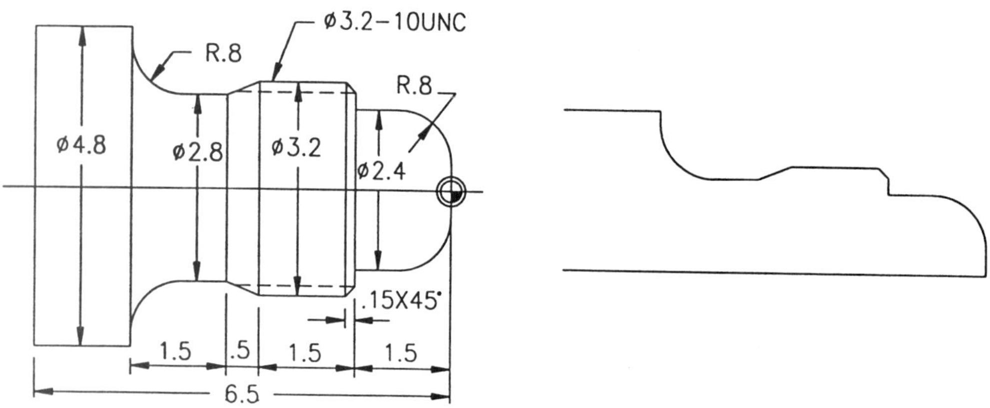

a. Dimensioned part
b. Part geometry
Figure 19.14 Lathe example 2

Step 1. Enter Mastercam lathe.

If you are already in the Lathe program: Skip to Step 2.

Type **Win** to enter Windows
Double-click the **Mastercam** lathe icon to enter the lathe system

Figure 19.15 Mastercam lathe Main Menu

Step 2. Create the line profile.

The line profile can be created easily by using the multiple-line command. It requires two endpoints to generate the first line, then from the second line and on, each line only requires its endpoint.

Select **MAIN MENU** → **Create** → **Line** → **Multi**
Specify endpoint 1: **2.4,-6.5** ←
Specify endpoint 2: **2.4,-5** ←
Specify endpoint 3: **1.4,-5** ←
Specify endpoint 4: **1.4,-3.5** ←
Specify endpoint 5: **1.6,-3.** ←
Specify endpoint 6: **1.6,-1.5** ←
Specify endpoint 7: **1.2,-1.5** ←
Specify endpoint 8: **1.2,0** ←
Specify endpoint 9: **0,0** ←

Press **Alt** + **F1,** then **F2** to fit the drawing on the screen

The drawing should look like Figure 19.16.

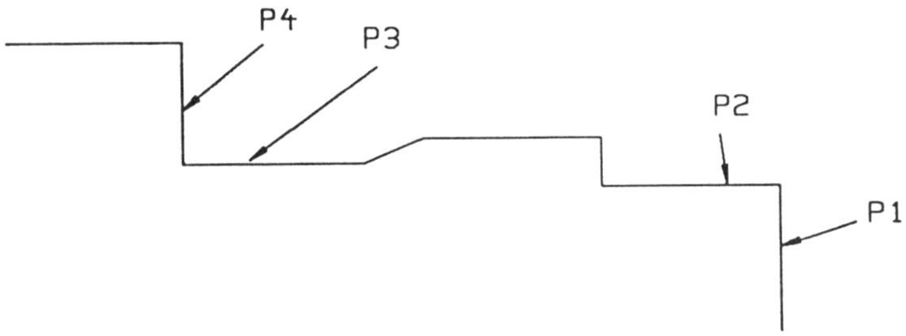

Figure 19.16

Step 3. Create two fillets. Use the pick points in Figure 19.16.
Select **MAIN MENU** → **Modify** → **Fillet** → **Radius**
Enter the fillet radius (0.25): **.8** ←
Pick at **P1** and **P2** to generate the first fillet
Pick at **P3** and **P4** to complete the second fillet

The drawing on the screen should resemble Figure 19.17.

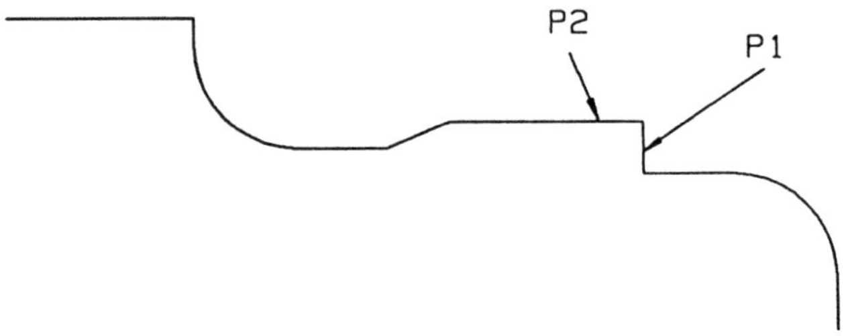

Figure 19.17

Step 4. Create a chamfer. Use the pick points in Figure 19.17.

Select **MAIN MENU → Create → Next Menu → Chamfer → Distances**
Enter the first distance (0.15): **.15** ←
Enter the second distance (0.15): **.15** ←
Pick at **P1** and **P2** to complete the chamfer

Your drawing now becomes Figure 19.18.

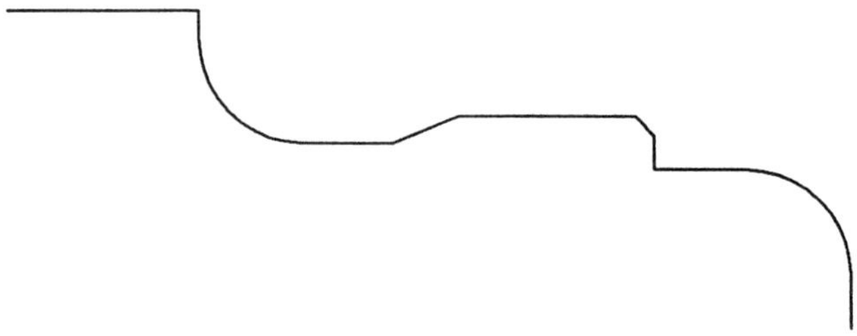

Figure 19.18

Step 5. Create a center line.

Select **MAIN MENU → Create → Line → Endpoints**
Specify the first endpoint: **0,.5** ←
Specify the second endpoint: **0,-7** ←

The complete geometry profile should appear as in Figure 19.19.

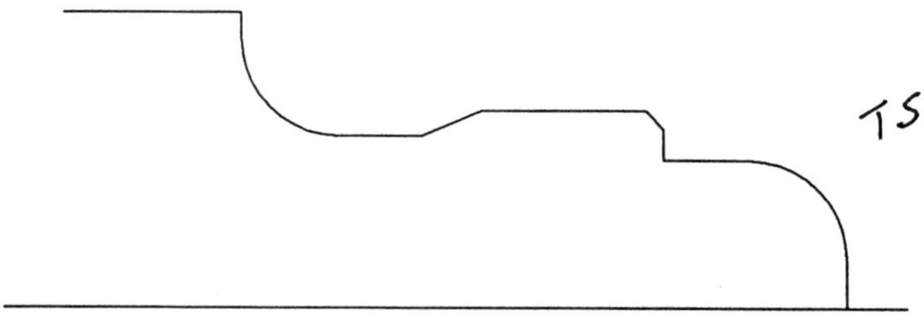

Figure 19.19

Step 6. Save the drawing. Use the file name **lathe2**.

Select **MAIN MENU → File → Save → Geometry**

Enter the file name **lathe2**

Project 3.

3

Figure 19.20a shows a part done with an internal bore. The geometry profile to be used for this part is shown in Figure 19.20b.

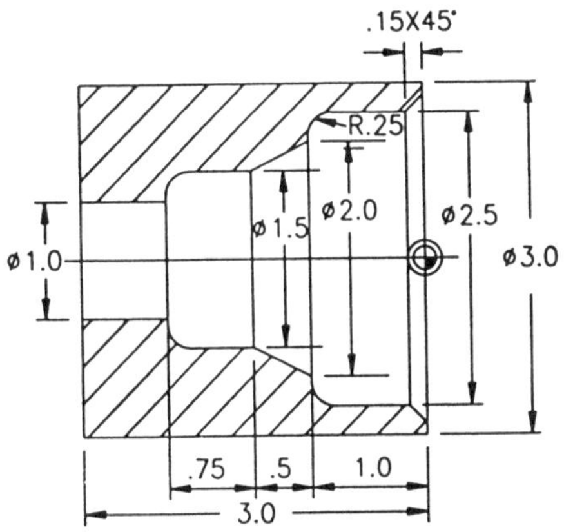

a. Dimensioned part

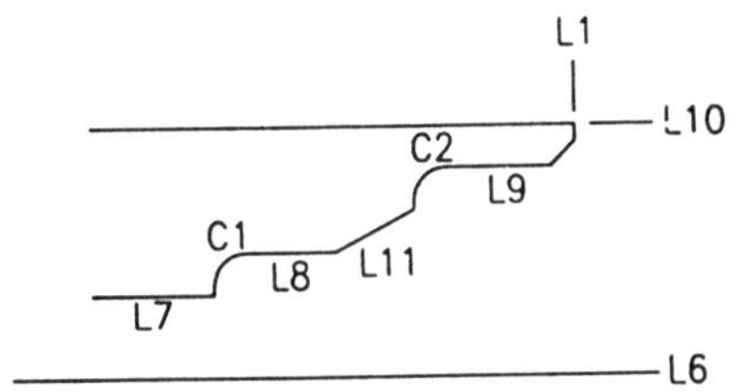

b. Part geometry

Figure 19.20 Lathe example 3

Step 1. Enter Mastercam Lathe.

If you are already in the Lathe program, go to Step 2.

Type **Win** to enter Windows

Double-click the **Mastercam** lathe icon to enter the lathe system.

Select lathe by typing **lathe386**

Step 2. Create the line profile.

Select **MAIN MENU → Create → Line → Multi**
To complete the line profile, enter the following coordinates sequentially as the system prompts:
1.5,-3 ←
1.5,0 ←
1.25,0 ←
1.25,-1 ←
1,-1 ←
.75,-1.5←
.75,-2.25 ←
.5,-2.25 ←
.5,-3 ←
Your drawing should appear as Figure 19.21.

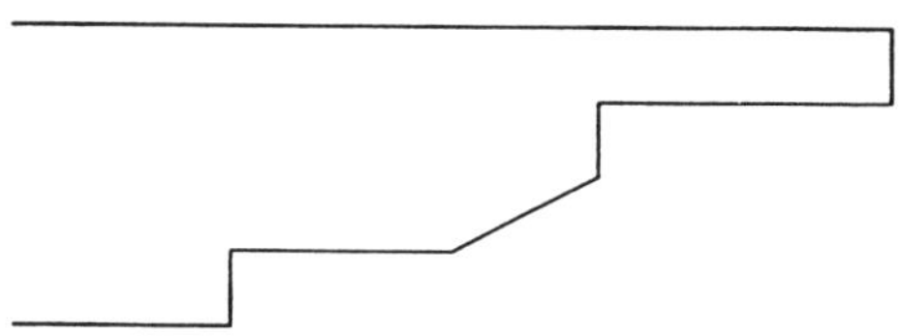

Figure 19.21

Step 3. Create the center line.

Select **BACKUP → Endpoints**
Specify the first point: **0,.5** ←
Specify the second point: **0,-3.5** ←
The drawing now looks like Figure 19.22.

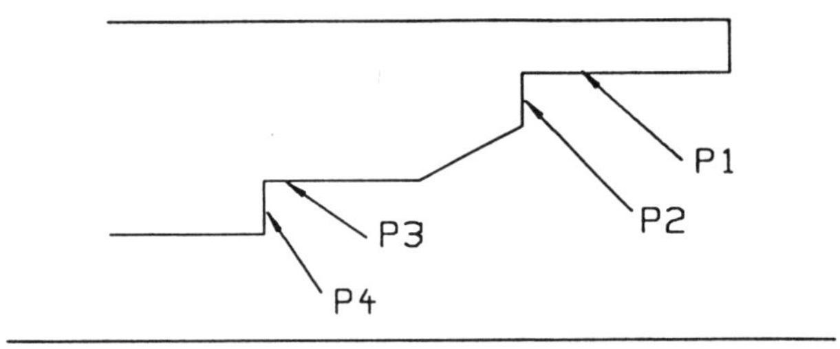

Figure 19.22

Step 4. Create two fillets. Use the pick points in Figure 19.22.

Select **MAIN MENU → Modify → Fillet → Radius**
Enter **.25** for radius value
Pick at **P1** and **P2** to complete the first fillet (Neglect the zero length line warning)
Pick at **P3** and **P4** to complete the second fillet

The drawing now should resemble Figure 19.23.

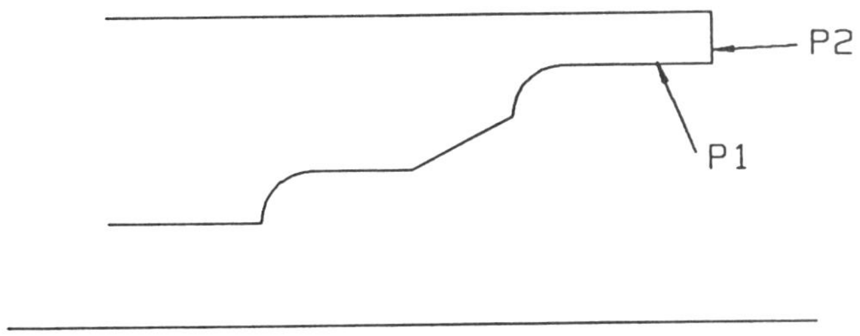

Figure 19.23

Step 5. Create a chamfer. Use the pick points in Figure 19.23.

Select **MAIN MENU → Create → Next Menu → Chamfer → Distances**
Enter first distance (.25): **.15** ←
Enter second distance (.25): **.15** ←
Pick at **P1** and **P2** to complete the chamfer

The complete geometry profile now appears in Figure 19.24.

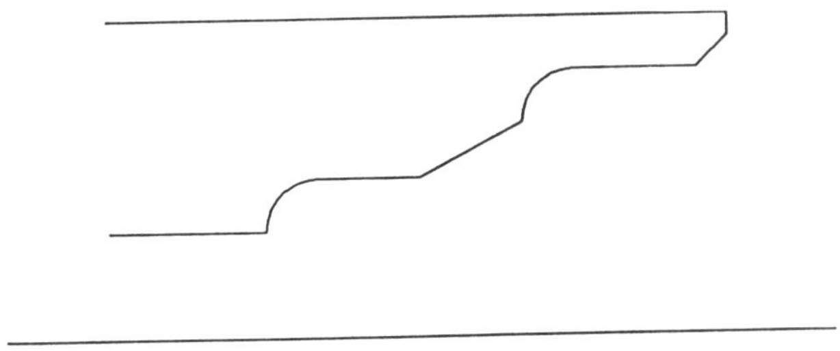

Figure 19.24

Step 6. Save the drawing. Use the filename **lathe3**.

Select **MAIN MENU → File → Save→ Geometry**
Enter the file name **lathe3** ← to complete the save

19.3 Toolpath Modules

Mastercam lathe system provides **five** toolpath modules to generate the toolpaths for producing a part. These modules include rough, finish, groove, thread, and drill. Table 19.2 on the next page summarizes the features and applications of these five toolpath modules. The detailed presentation of these modules is given after the common parameters section.

Table 19.2 Lathe toolpath modules

Module	Description	Application	Illustration
Rough	Generate the toolpaths to rough the part to its approximated shape and size for future finishing cuts.	Roughing external and internal part contours.	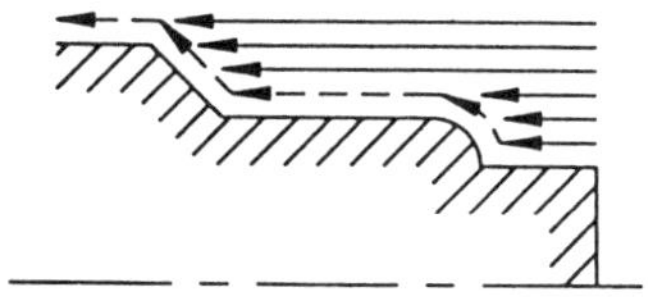
Finish	Generate the toolpaths to finishing cut the profiles.	Finishing cut along the OD, ID, or facing contours.	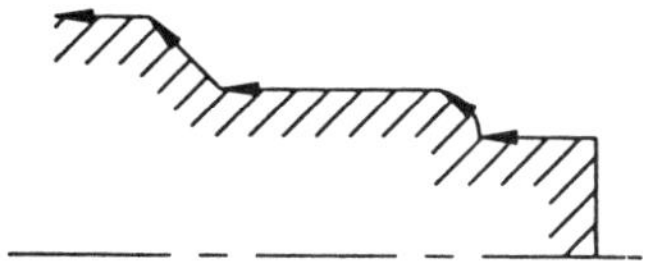
Groove	Generate the toolpaths to rough the grooves.	Grooving external or internal grooves. Roughing a casting by using the groove module.	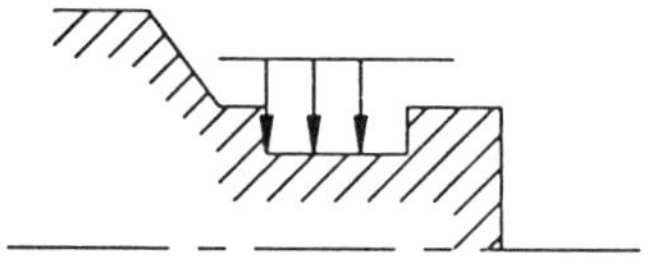
Thread	Generate the toolpaths to cut various types of threads.	Threading external or internal straight and taper threads.	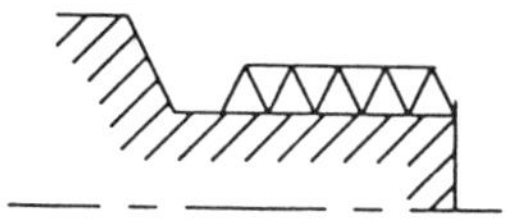
Drill	Generate the toolpaths to drill, bore, and tap holes.	Performing hole operations such as drilling, boring, and tapping.	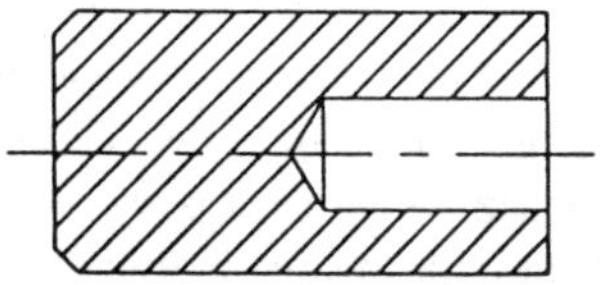

19.4 Lathe Common Parameters

Mastercam toolpath modules use **two** sets of parameters to define machining variables: common NC parameters and module specific parameters. As their names imply, common NC parameters are applied to all toolpath modules while module specific parameters are unique to a particular toolpath module. A sample of the lathe common NC parameter window is shown below. Although this parameter window is for roughing operations, you will find similar parameter windows for other operations.

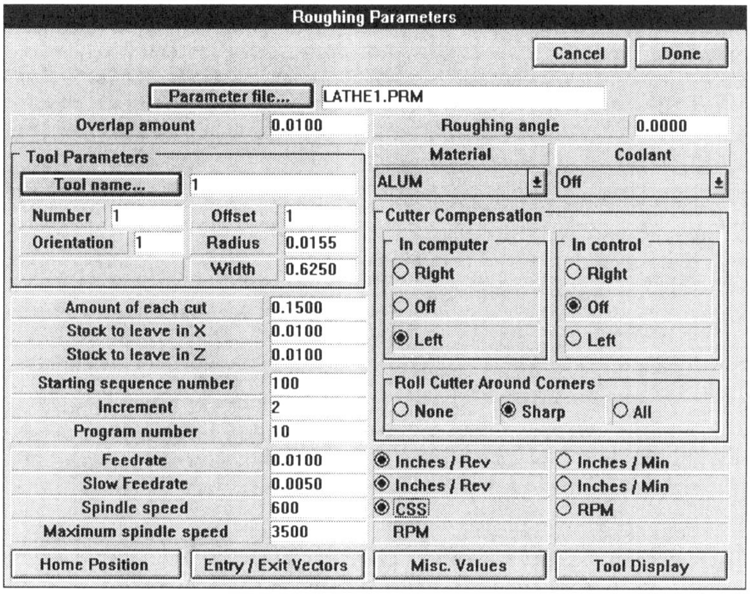

The lathe common parameters can be classified into **eight** groups:

Parameter and material file	Tool definition
Machining	Stock,
Cutter compensation	Miscellaneous
Tool positioning	Tool display

Parameter and Material File

Two parameters are in this category: parameter style and material file. The parameter file stores all the specific parameter settings for the current operation. The system automatically names the parameter file (a *.PRM file) to the *.GE3 file name. For example, LATHE1.PRM is assigned as the parameter file name for a part geometry file named LATHE1.GE3. The user can change the file name by clicking on the parameter file button, then selecting a name from the list that appears.

• Material File

The material file contains a list of material types and their default machining data (CSS and IPR) and saved in the file name LMATL.DOC (for inch unit system) or LMATL.MET (for the Metric unit system).

Click on the button underneathe the Material. The system will prompt with a list of materials as shown here ☞. Click on the desired material type. The value for these machining parameters will be automatically set when the material type is chosen.

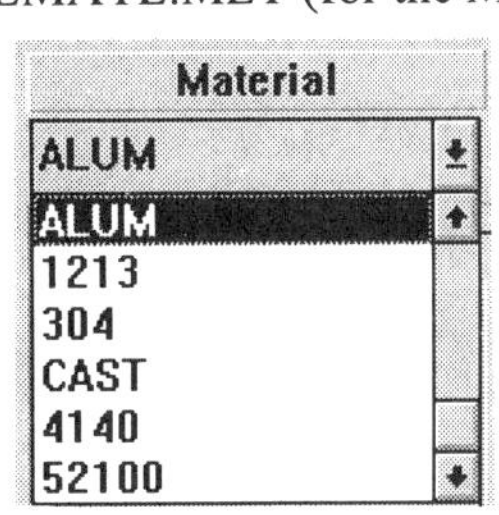

Tool Definition

Turning tools are made with a small, rounded nose at the tool tip to increase the strength of the tip, enhance tool life, reduce stress concentration, help heat dissipation, and produce a smooth surface. This small, rounded nose is referred to as the tool nose and its radius is called the tool nose radius (Figure 19.25).

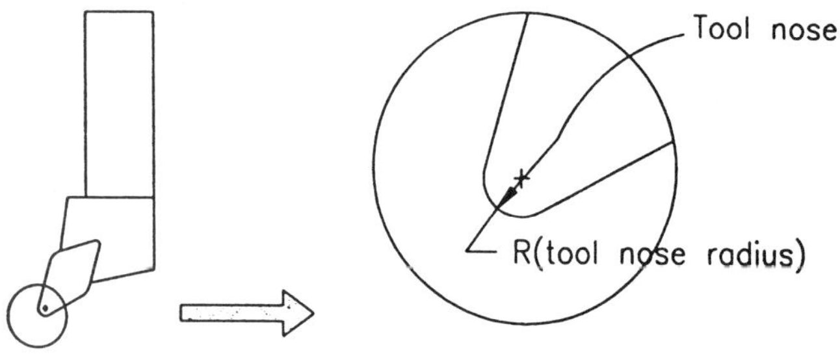

Figure 19.25 Tool nose definition

The imaginary tool nose is often used as the reference point for programming the tool path. It is defined as the intersection point between the two lines that are tangent to the tool nose and parallel to the X and Z axes, respectively (Figure 19.26). The use of an imaginary tool nose generates precise tool paths that are parallel to either the X or Z axis. However, it produces excessive cutting or insufficient cutting on taper and circular paths, depending on the orientation of the cutting vector. When the tool nose radius is very small, the cutter path error may be neglible. However, as the tool nose radius becomes larger, its effect on the actual cutting path should not be ignored. These cutting path errors can be compensated by using the TNR compensation command which is controlled by the cutter compensation in control parameter.

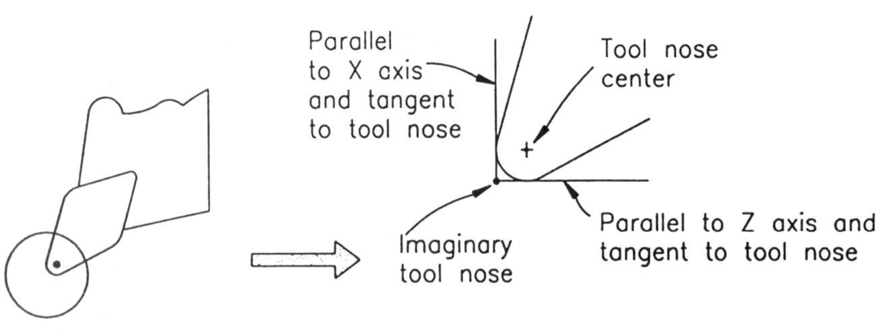

Figures 19.26 Imaginary tool nose definition

To properly use TNR compensation, a tool must be adequately defined by the following **six** variables: Tool name, Number, Offset number, Orientation, tool nose Radius and Width.

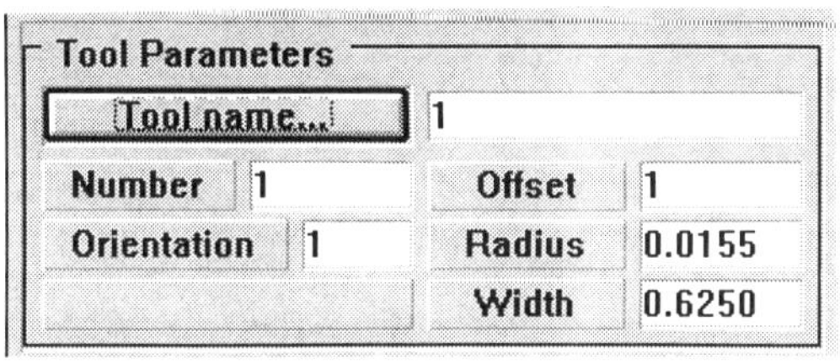

• Tool Name

This parameter is used to access the tool geometry (*.GE3) and definition (*.LTL) files. Mastercam Lathe System provides 35 tools in the tool library as shown in Figure 19.27.

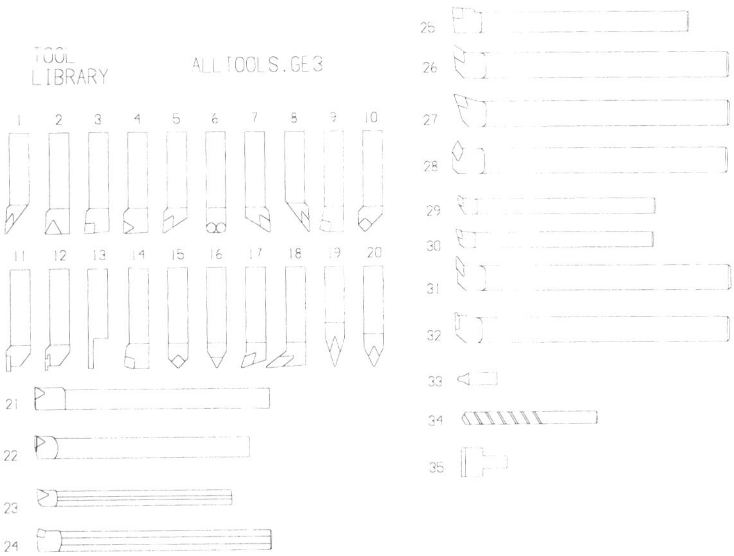

Figure 19.27

The system allows you to define new tools to generate toolpaths. See Chapter 20 for details on defining new turning tools.

Click on the Tool name button to select a tool number from the list. After entering the tool number, the other five parameters associated with the Chosen tool number will be automatically set.

• Number (Tool Number)

This variable is used to output a tool number to the part program. A number of 5, for example, will give the tool number command **T5** to the part program. A tool number normally represents the tool position in the turret or tool magazine. The tool position number ranges from 6 to 24 depending on the size of the machine and the number of turret used. It is recommended that the specified tool number must match the actual tool station on the turret.

• Offset (Offset Number)

This variable outputs a tool offset number to the part program. The tool offset number normally used together with the tool number is in the form

T0101

```
T0101
| | |_ tool offset number
| |_ tool number
|_ tool function
```

A tool offset number physically locates a register, which is a storage space, in the control and stores the following information there:

Offset number	Offset value in X axis (OFX)	Offset value in Z axis (OFZ)	Tool nose radius comp. value (OFR)	Direction of imaginary tool nose (OFT)
01	0	0	0.032	1
02	0.15	0.05	0.016	1

Note: A tool offset number can be different from the tool number (ex. T0105).

• Orientation (direction of imaginary tool nose)

The tool orientation is indicated by a number in the range of 1 to 8, with each number representing a tool nose vector. The vector is viewed from the tool nose center to the imaginary tool nose. Numbers 1 to 4 indicate a tool nose vector being in the first, second, third, or fourth quadrants, respectively (Figure 19.28). Their toolholders are held in the X direction. The numbers 5 to 8 are used to define the facing tools in the four quadrants, accordingly (Figure 19.29). Facing tools have their toolholders parallel to the Z axis.

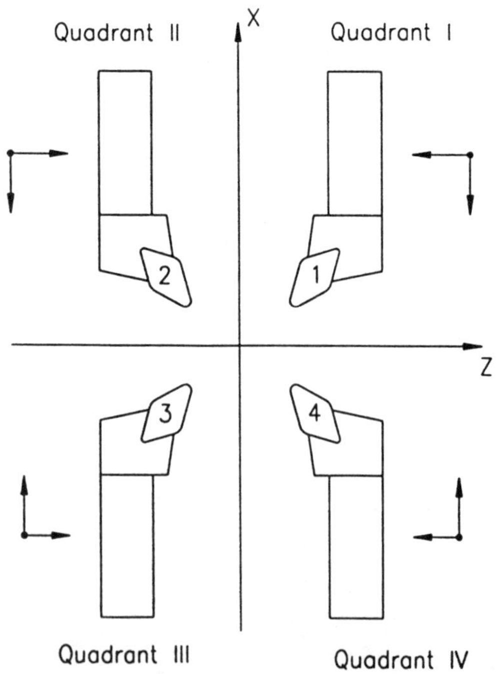

Figures 19.28 Orientation of turning tools

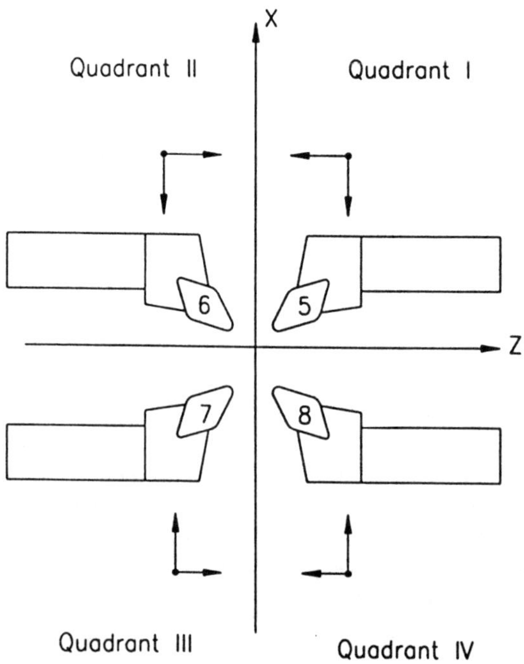

Figure 19.29 Orientation of facing tools

Figure 19.30 shows some typical turning tools used in the slant bed lathes that have the left-handed coordinate system. Figure 19.31 is for standard bed lathes that have the right-handed coordinate system.

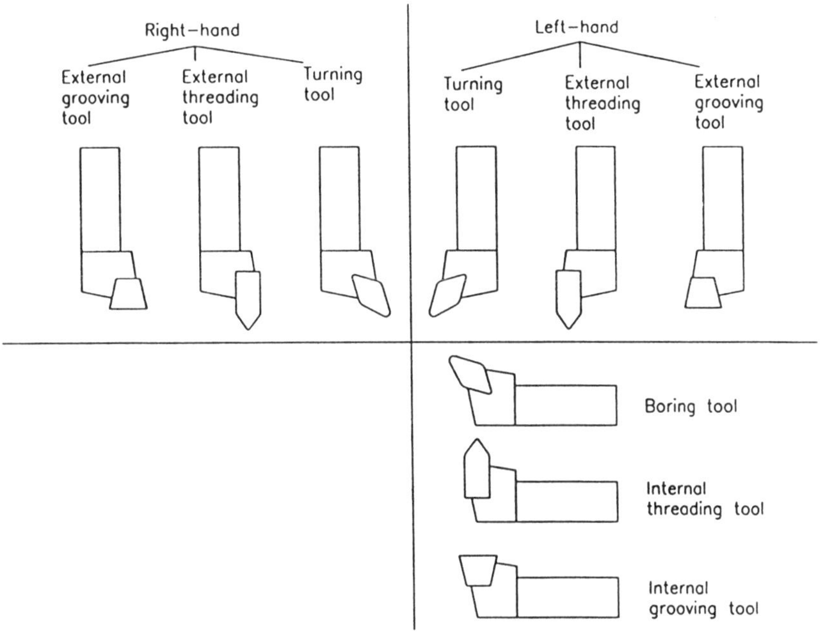

Figures 19.30 Typical slant bed lathe tools

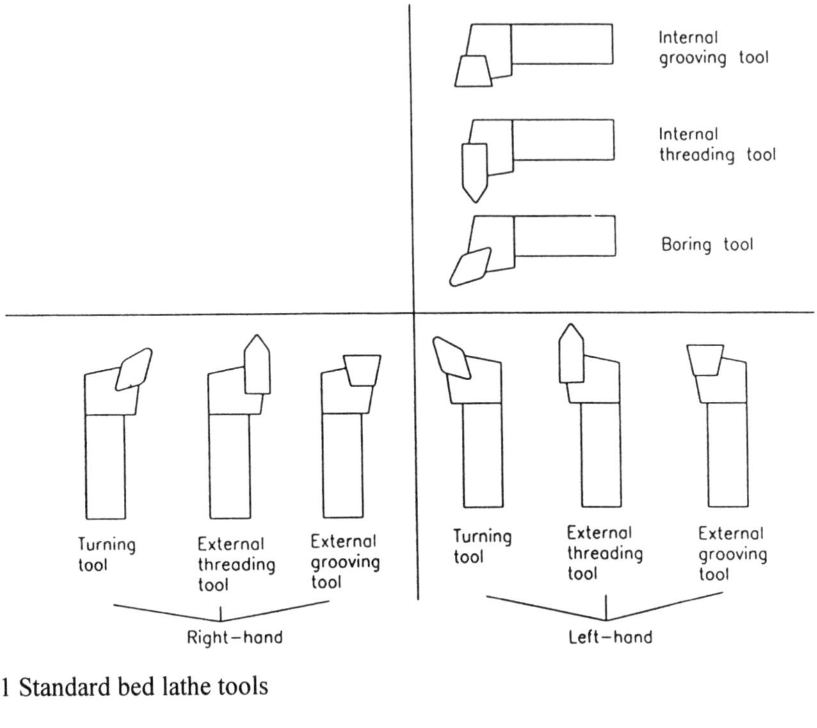

Figure 19.31 Standard bed lathe tools

• Radius (Tool Nose Radius)

This parameter indicates the tool nose radius at the tool tip. Typical tool nose radii used in turning are 1/64, 1/32, 3/64, and 1/16 in.

• Width

The tool width in Mastercam is defined as the distance across the radii of the tool, not the distance from center to center (Figure 19.32).

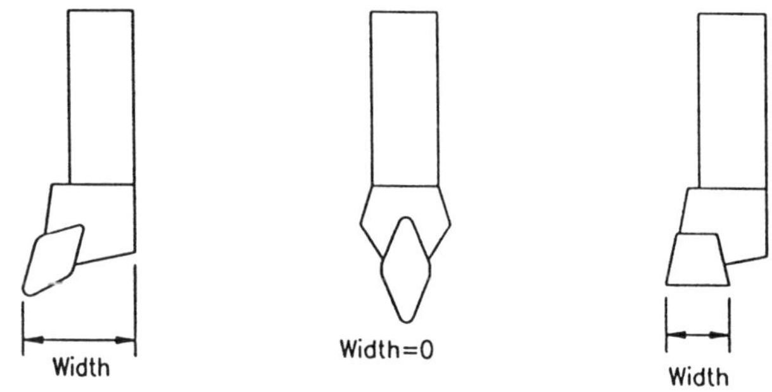

Figure 19.32

Machining Parameters

This group of parameters deal with the depth of cut, feed rate, and cutting speed.

•Amount of Each Cut

The amount of each cut parameter specifies the depth of cut for each tool pass. This distance is measured in the direction perpendicular to the cutting direction (Figure 19.33). The X value is expressed as the radius.

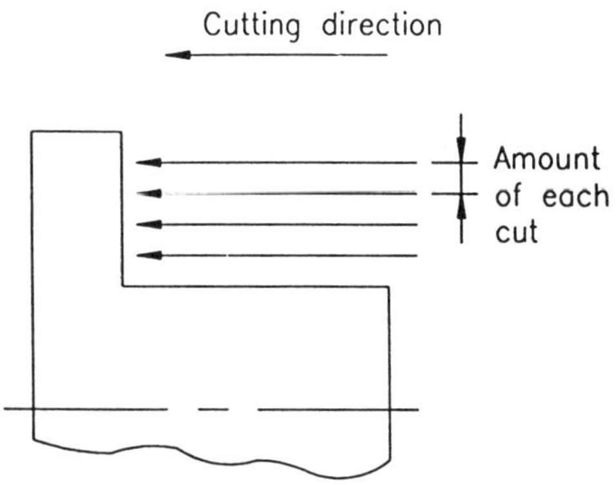

Figure 19.33a Cutting in the Z direction

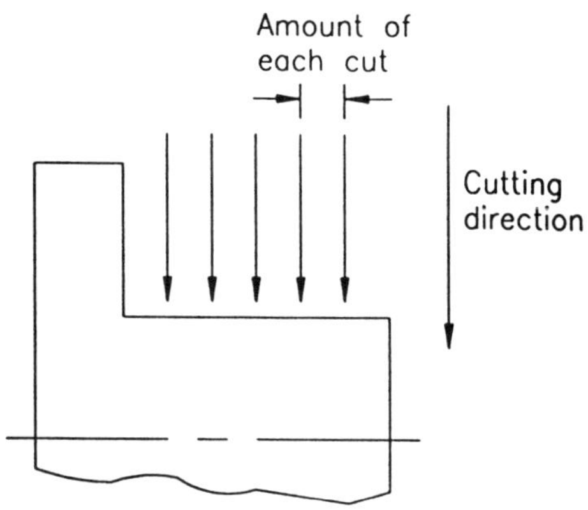

Figure 19.33b Cutting in the X direction

•Cutting Speed

The following three NC commands are used in lathes to control the spindle speed:

G50 Ss	maximum spindle speed in RPM
G96 Ss	constant surface speed in ft/min or m/min
G97 Ss	constant spindle speed in RPM

The constant surface speed is used in turning, boring, and grooving, while the constant spindle speed is utilized in drilling and threading.

A maximum speed limit must be specified when the constant surface speed mode is used. Figure 19.34 on the next page shows how the two commands G50 and G96 work together to provide proper speed control.

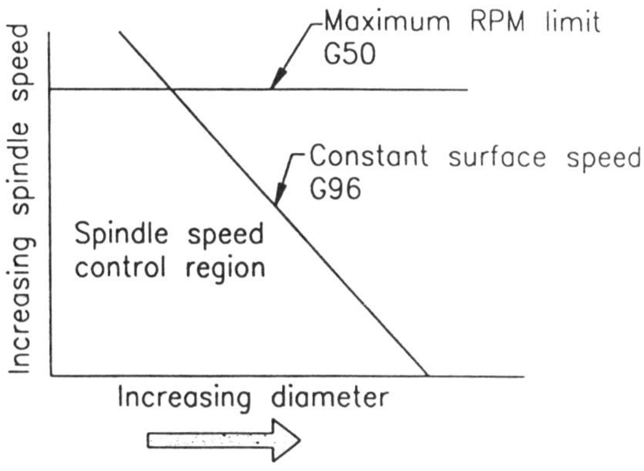

Figure 19.34 Spindle speed control

In Mastercam the spindle speed parameter can be toggled to constant RPM or constant surface speed in ft/min or m/min.

•Feedrate

The feedrate used in lathes is normally expressed in units of inches per revolution. This parameter can be toggled to inches per revolution or inches per minute.

Stock

The stock parameter specifies the amount of material to be left in both X and Z directions for subsequent finishing cuts (Figure 19.35). Although a negative value can be assigned to the stock parameter, it is recommended that only positive stock values are used in order to produce correct toolpaths. A negative value can result in an inaccurate toolpath as shown in Figure 19.36.

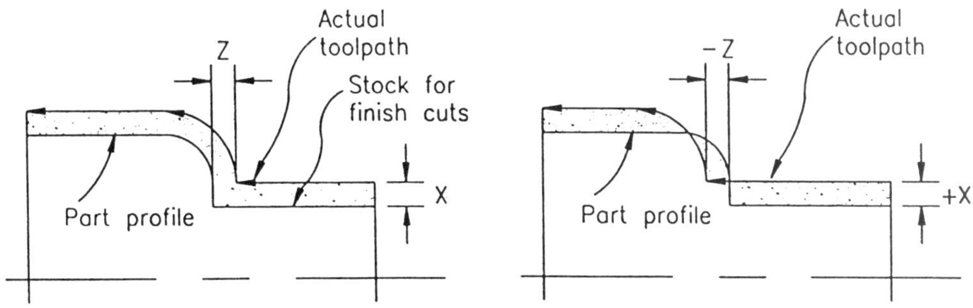

Figures 19.35 Stock in X and Z directions   Figure 19.36 Negative stock value in Z direction

Note: The stock parameter must be used in conjunction with the parameter of cutter compensation in computer.

Cutter Compensation

There are **two** types of cutter compensation used in Mastercam: cutter compensation in computer and cutter compensation in control.

•Cutter Compensation in Computer

This parameter can be selected from these options: **Off, Left** or **Right**. It is used to specify which side the cutter is offset in the direction of the cutting contour. The effect on the toolpath is illustrated in Figure 19.37. When this parameter is toggled to **off**, the actual toolpath coincides with the part profile even though a non-zero stock is specified (Figure 19.37a). The toolpath is displaced to the right of the part profile by a distance given in the stock parameter when this parameter is toggled to right (Figure 19.37b).

Note that when this parameter is set to left, the toolpath is displaced to the left of the part profile (Figure 19.37c). In other words, this changes the direction of the stock in both X and Z axes.

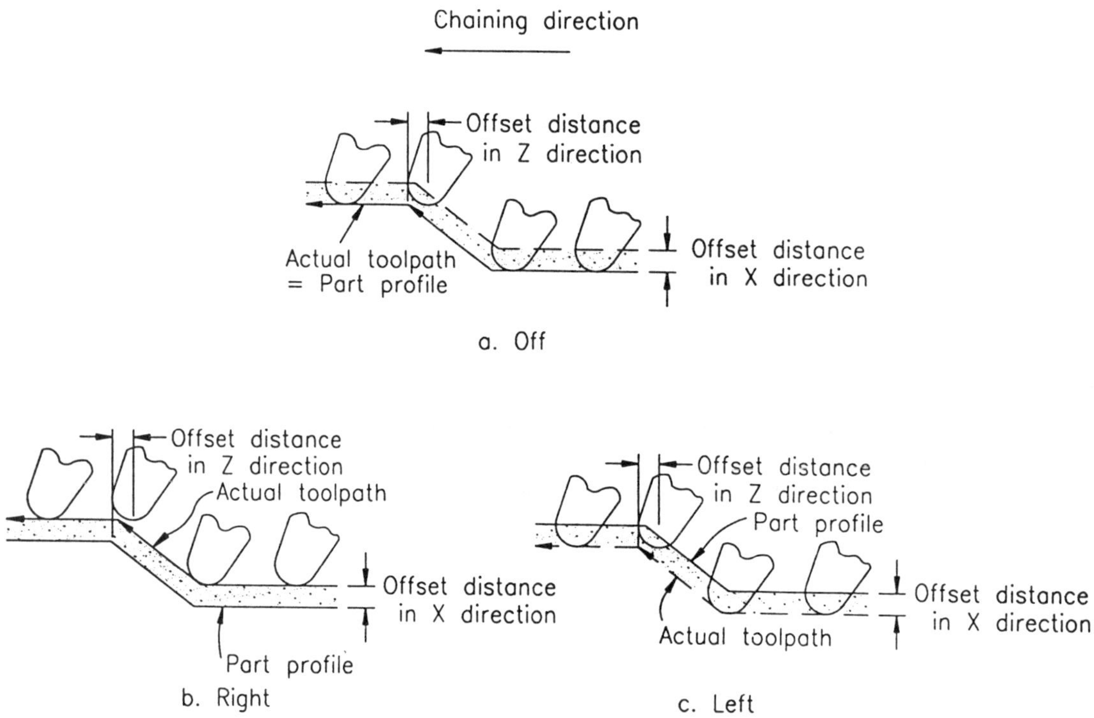

Figure 19.37 Effects of Cutter Compensation in Computer on the toolpath

The proper selection of a cutter compensation command depends on two factors: operation type and chaining direction. Table 19.3 on the following page summarizes compensation commands for various cases.

Table 19.3 Selection of Cutter Compensation Commands

Operation type	Chaining/Cutting direction	Compensation command	Toolpath Illustration
O.D. turning (Both roughing and finishing)	From right to left	Right	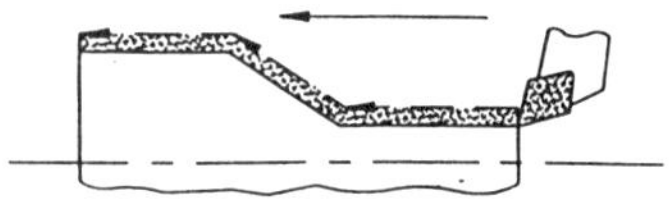
	From left to right	Left	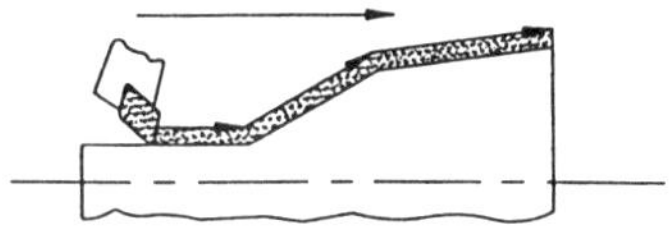
Facing	Inward	Left	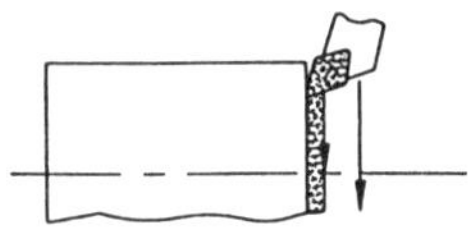
	Outward	Right	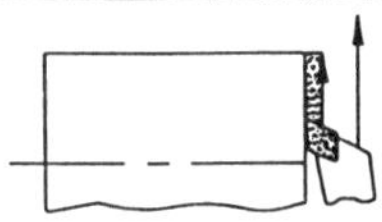
I.D. boring	From right to left	Left	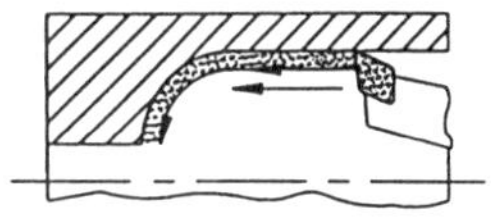
	From left to right	Right	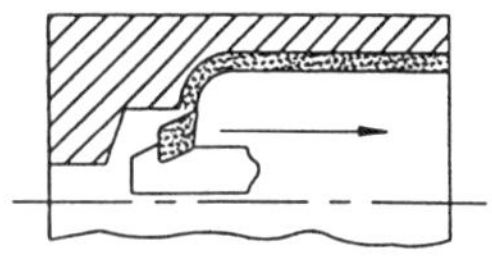
Drilling		Off	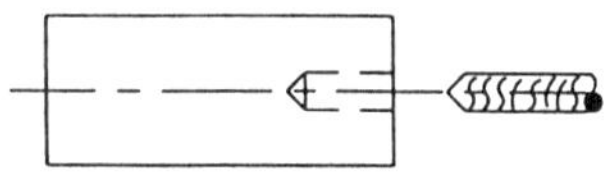

•Cutter Compensation in Control

This parameter can be selected from these options: **Off, Left** or **Right**. It outputs a tool nose radius (TNR) compensation command to the part program. Their corresponding TNR command is given below:

off	⇨	G40	(TNR off)
left	⇨	G41	(TNR left)
right	⇨	G42	(TNR right)

The consideration in selecting cutter compensation in control is the same as for cutter compensation in computer.

Cutter compensation in control is required when turning a slope surface or a curved surface while demanding a closed dimension. Figure 19.38 illustrates position errors encountered in turning a slope surface and a curved surface without using a proper TNR compensation.

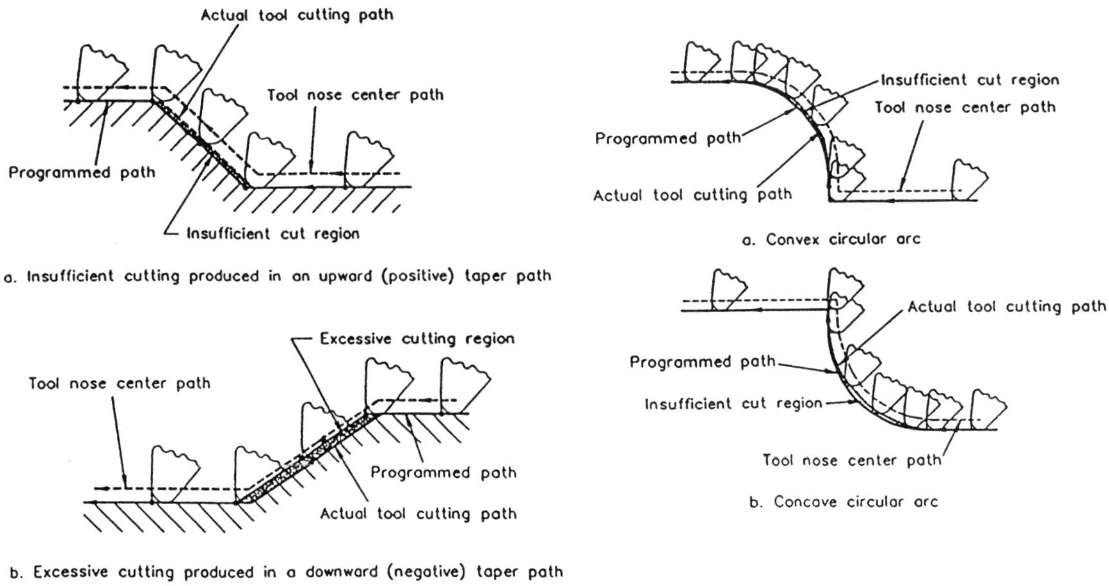

Figure 19.38 Toolpath errors encountered in slope surfaces and circular arcs
(Courtesy of Delmar Publishers, Inc.)

The status of this parameter does not affect the toolpath shown on the computer screen. It only inserts a TNR compensation command into the program. The tool vector and tool nose radius in the offset registers must be correctly specified in the CNC control in order to make the TNR command work properly.

Miscellaneous

There are three miscellaneous parameters: Coolant, Program number and Sequence number.

•Coolant

The coolant parameter can be selected from one of these three options:

Off, Flood and Mist as shown here ☞.
The selection of coolant parameter will generate a correspondent coolant control command to the part program as shown here.

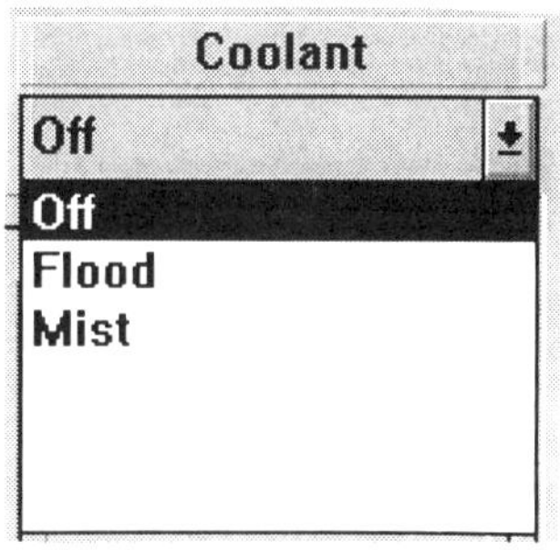

Off ⇨ MO9	
Flood ⇨ MO8	
MIST ⇨ MO7	

•Program Number

This parameter allows any value between 0 and 2,147,483,647 to be assigned to the post processor variable **progno.** This program number can be output to the part program for identification purpose.

•Sequence Number

Two parameters, starting sequence number and increment, are used to set the sequence number for the NC part program.

Tool Positioning

There are **three** parameters to be used to define the approaching and retracting toolpath pattern of each cutting pass: home position, entry vector and retraction vector.

•Home Position

This parameter specifies the intermediate position for the cutter to move to before returning to the reference return point. It can also be used as the tool change position. The procedure for defining home position is:

(1) Click on the Home Position button located at the left corner of the parameter window. A coordinates menu should appear as shown here: ☞

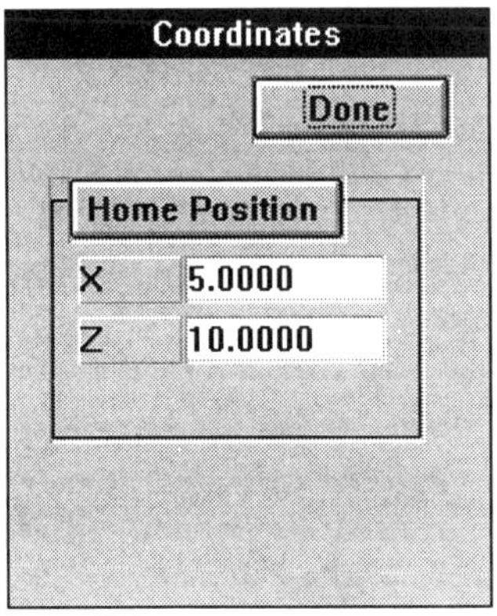

(2) Set X and Z coordinates as desired

(3) Click on the Done button to return to the parameters window.

•Entry Vector

This parameter specifies the toolpath pattern for the tool to enter the part for each cutting pass. It is defined by two vector components, the X component and the Z component. Both positive and negative values can be used. Figure 19.39 shows some examples of using an entry vector in O.D. turning and I.D. boring. The speed that the tool moves along the entry vector can be set to rapid rate or feedrate mode.

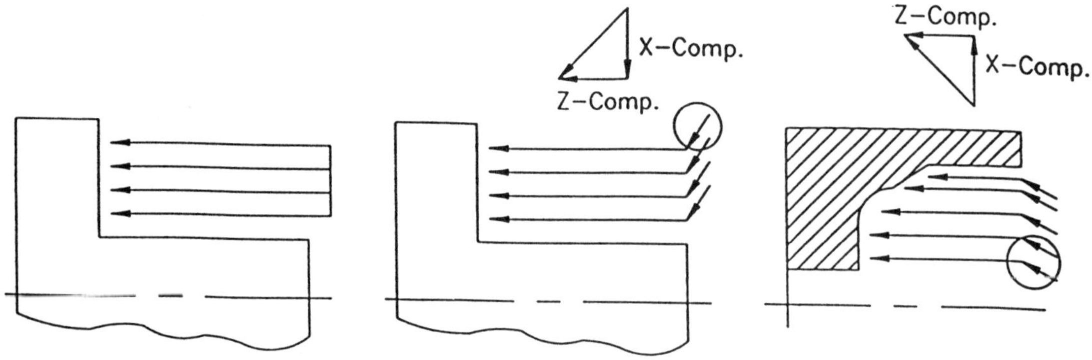

a. X = 0 Z = 0 b. O.D. Turning (-X, -Z) c. I.D. boring (+X, -Z)

Figure 19.39 Entry Vector

•Retraction Vector

This parameter defines how the tool retracts from the part at the end of each cutting pass. It also consists of two components. Some examples are given in Figure 19.40. The speed that the tool moves along the retraction vector can be set to rapid rate or feedrate mode.

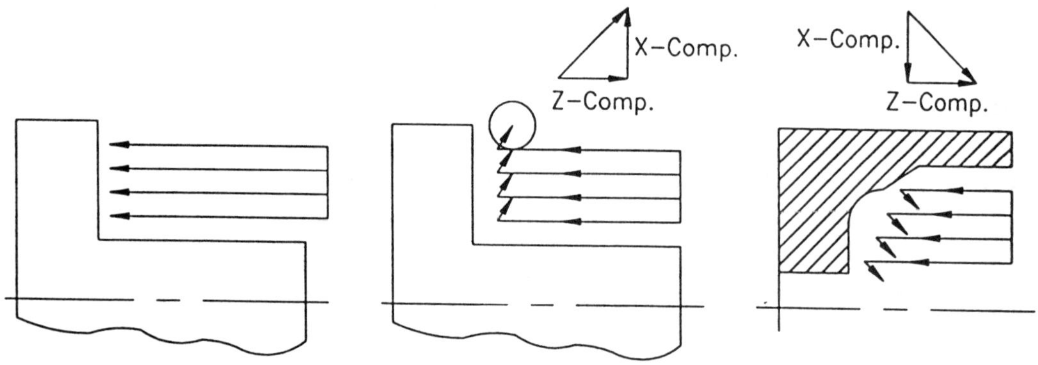

a. X = 0 Z = 0 b. O.D. Turning (-X, -Z) c. I.D. boring (+X, -Z)

Figure 19.40 Retraction vector

The procedure for defining entry and/or exit vectors is:

(1) Click on the "Entry/Exit Vectors" button located at the bottom of the Parameters windows. The Entry/Exit Vectors menu should appear ☞.

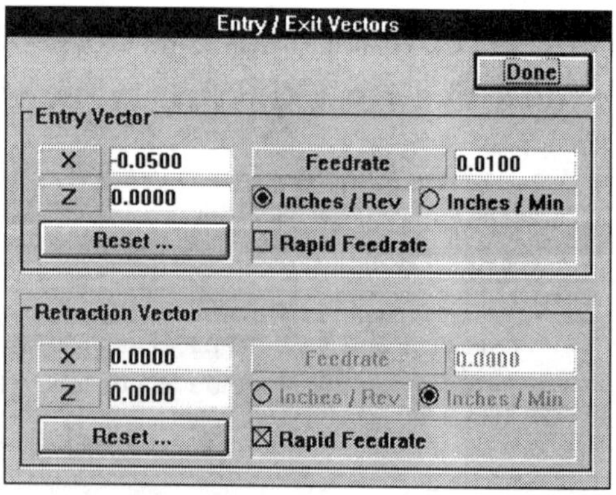

(2) Set the parameters to the appropriate value then Click on the Done button to return back to the Parameters window.

Tool Display

This set of parameters allows you to select the display mode for the tool and the toolpath. You can select to show both the tool and the toolpath, or only display either the tool or the toolpath. The procedure for defining tool display parameters is:

(1) Click on the "Tool Display" button located at the right bottom of the parameters window.

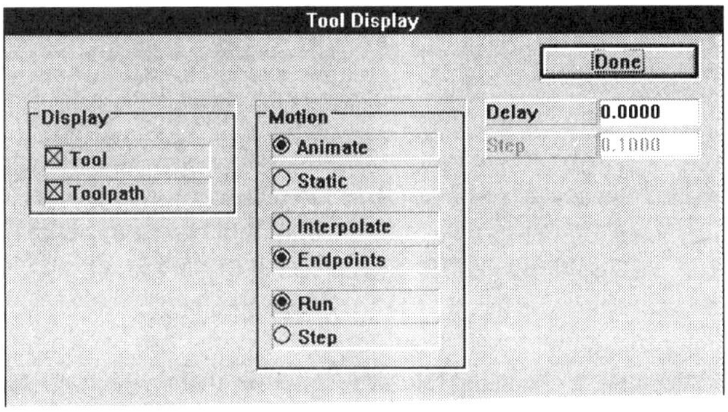

(2) Set the proper setting of each parameter then click on the Done button to return back to the Parameters window.

19.5 Rough Module

The rough module creates a set of toolpaths to rough the part to its approximate profile for future finishing cuts. This module is normally applied to outside diameter (O.D.) roughing (Figure 19.41a), inside diameter (I.D.) roughing (Figure 19.41b), and face roughing (Figure 19.41c).

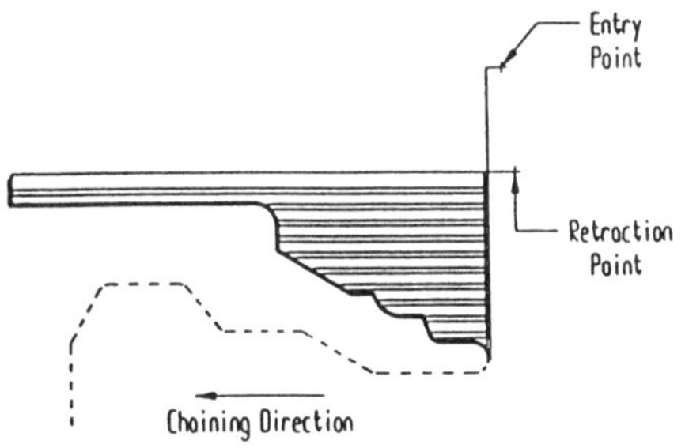

a. O.D. Roughing

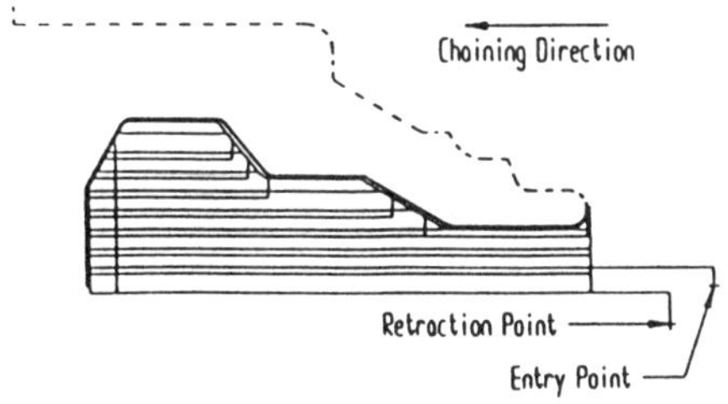

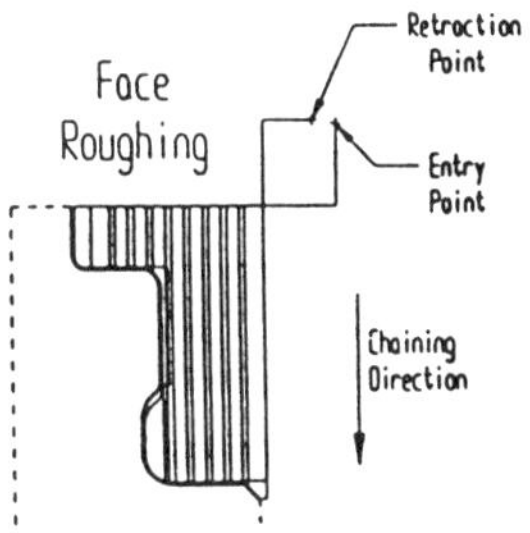

b. I.D. roughing

c. Face roughing

Figure 19.41 Roughing toolpaths (Courtesy of CNC Software, Inc.)

Rough Specific Parameters

In addition to the common parameters, the rough module has the following three unique parameters:

Overlap amount = 0.0100 Roughing angle = 0.0000 Fast feedrate = 0.0000 Slow feedrate = 0.0000 inches/rev

•Overlap Amount

This parameter specifies the amount of overlap between roughing cuts. This value determines the retraction distance of each pass. Retraction distance is equal to the sum of depth of cut and overlap value (Figure 19.42). For example, roughing an OD profile with a 0.1 in. depth of cut and a 0.015 overlap would result in a 0.115 in. (or 0.1 + 0.015) of the retraction distance. With no overlap, it will leave scallops on the profile. These scallops will be eliminated with the use of overlap. Therefore it produces a smooth finish cut because it is cutting the same amount of stock, but not hitting hills and valleys.

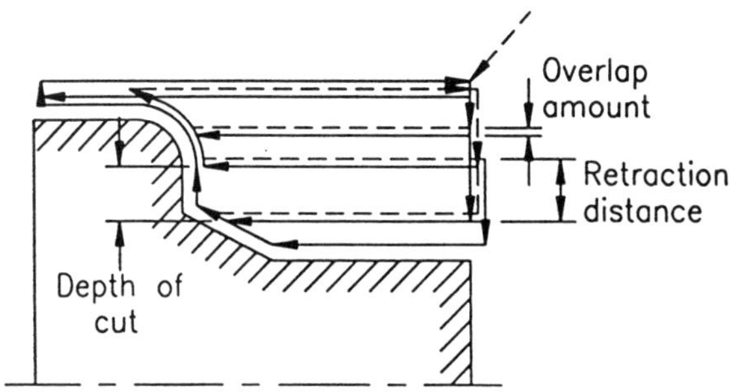

Figure 19.42

•Roughing Angle

This parameter determines the cutting direction of roughing passes. The definition of roughing angle is shown in Figure 19.43.

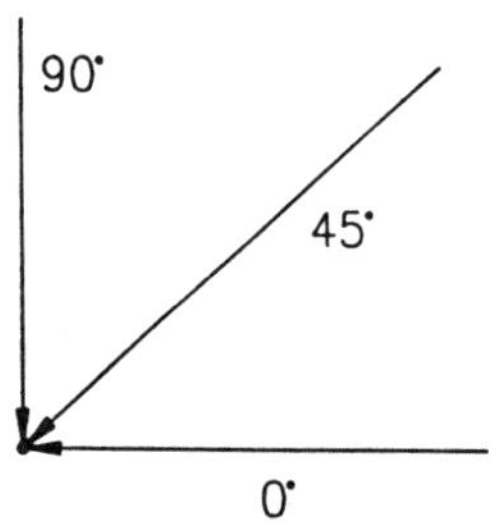

Figure 19.43

The roughing toolpaths for three roughing angles;0°, 45° and 90° are shown in Figure 19.44.

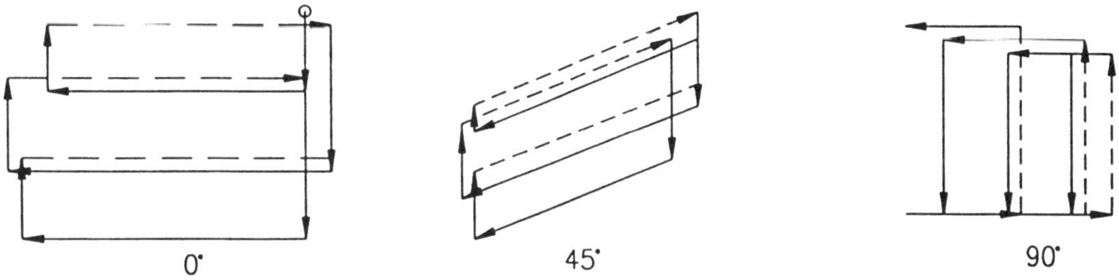

Figure 19.44

This angle can be set to any value ranging from 0 to 360°. It is recommended to use 0° for OD, or ID roughing, and 90° for face roughing. In addition to the roughing angle, the roughing toolpath pattern is also affected by the chaining direction, tool orientation number, and the cutter compensation direction. Figure 19.45 shows how to select a proper combination of chaining direction, roughing angle, cutter orientation number, and cutter compensation direction in some common applications.

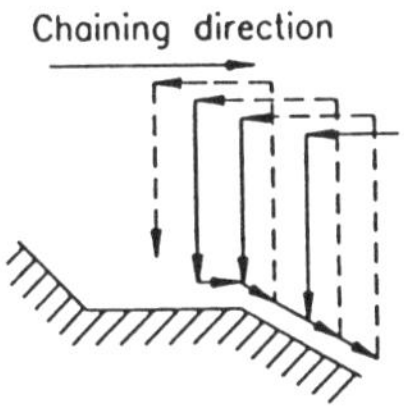

Offset = Left
O.D. Facing
Angle = 90^0
Orientation#=5

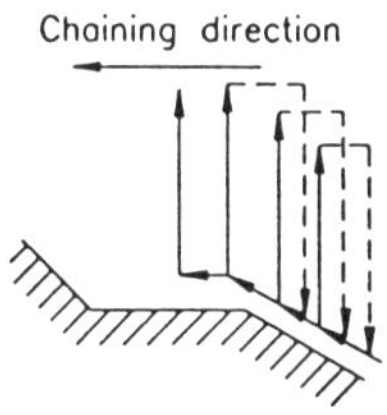

Offset = Right
O.D.Facing
Angle = 90^0
Orientation#=5

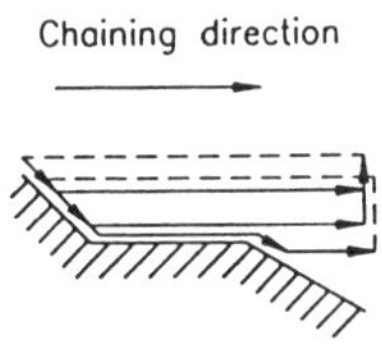

Offset = Left
O.D. Roughing
Angle = 0^0
Orientation#=1

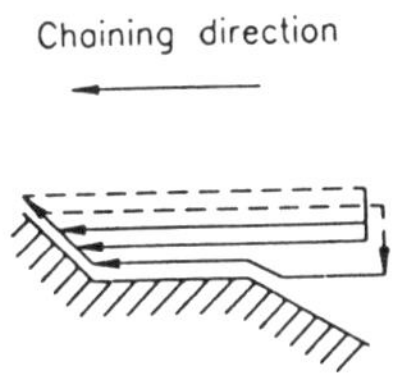

Offset = Right
O.D.Roughing
Angle = 0^0
Orientation#=1

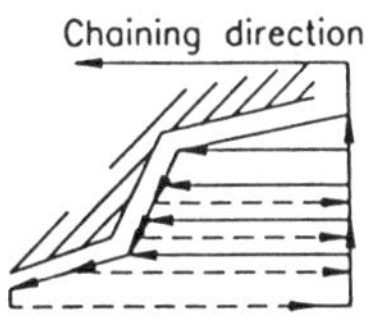

Offset = Left
Angle = 0^0
Orientation#=4

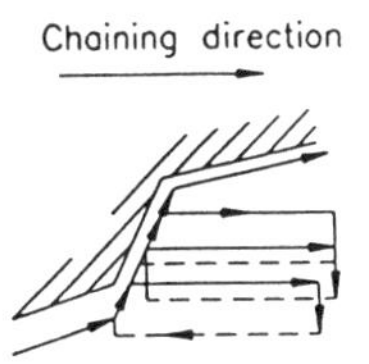

Offset = Right
Angle = 0^0
Orientation#=4

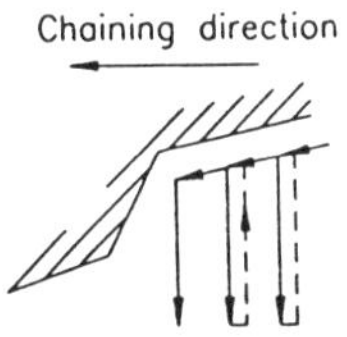

Offset = Left
Angle = 90^0
Orientation#=4

Offset = Right
Angle = 90^0
Orientation#=4

Figure 19.45

•Feedrate

Two feedrates can be specified in this roughing parameter; fast feedrate and slow feedrate. The slow feedrate refers to the plunge feedrate that is used on cuts where the tool plunges into the part. The fast feedrate is used in all other cuts beside plunging.

The feedrate unit can be toggled to either inches per revolution or inches per minute.

Tips 1. Extend the X-dimension to the rough stock diameter. This will make sure that the entire stock is to be roughed. If only the part profile is used, the first roughing pass may make too heavy a cut (Figure 19.46).

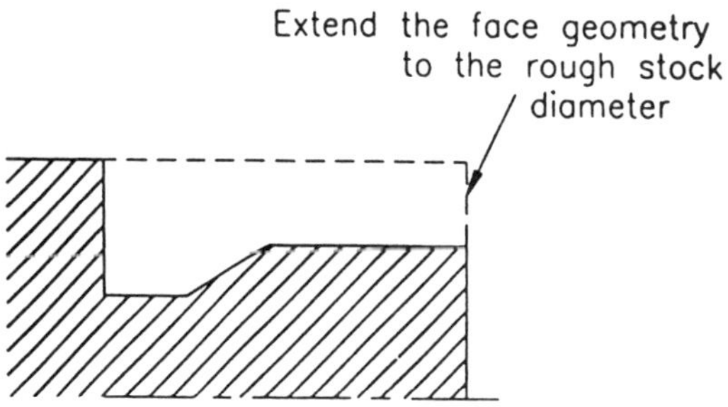

Figure 19.46

2. Extend the line to avoid the cutting of a recess or a groove in roughing (Figure 19.47).

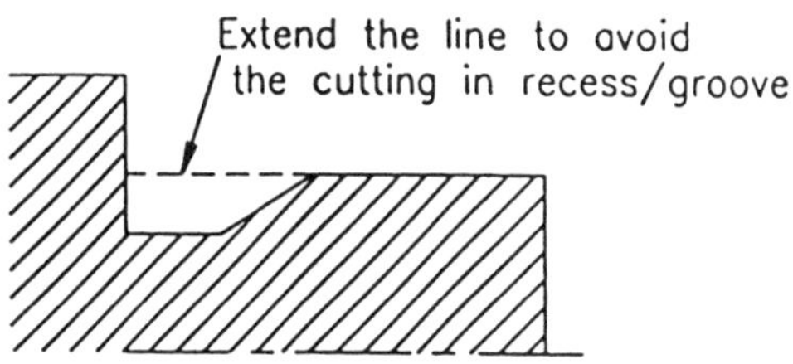

Figure 19.47

Project 1.

1

Rough the part geometry of lathe2.

The rough module is used to generate a set of toolpaths for roughing the part shown in Figure 19.48a. The toolpaths are shown in Figure 19.48b. The part geometry file is lathe2.ge3.

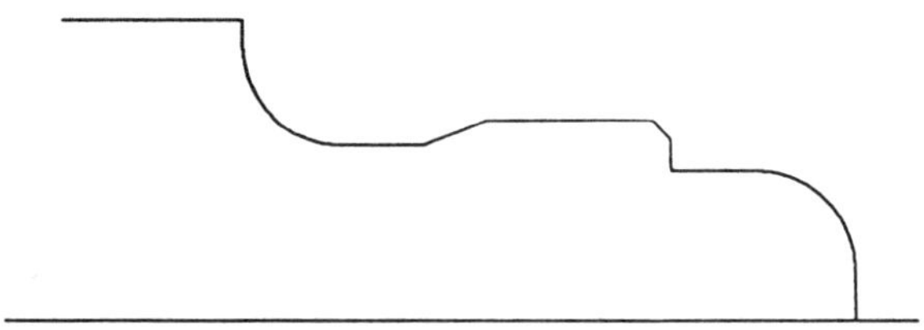

a. Part geometry

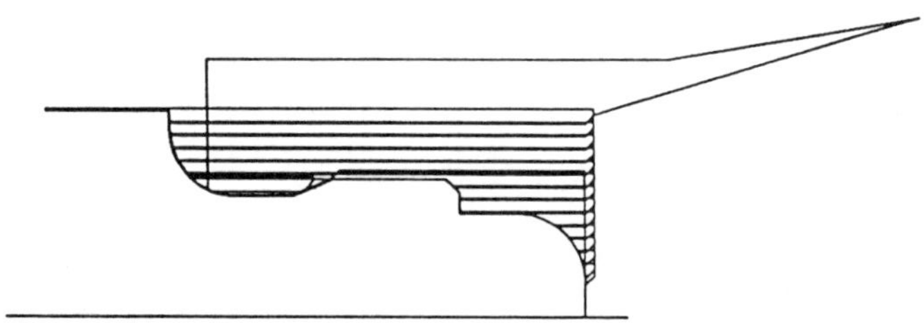

b. Toolpath

Figure 19.48

Tips 1. Part geometry file is **lathe2.ge3.**

2. Use the tool No. 5 in the tool library. This is an ideal tool for roughing.
   It has these parameters:

Tool no. (N) = 5 Offset number (ofs.) = 5 Tool orientation no. (O) = 1 Tool nose radius (R) = 0.031 (or 1/32") Width (W) = 0.6253.

3. Roughing parameters:

Overlap amount = 0.02 Amount of stock to leave: X=0.01 Z=0.01 Rounging angle = 0.0 Amount of each cut = 0.15

4. Set the entry vector the following settings:

X-0.1 Z-0.1 Feedrate = 0.01 inches / rev

This entry vector setting allows the cutter to start the cutting from 0.1" away from the part end face. This can remove the excess material. If X0.0 Z0.0 are an entry vector, it may cause a problem if the raw material of the part is slightly longer than the finish part.

5. Set the machining parameters to the following values:

Fast feedrate = 0.01 inches / rev Slow feedrate = 0.005 inches / rev Spindle speed = 800 CSS Maximum spindle speed = 4500 RPM

6. Set the two cutter compensations to the following settings:

Cutter compensation in control = off Cutter compensation in computer = right

7. Select the home position at (D7.0 Z4.0).

8. Select the retraction point at (D6.0 Z1.0).

Step 1. Load the part file lathe2 into the system.

Select **MAIN MENU → File → Get → Geometry**
Enter **lathe2** ← for file name
Select **Yes** to delete the current part if necessary

The part drawing for lathe1 should appear as Figure 19.49.

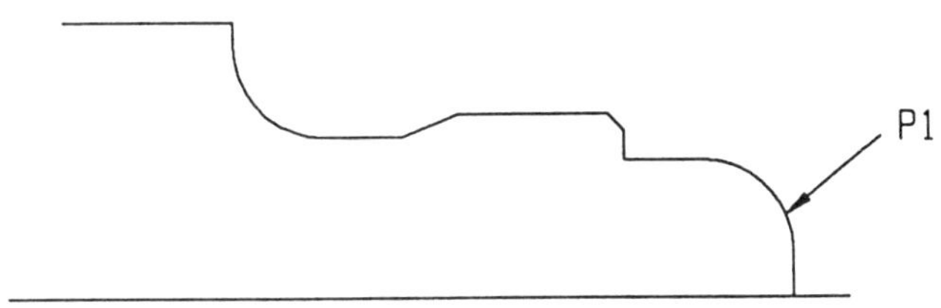

Figure 19.49

Step 2. Initiate Rough module.

Select **MAIN MENU → Toolpaths → Rough**
Enter file name: **lathe2 ←**

Step 3. Define the roughing contour using the pick point in Figure 19.49.

Select **Chain** from the Chaining method menu
Pick at **P1** for the first entity
Select **Close → End here**

Step 4. Select the retraction point.

Select **Point**
Enter **D6,1 ←**
Select **Done**

Step 5. Define rough parameters to the following settings.

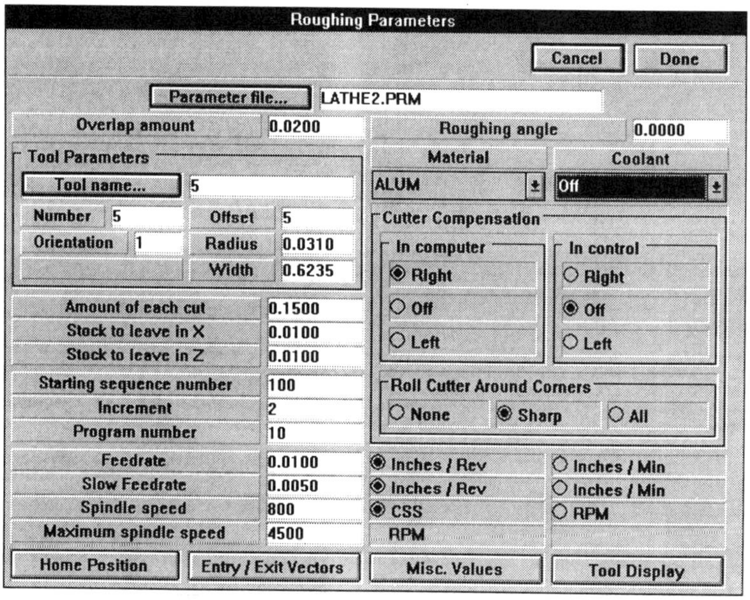

Step 6. Set the entry vectors.

Click on the "Entry/Exit Vectors" button
Set the entry vector parameters as shown below.

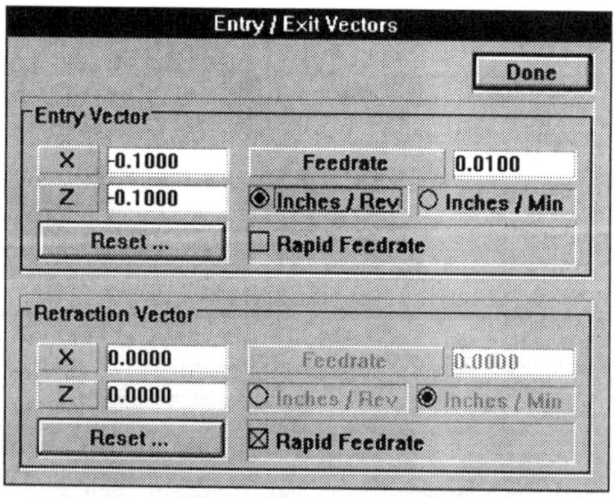

Click on the **Done button** to return back to the parameters window.

Step 7. Define tool display parameters.

Click on the "Tool Display" button
Set the parameters as shown below.

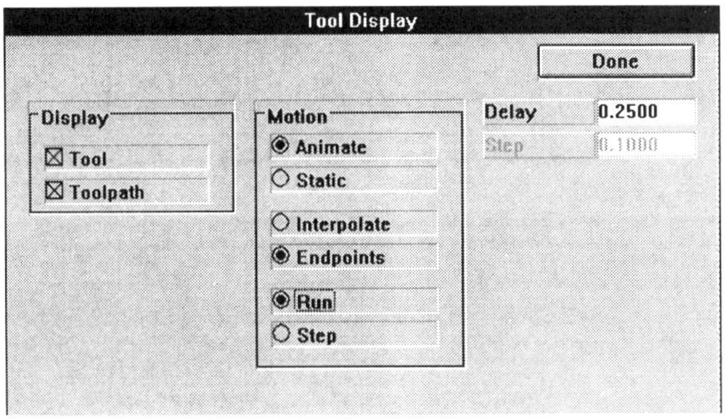

Click on the **Done button** to return to the parameters window.

Step 8. Set the home position at (D7.0, Z4.0).

Click on the "Home Position" button
Set the parameters as shown here ☞

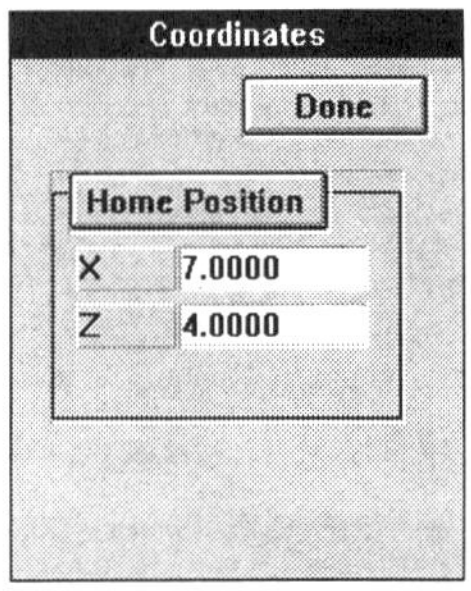

Click on the **Done button** to return to the parameters window.

Step 9. Accept and save the toolpaths.

Click on the **Done button** in the parameters window to generate toolpaths.

A warning “Entry vector is not perpendicular to the roughing direction. This may cause gouging” will appear. Ignore this warning. Press the **Enter key** to continue the process.

The toolapths should appear as in Figure 19.50.

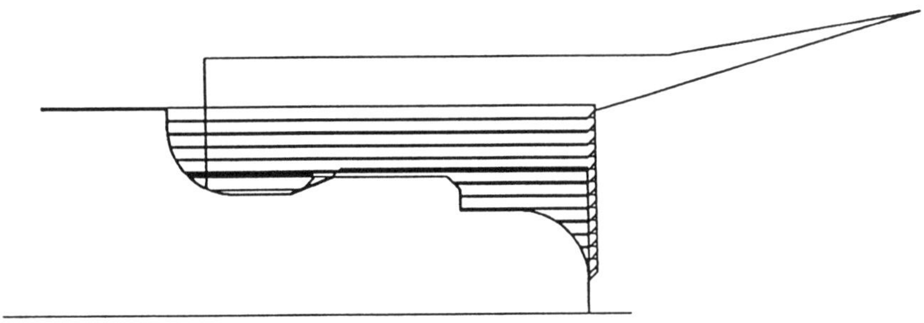

Figure 19.50

Step 10. Close the toolpath file and run the post processor.

Select **Yes** to accept the toolpath segment
Select **End program** to close toolpath file
Select **Yes** to “Run the post processor?”
Enter file name: **lathe2** ←

The system will convert the NCI file to a part program and list it on the screen as below.

```
%
O0010
(LATHE2)
N100G20
N102G50X10.Z10.
N104G0T0505
N106G50S4000
N108G97S0647M3
N110X4.72Z.11
N112G96S0800
N114G99G1X4.52Z.01F.01
N116Z-4.99
N118X4.738
N120G3X4.82Z-5.031R.041
N122G1Z-6.5
N124X4.86
N126G0Z.11
N128X4.42
N130G1X4.22Z.01
N132Z-4.9877
N134G2X4.338Z-4.99R.759
N136G1X4.56
N138G0Z.11
N140X4.12
N142G1X3.92Z.01
N144Z-4.9607
```

Double click the Window button located at the upper-left corner to Graphic View.

Step 11. Edit toolpath file.

Select **MAIN MENU → File → Edit → NC**
Enter file name: **lathe2**

The part program should appear on the screen. Do all necessary editing to reflect the requirements of your controller.

Step 12. Exit the Edit function.

Press **F10 → F10** to return back to graphic mode

Project 2. 2

Roughing an internal profile

The rough module is used to generate a set of toolpaths for roughing the internal profile of the part shown in Figure 19.51.

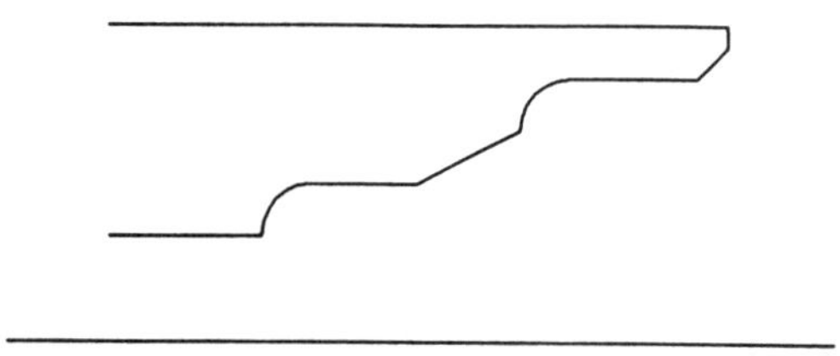

Figure 19.51

Tips 1. Part geometry file is **lathe3.ge3.**

2. Use the tool N0. 25 in the tool library. Set the tooling parameters to the following settings:

Tool No. (N) = 10 Offset number (Oft.) = 10 Tool orientation n. (O) = 4 Tool nose radius (R) = 0.0156 (or 1/64") Width (W) = 0.625

3. Set the roughing parameters to the following settings:

Overlap amount = 0.02 Amount of stock to leave: X = 0.01   Z = 0.01 Roughing angle = 0.0 Amount of each cut = 0.1

4. Set the entry and retraction vector to the following settings:

Entry vector (X0.1 Z-0.1)   Feedrate = 0.01 inches/rev Retraction vector (X-0.1 Z0.1)   Rapid feedrate

5. Set the machining parameters to the following settings:

Fast feedrate = 0.01 inches/rev   Slow feedrate = 0.005 inches/rev Spindle speed = 800 CSS Maximum spindle speed = 4500 RPM

6. Set two cutter compensations to the following settings:

Cutter compensation in control = off Cutter compensation in computer = left

7. Select the home position at (X2.5 Z2.5).

8. Select the retraction point at (D0.9,0.3).

Step 1. Load the part geometry file lethe3.ge3 or create one by following the instructions given in example 3 of this chapter.

Select **MAIN MENU → File → Get → Geometry**

Enter file name: **lathe3** ←

Select **Yes** to delete the current part if necessary

The part geometry drawing should appear as Figure 19.52.

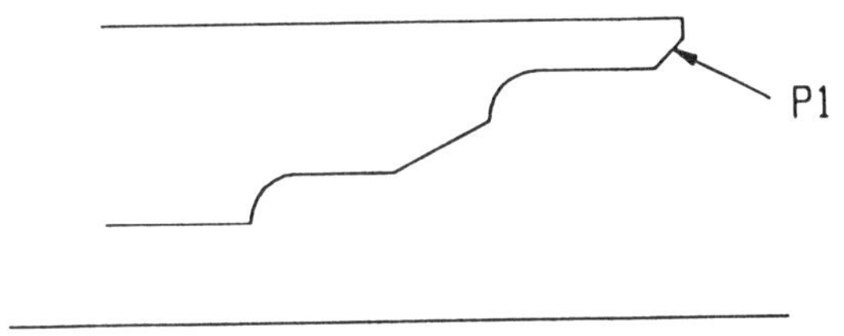

Figure 19.52

Step 2. Initiate the rough module.

Select **MAIN MENU → Toolpaths → Rough**

Enter file name: **lathe3** ←

Step 3. Define the roughing contour using the pick point in Figure 19.52 on the previous page.

Select **Chain** from the Chaining method menu
Pick at **P1** for the first entity
Select **Close → End here**

Step 4. Select the retraction point.

Select **Point**
Enter **D0.9,0.3** for the retraction point
Select **Done**

Step 5. Define rough parameters to the following settings.

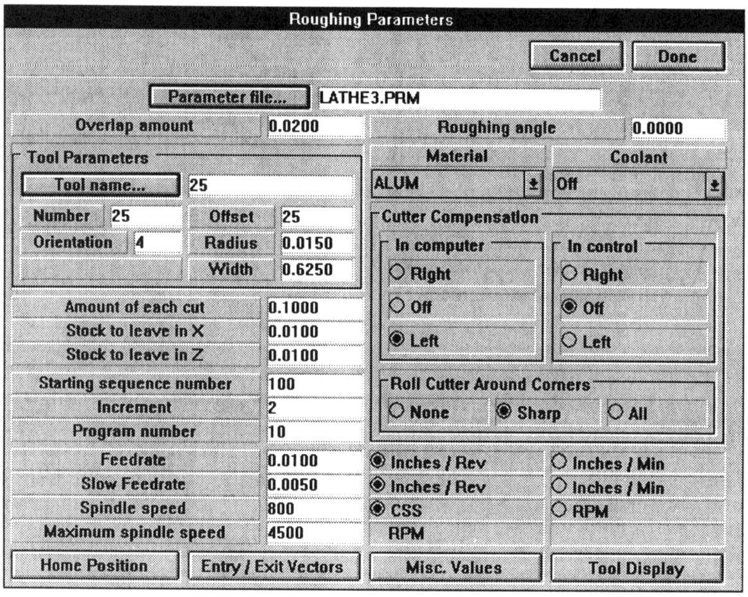

Step 6. Set the home position at (X2.5, Z2.5)

Click on the "Home position" button
Set two parameters to the following value: **X = 2.5, Z = 2.5**
Click on **Done**

Step 7. Set the entry and exit vectors;

Click on the "Entry/Exit Vectors" button

Set the parameters as shown here ☞

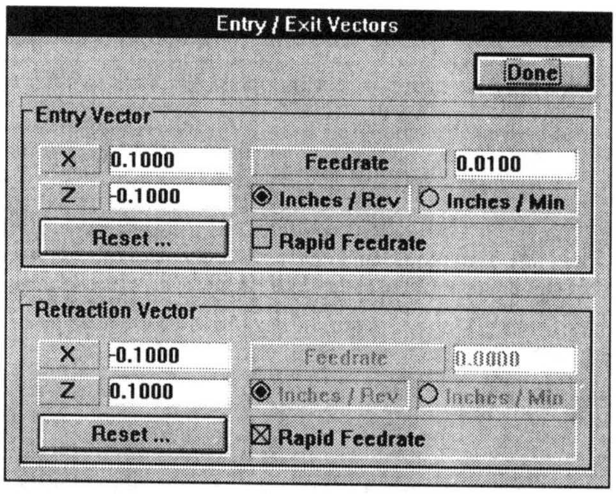

Click on the **Done button** to return to the parameters window.

Step 8. Accept and save the toolpaths.

Select **Done**

The toolpaths should appear as Figure 19.53.

Select **Yes** to accept this toolpath segment

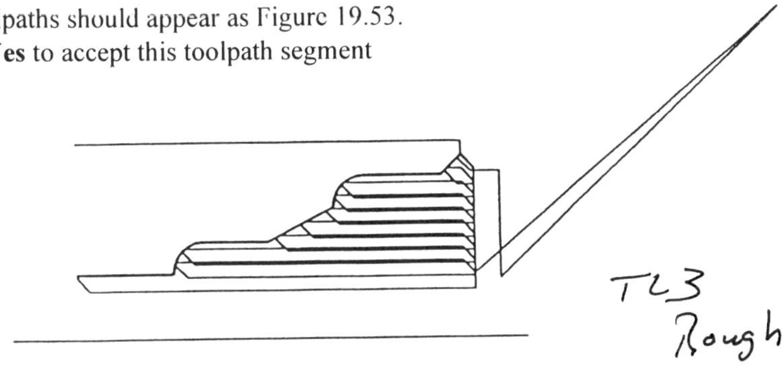

Figure 19.53

Step 9. Close the toolpath file and run the post processor.

Select **End program** to close toolpath file

Select **Yes** to "Run the post processor?"

Enter file name: **lathe3** ←

The system will convert the NCI file to a part program and list it on the screen.
Double-click the Window button in the upper-left corner to return to graphic mode.

19.6 Finish Module

The finish module creates a set of toolpaths to make one or more finish cuts along the OD, ID, or facing contours.

When to Use the Finish Module

When the rough module is first used to generate the roughing toolpaths, the finish module is then used to cut the part to its final finished shape and size (Figure 19.54).

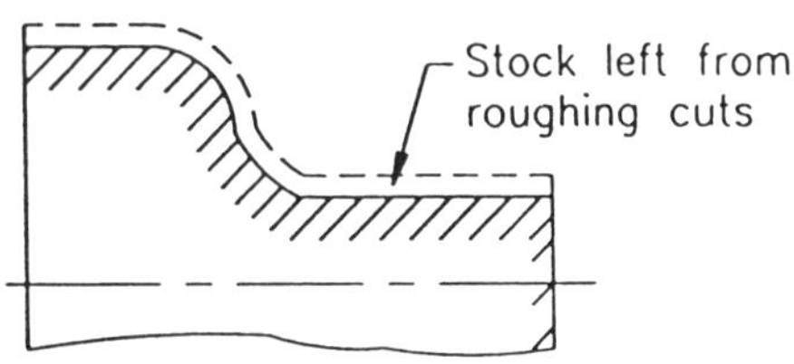

Figure 19.54

When the size of a part already has a close final dimension such as a casting or a forging, no roughing cuts are required. The finish module can be directly used to produce the final shape and size (Figure 19.55).

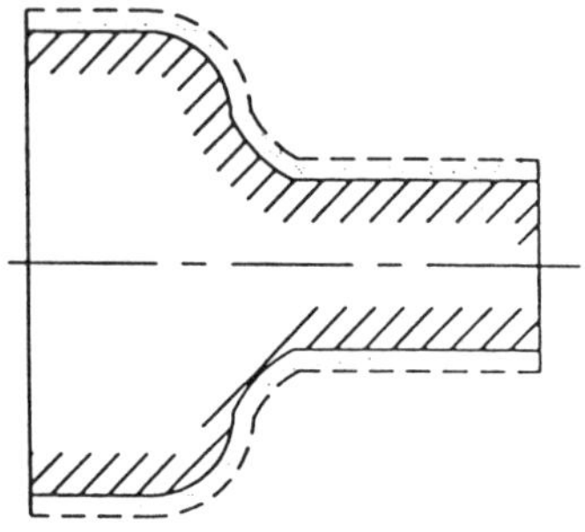

Figure 19.55

Finish Specific Parameter

There is only one unique finish parameter that specifies the number of cuts. If only one finish cut is specified, the cutter will cut to the given boundary. When the number of cuts is more than one, the cutter compensation in computer parameter should be set properly. If it is set to off, all the finishing cuts will overlap.

Cycle Parameters

Some CNC lathe controls provide a group of canned cycles for generating the toolpaths for roughing and finishing cuts. These controls are Fanuc-based and their compatible controls. The main advantage of using these canned cycles is to shorten part programs and programming time.

Mastercam lathe allows the following **four** roughing and finish cycles to be inserted into part programs:

G70:	Finish Cycle
G71:	Rough turning cycle
G72:	Rough facing cycle
G73:	Contour repeating cycle

Rough Turning Cycle (G71)

The rough turning cycle G71 is used to rough the part to a size that is slightly larger than its desired size in preparation for the finishing cut. This cycle specifies the range of instruction blocks to be included, the depth of cut per pass, and the amount and direction of stock left for the finishing cycle. Depending on the control model, it uses one or two command blocks for G71 programming. Fanuc T-6 uses a one-block format and other models such as T-10, T-11, or O-T use a two-block format.

•One-block format:

```
G71 Pp Qq Dd Uu Ww Ff
 |   |  |  |  |  |  └ roughing feedrate
 |   |  |  |  |  └ Z-axis finish stock
 |   |  |  |  └ X-axis finish stock
 |   |  |  └ depth of cut
 |   |  └ sequence number of cycle ending block
 |   └ sequence number of cycle starting block
 └ rough turning cycle command
```

•Two-block format:

G71 Dd Rr
└── retraction amount

G71 Pp Qq Uu Ww Ff

Figure 19.56 shows a typical toolpath pattern generated by using G71 command.

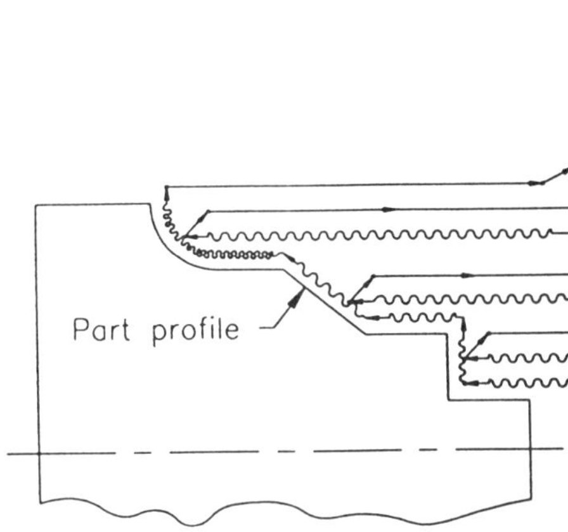

Figure 19.56

Rough Facing Cycle (G72)

The rough facing cycle G72 has a similar toolpath pattern to that of G71 except the main cutting direction is parallel to the X axis as shown in Figure 19.57.

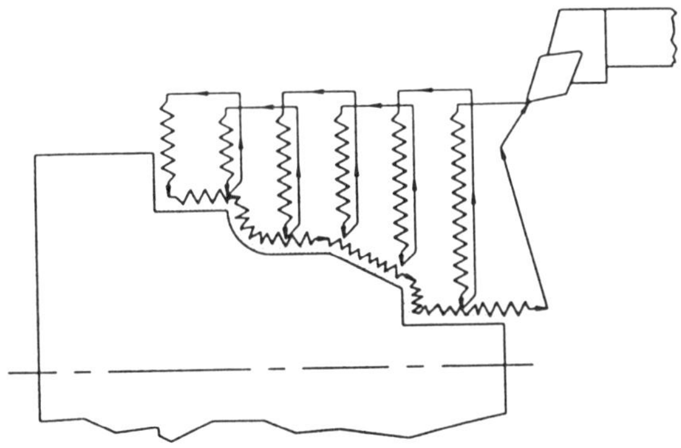

Figure 19.57

•One-block format:

G72 Pp Qq Dd Uu Ww Ff

•Two-block format:

G72 Ww Rr

G72 Pp Qq Uu Ww Ff

Contour Repeating Cycle (G73)

The contour repeating cycle (G73) generates a set of cutter paths that repeatedly move along with the part contour as many times as required. Each successive repeating path moves the cutter closer to the desired finished contour as shown in Figure 19.58.

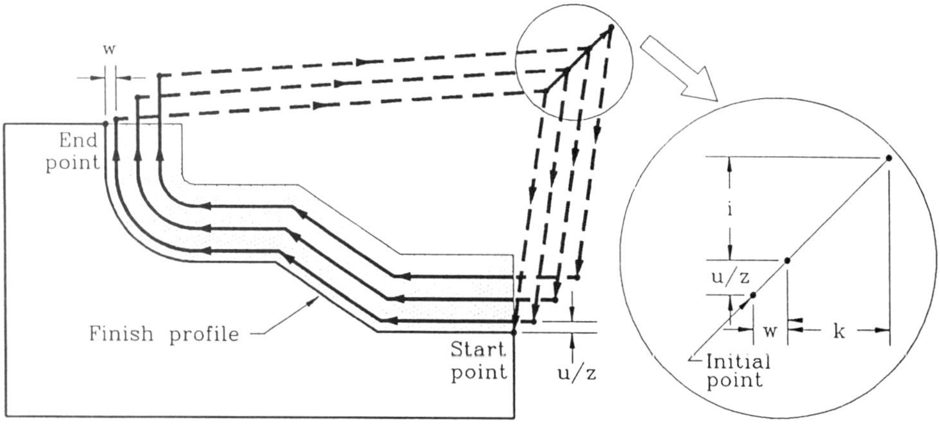

Figure 19.58

•One-block format:

G73 Pp Qq Uu Ww Rr Ff

└── number of repeated contours

•Two-block format:

G73 Ui Wk Rr

Wk ── Distance of retraction in the Z direction

Ui ── Distance of retraction in the X direction

G73 Pp Qq Uu Ww Ff

Finish Cycle (G70)

The finish cycle can be regarded as a single-pass contouring cycle. It must be used with one of two roughing cycles (G71 or G72). The G70 command is normally programmed after a roughing cycle. Its command indicates only the sequence numbers for the cycle start block and cycle ending block, and has the following format:

G70 Pp Qq

Procedure for Using Canned Cycles G71, G72 and G73

1. Enter the Rough toolpath module using the following commands:

   MAIN MENU → Toolpaths → Rough

2. Set roughing parameters to the following settings:

   a. Set the Roughing angle to either **0°** or **90°.** (Use 0° for G71 and 90° for G72).

   b. Turn Cutter Compensation in Computer to either **Left** or **Right**.

   c. Set the entry and exit vectors if desired.
      Select the Feedrate option, otherwise they will be omitted.

   d. Set the Overlap amount to **0**.

   e. Set the Miscellaneous Values to the following:

      Miscellaneous integer 2 (mi2) = **Canned cycle type selection.**

The miscellaneous integer 2 (mi2) is the variable used to set the roughing toolpath output either in the long or short format. The long format generates the actual command codes to rough the workpiece. The short format uses the canned cycle commands to shorten the roughing part programs.

mi2 = **0**: do not use canned cycle (output long code)
1: generate G71-G73 roughing canned cycle
2: generate G71-G73 roughing canned cycle and G70 finish cycle.
mr3 = enter value of G71-G73 clearance in canned cycle
f. Accept the toolpath.

3. Select the Finish module from the toolpaths menu.
Select **Last** from the chaining method menu
Set the finishing parameters:
a. Set the stock in both X and Z to 0
b. Keep the same tool radius size and geometry for both roughing and finishing
Note: Select Done to complete the Finish parameters settings.
Select Write to generate the toolpaths.
Select End program.

•For G73

The Finish module is used twice to generate a G73 for contour repeating roughing cycle and a G70 for the finish cycle. The procedure for generating G73 and G70 canned cycles are listed below:

1. Select **Toolpaths → Finish**

2. Set the Finishing parameters to the settings specifically for generating a G73 command:
a. Set the number of cuts and the depth of cuts to appropriate values.
b. Set the Stock in the X and Z to the appropriate finishing Stock value.
c. Select **Done** to generate roughing paths.
d. Accept the roughing paths.

3. Select **Finish** from the toolpaths menu again

4. Select **Last** from the chaining method menu

5. Set the **Finishing** parameters to the settings specifically for generating a G70 command:
a. Set both Stock in X and Z to **0**
b. Set the number of cuts to **1**

6. Generate finishing paths

7. Accept finishing paths.

Finish Set Menu

This menu writes the toolpath to the NCI file, including the options for changing feedrate at any point on the contour, inserting a rapid move at any point along a contour, and inserting comments or special codes into the NC program. This menu appears on the screen:

Finish - set:	
Write	causes the finish toolpaths to be written to the NCI file.
Feedrate	allows the feedrate to be changed at any point.
Rapid	causes a rapid move to be inserted to any point along a contour.
Manual ent	allows comments or special codes to be inserted at any point in the NC program.
Text 1	allows a character string to be output with the line of code.
Text 2	allows a character string to be output with the line of code.
Text 3	allows a character string to be output with the line of code.

Project 3.

Generating finish toolpaths for an external profile

The finish module is used to generate a set of toolpaths to cut the finish profile of the part shown in Figure 19.59. The geometry file is **lathe2.ge3**. This part geometry has been used in project 1 to generate the roughing toolpaths.

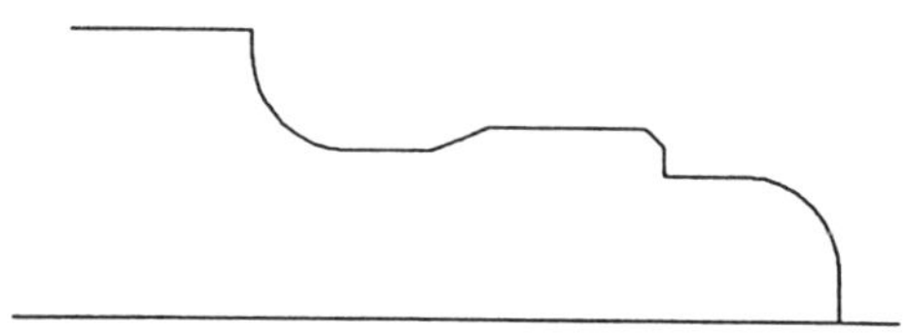

Figure 19.59a Part geometry

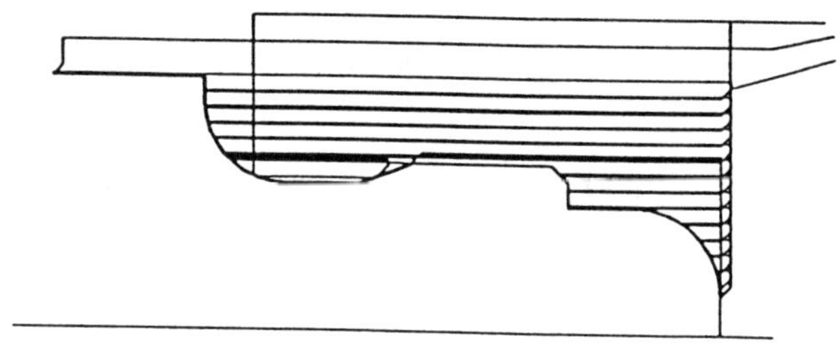

Figure 19.59b Toolpaths

Tips 1. The part geometry is **lathe2.**

2. The roughing toolpaths of this part were generated in project 1. Use the same NC file name for both roughing and finish toolpaths. Use the Append command to place the finish toolpaths after the rough toolpaths.

3. Use the tool number 5 with the following information:

   N = 5
   Ofs = 5
   O = 1
   R = 1/32
   W = 0.625

4. Set the cutter compensation in computer to right.

5. Set the machining parameters to the following settings:

Spindle speed = 1000 CSS Maximum spindle speed = 5000 RPM Feedrate = 0.005 inches/rev

Step 1. Load the part geometry.

Select **MAIN MENU → File → Get → Geometry**
Enter file name: **lathe2 ←**

Select **Yes** to delete the current part if necessary

The part geometry appears as Figure 19.60.

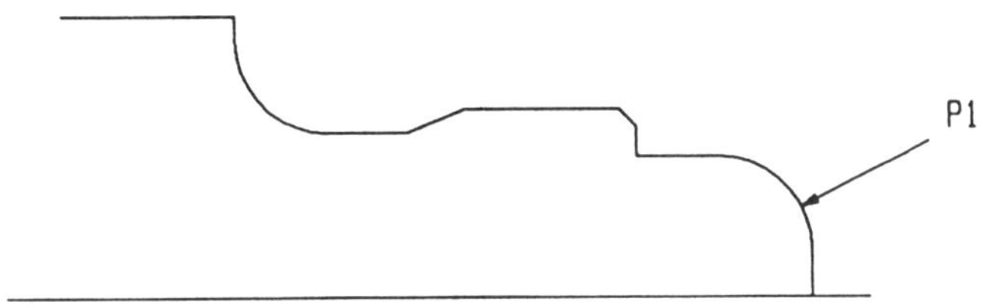

Figure 19.60

Step 2. Initiate the finish module.

Select **MAIN MENU** → **Toolpaths** → **Finish**
Enter file name: **lathe2** ←
Select **Append** to place the finishing toolpaths to the end of roughing toolpaths

Step 3. Define the contour using the pick point in Figure 19.60.

Select **Chain**
Pick at **P1**
Select **Close** → **End here** → **Point**
Enter **D5.5,0.5** ← for retraction point
Select **Done**

Step 4. Define the finish parameters to the following settings.

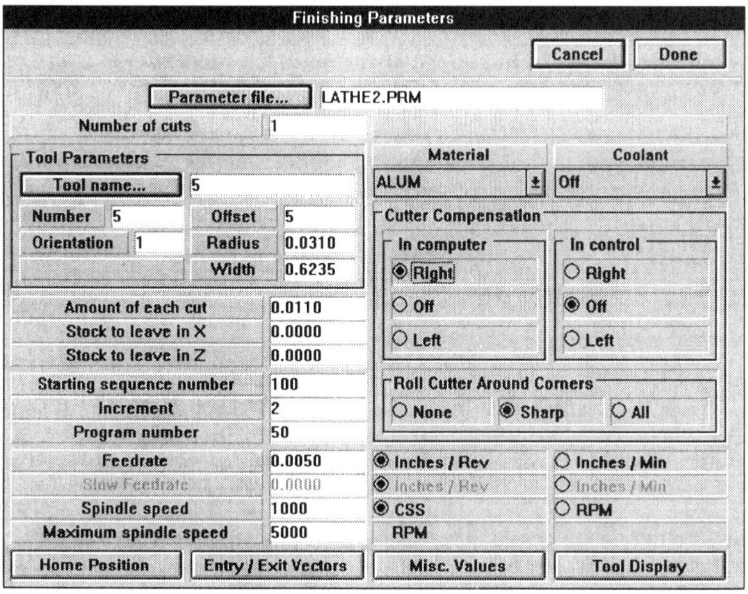

Step 5. Define home position.

Click on the Home Position button at the lower-left corner of the Finishing Parameters Window
Set the two Home position parameters to these values ☞

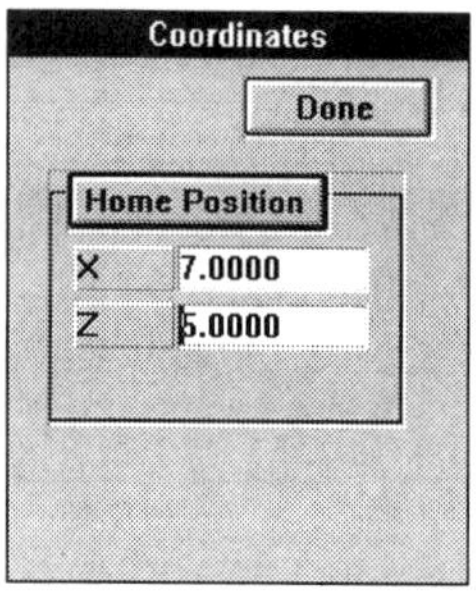

Select **Done** to return back to the Finishing Parameters Window

Step 6. Define the Entry/Exit Vectors.

Click on the Entry/Exit Vectors button at the bottom of the window
Set their parameters as shown here:

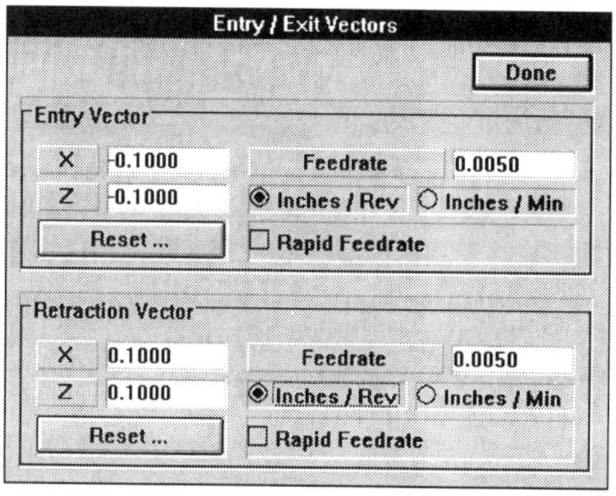

Select **Done** to return back to the Finishing parameters window.

Step 7. Set the Miscellaneous variables to their proper values.

Click on the Misc.Values button at the bottom of the window
Set the Miscellaneous Integer 2 to **0** (to generate a long program)
Select **Done** to return to the Finishing parameters window.

Step 8. Set the Display parameters

Click on the Tool Display button at the bottom of the window.
Set the Tool Display parameters as below:

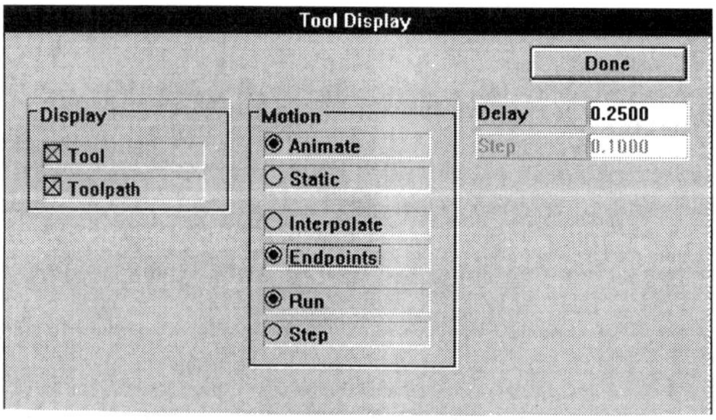

Select **Done** to return to the Finishing parameters window.

Step 9. Write the toolpaths.

Select **Done** from the Finishing parameters window
Select **Write** from the Finish-set menu
Press **F3** to repaint the screen
The toolpaths will be displayed as in Figure 19.61

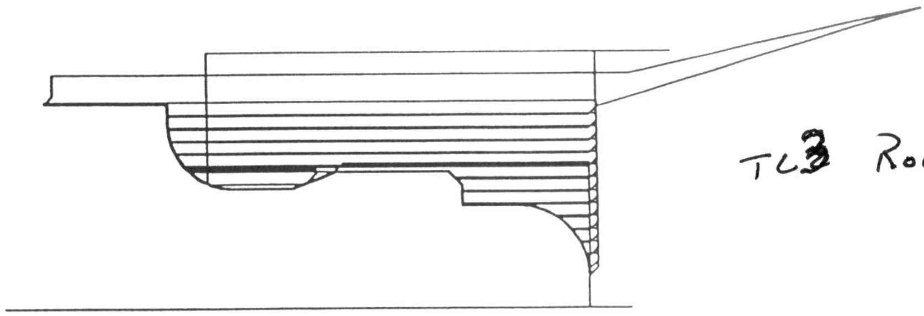

Figure 19.61

Step 10. Accept the toolpaths and run the post processor.

Select **Yes** to accept this toolpath segment
Select **End program**
Select **Yes** to "Run the post processor?"
Enter the file name: **lathe2**

The NC part program should be listed on the screen.
Double-click the upper-left window button to return back to the graphic mode.

Step 11. Edit the NC file.

Select **MAIN MENU → File → Edit → NC**
Enter the file name: **lathe2**

Do any necessary editing, the press **F10 → F10** to return back to graphic mode.

Project 4.

4

Using the finish module to generate a part program for roughing and finishing toolpaths

Generate roughing and finishing toolpaths with canned cycle commands for cutting the part shown in Figure 19.59. The part geometry file is **lathe2.** The finish module is used for this purpose.

Tip 1. The part geometry file is **lathe2.**

Step 1. Load the part geometry file (lathe2.ge3).

Select **MAIN MENU → File → Get → Geometry**
Enter file name: **lathe2**
Select **Yes** to delete the current part

The part geometry should appear as Figure 19.62.

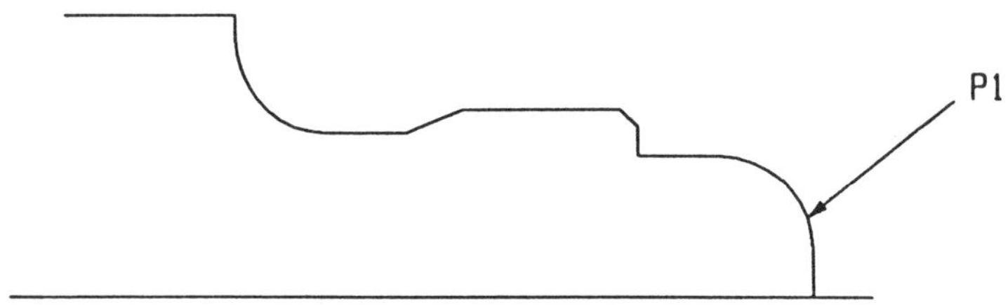

Figure 19.62

Step 2. Initiate the finish module.

Select **MAIN MENU** → **Toolpaths** → **Rough**
Enter file name: **lathe2c**

Step 3. Define the profile contour using the pick point in Figure 19.63.

Select **Chain** then pick at **P1**
Select **Close** → **End here** → **Point**
Enter **D5.5,0.5** ← for retraction point
Select **Done**

Step 4. Define finish parameters to the following settings.

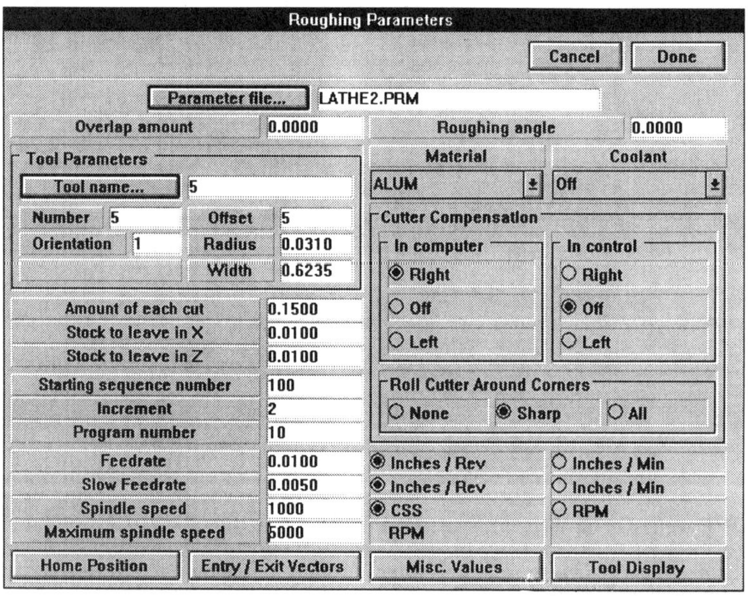

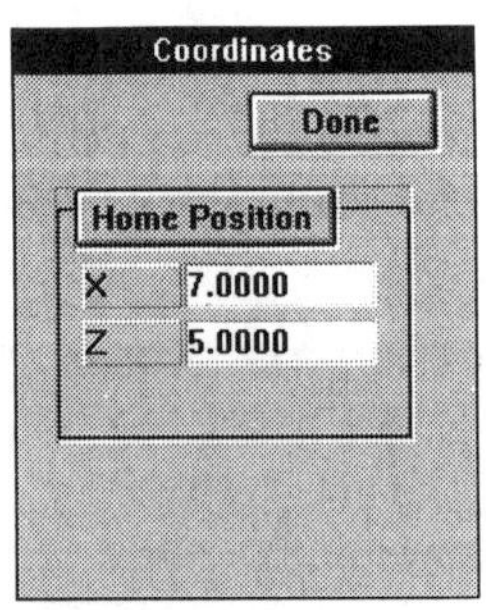

Step 5. Set the coordinate values.

Click on the **Home Position** button

Set the coordinate values as shown here ☞

Select **Done.**

Step 6. Set the Entry/Exit values.

Click on the Entry/Exit Vectors button

Set the vector values as shown here:

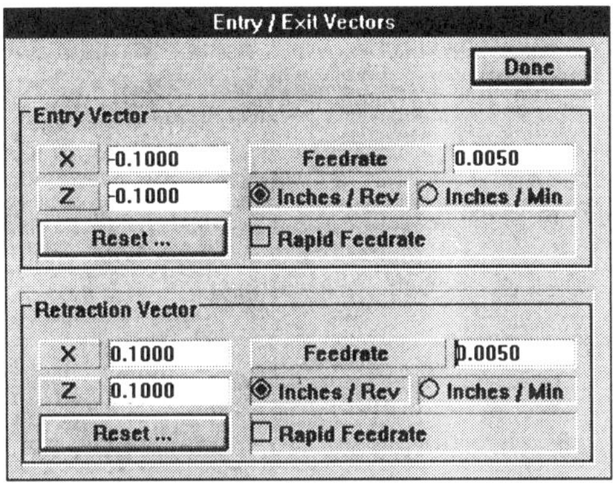

Select **Done**

Step 7. Set the Miscvellaneous values.

Click on the **Misc.Values** button.

Select the Miscellaneous Integer 2 = **2**

Select **Done**

Step 8. Set the display parameters.

Click on the Tool Display button

Set the display parameters as below:

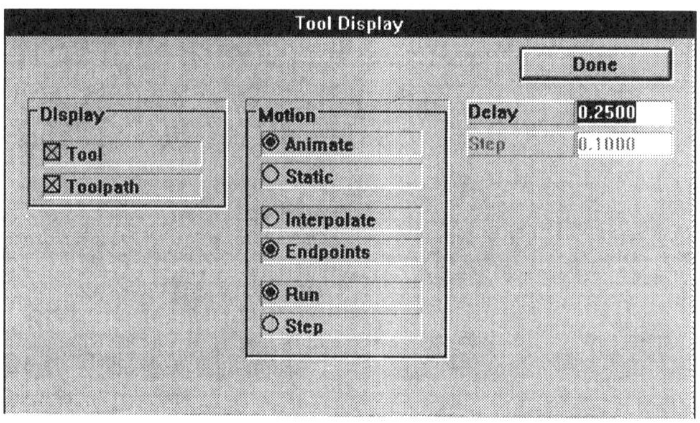

Select **Done**

Step 9. Generate the roughing toolpaths.

Select **Done** to complete the parameters setting

Press **Enter** to ignore the warning "entry vector is not perpendicular to the roughing direction"

The roughing toolpaths should be shown as Figure 19.63

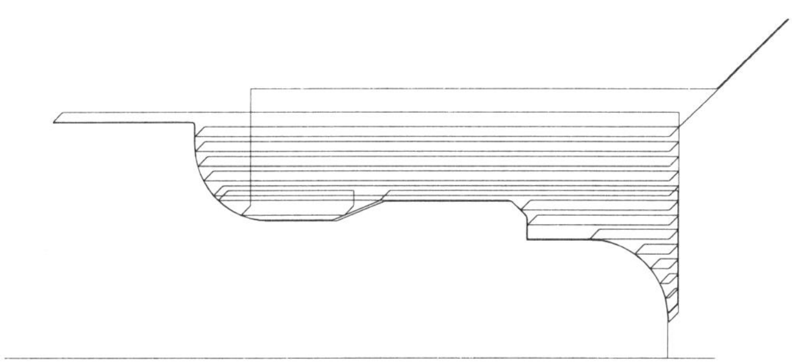

Figure 19.63

Step 10. Set the Finishing parameters.

Select **Finish → Last**

Set the Finishing parameters as shown here:

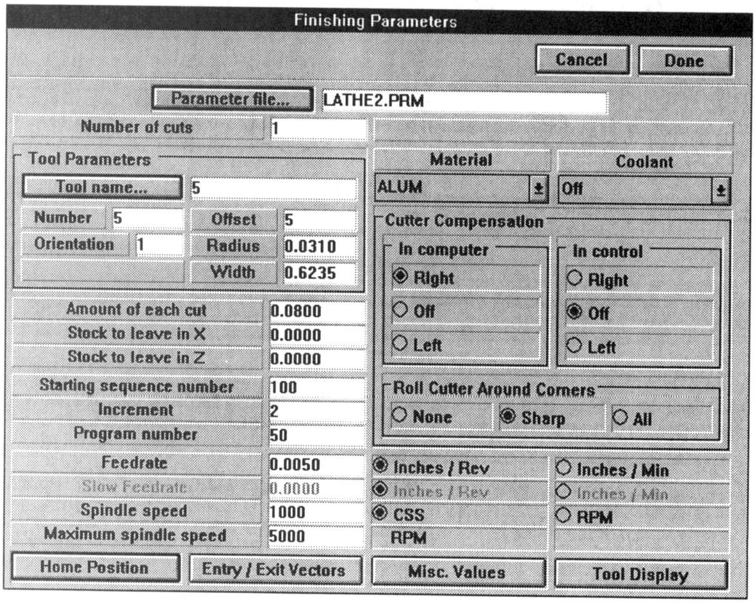

Step 11. Set the Home position.

Click on the Home Position button

Set **X = 7.0**

Z = 5.0

Select **Done** to return back to the Finishing parameters window

Step 12. Set the Final toolpaths.

Select **Done** to complete the parameters setting

Select **Write** from the Finish-set menu

The final toolpaths should resemble Figure 19.64

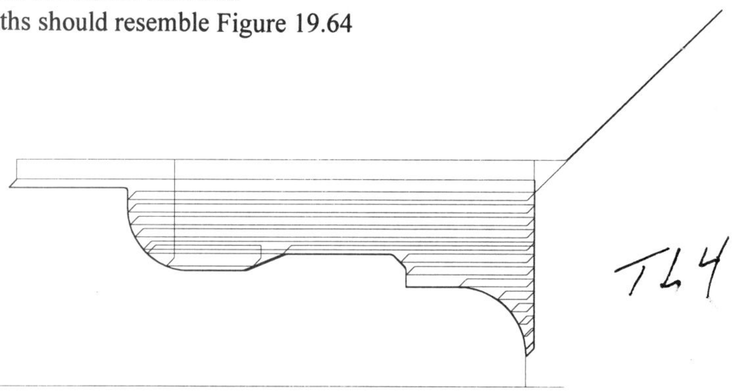

Figure 19.64

Step 13. Generate the part program.

Select **Yes** to accept the toolpath segment

Select **End program** to close the NCI file

Select **Yes** to run the post processor

Enter the File name: **lathec2**

The part program should appear like the example on the following page. Note that the G71 command appears in N116 and the G70 command in N150.

LATHEC2 Part Program

```
Mon Feb 27 19:11:20 1995
%
O0010
(LATHEC2)
N100G20
N102G50X14.Z5.
N104G0T0505
N106G50S4000
N108G97S0809M3
N110X5.5Z.11
N112G96S1000
N114G99
N116G71P118Q148U.02W.01D.1501F.01
N118G0X.938
N120G1X.738Z0.F.005
N122G3X2.4Z-.831R.831
N124G1Z-1.5
N126X2.838
N128G3X2.8818Z-1.5091R.031
N130G1X3.1818Z-1.6591
N132G3X3.2Z-1.681R.031
N134G1Z-3.037
N136X2.8Z-3.537
N138Z-4.231
N140G2X4.338Z-5.R.769
N142G1X4.738
N144G3X4.8Z-5.031R.031
N146G1Z-6.5
N148G1X5.Z-6.4
N150G70P118Q148
N152G0X5.5Z.11
N154G28U0.W0.
N156T0500
N158M5
N160M01
N162M30
%
```

19.7 Groove Module

The groove module generates a set of toolpaths for plunging the tool into the material to rough the part.

Groove Specific Parameter

Only **one** unique parameter is available in the groove module: cutting direction. The cutting direction can be specified in the vertical or the horizontal direction. The vertical cutting direction is used in stock grooving (Figure 19.65), while the horizontal cutting direction is used for face grooving (Figure 19.66).

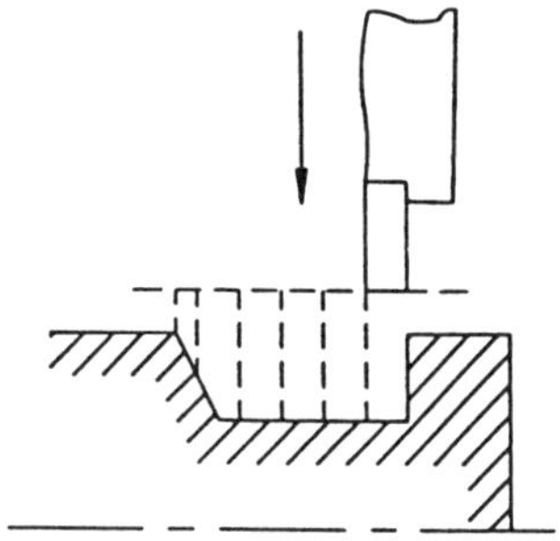

Figure 19.65

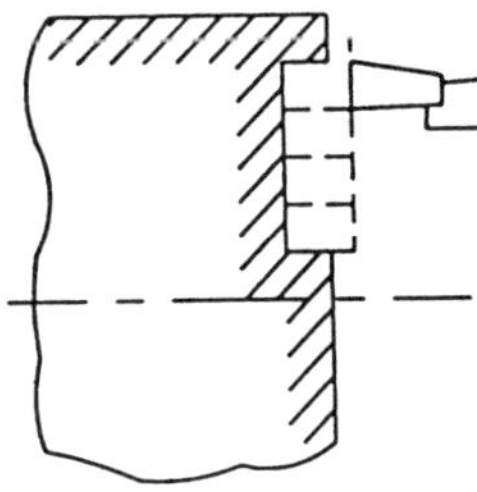

Figure 19.66

How to Define Grooving Toolpaths

Two boundaries, the inner boundary and outer boundary, are required to define the grooving toolpaths. The **inner boundary** is the desired part contour to be produced. The **outer boundary** defines the plunging start position and the retracting end position of each plunging cut. The outer boundary should be longer than the inner boundary in the Z direction for stock grooving, or longer in the X direction for face grooving. Figures 19.67 and 19.68 show typical examples of OD and ID grooving.

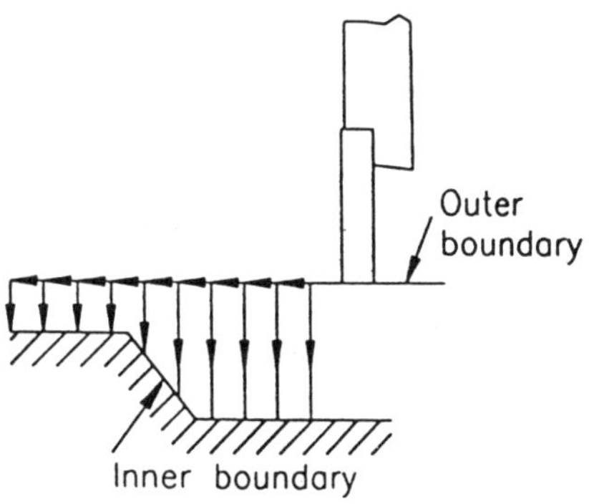

Figure 19.67 OD Grooving

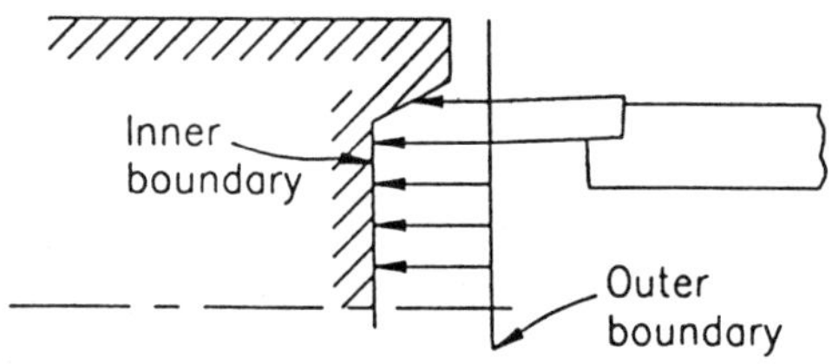

Figure 19.68 ID Grooving

G74 and G75 canned cycles can be used for grooving and drilling. They permit the tool to be automatically reliefed. The G74 canned cycle is used for ID grooving as shown in Figure 19.68 and G75 is used for OD grooving as shown in Figure 19.67.

These two canned cycles have the following command statement format:

•One-block format:

G74/G75 Xx Zz Pi Qk Rd Ff

- Rd — Relief amount
- Qk — Increment in the Z direction
- Pi — Increment in the X direction
- Xx Zz — X and Z coordinate of grooving end point

•Two-block format:

G74/G75 Re

- Re — Return amount

G74/G75 Xx Zz Pi Qk Rd Ff

Procedure for generating the Grooving Canned Cycle Command G74 or G75

1. Select Toolpaths → Groove
2. Define the inner and outer grooving boundary
3. Set the grooving parameters to the proper setting
4. Set the miscellaneous integer 2 to 1.

Project 5. 5

Cutting a groove

Use the grooving tool (#13) in the tool library to cut a groove shown in Figure 19.69. This grooving tool as shown in Figure 19.70 has a width of 0.125" with a radius of 0.003" at both corners.

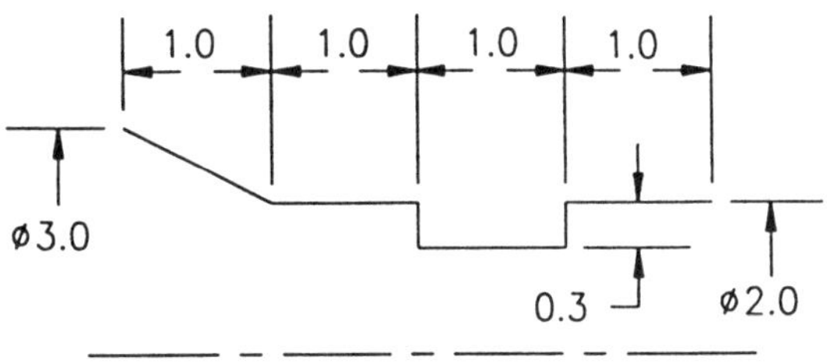

Figures 19.69

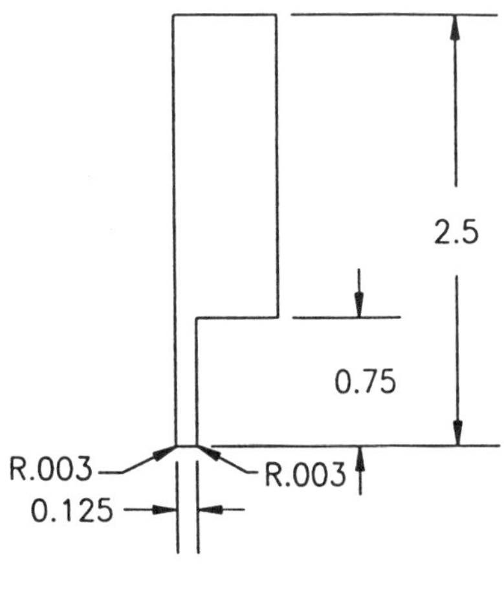

Figure 19.70

⌛**Tips** 1. Create the inner groove profile and outer boundary.

2. Change the line type to center to create the center line of the part geometry.

3. Use grooving tool #13 which has a width of 0.125".

4. Set the major grooving parameters to the following settings:

Cutter compensation in computer = right Amount of each cut = 0.1 Feedrate = 0.003 inches/rev Spindle speed = 500 CSS Maximum spindle speed = 3000 RPM

Step 1. Create the part profile.

Select **MAIN MENU → Create → Line → Multi**
Specify endpoint 1: **D2,0** ←
Specify endpoint 2: **D2,-1**←
Specify endpoint 3: **D1.4,-1** ←
Specify endpoint 4: **D1.4,-2** ←
Specify endpoint 5: **D2,-2** ←
Specify endpoint 6: **D2,-3** ←
Specify endpoint 7: **D3,-4** ←

The part profile should look like Figure 19.71.

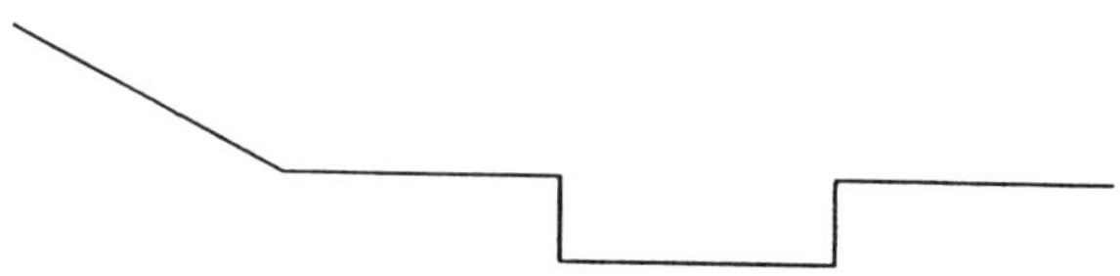

Figure 19.71

Step 2. Add a center line.

Select **-PM-** from the left menu column
The first page of the Drafting parameters menu should appear.
Click on the button **LineStyles** to get a list of linetype, then select **center**
Select **Done** to return to main menu
Select **MAIN MENU → Create → Line → Endpoints**
Specify the first endpoint: **0,0.25** ←
Specify the second endpoint: **0,-4.25**←

The center line is added as shown in Figure 19.72.

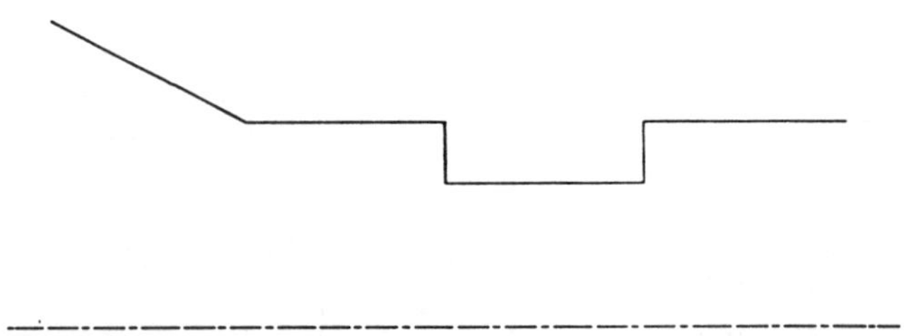

Figure 19.72

Step 3. Toggle the line style back to solid type.

Select **-PM-**
Click on the **Line Styles** button, then select **Solid** from the list
Select **Done**

Step 4. Create the outer boundary line.

Select **MAIN MENU → Create → Line → Endpoints**
Specify the first endpoint: **D2.5,-0.9** ←
Specify the second endpoint: **D2.5,-2.1** ←

The line is added as in Figure 19.73.

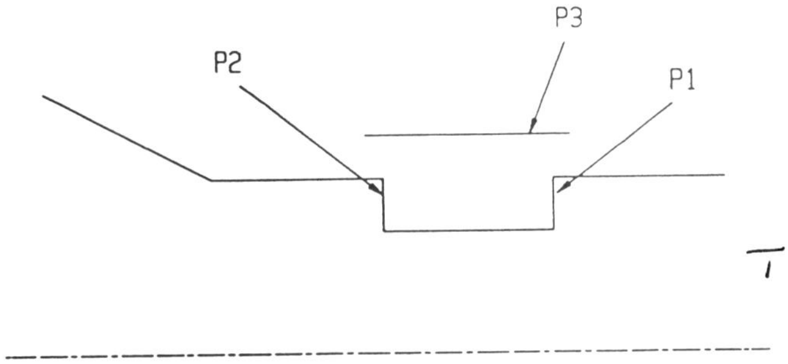

Figure 19.73

Step 5. Initiate the groove module.

Select **MAIN MENU → Toolpaths → Groove**
Enter file name: **groove** ←

Step 6. Define the inner and outer boundary using the pick points in Figure 19.73.

Select **Chain**, then pick at **P1** and **P2**
Select **End here** to complete the inner boundary
Select **Single** then pick at **P3** for the outer boundary
Select **Done**

Step 7. Define grooving parameters to the following settings.

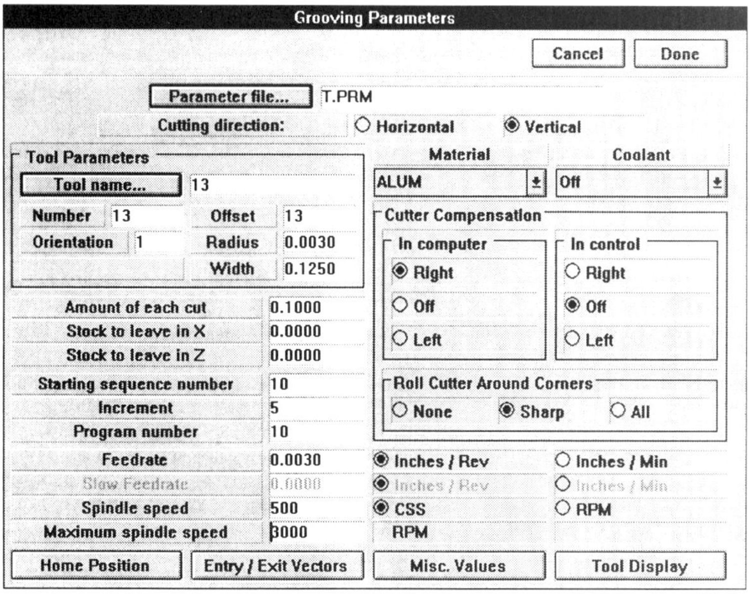

Step 8. Set the Home position.

Click on the **Home Position** button at the left-bottom of the window

Set **X = 3.0**

Z = 2.0

Select **Done**

Step 9. Set the Entry/Exit Vectors.

Click on the Entry/Exit vectors at the bottom of the parameters window

Set the parameters as indicated here ☞

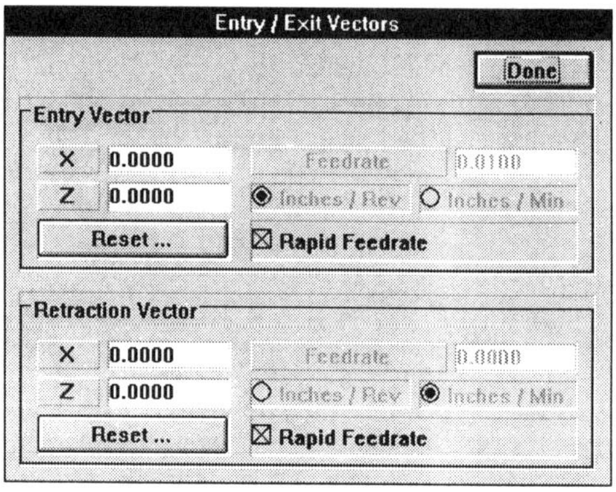

Select **Done**

Step 10. Set the Tool Display parameters.

Click on the Tool Display button at the right-bottom of the window

Set the parameters as below.

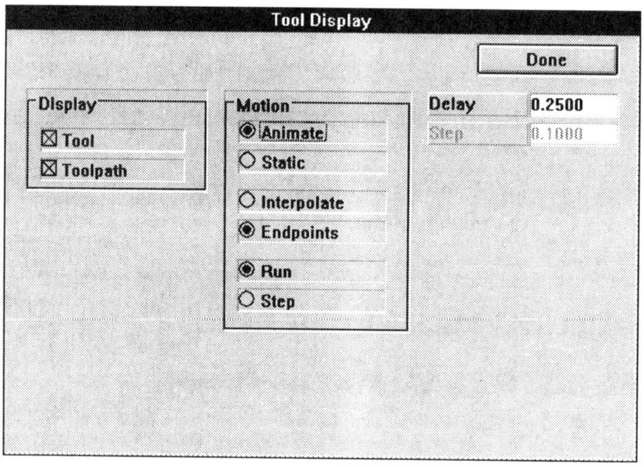

Select **Done** to return to the parameters window.

Step 11. Accept the toolpath.

The grooving toolpaths should appear as Figure 19.74.

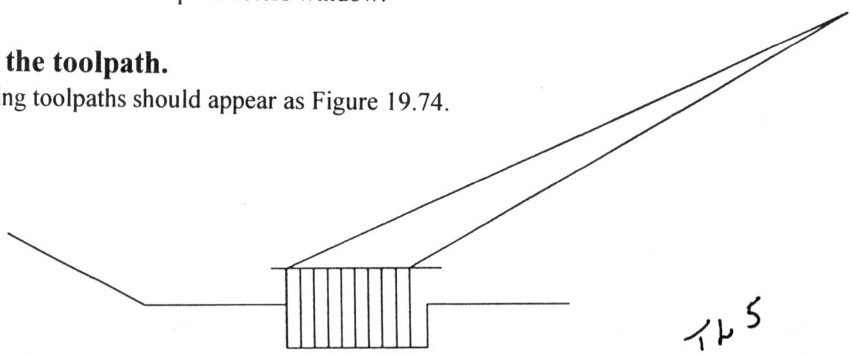

Figure 19.74

Select **Yes** to accept this toolpath segment
Select **End progrm** to close NCI file
Select **Yes** to "Run the post processor?"
Enter file name: **groove**

The part program should appear on the screen
Double-click the upper-left button of the window to return back to graphic mode.

Step 12. Save the Groove Geometry.

Select **MAIN MENU → File → Save → Geometry**
Enter file name: **groove**

Project 6. 6

Generating grooving toolpaths with the canned cycle command G74.

Use the groove geometry and tool used in project 5 to generate a "set of toolpaths" command to cut the groove.

Tips 1. The procedure for generating grooving the canned cycle command for the short program is identical to that generating the long program for grooving except setting three miscellaneous variables to proper values.

2. The three miscellaneous variables used to specify a grooving canned cycle and their proper values are:

Miscellaneous integer 2 = 1
Miscellaneous real 3 for clearance = 0.1 (for this project)
Miscellaneous real 4 for pecking depth = 0.15 (for this project)

Step 1. Load the groove geometry file (groove.ge3).

Select **MAIN MENU → File → Get → Geometry**
Enter the file name: **groove**
Select **Yes** to delete the current part if necessary
The part geometry should appear as in Figure 19.75

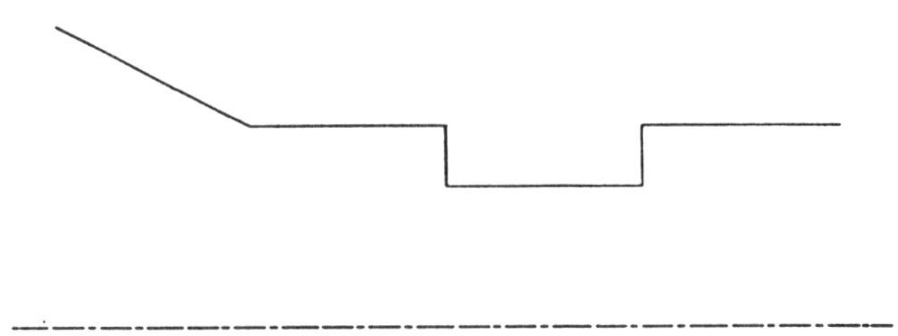

Figure 19.75

Step 2. Initiate the groove module.

Select **MAIN MENU → Toolpaths → Groove**
Enter the file name: **groove1**

Step 3. Repeat steps 6 - 10 in project 5.

Step 4. Set the Misc. Values to the proper values for grooving.

Click on the **Misc. Values** button located at the bottom of the parameters window.
Set the Miscellaneous Integer 2 to **1**
Miscellaneous Real 3 to **0.1**
Miscellaneous Real 4 to **0.15**

Step 5. Generate the grooving toolpaths.

Select **Done** from the parameters window
The grooving toolpaths should appear as in Figure 19.76

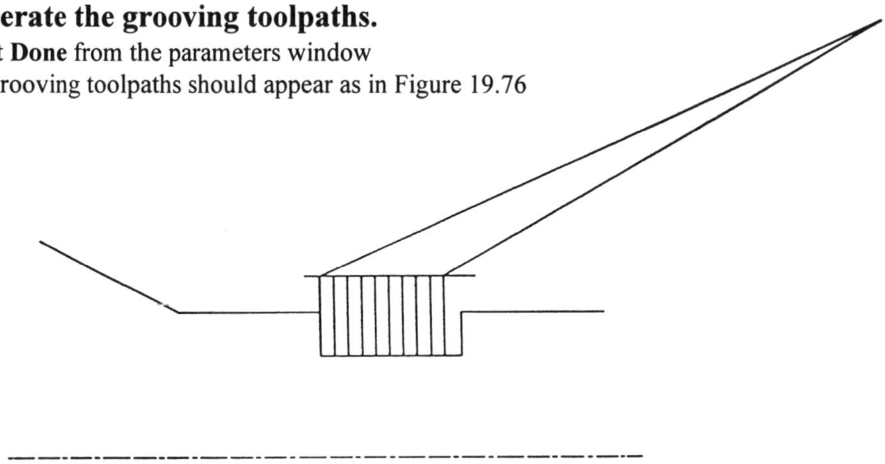

Figure 19.76

Select **Yes** to accept the toolpath segment
Select **End program** to close the NCI file
Select **Yes** to run the post processor
Enter the file name: **groove1.NC**
The part program should appear on screen as below in Figure 19.77.

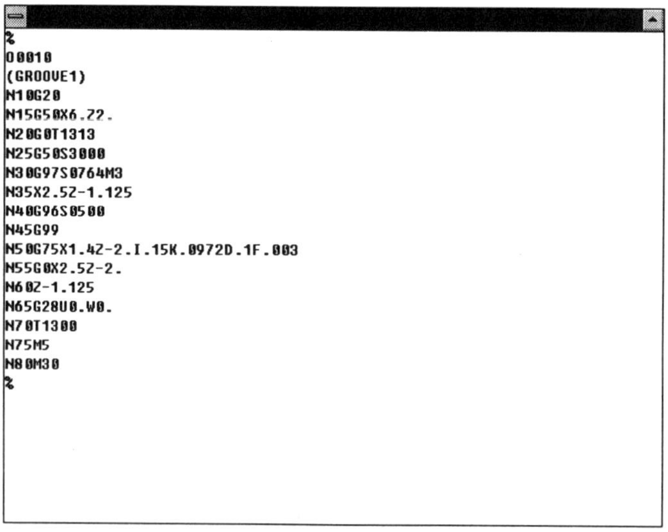

```
%
O0010
(GROOVE1)
N10G20
N15G50X6.Z2.
N20G0T1313
N25G50S3000
N30G97S0764M3
N35X2.5Z-1.125
N40G96S0500
N45G99
N50G75X1.4Z-2.I.15K.0972D.1F.003
N55G0X2.5Z-2.
N60Z-1.125
N65G28U0.W0.
N70T1300
N75M5
N80M30
%
```

Figure 19.77

Double-click the upper-left button of the window to return back to graphic mode.

19.8 Thread Module

The thread module is used to generate toolpaths to cut various types of threads including external and internal straight threads as well as taper threads.

Geometric Contour for Threading

Three pieces of information must be specified in defining geometry contour for thread cutting: major diameter, minor diameter, as well as thread length.

Mastercam uses a vertical line to define the major diameter and minor diameter of the thread (Figure 19.78). The end point with the larger X coordinate value specifies the major diameter, while the other end point with the smaller X coordinate value gives the minor diameter.

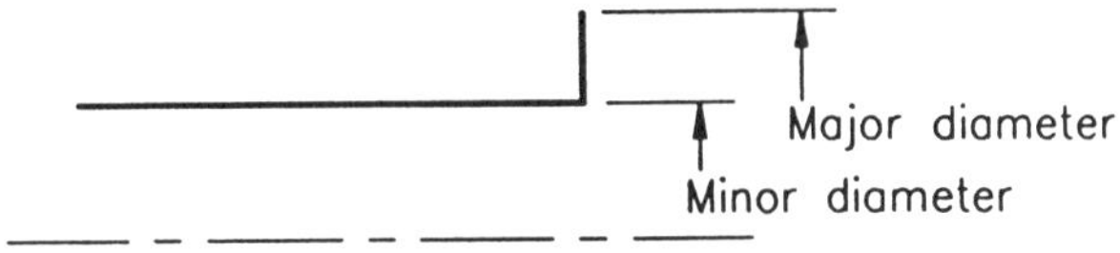

Figure 19.78

A horizontal line is used to define the thread length of the straight threads (Figure 19.79a and 19.79c). A taper line defines the thread length of taper threads (Figure 19.79b and 19.79d).

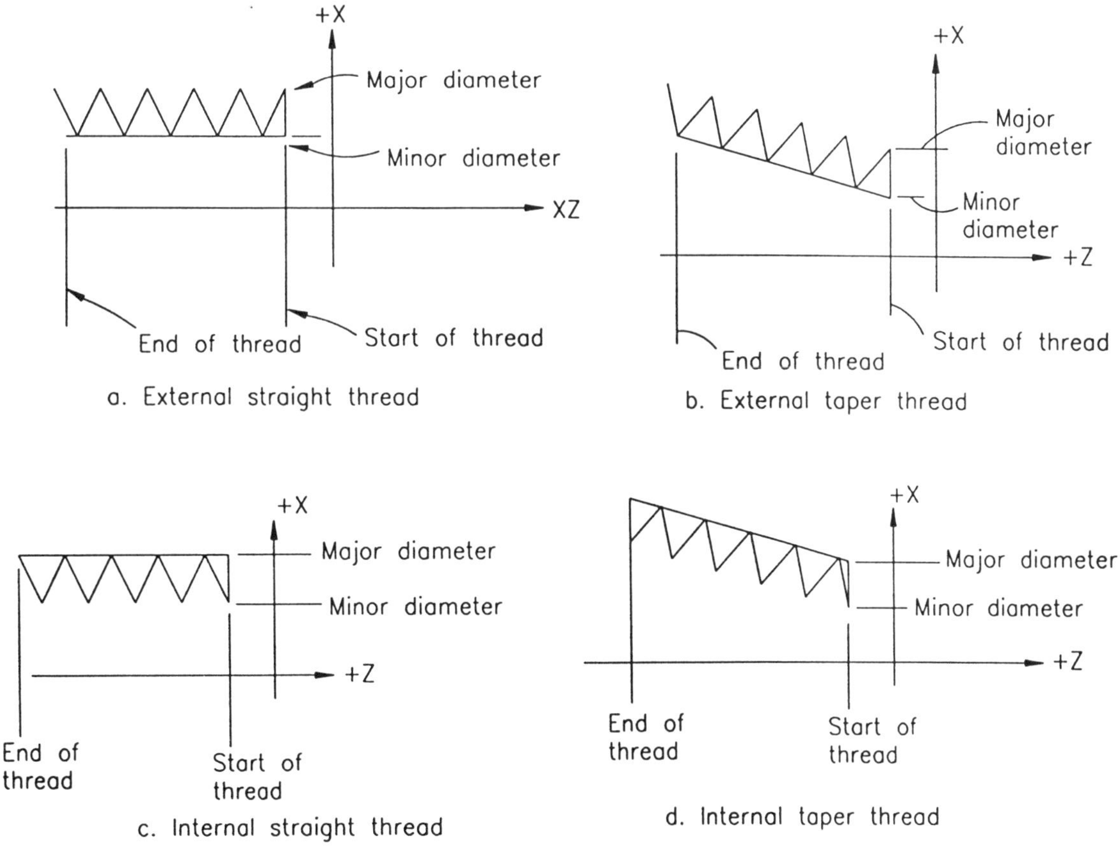

Figure 19.79

Thread Depth

The depth of threads varies according to thread form, thread series, and thread classes. Refer to Machinery's handbook or other references to obtain accurate thread dimensions. The formulas to calculate the thread height and minor diameter for two thread series, UNC and UNF, are given below:

UNC Threads:	External threads: Thread height h = 0.5952 P Minor diameter d = D - 1.1904 P where h = thread height P = thread pitch D = major diameter d = minor diameter Internal threads: Thread height h = 0.54125 P Minor diameter d = D - 1.0825 P
UNF Threads:	External threads: Thread height h = 0.599 P Minor diameter d = D - 1.198 P Internal threads: Thread height = 0.54125 P Minor diameter d = D - 1.0824 P

Example 1.

Calculate the thread height and minor diameter for the following three UNC threads.

	External thread		Internal thread	
	Thread height h=0.5952P	Minor diameter d= D-1.1904P	Thread height h=0.54125P	Minor diameter d=D-1.0825P
1/2-13-UNC	0.0458	0.4084	0.0416	0.4167
1-8-UNC	0.0744	0.8512	0.0677	0.8647
2-4½-UNC	0.1323	1.7355	0.1203	1.7594

Example 2.

Calculate the thread height and minor diameter for the following three UNF threads.

	External thread		Internal thread	
	Thread height h=0.5990P	Minor diameter d= D-1.198P	Thread height h=0.54125P	Minor diameter d=D-1.0824P
1/4-28-UNF	0.0214	0.2072	0.0193	0.2113
7/8-14-UNF	0.0428	0.7894	0.0387	0.7977
1½-12-UNF	0.0499	1.4002	0.0451	1.4098

Threading Specific Parameters

The unique parameters for threading are:

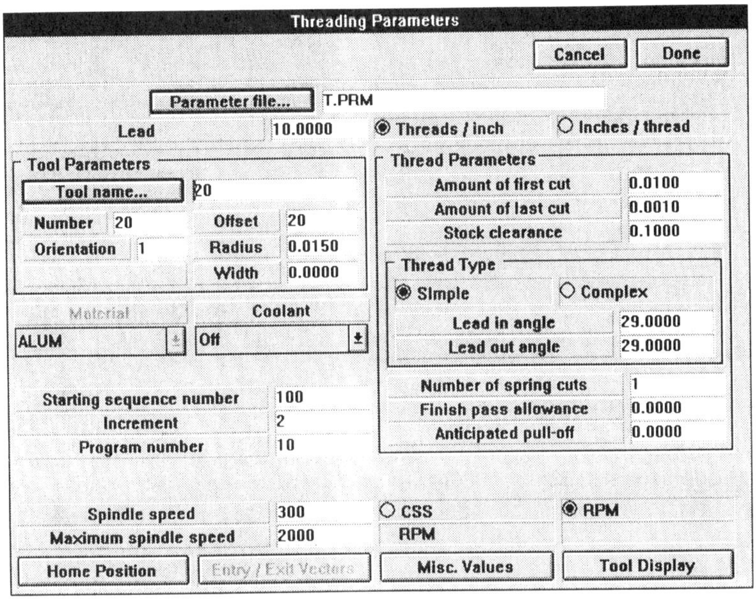

These parameters can be classified into the following **five** groups: thread lead, threading depth, acceleration and deceleration length, threading command type, and lead-in and lead-out angle.

Thread Lead

This command specifies the thread size which can be expressed in number of threads per inch or number of inches per thread.

Threading Depth

The depth of thread is one-half of the difference between the major diameter and minor diameter. As indicated previously, this depth is represented by a vertical line at the beginning of the thread. The required number of threading passes is determined by **three** factors; amount of first cut, amount of last cut, and the depth of the thread. Mastercam uses these three pieces of information to automatically determine the number of threading cuts and the depth of cut for each threading pass.

The two parameters that need to be specified in determining threading depth are amount of first cut and amout of last cut. The amount of first cut parameter specifies the amount of stock to be removed in the first threading pass. The amount of last cut parameter specifies the amount of stock to be removed in the last threading pass.

Tips 1. The amount of the first threading cut is suggested to be in the range of 0.03" to 0.045". The larger the number of threads per inch, the smaller the amount of first threading cut.
2. The amount of the last threading cut is about 0.005".

Acceleration Length and Deceleration Length

To produce accurate threads, an acceleration length and a deceleration length should be added at the start and at the end of the threading path, respectively (Figure 19.80). Acceleration length is the allowance distance for the servo control system to accelerate the drive from zero to the specified feedrate. Deceleration length is the allowance distance for the servo system to decelerate from the threading feedrate to zero.

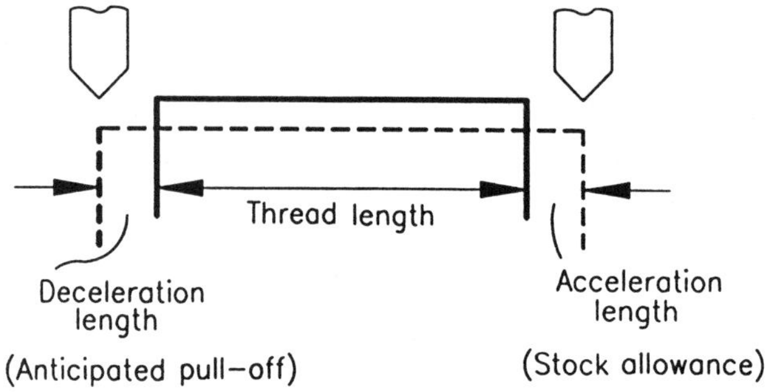

Figure 19.80

In Mastercam lathe, a stock clearance parameter is used to specify the acceleration length and the antipated pull-off parameter for deceleration length.

How to Determine Acceleration Length and Deceleration Length

The acceleration length (L_A) and deceleration length (L_D) can be found from the following two formulas:

$$L_D = \frac{LNT}{60}$$

$$L_A = -(1+\ln a) \times L_D$$

where
- L = thread lead (in.)
- N = spindle speed (RPM)
- T = time constant of the servo system (T = 0.033 s, 0.05 s, 0.067 s, 0.1 s with 0.067 s being most common)
- a = thread accuracy (a = dL/L)
- dL = error in thread lead
- ln = natural log

The acceleration length and deceleration length computed from the above two formulas are the minimum distances. Any distance greater than the computed value would satisfy the requirement.

Example 3.

Find the acceleration length and deceleration length for cutting a 1-8 UNC thread with the following operating conditions:

Time constant: 0.066 s
Spindle speed: 500 RPM
Thread accuracy: 0.01

Solution:

The deceleration length is found as

L_D = LNT/60 = (1/8)(500)(0.067)/60 = 0.07 in.

L_A = -(1+ln a) x L_D = -[1+ln (0.01)] x 0.07 = 0.252 in.

Threading Command Type

There are **three** common threading commands: G32, G92 and G76. G32 is the single-pass threading command and is generally used with the G00 code to complete the threading cycle. Note that some controllers use G33 as the single-pass threading command. Figure 19.81 illustrates the toolpath pattern of G32.

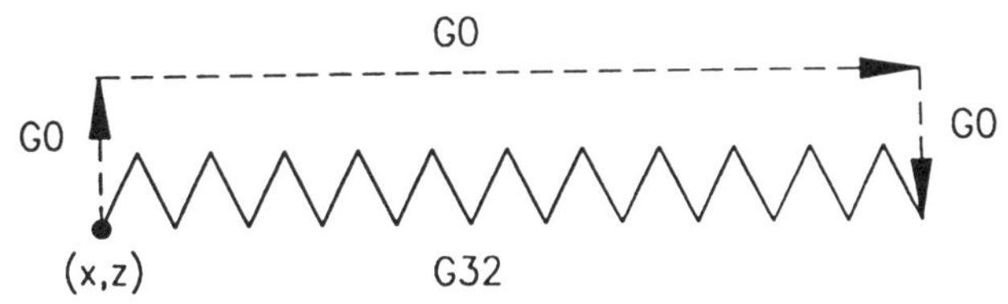

Figure 19.81

The G92 code is often referred to as a box threading cycle because it generates four toolpaths that form a box as shown in Figure 19.82. The use of G92 code reduces the number of part program blocks by 75 percent.

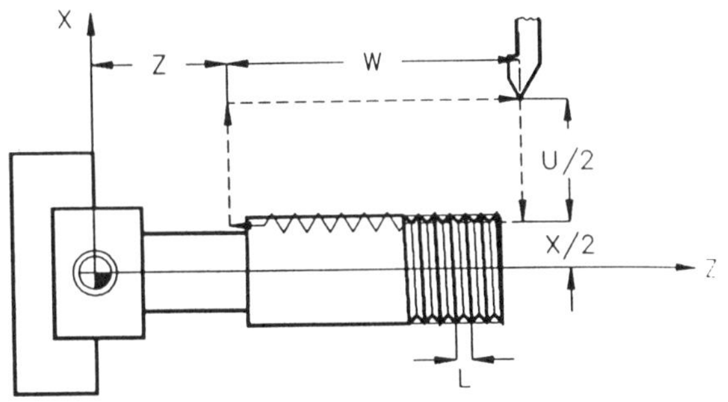

Figure 19.82

G76 is an automatic threading cycle. It generates several threading passes for cutting a thread in one G76 command block. Figure 19.83 depicts the threading toolpath pattern of G76 command.

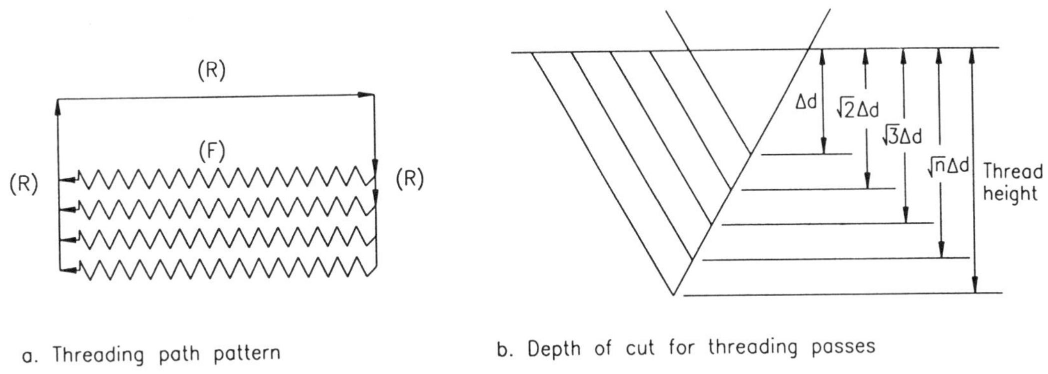

Figure 19.83

How to Select Threading Command

Mastercam Lathe uses **two** parameters for selecting the threading command to be output to the part program: thread type (simple or complex) and miscellaneous integer 4 (0 or 1). The proper parameter settings for each command are listed below.

Threading command	Thread Type parameter	Miscellaneous Integer 4
G32	Simple	0
G92	Simple	1
G76	Complex	--

Note: Not all CNC lathe controllers have the G92 and G76 threading commands.

The thread parameter in Mastercam lathe can be toggled to simple or complex to select the threading command type. The selection of simple indicates the G32 threading command is to be used, and complex identifies G76 to be used. Note that not all CNC lathe controllers have a G76 threading command.

Lead-in and Lead-out Angles

Lead-in angle and lead-out angle are only available when the complex command is chosen. The lead-in angle and lead-out angle allow the cutter to engage the part in one side only (Figure 19.84). These two angles normally are 29°.

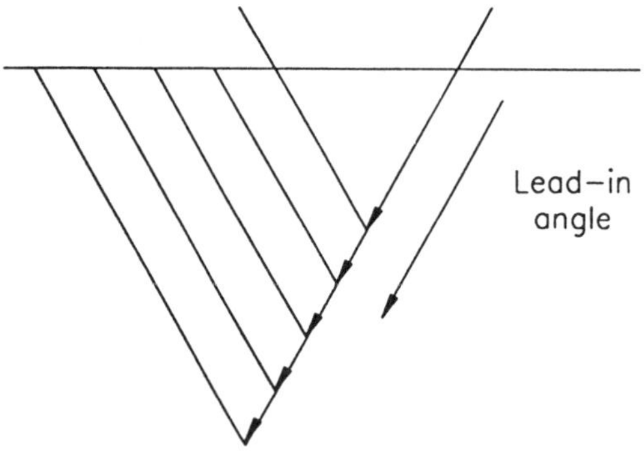

Figure 19.84

Spring Cuts

Spring cuts are those threading passes that cut the thread at the finish depth. In other words, no material is removed in those passes unless a non-zero value is given to the parameter of finish pass allowance.

Two parameters control the spring cuts: number of spring cuts and finish pass allowance. The value for the finish pass allowance is specified in the radius.

Project 7.

Cutting external threads

Use the thread module to cut external threads 1-8-UNC as shown in Figure 19.85. The threading tool is #16 in the tool library.

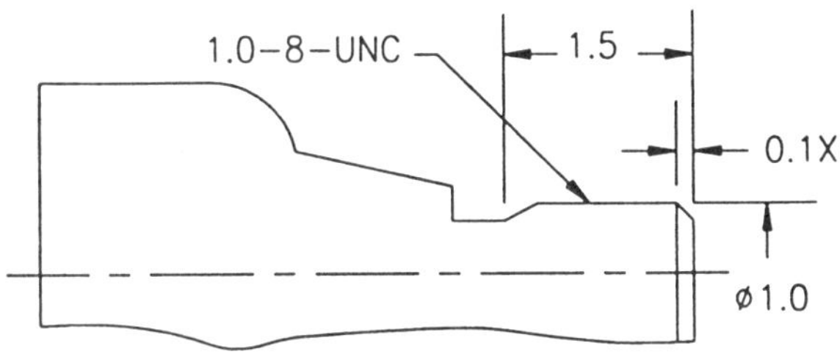

Figure 19.85

Tips 1. Create only two lines that represent major diameter, minor diameter, and the thread length.

2. Threading dimensions are calculated below:
   - Major diameter = D1.0
   - Pitch = 1/8 = 0.125"
   - Thread height h = 0.5952 P = 0.0744"
   - Minor diameter d = D - 1.1904 P = 0.8512"

3. Threading parameters are given below:
   - Retraction point: D1.5,0.2
   - Lead = 8.0 threads/inch
   - Amount of first cut = 0.02
   - Amount of last cut = 0.001
   - Stock clearance = 0.2
   - Thread = simple
   - Number of spring cuts = 1
   - Spindle speed = 500 RPM

4. Threading tool information:
   - Tool name = 16
   - N= 5
   - Ofs = 5
   - O = 1
   - R = 0.0155
   - W = 0

Step 1. Create threading geometry.

Select **MAIN MENU → Create → Line → Multi**
Specify endpoint 1: **D1.0,0.1** ←
Specify endpoint 2: **D0.8512,0.1** ←
Specify endpoint 3: **D0.8512,-1.55** ←

Press **Alt + F1** simultaneously, then press **F2** to fit the drawing on screen. The thread profile represented by two lines should appear as Figure 19.86.

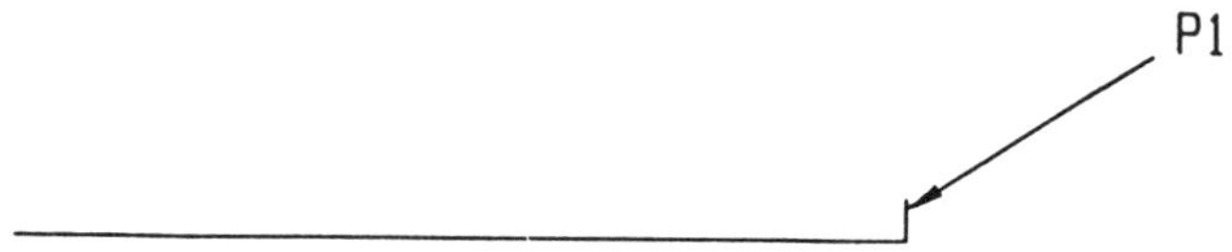

Figure 19.86

Step 2. Initiate the thread module.

Select **MAIN MENU** → **Toolpaths** → **Thread**
Enter file name: **thread1** ←

Step 3. Define the threading contours using the pick points in Figure 19.86.

Select **Chain**, then pick at **P1**
Select **Close** → **End here** → **Point**
Enter the retraction point: **D1.5,0.2** ←
Select **Done**

Step 4. Define the threading parameters to the following settings.

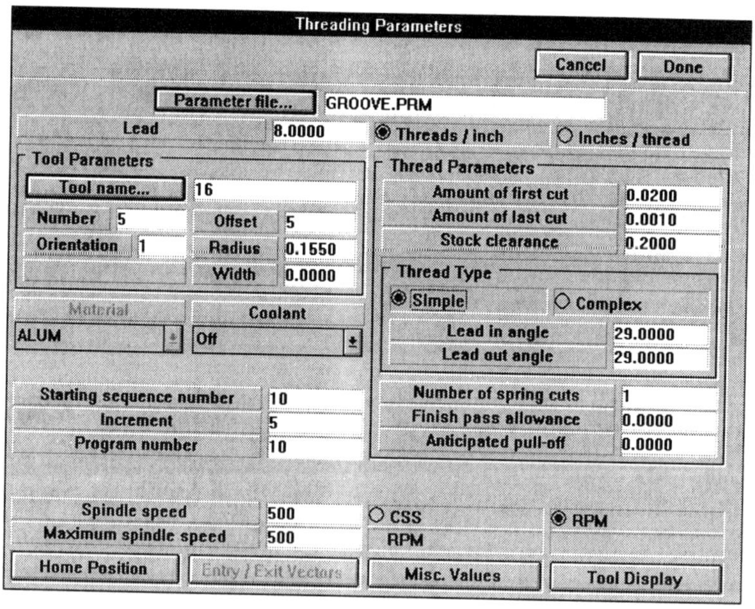

Step 5. Define the home position.

Click on the **Home Position** button
Set X and Z coordinates as below

X = **5.0**

Z = **3.0**

Select **Done**

Step 6. Set the variable Mi4 to 0 for output G32 codes.

Click on the **Misc. Values** button
Set the Miscellaneous Integer 4 to **0** if necessary
Select **Done**

Step 7. Set the tool display mode.

Click on the **Tool Display** button
Set the tool display parameters as below

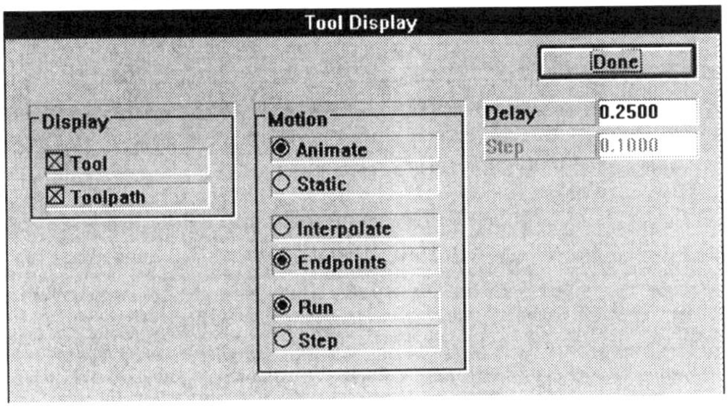

Select **Done** to return back to the parameters window.

Step 8. Generate and accept the threading toolpaths.

Select **Done** from the parameters window
The threading toolpaths should appear as Figure 19.87.

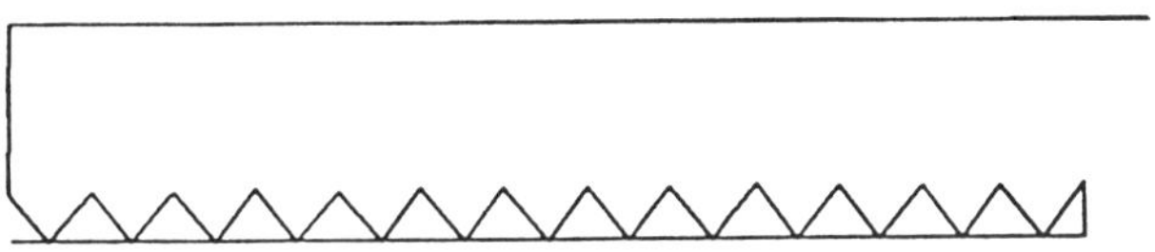

Figure 19.87

Select **Yes** to accept this toolpath segment
Select **End progrm** to close the NCI file
Select **Yes** to "Run the post processor?"
Enter file name: **thread1**
A partial part program is listed below.

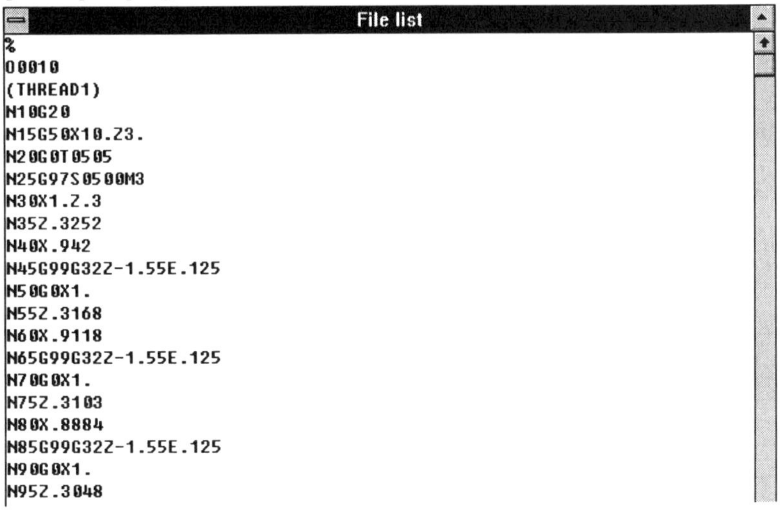

File list

```
%
O0010
(THREAD1)
N10G20
N15G50X10.Z3.
N20G0T0505
N25G97S0500M3
N30X1.Z.3
N35Z.3252
N40X.942
N45G99G32Z-1.55E.125
N50G0X1.
N55Z.3168
N60X.9118
N65G99G32Z-1.55E.125
N70G0X1.
N75Z.3103
N80X.8884
N85G99G32Z-1.55E.125
N90G0X1.
N95Z.3048
```

Double-click the upper-left button to return back to graphic mode.

Generate G92 Commands:

Step 9. Reinitiate the toolpath module.

Repeat steps 2-5.
Enter the file name: **thread1a** in step 2.

Step 10. Set the variable Mi4 to 1 for outputting G92 codes.

Click **Misc. Values** button
Set Miscellaneous Integer 4 to **1**
Select **Done**

Step 11. Generate and accept the threading toolpaths.

Select **Done** from the threading parameters window
The threading toolpaths should appear as Figure 19.87 on the previous page
Select **Yes** to accept the toolpath segment
Select **End program** to close the NCI file
Select **Yes** to run the post processor
Enter file name: **thread1a**

The part program with G92 commands should appear on screen as below:

```
%
O0010
(THREAD1A)
N10G20
N15G50X10.Z3.
N20G0T0505
N25G97S0500M3
N30X1.Z.3
N35G92X.942Z-1.55E.125
N40X.9118
N45X.8884
N50X.8687
N55X.8512
N60X.8512
N65G0X1.5
N70Z.2
N75Z.3
N80G28U0.W0.
N85T0500
N90M5
N95M30
%
```

Double-click the upper-left button to return to graphic mode.

Project 8.

Cutting internal threads

Use the thread module to generate a part program which cuts internal threads 1/8 -12-UNF.

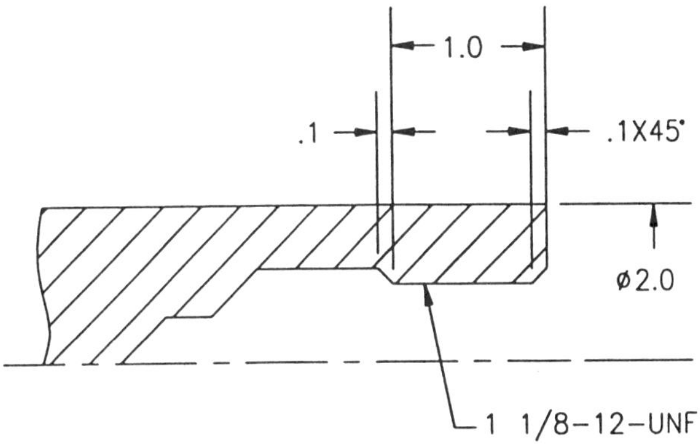

Figure 19.88

Tips 1. Generate two threading programs; one with the G32 command and the other with the G76 command.

2. Threading dimensions are given below:
   Major diameter = 1.125"
   Pitch = 1/12 = 0.0833"
   Thread height = 0.5412 P = 0.0451"
   Minor diameter = D - 1.0824 P = 1.0348"
3. Internal threading tool information:
   Tool name: 28
   Stored in position #10 in the turret. It has the following parameters:

N = 10	Ofs = 10	O = 4	R = 0.0	W = 0

4. Threading parameters are given below:

Lead = 12 threads/inch Amount of first cut = 0.02" Amount of last cut = 0.002" Thread = simple and complex, respectively Spindle speed = 450 RPM

Step 1. Create thread profile.

Select **MAIN MENU → Create → Line → Multi**
Specify endpoint 1: **D1.0348,0.15** ←
Specify endpoint 2: **D1.125,0.15** ←
Specify endpoint 3: **D1.125,-1.1** ←

Press **Alt** + **F1** simultaneously and then press **F2** to fit the drawing on the screen. The thread profile appears as Figure 19.89.

Figure 19.89

Step 2. Initiate the thread module.

Select **MAIN MENU** → **Toolpaths** → **Thread**
Enter file name: **thread2** ←

Step 3. Define the threading profile using the pick point in Figure 19.89.

Select **Point**, then enter **D1.0,0.25** ←for the entry point
Select **Chain**, then pick at **P1**
Select **Close** → **End here** to define the threading profile
Select **Point**, then enter **D1.0,0.25** ←for the retraction point
Select **Done**

Step 4. Set the threading parameters to the following settings.

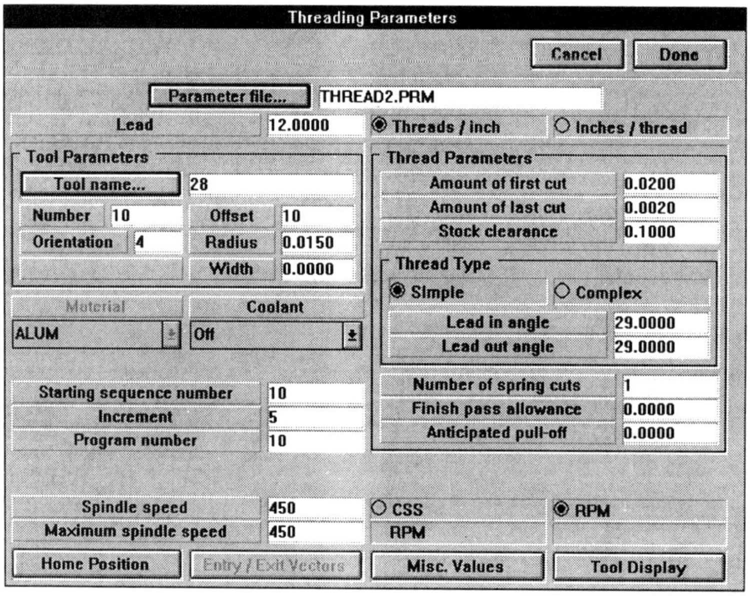

Step 5. Set Variable Mi4 to 0.

Click on the **Misc.Values** button
Set Miscellaneous Integer 4 to **0**
Select **Done** to return to the parameters window

Step 6. Generate and accept the toolpath.

Select **Done** to generate threading toolpath
The toolpath should appear as Figure 19.90.

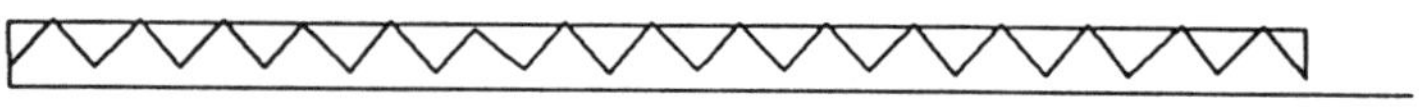

Figure 19.90

Select **Yes** to accept this toolpath segment
Select **End progrm** to close NCI file
Select **Yes** to "Run the post processor?"
Enter file name: **thread2**

The partial part program should appear on the screen as below.

```
%
O0010
(THREAD2)
N10G20
N15G50X10.Z10.
N20G0T1010
N25G97S0450M3
N30X1.
N35Z.25
N40Z.2649
N45X1.0713
N50G99G32Z-1.1E.08333
N55G0X1.0348
N60Z.2588
N65X1.0931
N70G99G32Z-1.1E.08333
N75G0X1.0348
N80Z.2541
N85X1.1103
N90G99G32Z-1.1E.08333
N95G0X1.0348
N100Z.25
N105X1.125
N110G99G32Z-1.1E.08333
N115G0X1.0348
N120Z.25
```

Step 7. Generate threading program in G76 (complex command).

Repeat steps 2 - 4 and 6 to generate another set of part program instrtuctions to cut these internal threads. (*Note:* set Thread = complex and save the file name as **thread2c.nc**).

The threading part program in G76 command format is listed below:

```
%
O0010
(THREAD2C)
N10G20
N15G50X10.Z10.
N20G0T1010
N25G97S0450M3
N30X1.
N35Z.25
N40X1.0348
N45G99
N50G76X1.125Z-1.1I0.K.0451D.02A29E.08333
N55G0X1.
N60Z.25
N65G28U0.W0.
N70T1000
N75M5
N80M30
%
```

19.9 Drill Module

The Mastercam drill module is used to generate fixed (or canned) cycle commands to perform drilling, boring, and tapping operations at the specified positions.

Drilling parameters

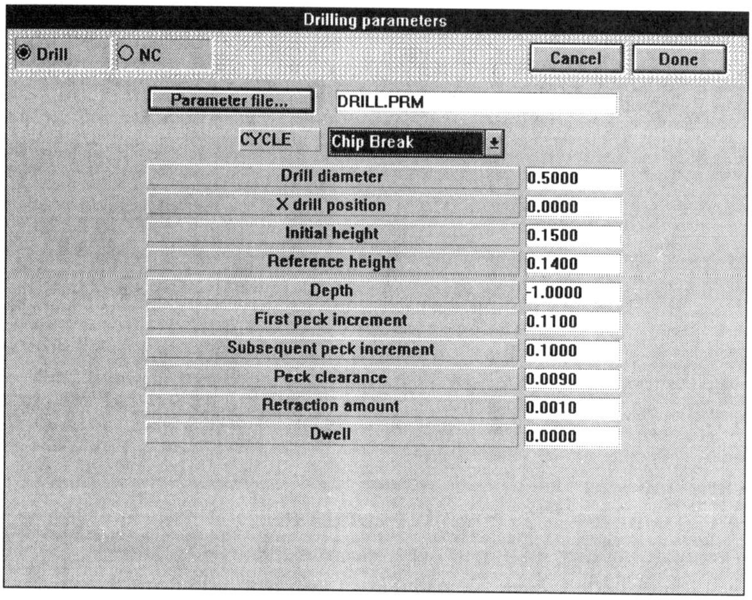

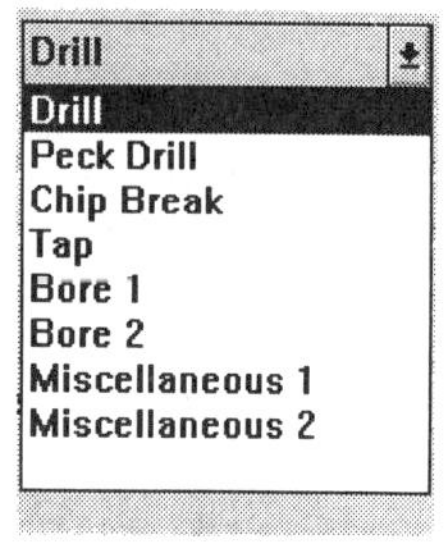

The above parameters can be classified into the following **five** groups: Cycle type, X-coordinate control, Z-coordinate control, peck drilling parameters and dwell.

Cycle Type

There are **eight** fixed cycles available in Mastercam lathe including drill, peck drill, chip break, tap, bore 1, bore 2, Miscellaneous 1 and Miscellaneous 2. Figure 19.91 on the following page, summarizes the feature and command statement of these cycle types. Note that not all lathe CNC controllers provide canned cycle commands. We can customize the post processor with G0, G1, and G4 (dwell command), and M3 (spindle clockwise), and M4 (spindle counterclockwise) commands to perform the tasks of drilling, boring, deep hole drilling, and tapping.

X-Coordinate Control

Two parameters are used to control the X-coordinate values:

drill diameter and X drill position.

The drill diameter parameter indicates the diameter of drill to be used. This value can be used to calculate the required spindle RPM from the given CSS found in the material table.

The X drill position parameter is used to specify the X-coordinate value at which the drilling operation is performed. Normally drilling is performed at the part center that has an X-coordinate setting of zero. When drilling is not performed in the part center ($X \neq 0$), a self-rotating tool should be used and the machine spindle should be indexed to the specified position. The X-coordinate value is specified in the radius.

Cycle type	G-code	Toolpath pattern	Application
Drill/counter bore	G81 Xx Yy Zz Rr Ff G81 no dwell G82 with dwell	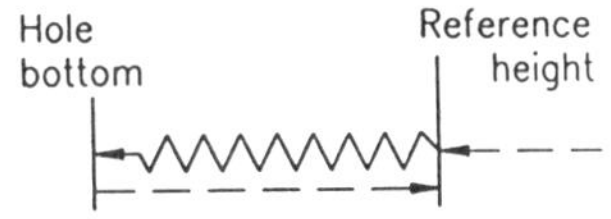	• Drilling holes
Peck drill	G83 both with/no dwell	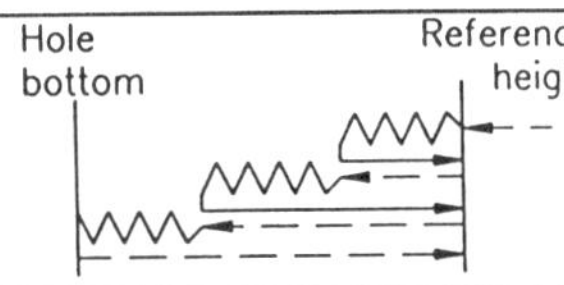	• Drilling deep holes
Chip breaker	G73 with/no dwell	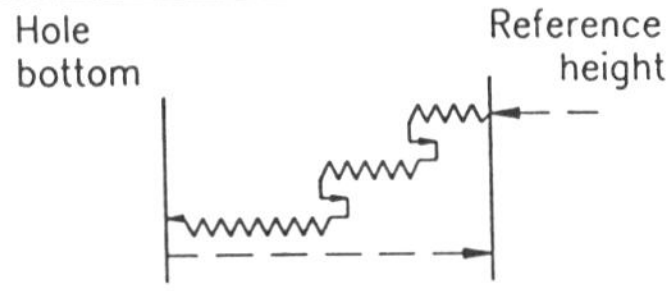	• Drilling deep holes
Tap	G84	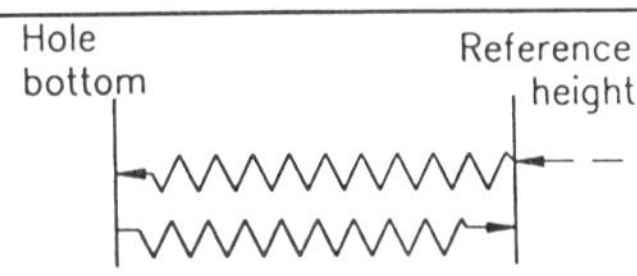	• Tapping internal threads
Bore #1	G85 – no dwell G89 – with dwell	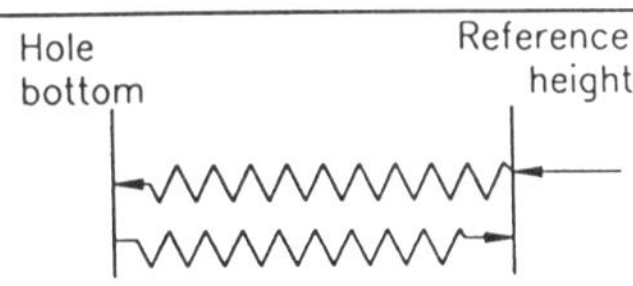	• Feed-in and feed-out
Bore #2	G86 – no/with dwell		• Feed-in and rapid-out

Figure 19.91 Drill cycle types

Z-Coordinate control

Three Z-coordinate values are normally required in defining the toolpath pattern of fixed cycles: initial height, reference height, and hole depth (Figure 19.92).

Initial height: specifies the z level at which the tool moves rapidly from a position to the hole center.

Reference height: indicates the level at which the feed changes from rapid to the programmed rate.

Hole depth: indicates the Z-coordinate value of the hole bottom.

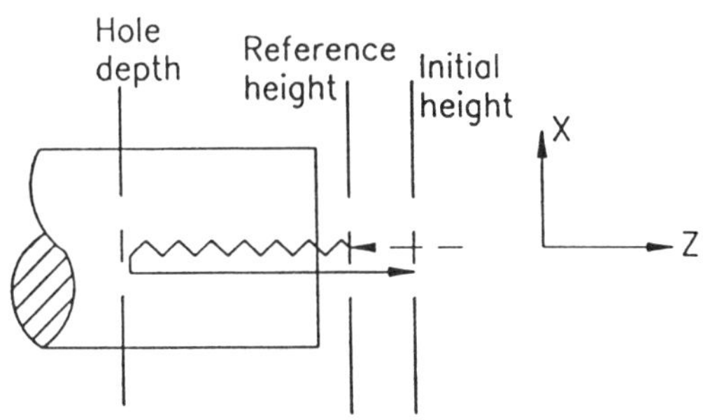

Figure 19.92

Dwell

This parameter specifies a period of time for temporary control of a total stop of the system.

Peck Drilling Parameters

This group of parameters is available for peck drilling and/or chip break cycle. They include first peck increment, subsequent peck increment, peck clearance, and retraction amount (Figure 19.93). Both peck clearance and retraction amount parameters are only available for the chip break cycle.

First peck increment: specifies the drilling depth on the first peck.
Subsequent peck increment: indicates the drilling depth on each peck after the first.
Peck clearance: specifies the distance above the metal to stop moving at rapid feedrate.
Retraction amount: indicates the amount to retract the tool between pecks.

Note: No geometry entity is required to define the X position and Z depth in using the drill module.

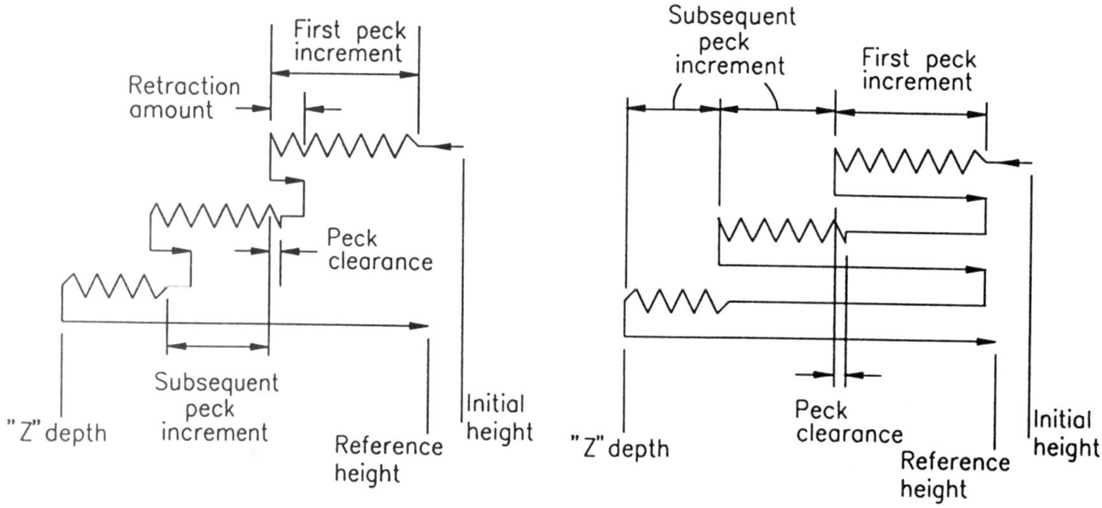

Figure 19.93

Project 9.

Drilling and tapping a hole at the center

Two operations are used to produce internal threads of 5/8-11. A 17/32" drill is used to drill the base hole, then a 5/8-11 tap is used to cut the threads. The thread length is 1".

Tips 1. Two tools are used in this project: 17/32" drill and 5/8-11 tap.

2. Major drilling parameters are:
   Cycle = drill/counterbore
   X drill position = 0
   Initial height = 0.5
   Reference height = 0.2
   Depth = -(thread length + 0.3 D + 0.1) = -(1 + 0.3(17/32) + 0.1) = -1.26

3. Drilling tool information:
   Tool name = 34
   N = 10
   Ofs = 10
   O = 1
   R = 17/64
   W = 0

4. Drilling parameters:
   Feedrate = 0.007 inches/rev
   Spindle speed = 2000 RPM

5. Major tapping parameters:
   Cycle = tap
   Dwell = 0.5
   initial height = 0.5
   Reference height = 0.2
   Depth = -1.0

6. Tapping tool information:
   Tool name = 34
   N = 12
   O = 12
   Ofs = 12
   R = 5/16
   W = 0

7. Tapping parameters:
   Feedrate = 0.909 inches/rev
   Spindle speed = 300 RPM

Step 1. Initiate the drill module.

Select **MAIN MENU → Toolpaths → Drill**
Enter file name: **drill**

Step 2. Define the drilling parameters to the following settings.

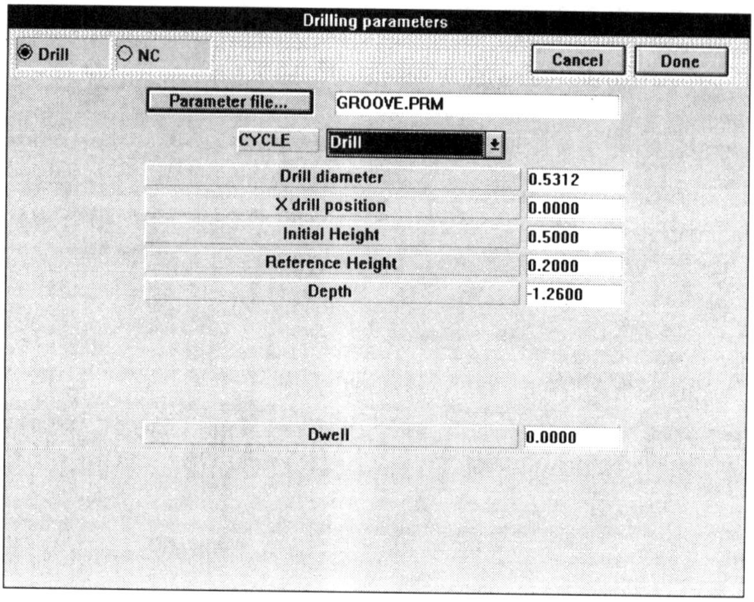

Select the **NC button** to advance to the NC parameters menu.

Step 3. Define the NC parameters to the following settings.

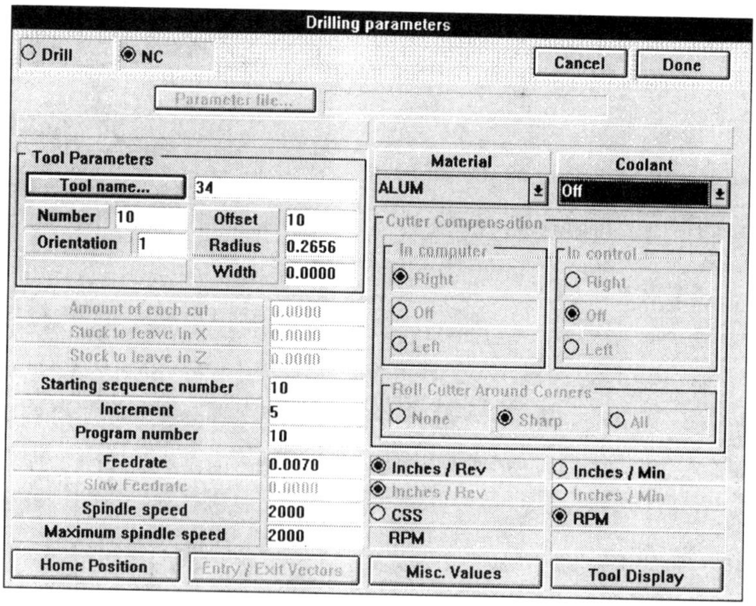

Step 4. Define the home position.

Click on the **Home** position button

Set the home position coordinate values as below

X = **4.0**

Z = **3.0**

Select **Done** to return back to the parameters window

Step 5. Generate and accept the drilling toolpath.

Select **Done** from the parameters window to generate the toolpath
Select **Yes** to accept this toolpath segment

Step 6. Select the drill module again for tapping.

Select **Drill** from the toolpaths menu

Step 7. Define the tapping parameters to the following settings.

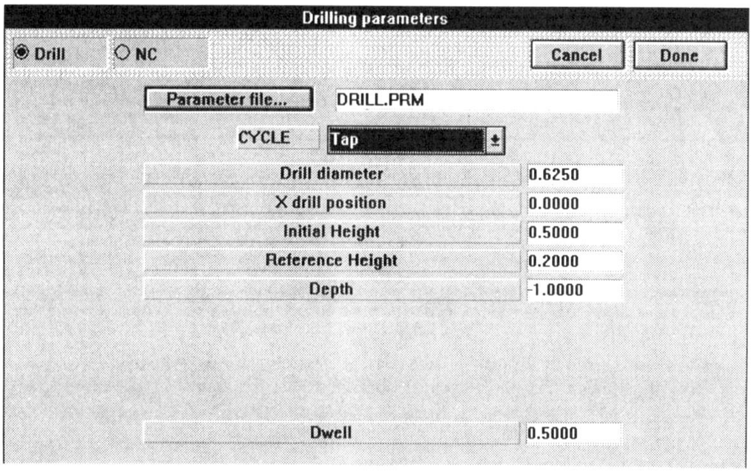

Select the **NC button** to advance to NC parameters menu

Step 8. Define NC parameters to the following settings.

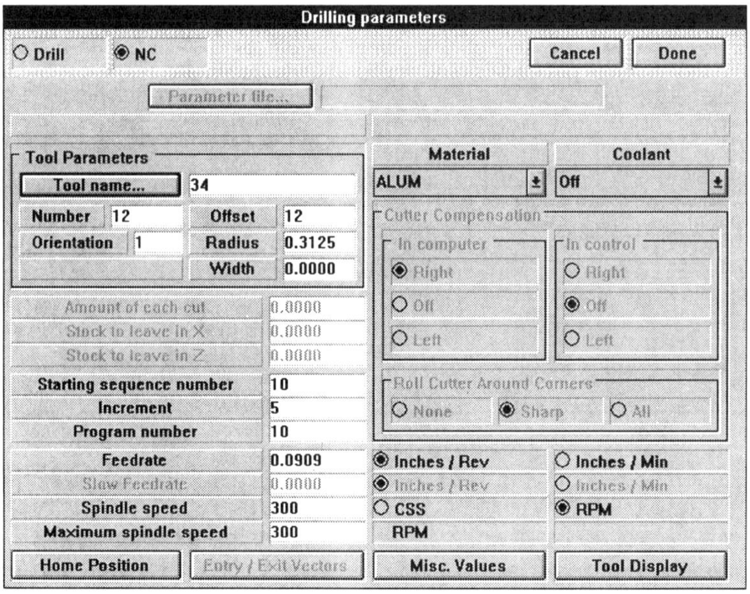

Step 9. Define the Home Position.

Click on the **Home** position button
Set the home position coordinate values as below

X = **4.0**
Z = **3.0**

Select **Done** to return back to the parameters window

Step 10. Accept the toolpath and run the post processor.

Select **Done** from the parameters window
Select **Yes** to accept this toolpath segment
Select **End progrm** to close NCI file
Select **Yes** to "Run the post processor?"
Enter file name: **drill**
The part program should appear on the screen.
Double-click the upper-left button to return to graphic mode

Project 10. 10

Final project

This project integrates the use of various lathe toolpath modules to generate the toolpaths to machine the part shown in Figure 19.94.

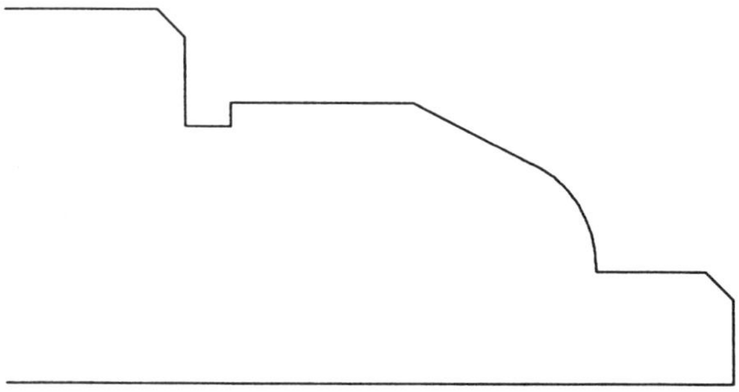

Figure 19.94

Tips 1. The part geometry file is lathe1.

2. The machining operations, their sequence, and module to use are given below:

Operation	Module
1. Facing	Finish
2. Roughing	Rough
3. Finishing	Finish
4. Grooving	Groove
5. Threading	Thread

3. Extend the right end face geometry entity to include the rough stock diameter.

4. Extend the entity over the groove. This allows the groove to be excluded in roughing and finishing cuts.

5. The tooling plan for this project is listed below:

Operation	Tool Type	Tool Name
Facing	Roughing tool	3
Roughing	Roughing tool	3
Finishing	Finishing tool	5
Grooving	Grooving tool	13
Threading	Threading tool	16

Step 1. Load the part geometry file lathe1.

Select **MAIN MENU → File → Get → Geometry**
Enter file name: **lathe1 ←**
Select **Yes** to delete the current part, if necessary

The part drawing of **lathe1** should appear as Figure 19.95.

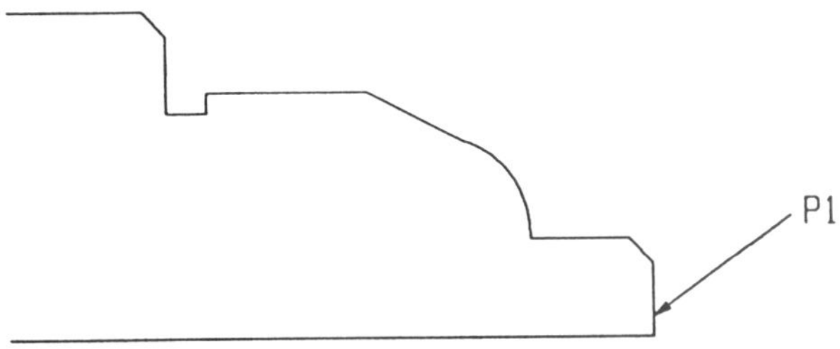

Figure 19.95

Step 2. Extend the face geometry to the rough stock diameter.

Select **MAIN MENU → Modify →Trim → To point**
Pick at **P1** to select the entity to trim
Indicate trim location: **D4.05, 0 ←**

The face geometry is extended as shown in Figure 19.96

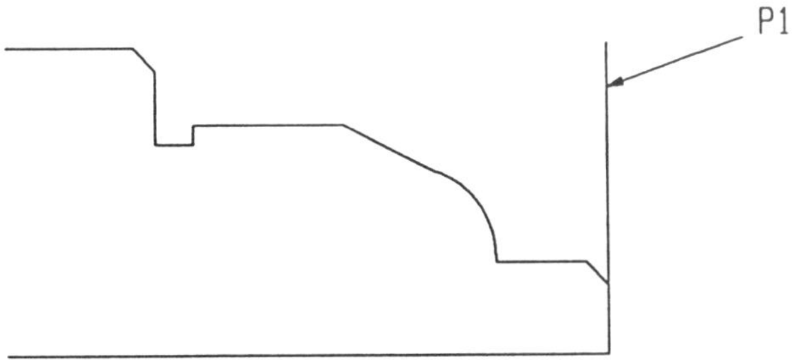

Figure 19.96

Step 3. Initiate the finish module for facing.

Select **MAIN MENU → Toolpaths → Finish**
Enter file name: **lathe1**

Step 4. Define the facing contour using the pick point in Figure 19.96.

Select **Single**, then pick at **P1**
Select **Point**
Enter **D4.2,2** for retraction point
Select **Done**

Step 5. Define the finish parameters to the following settings.

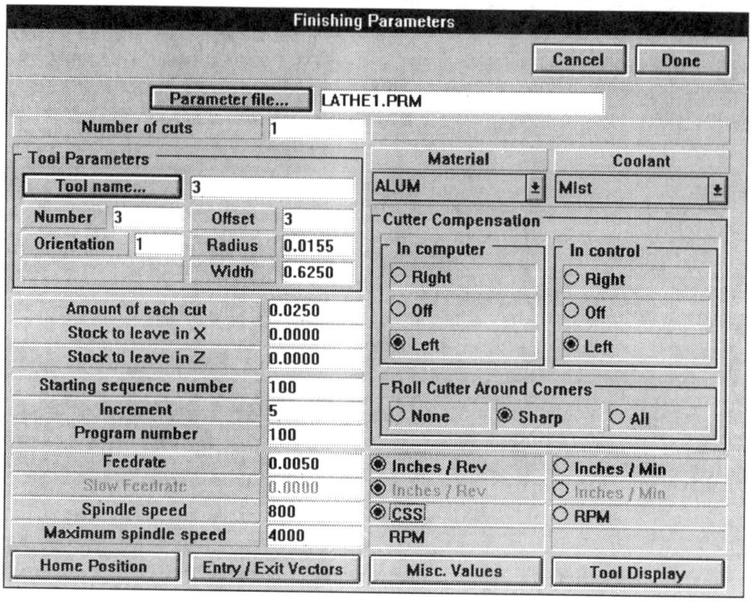

Step 6 Set the Home Position.

Click on the **Home** position button
Set the coordinate values as below

X = **3.0**
Z = **2.0**

Select **Done** to return back to the parameters window

Step 7. Set the entry and exit vectors parameters

Click on the **Entry/Exit Vectors** button
Set Vector values as below.

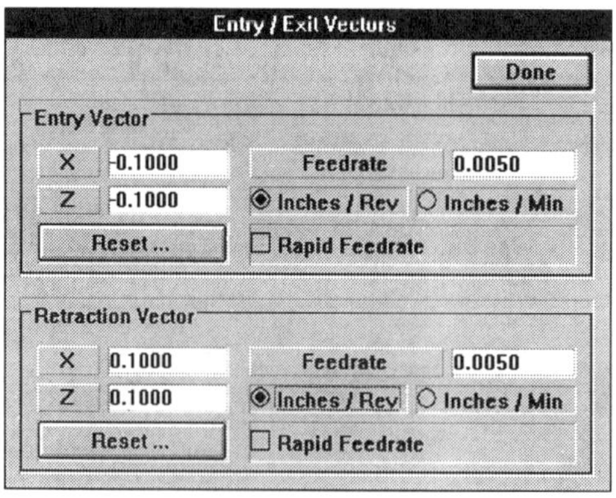

Select **Done** to return back to the parameters window

Step 8. Generate and accept the toolpath.

Select **Done** from the parameters window
Select **Write** from the Finish-set menu
Select **Yes** to accept the toolpath segment

The facing toolpath is shown as Figure 19.97.

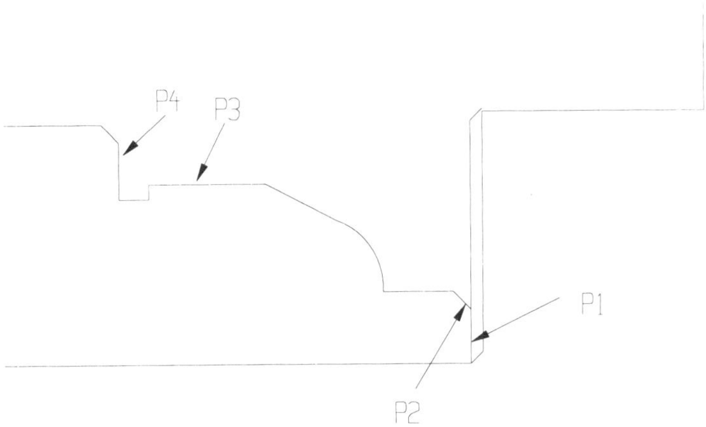

Figure 19.97

Step 9. Trim the groove entities and face entity for roughing. Use the pick points in Figure 19.97.

Press **Alt + T**, then **F3** to make the toolpaths visible
Select **MAIN MENU → Modify → Trim → 1 entity**
Select the entity to trim: pick at **P1**
Select the entity to trim to: pick at **P2**
Select **Backup → 2 entities**
Select the entity to trim: pick at **P3**
Select the entity to trim to: pick at **P4**
The trimmed drawing, without toolpaths, becomes Figure 19.98.

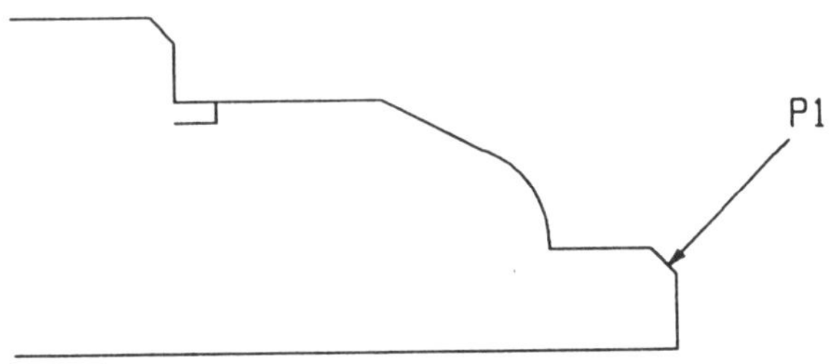

Figure 19.98

Step 10. Initiate the rough module and define the roughing contour. Use the pick point in Figure 19.98.

Select **MAIN MENU → Toolpaths → Rough**
Selcct **Chain**, then pick at **P1**
Select **Close → End here → Point**
Enter the retraction point: **D4.2,2**
Select **Done**

Step 11. Define the roughing parameters to the following settings.

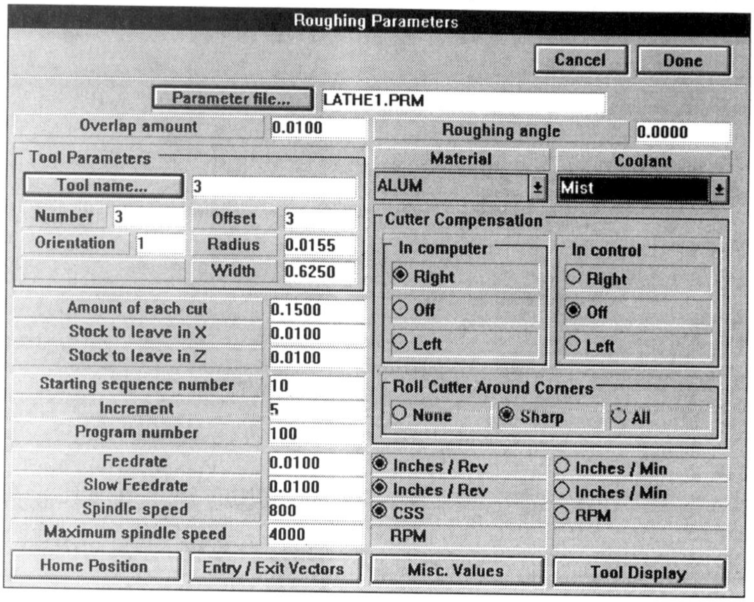

Step 12. Set the home position.

Click on the **Home position** button

Set these coordinate values:

X = **3.0**

Z = **2.0**

Select **Done**

Step 13. Accept the toolpaths.

Select **Done** from the parameters window to generate roughing toolpaths

The roughing toolpaths should look like Figure 19.99.

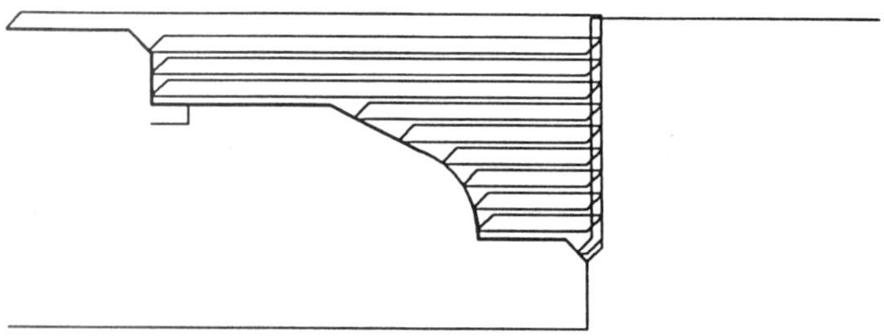

Figure 19.99

Select **Yes** to accept this toolpath segment

Step 14. Initiate the finish module.

The toolpaths will appear with the drawing on the screen. Press F3 to repaint the screen. The new drawing without the toolpaths is shown in Figure 19.100.

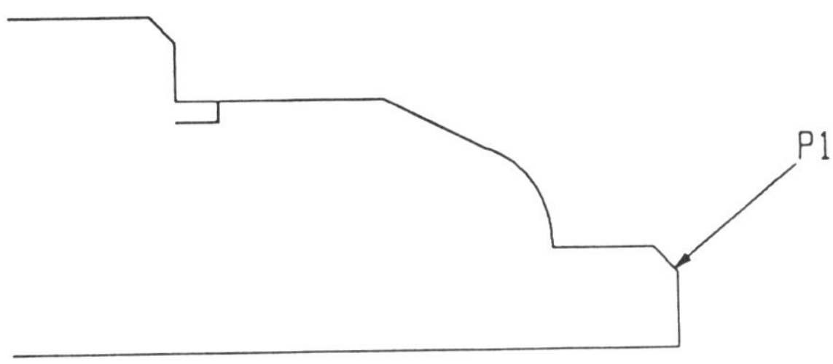

Figure 19.100

Select **Finish**

Step 15. Define the finishing contour using the pick point in Figure 19.100.

Select **Chain** then pick at **P1**
Select **Close** → **End here** → **Point**
Enter the retraction point: **D4.2,2**
Select **Done**

Step 16. Define the finish parameters to the following settings.

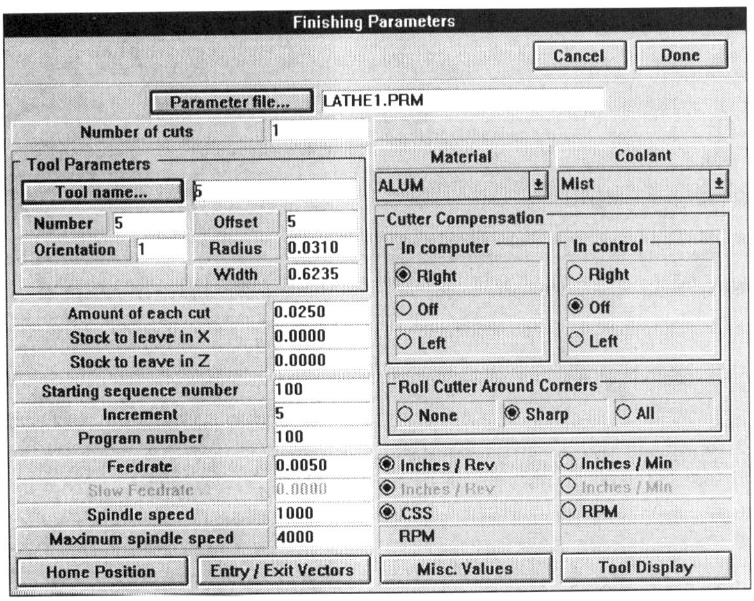

Step 17. Set the home position.

Click on the **Home position** button

Set the coordinate values as below:

X = **3.0**

Z = **2.0**

Select **Done**

Step 18. Generate and accept the finishing toolpaths.

Select **Done** from the parameters window

Select **Write** from the Finish-set menu

The finish toolpaths should appear as in Figure 19.101.

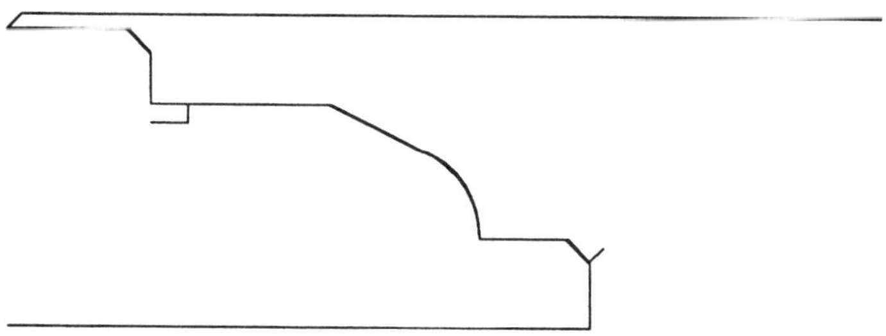

Figure 19.101

Select **Yes** to accept the toolpaths

Step 19. Create an offset line using the pick points in Figure 19.102.

Press **F3** to repaint the drawing. The new drawing is Figure 19.102.

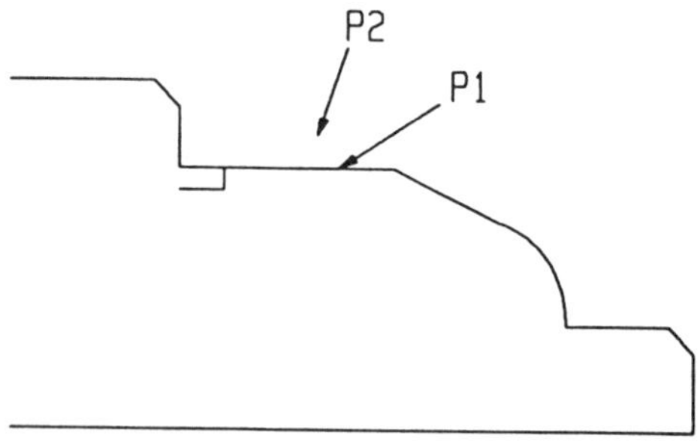

Figure 19.102

Select **MAIN MENU → Xform → Offset**

Set the Offset menu as shown here ☞

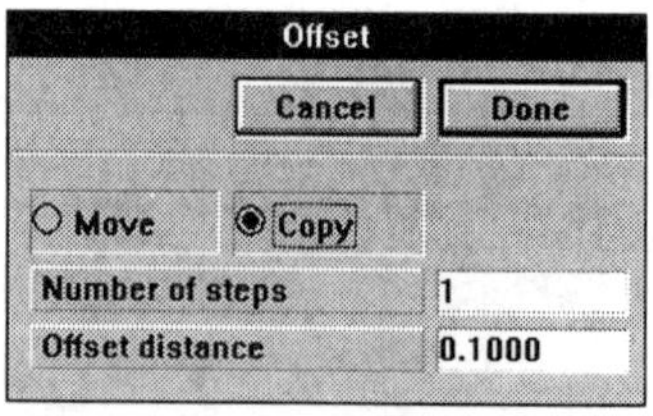

Select **Done**

Pick at **P1** to select the entity to offset

Pick at **P2** to indicate the offset direction

The offset line is added as in Figure 19.103.

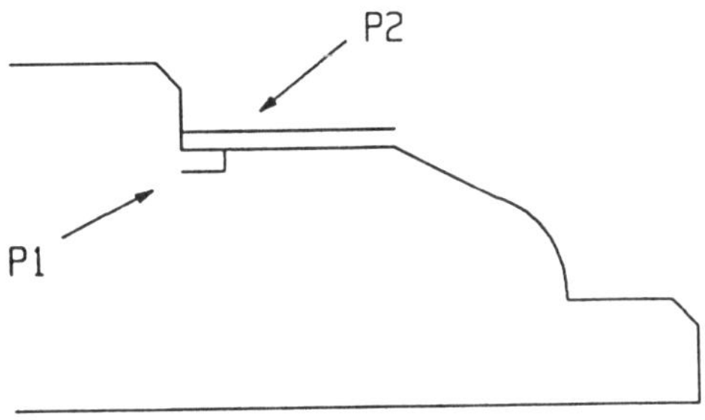

Figure 19.103

Step 20. Zoom the area for trimming using the pick points in Figure 19.103.

Press **F1**, then pick at **P1** and **P2**

The zoomed drawing, without toolpaths, is Figure 19.104.

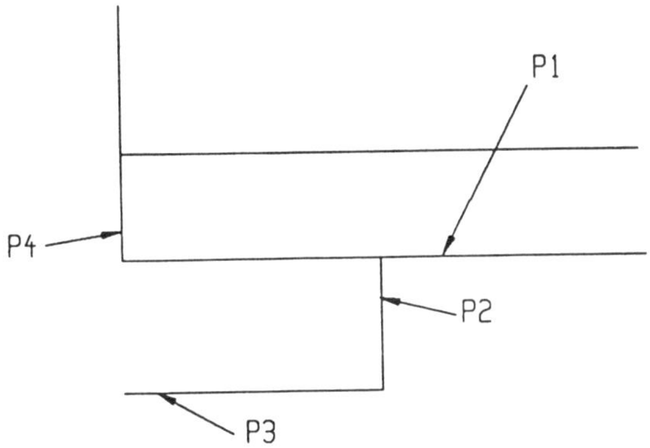

Figure 19.104

Step 21. Trim the entities using the pick points in Figure 19.104.

Select **MAIN MENU → Modify → Trim → 2 entities**
Sequentially pick at **P1 - P4** to trim entities for the grooves

The trimmed geometry, without toolpaths, should look like Figure 19.105.

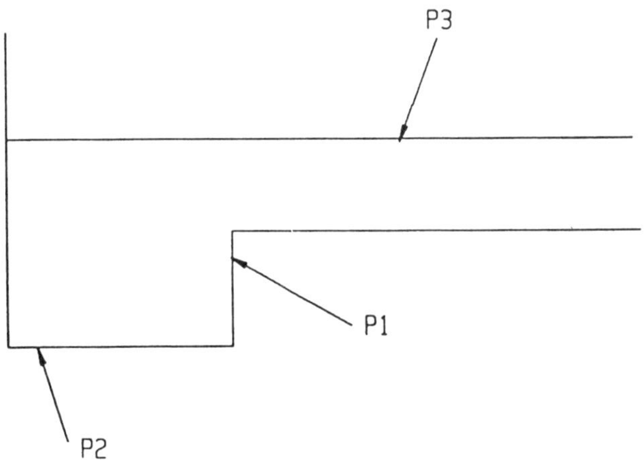

Figure 19.105

Step 22. Initiate the groove module and define the groove contour. Use the pick points in Figure 19.105 on the previous page.

Select **MAIN MENU → Toolpaths → Groove → Chain**
Pick at **P1** and **P2**
Select **End here** to define the inner boundary
Select **Single** then pick at **P3** to define the outer boundary
Select **Point** then enter **D3.75,-2.75** for the retraction point
Select **Done**

Step 23. Define the grooving parameters to the following settings.

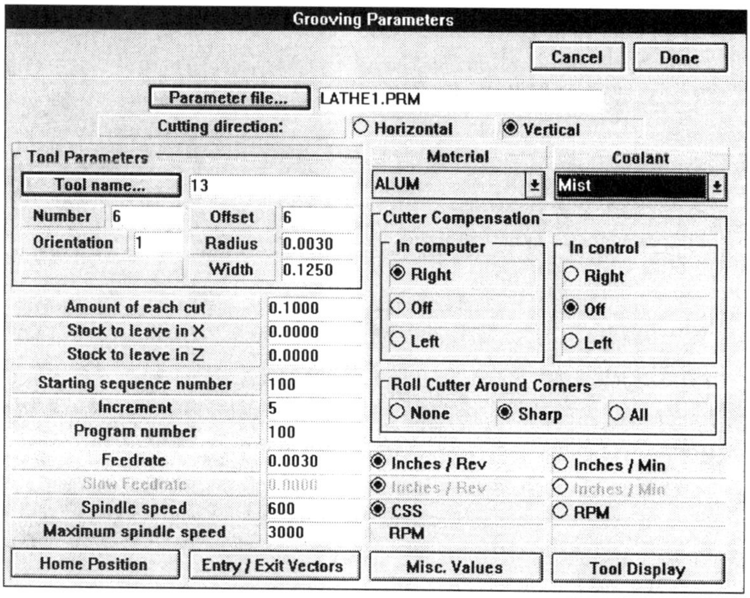

Step 24. Set the home position.

Click on the **Home position** button
Set these coordinate values:

X - **3.0**
Z = **2.0**

Select **Done**

Step 25. Generate and accept the grooving toolpaths.

Select **Done** from the parameters window
The grooving toolpaths should look like Figure 19.106.

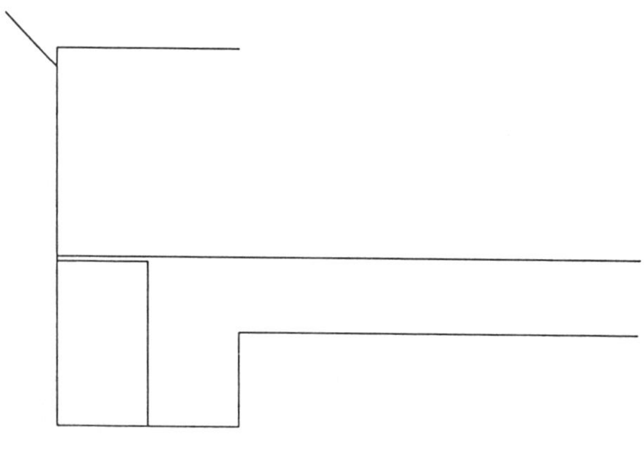

Figure 19.106

Select **Yes** to accept this toolpath segment
Press **Alt + F1** simultaneously and then press **F2** to fit the drawing,without the toolpaths, as shown in Figure 19.107.

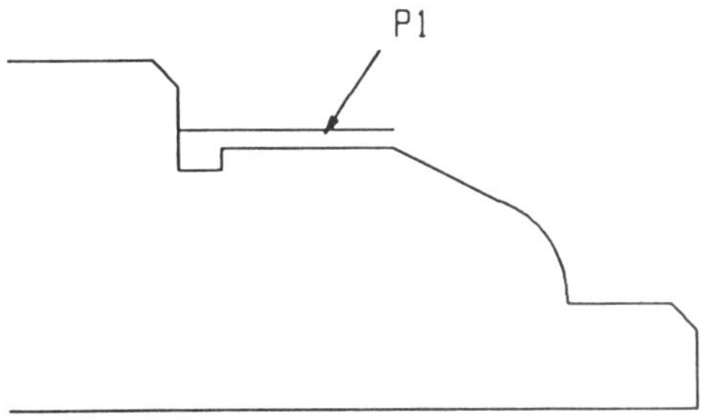

Figure 19.107

Step 26. Delete a construction line using the pick point in Figure 19.107.

Select **MAIN MENU → Delete**
Pick at **P1**

The new part drawing becomes Figure 19.108.

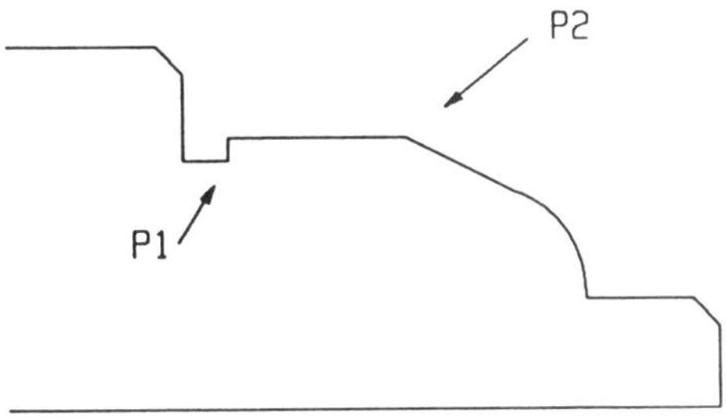

Figure 19.108

Step 27. Create the threading geometry.

Select **MAIN MENU → Create → Line → Multi**
Specify endpoint 1: D3,-1.5
Specify endpoint 2: D2.881,-1.5
Specify endpoint 3: D2.881,-2.875

Press **F1** then pick at **P1** and **P2** (using the pick points in Figure 19.108) to zoom the drawing

The added thread geometry is shown in Figure 19.109.

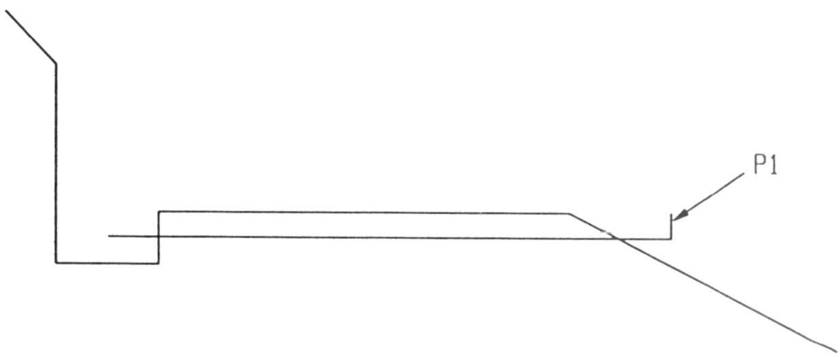

Figure 19.109

Step 28. Initiate the thread module.

Select **MAIN MENU → Toolpaths → Thread**

Step 29. Define the thread geometry. Use the pick points marked in Figure 19.109 on the previous page.

Select **Chain** then pick at **P1**

Select **Close → End here → Point**

Enter **D3.2,-1.3** for retraction point

Select **Done**

Step 30. Define the threading parameters to the following settings.

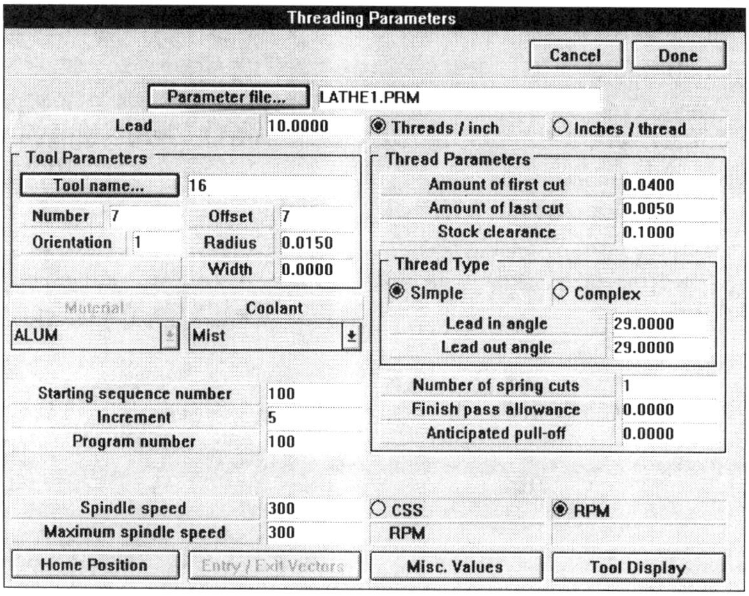

Step 31. Set the home position.

Click on the **Home position** button

Set these coordinate values:

X = **3.0**

Z = **2.0**

Select **Done**

Step 32. Generate and accept the threading toolpath.

Select **Done** from the threading parameters window

The threading toolpath should resemble Figure 19.110.

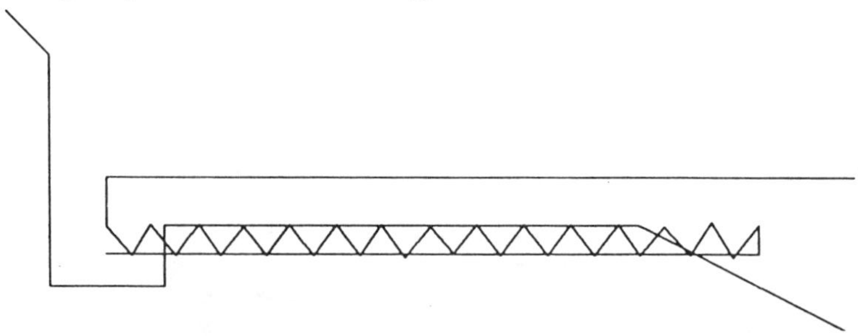

Figure 19.110

Select **Yes** to accept this toolpath segment

Step 33. Unzoom the part drawing.

Press **Alt + F1** simultaneously and then press **F2** to fit the drawing as shown in Figure 19.111.

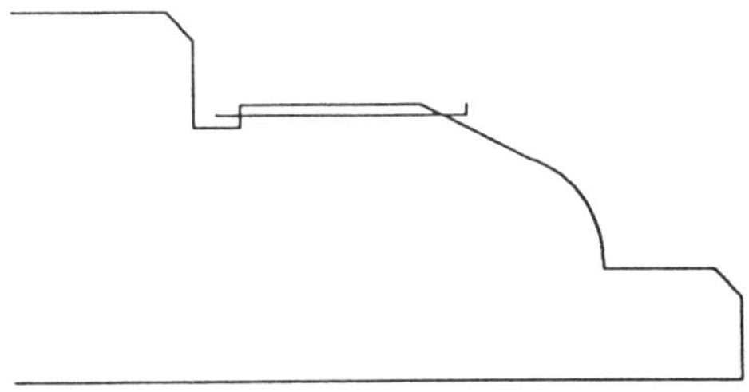

Figure 19.111

Step 34. Close NCI file and run the post processor.

Select **End progrm**
Select **Yes** to run the post processor
Enter file name: **lathe1**

The part program will appear on the screen.

Step 35. Backplot the complete toolpaths.

Select **MAIN MENU → NC utils → Backplot → Display**

Set the backplot parameters to the following settings:

```
Step mode = Endpoints                                           Tool motion = Animated
Spin tool = Yes              Delay = 0.2500                     Save geometry = No
Fit toolpath = No            Cleanup on NTC = No                Stop on NTC = No
Simulate cutter compensation in control = Yes
```

Select **Backup** to return to the Backplot menu
Set Backplot parameters as below:

Show Path	**Y**
Show Auto	**Y**
Show rEf	**Y**

Select **Run**

The toolpaths are backplotted as shown in Figure 19.112.

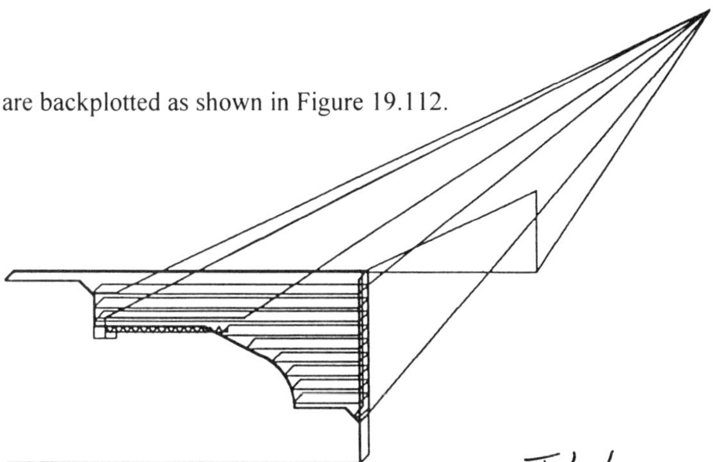

Figure 19.112

19.10 Exercises

1. Describe, with a drawing, how to determine the axis directions of a CNC lathe of the left-hand coordinate system.

2. Describe, with a drawing, how to determine the axis directions of a CNC lathe of the right-hand coordinate system.

3. What are the two methods of specifying the X coordinate values in the Mastercam lathe system?

4. Create a part geometry as shown in Figure 19.113. Save the part geometry as **lathep1.**

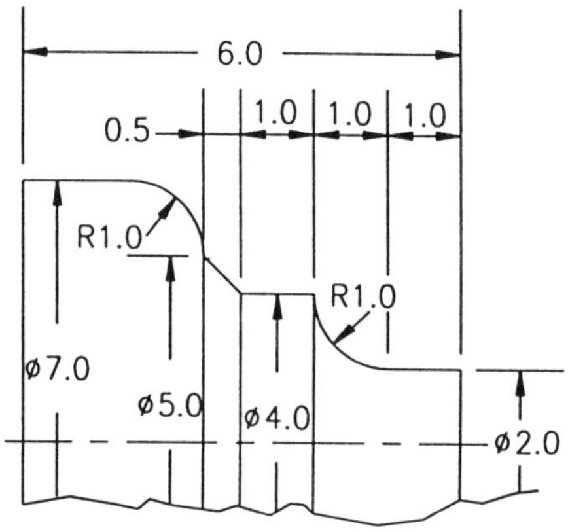

Figure 19.113

5. Create a part geometry as shown in Figure 19.114. Save the part geometry as **lathep2.**

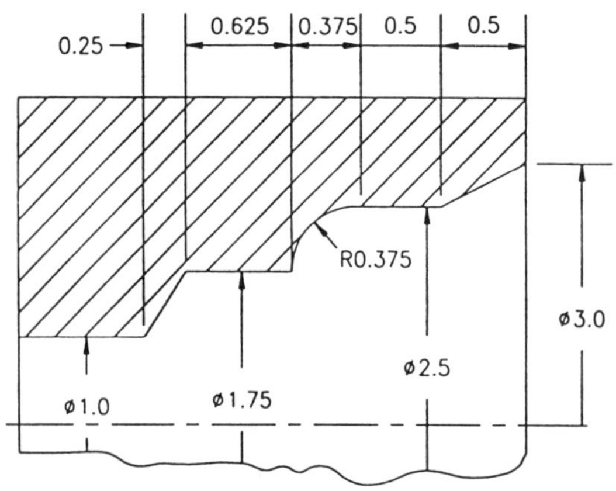

Figure 19.114

6. Create a part geometry as shown in Figure 19.115. Save the part geometry as **lathep3.**

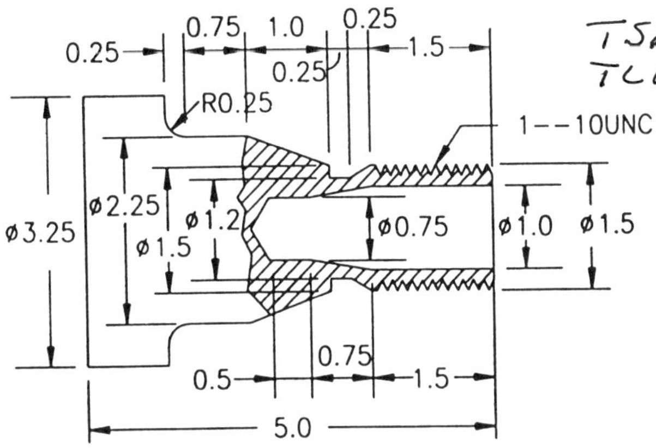

Figure 19.115

7. What are the five toolpath modules used in the Mastercam lathe? Describe when to use each of these modules.

8. What are the two sets of parameters used in the Mastercam lathe system?

9. Define the stock. Describe, with a drawing, how the stock affects the toolpath.

10. List the two types of cutter compensation used in Mastercam.

11. List the three possible toggle modes the cutter compensation in computer parameter.

12. Write the coorsponding G-codes for the following three modes of cutter compensation in computer:

Off:
Right:
Left:

13. Describe, with a drawing, how to select the proper mode of cutter compensation in computer.

14. What are the three NC commands used to regulate the spindle speed in CNC lathes?

15. List when to use constant surface speed.

16. List when to use constant spindle speed.

17. What are the two feedrate units used in CNC lathes?

18. Define the imaginary tool nose.

19. Describe the meaning of the T-code followed by four digits as below:

T0512

20. Define the following three angles in a turning tool:

Lead angle:
Insert angle:
Relief angle:

21. Find the relief angle for a turning tool having a -5° lead angle and 55° insert angle.

22. What are the four parameters used to define the approaching and retracting toolpath pattern of each cutting pass?

23. What are the three rough specific parameters?

24. What are the proper roughing angles for longitudinal roughing and face roughing, respectively?

25. What are the two types of feedrate used in the rough module? Describe when each is used.

26. Describe when to use the finish module.

27. What is the only finish specific parameter?

28. List the types of CNC lathe controllers that provide rough canned cycles (G71 and G72) and the finish canned cycle (G70).

29. Describe the advantages of using canned cycles for roughing and finishing operations.

30. List and describe the one-block format of the rough turning cycle (G71). What type of Fanuc-controllers used the one-block format?

31. List and describe the two-block format of the rough turning cycle (G71). What type of Fanuc-controllers used two-block format?

32. Use a drawing to show a typical toolpath pattern of the rough turning cycle (G71).

33. What is the major difference between the rough turning cycle (G71) and the rough facing cycle (G72)?

34. Use a drawing to show a typical toolpath pattern of the rough facing cycle (G72).

35. Describe the statement format of the finish cycle (G70).

36. Describe the procedure to insert the finish cycle command (G70) to the part program in Mastercam lathe.

37. What is the only groove specific parameter?

38. What are the two boundaries used in the groove module? Explain their purpose, respectively.

39. What three pieces of information must be specified in defining the geometry contour for thread cutting?

40. Describe how Mastercam defines the major diameter, minor diameter, and thread length.

41. Calculate the thread height and minor diameter for the following two UNC external threads:

    3/8-16 UNC

    1½-6 UNC

42. Calculate the thread height and minor diameter for the following two UNC internal threads:

5/8-11 UNC

2½-4 UNC

43. Calculate the thread height and minor diameter for the following two UNF external threads:

5/16-24 UNF

1-12 UNF

44. Calculate the thread height and minor diameter for the following two UNF internal threads:

7/16-20 UNF

1¼-12 UNF

45. Define the following two terms:

Thread lead:

Thread pitch:

46. What are the proper values for the amount of first cut and amount of last cut in threading?

47. Define the following two terms:

Acceleration length:

Deceleration length:

48. What parameters correspond to the acceleration length and deceleration length, respectively in Mastercam?

49. Find the acceleration length and deceleration length for cutting 1½-6 UNC threads with the following operation conditions:

Time constant = 0.066 s
Spindle speed = 300 RPM
Thread accuracy = 0.005

50. Explain, with a drawing, the threading toolpath pattern for G32.

51. Explain, with a drawing, the threading toolpath pattern for G76.

52. Describe how to specify the threading command G32 or G76 in Mastercam.

53. Explain the difference between peck drilling and chip breaker drilling.

54. Explain why the X drill position must be set to zero. List the conditions under which this parameter can be set to a non-zero value?

55. Define, with a drawing, the following three Z-coordinate parameters:

Initial height:

Reference height:

Hole depth:

56. Generate the part program to cut the part geometry created in problem 4.

57. Generate the part program to machine the part geometry created in problem 5.

58. Generate the part program to machine the part geometry created in problme 6.

Chapter 20

Turning Tools Construction and Definition

Objectives:

1. Identify commonly used cutting tools in turning operations.
2. Know how to select proper type of cutting tools for various turning operations.
3. Construct new tool drawings and define them in the tool database.
4. Modify existing tool drawings and redefine them in the tool database.

Overview

Many types of operations can be implemented with a turning machine. They include rough turning (external and internal), finish turning (external and internal), facing, grooving, threading (external and internal), drilling, boring, and milling (in mill-turn machines only). Each operation requires a particular kind of cutting tool. In other words, we must have a roughing tool to perform roughing, a boring tool for boring, and a threading tool for threading, etc. These commonly used cutting tools can be defined in the tool database to be retrieved when needed. The tool geometry can be constructed to allow the tool to be correctly displayed on the screen so that gouging checking and tool clearances with respect to the part geometry can be observed.

Four major sections are in this chapter: turning tools selection for various operations, tool definition, tool geometry construction, and existing tool geometry modification.

20.1 Turning Tools Selection

Turning tools, basically consist of two components: cutter and toolholder. In most cases, the cutters used in CNC turning are carbide inserts except for some drills and taps. Both carbide inserts and toolholders have been standardized by ANSI and ISO. They are presented in chapter 2.

Some typical turning tools are listed below.

Roughing tools:

Inserts:	C (80° diamond) shape or D (55° diamond) shape
Toolholders:	J (-3° lead angle) style or L (-5° lead angle) style

Figure 20.1 shows two combinations of above inserts and toolholders for roughing.

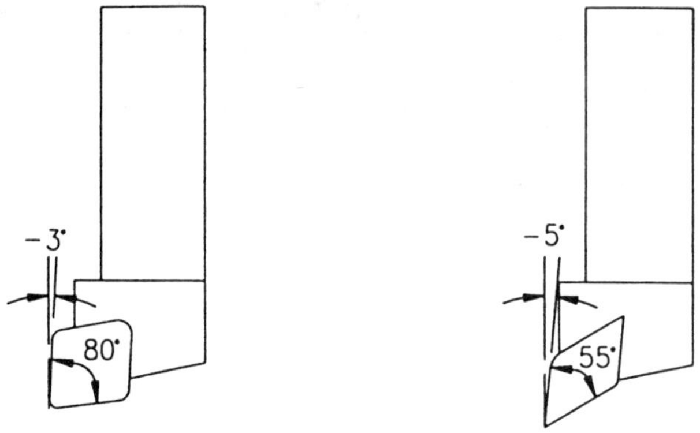

a. 80⁰ diamond insert J Style toolholder   b. 55⁰ diamond insert L Style toolholder

Figure 20.1

Finishing tools:

Inserts: D (55° diamond) shape or V (35° diamond) shape

Toolholders: J (-3° lead angle) style or L (-5° lead angle) style

Figure 20.2 gives two combinations of inserts and toolholders for finishing.

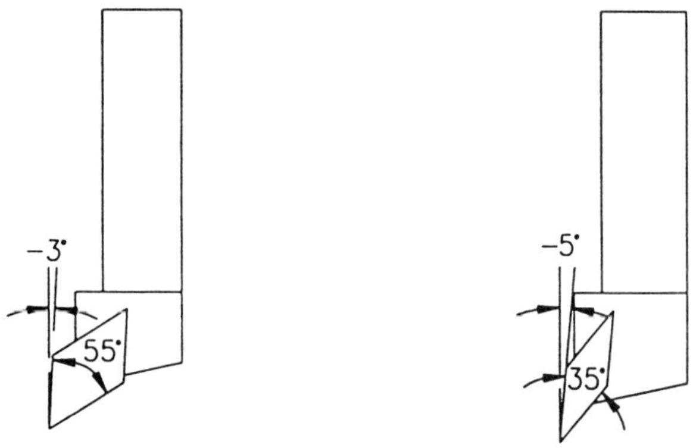

a. 53⁰ diamond insert J Style toolholder   b. 35⁰ diamond insert L Style toolholder

Figure 20.2

Boring tools:

The roughing and finishing tools for boring are the same as the roughing and finishing tools mentioned above. The only difference is that the toolholder shank is clamped in the Z direction for boring tools (Figure 20.3), while the turning tools are clamped in the X direction.

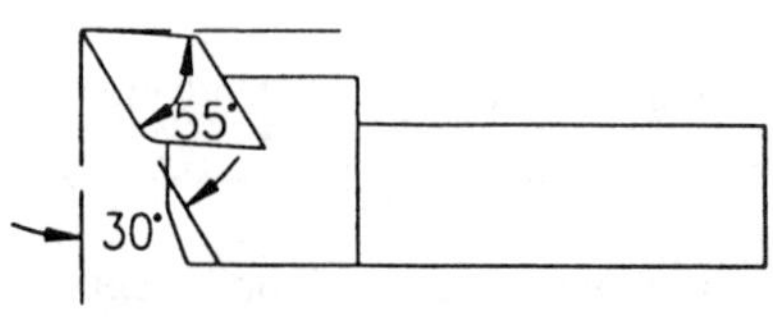

Figure 20.3

> **Facing Tools:**
> Normally, facing operations do not require to have a dedicated facing tool. Instcad, the roughing or finishing tools can be used to perform facing operations.

Tools for Other Operations

The selection of cutting tools for such operations as threading, grooving, drilling, tapping, etc., are self explanatory. Part feature specifications such as thread form, groove size, or hole diameter give the information to choose proper cutting tools.

Tool Hand Type

Turning tools are classified into **three** categories: right-hand, neutral, and left-hand tools (Figure 20.4).

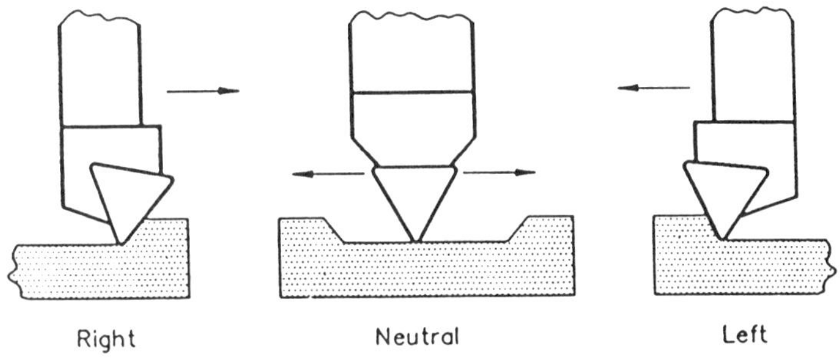

Figure 20.4

Actually, it is the toolholder cutting direction that determines the tool hand type. A right-hand tool is used to cut the workpiece to the right; a left-hand tool cuts to the left when the machine has the left-hand coordinate system as shown in Figure 20.5 or when the left-hand coordinate system is used in a turning machine.

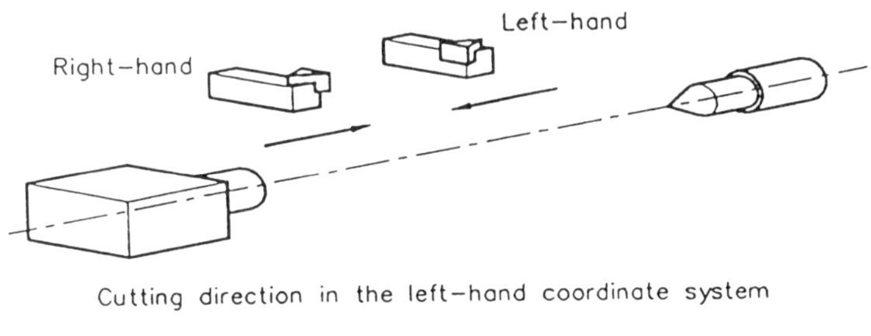

Figure 20.5 Cutting direction in the left-hand coordinate system
(Courtesy of Delmar Publishers, Inc.)

A neutral tool can cut in either direction. In a turning machine with a right-hand coordinate system (Figure 20.6 on the following page), a right-hand tool cuts the workpiece to the left, and a left-hand tool cuts to the right.

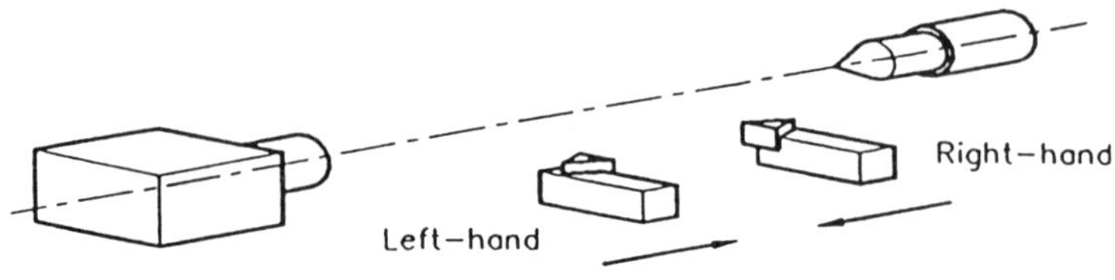

Figure 20.6 Cutting direction in the right-hand coordinate system
(Courtesy of Delmar Publishers, Inc.)

Slant-bed turning machines normally use the left-hand coordinate system. Standard flat-bed turning machines and desk-top lathes use the right-hand coordinate system.

20.2 Tool Definition

Mastercam uses a Def. tools function to define the necessary tool information for a particular tool. The following parameters are included in the Def. tools function:

Tool name:	the name of the tool geometry and tool definition files
Scan geo:	checking the geometry you want to define as a tool
Number :	the turret position number in which the tool is located
tN ofsN:	the offset register number used for a tool
Orient:	the orientation number used to indicate the direction of the tool
Angle:	the relief angle of the tool
Radius:	the radius of the tool nose
Width:	the distance of the tool measured across the radii of the tool
Home pos.:	the location for the tool to be retracted to
Center:	the location of the tool nose center
Save:	saving the current tool definition to a .LTL file

Tool Number and Offset number

The tool number and offset number are used with the T-code in the part program. A T-code is followed by a string of 4 digits. These four digits are arranged into two 2-digit groups. The first group indicates the tool number and the second group is the offset number as below:

```
T xxxx
| | └offset number
| └─tool number
└──T-code
```

Example 1: The command statement T0101 indicates the tool to be used is in the turret position 01, and the tool information is stored in the offset register #01.

Example 2: The command statement T0510 indicates the tool to be used is in the turret position 05, and the tool information is stored in the offset register #10.

Offset Register Parameters Setting

Cutting tools are installed in a specific position (or station) of the tool turret (or magazine). Each station on the turret is given a station number. A tool is identified by the station number. When a specific station number is used with the T-code, the tool change action will be implemented; the tool is selected from the specified turret station. The information related to the dimensions and features of a particular tool is stored in a register. A register is storage space for this information. The registers used for tooling information are referred to as offset registers.

Offset registers contain the following typical tooling information:

- Offset number
- Offset value in X axis (OFX)
- Offset value in Z axis (OFZ)
- Tool nose radius compensation value (OFR)
- Direction of imaginary tool nose (OFT)

Figure 20.7shows the definition of OFX, OFZ, and OFR.

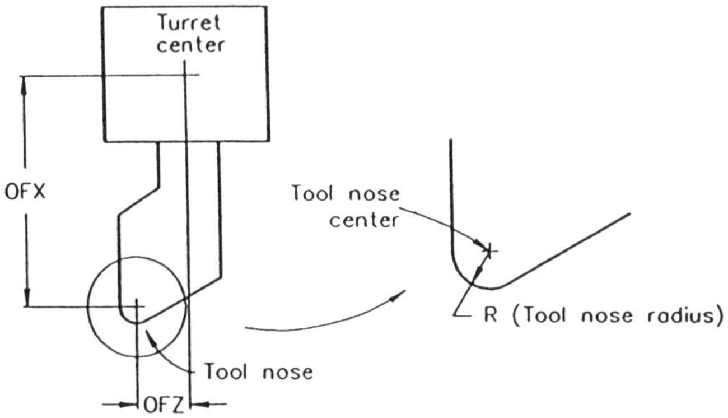

Figure 20.7 (Courtesy of Delmar Publishers, Inc.)

The imaginary tool nose is often used as the reference point for programming the tool path. It is defined as the intersecting point between two lines that are tangent to the tool nose and parallel to the X and Z axes, respectively (Figure 20.8).

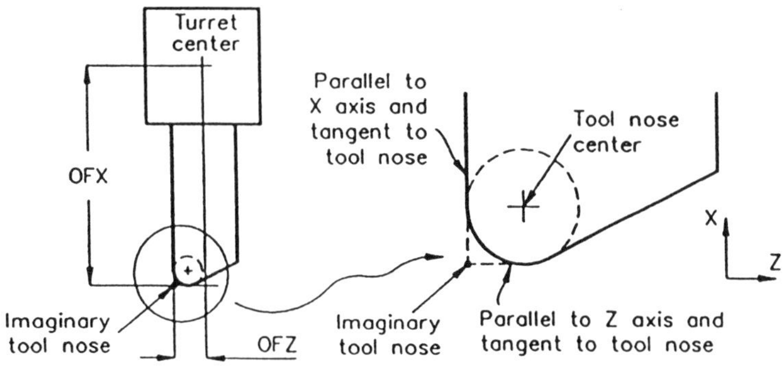

Figure 20.8 (Courtesy of Delmar Publishers, Inc.)

The direction of the imaginary tool nose (OFT) is indicated by a number ranging from 1 to 8, with each number representing a tool nose vector (Figure 20.9). The vector is viewed from the tool nose center toward the imaginary tool nose. Numbers 1 to 4 indicate a tool nose vector pointing to the first, second, third, and fourth quadrants, respectively. The numbers 5 to 8 denote a tool nose vector pointing to the +Z, +X, -Z, and -X directions, accordingly.

Table 20.1 gives a number of examples for defining tool information in the registers.

Table 20.1 Defining Tool Information

Offset number	Offset value in X axis	Offset value in Z axis	Tool nose radius compen.	Direction of Imaginary tool nose
01	0.05	0.10	0.032	1
02	0.15	-0.137	0.062	1
.	.	.	.	.
.	.	.	.	.
16	-0.37	1.50	0.032	4

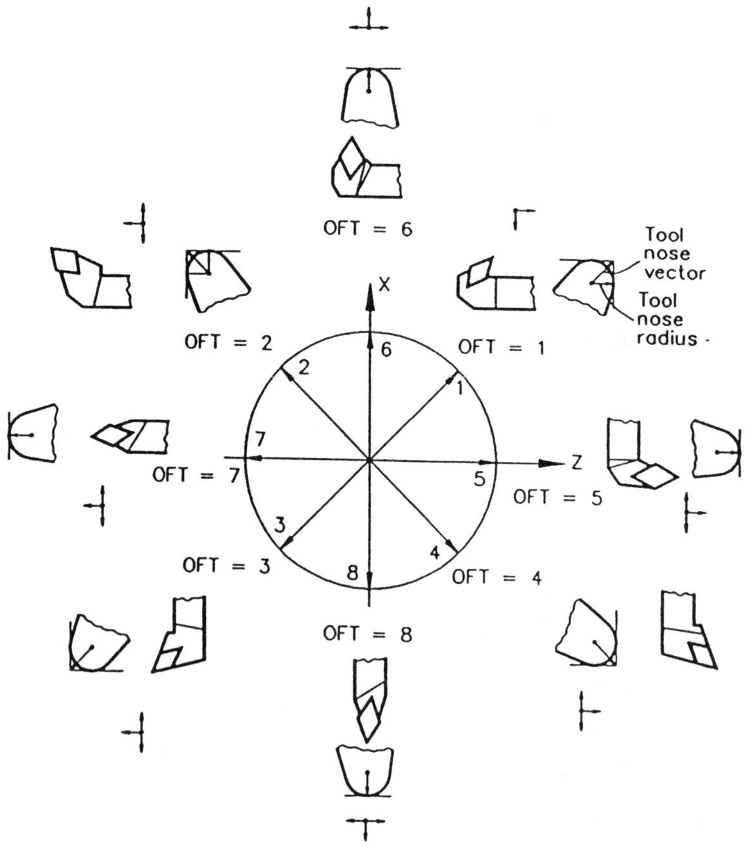

Figure 20.9 (Courtesy of Delmar Publishers, Inc.)

Orientation

Mastercam uses a special way to specify the direction of the cutting tools for turning. The number ranges from 1 to 8. See chapter 19 for details.

Angle

This parameter indicates the relief angle of the tool. The relief angle is formed between the relief edge of the insert and the cutting direction as shown in Figure 20.10. The relief angle of a tool is determined by two factors: lead angle and insert angle. The definition of the lead angle is illustrated in Figure 20.11. The lead angle can be positive or negative. The insert angle is the actual angle of the insert.

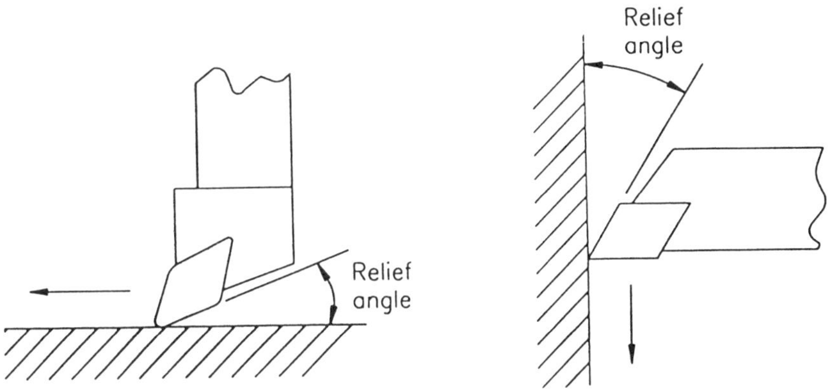

Figure 20.10

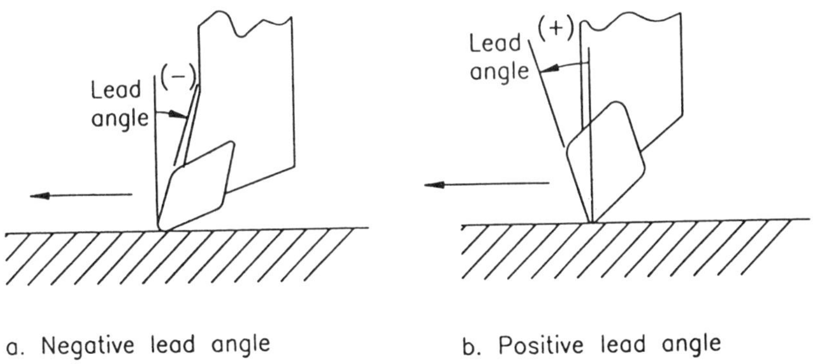

a. Negative lead angle   b. Positive lead angle

Figure 20.11

The formula given below can be used to determine the **relief angle of a tool**:

Relief angle = 90° + Lead angle - Insert angle

Example 3:

The relief angle for the tool shown in Figure 20.12 is

Relief angle = 90 + (-3) - 55 = 32°

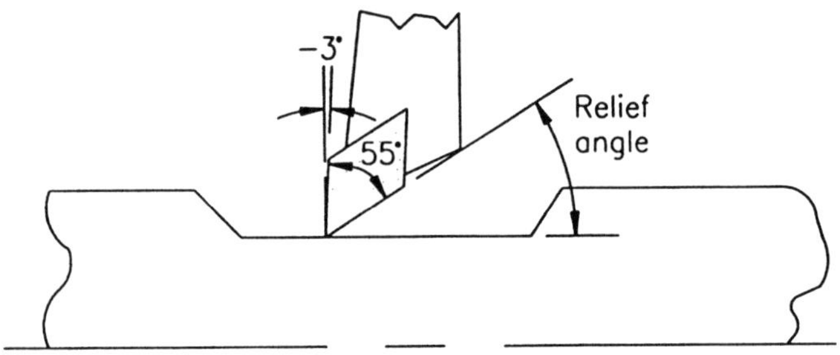

Figure 20.12

Example 4:

The relief angle for the boring tool shown in Figure 20.13 is

Relief angle = 90 + (-5) - 35 = 50°

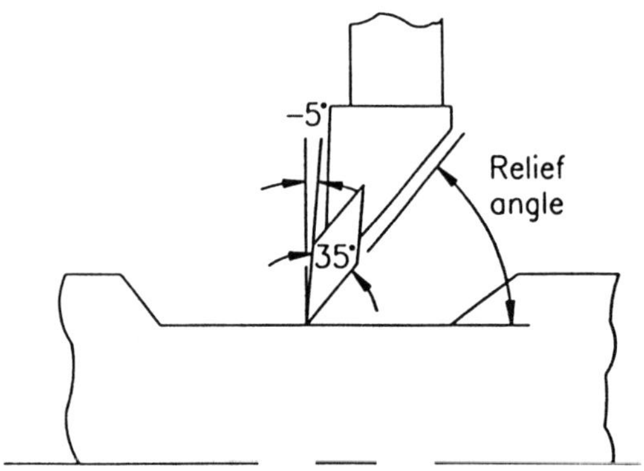

Figure 20.13

Width

This parameter denotes the distance across the radii of the tool. Figure 20.14 shows three examples of defining the width of tools.

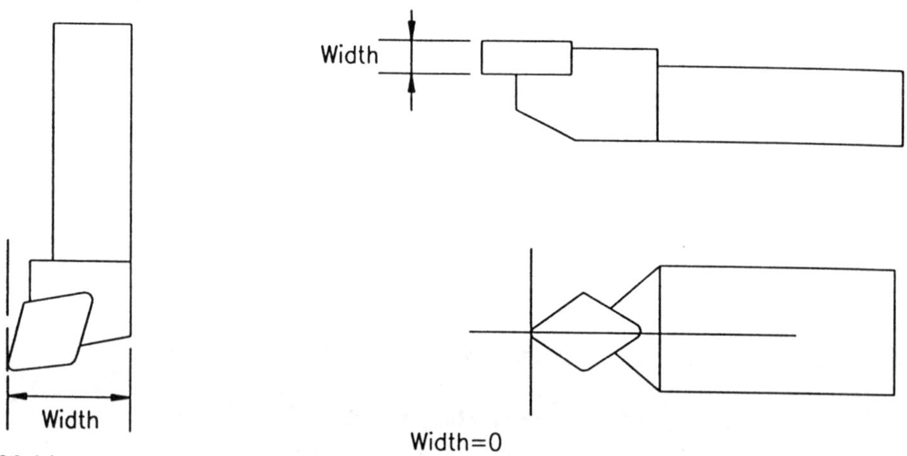

Figure 20.14

20.3 Turning Tools Construction

The tool geometry must bc cxactly constructed in order to allow this tool to be correctly displayed on the screen. The tool can be displayed on the screen in **two** situations: (1) the toolpaths are being generating and (2) the toolpaths are being backplotted. We can observe whether the tool and workpiece have any interference or undercut.

A tool geometry can be created as a new geometry or modified from an existing tool geometry. Mastercam provides a total of 35 tool geometries. You can load one tool geometry file and make necessary change to form the tool you are going to use. The way to create a tool geometry is the same as creating a part geometry.

Project 1. 1

Constructing a turning tool geometry

The turning tool shown in Figure 20.15 consists of an L style toolholder and an 80° diamond insert.

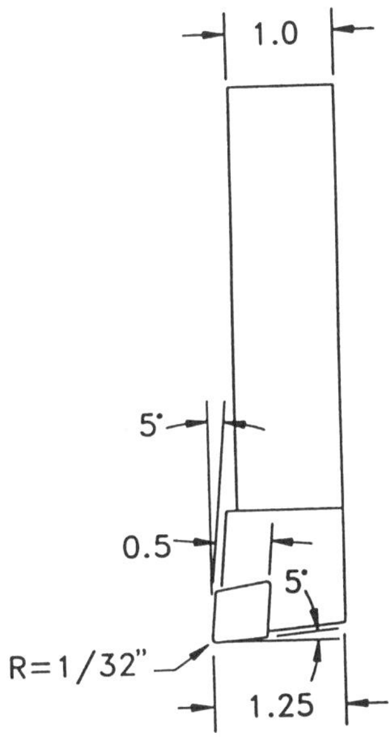

Figure 20.15

They have the following identification codes:

Insert: **CNMG432**

- tool nose radius = 1/32"
- IC thickness is 3/16"
- IC is 1/2"
- chipbreaker on both sides, with hole tolerance
- 0° clearance angle
- 80° diamond insert

Toolholder: **MCLNL164C**

- qualified length = 5"
- IC = 1/2"
- 1" square shank
- left-hand tool
- negative rake angle
- -5° lead angle style
- 80° diamond insert
- clamp and pin locking

Tips 1. Use the center of insert IC circle as the origin to construct the insert shape.

2. Create a point at the imaginary tool nose point by creating two construction lines tangent to the tool nose arc.
3. Translate the drawing origin from the IC center to the imaginary tool nose point.

4. Create the head of toolholder.

5. Construct the shank of toolholder.

6. Define the tool to the following settings:

Tool name = 36 Number = 10 Ofs. n = 10 Orientation = 1 Angle = 5 Radius = 1/32 Width = 1.25 Home postion = 5,4 Center = X0.03125 Z0.03125

Step 1. Create a circle for the insert IC circle.

Select **MAIN MENU → Create → Arc → pt Dia cir**
Enter the center point: **0,0** ←
Enter the diameter: **0.5** ←
Press **Alt** + **F1** simultaneously, then press **F2** to fit the drawing on the screen

The circle should appear as Figure 20.16.

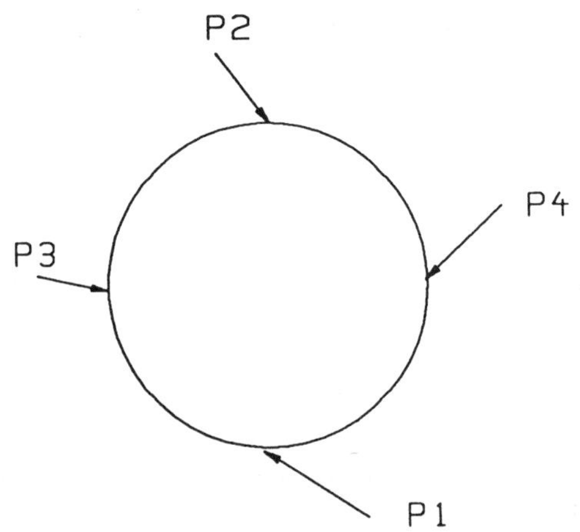

Figure 20.16

Step 2. Create four lines tangent to the IC circle. Use the pick points labeled in Figure 20.16 on the previous page.

Select **MAIN MENU → Create → Line → Tangent → Angle**
Select an arc: pick at **P1**
Enter the angle in degrees: **5** ←
Enter the line length: **0.5** ←

Two line segments appear collinearly and head in opposite directions.
Pick at the right segment to complete the first line.
Select an arc: pick at **P2**
Enter the angle in degrees: **5** ←
Enter the line length: **0.5** ←

Pick at the right segment for the second line
Select an arc: pick at **P3**
Enter the angle in degrees: **85** ←
Enter the line length: **0.5** ←

Pick at the upper segment for the third line
Select an arc: pick at **P4**
Enter the angle in degrees: **85** ←
Enter the line length: **0.5** ←
Pick at the upper segment for the fourth line

The four tangent lines are added as in Figure 20.17.

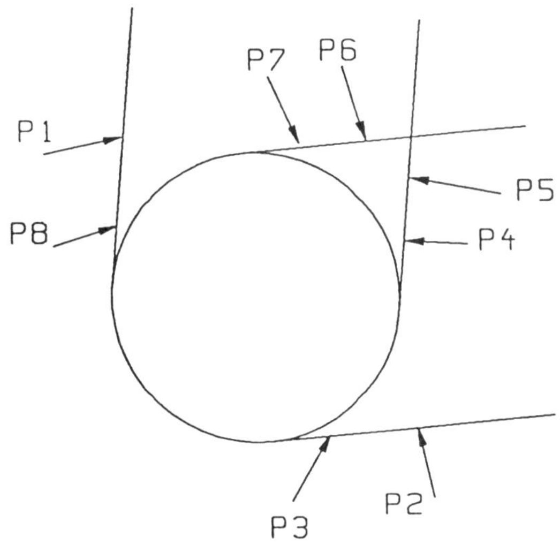

Figure 20.17

Step 3. Trim the four lines using the pick points in Figure 20.17.

Select **MAIN MENU → Modify → Trim → 2 entities**
Sequentially pick at **P1 - P8** to trim the four lines

The trimmed drawing appears as in Figure 20.18 .

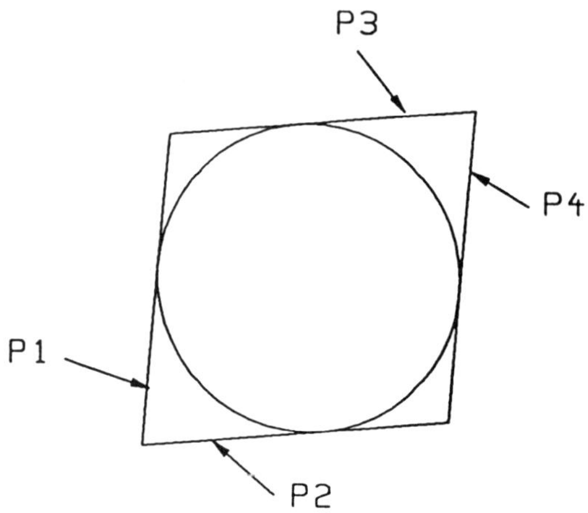

Figure 20.18

Step 4. Add two fillets to the drawings. Use the pick points in Figure 20.18.

Select **MAIN MENU → Create → Fillet → Radius**
Enter the fillet radius: **1/32** ←
Pick at **P1** and **P2** for the first fillet
Pick at **P3** and **P4** for the second fillet

The two fillets are added as shown in Figure 20.19.

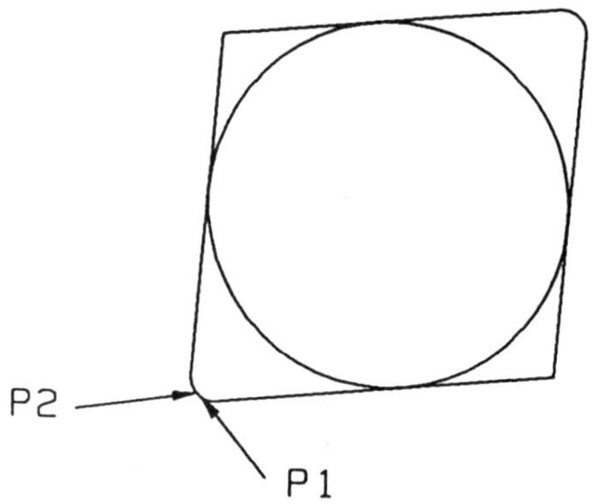

Figure 20.19

Step 5. Create two construction lines tangent to the tool nose arc. Use the pick points in Figure 20.19.

Select **MAIN MENU → Create → Line → Tangent → Angle**
Select an arc: pick at **P1**
Enter the angle in degrees: **0** ←
Enter the line length: **0.5** ←

Pick at the right segment for the horizontal line
Select an arc: pick at **P2**
Enter the angle in degrees: **90** ←
Enter the line length: **0.5** ←
Pick at the upper segment for the vertical line.

The new drawing becomes Figure 20.20.

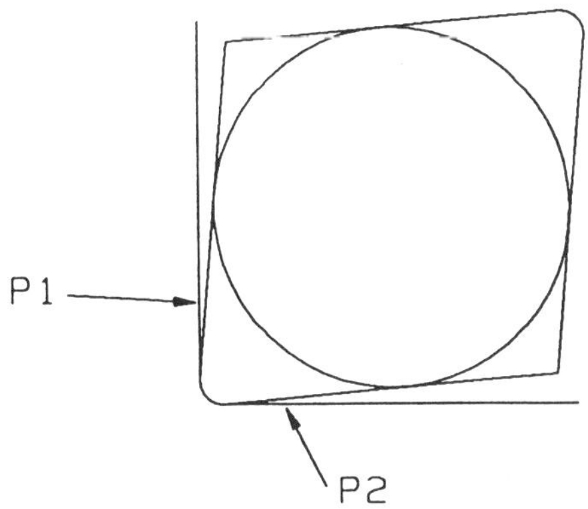

Figure 20.20

Step 6. Define the imaginary tool nose point using the pick points in Figure 20.20.

Select **MAIN MENU → Create→ Point → Position → Position → Intersec**
Pick at **P1** and **P2** to create a point

The point is added as shown in Figure 20.21.

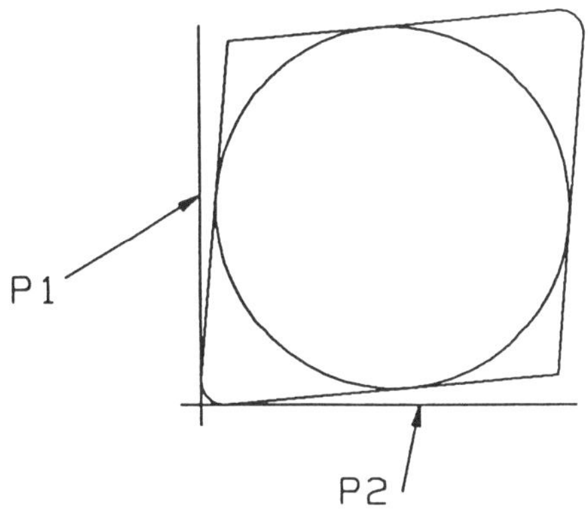

Figure 20.21

Step 7. Delete two construction lines using the pick points in Figure 20.21.

Select **MAIN MENU → Delete**
Pick at **P1** and **P2** to delete two lines

The new drawing should look like Figure 20.22.

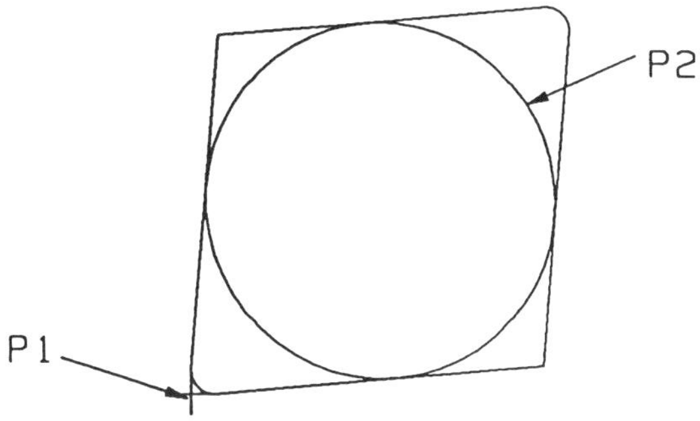

Figure 20.22

Step 8. Change the drawing origin from the IC center to the imaginary tool nose point. Use the pick points in Figure 20.22.

Select **MAIN MENU → Xform → Translate → All → entities → Done → Btween pts**
Enter the point to translate from:
select **Point** from the Point menu, then pick at **P1**
Enter the point to translate to:
select **Center** from the Point menu, then pick at **P2**

Set the Translate menu as shown here ☞

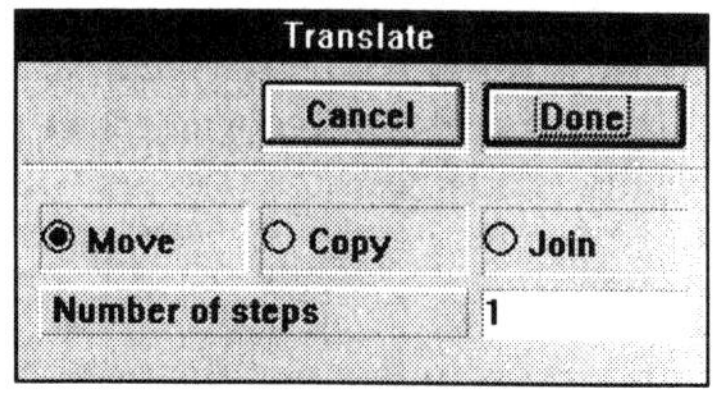

Select **Done** to complete the translation.

The geometry origin is shifted to the imaginary tool nose point now. The new drawing, as shown in Figure 20.23, only changes its position but not the shape and size.

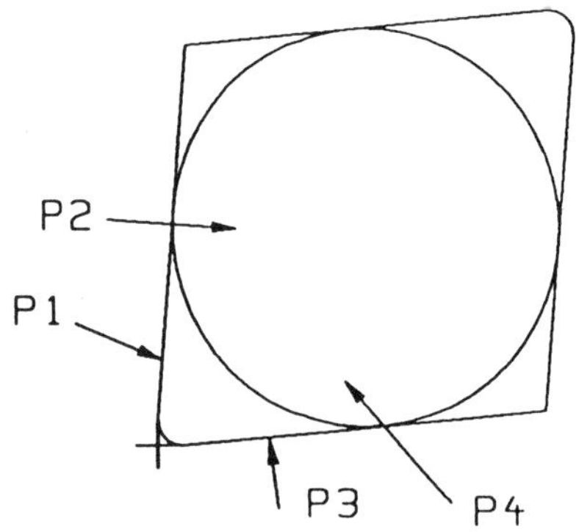

Figure 20.23

Step 9. Create two offset lines using the pick points in Figure 20.23.

Select **MAIN MENU → Xform → Offset**

Set the Offset menu as shown here ☞

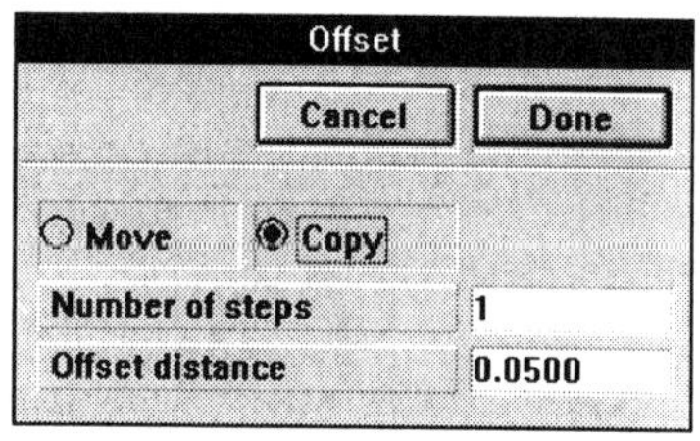

Select **Done** to return to graphic mode.

Select the line or arc to offset: pick at **P1**
Indicate the offset direction: pick at **P2** to complete the first offset line
Select the line or arc to offset: pick at **P3**
Indicate the offset direction: pick at **P4** to complete the second offset line

The two offset lines are added as in Figure 20.24.

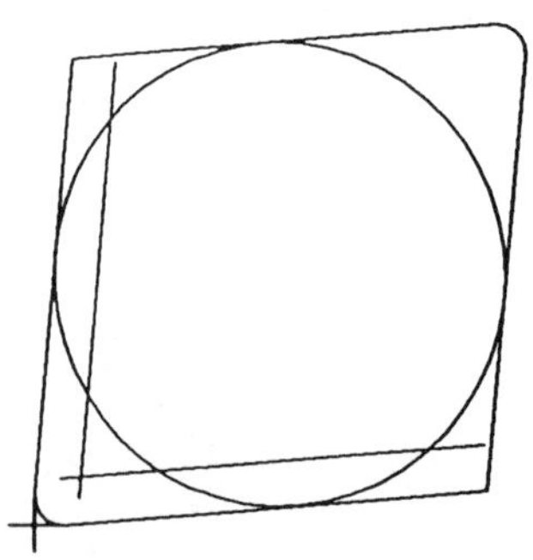

Figure 20.24

Step 10. Create two lines, one horizontal and one vertical.

Select **MAIN MENU → Create → Line → Endpoints**
Specify the first endpoint: **1.2,0**
Specify the second endpoint: **1.2,1.2** ← for the horizontal line
Specify the first endpoint: **0,1.25** ←
Specify the second endpoint: **1.5,1.25** ←
Press **Alt** + **2F1** simultaneously then **F2** to fit the drawing

The new drawing should look like Figure 20.25.

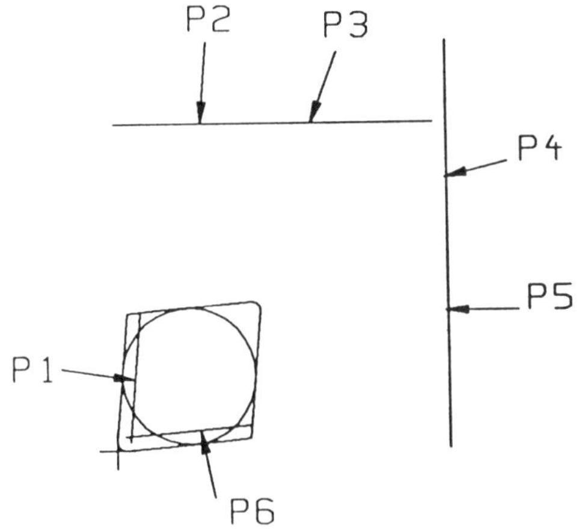

Figure 20.25

Step 11. Trim four lines to form the toolholder head. Use the pick points in Figure 20.25.

Select **MAIN MENU → Modify → Trim → 2 entities**
Sequentially select **P1 - P6** to trim the four lines

The drawing becomes Figure 20.26.

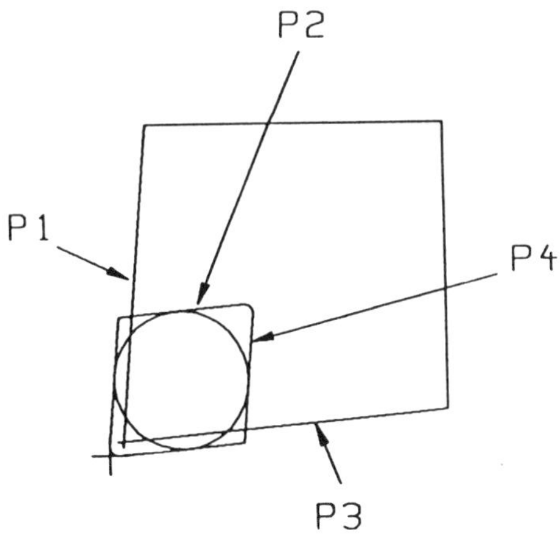

Figure 20.26

Step 12. Trim two lines using the pick points in Figure 20.26.

Select **BACKUP → 1 entity**
Select the entity to trim: pick at **P1**
Select the entity to trim to: pick at **P2**
Select the entity to trim: pick at **P3**
Select the entity to trim to: pick at **P4**

The trimmed drawing becomes Figure 20.27.

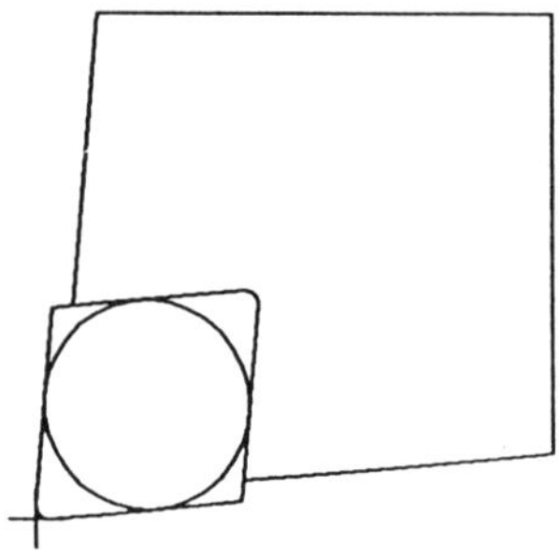

Figure 20.27

Step 13. Create two lines.

Select **MAIN MENU → Create → Line → Endpoints**
Specify the first endpoint: **5,0** ←
Specify the second endpoint: **5,1.5** ←
Specify the first endpoint: **5.5,0.25** ←
Specify the second endpoint: **1.0, 0.25** ←
Press **Alt** + **F1** simultaneously to fit the drawing

The two lines are added as shown in Figure 20.28.

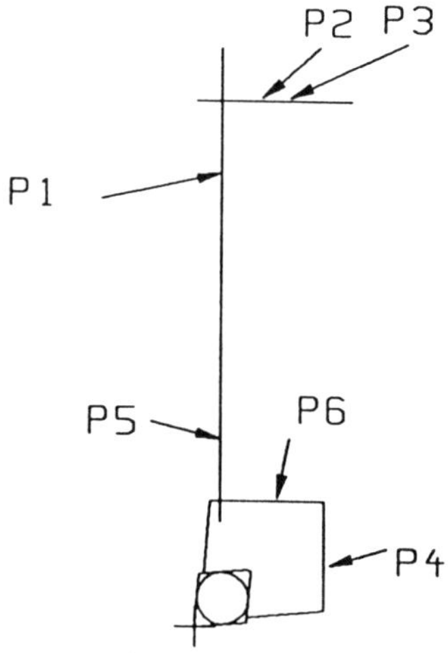

Figure 20.28

Step 14. Trim three lines using the pick points in Figure 20.28.

Select **MAIN MENU → Modify → Trim → 2 entities**
Sequentially pick at **P1 - P4**
Select **BACKUP → 1 entity**
Pick at **P5** to select the entity to trim
Pick at **P6** to select the entity to trim to

The shank of the toolholder is added as Figure 20.29.

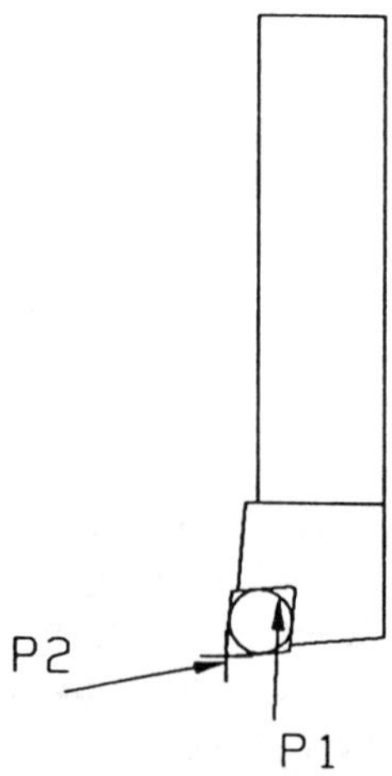

Figure 20.29 ☞

Step 15. Delete a construction circle and a point using the pick points in Figure 20.29 on the previous page.

Select **MAIN MENU → Delete**
Pick at **P1** and **P2** to delete two construction entities

The final tool geometry should appear as Figure 20.30.

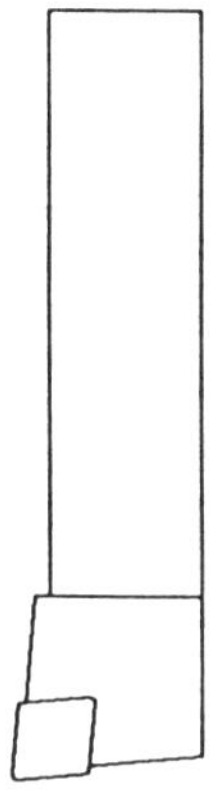

Figure 20.30

Step 16. Save the tool geometry.

Select **MAIN MENU → File → Save → Tool**
Enter file name(C:\NC\LTOOLS\1.GE3): **36** ←

Step 17. Define the tool.

Select **MAIN MENU → NC utils → Def. tools**

Note: A warning - "error opening C:\NC\LTOOLS\36.ltl" will appear. Ignore this warning and continue by clicking on the OK button.

Change the tool parameters to the following settings:

Tool:	36	Orientation:	4	Angle:	5.000	
Number:	10	Radius:	0.0312	Center:	X0.0312	Z0.0312
Offset n:	10	Width:	1.2500	Home position:	X5.0000	Z4.0000

Step 18. Save the tool parameters.

Select **Save** to save the tool information.
Filename = **36.LTL**

20.4 Modify An Existing Tool Geometry

An existing tool geometry either comes with the system, or is created by the user, and can be retrieved to be modified. The way to modify tool geometry is identical to editing part geometries.

How to Retrieve Tool Geometry Files from the Tool Library

Mastercam provides 35 tool geometry and information files in the tool library. They can be retrieved and displayed on the screen. In fact, any tool geometry file, either provided by the system or created by the user, can be retrieved and used. These 35 tool geometries provided in the tool library can be corporately or individually retrieved to the screen.

• The Procedure for Retrieving All 35 Tool Geometries

Select **MAIN MENU → File → Get → Tool**
Enter file pattern (C:\NC\LTOOLS*.GE3): **ALLTOOLS**
Select **Yes** to delete the current part if necessary

The drawing for all 35 tools should appear as Figure 20.31.

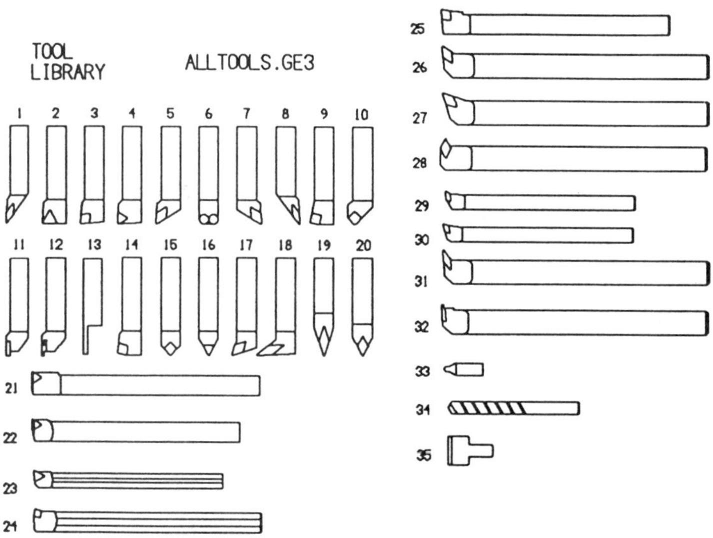

Figure 20.31

• The Procedure for Retrieving An Individual Tool Drawing

Select **MAIN MENU → File → Get → Tool**
Enter file pattern (C:\NC\LTOOLS*.GE3): **1 ←**
Select **Yes** to delete the current part if necessary

The tool drawing for tool #1 should look like Figure 20.32.

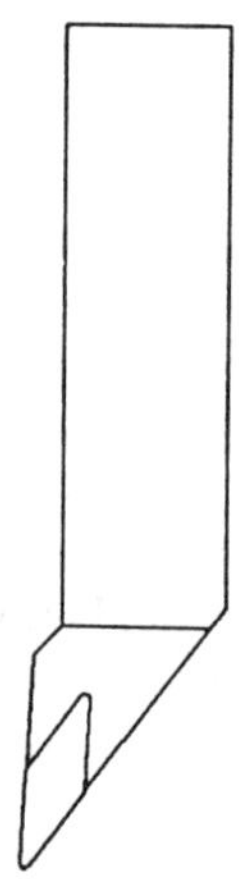

Figure 20.32 ☞

Project 2.

Modify the geometry of an existing boring bar

The existing boring bar (Tool #30), as shown in Figure 20.33a, is modified to become a larger tool. The modification is done by (1) scaled by a factor of 2, and (2) change the insert tool nose from 1/64" to 1/16". The modified tool appears as in Figure 20.33b.

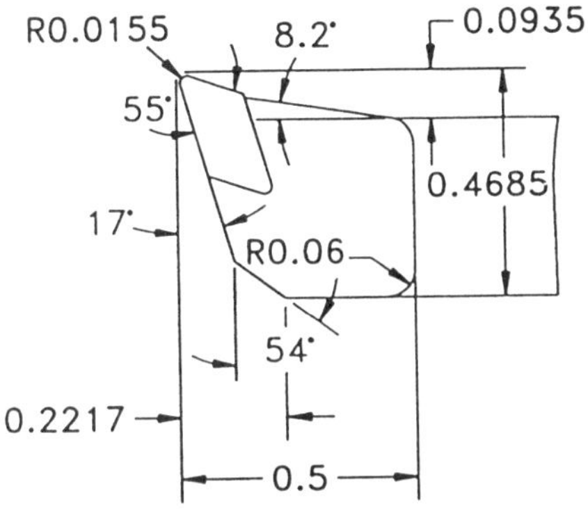

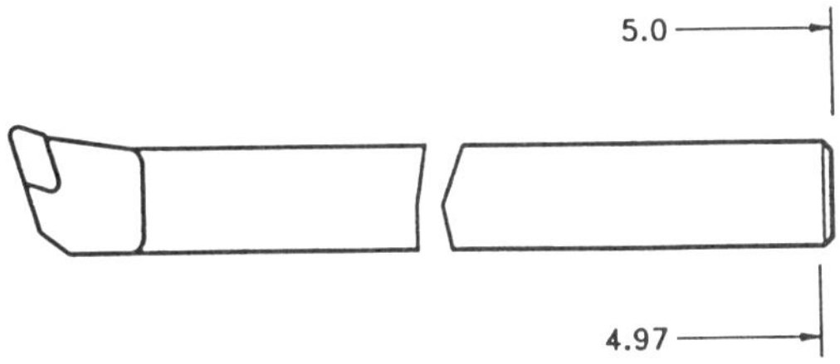

a. Existing boring bar b. Modified tool

Figure 20.33

Tips 1. Load the tool geometry file to be modified (30.ge3).

2. Scale the tool geometry by a factor of 2 and use the origin as the scaling center.

3. Add two fillets of 1/16" to the tool noses.

4. Determine the imaginary tool nose points for the new and old tool noses, respectively.

5. Change the drawing origin from the old imaginary tool nose point to the new imaginary tool nose point.

6. Define the modified tool to the following settings:

> Tool name = 37
> Number = 11
> Ofs. n = 11
> Orientation = 8
> Angle = 17
> Radius = 1/16
> Width = 0.92
> Home position = 7,5

Step 1. Load the boring tool geometry file (30.ge30).

Select **MAIN MENU → File → Get → Tool**
Enter file name(C:\NC\LTOOLS\1.GE3): **30 ←**
Select **Yes** to delete the current part

The boring tool should appear as Figure 20.34 on the following page.

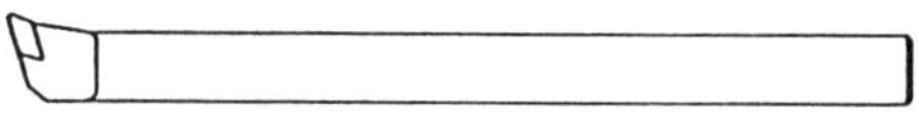

Figure 20.34

Step 2. Scale the tool geometry by a scaling factor of 2. Choose the origin as the scaling center.

Select **MAIN MENU → Xform → Scale → All → Entities → Done → Origin**

Set the Scale parameters as shown here ☞

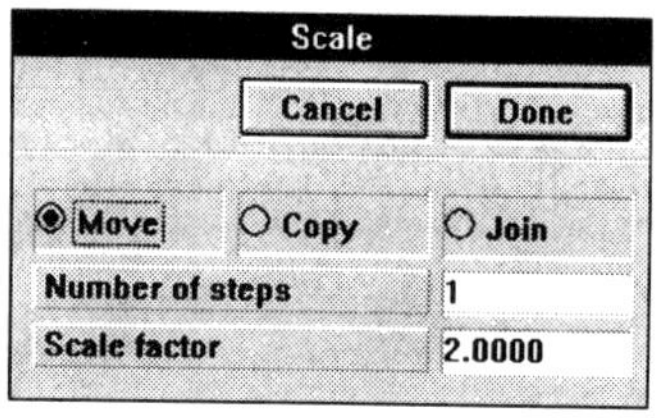

Select **Done** to enlarge the drawing.

Press **Alt** + **F1** simultaneously to display the enlarged tool drawing

The enlarged tool drawing shall appear as Figure 20.35.

Figure 20.35

Step 3. Zoom the insert to change the arc of tool nose. Use the pick points in Figure 20.35.

Press **F1** to initiate the Zoom function

Pick at **P1** and **P2** to zoom the insert

The zoomed insert appears as in Figure 20.36.

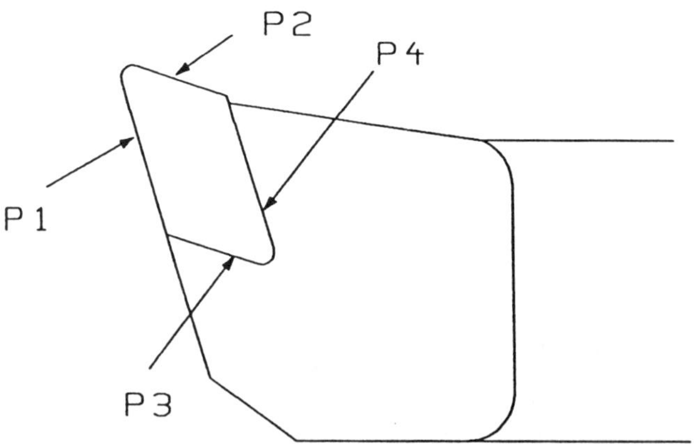

Figure 20.36

Step 4. Add two fillets at the two ends of the insert. Use the pick points in Figure 20.36 on the previous page.

Select **MAIN MENU → Modify → Fillet → Radius**
enter the fillet radius: **1/16** ←
Select an entity: pick at **P1**
Select another entity: pick at **P2** to complete the first fillet
Select an entity: pick at **P3**
Select another entity: pick at **P4** to complete the second fillet

The two fillets are added as Figure 20.37.

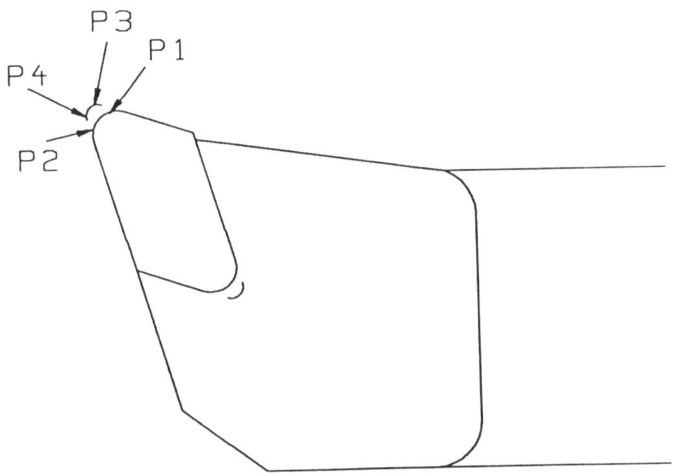

Figure 20.37

Step 5. Create four construction lines being tangent to the new tool nose. Use the pick points in Figure 20.37.

Select **MAIN MENU → Create → Line → Tangent → Angle**
Select an arc: pick at **P1**
Enter the angle in degrees: **0** ←
Enter the line length: **0.5** ←
Pick the right segment

Select an arc: pick at **P2**
Enter the angle in degrees: **270** ←
Enter the line length: **0.5** ←
Pick the bottom segment

Select an arc: pick at **P3**
Enter the angle in degrees: **0** ←
Enter the line length: **0.5** ←
Pick the right segment

Select an arc: pick at **P4**
Enter the angle in degrees: **270** ←
Enter the line length: **0.5** ←
Pick at the bottom segment

The four lines are added as shown in Figure 20.38.

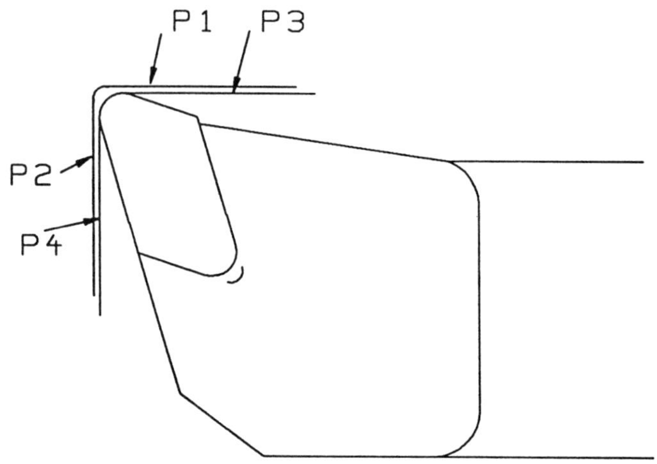

Figure 20.38

Step 6. Create two points for the old and new tool nose points.

Use the pick points in Figure 20.38.
Select **MAIN MENU** → **Create** → **Point** → **Position** → **Intersec**
Pick at **P1** and **P2** to define the old tool nose point
Pick at **P3** and **P4** to define the new tool nose point

The two points are added as in Figure 20.39.

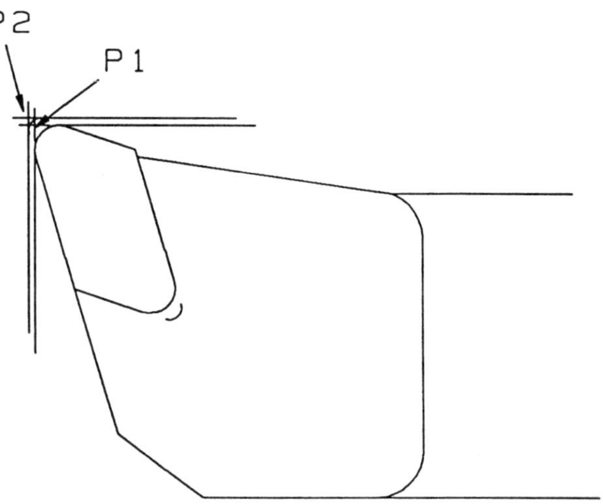

Figure 20.39

Step 7. Change the drawing origin from the old tool nose to the new tool nose. Use the pick points in Figure 20.39 on the previous page.

Select **MAIN MENU → Xform → Translate → All → Entities → Done → Btween pts**

Enter the point to translate from:

select **Point** from the Point menu, then pick at **P1**

Enter the point to translate to:

select **Point** from the Point menu, then pick at **P2**

Set the Translate parameters as here ☞

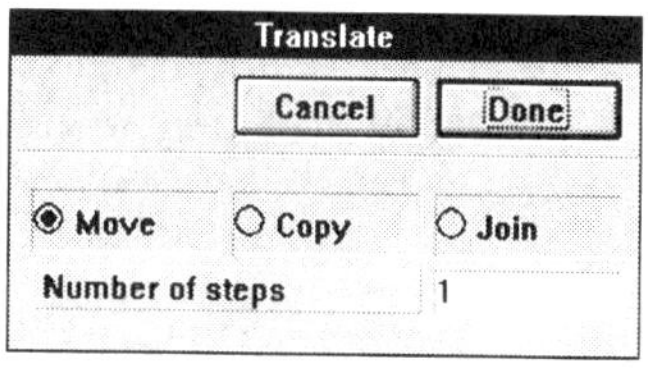

Select **Done** to complete the translation

The newly translated drawing should look the same as the one prior to translation, but the coordinates have been changed. The new drawing origin is located at the new tool nose point. The drawing is redisplayed as in Figure 20.40.

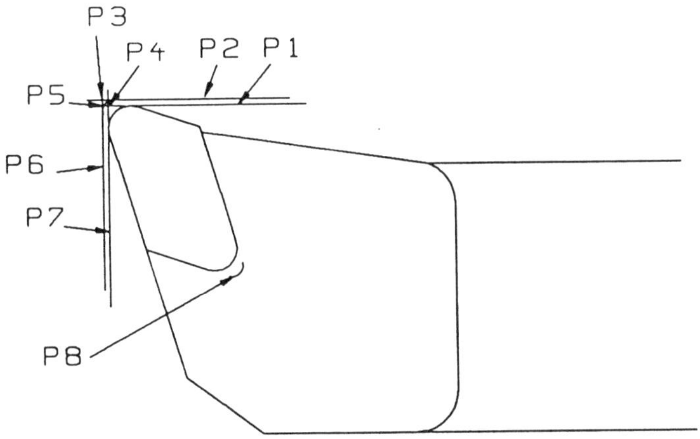

Figure 20.40

Step 8. Delete construction entities using the pick points in Figure 20.40.

Select **MAIN MENU → Delete**

Sequentially pick at **P1 - P8**

Press **Alt + F1** simultaneously to fit the drawing

The final tool drawing shall appear as Figure 20.41.

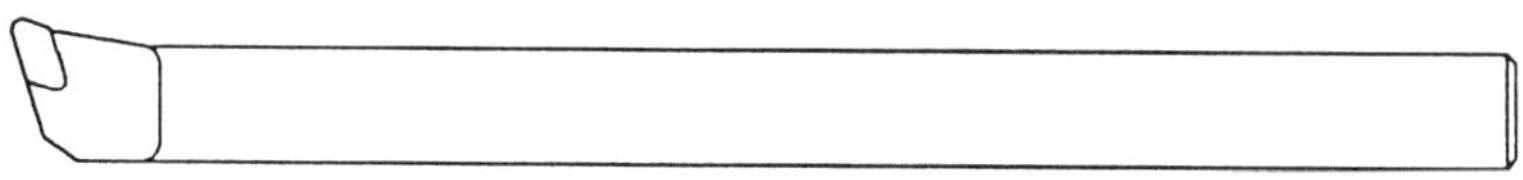

Figure 20.41

Step 9. Save the modified tool geometry.

Select **MAIN MENU → File → Save → Tool**

Enter file name (C:\NC\LTOOLS\30.GE3): **37** ←

Step 10. Define the modified tool.

Select **MAIN MENU → NC utils → Def.tools**

Note: A warning - “error opening C:\NC\LTOOLS\37.ltl” will appear. Ignore this warning and continue by selecting OK.

Change the tool parameters to the following settings:

Tool:	37	Orientation:	1	Angle:	17.000	
Number:	11	Radius:	0.0625	Center:	X0.0625	Z0.0625
Offset n:	11	Width:	0.9200	Home position:	X7.0000	Z5.0000

Step 11. Save the tool parameters.

Select **Save** to save the tool information.
Filename: **37.LTL**

20.5 Exercises

20.5.1 Short Answer

1. What are the two basic components of a turning tool?

2. Define the following tool hand types:

    Right-hand tool:
    Left-hand tool:
    Neutral tool:

3. Use drawings to illustrate the relationship between the cutting direction and the tool-hand type in a left-hand coordinate system.

4. Use drawings to illustrate the relationship between the cutting direction and the tool-hand type in a right-hand coordinate system.

5. What type of coordinate system is used by a slant-bed turning machine?

6. What type of coordinate system is used by a standard flat-bed turning machine?

7. Explain the following T-code statement with 4 digits: T0505

8. What relationship exists between the tool number and the actual position on the tool turret or magazine?

9. What are the five pieces of information contained in a tool offset register?

10. What is the imaginary tool nose? Use a drawing to show how to determine the imaginary tool nose.

11. Explain how to determine the tool nose vector.

12. What is the relief angle of a turning tool?

13. What are the two factors that determine the relief angle?

14. What is the relief angle for a turning tool that has a lead angle of -17° and an insert angle of 55°?

20.5.2 Problems

15. Create a roughing tool as shown in Figure 20.42. Save the tool geometry as 40.

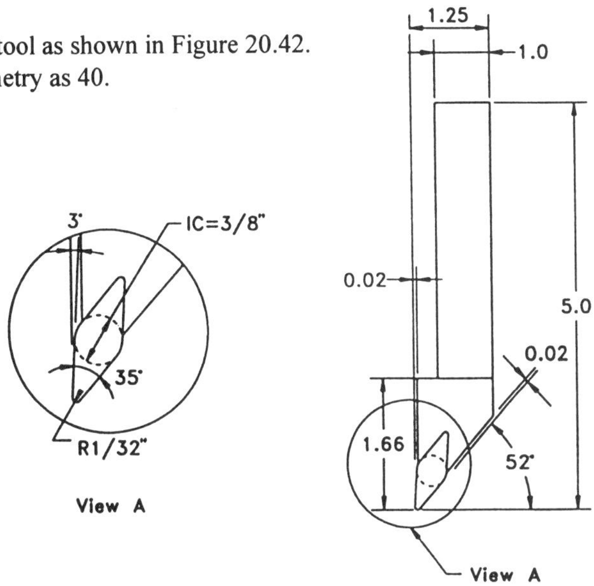

Figure 20.42

16. Create a boring tool as shown in Figure 20.43. Save the tool geometry as 41.

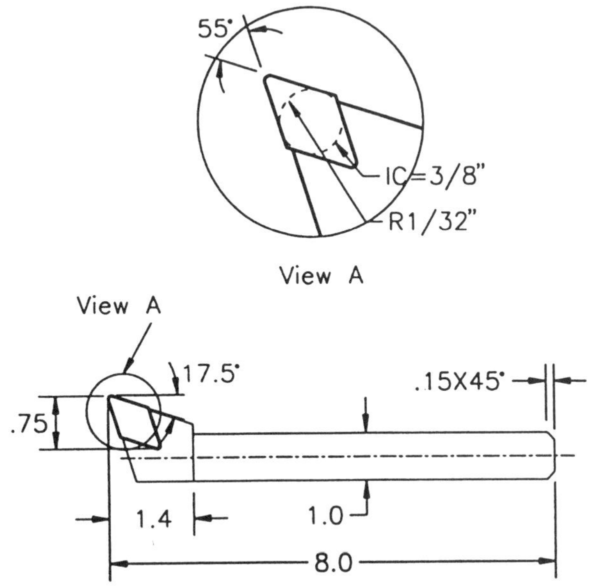

Figure 20.43

17. Modify a finishing tool that is already in the tool library. The tool name is 1. Change the tool nose radius to 1/16".

18. Modify a boring tool that is already in the tool library. The tool name is 23. Scale the tool size by a factor of 1.5. Also, change the tool nose radius to 1/64".

Chapter 21

Post Processor Customization

Objectives:

1. Know the file format of NCI and NC files.
2. Be familiar with the file structure of post processor files (.PST).
3. Know the commonly used variables for forming the NC programs.
4. Customize a post processor for a CNC mill or machining center.

Overview

The output of the CAM system is a toolpath file in generic form. The toolpath file in Mastercam is called the **NCI file**. This file can not be used directly in a CNC machine. It should be converted to the NC program acceptable to the CNC controller. The conversion of a generic toolpath file to the NC file is implemented in a software program called a **post processor**. A unique combination of machine and controller requires a dedicated post processor.

This chapter covers the structure of NCI and NC files, post processor structure, and post processor customization for a CNC mill. A sample customized post processor is given for the Fanuc-based controllers. This sample post processor is intended for 3-axis machining including rapid traverse, linear interpolation, circular interpolation, and canned cycles. Rotary-axis machining is not covered. This sample post processor is tested by a project having three machining operations including contouring, drilling, and tapping. The NC file of this project is then listed for checking its accuracy and correctness.

21.1 NCI Files and NC Files

The use of various toolpath modules in a CAM system generates a toolpath file that contains all information required to machine a part. This toolpath data is called an NCI file in Mastercam. It is written in a generic or intermediate format. NCI files are the input to all post processors. They are ASCII text files that contain all the necessary information to produce an NC program. *Note*, an NCI file can not be directly used as an input to a CNC controller. These NCI files must be converted into NC programs by a post processor which is another software program.

NCI file structure format

The data in an NCI file is arranged in pairs of lines. The first line is the operation line that contains a single number to indicate the type of operation such as a linear move, circular move, drill cycle, start of file, miscellaneous functions, etc. The second line is the data line that contains the information that defines the operation.

The data in the operation lines can be one of the following:

0: rapid traverse
1: linear interpolation
2: circular interpolation (clockwise)
3: circular interpolation (counter-clockwise)
11: five axis interpolation
80: cancel drill cycle
81: start drill cycle
100: drill hole
1000: null tool change
1001: start of file
1002: tool change
1011: define miscellaneous real numbers
1012: define miscellaneous integers
1013: define miscellaneous parameters

The above NCI operations can be classified into the following **four** groups:

- Motion operations
- Canned cycle operations
- File organization
- Miscellaneous operations

Motion operations

There are **two** motion operations: linear move and circular move. The linear move includes rapid traverse and linear interpolation.

• Linear move (rapid and linear interpolation)

The operation line contains only one digit, either 0 or 1. A zero indicates the rapid traverse and one linear interpolation. There are five pieces of information in the data line. The file format for the linear move is:

```
g (0 = rapid traverse, 1 = linear interpolation)
1  2  3  4  5
|  |  |  |  └── feedrate
|  |  |  └── Z-coordinate
|  |  └── Y-coordinate
|  └──X-coordinate
└─ cutter compensation in control
```

Keys for cutter compensation in control:

0 = no cutter compensation in control
40 = cancel cutter compensation in control
41 = cutter compensation in control (left)
42 = cutter compensation in control (right)
140 = last line or arc in the contour

Example 1:

The following pair of NCI lines defines the linear interpolation instruction that moves the cutter to a specified position (5.0,3.0,-1.0) with a feedrate of 10 inches/min and cutter compensation to left.

```
1
└──── G1 (linear interpolation)
41  5.0  3.0  -1.0  10.0
 │   │    │    │     └──── F10.0
 │   │    │    └──── Z-1.0
 │   │    └──── Y3.0
 │   └──── X5.0
 └──── G41 (cutter compensation left)
```

- **Circular move**

The operation line for the circular move also contains only one digit; either 2 or 3. A two indicates clockwise direction and three indicates the counter-clockwise direction. There are **eight** pieces of information in the data line to define the circular move as shown below.

```
g (2 = clockwise, 3 = counter-clockwise)

1  2  3  4  5  6  7  8
│  │  │  │  │  │  │  └──── feedrate
│  │  │  │  │  │  └──── Z-coordinate
│  │  │  │  │  └──── Y-coordinate of arc center
│  │  │  │  └──── X-coordinate of arc center
│  │  │  └──── Y-coordiante of arc end point
│  │  └──── X-coordiante of arc end point
│  └──── cutter compensation in control
└──── plane selection
```

Keys for plane selection

0 = XY-plane
1 = YZ-palne
2 = XZ-plane

Example 2:

The following two NCI lines move the cutter in a clockwise direction to cut a circular arc to (5,3,-0.5) with the arc center at (2,3).

```
2
└──── G2 (circular move (clockwise))
0  42  4.0  3.0  2.0  3.0  -0.5  7.5
│   │   │    │    │    │    │     └──── F7.5
│   │   │    │    │    │    └──── Z-0.5
│   │   │    │    │    └──── J3.0
│   │   │    │    └──── I2.0
│   │   │    └──── Y3.0
│   │   └──── X5.0
│   └──── G42 (cutter compensation right)
└──── XY-plane selection
```

Canned cycle operations

Three operations are involved in canned cycles:

1. start drill cycle (81)
2. drill hole (100)
3. cancel drill cycle (80)

•Start drill cycle (81)

The operation line of the start drill cycle is 81. There are twelve pieces of information in the data line. It has the following format.

81 (Start drill cycle)

1 2 3 4 5 6 7 8 9 10 11 12

height to retract cutter to after first peck
height to retract cutter to between holes
amount to retract for chip break
safety distance for chip break
amount of second peck increment
amount of first peck increment
feedrate (inches/minute)
dwell
Z-coordinate
Y-coordiante
X-coordinate
cycle type

Keys for cycle type:

0 = simple drilling
1 = peck drilling
2 = chip break
3 = tap
4 = bore #1
5 = bore #2
6 = misc. #1
7 = misc. #2

Example 3:

The pair of NCI file lines given below initiate the peck drilling cycle to drill a deep hole located at (3.5,4.0).

81 start drill cycle

1 3.5 4.0 -2.5 0.0 7.5 0.5 0.35 0.0 0.0 0.3 0.1

E = 0.1
R = 0.3
M = 0.0
Safety distance = 0.0
Q = 0.35
First peck amount = 0.5
F7.5
Dwell = 0.0
Z-2.5
Y4.0
X3.5
peck drilling cycle

•Drill hole (100)

When a canned cycle is used to drill more than one hole with the same operating conditions, the canned cycle instruction command (ex. G81) is used in drilling the first hole only because canned cycle commands are the **modal** type; the instruction commands for subsequent holes only require the specification of the coordinates of hole centers. Mastercam uses this procedure: use the start drill cycle (81) operation to define the location and operating conditions of the first hole and use the drill hole (100) operation to specify the center coordinates of the following holes.

The data format for drill hole is:

100 drill hole

1 2 3 4 5

not used
Z-depth
Y-coordinate of hole center
X-coordinate of hole center
not used

Example 4:

The following pair of data lines specifies that the drilling position is located at (5.5,3.0) and the drilling depth is -1.0.

100 drill hole

0 5.5 3.0 -1.0 0

- 5.5 — X5.5
- 3.0 — Y3.0
- -1.0 — Z-1.0

•Cancel drill cycle

The cancel drill cycle operation has a blank data line as shown below.

80 cancel drill cycle

blank line

File Organization

Two types of file structure data lines are used to organize the part program. One is for start of file and tool change, and the other is end of file.

•Start of file (1000, 1001, 1002)

The start of file data lines contain the information about tooling (size, offset, and compensation), coolant control, spindle speed, feedrate, home position, and rapid position. This set of information is required for tool change and start of part program. The start of file data lines have the following data format.

f (1000, 1001, or 1002)

1 2 3 4 5 6 7 8 9 10 11 12 13 14 15 16 17 18

- 1 — program number
- 2 — starting sequence number
- 3 — sequence number increment
- 4 — tool number
- 5 — tool diameter offset number
- 6 — tool length offset number
- 7 — cutter compensation
- 8 — spindle speed in RPM
- 9 — feedrate (inches/minute)
- 10 — coolant (0: off, 1:on)
- 11 — X-rapid position
- 12 — Y-rapid position
- 13 — Z-rapid position
- 14 — X-home position
- 15 — Y-home position
- 16 — Z-home position
- 17 — rotary axis orientation
- 18 — rotary axis diameter

Keys for f:

1000: null tool change
1001: start of file
1002: tool change

Example 5:

The data (1001) in the operation line for the pair of data lines given below indicates that it is the start of the file. The detailed information in the data line is described by notes.

1001 start of file

10 100 5 1 21 1 0 4000 10.0 1 -0.25 0. 0.5 0. 0. 0. 0 2.

- rotary axis diameter = 2
- none rotary axis
- Z0. (home position)
- Y0. (home position)
- X0. (home position)
- Z0.5 (rapid position)
- Y0. (rapid position)
- X-0.25 (rapid position)
- M7 (coolant on)
- F10.0 (feedrate 10.0 inches/min)
- S4000 (spindle speed 4000 RPM)
- G0 (rapid move)
- H1 (tool length offset number)
- D21 (tool length offset number)
- T1 (tool number)
- sequence number increment = 5
- starting sequence number (N=100)
- program number (O10)

•End of file

The data of the operation line for the end of file is 1003. Its data line contains only the X, Y and Z coordinates of the home position. Its data lines format is below:

1003 end of file

1 2 3

- Z home position
- Y home postion
- X home position

Miscellaneous Operations

Miscellaneous data lines are used to assign the values for miscellaneous real variables, miscellaneous integer variables, and miscellaneous parameters. Three operation line types are:

1011 (define miscellaneous real numbers)

1012 (define miscellaneous integers)

1013 (define miscellaneous parameters)

•Define miscellaneous real numbers (1011)

The values of the miscellaneous real variables are assigned in this statement. The data format for defining a miscellaneous real number is:

```
1011        define miscellaneous real number

1 2 3 4 5 6 7 8 9 10
|               | |
|               | L___ value of the miscellaneous real variable 10
|               L___ value of the miscellaneous real variable 9
|            -
|         -
|      -
L___ value of the miscellaneous real variable 1
```

• Define miscellaneous integers (1012)

The values of miscellaneous integer variables are assigned in this statement. The data format for defining a miscellaneous integer is:

```
1012    define miscellaneous intergers

1 2 3 4 5 6 7 8 9 10
|               | |
|               | L___ value of the miscellaneous integer variable 10
|               L___ value of the miscellaneous interger variable 9
|            -
|         -
|      -
L___ value of the miscellaneous integer variable 1
```

• **Define miscellaneous parameters (1013)**

Ten miscellaneous parameters are included in this definition statement. They have the following definition format:

```
1013    define miscellaneous parameters

1 2 3 4 5 6 7 8 9 10
| | | | | | | | | └── not used
| | | | | | | | └──── operation code
| | | | | | | └────── Z-coordinate of tool plane origin
| | | | | | └──────── Y-coordinate of tool plane origin
| | | | | └────────── X-coordinate of tool plane origin
| | | | └──────────── view number
| | | └────────────── compensation to (0: center,  1: tip)
| | └──────────────── tool corner radius
| └────────────────── tool diameter
└──────────────────── cutter compensation
```

Keys for operation modes (parameter 9):

1: 2D contour
2: 3D contour
3: drill
4: pocket
5: ruled
6: 2D swept
7: 3D swept
8: revolution
9: loft
10: coons
11: fillet

Example 6:

The following pair of data lines define the miscellaneous parameters used in a part program. The detailed description of each miscellaneous parameter is provided by a note.

```
1013    define miscellaneous parameters

42 1.0 0. 1 0 0 0 0 1 0
|   |  |  | | | | | └── 2D contour
|   |  |  | | | | └──── Z0 (tool plane origin)
|   |  |  | | | └────── Y0 (tool plane origin)
|   |  |  | | └──────── X0 (tool plane origin)
|   |  |  | └────────── view number = 0
|   |  |  └──────────── compensation to tool tip
|   |  └─────────────── tool corner radius = 0
|   └────────────────── tool diameter = 1.0
└────────────────────── cutter compensation (right)
```

Example 7:

The NCI file of the part program for machining the part shown in Figure 21.1 is listed below. The machining processes include 2D contouring and drilling.

Figure 21.1 ☞

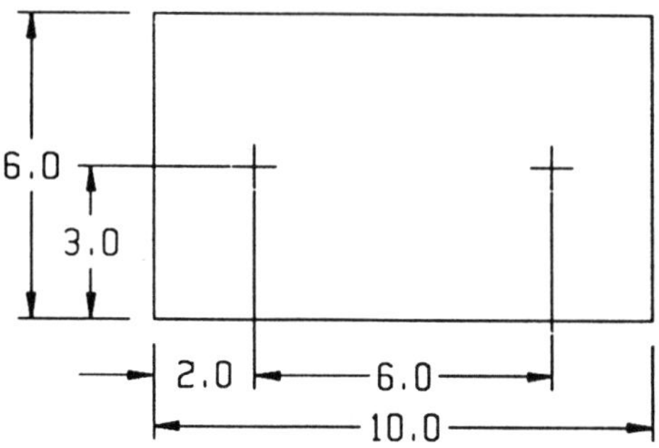

NCI file

1011	define miscellaneous real numbers
0. 118. 0. 0. 0. 0. 0. 0. 0. 0.	
1012	define miscellaneous integers
1 0 0 0 0 0 0 0 0 0	
1013	define miscellaneous parameters
41 1. 0. 0 0 0 0 0 1 0	
1001	start of file
10 100 2 1 21 1 0 2000 10. 1 -0.5 -0.5 0.5 0. 0. 0. 0 2.	
0	rapid traverse
0 -0.5 -0.5 0.5 -2.	
1	linear interpolation
0 -0.5 -0.5 -0.5 7.5	
1	linear interpolation
41 -0.5 6.5 -0.5 10.	
1	linear interpolation
0 10.5 6.5 -0.5 -1.	
1	linear interpolation
0 10.5 -0.5 -0.5 -1.	
1	linear interpolation
140 -0.5 -0.5 -0.5 -1.	
1004	cancel cutter compensation
0	rapid traverse
0 -0.5 -0.5 0.5 -1.	
1011	define miscellaneous real numbers
0. 118. 0. 0. 0. 0. 0. 0. 0. 0.	
1012	define miscellaneous integers
1 0 0 0 0 0 0 0 0 0	
1013	define miscellaneous parameters
0 0.5 0. 0 0 0 0 0 3 0	
1002	tool change
10 100 2 2 22 2 0 1000 7.5 1 2. 3. 1. 0. 0. 0. 0 2.	
81	start drill cycle
0 2. 3. -1. 0. 7.5 0.1 0.1 0.01 0. 1. 0.2	
100	drill hole
0 8. 3. -1. 0.	
80	cancel drill cycle
1003	end of file
0. 0. 0.	

The previous NCI file is converted into NC file by a post processor. This NC file is listed below for reference.

```
O O10
N100 G90 G80 G40 G0
N102 T1 M6
N104 G54 G0 X-.5 Y-.5
N106 S2000 M3
N108 G43 H1 Z.5 M08
N110 G1 Z-.5 F7.5
N112 G41 Y6.5 F10.0 D21
N114 X10.5
N116 Y-.5
N118 X-.5
N120 G40
N122 G0 Z.5 F7.5
N124 G91 G28 Z0 M5 M09
N126 G28 X0 Y0
N128 T2 M6
N130 G90 G80 G40 G00
N132 G54 G0 X2. Y3.
N134 S1000 M3
N136 G43 H2 Z1. M08
N138 G98 G81 X2. Y3. Z-1. R.2 F7.5
N140 X8.
N142 G91 G28 Z0 M5 M09
N144 G28 X0 Y0
N146 M30
%
```

21.2 Post Processors

A post processor is a software program that converts the generic toolpath (NCI) file into an NC part program. The combination of controller and machine requires a unique post processor. Therefore a post processor must be customized into a specific format for a particular controller/machine. Post processors consist of two files: the executable file (MP.DLL for Mill and MPL.DLL for lathe) and an ASCII customization file (.PST). The customization file provides a means of changing the way NC programs are written for a particular controller. The structure of Mastercam's customization file is organized into the following eleven sections:

Section 1:	Information	Section 2:	debugging aids
Section 3:	format statements	Section 4:	format assignments
Section 5:	initialization	Section 6:	question defined
Section 7:	lookup table	Section 8:	string lists
Section 9:	user-defined postblocks	Section 10:	pre-defined postblocks
Section 11:	system questions		

Table 21.1 summarizes the features and includes an example of each section of the customization file of post processors.

Table 21.1 Structure of customization file.

Section	Description	Example
Information	Contains notes and information pertinent to using the post. Typical information is the title block, revision notes and feature description. This part of the file is optional. Each line starts with a remark symbol # and is ignored by the post processor.	#PST file name: MPFAN.PST #Machine model: Generic
Debugging aids	Insert variables "bug1", "bug2","bug3","bug4", and "whatno" to help debugging the post processor by displaying data on the screen.	**bug1 : 0** └ No NC code is displayed **bug1 : 1** └ NC code is displayed on screen **bug1 : 3** └ NC code and leader characters are displayed on screen
Format statements	Define a numeric format to be used for variables. Always include the format statement before the format assignment.	**fs 1 2.4 l t n** - non modal └leave trailing zeros └ leave leading zeros └four places after decimal points └two places before decimal points └format number └format statement command
Format assignments	Assign a numeric format and prefix to a variable. If a variable is not output to the NC file, it is not required to format the variable.	**fmt x 1 x** └ variable to format └ format number └ prefix └ format assignment command
Initialization	Assign a specified value to a pre- or user-defined variable at the start of processing. Select canned cycles using short or long codes. Define global formulas.	**frrapid: 300** └300.0 in/min └ rapid feedrate variable **seqmax: 9999** └N9999 └ maximum sequence number
Question definitions	Insert a question to be posted during processing.	**FQ 1 seqno** (Enter starting sequence number)
Lookup Table	Define a lookup table to provide a way of selecting a number from a list of integers.	**flktbl** 1 12 table#1 with 12 items 58 63 #Code 1 Match 1 59 90 #Code 2 Match 2 " " " " " " " "
String lists	Select a string based on a numeric value. String labels must Start with 'S'. A string list consists of two or more string definitions, a target variable and a string select statement.	**SMO8** **MO8** String definition **SMO9** **MO9** String definition Scool Target variable fstrsel SM09 String selection coolant scool statement

Section	Description	Example
User-defined postblocks	A postblock consists of one or more postlines used to organize the structure of an NC part program. A postline represents a single line of NC codes. The postlines form is a collection of arguments separated by commas.	**Plin # linear line movement - at feedrate** **n sccomp sgcode x y z fr** feedrate Z-coordinate Y-coordinate X-coordinate G-code cutter compensation sequence number Ex.: N100 G41 G01 X1.0 Y9.0 F10.0
Pre-defined postblocks	Are pre-defined routines to format the most common areas of the NC program such as start of file, tool change, canned cycle, end of file, and tool move.	**peof #End of file for non-zero tool** n, "G91 G28 Z0 M5", pcooloff n, "G28 X0 Y0" n, "M30" "%"
System questions	Allow user to make slight configuration changes to the post processor.	**Rapid feedrate? 300.0** **Default X home position? 0.0** **Minimum arc length? 0.0002**

21.3 Post Processor Variables

Variables are important ingredients in a post processor. Some commonly used variables in customizing post processors are presented in this section. These variables can be classified into the following **six** groups:

- Position variables
- Compensation and offset variables
- Miscellaneous variables
- Motion and tool variables
- Canned cycle variables
- String and target variables

Position variables

X: X-coordinate of the new position
Y: Y-coordinate of the new position
Z: Z-coordinate of the new position

Xh: X-coordinate of the home position
Yh: Y-coordinate of the home position
Zh: Z-coordinate of the home position

Xr: X-coordinate of the first position in the NC program
Yr: Y-coordinate of the first position in the NC program
Zr: Z-coordinate of the first position in the NC program

I: arc center description in X-axis
J: arc center description in Y-axis
K: arc center description in Z-axis

Motion and tool variables

Gcode:	G code of the current operation
Plane:	Cutting plane of the current operation or circular move
fr:	feedrate of the current tool movement
frplunge:	feedrate for the current drilling cycle
t:	tool number

Compensation and offset variables

cc:	cutter compensation read directly from NCI file
ccomp:	cutter compensation in control status
tlngno:	tool length offset number
tloffno:	tool diameter offset number

Canned cycle variables

drillcyc:	canned drill cycle
initht:	initial height of the current drilling cycle
depth:	Z-coordinate of the current hole
dwell:	amount of dwell for the current drilling cycle
refht:	reference height of the current drilling cycle
retr:	retract amount of the current drilling cycle

Miscellaneous variables

ss:	spindle speed used for the current operation
n:	sequence number
coolant:	coolant status
progno:	program number as defined in the NC parameters
progname:	NC file name

String and target variables

sgcode:	target string for linear/circular motion G code
spdlon:	target string for spindle-on
smcool:	coolant code target string
sccomp:	cutter compensation target string
sgplane:	plane selection G-code target string
sgdrill:	target drill cycle G code

21.4 Post Processor Customization

To customize a post processor for a particular combination of controller/machine is a rather complicated task. The user must know the features, functions, and commands of the controller and the operation limitations of the machine, as well as file structure, variables, and commands of the post processor files. Fortunately, Mastercam has provided the executable files (MP.DLL for mill and MPL..DLL for lathe) and sample ASCII customization files (.PST) for most commonly used controllers. With the knowledge presented in previous sections and the reference material in the Mastercam manuals, the user should be able to modify an existing ASCII customization file to suit his own need.

In this section we modify a Fanuc generic customization file provided by Mastercam to create a new customization file. The intent is to provide a customization file that is much simpler and easy to understand than the original one. This new file is limited, it deals only with 3-axis machining and canned cycles. The main focus of modifying customization files is on user-defined postblocks and pre-defined postblocks.

User-defined Postblocks

A postblock consists of one or more postlines to implement a certain function. A postline is used to define the content of an NC program block. It consists of a collection of arguments separated by commas. Postline arguments can be of different types: boolean statements, formulas, functions, variables, forced variables, forced formulas, and special characters.

Here is a list of postlines that are used by this post processor. The lines handle cutter compensation and coolant control.

```
pccdia2       # Cutter Compensation2
              if ccomp <> 4, tloffno

pccdia        # Cutter Compensation
              if ccomp <> 0, pccdia2

pfr           # Feedrate W/O Negative Feedrates
              if fr > 0, fr

pcoolon       # Coolant on
              if coolant = 1, “M07” #FLOOD
              if coolant=2,"MO8"  #MIST

pcooloff      # Coolant off
              if prv_coolant = 1, “M09” #OFF

pwcs          #G54 + coordinate setting
              if mil >=4, *sgwcs

plinm         #Linear line  movement - at feedrate
              n,sccomp,pccdia,sgcode,x,y,z,pfr,pcam
```

Pre-defined Postblocks

NC part programs can be organized into modules according to their functions. Each module contains a series of commands to implement certain tasks. These modules are referred to as pre-defined postblocks in Mastercam. They include:

- File header
- Program start
- Tool change
- Machining process
- Canned cycle
- End of program

Each module consists of a fixed pattern of command blocks to execute certain tasks. What should be included in a particular module depends on the controller/machine requirements and the user's preference. Typical tasks performed by the above six modules are listed on the next page.

File header

- program number	O 100
- date	10/8/94
- part (or program) name	BLOCK

Program start

- safety features	G90 G80 G40 G00
- tool change	Tt M06
- work zero definition	G54 (or G92) Xx Yy
- tool length offset	G43 Zz Hh
- spindle speed control	Ss M03
- coolant control	M07

Tool change

- reference point return	G91 G28 Z0
	G28 X0 Y0
- spindle stop	M05
- tool change	Tt M06
- work zero definition	G54 (or G92) Xx Yy
- tool length offset	G43 Zz Hh
- safety feature	G90 G80 G40 G00
- spindle speed control	Ss M03

Machining operation

- rapid traverse	G0 Xx Yy Zz
- linear interpolation	G1 Xx Yy Zz Ff
- circular interpolation	G2 (or G3) Xx Yy (or Zz) Rr Ff
- cutter diameter compensation	G41/G42 (or G40) Dd

Canned cycle

- cycle type	G81/G82/G83 - -/G89 Xx Yy Zz Rr Ff
- retraction mode	G98/G99
- subsequent cycles	Xx Yy Zz

Program end

- reference point return	G91 G28 Z0
	G28 X0 Y0
- spindle stop	M05
- program end command	M30 (or M2)
- program end symbol	%

Example Procedures

The following procedures are written based on the tasks listed above, but the user can rewrite them in another way.

```
pheader        # File header
               "O",progno
```

psof

```
# Start of file for non-zero tool number
n, "G90 G80 G40 G0"
if t <> 0, n, t, "M6"
n, sgwcs, "G0", *xr, *yr, *speed,*spdlon
n, "G43", tlngno, *zr, pcoolon
```

ptlchg

```
# Tool change
n, "G91 G28 Z0 M5", pcooloff
n, "G28 X0 Y0"
n, t, "M6"
n, "G90 G80 G40 G00"
n, sgwcs, "G0", *xr, *yr. *speed,*spdlon
n, "G43", tlngno, *zr, pcoolon
```

peof

```
# End of file for non-zero tool
n, "G91 G28 Z0 M5", pcooloff
n, "G28 X0 Y0"
n, "M30"
"% "
```

prapid

```
# Linear line movement - at rapid feedrate
n,sccomp,sgcode,x,y,z,pfr
```

plin

```
# Linear line movement - at feedrate
n,sccomp,sgcode,x,y,z,pfr,pccdia
```

pz

```
# Linear movement in Z axis only - at feedrate
n, sgcode, z, pfr
```

pcir

```
# Circular interpolation
n,  sgplane, sccomp, sgcode, x, y, z, arcrad, pfr
```

pdrillref

```
# Determine G98 or G99
if initht <> refht, drillref = 98
if initht = refht, drillref = 99
```

pdwell

```
#Determine whether to output dwell
if dwell<> 0, *dwell
```

pdrill

```
#Canned Drill cycle
pdrillref
n,drillref,sgdrill, *x, *y, *depth, *refht, pdwell, *frplunge
```

ppeck

```
# Canned Peck Drill Cycle
pdrillref
n, drillref, *sgdrill, *x, *y, *depth, *peck1, *refht, pdwell, *frplunge
```

pchpbrk

```
# Canned Chip Break Cycle
pdrillref
n, drillref, *sgdrill, *x, *y, *depth, *refht, *peck1,pdwell, *frplunge
```

ptap	# Canned Tap Cycle pdrillref n, drillref, sgdrill, *x, *y, *depth, *refht, pdwell, *frplunge
pbore1	# Canned Bore #1 Cycle pdrillref n, drillref, *sgdrill, *x, *y, *depth, *refht, pdwell, *frplunge
pbore2	# Canned Bore #2 Cycle pdrillref n, drillref, *sgdrill, *x, *y, *depth, *refht, pdwell, *frplunge
pmisc1	# Canned Misc #1 Cycle (User Option) pdrill
pmisc2	# Canned Misc #2 Cycle (User Option) pdrill
pdrill_2	# Canned Drill Cycle n, x, y, depth
ppeck_2	# Canned Peck Drill Cycle pdrill_2
pchpbrk_2	# Canned Chip Break Cycle pdrill_2
ptap_2	# Canned Tap Cycle pdrill_2
pbore1_2	# Canned Bore #1 Cycle pdrill_2
pbore2_2	# Canned Bore #2 Cycle pdrill_2
pmisc1_2	# Canned Misc #1 Cycle pdrill_2
pmisc2_2	# Canned Misc #2 Cycle pdrill_2
pcanceldc	# Cancel canned drill cycle n,"G80"<prv_z=initht

pcancelcc	# Cancel cutter comp.
	ccomp = ccomp # dummy line to quiet ‘blank line’ message
	if mi2 = 0, n, “G40”
	if mi2 > 0, sn, “G40”

ptooltbl	# Tol table line format #”(“, *sopnote, “ OPER W /”, t, “ “,tldia, “DIA)”

Modifying the user-defined postblocks and pre-defined postblocks sections in the Fanuc 6M customization file to the above settings is recommended to the user. Then save the file to a new name such as LIN.PST. Finally, use the next project to test the new customized post processor. You can use any text editor or in Mastercam to edit the PST file.

Project:

Testing the customized post processor

This project uses the machining of a simple part shown in Figure 21.2 to test the newly customized post processor. The machining toolpaths consist of contouring, drilling, and tapping.

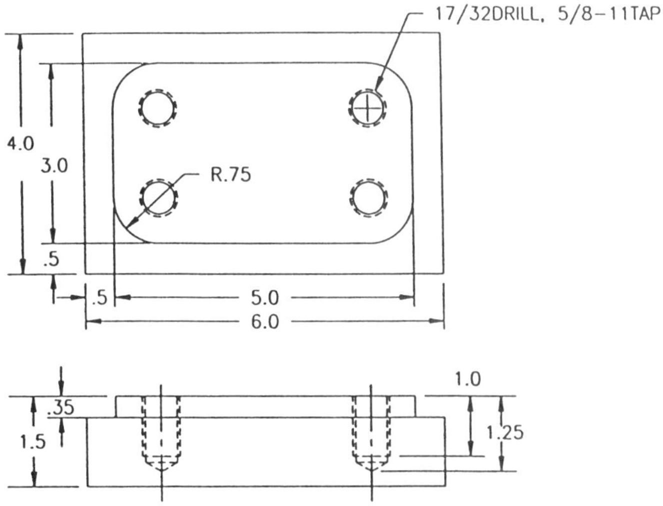

Figure 21.2

Tips 1. Use the contour module to cut the profile with tool T1 (1" end mill).

2. Use the drill/counterbore mode of the drill module to drill the four holes with tool T5 (17/32" drill).
3. Use the tap mode of the drill module to tap internal threads of the four holes with tool T7 (5/8-11 tap).

Step 1. Create two rectangles.

Select **MAIN MENU → Create → Rectangle → 2 points**
Enter the lower left corner: **0,0** ←
Enter the upper right corner: **6,4** ← for the first rectangle
Enter the lower left corner: **0.5,0.5** ←
Enter the upper right corner: **5.5,3.5** ← for the second rectangle

Press **Alt + F1** simultaneously, and then press **F2** to fit the drawing on screen

The drawing should look like Figure 21.3 on the next page.

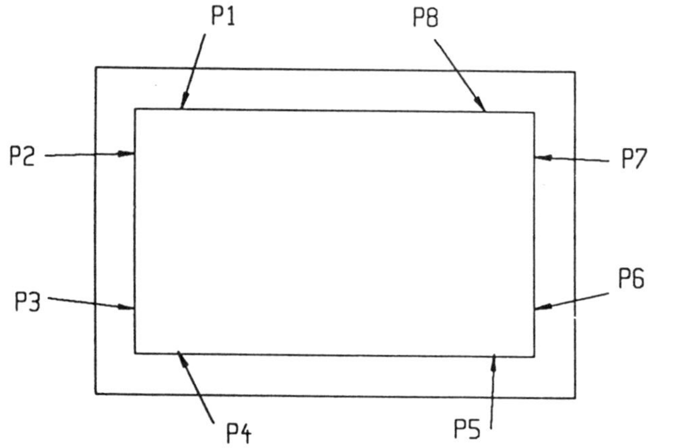

Figure 21.3

Step 2. Create four fillets at the corners of the inside rectangle. Use the pick points in Figure 21.3.

Select **MAIN MENU → Modify → Fillet → Radius**
Enter the fillet radius: **0.75 ←**
Sequentially pick at **P1 - P8** to complete the four fillets

The new drawing becomes Figure 21.4.

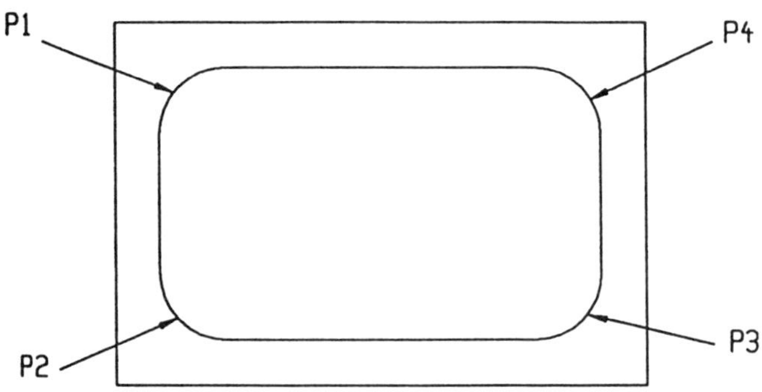

Figure 21.4

Step 3. Create four points for the hole centers using the pick points in Figure 21.4.

Select **MAIN MENU → Create → Point → Position → Center**
Pick at **P1 - P4** to define the four points

The four points are added as shown in Figure 21.5.

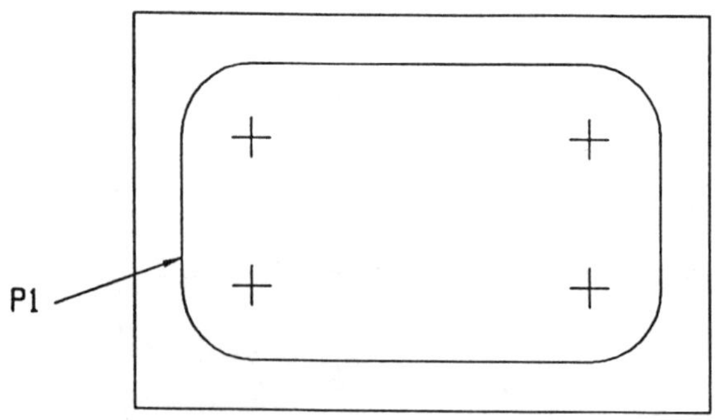

Figure 21.5

Step 4. Initiate the contour module.

Select **MAIN MENU** → **Toolpaths** → **Contour**

Enter file name: **pptest** ←

Step 5. Define the contour using the pick point in Figure 21.5.

Select **Chain** then pick at **P1**

Select **Close** → **End here** → **Done** → **Params**

Step 6. Set the contour parameters to the following settings.

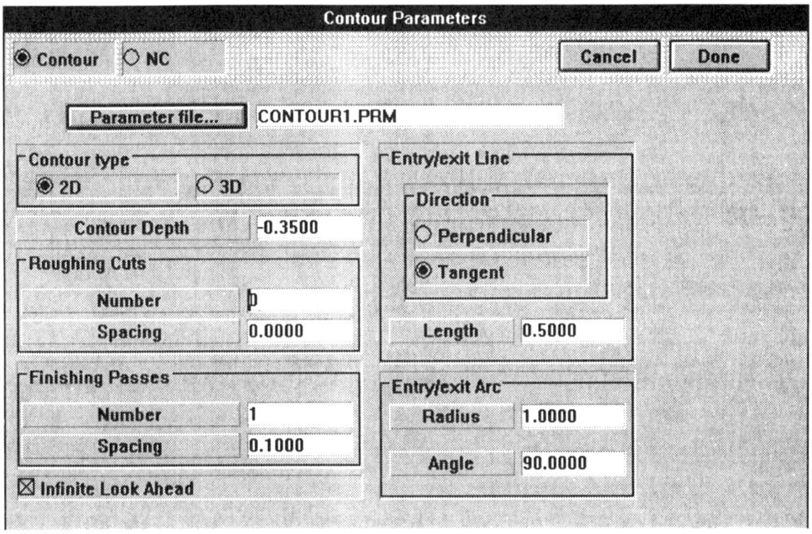

Click on the **NC button** to advance to the NC parameters menu.

Step 7. Set the NC parameters to the following settings.

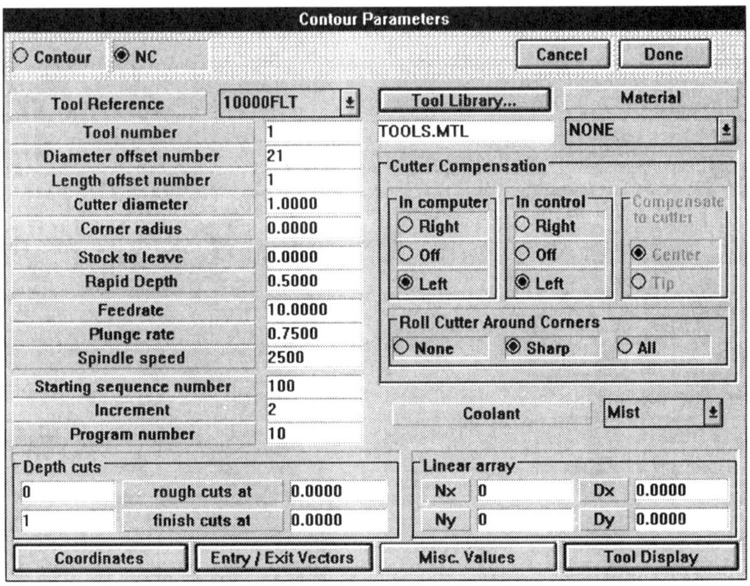

Select **Done** from the contour parameters menu.

Step 8. Accept the contouring toolpath.

Select **Write** to write the toolpath
Select **Yes** to accept this toolpath segment
Press F3 to repaint the screen

The contouring toolpath should resemble Figure 21.6.

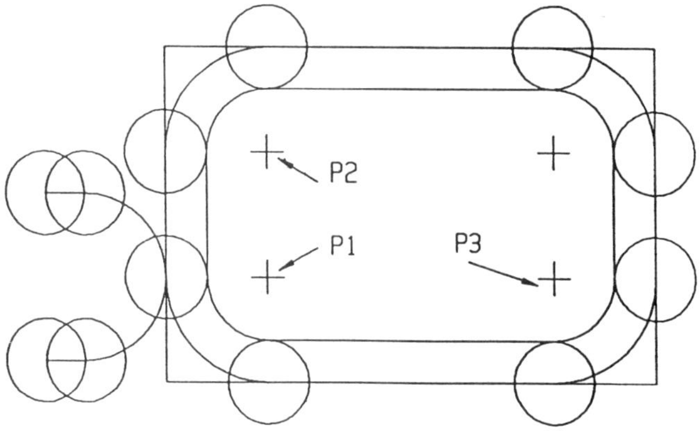

Figure 21.6

Step 9. Initiate the drill module.

Select **MAIN MENU → Toolpaths → Drill**

Step 10. Select the points for drilling using the pick points in Figure 21.6.

Select **Automatic**
Select the first point: pick at **P1**
Select the second point: pick at **P2**
Select the last point: pick at **P3**
Select **Yes** to draw the path between points
Select **Yes** to "Is the path OK?"

Step 11. Define the drill parameters to the following settings.

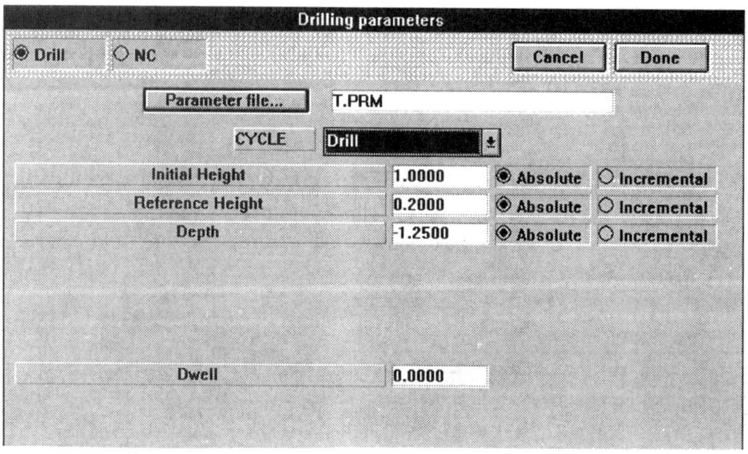

Select the **NC button**.

Step 12. Define the NC parameters to the following settings.

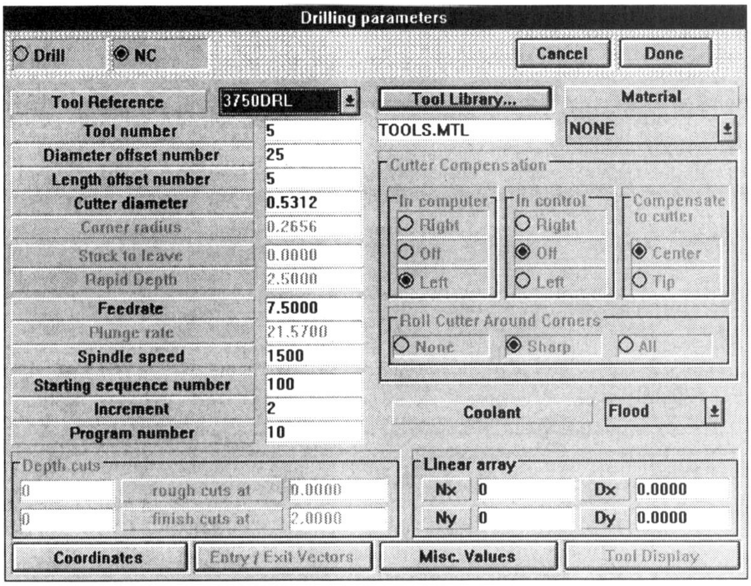

Select **Done** to complete the parameters settings.

Press F3 to remove the NC parameters menu from the screen.

Step 13. Accept the drilling toolpath.

Select **Write** → **Yes** to accept the toolpath

Select **Yes** to “Repeat with same points?” for tapping operations

Step 14. Define tapping parameters to the following settings.

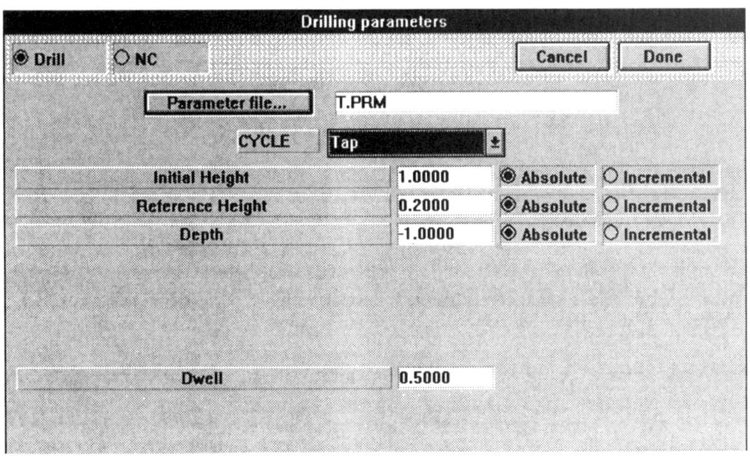

Select the **NC button** line to advance to the NC parameters menu.

Step 15. Define the NC parameters for tapping.

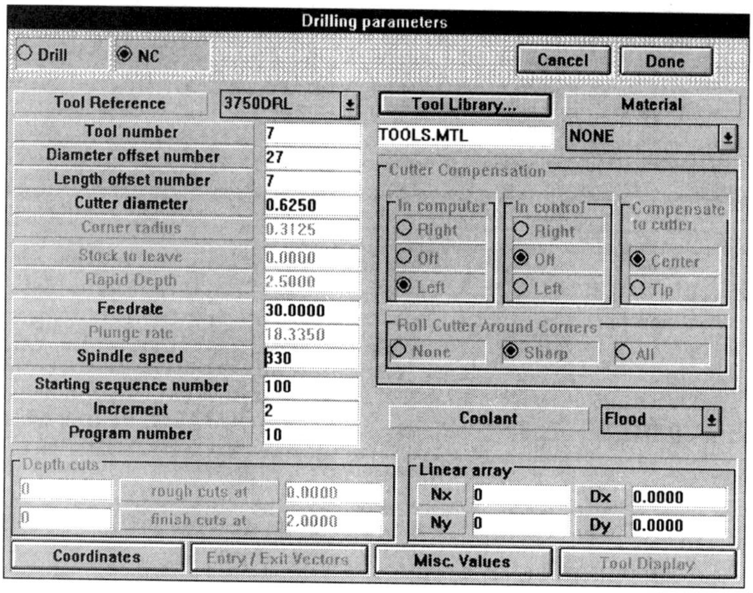

Select **Done** to complete the parameter settings.
Press F3 to repaint the screen

Step 16. Accept the tapping toolpath.

Select **Write** → **Yes** to accept the tapping toolpath
Select **No** to "Repeat with same points?"
Select **End progrm**
Select **No** to "Run the post processor?"

Step 17. Select the new customized post processor (LIN.PST).

Select **MAIN MENU** → **NC utils** → **Post proc** → **Change**
Enter file pattern (.pst): **lin** ←

Step 18. Run the post processor.

Select **Run**
Enter file pattern (.NCI): **pptest** ←
Enter file name (.NC): **pptest** ←

The NCI file should be converted to NC file and listed on the screen.
Double-click the upper-left window button to return back to graphic mode.

Step 19. Edit the NC file.

Select **MAIN MENU** → **File** → **Edit** → **NC**
Enter file pattern (.NC): **pptest** ←

The NC file should appear on the screen as below:

```
O O10                                       header (program number)
N100 G90 G80 G40 G0                         start of file
N102 T1 M6
N104 G54 G0 X-1.5 Y.25
N106 S2500 M3
N108 G43 H1 Z.5 M08
N110 G1 Z-.35 F7.5                          machining operation (contouring)
N112 G41 X-1. F10.0 D21
N114 G3 X0. Y1.25 R1.
N116 G1 Y2.75
N118 G2 X1.25 Y4. R1.25
N120 G1 X4.75
N122 G2 X6. Y2.75 R1.25
N124 G1 Y1.25
N126 G2 X4.75 Y0. R1.25
N128 G1 X1.25
N130 G2 X0. Y1.25 R1.25
N132 G3 X-1. Y2.25 R1.
N134 G1 X-1.5
N136 G40
N138 G0 Z.5
N140 G91 G28 Z0 M5 M09                      tool change (T5)
N142 G28 X0 Y0
N144 T5 M6
N146 G90 G80 G40 G00
N148 G54 G0 X1.25 Y1.25
N150 S1500 M3
N152 G43 H5 Z.2 M08
N154 G98 G81 X1.25 Y1.25 Z-1.25 R0. F7.5    canned cycle (drilling)
N156 Y2.75
N158 X4.75
N160 Y1.25
N162 G91 G28 Z0 M5 M09                      tool change (T7)
N164 G28 X0 Y0
N166 T7 M6
N168 G90 G80 G40 G00
N170 G54 G0 X1.25 Y1.25
N172 S330 M3
N174 G43 H7 Z1. M08
N176 G98 G84 X1.25 Y1.25 Z-1. R.2 P.5 F30.0 canned cycle (tapping)
N178 Y2.75
N180 X4.75
N182 Y1.25
N184 G91 G28 Z0 M5 M09                      end of file
N186 G28 X0 Y0
N188 M30
%
```

21.5 Exercises

1. What is the output file of the CAM system?

2. Explain the reason for using a post processor.

3. Describe how Mastercam uses a pair of lines to organize the data contained in NCI files.

4. Describe what the following numbers represent in the operation lines used in NCI files:

   0:
   1:
   2:
   3:
   11:
   80:
   81:
   100:
   1001:
   1002:
   1013:

5. What are the four groups of operations in NCI files?

6. Describe how the start drill cycle (81) and drill hole (100) operations are used together to specify the canned cycles for drilling, boring, or tapping multiple holes.

7. Define the term post processor.

8. What are the two files used in a post processor?

9. List the eleven sections of the post processor customization files. Briefly describe what they are.

10. What are main six groups of variables used in post processors?

Index